Egypt

written and researched by

Dan Richardson

with

Daniel Jacobs and Jessica Jacobs

with additional contributions from
**Michael Ackroyd, Jill and Enrik Franken,
Tony Howard and Di Taylor**

ROUGH
GUIDES

www.roughguides.com

SEA

Damietta

DELTA

Port Said

El-Mansura

Tanta

Ismailiya

West
Bank

Gaza

Rafah

El-Arish

ISRAEL

JORDAN

Petra

CAIRO

Suez

Eilat

Taba

Aqaba

SINAI

Fayoum

Beni Suef

Za'farana

Nuweiba

EGYPT

Mt. Sinai

Dahab

El-Tor

Gulf of Suez

Gulf of Aqaba

Minya

Ras Gharib

Tell el-Amarna

Sharm el-
Sheikh

SAUDI

ARABIA

Assyut

Hurghada

RED

Sohag

Qena

Port Safaga

SEA

Qus

El-Quseir

Luxor

Kharga
Oasis

Esna

Mersa Allam

RED SEA MOUNTAINS

Edfu

UPPER EGYPT

Kom Ombo

Aswan

The High Dam

Philae

Berenice

Bir Shalateen

Lake
Nasser

Abu Simbel

Halaib

Disputed Territory

Wadi Halfa

Disputed
Territory

Desert track

	metres
	2000
	1500
	1000
	400
	200
	0
	below
sea level

N

0   100 km

iii

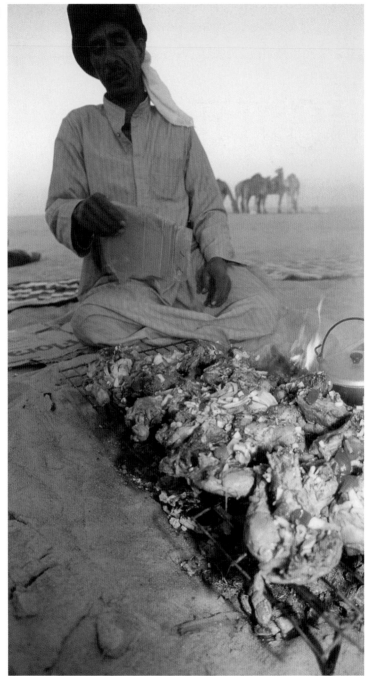

Introduction to

Egypt

Egypt is the oldest tourist destination on earth. Ancient Greeks and Romans started the trend, coming to goggle at the cyclopean scale of the Pyramids and the Colossi of Thebes. At the onset of colonial times, Napoleon and the British in turn looted Egypt's treasures to fill their national museums, sparking off a trickle of Grand Tourists that eventually became a flood of travellers, packaged for their Nile cruises and Egyptological lectures by the enterprising Thomas Cook.

Today, the attractions of the country are not only the monuments of the Nile Valley and the souks, mosques and *madrassas* of Islamic Cairo, but the natural wonders of the Red Sea, Sinai, and the Eastern and Western deserts: fantastic coral reefs and tropical fish, dunes and rockscapes – plus ancient fortresses, monasteries and rock art.

The land itself is a freak of nature, whose lifeblood is the River Nile. From the Sudanese border to the shores of the Mediterranean, the Nile Valley and its Delta are flanked by arid wastes, the latter as empty as the former are teeming with people. This stark duality between fertility and desolation is fundamental to Egypt's character and has shaped its development since prehistoric times, imparting continuity to diverse cultures and peoples over seven millennia. It is a sense of permanence and timelessness that is buttressed by religion, which pervades every aspect of life. Although the pagan cults of ancient Egypt are as moribund as its legacy of mummies and temples, their ancient fertility rites and processions of boats still hold their place in the celebrations of Islam and Christianity.

v

Fact file

• The Arab Republic of Egypt covers 1,001,450 square kilometres – roughly the size of France – of which 96.4 percent is desert; only the Nile Valley, its Delta and some oases are fertile.

• Egypt's population of 69 million is twice that of the next most populous Arab country (Algeria) and a quarter of the population of the Arab world. Its ethnic profile is Eastern Hamitic – Egyptians, Bedouin, Nubians and Berbers account for 99 percent – with tiny minorities of Greeks, Armenians and others. Arabic is universally spoken; Nubian or Siwi locally. Islam is the national religion, with some 96 percent followers; almost all the rest are Coptic Orthodox Christians. Average life expectancy is 64 years.

• A republic since 1952, Egypt is divided into 26 governorates or *muhafazat*. President Hosni Mubarak has been head of state since 1981. The National Democratic Party invariably wins 88 percent of the vote in elections to the People's Assembly (Maglis al-Shaab) and Advisory Council (Maglis al-Shura). Opposition parties and independent MPs are outspoken, but powerless to change anything.

• Tourism is Egypt's largest money-earner, followed by tolls on the Suez Canal, and exports of oil, petroleum products, cotton and textiles – soon to be joined by natural gas.

The result is a multi-layered culture, which seems to accord equal respect to ancient and modern. The peasants (*fellaheen*) of the Nile and Bedouin tribes of the desert live much as their ancestors did a thousand years ago. Other communities include the Nubians of the far south, and the Coptic Christians, who trace their ancestry back to pharaonic times. What unites them is a love of their homeland, extended family ties, dignity, warmth and hospitality towards strangers. Though most visitors are drawn to Egypt by its monuments, the enduring memory is likely to be of its people and their way of life.

Where to go

E gypt's capital, **Cairo**, is a seething megalopolis whose chief sightseeing appeal lies in its **bazaars** and medieval **mosques**, though there is scarcely less fascination in its juxtapositions of medieval and modern life, with fortified gates, villas and skyscrapers interwoven by flyovers whose traffic may be halted by donkey carts. The immensity and diversity of this "Mother of Cities" is as staggering as anything you'll encounter in Egypt, while just outside Cairo are the first of the **pyramids** that range across the desert to the edge of the Fayoum, among them the unsurpassable trio at **Giza**, the vast necropolis of **Saqqara** and the recently reopened pyramids at **Dahshur**. Besides all this, there are superb **museums** devoted to Ancient, Coptic and Islamic Egypt, and enough **entertainments** to occupy weeks of your time.

However, the principal tourist lure remains, as ever, the **Nile Valley**, with its **ancient monuments** and timeless river vistas – Nile **cruises** on a luxury vessel or a felucca sailboat being a great way to combine the two. The town of **Luxor** is synonymous with the magnificent temples of **Karnak** and the **Theban Necropolis**, which includes the **Valley of the Kings** where Tutankhamun and other pharaohs were buried. **Aswan**, Egypt's southernmost city, has the loveliest setting on the Nile

Ali or Aly?

There's no standard system of transliterating Arabic script into Roman, so you're sure to find that the Arabic words in this book don't always match the versions you'll see elsewhere. Maps and street signs are the biggest sources of confusion, so we've generally gone for the transliteration that's the most common on the spot. However, you'll often need to do a bit of lateral thinking, and it's not uncommon to find one spelling posted at one end of a road, with another at the opposite end. See p.835 for an introduction to the Egyptian language.

and a languorous ambience. From here, you can visit the island **Philae temple of Isis** and the rock-hewn colossi at **Abu Simbel**, or embark on a cruise to other temples around **Lake Nasser**. Other sites not to be missed are **Edfu** and **Kom Ombo** between Luxor and Aswan, and **Abydos** and **Dendara** north of Luxor.

Besides monuments, Egypt abounds in natural wonders. Edged by coral reefs teeming with tropical fish, the **Sinai Peninsula** offers superb **diving** and **snorkelling**, and palm-fringed **beaches** where women can swim unmolested. Resorts along the Gulf of Aqaba are varied enough to suit everyone, whether

The sheesha

The **sheesha** or water-pipe is an integral part of Egyptian life. Wherever you go, you'll see men chuffing away on them, whether in cafés or just on the street (though it'll be the café that's supplied them in either case). Women don't smoke them, as smoking isn't considered ladylike in Egypt.

The origin of the *sheesha* is something of a mystery. The name is Persian for "glass", a reference to the vase. Another name is *nargila*, Persian for coconut, which shows what the vase was originally, and both names tell us that the water pipe came to Egypt from Persia. But there were sophisticated water pipes in Persia almost as soon as tobacco arrived in the seventeenth century, and some have suggested that they must have been used there before tobacco arrived, presumably for smoking cannabis. Possibly the Persians got the idea from their trade with East Africa, where water pipes definitely were being used to smoke cannabis long before the arrival of tobacco.

Once strictly an old man's pastime, *sheesha*-smoking has gone through something of a renaissance of late, and flavoured tobacco (apple, strawberry, apricot and mint among other varieties) is now available as well as the traditional *ma'azil*, which is mixed with molasses. The water acts as quite an efficient filter, as you'll see from the state of it after use. Meanwhile, the smell of *ma'azil* is one of the great aromas of Egypt, guaranteed to take you right back there if you ever smell it again.

you're into the upmarket hotels of **Sharm el-Sheikh**, **Na'ama Bay** or **Taba**, or cheap, simple living at **Dahab** and **Nuweiba**. From there it's easy to visit **St Catherine's Monastery** and **Mount Sinai** (where Moses received the Ten Commandments) in the mountainous interior. With more time, cash and stamina, you can also embark on **jeep safaris** or **camel treks** to remote oases and spectacular wadis.

Egypt's **Red Sea Coast** has more reefs further offshore, with snorkelling and diving traditionally centred around **Hurghada**, while barely-touched island reefs further south from **Port Safaga** down to **Mersa Alam** beckon serious diving enthusiasts. Inland, the mountainous **Eastern Desert** harbours the Coptic **Monasteries of St Paul** and **St Anthony**, Roman quarries, and a host of pharaonic and **prehistoric rock art**, seen by few apart from the nomadic Bedouin.

While the Eastern Desert is still barely touched by tourism, the **Western Desert Oases** have been on the tourist trail for thirty years and nowadays host safaris into the wilderness. **Siwa**, out towards the Libyan border, has a unique culture and history, limpid pools and bags of charm. Another option is to follow the "Great Desert Circuit" (starting from Cairo or

Coral reefs

While the Nile Valley and the desert shaped its civilization, there's a third dimension to Egypt's environment. The Red Sea sustains an incredibly rich ecosystem of **coral reefs** and tropical fish, ranging from coastal mangrove swamps and coral gardens to deep-sea islands and underwater pillars. Since it was first explored by Jacques Cousteau in the 1960s, this undersea world has become the basis of a whole new tourist industry, with diving resorts all along the Red Sea Coast and south Sinai, and "liveaboards" venturing as far south as Eritrea. See p.684 for details of reef ecology, and p.683 for the essential facts of diving in Sinai; reefs from Hurghada to Mersa Alam are covered on p.758.

The ibis

Images of **ibises** appear on temples, tombs and billboards all over Egypt. The white-bodied, black-billed Sacred ibis that the ancient Egyptians revered as an incarnation of Thoth, the God of Knowledge, was last seen in Egypt in 1801 and is now only found as far north as Sudan – but in ancient times they were so abundant that literally millions were mummified at Tuna el-Gebel and other sites, despite it being a capital offence to kill one. Another species often depicted in tombs was the Crested ibis, used as the hieroglyph for *Akhu* (part of the soul) and known as the Akhu bird; while the Glossy ibis was painted in black, without its iridescent sheen. Nowadays, the main kinds seen in the Nile Valley are Amboseli's ibis – a near lookalike for the Sacred ibis – and two colourful cousins: the Scarlet ibis resembles a flamingo, but smaller, with blood-red plumage, while the Red-billed ibis has iridescent pink wings and a red beak.

Assyut) through the four "inner" oases. Though **Bahariya** and **Farafra** hold the most appeal, with the lovely **White Desert** between them, the larger oases of **Dakhla** and **Kharga** also have their rewards once you escape their modernized "capitals". And for those into serious desert expeditions, there's the challenge of exploring the **Great Sand Sea** or the remote wadis of the **Gilf Kebir** and **Jebel Uwaynat**, whose prehistoric rock art fea-

tured in the film *The English Patient*. In contrast to these deep-desert locations are the quasi-oases of the **Fayoum** and **Wadi Natrun**, with their diverse ancient ruins and **Coptic monasteries**.

Moving north to the **Mediterranean**, Egypt's second city, **Alexandria**, boasts a string of beaches to which Cairenes flock in summer, and excellent seafood restaurants. Despite being founded by Alexander the Great and lost to the Romans by Cleopatra, the city today betrays little of its ancient glory; however, the ongoing underwater excavation of (possibly) **Cleopatra's Palace** and the legendary **Lighthouse of Pharos** may once more bring an air of majesty to Alexandria. Famous, too, for its decadence during colonial times, romantics can still indulge here in a nostalgic exploration of the "Capital of Memory", while further along

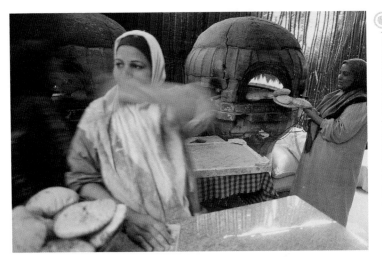

the Mediterranean coast lie the World War II battlefield of **El-Alamein** and the Egyptian holiday resort of **Mersa Matrouh**.

The Nile **Delta**, east of Alexandria, musters few archeological monuments given its major role in ancient Egyptian history, and is largely overlooked by tourists. However, for those interested in Egyptian culture, the Delta hosts colourful religious **festivals** at **Tanta**, **Zagazig** and other towns. Further east lies the **Canal Zone**, dominated by the Suez Canal and its three cities. **Port Said** and **Ismailiya** are pleasant, albeit sleepy places, where you can get a feel of "real Egypt" without tripping over other tourists. **Suez** is grim, but a vital transport nexus between Cairo, Sinai and the Red Sea Coast.

When to go

Deciding on the best time for a visit involves striking a balance between climatic and tourist factors. Egypt's traditional season runs from **late November to late February**, when the Nile Valley is balmy, although Cairo can be overcast and chilly. However, at these times, particularly during the peak months of December and January, the major Nile resorts of Luxor and Aswan get unpleasantly crowded. This winter season is also the busiest period for the Sinai resorts, while Hurghada is active year round.

With this in mind, **March or April** are good compromise options, offering decent climate and fewer visitors. In **May and June** the heat is still tolerable but, after that, Egyptians rich enough to do so migrate to Alex and the coastal resorts. From **July to September** the south and desert are ferociously hot and sightseeing is best limited to early morning or evening – though August still sees droves of backpackers. **October into early November** is perhaps the best time of all, with easily manageable climate and crowds.

Weather and tourism apart, the **Islamic religious calendar** and its related festivals can have an effect on your travel. The most important factor is **Ramadan**, the month of daytime fasting, which can be problematic for eating and transport, though the festive evenings do much to compensate. See "Public Holidays and Moulids" in the Basics chapter for details of its timing.

Average daily temperatures

	Jan	March	May	July	Sept	Nov
Alexandria *Mediterranean*						
°C Min/Max	11/18	13/21	18/26	23/29	23/30	17/25
°F Min/Max	51/65	55/70	64/79	73/85	73/86	62/77
Aswan *Southern Nile Valley*						
°C Min/Max	10/23	14/31	23/39	26/41	24/39	17/31
°F Min/Max	50/74	58/87	74/103	79/106	75/103	62/87
Cairo *Northern Nile Valley*						
°C Min/Max	8/18	11/24	17/33	21/36	20/32	14/26
°F Min/Max	47/65	52/75	63/91	70/96	68/90	58/78
Dakhla *Western Desert*						
°C Min/Max	5/21	8/28	20/37	23/40	21/36	12/28
°F Min/Max	41/70	47/82	68/99	74/104	70/96	53/82
Hurghada *Red Sea Coast*						
°C Min/Max	10/21	12/23	21/30	25/32	23/30	15/25
°F Min/Max	50/70	61/74	70/86	77/90	74/86	59/77

Note that these are *average* daily maximum/minimum temperatures. Summer peaks in Aswan, Hurghada or Sinai, for example, can hit the 120°s F (low 50°s C) in hot years. The dryness of the air and absence of cloud cover makes for drastic fluctuations, though they do also make the heat tolerably unsticky outside Cairo and the Delta.

The Mediterranean Coast can be windy and wet during wintertime.

30

things not to miss

It's not possible to see everything that Egypt has to offer in one trip – and we don't suggest you try. What follows is a selective taste of the country's highlights: outstanding temples and tombs, vibrant festivals, spectacular desertscapes, and good things to eat, drink and buy. It's arranged in five colour-coded categories, so that you can browse through to find the very best things to see, do and experience. All highlights have a page reference to take you into the guide, where you can find out more.

01 **Valley of the Kings** Page **388** • The descent into the Underworld, the Judgement of Osiris and the rebirth of the pharaoh are vividly depicted on the walls and ceilings of the royal tombs.

xiii

03 **The pyramids of Dahshur** Page **234** •
Less famous than the Giza trio but no
less fascinating – and far less crowded. The
Red and Bent pyramids contain elaborate
devices to foil tomb-raiders.

02 **Bellydancing** Pages **249** and **360** •
The centuries-old tradition of *raqs
sharqi* (oriental dance) is often debased in
hotel nightclubs, but the clubs frequented
by locals feature dancers and musicians
who'll set your pulse racing.

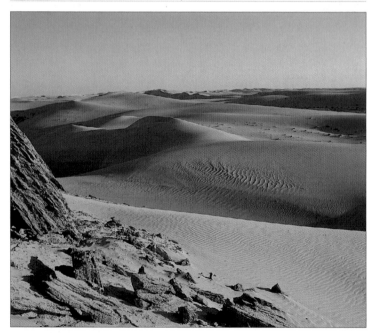

04 **Dunes** Pages **536**, **554** & **560** • From the crescent-shaped dunes of Dakhla to the
"whalebacks" of the Great Sand Sea or the red dunes of Wadi Hamra, their beauty
never fails to captivate.

06 **Birdwatching** Pages **478**, **502**, **650** & **704** • Egypt is a paradise for ornithologists, particularly Wadi Rayan, Lake Nasser, Lake Manzola and the Sinai Peninsula.

05 **Juice bars** Page **57** • On almost every street corner in Cairo, you can quench your thirst with whatever's in season, freshly pressed: from oranges and mangoes to strawberries and sugar cane.

07 **Abydos** Page **326** • One of the most ancient cult-centres in Egypt, its mortuary temple of Seti I contains magnificent bas-reliefs, the finest to have survived from the New Kingdom.

08 **The Pyramids of Giza** Page **212** •
The world's most famous monuments
have inspired scholarly and crackpot specu-
lations for centuries.

09 **Street food** Page **55** • Street snacks
such as *taamiya*, *kushari* and *fuul* are
tasty, cheap and nourishing.

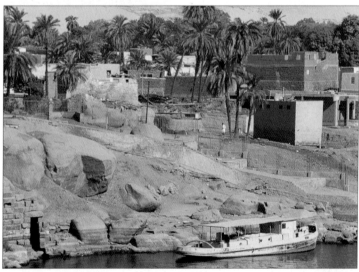

10 **Aswan** Page **434** • Egypt's gateway to Nubia since ancient times, Aswan's islands,
bazaars and riverside restaurants can keep you happy for days, even without visiting
Philae or Abu Simbel.

11 **Diving and snorkelling** Pages **683**, **690**, **758** & **760** • Amazing coral reefs, tropical fish and sunken wrecks make the Red Sea a paradise for scuba divers. All the resorts offer day-trips and longer diving safaris or "liveaboards", plus training courses to suit total novices or experienced divers – while snorkelling is so easy that you don't need any tuition at all to explore the ravishing coral gardens of Sinai.

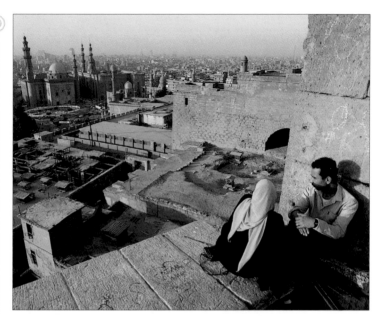

12 **Islamic Cairo** Page **132** • City of a thousand minarets, teeming with life, and chock-full of architectural masterpieces and historic monuments. Head for Khan el-Khalili bazaar, or the Citadel.

13 **Jeep or camel safaris** Pages **487**, **520**, **550** & **725** • Make tracks into the canyons of Sinai or the dunes of the Western Desert – overnight trips or major expeditions are easily arranged.

14 **Textiles and clothes** Pages **220**, **324**, **443** & **569** • Kerdassa and Harraniyya outside Cairo, Akhmim, Luxor and Aswan in the Nile Valley, Siwa and Bahariya oases and the Sinai Bedouin, each have their own styles and products – from camel-hair carpets to silk scarves.

15 **The Egyptian Antiquities Museum** Page **108** • Tutankhamun's treasures, monumental statues from the Old Kingdom and the Amarna era, and a dozen royal mummies are only some of the highlights of this amazing collection.

16 **Jewellery** Pages **262**, **362** & **569** • There's an endless choice of pharaonic, classical, Islamic and contemporary designs in the bazaars of Cairo, Luxor and Aswan, and oases such as Siwa.

17 **Na'ama Bay** Page **698** • Egypt's premier resort, teeming with bars, clubs and luxury hotels, with magnificent coral gardens nearby.

18 **Karkaday** Pages **57** & **444** • This infusion of hibiscus flowers makes a delicious hot or cold drink with medicinal properties. The flowers are graded by quality in Aswan's bazaar.

19 **Catacombs of Kom es-Shoqafa** Page **603** • The spookiest tombs in Egypt, located beneath the Karmous quarter of Alexandria, their bizarre fusion of pharaonic, Greek and Roman funerary motifs reflects the city's ancient diversity of cultures.

20 **Red Sea monasteries** Page **745** • Deep in the desert, the monasteries of St Anthony and St Paul are the oldest in Egypt – if not the world – dating back to the dawn of Christian monasticism.

21 **Feluccas** Pages **362**, **454** & **457** • Spend an afternoon sailing to Sehel or Banana island, or embark on a two- or three-day journey upriver from Aswan, visiting the temples at Kom Ombo and Edfu.

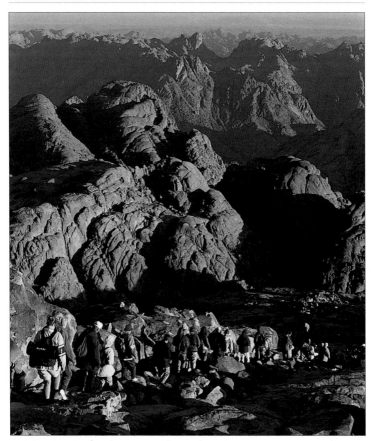

22 **Mount Sinai** Page **730** • This awesome peak is revered as the site where Moses received the Ten Commandments from God.

23 **Dahab** Page **707** • Sinai chill-out zone, renowned for its diving and laid-back beach cafés. Also a base for camel and jeep safaris into the rugged interior.

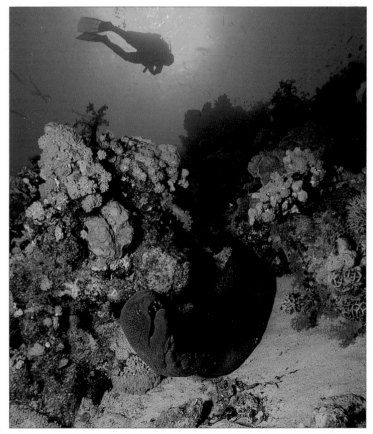

24 **Ras Mohammed** Page **690** • Egypt's oldest marine nature park boasts spectacular shark reefs and the wreck of the *Dunraven*.

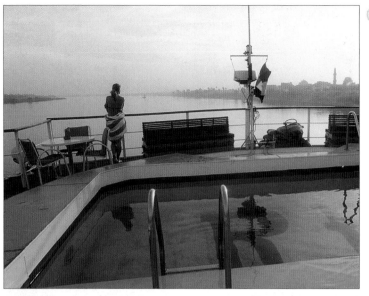

25 **Nile cruises** Pages **50** & **456** • Enjoy the river's scenery from a sundeck with a pool and bar at hand, delicious meals, and excursions to the temples each day.

26 **Karnak Temple** Page **366** • Dedicated to the Theban Triad of Amun, Mut and Khonsu, this vast complex reached its zenith during the New Kingdom.

27 **Oases** Pages **561**, **529**, **510** & **521** • Explore the palm groves, hot springs and medieval *qasrs* of Siwa, Dakhla, Bahariya and Farafra – ancient oases that are embracing modernity in their own way.

29 **Alexandria** Page **582** • With the ruins of Cleopatra's Palace and the Pharos lighthouse emerging from the seabed, and its dazzling new library, the Mediterranean port city founded by Alexander the Great is making waves again.

28 **Seafood** Pages **56**, **608** & **695** • The Mediterranean and Red seas and the River Nile yield a rich harvest of sea bass, lobster, prawns, squid and other delicacies. At many restaurants diners choose for themselves before it's grilled and served at your table.

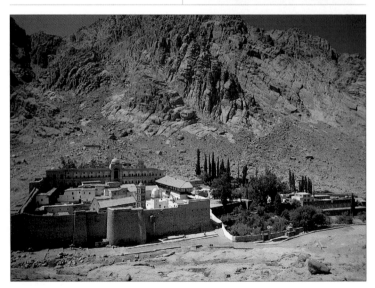

30 **St Catherine's Monastery** Page **726** • Secluded beneath Mount Sinai, St Catherine's harbours the burning bush that appeared to Moses, and other holy relics.

Contents

Using this Rough Guide

We've tried to make this Rough Guide a good read and easy to use. The book is divided into five main sections, and you should be able to find whatever you want in one of them.

Colour section

The front colour section offers a quick tour of Egypt. The **introduction** aims to give you a feel for the place, with suggestions on where to go. We also tell you what the weather is like and include a basic country fact file. Next, our authors round up their favourite aspects of Egypt in the **things not to miss** section – whether it's great food, amazing sights or a special hotel. Right after this comes a full **contents** list.

Basics

The Basics section covers all the **pre-departure** nitty-gritty to help you plan your trip. This is where to find out which airlines fly to your destination, what paperwork you'll need, what to do about money and insurance, about Internet access, food, security, public transport, car rental – in fact just about every piece of **general practical information** you might need.

Guide

This is the heart of the Rough Guide, divided into user-friendly chapters, each of which covers a specific region. Every chapter starts with a list of **highlights** and an **introduction** that helps you to decide where to go, depending on your time and budget. Likewise, introductions to the various towns and smaller regions within each chapter should help you plan your itinerary. We start most town accounts with information on arrival and accommodation, followed by a tour of the sights, and finally reviews of places to eat and drink, and details of nightlife. Longer accounts also have a directory of practical listings. Each chapter concludes with **public transport** details for that region.

Contexts

Read Contexts to get a deeper understanding of what makes Egypt tick. We include a brief history, a monumental chronology, articles about **Islam** and **Egyptian music**, and a detailed further reading section that reviews dozens of **books** relating to the country.

Language

The **language** section gives useful guidance for speaking Egyptian Arabic and pulls together all the vocabulary you might need on your trip, including a comprehensive menu reader. Here you'll also find a glossary of words and terms peculiar to the country.

Index + small print

Apart from a **full index**, which includes maps as well as places, this section covers publishing information, credits and acknowledgements, and also has our contact details in case you want to send in updates and corrections to the book – or suggestions as to how we might improve it.

Map and chapter list

Contents

Colour section

Basics

The Guide

Contexts

781–833

Language

835–846

Index and small print

847–858

Map symbols

maps are listed in the full index using coloured text

	Railway		⛏	Checkpoint
	Main road		★	Transport stop
	Minor road		Ⓜ	Metro station
- - - - -	Footpath/ track		◉	Hotel
= = = = =	Tunnel		ℂ	Telephone
	River		✉	Post office
– – –	Chapter division boundary		ⓘ	Information point
▬ ▬ ▪	International boundary		@	Internet access
⋔⋔⋔	Cliff face/ escarpment		⊞	Hospital
	Beach/ dunes		P	Parking
☾	Crescent dune			Building
✈	Airport		⊣	Church
⍦	Oasis/palm grove		⛪	Monastery/ convent
⚊	Spring		⊤	Christian cemetery
⚭	Viewpoint		✡	Synagogue
⬦	Point of interest		☾	Mosque
⌒	Mountain range			Muslim cemetery
▲	Mountain peak			Park/national park
☼	Crater			Farmland
◁	Pyramid			Delta
⌂	Cave			Saltpan
⊞	Temple			Coral reef
	Tomb			
✂	Battlefield			
⛽	Garage/ fuel station			

7

Basics

Basics

Getting there

Although it is possible to get to Egypt by land via Israel or Jordan, most visitors will want to fly. As a major air hub, Cairo is well served by international airlines, with direct scheduled flights from London and New York, and a large choice of indirect routes from pretty much anywhere. From the UK, major tourist resorts are also served by charter flights.

Airfares vary with the **season**: they are highest from June until the end of August, drop during the "shoulder" seasons – April, May, September and October – and you'll get the best prices during the low season, November to March (excluding Christmas and New Year, when prices are hiked up and seats are at a premium). Note also that flying at weekends can add as much as US$60/£40 to the round-trip fare; price ranges quoted below are for the cheapest round-trip tickets including airport departure tax, and assume midweek travel. Many of them will be subject to restrictions such as fixed dates, which cannot be changed once the ticket is booked, and some may require advance purchase (Apex tickets for example must be bought at least a week in advance).

You can often cut costs by going through a **specialist flight agent** – either a consolidator, who buys up blocks of tickets from the airlines and sells them at a discount, or a **discount agent**, who in addition to dealing with discounted flights may also offer special student and youth fares and a range of other travel-related services such as travel insurance, rail passes, car rentals, tours and the like. Some agents specialize in **charter flights**, which may be cheaper than anything available on a scheduled flight, but again departure dates are fixed and withdrawal penalties are high. You may even find it cheaper to pick up a bargain **package deal** to Luxor from one of the tour operators listed on pp.15–16.

Unfortunately, the likelihood of finding a **courier flight** (where you shepherd a parcel through customs in exchange for a heavily discounted ticket) is virtually nil for travel to Egypt. However, if Egypt is only one stop on a longer journey, you might want to consider buying a **Round-the-World (RTW) ticket**. Cairo is unlikely to feature on the cheaper "off-the-shelf" RTW itineraries offered by some agents, but can be visited on RTW mileage tickets issued by the airline consortiums Star Alliance and One World Alliance.

Booking flights online

Many airlines and discount travel websites offer you the opportunity to book your tickets online, cutting out the costs of agents and middlemen. Good deals can often be found through discount or auction sites, as well as through the airlines' own websites.

Online booking agents and general travel sites

Ⓦ **www.etn.nl/discount.htm** International hub for online consolidators, discount agents and bucket shops, maintained by the non-profit European Travel Network.

Ⓦ **www.geocities.com/Thavery2000** Has an extensive list of airline toll-free numbers.

Ⓦ **www.flyaow.com** Online air travel info and reservations site.

Ⓦ **www.smilinjack.com/airlines.htm** Lists an up-to-date compilation of airline website addresses.

Ⓦ **travel.yahoo.com** Incorporates a lot of Rough Guide material in its coverage of destination countries and cities across the world, with information about places to eat, sleep, etc.

Ⓦ **www.airfares.co.uk** Easy-to-use flight search, with online booking from Britain and Ireland only, plus city breaks and car rental.

Ⓦ **www.cheaptickets.com** Discount flight specialists.

Ⓦ **www.cheapflights.com** Bookings from Britain and Ireland only. Flight deals, travel agents, plus links to other travel sites.

Ⓦ **www.lastminute.com** Bookings from the UK only. Offers good last-minute holiday package and flight-only deals.

Ⓦ **www.expedia.com** Discount airfares, all-airline search engine and daily deals.

Ⓦ **www.travelocity.com** Destination guides, hot web fares and best deals for car rental, accommodation and lodging as well as fares. Provides access to the travel agent system SABRE, the most comprehensive central reservations system in the US.

Ⓦ **www.hotwire.com** Bookings from the US only. Last-minute savings of up to forty percent on regular published fares. Travellers must be at least eighteen and there are no refunds, transfers or changes allowed. Log-in required.

Ⓦ **www.priceline.com** Name-your-own-price website that has deals at around forty percent off standard fares. You cannot specify flight times (although you do specify dates) and the tickets are non-refundable, non-transferable and non-changeable.

Ⓦ **www.skyauction.com** Bookings from the US only. Auctions tickets and travel packages using a "second bid" scheme. The best strategy is to bid the maximum you're willing to pay, since if you win you'll pay just enough to beat the runner-up regardless of your maximum bid.

Ⓦ **www.travelshop.com.au** Australian website offering discounted flights, packages, insurance and online bookings.

Flights from Britain and Ireland

From London, there are regular direct scheduled flights to Cairo, Alexandria and Luxor, and highly competitive charters to Luxor, Hurghada (Red Sea) and Sharm el-Sheikh (Sinai). At the time of writing, there are no direct flights to Egypt from elsewhere in the UK or Ireland: you can either make your own way to London and fly from there, or take an indirect flight changing at London, Amsterdam, Paris or Frankfurt.

Flying direct to Cairo from London, you have a choice of **scheduled flights** on EgyptAir or British Airways, both of which fly daily from Heathrow. Fares vary according to the time of year (the most expensive being around Christmas) but depend more on the type of ticket – flexibility and duration being the main factors. BA currently charges £376 for a low-season return flight to Cairo (fixed-date, no advance purchase required), rising to £410 in high season, although discount agents may sell the same ticket for less. BA

also flies twice weekly to Alexandria. EgyptAir charges from £340 year-round for a similar ticket, and offers weekly direct flights to Luxor for £320. EgyptAir flights have in the past served Manchester, but do not currently do so. Sudan Airways stops at Cairo once a week on the way from London to Khartoum, but its tickets are more expensive, and standards of service somewhat lower.

Most other major **European airlines** can sell you flights to Egypt (almost always Cairo) travelling via their own "home" airport on the Continent. Standards vary enormously, from classy KLM to tatty TAROM, with most of the others somewhere in between. At the top end of the scale, prices are much the same as those of BA; at the other end you can pay well under £300 for a fixed-date or advance-purchase ticket. KLM tends to be pricey, but offers flights from a large number of **British airports outside London**, beaten only by BA. Lufthansa also offers flights from several British airports and serves Alexandria as well as Cairo. In addition, Air France, Austrian, Czech Airlines, Cyprus Airways, El Al and Swiss fly from Manchester; Air France, Cyprus and Swiss from Birmingham (though with a long wait at Larnaca airport in the last case); and Swiss from Edinburgh.

If a foreign airline flies via somewhere interesting, consider breaking the journey for a **stopover** there; if not, you'll want to spend as little time as possible in the airport (Bucharest is the worst) – a factor that might determine your choice of airline. Czech Airlines, Malev and Air Malta may offer the choice of a stopover in Prague, Budapest or Valetta respectively, and are also often the cheapest airlines from London to Cairo.

You'll generally get the best deals on flights through **discount agencies** or student/youth travel specialists like **STA Travel** (with a dedicated Africa desk at its London Euston Road branch), which offers return flights to Cairo from £224 year-round.

It's also possible to get flight-only deals on **charter flights** – often for less than £250. Another advantage is that they fly direct to destinations other than Cairo – to Luxor, Hurghada or Sharm el-Sheikh – and may depart from regional airports as well as from London. Various operators offer special one-off flight deals: check out Kuoni, Hayes and Jarvis, Thomas Cook and Libra Holidays (see p.15 for addresses). At present, the cheapest flight-only deals to Sharm el-Sheikh are offered by the dive companies; these are usually not advertised, so approach the company direct.

In addition to the recommended discount agents listed below, useful **sources for finding a flight** are classified advertisements in the travel sections of newspapers like *The Independent* and *The Guardian* (Saturday editions), *The Sunday Times* or – in London – *Time Out* and *The Evening Standard*. Bargains are also advertised on Teletext and the Internet, and high-street travel agents are worth checking for deals on package holidays and charter flights.

From **Ireland**, there are no direct flights to Egypt; the best option is to book a flight or package departing from Britain – either through your local travel agent or via the Internet – and get there on a budget flight. Return fares Dublin–London cost €38–250; Ryanair is usually the cheapest, but flies only to Stansted, Luton and Gatwick, leaving you with a two- to three-hour journey to Heathrow if your onward connection is from there. Aer Lingus, British Midland and British Airways cost a bit more but fly straight in to Heathrow, and BA will fly you on to Cairo for a total of €540–1000. Alternatively, Air France will take you from Dublin to Cairo via Paris for €613–727, and Lufthansa can get you there via Frankfurt for €1014–1114. Aer Lingus can also fly you from Dublin or Cork to Amsterdam for an onward connection with KLM. It is also possible to get there from Shannon with Royal Jordanian. From **Belfast**, your best bet is with BA via London (£444–478). These fares apply to tickets bought direct from the airlines, but will of course be cheaper from discount agents such as UsitNOW.

If you're pushed for time, or want to make things easier, buying a **package holiday** makes a lot of sense. There are still some amazing bargains to be had amongst the basic Luxor-plus-Cairo or Luxor-only packages. Besides these, many smaller independent operators feature felucca trips on the Nile, diving holidays on the Red Sea, or camel trekking in Sinai.

Airlines

Aer Lingus Ireland ☎01/886 8888, ⓦwww.aerlingus.ie. Several flights a day from Dublin, Shannon and Cork to London, and daily flights from Dublin and Cork to Amsterdam, for onward connections to Cairo.

Air France UK ☎0845/084 5111, Ireland ☎01/605 0383, ⓦwww.airfrance.co.uk. London, Dublin, Birmingham and Manchester to Cairo via Paris.

Air Malta UK ☎0845/607 3710, ⓦwww.airmalta.com. London to Cairo via Malta.

Alitalia UK ☎0870/5448 259, Ireland ☎01/677 5171, ⓦwww.alitalia.it. London and Dublin to Cairo via Rome or Milan.

Austrian Airlines UK ☎0845/601 0948, ⓦwww.aua.com. London and Manchester to Cairo via Vienna. Also from Dublin with a stopover in Vienna.

Balkan Airlines UK ☎020/7637 7637, ⓦwww.balkan.com. London to Cairo via Sofia. Cairo service temporarily suspended at last check but reinstatement expected.

British Airways UK ☎0845/7733 377, Ireland ☎1800/626 747, ⓦwww.britishairways.com. London to Cairo direct daily; London to Alexandria direct twice weekly.

British Midland UK ☎0870/607 0555, Ireland ☎01/407 3036, ⓦwww.flybmi.com. Flights from most British and Irish airports to London for onward connections to Cairo.

ČSA Czech Airlines London ☎020/7255 1898, Manchester ☎0161/498 8840, Dublin ☎01/814 4626, ⓦwww.csa.cz/en. London, Dublin and Manchester to Cairo via Prague.

Cyprus Airways UK ☎020/8359 1333, ⓦwww.cyprusairways.com. London, Birmingham and Manchester to Cairo via Larnaca.

EgyptAir UK ☎020/7734 2343 or 7734 2395, Ireland ☎01/370 011, ⓦwww.egyptair.com.eg. London to Cairo direct daily; London to Luxor direct once weekly. No alcohol served on flights, though if you take your own they'll supply mixers.

El Al UK ☎020/7957 4100, Ireland ☎ 01/670 4731, ⓦwww.elal.co.il. London, Manchester and Dublin to Cairo via Tel Aviv.

KLM UK ☎0870/507 4074, ⓦwww.klmuk.com. London (Heathrow, Stansted and City), Dublin, Aberdeen, Birmingham, Bristol, Cardiff, Edinburgh, Glasgow, Humberside, Leeds/Bradford, Manchester, Newcastle, Norwich and Teesside to Cairo via Amsterdam.

Lufthansa UK ☎0845/7737 747, Ireland ☎01/844 5544, ⓦwww.lufthansa.com. London,

Dublin, Birmingham, Edinburgh and Manchester to Cairo and Alexandria via Frankfurt.

Malév UK ☎020/7439 0577, ⓦwww.malev.hu. London, Dublin and Manchester to Cairo via Budapest. One of the better Eastern European airlines.

Olympic Airways UK ☎0870/606 0460, ⓦwww.olympic-airways.co.uk. London to Cairo via Athens.

Royal Jordanian UK ☎020/7878 6300, Ireland ☎061/712 871, ⓦwww.rja.com.jo. London and Shannon to Cairo via Amman.

Ryanair UK ☎0870/156 9569, Ireland ☎01/609 7800, ⓦwww.ryanair.com. Budget flights to London Stansted from many British and Irish airports; also from Dublin to London Gatwick and Luton.

Saudi Arabian Airlines UK ☎020/8995 7777, ⓦwww.saudiairlines.com. London to Cairo via Jeddah or Riyadh.

Sudan Airways UK ☎020/7631 3373, ⓦwww.sudanair.com. London to Cairo direct weekly.

Swiss Air Lines UK ☎0845/601 0956, Ireland ☎1890/200515, ⓦwww.swissairlines.com. London, Birmingham, Edinburgh and Manchester to Cairo via Zurich. Also from Dublin with a stopover in Zurich.

Syrian Arab Airlines UK ☎020/7493 2851, ⓦsyriaonline.com/syrair. London to Cairo via Damascus.

Tarom Romanian Airlines UK ☎020/7224 3693, ⓦtarom.digirow.net. London to Cairo via Bucharest. Unpredictable, with awful food and one of the worst airports in Europe, but sometimes offers rock-bottom prices.

Tunis Air UK ☎020/7734 7644, ⓦwww.tunisair.com.tn. London to Cairo via Tunis.

Turkish Airlines UK ☎020/7766 9300, ⓦwww.turkishairlines.com. London to Cairo via Istanbul.

Flight and travel agents

Airline Network ☎0870/241 0011, ⓦwww.airnet.co.uk. Discount flight consolidator.

Aran Travel International Ireland ☎091/562 595, ⓦhomepages.iol.ie/~arantvl/aranmain.htm. Good-value flights.

Bridge the World UK ☎020/7911 0900, ⓦwww.bridgetheworld.com. Specializing in round-the-world tickets, with good deals aimed at the backpacker market.

CIE Tours International Ireland ☎01/703 1888, ⓦwww.cietours.ie. General flight and tour agent.

Flightline Essex ☎0800/036 0777, ⓦwww.flightline.co.uk. Telephone and Internet discount flights consolidator.

International Flights UK ☎020/7631 1840. Flight consolidator.

Joe Walsh Tours Ireland ☎01/872 2555 or ☎021/427 7959, ⓦwww.joewalshtours.ie. General budget fares agent.

Lee Travel Ireland ☎021/277 111, ⓦwww.leetravel.ie. Flights and holidays worldwide.

McCarthy's Travel Ireland ☎021/427 0127, ⓦwww.mccarthystravel.ie. General flight agent.

North South Travel UK ☎ & ☎01245/608 291, ⓦwww.northsouthtravel.co.uk. Friendly, competitive travel agency, offering discounted fares worldwide – profits are used to support projects in the developing world, especially the promotion of sustainable tourism.

Soliman Travel 113 Earls Court Rd, London SW5 9RL ☎020/7370 5159, ⓦwww.solimantravel.co.uk. Well-established flight consolidators for scheduled flights, and also charters.

STA Travel UK ☎0870/160 6070, London ☎020/7361 6148, Bristol ☎0117/929 4399, Edinburgh ☎0131/226 7747, Glasgow ☎0141/338 6000, Leeds ☎0113/244 9212, Liverpool ☎0151/707 1123, Manchester ☎0161/834 0668, Newcastle ☎0191/233 2111, ⓦwww.statravel.co.uk. Worldwide specialists in low-cost flights and tours for students and under-26s, though other customers welcome. Branches on university campuses and in town centres throughout the country.

Top Deck UK ☎020/7370 4555, ⓦwww.topdecktravel.co.uk. Long-established agent dealing in discount flights.

Trailfinders UK ☎020/7628 7628, ⓦwww.trailfinders.com, Ireland ☎01/677 7888, ⓦwww.trailfinders.ie. One of the best-informed and most efficient agents for independent travellers; produce a very useful quarterly magazine worth scrutinizing for round-the-world routes.

Travel CUTS UK ☎020/7255 2082, ⓦwww.travelcuts.co.uk. British branch of Canada's main youth and student travel specialist.

usitNOW Ireland ☎01/602 1600, Northern Ireland ☎028/9032 7111, ⓦwww.usitnow.ie. Ireland's main student and youth travel specialists.

Package tours

Tour operators to Egypt come in many shapes and sizes. **Mainstream operators** offer traditional tours and cruises, as well as flight-plus-hotel packages to Luxor, Aswan and elsewhere which can cost little more than a flight – for example, seven nights in Luxor for around £350 (often less if booked at the last minute) – and share the same advantage of varied departure and destination points. Again, check the websites and newspapers listed below.

Other tour operators include small, independent **adventure holiday companies** priding themselves on modest-sized groups, adventurous itineraries or special interest activities – for all of which Egypt offers a lot of scope; and **diving holiday specialists**, who arrange trips to the Red Sea centres around Hurghada or Sharm el-Sheikh, usually inclusive of rental equipment and dives. All **prices quoted** below are inclusive of flights, unless otherwise stated.

Tour operators

Mainstream operators

Abercrombie & Kent UK ☎020/7730 9600, ⓦwww.abercrombiekent.co.uk. Upmarket firm with a number of Egypt tours including some led by Egyptologists; also creates custom packages.

Bales Worldwide UK ☎0870/241 3208 or 241 3212 (for tailor-made trips), ⓦwww.balesworldwide.com. Does nine- to fourteen-day Nile cruises (£895–2420); also nine-day (£799–1295) and fifteen-day (£795–1395) tours based in first-class hotels in Cairo, Luxor and Aswan.

British Airways Holidays UK ☎0870/242 4245, ⓦwww.baholidays.co.uk. Packages include seven nights in Luxor from £455, seven-day Nile cruises from £649, five-night city breaks in Cairo from £539, and a two-centre Cairo–Alexandria combination from £655.

Contiki UK ☎020/8290 6777, ⓦwww.contiki.com. Nine-day Egypt tours for 18–35-year-olds from £699 plus air fare.

Discover Egypt UK ☎ 020/7407 2111, ⓦwww.discoveregypt.co.uk. Charter flights, including "open-jaw" (flying into one airport and out from another), and tailor-made itineraries featuring Nile cruises and multi-centre holidays. Deals include a seven-night Essential Egypt tour from £659 and a ten-night Classic Egypt tour from £799.

Hayes & Jarvis UK ☎0870/898 9890, ⓦwww.hayes-jarvis.com. Mostly one-base hotel packages in Luxor (from £495) or on the beach at Dahab, Sharm or Hurghada (from £435); also two-centre holidays, and Nile cruises from £625.

Kuoni Travel UK ☎01306/742 888, ⓦwww.kuoni.co.uk. Experienced operator offering a wide variety of packages, including Nile cruises from £598, Cairo–Alexandria two-centre combinations from

£427, a week in Luxor from £359, in Hurghada from £525, or in Sharm el-Sheikh from £419 (with a three-day add-on to Petra from £320).

Libra Holidays UK ☎0870/241 1527, ⓦwww.libraholidays.co.uk. Seven nights in Luxor (from £399), Aswan (£698), Sharm el-Sheikh (£438), Hurghada (£299), or cruising the Nile (£599) in the Goldenjoy Worldwide brochure. Diving holidays at Sharm el-Sheikh or Hurghada are in the Goldenjoy Diving brochure.

Peltours UK ☎020/8343 0590, ⓦwww.peltours.com. Does a deluxe seven-day Cairo/Nile cruise package from £1199, four days in Cairo for £522 or seven days for £607. Also offers seven days in Taba Heights with weekly direct charter from £399.

Soliman Travel UK ☎020/7370 5159, ⓦwww.solimantravel.co.uk. One of the longest-established tour operators with a large range of packages and tailor-mades mainly in five-star accommodation. Nile cruises from £792; seven nights in Luxor from £499; seven-night diving holidays in Hurghada or Sharm el-Sheikh from £750 not including dive courses; and three-night city breaks to Alex or Cairo from £379.

Somak Holidays UK ☎020/8423 3000, ⓦwww.somak.co.uk. Offers five-night city breaks in Cairo from £619, a seven-night Luxor package from £619, seven nights in Hurghada from £799, and Nile cruises from £739.

Swan Hellenic UK ☎020/7800 2200, ⓦwww.swanhellenic.com. Upmarket cruises that include Egypt as part of an itinerary called "Spring in the Holy Land"; cruise takes in Cairo, Luxor and Aswan, as well as Petra and Jerusalem (from £3725).

Thomas Cook UK ☎01733/417 000, Ireland ☎01/677 1363, ⓦwww.thomascook.com. Thomas Cook more or less created tourism in Egypt with his first escorted tour in 1869, and the country remains a speciality. It offers a week in Luxor from £459, eight-day Nile cruises (from £739), four days in Cairo (from £439), or twin-centre deals featuring Aswan and Sharm el-Sheikh or Cairo and Hurghada.

Thomson UK ☎0870/550 2575. Reputable high-street tour operator offering two weeks in Hurghada from £625, a week in Luxor for £355, a week in Sharm from £539 (with add-ons for diving such as £200 for a 5-day PADI Open Water Course), and Nile cruises from £629 with the option of a seven-day add-on in Luxor from £809 for the whole package.

Tradewinds UK ☎0870/751 0003, ⓦwww.tradewinds.co.uk. Long-haul package specialist offering four-night Cairo city breaks from £519, a week in Luxor from £429, or Nile cruises from £699.

Travelscene UK ☎0870/777 4445,
Ⓦwww.travelscene.co.uk. City breaks in Cairo from £408 for three nights or £460 for five, or a week in Luxor from £478.

Voyages Jules Verne UK ☎020/7616 1000, Ⓦwww.vjv.co.uk. An interesting selection of upmarket holidays, including a seven-night cruise from Aswan to Abu Simbel from £675, four-night Cairo city breaks from £495, and eleven nights in Cairo, Sinai and Petra from £745.

Adventure and specialist tours

Adventures Abroad UK ☎0114/247 3400, Ⓦwww.adventures-abroad.com. Canadian-based company offering small group tours to Egypt or combined with Israel, Jordan, Syria, etc. Activities include camel rides, trekking and felucca cruises.

Ancient World Tours UK ☎ 01903/810 443, Ⓦwww.ancient.co.uk. In-depth archeological and historical tours led by experts (tour leaders have included David Rohl – see p.783). Include organized tours that take in Tel ed-Daba (Avaris), a site in the Delta as yet closed to the general public.

Exodus UK ☎020/8675 5550, Ireland ☎01/677 1029, Ⓦwww.exodus.co.uk. Its fourteen-day "Egyptian Discoverer" tour features a Nile cruise from Aswan to Luxor, a day in Hurghada and two nights in Cairo (from £749 plus flights and local charges of US$100), and they also offer a nine-day trip including three days on a felucca (from £579 plus flights and US$50), or a sixteen-day overland tour of Egypt, Jordan, Syria and Lebanon (from £1095 plus flights and US$125). Can also book Gecko's adventure tours (see p.21).

Explore Worldwide UK ☎01252/760 000, Ireland ☎01/677 9479, Ⓦwww.explore.co.uk. Highly respected small-groups operator with several Egyptian programmes, including a fifteen-day Nile Valley and Red Sea tour with four days on a felucca (from £745), a sixteen-day tour of the Nile and Western Desert (from £640), or sixteen days in the Nile Valley and Siwa (from £795). Prices include flights.

Guerba Expeditions UK ☎01373/826 611, Ⓦwww.guerba.co.uk. Long-established Africa-overland experts with a variety of Egyptian tours, such as nine days in Cairo, Luxor and Aswan from £515/€850, and a fourteen-day "Nile and Beyond" tour that includes a camel safari in Sinai, from £600/€990. Online bookings can be made from Britain, Ireland, Europe, North America and Australasia. Prices do not include flights.

Imaginative Traveller UK ☎020/8742 8612, Ⓦwww.imaginative-traveller.com. Offers 25 tours of Egypt, including fourteen-day Nile Valley and Red Sea trips (from £350/€1050); eight days in

Alexandria and Siwa Oasis (from £295/€495); and eight-day dive packages at Dahab and Hurghada (from £265/€445for divers, or £395/€665). Online bookings can be made from Britain, Ireland, Europe, North America and Australasia. Prices do not include flights.

Swim with Dolphins Ⓦwww.dolphinswims.co.uk. Swimming with dolphins at Nuweiba (from £440 for seven nights), Sinai desert adventure safaris (from £450 for seven days). Prices do not include flights.

Top Deck Travel UK ☎020/7370 4555, Ⓦwww.topdecktravel.co.uk. Youth-oriented tours favoured by Australians and New Zealanders include the fifteen-day felucca, Red Sea and Sinai "Pharaoh's Footsteps", from £454 (excluding flight), or eight days' diving at Sharm or Hurghada from £324 (excluding flight), or £504 including a diving course.

Dive holiday companies

Crusader Travel UK ☎020/8892 7606, Ⓦwww.crusadertravel.com. Experienced, specialist agent for diving holidays, which helps clients shop around the tour operators. Also does flight-only charter deals to Sharm, Hurghada or Luxor for £269–279.

Explorer Tours UK ☎01753/681 999, Ⓦwww.explorers.co.uk. Red Sea holidays with PADI courses from £425 including flight.

Oonasdivers UK ☎01323/648 924, Ⓦwww.oonasdivers.com. PADI courses (£525 for a package including flight and six dives, plus £120 for an open water course) and Red Sea safaris (from £595).

Regal Holidays UK ☎0870/220 1777, Ⓦwww.regal-diving.co.uk. Various dive packages at Hurghada, Safaga, Sharm el-Sheikh and other bases with a selection including courses for everyone from beginners to advanced, plus mini-safari add-ons and wreck trips. Seven nights in Sharm B&B costs from £359 including flight, plus £175 for a five-day PADI open water course including equipment rental.

Scubasnacks UK ☎0870/746 1266, Ⓦwww.scuba-diving-safaris.co.uk. Seven-day packages based at Dahab, Hurghada or Sharm el-Sheikh from £329 for flight and hotel, plus around £190 for a 5-day PADI open water course. Cheaper special offers are sometimes available, and there are also "liveaboard" diving holidays based on a boat in the Red Sea.

Flights from the US and Canada

The volume of North American travellers to Egypt is not great, and this is reflected in a relative dearth of flights. Only EgyptAir flies direct: failing that, you'll have to change planes somewhere on the way. North American travel agents can arrange flights with no problem, or – if you're heading to London – you can arrange connections yourself (see "Flights from Britain and Ireland" pp.12–14). If you are flying to Israel or Jordan to enter Egypt from there, see pp.23–25 for information on how to move on to Egypt.

EgyptAir flies to Cairo three times weekly from **New York** (11hr). Official round-trip fares (instant purchase, non-refundable) start at US$850 in the low season (winter), rising to US$1490 in the high season (summer). Failing that, a number of European and Middle Eastern airlines serve Cairo, offering a much wider range of departure points to choose from, though New York still offers by far the biggest choice of airlines. From the **West Coast**, several airlines serve LA, but only British Airways and Northwest/KLM fly from San Francisco, British Airways alone from Seattle. Ticket prices with most airlines are much the same as the fare for a direct flight from New York. Flights are routed via the airlines' hub cities, so you should check that you won't have to wait overnight for your onward connection. By shopping around discount agents and flight consolidators, you should be able to pick up a round-trip ticket for as little as US$775 in low season, US$915 high season.

From **Canada** there are currently no direct flights to Cairo, but many of the European carriers operate services via their hub cities from Toronto and Montreal (from around CDN$2000 in low season, CDN$2300 in high season). Vancouver is served by British Airways via London and Lufthansa via Frankfurt. Both BA and Lufthansa also offer flights to Alexandria, and Air Canada offers through tickets from Calgary and Edmonton, connecting with Lufthansa flights at Frankfurt.

Airlines

Air Canada ☎1-888/247-2262, ⓦwww.aircanada.ca. Flights from Calgary, Edmonton, Montreal, Toronto, Vancouver and most Canadian cities to Cairo and Alexandria via Frankfurt in combination with Lufthansa.
Air France US ☎1-800/237-2747, Canada ☎1-800/667-2747, ⓦwww.airfrance.com. Atlanta,

Boston, Chicago, Cincinnati, LA, Montreal, New York and Toronto to Cairo via Paris.
Alitalia US ☎1-800/223-5730, Canada ☎1-800/361-8336, ⓦwww.alitalia.com. Atlanta, Boston, Chicago, Miami, New York and Toronto to Cairo via Milan or Rome.
Austrian Airlines ☎1-800/843-0002, ⓦwww.aua.com. Montreal, New York and Washington DC to Cairo with an overnight stay in Vienna.
Balkan Airlines ☎1-800/852-0944, ⓦwww.balkanair.com. Cairo service suspended at last check but reinstatement expected.
British Airways ☎1-800/247-9297, ⓦwww.british-airways.com. Boston, Detroit, LA, Miami, Montreal, New York, Philadelphia, San Francisco, Seattle, Toronto, Vancouver and Washington DC to Cairo via London Heathrow. Flights from Atlanta, Baltimore, Charlotte, Dallas/Fort Worth, Denver, Houston, Orlando and San Diego involve changing airports in London, and flights from all of those plus Detroit involve either stopping over in London or a second change at New York on the way back.
Czech Airlines US ☎1-877/359-6629 or 212/765-6022, Canada ☎416/363-3174, ⓦwww.czechairlines.com. Montreal, New York and Toronto to Cairo via Prague.
Delta US ☎1-800/241-4141, Canada ☎1-800/221-1212, ⓦwww.delta.com. Atlanta, Boston, Chicago, Cincinnati, LA, Miami, New York, San Francisco and Washington DC to Cairo via Paris in conjunction with Air France. Connections from most US airports with a change at one of Delta's hubs.
EgyptAir US ☎1-800/334-6787 or 212/315-0900, Canada ☎416/960-0009, ⓦwww.egyptair.com.eg. Montreal and New York to Cairo direct three times weekly.
El Al ☎1-800/223-6700, ⓦwww.elal.com. Chicago, LA, Miami, New York and Toronto to Cairo via Tel Aviv.
Iberia ☎1-800/772-4642, ⓦwww.iberia.com. Chicago, New York and Miami to Cairo via Barcelona or Madrid.
Lufthansa US ☎1-800/645-3880, Canada ☎1-800/563-5954, ⓦwww.lufthansa-usa.com. Atlanta, Boston, Chicago, Dallas/Fort Worth, Denver, Detroit, Houston, LA, Miami, New York, Philadelphia, Phoenix, San Francisco, Vancouver and Washington DC to Cairo and Alexandria, and Toronto to Cairo via Frankfurt.
Malev Hungarian Airlines ☎1-800/223-6884 or 212/757-6446, ⓦwww.hungarianairlines.com. New York and Toronto to Cairo via Budapest.
Northwest/KLM ☎1-800/447-4747, ⓦwww.nwa.com. Boston, Chicago, Detroit,

Houston, LA, Memphis, Miami, Montreal, New York, San Francisco, Seattle, Toronto and Washington DC to Cairo via Amsterdam.

Olympic Airways ☎ 1-800/223-1226 or 718/896-7393, ⓦ www.olympic-airways.gr. New York to Cairo via Athens.

Royal Air Maroc ☎ 1-800/344-6726 or 212/750-6071, ⓦ www.royalairmaroc.com. New York to Cairo via Casablanca.

Royal Jordanian ☎ 1-800/223-0470 or 212/949-0050, ⓦ www.rja.com.jo. Chicago and New York to Cairo via Amman.

Swiss Air Lines ☎ 1-800/221-4750, ⓦ www.swissairlines.com. Boston, Chicago, LA, Miami, Montreal, New York and Washington DC to Cairo via Zurich.

Tarom Romanian Air ☎ 212/560-0840, ⓦ tarom.digiro.net/index_en.html. New York to Cairo via Bucharest. Rock-bottom service, but may also offer rock-bottom prices.

Turkish Airlines ☎ 1-800/874-8875, ⓦ www.thy.com. Chicago and New York to Cairo via Istanbul.

United Airlines ☎ 1-800/538-2929, ⓦ www.ual.com. Buffalo, Chicago, Minneapolis/St Paul, Orlando, San Francisco, Washington DC and most American cities to Cairo and Alexandria via Frankfurt in combination with Lufthansa.

Discount travel companies

Air Brokers International ☎ 1-800/883-3273 or 415/397-1383, ⓦ www.airbrokers.com. Consolidator and specialist in round-the-world tickets.

Airtech ☎ 1-877/247-8324 or 212/219-7000, ⓦ www.airtech.com. Standby seat broker; also deals in consolidator fares.

Council Travel US ☎ 1-800/226-8624, ⓦ www.counciltravel.com. Specializes mostly, but not exclusively, in student/budget travel.

Educational Travel Center ☎ 1-800/747-5551 or 608/256-5551, ⓦ www.edtrav.com. Student/youth discount agent.

High Adventure Travel ☎ 1-800/350-0612 or 415/912-5600, ⓦ www.airtreks.com. RTW specialist – its website features an interactive database that lets you build and price your own itinerary.

Now Voyager ☎ 212/459-1616, ⓦ www.nowvoyagertravel.com. Consolidator.

Skylink US ☎ 1-800/247-6659 or 212/573-8980, Canada ☎ 1-800/759-5465, ⓦ www.skylinkus.com. Consolidator.

STA Travel ☎ 1-800/777-0112 or 1-800/781-4040, ⓦ www.sta-travel.com. Specialist in independent travel; also student IDs, travel insurance, car rental, etc.

TFI Tours International ☎ 1-800/745-8000 or 212/736-1140, ⓦ www.lowestairprice.com. Consolidator.

Travac ☎ 1-800/872-8800, ⓦ www.thetravelsite.com. Consolidator and charter broker with offices in New York City and Orlando.

Travelers Advantage ☎ 1-877/259-2691, ⓦ www.travelersadvantage.com. Discount travel club; annual membership fee required (currently US$1 for three months' trial).

Travel Avenue ☎ 1-800/333-3335, ⓦ www.travelavenue.com. Full-service travel agent that offers discounts in the form of rebates.

Travel Cuts Canada ☎ 1-800/667-2887, US ☎ 1-866/246-9762, ⓦ www.travelcuts.com. Canadian student-travel organization specializing in student fares, IDs and other travel services.

UniTravel ☎ 1-800/325-2222 or 314/569-2501, ⓦ www.unitravel.com. Consolidator.

Worldtek Travel ☎ 1-800/243-1723, ⓦ www.worldtek.com. Discount travel agency.

Package holidays

There are many operators offering **packages** to Egypt or customized independent tours. Most package holidays concentrate on Cairo and the Pyramids (often with an experienced Egyptologist as the guide), or a Nile Valley cruise; there are also plenty of others that take in more of the country or offer specialist activities – for example, archeological trips or diving safaris. Check the Sunday travel sections of papers such as the *New York Times* and *Los Angeles Times* for special travel deals.

Tour operators

Mainstream tours

Abercrombie & Kent ☎ 1-800/323-7308 or 630/954-2944, ⓦ www.abercrombiekent.com. Upmarket firm with a number of Egypt tours, some led by Egyptologists, including a fourteen-day "Pharaohs and Pyramids" tour from US$4990 plus air fare, or a twelve-day "Splendors of the Nile" tour from US$3990 plus air fare. Can also create custom packages.

Contiki Tours ☎ 1-888/CONTIKI, ⓦ www.contiki.com. Nine-day Egypt tours for 18–35-year-olds from US$1099/CDN$1659.

Cox & Kings ☎ 1-800/999-1758, ⓦ www.coxandkingsusa.com. Upmarket customized tour operator offering tours such as a twelve-day

"Classical Egypt" package from US$2985 plus air fare.

Esplanade Tours ☎ 1-800/426-5492, ⓦ www.esplanadetours.com. Customized itineraries including city breaks in Cairo, Luxor and Aswan, Nile cruises or tours. A fourteen-day "Magical Egypt" tour costs from US$2100 plus air fare (from US$785).

General Tours ☎ 1-800/221-2216, ⓦ www.generaltours.com. Escorted tours include eight days in Cairo and Luxor from US$1899, Nile cruises from US$1999 for eight days, and a seventeen-day Adventure Tour of Lake Nasser, Aswan, Luxor, Cairo, the Sinai and Petra (in Jordan) from US$3999.

Globus Journeys ☎ 1-866/755-8581, ⓦ www.globusjourneys.com. Offers three fully escorted tours to Egypt, including a twelve-day Grand Tour from US$1643.

Homeric Tours ☎ 1-800/223-5570, ⓦ www.homerictours.com. Deluxe package tours, from an eight-day "Egyptian Escape" visiting Cairo, Aswan and Luxor with a four-day Nile cruise from US$1799, to a fourteen-day version with an added Lake Nasser cruise visiting Abu Simbel from US$2819. Greece and Israel extensions available.

Isram World of Travel ☎ 1-800/223 7460, ⓦ www.isram.com. Eight- to thirteen-day tours, all including Nile cruises. Eight-day "Jewel of the Nile" tours with a stay in Cairo, a Nile Cruise and an air-trip to Abu Simbel from US$2245; thirteen-day tours including three days in Sharm el-Sheikh from US$2745; Cairo city breaks from US$445; Sinai and Alexandria add-ons possible.

Maupintour ☎ 1-800/255-4266, ⓦ www.maupintour.com. Ten-day "Ancient Egypt" tours including a four-day Nile cruise from US$4590; seventeen-day versions from US$4590; five-day Red Sea add-ons based at Sharm el-Sheikh from US$765.

Megatrails ☎ 1-800/547-1211, ⓦ www.megatrails.com. Escorted small-group tours and customized packages; ten-day "Marvels of Egypt" tour including a four-day Nile cruise from US$835, can be combined with tours in Jordan, or Israel and Palestine.

Adventure and specialist tours

Adventure Center ☎ 1-800/228-8747 or 510/654-1879, ⓦ www.adventure-center.com. A large assortment of itineraries for small groups, including a Nile cruise, Red Sea diving, temples, the Pyramids and more, camping or in hotels. Can also book Gecko's adventure tours (see p.21).

Adventures Abroad ☎ 1-800/665-3998 or 604/303-1099, ⓦ www.adventures-abroad.com. Canadian company offering small-group tours to Egypt or combined with Israel, Jordan, Syria, etc.

Activities include camel rides, trekking and felucca cruises.

Archaeological Tours ☎ 212/986-3054, ⓔ archtours@aol.com. Small-group archeological/historical educational tours with renowned Egyptologist.

Exodus US ☎ 914/666-4417, Canada ☎ 416/260-0999, ⓦ www.exodus.co.uk. The fourteen-day "Egyptian Discoverer" tour features a Nile cruise from Aswan to Luxor, a day in Hurghada and two nights in Cairo (from US$850/CDN$1340 plus flights and local charges of US$100). There's also a nine-day trip including three days on a felucca (from US$545/CDN$860 plus US$50 plus flights), or a sixteen-day overland tour of Egypt, Jordan, Syria and Lebanon (from US$1295/CDN$2030 plus US$125 plus flights).

Insight International Tours ☎ 1-800/582-8380, ⓦ www.inusa.insightvacations.com. Nine- to thirteen-day cultural tours of Egypt starting at US$1360, or a seventeen-day tour of Egypt and Jordan starting at US$2835.

Mistress of Magic ⓦ egyptmagic.bizland.com. New Age tour led by a mystical High Priestess to uncover "the sacred secrets of Egypt" with ceremonies, readings and past-life regressions, visiting Cairo, Luxor, Aswan and Siwa; US$3731 from LAX, US$3481 from JFK.

Travcoa ☎ 1-800/992-2003, ⓦ www.travcoa.com. All-inclusive deluxe-accommodation tours led by experienced guides and prominent lecturers, who discuss history, politics, arts, etc. Offers several tours, including twelve-day "Classic Egypt" from US$4595, seventeen-day "Egypt Adventure" from US$6795, plus extensions to Jordan, Israel, Palestine, Kenya and Tanzania.

Wilderness Travel ☎ 1-800/368-2794, ⓦ www.wildernesstravel.com. Offers a small-group, sixteen-day cultural and archeological expedition (from US$4995 excluding flight), or an eleven-day tour and symposium with lectures by well-known Egyptologists (from US$5895 excluding flight).

Flights from Australia and New Zealand

Most Australians and New Zealanders visit Egypt as an extension of a European trip, usually buying a flight to London, plus an add-on fare to Cairo. However, you might want to consider taking in Egypt as a stopover on a Round-the-World (RTW) ticket, or take advantage of some very reasonable budget fares to Cairo from Asia. If you are planning to travel on to Egypt from Israel or Jordan, see pp.23–25.

The only airline **flying direct** from Australia to Egypt is EgyptAir, which runs two services a week (currently Wed and Fri) from Sydney to Cairo with a stop at Singapore. Obviously this is the most convenient route from Sydney, but it won't be the cheapest, though tickets can be had for as little as A$1650 off-season, A$1870 in winter (Egypt's summer).

No other airline flies direct from Australia or New Zealand to Egypt, but a number of European, Middle Eastern and Asian carriers offer **indirect flights**, changing planes at their hub airports. Travel agents may also be able to put you together a ticket using different airlines on different legs of the journey. Prices for a flight to Cairo via Southeast Asia, Europe or the Middle East start at around A$1540/NZ$2100 in low season (summer), A$1760/NZ$2370 in high season (winter).

For standards of comfort and service, plus the most direct route, your best bet is with Singapore Airlines via Singapore, and this is often one of the best-priced options too. Malaysia may offer a cheaper alternative, and both these airlines offer a choice of starting points, as to a lesser extent does Korean Air. A number of European airlines offer flights via Europe, which is only a slightly roundabout route. Austrian is one of the cheapest at present, and KLM is also a contender, and one with a generally good standard of service. From New Zealand, Air New Zealand offers combination tickets with Kuwait, Austrian, KLM and other airlines to get you there.

STA Travel is one of the best places to start **looking for a ticket** if you are under 26 or a student. Otherwise, Africa Bound tends to offer better fares. You can check fares and book online with both companies, but it's also worth comparing the price of a RTW ticket, which may offer better value (and sometimes even a lower price) than a straight return, especially from New Zealand.

Airlines

Alitalia Australia ☎ 1300/036 1400, ⊛ www.alitalia.com. Sydney to Cairo via Rome in conjunction with Qantas.
Air New Zealand Australia ☎ 13/2476, NZ ☎ 0800/737 000, ⊛ www.airnz.com. Through

tickets from New Zealand to Egypt in combination with other airlines.
EgyptAir Australia ☎ 02/9267 6979, ⊛ www.egyptair.com.eg. Sydney to Cairo direct (one stop) twice weekly.
Emirates Australia ☎ 02/9290 9700 or 1300/303 777, NZ ☎ 09/377 6004, ⊛ www.emirates.com. Melbourne, Perth and Sydney to Cairo with an overnight stop in Dubai.
Korean Air Australia ☎ 02/9262 6000, NZ ☎ 09/914 2000, ⊛ www.koreanair.com. Auckland, Brisbane and Sydney to Cairo via Seoul.
Malaysia Airlines Australia ☎ 13/2627, NZ ☎ 0800/657 472, ⊛ www.malaysia-airlines.com. Adelaide, Auckland, Brisbane, Melbourne, Perth and Sydney to Cairo via Kuala Lumpur.
Olympic Airways Australia ☎ 1800/221 663 or 02/9251 1040, ⊛ www.olympic-airways.com. Melbourne and Sydney to Cairo via Athens.
Qantas Australia ☎ 13/1313, NZ ☎ 09/357 8900, ⊛ www.qantas.com.au. Through tickets in combination with British Airways via London, Alitalia via Rome or Gulf Air via Bahrain.
Singapore Airlines Australia ☎ 13/1011, ⊛ www.singaporeair.com. Adelaide, Auckland, Brisbane, Christchurch, Melbourne, Perth and Sydney to Cairo via Singapore.

Travel agents

Africa Bound Holidays Australia ☎ 08/9361 2047, ⊛ www.africabound.com.au. Travel consultant covering the whole of Africa, with online fare quotes and bookings.
Anywhere Travel Australia ☎ 02/9663 0411 or 018/401 014, ✉ anywhere@ozemail.com.au. Discount ticket agent.
Budget Travel NZ ☎ 09/366 0061 or 0800/808 040, ⊛ www.budgettravel.co.nz. Facilities include online flight search.
Flight Centres Australia ☎ 02/9235 3522 or 13/3133, NZ ☎ 09/358 4310, ⊛ www.flightcentre.com.au. Online booking and branches across Australia and New Zealand.
Harvey World Travel Australia ☎ 02/9567 6099, ⊛ www.harveyworld.com.au, NZ ☎ 09-478 7118, ⊛ www.harveyworld.com.au. Branches nationwide in both Australia and New Zealand, plus online booking.
STA Travel Australia ☎ 1300/360 960, ⊛ www.statravel.com.au, NZ ☎ 0508/782 872, ⊛ www.statravel.co.nz. Worldwide specialist in low-cost flights and tours for students and under-26s, though other customers welcome. Branches throughout Australia and New Zealand, plus online booking.

Student Uni Travel (SUT) Australia ☏02/9232 8444, ⓦww.sut.com.au, NZ ☏09/379 4224, ⓦwww.sut.co.nz. Student and budget travel specialists.

Thomas Cook Australia ☏13/1771 or 1800/801 002, ⓦwww.thomascook.com.au; NZ ☏09/379 3920, ⓦwww.thomascook.co.nz. The same firm that pretty much started tourism in Egypt back in 1869 still offers a range of package tours there.

Topdeck Travel Australia ☏08/8410 1110. Adelaide-based discount agent.

Trailfinders Australia ☏02/9247 7666. Australian branch of the London-based independent travel specialists.

Travel Direct Pty Ltd Australia ☏07/3221 4933. Brisbane-based budget travel agent.

Tymtro Travel Australia ☏02/9223 2211.

Package tours

So far as **package holidays** go, many Australians and New Zealanders either sign up with a tour in Britain (see pp.14–16), or book a "land only" tour – which excludes the flight costs – and book their flight separately. There are, however, a few companies that organize flight-and-tour packages: see below for details (all offer land-only deals unless otherwise stated).

Tour operators

Adventure World Australia ☏02/9956 7766 or 1300/363 055, ⓦwww.adventureworld.com.au; NZ ☏09/524 5118, ⓦwww.adventureworld.co.nz. Agents for Explore Worldwide's seventeen-day escorted tour from Cairo to Luxor by bus, train, felucca and donkey, taking in the Valley of the Kings and the Pyramids.

Adventures Abroad Australia ☏1800/147 827, NZ ☏0800/800 434, ⓦwww.adventures-abroad .com. Canada-based company offering small group tours to Egypt or combined with Israel, Jordan, Syria, etc. Activities include camel rides, trekking and felucca cruises.

Allways PADI Travel Australia ☏1800/338 239 ⓦwww.allwaysdive.com.au. Eleven-day diving trip exploring wrecks and coral reefs around Sharm el-Sheikh and Ras Mohammed from aboard the *Wildcat*. Price (starting at A$4150) includes return air fares from east coast Australia and seven nights at sea, including all meals and two dives a day.

Contiki Holidays Australia ☏02/9511 2200, NZ ☏09/309 8824, ⓦwww.contiki.com. Nine-day Egypt tours for 18–35-year-olds from A$2049/NZ$2439 plus airfare.

Exodus Australia ☏03/9663 8611, ⓦwww.exodus.co.uk. The fourteen-day "Egyptian Discoverer" tour features a Nile cruise from Aswan to Luxor, a day in Hurghada and two nights in Cairo (from A$1510 plus flights and local charges of US$100). There's also a nine-day trip including three days on a felucca (from A$970 plus US$50 plus flights), or a sixteen-day overland tour of Egypt, Jordan, Syria and Lebanon (from A$2630 plus US$125 plus flights).

Gecko's Australia ☏1300/655 433 or 03/9663 8611, ⓦwww.geckos.com.au; NZ c/o Adventure Travel ☏09/379 9755. A variety of adventure tours, from an eleven-day "Felucca Safari" visiting Cairo, Aswan and Luxor (from A$800/NZ$1200) to a fifteen-day "Backroads of Egypt" journey including a Nile trip plus five days spent with Bedouins in the Western Desert (from A$1225/NZ$1555), and combined packages involving Egypt, Jordan and Israel. Prices do not include flights.

Made Easy Tours Australia ☏1800/673 337. A variety of packages, ranging from sightseeing in Alexandria and Aswan to Nile cruises for independent travellers or groups. Tours start from A$330/NZ$410 for three days with accommodation and meals.

Sun Island Tours Australia ☏02/9283 3840, ⓦwww.sunislandtours.com.au. Mainstream holiday packages including Cairo city breaks from A$382 for three days, and Nile cruises from A$1113 for eight days. Prices do not include flights.

Wiltrans/Maupintour, Australia ☏02/9255 0899 or 1800/251 174, ⓦwww.maupintour.com. Luxury historical tours guided by Egyptologists, including Nile cruises, the Pyramids, camel rides and desert treks. Ten-day tours start from US$3515, seventeen-day tours from US$4590, not including flights.

Overland from Britain

Travelling **overland from Britain to Egypt** only really makes sense if you intend to visit other countries en route. The two most obvious approaches are either **by land** through Turkey, Syria and Jordan, or **by ferry** from Greece. Greece and Turkey are both easily accessible by various combinations of train or bus from Britain, and it is even possible to hitch all the way from London to Istanbul in one lift if you have a very lucky thumb (though given the attendant risks, we don't recommend hitchhiking). In theory, you could get to Egypt via Italy, Tunisia and Libya, but for that you'd need a Libyan visa, not an easy thing to come by at the best of times.

By sea

The **boat service** from Greece via Cyprus and Israel is currently suspended due to the political situation in Israel and Palestine, though it is expected to resume at some time in the future. Run by Salamis Lines of Cyprus, the boat sailed weekly from Piraeus in Greece via the Greek islands of Patmos and Rhodes, then Limassol in Cyprus, and Haifa in Israel, to Port Said, taking three and a half days to complete the journey. Many passengers of course would take stopovers on the way, and not a few Egypt-bound travellers used to disembark at Haifa and continue by land. Last known fares from Piraeus to Haifa or Port Said were £82 low season, £98 high season including embarkation charges travelling steerage, or from £125/151 for a two-person cabin, plus £106/126 for a small car, £52/64 for a motorbike. Students got a twenty-percent discount. For the latest information, contact Hellas in Piraeus (details opposite).

By rail

The alternative is to travel by land through Turkey, Syria and Jordan. One of the most cost-effective ways to cover this, or indeed the sea route described above, while seeing some of Europe on the way is to get a European rail pass. For British, Irish and European residents, the **InterRail** pass is available from main stations and international rail agents (see opposite) in all the countries it covers. In theory it allows unlimited free travel on railways in the countries it covers, half-price in the country it was bought in, but in practice all the trains you'll want to use carry supplements which you will have to pay. There are eight zones, and a card covering zone E (France, Belgium, the Netherlands and Luxembourg) and zone G (Italy, Slovenia, Greece and Turkey, including the ferry from Italy to Greece) would get you all the way from Calais to Piraeus or the Syrian border. You can add more zones to cover other countries you want to visit, including zone A for Britain and Ireland, although it will probably be cheaper to get over to mainland Europe by other means and start using the card when you are over there. A two-zone card valid for a month costs £189 for under-26s, £265 for over-26s, rising to £209/299 for three zones, and £249/355 for all the zones. Officially, you need to have been resident in a participating country for at least six months to buy an InterRail pass. For further details, and price updates, see RailEurope's InterRail website at ⓦ www.inter-rail.co.uk.

Non-European residents aren't eligible for InterRail passes, though many agents don't in fact check residential qualifications. Non-residents can however buy a **Eurail pass**, which should be obtained outside Europe, but can be bought from RailEurope in London by non-residents who were unable to get it at home. Eurail gives unlimited travel in seventeen countries – Austria, Belgium, Denmark, Finland, France, Germany, Greece, Hungary, Ireland, Italy, Luxembourg, the Netherlands, Norway, Portugal, Spain, Sweden and Switzerland – and is valid for more express trains than InterRail, thus saving money on supplements. If you're 26 or over you'll have to buy a first-class pass, available in fifteen-day (US$572), 21-day (US$740), one-month (US$918), two-month (US$1298) and three-month (US$1606) versions. Under-26s can buy a **Eurail Youthpass**, costing US$401 for fifteen days, US$518 for 21 days, US$644 for one month, US$910 for two months, or US$1120 for three months. You stand a better chance of getting your money's worth out of a **Eurail Flexipass**, which is good for a certain number of travel days in a two-month period. This, too, comes in under-26 and first-class versions: ten days cost US$674 for first-class travel or US$473 for under-26s; and fifteen days, US$888 or US$622. There are also "Saver" versions of all these passes offering a discount of around fifteen percent for two to five people travelling together.

By bus

It is also possible to travel to Egypt by **bus** via Europe, Turkey, Syria and Jordan. The first leg, as far as Greece, can even be done in one journey from London with Eurolines (£90 one-way, £59 for under-26s), but it's a gruelling three-day trip. You would then continue on local buses or trains through Turkey and Syria into Jordan. To see a bit of Europe on the way, Eurolines also offer 15-, 30- or 60-day passes for unlimited travel between 31 European cities. Alternatively, between April and October, Busabout offers two-week, three-week, one-month, two-month and three-month passes for its own bus services around the Continent, and Flexipasses for any six, ten or fifteen days in two months, twenty days in three months, or 25 days in four months, with the possibility of adding extra days. Busabout passes can be bought in North America and Australasia as well as in Britain and Europe. The trouble with all these passes is that none of them will get you to Greece, though Busabout offers an Athens add-on; you can always use them as far as Brindisi (the Italian port for Greece) and make your own way on from there.

Overland travel contacts

Through tickets and rail passes in Britain and Ireland

Iarnród Éireann (Continental Rail Desk) Ireland ☎ 01/836 6222, ⊛ www.irishrail.ie. InterRail and some through tickets.
International Rail UK ☎ 01962/773 646, ⊛ www.international-rail.com. InterRail and through tickets to most of Europe.
Northern Ireland Railways Northern Ireland ☎ 028/9089 9411, ⊛ www.nirailways.co.uk. InterRail and some through tickets.
Rail Europe UK ☎ 0870/584 8848, ⊛ www.raileurope.co.uk. InterRail, Eurail and some through tickets.
Trainseurope UK ☎ 01354/660 222, ⊛ www.trainseurope.co.uk. InterRail and through tickets to most of Europe.

Eurail passes in North America

BritRail Travel US ☎ 1-888/BRITRAIL or 212/490-6688, Canada ☎ 1-800/361-RAIL, ⊛ www.raileurope.com.
European Rail Services Canada ☎ 1-800/205-5800 or 416/695-1211, ⊛ www.europeanrailservices.com.
DER Travel ☎ 1-888/337-7350, ⊛ www.dertravel.com/rail.
Online Travel ☎ 1-800/660-5300, ⊛ www.eurorail.com.
Rail Europe US ☎ 1-800/438-7245, Canada ☎ 1-800/361-7245, ⊛ www.raileurope.com/us. Official Eurail agent in North America.

Eurail passes in Australia and New Zealand

CIT World Travel Australia ☎ 02/9267 1255 or 03/9650 5510, ⊛ www.cittravel.com.au.
Rail Plus Australia ☎ 1300/555 003 or 03/9642 8644, ⓔ info@railplus.com.au, NZ ☎ 09/303 2484.
Trailfinders Australia ☎ 02/9247 7666, ⊛ www.trailfinder.com.au.

Bus tickets and passes

Busabout UK ☎ 020/7950 1661, US ☎ 1-800/664 4046, Canada ☎ 416/322-8468, Australia ☎ 1300/301 776, NZ ☎ 09/309 5973, ⊛ www.busabout.com.
Eurolines UK ☎ 0870/514 3219, Ireland ☎ 01/836 6111, ⊛ www.eurolines.co.uk. Tickets can also be purchased from any Eurolines or National Express agent (☎ 0870/580 8080, ⊛ www.nationalexpress.co.uk or ⊛ www.gobycoach.com).

Shipping companies

Salamis Lines Salamis House, 179 28th October Ave, PO Box 531, Limassol, Cyprus ☎ 2574 5666, ⊛ www.ferries.gr/salamis.
Viamare (UK agents for Salamis) Graphic House, 2 Sumatra Rd, London NW6 1PU ☎ 020/7431 4560, ⊛ www.viamare.com.
Hellas (Greek agents for Salamis) 12 Filellínon St, 18536 Piraeus ☎ 010/429 4325, ⓕ 429 4557, ⓔ info@salamis-hellas.gr.

Getting there from Israel and Jordan

If your travels include Israel or Jordan, moving on to Egypt is fairly straightforward. You can either fly – from Tel Aviv or Amman to Cairo – or, more cheaply, use one of the many bus and ferry services. From Israel and Palestine the quickest checkpoint for Cairo is the divided border town of Rafah, near the Mediterranean coast; for the resort towns of the Sinai peninsula, it's Taba, near Eilat. Which of these you use – if either of them – will depend on the current political situation in Israel and Gaza: keep your ear to the ground and steer clear of trouble spots. If you are travelling from Jordan, you can either go by ferry from Aqaba to the Sinai peninsula and then continue your journey by bus; or take the fast catamaran service that runs to Sinai's main resort, Sharm el-Sheikh, and on to Hurghada on the Red Sea Coast.

See pp.26–27 for details of Egyptian and Sinai-only visas and for addresses of Egyptian consulates in Israel and Jordan.

From Israel or the Gaza Strip

At time of writing the political situation is such that most travellers are steering clear of Israel, and even clearer of the Gaza Strip, and direct transport between Israel or Palestine and Egypt has all but dried up. In the hope that things will improve, however, we offer the following information.

Entering Egypt via Rafah, you're subject to an **Israeli departure tax** of US$32 and an **Egyptian entry tax** of US$6. Entering via Taba, departure and entry taxes are US$15 and US$8 respectively.

In the past, a number of firms offered daily bus services from Tel Aviv or Jerusalem to Cairo, but currently the only company operating buses is Mazada Tours (see below), which runs three a week. One-way tickets are US$35, return tickets US$50, and it's best to book (and confirm return journeys) at least three days in advance. The same company will also get your visa for you on request, but the Egyptian embassy is just around the corner from its office (see p.27 for the address), and it is cheaper to do it yourself.

To reach Rafah under your own steam, there are once-daily Israeli Egged buses from Tel Aviv, Ashqelon and Beersheba to the border. Otherwise the journey would involve travelling by service taxi through the Gaza Strip and changing at several points. Whether you can use this route will of course depend on the current political situation between Israel and the Palestinians, but when things are good, there are service taxis (*sherut* in Hebrew) from Jaffa to the Israel–Gaza border at Erez (Israeli buses from Tel Aviv and Ashqelon will leave you 4km short at Yad Mordecai), and from there to Gaza City and then on to Rafah. You may have to walk or charter a "special" (private taxi) for the 5km from Rafah town to the border post. Once across the border (open daily 24hr), the Egyptian guards will examine your passport and visa (which cannot be issued here), and demand the entry tax. The exchange office on the Egyptian side is open 24 hours. Rafah and nearby El-Arish in themselves have little to offer apart from bus and service taxi connections to Cairo.

Taba makes a fine jumping-off point for the Sinai coast resorts, St Catherine's Monastery or Cairo. From Eilat, a taxi (NIS20) or a much cheaper #15 bus (which doesn't run on *Shabbat*) will get you to the Israeli checkpoint at Taba for an exit stamp; you then walk for fifteen minutes across no-man's-land to the Egyptian side (ignore taxi drivers who tell you it's too far to walk), where proceedings are similar to those at Rafah, except that **Sinai-only visas** can be obtained on the spot. It usually takes a good hour to cross the border (longer at holiday times). If you're carrying any Israeli shekels, the bank at the *Taba Hilton,* a few banks in Sharm el-Sheikh and one or two banks and Forex bureaux in Cairo are the only places in Egypt where you can legally exchange them. However, Israeli shekels are now common currency in the Sinai as far south as Dahab and many businesses will accept them at an exchange rate of NIS1 to £E1.

Travelling on from Taba (see p.723), there is one bus daily for Dahab and Sharm el-Sheikh (at 3pm; £E10 and £E15; four to Nuweiba (6.30am, 9am, 2pm and 3pm; £E10) and two to Cairo (9am and 2pm; £E65 and £E75). **Taxis** take full advantage of the fact that there's no bus to St Catherine's, and also demand premium rates for Nuweiba or places further down the Gulf of Aqaba. **Service taxis** are a bit cheaper, with per person rates £E25 to Nuweiba or Tarabin, £E35 to Dahab and £E50 to Sharm el-Sheikh. Prices for both drop immediately before the bus departs, and soar once it has departed. Try to resist being cajoled into the limousine services of Europcar and Aquasun, which have recently pushed out local taxi drivers.

You are not allowed to drive **rented cars** or 4WDs across the Israeli–Egyptian border.

Bus operators

Mazada Tours 141 Rehov Ibn Givrol, Tel Aviv ☎03/544 4454; 19 Jaffa Rd, Jerusalem ☎02/623 5777, ⊛www.mazada.co.il.

Israeli tour operators

ISSTA (Israel Students Travel Company) 5 Yoel Salomon St, Nahalat Shiva'a, Jerusalem ☎02/624 3177, ⓕ624 2996.

Neot Ha Kikar Touring Company 78 Rehov Ben Yehuda St, Tel Aviv ☎03/522 8161; 36 Keren HaYesod St, Jerusalem ☎02/636 494; Sederot HaTemarim, Eilat ☎07/371 329. Specializes in Sinai treks.

SPNI (Society for the Protection of Nature in Israel) 19 Rehov HaShfela, Tel Aviv 66183 ☎03/638 8662, ⓦ www.spni.org.il (but for information in English, see the site of its US representatives AMI Travel at ⓦ www.amitravel.com/spni). Organizes four-day jeep safaris (from US$295) and a five-day hiking, snorkelling and camel-trekking adventure (from US$360) departing from Eilat.

From Jordan

Starting out at Amman, there are **direct buses** to Cairo but they are neither very pleasant nor very economical. Unless speed is absolutely of the essence (in which case flying is a better option), you'd do far better to break the 21-hour journey at Aqaba or in the Sinai. The main operator is JETT (north of Abdali station ☎06/569 6191; Tues & Sat 6.30am; around US$57), whose service terminates rather inconveniently at the office of the Arab Union Bus Company at Midan Almaza in Heliopolis, some way from central Cairo. Plenty of other Abdali-based firms compete, undercutting JETT. One such is Afana (next door to JETT and at Abdali station; daily 7am & 10pm; JD27), whose buses leave from Middle East Circle (*Duwaar ash-Sharq al-Aswat*).

From Aqaba, the quickest route is by land via Eilat in Israel, using local buses. Disincentives are that telltale Taba border stamp, and the hefty exit and entry taxes (totalling around US$23) which are payable at Taba. **By sea**, the Arab Bridge Maritime Company operates ferry and catamaran services to Nuweiba. You can buy tickets for all services from the company's offices, downtown near the *China* restaurant (daily 7am–midnight; ☎03/201 3237), from agents

in town, or up to an hour before departure at the passenger terminal itself, 9km south of town (open daily 24hr; ☎03/201 3240). The terminal is served by local buses from the Corniche, or costs about JD3 by taxi. There's a duty-free shop by the terminal in case you need a bottle of whisky to take with you.

The ordinary **ferry** takes three hours and costs US$22 or JD15. For years it has been notoriously unpunctual, and now the company has finally given up on its own timetable. On days when there's one ferry, it usually leaves at about 3pm; on other days there are two sailings at about noon and 6pm – call the port (☎03/201 3240) on your day of departure to find out which it's to be. The ferry will carry bicycles (free), motorbikes (around JD14/US$20), small cars (JD75/US$105) and 4WDs (JD105/US$157). The **catamaran**, on the other hand, carries people only (JD21/US$30), but takes just an hour to complete the crossing. Whether by ferry or by catamaran, a tax of JD6 is payable on departure. Egyptian visas are available on board for US$17, but it's easier to get them ahead of time in Amman or Aqaba. On arrival in Nuweiba you can obtain a Sinai-only visa at the port. See p.715 for information on Nuweiba itself, and on travelling in the opposite direction, towards Aqaba.

If you prefer to **fly**, Royal Jordanian (☎06/567 8321) and EgyptAir (☎06/463 0011) operate expensive daily flights from Amman to Cairo, with discounted charter flights from Amman to Sharm el-Sheikh and Hurghada on Royal Wings (☎06/487 5201) available from National Tours (☎06/568 2054) and Dakkak Tours (☎06/567 0289). There are sometimes charters to the same destinations from Aqaba – check with Royal Wings at Aqaba airport (☎03/201 4477) for the latest information.

For further details, see the *Rough Guide to Jordan*.

Red tape and visas

Bureaucracy has flourished in Egypt for five thousand years, pervading most aspects of life. Nasser's promise of a civil service job for every graduate has led to a vastly overstaffed, inefficient administration, which you'll come up against when obtaining travel permits or visa extensions, and which may well defeat you if you try to do anything more complicated. Rules change from place to place and individual bureaucrats may interpret them differently, or introduce new regulations, or simply be obstructive through caprice. Remain patient and good-humoured no matter what.

Passports and visas

All visitors to Egypt must hold **passports** that are valid for at least **six months** beyond the proposed date of entry to the country. Citizens of most countries, including the UK, Ireland, the USA, Canada, Australia, New Zealand and all European countries, must also obtain **tourist visas** (see below).

Tourist visas

Regular tourist visas are available from Egyptian consulates abroad (see opposite). For most nationalities, including British, Irish, Americans, Canadians, Australians, New Zealanders and all EU citizens, they can also be obtained on arrival at Cairo, Luxor and Hurghada airports. The process is generally painless, and cheaper than getting one through a consulate, but bear in mind that visas issued at the airport are only valid for one month. You *cannot* get them at overland border crossings, or at Aswan, Suez or Nuweiba (apart from Sinai-only visas – see below). From an embassy or consulate the **single-visit** and **multiple-entry** types of visa entitle you to stay in Egypt for three months; the latter allows you to go in and out of the country three times within this period. Don't be misled by statements on the application form that it is "valid for six months"; this simply means that it must be used within that period (validated from the day of issue).

Visa applications can be made in person or by post. Applying in person, you can normally get a visa the same day in Britain, North America, Australia, Israel or Jordan. Always turn up early in the day and expect to pay in cash – postal applications take between seven working days and six weeks to process. When returning the form, you need to include a registered or recorded SAE, your passport, one photo, and a postal or money order (not a personal cheque).

The **cost** varies according to your nationality, and from place to place. Getting a standard visa on arrival costs US$15, irrespective of your nationality. Abroad, the price varies according to where you buy it, and sometimes your nationality. **In Israel**, US, German and Scandinavian nationals are charged NIS60, most other nationalities NIS80. Some consulates may demand that you pay in US$ instead of local currency, or ask you to supply extra photos (and maybe glue to stick them down!). It's wise to allow for all these eventualities.

If you don't mind being limited to Sinai, you can obtain special **Sinai-only visas** (free of charge) at Taba on the Israeli–Egyptian border, St Catherine's Monastery or Sharm el-Sheikh airport, or the seaports at Sharm el-Sheikh and Nuweiba. Valid for fourteen days only, this visa restricts you to the Aqaba coast down to Sharm el-Sheikh, and the vicinity of St Catherine's; it is **not valid** for Ras Mohammed, the mountains around St Catherine's (except for Mount Sinai), or any other part of Egypt. It can't be extended, and there's no period of grace for overstaying. Note that neither regular nor Sinai-only visas are available at Rafah, the other crossing between Israel and Egypt.

Egyptian embassies and consulates abroad

For visa applications in person, submit your passport and application in the morning and collect the visa that afternoon (applications cannot be submitted then). Current lists of Egyptian embassies can be found at ⓦwww.mfa.gov.eg/frames.asp?id=05 and ⓦwww.arab.net/egypt/govt/et_embassies .html.

Australia 1 Darwin Ave, Yarralumla, ACT 2600 ☎02/6273 4437 (Mon–Fri 9am–4pm); 112 Glenmore Rd, Paddington, NSW 2021 ☎02/9332 3388 (Mon–Fri 9am–3pm); Level 9, 124 Exhibition St, Melbourne, Vic 3000 ☎03/9654 8869 (Mon–Fri 10am–2pm). Single-entry visa A$35, multiple-entry A$42.

Canada 454 Laurier Ave E, Ottawa, ON K1N 6R3 ☎613/234 4931 (Mon–Fri 9am–3pm); 1 Pl Ville Marie, Suite 2617, Montreal PQ H3B 4S3 ☎514/866 8455 (Mon–Fri 9.30am–1pm). Single-entry visa CDN$25, multiple-entry CDN$31.

Cyprus PO Box 21752, Éyíptou 3 (near Paphos Gate), 1097 Nicosia ☎2268 0650 or 0651.

Denmark Kristianiagade 19, 2100 Copenhagen Ø ☎3526 3026.

Greece 3 Leoforos Vassilissis Sofias, 10671 Athens ☎0301/361 8612–3.

Ireland 12 Clyde Rd, Dublin 4 ☎01/660 6566.

Israel 54 Rehov Basel, Tel Aviv 62744 ☎03/546 5152 (Mon–Thurs & Sun 9–11am); 68 Rehov HaEfrony, Bnei Betkha, Eilat ☎08/637 6882 (Mon–Thurs & Sun 9am–2pm).

Jordan Qurtubah St, Amman (between 4th and 5th circles, next to *Dove Hotel*) ☎06/560 5175 (daily except Fri 10am–3pm); Al-Wahdat Al-Jarbiyya, Sharia al-Istiqlal, Aqaba ☎03/201 6171 (Mon–Thurs & Sun 10am–1pm). Multiple-entry visa JD18; Sinai-only visas are issued free.

Libya Sharia el-Shatt, 1105 Tripoli ☎021/444 8909; Sharia el-Awarsi, Western Fuwaihat, 2148 Benghaz ☎061/222 3099.

Netherlands Badhuisweg 92, 2587CL The Hague ☎070/354 2000.

New Zealand *There is no Egyptian embassy or consulate in New Zealand; contact one of the consulates in Australia.*

Norway Drammensvn 90a, 0244 Oslo ☎2254 0800.

Palestine 204/55 Sharia Omar al-Mukhtar, PO Box 1234, Gaza City ☎07/282 4274 or 84 or 94.

South Africa 270 Bourke St, Muckleneuk 0002 ☎012/343 1590.

Sudan Sharia al-Gamma, PO Box 1126, Khartoum ☎011/772836; Midan al-Kabir, El Obeid ☎0249/4167; Sharia Kabbashi Eissa, Port Sudan ☎0249/2036.

Sweden Strandvägen 35, PO Box 14230, 10440 Stockholm ☎08/662 9603.

UK 2 Lowndes St, London SW1X 9ET ☎020/7235 9777, ⓔegypt@freenetname.co.uk. Applications received Mon–Fri 9.30am–12.30pm, collection 2.30–4pm. Single-entry visa £15, multiple-entry £18.

USA 3521 International Court NW, Washington DC 20008 ☎202/895-5400 (Mon–Fri 9.30am–1pm); 1110 Second Ave, Suite 201, New York, NY 10022 ☎212/759-7120–2, ⓦwww.egyptandus.net (Mon–Fri 9am–2pm); 3001 Pacific Ave, San Francisco, CA 94115 ☎415/346-9700 (Mon–Fri 9.30am–3pm); 500 N Michigan Ave, Suite 1900, Chicago, IL 60611 ☎312/828-9162-4 (Mon–Fri 9am–noon); 1990 Post Oak Blvd, Suite 2180, Houston, TX 77056 ☎713/961-4915-6 (applications 9.30am–12.30pm, collection 2–2.30pm, 4 days to issue). Single-entry visa US$15 for US nationals, US$20 for others; multiple-entry US$23.

Israeli passport stamps

Politics may yet change this, but at time of writing, most Arab countries except Egypt and Jordan will deny entry to anyone whose **passport shows evidence of a visit to Israel**. In particular this applies to Syria, Lebanon, Libya and Sudan. Although Israeli immigration officials will usually give you an entry stamp on a separate piece of paper if you ask them to, an Egyptian entry stamp at Taba or Rafah in the Sinai will give you away – and the Egyptians insist on stamping your passport. So if you are travelling around the Middle East, be sure to visit Israel *after* you have been to Syria, Lebanon, or wherever. If you enter Egypt from Israel with the intention of travelling on to Libya or Sudan, you are going to have big problems trying to get an onward visa. Even if you have more than one passport, and apply for your Sudanese or Libyan visa on a passport with no Egyptian entry stamp, the embassy will want to know why it doesn't have one. Similarly, if you trade your old passport and get a new one issued by your embassy in Cairo, it is unlikely to pass muster with the Sudanese or Libyan authorities.

Passport precautions

Once **in Egypt**, you should always carry your passport with you: you'll need it to register at hotels, change money, collect mail, and possibly to show at police checkpoints. If you're travelling for any length of time, you may find it worthwhile to **register with your embassy** on arrival in Cairo, which will help speed things up if you lose your passport. At the least, it's a wise precaution to **photocopy** the pages recording your particulars and keep them separately. If you are travelling to areas of the country that require permits, spare sets of photocopies are useful for producing with your application.

Overstaying and extensions

Tourists who **overstay** their (regular) visa are allowed a fifteen-day period of grace in which to renew it. After this, they're fined £E60 unless they can present a letter of apology from their embassy (which may well cost more).

Visa extensions are obtainable from the Mugamma in Cairo (see p.272) or offices in Alexandria, Luxor, Aswan, Suez, El-Tor, Mersa Matrouh and Ismailiya (addresses are detailed under their respective entries). Depending on how long you wish to extend by, and on the whim of the official, you may have to produce exchange receipts proving that you've cashed US$180 during the last month. You'll have to supply one or two photos, and pay around £E12. Procedures vary slightly from office to office, but shouldn't take longer than an hour.

Visitors anticipating an extended stay may apply for a **tourist residence visa**, valid for up to a year. Applications are made to the same offices as for ordinary extensions. The current cost in fees and duty amounts to around £E50, and you will need to supply two passport photos.

If you have a single-entry visa and want to leave Egypt and return within the period of its validity, you will need a **re-entry visa**. Procedures for obtaining these are much the same as for a visa extension, and the cost is around £E14.

Customs

Egyptian **customs** allows you to bring in 200 cigarettes (or 250g of tobacco) and one litre of **alcohol**. It's worth bearing in mind that Cairo and Luxor airports have **duty-free shops** for arriving passengers before *and* after customs. You can in fact buy up to three more litres of spirits, or two litres and a case of two dozen cans of beer, at the duty-free shop after customs clearance on arrival or within 24 hours. If you don't want to buy at the airport, or if you enter by land, you can get the same allowance, for about a dollar a bottle more, at duty-free shops in Cairo, Alexandria, Port Said, Luxor, Aswan, Sharm el-Sheikh, Nuweiba and Hurghada. There is a black market for the duty-free booze, but scams abound (see p.270), so beware.

Though personal effects and cameras are exempt from duty, items such as electronic equipment and video cameras should be declared and listed on a Form D. If you lose them during your visit, they will be assumed "sold" when you come to leave and (unless you have police documentation of theft) you will have to pay 100 percent duty. On items with a high resale value (for example, laptop

Travel permits

You can travel without restriction through most areas of Egypt. However, **special travel permits** are required for the Red Sea Coast beyond Mersa Alam, for desert travel between Bahariya and Siwa oases (permits available in Siwa), to Ain Della and the Gilf Kebir/Jebel Uwaynat (permits available in Cairo only), as well as sometimes – depending on relations with Libya – between Mersa Matrouh and the border. You can make your applications through Misr Travel (1 Sharia Talaat Harb; ☎02/393 0010, ✉misrtrav@link.com.eg). Other border areas may also become problematic, so if you're thinking of visiting such areas, check beforehand. For further information, contact the tourist police in Cairo (see p.93); if you do need a permit, they can take from five to fourteen days to process.

computers or video cameras) you may be required to pay a deposit against possible duty charges, which is refundable on departure. If customs insists on impounding goods, get a receipt and contact your consulate. Customs duty is also likely to be payable on goods posted to you from abroad, which may be impounded at the post office (without notice to you) until it is paid.

Information, websites and maps

Besides this book, readily available sources of information include the Egyptian Tourist Authority (which has offices abroad and in Egypt), the Internet, travel agencies, hotels and local, often self-appointed, guides (see p.66).

Tourist offices

The **Egyptian Tourist Authority** (sometimes abbreviated as EGAPT) maintains general information offices in several countries (see below), where you can pick up a range of pamphlets. However, most are simply intended to whet your appetite, and few hard facts can be gained from offices abroad.

In Egypt itself, you'll get a variable response from **local tourist offices** (addresses are given throughout the guide). The most knowledgeable and helpful ones are in Aswan, Luxor, Alexandria, and the oases of Siwa and Dakhla. Staff in Cairo are also well informed, but may need prodding. Elsewhere, most provincial offices are good for a dated brochure, if nothing else.

Egyptian tourist offices abroad

Canada 1253 McGill College Ave, Suite 250, Montreal, PQ H3B 2Y5 ☎514/861-4420, ✉eta@total.net.
Greece 10, Amerikis St, 6th floor, 10671 Athens ☎01/360 6906.
South Africa 1st Floor, Regent Palace Building, Mutual Gdns, Cradock Ave, Rosebank, Johannesburg, PO Box 6298 ☎11/880 9602–3.
Sweden Drottninggatan 65, S-11136 Stockholm ☎08/102548.
UK 170 Piccadilly, London W1V 9DD ☎020/7493 5283.
USA 630 Fifth Ave, Suite 1706, New York, NY 10111 ☎212/332-2570, ✉info@egypttourism.org; 8383 Wilshire Blvd, Suite 215, Beverly Hills, CA 90211 ☎323/653-8815, ✉egypt@etala.com; 645 N Michigan Ave, Suite 829, Chicago, IL 60611☎312/280-4666, ✉egyptmdwst@aol.com. Toll-free enquiries ☎1-877/77-EGYPT.

Travel agencies and hotels

Found in towns and cities, **travel agencies** can advise on (and book) transport, accommodation and excursions. Just remember that they are in business for themselves, so their advice may not be exactly unbiased.

The most ubiquitous agency is **Misr Travel**, the state-run tourist company, which operates hotels, buses and limos, and can make bookings for most things. Its head office is in Cairo (1 Sharia Talaat Harb ☎02/393 0010, ✉misrtrav@link.com.eg), with a walk-in office just up the street (7 Sharia Talaat Harb), and branches in Alexandria, Luxor, Aswan, Port Said, Suez, Hurghada, El Arish, Sharm el-Sheikh and Taba. Misr Travel is also represented in London (2nd floor, 308 Regent St, W1B 3AT ☎020/7255 1087) and New York (630 Fifth Ave, Suite 1460, New York, NY 10011 ☎1-800/223-4978 or 212/582-9210-1). **American Express** and **Thomas Cook** (see pp.43–44) offer various services besides currency exchange.

Receptionists at **hotels** can also be a source of information, and maybe practical assistance. In Luxor, Hurghada and some of the Western Desert oases, most *pensions* double as information exchanges and all-round "fixers"; likewise, campsites and backpackers' hotels in Sinai.

Tourist publications

A series of **regional tourist booklets** under the generic heading *"Night & Day"* are sporadically available free of charge at tourist offices and hotels. Currently there are four, covering Cairo, Alexandria, Upper Egypt and the Red Sea, and the Canal Zone. Each contains a dubious map, notes on local sites and listings of hotels, restaurants, agencies and banks – usually years out of date.

The best guide to **what's on** can be found in the monthly magazine *Egypt Today*, which lists activities, entertainment and exhibitions in Cairo and Alexandria, and events in Luxor and Aswan. Its feature articles cover diverse aspects of Egyptian culture and travel in Egypt. It's sold in Cairo and Alexandria. Selected events are also listed in the daily *Egyptian Gazette*, which is more widely available (see also p.62).

Useful websites

Government advisories
UK Foreign Office Ⓦ www.fco.gov.uk/travel/
countryadvice.asp?EG
US State Department Ⓦ travel.state.gov/egypt.html
Canadian Foreign Affairs Department
Ⓦ www.dfait-maeci.gc.ca/menu-e.asp
Australian Foreign Affairs Department
Ⓦ www.dfat.gov.au/geo/egypt/index.html
The latest information and advice on travel in Egypt put out by Western governments for their citizens, sometimes over-cautious, but well-informed, regularly updated, and always worth reading before making travel plans, and again before departure.

Egyptian National Tourist Organization
Ⓦ www.egypttourism.org
Aimed at tourists from North America, covering the major sights, and illustrating them with a "slideshow". Handy features include a list of diving centres, sound and light show schedules, a short page of links, and – if it isn't out of date – a calendar of events.

The Official Ministry of Tourism Site
Ⓦ www.touregypt.net
Far more informative than the Egyptian National Tourist Organization site, well put-together and jam-packed with useful information, including details of all the main tourist attractions, listings of hotels, nightclubs and Internet cafés, plus travel articles, a

virtual dive centre, and even a page that will translate your name into hieroglyphics.

Egypt Links
Ⓦ ce.eng.usf.edu/pharos
The biggest list of links to websites about Egypt, covering a huge variety of topics including tourism, art and culture, dive sites, history, politics, business, and towns and regions of the country. Unfortunately this massive garden of sites is not weeded too often, and half of them turn out to be off-line.

Guardian's Egypt
Ⓦ www.guardians.net/egypt
An excellent non-commercial site run by an American Egypt enthusiast, and a good one to visit for information on Ancient Egypt and the latest archeological finds. Features include a virtual tour of the pyramids at Giza and Dahshur, inside and out, plus everything you wanted to know about mummies, and masses of links.

Egyptology Resources
Ⓦ www.newton.cam.ac.uk/egypt
If you're serious about Egyptology, this site from the Newton Institute in Cambridge has helpful academic articles and links, plus an Egyptology FAQ, latest Egyptology news, and listings of booksellers, publishers, organizations and museums specializing in Ancient Egypt.

Egyptology On Line
Ⓦ www.egyptologyonline.com
A layperson's potted Egyptology site, with features on famous pharaohs, famous Egyptologists, the main Egyptian gods, and the most important pyramids.

Paranormal Egyptology
Ⓦ paranormal.about.com/cs/ancientegypt
Links to pages on assorted unorthodox theories about the Sphinx and the Pyramids, from the one that they were part of Atlantis to the one that they were built by Martians.

The Egyptian Press
Ⓦ www.start4all.com/newspapers/egypt.htm
Links you up to all the Egyptian publications that have websites, with the advantage that you can read articles – including those critical of the Egyptian government – before the censors get to them.

Egypt Today
Ⓦ www.egypttoday.com
One of Egypt's best monthly English-language magazines, with news, arts and culture sections and

especially good listings and reviews of restaurants, films and events.

Al-Ahram
ⓦ www.ahram.org.eg/weekly
The weekly edition of *Al-Ahram*, Egypt's main newspaper, online in English, for the latest Egyptian news, and an Egyptian take on the Middle East and the world.

Legal Research and Resource Center for Human Rights
ⓦ www.geocities.com/lrrc.geo
Information you won't find in the tourist brochures, on human rights, women's rights, religious freedom and environmental issues – a reminder of the unjustified abuse that ordinary Egyptian people can face from government, police, religious organizations, or even their own families and neighbours.

Ibn Khaldun Center for Development Studies
ⓦ www.ibnkhaldun.org
The website of an independent social science and development research institute, whose championing of human rights and democracy has led to the imprisonment of its director for "defaming Egypt's reputation abroad".

Amnesty International
ⓦ web.amnesty.org/ai.nsf/countries/egypt
Amnesty's latest reports on human rights and prisoners of conscience in Egypt.

Digital Freedom Network
ⓦ www.dfn.org
An international anti-censorship site, containing articles from the *Middle East Times* that were cut by government order – to find them, type "Egypt" into the search box in the top right-hand corner of the screen.

Egyptian Presidency
ⓦ www.presidency.gov.egypt
Mubarak's own website, where you can see interior views of his palaces.

Go Red Sea
ⓦ www.goredsea.com
An excellent site on Red Sea diving, with maps and detailed information on dive locations, resorts and hotels, plus a magazine section and online hotel booking.

Egyptian Football
ⓦ www.egyptiansoccer.com
Latest major match results and reports from Egypt's

football (soccer) league, plus league tables, and information on the country's top clubs and national team.

Weather Report
ⓦ weather.noaa.gov/weather/EG_cc.html
The US government National Weather Service page on Egypt, giving the latest weather conditions in Cairo, Alexandria, Aswan, Luxor, Mersa Matrouh, Port Said and Sharm el-Sheikh.

Maps

The best **general map of Egypt**, published by Freytag & Berndt (1:1,000,000), is not easy to find in Egypt, but should be on sale at good map shops abroad. If it is unavailable, Kümmerly & Frey (1:950,000; published in Egypt by Lenhert & Landrock) makes a decent substitute, but the more common Bartholomew map (1:1,000,000) has rather less detail. Michelin map #154 covers Egypt and the Sudan; its coverage of Sudan is excellent, but the Egypt section is nothing special. Berndtson & Berndtson's 1:1,550,000 map is less detailed, but a handier size, and cheaper. If you plan to do any serious motoring, the Shell/AA Road Atlas of Egypt covers the country comprehensively, with 1:500,000 maps of the Nile Valley and Delta, and 1:1,000,000 maps of the rest of the country. Along with many of the maps mentioned above, it is available from good bookshops in Cairo (see p.268) and sometimes elsewhere in the country.

Taken together, several local **city plans** cover Cairo in comprehensive detail (see p.93). Elsewhere, however, coverage is poor or non-existent. Aside from fairly crude maps of Alexandria, Luxor, Aswan, Hurghada and Port Said, and photocopied handouts in Mersa Matrouh and Siwa Oasis, there are no town plans to be had. Those in this book are as good as any. **Diving maps** of the Red Sea are available in Egypt, but many of these do not cover sites in the Sinai, which for most people is the main diving area.

Full-blown desert expeditions require **special maps**. Recommended are those published by the Geological Survey and Mining Authority in Cairo (3 Sharia Salah Salem, Abbassiya; Mon–Thurs & Sun 8am–3pm); or equally those from the Desert Survey, also in Cairo (Midan Mesaha, Dokki; same hours).

Map outlets

In the UK and Ireland

Blackwell's Map and Travel Shop 50 Broad St, Oxford OX1 3BQ ☏01865/793 550, ⓦmaps.blackwell.co.uk/index.html.

Easons Bookshop 40 O'Connell St, Dublin 1 ☏01/873 3811, ⓦwww.eason.ie.

Heffers Map and Travel 20 Trinity St, Cambridge CB2 1TJ ☏01223/568 568, ⓦwww.heffers.co.uk.

Hodges Figgis Bookshop 56–58 Dawson St, Dublin 2 ☏01/677 4754, ⓦwww.hodgesfiggis.com.

James Thin Booksellers 53–59 South Bridge Edinburgh EH1 1YS ☏0131/622 8222, ⓦwww.jthin.co.uk.

John Smith & Son 100 Cathedral St, Glasgow G4 0RD ☏0141/552 3377, ⓦwww.johnsmith.co.uk.

The Map Shop 30a Belvoir St, Leicester LE1 6QH ☏0116/247 1400, ⓦwww.mapshopleicester.co.uk.

National Map Centre 22–24 Caxton St, London SW1H 0QU ☏020/7222 2466, ⓦwww.mapsnmc.co.uk.

Newcastle Map Centre 55 Grey St, Newcastle-upon-Tyne, NE1 6EF ☏0191/261 5622.

Stanfords 12–14 Long Acre, London WC2E 9LP ☏020/7836 1321, ⓦwww.stanfords.co.uk, ⓔsales@stanfords.co.uk. Maps available by mail, phone order or email. Other branches within British Airways offices at 156 Regent St, London W1R 5TA ☏020/7434 4744 and 29 Corn St, Bristol BS1 1HT ☏0117/929 9966.

The Travel Bookshop 13–15 Blenheim Crescent, London W11 2EE ☏020/7229 5260, ⓦwww.thetravelbookshop.co.uk.

In the USA and Canada

Adventurous Traveler Bookstore 102 Lake St, Burlington, VT 05401 ☏1-800/282-3963, ⓦwww.adventuroustraveler.com.

Book Passage 51 Tamal Vista Blvd, Corte Madera, CA 94925 ☏1-800/999-7909, ⓦwww.bookpassage.com.

Distant Lands 56 S Raymond Ave, Pasadena, CA 91105 ☏1-800/310-3220, ⓦwww.distantlands.com.

Elliot Bay Book Company 101 S Main St, Seattle, WA 98104 ☏1-800/962-5311, ⓦwww.elliotbaybook.com.

Forsyth Travel Library 226 Westchester Ave, White Plains, NY 10604 ☏1-800/367-7984, ⓦwww.forsyth.com.

Globe Corner Bookstore 28 Church St, Cambridge, MA 02138 ☏1-800/358-6013, ⓦwww.globercorner.com.

GORP Books & Maps ☏1-877/440-4677, ⓦwww.gorp.com/gorp/books/main.htm.

Map Link 30 S La Patera Lane, Unit 5, Santa Barbara, CA 93117 ☏805/692-6777, ⓦwww.maplink.com.

Rand McNally ☏1-800/333-0136, ⓦwww.randmcnally.com. Around thirty stores across the US; dial ext 2111 or check the website for the nearest location.

Travel Books and Language Center 4437 Wisconsin Ave NW, Washington DC 20016 ☏1-800/220-2665, ⓦwww.bookweb.org/bookstore/travelbks.

The Travel Bug Bookstore 2667 W Broadway, Vancouver, BC V6K 2G2 ☏604/737-1122, ⓦwww.swifty.com/tbug.

World of Maps 1235 Wellington St, Ottawa, ON K1Y 3A3 ☏1-800/214-8524, ⓦwww.worldofmaps.com.

In Australia and New Zealand

The Map Shop 6–10 Peel St, Adelaide, SA 5000 ☏08/8231 2033, ⓦwww.mapshop.net.au.

MapWorld 173 Gloucester St, Christchurch, New Zealand ☏0800/627 967 or 03/374 5399, ⓦwww.mapworld.co.nz.

Mapland 372 Little Bourke St, Melbourne, Victoria 3000 ☏03/9670 4383, ⓦwww.mapland.com.au.

Perth Map Centre 1/884 Hay St, Perth, WA 6000 ☏08/9322 5733, ⓦwww.perthmap.com.au.

Specialty Maps 46 Albert St, Auckland 1001 ☏09/307 2217, ⓦwww.ubdonline.co.nz/maps.

Insurance

Travel insurance can buy you peace of mind as well as save you money. Before paying for a new policy, however, it's worth checking whether you are already covered: some all-risks home insurance policies may cover your possessions when overseas, and many private medical schemes include cover when abroad. In Canada, provincial health plans usually provide partial cover for medical mishaps overseas, while holders of official student/teacher/youth cards in Canada and the US are entitled to meagre accident coverage and hospital in-patient benefits. Students will often find that their student health coverage extends during the vacations and for one term beyond the date of last enrolment.

After exhausting the possibilities above, you might want to contact a specialist travel insurance company, or consider the travel insurance deal we offer (see box). A typical travel insurance policy usually provides cover for the loss of baggage, tickets and – up to a certain limit – cash or cheques, as well as cancellation or curtailment of your journey. Most of them exclude so-called dangerous sports unless an extra premium is paid. This can include scuba-diving, and you should be sure if you intend to do any diving that your policy covers you for it: treatment in a recompresssion chamber can cost US$1000 a day.

Many policies can be chopped and changed to exclude coverage you don't need – for example, sickness and accident benefits can often be excluded or included at will. If you do take medical coverage, ascertain whether benefits will be paid as treatment proceeds or only after return home, and whether there is a 24-hour medical emergency number. When securing baggage cover, make sure that the per-article limit – typically under £500/US$700 – will cover your most valuable possession. If you need to make a claim, you should keep receipts for medicines and medical treatment, and in the event you have anything stolen, you must obtain an official theft report from the police (called a *mahdar*).

Rough Guides travel insurance

Rough Guides offers its own travel insurance, customized for our readers by a leading UK broker and backed by a Lloyds underwriter. It's available for anyone, of any nationality and any age, travelling anywhere in the world.

There are two main Rough Guide insurance plans: **Essential**, for basic, no-frills cover; and **Premier** – with more generous and extensive benefits. Alternatively, you can take out **annual multi-trip insurance**, which covers you for any number of trips throughout the year (with a maximum of 60 days for any one trip). Unlike many policies, the Rough Guides schemes are calculated by the day, so if you're travelling for 27 days rather than a month, that's all you pay for. If you intend to be away for the whole year, the Adventurer policy will cover you for 365 days. Each plan can be supplemented with a "Hazardous Activities Premium" to cover things like scuba diving.

For a policy quote, call the Rough Guide Insurance Line on UK freefone ☏0800/015 0906; US freefone ☏1-866/220-5588, or, if you're calling from elsewhere ☏+44 1243/621 046. Alternatively, get an online quote or buy online at ⊛www.roughguides.com/insurance.

Health

Despite the potential health hazards of travel in Egypt, the majority of visitors experience nothing worse than a bout or two of diarrhoea. For minor health complaints, a visit to a pharmacy is likely to be sufficient. Egyptian pharmacists are well trained and dispense a wide range of drugs, including many normally on prescription in Europe. If they feel you need a full diagnosis, they can usually recommend a doctor – sometimes working on the premises. Most doctors speak English or French.

Although the change of diet and climate accounts for most health problems, **individual responses** vary. While some people adapt quickly to the heat and consume local food with impunity, others get sick and stay poorly (children and the elderly are likely to suffer the worst effects). If you're only here for a week or two, it makes sense to be cautious, but longer-staying visitors might prefer to get ill early, acclimatize, and worry less thereafter – a lot depends on your constitution. Bearing this in mind, take whatever precautions seem appropriate.

For comprehensive coverage of the health problems encountered by travellers worldwide, consult the *Rough Guide to Travel Health* by Dr Nick Jones.

Medical resources for travellers

Websites

Ⓦ **health.yahoo.com** Information on specific diseases and conditions, drugs and herbal remedies, as well as advice from health experts.
Ⓦ **www.istm.org** The website of the International Society for Travel Medicine, with worldwide listings of clinics specializing in travel health.
Ⓦ **www.tripprep.com** Travel Health Online provides an online-only comprehensive database of necessary vaccinations, with a page of information specific to Egypt.
Ⓦ **www.fitfortravel.scot.nhs.uk** Scottish NHS website with general information about travel-related diseases and how to avoid them, and also pages on specific countries including Egypt.

In the US and Canada

Canadian Society for International Health 1 Nicholas St, Suite 1105, Ottawa, ON K1N 7B7 ☎613/241-5785, Ⓦ www.csih.org. Distributes a free pamphlet, "Health Information for Canadian Travellers", containing an extensive list of travel health centres in Canada, which can also be found on its website.
Centers for Disease Control 1600 Clifton Rd NE, Atlanta, GA 30333 ☎1-800/311-3435 or 404/639-3534, Ⓕ1-888/232-3299, Ⓦ www.cdc.gov. Publishes outbreak warnings, suggested inoculations, precautions and other background information for travellers. Useful website plus International Travelers Hotline on ☎1-877/FYI-TRIP.
International Association for Medical Assistance to Travellers (IAMAT) 417 Center St, Lewiston, NY 14092 ☎716/754-4883, Ⓦ www.sentex.net/~iamat; and 40 Regal Rd, Guelph, ON N1K 1B5 ☎519/836-0102. Can provide members with a list of English-speaking doctors in Egypt, climate charts and leaflets on various diseases and inoculations.
International SOS Assistance Eight Neshaminy Interplex Suite 207, Trevose, PA 19053-6956 ☎1-800/523-8930, Ⓦ www.intsos.com. Members receive pre-trip medical referral information, as well as overseas emergency services designed to complement travel insurance coverage.
Travel Medicine ☎1-800/872-8633, Ⓕ1-413/584-6656, Ⓦ www.travmed.com. Sells first-aid kits, mosquito netting, water filters, reference books and other health-related travel products.
Travelers Medical Center 31 Washington Square West, New York, NY 10011 ☎212/982-1600. Consultation service on immunizations and treatment of diseases for people travelling to developing countries.

In the UK and Ireland

British Airways Travel Clinics 28 regional clinics (call ☎01276/685 040 for the nearest, or consult Ⓦ www.britishairways.com), with several in London (Mon–Fri 9.30am–5.15pm, Sat 10am–4pm), including 156 Regent St, London W1B 5LB (☎020/7439 9584; no appointment necessary). There are appointment-only branches at 101 Cheapside, London EC2V 6DT (☎020/7606 2977) and at the BA terminal in London's Victoria Station (☎020/7233 6661). All clinics offer vaccinations, tailored advice from an online database and a complete range of travel healthcare products.

Dun Laoghaire Medical Centre 5 Northumberland Ave, Dun Laoghaire, Co. Dublin ☎01/280 4996, ⓕ280 5603. Advice on medical matters abroad.

MASTA (Medical Advisory Service for Travellers Abroad) London School of Hygiene and Tropical Medicine ⊛www.masta.org. Operates a pre-recorded 24-hour Travellers' Health Line (☎0906/822 4100; 60p per min), giving written information tailored to your journey by return of post.

Nomad Pharmacy surgeries 40 Bernard St, London, WC1N 1LE and 3-4 Wellington Terrace, Turnpike Lane, London N8 0PX (Mon–Fri 9.30am–6pm; ☎020/7833 4114 to book vaccination appointment). Free advice to personal callers, or a telephone helpline on ☎0906/863 3414 (60p per minute). Information tailored to specific travel needs.

Trailfinders Immunization clinic (no appointments necessary) at 194 Kensington High St, London W8 7RG ☎020/7938 3999 (Mon–Fri 9am–5pm except Thurs to 6pm, Sat 9.30am–4pm).

Travel Health Centre Department of International Health and Tropical Medicine, Royal College of Surgeons in Ireland, Mercers Medical Centre, Stephen's St Lower, Dublin 2 ☎01/402 2337. Expert pre-trip advice and inoculations.

Travel Medicine Services PO Box 254, 16 College St, Belfast BT1 6BT ☎028/9031 5220. Offers medical advice before a trip and help afterwards in the event of a tropical disease.

In Australia and New Zealand

Travellers' Medical and Vaccination Centres 27–29 Gilbert Place, Adelaide, SA 5000 ☎08/8212 7522.
1/170 Queen St, Auckland ☎09/373 3531.
5/247 Adelaide St, Brisbane, Qld 4000 ☎07/3221 9066.
5/8–10 Hobart Place, Canberra, ACT 2600 ☎02/6257 7156.
147 Armagh St, Christchurch ☎03/379 4000.
5 Westralia St, Darwin, NT 0800 ☎08/8981 2907.
270 Sandy Bay Rd, Sandy Bay, Hobart, Tas 7000 ☎03/6223 7577.
2/393 Little Bourke St, Melbourne, Vic 3000 ☎03/9602 5788.
5 Mill St, Perth, WA 6000 ☎08/9321 1977, plus branch in Fremantle.
7/428 George St, Sydney, NSW 2000 ☎02/9221 7133, plus branches in Chatswood and Parramatta.

Shop 15, Grand Arcade, 14–16 Willis St, Wellington ☎04/473 0991.

Preventative medicine

Although visitors to Egypt are not required to have **inoculations** unless coming from an infected area, you should always be up to date with **polio** and **tetanus**. It's also worth being vaccinated against **typhoid**, which occasionally flares up in parts of Egypt – although the **cholera** shot is generally acknowledged to be worthless. If you're hoping to visit southern Egypt, Sudan or sub-Saharan Africa, a vaccination against **meningitis** is essential.

While not an issue for most tourists, visitors planning to stay a long time in Egypt or the Middle East should consider vaccination against **hepatitis**. The new shot for Hepatitis A (Havrix monodose) is expensive at about £50/US$70 (though your doctor may provide it free), but with a booster a year later it lasts for ten years. Hepatitis B is transmitted like HIV, through body fluids, so you will be protected from it by the same precautions that you take against HIV infection (see p.38); immunization is only really necessary for medical workers. Though all these vaccinations can be obtained in Cairo (see p.276), it is vital to ensure that any injections are done with sterile needles. If necessary, supply your own disposable syringe, sold at pharmacies.

Other precautions are fairly obvious, though whether all of them are justified is debatable. Guard against **heatstroke** (see overleaf) and **food poisoning**. Rare meat and raw shellfish top the danger list, which descends via creamy sauces down to salads, juices, raw fruit and vegetables – and if slavishly followed would prevent you from eating most of what's on offer. Visitors who insist on washing everything (and only cleaning their teeth) in mineral water are overreacting. Just use common sense, and accustom your stomach gradually to Egyptian cooking. Asking for dishes to be served very hot (*sukhna awi*) will reduce the risk of catching anything. Take prompt care of **cuts and skin irritations**, since flies can quickly spread infections. Anthisan cream (available abroad) is good for bites, swellings and rashes.

Pharmacies, doctors and hospitals

Pharmacies, found in every town, form the advance guard of Egypt's health service. Pharmacists usually speak English, and can dispense most drugs without a prescription. Private **doctors** are equally common, but charge for consultations: expect to pay about £E100 (roughly £15/US$22) a session, excluding the price of any drugs you are prescribed. If you get seriously ill, private **hospitals** are generally preferable to public sector ones. Those attached to universities are usually well equipped and competent, but small-town hospitals are often abysmal. Many hospitals (*mustashfa*) require a **deposit** at the very least, and often payment on the spot; you will then have to claim it back from your insurance provider. Despite several good hospitals in Cairo and Alexandria, Egypt is no country to fall seriously ill in. In particular, if you need surgery, it is best to get back home for it if you can.

Health hazards

The **tap water** in Egyptian towns and cities is heavily chlorinated and mostly safe to drink, but unpalatable and rough on tender stomachs. In rural areas, Sinai campsites and desert rest-houses there's a fair risk of contaminated water.

Consequently, most tourists stick to **bottled mineral water**, which is widely available, tastes better, and won't upset sensitive tums. However, excessive fear of tap water is unjustified, and hard to sustain in practice if you're here for long. Once your guts have adjusted, it's usually okay to drink it without further purification (Halazone tablets, iodine crystals, or by boiling).

What you should avoid is any contact with stagnant water that might harbour **bilharzia** (schistosomiasis) flukes. Irrigation **canals** and the slower stretches of the **River Nile** are notoriously infested with these minute worms, which breed in the blood vessels of the abdomen and liver (the main symptom is blood in the urine). Don't drink or swim there, nor walk barefoot in the mud, or even on grass that's wet with Nile water. But it's okay to bathe in the saline pools of the desert oases.

Heat and dust

Many visitors experience problems with Egypt's intense **heat**, particularly in the south. Because sweat evaporates immediately in the dry atmosphere, you can easily become dehydrated without realizing it. **Dehydration** is exacerbated by both alcohol and caffeine. Drink plenty of other fluids (at least three litres per day; twice as much if you're exerting yourself) and take a bit of extra salt with your food. Wear a hat and loose-fitting clothes (not synthetic fabrics), and a high-factor sunscreen to protect yourself from **sunburn**, especially during summer. Try to avoid going out in the middle of the day and wear a T-shirt when snorkelling, as the sun burns you even quicker in the water.

Heat exhaustion – signified by headaches, dizziness and nausea – is treated by resting in a cool place and drinking plenty of water or juice with a pinch of salt. An intense headache, heightened body temperature, flushed skin and the cessation of sweating are symptoms of **heatstroke**, which can be fatal if not treated *immediately*. The whole body must be cooled by immersion in tepid water, or the application of wet towels. Seek medical assistance. If walking for long distances in the sun, it is vital to carry drinking water and wear a sunhat; a cotton sunhat can also be drenched with water, wrung to stop it dripping, and worn wet so that the evaporation of the water cools your head – you'll be amazed at how quickly it dries out.

Less seriously, visitors from cooler climates may suffer from **prickly heat**, an itchy rash caused by excessive perspiration trapped beneath the skin. Wearing loose clothing, keeping cool and bathing often will help relieve the symptoms until your body acclimatizes.

In non-air-conditioned environments, you might employ the traditional Egyptian method of sprinkling water on the ground to cool the surrounding area by evaporation – it also levels the dust.

Desert **dust** – or grit and smog in Cairo – may cause your **eyes** to itch and water. **Contact lens-users** should wear glasses instead, at least part of the time. If ordinary eye drops don't help, try antihistamine decongestant eye drops such as Vernacel, Vascon-A or Optihist. Persistent irritation may indicate **trachoma**, a contagious infection which is easily cured by antibiotics at an early stage, but eventually causes blindness if left untreated. Its prevalence in Egypt explains the number of older folk with cloudy eyes, and the ophthalmologists in every town.

Spending time in the desert, you might find that your **sinuses** get painfully irritated by wind-borne dust. Covering your nose and mouth with a scarf helps prevent this, while olbas oil or a nasal decongestant spray (available at pharmacies) can relieve the symptoms.

Diarrhoea and worse...

Almost every visitor to Egypt gets **diarrhoea** at some stage. Unless you're stricken by cramps, the best initial treatment is to simply adapt your diet, using drugs only as a last resort. Plain boiled rice and vegetables are the best things to eat, and you should try to avoid greasy or spicy food, caffeine, alcohol, and most fruit and dairy products (although some say that bananas and prickly pears can help, while yoghurt provides a form of protein that your body can easily absorb). Most importantly, keep your bodily fluids topped up by drinking plenty of bottled water (perhaps mixed with a rehydration sachet or, failing that, salt and sugar). Drugs like Imodium or Lomotil will plug you up, undermining your body's efforts to rid itself of infection, but can be handy as a stop-gap measure if you have to travel. Avoid Enterovioform, which is still available in Egypt despite being suspected of damaging the optic nerve. Antinal (nifuroxazide) is widely prescribed against diarrhoea in Egypt, and available over the counter in pharmacies, but should not be used for more than a couple of days. Don't give any of these quite powerful drugs to children. Also note that having diarrhoea can make drugs less effective if taken orally (contraceptive pills for example), as they pass straight through your system without being absorbed.

If symptoms persist longer than a few days, or if you develop a fever or pass blood in your faeces, get medical help immediately, since diarrhoea can also be a symptom of serious infection. Accompanied by vomiting

and fever, it may indicate **typhoid**, which responds well to antibiotics. Rarer is **cholera**, which requires urgent treatment with antibiotics and rehydration fluids; it is marked by a sudden onset of acute diarrhoea and cramps, and tends to occur in epidemics rather than isolated cases. Except for the "rice-water shits" typical of cholera, similar symptoms occur with bacilliary **dysentery**, which is treated with antibiotics. Amoebic dysentery is harder to shift and can cause permanent damage if untreated. The normal remedy is the heavy-duty antibiotic metronidazole (Flagyl), which should only be taken under medical supervision.

Rabies and malaria

Rabies is endemic in Egypt, where many wild animals (including bats, sometimes found in temples and tombs) carry the disease. Avoid touching *any* strange animal, wild or domestic. Treatment must be given between exposure to the disease and the onset of symptoms; once these appear, rabies is invariably fatal. If you think you've been exposed, return home and seek help immediately. To err on the side of caution, consider having a rabies jab before coming to Egypt. It doesn't confer any protection, but fewer injections will be required should you become infected and need treatment.

Currently resurgent throughout Africa, **malaria**, spread by the anopheles mosquito, could become a problem in Egypt in the future, but isn't currently a threat – it does exist during the summer months in the Fayoum, but not to the extent that warrants the use of malaria pills, although you should take extra steps to avoid mosquito bites while you are there (use repellent and cover bare skin, especially feet and ankles, after dusk – see below). Consult your doctor, or enquire at a Medical Advisory Service (see pp.34–35) for latest information on malaria risk and prevention. The first signs of infection are muscular soreness and a low fever; four to eight days later, the characteristic bouts of chills and fever appear. If you suspect that you have it, seek treatment immediately.

Mosquitoes and bugs

Besides the risk of malaria, **mosquitoes** can

make your life a misery. Horribly ubiquitous over the summer, these blood-sucking pests are never entirely absent – even in Cairo, despite locals' assertions to the contrary. The only solution is total war, using fans, mosquito coils, rub-on repellent, and perhaps a plug-in Ezalo device, sold at pharmacies. A lot of people in Egypt use citronella oil, obtainable from many pharmacies, as a mosquito repellent, but tests have shown it to be much less effective than repellents containing DEET (diethyltoluamide), which are the ones recommended by medical authorities. X-gnat skin gel is an effective natural alternative. You can also reputedly make yourself less attractive to mosquitoes by taking Vitamin B-12 tablets, starting before you leave home. The theory is that after two weeks of 50mg per day, your blood begins to smell bad to them, but again, medical authorities in general are sceptical. The best guarantee of a bite-less night's sleep is to bring a mosquito net with long tapes, to pin above your bed. Mosquitoes favour shady, damp areas, and anywhere around dusk. Feet are the part of the body that most attracts them, and you should always be sure to put repellent on your ankles if they are uncovered when you go out in the evening.

Equally loathsome – and widespread – are **flies**, which transmit various diseases. Only insecticide spray or air conditioning offers any protection. Some cheap hotels harbour fleas, scabies, mites, giant roaches and **other bugs**. Consult a pharmacist if you find yourself with a persistent skin irritation.

Scorpions and snakes

The **danger** from scorpions and snakes is minimal, as most species are nocturnal, hide during the heat of the day, and generally avoid people. However, you shouldn't go barefoot, turn over rocks or stick your hands into dark crevices anywhere off the beaten track. Whereas the sting of larger, darker **scorpions** is no worse than a bad wasp sting, the venom of the pale, slender-clawed *Buthridae* is highly toxic. If stung, cold-pack the affected area and seek medical help immediately.

Egypt has two main types of poisonous snake. **Vipers** vary in colour from sandy to reddish (or sometimes grey) and leave two fang punctures. The horned viper, Egypt's deadliest snake, is recognizable by its horns. **Cobras** are recognizable by their distinctive hood and bite mark (a single row of teeth plus fang holes). The smaller Egyptian cobra (coloured sandy olive) is found throughout the country; the longer black-necked cobra (which can spit its venom up to three metres) only in the south. Be somewhat reassured that snakes come out to drink usually at night, and hibernate in the winter. All snakebites should be washed immediately. Stay calm, as panicking sends the venom through your bloodstream more quickly, and get immediate medical help.

HIV and AIDS

Despite a TV campaign, the level of **AIDS** awareness is low, and most Egyptians still perceive it as a Western problem. Tourists likewise may not think of Egypt as the sort of country that would have an AIDS problem, but the few hundred cases reported here are almost certainly the tip of an iceberg. Prostitution, homosexuality and extra-marital sex in general are so clandestine and taboo that levels of education about them are low, and few Egyptian men take any precautions. As throughout the world, the need for extreme caution, and safe sex, cannot be overstressed. This particularly applies to Western women having a fling in places like Luxor (see p.347), who may not be aware of just how much of an industry that is. Anyone of either sex or orientation, contemplating any kind of casual affair, whether with Egyptians or with fellow tourists, should always carry condoms and insist on using them. Likewise, be absolutely sure that any injections, tattooing or acupuncture is done with sterile instruments, and that barbers use a new blade if you go to them for a shave. Pharmacies in cities plus a few shops in Hurghada and Sinai are the only places in Egypt to sell **condoms** (*kabout*) – either Egyptian-made *Tops* (liable to rip) or US imports (thick and short). It's best to bring your own supply.

Women's health

Travelling in the heat and taking antibiotics for an upset stomach, you are liable to **vaginal infections** even if you wash regularly with mild soap, wear cotton underwear and loose clothing. Yeast infections are treatable with Nystatin pessaries (available at pharmacies; "one-shot" Canesten pessaries (bring some from home if you're prone to thrush; or douches of a weak solution of vinegar or lemon juice. Sea bathing can also help. Trichomonas is usually treated with Flagyl, which should only be taken under medical supervision.

Sanitary protection is available from pharmacies in cities and tourist resorts, but seldom anywhere else, so it's wise to bring a supply for your trip.

Bring your own **contraceptives**, since the only forms widely available in Egypt are old-fashioned, high-dosage pills, the coil, and not too trusty condoms (see above). Cap-users should pack a spare, and enough spermicide and pessaries. If you're on the pill, beware that persistent diarrhoea can render it ineffective.

Costs, money and banks

Once you've arrived, Egypt is an inexpensive and good-value destination – except perhaps for Sinai and Hurghada, which are pricier than other parts of the country. As a rule, though, providing you avoid luxury hotels or tourist-only services, costs for food, accommodation and transport are low by European standards. The currency is the Egyptian pound (£E), divided into a hundred piastres (pt), and the rate of exchange currently stands at just over six and a half Egyptian pounds to one pound sterling, and just over four and a half to the US dollar and the euro.

Average costs

Accommodation ranges from about £3–7/US$5–10 a night for a double room in a basic, unclassified hotel to £70–180/US$100–250 in Egypt's most luxurious establishments. On a limited budget, you can expect to get a decent double room in a one- or two-star hotel for £5–10/US$7–15. The occasional splurge in a three-star hotel, with a pool, will cost £20–70/US$30–100 for a double room off season, or £30–100/US$40–140 at peak periods. To some extent, all these costs are affected by **where you are and when**. Though low-budget options exist, the cost of hotels is higher in Cairo, Sinai and Hurghada throughout the year; in Alexandria during the summer; and in Luxor and Aswan over winter.

The price of a **meal** reflects a similar span, but the basic Egyptian staple of *fuul* and *taamiya* (beans and felafel) or *kushari* (noodles, rice and lentils with hot sauce) can be had in a local eatery for about 50p/70¢. Egyptian pizzas, chicken or kebabs cost about £2–4/US$3–6, and European-style meals in restaurants from around £5/US$7.

Locally manufactured **drinks** are reasonably cheap – a bottle of Stella beer costing about £1.20/US$2.50, native spirits or wines under £4/US$6 – but imported booze is more expensive than back home in hotels and restaurants, which are generally the only outlets serving alcohol (though you can buy it cheaply in duty-free shops). Everyday items tend to be pricier in Sinai, Hurghada and the desert oases, where goods have to be trucked in from distant centres.

Unless you take domestic flights or rely heavily on private taxis, **transport** is likewise cheap. You can rent a car for £45/US$65 a day, including petrol (which costs less per litre than mineral water). The cost of buses, trains and collective taxis is generally absurdly low. For instance, the 885km journey from Cairo to Aswan costs £12.50/US$18 by train in first class, £7.50/US$11 in air-conditioned second class, and £10.50/US$15 by bus. In fact, these train fares are high by Egyptian standards as tourists may only use specific air-conditioned trains on this route (see p.262) – if you could use ordinary second- and third-class trains, the fares would cost less than half that.

Hidden costs

Hidden costs in Egypt are fourfold. Most restaurant and hotel bills are liable to a **service charge** plus local taxes (Luxor and Hurghada have the highest), which increase the final cost by 17–25 percent (unless already included in the price, or irrelevant, as in really cheap hotels and cafés). Visiting the Pyramids and the monuments of the Nile Valley entails spending a lot on **site tickets** (£2–5/US$3–7), unless you have a student card (see below) entitling you to a fifty percent discount (which many non-students obtain in Cairo, see p.273). The custodians of tombs and temples and the medieval mosques of Islamic Cairo also expect to be tipped. For more on admission prices, see p.66.

A harder aspect to come to terms with is that you'll be confronted with real **poverty**. As a tourist, you're not going to solve any problems, but with an average Egyptian's wage at around £E120 a month (less than £20/US$30), even a small tip can make a difference to individual family life. For Egyptians, giving money and goods to the needy is a natural act – and a requirement of Islam. As a presumed-rich *khawaga* (the Egyptian term for a foreigner), you will be expected to be liberal with **baksheesh**, which can be divided into three main varieties.

The most common is **tipping**: a small reward for a small service, which can encompass anyone from a waiter or lift operator to someone who unlocks a tomb or museum room at one of the ancient sites. The sums involved are often paltry (see below) – and you needn't feel railroaded into giving more; but try to strike a balance between defending your own wallet and acquiescing gracefully when appropriate. There's little point in spoiling your mood and offending people over what are trifling sums

for a Western tourist, but often an important part of people's livelihood in Egypt.

Typical tips might be 50pt–£E1 for looking after your shoes while you visit a mosque; £E2–5 to a custodian for opening up a door to let you enter a building or climb a minaret. In restaurants, you do not usually leave a percentage of the bill: typical tips (regardless of whether the bill claims to include "service") are as little as 50pt in an ultra-cheap place such as a *kushari* joint, £E2 in a typical cheap restaurant, or £E5 in a smarter establishment. Customers also usually give tips of 10–25pt in a juice bar, and 50pt in a café.

A second common type of *baksheesh* is more expensive: rewarding the **bending of rules** – many of which seem to have been designed for just that purpose. Examples might include letting you into an archeological site after hours (or into a vaguely restricted area), finding you a sleeper on a train when the carriages are "full", and so on. This should not be confused with bribery, which is a more serious business with its own etiquette and risks – best not entered into.

The last kind of *baksheesh* is simply **almsgiving**. The disabled are traditional recipients of such gifts, and it seems right to join locals in giving out small change. Children, however, are a different case, pressing their demands only on tourists. If someone offers some genuine help and asks for an *alum* (pen), it seems fair enough, but to yield to every request might encourage a cycle of dependency that Egypt could do without.

Since most Egyptian money is paper, often in the form of well-used banknotes that can be fiddly to separate out, it can make life easier if you keep small bills in a separate "*baksheesh* pocket" specifically for the purpose. If giving *baksheesh* in foreign currency, give notes rather than coins (which are useless to Egyptians). Bringing a wad of one-dollar bills can be useful for this.

Youth and student discounts

Full-time students are eligible for the **International Student ID Card** (**ISIC**), which entitles the bearer to special air, rail and bus fares and discounts at museums, theatres and other attractions. For Americans there's also a health benefit, providing up to

US$3000 in emergency medical coverage and US$100 a day for up to sixty days' hospital care, plus a 24-hour hotline to call in the event of a medical, legal or financial emergency. The card costs £6 in the UK, €12.70 in Ireland, US$22 in the USA, CDN$16 in Canada, Aus$16.50 in Australia, or NZ$21 in New Zealand. You can also buy an ISIC card at the Medical Scientific Centre in Cairo for £E50 – but you still require a valid student ID card or proof of student status (see p.273 for further details). It is possible to buy a card without any student ID at some of the budget hotels in Cairo, but this unofficial practice has been cracked down on in recent years, and obvious non-students brandishing dodgy student cards for reductions at archeological sites may end up having to explain themselves to the tourist police. The ISIC card entitles you to a fifty-percent discount on most of Egypt's museums and sites, a thirty-percent discount on rail fares and around fifteen percent on ferries.

An alternative available to anyone under 26 is the **International Youth Travel Card**, which costs £7/US$22 and entitles holders to the same discounts (within Egypt) as the ISIC card. This card is also available for £E50 from the Medical Scientific Centre in Cairo (see above).

Teachers qualify for the **International Teacher Identity Card**, offering similar discounts. All these cards are available from youth travel specialists such as Council Travel, STA, Usit and Travel CUTS. Basically, it's worth flashing one or the other at every opportunity to see what you can get.

Prices and inflation

Most of the **prices** in this book are given in local currency (see below). The main exceptions to this rule – air fares, top-flight accommodation and special packages – are reckoned in US$, although most are actually payable in Egyptian pounds backed by an exchange receipt.

Both of these price indications will certainly change, so costs quoted in this guide can't be taken for granted. However, the cost for tourists in real terms shouldn't rise so much compared to local prices, and might even decrease if your own currency is riding high.

Although Egyptian **inflation** is currently running at around three percent, it's unevenly distributed. Prices for luxury goods and services (ie, most things in the private sector) rise faster than the cost of public transport, petrol and basic foodstuffs, which is held down by subsidies that the government dare not abolish.

Money

Egypt's basic unit of **currency** is the **Egyptian pound** (called a *ginay* in Arabic, and written as £E or LE). It has been sliding of late against hard currencies, and currently rates at around £6.60 sterling, US$4.50 or €4.40.

Egyptian **banknotes** bear Arabic numerals on one side, Western numerals on the other, and are colour coded: £E1 (brown), £E5 (blue), £E10 (red), £E20 (green), £E50 (red), £E100 (green). The £E50 has been suspect since forgeries came to light, while the £E100 is never used in everyday life.

The Egyptian pound is divided into 100 **piastres**, called *'urush* (singular *'irsh*) in Arabic and written as ﻕ (abbreviated by Westerners to pt). There are 10pt, 25pt and 50pt notes, and variously sized **coins** to the value of 5pt, 10pt, 20pt, 25pt and 50pt; some 25pt coins have a hole in the middle.

Many of the notes in circulation are so ragged that merchants refuse them. Trying to palm off (and avoid receiving) decrepit notes can add spice to minor transactions, or be a real nuisance. Conversely, many vendors won't accept high-denomination notes (£E20 upwards) due to a shortage of **change**. While some offer sweets in lieu of coins, others round prices up. Try to hoard coins and small-value notes for tips, fares and small purchases.

Carrying your money

Arriving in Egypt, it is useful to have at least three days' survival money in **cash**, although you will not need local currency if arriving by air, as bank kiosks offering normal rates are open round the clock at the airport. Arriving by land or sea, you should have no trouble changing money at the border. It is illegal, and unnecessary, to import or export more than £E1000 in local currency.

US dollars, euros and English sterling notes are easy to exchange almost anywhere – though due to **forgeries**, banks are often unwilling to accept US$100 notes issued before 1992, or in less than mint condition. Aside from ordinary spending, hard cash (usually US$) may be required for visas, border taxes and suchlike. In Cairo, Forex bureaux (see below) will also change Canadian, Australian, Cypriot, Jordanian and Libyan currency (though notes must be in mint condition), and some banks will change all but the last – branches in five-star hotels are your best bet. **Do not bring** New Zealand dollars, or Scottish or Northern Irish sterling banknotes, which are not accepted by banks or Forex bureaux. Sudanese pounds likewise cannot be changed in Egypt except perhaps on arrival by boat at Aswan, and Israeli shekels can only be changed at the Taba border crossing, and at one or two banks (in five-star hotels) and some Cairo Forex bureaux.

The rest of your money should, ideally, be spread around different forms and currencies for the sake of security. You may wish to carry the bulk of it in a well-known brand of **travellers' cheque**, with **credit cards** and/or **Eurocheques** for backup. It is worth bearing in mind, however, that a number of banks now have **ATM** facilities, which enable you to draw directly from your bank account (see below). It therefore may not be necessary to carry too big a wad of travellers' cheques, or even a credit card. Note too that by taking cash in one currency and cheques in another, you can choose to exchange whichever offers the better rate.

American Express, Barclays, Citibank and Bank of America **travellers' cheques** are accepted by most banks and exchange offices. Thomas Cook cheques are usually good, though they may present problems in untouristed places – and, like Amex in Egypt, have a reputation for delaying refunds. Any other brand will prove more trouble than it's worth. **Eurocheques** backed by a Eurocard can be cashed at most branches of the Banque Misr. Cashing International Girocheques at major post offices entails an incredible rigmarole.

Credit, debit and ATM cards

Credit cards are accepted at major hotels, top-flight restaurants, some shops and airline offices, but virtually nowhere else. American Express, MasterCard and Visa are the likeliest to be accepted. Beware of people making extra copies of the receipt, to fraudulently bill you later; insist that the transaction is done before your eyes. **Cash advances** on Visa and MasterCard can be obtained at most branches of the Banque Misr (up to US$1000 daily with 1.5 percent commission), while American Express cardholders can cash personal cheques at the main Amex branches (see p.44).

In Cairo, Alexandria, Luxor, Hurghada and an increasing number of towns throughout Egypt, branches of major banks have **ATMs** (hole-in-the-wall cash machines) that allow you to draw cash using Visa, MasterCard, Plus or Cirrus **cash cards** – though the machines do have an annoying habit of swallowing cards. The ATMs are usually situated outside the banks, inside airports and some shopping centres, so you can use them at any time. Be warned, however, that Cirrus charges US$5 for each withdrawal, and others may charge more – check with your card-issuer before leaving. The Egyptian British Bank's ATMs also accept cards showing Electron, Express Net, Global Access, Electro Bank and Marine Machine.

A compromise between travellers' cheques and plastic is **Visa TravelMoney**, a disposable pre-paid debit card with a PIN which works in all ATMs that take Visa cards. You load up your account with funds before leaving home, and when they run out, you simply throw the card away. You can buy up to nine cards to access the same funds – useful for couples or families travelling together – and it's a good idea to buy at least one extra as a back-up in case of loss or theft. In case of loss, there is a 24-hour emergency customer assistance number in the United States which can be called collect: ☎410/581-9994. The card is available in most countries from branches of Thomas Cook and Citicorp. For more information, check the Visa TravelMoney website at ⓦhttp://usa.visa.com/personal/cards/visa_travel_money.html.

Emergency numbers for lost cards and travellers'cheques

American Express ☎02/570 3153
Diners Club ☎02/738 2638
MasterCard and Visa ☎ 02/797 1148-9

Banks and exchange

Exchange rates at the main **Egyptian banks** (Bank of Alexandria, Banque Misr, Banque du Caire and National Bank of Egypt) and **Forex bureaux** (private money changers) vary enough to make a difference to people changing a lot of money at once, or bent on saving every penny – but not enough to worry about otherwise. In most towns there isn't much choice anyway; because their use by currency speculators helped put the skids under the pound, they have been closed down everywhere except Cairo. There, they offer the best rates for cash, but may not take travellers' cheques, and will offer lower rates than banks if they do. They are open longer hours and transactions are faster than in banks, where forms are passed among a bevy of clerks and counters.

Such extended transactions are less likely at **foreign banks** (found only in Cairo and Alexandria) or branches **in hotels**, but there are plenty of exceptions in practice. If you're carrying **American Express** or **Thomas Cook** travellers' cheques (or cash) it's often quicker to do business at their own local branches (see below).

Opening hours for Egyptian banks are generally Monday to Thursday 8.30am to 2pm, plus an evening shift (5–8pm in winter, 6–9pm in summer); some also open similar hours on Saturday, and from 10am to noon on Sunday (details are given as relevant in the text). Most foreign banks are open from 8.30am to 1pm Monday to Thursday, and sometimes on Sunday. For arriving visitors, the banks at Cairo Airport and the border crossings from Israel are open 24 hours daily, and those at ports whenever a ship docks.

With the recent run on the Egyptian pound, the **black market**, which had with-ered with the introduction of legal Forex bureaux, has returned. It remains extremely clandestine, and you are unlikely to encounter illegal street money changers, who are best avoided if you do, as they are very likely to be rip-off artists or *agents provocateurs*. The current black market rate is £E5.10 to the US dollar, which is about twenty percent higher than the bank rate. Whether this illegal market survives or not remains to be seen, but the government is trying its best to clamp down hard on it, and tourists are best off avoiding it. That said, you might find it expedient to change some cash unofficially in the Sinai or the desert oases, where banks are thin on the ground and the risk factor is lower.

B

BASICS | Costs, money and banks

Commission and receipts

Commission is not generally charged on straight exchanges, but there might be 40pt stamp duty, which you can either pay on the spot or have them deduct from the amount issued. Even if you're not planning to use them, it's wise to **keep all receipts** until you leave Egypt.

Rather than going through the hassle of **re-exchanging Egyptian pounds** into hard currency, it's better to spend it all before leaving (you can't use it at Cairo Airport's duty-free shop, but you can in the café). While minor sums may not incur any forfeit, exchanging large amounts back into hard currency entails a "deduction" of £E30 per day from the sum total of your exchange receipts; what remains is in theory eligible for conversion, but in practice you will find that airport banks rarely have any hard currency in stock. If you really need to change back any currency before leaving, a Forex bureau is your best bet.

American Express and Thomas Cook

American Express has several offices in Cairo and branches in Alexandria, Luxor, Aswan and Ismailiya. All of them can hold client mail and cash Amex travellers' cheques, paying out in Egyptian pounds. Money may be wired to any branch, most of which also allow Amex cardholders to buy travellers' cheques, or cash personal cheques. Green cardholders may draw up to US$1000 every three weeks; gold cardhold-ers can take out US$5000 over the same period, and if your card is platinum, it's US$10,000.

43

Amex's old-established rival, **Thomas Cook**, will cash most brands of travellers' cheque, and sell its own cheques (in whatever hard currency you buy them with). Like Amex, it can also receive money wired from abroad (see below).

American Express offices

Cairo (downtown): 15 Sharia Qasr el-Nil ☎02/574 7991–2, ℱ574 799; *Nile Hilton* ☎02/578 5001, ℱ578 5002; 10th Floor, 21 Sharia Giza ☎02/567 2216, ℱ570 3146 (Mon–Fri 9am–5pm).
Cairo (Heliopolis): 11 Sharia Almaza ☎02/418 2114, ℱ290 9157.
Aswan: Corniche el-Nil ☎097/306 983, ℱ302 909.
Luxor: c/o *Winter Palace Hotel* ☎095/372 862, ℱ378 833.

Thomas Cook offices

Cairo (downtown): 17 Sharia Mahmoud Bassiouny ☎02/574 3955, ℱ576 2750; also at the old airport ☎02/265 3147, ℱ290 4856; the *Semiramis Intercontinental Hotel* ☎02/795 8544, ℱ795 7061; and the World Trade Centre, 1191 Corniche el-Nil ☎02/578 0808, ℱ578 0809.
Cairo (suburbs): 10 26th July St, Mohandiseen ☎02/346 7187, ℱ303 4530; 7 Sharia Baghdad, Heliopolis ☎02/417 3511 or 2, ℱ418 5406; 33 Sharia Nabil el Wakkad, Heliopolis ☎02/419 4082, ℱ414 8601; 88 St 9, Station Sq, Ma'adi ☎02/359 1419, ℱ358 2651.
Alexandria: 15 Midan Saad Zaghloul ☎03/484 7830, ℱ487 4073.
Aswan: 59 Sharia Abtal el-Tahrir, Corniche el-Nil ☎097/304 011, ℱ306 209.
Luxor: c/o *Winter Palace Hotel*, ☎095/372402, ℱ376502.
Port Said: 43 Sharia el-Gumhorriya ☎066/227 559, ℱ236 111.
Hurghada: 8 Sharia El Sheraton ☎ & ℱ065/443 500.
Sharm el-Sheikh: Gafy Mall, Gafy Land ☎ & ℱ062/601 808.

Wiring money from abroad

Having **money wired** from home is never cheap, and should be considered as a last resort. Funds can be sent via MoneyGram or Western Union. Both companies' fees depend on the amount being transferred, but as an example, wiring £700/US$1000 will cost around £40/US$60. The funds can be collected (in Egyptian pounds or, paying one percent commission, in US dollars) from the company's Egyptian agent: MoneyGram's are branches of Thomas Cook, American Express and Sphinx Trading; Western Union's are branches of Misr America Intel Bank and Intel Business Associates. The money can be sent in person at the company's nearest office (in the UK all post offices are agents for MoneyGram), or in the case of Western Union, over the phone using a credit card; it should be available at the other end within minutes.

It's also possible, and slightly cheaper, to have money sent by **bank-to-bank transfer** from a bank in your home country to one in Egypt, but this is much slower (you could be waiting weeks) and much less reliable. First, you would need to find an Egyptian bank prepared to accept a wire; then write or fax your own home bank, giving your own account number, the name and address of the recipient bank, and a routing number; you'll also need to specify the form of ID that the recipient bank will accept before paying out your money. A compromise option is Thomas Cook's **Telegraphic Transfer service**, which costs £15 plus one percent of the amount to be sent (minimum charge £25), and takes one to two days to arrive.

Money-wiring companies

MoneyGram UK ☎0800/018 0104, Ireland ☎1850/205 800, US and Canada ☎1-800/926-9400, Australia ☎1-800/230 100, New Zealand ☎09/379 8243 or 0800/262 263, international toll-free number ☎+800/8971 8971, ⓦwww.moneygram.com.
Thomas Cook UK ☎01733/318 922, Ireland ☎01/677 1307, Northern Ireland ☎028/9055 0030, US ☎1-800/287-7362, Canada ☎1-888/823-4732, ⓦwww.thomascook.com.
Western Union UK ☎0800/833 833, Ireland ☎1800/395 395, US and Canada ☎1-800/325-6000, Australia ☎1-800/649 565, New Zealand ☎09/270 0050, ⓦwww.westernunion.com.

Getting around

Egyptian public transport is, on the whole, pretty good. There is an efficient rail network linking the Nile Valley, Delta and Canal Zone, and elsewhere you can travel easily enough by bus or collective (service) taxi. On the Nile you can indulge in feluccas or cruise boats, and in the desert there's the chance to test your camel-riding prowess. For the hurried, EgyptAir and Air Sinai also provide a network of flights.

By rail

Covering a limited network of routes, **trains** are best used for long hauls between the major cities, when air-conditioned services offer a comfier alternative to buses and taxis. For shorter journeys, however, trains are slower and less reliable. There's a crucial distinction between relatively fast **air-conditioned (a/c) trains** (including **wagons-lits** services) and the snail-like **non-a/c local-stop services**. For reasons of security, the authorities want tourists to use only specially designated a/c trains between Cairo and Upper Egypt, so railway clerks have been instructed not to sell tickets for other trains (see p.68). Most tourists abide by this but, if you have good reasons not to, it's possible to get an Egyptian to buy your ticket, or simply board a non-a/c train without a ticket, and buy one from the conductor.

Students with ISIC cards (see p.40) get thirty-percent reductions on all fares except sleepers and *wagons-lits*. Train **timetables** are posted online at ⓦ touregypt.net/trains.htm.

A/C trains

Air-conditioned trains nearly always have two classes of carriage. The most comfortable option is **first class** (*daraga oola*), which has a/c, waiter service, reclining armchairs and no standing in the aisles. Unfortunately for those trying to sleep, they also screen videos until midnight. Air-conditioned **second class superior** (*daraga tania mumtaaza*) is less plush and more crowded – but at two-thirds of the price of first class it's a real bargain. Occasionally a/c trains will be first or second class only.

Travelling between Cairo, Luxor and Aswan, foreigners are only allowed to use four **"tourist trains"** (three with seats including one that runs in the summer only, plus one sleeper train), whose compartments are guarded by plain-clothes cops toting Uzis. The regular **sleepers** attached to some services along the Nile Valley used to be an economical way of travelling overnight to Luxor or Aswan, but the only sleeper trains that tourists are now permitted to use are the far costlier *wagons-lits* (see below). If you baulk at this, an ordinary first- or a/c second-class carriage should be comfortable enough to allow sleeping on an overnight journey, at a fraction of the cost.

Seats are **reservable** up to seven days in advance. There is occasional double booking but a little *baksheesh* to the conductor usually sorts out any problem. One common difficulty is that **return bookings** can't be arranged at the point of origin, so if you're travelling back to Cairo from Aswan/Luxor (or vice versa), it's best to book a seat the day you arrive. Most **travel agencies** sell first-class tickets for a small commission, saving you from having to queue.

To give an idea of **fares**, a first-class ticket from Cairo to Aswan costs about £12.50/US$18; a/c second-class £7.50/US$11.

Non-a/c trains

Non-air-conditioned trains divide into **ordinary second class** (*daraga tania aadia*), which has padded bench seating, and **third class** (*daraga talata*), which is just wooden benches and open doors and windows for ventilation. Both classes are invariably crowded, the rolling stock is ancient and often filthy, and schedules fanciful. Few foreigners use them, and the only reason to do so for a long journey is to save money. Over short distances, however, some might enjoy the funky disorder, with peasants and vendors getting on and off at every stop.

There is no advance booking for seats on these services and you needn't queue for a ticket at the station. You simply walk on and buy a ticket from the conductor, paying a small penalty fee (about 20p/30¢).

Wagons-lits

The ban on using regular sleepers persuades many tourists to cough up for snazzier *wagons-lit*; these may comprise an entire train, or be limited to a couple of carriages tacked on to a regular service. However, *wagons-lits* have also been shot at on occasion, though again not recently. If you do decide to book one, the fare is a hefty sum (currently £E331.50 – £50/US$72 – per person from Cairo to Luxor or Aswan) for anyone on a low budget – though still cheaper than a flight. Passengers get a comfortable two-bed cabin with a sink, breakfast in bed, a dining car, a bar and sometimes a disco.

Booking of *wagons-lit* is best done through branches of Thomas Cook or American Express, or in Cairo through the cash-only reservations centre (daily 9am–3pm; ☎02/574 9474) in Ramses station, online with Wagons Lits (✪www.sleepingtrains.com), or through Hamis Travel by Ramses Station (☎02/574 9275, ✪www.hamis.com.eg), who will accept credit-card bookings online.

By bus

Inter-city **buses** are an inexpensive way to travel, and often preferable to trains. Besides being quicker for short trips along the Nile Valley, buses serve areas beyond the rail network, such as Sinai, the oases, Abu Simbel and Hurghada. Travelling in Egypt for any length of time, you are likely to make considerable use of the various networks.

Bus services

Egypt's bus network is divided between three main operators, based in Cairo. The **Upper Egypt Bus Company** serves all points along the Nile Valley, the Fayoum and inner oases, and the Red Sea Coast as far

down as El-Quseir. Sinai and the Canal Zone are covered by the **East Delta Bus Company**, whose livery is orange and white. The **West Delta Bus Company**'s blue vehicles serve Alexandria, Mersa Matrouh, Siwa Oasis and the Nile Delta. As bus services are deregulated, other operators are entering the field, such as El Gouna in Aswan.

Major routes are plied by **air-conditioned (a/c)** buses – which are usually new(ish) and fast – while local routes usually have **non-a/c** ones, generally old rattletraps. The former are invariably more expensive, but whether their a/c actually works depends on the bus company and the route.

Key routes (from Cairo to Alexandria, Sharm el-Sheikh and Hurghada) are also covered by the **Superjet** company, whose a/c buses have toilets, videos and expensive snacks. Their red, black and gold livery explains their nickname, the "Golden Arrows" or "Golden Rockets". Superjet is a subsidiary of the **Arab Union Transport Company**, which operates international services to Libya, Jordan, Syria and Saudi Arabia.

Terminals and bookings

Though most towns have a single bus depot for all destinations, cities such as Cairo, Alexandria, Port Said and Ismailiya have several **terminals** (detailed in the guide). English- or French-speaking staff are fairly common at the larger ones, but rare in the provinces. **Schedules** – usually posted in Arabic only – change frequently, so information in this guide should be verified in person. Hotels in Sinai and the oases, and the tourist offices in Luxor, Aswan and the oases can also supply information.

At city terminals, **tickets** are normally sold from kiosks, up to 24 hours in advance for a/c or long-haul services. In the provinces, tickets may only be available an hour or so before departure, or on the bus itself in the case of through-services, which are often standing-room only when they arrive. Passengers on a/c services are usually assigned a seat (the number is written in Arabic on your ticket), but seats on "local" buses are taken willy-nilly.

By service taxi

Collective **service taxis** (*servees*) are one of the best features of Egyptian transport. They operate on a wide variety of routes, are generally quicker than buses and trains, and fares are very reasonable. On the downside, maniacal driving on congested roads calls for strong nerves and a certain fatalism. Accidents are not uncommon.

The taxis are usually big **Peugeot saloons** carrying seven passengers or **microbuses** seating a dozen people. Most business is along specific routes, with more or less non-stop departures throughout the day on the main ones, while cross-desert traffic is restricted to early morning and late afternoon. You just show up at the terminal (locations are detailed, city by city, in the guide) and ask for a *servees* to your destination. As soon as the requisite number of people (or less, if you're willing to pay extra) are assembled, the taxi sets off. As fewer people travel after dark in winter, you might have to wait a while for a ride to a distant town; catching a *servees* to somewhere nearer, and then another one to your final destination, could be quicker. Fridays are bad for travel, too.

On established routes service taxis keep to **fixed fares** for each passenger (detailed in the guide). You can ascertain current rates by asking at your hotel (or the tourist office), or observing what Egyptians pay at the end of the journey.

Alternatively, you can **charter a whole taxi** for yourself or a group – useful for day excursions or on odd routes. You will have to bargain hard to get a fair price (see entries in the guide).

Driving, biking and hitching

Driving in Egypt is not for the faint-hearted or inexperienced motorist. Cities, highways, backroads and *pistes* each pose a challenge to drivers' skills and nerve. Pedestrians and carts seem blithely indifferent to heavy traffic. Though accidents are less frequent than you'd think, the crumpled wrecks alongside highways are a constant reminder of the hazards of motoring.

Although driving on the right is pretty much universal, other **rules of the road** vary. Traffic **in cities** is relentless and anarchic, with vehicles weaving to and fro between lanes, signalling by horn. Two beeps means "I'm alongside and about to overtake." A single long blast warns "I can't (won't) stop and I'm coming through!" Extending your hand, fingers raised and tips together, is the signal for "Watch out, don't pass now"; spreading your fingers and flipping them forwards indicates "Go ahead." Although the car in front usually has right of way, buses and trams always take precedence.

On country roads – including the two-lane east- and west-bank "highways" along the Nile Valley – trucks and cars routinely overtake in the face of incoming traffic. The passing car usually flashes its lights as a warning, but not always. Most roads are bumpy, with deep potholes and all manner of traffic, including donkey carts and camels. Beware, especially, of children darting into the road. If you injure someone, relatives may take revenge on the spot. Avoid driving **after dark**, when Egyptians drive without lights, only flashing them on to high beam when they see another car approaching. Wandering pedestrians and animals, obstructions and sand drifts present extra hazards. During spring, flash floods can wash away roads in Sinai. On **pistes** (rough, unpaved tracks in the desert or mountains) there are special problems. You need a good deal of driving and mechanical confidence – and shouldn't attempt such routes if you don't feel your car's up to scratch. **Desert driving** is covered in detail on p.484.

One danger to be aware of is that of **unexploded mines** left over from the Middle East's many conflicts. These exist in several parts of the country and have taken the lives of a number of tourists. Because of this, off-road driving is best avoided, especially in the Sinai and along the Red Sea coast. Minefields are usually surrounded by barbed wire (often old and rusty), but are not generally signposted.

Police checkpoints – signposted in English as "Traffic Stations" – occur on the approach roads to towns and oases and along major trunk routes. Foreign motorists are usually waved through, but you might be asked to show your passport or driving licence. In Middle Egypt the checkpoints are militarized, and Egyptian vehicles may be searched for weapons.

The official **speed limit** outside towns is 90km per hour (100km on the Cairo–Alexandria Desert Road), but on certain stretches it can be as low as 30km per hour. Road signs are similar to those in Europe, but speed limits are posted in Arabic numerals, which it would be wise to learn (see p.840). The **minimum age** for driving in Egypt is 25 years; the **maximum age** limit is seventy years. Foreigners require an International Driving Licence (obtainable from motoring organizations, see below).

Car rental

Renting **a car** pays obvious dividends if you are pushed for time or plan to visit remote sites (you cannot bring rented cars across the border), but whether you'd want to drive yourself is another matter (see above) – it's not much more expensive to hire a car and driver.

Any branch of Misr Travel (see p.29), and numerous local tour agencies, can fix you up with a **car and driver**. An alternative is simply to negotiate with local taxi drivers (see p.51).

For a **self-drive car**, visitors can make arrangements abroad through Hertz, Avis or Budget, or directly with local car rental companies in Egypt (addresses given where relevant in the guide). It's worth shopping around for the best deal, since rates and terms vary considerably. At the cheaper end of the market, you can get a car with unlimited mileage for about £40/US$60 a day. Of the international agencies, Budget offers the best rates. Most companies require a hefty deposit, and not all accept credit cards.

Before making a reservation, be sure to find out if you can pick up the car in one city and return it in another. Generally, this is only possible with cars from Hertz, Avis or Budget, found in the main cities and tourist centres. And before setting out, make sure the car comes with spare tyre, tool kit and full documentation – including insurance cover, which is compulsory issue with all rentals.

Car rental agencies

Avis UK ☎0870/606 0100, Ireland ☎01/605 7500, US ☎1-800/331-1084, Canada ☎1-800/272-5871, Australia ☎13/6333, New Zealand ☎0800/655 111 or 09/526 2847, ⊛www.avis.com

Budget UK ☎0800/181 181, Ireland ☎1850/575 767, US & Canada ☎1-800/527-0700, Australia ☎1300/362 848, New Zealand ☎0800/652 227 or 09/976 2222, ⊛www.budgetrentacar.com

Europcar UK ☎0845/722 2525, Ireland ☎01/614 2800, US & Canada ☎1-877/940-6900, Australia ☎1300/131390; ⊛www.europcar.com

Hertz UK ☎0870/848 4848, Ireland ☎01/813 3416, US ☎1-800/654-3001, Canada ☎1-800/263-0600, Australia ☎13/3039, New Zealand ☎0800/654 321, ⊛www.hertz.com

Motoring organizations

American Automobile Association (AAA) US ☎1-800/222-4357, ⊛www.aaa.com

Australian Automobile Association Australia ☎02/6247 7311, ⊛www.aaa.asn.au

Automobile Association (AA) UK ☎0800/444 500, ⊛www.theaa.co.uk

Automobile Association of Ireland (AA) Ireland ☎01/617 9988, ⊛www.aaireland.ie

Canadian Automobile Association (CAA) Canada ☎613/247 0117, ⊛www.caa.ca

New Zealand Automobile Association New Zealand ☎09/377 4660, ⊛www.nzaa.co.nz

Royal Automobile Club (RAC) UK ☎0800/550 055, ⊛www.rac.co.uk

Motorbikes and bicycles

Motorcycling could be a good way to travel around Egypt, but the red tape involved in bringing your own bike is diabolical (ask your national motoring organization and the Egyptian consulate for details). It's difficult to rent a machine except in Luxor or Hurghada. Bikers should be especially wary of potholes, sand and rocks, besides other traffic on the roads.

Useful for getting around small towns and reaching sites or beaches in the vicinity, **bicycles** can be rented in Luxor, Aswan, Hurghada, Siwa Oasis and other places for a modest sum. Cycling in big cities or over long distances is not advisable. Traffic is murderous, the heat brutal, and foreign cyclists are sometimes stoned by children (particularly in the Delta). If you're determined to cycle the **Nile Valley**, the new east bank expressway that runs down as far as Aswan is the safer route.

Most towns have a wealth of **general repair shops**, well used to servicing local bikes and mopeds. Though unlikely to have the correct spare parts for your make of bike, they can usually sort out some kind of temporary solution.

Fuel and breakdowns

Petrol (*benzene*) and diesel stations are plentiful in larger towns but few and far between in rural and desert areas. Always fill your tank to the limit. Replace oil/air filters regularly, lest impurities in the petrol, and Egypt's ubiquitous dust, clog up the engine.

Egyptian **mechanics** are usually excellent at coping with breakdowns, and all medium-sized towns have garages (most with a range of spare parts for French, German and Japanese cars). But be aware that if you break down miles from anywhere you'll probably end up paying a lot to get a truck to tow you back.

If you are driving your own vehicle, there is also the problem of having to re-export any car that you bring into the country (even a wreck). You can't just write off a car; you'll have to take it out of Egypt with you.

Vehicle insurance

All car-rental agreements must be sold along with third-party liability insurance, by law. Though accident and damage insurance should be included in the package, always make sure. In the case of an **accident**, get a written report from the police and from the doctor who first treats any injuries, without which your insurance may not cover the costs. Reports are written in Arabic.

Driving your own vehicle, you will need to take out **Egyptian insurance**. Policies are sold by the Al-Shark, Misr and Al-Ahlia insurance companies; offices are found in most towns and at border crossings. Premiums vary according to the size, horsepower and value of the vehicle.

Hitching

Hitching is largely confined to areas with minimal public transport (where anything that moves is considered fair game) or trunk routes (where hopefuls wait by the roadside for passing service taxis or scheduled buses). Since you'll probably end up paying anyway, there's no point in hitching unless you have to. Indeed, foreigners who hitch where proper transport is available may inspire contempt rather than sympathy. As few tourists have their own car in Egypt, you can't expect much help from that quarter, either. Women should never hitch without a male companion.

In the countryside and the desert, where buses may be sporadic or non-existent, it is standard practice for **lorries** (*camions*) and **pick-up trucks** (*bijous*) to carry and charge passengers. You may be asked to pay a little more than the locals, or have to bargain over a price, but it's straightforward enough. Getting rides from tractors is another possibility in rural areas.

Also noteworthy are **pilgrim convoys**, bound for the monasteries of Wadi Natrun, St Paul or St Anthony, or remoter sites to celebrate a festival such as the moulid of St Damyanah (p.649) or Sheikh al-Shazli (p.778).

By air

Egyptian domestic air fares are average by international standards, but probably too expensive for most low-budget travellers. In general, it's only worth flying if your time is very limited, or for the view – the Nile Valley and Sinai look amazing from the air.

EgyptAir, the national airline, enjoys a near monopoly so it has no incentive to offer discounts. **Air Sinai** was specially created to serve the Sinai and Israel, in order to protect EgyptAir from the withdrawal of landing rights in other Arab countries, but is really just the same outfit under another name. Details of flights and the addresses of local offices appear in the text.

Fares are calculated in US$ but payable in Egyptian currency, backed by an exchange receipt. As a rough guide to prices, a one-way economy-class ticket from Cairo to

Luxor costs about £85/US$125. In the winter season, you would be lucky to get any kind of flight between Cairo and Luxor, Aswan, Abu Simbel or St Catherine's Monastery, without booking at least a week ahead. Always reconfirm 72 hours prior to the journey, as overbooking is commonplace.

By boat

The colonial tradition of **Nile cruises**, familiar from films and novels, has spawned an industry deploying 240 steamers. Before the 1997 Luxor massacre, most cruise boats were booked months in advance by tour companies and it was difficult for individuals to make bookings in Egypt – but right now, it's much easier. See the box under Aswan on p.456 for more details.

There are also some excellent cut-price offers available. Package deals from abroad cost as little as £600/US$850 for a week's cruise (see pp.15–16, 18–19 & 21 for tour company details); while in Egypt you can arrange a four-day trip on the spot for as little as £100/US$140 (see p.456; all prices are per person, in a twin cabin). Prices escalate dramatically with the luxury quotient. Most boats start off in Luxor, sailing down to Aswan (others start here), with stops at Esna, Edfu and Kom Ombo, over three to five days.

If you're looking for a cruise in Egypt, shop around and don't necessarily go for the cheapest deal – some boats leave a lot to be desired in terms of hygiene and living conditions. The luxurious boats with swimming pools can be wonderful, but you need to pick with care. If at all possible, try to look around the vessel first. The best deals are available from local agents (or directly from the boats) in Luxor and Aswan. Particularly beware of overpriced trips sold by touts and some hotels in Cairo (see p.103). The most reliable cruises are generally those sold in association with package holidays.

Feluccas, the lateen-sailed boats used on the Nile since antiquity, still serve as transport along many stretches of the river. Favoured by tourists for sunset cruises, they allow you to experience the changing moods and scenery of the Nile while lolling in blissful indolence.

> **Dive safaris** are the boom tourist industry in Hurghada and Sinai (where they are called "liveaboards"). Private charter boats take divers to remote reefs, on trips lasting from several days to two or three weeks. Most are pre-booked by groups, which may not welcome individuals joining them at the last moment, so it's better (and cheaper) to buy a package deal at home (see pp.16, 19 & 21 for lists of operators). Read the "Sinai" and "Red Sea Coast" chapters for an idea of the dive sites on offer.

Many visitors opt for longer **felucca cruises**, stopping at the temples between Aswan and Luxor – heading downriver from Aswan. While it's easy to arrange a cruise yourself (see p.454), several tour operators also offer packages.

Local **ferries** cross the Nile and the Suez Canal at various points (specified as relevant in the guide). They are generally cheap, battered and crowded. There are also smarter tourist ferries between Luxor and the West Bank, but it's more fun to use the ordinary boats.

Long-distance services are confined to the Red Sea and the Gulf of Aqaba, where the slow boats of yore have been superseded by a deluxe high-speed **catamaran** that zips over from Hurghada to Sharm el-Sheikh three times a week, in just ninety minutes. The US$40 (£27) fare isn't much more than is charged by the last of the old boats (which take over five hours), and is worth it to avoid the long overland journey via Suez, which requires the best part of a day. Another catamaran runs from Nuweiba to the Jordanian port of Aqaba.

Horses, donkeys and camels

Around the Pyramids and the major Nile sites, donkeys, horses and camels are all available for rental. **Horses** are fun if you want to ride across stretches of sand between the Pyramids or gallop in the desert in Sinai. **Donkeys** are best used for visiting the Theban Necropolis, where they traverse mountains that you'd never cross on foot, and enliven the trip no end. Elsewhere they have less appeal, but you might rent a *caretta* (donkey-drawn taxi cart) to explore the pools and ruins in Siwa Oasis. The Arabic word for donkey is *humár* (plural *hameer*; a donkey-guide is called a *hámar*.

Camels (the one-humped Arabian variety, also called a dromedary) make for pretty rigorous but exhilarating riding, and you'll probably want to try them at least once. They are good for short rides around Aswan, to the monastery of St Simeon, for example, but where they really come into their own is in Sinai or the Western Desert oases, where you can go trekking up wadis or across dunes that horses could never cope with. Trips – lasting anything from a half-day to a week – are easily enough arranged with local operators, or as part of "adventure holiday" packages before you set off.

Camel riding is a real art, which gets a little easier on the body with experience. The mounting is done for you but be sure to hold on to the pommel of the saddle as the camel raises itself in a triple-jerk manoeuvre. Once on, you have a choice of riding it like a horse or cocking a leg around the pommel, as the Bedouin do. Be sure to use a lot of padding around the pommel: what begins as a minor irritation can end up leaving your skin rubbed raw.

Beware also of being palmed off with a male (bull) camel that's in heat – they can be quite vicious. Bad signs are an inflated mouth sac, aggressive behaviour towards its mates, and lots of noise and slobbering. When enraged, camels can launch a fierce attack – they've been known to grip someone's neck and shake them like a rag doll, or crush the bones in a leg.

City transport

Most Egyptian towns are small enough to cover on foot, especially if you stay in a hotel near the centre. In larger cities, however, local transport is definitely useful. Learn to recognize Arabic numerals and you can take full advantage of the cheap **buses, minibuses and trams** that cover most of Alexandria and Cairo (which also has river taxis and an excellent metro). Bus and tram routes are detailed under individual entries in the guide.

Equally ubiquitous are four-seater **taxis**

(black and white in Cairo, black and yellow in Alex), which often pick up extra passengers heading in the same direction. As meters are rarely used (or work), the trick is to know the fare and pay on arrival, rather than ask or haggle at the beginning. Above all, don't confuse these cabs with larger *special* taxis (usually Peugeot 504s or Mercedes), which cost three times more and prey on tourists. If you do rent a *special*, establish the price – and bargain it down – before you get in. The section on Cairo taxis (p.96) contains some more advice.

You will also come across **caleches** – horse-drawn buggies, also known as **hantours**. These are primarily tourist transport, and you'll be accosted by drivers in Alexandria, a few parts of Cairo, and most of all in Luxor and Aswan. Fares are high by local taxi standards and, despite supposed tariffs set by the local councils, are in practice entirely negotiable. In a few small towns, mostly in Middle Egypt, *hantours* remain part of local city transport. Ask locals the price of fares before climbing on board, or simply pay what you see fit at the end. Some of the horses and buggies are in pristine condition; others painful to behold. Tourists can help by boycotting drivers who abuse their animals, and by contributing to the Brooke Hospital for Animals (see box below).

Founded in 1934, the **Brooke Hospital for Animals** now has clinics in Cairo, Luxor, Edfu, Aswan, Alexandria and Mersa Matrouh, as well as in Jordan, India and Pakistan. They provide free treatment for any animal brought to the clinic, and rescue abandoned ones. Tourists are asked to help by admonishing drivers who gallop their horses, and not travelling more than four to a carriage. Boycotting the worst offenders may work, but it would be wrong to judge all owners of neglected animals harshly, for many simply can't afford to take their horses off the streets. Tourists are welcome to visit the Brooke clinics in Egypt. Donations can be sent to the Brooke Hospital for Animals, Broadmead House, 21 Panton St, London SW1Y 4DR ☏ 020/7930 0210.

Accommodation

The main tourist centres offer a broad spectrum of accommodation, with everything from luxury palaces – familiar from movies such as *Death on the Nile* – to homely pensions and flea-ridden dives. Even in high season, in Cairo, Sinai or the Nile Valley, you should be able to find something in your preferred range. Elsewhere, the choice is generally more limited, with only basic lodgings available in most of the desert oases.

Hotels

Egyptian hotels are loosely categorized into **star ratings**, ranging from five-star deluxe class down to one-star. Below this range, there are also unclassified hotels and *pensions*, some of them tailored to foreign backpackers, others mostly used by Egyptians.

Standards vary within any given category or price band – and from room to room in many places. The categorizations tend to have more meaning in the higher bands; once you're down to one or two stars, the differences are almost negligible.

Deluxe hotels are almost exclusively modern and chain-owned (*Sofitel*, *Mövenpick*, *Hilton*, etc), with swimming pools, bars, restaurants, air conditioning and all the usual international facilities. **Four-star** hotels can be more characterful, including some famous (and reconditioned) names from the old tradition of Egyptian tourism: places like the *Old Cataract* in Aswan and the *Winter Palace* in Luxor. Again, all hotels in this class are air conditioned, with a pool, café and restaurant, etc. They merge into **three-star** hotels, among which there is again the odd gem, though most are 1970s-style towers, now becoming a little shabby. Facilities like plumbing and air-conditioning get a lot less reliable, too.

Down on the **two- and one-star** level, you rarely get air conditioning, though better places will supply fans, and old-style buildings with balconies, high ceilings and louvred windows are well designed to cope with the heat. Conversely, these places can be distinctly chilly in winter, as they scarcely ever have any form of heating.

Some of the cheaper hotels are classified as **pensions**, which makes little difference in terms of facilities, but tends to signify family ownership and a friendlier ambience. Cairo, in particular, has some wonderful *pensions*.

At the cheap end of the scale, in the most popular tourist towns, like Luxor and Hurghada, you also get **"student hotels"**, specifically aimed at backpackers. They are often quite well run and equipped, if a bit cramped.

Booking and charges

Bookings for the **four- and five-star hotels** are best made through the central reservations office of the chain owning the hotel, or by fax. Simply turning up at a ritzy hotel, or even phoning ahead, you may find a reluctance to book you in, with staff even sometimes claiming the hotel is full. Many rely on tour groups for their business and are not very interested in individual travellers. You may alternatively prefer to book as part of a package, through one of the many companies detailed on pp.15–16, 18–19 & 21. Package tourists get greatly **reduced rates**, while modest **discounts** may also be available to independent travellers who book from abroad.

At **mid-range hotels**, it is worth trying to book ahead if you want to stay in a particular place in **Cairo**, **Alex**, **Aswan or Luxor**. Elsewhere – and at all the **cheaper hotels** – most people just turn up. Phoning may itself prove unrewarding (see p.60).

Most hotels levy a **service charge** (12 percent) plus **local taxes** (2–15 percent) on top of their quoted rates. **Breakfast** is often obligatory and may or may not be included in the room rate. It's not usually anything to get excited about. **Extra charges** most commonly turn up at mid-range hotels, which may add on a few pounds for a fan or air conditioning, or a TV that doesn't work, or may only show Egyptian channels. Throughout this book we have indicated prices according to the system outlined in the box above.

International booking for luxury hotel chains

Four Seasons UK & Ireland ☎0800/6488 6488, US ☎1-800/332-3442, Canada ☎1-800/268-6282, Australia ☎1800/142 163, New Zealand ☎0800/449 286, ✆www.fourseasons.com.

Accommodation price codes

All the establishments listed in this book have been graded according to the categories listed below.

Prices given are for the **cheapest double room** in each establishment in high season (winter in Upper Egypt and Sinai, summer in Alexandria), including tax. Bear in mind, however, that Cairo is generally more expensive for accommodation of all types than most other places in Egypt; thus, a category ❶ place in Cairo may be pretty dire, while a room in Siwa Oasis at the same price may be quite comfortable. For places that offer **dorm beds** or charge on a singles basis, rates per person are given in £E.

For the purposes of ready reckoning, we have taken the exchange rate as *roughly* US\$1 = £E4.50; £1 = £E6.60. Please note that most hotels in categories ❻ to ❾ quote rates in US\$, but will accept payment in £E.

❶ **under £E25/US\$6**. This could be a fleapit in Cairo, a bed in a spartan resthouse in the Western Desert, or a room in a no-star hotel in Luxor or Hurghada. Electricity is certain, hot water less so.

❷ **£E25–50/US\$6–11**. The rate for a basic room year-round in Cairo, or during peak times in Luxor, Aswan or Alexandria. No-star *pensions* and "student hotels" are generally a better deal than the bleak official youth hostels in most parts of Egypt, but as singles are rare, solo travellers may have to share with strangers or pay for a double room. Facilities are shared, with a good chance of hot water.

❸ **£E50–75/US\$11–16**. An average one-star hotel, containing a mixture of rooms with shared and private facilities, and in most cases comfortable enough for a shortish stay.

❹ **£E75–100/US\$16–22**. Mostly two-star hotels, with the odd three-star place: the facilities may amount to no more than in the previous category, or be considerably better, depending on the age and location of the hotel. Hotels in this category in Luxor and Hurghada will probably have a restaurant.

❺ **£E100–150/US\$22–33**. Largely three-star places, some rather aged, but there are many new ones in Hurghada, Luxor and Aswan. Rooms should have a/c, a phone, TV and fridge. There's certain to be a restaurant on the premises, and possibly a disco.

❻ **US\$33–65/£E150–300**. Posher three-star places, which in Luxor, Sinai or Hurghada could well have a pool.

❼ **US\$65–108/£E300–500**. The border line between three- and four-star hotels, where you can usually take a pool and a/c for granted, although the odd place with neither may charge such rates for half- or full-board accommodation.

❽ **US\$108–217/£E500–1000**. At this level, prices are posted in US\$, and you're talking somewhere pretty classy, like a top-flight chain hotel or holiday village. There are scores along the Red Sea Coast, where the deal may include half-board.

❾ **US\$217/£E1000 upwards**. The ritziest chain hotels and holiday villages, including such extravagances as the Agatha Christie suite of the *Old Cataract* in Aswan (US\$1215 a night).

Intercontinental UK ☎0800/028 9387, Ireland ☎1-800/709 300, US & Canada ☎1-800/327-0200, Australia ☎1-800/221 355 or 02/9232 1199, New Zealand ☎0800/442 215, ⓦwww.intercontinental.com.
Hilton UK ☎0800/856 8000, US & Canada ☎1-800/HHONORS, Australia ☎1-800/222 255 or 02/9209 5209, ⓦwww.hilton.com.
Marriott UK ☎ 0800/221 222, US & Canada ☎1-888/236-2427, Australia ☎ 1800/251 259, New Zealand ☎ 0800/441035, ⓦwww.marriott.com.
Meridien UK ☎0800/500 500, US & Canada ☎1-800/543-4300, Australia ☎1-800/622 240, international toll-free number ☎+800/3738 3940, ⓦwww.lemeridien.com.
Oberoi UK ☎0800/181 123, US & Canada ☎1-800/223 6800, Australia ☎1-800/222 033, New Zealand ☎0800/441 016, ⓦwww.oberoihotels.com.
Sheraton UK & Ireland ☎0800/325 353535, US & Canada ☎ 1-800/325-3535, Australia ☎1-800/073 535, New Zealand ☎0800/3253 5353, ⓦwww.sheraton.com.

Hotel touts

"Fishing" for guests (as Egyptians call it) is common practice in the main tourist centres, where new arrivals are approached by hotel touts at train and bus stations, airports and docks. Though some actually work in the hotel they're touting, most are simply hustling for commissions and quite prepared to use trickery to deliver clients to "their" establishment – swearing that other places are full, or closed, or whatever. In some cases, the hotel being touted may be agreeable, or even the best deal going; all too often, however, it's the grotty or overpriced places that depend on touts. In any case, their commission will usually be added to your bill – another reason to avoid using them. In Cairo especially, some of these places exist purely for the purpose of housing foreigners so that they can be sold overpriced excursions or souvenirs.

By studying the hotel listings and town plans in this book, you should be able to detect most scams. Advice for travellers flying into Cairo appears on p.103.

Hostels

Egypt's **youth hostels** are cheap but their drawbacks are considerable. A daytime lock-out and nighttime curfew are universal practice; so, too, is segregating the sexes and (usually) foreigners and Egyptians (which you might appreciate when riotous groups are in residence). The most salubrious hostels are in Cairo, Sharm el-Sheikh and Ismailiya. These, however, are far from where the action is, as are grungier places in Alexandria, Mersa Matrouh, Luxor, Assyut and Sohag. Only Aswan's hostel is smack in the centre.

It seems to be up to individual hostels whether you need an **Hostelling International (HI) card**, and their rulings change constantly. If admitted, non-HI members are usually charged £E1 extra per night, and may be granted automatic membership after six days. For more information, contact the Egyptian Youth Hostel Association in Cairo (1 Sharia el-Ibrahimy, Cairo; ☎02/354 0527, ⓔeyhaho@usa.net; annual membership £E25). Addresses for all hostels appear in the text.

Also worth noting are a couple of **YMCA hostels**, which admit anyone. The one in Port Said is nothing special, but the YMCA in Assyut is positively luxurious and excellent value – not that any tourists are likely to visit Assyut.

Resthouses

In the Western Desert oases, there are still a couple of government **resthouses**, with basic triple-bed rooms and cold showers for about £E5 per person. Guests may have to share with strangers unless they're willing to pay for beds to be kept unoccupied. Aside from tourists making the "Great Desert Circuit", resthouses are mostly used by truckers.

Camping

Egypt is not established camping territory. Such campsites as there are in the country tend to be **on the coast**, often shadeless and with few facilities, catering for holidaying Egyptian families. You'd have to be desperate to stay at these places.

Rather better are the occasional **campsites attached to hotels**, which may offer ready-pitched tents with camp beds, plus use of the hotel shower and toilet facilities. As for **camping wild**, you should always check with the authorities about any coastal site – some beaches are mined, others patrolled by the military. In the oases it's less

of a problem, though any land near water will belong to someone: so again, ask permission.

Eating and drinking

Egyptian food combines elements of Lebanese, Turkish, Syrian, Greek and French cuisines, modified to suit local conditions and tastes. Dishes tend to be simple and wholesome, made only with fresh ingredients, and therefore vary with the seasons. Nubian cooking, found in southern Egypt, is spicier than food in the north; in Alexandria, Mediterranean influences prevail. Cairo offers every kind of cuisine in the world.

Eating out falls into two camps. At a local level, there are cafés and diners, and loads of street stalls, which sell one or two simple dishes. More formally and expensively, restaurants cater to middle-class Egyptians and tourists. The latter have menus (most cafés don't) offering a broader range of dishes, and sometimes specializing in foreign cuisine. They will also invariably add a service charge and taxes to your bill, which usually increases the total by seventeen percent. You are also expected to tip – conventions for which are byzantine. Basically, you tip in proportion to the size of the bill; below ten percent in expensive places, more where the sums involved are trifling. In juice bars and diners, customers simply put 10–25pt on a plate by the exit.

Cafés and street food

The staples of the Egyptian diet are bread (*'aish*, which also means "life"), *fuul* and *taamiya*. **Bread** is eaten with all meals and snacks and comes either as pitta-type *'aish shamsi* (sun-raised bread made from white flour) or *'aish baladi* (made from coarse wholewheat flour).

Native beans or **fuul** (pronounced "fool") can be prepared in several ways. Boiled and mashed with tomatoes, onions and spices, they constitute *fuul madammes*, which are often served with a chopped boiled egg for breakfast. A similar mixture stuffed into *'aish baladi* constitutes the pitta-bread sandwiches sold on the street.

Deep-fried patties of green beans mixed with spices are called **taamiya** (or sometimes **felafel**) and are again served in pitta bread, often with a snatch of salad, pickles and **tahina** (a sauce made from sesame paste, tahini).

A common appetizer is **torshi**, a mixture of pickled radishes, turnips, gherkins and carrots; luridly coloured, it is something of an acquired taste, as are pickled lemons, another favourite.

Another cheap café perennial is **makarona**, a clump of macaroni baked into a cake with minced lamb and tomato sauce inside. It's rather bland but very filling. Similarly common is **kushari**, which is a mixture of noodles, rice, macaroni, lentils and onions, in a spicy tomato sauce (another sauce, made of garlic, is optional). These are sold in tiled stand-up diners, also called *kushari*.

More elaborate, and pricier, are **fatir**, which can be either sweet or savoury. These are a cross between pizza and pancake, consisting of flaky filo pastry stuffed either with white cheese, peppers, mince, egg, onion and olives, or with raisins, jams, curds or just a dusting of icing sugar. They are served at café-like establishments known as *fatatri*.

Most **sandwiches** are small rolls with a minute portion of *basturma* (pastrami) or cheese. Other favourites include: grilled liver (*kibda*) with spicy green peppers and onions; tiny shrimps; and *mokh* (crumbed sheep's brains).

Lastly, there are **shawarma** – slices of marinated lamb, stuffed into pitta bread and garnished with salad and *tahina* – which are usually superior to the doner kebabs sold abroad, though foreigners often assume they are the same.

On the **hygiene** front, while cafés and tiled eateries with running water are generally safe, street grub is highly suspect unless it's peelable or hot.

Restaurant meals

The classic Egyptian restaurant or café meal is either a lamb **kebab** or **kofta** (spiced mince patties), accompanied or preceded by a couple of dips. The dips usually comprise **hummus** (made from chickpeas), *tahina* and **babaghanoug** (*tahina* with aubergine).

In a basic place, this is likely to be all that's on offer, save for a bit of salad (usually lettuce- and tomato-based), *fuul* and bread. However, you may also find other grilled meats. **Chicken** (*firakh*, pronounced "frakh" in Upper Egypt) is a standard, both in cafés and as takeaway food from spit-roast stands. **Pigeon** (*hamam*) is common too, most often served with *freek* (spicy wheat) stuffing. There's not much meat on a pigeon, so it's best to order a couple each. In slightly fancier places, you may also encounter pigeon in a **tageen** or *ta'gell*, stewed with onions, tomatoes and rice in an earthenware pot.

More expensive restaurants feature these same dishes, plus a few that are more elaborate. Some may precede main courses with a larger selection of dips, plus olives, stuffed vine leaves and so on – a selection known, as in Greek, as **mezzes**. Soups, too, are occasionally featured, most famously **molukhiyya**, which is made from stewing Jew's mallow in chicken stock – a lot tastier than its disconcertingly slimy appearance suggests. Two common main dishes are **mahshi**, comprising stuffed vegetables (tomatoes, aubergines, etc), and **torly**, a mixed vegetable casserole with chunks of lamb, or occasionally beef (which in reality may be donkey, water buffalo or camel meat).

Fish (*samak*) is featured on restaurant menus in Alexandria, Aswan, the Red Sea Coast and Sinai. It is invariably grilled or fried, served with salad and chips, and usu-ally very tasty. There are many types, ranging from snapper to Nile perch; you're usually invited to pick your own fish from the ice box and it'll then be priced by weight. You may also find squid (*calamari*), shrimps (*gambari*) and octopus (*kaborya*).

One confusion you'll often run up against is the notion that **pasta**, **rice**, **chips** (French fries) and even **crisps** (potato chips) are interchangeable. Order rice and you'll get chips, and your querying of the matter will be regarded as inexplicable.

Vegetarian eating

Most Egyptians eat vegetables most of the time – meat and fish are seen as luxuries. However, the concept of **vegetarianism** is totally incomprehensible to most people, and you'll be hard pushed to exclude meat stock from your diet. If you do get across the idea that you "don't eat meat", you're as likely as not to be offered chicken or fish as a substitute.

Cheese, cakes and nuts

You can supplement regular cooked meals with a variety of fare available from corner shops, delicatessens, patisseries and street stalls.

There are two main types of Egyptian **cheese**: *gibna beyda* (white cheese), which tastes like Greek feta, and *gibna rumi* (Roman cheese), a hard, sharp, yellow cheese. For breakfast you will often be given imported processed cheeses such as *La Vache qui Rit* ("The Laughing Cow" – a popular nickname for President Mubarak).

Nut shops (*ma'la*) are a high-street perennial, offering all kinds of peanuts (*fuul sudani*) and edible seeds. *Lib abyad* and *lib asmar* are varieties of pumpkin seeds, *lib battikh* come from watermelon, and chickpeas (*hummus*) are roasted and sugar-coated or dried and salted; all of these are sold by weight. Most nut shops also stock candies and mineral water.

Cakes are available at patisseries (some of which are attached to quite flash cafés) or from street stalls. The classics will be familiar to anyone who has travelled in Greece or Turkey: *baklava* (filo pastry soaked in honey and nuts) – called *basbousa* in Upper Egypt;

katif (similar but with shredded wheat; and a variety of milk- or cornflour-based puddings, like *mahallabiyya* (sweet rice or cornflour, topped with pistachio nuts) and most famously *Umm Ali* (corn cake soaked in milk, sugar, coconut and cinnamon and served hot).

Fruits in Egypt are seasonal and wonderful. In winter there are oranges, bananas and pomegranates, followed by strawberries in March. In summer you get mangoes, melons, peaches, plums and grapes, plus a brief season (Aug–Sept) of prickly pears (cactus fruit). Fresh dates are harvested in late autumn. Only apples are imported, and thus expensive. All are readily available at street stalls, or can be drunk as juices at juice bars (see below).

Drinks

As a predominantly Muslim country, Egypt gives alcohol a low profile. Drinks consist primarily of tea, coffee, fruit juices and familiar brands of soft drinks. Invitations to drink tea (*shurub shai?*) are as much a part of life in Egypt as they are in Britain, although the drink itself is served quite differently. Many Egyptian men accompany it with a *sheesha* (see box).

Tea, coffee and karkaday

Egypt's national beverage, **tea** (*shai*), is generally made by boiling the leaves, and served black and sugared to taste – though an increasing number of cafés use tea-bags and may supply milk. Tea with milk is *shai bi-laban*, tea-bag tea is *shai libton* – to avoid it ask for loose-leaf tea (*shai kushari*). Tea with a sprig of mint (*shai bi-na'ana*) is refreshing when the weather is hot.

Coffee (*'ahwa*) is traditionally of the "Turkish" kind, served in tiny cups or glasses and pre-sugared as customers specify: *saada* (unsugared), *'ariha* (slightly sweetened), *mazboot* (medium sweet) or *ziyaada* (syrupy). In some places you can also get it spiced with cardamom (*'ahwa makhaweka*). Most middle-class or tourist establishments also serve **European-style** coffee, made from Nescafé (or, worse, Misrcafé, an inferior local brand) rather than the real thing; with the option of having it with milk (*'ahwa bi-*

> The **sheesha**, or water-pipe, is inseparable from Egyptian café society. It takes a special kind of tobacco mixed with molasses, which has a distinctive taste and aroma. Posh coffee houses may also stock apple-flavoured tobacco and provide disposable plastic mouthpieces for their clients' waterpipes. A *sheesha* is normally shared among friends, but you can decline to partake without causing offence. Don't call it a "hubbly bubbly", as the term in Egypt specifically refers to hashish, which is illegal. See p.viii of the colour section for more.

laban). Increasingly, however, five-star hotels and other upmarket places are investing in espresso machines.

Beverages are widely consumed in traditional **coffee houses** or **tearooms** (called *'ahwa*), which are exclusively male territory. Foreign women won't be turned away but may feel uneasy, especially if unaccompanied by a man. For a more relaxed tea or coffee, try one of the middle-class places (in larger towns), which are often attached to patisseries, and where Egyptian women may also be found.

A third drink, characteristic of Egypt, is **karkaday** (or *karkadé*), a deep-red infusion of hibiscus flowers. Most popular in Luxor and Aswan, it is equally refreshing drunk hot or cold. Elsewhere, alas, they tend to use dehydrated extract instead of real hibiscus, so it doesn't taste so good. You may also enjoy **other** infusions such as *helba* (a bright yellow infusion of fenugreek), *yansoon* (aniseed) or *'irfa* (cinnamon).

On cold winter evenings you might enjoy **sahleb**, a thick, creamy drink made from milk thickened with ground orchid root, with cinnamon and nuts sprinkled on top. In hot weather Egyptians imbibe **rayeb** (soured milk), which is something of an acquired taste.

Fruit juices and soft drinks

Every main street has a couple of stand-up **juice bars**, recognizable by their displays of fruit. Normally, you order and pay at the cash desk before exchanging a plastic token for your drink at the counter.

Juices made from seasonal fruit include *burtu'an* (orange), *mohz* (banana; with milk *mohz bi-laban*), *manga* (mango), *farawla* (strawberry), *gazar* (carrot), *rumaan* (pomegranate), *subia* (coconut) and *'asab* (the sickly-sweet, creamy light-green juice of crushed sugar cane). You can also order blends; *nus w nus* (literally "half and half") usually refers to carrot and orange juice, but other combinations can be specified.

Street vendors also ladle out iced *'asiir limoon* (strong, sweet lemonade), bittersweet liquorice-water, and deliciously refreshing *tamar hindi* (tamarind cordial).

Despite this profusion of cheap fresh juices, the usual brands of **soda** are widely available, including Coca-Cola, Fanta, Sprite and 7-Up (called "Seven"), all in both bottles and cans. Bottled sodas are normally drunk on the spot; you'll have to pay a deposit on the bottle to take one away.

Mineral water

Bottled **mineral water** (*mayya ma'adaniyya*) is widely available, particularly Baraka ("Blessing"; the company is owned by Nestlé); the brands Siwa and Hyat (from Siwa Oasis) are less widely distributed. Baraka comes in 1.5-litre, one-litre and half-litre bottles. If tourists request water, it is assumed that they mean mineral water unless they specifically ask for **tap water** (*mayya baladi*), which is safe to drink in major towns and cities, but too chlorinated for the average visitor's palate; people with sensitive stomachs should definitely stick to bottled water. When buying mineral water, it is wise to check that the seal is intact; unsuspecting tourists may be palmed off with tap water – a favourite trick in the backpackers' resort of Dahab.

Alcohol

Alcohol can be obtained in most parts of Egypt, but the range of outlets is limited. In the Western Desert oases or Middle Egypt its sale is severely restricted or entirely prohibited. If there are no bars, hotels or Greek restaurants are the places to try; if you can't

see anyone drinking it, there's none to be had. When you do manage to locate a drink, keep in mind that the hot, dry climate makes for dehydration, and agonizing hangovers can easily result from overindulgence. Public drunkenness is totally unacceptable in Egypt. In deference to the non-drinking Muslim majority, the sale of alcohol is prohibited on the Prophet Mohammed's birthday and the first and last days of Ramadan (if not during the whole month).

Beer, whose consumption goes back to pharaonic times, is the most widely available form of alcohol. Native Stella beer is a light lager (4 percent ABV) in half-litre bottles, which is okay if it hasn't sat in the sun for too long, and also in cans. To check that bottled beer hasn't gone flat, invert the bottle before opening and look for a fizzy head. Stella retails in most places for £E6–10, though discos may charge as much as £E15 and cruise boats £E20 or more. In competition with Stella, a new brand called Sakkara has hit the market, a similarly light lager (4 percent) that most foreigners seem to prefer. Premium or "export" versions of both Stella and Sakkara (4.7 percent) are available, which have a slightly fuller flavour. There are also Egyptian versions of Carlsberg, Löwenbrau and Meister, none of which is worth the extra cost, and kamikaze (7 percent) versions of Sakkara and Meister, which are worth avoiding. Marzen, a dark bock beer, appears briefly in the spring; Aswali is a dark beer produced in Aswan. Imported beer, which is the most expensive (£E15–20), only appears in bars, flash hotels and restaurants. There is also Birrel, a non-alcoholic beer.

A half-dozen or so **Egyptian wines** are produced near Alexandria and have improved a lot since French specialists started supervising production. The most commonly found are Omar Khayyam (a very dry red), Cru des Ptolémées (a decent dry white) and Rubis d'Egypte (an acceptable rosé). A new range of wines called Obélisque emerged in 1999, whose Rouge des Pharoahs is pretty good, though the rosé and white are less so. In most restaurants all these wines retail for about £E30 a bottle (but more like £E45 on a cruise boat).

For serious drinking, Egyptians get stuck

into spirits, mixed with beer. The favoured tipple is **brandy**, known by the slang name of *jaz* (literally, "bottle"), which comes under three labels: Ahmar (the cheapest), Maa'tak (the best) and Vin (the most common). **Zibiba** is similar to Greek ouzo, but drunk neat. Avoid vile Egyptian-made **gin** and **whisky**, whose labels are designed to resemble famous Western brands; in fact they may even contain wood alcohol and other poisons, and can be dangerous if drunk to excess. Imported spirits are sold at **duty-free shops** in the main resorts for modest sums (Johnny Walker Red Label US$12; Stolichnaya vodka US$10). Beware of touts conning you into buying them duty-free liquor for resale on the **black market** (see p.270).

Communications

Communications in Egypt are generally less reliable than they are in the West, but you should have no trouble sending ordinary letters or postcards, making phone calls or sending email. Receiving mail and sending packages is a little more complicated, but all that means in practice is that it will take a little longer and require a bit more patience, although some mail does fail to get through.

Mail

Airmail letters between Egypt and Western Europe (including Britain and Ireland) generally take around a week to ten days, two to three weeks for North America or Australasia. Sending mail from Egypt, it speeds up the delivery if you get someone to write the name of the country in Arabic. As a rule, around fifteen percent of correspondence (in either direction) never arrives; letters containing photos or other items are especially prone to go astray.

It's best to send letters from a major city or hotel; blue **mailboxes** are for overseas airmail, red ones for domestic post. Airmail (*bariid gawwi*) **stamps** can be purchased at post offices, hotel shops and postcard stands, which may charge 5–10pt above the normal rate (£E1.25 for a postcard/letter to anywhere in the world). **Registered mail**, costing £E1 extra, can be sent from any post office. Selected post offices in the main cities also offer an **Express Mail Service** (48hr delivery, costing £E57.10 for up to half a kilo to the British Isles, £E66 to North America, Australia or New Zealand). **Private courier firms** such as Federal Express or DHL are limited to a few cities, and a lot more expensive.

To **send a parcel**, take it unsealed to a major post office for customs inspection, weighing and wrapping. The procedure – explained in the Cairo section (p.277) – is much the same throughout Egypt.

Post office hours are generally daily except Friday 8am to 2pm (Ramadan 9am–3pm), though central offices may stay open until 8pm. Almost invariably, offices are closed on Fridays.

Poste restante

Receiving letters **poste restante** (general delivery) is a bit of a lottery, since post office workers don't always file letters under the initials you might expect. Ask for all your initials to be checked (including *M* for Mr, Ms, etc), and, if you're half expecting anything, suggest other letters as well. To have mail sent to you, it should be addressed (preferably with your surname underlined and/or highlighted) to *Poste Restante* at the central post office. To pick up mail, you'll need your passport.

A better option is to have mail sent to a major **hotel** (anything with three or more stars should be reliable) or **c/o American Express** (branches in Cairo, Alexandria, Luxor and Aswan; see p.44 for addresses). The latter service is officially only for Amex travellers' cheque- or cardholders. Note that

parcels sent c/o American Express will be held at the post office (in the case of Cairo, at the branch on Sharia Mohammed Farid).

Telecommunications

All towns and cities have at least one 24-hour **telephone and telegraph office** (*maktab el-telephonat*, or *centraal*) for calling long-distance and abroad. Many of these feature orange direct-dial phones that take phonecards (you'll need one for at least £E20 or £E30 to make an international call), enabling you to avoid the old system of booking calls through the exchange (which entailed giving the number to a clerk and paying for the call in advance, either for a set amount of time or £E30–40 for an open line, and settling the bill afterwards). Expect to queue and hang around a while. It's also possible to book (and prepay) a call that is routed through to your hotel or some other number. Alternatively, you can **make calls through a hotel** with a trunk or direct international line (most places with three or more stars have them), which entails paying up to 100 percent above the normal rate. Always ascertain the rate first.

Regular **phone boxes** really only serve for local calls, which cost 10pt (though some kiosks only accept the old 5pt coins). You can also make local calls on semi-public phones owned by shopkeepers or hoteliers, who charge 25–50pt. **Phonecard booths** (Menatel, Ringo or Nile Phone) are becoming increasingly common – shops which sell the cards usually display the companies' signs. Menatel (£E5, £E10, £E20 & £E30 cards) is the main company, and charges 10pt for the first minute and 9pt for subsequent minutes for local calls, 40pt and 30pt for long-distance, 80pt and 66pt to a mobile or pager in Egypt, £E4.20 and £E1.30 to North America, £E4.80 and £E1.50 to the British Isles and Europe, and £E6.20 and £E2 to Australia and New Zealand. It offers discounts for higher-value cards, and its latest rates can be found on its website at Ⓦwww.menatel.com.eg.

Better still, cards which have a scratch-off panel with a PIN number underneath can be used from any phone by dialling a toll-free number, then the PIN number on the card, and finally the number you wish to call. The card just carries the PIN number – you don't actually insert it into the phone. These usually work out cheaper than ordinary phonecards.

Dialling

Overloaded exchanges and antiquated equipment make **local calls** a hit-and-miss affair, especially during peak hours. Even dialling slowly, you'll often get a wrong number. The **ringing tone** is a double purr, similar to the one used in Britain; the **engaged (busy) tone** consists of two-second bursts of tone separated by one second's silence. A persistent whine or silence indicates that the number is unobtainable, or the local exchange is overloaded.

Long-distance calls within Egypt must be prefixed by a two- or three-digit area code number (listed under the appropriate chapters in this book) and are best made from a phonecard kiosk or arranged through your hotel or a telephone office.

International calls can be made using phonecards at Menatel and Nile kiosks or using the orange direct-dial phones at telephone and telegraph offices and other locations. Although using a phonecard may be easier, it remains slightly cheaper to go to a telephone office, where calls are booked and paid for in advance, and can either be taken in a booth or directed to an outside number such as a hotel. From Cairo, a three-minute call to the British Isles, North America or Europe costs £E12.50 during peak hours (8am–midnight local time), to Australia or New Zealand £E20; outside peak time prices are around twenty percent less.

Direct dialling involves punching 00 for an international line, then the country code, the area code (leaving out the initial zero in calls to most countries outside North America), and finally the subscriber number.

If you have a **telephone charge card** from your phone company back home, you can use it from any international public telephone, and the call will be charged to your account. The benefit of calling cards is mainly one of convenience, as rates aren't necessarily cheaper than calling from a public phone. Check that the issuing company's charge card works from Egypt, as not all do.

Dialling abroad from Egypt

Australia 00-61+ area code (without initial zero) + number
Canada 001+ area code + number
Ireland 00-353 + area code (without initial zero) + number
New Zealand 00-64 + area code (without initial zero) + number
UK 00-44 + area code (without initial zero) + number
US 001+ area code + number

Dialling Egypt from abroad

Australia 0011-20 + area code (without initial zero) + number
Canada 011-20 + area code (without initial zero) + number
Ireland 00-20 + area code (without initial zero) + number
New Zealand 00-20 + area code (without initial zero) + number
UK 00-20 + area code (without initial zero) + number
USA 011-20 + area code (without initial zero) + number

Numbers to dial for charge card calls

BT ☎02/365 3644
AT&T ☎02/510 0200
MCI ☎02/355 5770
Sprint ☎02/365 4777
Canada Direct ☎02/365 3643
Telecom NZ ☎02/365 3764

Emergencies and information

Directory enquiries ☎140 or 141
International operator ☎144
Police ☎122
Tourist police ☎126
Ambulance ☎123
Fire department ☎125

Mobile phones

If you want to use your mobile phone in Egypt, you'll need to check with your phone provider whether it will work there, and what the call charges are. In the UK, for all but the very top-of-the-range packages, you'll have to inform your phone provider before going abroad to get international access switched on. You may get charged extra for this depending on your existing package. You are also likely to be charged extra for incom-

The commonest **mobile phone prefixes** in Egypt are 010 and 012.

ing calls in Egypt, as the people calling you will be paying the usual rate. If you want to retrieve messages while you're away, you'll have to ask your provider for a new access code, as your home one is unlikely to work abroad.

If you're planning to use your phone a lot in Egypt, especially for local calls, it's worth getting on to one of the **two Egyptian networks** – Mobinil or Click. To do this, get your mobile "unlocked" by a dealer before leaving home; then, once in Egypt, go to a Mobinil or Click retailer (they're everywhere) and buy a simcard. First-time subscribers usually get £E200 worth of calls; expect to pay about £E280 to get on to the network.

For further information about using your phone abroad, check out ❀www.telecomsadvice.org.uk/features/using_your_mobile_abroad.htm.

Telegrams and faxes

Telegrams can be sent from any telephone office and are charged per word (including the address).

Most hotels with three or more stars have **fax machines**, making this the best way to reserve a room from abroad. The procedure is the same as for phoning from abroad (see above; individual fax numbers appear in the text). Faxes can be sent from (and received at) certain telephone offices in the main cities; you can also have them sent to American Express offices, who'll hold them like client mail but won't notify the recipient. See p.280 for details of fax points in Cairo.

Email and Internet access

There is currently an Internet boom in Egypt, both in terms of access and in the number of Egyptian websites. New servers are constantly being added to cope with demand, even as competing websites merge or disappear altogether. Useful Egyptian websites are listed on pp.30–31. The biggest index of Egyptian sites is at ❀ce.eng.usf/pharos/index.html.

BASICS | Communications

Internet access is available in almost all the main tourist destinations, with Internet cafés sprouting everywhere and hotels providing computers for guests to use. The government recently introduced a free Internet service, with only the phone call to paid for, which has brought charges at Internet cafés right down. The charge for access is £E5–10 an hour, although five-star hotels may charge up to £E50, and some places charge as little as £E3.

One of the best ways to keep in touch while travelling is to sign up for a free Internet email address that can be accessed from anywhere, such as YahooMail (accessible through Ⓦ www.yahoo.com). Hotmail (Ⓦ www.hotmail.com) can be very slow. Once you've set up an account, you can log into the same website to pick up and send mail from any Internet café, or hotel with Internet access.

Ⓦ www.kropla.com is a useful website giving details of how to plug your laptop in when abroad, phone country codes around the world, and information about electrical systems in different countries.

The media

Various British, US, French and German newspapers are available in Cairo, Alexandria, Luxor and Aswan, as are *Newsweek* and *Time* magazines. Elsewhere, however, you'll be lucky to find even the *Egyptian Gazette* (see below).

If you have a short-wave radio, you can pick up the **BBC World Service**, which is broadcast on various frequencies depending on the time of day. The main ones are 1323KHz, 11,760KHz, 12,095KHz and 15,575KHz. Full details of programmes and frequencies can be found on the BBC website at Ⓦ www.bbc.co.uk/worldservice. Reception is best in the north. The **Voice of America** broadcasts 24 hours on a number of frequencies including 1197KHz, 1548KHz, 9700KHz, 9760KHz and 15,205KHz (full details of schedules and frequencies at Ⓦ www.voa.gov). Both services carry news on the hour. Radio Canada can be picked up at 10pm–midnight in winter, 11pm–1am in summer, on 5850kHz (details at Ⓦ www.rcinet.ca), and in Cairo, FM95 broadcasts English-language news daily at 7.30am, 2.30pm and 8pm.

Television

Egypt has a plethora of terrestrial **television** channels, all state-controlled. Local football matches and Koranic recitations account for the bulk of programming, so it's not worth paying extra for a TV set in your hotel room unless it receives cable or satellite TV – and

even then, chances are that half the channels will be Turkish, Kuwaiti or something equally dull.

Channels 1 and 2 both screen American films (generally after 10pm or during Ramadan between midnight and 4.30am) and **Nile TV** has English subtitles on most programmes, plus news in English and French. In addition to these, some hotels receive **satellite channels** like *BBC World*, *CNN*, *Star Plus*, *Prime Sports*, *EuroNews* or *MTV*. Daily TV **schedules** appear in the *Egyptian Gazette*, whose Monday edition lists all the movies for the forthcoming week.

The press

The **Egyptian** press encompasses a range of daily papers and weekly magazines, chiefly published in English, French or Arabic.

The **English-language** *Egyptian Gazette* (on Saturday, the *Egyptian Mail*) carries agency reports, articles on Middle Eastern affairs and tourist features. For more serious journalism, look out for the English weekly edition of *Al-Ahram* (see opposite), which has interesting opinion pieces on politics, sociology and international affairs. There are also a couple of regional English-language journals: the informative weekly *Middle East Times* and the Saudi *Arab News*. The **French-language** counterparts of the *Egyptian Gazette/Egyptian Mail* are *Le Journal d'Egypte* and *Le Progrès Egyptien*; there is also a French edition of *Al-Ahram*, called *Hebdo*. All of them are fairly bland and heavily censored.

There's more diversity of opinion **in Arabic**. Egypt's oldest newspaper, *Al-Ahram* ("The Pyramids"), reflects official thinking, as do *Al-Akhbar* and *Al-Gomhouriya*. Other dailies with a party affiliation include *Al-Wafd* ("The Delegation"; conservative); *Al-Ahly* ("The Nation"; socialist); and *Al-Da'wa* ("The Call"; the journal of the Muslim Brotherhood). The left-wing Islamist-oriented *Al-Shaab* ("The People") is Egypt's most provocative paper; its editor and journalists are regularly jailed for exposing corruption.

Public holidays and festivals

Egypt abounds in holidays and festivals of all kinds, both Muslim and Christian, national and local. Coming across a local moulid can be one of the most enjoyable experiences Egypt has to offer, with the chance to witness music, dancing and other entertainments.

Even if you're not interested in such festivals, it's important to be aware of **Ramadan**, when all Muslims (which means 90 percent of Egyptians) observe a total fast from sunrise to sunset for a month. This can pose big problems for travellers but the celebratory evenings are again good times to hear music and to share in hospitality.

Islamic holidays

Most Islamic holidays and festivals follow the Islamic calendar. This is lunar-based, so dates vary each year in relation to the Western calendar. You may find it useful to get hold of an annual prayer calendar from a local Islamic cultural centre in your own country.

The twelve **months** are *Moharrem* (30 days), *Safar* (29 days), *Rabi el-Awwal* (30 days), *Rabi el-Tani* (29 days), *Gumad el-Awwal* (30 days), *Gumad el-Tani* (29 days), *Ragab* (30 days), *Sha'ban* (29 days), *Ramadan* (30 days), *Shawwal* (29 days), *Zoul Qiddah* (30 days) and *Zoul Hagga* (29 days – or 30 days in leap years).

See overleaf for the estimated **starting dates of Moharrem** (which begins on *Ras el-Sana el-Hegira*) for the next few years. Note that a day in the Islamic calendar begins at sundown, as a consequence of which Islamic festivals start on the evening before you'd expect.

Ramadan

Ramadan, in a sense, parallels the Christian Lent. The ninth month of the Islamic calendar, it commemorates the time in which the Koran was revealed to Mohammed. In contrast to the Christian West, though, the Muslim world observes the fast rigorously.

What **the fast** involves is abstention from food, drink and smoking during daylight hours, and abstinence from sex throughout the month. Strict Muslims will even refrain from swallowing, lest they "drink" their own saliva.

With all opening times and transport schedules going haywire, and most local cafés and restaurants closing during the day (or remaining open, but not selling food), Ramadan is in many respects a bad time to travel. (We have given the Ramadan opening times where available throughout the text.) It is certainly no time to try camel trekking in the Sinai – no guide would undertake the work – and it is probably safer to travel by bus during the mornings only, as drivers will be fasting, too. (Airline pilots are forbidden to observe the fast.)

But there is a compensation in witnessing and becoming absorbed in the pattern of the fast. At sunset, signalled by the sounding of a siren and the lighting of lamps on the minarets, an amazing calm and sense of well-being fall on the streets, as everyone eats *fuul* and *taamiya* and, in the cities at least, gets down to a night of celebration and entertainment. Throughout the evening, urban cafés – and main squares – provide venues for live music and singing, while in small towns and poorer quarters of big cities, you will often come across ritualized *zikrs* – trance-like chanting and swaying.

If you are a **non-Muslim** outsider you are not expected to observe Ramadan, but it is good to be sensitive about not breaking the fast (particularly smoking) in public. In fact, the best way to experience Ramadan – and to benefit from its naturally purifying rhythms – is to enter into it. You may not be able to last without an occasional glass of water, and you'll probably breakfast later than sunrise, but it is worth an attempt – and you'll win local people's respect.

Other Islamic holidays

At the end of Ramadan comes the feast of **Eid el-Fitr**, a climax to the festivities in Cairo, though observed more privately in the villages. Equally important in the Muslim calendar is **Eid el-Adha** (aka *Eid el-Kabir* or *Corban Bairam* – the Great Feast), which celebrates the willingness of Ibrahim (Abraham) to obey God and sacrifice his son. The *Eid el-Adha* is followed, about three weeks later, by **Ras el-Sana el-Hegira**, the first day of the month of Moharrem, which marks the Muslim new year.

Both *eids* are traditional family gatherings. At the *Eid el-Adha* every household that can afford it will slaughter a sheep. You see them tethered everywhere, even on rooftops, for weeks prior to the event. The slaughtering is often done on the streets.

The fourth main religious holiday is the **Moulid el-Nabi**, the Prophet Mohammed's birthday. This is widely observed, with processions in many towns and cities.

Moulids

Moulids are the equivalent of medieval European saints' fairs: popular events combining piety, fun and commerce. Their ostensible aim is to obtain blessing (*baraka*) from the saint, but the social and cultural dimensions are equally important. Moulids are an opportunity for people to escape the monotony of their hard-working lives in several days of festivities, and for friends and families from different villages to meet. Farming problems are discussed, as well as family matters – and marriage – as people sing, dance, eat and pray together.

Ramadan and Islamic holidays

Islamic religious holidays are calculated on the lunar calendar, so their dates rotate throughout the seasons (as does Ramadan's). Exact dates in the lunar calendar are impossible to predict – local Islamic centres can supply the current year's calendar only – but approximate dates for the next few years are:

	2002	2003	2004	2005	2006
Eid el-Adha	Feb 22	Feb 11	Jan 31	Jan 19	Jan 8
Ras el-Sana el-Hegira	March 15	March 4	Feb 21	Feb 10	Jan 30
Moulid el-Nabi	May 24	May 13	May 1	April 20	April 9
1st of Ramadan	Nov 5	Oct 25	Oct 13	Oct 2	Sept 21
Eid el-Fitr	Dec 5	Nov 24	Nov 12	Nov 1	Oct 21

Public holidays

January 1 New Year's Day
April 25 Liberation Day
Monday after Easter Sham el-Nessim
May 1 Labour Day

July 23 Revolution Day
October 6 Armed Forces Day
October 23 Suez Day
December 23 Victory Day

The largest events draw crowds of over a million, with companies of *mawladiya* (literally, "moulid people") running stalls and rides, and music blaring into the small hours. Smaller, rural moulids tend to be heavier on the practical devotion, with people bringing their children or livestock for blessing, or the sick to be cured.

Dates...

With the exception of the *Moulid el-Nabi* (the Prophet's Birthday – see opposite), which is celebrated throughout Egypt, most moulids are localized affairs, usually centred around the mosque or tomb (*qubba*) of a holy man or woman. Most are scheduled according to the Islamic calendar, so dates vary from year to year when reckoned by the Western calendar.

To complicate matters further, certain moulids start (or finish) on a particular day (eg a Tuesday in a given month), rather than on any specific date. However, a minority of festivals occur at the same time every year, generally following the local harvest. If you're planning to attend a moulid, it's wise to verify the (approximate) dates given in this guide by asking local people or the tourist office.

...and spectacles

At the heart of every moulid is at least one **zikr** – a gathering of worshippers who chant and sway for hours, striving to attain a trance-like state of oneness with God.

Frequently, the *zikr* participants belong to one of the **Sufi brotherhoods**, which are differentiated by coloured banners, sashes or turbans, and named after their founding sheikh. The current incumbent of this office may lead them in a **zaffa** (parade) through town, and in olden times would ride a horse over his followers – a custom known as "the Treading".

Luxor's own festival features a parade of boats; elsewhere, the procession may be led by camels or floats. Accompanying all this are **traditional entertainments:** mock stick fights, conjurers, acrobats and snake charmers; horses trained to dance to music; and, sometimes, belly dancers. Music and singing

are a feature of every moulid and locals often bring tape recorders to provide sounds for the rest of the year. If you are lucky enough to catch one of the major events, you'll get the chance to witness Egyptian popular culture at its richest.

The largest moulids are in Cairo, Tanta and Luxor. **Cairo** hosts three lengthy festivals in honour of El-Hussein, Saiyida Zeinab and the Imam el-Shafi'i (held during the months of *Rabi el-Tani*, *Ragab* and *Sha'ban*, respectively), plus numerous smaller festivals (see p.254). Following the cotton harvest in October, the Moulid of El-Bedawi in **Tanta** starts a cycle of lesser **Nile Delta festivals** that runs well into November (see p.636). Equally spectacular is the Moulid of Abu el-Haggag in **Luxor**, held during the month of *Sha'ban* (p.361).

Coptic festivals

Egypt's Christian Coptic minority often attend Islamic moulids – and vice versa. **Coptic moulids** share some of the social and market functions of their Islamic counterparts and, similarly, at their core is the celebration of a saint's name-day. As you'd expect, the major Christian events of the year are also celebrated.

The dates of **Christmas** (January 6/7), **Epiphany** (January 19) and the **Annunciation** (March 21) are as specified in the Julian calendar used by the Orthodox Church, but **Easter** and its related feast days are reckoned according to the solar Coptic calendar, and therefore differ from both the Orthodox and Western dates by up to one month.

Major **saints' day events** include the Moulid of St Damyanah (May 15–20), the Feast of the Apostles Peter and Paul (July 12), and various moulids of the Virgin and St George during August. Many of these are held at monasteries in Middle Egypt, the Delta and the Red Sea Hills.

Lastly, a Coptic festival (of pharaonic origin) celebrated by all Egyptians is the **Sham el-Nessim**, a coming-of-spring festival which provides the excuse for mass picnics in parks and on riverbanks throughout the country. Its name literally means "Sniffing the Breeze".

Monuments and sites

The price of admission to Egypt's monuments skyrocketed in the 1990s, and entry costs now form a significant part of travel expenses. At major sites like the Theban Necropolis you could spend £40/US$65, taking into account such costly one-offs as Tutankhamun's tomb and the tomb of Nefertari – not to mention extra charges for the right to take photos inside tombs, or use a video camera. However, visitors qualify for fifty-percent reductions on the price of admission tickets (but not photo permits) if they can present an ISIC student card (see p.40).

Guides

Official **guides** can be engaged through branches of Misr Travel, American Express and Thomas Cook, local tourist offices and large hotels. You can also hire them on the spot at the Antiquities Museum in Cairo and the Pyramids of Giza. They normally charge a fixed hourly rate, which can be shared among a group of people, though obviously a group would be expected to make some additional tip.

Such professional guides can be useful at **major sites**, like the Valley of the Kings, where they will be able to ease your way through queues at the tombs. If you feel intimidated by the culture, too, you might welcome an intermediary for the first couple of days' sightseeing. In general, however, there's no special need to employ anyone: they tend to have enough work already with tour groups.

Far more common are **local, self-appointed guides**, who fall into two main categories. At ancient sites, there are always plenty of hangers-on, who will offer to show you "secret tombs" or "special reliefs", or just present themselves in tombs or temples, with palms outstretched. They don't have a lot to offer you, and encouragement makes life more difficult for everyone following. You can usually get rid of them by reading aloud from a guidebook.

The other kind – most often encountered in a small town or village – are people who genuinely want to help out foreigners, and maybe practise their English at the same time. They are often teenagers. Services offered could be escorting you from one taxi depot to another, or showing you the route to the souks or to a local site. The majority of people you meet this way don't expect money – children included – and you could risk offence by offering. If people want money from you for such activities, they won't be shy about asking.

An official version of this kind of guiding is offered by members of the **Tourist Friends Association**, who often approach lost-looking foreigners at bus and train stations, and will swiftly produce their identity cards. They are generally students, very friendly and helpful, and not on the make. Be courteous even if you don't want their help.

Ancient monuments

Egypt's **ancient sites and monuments** are maintained by the **Supreme Council of Antiquities** (SCA; formerly known as the Egyptian Antiquities Organization or EAO). Most are kept open on a daily basis, with caretakers on hand to unlock tombs and point you towards the salient features. Local opening hours are detailed in individual entries; for a few hints on *baksheesh*, see pp.40 & 135.

If you're a committed Egyptologist and want to visit sites that are under excavation or closed for repairs, you may want to contact the local branch of the SCA for a **special permit**. This is usually quite routine and you'll just be given a scrawled note in Arabic to show to the guards on site.

Religious buildings

Most of the **mosques** and their attached **madrassas** (Islamic colleges) that you'll want to visit are in Cairo, and, with the exception of the El-Hussein and Saiyida Zeinab mosques, are classified as "historic monuments". They are open routinely to non-Muslim visitors, although anyone not worshipping should avoid prayer times, especially the main service at noon on Friday. Elsewhere in the country, mosques are not used to seeing tourists and locals may object to your presence. Tread with care and if at all possible ask someone to take you in.

At all mosques, **dress** is important. Shorts (or short skirts) and exposed shoulders are out, and in some places women may be asked to cover their hair (a scarf might be provided). Above all, remember to remove your **shoes** upon entering the precinct. They will either be held by a shoe custodian (small *baksheesh* expected) or you can just leave them outside the door, or carry them in by hand (if you do this, place the soles together, as they are considered unclean).

Egyptian **monasteries** (which are Coptic, save for Greek Orthodox St Catherine's, in Sinai) admit visitors at all times except during the Lenten or other fasts (local fasts are detailed in the guide where appropriate). Similar rules of dress etiquette to those for mosques apply, though unless you go into the church itself you don't need to remove your shoes.

Cultural hints

If you want to get the most from a trip to Egypt, it is vital not to assume that anyone who approaches you expects to profit from the encounter. Too many tourists do, and end up making little contact with an extraordinarily friendly people.

Behaviour and attitude on your part are important. If some Egyptians treat tourists with contempt, it has much to do with the way the latter behave. It helps everyone if you can avoid rudeness or aggressive behaviour in response to insistent offers or demands. And be aware, too, of the importance of **dress**: shorts are socially acceptable only at beach resorts (and for women only in private resorts or along the Aqaba coast; shirts (for both sexes) should cover your shoulders. Many tourists ignore these conventions, unaware of how it demeans them in the eyes of the Egyptians.

Photography needs to be undertaken with care. If you are obviously taking a photograph of someone, ask their permission – especially in the more remote, rural regions where you can cause genuine offence. You may also find people stop you from taking photos that show Egypt in a "poor" or "backward" light. On a more positive front, taking a photograph of (and later sending it to) someone you've struck up a friendship with, or exchanging photographs, is often – in the towns at least – greatly appreciated. As ever, be wary of photographing anything militarily sensitive (bridges, train stations, dams, etc).

When **invited to a home**, it's normal to take your shoes off before entering the reception rooms. It is customary to take a gift: sweet pastries (or tea and sugar in rural areas) are always acceptable.

One important thing to be aware of in Egypt is the different functions of the two hands. Whether you are right- or left-handed, the **left hand** is used for "unclean" functions, most importantly wiping your bottom, but also doing things like putting on and taking off shoes. This means that it is considered unhygienic to eat with your left hand. You can hold things like bread in your left hand in order to tear a piece off with your right hand, but you should never put food into your mouth with your left hand, and certainly never put it into the bowl when eating communally. You should also avoid passing things to people or accepting them with your left hand.

Crime and personal safety

During the 1990s, Egypt's image as a safe country to visit was shattered by a wave of terrorism, culminating in the 1997 Luxor massacre. Although it ceased shortly afterwards and shows no signs of resuming, security at all tourist sites remains extremely heavy, giving first-time visitors an unnerving impression.

Petty crime

While relatively few in number, **pickpockets** are skilled and concentrate on tourists. Most operate in Cairo, notably in queues and on the crowded buses to the Pyramids. To play safe, keep your valuables in a **money belt** or a pouch under your shirt (leather or cotton materials are preferable to nylon, which can irritate in the heat). Overall, though, **casual theft** is more of a problem. Campsites, hostels and cheap hotels often have poor security, making it unwise to leave valuables there. At most places, you can deposit them at the reception (always get a receipt for cash).

If you are **driving**, it goes without saying you should not leave anything you cannot afford to lose visible or accessible in your car.

Terrorism

Between 1992 and 1997, Islamist militants murdered tourists, police and government officials in a series of bombings and shootings. Middle Egypt became a no-go zone for foreigners and tourism expired nationwide after the Luxor massacre. Egyptians were so revolted by the atrocity that even the *Gamaat Islamiya* disowned it as an act by wayward members, and their imprisoned leadership announced an end to violence in 1998. Meanwhile, thousands were detained under the emergency laws until the state saw fit to release them, and the combination of force and inducements seems to have worked, for there has been no terrorist act in Egypt since then.

But the authorities are taking no chances, and security has been reinforced since the September 11 and Bali outrages. There are armed police at all tourist sites, stations and checkpoints; scanners in hotels, plainclothes agents in bars and bazaars. More relevant to visitor's movements, travel restrictions apply in the Nile Valley (see box on p.292).

In Cairo and Luxor, railway clerks have been told not to sell tickets for any **trains** up or down the Nile Valley except on those services designated for tourists, which have plainclothes guards riding shotgun. Tourist buses between Cairo and Israel, and from Aswan to Luxor or Abu Simbel, must travel in a **convoy** (*kol*) with a police escort. Perversely, there is no formal ban on visiting once "risky" areas, but the local police will certainly keep a close eye on you, and may insist on accompanying you to sites like Abydos or Dendara.

Another wise move is to **respect local customs** (in public, anyway). The less you stand out and cause offence, the smaller the chance of attracting any hostility. By going with the swim of society, you'll gain a measure of protection. There are also armed police everywhere, whose mission includes keeping an eye on your safety, but as their usual response to trouble is to let rip with Kalashnikovs, this is a somewhat mixed blessing. In the event of **real trouble**, hit the deck or get off the streets *immediately*.

It goes without saying that certain subjects – Palestine, Israel and Islam, for instance – should be diplomatically should they come up in conversation. Some Egyptians are keen to discuss them, others not.

The police

Egypt has a plethora of police forces whose high profile in Cairo (which has more cops per thousand citizens than any other capital in the world) and at checkpoints on trunk roads strikes first-time visitors as a sign of recent trouble, although it has actually been the rule since the 1960s. Whereas Egyptians fear police brutality, foreign visitors are usually treated with kid gloves and given the benefit of the doubt unless drugs or espionage are suspected.

The **Municipal Police** handle all crimes, and have a monopoly on law and order in smaller towns. Their uniform (khaki in winter, tan or white in summer) resembles that of the **Traffic Police**, who wear striped cuffs. Both get involved in accidents and can render assistance in emergencies. However, relatively few officers speak anything but Arabic.

If you've got a problem or need to report a crime, always go to the **Tourist and Antiquities Police**. The ordinary ranks wear the regular khaki police uniform with a "Tourist Police" armband; officers wear black uniforms in winter and white in summer. Found at tourist sites, museums, airports, stations and ports, they are supposedly trained to help tourists in distress, and speak a foreign language (usually English). In practice, the odds of getting such an officer are fifty-fifty – but it's worth trying them first. The more senior the officer, the better the chance they'll speak English.

The fourth conspicuous force is the **Central Security** force (dressed all in black and armed with Kalashnikovs), who guard embassies, banks and highways. Though normally genial enough, this largely conscript force will shift rapidly from tear gas to live rounds when ordered to crush demonstrations or civil unrest. If you find yourself getting caught up in anything, clear out quick. Ordinarily, though, they are nothing to worry about.

To guard vital utilities, there are also Electricity, Airport and **River Police** forces; the last is responsible for overseeing felucca journeys between Aswan and Luxor, though the formalities are usually handled by the captain of the boat rather than the passengers.

The **Military Intelligence** (the Mukhabarat) is only relevant to travellers who wish to visit remote parts of the Western Desert or go down beyond Mersa Alam on the Red Sea Coast, for which you need permission (details in the text). Their offices in Mersa Matrouh and the oases are signposted in English and quite tourist-friendly, whereas in Sinai they have secret agents stationed in Dahab, Nuweiba, Na'ama Bay and Sharm el-Sheikh, whose brief includes watching Israeli tourists, and Egyptians who visit Israel.

Finally there is the **State Security**, who may take an interest in tourists in border areas or Middle Egypt, but are generally irrelevant as far as most tourists are concerned. All of these forces deploy **plainclothes agents** who hang around near government buildings and crowded places, dressed as vendors or peasants – hence their nickname, the "Galabiyya Police". Aside from the sport of spotting agents in Cairo (where they dress quite snappily), tourists needn't think about them – though in hotels or bars, you might be disconcerted to find yourself chatting with a guy who suddenly announces that he's a cop. There are lots of them around.

Addresses and phone numbers of local police stations appear in the text.

Drugs

Most of Egypt's hashish came from Lebanon until the destruction of that country's industry by the Syrians at the end of the 1980s, when it was replaced by *bango* (marijuana) from Sudan. Since then, Egypt's own marijuana industry, based in the Sinai (see p.710), has seen a vast increase in both quantity and quality, supplemented by the recent, though still small-scale, return of Lebanese hash. A small amount of opium is also produced in the Sinai.

Despite a tradition of use stretching back to the thirteenth century, Egypt was the first country in modern times to ban cannabis, back in 1879. The prohibition was not strictly enforced under President Sadat (who smoked dope himself), but the country now has draconian anti-drugs laws that make hanging or life imprisonment mandatory for convicted smugglers and dealers (which could be interpreted to mean somebody caught with a few sachets of the stuff), and the law against cannabis is much more strictly enforced than it ever used to be. Mere possession or use merits a severe prison sentence and a heavy fine, plus legal costs, upwards of US$1000. Despite this, hashish and bango are still consumed by Egyptians who can afford it, and by tourists in Dahab, Luxor, Aswan, Hurghada and

Cairo – where police usually turn a blind eye if people smoke indoors and behave themselves on the street. In practice, the least you can expect if caught with a smoke is immediate deportation, and a ban from ever visiting the country again. You may be able to buy your way out of trouble, but this should be negotiated discreetly and as soon as possible, while the minimum number of officers are involved: once you are taken in, it will be a lot more difficult. Needless to say, your embassy will be unsympathetic. The best advice is to steer well clear of all illegal drugs while you are in the country.

Foreign consulates in Egypt

If you do find yourself in trouble – or simply need a visa – there are **consulates** for most nationalities in **Cairo** (see p.274). Britain and several other European countries also maintain consulates in **Alexandria** (p.614) and **Port Said** (p.672). Consulates can advise on legal matters and replace missing passports, but are unsympathetic towards drug offenders and will not make loans to penniless travellers (though they will repatriate you as a last resort).

Working and studying

Cairo offers work possibilities for teaching English as a foreign language, journalism or modelling, while the American University in Cairo (AUC) is a rewarding if expensive place to study Arabic, Middle Eastern affairs or Egyptology. To a lesser extent, opportunities to teach or study also exist in Alexandria. Elsewhere, you might find work as a tour rep or salesperson at one of the main resorts, as a diving instructor in Hurghada or Sinai, or a belly dancer in a hotel nightclub.

Teaching English

Teaching in Egypt largely means working in Cairo or Alexandria, where there are many private language schools, generally catering to adults. There's quite a big market for people wanting to learn both conversational and business English. Try contacting one of the following:

British Council 192 Corniche el-Nil, Aguza, Cairo ☎ 02/303 1514; 9 Sharia El-Batalassa, Alexandria ☎ 03/482 0199, ⓦ www.britishcouncil.org.eg. An RSA TEFL certificate is required for jobs at the British Council, which recruits most of its staff in Britain (head office: 10 Spring Gdns, London SW1A 2BN; to check vacancies call ☎ 020/7389 4931, or look up ⓦ trs.britishcouncil.org/vacancies). Vacancies do occur locally from time to time, however. Pays good rates.

International Language Institute (ILI) 2 Sharia Mohammed Bayoumi, Heliopolis, Cairo, ☎ 02/291 9295, ⓔ ili@idsc.net.eg. Affiliated to International House. ILI require an RSA TEFL certificate and a university degree. High turnover of staff, so a good chance of work. Rates are slightly lower than at the British Council.

Journalism

Cairo has been the launch pad for several journalistic careers, for it is easy to place work with the local English-language media. Egypt Today takes travel articles and photos, while the Egyptian Gazette may need subeditors from time to time. International press agencies may also accept material and possibly employ stringers.

Acting and modelling

Westerners are often required as extras in Egyptian films, TV shows or advertisements. You aren't expected to be a professional model, nor are you paid like one: this is simply a day-to-day job for any face that fits; you'll spend most of your time just hanging around doing nothing and earn about £E40–50 a day, which agents may well try to worm their way out of paying you. You can make contact with agents at the *New Sun Café* in Cairo (see p.240). Women should keep their wits about them – and preferably a male escort.

Diving instructors

Divers with Divemaster or Instructor certificates can often find work with diving centres in Hurghada or Sinai, which may also take on less qualified staff and let them learn on the job, at reduced rates of pay or in return for free tuition. Dive centres commonly turn a blind eye to the lack of a work permit, or might procure one for a valued worker. As with language schools, you should be wary about surrendering your passport, and ask other foreigners working in the same job about the potential drawbacks.

Bellydancing

Foreign bellydancers are much in demand in nightclubs in Cairo, Alexandria, Luxor and Hurghada. The work can be well paid, but you have to be careful: financial or sexual exploitation are real hazards. Aside from work, many foreign dancers come to Egypt to improve their art or buy costumes. Finding a teacher is surprisingly difficult, as there are no schools as such; instruction takes place in people's homes and the addresses are hard to obtain. If you're interested, start making enquiries at the specialist shops in Cairo, where you can buy costumes, music tapes and videos of top performers (see p.268).

Tourism

Though most jobs in the tourism field are restricted to Egyptian nationals, and locally based companies usually insist on a work permit, you can sometimes fix up a season's work with a foreign tour operator abroad as a rep or tour guide. See the lists on pp.15–16, 18–19 and 21 for companies to approach.

In Sinai, Hurghada and Luxor there may be a demand for people with foreign languages to sell dive courses or work on hotel reception desks. The most useful languages to have are German, French, Italian, Japanese or Russian (the last only in Hurghada). Ask around dive centres or upmarket hotels if you're interested.

Studying

The American University in Cairo (113 Sharia Qasr el-Aini, near Midan Tahrir ☏02/355 2965, ⊛www2.aucegypt.ed) offers year-abroad and non-degree programmes, a summer school and intensive Arabic courses. A full year's tuition costs roughly US$12,000. US citizens may apply to the Stafford Loan Program; contact the Office of Admissions, 420 Fifth Ave, 3rd Floor, New York, NY 10018-2729 (☏212/730-8800, ⊛www.auc-egypt.edu). For one-month courses, it is less expensive to study Arabic at the British Council (£E400) or ILI (£E350; see "Teaching English", above, for addresses).

Foreign students may also attend one- or two-term programmes at three Egyptian universities: Cairo, Ain Shams and Al-Azhar. These are valid for transferable credits at most American and some British universities. In the US, contact the Egyptian Cultural and Educational Bureau, 1303 New Hampshire Ave NW, Washington DC 20036 (☏202/296-3888) or AmidEast, 1730 M St NW Suite 1100, Washington DC 20036 (☏202/776-9600).

Travellers with disabilities

Disability is common in Egypt; many conditions that would be treatable in the West, such as cataracts, cause permanent disabilities here because people can't afford the treatment. Disabled people are unlikely to get jobs (though there is a tradition of blind singers and preachers), so the choice is usually between staying at home being looked after by your family, and going out on the streets to beg for alms. For the disabled traveller, this has its advantages; disability and disfigurement do not get the same embarrassed reaction from Egyptians that they do from able-bodied Westerners. Disability carries no stigma, it is simply God's will, to be accepted and made light of – as Egyptians say, *Allah karim* (God is generous).

On the other hand, you'll be lucky to see a wheelchair or a disabled toilet, and the streets are full of all sorts of obstacles that would be hard for a blind or wheelchair-bound tourist to negotiate independently. Recently constructed hotels and other tourist facilities tend to be wheelchair-friendly, but few other places have ramps, which are intended for moving baggage rather than people, if they exist at all. If you walk with difficulty, you will find street obstacles and steep stairs hard going. Queuing, and the heat, will take it out of you if you have a condition that makes you tire quickly. A light, folding camp-stool could be invaluable if you have limited walking or standing power.

The **monuments** are a mix of the accessible and the impossible. Most of the major temples are built on relatively level sites, with a few steps here and there – manoeuvrable in a wheelchair or with sticks if you have an able-bodied helper. Your frustrations are likely to be with the tombs, which are almost always a struggle to reach – often sited halfway up cliffs, or down steep flights of steps. In the Valley of the Kings, for example, the only really straightforward tomb is that of Ramses VI. The Pyramids of Giza are accessible to viewing but not entry; Saqqara is difficult, being so sandy.

Cairo itself is bad news, especially Islamic Cairo, with its narrow, uneven alleys and heavy traffic, but with a car and helper, you could still see the Citadel and other major monuments. There's a lift in the Egyptian Antiquities Museum. Some **diving centres** in Sinai and Hurghada accept disabled students on their courses, and the hotels in these resorts tend to be wheelchair-friendly.

Taxis are easily affordable and quite adaptable; if you rent one for the day, the driver is certain to help you in and out, and perhaps even around the sites you visit. If you employ a guide, they may well also be prepared to help you with steps and other obstacles.

Planning a holiday

There are **organized tours and holidays** specifically for people with disabilities; see the listings opposite for contacts – who will be able to put you in touch with any specialists for trips to Egypt – and tour operators. If you want to be more independent, it's important to become an authority on where you must be self-reliant and where you may expect help, especially regarding transport and accommodation. It is also vital to be honest – with travel agencies, insurance companies and travel companions.

People with a pre-existing medical condition are sometimes excluded from **travel insurance policies**, so read the small print carefully. To make your journey simpler, ask your travel agent to notify airlines or bus companies, who can cope better if they are expecting you, with, for example, a wheelchair provided at airports, and staff primed to help. A **medical certificate** of your fitness to travel, provided by your doctor, is also extremely useful; some airlines or insurance companies may insist on it.

Make sure that you have extra supplies of drugs – carried with you if you fly – and a prescription including the generic name in case of emergency. It's also a good idea to carry spares of any clothing or equipment that might be hard to find; if there's an association representing people with your disability, contact them early in the planning process.

Contacts for travellers with disabilities

In the USA and Canada

Access-Able ⓦ www.access-able.com. Online resource for travellers with disabilities.
Directions Unlimited 123 Green Lane, Bedford Hills, NY 10507 ⓣ 1-800/533-5343 or 914/241-1700. Tour operator specializing in custom tours for people with disabilities.
Mobility International USA 451 Broadway, Eugene, OR 97401, voice and TDD ⓣ 541/343-1284, ⓦ www.miusa.org. Information and referral services, access guides, tours and exchange programmes. Annual membership US$35 (includes quarterly newsletter).
Society for the Advancement of Travelers with Handicaps (SATH) 347 Ffth Ave, New York, NY 10016 ⓣ 212/447-7284, ⓦ www.sath.org. Non-profit educational organization that passes queries on to its members as appropriate; allow plenty of time for a response.
Travel Information Service ⓣ 215/456-9600. Telephone-only information and referral service.
Twin Peaks Press Box 129, Vancouver, WA 98661 ⓣ 360/694-2462 or 1-800/637-2256, ⓦ www.twinpeak.virtualave.net. Publisher of the *Directory of Travel Agencies for the Disabled* (US$19.95), listing more than 370 agencies worldwide; *Travel for the Disabled* (US$19.95); the *Directory of Accessible Van Rentals* (US$12.95); and *Wheelchair Vagabond* (US$19.95), loaded with personal tips.
Wheels Up! ⓣ 1-888/389-4335, ⓦ www.wheelsup.com. Provides discounted air fare, tour and cruise prices for disabled travellers,

also publishes a free monthly newsletter and has a comprehensive website.

In the UK and Ireland

Disability Action Group 2 Annadale Ave, Belfast BT7 3JH ⓣ 028/9049 1011. Provides information about access for disabled travellers abroad.
Holiday Care 2nd floor, Imperial Building, Victoria Rd, Horley, Surrey RH6 7PZ ⓣ 01293/774 535, Minicom ⓣ 01293/776 943, ⓦ www.holidaycare .org.uk. Provides free lists of accessible accommodation abroad. Information on financial help for holidays available.
Irish Wheelchair Association Blackheath Drive, Clontarf, Dublin 3 ⓣ 01/833 8241, ⓕ 833 3873, ⓔ iwa@iol.ie. Useful information provided about travelling abroad with a wheelchair.
Tripscope Alexandra House, Albany Rd, Brentford, Middlesex TW8 0NE ⓣ 08457/585 641, ⓦ www.justmobility.co.uk/tripscope. This registered charity provides a national telephone information service offering free transport and travel advice for people with a mobility problem.

In Australia and New Zealand

ACROD (Australian Council for Rehabilitation of the Disabled) PO Box 60, Curtin ACT 2605 ⓣ 02/6282 4333; 24 Cabarita Rd, Cabarita NSW 2137 ⓣ 02/9743 2699. Provides lists of travel agencies and tour operators for people with disabilities.
Disabled Persons Assembly 4/173–175 Victoria St, Wellington ⓣ 04/801 9100. Resource centre with lists of travel agencies and tour operators for people with disabilities.

In Egypt

Misr Travel (See p.29 for details.) Can be helpful with transport and accommodation arrangements.
Peace Tourism 4 Sharia Ismail Sabry, Heliopolis, Cairo ⓣ 02/637 3833, ⓕ 635 1919, ⓔ peacetourism@attmail.com. Can offer the same sort of assistance as Misr Travel.

Women travellers

The biggest problem women travellers face in Egypt is the perceptions that Egyptian men have. Unless accompanied by husbands, women tourists are seen as loose, willing to have sex at the most casual opportunity, and – in Egyptian social terms – virtually on a par with prostitutes. While Hollywood films are partly to blame for this view, the root cause is the vast disparity between social norms in Islamic and Western countries.

Many women visitors do a range of things that no respectable Egyptian woman would consider: dressing "immodestly", showing shoulders and cleavage; sharing rooms with men to whom they are not married; drinking alcohol in bars or restaurants; smoking; even travelling alone on public transport, without a relative as an escort. While well-educated Egyptians are familiar with Western culture can take these in their stride, less sophisticated ones are liable to assume the worst. Tales of affairs with tourists, and the scandalous Russians of Hurghada, are common currency among Egyptian males. In Sinai, however, unaccompanied women experience few hassles, except from construction workers from "mainland" Egypt.

Without compromising your freedom too greatly, there are a few steps you can take to **improve your image**. Most important and obvious is *dress*: *loose* opaque clothes that cover all "immodest" areas (thighs, upper arms, chest) and hide your contours are a big help, and essential if you are travelling alone or in rural areas (where covering long hair is also advisable). On public transport (buses, trains, service taxis), try to sit with other women – who may often invite you to do so. On the Cairo metro and trams in Alexandria there are carriages reserved for women. If you're **travelling with a man**, wearing a wedding ring confers respectability, and asserting that you're married is better than admitting to being "just friends".

As anywhere, looking confident and knowing where you're going is a major help in avoiding hassle. It's also a good idea to avoid making eye contact with Egyptian men (some women wear sunglasses for the purpose), and it is best to err on the side of standoffishness, as even a friendly smile may be taken as a come-on. Problems – most commonly hissing or groping – tend to come in **downtown Cairo** and in the public **beach resorts** (except Sinai's Aqaba coast, or Red Sea holiday villages, which are more or less the only places where you'll feel happy about sunbathing). In the **oases**, where attractions include open-air springs and hot pools, it's okay to bathe – but do so in at least a T-shirt and leggings: oasis people are among the most conservative in the country.

Your **reaction to harassment** is down to you. Some women find that verbal hassle is best ignored, while others may prefer to use an Egyptian brush-off like *khalás* (finished) or *úsqut* (be quiet). If you get groped, the best response is to yell *áram!* (evil!) or *sibnee le wadi* (don't touch me), which will shame any assailant in public, and may attract help. Groping an Egyptian woman would be judged totally unacceptable behaviour, so there's no reason why you should put up with it, either. Some women find that it occasionally helps to clout gropers, if only to make themselves feel better.

Conversely, enough foreign women have relationships with Egyptian men to justify a warning about **gigolos**. Every year, dozens of women are persuaded to invest money in Egypt and find themselves exploited due to ignorance of the language and local law. Although foreign women needn't be married to an Egyptian to buy property or become a partner in a business, it's vital to find a good lawyer whom they can trust as an intermedi-

See p.39 for advice on women's health issues while travelling in Egypt.

ary; preferably one who has worked abroad and is familiar with western ways.

Many women in relationships with Egyptian men enter into so-called **Orfi marriages** (aka "Dahab marriages"), arranged by a lawyer, to circumvent the law that prohibits unmarried couples from sleeping under the same roof, or public displays of affection. These allow couples to rent a flat without hassle from the Vice Squad (thereby also providing cover for prostitution) and can be annulled without a divorce. They don't confer the same legal rights as a **full marriage** in special registry office (*Sha'ar el-Aqari*) in Cairo, which is the only kind that allows women to bring their spouse to their own country or gives them any rights in child custody disputes. Women can bolster their position by insisting on a marriage contract (pre-nuptial agreement). A useful factsheet, *Notes on Marrying an Egyptian,* is available from the British Embassy in Cairo.

On the positive side, **spending time with Egyptian women** can be a delight, if someone decides to take you under their wing. The difficulty in getting to know women is that fewer women than men speak English, and that you won't run into women in cafés or tourist facilities. However, public transport can be good meeting ground, as can shops and, best of all, local schools (Egypt has a high proportion of women teachers). If asking directions in the street, it's always better to ask a woman than a man.

Travelling with children

Children evoke a warm response in Egypt and are welcome more or less everywhere. It's not unusual to see Egyptian children out with their parents in cafés or shops past midnight. The only child-free zones tend to be bars and clubs frequented by foreigners. Most hotels can supply an extra bed and breakfast (which should be supplemented for variety). Pharmacies sell formula milk, baby food and disposable nappies, and the last two may also be stocked by corner stores in larger towns. Things worth bringing, depending to a certain extent on the child's age, are a mosquito net for a buggy or crib and a parasol for sun protection.

From an adult minder's standpoint, most hazards can be minimized or avoided by taking due precautions. Traffic is obviously dangerous, while stray animals (possible disease carriers), fenced-off beaches (probably mined – see p.79), elevators with no inner doors (keep small hands away!), and poisonous fish and coral in the Red Sea (see p.687) are other potential hazards.

Children (especially young ones) are more susceptible than adults to **heatstroke and dehydration** and should always have a sunhat, and high-factor sunscreen on exposed skin. Certainly for the first few days, if swimming at a beach resort, they should do so in a T-shirt.

The other thing that children are very susceptible to is an **upset tummy** and, while this is to be expected to some extent, especially with an unfamiliar diet, bear in mind that diarrhoea can be much more dangerous to a child than it is to an adult. If diarrhoea strikes, keep your child on a sensible diet (boiled vegetables, yoghurt, bananas), and be sure to maintain their salt and fluid levels, by giving them plenty of mineral water, preferably with oral rehydration salts ("Rehydran", available very cheaply at most pharmacies and worth carrying).

Incidentally, if children baulk at unfamiliar food, outlets of all major American fast-food chains, as well as the British chain *Wimpy*, are always close at hand as a last resort. Egyptian sweets are unlikely to appeal much to Western kids, but ice cream is cheap and ubiquitous, as is rice pudding.

On a more positive note, there are plenty of aspects to life in Egypt that children

75

should enjoy, among them camel, horse and donkey rides (but choose carefully – AA Stables in Cairo for example (see p.257) has a good reputation), and felucca rides, snorkelling and (a few of) the great monuments. All the main resorts have discos and sports facilities, and the hotel pool is bound to be a big favourite with younger holidaymakers. We've listed a number of activities in Cairo that will especially appeal to younger travellers (see p.259).

For younger readers, Hoopoe Books publishes a series called "Pictures of Egypt" featuring photographs of daily life at the market, on the river, in the desert and so on, with brief and easy-to-read text, concentrating on things that children can see around them while in Egypt.

Senior travellers

A lot of retired people visit Egypt, which is hardly surprising considering that a visit here has been many people's lifelong dream. However, this is not a country to rush around in, even if you had the inclination to do so, nor is it likely to be, unless you are very intrepid indeed, a country where you will want to rough it.

Luckily, your money will go a lot further in Egypt than it would at home, so a bit of luxury should not be beyond your reach, and you can afford to do things the easy way. There is no need to fight your way onto city buses for example, when you can take a taxi for a dollar, or hire one for a whole day, should you so wish, for less than £10/US$15. Nor need you stay in a cheap city hotel when as little as £25/US$40 will get you a double room with breakfast in a very nice three-star establishment like the *Grand* or the *Victoria* in Cairo, for example.

Especially if you intend to visit a number of widely spread-out sites, it is definitely worth taking it easy and using **taxis** to get around. This particularly applies if you plan to go to a number of the pyramid sites around Cairo (say, Giza, Saqqara and maybe Dahshur), or sites on the west bank of the Nile at Luxor. If you do not, the heat can really take it out of you in a surprisingly short time. Don't underestimate the sun, which can be absolutely roasting, and always take a sunhat and sufficient drinking water.

Most older people visiting Egypt prefer to take a **package tour** than travel independently, and while there is absolutely no reason why you should not travel on your own, a package tour does make it very much easier. When choosing a package, it is worth considering one that is specifically aimed at travellers of a certain age, and particularly if you are single or widowed, it can be a whole lot more sociable. Operators running tours aimed specifically at the over-50 age group are listed below, while among the tour operators listed on pp.15–16, 18–19 and 21, the more upmarket firms are the ones most likely to appeal to mature readers.

Contacts for senior travellers

In the US and Canada

American Association of Retired Persons 601 E St NW, Washington DC 20049 ☎1-800/424-3410, membership hotline ☎1-800/515-2299 or 202/434-2277, ⓦwww.aarp.org. Can provide discounts on accommodation and vehicle rental. Membership open to US and Canadian residents aged 50 or over for an annual fee of US$10 or US$27 for three years. Canadian residents only have the annual option.
Elderhostel 75 Federal St, Boston, MA 02110 ☎1-877/426-8056, ⓦwww.elderhostel.org. Runs an extensive worldwide network of educational and activity programs, cruises and homestays for people over 60 (companions may be younger).
Saga Holidays 222 Berkeley St, Boston, MA 02116 ☎1-800/343-0273, ⓦwww.sagaholidays.com. Specializes in worldwide group travel for seniors. Saga's Smithsonian Odyssey Tours have a more educational slant.

In the UK

Saga Holidays ☎01303/771 111,
Ⓦwww.sagaholidays.com. The UK's biggest and
most established specialist in tours and holidays
aimed at older people.

Thomson Young at Heart ☎0870/550 2575,
Ⓦwww.thomson-holidays.com. A range of holidays
from one of Britain's most reputable high-street tour
operators, selected to cater for over-55s, including
Nile cruises from £629, or a week in Luxor from
£355.

Gay and lesbian travellers

Male homosexuality is common in Egypt, but attitudes towards it are schizo-
phrenic. No Egyptian will declare himself gay – which has connotations of femi-
ninity and weakness – and the dominant partner may well not consider himself
to be indulging in a homosexual act. Rather, it is tacitly accepted as an outlet for
urges that can't otherwise be satisfied: few men can afford marriage until their
thirties, and boys have little other means of gaining sexual experience. Despite
this, people are mindful that homosexuality is condemned in the Koran and the
Bible, and reject the idea of Egypt as a "gay destination" (although male prostitution is an open secret in Luxor and Aswan).

In practice, this means that men travelling
alone are liable to be propositioned (whatever
their sexual orientation), but actively seeking
partners can cause offence and lead to trouble. So far as propositions go, the crucial
phrase to remember is *"Anna (mish) elk"* –
"I'm (not) gay".

Homosexuality as such is not illegal in
Egypt, but that does not stop the authorities
from persecuting gay men, usually on
charges of "habitual debauchery". Indeed,
there has recently been a wave of such persecution, which hit the headlines worldwide
when Egyptian police raided the *Queen Boat*
floating discoteque in May 2001. The disco
was frequented by heterosexual couples as
well as by gay Egyptian and foreign men,
but only Egyptian men alone or with male
partners were arrested. Most were eventually
tried for "habitual debauchery", and two for
"contempt of religion". Those convicted
received sentences of one to five years in
jail. Foreigners seem to be safe from such
persecution, but if you have a gay relationship with an Egyptian man, be aware that
discretion is vital to avoid putting him in
serious danger.

As emphasized under "Health" (see p.38),
AIDS is a real threat in Egypt, despite the

minuscule number of reported cases. There
is some awareness of AIDS amongst
Egyptians but most are steadfast in seeing it
as a "disease for foreigners" and the concept, let alone the practice, of "safe sex" has
yet to emerge.

There is almost no public perception of
lesbianism in Egypt, and as a Western
woman, your chances of making contact are
virtually zilch.

Two **websites** deal with gay issues in
Egypt. Gay Egypt in Private at Ⓦwww
.geocities.com/westhollywood/5884 covers
the *Queen Boat* case in some detail, and
also reports on other instances of persecution of gays by the Egyptian authorities. Gay
Egypt at Ⓦwww.gayegypt.com offers more
in the way of practical advice and contacts.
Warning: don't log on to these sites in
Egypt, where they are monitored by the
Security Police.

Contacts for gay and lesbian travellers

Ferrari Publications PO Box 37887, Phoenix, AZ
85069, USA Ⓦwww.ferrariguides.com. Publishes
Ferrari Gay Travel A to Z, a worldwide gay and
lesbian guide; *Inn Places*, a worldwide

accommodation guide; the guides *Men's Travel in Your Pocket* and *Women's Travel in Your Pocket*.

Gay and Lesbian Travel Australia ⓦwww.galta.com.au, New Zealand ⓦwww.nz.glta.org.nz/index.html. Directory and links for gay and lesbian travel from Australia and New Zealand.

Gay Travel ⓦwww.gaytravel.com. Site for trip planning, bookings and general information about international travel.

Madison Travel 118 Western Rd, Hove, East Sussex NN3 1DB, UK ☎01273/202 532, ⓦwww.madisontravel.co.uk. Established travel agents specializing in packages to gay- and lesbian-friendly mainstream destinations, and also to gay/lesbian destinations.

Parkside Travel 70 Glen Osmond Rd, Parkside, SA 5063, Australia ☎08/8274 1222 or 1800/888 501, ⓔhwtravel@senet.com.au. Gay travel agent associated with local branch of Hervey World Travel; all aspects of gay and lesbian travel worldwide.

Pinkstay ⓦwww.pinkstay.com. Australian-based organization with information on everything from visa

information to finding accommodation and work around the world.

Silke's Travel 263 Oxford St, Darlinghurst, NSW 2010, Australia ☎02/8347 2000 or 1-800/807 860, ⓦwww.silkes.com.au. Long-established gay and lesbian specialist, with the emphasis on women's travel.

Spartacus Gay Guide Bruno Gmünder Verlag, PO Box 610104, 10921 Berlin, Germany (☎49-30/6100 1120); at Bookazine Co, 75 Hook Rd, Bayonne, NJ 07002, USA (☎1-800/548-3855); at Turnaround, Unit 3, Olympia Trading Estate, Coburg Rd, London N22 6TZ, UK (☎020/8829 3000); at Bulldog Books, PO Box 300, Beaconsfield, NSW 2014, Australia (☎02/9699 3507). International gay guide with information on meeting and cruising spots for gay men, but nothing much for lesbians.

Tearaway Travel 52 Porter St, Prahan, Vic 3181, Australia ☎03/9510 6344, ⓔtearaway@bigpond.com. Gay-specific business dealing with international and domestic travel.

Directory

ABU AND UMM Literally "father of" and "mother of", *Abu* and *Umm* are used both as honorific titles and also figuratively as a nickname, picking out the salient characteristic of a person or object. They can also be used metaphorically, as in "The Mother of Battles".

ADDRESSES The words for street (*sharia*), avenue (*tariq*) and square (*midan*) always precede the name. Whole blocks often share a single street number, which may be in Arabic numerals (see also p.840). Elsewhere, street numbers may not be used at all.

CIGARETTES Almost the entire adult male population of Egypt smokes, and offering cigarettes around is common practice. The most popular brand is Cleopatra (£E1.65; £E1.75 in a crush-proof pack). Locally produced versions of Marlboro, Rothmans and Camel (typically retailing at around £E5.50) have a much higher tar content than their equivalents at home; the genuine article can be found in duty-free shops.

Matches are *kibreet*; a cigarette lighter is a *wallah*. Respectable women don't smoke, and certainly not in public.

Metric weights and measures

1 kilo = approx 2.2lb; 1lb = approx 454g/0.454kg; 1oz = approx 28.3g.
1 centimetre = approx 0.394 inches;
1 inch = approx 2.5cm;
1 foot = approx 30cm.
1 metre = approx 1.094 yards or 39 inches; 1 yard = approx 0.914m.
1 kilometre = approx 0.621 miles;
1 mile = approx 1.609km;
5 miles = approx 8km.
1 litre = approx 1.76 UK pints;
1 UK pint = approx 0.568 litres;
1 UK gallon = approx 4.54litres.
1 litre = approx 2.11 US pints;
1 US pint = approx 0.473 litres;
1 US quart = approx 0.946 litres.
1 litre = approx 0.264 US gallons;
1 US gallon = approx 3.785 litres.

ELECTRICITY The current in Egypt is 220V, 50Hz. North American travellers with appliances designed for 110V should bring a converter. Most sockets are for round-pronged plugs, so you'll also need an adapter. Brief power cuts are quite common in Egypt.

FOOTBALL (*kurat 'adem*) is Egypt's national sport. The two Cairo-based rivals, Ahly and Zamalek, are the major teams and contributed most of the country's 1998 squad which won the Cup of Nations as well as the Arabic Super-Cup. Clashes between the two teams can be intense – and occasionally have led to rioting – but games are in general relaxed. Should their team win, thousands of jubilant supporters drive around Cairo honking horns and waving flags attached to lances – beware of being run over or impaled. Two other teams currently on the rise are Ismailiya and Masry, while Santa Katerina is a team composed entirely of Sinai Bedouin who train by running up Mount Sinai twice a day. You can find detailed information about all aspects of Egyptian football at ⓦ www.egyptiansoccer.com.

LAUNDRY In Egypt no one goes to the laundry: if they don't do their own, they send it out to a *mahwagi*. Wherever you are staying, there will either be an in-house *mahwagi*, or one close by to call on. Some low-budget hotels in Luxor, Aswan and Hurghada allow guests to use their washing machine for a small charge, or gratis. You can buy washing powder at most pharmacies. Dry cleaners are confined to Cairo, Aswan and Hurghada.

MINEFIELDS still exist from World War II along the Mediterranean coast, and from Israeli conflicts in the interior of Sinai and along the Red Sea Coast. Do not take any risks in venturing into fenced-off territory, unless local people go there often.

Useful things to bring

❏ **Alarm clock** Vital for early-morning buses.

❏ **Binoculars** Perfect for observing reliefs high up on temple facades – or birdlife.

❏ **Clothes** Keep both practicality and sensitivity in mind. As emphasized on p.74, Egypt is a deeply conservative nation; the more modest your dress the less hassle you will attract.

On the practicalities front, bear in mind that northern Egypt can be cold and damp in the winter, while the desert gets freezing at night, even in the spring and autumn. A warm sweater is invaluable. So, too, are a solid pair of shoes: burst pipes are commonplace, and wandering around muddy streets in sodden sandals is a miserable experience.

❏ **Earplugs** Help muffle the noise of videos on long-distance buses and trains, if you're trying to sleep.

❏ **Film** Kodak and Fuji film is available in most towns and major resorts, but it may well be pretty old stock. It's best to bring adequate supplies. For photography in dark alleyways, tombs and hidden corners, fast film (400–800 ASA) is useful. If you're looking for good landscape photographs, slow film (and/or getting out of bed early) is a must. For cautions on taking photographs, see p.67.

❏ **Mosquito net** The best guarantee of a mosquito-free night's sleep. Alternatively, you can buy a plug-in device at any Egyptian pharmacy.

❏ **Plug** If you like your water to fill a basin, it is worth remembering to pack an omnisize plug: few hotels (even relatively upmarket ones) have sink plugs.

❏ **Sleeping bag** A decent bag is invaluable if you're planning to sleep out in the desert in spring or autumn, or in any low-budget hotel over winter. In the summer, a sheet sleeping bag is handy if you're staying at cheaper hotels.

❏ **Snaps** of your family, home town, football team (or whatever) help bridge the language barrier. Locals will proudly show you their own.

❏ **Torch/flashlight** For exploring dark tombs, and for use during power cuts.

SPELLINGS Arabic is notoriously hard to transliterate into Roman script. The existence of several systems, and the popular familiarity of certain spellings, make consistency a nightmare. Egyptians themselves employ English spelling loosely; basically, you get accustomed to different variations on the same Arabic name.

TIME Egypt is on GMT+2 in winter, which means that in principle it is two hours ahead of the British Isles, seven hours ahead of the US East Coast (EST), eleven hours ahead of the North American West Coast (PST), six hours behind Western Australia, eight hours behind east Australia and ten hours behind New Zealand. Clocks move forward for Daylight Saving Time on the last Friday in April, and the swap to DST in Egypt or your home country can add or subtract an hour from the time difference. Time in Egypt is a more elastic concept than Westerners are used to. In practice, "five minutes" often means an hour or more; *bahdeen* ("later") the next day; and *bukkra* ("tomorrow") an indefinite wait for something that may never happen. Besides hinting that it won't, *inshallah* ("God willing") can be a polite way of backing away from unwanted commitments – a game which foreigners can also play. Remember, too, that Western abruptness strikes Egyptians as rude; never begrudge the time it takes to say *Salaam aleikum*, or return a greeting.

TOILETS Public ones are almost always filthy, and there's never any toilet paper (though someone may sell it outside). They're usually known as *Toileta*, and marked with WC and Men and Women signs. Expect squat toilets in bus stations, resthouses and fleapit hotels; on sit-down toilets, beware of pranging yourself on the nozzle of the curly waterpipe, intended to assist the ablutions of devout Muslims, to whom toilet paper is anathema. Though it's wise to carry toilet paper (£E1 per double roll in pharmacies) at all times, paper tissues, sold on the streets (50pt), will serve at a pinch.

Guide

Guide

Cairo and the Pyramids

CHAPTER 1

Highlights

* **The Pyramids of Giza**
The sole surviving wonder of the ancient world, and still a wonder to this day. If you only ever travel to one tourist sight in the whole world, this should be it. **See p.212**

* **The Egyptian Antiquities Museum** One of the world's few truly great museums, with a massive collection of ancient statues, sarcophagi, frescoes and reliefs, and incredible treasures from the tomb of Tutankhamun. Unmissable. **See p.108**

* **Islamic Cairo** Salah al-Din's medieval city is Cairo's true heart, teeming with life, and chock-a-block with stunning architecture. **See p.132**

* **Old Cairo** A compact quarter containing the city's most ancient Coptic churches, and its oldest synagogue to boot. **See p.174**

* **The Citadel** Dominating Cairo's skyline, the great fort commissioned by Salah al-Din harbours a plethora of quirky museums, a classic Ottoman mosque, and commanding views of the city. **See p.159**

* **The Pyramids of Dahshur** Not the famous pyramids of Giza – harder to get to and not quite as impressive – but if anything even more fascinating, and still largely unknown to tour groups and their hangers-on. **See p.234**

Cairo and the Pyramids

T he twin streams of Egypt's history converge just below the Delta at **Cairo**, where the greatest city in the Islamic world sprawls across the Nile towards the **Pyramids**, those supreme monuments of antiquity. Every visitor to Egypt comes here, to reel at the Pyramids' baleful mass and the seething immensity of Cairo, with its bazaars, mosques and Citadel, and extraordinary Antiquities Museum. It's equally impossible not to find yourself carried away by the streetlife, where medieval trades and customs coexist with a modern, cosmopolitan mix of Arab, African and European influences.

Cairo has been the largest city in Africa and the Middle East ever since the Mongols wasted Imperial Baghdad in 1258. Acknowledged as *Umm Dunya* or **"Mother of the World"** by medieval Arabs, and as Great Cairo by nineteenth-century Europeans, it remains, as Jan Morris writes in *Destinations*, "one of the half-dozen supercapitals – capitals that are bigger than themselves or their countries … the focus of a whole culture, an ideology or a historical moment". As Egypt has been a prize for conquerors from Alexander the Great to Rommel, so Cairo has been a fulcrum of power in the Arab world from the Crusades unto the present day. The *ulema* of its thousand-year-old Al-Azhar Mosque (for centuries the foremost centre of Islamic intellectual life) remains the ultimate religious authority for millions of Sunni Muslims, from Jakarta to Birmingham. Wherever Arabic is spoken, Cairo's cultural magnetism is felt. Every strand of Egyptian society knits and unravels in this febrile megalopolis.

Finding your way around this chapter

Egyptians have two names for the city, one ancient and popular, the other Islamic and official. The foremost is **Masr**, meaning both the capital and the land of Egypt – "Egypt City" – an ur-city that endlessly renews itself and dominates the nation, an idea rooted in pharaonic civilization. (For Egyptians abroad, "Masr" refers to their homeland; within its borders it means the capital.) Whereas *Masr* is timeless, the city's other name, **Al-Qahira** (The Conqueror), is linked to an event: the Fatimid conquest that made this the capital of an Islamic empire that embraced modern-day Libya, Tunisia, Palestine and Syria. The name is rarely used in everyday speech.

Both archetypes still resonate and in monumental terms are symbolized by two dramatic **landmarks**: the **Pyramids of Giza** at the edge of the Western Desert and the great **Mosque of Mohammed Ali** – the modernizer of Islamic Egypt – which broods atop the Citadel. Between these two monuments sprawls a vast city, the colour of sand and ashes, of diverse worlds and time zones, and gross inequities. All is subsumed into an organism that somehow thrives in the terminal ward: medieval slums and Art Deco suburbs, garbage-pickers and marbled malls, donkey carts and limos, piousness and "the oaths of men exaggerating in the name of God". Cairo lives by its own contradictions.

This is a city, as Jan Morris put it, "almost overwhelmed by its own fertility". Its **population** is today estimated at around eighteen million and is swollen by a further million commuters from the Delta and a thousand new migrants every day. Today, one third of Cairene households lack running water; a quarter of them have no sewers, either. Up to three million people reside in squatted cemeteries – the famous **Cities of the Dead**. The amount of green space per citizen has been calculated at thirteen square centimetres, not enough to cover a child's palm. Whereas earlier travellers noted that Cairo's air smelt "like hot bricks", visitors now find throat-rasping air **pollution**, chiefly caused by traffic. Cairo out-pollutes LA every day of the week: breathing the atmosphere downtown is reputedly akin to smoking thirty cigarettes a day.

A brief historical outline

Cairo reveals its history in a succession of sights and quarters and it's in the descriptions of these areas that we've provided the relevant background. What follows is the briefest of outlines, with page references for the main accounts.

Cairo is an agglomeration of half a dozen cities, the earliest of which came into existence 2500 years *after* ancient **Memphis**, the first capital of pharaonic Egypt, was founded (c.3100 BC) across the river and to the south. During the heyday of the Old Kingdom, vast necropolises developed along the desert's edge as the pharaohs erected ever greater funerary monuments, from the first Step Pyramid at **Saqqara** to the unsurpassable **Pyramids of Giza** (for more on this part of the history, see p.209). Meanwhile, across the Nile, there flourished a sister-city of priests and solar cults known to posterity as **Ancient Heliopolis** (see p.206).

It took centuries of Persian, Greek and Roman rule to efface both cities, by which time a new fortified town had developed on the opposite bank. **Babylon-in-Egypt** was the beginning of the tale of cities that culminates in modern Cairo, the first chapter of which is described under "Old Cairo" (see p.175). Oppressed by foreign overlords, Babylon's citizens almost welcomed the army of Islam that conquered Egypt in 641. For strategic and spiritual reasons, their general, Amr, chose to found a new settlement beyond the walls of Babylon – **Fustat**, the "City of the Tent" (see "Old Cairo", p.187), which evolved into a sophisticated metropolis while Europe was in the Dark Ages.

Under successive dynasties of *khalifs* who ruled the Islamic Empire from Iraq, three more cities were founded, each to the northeast of the previous one, which itself was either spurned or devastated. When the schismatic Fatimids won the khalifate in 969, they created an entirely new walled city – **Al-Qahira** – beyond this teeming, half-derelict conurbation. **Fatimid Cairo** formed the nucleus of the later, vastly expanded and consolidated capital that Salah al-Din (Saladin) left to the Ayyubid dynasty in 1193. But the Ayyubids' reliance on imported slave-warriors – the Mamlukes – brought about their downfall: eventually, the Mamlukes simply seized power for themselves, ushering in a new era.

Mamluke Cairo encompassed all the previous cities, Salah al-Din's Citadel (where the sultans dwelt), the northern port of Bulaq and vast cemeteries and rubbish tips beyond the city walls. Mamluke sultans like Beybars, Qalaoun, Barquq and Qaitbey erected mosques, mausoleums and caravanserais that still ennoble what is now known in English as "Islamic Cairo". The like-named section of this chapter relates their stories, the Turkish takeover, the decline of **Ottoman Cairo** and the rise of Mohammed Ali, who began the modernization of the city. Under Ismail, the most profligate of his successors, a new, increasingly **European Cairo** arose beside the Nile (see "Central Cairo", p.108). By 1920, the city's area was six times greater than that of medieval Cairo, and since then its residential suburbs have expanded relentlessly, swallowing up farmland and desert. The emergence of this **Greater Cairo** is charted under "Gezira and the West Bank" and "The northern suburbs".

Cairo's genius is to humanize these inescapable realities with **social rituals**. The rarity of public violence owes less to the armed police on every corner than to the *dowshah*: when conflicts arise, crowds gather, restraining both parties, encouraging them to rant, sympathizing with their grievances and then finally urging "*Maalesh, maalesh*" ("Let it be forgiven"). Everyday life is sweetened by flowery gestures and salutations; misfortunes evoke thanks for Allah's dispensation (after all, things could be worse!). Even the poorest can be respected for piety; in the mosque, millionaire and beggar kneel side by side.

Extended-family values and neighbourly intervention prevail throughout the *baladi* quarters and **urban villages** where millions of first- and second-generation rural migrants live, whilst arcane structures underpin life in Islamic Cairo. On a city-wide basis, the colonial distinction between "native quarters" and *ifrangi* (foreign) districts has given way to a dynamic stasis between rich and poor, westernization and traditionalism, complacency and desperation. In the closing decade of the twentieth century, the city's tolerance was further strained by natural and man-made calamities. In October 1992, up to a thousand people died in an **earthquake**, when shoddily built high-rises and hovels collapsed across the city. Its image took a worse battering abroad after the shooting of seventeen Greek tourists in 1996 and the firebombing of a German tour bus a year later – although the tourists didn't take long to make a cautious return. Every year its polarities intensify, safety margins narrow and statistics make gloomier reading. The abyss beckons in prognoses of **future trends**, yet Cairo confounds doomsayers by dancing on the edge.

Arrival, orientation and information

Setting foot in a big city can be a daunting experience, but you needn't worry about Cairo. Being overcharged by a taxi driver and spending your first night in a second-rate hotel is the worst that can happen to newcomers. Hustlers might try to lure you into overpriced perfume shops, but elaborate swindles are rare and robbery with violence is unheard of.

Cairo International Airport has two main terminals, roughly 3km apart. **Terminal 1** (known as the old airport) is used by Egyptian carriers, El Al and most Arab, African and Eastern European airlines. Western European, East Asian and Gulf airlines use **Terminal 2** (aka the new airport). For **airport information** call ☏02/291 4255. You'll find 24-hour currency exchange as well as **ATMs** that accept Visa, Plus, Cirrus and MasterCard at both terminals.

Emerging from customs, you'll be waylaid by taxi drivers who'll swear that they're the only way of **getting into town**. Usually, this isn't so, but you might prefer going by **taxi** anyway. Cab drivers will probably demand £E50, but Cairenes usually pay around half that – to get a taxi into town for £E30 or so, head out beyond the airport car park and pick up a taxi outside its precincts. Another ploy of airport taxi drivers is to swear blind the hotel you want to go to is closed, full or a terrible place. They then take you to another hotel where they pick up a hefty commission, which will be quietly added to the cost of your room.

On one side of Terminal 1's forecourt is the parking area for **buses** and **minibuses** into the centre. The most comfortable of the bus services is the a/c bus #356 (£E2), which stops at Terminal 2 before continuing to Midan Ramses, and Abdel Mouneem Riyad terminal by Midan Tahrir in downtown Cairo. This service runs from about 7am to 11pm, as does minibus #27 (50pt), which follows the same route. After hours, your choice is between bus #400 (25pt), which plies the same route round the clock, though it is less comfortable and takes somewhat longer to get downtown – easily over an hour during rush hours, about forty minutes at night. There is another 24-hour service – bus #948 – to Midan Ataba, on the northern edge of downtown. Note that **touts** work the buses, posing as friendly locals to try to get you into hotels that

GREATER CAIRO

SHUBRA EL-KHEIMA

River Nile

Shubra Palace

Ismailiya Canal

IMBABA

SHUBRA AL-BALAD

HADA'IQ AL-QUBBA

ROD EL-FARAG

Aboud Bus Terminal

Ain Shams University

Conrad Hotel

World Trade Centre

ZAMALEK

Sakakini Palace

SAHAFAYEEN

Turgoman Garage

Ramses Station

Mosque of Beybars the Crossbowman

4 9

BULAQ 2

1

3

MOHANDISEEN

GEZIRA

MIDAN ATABA

AGUZA

MIDAN TAHRIR

5

Agricultural Museum

6

DOKKI

BULAQ AL-DAKHROUR 11

SAIYIDA ZEINAB

Citadel

7

Zoo

RODA

OLD CAIRO (MASR AL-QADIMA)

8

GIZA

Giza Station 10

Site of Fustat

EL KHALIFA

River Nile

CORNICHE

SHARIA BUR SAID

SHARIA AL-MATARIYYA

SHARIA SHUBRA

SHARIA RAMSES

SHARIA EL-GISH

SHARIA PORT SAID

26TH JULY STREET

SHARIA AL-SUDAN

ARAB LEAGUE

SHARIA BUR SAID

SHARIA PORT SAID

SHARIA SALAH SALEM

SHARIA EN NASR

SHARIA TAHA HUSSEIN

PYRAMIDS ROAD

N

▲ Tanta   Port Said ▲

◄ Sadat City

◄ Pyramids

▼ Nile Valley   ▼ Ma'adi, Helwan & Minya   ▼ al-Basatin

pay them a commission. The airport terminals are connected to each other by a free Egyptair **shuttle bus**, running all through the night. Besides the above options, there's a **limousine taxi service** next to Terminal 1's Masr Travel stand; prices are fixed and posted, though higher than regular taxi rates.

Buses from Israel, Jordan and Sinai still wind up at the old **Sinai Bus Terminal** (aka Abbassiya Station), 4km from the centre. Taxis outside grossly

Virgin's Tree ▲ & Obelisk   ▲ Ismailiya

MATARIYYA   EL-ZEITUN

Buses for Cairo   Terminal 1
Cairo International Airport
Terminal 2

HELIOPOLIS
(MASR EL-GADIDA)

Merryland   MIDAN TRIOMPHE

Qubba Palace

SHARIA AL-HIGAZ

MIDAN ISMAILIYA
SHARIA AL-AHRAM

MIDAN ROXI   Urubah Palace

SHARIA AL-URUBAH

NOUZHA

SHARIA EL-NOUZHA

SHARIA MERGHANI

Heliopolis Sporting Club   Baron Empain's Palace   ILI

Nasser's Tomb

Sadat's Tomb and October War Panorama

SUEZ DESERT ROAD

▶ Suez

ABBASSIYA

Misr Travel Tower

Cairo Stadium

Sinai Bus Terminal

SHARIA RAMSES

MEDINET NASR

MAP ENLARGEMENTS
1 Central Cairo (see pp.110–111)
2 Around Ramses Station (p.131)
3 Around Khan el-Khalili & al-Azhar (p.137)
4 To the Northern Gates (p.142)
5 Between Al-Azhar & the Bab Zwayla (p.149)
6 Between Bab Zwayla & The Citadel (p.156)
7 The Citadel (p.160)
8 Around Ibn Tulun & S. Cemetery (p.166)
9 The Northern Cemetery (p.172)
10 Old Cairo & Roda Island (pp.176–177)
11 Gezira & The West Bank (pp.192–193)

M u q a t t a m   H i l l s   Petrified Forest

0   Kilometres   2

overcharge newcomers and try to inveigle them into hotels: resist them – Cairenes would feel generous if they paid £E5 for a black-and-white cab, or £E1.50 per person for a full seven-seater "special" taxi into the centre from here. Alternatively, cross the street (Sharia Ramses) outside the station and from the bus stop 20m to your right you can catch minibuses or buses to Midan Ramses and Midan Tahrir (see p.97 for bus numbers); or turn left outside the station and walk 300m on past the flyover to the hospital, where you have an even wider choice of buses and minibuses to Ramses, Tahrir and Ataba. The tickets on nearly all of the buses and minibuses plying these routes cost 25–50pt.

In the not-too-distant future, these buses should arrive at the same place as where they leave: **Turgoman Garage**, in Bulaq. As it's still relatively newly opened, transport from Turgoman into downtown Cairo is somewhat disorganized; the simplest option is to take a taxi (£E1.50 to Midan Ramses, £E2–3 to central Cairo), unless you fancy walking the 600m to Midan Ramses and catching a bus from there.

Coming from Alexandria and the Delta, and sometimes by bus from Upper Egypt, you'll probably end up at **Aboud Terminal** in Shubra. By far the easiest way into town from here is to climb up the steps to the main road where minibus service taxis await to take you straight to Midan Ramses by the train station (see below).

All **trains** into Cairo stop at **Ramses Station** (see map on p.131 for the station). There are hotels nearby, but the neighbourhood is so grotty that most visitors prefer to head downtown by metro (Mubarak Station is beneath Midan Ramses), taxi (£E3–5), or a bus along Sharia Ramses. Alternatively, it's a twenty-minute walk down Sharia Ramses, taking a left at Sharia Emad el-Din or Sharia Orabi, into the main downtown area, where most of the budget hotels are located.

Orientation

Greater Cairo consists of two metropolitan governorates: **Cairo**, on the east bank of the Nile, and **Giza**, across the river. The **River Nile** (*Bahr el-Nil*, or simply *El-Nil*) is the prerequisite of their existence and fundamental to basic orientation. Bear in mind that it flows northwards through the city, so that "downriver" means north, and "upriver" south, a reversal of the usual associations. The city's waterfront is dominated by the **islands** of Gezira and Roda and the **bridges** that connect them to the **Corniche** (embankment) on either side of the Nile. There are four major divisions of the city:

• **Central Cairo** spreads inland to the east of the islands. Its **downtown** area – between Ezbekiya Gardens and **Midan Tahrir** – bears the stamp of Western planning, as does **Garden City**, the embassy quarter further south. At the northern end of central Cairo (beyond the downtown area) lies **Ramses Station**, the city's main train terminal. Most of the banks, airlines, cheap hotels and tourist restaurants lie within this swathe of the city.

• Further east sprawls **Islamic Cairo**, encompassing **Khan el-Khalili** bazaar, the Gamaliya quarter within the **Northern Walls**, and the labyrinthine Darb al-Ahmar district between the **Bab Zwayla** and the **Citadel**. Beyond the latter spread the eerie **Cities of the Dead** – the Northern and Southern cemeteries.

• The Southern Cemetery and the populous **Saiyida Zeinab** quarter merge into the rubbish tips and wasteland bordering the **ruins of Fustat** and the **Coptic quarter** of **Old Cairo**, further to the south. From there, a ribbon of development follows the metro out to **Ma'adi**, Cairo's plushest residential suburb, and **Helwan**, the city's heaviest industrial centre. Except for stylish **Heliopolis**, the **northern suburbs** likewise hold little appeal for visitors.

●Across the river on the **west bank**, the residential neighbourhoods of **Aguza** and **Dokki** aren't as smart as nearby **Mohandiseen** or the high-rise northern end of **Gezira** island, known as **Zamalek**. The **Imbaba** district, just to the northeast, was once notable for its weekly **camel market**, but this has now moved slightly further out to Bil'esh. The dusty expanse of **Giza** (which lends its name to the west bank urban zone) is enlivened by **Cairo Zoo** and the nightclub-infested **Pyramids Road** leading to the **Pyramids of Giza**.

Information

Cairo's downtown **tourist office**, at 5 Sharia Adly (daily 8.30am–8pm; ☎02/391 3454), can supply a rather useless free map and out-of-date brochures, and little in the way of hard facts. There are also tourist offices at both airport terminals: Terminal 1 (open 24hr; ☎02/291 4255 ext 2223); Terminal 2 (open 24hr; ☎02/291 4255). Tourist information is also available at Ramses Station (daily 8am–8pm; ☎02/579 0767), Manial Palace (daily 9am–3pm; ☎02/531 5587), Giza train station (daily 9am–3pm; ☎02/570 2233), and the Giza Pyramids (daily 8am–5pm; ☎02/383 8823).

Should the need arise, an alleyway to the left of the Sharia Adly office gives access to the headquarters of the **tourist police** (open 24hr; ☎02/395 9116). Whether they're helpful or a waste of time largely depends on who you encounter. Other tourist police stations can be found at Ramses Station (☎02/579 0767), the Giza Pyramids (☎02/335 0259), Khan el-Khalili (☎02/590 4827) and the Manial Palace (☎02/363 6707).

Maps and addresses

Cairo's more interesting areas are mapped in detail alongside their descriptions in this chapter. These **maps** – and the general plan on pp.90–91 – should suffice for most sightseeing needs, although for an overview of the city they can't match that provided by the maps on sale at bookshops such as Lenhert & Landrock (44 Sharia Sherif) and Shorouk (1 Midan Talaat Harb). Of these, Condor's *City Map of Cairo* is generally the best, though it doesn't cover outlying areas. Alternatives include the Cairo Engineering and Manufacturing Company's *Cairo Tourist Map*, which extends out to Heliopolis, and Lenhert & Landrock's map of the same name, which is better for downtown. The *Handy Map of Cairo* comes in a close third. The free "souvenir" map issued by the tourist office conveys the city's general layout, but can't be relied upon for navigation. Of more use for longer stays are the American University in Cairo's (AUC) *Cairo: The Practical Guide Maps* (£E20), which contains a useful set of maps; and the weighty *Cairo A–Z* (£E40).

It helps to memorize a few **geographical terms**. *Sharia* means "street" and always precedes the name (for example, Sharia Talaat Harb); narrower thoroughfares may be termed *Darb*, *Haret*, *Sikket* or *Zuqaq*, instead of Sharia. *Midan* denotes a square or open space. *Bab* signifies a medieval gate, after which certain quarters are named (for example, Bab el-Khalq); *Kubri* a bridge; and *Souk* a market. However, some of these words have more than one English transliteration (for example, *Sharia* is also spelt *Sharic* and *Chareh*), or may be inconsistently transliterated. **Street names** are posted in English (or French) and Arabic in central Cairo and Zamalek; almost everywhere else in Arabic only, or not at all. The same goes for **numbers**, rendered in Western and Arabic numerals (see p.840), or just the latter; a single number may denote a whole block with several entrance passageways – something to remember when you're following up addresses.

Don't expect Cairenes themselves to relate to maps; they comprehend their city differently. That said, however, people are remarkably helpful to visitors, going out of their way to steer them in the right direction; offer profuse thanks, but never *baksheesh*, which will offend in this situation.

City transport

Getting around Cairo is relatively straightforward; Midan Tahrir is the main transport hub, with several other terminals in the centre connecting up the city (see "Buses", p.97). The metro is simple to use, and taxis are inexpensive once you understand their system. Familiarize yourself with Arabic numerals (see "Language", p.840) and you can also use buses and minibuses, which reach most parts of the city.

You might as well resign yourself to the fact that everyone here drives like participants in the Paris–Dakar Rally, but accidents are surprisingly rare, all things considered. The streets are busy from 8am to midnight, and, unless you enjoy sweltering in traffic jams, it's best to try and avoid travelling during **rush hours** (7–10am & 4–7pm), when the streets are choked. An additional cause of confusion at the moment is the extensive drilling operations related to the Cairo Wastewater Project, which impede traffic at many points around the city.

The metro

Cairo's **metro** (the first in the Arab world) works like nothing else in the city: pristine and efficient, with a well-enforced ban on littering and smoking. Trains run every few minutes from 6am to midnight; outside of the rush hours (as above) they're no more over-crowded than in other cities around the world. The front carriage of each train is reserved for women, worth keeping in mind if you're a lone female traveller.

Stations are signposted with a large "M"; signs and route maps appear in Arabic and English. **Tickets** are purchased in the station (55pt for up to eight stops; 80pt from the centre to the end of the line; £E1.20 from one end of the line to the other); twin sets of booths cater for passengers heading in opposite

Useful metro stations

From a tourist's standpoint, there are seven **crucial stations** (listed here from north to south):

MUBARAK, beneath Midan Ramses, is for reaching or leaving Ramses Station.

NASSER, two stops on, leads onto 26th July Street near the top end of Talaat Harb (take the High Court exit).

SADAT, the most used (and useful) station, is set beneath Midan Tahrir, and doubles as a pedestrian underpass.

SAIYIDA ZEINAB, two stops beyond, lies midway between that quarter and the northern end of Roda Island.

EL-MALEK EL-SALEH, the next stop, can usefully serve for exploring parts of Old Cairo.

MARI GIRGIS is the most useful stop for Coptic Cairo and Amr's Mosque.

GEZIRA/OPERA connects directly into the Opera Complex in south Gezira.

directions, sometimes with separate queues for either sex. Hang onto your ticket to get through the automatic barriers at the other end. Travelling without a ticket will result in a fine (£E5).

The red metro line connects the northeastern suburb of **El-Marg** with the southern industrial district of **Helwan** (via Mubarak, Sadat, Saad Zaghoul, Saiyida Zeinab, Mar Girgis and Maadi), with the green line running from **Shobra** in the north to **Giza** (via Mubarak, Ataba, Sadat and Gezira). The yellow **Salah Salim** to **Imbaba** line (via Al-Azhar, Ataba and Zamalek) is still under construction, and an extension of the green line from Giza to Fazal is also being built.

Taxis

The city has three kinds of taxi: **black–and–white cabs**, **service taxis** and "**specials**". Though each requires different handling, some general rules apply. Firstly, choose the right sort of taxi. Secondly, try to discover the fare in advance of travelling (see below for a general guideline to fares); never start by asking the driver how much. Thirdly, don't expect drivers to speak English or know the location of every street; identify a major landmark or thoroughfare in the vicinity and state that instead. If your destination is obscure or hard to pronounce, get it written down in Arabic.

The best kind to use are four-seater **black–and–white taxis** (Fiats or Ladas), which often carry passengers collectively. Pick a major thoroughfare with traffic heading in the right direction, stand on the kerb, and wave and holler out your destination (for example, "Mohandiseen") as one approaches; if the driver's interested he'll stop and wait for you to run over. State your destination again, in more detail. If the driver starts talking money, say "*maalesh*" (forget it) and look for another cab; otherwise jump in. Don't be alarmed by the circuitous routes taken to avoid bottlenecks, nor by other people getting in along the way. Near the end, direct him to stop where you want (bearing in mind one-way systems and other obstacles) with "*hina/hinak kwayes*"(here/there's okay).

Ideally, you know the correct fare and just hand over the money with "*itfuddel, shukran*" (here you are, thank you) and that's the end of it. If the driver protests, either he's trying it on and will back down if you invoke the police, or you've misjudged the fare and should pay more with good grace. **Fares** are determined by market rates rather than by meters (which are rarely switched on). Cairenes normally pay a £E1 minimum; £E3–5 for a downtown hop (for example, Midan Tahrir to Al-Azhar, Zamalek or Mohandiseen); and more if heading further out, especially to a prosperous area (for example £E8–10 to Heliopolis, £E15 to the Pyramids). For each extra person, you pay 25 percent again. After midnight, fares increase by 50–100 percent. Though foreigners can get away with **local rates**, drivers expect you to pay over the odds, especially if you are well dressed or staying in an expensive hotel: say £E5 minimum, £E5–8 across downtown or the Nile, and £E10–15 further out. The airport and the Pyramids are special cases (see p.89 and "The Pyramids of Giza" on p.212). Fares given in the text are for a single person at **tourist rates**, unless indicated otherwise. Remember that taxi drivers don't generally deal with change so it's best to have the exact fare ready.

Another form of collective transport is the **service taxi**, which can be flagged down anywhere along its set route (see box below for some of the most useful). Service taxis are usually vans (known as *arrabeya bil nafar*) or microbuses; service taxi – in Arabic, *servees* – is the generic term for all such transport.

Useful service taxi routes

ABDEL MOUNEEM RIYAD (in front of *Ramses Hilton*) to the Pyramids, Faisal (near the Pyramids), Midan Giza, Mohandiseen, Bulaq, Bulaq al-Dakrour, Imbaba, Ma'adi and Helwan.

RAMSES to Aboud terminal, Midan Giza, Giza train station, Pyramids, Sharia Sudan (via Zamalek and Mohandiseen), Imbaba, Waraq, Ma'adi, Helwan, Dirasa (via Al-Azhar); to Dahshur on Thursday and Friday only.

MIDAN ATABA to the Pyramids, Dirasa (via Al-Azhar).

GIZA TRAIN STATION to Ramses, Badrasheen (for Saqqara), Dahshur, Abu Ruash.

MARYOTTEYA CANAL (Pyramids Road) to Tahrir, Ataba, Ramses, Saqqara, Badrasheen, Abu Sir, Shabramant.

There are some 60,000 service taxis which transport over a million Cairenes to work every day, causing appalling pollution, traffic jams (because they'll stop anywhere) and accidents. Fares range from 25pt to £E1 per person, according to the distance travelled (inter-city versions, which are usually Peugeot saloons, are covered at the end of this chapter; see p.284).

The third type – not to be confused with either of the above – are **"special" taxis**, usually seven-seater Peugeot 504s. Found around all the major terminals and hotels, they specialize in fleecing unwary tourists and charge at least triple the rates of black-and-white cabs. Even for a short ride, they demand the **"tourist minimum"** (currently around £E10). Their ample seating and luggage racks are their only advantages. See "Driving" (p.99) for details on renting taxis for the day.

Buses

Cairo's **buses** are battered, exhaust-spewing workhorses, active from 5.30am to 12.30am daily (6.30am–6.30pm & 7.30pm–2am during Ramadan). Fares are cheap enough to be affordable by everyone, so buses are usually full, and overflow during the 7–10am and 4–7pm rush hours, when passengers hang from doorways or each other and clamber in and out through windows. Though many foreigners are deterred from using buses by the risk of pickpockets and gropers, there's no denying that the network reaches virtually everywhere.

Buses are painted blue-and-white or red-and-white (the former being slightly more comfortable and more expensive), with **route numbers** in Arabic on the front, side and back. Those with slashed numbers (for example, #13/) may follow different routes from buses with the same number unslashed. Aside from the numbered bays on Midan Tahrir, few **stops** are clearly signposted (look for metal shelters, plaques on lampposts or crowds waiting), and buses generally slow down instead of halting, compelling passengers to board and disembark on the run. Except at terminals, you must enter through the rear door (which

Bus and minibus destinations

From / To	Tahrir/ Abdel Mouneem Riyad	Midan Ramses	Midan Ataba
Amr Mosque (Coptic Cairo)	#93//, #134	#93//, #134	minibus #156
Citadel (Bab Gabal)	#755	#416, #755	#160
Heliopolis (Midan Roxi)	#400, #400/, #500/, minibuses #24, #27, #35, #35/		#948, minibus #21
Mohandiseen (Arab Laeague St)	#337	minibuses #30, #83	#17, #19, #91, #103, #815
Midan Giza	#355, #357, minibuses #82, #83	#9, #987, minibuses #30, #83	#6, #7, #106, #107, minibus #84
Giza Pyramids	#355, #357, #900	#30, #355, #357, #900	minibus #183
Airport	#346, #400 (24hr), minibus #27	#346, #400 (24hr), minibus #27	#948 (24hr)
Zamalek	#13, minibus #49	minibus #47	minibus #48
Badrasheen	#987	#987	
Other useful destinations	#951 to Muqattam Hills #214 to Manashi		

Bus numbers in Arabic

13	١٣	63	٦٣	93//	٩٣//	400	٤٠٠	904	٩٠٤
17//	١٧/	64	٦٤	99(/)	٩٩(/)	401	٤٠١	913	٩١٣
21	٢١	65	٦٥	108	١٠٨	404	٤٠٤	924	٩٢٤
24	٢٤	66	٦٦	134/	١٣٤	500	٥٠٠	945/	٩٤٥/
27	٢٧	68	٦٨	135	١٣٥	609	٦٠٩	948	٩٤٨
30	٣٠	69	٦٩	174	١٧٤	611	٦١١	949	٩٤٩
33	٣٣	71	٧١	186	١٨٦	710	٧١٠	958	٩٥٨
35	٣٥	72(/)	٧٢(/)	194	١٩٤	811	٨١١	983	٩٨٣
50	٥٠	73	٧٣	210	٢١٠	814	٨١٤	987	٩٨٧
53	٥٣	76	٧٦	214	٢١٤	815	٨١٥	997	٩٩٧
54	٥٤	77	٧٧	235	٢٣٥	888	٨٨٨	998	٩٩٨
57	٥٧	83	٨٣	307	٣٠٧	900	٩٠٠		

is often removed to facilitate access); at official stops, you're supposed to exit from the front. Conductors sell **tickets** (the flat fare on most routes is 25pt, or 50pt on longer routes) from behind a crush-bar by the rear door. The front of the bus is usually less crowded, so it's worth squeezing your way forwards; start edging towards the exit well before your destination.

New blue-and-white **a/c buses** are now being introduced on some routes for those who want to travel in comfort and avoid the crowds (flat fare £E2). At the moment, they serve only prosperous suburbs such as Heliopolis and Medinet Nasr and tourist sites like the Pyramids, but other routes will be added.

Most buses start from (or pass through) at least one of the main city-centre nucleii at Midan Tahrir, Abdel Mouneem Riyad terminal (behind the Antiquities Museum), Midan Ramses or Midan Ataba. At each of these locations, there are several bus stops, and where exactly you pick up your bus will depend on which direction it is going in, and whether it starts there or is simply passing through. If possible, ask the conductor "*Rayih...?*" (Are you going to...?) to make sure.

Minibuses

During the early 1980s, the Cairo governorate introduced **minibuses** along many of the existing bus routes. Besides making better headway through traffic and actually halting at stops, they are far more comfortable and never crowded, as standing is not permitted. Tickets (25–50pt) are bought from the driver. Minibuses should not be confused with service taxis (usually smaller microbuses, see p.96). There are minibus **terminals** alongside the big bus stations in Midan Tahrir (by the *Nile Hilton* and near Arab League/Omar Makram Mosque) and Midan Ataba, and minibuses usually use the same bus stops as ordinary buses.

Trams and river-taxis

As the metro and minibus systems expand, Cairo's original **tram network** (built in colonial times) is being phased out. The Heliopolis tram system remains in use throughout that area (see "The northern suburbs", p.207, for details), but all the other lines have been withdrawn. Like buses, the trams are cheap and battered, with standing room only; their Arabic route numbers are posted above the driver's cab.

The most relaxing way to reach Old Cairo is by river-taxi. **River-taxis** (aka waterbuses) leave from the Maspero Dock outside the Television Building, 600m north of the Antiquities Museum. Boats run every hour from 7am until

4pm to Old Cairo via Giza and Roda (other services, and all after 4pm, run only as far as El Gama'a Bridge; frequencies may be slightly different during Ramadan); you can buy tickets (£E1 flat fee) at the dock. On Fridays and Sundays, they also run up to the Nile Barrages at Qanatir (£E2 each way; see "Excursions from Cairo", p.278).

Driving

The only thing scarier than **driving in Cairo** is cycling, which is tantamount to suicide. Dashes, crawls and finely judged evasions are the order of the day; donkey carts and jaywalkers trust in motorists' swift reactions. Any collision draws a crowd. Minor dents are often settled by on-the-spot payoffs, but should injury occur, it's wise to involve a cop right away. Multistorey car parks, such as the one on Midan Ataba, are ignored as motorists park bumper-to-bumper along every kerb, leaving their handbrakes off so vehicles can be shifted by the local *minairdy* (street parking attendant), whom they tip 50pt–£E1. Given all this, it's no surprise that few foreigners drive in Cairo.

To rent a car you must be at least 25 years old and have an International Driving Licence, held for at least a year. The cheapest of the big agencies is Budget, which has Suzuki Swifts at US$62 per day unlimited mileage if you rent for three days or more. Hertz, Avis and Europcar (all with offices at the airport and in big hotels) are worth trying, but will probably be pricier.

Many of these agencies offer the preferable and reasonably priced option of **rented cars with drivers**. Budget, for example, charge $10 per day for the driver on top of the car rental for up to eight hours, with $2 more for each additional hour after that. Thrifty offer cars with driver from £E220 per day including up to ten hours and 120km.

Car rental agencies

Avis 16A Sharia Maamal el-Sukar, Garden City ☎02/368 9400, ✉ruavais@rusys.eg.net.
Budget 5 Sharia el-Makrizi, Zamalek ☎02/735 0070, New Airport ☎02/265 2395.
Europcar 22 Sharia el-Qods el-Sharif, Mohandiseen ☎02/303 5630.

Hertz 8th floor, 195 26th July St, Mohandiseen ☎02/347 2238, ℗344 6627.
J Car 33 Sharia Missaha, Dokki ☎02/335 0521, ℗360 3255.
Thrifty 211 Sharia Ramses ☎02/589 0414.

Walking

The one advantage of Cairo's density is that many places of interest are within **walking** distance of Midan Tahrir or other transport ganglions. You can walk across downtown Cairo from Tahrir to Midan Ataba in fifteen to thirty minutes; the same again brings you to Khan el-Khalili in the heart of Islamic Cairo. Starting from here or the Citadel, you can make fascinating walks through the medieval quarter, which doesn't suit other methods of exploration.

Arguably, walking is the only way to experience the city's pulsating streetlife. Though pavements are congested with vendors and pedestrians, they weave gracefully around each other, in contrast with the bullish jostlings of Western capitals. The commonest irritants are rubbish, noxious fumes and puddles, uneven pavements and gaping drains; in poorer quarters, the last two may not even exist. Women travellers must also reckon with gropers, who strike chiefly along Talaat Harb and around the Khan. Close proximity to a male escort confers some immunity, but the best solution is to develop an instant response (see "Women travellers", p.74).

To make faster headway you can walk along the edge of the road – obviously, always facing oncoming traffic. **Traffic** is heavy from 8am to midnight, and ceases for a few hours before dawn. Its daytime flow only diminishes during Ramadan celebrations, major football matches, and the midday prayer on Fridays, when many side streets are carpeted over and used as outdoor mosques.

At all times, **crossing the road** takes boldness. Drivers will slow down to give people time to dart across, but dithering or freezing midway confuses them and increases the risk of an accident. A prolonged horn burst indicates that the driver can't or won't stop. Remember that motorists obey police signals rather than traffic lights, which were only installed in the 1980s and have still to acquire any local credibility.

Accommodation

Cairo is packed with **accommodation** to suit every tourist's taste and budget. When tourism is at its normal level, most hotels are busy or full throughout December and January, while the cheaper ones are flooded with backpackers over the summer. When tourism is down, however – as it invariably is following any kind of ruction in the Middle East – you can be certain of a vacancy almost anywhere. Consequently, **hotel touts** compete more fiercely than ever (see box, p.103). At the airport they masquerade as blazered "tourist officials" and are keen to book you into the most expensive hotel that will wash (say, £E75/US$25 a night for backpackers); downtown, they're more likely touting budget hotels. Taxi drivers are also in on the game and may claim a split from both parties. Yet **finding a room** needn't be traumatic if you take control of the situation. All you need to do is hop on a bus or hail a taxi and begin visiting downtown hotels (all the downtown hotels are marked on the map of Central Cairo on p.110; others are shown on maps specified).

Hotels and pensions

Cairo's hotels reflect the city's diversity: deluxe chains overlooking the Nile; functional high-rises; colonial piles and homely *pensions* with the same raddled facades as bug-infested flophouses. **Standards** vary within any given price range or star rating – and from room to room in many places. Try to inspect the facilities (a/c denotes airconditioning) before checking in. Also establish the price and any service tax or extra charges (which should be posted in reception) at the outset. Guests at deluxe hotels or certain budget places such as the *Ismailia House*, *Magic*, *Luna* and the *Pensione Roma* can avail themselves of **laundry services** charged at piece rates; in budget places, prices should be around £E4 for a dress, £E2 for a skirt, shirt or trousers, and 50pt for socks or underwear. Elsewhere, hotel receptionists or building janitors can probably put you in touch with the local *makwagi*, who does washing and ironing also at piece rates.

Hotels with three or more stars require payment in US$, or Egyptian currency backed by an exchange receipt. Officially, rates are the same all year, with an annual rise in early October.

Deluxe and four-star hotels – city-wide

All the international chains are represented in Cairo, which has over thirty hotels with a four- or five-star (deluxe) rating. Though package tourists may get hefty reductions, the regular rates for such places start at around US$150 for a double. Our **city-wide selection** boasts fine locations, superlative facilities or splendid decor; none of the deluxe or four-star hotels include breakfast in their price.

Conrad 1191 Corniche el-Nil, Bulaq ☎02/580 8000, ⑥580 8080, ⑥conrad@conradcairo.com.eg (international reservations via Hilton, see p.54). A new hotel, run by the Hilton chain, but calmer and more sedate than its city-centre counterparts, with some of the most comfortable rooms in town. It has international dining, palm trees in the lobby, a pool and health club, but no disco or nightclub except during festivals. ❽

Four Seasons 35 Sharia Giza ☎02/573 1212, ⑥568 1616, ⑥cairo.reservations@ fourseasons.com (see map p.174; for international reservations, see p.53). Cairo's swankiest hotel, luxurious to a fault, though decor is a little on the gaudy side and security a tad too obvious. ❾

El-Gezirah Sheraton southern end of Gezira Island ☎02/737 3737, ⑥736 3640, ⓦwww.sheraton.com/elgezirah (see map p.192; for international reservations, see p.53). Overlooking the Nile from the southern end of Gezira Island, with Middle Eastern and Italian restaurants, *Rumours* piano bar, a casino, bank and the expensive *le Disco* nightclub. ❾

Helnan Shepheard's Hotel Corniche el-Nil, ☎02/792 1000, ⑥792 1010, ⑥saleshs@helnan .com. Five-star, Nile-side version of the famous nineteenth-century establishment that stood on Midan Opera. Rooms on the quieter side facing the Muqattam Hills are cheaper. ❽

Cairo Marriott Sharia Saraya el-Gezira, off 26th July St, Zamalek ☎02/735 8888, ⑥735 6667, ⑥reservation@cairomarriott.com (see map p.192; for international reservations, see p.53). Modern guest rooms built around the lavish palace constructed to house Empress Eugénie. Offers fine restaurants and bars, a casino, nightclub and pool; non-residents can drink or dine in the khedival salons and billiard room. Good value at last check compared with other hotels in this bracket. ❻/❼

Mena House Oberoi ☎02/383 3222, ⑥383 7777, ⑥obmhobc@oberoi.com.eg (for international reservations, see p.53). Set in lush grounds near the Giza Pyramids (of which some rooms have a view), this one-time khedival hunting lodge wit-

nessed Roosevelt and Churchill initiate the D-Day plan, and the formal signing of the peace treaty between Israel and Egypt. Its renovated arabesque halls and nineteenth-century rooms are delightful; the modern Mena Gardens annexe isn't. Facilities include the *Moghul* restaurant (the best Indian restaurant in Egypt), pool, golf course and tennis courts. ❽/❾

Nile Hilton ☎02/578 0444 or 0666, ⑥578 0475 or 6, ⑥nhilton@internetegypt.com (for international reservations, see p.54). Sited between Midan Tahrir and the Nile, this refurbished 1950s building is one of the first landmarks you'll get to recognize in Cairo, and boasts the biggest hotel rooms in town. It also contains a range of cafés and restaurants: the *Taverne du Champs de Mars*, *Ibis Café*, *Da Mario* and *Rotisserie Belvedere*. River-facing doubles cost more than rooms overlooking Tahrir. Bar and winter nightclub on the roof; during summer, action revolves around the pool. ❾

Ramses Hilton ☎02/574 4400, ⑥575 7152, ⑥rhinet@intouch.com (for international reservations, see p.54). Just north of the Antiquities Museum, this is Cairo's tallest hotel, with 3-storey atrium and glass elevator, pool, bars, restaurants and a casino, but standards of service are not upto scratch. ❽

Royal Meridien ☎0800/448 888 or 02/362 1717, ⑥362 1927, ⑥mail@leroyalmeridien-cairo.com (see map p.174; for international reservations, see p.54). French-managed pile at the northern tip of Roda Island, recently set up in a sumptuous new wing with very stylish rooms (north-facing ones offer killer views of central Cairo and the Nile). The pool, health club and nightclub are still in the process of transfer from the old wing, but should be up and running by the time this book goes to press. ❽

Semiramis Intercontinental ☎02/795 7171, ⑥796 3020, ⑥cairo@interconti.com (for international reservations, see p.54). Just south of Midan Tahrir, elegant rooms with every facility, including Internet access and some with Nile views. There's also a gym, pool, Al-Rashid nightclub and a host of restaurants offering every type of cuisine. ❽/❾

Mid-range and cheap places: hotels and pensions

The mid-range of the budget spectrum chiefly consists of **three-star hotels** whose rooms have private bathrooms and a/c, perhaps also fridges, phones and TV. If facilities fall short of what's advertised (and charged for), you're entitled to raise a stink. However, a couple of places in the centre are (more or less) refurbished colonial edifices whose old-world charm makes up for any lack of modern gadgetry.

Budget travellers usually go for the **cheap hotels and pensions** on the upper floors of downtown office buildings. Designed to exclude sunlight and circulate air during summer, the unheated ones can be damp and draughty in winter. During the summer, bedbugs and mosquitoes may infest seedier places where hot water (or any water at all) is often lacking. By way of compensation, some feature Art Deco rooms with sweeping balconies, and all can provide bottled water, tea and soft drinks. Most are reached from street level via an alleyway and/or lobby serving the entire building; many are locked at midnight, so if you arrive late at night you'll have to roust the doorman (*bowab*) who will probably expect some modest *baksheesh* for his trouble. Riding the elevators can feel like playing Russian roulette, but we've never heard of a serious accident.

The following rundown is by no means exhaustive, focusing as it does on places that are cheap, agreeable or conveniently located (a few combine all these assets) – or bad enough to merit a warning. Note that accommodation in the areas around Midan Tahrir and Midan Talaat Harb, although convenient for the Antiquities Museum and downtown, is a honey-pot for every type of tout and con artist in Cairo. Notices in all the hotels in this area give due warning, but the constant harassment can give you a bad impression of Egyptian people.

The hotels are listed according to location, the areas corresponding to descriptive sections (and maps) in this chapter; the downtown ones are all shown on the map on pp.110–111, mostly keyed in by number. Breakfast is included in the price unless otherwise stated.

Downtown – between Tahrir and Ezbekiya

Talaat Harb, Mahmoud Bassiouni and Qasr el-Nil streets offer the widest range of **budget** hotels. A few are excellent, a few really squalid, but the majority fall somewhere in between. Richer tourists can choose between comfortable modern hotels or a number of vintage establishments redolent of prewar high society.

Amin 38 Midan Falaki ☎02/393 3813. Reasonable rooms with fans on the 6th, 7th and 10th floors; it's worth paying £E5 more for a room with private bathroom and constant hot water – the shared facilities aren't so clean. Opposite Bab al-Luq market. Breakfast not included. ❷

Berlin Hotel 2 Sharia el-Shawarby ☎ & ℱ02/395 7502, ✉berlinhotelcairo@hotmail.com. A small hotel on the 4th floor, just off Qasr el-Nil, with lofty double and triple rooms, each with its own shower stall, quiet split-unit a/c, plus Art Nouveau-style fittings, and friendly and helpful management. Services include cheap Internet access (£E5 per hour), airport pick-ups, and their own drivers to take you round the pyramid sites or elsewhere at decent rates. ❹

Carlton 21 26th July St ☎02/575 5022, ℱ575 5323. Built in 1935 and still retaining some wood-panelled period charm, albeit rather worn around the edges. Modern facilities include a/c and TV with satellite reception in every room, but don't bother to pay the £E15 extra for a minibar. Has a restaurant on the seventh floor and a very pleasant rooftop garden with coffee shop. ❹

Cosmopolitan Sharia el Kady el Fadel, off Qasr el-Nil ☎02/392 3956, ℱ393 3531. This refurbished and rather grand monumental Art Nouveau building has a European restaurant, Olde-English bar, bank and international calls facility, but avoid the tours sold at the travel desk. All rooms have a/c and private baths. ❻

Crown 9 Sharia Emad el-Din ☎020/591 8374, ℱ735 0424, ✉crowncairo@yahoo.com. Salubrious and roomy, with hot water in shared bathrooms on 4th floor. Sufferers of bad backs will appreciate the firmness of the beds, but standards have been slackening lately, and the place is becoming a little bit grubby, although all rooms are a/c and some are en suite (with no price difference). Breakfast not included. Twenty percent off for *Rough Guide* readers. ❸

Dahab Hotel 26 Sharia Bassiouny ☎02/579 9104, ✉dahabhotel@hotmail.com. A Dahab tourist camp transported – surprisingly convincingly – to

Hotel touts and excursion rackets

There's a big racket going on in Cairo, and newly arrived tourists are the victims. It starts at the airport and bus terminals, and you need to be aware of it if you are to avoid it. The aim is to steer tourists into hotels which will pay a commission to the person bringing them, usually a taxi driver or street tout. The commission will of course be added to your bill. The same hotels will then try to sell you overpriced tours to Luxor and Aswan, or steer you into perfume or papyrus shops, taking a commission in turn on all sales. Some of them are less than subtle in their sales techniques. Most places in Cairo are reputable and above board, but it pays to know that some are not, and how to avoid those places and their scams.

As soon as you arrive at Cairo airport, and before you even clear customs, you will probably be approached by "travel agents" wearing official badges with their photo, on which the only thing written in English is the words "Ministry of Tourism". This does not mean, despite what these people may tell you, that they work for the ministry of tourism, simply that they have a licence to operate in the airport. They will try to dissuade you from going to the hotel you had in mind, and they may even appear to call the hotel to check if there is room. A voice on the other end of the phone may say, "Sorry, we are full today." Don't believe it. Nor should you believe these "travel agents" if they tell you that your hotel has closed or is no good. Similarly, do not believe taxi drivers (especially the taxi drivers who accost you before you leave the airport), or any "friendly stranger" who gets talking to you on the bus into town, or in the street in downtown Cairo, if they ask where you are going and then proceed to tell you that the hotel you want has closed, or is dirty or expensive, "but I know a better one." If a taxi driver tells you that the hotel you want has closed, take another taxi. If you are already on your way into town, ask to be dropped off at Midan Tahrir or on Sharia Talaat Harb and walk the rest of the way. Other touts will approach you on the street and try to steer you into a different hotel from the one of your choice. Some of these hang around downstairs below popular hotels when certain flights have just come in and may even claim to be the manager! Remember, while you have your baggage with you, you are an obvious new arrival and you will attract every tout in town.

A number of hotels that work with touts also subject their guests to a sales campaign with the aim of getting them to buy papyruses, perfumes, horse and camel trips and, most of all, excursions to Luxor and Aswan. These hotels will take a cut of whatever the tourist pays. Most hotels in town will of course sell sightseeing tours, either within Cairo or further afield, and these tours will be advertised in reception, but no reputable hotel will use sales techniques to persuade their guests to buy such tours, nor overcharge to the extent that some do. In places where sales techniques are used, the tour will almost certainly be priced well over the odds, and large parts of it will be spent visiting papyrus and perfume shops (often referred to as "museums") rather than the sites you came to see.

The tour that is usually sold and adapted by dubious operators is that of Amigo Tours in Aswan, which is frequently sold to unsuspecting tourists with a mark-up of 300 percent or more. As well as budget places, the travel desks in the lobbies of hotels such as the *Cleopatra Palace* are among those selling Amigo Tours trips with a huge mark-up.

Our advice is: first of all, never stay in a hotel that is recommended by a taxi driver or street tout in preference to the one you have already decided on. Secondly, never buy any tour without first shopping around. Thirdly, check out of any hotel that starts putting pressure on you to buy a tour, or that allows in touts who will try to take you to papyrus or perfume shops. And fourthly, don't pay for more than one night upfront, so that you can leave if necessary the next day.

For more on touts, see p.123.

a downtown roof, this place has clean but poky rooms, dorm beds (£E10) – and lots of backpackers. Friendly staff and plenty of vegetation make it a pleasant hang-out, where facilities include a bedouin-style café, communal kitchen, laundry service, 24-hour hot water and cheap Internet access. ❷

Garden City House 26 Sharia Kamal al-Din Salah ☎02/354 4969 or 354 4126. Refurbished 3rd-floor 1930s *pension* on the edge of the Garden City, behind the *Semiramis*. Some rooms have Nile views, some have en-suite bathrooms, some have a/c, and all have satellite TV. On the downside, the location is rather noisy. ❸

Grand 17 26th July St ☎02/575 7700 or 16 or 47, ☎575 7593, ✉grandhotel@themail.com. Characterful and very comfortable Art-Deco edifice featuring original lifts and furniture, a fountain, *Valley of the Kings* restaurant, coffee shop and old-fashioned, homely rooms with immaculately varnished wooden floors, attached to large, spotless and bright tiled bathrooms. Entrance in the alley off Sharia Talaat Harb. Very good value. ❻

Happyton 10 Sharia Ali el Kassar ☎02/592 8671 or 6. Two-star hotel with en-suite rooms with a/c. The rooms are all well kept but vary in size, with some of them quite large, and there's also a bar and a disco. A TV in your room costs £E5 extra, so specify if you don't want one. ❸

Ismailia House 1 Midan Tahrir ☎02/796 3122. Advance booking is advisable for this cool, clean and cheerful 7th-floor haven, with singles, doubles, triples, dorm beds (£E15), 24-hr hot water and CNN on tap. The Tahrir-facing rooms are noisy at night but do have great views. ❷

Lotus 12 Sharia Talaat Harb ☎02/575 0627, ☎575 4270, ⊛www.lotushotel.com. Reception on the 7th floor, reached via an arcade. Clean, with friendly staff, a restaurant and a bar, but avoid buying tours here. Some rooms with a/c and private baths. Hot water 6–10am and 6–10pm. ❹

Luna 27 Talaat Harb ☎02/396 1020, ✉lunapension@hotmail.com. Excellent-value hotel with standards far higher than you would expect for the price, friendly, helpful staff, and an Egyptian breakfast that you'll be hard-put to finish. Free airport pick-up if you stay three days or more. Large, clean rooms, some en suite with a/c, others with fans. ❸

Magic Hotel 10 El Bustan St, a quiet street near Midan El Tahrir ☎ & ☎02/579 5918, ⊛www.geocities.com/magichotel. Very helpful and welcoming place with clean and comfortable, though small, rooms. Has a plush satellite TV lounge with all the international channels and Internet access at £E10 per hour. Call beforehand

and someone will pick you up from the airport. ❷

New Hotel 21 Sharia Adly ☎02/392 7065, ☎392 9555. A reasonable mid-range place with a 24-hr café and slightly worn, carpeted rooms, some with a/c, and all with en-suite shower and toilet. ❸/❹

Odeon Palace 6 Sharia Abdel Hamid Said ☎02/577 6637, ☎576 7971. Modern three-star tower with restaurant and 24-hour roof garden bar, just off Sharia Talaat Harb; breakfast not included. ❻

Orient Palace 14 26th July St ☎02/393 9375 or 6. A friendly place, with the cheapest singles (£E12) in town, but rather dingy rooms. On the 10th floor (use the right-hand elevator), with a rooftop café. ❷

Oxford 32 Sharia Talaat Harb ☎02/575 8173. Once one of the world's great travellers' hotels, but now just a filthy dive that has featured regularly in the crime pages of the local press. On one famous occasion in 1985, half its British guests were rounded up and jailed for dealing marijuana and LSD, only to escape during a prison riot and slip across the border to Israel. Since then it has degenerated into a sleazy knocking shop, whose bedbugs and squalor are definitely not worth braving just for a bit of underground history. Its notoriety earns it a place in our list, however. ❷

Pensione Roma 169 Sharia Mohammed Farid – entrance around the side of the Gattegno department store ☎02/391 1088 or 391 1340, ☎579 6243. The stylish 1940s ambience, immaculately maintained by Madame Cressaty, comes highly recommended and it's a wise idea to book in advance (call at 9am or the night before). Constant hot water, shared and private bathrooms; laundry service. ❸

Hotel Select Sharia Adly, beside the synagogue ☎02/393-3707. Palestinian-run, with simple, mostly triple rooms and hot-water bathrooms, 8 floors up in a 1930s building with period touches. ❷

Sultan ☎02/577 2258, **Safary** ☎02/577 8692 and **Venice** hotels ☎02/575 1171, 4 Sharia Tawfiqia. Trio of ultra-cheapies in a building opening onto a colourful market street near Midan Orabi, very handy for inexpensive eating and groceries, and just the right distance away from the centre of downtown. All are very friendly, and offer hot water and use of kitchen facilities, but none of them is especially clean. The *Venice* is the best, and the only one to offer single and double rooms as well as dorms. The *Sultan* has dorms on three floors, those at the top (no elevator) being the cheapest. The *Safary* is popular with Japanese backpackers, despite being the least appealing of the three. Dorm beds £E6–8. ❷

Tulip 3 Midan Talaat Harb ☎02/393 9433, ☎361 1995, ✉tuliphotel@yahoo.com. Decent old-style place facing *Groppi's*. The singles, doubles and triples – with and without private baths – have firm mattresses. Also has a restaurant/bar. ❸

Windsor 19 Sharia Alfi Bey ☎02/591 5810, ℱ592 1621, �🖥www.windsorcairo.com Colonial hotel that retains much character, and one of the nicest bars in Cairo, but has definitely seen better days and is overpriced (trading on the fact that

Michael Palin slept here when filming a travel documentary). The patron's father, Ramses Wissa Wassef, founded Harraniyya's weaving school (see below, p.220). All rooms have a/c and satellite TV; all but the very cheapest have private bathroom. Offers fifteen percent discount for *Rough Guide* readers, but avoid buying tours here. ❷/❸

Downtown – nearer Ramses Station

Arriving late or leaving early from one of the terminals around Midan Ramses, the following places commend themselves despite their grim surroundings. They're marked on the map on p.131.

Big Ben 33 Sharia Emad el-Din ☎02/590 8881. Singles, doubles and triples with fans, soft beds and a few with private bath – some even have balconies with a view of the mosque next door. Take the left-hand elevator in the foyer to the 7th floor. Breakfast not included. ❷

Fontana off Midan Ramses ☎02/592 2321, ℱ592 2145. Comfortable and well kept, with a swimming pool, bar, restaurant, patisserie, and disco or bellydancing in its nightclub. The rooms have TV, fridge and a/c, and some have views of the Citadel. ❺

New Cicil 29 Sharia Emad el-Din, 4th floor ☎02/591 3859. Clean-ish, with fans and shared hot-water bathrooms. Breakfast not included. ❷

Venus Hotel 38 Sharia Ramses ☎02/577 5186, ℮venus_hotel@yahoo.com. The best budget option near Ramses, the rooms are clean and comfortable although they are small; some are en suite with a/c. There's also a TV lounge and laundry service, they store luggage, and give a twenty percent discount to students. ❷

Victoria 66 Sharia el-Gumhorriya ☎02/589 2291–4, ℱ591 3008, ℮info@victoria.com.eg. A three-star 1930s hotel once frequented by George Bernard Shaw. The large recently renovated a/c rooms (many with mahogany furniture), bar and restaurant make this one of the best deals in town. Bank and hairdresser on the premises; international calls. Takes Amex, MasterCard and Visa. ❺

Islamic Cairo

Islamic Cairo rubs shoulders with its medieval past: noises, smells and insects penetrate one's room, while outside the quarter's values and customs demand recognition. Excluding numerous bug-ridden dives around Saiyida Zeinab and Khan el-Khalili, three hotels are worth considering.

El-Hussein Muski (map p.137) ☎02/591 8089 or 591 8664. Entered via a passage into *Fishawi's*, the hotel's balcony rooms overlooking the square are harangued by Cairo's loudest muezzins, while the upper floors shake from wedding parties in its rooftop restaurant (great views, awful food). Sleep is impossible during festivals (bring earplugs), when the square bops all night. Pleasant singles and doubles, but it's worth paying £E15 extra for a/c and a private bathroom. Fine for women alone. Reservations advisable. ❹

New Rich 74 Sharia Abdel Aziz, off Midan Ataba (map p.111) ☎02/390 0145, ℱ390 6390. Roughly midway between downtown and Islamic Cairo. Quite large but rather gloomy rooms with fans in lieu of failed a/c. ❸

Radwan Muski (map p.137) ☎02/786 5180 or 2, ℱ592 5287, ℮said19480@yahoo.com In an excellent location just across the Muski from the *El-Hussein*, so equally noisy, but with smaller rooms and less character. Singles, doubles and triples with shared or private baths. Sporadic hot water. Not advisable for women alone. ❸

Zamalek

The northern half of Gezira Island is quieter and fresher than central Cairo, except along 26th July Street, where buses and service taxis shuttle between downtown and the west bank, with an elevated roadway for through traffic. Besides its *Cairo Marriott* and *Gezirah Sheraton* (see p.101), the island has a few modern **three-star hotels**, plus a couple of **cheaper options**. Below are our top choices; all are keyed on the map on pp.192–193.

El-Nil Zamalek 21 Sharia Aziz Abaza ⓣ 02/735 1846, ⓕ 735 0220. Spacious modern rooms with bath, phone, TV and a/c, and maybe a balcony overlooking the Nile. ❹

Mayfair Clean, comfortable rooms in a quiet location, with a great Art Deco entrance lobby and a ten percent discount for *Rough Guide* readers, but avoid buying tours here. ❸

Longchamps 21 Sharia Ismail Muhammed, 5th floor ⓣ 02/735 2311 or 2, ⓕ 735 9644, ⓦ www.hotellongchamps.com. Spotless, quiet and well-run three-star hotel with a/c, satellite TV and a minibar in all rooms, plus a pleasant terrace and the choice of B&B, half- or full-board. Larger rooms with their own Internet access are also available. If it's full, the *Horus House* downstairs isn't a bad fall-back option. ❻

Pension Zamalek 6 Sharia Salah el-Din ⓣ 02/735 9318, ⓕ 735 3773. Very much a *pension*: clean, quiet and secluded with a pleasant family atmosphere. ❹

Hostels and camping

Hostelling and camping offer meagre rewards by comparison with downtown hotels, and any gains in clean air or seclusion tend to be negated by the extra travel involved in sightseeing from an outlying base.

That said, the **HI youth hostel** near the El-Gama'a Bridge on Roda Island (ⓣ 02/364 0729, ⓕ 368 4107; see map on pp.176–177) is readily accessible by #82 minibus from Tahrir. Buses #355 and #357 also run nearby, or you can catch a river-taxi to the Giza University stop and walk back across the bridge. There is a choice between three-person dorms or cheaper six-person ones (£E20.10 or £E15.10; breakfast included) and it's open year-round. Non-HI members pay £E1 extra, or can take out membership for £E25. Doors are closed midnight to 8am, so no carousing unless you aim to make a full night of it.

Salma Camping in Harraniyya, outside Giza (ⓣ & ⓕ 02/384-9152), attracts tourists with camper-vans or bikes. Camping or caravanning, it costs £E15 per person, including free hot showers with no extra tent or vehicle charge. Alternatively, you can rent a hut: £E35 for a small two-person cabin, £E50 for a cabin with two double beds, £E60 for a two-person hut with bathroom; breakfast is not included, but there is use of a kitchen. There are also small but clean and pleasant double rooms (£E50), which are better value than the huts. Despite its friendly staff, bar, delightful garden and view of the Pyramids, the site's distance from everywhere but the Wissa Wassef School (next door) is bound to cause difficulties, though it is obviously handy for the Pyramid sites at Giza, Abu Sir and Saqqara. It's reached by turning off Pyramids Road towards Saqqara at Maryotteya Canal (1km before the pyramids), and then after 4km taking a signposted turn-off at Harraniyya village; continue for 100m, and the site is about 100m away on your right. Buses and service taxis run from town to the junction of Maryotteya Canal with Pyramids Road, where you can catch regular service taxis to the Harraniyya turn-off.

Long stays and flat-hunting

Should you decide to stay a while, it's worth remembering that many hotels reduce their rates by ten percent after fifteen days' occupation. Depending on demand for rooms and your rapport with the management, it may be possible to negotiate further discounts for **long stays at pensions**. Unfortunately, smart places like the *Roma* are less open to persuasion than dives like the *Oxford*, which allows long-stay residents to customize their rooms and cook on the premises.

In the longer term it's better **to rent a flat**; a base with a phone makes working or socializing in Cairo a lot easier. Given the range of localities and amenities, expect to look at half a dozen places before settling on one. Check the small ads in *Cairo Today*, the *Maadi Messenger*, *British Community News*, *Egyptian Gazette* and *Community Times*; and notice boards at English-language institutes and cultural centres (see p.275), and the American University. It's also possible to see what's available and check prices online via the websites of firms like E-dar (Ⓦ www.e-dar.com) and Gomhoria (Ⓦ www.algomhoria.com). Foreigners working or studying in Cairo often seek flatmates or want to sublet during temporary absences. With luck, you can move into a fully furnished flat with little ado. As a general guide to **prices**, you can rent a flat in the centre for around £E400 per month per person, or a houseboat for two moored on the Nile at Aguza for £E750.

Another way involves using a *simsar* (flat agent), who can be found in any neighbourhood by making enquiries at local shops and cafés. Unless you spend a long, fruitless day together, he's only paid when you settle on a place; ten percent of your first month's rent is the normal charge. Flat agencies in Ma'adi levy the same commission on both tenant and landlord. Additional "key money" is illegal, but often demanded.

Before agreeing to **sign a lease**, **check** plumbing, water pressure, sockets, lighting, phone, stove and water-heater (*buta* gas cylinders need changing), and ask if power or water cuts are regular occurrences. Also determine whether utilities (phone, gas, electricity) and services (the *bowab*, garbage collector) are included in the rent, and paid up to date when you move in (ask to see receipts if necessary). All the flat's contents should be accurately noted on an inventory, and the responsibility for repairs and the size of the deposit established. A flat without a phone isn't likely to acquire one, whatever the landlord promises.

Cairo's **residential neighbourhoods** range from smart Western enclaves to countrified *baladi* quarters. Quietly spacious **Ma'adi**, thirty minutes by metro from the centre, is home to most of Egypt's American community, and mega-wealthy natives. **Zamalek**, favoured by embassies and European expats, is likewise costly, but always has vacancies. Another focus for the foreign community is **Heliopolis**, a self-contained suburb where palatial Art Deco flats jostle with air-conditioned high-rises. Rents here are lower than in downtown Cairo, where few flats are available at any price unless you move into **Bulaq** or plumb the Qasr al-Aini side of **Garden City**.

Across the Nile, middle-class **Dokki** merges into *baladi* market quarters, while **Mohandiseen** parades blocks of flats and shopping centres along its shiny boulevards. Single males with a grasp of Arabic and Egyptian ways might enjoy living in **baladi quarters** (Islamic Cairo, Bulaq, Imbaba), which are cheap and cheerful, unhygienic and noisy. Foreigners are expected to contribute to the incessant drama of local life and do (verbal) battle when necessary – personal privacy doesn't exist in these urban villages.

The City

With so much to see (and overlook, initially), you can spend weeks in **CAIRO** and merely scratch the surface. But as visitors soon realize, there are lots of reasons why people don't stay for long. The city's density, climate and pollution conspire against it, and the culture shock is equally wearing. Tourists unfamiliar with Arab ways can take little for granted, regular visitors expect to be baffled, and not even Cairenes comprehend the whole metropolis. The downside weighs especially on newcomers, since it's the main tourist sites that generate most friction. A day at Khan el-Khalili bazaar can feel like a course in sales resistance and *baksheesh* evasion. Generally, however, Cairenes are the warmest, best-natured city dwellers going. They have to be to live in such a pressure cooker without exploding. Their sly wit and prying render pretension and secrecy impotent; their spirited ingenuity transcends horrendous conditions. Potential riots are defused by tolerance and custom; a web of ties resists alienation. Once you have something of the measure of this, Cairo feels an altogether different and more enjoyable place.

Central Cairo

Most people prefer to get accustomed to **central Cairo** before tackling the older, Islamic quarters, for even in this Westernized downtown area known as *wust al-Balad*, the culture shock can be profound. Beyond the sanctuary of the luxury hotels beside the Nile, crowds and traffic jostle for space in the fume-laden air; whistling cops direct weaving taxis and limousines, donkey carts and buses; office workers rub shoulders with *baladi* folk, Nubians and soldiers. The pavements and shadowy lobbies of cavernous Art Deco or Empire-style apartment buildings are a lifetime's world for many vendors and doormen – both major contributors to Cairo's grapevine. Above the crumbling pediments and hoardings, pigeon lofts and extra rooms spread across the rooftops – a spacious alternative to the streets below, forming a city above the city centre.

The area is essentially a lopsided triangle, bounded by **Ramses Station**, **Midan Ataba** and **Garden City**, and for the most part it's compact enough to explore on foot. Only the Ramses quarter and the further reaches of Garden City are sufficiently distant to justify using transport. At the heart of central Cairo is the broad, bustling expanse of **Midan Tahrir** (for an account of the square, see p.122); aside from being the city's main transport terminal, Tahrir's most famous landmark is the domed **Museum of Egyptian Antiquities**, which houses the finest collection of its kind in the world.

The Museum of Egyptian Antiquities

At the northern end of Midan Tahrir, the **Museum of Egyptian Antiquities** (daily 9am–4.45pm; during Ramadan 9am–3pm; £E20, students £E10, camera £E10, camcorder £E100; no flashes or tripods) feels almost as archaic as the civilization it records. Founded in 1858 by Auguste Mariette, who excavated the Serapeum at Saqqara and several major temples in Upper Egypt (and was later buried in the museum grounds), it has long since outgrown its present

On your way to the museum, beware of a "friendly local" who may accost you and try to persuade you that the museum is closed for a couple of hours. Instead, he will invite you to spend the time enjoying "Egyptian hospitality" at a local papyrus shop (or "papyrus museum" as he will probably call it). Needless to say, you will have then to endure an hour's worth of time-wasting hard-sell, and the papyruses will be outrageously overpriced.

Although Cairo has more than a dozen museums, most visitors limit themselves to the big three, devoted respectively to **Egyptian Antiquities** (see p.108), **Coptic** (see p.178) and **Islamic Art** (see p.152). Of these, the Antiquities Museum is the most popular and by far the largest, necessitating at least two visits to do it any kind of justice. The Coptic and Islamic Art museums can each comfortably be seen in a couple of hours and make fitting adjuncts to exploration of their quarters of the city.

On a practical note, unless you're planning to buy a photo permit, it's best to leave your **camera** at the hotel. Otherwise you'll have to check it in at the entrance to all three main museums, a process which occasionally leads to the wrong camera being returned to the wrong owner. For the smaller museums, given temporary closures and erratic opening hours, it's worth telephoning the distant ones before setting out.

building, which now scarcely provides warehouse space for the pharaonic artefacts. Allowing one minute for each, it would take about nine months to view its 136,000 exhibits. Forty thousand more items lie crated in the basement, where many have sunk into the soft ground, necessitating excavations beneath the building itself. Plans are afoot for a new museum, beyond the Pyramids of Giza, which will house some or all of the exhibits in the current building, but construction is still some years away. Yet for all the chaos, poor lighting and captioning of the old museum, the richness of the collection makes this one of the great museums of the world.

Before you enter the museum, check the pond in front of the main entrance: the water lilies growing here are the now-rare blue lotus, a psychoactive plant used as a drug by the ancient Egyptians – which they are depicted using (by dipping the flowers into their wine) on several frescoes and reliefs. Once inside the museum you'll probably be offered a **guided tour**, which generally lasts two hours (at around £E50 an hour), though the museum deserves at least six. The guides are extremely knowledgeable and they do help you to make sense of it all – if you are in a small group it really isn't that expensive. It's best to come on successive days or at the beginning and end of your trip, so as to get a fuller appreciation. A single visit of three to four hours suffices to cover the Tutankhamun exhibition and a few other **highlights**. The Amarna gallery on the ground floor and the selection of masterpieces on the other are all impressive, but everyone has their own favourites. A reasonable shortlist might include the cream of statuary from the Old, Middle and New kingdoms (**rooms 42, 32, 22 and 12**) and the Nubian funerary cache (**Room 44**) downstairs; on the first floor, the Fayoum Portraits (**Room 14**) and model figures (**rooms 37, 32 and 27**), and, of course, the Mummy Room (**Room 56**) – though it costs extra.

The best guide to the museum's contents is the AUC's *Illustrated Guide to the Egyptian Museum* (£E120), with lavish illustrations of some of the museum's top exhibits. Inevitably, however, it omits some of our favourites and, though it gives room numbers, it doesn't put the exhibits in order, so you can't easily use it when going from room to room. Exhibits are numbered on at least two different systems, so many have two numbers, and often they have no other labelling (in such cases, we have identified exhibits by their most prominent number). Should you want running commentary, it's easy to tag along behind a tour group. The first-floor **café–restaurant** is entered via the souvenir shop from outside the museum.

World Trade Centre & Conrad Hotel ▲   ▲ Zamalek

◀ Zamalek

◀ Aguza

◀ Cairo Tower

◀ Opera House

◀ Doldei

N

BULAQ

26TH JULY STREET

6TH OCTOBER FLYOVER

Royal Carriage
Museum

Mosque of
Abu'l'Ila

Television
Building

River Taxi (Fri & Sun only)

Maspero
Dock

Qanatir
Boats

Ramses
Hilton

NASSER Ⓜ

SHARIA RAMSES

SHARIA ABDEL KHALID

SHARIA ABDEL
HAMID SAID

SHARIA MANSUR

CHAMPOLLION

SHARIA BARHA

SHARIA MIRIT

⑫

6TH OCTOBER BRIDGE

GEZIRA

Andalusian
Garden

River Taxi

Quay

Nile
Hilton

Arab
League

City Buses ★

Service ★
Taxis   City ★
       Buses

Egyptian
Antiquities
Museum

★ Pyramids Buses

SHARIA BASSIOUNI

Thomas
Cook

American
Express

SHARIA ABDEL SALAM ARIF

⑳

⑲

⑯

MIDAN
TALAAT
HARB

⑱

SHARIA TALAAT HARB

SHARIA EL-BUSTAN

MIDAN
TAHRIR

Ⓜ SADAT

NZ Consulate

SHARIA TAHRIR

⑫

AUC
Library

SHARIA MOHAMMED

TAHRIR BRIDGE

Semiramis
Intercontinental

⑳

Omar
Makram
Mosque

Mugamma

American
University
(AUC)

CORNICHE EL NIL

Helnan
Shepheard
Hotel

US Embassy

SHARIA QASR AL-AINI

SHARIA SHEIKH RIHAN

National
Assembly

SHARIA FALAKI

River Nile

Feluccas

British
Embassy

Canadian
embassy

GARDEN CITY

SHARIA AMERICA LATINA

CORNICHE EL NIL

Sudanese
Consulate

SHARIA MAGLIS AL-SHAAB

Turkish
embassy

River Taxi

0   Metres   250

SA'AD Ⓜ
ZAGHLOUL

CENTRAL CAIRO

Ramses Station

SHARIA RAMSES
SHARIA TAWFIQIA
SHARIA EMAD EL-DIN
SHARIA SOLIMAN EL HALABY
SHARIA EL-GUMHORRIYA
SHARIA ALFI BEY
SHARIA KHULUD (CLOT BEY)
SHARIA KHIUUD

MIDAN ORABI

26TH JULY STREET

High Court

Indian Consulate

SHARIA TALAAT HARB
SHARIA ADLY
SHARIA SHERIF
SHARIA ABDEL
KHALIQ SARWAT
SHARIA SARWAT

Continental-Savoy

Garden Groppi's

SIKKET AL MANAKH
SHARIA EL-GUMHORRIYA

Bookstalls

Ezbekiya Gardens

ATABA

SALAH SALEM TUNNEL (EXIT)

Puppet Theatre

City Buses & Minibuses

★ **Pyramids Microbuses**

Khan el-Khalili ▶

Al-Azhar Bus Terminal & Mosque ▶

Opera Square

MIDAN ATABA

SALAH SALEM TUNNEL (ENTRANCE)

★ **Libya Service Taxis**

Central Post Office

SHARIA DALAA

SHARIA EL-GEISH

MUSKI

SHARIA QASR EL-NIL
SHARIA SHERIF
SHARIA MOHAMMED FARID
SHARIA RUSHDI
SHARIA EL-GUMHORRIYA
SHARIA ABDEL AZIZ

Gumhorriya Theatre

SHARIA MOHAMMED SABRI AIN KATOM
SHARIA HODA SHAARAWI

MIDAN FALAKI

SHARIA TAHRIR

Bab al-Luq Market

MAHMOUD

SHARIA MANSUR
SHARIA NUBAR

ABDEEN

SHARIA SAMI EL BARUBI

MIDAN EL-GUMHORRIYA

Abdin Palace

SHARIA MOHAMMED FARID

SHARIA BUR SAID

Islamic Art Museum

MIDAN AHMED MAHER

Bab Zwayla ▶

Citadel ▶

Interior Ministry

ABDEEN

MIDAN LAZOGHLI

Saiyida Zeinab ▼   ▼ Saiyida Zeinab   ▼ Saiyida Zeinab

ACCOMMODATION

Amin	21	Ismailia House 22	Pensione Roma 8
Berlin	14	Lotus 19	Safary 4
Carlton	5	Luna 13	Select 10
Cosmopolitan	17	Magic 20	Sultan 4
Crown	2	New 9	Tulip 18
Dahab	16	New Rich 15	Venice 4
Garden City House	23	Odeon Palace 12	Windsor 3
Grand	6	Orient Palace 7	
Happyton	1	Oxford 11	

Ground floor

Exhibits are arranged more or less chronologically, so that by starting at the entrance and walking in a clockwise direction round the outer galleries you'll pass through the Old, Middle and New kingdoms, before ending up with the Late and Greco-Roman periods in the east wing. This approach is historically and artistically coherent but rather plodding. A snappier alternative is to proceed instead through the Atrium – which samples the whole era of pharaonic civilization – to the superb Amarna gallery in the northern wing; then backtrack to cover sections that sound interesting, or instead head upstairs to Tutankhamun.

To suit either option, we've covered the ground floor in six sections: the Atrium, Old, Middle and New Kingdom galleries, the Amarna gallery, and the East Wing. Whichever approach you decide on, it's worth starting with the Atrium foyer (**Room 43**), where the dynastic saga begins.

The Rotunda and Atrium

The **Rotunda**, inside the museum entrance, kicks off with a highlighted "piece of the month" and **monumental sculptures** from various eras, notably (in the four corners) three colossi of Ramses II (XIX Dynasty) and a statue of

EGYPTIAN ANTIQUITIES MUSEUM:
GROUND FLOOR

Amenhotep, son of the XVIII Dynasty royal architect Hapu. Also here are six-teen small wooden and stone statues of a 24th-century BC official named Iby showing him at various stages in his life. Just to the left of the door as you enter sits the limestone **statue of King Zoser** (#6008), installed within its *serdab* beside his Step Pyramid at Saqqara in the 27th century BC, and removed by archeologists 4600 years later. Those who regard Zoser's reign as the start of the Old Kingdom categorize the preceding era as the Early Dynastic or **Archaic Period**.

The actual forging of dynastic rule is commemorated by a famous exhibit in **Room 43**, as you enter the Atrium. The **Palette of Narmer**, a decorative ver-sion of the slate palettes used to grind kohl, records the unification of the Two Lands (c.3100 BC) by a ruler called Narmer or Menes. One side of the palette depicts him wearing the White Crown of Upper Egypt, smiting an enemy with a mace, while a falcon (Horus) ensnares another prisoner and tramples the heraldic papyrus of Lower Egypt. The reverse face shows him wearing their Red Crown to inspect the slain, and ravaging a fortress as a bull; dividing these tableaux are mythical beasts with entwined necks, restrained from conflict by bearded men, an arcane symbol of his political achievement. Two XII Dynasty **funerary barques** from the pyramid of Senusert III at Dahshur stand on either side of the room.

Descending into **Room 33**, which is the museum's atrium, you'll find **pyra-midions** (pyramid capstones) from Dahshur, and more sarcophagi from the New Kingdom. Overshadowing those of Tuthmosis I and Queen Hatshepsut (before she became pharaoh), the **sarcophagus of Merneptah** is surmounted by a figure of the king as Osiris and protectively embraced from within by a relief of Nut, the sky goddess. But Merneptah's bid for immortality failed: when discovered at Tanis in 1939, his sarcophagus held the coffin of Psusennes, a XXI Dynasty ruler whose gold-sheathed mummy now lies upstairs.

At the centre of the Atrium is a **painted floor from the royal palace at Amarna** (XVIII Dynasty). A river brimming with ducks and fish is framed by reeds where waterfowl and cows amble, a fine example of the lyrical natural-ism of the Amarna period. For more of this revolutionary epoch in pharaonic history, head upstairs past the **colossal statues of Amenophis III, Queen Tiy and their three daughters**, which serenely presage Akhenaten and Nefertiti in the northern wing.

But first you must pass through **Room 13**, containing Merneptah's Victory Stele on the right, also called the **Israel Stele**. Its name derives from the boast "Israel is crushed, it has no more seed", from among a list of Merneptah's con-quests at the temple of Karnak – the sole known reference to Israel in all the records of ancient Egypt. Partly on the strength of this, many believe that Merneptah, son of Ramses II, was the Pharaoh of the Exodus (XIX Dynasty) – although this view has come under increasing criticism of late (see box on p.185). The other side carries an earlier record of deeds by Amenophis III (Akhenaten's father) in the service of Amun, whom his son later repudiated.

The hall beyond is part of the **New Kingdom galleries**. Straight ahead (heading towards Room 8) lies a **model of a typical Egyptian house**, as excavated at Amarna, the short-lived capital of Akhenaten and Nefertiti – who are honoured with their own gallery across the hall.

Old Kingdom Galleries

The southwest corner of the ground floor is devoted to the **Old Kingdom** (c.2700–2181 BC), when the III–VI dynasties ruled Egypt from Memphis and built the Pyramids. Lining the central aisle of **rooms 46–47** are funerary statues of deceased VIPs and servants (the custom of burying retainers alive ended with the II Dynasty). In Room 47, the **panel from Userkaf's temple**, by the north side of the doorway to Room 48, is the first known example of natural scenes being used as decoration within a royal funerary edifice. A pied king-fisher, purple gallinule and sacred ibis are clearly recognizable. Also in Room 47 are statuettes of *shabti* (worker) figures, depicted preparing food (Case D, also labelled #52 and 53).

Among the more striking exhibits in Room 46 are **statuettes** of the dwarf Khnumhotep, Overseer of the Wardrobe, a man with a deformed head and a hunchback afflicted by Pott's disease (Case B, also labelled #54 and 65). To the north and south are three **slate triads of Menkaure flanked by Hathor** and the goddess of the Aphroditopolis nome, from the Mycenius valley temple at Giza. The pair of alabaster **lion tables** by the fourth pillar on the north side were probably used for sacrifices or libations towards the end of the II Dynasty.

Fragments of the **beard of the Sphinx** are at the end of the hall (**Room 51**), to the left below the stairs (#6031). The British Museum in London pos-sesses another metre-long chunk; the beard was probably five metres long before it was shot to pieces by Mamluke and Napoleonic troops during target practice. Also in Room 51, a sculptured head of V Dynasty pharaoh Userkaf (#6051) represents the earliest known larger-than-life-size statue in the world.

At the entrance to **Room 41**, **reliefs** from a V Dynasty tomb at Maidum (#25) depict a desert hunt and other rural activities. Another panel (#59), from a V Dynasty tomb at Saqqara, shows grain being weighed out, milled and grad-ed, as well as glass being blown and statues carved. The women on these reliefs wear long chemises, the men loincloths or sometimes nothing (revealing them to be circumcized, according to Egyptian custom). **Room 42** boasts a superb **statue of Chephren**, his head embraced by Horus (#31). Carved from black diorite, whose white marbling emphasizes the sinews of his knee and clenched fist, the statue comes from Chephren's valley temple at Giza. Equally arresting on the left is the wooden **statue of Ka-aper** (#40), a plump figure with an introspective gaze, which Arab diggers at Saqqara called "Sheikh al-Balad" because it resembled their own village headman. The **statue of a scribe**, poised for notation with an open scroll across his knees, is also memorable.

On the left-hand side of **Room 31**, six **wooden panels** from the tomb of **Hesy-Re** portray this senior scribe of the III Dynasty, who was also a dentist – the earliest known to history. On the wall are sandstone reliefs from Wadi Maraghah, near the ancient turquoise mines of Sinai. Twin limestone **statues of Ra-Nufer** signify his dual role as Memphite high priest of Ptah and Sokar; aside from their wigs and kilts, they look virtually identical. Both were created in the royal workshops, possibly by the same artist.

Room 32 is dominated by life-size seated **statues of Prince Rahotep and Princess Nefert**, from their *mastaba* at Maidum (IV Dynasty). His skin is painted brick-red, hers a creamy yellow – a distinction common in Egyptian art. Nefert wears a wig and diadem and swathes herself in a diaphanous wrap; the prince is simply clad in a waist cloth. Look out for the **tableau of the dwarf Seneb and his family** on the left (#39). Embraced by his wife, this Overseer of the Wardrobe seems contented; his naked children hold their fin-gers to their lips. In the second niche on the left-hand wall hangs a perfectly observed, vividly stylized mural, known as the **Maidum Geese** (III/IV Dynasty). Although the heyday of the Old Kingdom is poorly represented by a **statue of Ti**, also on the left (#49), its twilight era boasts, just by the door-way, the first known metal sculptures (c.2300 BC): two **statues of Pepi I and**

his son, made by hammering sheets of copper over wooden armatures (one of which was away for restoration at the time of writing).

In **Room 37**, next door, the **furniture of Queen Hetepheres** has been expertly reconstructed from heaps of gold and rotten wood. As the wife of Snofru and mother of Cheops, she was buried near her son's pyramid at Giza with a sedan chair, gold vessels and a canopied bed. Also in the room, in a cabinet of its own, is a tiny **statuette of Cheops**, the only known likeness of the Great Pyramid pharaoh.

Middle Kingdom Galleries

With **Room 26** you enter the **Middle Kingdom**, when centralized authority was restored and pyramid-building resumed under the XII Dynasty (c.1991–1786 BC). A relic of the previous era of civil wars (termed the First Intermediate Period) sits on the right, glum-faced. Endowed with hulking feet to suggest power, and black skin, crossed arms and a curly beard to link it to Osiris, this **statue of Mentuhotpe Nebhepetre** was buried near his funerary shrine at Deir el-Bahri and discovered by Howard Carter – whose horse fell through the roof. If the Mummy of Dagi were still around, it could use the pair of "eyes" painted inside its sarcophagus across the hall (#34) to espy two statues of Queen Nofret wearing a sheath dress and a Hathor wig, flanking the entrance to Room 21.

The statuettes at the back of **Room 22** are striking for the uncharacteristic expressiveness of their faces, in contrast to the manic staring eyes of the wooden sculptures on the right. Also in the room are likenesses of Amenemhet III and Senusert I, but your attention is grabbed by the **burial chamber of Harhotpe** from Deir el-Bahri, in the middle of the room and covered inside with pictorical objects, charms and texts. Surrounding the chamber are ten limestone **statues of Senusert** from his pyramid complex at Lisht, stiffly formal in contrast to his cedarwood figure in the case to your right as you enter the room. The sides of these statues' thrones bear variations of the *sema-tawy* symbol of unification: Hapy the Nile-god, or Horus and Seth, entwining the heraldic plants of the Two Lands.

This basic imperative of statecraft might explain the unique **double statue of Amenemhat III** (#508) in **Room 16**. Personified as the Nile god bringing his people fish on trays, the dual figures may represent Upper and Lower Egypt, or the living king and his deified *ka*. On the left, five **lion-headed sphinxes with human faces** watch your exit from the Middle Kingdom; the anarchic Second Intermediate Period and the Hyksos invasion go uncommemorated.

New Kingdom Galleries

With **Room 11** you pass into the **New Kingdom**, an era of renewed pharaonic power and imperial expansion under the XVIII and XIX dynasties (c.1567-1200 BC). Egypt's African and Asian empires were forged by Tuthmosis III, who had long been frustrated while his unwarlike stepmother, Hatshepsut, ruled as pharaoh. From one of the Osiride pillars of her great temple at Deir el-Bahri comes a commanding crowned **head of Hatshepsut**, while in **Room 12** you'll find a grey schist statue of **Tuthmosis III** (#400), and other masterpieces of XVIII Dynasty art. Also in Room 11, on the left, stands an unusual *ka* statue of Pharaoh Hor (#75), mounted on a sliding base to signify his posthumous wanderings. At the back of the room, the **Hathor Shrine** from Tuthmosis III's ruined temple at Deir el-Bahri contains a statue of the goddess in her bovine form, emerging reborn from a papyrus swamp. Tuthmosis stands beneath her cow's head, and is suckled as an infant in the fresco behind Hathor's statue, overshadowed by a star-spangled ceiling. To the right of the shrine is a block statue (#418) of Hatshepsut's vizier, Senenmut, with the queen's daughter Neferure, with a smaller statue of the same duo in the second recess on the right. The relationship between the queen, her daughter and her vizier has inspired much speculation. From the same period comes a section of the Deir el-Bahri "**Punt relief**" (in the second niche on the left), showing the Queen of Punt, who suffered from elephantiasis, and her donkey, observed by Hatshepsut during her expedition to that fabled land.

To the right of the Punt relief stands a grey granite **statue of the god Khonsu** with a sidelock denoting youth, and a face thought to be that of the boy pharaoh Tutankhamun, which was taken from the temple of the moon-god at Karnak. Flanking this statue and the Punt relief, two **statues** of a man named **Amenhotep** portray him as a young scribe of humble birth, and as an octogenarian priest, honoured for his direction of massive works like the Colossi of Memnon.

Before turning the corner into the northern wing, you encounter two **lion-headed statues of Sekhmet**, found at Karnak. **Sphinxes** with the heads of Hatshepsut and her family dominate the central aisle of **rooms 6** and **7**. Some of the reliefs along the southern wall come from the Tomb of Maya at Saqqara, which was uncovered last century but subsequently lost until its rediscovery in 1986. From **Room 8**, most visitors check out the Amarna gallery (see below) before walking through the cast of statues and sarcophagi in **Room 9**.

To the left of the stairs, in **Room 10**, note the **relief** on a block from Ramses II's temple at Memphis (#769), which shows him subjugating Egypt's foes. In a motif repeated on dozens of temple pylons, the king grabs the hair of a Libyan, Nubian and Syrian, and wields an axe. Ramessid pharaohs who never fought a battle were especially keen on such reliefs. The room ends with a pun (#6245): a **statue of Ramses II** as a child, finger to mouth, holding a plant while protected by the sun-god *Re* or *Ra*, which combines with the word for child (*mes*) and the word for the plant (*su*) to form his name. From Room 10 you can follow the New Kingdom into the east wing (covered opposite), or climb the stairs to the Tutankhamun galleries on the upper floor.

The Amarna Gallery

Room 3 focuses on the **Amarna period**: a break with centuries of tradition which barely outlasted the reign of Pharaoh Akhenaten (c.1379–1362 BC) and Queen Nefertiti. Rejecting Amun and the other deities of Thebes, they decreed the supremacy of a single god, the Aten; built a new capital at Amarna in Middle Egypt to escape the old bureaucracy; and left enigmatic works of art that provoke a reaction.

Staring down from the walls are four **colossi of Akhenaten**, whose attenuated skull and face, flaring lips and nostrils, rounded thighs and belly are suggestive of a hermaphrodite or a primeval earth goddess. Because these characteristics are carried over to the figures of his wife and daughters on certain **steles** (in the left-hand niche and the cases in front of it) and tomb reliefs, it has been argued that the Amarna style pandered to some physical abnormality in Akhenaten (or the royal family) – the captions hint at perversions. Others retort that the exquisite **head of Nefertiti**, in Berlin, proves that it was just a stylistic device. Another feature of Amarna art was its note of intimacy: a **stele of the royal family** (#167) portrays Akhenaten dandling their eldest daughter, Meritaten, whilst Nefertiti cradles her sisters. For the first time in Egyptian art, breakfast was depicted. The Amarna focus on this world rather than the afterlife infused traditional subjects with new vitality – witness the freer brush strokes on the fragments of a **marsh scene**. To the left of the entrance, display case A contains some of the **Amarna Letters**, recording pleas for troops to aid the pharaoh's vassals in Palestine, the impact of his death, and Nefertiti's search for allies against those who pressed Tutankhamun to reverse the Amarna revolution. Originally baked into earthen "envelopes" for delivery, these cuneiform tablets were stored in the Foreign Office archives at Amarna.

Akhenaten's carnelian-, gold- and glass-inlaid **coffin** is back in **Room 8**, the upper half displayed alongside the gilding from the bottom part of the coffin. This gilding disappeared from the museum at some time between 1915 and 1931, but resurfaced in Switzerland in the 1980s. It has now been restored and mounted on a plexiglass cast in the presumed shape of the original coffin.

The East Wing

As an inducement to follow the New Kingdom into the east wing, **Room 15** holds a sexy statue of the wife of Nakht Min (Case 195). Inside **Room 14** is a huge alabaster **statue of Seti I**, whose sensitive facial modelling recalls Nefertiti's head. Originally, it would have worn a *nemset* headdress like the one on Tutankhamun's funerary mask. More striking, however, is the restored pink granite triple statue of Ramses III being crowned by Horus and Set, representing order and chaos respectively.

Waning with the XX Dynasty and expiring with the XXI, the New Kingdom was followed by the so-called **Late Period** of mostly foreign rulers. From the same period, in the middle of the room, comes an alabaster **statue of Amenirdis the Elder**, whom the pharaoh made divine votaress of Amun to watch over the Theban priesthood (**Room 30**). Dressed as a New Kingdom queen, Amenirdis wears a falcon headdress crowned with *uraei*, originally topped by a Hathor crown bearing a solar disc and horns. Of the diverse **statues of deities** in **Room 24**, it's Taweret (or Tweri), the pregnant-hippopotamus goddess of childbirth, that most visitors remember.

Rooms 34 and **35** cover the **Greco–Roman Period** (332 BC onwards), when Classical art engaged with Ancient Egyptian symbolism. The meld of styles is typified by the bizarre **statues and sarcophagi** down the corridor in **Room 49**, especially that of Alexander II at the threshold of the room. Room 44, on your way, is used for temporary exhibitions.

First floor

The upper floor is dominated by the Tutankhamun galleries, which occupy the best part of two wings. Once you've seen Tut's treasures, everything but the Mummy Room and the display of masterpieces seems lacklustre – even though the other galleries feature artefacts just as fine as those downstairs. Come back another day and check them out.

Tutankhamun Galleries

The funerary impedimenta of the boy-king **Tutankhamun** numbers 1700 items and fills a dozen rooms. Given the brevity of his reign (1361–1352 BC) and the paucity of his tomb in the Valley of the Kings, one's mind boggles at the treasure that must have been stashed with great pharaohs like Ramses or Seti. Tutankhamun merely fronted the Theban counter-revolution that effaced Amarna and restored the cult of Amun and its priesthood to their former primacy. However, the influence of Amarna is apparent in some of the **exhibits**, which are laid out roughly as they were packed into his tomb: chests and statues (**Room 45**) preceding furniture (**rooms 40, 35, 30, 25, 20, 15 and 10**), shrines (**rooms 9–7**) and gold appurtenances (**Room 3**). Adjacent to this are

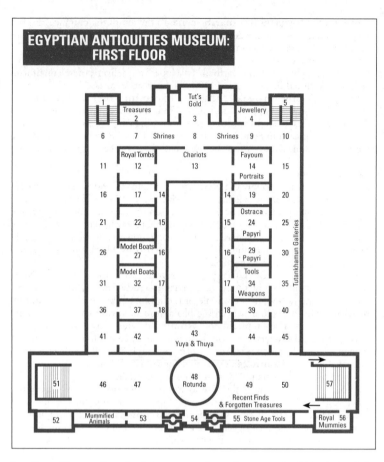

jewellery (**Room 4**) and other treasures from diverse tombs (**rooms 2 and 13**). Most visitors make a beeline for the last four (2, 3 and 4 close fifteen minutes early), ignoring the sequence just outlined. If that includes you, skip ahead through the following rundown.

When Carter's team penetrated the sealed corridor in 1922 they found an antechamber stuffed with caskets and detritus ransacked by robbers, and two life-size **ka statues of Tutankhamun** (flanking the doorway to Room 45), whose black skin symbolized his rebirth. Pass between these to see the worldly goods that the boy pharaoh was to carry with him into the next world. Among the things he packed, for example, are an ebony and ivory **gaming set** for playing *senet*, a game similar to draughts (#49 in Room 35), and a host of **shabti figures** to fulfil any tasks the gods might set him (in Room 35, flanking the door to Room 34). The king's clothes and unguents were stored in two magnificent **chests**. On the lid and sides of the "Painted Chest" (#186 between rooms 40 and 35), he is depicted hunting ostriches and antelopes and devastating ranks of Syrians in his war chariot, larger than life; the end panels show him trampling other foes in the guise of the sphinx.

In the corridor (Room 33) on the other side of Room 34, two interesting seats are displayed: an Amarna toilet seat in Case O by the door, and in Case S, a seat used for childbirth in a form that astoundingly resembles seats used for the same purpose today.

In Room 30, in contrast to the warlike figures of Tutankhamun elsewhere in the gallery, the lid of the "Inlaid Chest" bears a gentle, Amarna-style vignette of Ankhesenamun (daughter of Nefertiti and Akhenaten) offering lotus, papyrus and mandrake to her husband, framed by poppies, pomegranates and cornflowers. Note the **statues of Tutankhamun hunting with a harpoon** between **rooms 45 and 40**. The **golden shrine** covered in repoussé scenes of conjugal harmony once held statues of Tut and his wife Ankhesenamun that were stolen in antiquity.

Next come thrones and chairs (rooms 30, 25 and 20). On the back rest of the **gilded throne** with winged-serpent arms and clawed feet (#179 in Room 35), the royal couple relax in the rays of the Aten, their names given in the Amarna form – dating it to the time when Tutankhamun still observed the Amarna heresy. The "**ecclesiastical throne**", the prototype for episcopal thrones of the Christian Church (#181 in Room 25), is exquisitely inlaid with ebony and gold, but looks uncomfortable. More typical of pharaonic design are the wooden *Heb* chair and footstools, and a commode that wouldn't look amiss at Harrods. **Room 30** has a case of "**Prisoners' Canes**" (#187), whose ebony- and ivory-inlaid figures symbolize the unity of north and south.

From ivory headrests in **Room 15**, it's a natural progression to **gilded beds** dedicated to the gods whose animal forms are carved on their bedposts (#183, 221 and 732 in Room 10). Beyond these in Room 9 is a **shrine of Anubis** (#54), carried in the pharaoh's cortege: the protector of the dead depicted as a vigilant jackal with gilded ears and silver claws. Next along, four alabaster canopic jars in an alabaster chest (#176) contained the pharaoh's viscera, and were themselves contained in the next exhibit, a golden **canopic chest** protected by statues of the goddesses Isis, Nephthys, Selket and Neith (#177). Ranged along **rooms 7 and 8** are four boxy **gilded shrines**, which fitted one inside another like Russian dolls, enclosing Tutankhamun's sarcophagus.

The always packed-out **Room 3** contains **Tutankhamun's gold**, some of which may be on tour abroad. Assuming it's in Cairo, the centrepiece is his haunting **funerary mask**, wearing a *nemset* headdress inlaid with lapis lazuli, quartz and obsidian. The middle and innermost layers of his mummiform **coffin**, adorned with the same materials, come a close second, showing the boy king with his hands clasped in the Osiride position, is protected by the cloisonné feathers of Wadjet, Nekhbet, Isis and Nephthys. On Tutankhamun's mummy (which remains in his tomb at the Valley of the Kings) were placed scores of **amulets**, a cloisonné **corselet** spangled with glass and carnelian, gem-encrusted **pectorals** and a pair of golden **sandals** – all displayed here.

The **Jewellery Room** next door is equally overpowering. A VI Dynasty golden **head of a falcon** (once attached to a copper body) from Hieraconpolis rates as the star attraction, but there's stiff competition from the **crown and necklaces of Princess Khnumyt** and the **diadem and pectorals of Princess Set-Hathor**. Buried near the latter at Dahshur were the **amethyst belt and anklet of Mereret**, another XII Dynasty princess. The ceremonial **axe of Ahmosis**, commemorating his expulsion of the Hyksos from Egypt, was buried in the tomb of his mother, Queen Ahhotep. From the same cache (found by Mariette in 1859) came a hinged bracelet of lapis lazuli and the bizarre **golden flies** of the Order of Valour – bug-eyed decorations for bravery.

From the XXI–XXII Dynasty, when northern Egypt was ruled from the Delta, comes the Treasure of Tanis, displayed in **Room 2**. Of the three royal caches unearthed by Montet in 1939, the richest was that of Psusennes I, whose electrum coffin was found inside the sarcophagus of Mernepth (which is downstairs). His gold necklace is made from rows of discs, in the New Kingdom style.

Between **Room 8** and the Atrium stand two wooden **chariots**, found in the antechamber of Tutankhamun's tomb. Intended for state occasions, their gilded stucco reliefs show Asiatics and Nubians in bondage; pharaonic war chariots were lighter and stronger.

Having finished with Tut, you can either head down the western wing to the Mummy Room, or tackle the other galleries (see below).

Mummies

The southern end of the museum's upper floor harbours two rooms full of mummies. **Room 53** exhibits **mummified animals and birds** from necropolises across Egypt, evincing the strength of animal cults towards the end of the pagan era, when devotees embalmed everything from bulls to mice and fish.

Modern Egyptians regard these relics of ancestral superstition with equanimity, but the exhibition of human remains offended many – hence Sadat's closure of the famous **Mummy Room** (previously Room 52) in 1981. Since then, the Egyptian Museum and the Getty Institute have been working to restore the badly decomposed royal mummies. The results of their work are now displayed in Room 56, where you have to buy another ticket (£E40, students £E20; closes 4.20pm) to see them. Altogether eleven royal mummies are displayed here (clearly labelled and arranged chronologically anticlockwise around the room), including the mortal remains of some of the most famous pharaohs, in particular the great conquerors of the XIX Dynasty, Seti I and his son Ramses II, the latter looking rather slighter in the flesh than the massive statue of him outside the train station. Also here is Ramses's son, Mernepth, whom many believe to be the pharaoh of the Biblical exodus (see box p.159). Unless you have a keen interest in mummies, it's probably not worth the high price you have to pay to see them – a reaction echoed by many readers' letters.

All the mummies are kept in sealed cases at controlled humidity, and most of them look remarkably peaceful – Tuthmosis II and Tuthmosis IV could almost be sleeping – and many still have hair. Queen Henuttawi's curly locks and handsome face suggest Nubian origin. In deference to the deceased, no photography or guiding are allowed, and the low hum of *sotto voce* chatter is only broken by the attendant periodically calling for "Silence, please!" The mummies were found in the royal cache at Deir el-Bahri (see p.405) and in a spare chamber in the tomb of Amenophis II (see p.399), where they had been reburied during the XXI Dynasty to protect them from grave robbers. For a description of the mummification process, see p.390; and for a graphic demonstration of the hollowness of a mummy, take a look up Ramses V's right nostril – from this angle you'll be able to see straight out through the hole in his skull.

The Other Galleries

To view the other galleries in approximate chronological order you should start at **Room 43** (overlooking the Atrium) and proceed in a clockwise direction, as on the ground floor. However, since most visitors wander in from Tut's galleries, we've described the western and eastern wings from that standpoint.

Starting with the **western wing**, notice the "**Heart Scarabs**" that were placed upon the throats of mummies, bearing a spell that implored the deceased's heart not to bear witness against him or her during the Judgement of Osiris (**Room 6**). **Room 12**'s hoard of **objects from XVIII Dynasty royal tombs** includes the mummies of a child and a gazelle (Case I); priestly wigs and wig boxes (Case L); two leopards from the funerary cache of Amenophis II (#3842); and the chariot of Tuthmosis IV (#4113). **Room 17** holds the **contents of private tombs**, notably that of Sennedjem, from the Workmen's village near the Valley of the Kings. With skills honed on royal tombs, Sennedjem carved himself a stylish vault; its door (#215) depicts him playing *senet*. The sarcophagus of his son Khonsu carries a design showing the lions of Today and Yesterday supporting the rising sun, while Anubis embalms his mummy under the protection of Isis and Nephthys.

While the corridor displays **canopic chests and coffins**, the inner rooms feature **Middle Kingdom models**. From Meketre's tomb at Thebes come marvellous domestic figures and tableaux in **Room 27**: a woman carrying wine jars on her head (#74), peasants netting fish from reed boats (#75), and cattle being driven past an estate-owner (#76). In **Room 32** compare the fully crewed model boats in Case F with the unmanned solar barques for voyaging through eternity in Case E. Model-soldier buffs will delight in the phalanxes of Nubian archers and Egyptian pikemen from the tomb of Prince Mesehti at Assyut, in **Room 37**.

The museum's **southern wing** is best seen at a trot. The middle section contains a **model of a funerary complex** showing how the pyramids and their temples related to the Nile (**Room 48**), and the cubic **leather funerary tent** of an XXI Dynasty queen, decorated in red-and-green checkered squares (#3846, by the southeast stairway). More striking are two exhibitions in the central section: **recent finds and forgotten treasures**, which are showcased outside Room 54; and in Room 43, **objects from the tomb of Yuya and Thuya**. The finest of these are Thuya's gem-inlaid gilded mask, their mummiform coffins and statues of the couple. As parents of Queen Tiy (wife of Amenophis III), they were buried in the Valley of the Kings; their tomb was found intact in the late nineteenth century. Hidden away by the entrance to Room 42 is a panel of blue faïence tiles from Zoser's burial hall at Saqqara (#17).

Also in Room 48, on the east side by the banister over the Rotunda, is a display case (#144) containing a stone head of Akhenaten's mum Queen Tiy that prefigures the Amarna style, and "dancing dwarves" modelled on equatorial pygmies. The same case also holds a beautiful, very lifelike wooden statuette of a Nubian woman, possibly Queen Tiy, with her hair in braids, looking strikingly modern.

If approached from the north, the **eastern wing** begins with **Room 14**, containing a couple of mummies and the superbly lifelike but sadly ill-lit "**Fayoum Portraits**" found by archeologist Flinders Petrie at Hawara. Painted in encaustic (pigments mixed into molten wax) while their sitters were alive, the portraits were glued onto Greco-Roman mummies (100–250 AD). The staggering diversity of Egypt's pantheon by the late pagan era is suggested by the **statues of deities** in **Room 19**. The tiny statuettes are worth a closer look, especially those of the pregnant hippo goddess Sekhmet (in Case 7), Harpocrates (Horus as a child), Ibis-headed Thoth and the dwarf god Ptah-soker (all in Case 5), and the almost Mexican-looking Bes (in Case 3). Next door and the room after are devoted to **ostraca and papyruses**. Ostraca were limestone flakes or potshards, on which were scratched sketches or ephemeral writing; papyrus was used for finished artwork and lasting **manuscripts**. Besides the *Book of the Dead* (**rooms 1 and 24**) and the *Book of AmDuat* (depicting the Weighing of the Heart ceremony; #6335 on the south side), note the *Satirical Papyrus* (#232 in Cabinet 9 on the north side), showing mice being served by cats. Painted during the Hyksos period (see p.787), the cats represent the Egyptians, the mice their rulers, who came from countries that were part of Egypt's former empire. The implication is that rule of Egyptians by foreigners is not the natural order of things: we may be serving you now, but come the day, we'll be serving you up. **Room 29** also displays a scribe's writing kit and an artist's paints and brushes (#233). The **miscellaneous and everyday objects** in **rooms 39 and 34** are hardly thrilling, but it's worth popping into **Room 44** to see the faïence panels from the palaces of Ramses II and III.

Midan Tahrir and around

The centre of modern Cairo is a concrete assertion of national pride, which threatens to burst as it pumps traffic around the city. Created on the site of Britain's Qasr el-Nil Barracks after the 1952 revolution, **Midan Tahrir** (Liberation Square) embodies the drawbacks of subsequent political trends. During the 1960s, two bureaucratic monoliths and several transport depots responsible for much of Egypt and all of Greater Cairo were concentrated here, as Nasser adopted Soviet-style centralization. A decade later, Sadat rejected his mentor's "Arab Socialism" in favour of an *Infitah* (Open Door) to Western capitalism, causing private car ownership to soar almost as fast as Cairo's population. Impending gridlock was only averted by digging a metro; in spite of which, buses and roads are still grossly overcrowded.

The entrances to **Sadat metro station** serve as pedestrian underpasses linking these depots and buildings with the main roads leading off Tahrir. Despite clear labelling in English, it's easy to go astray in the maze of subways and surface at the wrong location. Many Cairenes prefer to take their chances crossing by road – a nerve-wracking experience for newcomers. Though some **landmarks** are obvious, rooftop billboards and neon signs flanking the end of streets like Talaat Harb or Qasr el-Nil (beside the *Cleopatra Hotel*) also help with orientation. To watch the square over tea, try one of the Arab cafés between Talaat Harb and El-Bustan; the café nearest to Sharia Talaat Harb, the *Wadi el-Nil*, was bombed by Islamic radicals in 1993.

Tahrir landmarks

Abutting the grounds of the Antiquities Museum to the south, the blue-and-white **Nile Hilton** – the first modern "international" hotel built along the Corniche – stretches down to where the Tahrir Bridge runs between guardian lions towards Gezira Island. The tan-coloured edifice just beyond the *Hilton*, built during the 1960s to serve as the secretariat of the Arab League, now stands as a vestige of the time when Egypt was acknowledged leader of the "progressive" Arab cause. After Sadat's treaty with Israel, the headquarters of the **Arab League** moved to Tunis and most of its members severed relations with Egypt. Mubarak's policy of rapprochement was finally rewarded in 1992, when the League returned to Cairo and, with it, posses of limos and gun-toting guards. Further down the Corniche, roughly opposite the new **Helnan Shepheard Hotel**, was the site of the Thomas Cook landing stage, where generations of tourists embarked on Nile cruises and General Gordon's ill-fated expedition set off for Khartoum in 1883.

Across the Tahrir Bridge ramp from the Arab League building, Egypt's Ministry of Foreign Affairs is less conspicuous than the **Omar Makram Mosque**, where funeral receptions for deceased VIPs are held in brightly coloured marquees. But dominating the southern end of Midan Tahrir is a concave office block that inspires shuddering memories: **the Mugamma**. A "fraternal gift" from the Soviet Union in the 1960s, this Kafkaesque warren of gloomy corridors, dejected queues and idle bureaucrats houses the public departments of the Interior, Health and Education ministries, and the Cairo Governorate. How many of the 50,000 people visiting *El-Mugamma* each day suffer nervous breakdowns from sheer frustration is anyone's guess; an African supposedly flung himself through a window several years ago (for advice on handling the Mugamma, see p.272). On the corner of Sharia Qasr al-Aini,

Tout trouble

Common on the streets of downtown Cairo, especially Talaat Harb, are **tourist touts**. These are petty crooks and confidence tricksters, not by any means all young, who attach themselves to tourists, posing as friendly strangers. Their aim is either to work various scams on you, to persuade you to buy overpriced tours (see p.103), or to steer or follow you into shops, where they will tell the shopkeeper, in Arabic of course, that they are your guide and entitled to a commission on whatever you buy, added to your bill of course. And we are not just talking ten percent. In general, touts favour particular perfume and papyrus shops with whom they regularly work, but they can go with you into any shop, and in general the shopkeeper will go along with them to avoid trouble – you will be gone next week after all, but the tout will still be around.

Touts tend to come up behind you to start a conversation. Each has their own line. Some will compliment you on your clothing, others will simply ask what you are looking for – if anyone asks you this when you are not obviously looking for anything, you can be sure it's a tout. Once they've gained your confidence they can be very hard to shake off. Should you make the mistake of telling one of them your name and hotel, you may find them turning up there asking for you, or you may even be greeted on the street by name by a different tout (who may even say, "Don't you remember me?" as if you had met before), since they often work in teams.

Trouble is, Cairo is full of friendly people who greet you on the street with no ill intent whatsoever. "Welcome in Egypt" is a common refrain, and it usually means just that. So how do you tell who's a tout and who's just being friendly? The first rule of thumb is, whoever it is, there's no need to be rude: just smile and say hello, or nod or wave, but never slacken your pace. Just carry on walking. An ordinary Egyptian will not be offended. A tout will probably try to stop you by demanding to know why you are in such a hurry, or why you are angry or upset, or they may accuse you of being rude. Similarly, ordinary Egyptians do not usually walk up behind you to strike up a conversation, but will call to you as you pass, though touts may also do this. In general you can get rid of touts by being noncommittal. If asked where you are going for example, you can reply airily, "Nowhere." Sometimes you may get abuse for this, but it is better than getting one of them attached to you. As a last resort, bear in mind that it is illegal for touts to harass tourists, and you can expect ordinary Egyptians to take your side if you have any serious problems. It is not usually necessary, however, to be rude or have an argument: so long as you are aware of the situation from the start, you should be able to get rid of them relatively quickly.

Touts favour **specific areas**. One such is Sharia Talaat Harb, especially between Midan Tahrir and Midan Talaat Harb, where outside *Felfela* is a favourite place, as are road junctions (where they will often accost you while crossing the street). Other places where touts currently gather include the Ghuriya and Spice Bazaar in Islamic Cairo (see p.148), and the road from there to Bab Zuweila, and some also work Sharia Tahrir on Gezira Island. People who greet you in areas with few tourists on the other hand are most unlikely to be touts, and indeed ordinary Egyptians are much more likely to take an interest in you in such areas, much less so by Khan el-Khalili or the Antiquities Museum, where tourists are two-a-penny.

opposite the Mugamma, a handsome pseudo-Islamic facade masks the old campus of the **American University in Cairo** (entered via Sheikh Rihan Street; the Library is one block northeast). Responsible for publishing some of the best research on Egypt in the English language, the AUC is also a Western-style haven for wealthy Egyptian youths and US students doing a year abroad, its shady gardens and preppy ambience seeming utterly remote from everyday life in Cairo. Visitors might experience a premonitory shiver that Iran's gilded youth probably looked pretty similar before the Islamic Revolution. Egyptian Marxists and Islamic fundamentalists regard the AUC as a tool of US and Zionist imperialism.

Five or so minutes' walk north from the main AUC entrance, near the University Library at **Midan Falaki** (or walk along Sharia Tahrir from the square), you'll find a pedestrian bridge of the kind that circumvented Midan Tahrir before its subways were dug. Off to the right, a broad street awash with fruit and vegetable stalls runs alongside **Bab al-Luq market**. Not a place for the squeamish, and overpriced compared to other markets, it's still an interesting spot to watch haggling and gossiping over trussed poultry or tea and *shee-shas*. It also holds a number of extremely cheap eating places. Across the bridge, a coffee merchant's store fills the square with the fine aroma of cardamom-spiced *'ahwa mahaweka*.

Moving on from Tahrir you can continue south and east to explore the Garden City and the Abdin quarter (see below), or walk back to the square and take either Sharia Talaat Harb or Qasr el-Nil to head for the shops and restaurants of downtown Cairo (see pp.126–129).

Garden City and the Abdin quarter

Spreading south from the square towards Old Cairo and the Islamic districts are two very different, yet historically interlinked, quarters. Deluxe hotels follow the Corniche towards Roda Island, separating the old diplomatic quarter from the Nile just as Sharia Qasr al-Aini divides the leafy winding streets of **Garden City** from the grid of blocks where Egypt's ministries and parliament are located. Like a spider in its web, the ex-royal, now presidential Abdin Palace lends its name to the convoluted **Abdin quarter** that merges into Saiyida Zeinab.

Since Garden City and Abdin meet around Midan Tahrir, both can claim to host Egypt's **National Assembly** (*Maglis al-Shaab*). During the late 1980s, Cairenes were agog over abusive exchanges and fisticuffs in parliament, as the hardline minister Zaki Badr replied to allegations of torture, wrongful arrest and bugging by the **Interior Ministry**, sited a couple of blocks to the west in Abdin. Badr has long since gone, but the ministry's repressive activities continue: Amnesty International reports cases of torture from Alexandria to Aswan. The road on which both buildings stand is barricaded at either end against suicide car bombers, floodlit at night and perpetually guarded by machine-gunners.

Garden City

When Ibrahim Pasha's al-Dubbarah Palace was demolished in 1906, British planners developed the site for diplomatic and residential use, laying down crescents and cul-de-sacs to create the illusion of lanes meandering through a **Garden City**. Until the Corniche road was ploughed through, embassies and villas boasted gardens running down to the Nile; nowadays, fishermen's shacks and vegetable plots line the river's edge.

War stories

During World War II, much of Garden City was commandeered by military organizations. At GHQ – which rapidly outgrew "Grey Pillars" to fill an entire neighbourhood – **R.A. Bagnold** proposed the formation of the Long Range Desert Group, whose daring raids (with David Stirling's SAS) behind enemy lines were the genesis of a martial legend.

On Sharia Rustrum, the Middle Eastern headquarters of the **SOE** (Special Operations Executive) plotted operations from Yugoslavia to Libya, involving Fitzroy McLean, Evelyn Waugh and Patrick Leigh Fermor, among others. At no.13 Sharia Ibrahim Pasha Naguib, novelist **Olivia Manning** and her husband Reggie (the model for Guy Pringle in *Fortunes of War*) lived beneath Stirling's brother, Peter, who hosted wild parties in a flat crammed with captured ammunition.

British sang-froid only cracked once, when the Afrika Korps seemed poised to seize Alexandria and advance on Cairo. On **"Ash Wednesday"** (July 1, 1942) GHQ and the Embassy burned their files, blanketing Garden City with smoke. Half-charred classified documents were wafted aloft to fall on the streets, where peanut vendors twisted them into little cones.

Aside from the traffic, it's a pleasant walk along the Corniche towards Roda Island, past a cluster of **feluccas** available for Nile cruises (see p.257). Further inland, Art Deco residences mingle with heavily guarded **embassies** (for addresses, see pp.274–275). Despite being outsized by the US – whose embassy here is the largest in the world – the British enjoy grander buildings with more spacious grounds, a legacy of their pre-eminence in the days of Lord Cromer and Sir Miles Lampson. The main artery, running south from Tahrir towards Old Cairo, is **Sharia Qasr al-Aini**, which goes from riches to rags, banks and villas yielding to cheap backstreet eating places near the Sayala Bridge. A bygone "Palace of the Spring" lends its name to the mixed neighbourhood between Garden City and the slaughterhouse district (see "Old Cairo", p.188), and to Cairo's largest public **hospital**, erected in the 1960s, where Yusuf Idris practised as a doctor before devoting himself to writing. **Roda Island** and the mainland **further south** are described under "Old Cairo" (see pp.174–191).

The Abdin quarter

With hindsight, several rulers must have regretted that Ismail moved the seat of state from the Citadel to what is now the **Abdin quarter**, where tenements surrounded the palace enclave long ago. When Ismail began building the European-style **Abdin Palace**, in the 1860s, a worldwide scarcity of cotton had raised the value of Egypt's export crop to £25 million a year, and his own civil list was double that of Queen Victoria. After prices slumped and creditors gathered, the palace was bequeathed to his successors together with vast debts that reduced them – and Egypt – to near vassal status.

The nadir of humiliation came in February 1942, when British armoured cars burst through the palace gates and Ambassador Lampson demanded that King Farouk sack the prime minister or abdicate himself. It was this that resolved Nasser to assemble the Free Officers, seize power and redeem Egypt. Ten years later, as Farouk displayed his long-awaited son at a magnificent reception, rioters burned downtown Cairo within earshot of the palace; six months afterwards, the Free Officers deposed him and declared a Republic.

Another mass protest – against Sadat's abolition of subsidies on bread and other essentials in January 1977 – actually happened outside the palace on

Midan el-Gumhorriya (Square of the Republic). Chanting "Thieves of the *Infitah*, the people are famished", crowds overwhelmed Central Security and rampaged against symbols of wealth and authority until the subsidies were restored. Still the state headquarters of Egypt's president, the Abdin Palace is flanked to the north by the Cairo Governorate building. During Ramadan a large tent is pitched in the middle of the square, in which virtuoso performers recite the Koran.

Behind the palace grounds are blocks of crumbling tenements where families lower baskets from the upper windows to passing street vendors. The neighbourhood is chiefly residential, with many Nubians and Sudanese, several street **markets** (around Midan Lazoghli) and a reputation for *ghorzas* (see p.140). **Sharia Bur Said** (Port Said), which divides it from the Saiyida Zeinab quarter, marks the course of the Khalig al-Masri canal that was filled in early last century after the Aswan Dam reduced Cairo's dependency on Nile flood-water. Various stretches of Bur Said carry buses and minibuses to diverse locations around the city, but you need to know the routes well to take advantage of them. Easier to suss is the Saiyida Zeinab to Matariyya tram service, which runs along the street.

Downtown Cairo

The layout of **downtown Cairo** goes back to the 1860s, when Khedive Ismail had it rebuilt in the style of Haussmann's new Paris boulevards to impress dignitaries attending the inauguration of the Suez Canal. Cutting an X-shaped swathe through the area are the main throughfares of **Talaat Harb** and **Qasr el-Nil** (each about 1km long), which contain most of the city's budget hotels, airlines and travel agencies. Almost every visitor gravitates here at least once, while many spend a lot of time checking out the restaurants, shops and bars. Inevitably, hustling tourists is a major industry; the guys touting for perfume shops are especially adept at distinguishing gullible newcomers from *khawaga*s who've been around a while. But don't brush off every approach as a sales ploy – passers-by may bid you "Welcome in Egypt" with no motive other than courtesy.

Although overshadowed by Talaat Harb and Qasr el-Nil, four streets running east off the northern end of Talaat Harb are equally integral to downtown Cairo: **Sharia Abdel Khaliq Sarwat**, **Sharia Adly**, **26th July Street** and **Sharia Alfi Bey**.

Talaat Harb

Fifty years ago, Suleyman Pasha Street was lined with trees and sidewalk cafés, a gracious ornament to the Europeanized city centre built in the late nineteenth century. Since being renamed **Sharia Talaat Harb**, the street's once elegant facades have been effaced by grime and neglect, tacky billboards and glitzy facings – yet its vitality and diversity have never been greater. Overflowing the pavements, thousands of Cairenes window-shop, pop into juice bars and surge out of cinemas. Imelda Marcos would drool over the profusion of shoe shops, some devoted to butterfly creations fit only for a boudoir. In the shadows of Western-style affluence, beggars lie with palms outstretched and barefoot urchins hump garbage pails onto donkey carts – an accepted part of Cairo's streetlife.

Almost every tourist seeks a break from the crowds and culture shock at one of three places along the initial stretch of Talaat Harb. **Felfela's Restaurant**, just around the corner of Hoda Shaarawi, is followed shortly by the **Café** bread riots of 1977, nightclubs and boutiques were specifically targeted by the radical Islamic group *Al-Taqfir w'al-Higrah* (Repentance and Holy Flight).

Midan Ataba

Behind Midan Opera car park, a minibus depot and split-level thoroughfares render **Midan Ataba** just as Yusuf Idris described it in *The Dregs of the City*: "a madhouse of pedestrians and automobiles, screeching wheels, howling klaxons, the whistles of bus conductors and roaring motors". Originally called the Square of Green Steps, Ataba should rightly be renamed the Square of Flyovers.

There is one attraction, however, that you might want to visit, the **Post Office Museum** on the second floor of the Central Post Office (daily except Fri 9am–1pm; 10pt; tickets sold in the post office itself, near the commemorative stamps office, then go upstairs through the guarded entrance on the east side of the building). The museum houses exhibits from Egypt's postal service through the ages, with stamps galore (including the rare Suez Canal commemorative issue), Egypt's oldest mailboxes, and a picture of the Sphinx and Pyramids composed entirely of stamps bearing an image of the same.

The minibus terminal is around the back of the multistorey car park; for local **transport** details, see p.97.

From Midan Ataba you can also take a number of **walking routes into Islamic Cairo** (see pp.134–135).

Ezbekiya Gardens and north to Ramses

The **Ezbekiya Gardens**, to the north of Opera and Ataba squares, were laid out in the 1870s by the former chief gardener of Paris, forming a twenty-acre park. Subsequent extensions to 26th July Street reduced them to trampled islands amidst a sea of commerce and traffic, but the western half has now been enclosed to preserve its magnificent banyan tree, while much of the eastern side remains a pitch for hawkers of Islamic arts, gewgaws and incense, as well as a market for second-hand books. Beyond the clothes stalls on the east side stands the **Cairo Puppet Theatre** (see p.260).

In medieval times a lake fed by the Nasiri Canal and surrounded by orchards existed here, but in 1470 the Mamluke general Ezbek built a palace, inspiring other beys and wealthy merchants to follow suit. During the French occupation Napoleon commandeered the sumptuous palace of Alfi Bey, and his successor Kléber promoted Western innovations such as windmills, printing presses, and a balloon launch which embarrassingly failed. Another novelty was *Le Tivoli* club, where "ladies and gentlemen met at a certain hour to amuse themselves" – unheard of in a society where men and women socialized separately.

During Mohammed Ali's time, visitors could still witness Cairenes celebrating the Prophet's Birthday here (12 *Rabi al-Awwal*) with unrestrained fervour. Sufi dervishes entranced by *zikr*s lay prostrate to be trampled by their mounted sheikh in the famous *Doseh* (Treading) ceremony. However, snake-swallowing had already been ruled "disgusting and contrary to their religion" by the sheikh of the Sa'adiya, and under British rule popular festivals were discouraged and dispersed around the city. Nowadays, El-Hussein and other squares are more active during the *Moulid al-Nabi*.

Though nothing remains of them today, two bastions of colonialism once overlooked Ezbekiya from a site bounded by Alfi Bey and El-Gumhorriya, where Scottish pipers once played. Here, *Shepheard's Hotel* (founded in 1841) flourished alongside the Thomas Cook Agency, which pioneered tourist "expeditions" in the 1870s. Rebuilt more grandly in 1891, *Shepheard's* famous terrace, Moorish Hall, Long Bar and Ballroom (featuring "Eighteenth Dynasty Edwardian" pillars modelled on Karnak) were destroyed by Black Saturday rioters in 1952 (see p.128).

Between Ezbekiya and Ramses

When Mohammed Ali created a military high road to link the Citadel with Cairo's new railway station, and named it after the French physician Antoine Clot – whom he ennobled for introducing Western ideas of public health to Egypt – nobody foresaw that **Sharia Clot Bey** (spelt Klot Bek on newer street signs) and the fashionable area north of Ezbekiya would degenerate into a vice-ridden "Open Land". By World War I, however, the quarter was full of honky-tonk bars, backstreet porn shows and brothels; shacks and plush establishments alike paying tribute to Ibrahim el-Gharby, the fearsome transvestite "King of the *Wasa'a*". In the Mahfouz novel and classic Egyptian movie *The Beginning and the End*, the main character's hash-dealing brother set up shop here. During World War II, activities centred around Wagh el-Birket, known to troops as "**the Berka**": a long street with curtained alleys leading off beneath balconies where the prostitutes sat fanning themselves. Only after the killing of two Australian soldiers (who were notorious for throwing women and pianos out of windows) was the Berka closed down in 1942.

Nowadays the area is shabbily respectable, with cheap shops and cafés. Any bus heading up it from the gardens towards Ramses will take you past the hulking nineteenth-century **Cathedral of St Mark**, now superseded by the new Coptic cathedral in Abbassiya. The derelict Moorish pile at the Ramses end of **Sharia el-Gumhorriya** (which runs up from the west side of the gardens) was the original premises of *Al-Ahram* (The Pyramids), the first – if not still the foremost – newspaper in the Arab world.

Ramses Station and around

The Ramses Station area is the northern ganglion of Cairo's transport system. Splayed flyovers and arterial roads haemorrhage traffic onto darting pedestrians, keeping **Midan Ramses** busy round the clock. Its main focus is **Ramses Station** itself, a quasi-Moorish shoe box to which a major **post office** and the **Egyptian Railways Museum** are appended. The museum (Tues–Sun 8am–1pm; £E10, £E20 on Fri & public holidays), at the east end of the station, houses a cast of antique steam engines, headed by Ismail's private train.

In ancient times, when the Nile ran further east, Ramses was the site of *Tendunyas*, the port of Heliopolis. Renamed *Al-Maks* (the Customs Point) by the Arabs, it was incorporated within Cairo's fortifications by Salah al-Din, whose Iron Gate was left high and dry as the Nile receded westwards, and was pulled down in 1847 to make way for the station. A nine-metre-high red-granite **Colossus of Ramses II**, moved here from Memphis in 1955, now stands diminished by the Heliopolis flyover and an overhead walkway; it is becoming so corroded by pollution that experts have long been insisting it be removed. It was due to be transported to the junction of Pyramids Road and the Alexandria Desert Road, out by the Giza Pyramids, despite lobbying from local Egyptologists to have it returned to its original site – pehaps this wrangling is why it's still slowly dissolving *in situ*. A modern replica of this colossus stands beside the airport road.

Near Rameses station is the main intercity bus terminal – Turgoman Garage (see p.282) – plus departure points for service taxi microbuses to destinations in and around Cairo (see p.96) and to the Canal Zone (seep.284). You may also find microbuses to Alexandria and the Delta here. For most of these, you have

AROUND RAMSES STATION

Shubra

Former Army Surplus Market

Egyptian Railways Museum

Airport

Ramses Station

Turgoman Garage

SHARJA EL-SABTIYA

SHARJA ORABI

Service Taxis

Pyramids Microbuses ★

Ⓜ MUBARAK

Footbridge

Heliopolis Trams ★

Colossus of Ramses II

Aboud Microbuses

N

MIDAN RAMSES

Ma'adi Microbuses

Fontana Hotel

Abbassiya

City Buses ★

Everest Hotel

P

Gezira

East Delta Buses ★

Venus Hotel

SHARIA RAMSES

Al-Fath Mosque

Al-Azhar Microbuses ★

SHARIA FAGGALA

SHARIA BAYN AL-HARET

6th OCTOBER (AL-GALA') FLYOVER

Big Ben Hotel

SHARIA EMAD EL-DIN

SHARIA RAMSES

SHARIA KHULUD (CLOT BEY)

New Cecil Hotel

Ⓜ ORABI

SHARIA EL-GUMHORRIYA

Victoria Hotel

St Mark's Cathedral

Midan Ataba

SHARIA NAGIB AL-RIHANY

SHARIA ORABI

SHARIA ALI AL-KASSAR

0   Metres   100

El-Tabei

Happyton Hotel

▼ 26th July Street

▼ Ezbekiya Gardens

to cross the humpbacked iron bridge. This used to overlook Cairo's army surplus market, which had to be removed to prevent fundamentalists from donning uniform in order to impersonate military officers. The *Fontana*, a **hotel** south of Midan Ramses, deserves a mention for its facilities: it lets non-residents use its rooftop swimming pool. Overlooking Midan Ramses from its southern end, the terrace café of the otherwise rather down-at-heel fifteenth-floor *Everest Hotel* is open round the clock and offers a superb vista over the square.

Islamic Cairo

> The core of the city itself was circumscribed by the river and hills of refuse, the castle, the aqueduct and the abandoned slums. Most of the bazaars lay in the densely packed quarters of the North-East, nestling in amongst and parasitic upon the rubble of the old Fatimid palaces, and behind the commercial streets one found small courtyards and large tenements, into which were crowded communities of closely knit creeds and tribes ... The city was like a disordered mind, an expression of archaic wishes and half-submerged memories of vanished dynasties.
>
> Robert Irwin, *The Arabian Nightmare*

Islamic Cairo sustains fantasy and confounds certainty. Few foreigners enter its maw without equal measures of excitement and trepidation. Streets are narrow and congested, slimy underfoot with donkey shit and burst water mains, over-hung with latticed balconies. Mosques, bazaars and medieval lanes abound; the smell of *sheeshas* and frying offal wafts through alleys where muezzins wail "*Allahu Akbar!*" (God is Greatest) and beggars entreat "*Ya Mohannin, ya Rabb*" (O Awakener of Pity, O Master) – as integral to streetlife as the artisans and hawkers. The sights, sounds, smells and surprises draw you back time after time, and getting lost or dispensing a little *baksheesh* is a small price to pay for the experience.

You can have a fascinating time exploring this quarter of the city without knowing anything about its history or architecture, but to describe Islamic Cairo one has to refer to both. Islamic architecture has its own conventions, terminology and stylistic eras, which we've attempted to summarize in the glossary on p.843. The potted history section provides a general context, with many of the personalities and events mentioned in more detail under the appropriate monument. Most of these are named after their various founders; modern-day Islamic fundamentalists shun them as *mesjid el-derar* – mosques built for self-glorification.

A brief history of Islamic Cairo

Islamic Cairo is the sum total of half a dozen cities whose varied names, ages and locations make for an unusually complex urban history. One helpful constant is that new cities have invariably been constructed to the north of the old, for quite simple reasons: an east–west spread was constrained by the Muqattam Hills and the Nile (which ran further east than nowadays), while the prevailing northerly wind blew the smoke and smell of earlier settlements away from newer areas.

Thus when the Muslim troops of Amr conquered Egypt for Islam in 641 AD, they sited their city, **Al-Fustat**, just north of Coptic Babylon (see "Old Cairo", p.185). Here it grew into a powerhouse of religious conversion, surpassing Alexandria as Egypt's leading city, though remaining a mere provincial capital in the vast Islamic empire ruled from Damascus by the khalifs, whose only direct contact occurred when the last of the **Umayyads** (661–750) fled to Al-Fustat, and then burned it. Their successors, the **Abbasids** (750–935), ordered the city to be rebuilt further north, and so *Medinet al-Askar* (City of Cantonments) came into being. More important in the long term was the Abbasid reliance on Turkish-speaking warriors, who were granted fiefdoms throughout the empire, including Egypt.

In 870, encouraged by popular discontent, the Abbasids' viceroy in Egypt asserted his independence, and went on to wrest Syria from their control. Like his predecessors, Ahmed **Ibn Tulun** founded a new city, reaching from Medinet al-Askar towards a spur of the Muqattam. Inspired by the imperial capital of Samarra, it consisted of a gigantic congregational mosque, palace and hippodrome, surrounded by "the Wards" (*Al-Qitai*) or military quarters after which the city was named. However, when the Abbasids invaded Egypt in 905, Al-Qitai was razed and ploughed under, sparing only the great Mosque of Ibn Tulun, which stands to this day.

The city regained a shadow of its former importance under the **Ikhshidids** (935–969), who seceded from the later Abbasid khalifs. But the impetus for its revival, and that of the Islamic empire, came from Tunisia, where adherents of Shia Islam had created their own theocracy, ruled by a descendant of Ali and Fatima – the dynasty of **Fatimids**. Aiming to seize the khalifate, they hit upon Egypt as an ill-defended yet significant power base, and captured it with an army of 100,000 in 969. The Fatimid general, Gohar (Jewel), a converted Greek, immediately began a new city where the dynasty henceforth reigned (969–1171).

By this time distinctions between the earlier cities had blurred, as people lived wherever was feasible amidst the decaying urban entity known as **Masr** (which also means "Egypt"). The Fatimids distanced themselves from Masr by building their city of **Al-Qahira** (The Conqueror) further north than ever, where certain key features remain. It was at the Al-Azhar Mosque that Al-Muizz, Egypt's first Fatimid ruler, delivered a sermon before vanishing into his palaces (which, alas, survive only in name); while the Mosque of Al-Hakim commemorates the khalif who ordered Masr's destruction after residents objected to proclamations of his divinity. You can also see the great Northern Walls and the Bab Zwayla gate, dating from Al-Gyushi's enlargement of Al-Qahira's defences. But as the Fatimid city expanded, Fustat began disappearing as people scavenged building material from its abandoned dwellings; a process that spread to Masr, creating great swathes of *kharab*, or derelict quarters.

The disparate areas only assumed a kind of unity after **Salah al-Din** (Saladin to the Crusaders) built **the Citadel** on a rocky spur between Al-Qahira and Masr, and walls which linked up with the aqueduct between the Nile and the Citadel, so as to surround the whole. Salah al-Din promoted Sunni, not Shia, Islam and built madrassas to propagate orthodoxy; he ruled not as khalif, but as a secular *sultan* (power). His successors, the **Ayyubids**, erected pepperpot-shaped minarets (only one remains, on Sultan Ayyub's Madrassa and Mausoleum; see p.169) and the magnificent tombs of the Abbasid Khalifs and Imam al-Shafi'i (which still exist) in the Southern Cemetery, but they made the same error as the Abbasids: depending on foreign troops and bodyguards. When the sultan died heirless and his widow needed help to stay in power, these troops, the Mamlukes, were poised to take control.

The **Mamlukes** were a self-perpetuating caste of slave-warriors, originally from Central Asia but later drawn from all over the Near East and the Balkans. Their price in the slave markets reflected the "value" of ethnic stock – 130–140 ducats for a Tartar, 110–120 for a Circassian, 50–80 for a Slav or Albanian – plus individual traits: sturdy, handsome youths were favoured. Often born of concubines and raised in barracks, Mamlukes advanced through the ranks under amirs who sodomized and lavished gifts upon their favourites. With the support of the right amirs, the most ruthless Mamluke could aspire to being sultan. Frequent changes of ruler were actually preferred, since contenders had to spread around bribes, not least to arrange assassinations. The Mamluke era is divided into periods named after the garrisons of troops whence the sultans intrigued their way to power: the Qipchak or Tartar **Bahri Mamlukes** (1250–1382), originally stationed by the river (*bahr* in Arabic); and their Circassian successors, the **Burgi Mamlukes** (1382–1517), quartered in a tower (*burg*) of the Citadel.

Paradoxically, the Mamlukes were also renowned as aesthetes, commissioning mosques, mansions and *sabil-kuttabs* that are still the glory of today's Islamic Cairo. They built throughout the city, from the Northern to the Southern

Approaching and exploring Islamic Cairo: practicalities

The best (if not only) way **to explore Islamic Cairo** is by walking. Basically, you decide on a starting point that's readily accessible from downtown Cairo, and then follow an itinerary on foot from there. The most obvious **starting points** are Khan el-Khalili, the Bab Zwayla and the Citadel; see the beginning of each of these sections for details on getting there by public transport (also see the bus/minibus information on p.97). If you want to walk from the downtown area, there are four approaches to Islamic Cairo from **Midan Ataba** (see p.129), using the Ataba post office and fire station for orientation.

THE MUSKI is the classic approach to **Khan el-Khalili**: a narrow bazaar, identifiable by the crowds passing between the *El-Mousky* hotel and a clump of luggage stalls. For more details, see "Around Khan el-Khalili and Al-Azhar", p.136.

SHARIA AL-AZHAR. Overshadowed by a flyover running from Midan Ataba to the heart of Islamic Cairo, Sharia al-Azhar – which runs parallel to the Muski – buzzes with traffic and cottage industries. Buses and minibuses push their way through the crowds and traffic, past **Al-Azhar bus terminal** (for the Western Desert Oases) and across one of Cairo's few remaining tram routes at the Bur Said overpass, taking you on to the **Al-Azhar Mosque**, just south of **Midan el-Hussein**. By walking back from the square along the Muski to the junction with Sharia al-Muizz, you can go south to **Bab Zwayla**.

SHARIA QALAA (formerly Boulevard Mohammed Ali), across from the fire station. This street runs directly to the **Citadel** (2km). When Ismail's Minister of Public Works ordered the thoroughfare ploughed through the old quarter, he asked rhetorically: "Do we need so many monuments? Isn't it enough to preserve a sample?" The stretch down to Midan Ahmed Maher – where the **Islamic Arts Museum** is located – features musical instrument shops, all-night stalls and cafés. In pre-revolutionary times, brothels and hashish dens infested the stepped lanes that rise between its tenements.

SHARIA EL-GEISH. Also topped by a flyover, "Army Street" runs out towards Abbassiya and Heliopolis. The main reason for venturing beyond the Paper Market is to visit the Mosque of Beybars the Crossbowman on Midan Zahir, and the Sakakini Palace beyond.

Many of the **itineraries** given on the following pages can be linked up or truncated; the main limitations on how much you can see are time and your own stamina. It makes sense to read up on an area before striking out on foot. The streets of Islamic Cairo are labyrinthine and, while getting lost among them can result in the richest experiences, some visitors prefer to be shown round by a **guide**. The tourist office can put you in touch with authorized guides, and unofficial ones may accost you on the street. If you are in an official or student group you could try the Tourist Friends Association (9th floor, 33 Sharia Qasr el-Nil; ☎02/392 2036); its tours are free, as the main motive of its members – all students – is to practise their English.

Most of Islamic Cairo's **monuments** are self-evident and often identified by little green plaques with Arabic numbers; these correspond to the numbers on Lehnert & Landrock's map of Cairo and the listings in the exhaustive *Islamic Monuments in Cairo: A Practical Guide*, published by the AUC. Although the area **maps** printed in this book should suffice, the AUC book and four fold-out maps published by SPARE (the Society for the Preservation of the Architectural Resources of Egypt) have the advantage of greater detail.

Likewise, we can't hope to match the wealth of detail or evocations of time and place in certain **books**. Edward Lane's *The Manners and Customs of the Modern*

Cemetery, and the Citadel to the Nile, and although urban life was interrupted by their bloody conflicts, the city nevertheless maintained civilized institutions: public hospitals, libraries and schools bequeathed by wealthy Mamlukes

Egyptians illuminates life during Mohammed Ali's time. The changes wrought last century underlie Naguib Mahfouz's *Midaq Alley* and *Cairo Trilogy*. Mamluke Cairo is the setting for Robert Irwin's surreal *The Arabian Nightmare*, whereas its fevered demise haunts *Zayni Barakat* by Gamal al-Ghitani. Life in the Cities of the Dead is captured in *Down to the Sea* by Gamil Attiyah Ibrahim. For straight – but never dull – history, try James Aldridge's *Cairo* or, if you can get your hands on a copy, Desmond Stewart's *Great Cairo, Mother of the World*. All of these works are reviewed under "Books" in the Contexts chapter and a selection is available at bookstores such as Al-Shorouk on Midan Talaat Harb, the Anglo-Egyptian Bookshop at 169 Sharia Mohammed Farid and the AUC bookstore at the back of the main campus. Al-Shorouk, AUC and Lenhert & Landrock (44 Sharia Sherif) are the best places to look for the SPARE maps, which are not always easy to come by.

The buildings you will most want to visit are **mosques**, **madrassas** (theological schools) and **wikalas** (caravanserais, see p.148). On occasion, former private **mansions** are also open to the public. Mosques and most religious buildings no longer charge any **entrance fee** – these were abolished after complaints by Muslim visitors who felt that they should not have to pay to pray. This has not stopped certain unscrupulous custodians and other opportunists from attempting to charge visitors for entry. If somebody tries to charge you for entering a mosque, demand an official ticket – if they have none, the charge is spurious and you should refuse to pay it. **Opening hours** are roughly 9am to 7pm daily, though they may well open up later, depending on when the guardian turns up, and will probably close an hour or two earlier in winter. During Ramadan, when everybody wants to be at home by sunset in order to eat, you will not be able to visit after about 4pm. Entry charges and opening hours are only given in the text when they differ significantly from the above. You will also not be welcome during **prayer times** and the Friday noon assembly, which lasts over an hour but should be finished by 2.30pm. A couple of mosques are permanently closed to non-Muslims (as indicated in the text).

Despite entry charges having been abolished for visiting mosques, custodians generally expect **baksheesh**. The amount Egyptians pay for looking after shoes is 50pt, though you may wish, as a tourist, to be more generous than that. Someone who opens a place up, takes you into a tomb or lets you up a minaret rates £E2–5 (which you should pay after your visit). Excessive demands should be politely resisted, and asking for change is awkward, so bring lots of small bills.

How you **dress** is important. Wearing shorts automatically diminishes prestige in Egyptian eyes, and women wearing halter-necks, skimpy T-shirts, miniskirts, etc, will attract gropers and the disapproval of both sexes. Mosques baulk at admitting the "immodestly" dressed, and for Muslims and unbelievers alike it's obligatory to remove shoes (or don overshoes) to avoid sullying the sacred precincts. Comfortable, easy to slip off footwear is recommended; sandals offer scant protection against manure and leaking drains. Women may feel more comfortable with a male companion, and covering their hair and shoulders with a shawl or headscarf.

It shouldn't need saying that intimate **behaviour** in public is a definite no-no. By remaining courteous and alert, you minimize the risk of hassles on the crowded streets. An effective yet graceful way of brushing off hustlers is to intone "*la shukran*" (no thank you) while smiling, touching your heart (a gesture of sincerity) and hurrying on. But never begrudge the effort of politeness, nor mistake every approach for a sales ploy. Ordinary Egyptians enjoy welcoming *khawagas* with the right attitude as much as they like watching arrogant tourists get misdirected and cheated.

and merchants. The caravanserais overflowed with exotica from Africa and the spices of the East, and with Baghdad laid waste by the Mongols, Cairo had no peer in the Islamic world, its wonders inspiring many of the tales in the *Thousand and One Nights*.

But in 1517 the **Ottoman Turks** reduced Egypt from an independent state to a vassal province in their empire, and the Mamlukes from masters to mere overseers. When the French and British extended the Napoleonic War to Egypt they found a city living on bygone glories: introspective and archaic, its population dwindling as civil disorder increased. Eighteenth-century travellers like R.R. Madden were struck by "the squalid wretchedness of the Arabs, and the external splendour of the Turks", not to mention the lack of "one tolerable street" in a city of some 350,000 inhabitants.

The city's renaissance – and the ultimate shift from Islamic to modern Cairo – is owed to **Mohammed Ali** (1805–48) and his less ruthless descendants. An Ottoman servant who turned against his masters, Mohammed Ali effortlessly decapitated the vestiges of Mamluke power, and raised a huge mosque and palaces upon the Citadel. Foreigners were hired to advise on urban development, and Sharia Qalaa (Blvd Mohammed Ali) was ploughed through the old city. As Bulaq, Ezbekiya and other hitherto swampy tracts were developed into a modern, quasi-Western city, Islamic Cairo ceased to be the cockpit of power and the magnet for aspirations. But as visitors soon discover, its contrasts, monuments and vitality remain as compelling as ever.

Around Khan el-Khalili and Al-Azhar

Khan el-Khalili bazaar and the Mosque of Al-Azhar form the commercial and religious heart of Islamic Cairo, and the starting point for several walking tours. **To get there from downtown Cairo** you can take a taxi, bus, or walk. Taxis (which usually go via the Al-Azhar flyover) shouldn't cost more than £E3–5, although drivers normally try to overcharge tourists bound for Midan el-Hussein – the main square adjoining Khan el-Khalili that's best given as your destination. For details of the buses from downtown, see p.97.

Approaching on foot: the Muski

Walking **from Midan Ataba** there are two basic routes: along Sharia al-Azhar (beneath the flyover), which takes ten to fifteen minutes; or via the Muski, a more interesting, slightly longer approach. It's best to go one way and return by the other.

The Muski is a narrow, incredibly congested street running eastwards from Midan Ataba; look for the faded Arabic sign of the *El-Mousky Hotel* on the corner. Worming your way through the crowds – past windows full of wedding gear, tape decks and fabrics, and vendors peddling everything from salted fish to socks – beware of mopeds and other traffic thrusting up behind. Barrowmen still yell traditional warnings – "*Riglak!*" (Your foot!), "*Dahrik!*" (Your back!), "*Shemalak!*" (Your left side!). Itinerant drinks-vendors are much in evidence: although the *saqi* (water-sellers) have been made redundant by modern plumbing, *susi* dispensing liquorice-water and *sherbutli* with their silver-spouted lemonade bottles remain an essential part of streetlife.

Halfway along the Muski you'll cross Sharia Bur Said, which you cannot cross directly (you'll have to take a right and dodge under the flyover). Beyond here the Muski turns touristy, with hustlers emerging as it nears Khan el-Khalili.

AROUND KHAN EL-KHALILI AND AL-AZHAR

RESTAURANTS

Cafeteria Khan el-Khalili	A
Dahan	C
Egyptian Pancake House	D
Fishawi's	B

ACCOMMODATION

El Hussein	1
Radwan	2

Midan el-Hussein

Midan el-Hussein, framed by an eclectic mix of architecture, is a central point of reference. To the north stands the tan-coloured **Mosque of Saiyidna Hussein**, where the Egyptian president and other dignitaries pray on special occasions; it's a sacred place, off-limits to non-Muslims. Its cool marble, green and silver interior guards the relic of a momentous event in Islamic history: the **head of Hussein**. The grandson of the Prophet Mohammed, Hussein was killed in Iraq in 680 by the Umayyads, who had earlier been recognized as Mohammed's successors against the claims of his son-in-law, Ali, Hussein's father, whom they had murdered. This generational power struggle over the khalifate caused an enduring schism within Islam. The Muslim world's *Sunni* ("followers of the way") majority not only recognized the khalifate, but forbade the office to anyone of Ali's line. Conversely, the *Shia* ("partisans of Ali") minority refused to accept any khalif but a descendant of Ali, and revered Hussein as a martyr. In predominantly Sunni Muslim Egypt, he's nevertheless regarded as a popular saint, ranked beside Saiyida Zeinab, the Prophet's grand-daughter.

Hussein's annual moulid is one of Cairo's greatest **festivals** – a fortnight of religious devotion and popular revelry climaxing on the *leyla kebira* or "big night", the last Wednesday in the Muslim month of *Rabi al-Tani*. Here the Sufi brotherhoods parade with their banners and drums, and music blares all night, with vast crowds of Cairenes and *fellaheen* from the Delta (each of whose villages has its own café and dosshouse in the neighbourhood). El-Hussein is also a focal point during the festivals of *Moulid al-Nabi, Eid al-Adha, Ramadan* and *Eid al-Fitr*, all well worth seeing. A balcony room at the *El-Hussein Hotel* provides a perfect vantage point, but don't expect to get any sleep. Ablaze with neon lights (including green "Allahs"), the minarets boom sleepers into wakefulness around dawn with their amplified muezzins – and that's on ordinary nights of the year.

The Khan el-Khalili bazaars

Above all, the **Khan el-Khalili** quarter pulses with commerce, as it has since the Middle Ages. Except on Sundays, when most shops are shut, everything from spices to silk is sold in its bazaars. What follows is primarily a guide to the sights; for hard facts about merchandise, dealers and bargaining, see "Shopping", pp.260–270. Generically speaking, all the bazaars around here are subsumed under the name Khan el-Khalili – after Khalil, a Master of Horse who founded a caravanserai here in 1382. However, the Khan itself is quite compact, bounded by Hussein's Mosque, Sharia al-Muizz and the Muski, with two medieval lanes (Sikket al-Badestan and Sikket Khan el-Khalili) penetrating its maze-like interior.

Most of the shop fronts conceal workshops or warehouses, and the system of selling certain goods in particular areas still applies, if not as rigidly as in the past. **Goldsmiths**, jewellers and souvenir-antique shops mostly congregate along the lanes, which retain a few arches and walls from Mamluke times. When you've tired of wandering around, duck into **Fishawi's** via one of the passages off the Muski or the square. Showing its age with tobacco-stained plaster and cracked gilded mirrors, this famous café has been open day and night every day of the year for over two centuries, an evocative place to sip mint tea, eavesdrop, and risk a *sheesha*.

South off the Muski, along Sharia al-Muizz, you'll find the *Souk al-Attarin* or **Spice Bazaar**, selling dried crushed fruit and flowers besides more familiar spices. On the corner of the same street, screened by T-shirt and *galabiyya* stalls, stands the **Madrassa of Sultan al-Ashraf Barsbey**, who made the spice trade a state monopoly, thus financing his capture of Cyprus in 1426.

Sharia Sanadiqiya (off Sharia al-Muizz) will take you into the **Perfume Bazaar**, a dark, aromatic warren sometimes called the *Souk es-Sudan* because much of the incense is from there; in the last century, Baedeker's *Guide for Travellers* also noted "gum, dum-plant nuts" and "ill-tanned tiger-skins" amongst the merchandise. Mamluke sultans appointed a *Muhtasib* to oversee prices, weights and quality. Empowered to inflict summary fines and corporal punishments, he was also responsible for public morals – "enjoining what is right and forbidding what is wrong". The first passage on your left off Sharia Sanadiqiya leads up a flight of steps to a tiny cul-de-sac. This is Zuqaq al-Midaq, or **Midaq Alley**, immortalized by Naguib Mahfouz in his novel of the same name, and made into a film, which was shot here. There is no street sign apparent; it's kept in the tiny (and easy to miss) café, where they'll ask if you want to photograph it – for *baksheesh*, of course.

△ The Ghuriya, Islamic Cairo

Al-Azhar Mosque

To the southwest of Midan el-Hussein, a pedestrian underpass leads towards the **Mosque of Al-Azhar** (pronounced "Al-*Az*har"), whose name can be translated as "the radiant", "blooming" or "resplendent". Founded in 970, as soon as the enclosure walls of Fatimid Al-Qahira were completed, Al-Azhar claims to be the world's oldest university (a title disputed by the Kairaouine Mosque in Fez, Morocco). For more than a millennium, though, Al-Azhar has provided students from all over the Muslim world with free board and with an education that, despite Nasserite reforms, remains largely as it was during the classical Islamic era. *Muqawrin* study every facet of the Koran and Islamic jurisprudence (*fiqh*); logic, grammar and rhetoric; and how to calculate the phases of the lunar Muslim calendar. Much of this involves listening in a circle (*halqa*) at the feet of a sheikh, and rote memorization; but with greater knowledge, students may engage in Socratic dialogue with their teachers, or instruct their juniors.

Given this, and the Sheikh al-Azhar's status as the ultimate theological authority for Egyptian Muslims, it's unsurprising that the mosque has always been politically significant. Salah al-Din changed it from a Shi'ite hotbed into a bastion of Sunni orthodoxy, while Napoleon's troops savagely desecrated it to demonstrate their power. (Omitting any mention of this, Baedeker cautioned visitors to this "fountain-head of Mohammedan fanaticism... not to indulge in any gestures of amusement or contempt".) A nationalist stronghold from the nineteenth century onwards, Al-Azhar was chosen by Nasser as the venue for his speech of defiance during the Suez invasion of 1956. When Saudi King Fahd prayed here with Mubarak in 1989 it symbolized Egypt's return to the conservative Arab fold; yet, paradoxically, many of Al-Azhar's 90,000 students revere the blind fundamentalist sheikh Omar Abd al-Rahman, currently serving a life sentence in the US for his part in the 1993 World Trade Center bombing.

The Mosque

The **mosque** itself (open for tourists Mon–Thurs & Sun 9am–6pm, Fri 3–6pm; open for prayer daily 9am–9pm) is an accretion of centuries and styles, harmonious if confusing. You come in through the fifteenth-century **Barber's Gate**, where students traditionally had their heads shaved, onto a great **sahn** (courtyard) that's five hundred years older, overlooked by three minarets. The *sahn* facade, with its rosettes and keel-arched panels, is mostly Fatimid, but the latticework-screened *riwaqs* (residential quarters) of the **madrassas** (theological schools) on your right-hand side date from the Mamluke period. Unfortunately, these are rarely opened for visitors, but you can walk into the carpeted, alabaster-pillared **qibla liwan** (prayer hall), where the *mihrab*, or prayer niche facing Mecca, is located.

The **roof** and minarets (closed to visitors at last check, but worth asking) offer great views of Islamic Cairo's timeless vista of crumbling, dust-coloured buildings that could have been erected decades or centuries ago, the skyline bristling with dozens of minarets.

Butneya – and leaving Al-Azhar

The warren of lanes and tenements behind Al-Azhar – an area known as **Butneya** – could be described as Cairo's "Thieves' Quarter", except that racketeering and drugs are more important. Until 1988, the main business was hashish: sold from "windows" and "green doors", it could be smoked with impunity in *ghorzas* (literally "stitches", small and hidden places) throughout the quarter. Local drugs barons like Kut Kut and Wilad Nasare entered Cairene folklore for their ostentatious wealth and devotion to their neighbourhood; Mustafa Marzuaa built a fifteen-room villa, with VCRs in every room, smack in the middle. After the great crackdown in December 1988, when scores of corrupt officials were arrested, the drugs "mafiosi" decamped to the suburbs, leaving Butneya to local racketeers. Some gangs cream the profits from organized garbage collection and begging; others extort money from shops or restaurants, and one gang even specializes in weddings: families pay them to stay away rather than risk disturbances – to hire bouncers would be a shameful admission of family weakness.

None of this should affect foreigners who stay outside the quarter (though you might be offered hashish, or even regaled with stories of the "good old days" when slabs were carved up on tables outdoors). In any case, the well-defined tourist trail leads elsewhere. **Leaving Al-Azhar** by the Barber's Gate, you can turn left down an alley to reach the Wikala of al-Ghuri and other monuments described in the next-but-one walking tour; or return to Midan el-Hussein and check out the following itinerary.

To the Northern Gates and back again

As described below, this itinerary covers an array of monuments from different eras, occupying the one-time heart of Fatimid Cairo. Although one can walk the route – from Midan el-Hussein to the Northern Gates and back again – within an hour, checking out the interiors of all the monuments could take half a day or more, so you might wish to be selective. If your time is limited, it's probably best to concentrate on the three big attractions: the Qalaoun–al-Nasir–Barquq complex, Al-Hakim's Mosque and the Beit al-Sihaymi.

Midan el-Hussein to Bayn al-Qasrayn

Starting from Midan el-Hussein (see the map p.137), walk 200m west along the Muski to a crossroads with two mosques, and then turn right onto the northern extension of **Sharia al-Muizz**. Here, jewellers' shops overflowing from the Goldsmiths Bazaar soon give way to vendors of pots, basins and crescent-topped finials, after whom this bit of street is popularly called *Al-Nahaseen*, the **Coppersmiths Bazaar**.

In Fatimid times this bazaar was a broad avenue culminating in a great parade ground between khalifal palaces – hence its name, **Bayn al-Qasrayn** (Between the Two Palaces), which is still used today although traces of the palaces are long gone. Robert Irwin writes evocatively of the place as it was during the Mamluke era, when it was customary "for the men and even a few of the women to promenade in the cool twilight. Later, when respectable people had gone back to their homes, the streets were left to the lamplighters, carousing mamlukes, prostitutes and the sleepers." More recently, the street has given its name to the first novel of Naguib Mahfouz's *Cairo Trilogy*, where it is usually translated as "Palace Walk".

To the right of the bazaar, a minaret poking above a row of stalls gives away the unobtrusive **Madrassa and Mausoleum of Sultan Ayyub**, more interesting for its historical associations than anything else. Its founder, the last Ayyubid sultan, was responsible for introducing Mamlukes, or foreign slave troops (originally Qipchaks, from an ethnic group related to the Tartars, who lived in Russia's lower Volga region), an act pregnant with consequences for Egypt. As related under "Cities of the Dead" (see p.170), the sultan's widow's daring bid for power made the Mamlukes aware that they were kingmakers – whence it was a short step to ruling Egypt themselves, as they did from 1250

TO THE NORTHERN GATES

Glass Factory ▲

Bab el-Futuh

Bab el-Nasr Cemetery

Mosque of el-Hakim

Bab el-Nasr

SHARIA BAYN EL-SAYARIG

N

SHARIA AMIR EL-GYUSHI

SHARIA EL-MUIZZ

Wikala of Qaitbey

Northern Walls

Hammam el-Malyatah

HARET

SHARIA BAB AL-NASR

Mosque of Bargouan

BARDUAN

SIKET BARGOUAN

Kahla Wikala

EL-GAMALIYA

Mosque of Suleyman el-Silahdar

Beit Gaafar

Beit el-Sihaymi

Beit Kharazati

DARB EL-ASFUR

Qitus

Mosque of el-Aqmar

SHARIA GAMALIYA

Khanqah of Beybars el-Gashankir

Sabil-Kuttab of Abd el-Rahman Katkhuda

SHARIA EL-KHRUNFISH

Wikalas

Hammam el-Sultan

Wikala

Madrassa el-Kamiliya

Qasr Bashtak

BAYN EL-QASRAYN

SHARIA GAMALIYA

Madrassa-Khanqah of Sultan Barquq

Mosque of el-Nasir Mohammed

MIDAN BEIT EL-QADI

QASR EL-SHOOK

Musafirkhana Palace

Maristan, Madrassa & Mausoleum of Sultan Qalaoun

House of Uthman Katkhuda

SHARIA BEIT EL-QADI

Madrassa-Mausoleum of Sultan Ayyub

SHARIA EL-MUIZZ

0 Metres 50

Wikala

▼ The Muski

▼ Midan el-Hussein

▲ Northern Cemetery

onwards. From an architectural standpoint, Ayyub's madrassa (built 1242–50) was the first to incorporate all four *mahhabs* (rites) of Sunni Islam, and be linked to its founder's mausoleum, thus serving as the prototype for the Mamlukes' great mosque-madrassa-mausoleum complexes. Beneath the minaret, whose *mabkhara* (incense burner) or "pepperpot" crown is the sole example of this Ayyubid motif left in Cairo, an alleyway with a gate (on the left) leads into the courtyard of what used to be the madrassa. A sixteenth-century *sabil-kuttab* (Koranic school and fountain) protrudes from the wall between the minaret and Ayyub's domed mausoleum (usually locked), further up the street.

The Qalaoun–Al-Nasir–Barquq complex

Across the road from the madrassa, the medieval complex of buildings endowed by the sultans **Qalaoun**, **Al-Nasir** and **Barquq** forms an unbroken and quite breathtaking 185-metre-long facade. Founded by three of the most significant of the Mamlukes, each of these building groups was designed to serve several functions, yet to form a harmonious whole. As all are under restoration, most parts of the buildings will probably be off-limits to visitors, but it's worth trying to see as much as you can.

The Qalaoun Complex

Influenced by the Syrian and Crusader architecture its founder had encountered while fighting abroad, **Sultan Qalaoun's Maristan, Madrassa and Mausoleum** arguably inaugurated the Burgi Mamluke style, which is typified by lavish ornamentation and execution on a grand scale. If modern visitors are impressed by the fact that these structures were completed in thirteen months (1284–85), Qalaoun's contemporaries were amazed. Unfortunately, at time of writing, the complex was undergoing heavy restoration work and closed to public access.

The **Maristan** provided free treatment for every known illness (including cataract removals), storytellers and musicians to amuse the patients, and money to tide them over following their discharge. A modern eye clinic now occupies the site of Qalaoun's hospital, of which only three *liwans* remain; to see them, walk down the tree-shaded lane that starts opposite the *sabil-kuttab* mentioned above.

Further up the street, a main door clad in bronze with geometric patterns gives access to a corridor running between the madrassa and the mausoleum. The damaged **Madrassa** (entered to the left off this corridor) has a sanctuary *liwan* recalling the three-aisled churches of northern Syria, with Syrian-style glass mosaics around its prayer niche.

But the real highlight of the ensemble is Qalaoun's **Mausoleum**, across the corridor. First comes an atrium court with a *mashrabiya* doorway, surmounted by a beautiful stucco arch worked with interlocking stars, floral and Koranic motifs, as intricate as lace. Beyond is the tomb chamber, thirty metres high, with its soaring dome pierced by stained-glass windows in viridian, ultramarine and golden hues. Elaborately coffered, painted ceilings overhang walls panelled in marble, with mother-of-pearl mosaics spelling out "Mohammed" in abstract calligraphy. Until this century the *mihrab* was credited with healing powers, so supplicants could be seen "rubbing lemons on one of its pilasters, and licking up the moisture", while a stick hanging from the tomb's railings was used "to cure fools or idiots by striking them on the head".

Qalaoun himself was a handsome Qipchak, purchased for one thousand dinars during Ayyub's reign. He rose through the ranks due to the patronage of Sultan Beybars al-Bunduqdari, whose seven-year-old son he eventually deposed in 1279. Qalaoun's sonorous titles *Al-Mansour* and *Al-Alfi* ("the Thousand", after his high price) were mocked by his name, which sounds comical in Arabic; it's supposedly derived from the Mongolian word for "duck", or an obscure Turkish noun meaning "great ransom" or "rich present". A tireless foe of the Crusaders – he died en route to Acre fortress in 1290, aged 79 – Qalaoun imported Circassians to offset Qipchak predominance amongst the Mamlukes, and founded a dynasty that ruled for almost a century (barring hiccups).

The Al-Nasir Complex

Qalaoun's second son, responsible for the **Mosque of Al-Nasir Mohammed** next door, had a rough succession. Only nine years old when elected, he was deposed by his regent, then restored but kept in miserable conditions for a decade by Beybars al-Gashankir. He finally had Beybars executed and subsequently enjoyed a lengthy reign (1293–1340, counting interregnums), which marked the zenith of Mamluke civilization.

The building of thirty mosques, the great aqueduct and a canal north of Cairo attests to Al-Nasir's enthusiasm for public works (matched apparently by his devotion to horses and sheep). The **minaret** is a superb ensemble of stuccoed kufic and naskhi inscriptions, ornate medallions and stalactites, probably made by Moroccan craftsmen. Al-Nasir is actually buried in Qalaoun's mausoleum, and his own son occupies the **mausoleum** intended for him.

At the time of writing, the complex was undergoing heavy restoration work and closed to public access.

The Barquq Madrassa and Khanqah

The adjacent **Madrassa and Khanqah of Sultan Barquq** appears in a much reproduced nineteenth-century drawing by Owen Carter, which also depicts the Sabil-Kuttab of Ismail Pasha, opposite Al-Nasir's. Its broad facade, divided into shallow recesses, echoes Qalaoun's madrassa, although Barquq's complex (1384–86) has the taller dome, and also boasts a minaret.

Barquq was the first Circassian sultan (1382–98), a Burgi Mamluke who seized power by means of intrigue and assassination. His name, meaning "plum" in Arabic, appears on the raised boss in the centre of the bronze-plated doors, behind which a vaulted passageway leads to an open court. The **madrassa**'s sanctuary *liwan* (on the right as you enter) has a beautiful ceiling supported by porphyry columns of pharaonic origin; upstairs are the cells of the Sufi monks who once inhabited the **khanqah** (monastery). To one side of the *qibla liwan*, a splendid domed mausoleum upheld by gilded pendentives contains the tomb of Barquq's daughter. At the time of writing, however, the complex was undergoing heavy restoration work and closed to public access.

Mansions and Sabil-Kuttabs

The domestic architecture of the Mamlukes was no less sophisticated: perfectly adapted to Cairene conditions, it offered greater comfort than contemporary European homes – for the well-to-do, at least. An example close at hand is the **House of Uthman Katkhuda**, so called after an eighteenth-century resident, although the mansion itself dates from 1350. You'll find it on Sharia Beit al-Qadi, which runs eastwards opposite Qalaoun's mausoleum; it's halfway along the north side of the street at no.9, but currently closed for restoration. The entrance leads into the *qa'a*, a narrow, sixteen-metre-high reception hall with a handsome fountain and wainscoting, cooled by a north-facing *malqaf*, or air scoop, on the roof.

Back on Sharia al-Muizz, walk past Barquq's complex (beyond which the street is known as Bayn al-Qasrayn, meaning "between the two palaces" – see p.141) and cross the road, turning into a muddy alleyway on the right, where the second door on the left opens onto the fourteenth-century **Qasr Bashtak**. Here the *qa'a* is upstairs, with *mashrabiya*-screened galleries that permitted ladies to witness the amir's parties, and similar devices overlooking the street. Amir Bashtak was married to Al-Nasir's daughter, so he could afford a five-storey palace with running water on every floor; alas, only a section has survived.

The entrance to Qasr Bashtak is round the side on Derb Kermez, just before the bend, but it is currently closed for restoration.

Back on Bayn al-Qasrayn and situated on a fork in the road just beyond the Qalaoun, Al-Nasir and Barquq complex, the **Sabil-Kuttab of Abd al-Rahman Katkhuda** rises in tiers of airy wooden fretwork above solid masonry and grilles at street level. Founded by an eighteenth-century amir who wished to make amends for roistering, this is an Ottoman-influenced example of a type of building once widespread throughout Cairo, intended to provide the "blessings" of water and education, mentioned in the Holy Koran. Thus, local people could draw water from the *sabil* (public fountain) on the ground floor (where the Ka'ba at Mecca is depicted in Syrian tilework), while their sons learned Koranic precepts in the *kuttab* upstairs. (Girls were deemed unworthy of schooling.) An old proverb suggests that teaching methods were simple: "A boy's ear is on his back – he listens when he is beaten."

By taking the left-hand fork at the *sabil-kuttab* and walking 70m north you reach the **Mosque of Al-Aqmar** (on the right; daily 7.30am–9pm). Newly restored, its most salient feature is the facade, whose ribbed shell hood, keel arches and stalactite panels were the first instance of a decorated mosque facade in Cairo. Built between 1121 and 1125 by the Fatimid khalif's grand vizier, the mosque gets its name – "the moonlit" – from the glitter of its masonry under lunar light. Notice the intricate medallion above the door; the way that the street level has risen well above the mosque's entrance; and the "cutaway" corner up the road, designed to facilitate the manoeuvring of loaded camels.

One block further north, turn right into **Darb al-Asfur**. This whole street has now emerged from years of major restoration work, which has left it in such a pristine state that it no longer seems part of the surrounding district. In fact it looks more like a modern imitation than a genuine Gamaliya street. The first three houses on the left are all open to the public (daily 9am–6pm; £E20, students £E10, camera £E10), entered through the broad wooden door of no.19, **Beit al-Sihaymi**, which is the finest of the three. Its rooms, all open to visitors, surround a lovely courtyard filled with bird noises and shrubbery, overlooked by a *maq'ad* or loggia, where males enjoyed the cool northerly breezes; the ground-floor reception hall with its marble fountain was used during winter, or for formal occasions. The *haramlik* section, reserved for women, is equally luxurious, adorned with faïence, stained glass, painted ceilings and delicate latticework. From here, you pass through the similarly restored early eighteenth-century **Beit Gaafar**, to emerge via the smaller, nineteenth-century **Beit Kharazati** on the corner at no.25. The three houses offer a unique chance to see what lies behind the walls of these old-city streets, and view the interior of a traditional wealthy Cairene's home, although the family life that once filled it is missing.

Returning to the main street and continuing north brings you to the **Mosque of Suleyman al-Silahdar**, recognizable by its "pencil" minaret, a typically Ottoman feature. Built in 1839, the mosque reflects the Baroque and Rococo influences that reached Cairo via Istanbul during Mohammed Ali's reign – notably the fronds and garlands that also characterize *sabil-kuttabs* from the period. Shortly afterwards the street widens into a triangular square, beyond which it's busy with the colourfully painted carts of garlic- and onion-sellers who roll in through the mighty gate ahead.

Al-Hakim's Mosque and the Northern Gates

The **Mosque of Al-Hakim**, abutting the Northern Walls, commemorates one of Egypt's most notorious rulers. **Al-Hakim bi-Amr Allah** (Ruler by God's

Command) was only eleven years old when he became the sixth Fatimid khalif, and fifteen when he had his tutor murdered. His reign (996–1021) was capricious and despotic by any standards, characterized by the persecution of Christians, Jews and merchants and by a rabid misogyny: Al-Hakim forbade women to leave their homes (banning the manufacture of women's footwear to reinforce this) and once had a group of noisy females boiled alive in a public bath. His puritanical instincts were also levelled at wine, chess and dancing girls – all of which were prohibited – and all the city's dogs were exterminated as their barking annoyed him. Merchants found guilty of cheating during Al-Hakim's inspections were summarily sodomized by his Nubian slave, Masoud, while the khalif stood upon their heads – comparatively restrained behaviour from a man who once dissected a butcher with his own cleaver.

In 1020, followers proclaimed Al-Hakim's divinity in the Mosque of Amr, provoking riots which he answered by ordering Fustat's destruction, watching it burn from the Muqattam Hills, where he often rode alone at night. However, legend ascribes the conflagration to Al-Hakim's revenge on the quarter where his beloved sister, **Sitt al–Mulk** (Lady of Power), took her lovers. Only after half of Fustat-Masr was in ruins was she examined by midwives and pronounced a virgin, whereupon he surveyed the devastation and asked, "Who ordered this?" Allegedly, it was his desire for an incestuous marriage that impelled her to arrange Al-Hakim's "disappearance" during one of his nocturnal jaunts.

By governing as regent for the child-khalif Zahir and dying peacefully in her bed, Sitt al-Mulk forfeited the eternal fame that later accrued to Shagar al-Durr, renowned as the only female ruler of Egypt since Cleopatra (see p.170). Meanwhile, Al-Hakim's follower Hamza Ibn Ali, and his disciple, Mohammed al-Durzi, persuaded many foreign Muslims that Al-Hakim was a manifestation of God similar to the Christian Messiah. This idea is the origin of the **Druze** faith, whose tightly knit communities still exist in Syria, Lebanon and Israel, and who subscribe to doctrines the details of which are secret. Conversely, the Copts maintain that Al-Hakim experienced a vision of Jesus, repented, and became a monk.

At all events, though, his huge **mosque** was thereafter shunned or used for profane purposes until 1980, when it was restored by a sect of Isma'ili Shi'ites from Brunei who venerate Al-Hakim. The sect's addition of brass lamps, glass chandeliers and a new *mihrab* outraged purists, but the original wooden tie-beams and stucco frieze beneath the ceilings remain. From the roof, you can gaze over Bab al-Nasr Cemetery (see below) and admire the mosque's minarets, which resemble bastions and are its only original features.

The Northern Gates

In times past, the annual pilgrim caravan returning from Mecca would enter Cairo via the **Bab al-Futuh** (Open Gate), drawing huge crowds to witness the arrival of the *Mahmal*. This decorative camel litter once carried Ayyub's widow on her pilgrimage, but thereafter it symbolized rather than signified the sultan's participation. Islamic pageantry is still manifest during the **Moulid of Sidi Ali al-Bayoumi**, in early October, when the Rifai brotherhood parades behind its mounted sheikh with scarlet banners flying. The procession starts from El-Hussein, passes through the Bab al-Futuh and north along Sharia Husseiniya, where locals bombard the sheikh and his red-turbanned followers with huge sweets called *arwah*.

From Al-Hakim's Mosque, you can gain admission to a **prison** in the dark interior of the **Northern Walls**, whose custodian will point out archers' slits and bombardiers' apertures, shafts for pouring boiling oil onto enemies entering through the Bab al-Futuh below, and bits of pharaonic masonry (featuring Ramses II's cartouche and a hippo) filched from Memphis, striking matches if you haven't brought a torch. The ceiling of the 200-metre tunnel is vaulted, which allowed mounted guards passage through. At its end lies a grim and cavernous judgement room where the condemned, if found guilty, were hanged immediately, their corpses unceremoniously dumped through a hole in the floor, into the waters of the moat.

Erected in 1087 to replace the original mud-brick ramparts of Fatimid Al-Qahira, the walls were intended to rebuff the Seljuk Turks, but never put to the test, although they later provided a barracks for Napoleonic, and then British, grenadiers. The French attempted to rename the bastions of Bab al-Futuh and the next gate along, **Bab al-Nasr** (Gate of Victory), and titles such as "Tour Julien" and "Tour Pascal" are still inscribed on them. Bab al-Nasr can be reached, like Bab al-Futuh, from the roof of Al-Hakim's Mosque. The gate's inscription – "No deity but Allah; Mohammed is the Prophet of God" – includes a defiant Shi'ite addition, "And Ali is the Deputy of God". It was after entering this gate in 1517 that the victorious Ottoman sultan Selim the Grim had eight hundred Mamlukes decapitated, and their heads strung on ropes on Gezira Island. Directly opposite the gate lies **Bab al-Nasr Cemetery**, nowadays so overbuilt with houses that you can hardly see the tombs. At the top end of Haret al-Birkhader is a primitive glass factory where they hand-blow Muski glass.

From Bab al-Nasr you could catch a taxi or walk 1500m east, following the Walls and then Sharia Galal, to reach Barquq's complex in the Northern Cemetery (see p.173). Alternatively, minibus #10 runs from here in one direction to Dirasa, and the other way to Midan Ramses via the Mosque of Beybars (see p.204) and Midan Ataba.

Heading back along Sharia Gamaliya

Re-entering Islamic Cairo along Sharia Bab al-Nasr you pass into **El-Gamaliya**, whose name derives from the old camel road, Sharia Gamaliya, off which the quarter's alleys run; in one of them, Nobel prize-winning author Naguib Mahfouz was born in 1911. Immediately to your right stands the sturdy fifteenth-century caravanserai or **Wikala of Qaitbey**, currently undergoing restoration. Such caravanserais naturally clustered near the city gates, and the facades of three more *wikalas* (the last reduced to a mere portal) are visible beyond a small domed mausoleum on the other side of Sharia Gamaliya.

Beyond these *wikalas* stands the **Khanqah of Beybars al-Gashankir**, with its unmistakably bulbous dome and stumpy minaret (daily 11am–9pm; entry free but *baksheesh* expected). Founded in 1310, and thus the oldest Sufi monastery in Cairo, the *khanqah* is entered via a "baffled" corridor that excludes street noises from the inner courtyard. Without tiles or mosaics, the courtyard escapes severity by the variety of its windows: ribbed, S-curved or keel-arched in styles derived from the Fatimid era. Al-Gashankir's tomb (off the corridor) is spectacular by comparison, with sunbeams falling through stained glass onto marbled walls inset with radiating polygons, and his cenotaph within its ebony *mashrabiya* cage. Sultan for one year only, Beybars was dubbed *Al-Gashankir* (the Taster) to distinguish him from Beybars al-Bunduqdari (the Crossbowman), a mightier predecessor.

The next street on the left is Darb al-Asfur (see p.145), which starts opposite the *khanqah*. The little building on the corner, **Qitus**, is a *sabil* built in 1630 and, like the rest of the street, now lovingly restored. Otherwise, continue south along Sharia Gamaliya for 100m, past a ruined *wikala*, a fifteenth-century mosque built above shops (whose rent finances the mosque's maintenance), and then another mosque. Immediately after this, turn left into Qasr el-Shook, an alleyway that bends left around a high stone wall to reach the **Musafirkhana Palace**. Though semi-derelict and undergoing slow restoration, this eighteenth-century mansion (where Khedive Ismail was born) retains beautiful *mashrabiyas*, decorative ceilings, a fountain in the reception hall, and a peaceful atmosphere rarely disturbed by visitors. Though still closed to the public at the time of writing, the custodian may let you in for a small tip if you can locate him.

Returning to the main street, you'll find that it narrows and forks as it runs south. Precise directions are difficult, but by turning right at one fork and passing through a medieval-looking gate, you should emerge onto a square with shops selling scrap metal and weighing machines, behind the El-Hussein Mosque.

Between Al-Azhar and the Bab Zwayla

Some of the most arresting sights in Islamic Cairo cluster between **Al-Azhar Mosque** and the medieval gate known as the **Bab Zwayla** – a fairly brief itinerary (20–60min) that can be followed in either direction. We've described the sequence of places starting from Al-Azhar and finishing at the gate, but you could equally well start at the Bab Zwayla (a short walk from the Islamic Art Museum) and work north from there. Be aware that this section of the old city, and particularly the area around the Al-Ghuri complex, is currently infested with **touts** (see p.123), who aim to steer or follow you into shops so as to garner a commission on anything you buy.

Bab Zwayla is also the starting point for **longer walking tours** of the Qasaba and Darb al-Ahmar, winding up beneath the Citadel, as described in the section following; so you could also take this itinerary in reverse from there.

The Wikala, Mosque-Madrassa and Mausoleum of Al-Ghuri

The **Wikala of Al-Ghuri** is Cairo's best-preserved merchants' hostel (twenty such squatted or derelict structures remain, out of the 200 active in 1835). Its upstairs rooms have been converted into artists' studios (officially closed for restoration at time of writing, though the custodian will show you around for a small consideration). With its stables and lock-ups beneath tiers of spartan rooms, the *wikala* is uncompromisingly functional, yet the rhythm of *ablaq* (striped) arches muted by the sharp verticals of shutters, and the severe masonry lightened by *mashrabiyas* and a graceful fountain, achieves elegance.

Although it was built (in 1505) just as the new Cape route to the East Indies was diminishing Cairo's role as a spice entrepôt, the *wikala* doubtless witnessed the kind of scenes described in *The Arabian Nightmare*:

The Muhtasib stood immovable, flanked by two huge Turks who carried lanterns on great staves. Black slaves staggered under trunks of merchandise that were being fought over. A party of men were unsuccessfully trying to persuade a camel to leave by the same gate that it had come in by. A sheep was being roasted in the centre of the compound.

Located on a side street off Sharia al-Azhar, the *wikala* can be reached by turning left on leaving the Mosque of Al-Azhar, then following the alley round past a market; or you can visit it after seeing the **Ghuriya** – the mausoleum and mosque-madrassa of Al-Ghuri. Boldly striped in buff and white, this pair of buildings forms a set piece at the junction of Sharia al-Muizz and the Al-

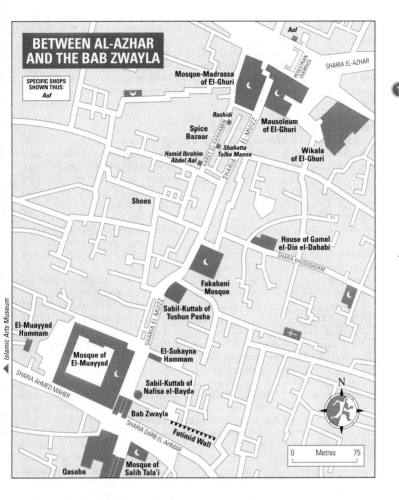

BETWEEN AL-AZHAR
AND THE BAB ZWAYLA

SPECIFIC SHOPS
SHOWN THUS:
Auf

Auf

SHARIA EL-AZHAR

PEDESTRIAN OVERPASS

Mosque-Madrassa
of El-Ghuri

Rashidi

Spice
Bazaar

Mausoleum
of El-Ghuri

Shahatta
Talba Manna

Hamid Ibrahim
Abdel Aal

Wikala
of El-Ghuri

HARET EL-FAHAMIN

SHARIA EL-MUIZZ

Shoes

House of Gamal
el-Din el-Dahabi

SHARIA KHUSHQADAM

Fakahani
Mosque

SHARIA EL-MUIZZ

Sabil-Kuttab of
Tushun Pasha

El-Muayyad
Hammam

El-Sukayna
Hammam

Mosque of
El-Muayyad

Islamic Arts Museum

SHARIA AHMED MAHER

Sabil-Kuttab of
Nafisa el-Bayda

Bab Zwayla

N

SHARIA DARB EL-AHMAR

Fatimid Wall

0   Metres   75

Qasaba

Mosque of
Salih Tala'i

CAIRO AND THE PYRAMIDS | Between Al-Azhar and the Bab Zwayla

Azhar high road, plainly visible from the footbridge. To the right (west) of the
bridge stands the **Mosque-Madrassa**, now restored to its full glory. The
rooftop offers glimpses of the Spice Bazaar and a grand view of the neighbourhood – the door is diagonally opposite the entrance to the main part of
the mosque, but is often closed, so you may have to ask a custodian for access.
Across the way is Al-Ghuri's domed **Mausoleum** (closed for restoration) and
the Al-Ghuri Palace, which has become an adult educational centre. Currently
closed for restoration, it held an exhibition area and a theatre with a splendid
ceiling, where performances by whirling dervishes were held, though these
have temporarily moved to the Citadel (see p.256).

Sixty years old when he became the penultimate Mamluke sultan in 1500,
Qansuh al-Ghuri remained vigorous into his seventies, playing polo, writing
poetry and discoursing with Sufis – not forgetting traditional pursuits like
building, intrigue and arbitrary justice. Though not averse to filching marble
for his mosque-madrassa, Al-Ghuri wished to be remembered for his strict

149

enforcement of Koranic precepts: sentencing a dervish accused of "atheism, sorcery, and the use of milk for his ablutions and intimate toilet" to be paraded naked on a camel, and then hanged; and berating his judges for laxity. Al-Ghuri was killed in 1516 fighting the Turks outside Aleppo; his body was never found and his intended tomb was occupied by his luckless successor, Tumanbey (see below). Gamal al-Ghitani's novel *Zayni Barakat* is a fictionalized account of this Mamluke twilight.

Towards the Bab Zwayla

In olden times the **Sharia al-Muizz**, the street between the Ghuriya buildings, was roofed over, forming the Silk Bazaar where carpets were sold, the subject of a famous drawing by David Roberts. Nowadays, shops along here sell mostly household goods, making fewer concessions to tourism than Khan el-Khalili. At the time of writing, the last fez★ workshop in Cairo was situated on the right, 75m past Al-Ghuri's Mosque, kept just alive by sales to five-star hotels and tourists. The street is named after the conquering Fatimid khalif and it was the chief thoroughfare of Islamic Cairo, running from the Northern Gates down towards the Citadel, and meeting another main road – the Darb al-Ahmar – at the Bab Zwayla. Traditionally, each stretch of Al-Muizz had its own name, usually derived from the merchandise sold there.

Roughly 200m down the street you'll find the "Fruit Seller" or **Fakahani Mosque**, whose arabesque-panelled doors are all that remain of the twelfth-century original after its reconstruction in 1735. The nearby **House of Gamal al-Din al-Dahabi**, at no.6 Sharia Khushqadan (aka "Haret Hoche Kadam"), was the home of seventeenth-century Cairo's foremost gold merchant. Its magnificent interior is under restoration but will eventually open to the public.

South of the Fakahani Mosque, Sharia al-Muizz curves around the Rococo facade of the **Sabil-Kuttab of Tusun Pasha**, adorned with wrought-iron sunbursts, garlands and fronds. Shortly afterwards the street passes between two buildings structurally adjacent to the Bab Zwayla, whose formidable outline dominates the view ahead. To your left, the wall of a *mashrabiya*-fronted *wikala* is preceded by an unobtrusive door (next to a jewellers' shop) that leads into the eighteenth-century **as-Sukanya Hammam**. The fires that heat the water for this grubby men's bathhouse are also used to cook *fuul madammas* (broad beans) for the neighbourhood's breakfast. The traditional extra allure of such baths was described by Flaubert in 1839: "You reserve the bath for yourself (five francs including masseurs, pipe, coffee, sheet and towel) and you skewer your lad in one of the rooms." Today, such practices continue more furtively, with none of Flaubert's "naked *kellaas* … turning you over like embalmers preparing you for the tomb" (see "Hammams", p.258), although many bathhouses still double as gay brothels (see "Hammams", p.258).

Across the way, the **Mosque of Al-Muayyad** – also known as the "Red Mosque" for the colour of its exterior – occupies the site of a prison where its founder was once incarcerated for plotting against Sultan Barquq. Plagued by lice and fleas, he vowed to transform it into a "saintly place for the education of scholars" once he came to power. When he did, 40,000 dinars were dutifully lavished on the mosque's construction (1415–22).

★ The **fez**, called a *tarboush* in Egypt, was originally a mark of Ottoman allegiance, which came to represent the secular, Westernized *effendi*, as opposed to the turbaned traditionalist. Still later, the *tarboush* was stigmatized as a badge of the *ancien régime* that the Nasserite revolution aimed to dispossess. Waiters and entertainers are the main wearers nowadays, but demand is so small that the craft of fez-making seems likely to perish.

The building is entered via a nine-tiered stalactite portal with a red-and-turquoise geometric frame around its bronze door. Off the vestibule lies a mausoleum where Al-Muayyad and his son are buried in befittingly sized cenotaphs. The kufic inscription on Al-Muayyad's reads: "But the god-fearing shall be amidst gardens and fountains: Enter you them, in peace and security" – which seems appropriate for the mosque's courtyard, half filled with palms and open to the sky. Beneath the roofed section a thickly carpeted sanctuary precedes the *qibla* wall, niched and patterned with polychrome marble and mosaic. But best of all is the **view** from one of the minarets, built atop the turrets of Bab Zwayla (*baksheesh* expected, though you may be asked to pay this as an extra £E4 charge on entry).

The Bab Zwayla

The Al-Muayyad's minarets, added four hundred years after the turrets were built, make **Bab Zwayla** look far mightier than the Northern Gates. The gate itself was constructed when the Fatimid city's defences (including sixty gates) were reinforced during the 1090s, using Anatolian or Mesopotamian Christian architects and Egyptian labour. Originally the main south gate, Bab Zwayla later became a central point in the Mamluke city, which had outgrown the Fatimid walls and pushed up against Salah al-Din's extensions. Nevertheless, the practice of barring the gates each night continued well into the nineteenth century, maintaining a city within a city. There's a strikingly medieval passage just on the north side of the gate, but the full awesomeness of the Bab itself is best seen from the south side. Note the barbells high up on the western gate-tower: a relic of medieval keep-fit enthusiasts.

The gate was named after Fatimid mercenaries of the Berber al-Zwayla tribe, quartered nearby, whom the Mamlukes displaced. Through the centuries it was the point of departure for caravans to Mecca and the source of the drum rolls that greeted the arrival of senior "Amirs of One Hundred". Dancers and snake charmers also performed here, and from the fifteenth century onwards punishments provided another spectacle. Dishonest merchants might be hung from hooks or ropes; garrotting, beheading or impalement were favoured for common criminals; while losers in the Mamluke power struggles were often nailed to the doors. It was here that Tumanbey, the last Mamluke sultan, was hanged in 1517, after a vast crowd had recited the *Fatah* and the rope had broken twice before his neck did. However, Bab Zwayla's reputation was subsequently redeemed by its association with Mitwalli al-Qutb, a miracle-working local saint said to manifest himself to the faithful as a gleam of light within the gatehouse.

A whole slew of places to the south of the Bab are covered by the next itinerary (see p.155), but it's worth mentioning an alternative: namely, heading westwards along Sharia Ahmed Maher **towards the Islamic Art Museum** (see below). En route you'll pass stalls selling waterpipes and braziers, piles of logs destined for the **Al-Muayyad Hammam** (another dubious men's bathhouse, see p.258), a nineteenth-century *sabil-kuttab* and a fifteenth-century mosque. It's a ten-minute walk or a short minibus ride (#68) to the museum. The neighbourhood between Bab Zwayla and the Abdin district is known as the **Bab el-Khalq quarter**, after a long-since-vanished medieval gate. On your right off Sharia Ahmed Maher, just before Sharia Bur Said (the entrance to the museum is off this street), is Derb es-Saada, a street of carpenters' workshops, which backs onto a local remand prison. Relatives of the inmates can often be seen on unofficial visits, lining the street and calling up to the windows of the cells.

The Museum of Islamic Art

Try to visit the **Museum of Islamic Art** (daily 9am–3pm, Friday closed for prayer: May–Sept 12.30–2pm, Oct–Apr 11.30am–1pm; £E16, students £E8, camera £E10, video £E200) midway through exploring Islamic Cairo, since the historic architecture lends meaning to the museum's artefacts, which, in turn, enhance your appreciation of the old city. It was the ruinous state of many of its mosques and mansions that impelled Khedive Tewfiq and the historians Herz and Cresswell to establish an Islamic collection in 1880. Pieces were stored in Al-Hakim's Mosque until 1902, when a museum was created on the ground floor of the imposing neo–Mamluke *Dar al-Kutub* (National Library) at the junction of Bur Said and Qalaa streets, 600m west of the Bab Zwayla (see map on p.149).

The museum is entered from Sharia Bur Said via its garden door, which messes up the already confusing arrangement of **exhibits** by period and medium. To view them in order, walk straight through rooms 7, 10, 4B and 2 (which contain some of the finest work) and begin with Room 1. However, the cool, deserted halls tempt one to wander through the collection, which can be seen in around ninety minutes. Although the rooms are numbered, the numbers are nowhere displayed, so you will have to work them out from the plan.

Because Sunni Muslims extended the Koranic strictures against idolatry to any images of humans or animals, these are largely absent. Instead of paintings and statues, there are exquisite designs based on geometry, Islamic symbolism, plant motifs and Arabic calligraphy – a totally different aesthetic. You'll also notice that dates are given as *AH* – After the Hegira (Mohammed's flight from Mecca) – the starting point of Islamic chronology (622 AD by Western reckoning).

Touring the museum

Assuming you proceed through the central halls without getting sidetracked by the marvellous woodwork and fountains, the exhibition starts with some of the museum's most **recent acquisitions** in **Room 1**. Surrounded by Ottoman mosaics of polychrome marble, a single display case in **Room 2** contains objects from the **Umayyad period** (661–750). Among them is a bronze ewer with a spout in the form of a crowing cockerel, which probably belonged to the last Umayyad khalif of the Arab Empire, Marwan II, who was slain near Abu Sir. On his death, the Ummayads were succeeded by the Abbasid dynasty, who moved the capital of the khalifate from Damascus to Baghdad.

Brassware from the **Abbassid** period in **Room 3** includes the figure of a deer, not an animal much associated with the Middle East. Also here are ninth- and tenth-century Persian imitations of Chinese ceramics, showing how Chinese art influenced the Islamic world. The examples of **stucco** on the walls here show how it was developed into a high art form under the Abbassids, and especially in Iraq. From being deeply cut and crisply textured with relatively naturalistic vines and acanthus scrolls, stucco panels became increasingly abstract and flowing, no longer carved but moulded. Meanwhile under **Tulunid** rule in Egypt (868–905), three different styles from Samarra were also imitated in wood; compare the stucco panels with the woodwork from Al-Qitai.

Passing through a huge door from Sultan Qalaoun's *Maristan* into **Room 4**, you enter the **Fatimid era** (969–1171). As Shi'ites, the Fatimids had no doctrinal objection to depicting animals and birds (a theme popular amongst their co-religionists in Persia), as attested by **panels from the Western Palace**. Also exhibited are inlaid ivory and jewellery, rock crystal, painted **glassware**, and early **lustre ware** ceramics from Fustat. On the southern wall, **frescoes** from a Fustat bathhouse depict people and animals, not yet taboo at this time in Islamic art.

Room 4B (part of the main hall) is a lovely composite of Mamluke columns, an Ottoman fountain and floor, and intricate *mashrabiya* work from the **Ayyubid** period (1171–1250).

From Room 4, you enter **Room 5** under a collection of Ottoman-period stained-glass "moon windows" set in open plasterwork. Also in the doorway (on the right), a stone medallion once embedded in the wall of a building depicts a two-headed eagle and fire-breathing bull amongst a confusion of animal forms that all seem to belong to one body. The room itself covers the **Mamluke period** (1250–1517) and centres upon a lovely sunken mosaic fountain. Round about are displayed **mosque lamps** and stucco *mihrabs*; woven and printed textiles of linen and cotton; inlaid metalwork, polychrome pottery and a wooden **cenotaph from the El-Hussein Mosque**. At the far end of the room is a wooden door from the Mosque of Sultan Ayyub, bearing square *kufic* and cursive *naskhi* inscriptions. The **glassware** here is noticeably more sophisticated, painted with ornate calligraphy.

A pair of doors from the Al-Azhar Mosque leads into **Room 6**, the first of three rooms devoted to **woodwork**, whose evolution paralleled that of stuccos. The deeply incised, naturalistic forms of Umayyad woodcarving gave way to interlocking arches and concentric circles under the Abbassids, followed by bevelled, stylized birds and animals in Tulunid times. Gradually confined to small areas during the Fatimid era, figures were then progressively simplified into arabesques by Ayyubid craftsmen. However, representational art could still be found under the early Mamlukes, as evinced by a **frieze from Qalaoun's Maristan**, which shows hunting, music and dancing. Also featured in Room 6 are carved panels from the Western Palace, the original *mihrab* from Saiyida Ruqayya's Mashrad, and a portable prayer niche for use on military campaigns.

Room 7, opposite the entrance, contains a series of *mashrabiyas*, and a high-lighted **object of the month**. Hanging from the ceilings of rooms 7 to 11 are examples of the brass lanterns traditionally hung in mosques, though out of use in these days of electricity.

Room 8's treasures include three wooden **minbars** (pulpits), a panelled ceiling and a case of pieces originally inlaid in the geometric designs of *minbars*, ceilings, doors and furniture. The objects in the room's other display cases include wooden combs, ivory boxes, and a beautiful bone-inlaid panel depicting a hawk attacking a hare. Among the wooden panels on the wall, a frieze in Hebrew commemorates the building of a synagogue in the twelfth century by one Ibrahim el-Amshati.

Wooden panels overspill into **Room 9**, where caskets inlaid with ivory and mother-of-pearl rather show up the shoddy workmanship of the goods nowadays sold to tourists in the *khan*. Bronze **mirrors** and brass lamps inaugurate the museum's **metalwork** section, but the room's most striking pieces are a Persian brass candlestick in the form of two intertwined snakes and, among the **figurines** by the west wall, a little man on a horse saying "Look, no hands!". What looks like a horse-headed cigar-cutter in the same case is in fact a chopper for betel nut, a stimulant much used in India and Southeast Asia, but not in the Middle East.

Room 10, next door, reflects Ottoman tastes in interior design. Beneath an **exquisitely coffered ceiling**, guests could socialize around a graceful fountain, secretly overlooked by the women of the household. The furnishings in here date from the seventeenth and eighteenth centuries.

From Mosul in Iraq came the technique of inlaying copper or silver into bronze, which was to characterize Egyptian **metalwork**. A brass-plated door from the Mosque of Salih Tala'i stands at the entrance to **Room 11**. Inside you'll find candlesticks and caskets; incense burners inlaid with gold and silver (some with Christian symbols); a fourteenth-century hand-warmer; and a case of astrolabes, used by Muslim navigators.

Room 12 contains a fraction of the Mamluke **Armoury** (most of which was taken to Istanbul by Selim the Grim). Case 7, on the left of the door to Room 11, holds the swords of Mehmet II and Suleyman the Magnificent (the respective conquerors of Constantinople and the Balkans). Daggers on the west wall include one with an exquisite enamelled Persian scabbard of the fifteenth or sixteenth century.

Room 13 takes us back to the Fatimid period, with a display of lustreware decorated with people and animals in the northeasterly of the room's four main display cases. The relatively primitive nature of this decoration is shown up by the metallic blue Mina'i ware in the southwest case. In the northwest case, and on the west wall, tiny glass vessels are the ancestors of today's ornate perfume bottles.

Room 14 contains more ceramics, mainly Persian, including blue wall-tiles. Ceramics in **Room 15** include tiles found at Fustat that originated in Tunisia, Andalusia and Christian Europe, showing the extent of the city's commercial reach, and including blue Delft tiles from Holland. Also here are **stone moulds** used for casting metal ornaments.

The dominant exhibit in **Room 16** is a blue-tiled nineteenth-century **Turkish fireplace**. At the southern end of the room, a section of an old **kuttab** (Koranic school) from Rosetta incorporates a niche for the teacher to sit beneath its *murqana*'d ceiling. Among the ceramics, notice the *ahlaq* (chokes) that were inserted in the necks of Fatimid water jars to regulate their flow, fretted with bird, animal and calligraphic motifs. The room also contains stucco *mihrabs* and nineteenth-century Turkish prayer rugs. A diversion from Room 16 takes you down a passage whose walls are decked with stone inscriptions, to **Room 16B**, used to display coins, weights, medals and glass seals, but currently closed.

At the museum's southern end, **Room 19** showcases **calligraphy and bookbinding**, including Persian and Indian illustrated manuscripts, but primacy is accorded to the word of God, with numerous medieval Korans from the collection of King Farouk. The first mass-produced, totally standardized Korans were made in Egypt following Napoleon's introduction of the printing press; Cairo is still the main publishing centre of the Arab world.

Room 20 is stuffed with **Ottoman material**, including seventeenth- and eighteenth-century wall-tiles depicting the Kaaba at Mecca, Islam's holiest site, and the Prophet's Mosque at Medina, Mohammed's burial place. Among the room's less pious offerings is a beautifully made *sheesha* pipe from Istanbul.

Room 21 is devoted to Egyptian **glass**. Various techniques perfected in ancient times continued to be used; lustreware (a Fatimid speciality) and enamelled glass were the chief innovations in the Islamic period. Among the mosque lamps and eighth- to fourteenth-century perfume jars, a large hour-glass stands out as the most prominent exhibit.

Amongst the **Persian objects** of the ninth to seventeenth centuries in **Room 22** are three ceramic figurines of animals: a camel with a litter on its back by the west wall and a lion by the east wall, both in cobalt blue; plus, by the east wall, a hoopoe glazed in turquoise.

Like the neighbouring *metkhal* (entrance hall), **Room 23** is used for **temporary exhibitions**.

Between the Bab Zwayla and the Citadel

There are two basic walking **routes between Bab Zwayla and the Citadel**: via the Qasaba, Sharia al-Muizz and Sharia Qalaa; or following the old **Darb al-Ahmar** (after which this quarter of Islamic Cairo is named). It's possible to get the best of both worlds by combining the Darb al-Ahmar with a detour into the **Qasaba** and **Saddlemakers Bazaar**, located on the other route: a total distance of about 1500m. Assuming you're **starting from the Bab Zwayla** as in the itinerary below, it's logical to visit the Qasaba before embarking on the Darb al-Ahmar; whereas the reverse holds true if you're **coming from the Citadel**. Starting with the "Blue Mosque" of Aqsunqur on Sharia Bab al-Wazir (the Citadel end of Darb al-Ahmar), you can backtrack through the text from there.

From the Bab Zwayla into the Qasaba

Emerging from the Bab Zwayla, you'll see a cluster of Islamic monuments across the street, which is often flooded by burst water mains. On the right-hand corner stands a Sufi establishment, the **Zawiya of Farag ibn Barquq** (currently closed for restoration), whose inlaid marble lintels and *ablaq* panels may be hidden by stalls. Opposite the *zawiya*, the **Mosque of Salih Tala'i** withdraws behind an elegant portico with five keel arches – a unique architectural feature. The shops around its base (whose rents contributed to the mosque's upkeep) were once at street level, but this has risen well over a metre since the mosque was built in 1408. The last of Cairo's Fatimid mosques, the building shows an assured use of the motifs that were first employed on the Mosque of Al-Aqmar: ribbed and cusped arches and panels, carved tie beams and rosettes. Notice the capitals, plundered from pre-Islamic buildings, and the "floriated kufic" script around the arches.

Straight ahead lies the **Qasaba**, where colourful fabrics, appliqué and leather-work are piled in dens ranked either side of a gloomy, lofty passageway. Erected by Ridwan Bey in 1650, this is one of the best-preserved examples of a covered market left in Cairo. It is popularly known as the *Khiyamiyya*, or

BETWEEN BAB ZWAYLA
AND THE CITADEL

0   Metres   100

Midan Ataba

Zawiya of
Farag ibn
Barqaq

Bab
Zwayla

Qasaba

Mosque of
Salih Tala'i

Zawiya of
Radwan Bey

Tentmakers' Bazaar

Palace of
Radwan Bey

Mosque of
Mahmoud el-Kurdi

Mosque of
Qajamas el-Ishaqi

Mosque of
Inal el-Atabaki

DARB EL-AHMAR

Mosque of
Gani Bak

Mosque of
el-Maridani

Saddlemakers'
Bazaar

Beit
el-Razzaz

Takiya of
Suleyman

Madrassa of Umm
Sultan Sha'ban

Hammam
Bashtak

'Blue' Mosque
of Aqsunqur

Sabil-Kuttab of
Ruqayya Dudu

Bab el-Wazir
Cemetery

Madrassa of
al-Yusufi

BAB EL-WAZIR

Rifai
Mosque

Mosque of
Sultan Hassan

Mahmudiyya
Mosque

MIDAN
SALAH EL-DIN

THE CITADEL

SHARIA EL-MU'IZZ

BOULEVARD MOHAMMED ALI

SHARIA EL-MARIDANI

SHARIA TABBANA

SHARIA DARB EL-AHMAR

SHARIA QALAA

SHARIA SOUK ES-SILAH

SHARIA TABBANA

SHARIA BAB EL-WAZIR

SHARIA BAB EL-GADID

'Walls of Salah el-Din'

Mosque of Aslam al-Silander

N

156

Tentmakers Bazaar, as colourful printed fabrics are used here to make tents for moulids and weddings, and to screen unsightly building work – a big improvement on tarpaulins. Printed fabric is sold by the metre, quite cheaply; labour-intensive appliqué work is much pricier (see "Shopping", p.264).

Beyond the Qasaba

Emerging from the southern end of the Qasaba, **Sharia al-Muizz** extends its path between two mosques and the facade of Ridwan Bey's former palace, beyond which the monuments thin out as vegetable stalls and butchers congest the narrow street – some of which is still supported by scaffolding, following earthquake damage in 1991. By Mamluke times most of the older quarters here were semi-derelict, merging into the "Tartar Ruins" near the Citadel. The Tartars, recruited by Sultan Kitbugha (1296–96), were despised by other Mamlukes as horse-eaters, and billeted in a quarter that's long since disappeared. About 150m on you'll pass the **Mosque of Gani Bak**, a protégé of Sultan Barsbey, who was poisoned by rivals at the age of twenty-five. Beyond, a few stalls selling donkey- and camel-wear constitute what remains of the *Souk es-Surugiyyah*, or **Saddlemakers Bazaar**, formerly the centre of Cairo's leather industry.

Assuming you don't turn back here to pursue the Darb al-Ahmar, it's a fairly mundane 350-metre walk to Al-Muizz's junction with **Sharia Qalaa**. The Sultan Hassan and Rifai mosques below the Citadel are plainly visible at the boulevard's southern end, 300m away. Alternatively, use bus services in the opposite direction to reach the Islamic Arts Museum, 1km up Sharia Qalaa. Some of the buses continue on to Midan Ataba, others to Abdin or Al-Azhar.

Adventurous types might consider visiting the **Hammam Bashtak** bathhouse (women 10am–5pm, men 6pm–8am), deep in the Darb al-Ahmar quarter. To get there, follow the backstreet running eastwards behind the Takiya of Suleyman, a block before Al-Muizz's junction with Sharia Qalaa. After 250m it reaches a square, where you'll recognize the baths on the western side by their elaborate portal, whose ribbed keel arch bears the napkin symbol of a *jamdar* or "Master of Robes". In Mamluke society, this position ranked below the "Men of the Sword" (cabinet ministers, chosen from the Amirs of One Hundred), but was on a par with the sultan's Taster, Cup-Bearer, Slipper-Holder and Polo-Stick Keeper. Several Mamlukes who became sultans included their former rank (or slave price) among their titles. Nowadays the bath serves people from the neighbourhood whose own tenements lack washing facilities.

To reach the Citadel from the hammam, walk 300m down **Sharia Souk es-Silah** (formerly the Weapons Bazaar, now a secondhand ballbearings market), past the neglected gingerbread facade of the **Sabil-Kuttab of Ruqayya Dudu** at no.41, and then the **Madrassa of al-Yusufi**, whose founder was a Cup-Bearer.

Along the Darb al-Ahmar

An alternative, more picturesque route towards the Citadel follows the "Red Road", or **Darb al-Ahmar**. Originally a cemetery beyond the southern walls of the Fatimid city, this quarter became a fashionable residential area in the fourteenth century, as Al-Nasir developed the Citadel. The thoroughfare acquired its present name in 1805, when Mohammed Ali tricked the Mamlukes into staging a coup before slaughtering them. Stuffed with straw, their heads were sent to Constantinople as a sign of his power; six years later the surviving Mamlukes fell for another ruse, and were massacred on the Citadel (see below, p.161).

Start by walking 150m east from Salih Tila'i's Mosque near the Bab Zwayla. On the corner where the Darb turns south, the **Mosque of Qajmas al-Ishaqi** looms over workshops sunk beneath street level. Its founder's blazon – a napkin, penbox, cup and horn of plenty – appears on the knots of the window grilles, indicating the various positions that Qajmas held under Sultan Qaitbey. A marble panel with swirling leaf forms in red, black and white surmounts the entrance to a vestibule with a gilded ceiling; left off this is the mosque itself. Notice the sinuous decorations on the *mihrab* (incised grooves filled with red paste or bitumen) and the fine panelling on the floor near the *qibla* wall (ask the custodian to lift a mat). Best of all are the stained-glass windows in the tomb chamber occupied by one Abu Hurayba. A raised passage connects the mosque with a *sabil-kuttab* across the street; both were built in the 1480s.

A short detour: Al-Silahdar's Mosque

If you're not pushed for time, consider detouring off the Darb to visit the **Mosque of Aslam al-Silahdar**. From Qajmas's Mosque, walk through the tunnel around the side and on past a shrine where the street forks (either one will do); Al-Silahdar's Mosque lies 250m ahead. The marble panel outside is typical of exterior decoration during the Bahri Mamluke period; inside, the layout is that of a cruciform **madrassa**. Students used to live in rooms above the north and south *liwans*, behind an ornate facade of stucco mouldings and screened windows. The mosque's founder was a Qipchak Mamluke who lost his position as Swordbearer after Sultan al-Nasir believed rumours spread by his enemies, and imprisoned him, only to reinstate Aslam as *silahdar* (swordbearer) six years later. To return to the Darb, either retrace your steps or take the street running southwest off the square, which joins the Darb further south, beyond Al-Maridani's Mosque.

South along the Darb Al-Ahmar

South from the Qajmas Mosque, the Darb al-Ahmar passes the **Mosque of Al-Maridani**, built in 1340 and still a peaceful retreat from the streets. The mosque is usually entered via its northern portal, offset by a stalactite frieze with complex patterns of joggled voussoirs and *ablaq* panels. Inside, a splendid *mashrabiya* screen separates the open courtyard from the *qibla riwaq*, whose stained-glass windows and variegated columns (Mamluke, pre-Islamic and pharaonic) can be glimpsed through the lattice. Because it was economical with wood, and minimized the effect of warping in a hot, dry climate, *mashrabiya*-work was an ideal technique for Egyptian craftsmen. Architecturally speaking, the minaret marks the replacement of the Ayyubid "pepperpot" finial by a small dome on pillars, which became the hallmark of Mamluke minarets. Below the dome and above the *minbar*, arboreal forms in stucco may allude to the Koranic verse, "A good word is as a good tree – its roots firm, its branches in heaven".

Leaving via the southern entrance, you'll need to turn left to rejoin the Darb – or **Sharia Tabbana** as it's called at this point. Roughly 200m on, past a small Turkish mosque, stands the hulking **Madrassa of Umm Sultan Sha'ban**. *Umm* (Mother of) Sha'ban was the concubine of a son of Al-Nasir, whose own son erected the madrassa (1368–69) as a gesture of gratitude after he became sultan at the age of ten; murdered in 1376, he preceded her to the grave and was buried here since his own madrassa was unfinished. A wealth of *murqanas* and *ablaq* rims the entrance, which is flanked by a *sabil* and a drinking trough. Watering animals was meritorious in the eyes of Islam; the Prophet himself had seen a prostitute give water to a thirsty dog, and promised her, "For this action you shall enter paradise"; but if you want to enter the mosque, you'll have to find the guardian, which is easier said than done. Behind it, and entered by the neighbouring doorway (no.56), lurks the **Beit al-Razzaz**, a rambling, derelict palace which the Supreme Council for Antiquities is currently restoring in conjunction with the American Research Center.

The Blue Mosque

Further along the street, now called **Sharia Bab al-Wazir** after the Gate of the Vizier that once stood here, lies the **"Blue Mosque"** or **Mosque of Aqsunqur**, which is directly accessible via #68 minibus from Midan Ramses and the Bab Zwayla, or #75 from Midan Tahir, but was closed for restoration at last check. When originally built in 1347, the mosque was plainer, its *ablaq* arches framing a *sahn*, now battered and dusty, with a palm tree and chirping birds. The Iznik-style tiles (imported from Turkey or Syria) were added in the 1650s by Ibrahim Agha, who usurped and redecorated the fourteenth-century mosque. The indigo and turquoise tiles on the *qibla* wall – with cypresses, tulips and other floral motifs either side of the magnificently inlaid *mihrab* – were added at the same time. Along with similar tiles around the tomb of Ibrahim Agha in the mosque's southwest corner, they were probably made in Damascus, and explain the mosque's name and its popularity with tourists.

The marble *minbar*, inlaid with salmon, plum, green and grey stone is from the original building. The recently restored circular minaret, also original, affords a superb **view** of the Citadel, and on a clear day you can even make out the Pyramids on the far side of the city.

The mosque's founder, Shams al-Din Aqsunqur, intrigued against the successors of Sultan al-Nasir, his father-in-law – whose son Al-Ashraf Kuchuk (Little One) was enthroned at the age of six, "reigned" five months, and was strangled by his brother three years later. The reign of Al-Kamil Sha'ban (not to be confused with Sha'ban II, who erected the madrassa) lasted a year, ending in a palace coup and the crowning of his brother-in-law, Muzaffar Hadji. Recalling how Aqsunqur had manipulated Kuchuk (who's buried just inside the mosque's entrance) and deftly organized the coup against Sha'ban, Muzaffar promptly had him garrotted.

From this mosque, Bab al-Wazir gradually slopes up to meet the approach road **to the Citadel**. If that's your destination, turn left and keep climbing.

The Citadel and around

The Citadel is the natural focus of a visit to Islamic Cairo; while the area just below it, around Midan Salah al-Din, features two of the city's greatest monuments – the **Sultan Hassan** and **Rifai mosques**. To do justice to these, and to the Citadel itself, you need a good half a day.

To reach the Citadel area, you can either catch a taxi from downtown (£E5–7), or a bus (see p.97 for bus routes) – if you've got the energy, it's also an interesting walk. Any of these approaches will leave you beneath the Citadel, either on Midan Salah al-Din or lower down behind the Sultan Hassan and Rifai mosques. Note, however, that the actual **entrance** to the Citadel is over a kilometre's walk from Midan Salah al-Din, which is where most Cairenes will assume you want to go if you just ask for the Citadel (*al-Qalaa* – usually pronounced "al-'Alaa").

Depending on how much time you have, you may only want to visit the Citadel, but it is well worth stopping in Midan Salah al-Din to take in the arresting mix of sounds and the views (see below). For information on moving on from the Citadel and connecting up with other walking itineraries, see p.164.

SHARIA QAL'AA · Rifai Mosque · Mosque of Gawhar Lak · Akhur Mosque · SHARIA BAB AL-WAZIR · BAB AL-WAZIR · SHARIA BAB AL-GADID · Mosque of Sultan Hassan · MIDAN SALAH AL-DIN · Bab al-Gadid (closed) · Mosque of Mahmudiyya · Bab al-Azab (closed) · LOWER ENCLOSURE (closed to public) · Police National Museum · British Prison Cells · Military Museum · Mosque of Suleyman Pasha · Tomb of Sheikh Mohammed al-Kahki · NORTHERN · Garden Museum · SHARIA SALAH AL-DIN · Qasr al-Ablaq (remains) · Mosque of Sultan al-Nasir · Bab al-Qullah · Carriage Museum · ENCLOSURE · Seized Museum · SHARIA SALAH AL-DIN · SOUTHERN · Mohammed Ali Mosque · ENCLOSURE · Yussef's Well · Bab al-Gabal · Burg Kurkilyan · Burg al-Turfa · Burg al-Matar · P · SHARIA SALAH SALEM · Muqattam Hills · Mosque of Ibn Tulun ▲ · N · Tourist Police · Al-Gawhera Palace · 0 Metres 200 · **THE CITADEL**

Midan Salah al-Din

Humdrum traffic islands and monumental grandeur meet beneath the Citadel on **Midan Salah al-Din**, where makeshift swings and colourful tents are pitched for local moulids. With an audience of lesser mosques on the sidelines, the scene is set for a confrontation of the square's two behemoths, given voice when the **muezzins** call. Both the **Rifai** and **Sultan Hassan mosques** have powerfully voiced muezzins whose duet echoes off the surrounding tenements. This amazing aural experience is best enjoyed seated in the **outdoor café** beside Sultan Hassan's Mosque; never mind that its tea is vastly overpriced. From this café vantage point you can survey both mosques, built so close as to create a knife-sharp, almost perpetually shadowed canyon between them. The dramatic angles and chiaroscuro, coupled with the great stalactite portal on this side of the Rifai, make this facade truly spectacular, although the view from the Citadel itself takes some beating. A few centuries ago, all this area would have been swarming with mounted Mamlukes, escorting the sultan to polo matches or prayers.

The Citadel

The Citadel (daily 8am–5pm; mosques closed Fri except for prayer; museums refuse entry 30min before closing; £E20, students £E10) presents the most dramatic feature of Cairo's skyline: a centuries-old bastion crowned by the needle-like minarets of the great Mosque of Mohammed Ali. The entrance at Bab al-Gabal is on the opposite side of the Citadel, a good kilometre's walk from Midan Salah al-Din, but can be reached by bus #416 or #755 from Midan Ramses, #755 from Tahrir, or #160 from Ataba, as well as *servees* microbuses from both Ramses and Ataba along Sharia Salah Selim.

The whole fortified complex was begun by **Salah al-Din**, the founder of the Ayyubid dynasty – known throughout Christendom as Saladin, the Crusaders' chivalrous foe. Salah al-Din's reign (1171–93) saw much fortification of the city, though it was his nephew, Al-Kamil, who developed the Citadel as a royal residence, later to be replaced by the palaces of Sultan al-Nasir.

The main features of the Citadel as it is today, however, are associated with **Mohammed Ali**, a worthy successor to the Mamlukes and Turks. In 1811 he feasted 470 leading Mamlukes in the Citadel palace, bade them farewell with honours, then had them ambushed in the sloping lane behind the **Bab al-Azab**, the locked gate (now closed to the public) opposite the Akhur Mosque. An oil painting in the Manial Palace on Roda Island depicts the apocryphal tale of a Mamluke who escaped by leaping the walls on his horse; in reality he survived by not attending the feast.

On entering the Citadel, you keep the wall to your right and follow it round into the southern courtyard of the **southern enclosure**, most of whose buildings are currently closed for restoration, among them the former **Mint**. Also in the enclosure are refreshments, toilets and a police post. A passage from the courtyard's north side leads through to the central courtyard; to the left of this passage, stairs lead up to the back of the Citadel's most dominant structure, the Mosque of Mohammed Ali.

Mohammed Ali's Monuments

The **Mohammed Ali Mosque**, which so ennobles Cairo's skyline, disappoints at close quarters: its domes are sheathed in tin, its alabaster surfaces grubby. Nonetheless, it exudes *folie de grandeur*, starting with the ornate clock given by Louis Philippe (in exchange for the obelisk in the Place de la Concorde, Paris), which has never worked; and the Turkish Baroque ablutions fountain, resembling a giant Easter egg. Inside the mosque, whose lofty dome and semi-domes are decorated like a Fabergé egg, the use of space is classically Ottoman, reminiscent of the great mosques of Istanbul. A constellation of chandeliers and globe lamps illuminates Thuluth inscriptions, a gold-scalloped *mihrab* and two *minbars*, one faced in alabaster, the other strangely Art Nouveau. Mohammed Ali is buried beneath a white marble cenotaph, behind a bronze grille on the right of the entrance. The mosque itself was erected between 1824 and 1848, but the domes had to be demolished and rebuilt in the 1930s.

Due south of Mohammed Ali's Mosque is the entrance to what remains of his **Al-Gawhara Palace**, where he waited while the Mamlukes were butchered. Also known as the *Bijou* (Jewelled) Palace, its French-style salons contain a dusty display of nineteenth-century dress, royal furniture and tableware. Its most notable exhibit, however, is a mother-of-pearl model of Jerusalem's Dome of the Rock. Somewhere in this vicinity is the spot where St Francis of Assisi attempted to preach Christianity to the Ayyubid ruler Al-Kamil.

Medieval remains

For an idea of the Citadel's appearance before Mohammed Ali's grandiose reconstruction programme, descend from the Mohammed Ali Mosque's front entrance into the Citadel's central courtyard. On your right, at the end of the passage from the southern courtyard, is the **Mosque of Sultan al-Nasir** (also called the Mosque of Ibn Qalaoun, after Al-Nasir's father). Unlike other Citadel mosques, this one is exempt from Friday closure to sightseers as it is not used for prayers.

The Mamlukes and the Mongols of Persia enjoyed good relations when the mosque was constructed (1318–35), and a Tabriz master mason probably designed the corkscrew minarets with their bulbous finials and faïence decorations, if not the dome, which also smacks of Central Asia. Since Selim the Grim carted its marble panelling back to Turkey, the mosque's courtyard has looked ruggedly austere, with rough-hewn pillars supporting *ablaq* arches linked by Fatimid-style tie-beams – although the *mihrab* itself is a feast of gold and marble. Notice the stepped merlons around the parapet, and the blue, white and silver decorations beneath the sanctuary *liwan*.

If you leave the mosque, turn right and walk clockwise around it, you'll find a wasteland with barbicans at the far end. There, a locked gate prevents admission to **Yussef's Well**, which spirals down 97m to the level of the Nile, whence water percolates through fissures in the bedrock. Dug by prisoners between 1176 and 1182, this so-called "Well of the Snail" had its steps strewn with soil to provide a footing for the donkeys that carried up water jars. The Citadel's infamous Jubb dungeon, "a noisome pit where foul and deadly exhalations, unclean vermin and bats rendered the pitchy darkness more horrible", was blocked up by Al-Nasir in 1329, but reactivated under the latterday Mamluke sultans.

The Police National Museum

On the northwestern side of the central enclosure, a gate leads through to another courtyard, at whose northern end is the **Police National Museum**. As you pass through the gateway, notice the door in its northern side. This leads through to **cells** that were used when the Citadel was a prison. Famous detainees included Anwar Sadat, arrested by the British for wartime espionage (see p.199). Although it is closed to the public, you will probably be allowed in if you show an interest, in exchange for a little lubrication of the relevant palms.

The quirky exhibition in the **Police National Museum** covers some of Egypt's most sensational murders and assassinations, although the most infamous of all – Awar Sadat's – is conspicuously absent. The main hall features portraits of interior ministers since 1878, and its rooms (going round clockwise) begin with one on Pharaonic Egypt, including weapons of the time and an explanation of the conspiracy to assassinate Ramses III. The next room, incongruously labelled "Islamic", shows photos taken after the assassination of Lord Moyne by members of the maverick Zionist paramilitary group, the Stern Gang, in Zamalek in 1944. Also featured here are 1940s Assyut gangster Al-Khott, and female serial killers Rayya and Sakina, whose grizzly murders of nearly thirty young girls for their jewellery led to the duo's execution in 1921. The next room has a scale model of Ismailiya barracks illustrating the 1952 Battle of Ismailiya (see p.661) that galvanized public opinion against the British occupation. The incident is further illustrated with photos and artefacts. The "Forgery and Counterfeiting" room contains the death mask of murderer Mahmoud Amin Mahmoud Soleiman, as well as a press for counterfeiting banknotes; forged coins and bills further illustrate the theme. Fake ancient coins appear in the "Confiscations" room, along with ancient artefacts seized from smugglers attempting to export them illegally.

There is a superb **view** of the entire city from the terrace outside the Police Museum. At the southern end, in a pit, are the **excavated remains of the Qasr al-Ablaq**, or Striped Palace of Sultan al-Nasir. For many of the hapless boy-sultans chosen by the Mamlukes, the palace amounted to a luxury prison, and finally an execution cell. Nevertheless, the Citadel remained the residence of Egypt's rulers for nearly 700 years, and Mohammed Ali prophesied that his descendants would rule supreme as long as they resided here. Ismail's move to the Abdin Palace did indeed foreshadow an inexorable decline in their power.

The Northern Enclosure

Passing through the Bab al-Qullah, you'll enter the Citadel's northern enclosure, open to visitors despite a military presence. Straight ahead, beyond a parade of Soviet- and US-made tanks from four Arab–Israeli Wars, Mohammed Ali's old Harim Palace is occupied by the **Military Museum** (no extra entry charge, but £E1 to take in a camera). This vast exhibition devotes more space to ceremonial accoutrements than the savage realities of war, and even pacifists should enjoy the main salon, with its spectacular trompe l'oeil. While in a military vein, it's worth recalling that the Citadel fell to Mohammed Ali after he stationed cannons on the Muqattam heights. The military electronics that festoon them now are a reminder that strategic ground seldom loses its utility.

By turning right at the barracks near the enclosure entrance and following the lane around, you'll come out into a compound with a formal garden. This "**Garden Museum**" is unshaded but decorated with assorted columns, the odd nineteenth-century gateway, and – its centrepiece – the top of a minaret from the 1441 mosque of Qaitbey al-Jatkasi. To its south is the **Carriage Museum**, with its row of horseheads. Inside are six royal carriages and two picnic buggies, one of them an infant prince's; the largest state carriage – heavy with gold – was presented as a gift to Khedive Ismail by Emperor Napoleon and Empress Eugénie.

Just beyond is the small **Seized Museum**, displaying various pharaonic, Roman, Coptic and Islamic antiquities recovered from smugglers before they left Egypt. Exhibits in the first room include, in the first display case on the right, the mummy of an ibis before which sits a little man in supplication, plus whole sarcophagi from the late Pharaonic period. The second room contains Coptic icons, antique manuscripts, glassware and pistols, all charmingly labelled "misdemeanor no. 738", "misdemeanor no. 1296" and the like.

Behind here are two of the many bastions along the Citadel's ramparts, each with evocative names. Although the derivation of **Burg Kirkilyan** (Tower of the Forty Serpents) is unknown, the **Burg al-Matar** (Tower of the Flight Platform) probably housed the royal carrier pigeons. Neither can be entered, but it's worth visiting a neglected treasure at the other end of the compound. A cluster of verdigris domes and a pencil-sharp minaret identify the **Mosque of Suleyman Pasha** as an early sixteenth-century Ottoman creation, borne out by the lavish arabesques and rosettes adorning the interior of the cupola and semi-domes. Inside, cross the courtyard to find a **mausoleum** where the tombs of amirs and their families have *tabuts* indicating their rank: turbans or hats for the men, floral-patterned *lingam*-like rods for the women. Adjacent to the courtyard is a **madrassa** where students took examinations beneath a *riwaq* upheld by painted beams.

The Mosque of Sultan Hassan

The **Mosque of Sultan Hassan** (daily 8am–10pm) stands on Midan Salah al-Din, facing the Citadel. If you are asked to pay an entry fee here, remember that there's no charge to enter this or any other mosque in Cairo and you should refuse to pay unless they can give you an official ticket.

Raised at the command of a son of Al-Nasir, the Sultan Hassan Mosque was unprecedentedly huge in scale when it was begun in 1356, and some design flaws soon became apparent. The plan to have a minaret at each corner was abandoned after the one directly above the entrance collapsed, killing 300 people. Hassan himself was assassinated in 1391, two years before the mosque's completion. After another minaret toppled in 1659, the weakened dome collapsed; and if this wasn't enough, the roof was also used as an artillery platform during coups against sultans Barquq (1391) and Tumanbey (1517). But the mosque is big enough to withstand a lot of battering: 150m long, covering an area of 7906 square metres, its walls rise to 36m and its tallest minaret to 68m.

The mosque is best seen when the morning sun illuminates its deep court-yard and cavernous mausoleum, revealing subtle colours and textures disguised by shadows later in the day. Entering beneath a towering stalactite hood, you're drawn by instinct through a gloomy domed vestibule with *liwans*, out into the central **sahn** – a stupendous balancing of mass and void. Vaulted **liwans** soar on four sides, their height emphasized by hanging lamp chains, their maws by red-and-black rims, all set off by a bulbous-domed ablutions fountain (proba-bly an Ottoman addition). Each *liwan* was devoted to teaching a rite of Sunni Islam, providing theological justification for the cruciform plan the Mamlukes strove to achieve regardless of the site. At Sultan Hassan, four **madrassas** have been skilfully fitted into an irregular area behind the *liwans* to maintain the internal cruciform.

Soft-hued marble inlay and a band of monumental kufic script distinguish the sanctuary *liwan* from its roughly plastered neighbours. To the right of the *mihrab* is a bronze door, exquisitely worked with radiating stars and satellites in gold and silver; on the other side is **Hassan's mausoleum**. Cleverly sited to derive *baraka* from prayers to Mecca, while overlooking his old stamping grounds, the mausoleum is sombre beneath its restored dome, upheld by stalactite penden-tives. Around the chamber runs a carved and painted *Thuluth* inscription, from the Throne verse of the Koran. Note also the ivory-inlaid *kursi*, or Koranic lectern.

The Rifai and Amir Akhur mosques

Adjoining Sultan Hassan, the **Rifai Mosque** (daily 8am–5pm; no entry charge) is pseudo-Mamluke, built between 1869 and 1912 for Princess Khushyar, the mother of Khedive Ismail. With the royal entrance now closed, you enter on the side facing Sultan Hassan. Straight ahead in a sandalwood enclosure lies the **tomb of Sheikh Ali al-Rifai**, founder of the Rifai *tariqa* of dervishes, whose moulid occurs during the sixth month of the Muslim calen-dar, *Gumad el-Tani*. Off to your left are the *mashrabiya*-screened **tombs of King Fouad** (who reigned 1917–36), his mother, the last **Shah of Iran** and **King Farouk** of Egypt (who likewise died in exile). The monumental sanctu-ary (on the left) is impressive, but after Ismail's chief eunuch had overseen its forty-four columns, nineteen types of marble, eighteen window grilles costing £E1000 apiece, and £E25,000 dispersed on gold leaf, dowdiness was scarcely possible: what it lacks is the power of simplicity embodied by the mosques of Ibn Tulun and Sultan Hassan.

Finally, facing the Citadel, you can't miss the **Mosque of Amir Akhur** (on the left), with its bold red-and-white *ablaq*, breast-like dome and double minaret finial, incorporating a *sabil-kuttab* at the lower end of its sloping site.

On from the Citadel

Of the various itineraries emanating from the Citadel, the shortest (covered on p.165) takes you to the awesome Mosque of Ibn Tulun, whilst the longest ones (requiring transport, and covered on pp.169–171) involve the Cities of the Dead. The route along the Darb al-Ahmar/Sharia Bab al-Wazir from the Bab Zwayla is covered on pp.155–159; you could pick up the trail at the Blue Mosque (p.159) and follow the directions in the text in reverse.

The Mosque of Ibn Tulun and the Saiyida Zeinab quarter

Two aspects of Islam are strikingly apparent in the great **Mosque of Ibn Tulun** and the quarter of the city named after Egypt's beloved saint, **Saiyida Zeinab**. The mosque evokes the simplicity of Islam's central tenet, submission to Allah, whereas the surrounding neighbourhoods are urban stews seething with popular cults. **Zeinab's moulid** is the wildest festival in Cairo, sucking 500,000 people into a pulsing vortex around her mosque, 1km west of Ibn Tulun's. Its high-octane blend of intense devotion and sheer enjoyment is also characteristic of **other moulids** honouring Saiyida Nafisa, Ruqayya and Aisha, whose shrines lie between Ibn Tulun and El-Khalifa (the Southern Cemetery).

The following section covers only Ibn Tulun, Saiyida Zeinab and sites along Sharia Saliba, which are shown in relation to the Citadel and Southern Cemetery on the **map** on p.166. Conceivably, you could visit all of them in a single day – though a more leisurely approach would allow you more time to take them in.

Approaches to the quarter

Buses #72/ and #160/ provide the easiest access to Saiyida Zeinab **from Midan Tahrir**, running through the quarter past its namesake shrine and within sight of Ibn Tulun's Mosque, towards the Citadel, and on to the Mausoleum of Al-Shafi in the Southern Cemetery. Alternatively, bus #840 runs **from Midan Ataba**. There is also a **metro station** within five to ten minutes' walk from Midan Saiyada Zeinab.

Alternatively, the fifteen-minute walk **from the Mosque of Sultan Hassan** to Ibn Tulun takes you along **Sharia Saliba**, past a prison that serves as a barometer of law and order: whenever there's been a crackdown you can see several arms thrust from each cell window. Next comes the lofty **Sabil-Kuttab of Qaitbey**, with its bold red, white and black facade, now beautifully restored. Further along, beyond the **Khanqah of Shaykhu**, Sharia al-Khalifa turns off **towards the Southern Cemetery**, as described in the following section, "Cities of the Dead". By ignoring this and carrying on past the nineteenth-century *sabil* **of Umm Abbas**, with its blue-and-red panels and gilt calligraphy, you'll see the huge walls of Ibn Tulun's Mosque on the left. Its entrance is that way, too. The portal on the main street belongs not to Ibn Tulun but to the adjoining **Madrassa of Sarghatmish**, which has recently been restored and should be open to the public. The courtyard, resplendent in white marble inlaid with red, black and green porphyry, is absolutely stunning, with a cool, light feel that makes a pleasant change from the rather heavy architecture of Cairo's classic mosques. It centres around a fountain surmounted with an *oba* (canopy), and surrounded by the cell-like quarters formerly used by its students.

The Mosque of Ibn Tulun

Ibn Tulun's Mosque (daily 7am–5pm; no entry fee) is a rare survivor of the classical Islamic period of the ninth and tenth centuries, when the Abbassid khalifs ruled the Muslim world from Iraq. Their purpose-built capital, Samarra, centred upon a congregational mosque where the entire population assembled for Friday prayer, and this most likely provided the inspiration for the Ibn Tulun. You enter the mosque via a **ziyada**, or enclosure, designed to distance the mosque from its surroundings; to the left stands the Gayer-Anderson

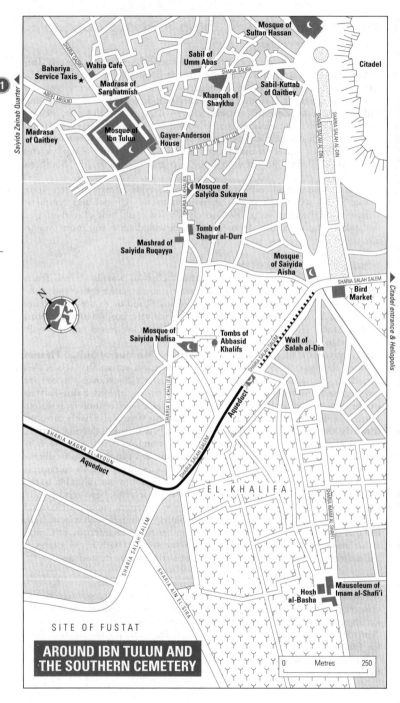

Mosque of
Sultan Hassan

Citadel

Sabil of
Umm Abas

SHARIA SALIBA

Bahariya
Service Taxis

Wahia Café

Sabil-Kuttab
of Qaitbey

Madrasa of
Sarghatmish

ABDEL MEGUID

Khanqah of
Shaykhu

Saiyida Zeinab Quarter

SHARIA QADRY

SHARIA SALAH AL-DIN

Madrasa
of Qaitbey

Mosque of
Ibn Tulun

Gayer-Anderson
House

SHARIA IBN TULUN

Mosque of
Saiyida Sukayna

SHARIA EL-KHALIFA

Tomb of
Shagur al-Durr

Mashrad of
Saiyida Ruqayya

Mosque
of Saiyida
Aisha

SHARIA SALAH SALEM

Citadel entrance & Heliopolis

Bird
Market

Mosque of
Saiyida Nafisa

Tombs of
Abbasid
Khalifs

Wall of
Salah al-Din

SHARIA EL-KHALIFA

Aqueduct

SHARIA MAGRA EL-AYDUN

Aqueduct

SHARIA SALAH SALEM

E L - K H A L I F A

SHARIA IMAM AL-SHAFI

SHARIA SALAH SALEM

SHARIA AIN EL-SIRA

Hosh
al-Basha

Mausoleum of
Imam al-Shafi'i

SITE OF FUSTAT

**AROUND IBN TULUN AND
THE SOUTHERN CEMETERY**

0   Metres   250

Ibn Tulun and Al-Qitai

It was from Iraq that the Abbassids made **Ahmed Ibn Tulun** governor of Fustat in 868, and smarted as he declared his independence. Ibn Tulun (the "Son of Tulun", a Turkish slave) founded the Tulunid dynasty that ruled Egypt until 905, and established a new city to the northeast of Fustat. According to legends, Noah's Ark had come to rest on this site when the Flood receded; Moses confronted the pharaoh's magicians here; and Abraham had been ready to sacrifice his son on a nearby hillock. Unperturbed by this, nor by the existence of Christian and Jewish cemeteries on the site, he dictated the construction of **Al-Qitai**, called "the Wards" after its division into military cantonments.

Ibn Tulun's performance on the polo field filled his doctors with foreboding, for in sickness he "refused to follow their orders, flouted their prescribed diet, and when he found himself still sinking, he had their heads chopped off, or flogged them till they died". But under his soft-living successor the Al-Qitai midan was converted into a garden with a quicksilver lake, where the insomniac Khomaruya lolled on an airbed guarded by a blue-eyed lion. The Tulunids could afford such luxury, for their annual revenue amounted to 4,300,000 dinars.

When the Abbassids subsequently reconquered Egypt in 905, they destroyed everything here but the mosque, which became derelict. Exploited as a makeshift caravanserai, and a hideout for bodysnatchers during the terrible famine of 1200, it was belatedly restored in 1296 by Sultan Laghin, who had hidden there as an amir suspected of murdering the sultan.

House (see below). It's only within the inner walls that the vastness of the mosque becomes apparent: the courtyard is 92 metres square, while the complex, measuring 140m by 122m, covers six and a half acres.

Besides its sheer size, the **mosque** impresses by its simplicity. Strewn with pebbles and open to the sky, its vast court has the grandeur of a desert where all of Allah's worshippers are prostrated equally beneath the sun. Ibn Tulun's architects understood the power of repetition – see how the merlons echo the rhythm of the arcades – but also restraint: small floral capitals and stucco rosettes seem at first glance to be the only decorative motifs. Beneath the arcades you'll find a sycamore-wood frieze over two kilometres long, relating roughly one fifth of the Koran in kufic script. The severely geometric *mida'a*, an inspired focal point, was added in the thirteenth century, when the *mihrab* was also jazzed up with marble and glass mosaics – the only unsuccessful note in the complex.

The **minaret** (entered from outside the mosque) is unique for its exterior spiral staircase, which gives the structure a helical shape. Supposedly, Ibn Tulun twisted a scrap of paper into a spiral, and then justified his absent-minded deed by presenting it as the design for a minaret. But the great minaret at Samarra (itself influenced by ancient Babylonian ziggurats) seems a likelier source of inspiration. Payment of *baksheesh* to climb the minaret is fair enough, as it is for looking after shoes or providing shoe covers, but resist excessive demands, especially if you are told (falsely) that they are official charges.

The Gayer-Anderson House

From the *ziyada* of the Ibn Tulun Mosque a sign directs you to the **Gayer-Anderson House** (daily 8am–4.30pm; £E16, students £E8, camera £E4, video £E100), otherwise known as the *Beit al-Kritiliya* (House of the Cretan Woman), which abuts the southeast corner of the mosque.

Gayer-Anderson was a retired British major who, during the 1930s and 1940s, refurbished two mansions dating from the sixteenth and eighteenth centuries, filling them with his Orientalist bric-a-brac. Amongst the many paintings here is a self-portrait of Gayer-Anderson wearing a pharaonic headdress. **Tours** of the house (the buildings are linked by a passage on the third floor) are conducted by charming curators. There are Persian, Chinese and Queen Anne rooms, and an amazing guest bedroom named after Damascus, whence its opulent wooden panelling originated. Women can sneak through a camouflaged *dulap* (wall cupboard) into the screened gallery overlooking the *salamlik*, as in olden days. With its polychrome fountain, decorated ceiling and kilim-covered pillows, this is the finest reception hall left in Islamic Cairo. It was the set for a tryst and murder in the James Bond film *The Spy Who Loved Me*.

Saiyida Zeinab

The backstreets west of Ibn Tulun harbour another gem of Islamic architecture in the **Madrassa of Qaitbey**. Ignore the dust and grime and tip the curator to unlock the building, whose mosaic floors and *minbar* are superb examples of fifteenth-century craftsmanship.

Real aficionados can also track down other monuments in the area, detailed in the AUC guide. Otherwise, ride further west into the densely populated **Saiyida Zeinab quarter**, where Islamic and modern Cairo merge in a confusion of tenement blocks and **markets**. Midan Lazoghli, on the edge of the Abdin quarter, hosts a daily car spares and repairs souk, while a **bird market** is held beneath an overpass in the direction of Qasr al-Aini Hospital on Mondays and Thursdays – hence its name, the *Souk Itnayn w Khamibs*.

Like Saiyida Zeinab metro station, the market is on the quarter's periphery, where it merges with Garden City and Old Cairo (see the map on p.176). To the northeast of the slaughterhouse district and the Al-Abdin Mosque lies the **Brooke Hospital for Animals**. Founded by Dorothy Brooke in 1934, the hospital treats infirm donkeys and other beasts of burden free of charge, purchases the incurables and puts them out to grass. Egyptians find the whole idea bizarre, but appreciate the service; a stream of patients wends its way up Sikket el-Masbah, off Sharia Bayram el-Tonsi. Phone if you want to visit (℡02/364 9312).

The quarter's highlight is the annual **Moulid of Saiyida Zeinab**, which features parades of Sufi orders by day, and nocturnal festivities that attract half a million people. Ecstatic devotion and pleasure rub shoulders (and other parts of the anatomy, if you're a woman) in this seething, mostly male crowd, transfixed by the music and spectacles. To see the *zikrs*, snake charmers, conjurers, nail-swallowers and dancing horses performing, you'll have to force your way through a scrum of people and tents – don't bring any valuables. The fifteen-day event takes place during *Ragab*, the seventh month of the Muslim calendar.

The focal point for these celebrations is the **Mosque of Saiyida Zeinab** (closed to non-Muslims), off Sharia Bur Said. Born in 628 AD, Zeinab, the Prophet's granddaughter, emigrated to Fustat after the Umayyads slew her brother, Hussein, and died there shortly afterwards. For Egyptian Muslims – especially women – Zeinab is a protectress whose *baraka* (blessing) is sought in matters of fortune and health; in other words, a popular saint. Although the Koran forbids the deification of mortals, the human urge to anthropomorphize religious faith seems irresistible. Every Muslim nation has its own "saints" (chosen by popular acclaim rather than a supreme authority), and respects bloodlines descended from the Prophet or his immediate kin. For the Shia, the martyrdom of Ali and Hussein is a parable of their own oppression, while Zeinab (whose moulid attracts foreign Shia) is honoured as their closest kinswoman.

Before heading back into town, you might want to try one of Saiyida

Zeinab's many cheap but renowned **eating places**, for more on which see p.243. To return to downtown Cairo from here, catch a bus or minibus from near Zeinab's Mosque (see above for bus numbers), or ask for directions to the nearest metro entrance (ten minutes' walk). From Saiyida Zeinab station you can ride two stops north to Tahrir, or two stops south to reach Old Cairo (Mari Girgis station).

Cities of the Dead

It's thought that at least 300,000 Cairenes live amid the **Cities of the Dead**: two vast cemeteries that stretch away from the Citadel to merge with newer shantytowns below the Muqattam. The Southern Cemetery, sprawling to the southeast of Ibn Tulun's mosque, is only visible from the Muqattam, or at close quarters. The Northern Cemetery, by contrast, is an unforgettably eerie sight, with dozens of mausolea rising from a sea of dwellings along the road from Cairo Airport.

Although tourists generally – and understandably – feel uneasy about viewing the cemeteries' splendid **funerary architecture** with squatters living all around or in the tombs, few natives regard the Cities of the Dead as forbidding places. Egyptians have a long tradition of building "houses" near their ancestral graves and picnicking or even staying there overnight; other families have simply occupied them. By Cairene standards these are poor but decent neighbourhoods, with shops, schools and electricity, maybe even piped water and sewers. The saints buried here provide a moral touchstone and *baraka* for their communities, who honour them with **moulids**.

Though generally not a dangerous quarter, it's best to exercise some caution when **visiting**. Don't flaunt money or costly possessions, and be sure to dress modestly; women should have a male escort, and will seem more respectable if wearing a headscarf. By responding to local kids (who may request *baksheesh*) with the right blend of authority and affection, you can win the sympathy of their elders and seem less of an intruder; react wrongly, and you might be stoned out of the neighbourhood. You'll be marginally less conspicuous on Fridays, when many Cairenes visit their family plots; but remember that mosques can't be entered during midday prayers. At all events, leave the cemeteries well before dark, if only to avoid getting lost in their labyrinthine alleys – and don't stray to the east into the inchoate (and far riskier) slums built around the foothills of the Muqattam.

The Southern Cemetery (Al-Qarafah al-Kubra)

The older and larger **Southern Cemetery** is broadly synonymous with the residential quarter of **El-Khalifa**, named after the Abbassid khalifs buried amidst its mud-brick tenements. The area is noted for drug dealing and quite unsafe after dark. Although the Abbassid tombs aren't half as imposing as those of the Mamlukes in the Northern Cemetery, one of the approach routes passes several shrines famous for their moulids, while another moulid is held at the beautiful **Mausoleum of Imam al-Shafi'i**, best reached by bus as a separate excursion. For this reason, we've described two different routes into what Egyptians call "the Great Cemetery" (*Al-Qarafah al-Kubra*).

Sharia Saliba to the Tomb of the Abbassid Khalifs

This walking route passes through one of the oldest poor neighbourhoods in Cairo, where it's thought that people started settling around their saints' graves as early as the tenth century. None of the tombs are remarkable visually, but the stories and moulids attached to them are interesting. The trail begins where

Sharia el-Khalifa turns south off Sharia Saliba, just after the Khanqah of Shaykhu (see map p.166).

Heading south along this narrow street, full of commerce and capering children, you'll be pestered past a succession of tombs. The second on the left, within a green-and-white mosque, is that of **Saiyida Sukayna**, a daughter of Hussein, whose moulid (held during *Rabi el-Tani*) is attended by several thousand locals and features traditional entertainments like dancing horses and stick-twisters.

Such saintly graves invariably acquired an oratory (*mashrad*) or mosque, unlike the **Tomb of Shagar al-Durr**, 100m further on: a derelict edifice sunk below street level. Shagar al-Durr (Tree of Pearls) was the widow of Sultan Ayyub, who ruled as *sultana* of Egypt for eighty days (1249–50) until the Abbassid khalif pronounced "Woe unto nations ruled by a woman", compelling her to marry Aybak, the first Mamluke sultan, and govern "from behind the *mashrabiya*". In 1257 she ordered Aybak's murder after learning that he sought another wife, but then tried to save him; the assassins cried, "If we stop halfway through, he will kill both you and us!" Rejecting her offer to marry Qutuz, their new leader, the Mamlukes handed Shagar al-Durr over to Aybak's former wife, whose servants beat her to death with bath clogs and threw her body to the jackals. Now totally gutted, her locked tomb once contained a *tabut* inscribed: "Oh you who stand beside my grave, show not surprise at my condition. Yesterday I was as you, tomorrow, you will be like me".

Slightly further down and across the street, three shrines are grouped within a compound entered via a green-and-white doorway. The **Mashrad of Saiyida Ruqayya**, on the left, commemorates the stepsister of Saiyida Zeinab, with whom she came to Egypt; the name of her father, Ali, adorns its rare Fatimid *mihrab*, and the devotion she inspires is particularly evident during Ruqayya's moulid.

Ruqayya's devotion doesn't, however, compare with that accorded to the **Mosque of Saiyida Nafisa**, 100m to the south, past the market square. This, Egypt's third-holiest shrine, is closed to non-Muslims, though visitors can still appreciate the good-natured crowd that hangs around after Friday noon prayers, or Nafisa's moulid, usually held in the middle of the month of *Gumad al-Tani* (see p.255). Honoured during her lifetime as a descendant of the Prophet, a *hafizat al-Qur'an* (one who knows the Koran by heart) and a friend of Imam al-Shafi'i, Nafisa was famed for working miracles and conferring *baraka*. Her shrine has been repeatedly enlarged since Fatimid times – the Southern Cemetery possibly began with devotees settling or being buried near her grave – and the present mosque was built in 1897.

If you walk through the passage to its left, turn right at the end and then right again, you should find yourself outside the compound enclosing the **Tombs of the Abbassid Khalifs** (open 24hr). Having been driven from Baghdad by the Mongols, the khalifs' surviving relatives gratefully accepted Beybars' offer to re-establish them in Egypt, only to discover that they were "No longer Commander of the Faithful, but Commander of the Wind". Beybars appropriated the domed mausoleum (usually kept locked) for his own sons; the khalifs were buried outdoors in less than grandiose tombs. Notice the beautiful foliate kufic inscription on the cenotaph of Khadiga, under the wooden shed. In 1517 the last Abbassid khalif was formally divested of his office, which the Ottomans assumed in 1538, and Ataturk abolished in the 1920s.

An alternative route back towards the Citadel passes the **Mosque of Saiyida Aisha**, whose **moulid** occurs during *Sha'ban*. To get there, retrace your steps to the market square south of Ruqayya's shrine and take the road leading off to the right. It's roughly 500 metres' walk to Aisha's Mosque. From there, Sharia Salah Salem runs southwest alongside the medieval **Wall of Salah al-Din**, and northeast to the Citadel entrance at Bab al-Gabal, while Sharia Salah al-Din leads north to Midan Salah al-Din. If you happen to be here on Friday, consider making a detour to the **bird market** (*Souk al-Asafeer* or *Souk al-Gom'a*), held on a side street to the south of the Salah Salem overpass.

The Mausoleum of Imam Al-Shafi'i

Imam al-Shafi'i, revered as the founder of one of the four rites of Sunni Islam, occupies a great mausoleum 2km from the Citadel. Aside from catching a taxi from there (for about £E3–5), the mausoleum is accessible by bus #81 or #89 from Midan Ataba, or bus #160 from Midan Ramses, or more comfortable #54 minibuses from Tahrir, which turn off Sharia Imam al-Shafi'i, 100m beforehand. If you miss the turn-off, ride on to the terminal, have a glass of tea with the driver, and get dropped at the corner on the way back.

Recognizable by its graceful dome, crowned by a metal boat like a weather vane, the **Mausoleum of Imam al-Shafi'i** lurks beside a mosque at the end of the street (free but *baksheesh* appropriate). The largest Islamic mortuary complex in Egypt, it was raised in 1211 by Al-Kamil, Salah al-Din's nephew, a propagator of Sunni orthodoxy like the Imam himself, who died in 820. Al-Shafi'i's teak cenotaph – into which the faithful slip petitions – lies beneath a magnificent dome perched on stalactite squinches, painted red and blue, with gilt designs. The walls are clad in variegated marble, dating from Qaitbey's restoration of the building in the 1480s. In times past, the boat on the roof was filled with birdseed and water; boats are vehicles of spiritual enlightenment in Islamic symbolism, while birds are associated with souls.

Al-Shafi'i's **Moulid** attracts many sick and infirm people, seeking his *baraka*. The festival occurs in *Sha'ban*, the eighth month of the Muslim calendar, but the starting date varies. Normally it's the first Wednesday of the month; however, if this falls on the first or second day of *Sha'ban*, the moulid is delayed until the following Wednesday. Either way, it ends on Wednesday evening the following week. More prosaically, the street leading northwards to the mausoleum from the Al-Basatin quarter is used for scrap, clothing and livestock **markets** every Friday morning.

By walking clockwise around the block in which the Imam's mausoleum is located, you'll find a five-domed complex directly behind it. Inside the courtyard are clumps of cenotaphs decorated with garlands and fronds, topped by a turban, fez or other headdress to indicate the deceased's rank. These constitute the **Hosh al-Basha**, where Mohammed Ali's sons, their wives, children and retainers are buried. The conspicuously plain cenotaph belongs to a princess with radical sympathies, who abhorred ostentation. The body of King Farouk himself, who died in exile, now reposes in the Rifai Mosque. In a separate room, forty statues commemorate the 470 Mamlukes butchered by Mohammed Ali in the Citadel (see p.161).

The Northern Cemetery (Al-Qarafat al-Sharqiyyah)

The finest of Cairo's funerary monuments – erected by the Burgi Mamlukes from the fourteenth to sixteenth centuries – are spread around the **Northern Cemetery**. The majority of tourists who venture in from Sharia Salah Salem are content to see three main sites, plus whatever crops up in between, over an hour or so.

Aside from catching a taxi (ask for the *Qarafat al-Sharqiyyah* – Eastern Cemetery – in Arabic), the surest way of **getting there** is to walk **from**

Al–Azhar. This will take around ten to fifteen minutes, following the dual carriageway Bab al–Ghuriyab past university buildings and uphill to its round-about junction with Salah Salem. Although the tombs of Anuk and Tulbey are amongst the nearby mausolea, you might prefer to head 250m north along the highway to Dirasa – also accessible by bus #102 **from Midan Falaki** or minibus #10 **from Ramses and Ataba** – and then cut east into the ceme-

Map labels:

Heliopolis

NORTHERN CEMETERY

MIDAN BARQUQ

Bab al-Nasr Cemetery

SHARIA GALAL

Military Cemetery

Bab al-Nasr   Northern Walls

Tomb of 'Asfur

Sultan Barquq's Mausoleum

Tombs of al-Bagasi & Amir Suleyman

SHARIA GAMALIYA

Tomb of al-Saba Banat

Tomb of Gani Bak

Tomb of al-Rifai

Sultan Barsbey's Mausoleum

Al-Azhar

Footbridge

Dirasa

Qaitbey's Rab

TUNNEL TO MIDAN OPERA

Sultan Qaitbey's Mausoleum

N

Tombs of Umm Anuk & Tulbey

SHARIA SALAH SALEM

Muqattam Hills

0   Metres   250

Sharia Bab al-Wazir ▼   ▼ Citadel & Southern Cemetery

tery. That way you start with Qaitbey's Mausoleum (a known point on the circuit), whose ornate dome and minaret are clearly visible. Dirasa can also be reached by tram from Midan Triomphe in Heliopolis, and there will be a metro station here when the new cross-town line finally opens (see map on p.95).

Sultan Qaitbey's Mausoleum

Sultan Qaitbey was the last strong Mamluke ruler, and a prolific builder of monuments from Mecca to Syria; his funerary complex (depicted on £E1 notes) is among the grandest in the Northern Cemetery. His name means "the restored" or "returned", indicating that he nearly died at birth; as a scrawny lad, he fetched only fifty dinars in the slave market. The rapid turnover in rulers after 1437 accelerated his ascent, and in 1468 he was acclaimed as sultan by the bodyguard of the previous incumbent, an old comrade-in-arms who parted from Qaitbey with tears and embraces. His 28-year reign was only exceeded by Al-Nasir's, and Qaitbey remained "tall, handsome and upright as a reed" well into his eighties, still attentive to citizens' complaints at twice-weekly *diwaniyyas*.

An irregularly shaped complex built in 1474, the **Mausoleum of Sultan Qaitbey** (daily 11am–9pm) is dynamically unified by the bold stripes along its facade, which is best viewed from the north. The trilobed portal carries one's eye to the graceful **minaret**, soaring through fluted niches, stalactite brackets and balconies to a teardrop finial. Inside, the **madrassa** *liwans*, floors and walls are a feast of marble and geometric patterns, topped by elaborately carved and gilded ceilings, with a lovely octagonal roof lantern. Qaitbey's **tomb chamber** off the *qibla liwan* is similarly decorated, its lofty dome upheld by squinches. Ask to climb the minaret for a close view of the marvellous stone carving on the dome's exterior. A raised star-pattern is superimposed over an incised floral one, the two designs shifting as the shadows change. From this minaret vantage point you could also plot a course to Barsbey's complex, further up the narrow, winding street.

The Barsbey and Barquq complexes

As the street jinks northwards from Qaitbey's Mausoleum it passes (on the left) the apartment building that Qaitbey deeded to provide income for the building's upkeep and employment for poor relations. Such bequests could not be confiscated, unlike merchants' and Mamlukes' personal wealth, which partly financed the **Mausoleum of Sultan al-Ashraf Barsbey** (daily 11am–9pm), 200m beyond the building. Based on a now-ruined *khanqah*, the complex was expanded to include a mausoleum and mosque-madrassa (1432) after Barsbey's funerary pile near Khan el-Khalili was found lacking. If there's a curator around, ask him to lift a mat hiding the marble mosaic floor inside the long mosque, which also features a superb *minbar*. At the northern end, a great dome caps Barsbey's tomb, its marble cenotaph and mother-of-pearl-inlaid *mihrab* softly lit by stained-glass windows, added at a later date. The stone carving on the dome's exterior marks a transition between the early chevron patterns and the fluid designs on Qaitbey's Mausoleum.

Barsbey was the sultan who acquired young Qaitbey at a knockdown rate. He himself had been purchased in Damascus for eight hundred dinars, but was "returned to the broker for a filmy defect in one of his blue eyes". Unlike other sultans who milked the economy, Barsbey troubled to pay his Mamlukes regularly and the reign (1422–38) of this well-spoken teetotaller was characterized by "extreme security and low prices". Fifty metres up the street, another finely carved dome surmounts the **Tomb of Gani Bak**, a favourite of Barsbey's, whose mosque stands near the Saddlemakers Bazaar.

The third – and oldest – of the great funerary complexes can be found 50m further north, on the far side of a square with a direct through road onto Sharia Salah Salem. Recognizable by its twin domes and minarets, the **Mausoleum of Sultan Barquq** (daily 8am–8pm) was the first royal tomb in a cemetery that was previously noted for the graves of Sufi sheikhs. Its courtyard is plain, with sere, stunted tamarisks, but the proud chevron-patterned domes above the sanctuary *liwan* uplift the whole ensemble. Barquq and his son Farag are buried in the northern tomb chamber; his daughters Shiriz and Shakra in the southern one, with their faithful nurse in the corner. Both are soaring structures preceded by *mashrabiyas* with designs similar to the window screens in Barquq's madrassa, "Between the Two Palaces". The sinuously carved *minbar* was donated by Qaitbey to what was then a Sufi *khanqah*; stairs in the northwest corner of the courtyard lead to a warren of dervish cells on the upper floors, long since deserted.

The complex was actually erected by Farag, who transferred his father's body here from the madrassa on Sharia al-Muizz. Farag was crowned at the age of ten and deposed and killed in Syria after thirteen years of civil strife: it's amazing that the mausoleum was ever completed in 1411.

Depending on your route out, you might pass the minor **tombs of Barsbey al-Bagasi and Amir Suleyman**, or those of **Princess Tulbey and Umm Anuk**, nearer Bab al-Ghuriyab and visible from the highway.

Old Cairo, Roda Island and the southern suburbs

The southern sector of the city is divisible into three main areas, the most interesting of which is **Old Cairo** (*Masr al-Qadima*), the historic link between Egypt's pharaonic and Islamic civilizations. Here, the fortress-town of **Babylon**, where the Holy Family is thought to have taken refuge, developed into a powerhouse of native Christianity which today remains the heart of Cairo's **Coptic community**. Featuring several medieval churches, the superb **Coptic Museum** and an atmospheric synagogue, it totally eclipses the site of **Fustat** – Egypt's first Islamic settlement, of which little remains but the much-altered **Mosque of Amr** – or the largely uninteresting **southern suburbs** of Ma'adi and Helwan.

Connected by bridge to Old Cairo – and so covered in this section, too – is **Roda Island**, which boasts a venerable Nilometer and the wonderfully kitsch Manial Palace. The Nilometer is best visited in combination with Coptic Cairo, but the palace is more easily accessible from central Cairo.

Approaching Old Cairo: transport links

Depending on whether it's broadly or narrowly defined, **Old Cairo** covers everything south of Garden City and Saiyida Zeinab – from the slaughterhouse district beside the Mamluke Aqueduct out to the ancient Jewish cemetery of Al-Basatin – or a relatively small area near the Mari Girgis metro station, known to foreigners as **"Coptic Cairo"**. Cairenes themselves distinguish between the general area of *Masr al-Qadima* and specific localities such as *Fumm al-Khalig* (Mouth of the Aqueduct) or *Qasr el-Sham'ah* (the erstwhile fortress of Babylon). Most tourists concentrate on Coptic Cairo, followed by a brief look at the Mosque of Amr.

The Coptic quarter is rapidly accessible by taking the **metro** from downtown Cairo to the **Mari Girgis** station (four stops from Midan Tahrir in the

Helwan direction; 55pt). Another possibility is the **river-taxis** (aka water buses; £E1) that leave from the Maspero Dock (see p.98), zigzagging southwards upriver. Note, however, that not all of them run as far as Mari Girgis, and services end at 4pm. The Mari Girgis stop is the fifth one; to reach the Coptic quarter from there, head inland, turn left and then cross the tracks at the end of the road. **Taxis** from downtown Cairo are reluctant to accept less than £E10, while **buses** from Tahrir and **minibuses** from Midan Ataba to Amr's Mosque (see p.97 for bus numbers) are usually packed on the outward journey but fine for getting back. To reach other points, see the directions below.

Coptic Cairo

Coptic Cairo recalls the millennial interlude between pharaonic and Islamic civilization, and the enduring faith of Egypt's Copts (see below). Though not a ghetto, the quarter's huddle of dark churches suggests a mistrust of outsiders – an attitude of mind that has its roots in the Persian conquest and centuries of Greek or Roman rule.

Perhaps as early as the sixth century BC, a town grew up in this area, built around a fortress intended to guard the canal linking the Nile and the Red Sea. Some ascribe the name of this settlement – **Babylon-in-Egypt** – to Chaldean workmen pining after their home town beside the Euphrates; another likely derivation is *Bab il-On*, the "Gate of Heliopolis". Either way, it was Egyptian or Jewish in spirit long before Emperor Trajan raised the existing fortress in 130 AD. Resentful of Greek domination and Hellenistic Alexandria, many of Babylon's inhabitants later embraced Christianity, despite bitter persecution by the pagan Romans. Subsequently, after the emperor Constantine's conversion, the community was further oppressed by Byzantine clerics in the name of Melkite orthodoxy. Thus when the Muslim army besieged Babylon in 641, promising to respect Copts and Jews as "People of the Book", only its garrison resisted.

The Roman fortress

Almost opposite the **Mari Girgis** (St George) metro station you'll see the twin circular **towers** of Babylon's western gate. In Trajan's day, the Nile lapped the base of this gate and was spanned by a pontoon bridge leading to the southern tip of Roda. Today, Babylon's foundations are buried under ten metres of accumulated silt and rubble, so the churches within the compound and the streets outside are nearly at the level of the fortress's ramparts. The right-hand tower is ruined, exposing a central shaft buttressed by masonry rings and radial ribs, which enabled it to withstand catapults and battering rams. Atop the other tower stands the Orthodox Church of St George (see below). Both towers are encased in alternating courses of dressed stone (much of it taken from pharaonic temples) and brick, a Roman technique known as *opus mixtum* or "mixed work".

By purchasing a ticket for the Coptic Museum, you can walk through the fortress's inner courtyard and down into the old **Water Gate** beneath the Hanging Church. The gate is now partly flooded and, though its arches and walls are visible from precarious walkways, the interior is only accessible by a stairway behind the three stone piers supporting the back of the church (bring a torch). It was through this gate that the last Byzantine viceroy, Melkite bishop Cyrus, escaped by boat under cover of darkness before Babylon surrendered to the Muslims.

While exploring the Coptic quarter, you'll also notice various sections of Babylon's Roman **walls**, rebuilt during the fourth and fifth centuries.

OLD CAIRO AND RODA ISLAND

Metres 0 250

N

Saiyida Zeinab Mosque

Institut Français

SAIYIDA ZEINAB

M

Lux

Saudi Consulate

GARDEN CITY

Fontana

Abou Shakra

Qasr al-Aini Hospital

Bird Market

SHARIA MANSUR

SHARIA BAYRAM EL-TONSI

SHARIA BUR SAID

AL-BARRANI

Monastery of St Menas

SHARIA AL-SAID

SHARIA MANSUR

Al-Abdin Mosque

Slaughter House

Mamluke Aqueduct

MANIAL BRIDGE

Manial Palace

SHARIA SARAI

Cairo University Medical Faculty

Meridien Hotel

EL CORNICHE

EL CORNICHE

Fumm al-Khalig

i

Youth Hostel

SHARIA EL-MANIAL

RODA ISLAND

River Nile

EL-GAMA'A BRIDGE

Dr Ragab's Papyrus Institute

Mahmoud Khalil Museum

SHARIA EL-GIZA

Nasr Building

El-Mashrabiah

Saudi-Arabian Embassy

Israeli Consulate

Gate

El-Urman Garden

Gate

Four Seasons Hotel

Zoological Garden

Gate

Pharaohs Floating Restaurants

River Nile

Tanneries

EL-MALEK
EL-SALEH Ⓜ

SHARIA SALAH SALEM

SHARIA MANSUR

OLD CAIRO

Deir Abu'l-Sayfayn

Mosque
of Amr

SITE OF FUSTAT

See inset
for detail

Museum

MARI
GIRGIS Ⓜ

OLD CAIRO

EL-SALIH BRIDGE

SHARIA EL-QADWA

EL CORNICHE

Nile Peking
Restaurant

▼ Ma'adi & Helwan

SHARIA EL-MANIAL

Student
Cards

Umm
Kalthoum
Museum

Monastirli Palace
Nilometer

River taxi routes

EL-GIZA BRIDGE

SHARIA EL-GIZA

SHARIA MURAD

GIZA

SHARIA GAMI'AT EL-QAMIRA

COPTIC CAIRO

Church of
the Virgin

Church of
St George

Church of
St Barbara

Convent of
St George

Nuptial
Hall

Church of
St Sergius

Ben Ezra
Synagogue ✡

Roman Walls

Monastery of
St George

Church of
St George

Coptic
Museum

Footbridge

MARI
GIRGIS Ⓜ

Roman
Towers

Hanging
Church

Water Gate

▼ Pyramids

177

The Coptic Museum

Nestled between the Hanging Church and the Roman towers of Babylon, the **Coptic Museum** is one of the highlights of Old Cairo (daily 9am–5pm; Ramadan 9am–3pm; £E16, students £E8, camera permit £E10, video permit £E100; tickets are sold even after the museum stops admitting visitors one hour before closing). Its peerless collection of Coptic artefacts is enhanced by the beautiful carved ceilings, beams and stained-glass domes inside its *mashrabiya*'d wings, which enclose peaceful gardens. Founded in 1908 under the patronage of Patriarch Cyril V and Khedive Kamil, the museum was intended to save Christian antiques from the ravages of neglect and foreign collectors, but soon widened its mandate to embrace secular material. With artefacts from Old Cairo, Upper Egypt and the desert monasteries, the museum traces the evolution of Coptic art from Greco-Roman times into the Islamic era (300–1000 AD). Notwithstanding debts to pharaonic and Greco-Roman culture, its spirit was refreshingly unmonumental: "realistic, at times humorous",

The Copts

While most Egyptians are Muslims, about ten percent of the population are Coptic Orthodox Christians. **The Copts** share a common national culture with their Muslim compatriots, but remain acutely conscious of their separate identity. Because intercommunal marriages are extremely rare, it's often said that the Copts are "purer" descendants of the ancient Egyptians than the Muslims – overlooking the infusions of Nubian, Greek, Jewish and Roman blood that occurred centuries before the Arab conquest. Though some maintain that they have higher cheekbones or almond-shaped eyes, Copts are rarely recognizable other than by tokens of their faith (wearing a cross around their neck, or tattooed on their wrist) or by forenames such as Maria, Antunius (Antony), Girgis (George) and Ramses.

Coptic Christianity differs from the Eastern Orthodox and Roman churches over doctrine and ritual. The Coptic Orthodox Church and its pope (chosen from the monks of Wadi Natrun) are totally independent from the Vatican, which only recently agreed to disagree for the sake of ecumenical harmony. The Coptic Bible (first translated from Greek c.300 AD) antedates the Latin version by a century. While Coptic services are conducted in Arabic, portions of the liturgy are sung in the old Coptic language descended from ancient Egyptian, audibly prefiguring the Gregorian chants of Eastern Orthodoxy. However, the Coptic influence goes well beyond music, for it was in Egypt that the monastic tradition, the cult of the Virgin and – arguably – the symbol of the cross originated.

Christianity reached Egypt early: tradition holds that **St Mark** made his first convert (a Jewish shoemaker of Alexandria) in 45 AD. From Jews and Greeks the religion spread to the Egyptians of the Delta – which teemed with Christian communities by the third century – and thence southwards up the Nile. The persecution of believers began under Emperor Decius (249–51) and reached its apogee under Diocletian, whom the Copts accuse of killing 144,000 Christians; the Coptic Church dates its chronology from his accession (284). During this **Era of Martyrs** many believers sought refuge in the desert. Paul of Thebes, Antony and Pacome – the sainted "**Desert Fathers**" – inspired a multitude of hermits and camp followers whose rude communities became the first **monasteries**.

The Christian faith appealed to Egyptians on many levels. Its message of resurrection offered ordinary folk the eternal life that was previously available only to those who could afford elaborate funerary rituals. And much of the new religion's **symbolism** fitted old myths and images. God created man from clay, as did Khnum on his potter's wheel, and weighed the penitent's heart, like Anubis; Confession echoed the Declaration of Innocence; the conflict of two brothers and the struggle against Satan the myth of Osiris, Seth and Horus. Scholars have traced the **cult of**

Coptic art reflected "plebian or agricultural concerns" (Stewart) and often seems homespun compared to pharaonic and Islamic craftsmanship; appropriately enough, its finest expression was in textiles.

Though spread over three floors, the collection isn't so large that visitors become jaded. You can do it justice within a couple of hours, or cover it at a trot in half that time. A **café** in the grounds sells tea and biscuits; the gateway beyond gives access to the courtyard of the Hanging Church (see p.182).

New Wing

Entering the museum grounds from Mari Girgis street, you'll find the **New Wing**, built in 1937, straight ahead. The **ground floor** is arranged in chronological order in an anticlockwise direction, starting with Room 1. The other exit from this room leads into a garden containing tombstones and funerary steles, although at the time of writing this area was still a bit of a building site; when its garden-state is restored, you should be able to access stairs from here

the **Virgin** back to that of the Great Mother, Isis, who suckled Horus. The resemblance between early **Coptic crosses** and pharaonic *ankhs* has also led some to argue that Christianity's principal symbol owes more to Egypt than Golgotha.

Although Emperor Constantine converted to Christianity and legalized his adopted faith throughout the empire (313–30), Byzantine converts known as **Melkites** continued to oppress the Copts. Political tensions were expressed in bitter theological disputes between **Arius** and **Athanasius** of Alexandria, which the Nicene Council (325) failed to resolve. When the Copts rejected the compromise verdict of the Council of Chalcedon (451) that Christ's human and divine natures were both unmixed and inseparable, and insisted that his divinity was paramount, they were expelled from the fold for this **Monophysite heresy** (monophysite meaning "single nature", a misrepresentation of their stance on Christ's divinity).

The association between Coptic Christianity and proto-nationalism was plain to Egypt's foreign rulers. "Copt" derives from the Greek word for Egypt, *Aigyptos*, truncated to *gibt* in Egyptian Arabic. Most Egyptians remained Christian long after the Arab conquest (640–41) and were treated justly by the early Islamic dynasties. Mass **conversions to Islam** followed harsher taxation, abortive revolts, punitive massacres and indignities engendered by the Crusades, until the Muslims attained a nationwide majority (probably during the thirteenth century, though earlier in Cairo). Thereafter Copts still participated in Egyptian life at every level, but the community retreated inwards and its monasteries and clergy stagnated until the nineteenth century, when Coptic reformists collaborated with Islamic and secular nationalists bent on overhauling Egypt's institutions.

In recent decades the Coptic community has undergone a **revival** under the dynamic leadership of its current pope, **Shenouda III**. The monasteries have been revitalized by a new generation of highly educated monks; community work and church attendances flourish as never before. Undoubtedly, this Coptic solidarity also reflects alarm at rising Islamic fundamentalism: what frightens the Copts is the state's strategy of wooing Islamist opinion by discriminating against non-Muslims. Merely to open a new church requires presidential permission; one in Ma'adi was closed by security forces backed up by armoured cars. Over 200 converts to Christianity have been arrested under the National Security Act, and in 1999, a local bishop accused the security forces of atrocities against the Copts of El-Qusiya, in Middle Egypt.

Fortunately, it's relatively few Muslims that actively support this kind of sectarian repression – which is at least a source of comfort for Egypt's six million Copts and 200,000 **Christians of other denominations** (Greek Orthodox, Maronite, Armenian, Catholic, Anglican and Baptist).

that lead down to the Water Gate beneath the Hanging Church and up into the old wing.

Centred upon a fountain from one of the old houses of the quarter, **Room 1** displays **pagan reliefs and statues** of figures from Classical mythology. Their squat proportions and oversized heads make Aphrodite, Daphnae, Pan, Leda and the Swan look more African than Greco-Roman. The tendency to superimpose two flat layers, and the motif of a broken pediment with a shell, were both characteristic of proto-Coptic art. Artefacts in **Room 2** evince a **shift towards Christian symbolism** from the third century onwards. Pharaonic *ankhs* (see p.294) are transmuted into looped crosses, while true crosses appear on the shell pediments and coexist with Horus hawks on a basket-weave capital.

Coptic artistry reached its zenith between the sixth and ninth centuries, as exemplified by the **stone-carvings and frescoes from Bawit Monastery**, near Assyut. In the middle of the righthand wall of **Room 3** is a splendid apse niche depicting Christ enthroned between the creatures of the Apocalypse and the moon and sun; below, the Virgin and Child consort with Apostles whose homely faces can still be seen in any Egyptian city today. In **Room 4**, whose contents are described as "Miscellaneous", notice the eagle on the right, an early Christian symbol of resurrection (as was the peacock). **Room 5** is also filled with miscellaneous objects, its centrepiece a painted capital carved with sinuous acanthus leaves, a motif borrowed from the Greeks and Romans but apparently devoid of symbolic meaning for the Copts.

Entering **Room 6**, dedicated to **objects from the Monastery of St Jeremiah** at Saqqara, you walk between an avenue of capitals with acanthus leaves and grapevines that mingle with pharaonic palm fronds and lotus motifs. At the end is the earliest known example of a stone pulpit, possibly influenced by the *heb-sed* thrones of Zoser's funerary complex. The fresco to its right, like the Bawit apse, subtly identifies the Virgin Mary with Isis. Other instances of recycled iconography can be seen around the corner in **Room 7**: a frieze of the grape harvest (a theme favoured by pharaonic nobles) and a small sphinx-like lion figure between two stylized versions of itself.

Room 8 moves on to **Biblical scenes** (Abraham and Isaac, Christ with angels) and **friezes** of animals offset in plant rondels – a motif that was later adopted by Fatimid woodcarvers. Entering **Room 9** you'll encounter on your right a tenth-century panel from Umm al-Birgat (in the Fayoum), depicting Adam and Eve before and after the Fall, for which he blames her in the latter scene while a serpent relishes the denouement. In the centre of the hall is an elaborate papyrus and lotus basket-weave capital, hollowed out to form a **baptismal font**.

Climbing the staircase to the **upper floor**, you come to casefuls of *ostraca* (inscribed shards of pottery, stone, bone and wood) and manuscripts produced by monastic scriptoria, including several papyrus sheets from the **Gnostic Gospels of Nag Hammadi**, whose 1200 pages shed light on the development of early Christianity and its mystic tradition. The Gospels (translated from Greek into Coptic) were probably buried during the purges against Gnostics in the fourth and fifth centuries; farmers unearthed the sealed jar in 1945 (see p.335).

Proceeding clockwise from **Room 10**, a 1600-year-old towel by the doorway to Room 11 – and next to the oldest book ever to be found complete with its cover – presages a host of **textiles**. From the third or fourth century onwards, Coptic weavers (chiefly women) developed various techniques to a pitch of sophistication. Tapestry and pile-weave designs blended human and bird forms with plant motifs; tunics were appliquéd with bands and rondels. In **Room 12** there's a magnificent silk robe embroidered with pictures of the Apostles, dating from the eighteenth century.

Room 13 displays Alexandrian-style **ivorywork** and cruder efforts from Upper Egypt, alongside a selection of **icons** from Old Cairo, Aswan and Kharga Oasis. Some believe that the change from murals to painted icons resulted from the need to hide sacred treasures from hostile interlopers. The next three rooms showcase **metalwork**, ranging from crosses and censers to musical instruments and tools. In **Room 15** are patriarchal crowns, a lamp emblazoned with both a Christian cross and an Islamic crescent, and an eagle from the Fortress of Babylon.

The upper floor concludes with an exhibition in **Room 17** (currently under renovation) of **Nubian paintings** salvaged during the 1950s and 60s from villages about to be drowned by Lake Nasser. Like Isis-worship in ancient times, Christianity persisted as the dominant religion in Nubia for several centuries after it had waned in Egypt. The figures are darker, with larger eyes and rounder heads than the Copts.

Old Wing

Entered via stairs from the sculpture garden, the **Old Wing**, with its even finer ceilings and *mashrabiyas*, is currently closed for renovation. If it has reopened by the time of your visit, the items on show and their layout may be slightly different from this description.

On the left as you enter **Room 22** are the original **fourth-century altar** and a Fatimid-era dome from the Church of St Sergius. In the other direction lie two halls full of Nubian wall paintings, plus a pair of lunettes (semicircular paintings) from Bawit Monastery (**Room 23**). Rounding the corner, an original screen from the Church of St Barbara inaugurates the **woodwork** section. Fragments in the following alcove show a similar mixture of Hellenistic mythology, pharaonic symbolism and Coptic naturalism to the stone-carving in the other wing, while later pieces feature human activities. A **panel depicting Christ's entry into Jerusalem**, taken from the Hanging Church, is the high point of **Room 25**.

Sharing **Room 26** with Coptic toys and domestic utensils are several **mummy portrait panels**, latter-day versions of the Roman "Fayoum Portraits" displayed in the Egyptian Antiquities Museum. In the far right-hand corner is a remarkable **Early Coptic crucifix** (one of the few in existence), which combines a beardless Christ with a Horus hawk and sun disc. Byzantine and Sassanid (Persian) influences underlie the **friezes** of hunting scenes and fabulous creatures – motifs which continued into Islamic times until the Sunni restoration. The episcopal chairs in the annexe to **Room 27** are similar to the reception thrones used by wealthy amirs.

The last quarter of the wing displays **pottery**, arranged by type or form rather than antiquity. Ancient motifs such as fish, ducks and plants are widely employed. At the end of **Room 29** are **Pilgrims' flasks** showing St Menas between two camels (see p.620). Amongst the later work in **Room 30** are lustreware pieces like those made by Muslim potters at Fustat, but here emblazoned with a Coptic fish or cross. The annexe beyond contains a small collection of **glassware**.

The Hanging Church

Built directly above the water gate, the **Hanging Church** (*Al-Mu'allaqah*, "The Suspended" in Arabic) can be reached via an ornate portal on Mari Girgis street. Ascending a steep stairway, you enter a nineteenth-century vestibule displaying cassettes and videos of Coptic liturgies and papal sermons. Above this are the monks' quarters; beneath it lies a secret repository for valuables, only discovered last century.

The main **nave** – whose ceiling is ribbed like an upturned boat or ark – is separated from its side aisles by sixteen pillars, formerly painted with images of saints. Behind the marble pulpit, beautifully carved screens hide three **haikals** (altar areas) from the congregation. Accentuated by inlaid bone and ivory, their star patterns are similar to those found in mosques. Both pulpit and screens date from the thirteenth century, but the church was founded at least six hundred years earlier and may even have originated in the fourth century as a chapel for the soldiers of the bastion. Amongst its relics, the church once claimed to own an olive stone chewed by the Virgin Mary, to whom *Al-Mu'allaqah* is dedicated.

Coptic Masses are held on Fridays (8–11am) and Sundays (7–10am).

The Monastery of St George and into the Old Quarter

Returning to the Coptic Museum and heading north, go through the first gateway beyond the Coptic Museum entrance (ignoring any demands for cash from "doormen") to reach the precincts of the **Monastery of St George**, now the seat of the Greek Orthodox Patriarchate of Alexandria. The monastery itself rarely admits tourists, but it's worth looking into the neighbouring **Church of St George** (daily 8am–5pm). The only round church in Egypt, its dark interior is perfumed with incense and pierced by sunbeams filtered through stained glass. A (barred) flight of steps descends into the bowels of the Roman tower, once believed to be "peopled by devils". The present church was built in 1904 after a fire destroyed the original tenth-century structure. Notwithstanding the church's Orthodox allegiance, its **Moulid of Mari Girgis** (on St George's Day – April 23) is one of the largest Coptic festivals in Cairo.

Further up the main road, a **subterranean gateway** leads into the oldest part of Old Cairo, whose cobbled lanes flanked by high-walled houses wend between **medieval churches and cemeteries**. In 1929, Evelyn Waugh wrote disparagingly of a "constricted slum" whose Coptic residents hardly differed from their Muslim neighbours: "the only marked sign of their emancipation from heathen superstition was that the swarm of male and juvenile beggars were here reinforced by their womenfolk, who in the Mohammedan quarters maintain a modest seclusion." Since the late 1970s, the quarter has been gradually sanitized and tarted up for tourists, and now seems quite spruce compared to Islamic Cairo.

The most interesting of the churches is reached through the first gate on the left, after you pass through the subterranean gateway. This is the Coptic **Convent of St George** (*Deir Mari Girgis*), whose main building, still a nunnery, is closed to visitors. However, you can walk down into a lofty hall that once belonged to a Fatimid mansion and into the chapel beyond, with its tall, narrow wooden doors, which boasts a cedarwood casket containing relics of St George. To the left of this building is a small room used for the "**chain-wrapping ritual**", symbolizing the saint's persecution by the Romans. Several of the nuns speak English and welcome questions about their faith; they might even wrap you in chains for a souvenir photo.

Upon leaving the convent, walk on to the end of the lane, where it meets another thoroughfare. At this intersection, turn right around the corner to stumble upon the Church of St Sergius, or head left to explore the quarter's northern reaches.

North to the churches of St George and the Virgin

The north part of the Coptic quarter contains nothing special, but its solitude is refreshing and you might enjoy wandering around the overgrown **cemeteries** – so far unsquatted Cities of the Dead.

Fifty metres up the road from the intersection, an alley to the right leads to yet another **Church of St George**, founded in 681 by Athanasius the Scribe. From the original foundation only the Hall of Nuptials survived a conflagration in the mid-nineteenth century, after which the current structure was erected.

Beyond it, at the end of the road, stands the smaller **Church of the Virgin**, also known as *Qasriyyat al-Rihan* (Pot of Basil) after the favourite herb of the Orthodox Church. Because Al-Hakim's mother was of that faith, the church was given to the Greek community for the duration of his reign, but later returned to the Copts. Largely rebuilt in the eighteenth century, it's chiefly notable for several icons painted by John the Armenian in 1778.

The churches of St Sergius and St Barbara

Heading right from the intersection beyond the convent, you pass a tourist bazaar before reaching the **Church of St Sergius** (daily 8am–4pm), whose site below street level attests to its great age. Probably founded in the fifth century and continuously rebuilt since medieval times, *Abu Serga* retains the basilical form typical of early Coptic churches. The low ceiling and the antique columns topped with Corinthian capitals support the women's gallery, where you can inspect its thirteenth-century *haikal* screen and bits of frescoes and mosaics in the central apse. Steps to the right of the altar descend into a **crypt** where the Holy Family are believed to have stayed. A Coptic **festival** (June 1) commemorates their sojourn.

From St Sergius, you can wander along to the end of the lane where another thoroughfare leads to the Church of St Barbara (to the left) and Ben Ezra Synagogue (on the right).

The eleventh-century **Church of St Barbara** (daily 7am–4.30pm, extended to 8pm on Sat) replaced an earlier Church of SS Cyrus and John, which was razed during Al-Hakim's assault on Fustat. Unlike others in the quarter, its wooden-vaulted roof is lofty, with skylights and windows illuminating a nave flanked by Arabic arches with Fatimid tie-beams. Nor would its *minbar*-esque pulpit and inlaid *haikal* screen look amiss in a mosque. The western sanctuary contains the relics of *Sitt Barbara*. Tradition holds that she was the daughter of a pagan merchant who was murdered for preaching Christianity in the third century, but sceptics might note that her belated recognition followed another questionable case (see p.732).

The Ben Ezra Synagogue

Down the road, behind a wrought-iron fence, the **Ben Ezra Synagogue** is a unique relic of Cairo's ancient Jewish community. Bereft of its former host of worshippers (see the box below), the synagogue would have crumbled away were it not for the efforts of one "Rabbi" Cohen, who shamelessly overcharged for souvenir postcards to fund repairs for twenty years, until the American Jewish Congress and the Egyptian government stepped in to restore it. Today it is as good as new again.

In form, the synagogue resembles a basilical church of the kind that existed here between the fourth and ninth centuries. Sold to the Jews in order to pay taxes raised from the Copts to finance Ibn Tulun's Mosque, this church was either demolished or incorporated within the synagogue, which Abraham Ben Ezra, the Rabbi of Jerusalem, restored in the twelfth century. The inlaid marble and gilded stalactite niche date from around then, but most of the graceful mouldings and floral swirls are the result of nineteenth-century repairs, which unearthed a huge cache of medieval manuscripts, including a sixth-century Torah written on gazelle hide (now dispersed around Western libraries).

Nevertheless, Jewish and Coptic traditions invest the site with ancient significance. Here, the pharaoh's daughter found Moses in the bulrushes; Jeremiah gathered survivors after Nebuchadnezzar destroyed Jerusalem; and the temple named after him provided a haven for the Holy Family, who lived amongst the Jews of Babylon for three months. Moreover, the Copts believe that Peter and Mark pursued their apostolic mission in Egypt, whence Peter issued the First Epistle General. The rest of Christendom disagrees, however, arguing that the Biblical reference to Babylon (I Peter 5:13) is only a metaphor for Rome.

Around the back of the synagogue are a newly restored chunk of the Roman walls and a derelict Jewish Refuge founded by one Ralph Green.

Egypt's Jewish community is dying out: fewer than two hundred *Yahud* remain in Alexandria, Old Cairo and the Jewish Old People's Home in Heliopolis. The three synagogues that still exist will become empty memorials within a decade or so – a melancholy end to a story that begins in the **Old Testament**. The book of Genesis relates how the descendants of Abraham escaped famine in Canaan (Palestine) by migrating to Egypt at the behest of Joseph, the pharaoh's favourite. Settling in the "Land of Goshen", they "multiplied and waxed mighty" until a new pharaoh enslaved them to build "the treasure-cities, Pithom and Raamses". Their flight from Egypt to the Promised Land is described in Exodus.

Squaring this with ancient Egyptian **history** presents difficulties. Whereas numerous sites are suggestive of Pithom and Raamses, there's no mention of the Exodus in pharaonic records. Assuming the Old Testament is based on genuine history, the Jews probably arrived sometime in the Ramessid era (c.1320–1237 BC), while the Exodus is generally ascribed to the reign of Merneptah (1236–1223 BC). There's some evidence for the Prophet Jeremiah's foundation of a new community at Babylon-in-Egypt after the destruction of Jerusalem (585 BC), but there is no firm historical ground until the second century BC, when it is known that the Ptolemies encouraged an influx of Jews into Alexandria.

In contrast to the Alexandrian fusion of Greek and Jewish culture, the Jews of Babylon were more akin to native Egyptians. Mutual sympathies were strengthened by the **Jewish revolt** against Roman rule (115–17 AD) and the Coptic belief in the **Egyptian exile of the Holy Family**. Babylon's Jewish community would have been a natural haven for Mary, Joseph and the baby Jesus when Herod's wrath made Palestine too dangerous (it's harder to see why they should have hidden out near Assyut, as is also claimed).

As "People of the Book", Egypt's Jews were treated about as well (or badly) as the Copts **during the Islamic period**, acting as small traders, gold- and silversmiths, moneychangers or moneylenders. In Mohammed Ali's day, E.W. Lane (see p.820) estimated that they numbered about five thousand. The British, however, introduced a new element: Jews who came as Europeans and shared the Brit-colonial disdain for the natives. Most of these new arrivals were merchants or professionals and settled in Alexandria or Cairo. A few families of *haute Juiverie* – the Menasces, Rolos, Hararis and Cattauis – were financiers who moved in royal circles. These **foreign Jews** lamented post-revolutionary restrictions on business and left en masse before and after the Suez Crisis (1956).

Meanwhile, native Jews were torn between Egypt and **Israel** as each war eroded their security. By the time of the 1967 war their numbers had declined from 75,000 to 2600 (mostly living in Cairo), though the capital still had 26 working synagogues, until mobs attacked them for the first time during the conflict. Thereafter, all but a few hundred Jews emigrated, leaving the poor, now aged, community that remains today.

The Mosque of Amr, Deir Abu'l-Sayfayn and Fustat

To get a feel for what happened after Babylon and Egypt surrendered to Islam, return to Mari Girgis Street and follow it northwards, past the turning for Fustat and a small bus depot, to the **Mosque of Amr**. Though continuously altered, not to mention doubled in size in 827, this boasts direct descent from Egypt's first-ever mosque, built in 641. A simple mud-brick, thatch-roofed enclosure without a *mihrab*, courtyard or minaret, it was large enough to contain the Muslim army at prayer. At its inauguration, **Amr Ibn al-As** told his 3500 Arab warriors:

The Nile floods have risen. The grazing will be good. There is milk for the lambs and kids. Go out with God's blessing and enjoy the land, its milk, its flocks and its herds, and take good care of your neighbours, the Copts, for the Prophet of God himself gave orders for us to do so.

Until the fratricidal struggle between Sunni and Shia, this injunction was honoured: aside from paying a poll tax, non-Muslims enjoyed equal rights. It was Ibn Tulun and Al-Hakim who introduced the discrimination (or worse), that later rulers either foreswore on principle or practised for motives of bigotry, fear or greed. But on an everyday level, citizens of each faith amicably coexisted within the city of Fustat-Masr, as they do in modern Cairo.

The site of the mosque was indicated by Allah, who sent a dove to nest in Amr's tent while he was away at war; on returning he declared it sacrosanct, waited until the dove's brood was raised, then built a mosque. The existing building follows the classic congregational pattern, arched *liwans* surrounding a pebbled *sahn* centred on an ablutions well. Believers pray or snooze on fine carpets in the sanctuary *liwan*, whose original *mihrab* is misaligned towards Mecca. When Amr introduced a pulpit, he was rebuked by Khalif Omar for raising himself above his Muslim brethren. The *mashrabiya*'d **mausoleum** of his son, Abdullah, marks the site of Amr's house in Fustat. A nearby column bears a gash caused by people licking it until their tongues bled, to obtain miraculous cures. The pair of columns on the left as you come in are said to part to allow the truly righteous to squeeze through, and another was whipped from Mecca by Omar. From the mosque's **well**, it is said, a pilgrim retrieved a goblet dropped into the Well of Zemzem in the Holy City.

Deir Abu'l-Sayfayn

If the Coptic quarter hasn't satisfied your curiosity about medieval churches, pay a visit to **Deir Abu'l-Sayfayn**, northwest of Amr's Mosque. This high-walled enclosure (currently closed for renovation, though you may be able to enter when it opens for prayers) is entered via a humble wooden door; the original iron-bound door is now in the Coptic Museum. Within the compound are several churches of indeterminate age. First mentioned in the tenth century (when it served as a sugar-cane warehouse) and totally rebuilt after the burning of Fustat, the **Church of St Mercurius** claims older antecedents. Beneath its northern aisle lies a tiny crypt where St Barsum the Naked lived with a snake until his death in 317; a special Mass is held here on his nameday (September 10).

A doorway beside the crypt stairway leads through into the rest of the complex. The Upper Church, reached by steps, contains five disused chapels. Of more interest are the Small Church with its *haikal* dedicated to St James the Sawn-asunder, and the early seventh-century **Church of St Shenute**, featuring beautiful cedarwood and ebony iconostases. From the same period comes the diminutive, icon-packed **Church of the Holy Virgin**, beyond which stands the **Convent of St Mercurius**, still inhabited by nuns. The liturgy is celebrated in all the churches (Wed 8am–noon, Fri 7–11am & Sun 6–10am). Adjacent to Deir Abu'l-Sayfayn are extensive Protestant and Maronite **cemeteries**.

The remains of Fustat and Cairo's zebaleen

En route to Amr's Mosque you'll pass a turn-off to the right, lined with piles of earthenware pots, jars and waterpipes. Behind them, smouldering rubbish tips and hovels sprawl beneath a pall of smoke, seemingly as far as the Citadel. The hundred-year-old shantytown on the site of ancient Fustat looks – and smells – daunting, but is actually a success story in Third World terms. Its US-sponsored health centre is the most conspicuous example of many recent improvements in a community that used to be at the bottom of the Cairene heap. Should you care to explore, a twenty-minute walk alongside the shanty-town will bring you to the **remains of Fustat**. Bring water, a few stones to deter dogs, and above all tread carefully – much of the site consists of centuries-old rubbish tips and kilns, prone to caving in. The foundation walls and water system (still being excavated by the American University) hardly do justice to Fustat's past, though the pottery shards that blanket the site are evocative; some fine early medieval and imported Chinese ware can be seen in the Islamic Arts Museum.

Originally a cluster of tribal encampments around Amr's Mosque, Fustat (City of the Tent) evolved into a mud-brick beehive of multistorey dwellings with rooftop gardens, fountains, and a piped water and sewage system unequalled in Europe until the eighteenth century. As the Abbassids, Tulunids and Ikhshidids also built their own cities ever further to the northeast, a great conurbation known as **Fustat–Masr** was formed. Its decline began in Fatimid times, as the noxious potteries encouraged migration towards Al-Qahira; thieves moved in and dereliction spread like cancer. In 1020, the mad khalif Al-Hakim ordered his troops to sack Fustat-Masr for reasons worthy of Caligula (see p.146). Yet even in 1168, what remained was so vast that Vizier Shawar decided to evacuate and burn it rather than let the Crusaders occupy the old city beyond Al-Qahira's walls. Set ablaze with 10,000 torches and 20,000 barrels of naphtha, Fustat smouldered for 55 days.

Today the Fustat shantytown is inhabited by seventeen thousand people whose filthy work keeps Cairo tolerably clean. Whole families of **potters** slave over beehive kilns, churning out domestic ware for *baladi* households and piping for sewers and water mains. Even more important are the *zebaleen* or **rubbish-gatherers**. These families collect and sift Cairo's rubbish for anything edible or recyclable. All the glass, cardboard, metal, rags and leather are sold as raw materials to over five hundred factories. Though previously regarded as an embarrassment by the authorities, the *zebaleen* have made an indispensable contribution to Cairo's ecology, recognized by the award of a prize at the World Earth Summit and an official government contract in 1991. Community amenities are being improved through self-help projects with foreign backing, in a development programme that could be a model for others in the Third World.

Fustat is served by bus #83 from Midan Ramses. Otherwise, **to return to central Cairo**, walk to El-Malek el-Saleh metro station, or head back to the Amr's Mosque and catch a bus (#134/ and #27 to Midan Tahrir, #825 to Ataba, all of those to Ramses).

North to the Aqueduct

Travelling between Coptic and central Cairo by bus or taxi, you'll catch sight of the great **Aqueduct** that carried water to the Citadel. Originally a mere conduit supported by wooden pillars, it was solidly rebuilt in stone by Sultan al-Nasir in 1311 and subsequently extended in 1505 by Al-Ghuri to accommodate the Nile's westward shift, to a total length of 3405m. River water was lifted by the **Burg al-Saqiyya**, a massive hexagonal water-wheel tower near the Corniche. On its western wall can be seen Al-Ghuri's heraldic emblem and slots for engaging the six oxen-powered water wheels, which remained in use until 1872.

The site of this tower is known as **Fumm al-Khalig** (Mouth of the Canal), after the waterway that once ran inland to meet the walls of Fatimid al-Qahira. This *Khalig Masri* (Egyptian Canal) supplied most of Cairo's water during Mamluke and Ottoman times, and was also linked to the ancient Nile Delta–Red Sea waterway, re-dug by Amr and Al-Nasir. In an annual ceremony to mark the *Wafa el-Nil*, or Nile flood, the dike that separated it from the river was breached, sending fresh water coursing through the city. Pleasure boats were launched onto the lakes near Bab al-Luq and Ezbekiya, while fireworks heralded nocturnal revelries. But the taming of the Nile spelt the end of this practice, and after piped water was introduced early last century the canal was filled in to create Bur Said and Ramses streets.

Further inland

From the Fumm al-Khalig roundabout, Sharia al-Sadd al-Barrani runs up to Saiyida Zeinab (2km) past a swathe of **Christian cemeteries**. Within the northernmost cemetery, high walls enclose the **Monastery of St Menas** (*Deir Abu Mina*), whose sunken basilical church has been endlessly rebuilt since 724. Having returned the holy remnants of St Menas to his desert monastery (see p.620), the church now gives pride of place to the relics of saints Behnam and Sarah, who were martyred by their own father. The monastery receives very few visitors and has no set opening hours.

Further south, the Aqueduct bestrides a medieval slum centred around a huge **slaughterhouse** and reeking **tanneries**. To outsiders, stark poverty seems all-pervasive; yet among those who live here, social distinctions are keenly felt. A slaughterhouse worker and his boss will both wear bloodstained *galabiyyas* during working hours, and possibly live on the same street – but the former can only speculate on what riches the latter keeps indoors. Conversely, people will salvage designer-label bags and boxes to flaunt on the streets as if they were returning with a purchase.

Unlike the tanneries of Morocco, this is hardly on the tourist trail, although French writer Gustave Flaubert spent an afternoon here in 1850, shooting birds of prey and "wolf-like dogs". However, the odd tourist has been known to attend Saturday evening *zikrs* outside the **Mosque of Sidi Ali Zein al-Abdin**, on the periphery of the quarter of Saiyida Zeinab (see p.168).

Roda Island

The narrow channel between **Roda Island** and the mainland is bridged in such a way that the island engages more with Garden City than with Old Cairo – a reversal of historic ties. As its much-rebuilt **Nilometer** suggests, it was the southern end of Roda that was visited by ferries en route between Memphis and Heliopolis, and Roman ships bound for Babylon-in-Egypt. However, nothing remains of the Byzantine fortress that defied the Muslim invasion, nor the vaster Ayyubid *qasr* where the Bahri Mamlukes were garrisoned, since Roda reverted to agricultural use as Cairo's focus shifted north-eastwards. The island's main sight, the **Manial Palace**, re-established a fashion for palatial residences early this century, though it wasn't until the 1950s that Roda experienced a building explosion similar to Zamalek's.

Approaching the sights

With Roda's tourist attractions sited 3km apart, choice of **transport** is a major consideration. The Nilometer is best reached on foot from Old Cairo via the footbridge from the Corniche. You can take a minibus or service taxi down the Corniche from the centre to Old Cairo; alternatively Mari Girgis metro station is just two blocks southeast of the footbridge. Should you decide to settle for only one site, make it the palace, which is easily accessible from central Cairo. Aside from a taxi (£E4–5), a #58 minibus is the fastest way of getting there from Midan Tahrir (Abdel Mouneem Riyad terminal), or minibus #56 from Ramses: alight on Sharia Sayala, near the palace gates. Walking takes about half an hour from downtown Cairo, and on hot days can leave you totally bushed.

The first bridge, coming from downtown, leads to the **Meridien Hotel**, a deluxe five-star job with some of the best views in Cairo. The next crossing, Qasr al-Aini Bridge, leads down to **Cairo University Medical Faculty**. By walking 150m south from here you can reach the palace gates without crossing the Manial Bridge, used by traffic heading for Giza. Cairo's **youth hostel** overlooks the El-Gama'a Bridge, 500m further west.

The Manial Palace

The **Manial Palace** (daily 9am–4.30pm; £E10, students £E5) is a Cairo must. Built in 1903, its fabulously eclectic architecture reflects the taste of King Farouk's uncle, Prince Mohammed Ali, author of *The Breeding of Arabian Horses* and the owner of a flawless emerald that magically alleviated his ill health (so legend has it). Each of the main buildings manifests a different style – Persian, Syrian, Moorish, Ottoman and Rococo – or mixes them together with gay abandon.

Having bought your ticket, make a beeline for the **Reception Palace** just inside the gateway. Its magnificent *salamlik*, adorned with stained glass, polychrome tiles and ornate woodcarving, prepares you for the opulent guest rooms upstairs; the finest is the Syrian Room, which was quite literally transplanted from Damascus. On the stairs you'll notice a scale model of Qaitbey's Mausoleum, made entirely of mother-of-pearl.

Leaving the Reception Palace and turning right, you come upon a pseudo-Moroccan tower harbouring the prince's **mosque**, whose lavish decor is reminiscent of the great mosque of his namesake in the Citadel. Further along, the grotesque **Hunting Museum** features scores of mounted ibex heads, gorgeous butterflies and ineptly stuffed fowl, a hermaphrodite goat, a table made from elephants' ears and a vulture's claw candlestick.

The **Prince's Residence**, deeper into the banyan-shaded garden, is richly decorated in a mixture of Turkish and Occidental styles. The drab-looking building out back contains a long **Throne Hall** whose red carpet passes life-size royal portraits hung beneath a sunburst ceiling. Around the outside of this hall are the skeletons of the prince's horse and camel, and a stairway to the upper level (often closed). If accessible, visitors can admire its Obsidian Salon and the private apartments of the prince's mother, enriched by a silver four-poster bed from the Abdin Palace. Lastly, follow the signs to the **Private Museum**, a family hoard of manuscripts, carpets, glassware and silver plate – notice the huge banqueting trays.

The Nilometer and Umm Kalthoum Museum

The southern tip of Roda Island, most easily accessed via a footbridge from the Corniche west of Mari Girgis and Old Cairo, features a new **museum** dedicated to the life and work of Egypt's most popular singer, **Umm Kalthoum** (daily 10am–6pm; £E5). Through audiovisual clips, photos, press cuttings and a filmshow, the museum attempts to recreate the life of this giant of Arabic music (see p.815). Though she died in 1975, her songs, invariably backed by an orchestra of violins, remain massively popular throughout the Arab world. Exhibits include 78rpm wax records, letters from Egyptian and other Arab heads of state including Nasser, Sadat and King Farouk, and, most poignantly, her trademark pink scarf and dark glasses. Unfortunately, however, all explanation is in Arabic only.

In the same compound is the **Nilometer** (daily 9am–5pm; £E6). From ancient times into the present century, Egyptian agriculture depended on the annual **flooding of the Nile**. Crop yields were predicted and taxes were set according to the river's level in August, as measured by Nilometers. A reading of 16 *ells* (8.6m) foretold the valley's complete irrigation; significantly more or less meant widespread flooding or drought. Public rejoicing followed the announcement of the *Wafa el-Nil* (Abundance of the Nile), while any other verdict caused gloom and foreboding.

Although the southern tip of Roda has probably featured a Nilometer since pharaonic times, the existing one dates from 861 and its Turkish kiosk is actually a modern replica, built in 1947 and recently restored. Descending well below the level of the Nile, its stone-lined shaft was connected to the river by three tunnels (now sealed) at different heights – the uppermost is still accessible. Around the shaft's interior are Koranic verses in kufic script, extolling rain as God's blessing; its central column is graduated into 16 *ells* of roughly 54cm each. The Nilometer is often locked, but its caretaker will turn out for rare visitors.

The ticket for the Nilometer or the Umm Kalthoum Museum also admits you to the neighbouring **Monastirli Palace**, a Rococo confection dating from 1850. Built as a conference centre, the palace has now been transformed into an International Music Centre, with a theatre, exhibition hall and library (ⓦ www.manasterly.com).

The southern suburbs

South of Old Cairo, a ribbon of development follows the east bank of the Nile down to Helwan. Though easily reached by metro, these **southern suburbs** hold little attraction for tourists, notwithstanding Ma'adi's popularity as an expatriate residential area. However, even the least-favoured quarters cast some light on various facets of Egyptian life.

Al-Basatin: the Jewish cemetery

A case in point is the **Jewish cemetery of Al-Basatin**, 3km beyond El-Khalifa (minibus #54 or bus #160/ from Midan Tahrir; bus #72 from Midan Ramses; or minibus #57 from Midan Ataba). Tens of thousands of graves, up to nine hundred years old, have been stripped of their marble slabs, while squatters have occupied any mausolea going (Al-Basatin has few of these compared to the Muslim and Coptic cemeteries). During the late 1980s, the elders of Cairo's depleted Jewish community agreed to accept US$80,000 in return for allowing a highway to be ploughed through Al-Basatin. When foreign rabbis intervened, the whole affair acquired diplomatic overtones and turned into a massive legal wrangle. In the end the government reached an agreement with an American Jewish organization to rehouse the squatters, restore the cemetery and build a flyover to carry the ring road over it.

Ma'adi and the quarries of Tura

With its Corniche boutiques and takeaways, and acres of villas set amidst luxuriant grounds, **Ma'adi** is unmistakably wealthy. Besides native millionaires and Gulf Arabs, most of Egypt's American community lives here. Trendy **restaurants** include the Thai *Bua Khao*, at 9 Road 151 (daily noon–11pm; ☎02/358 0126), and the *Seahorse* on Ma'adi's Corniche, near the **As-Salam International**

Hospital (☎02/524 0360). Ma'adi also has a handful of Chinese restaurants, including a branch of the city-wide *Peking* chain at 29 Sharia el-Nasr/Road 257 (daily noon–1am; ☎02/516 4218); an Indian, the *Bukhara*, 43 Sharia Misr Helwan (daily noon–1am; ☎02/380 5999); and an outpost of posh patisserie *La Poire*, in the Pico Building at 24 Sharia Wadi el-Nil.

The **Military Hospital**, on the Corniche further north, is the largest of its kind in the Middle East. It was here that the ex-Shah of Iran died of cancer, and President Sadat was rushed by helicopter from the blood-soaked reviewing stand in Medinet Nasr. As a young officer during World War II, Sadat was actually stationed in Ma'adi when he became embroiled in a Nazi spy ring (see p.199). Ma'adi is directly accessible from Tahrir or Ramses by microbus service taxi or metro (25min).

Further south amidst the Muqattam foothills, the **quarries of Tura** have yielded fine limestone since pharaonic times (it was here that pyramid casing blocks were quarried), and now also produce cement.

Helwan

The once-fashionable spa of **Helwan** is now grossly polluted by a gigantic **iron- and steelworks** that exploits power from the Aswan Dam and iron ore from the Western Desert. The steelworks wreak eco-death on a nineteenth-century **Japanese Garden** (daily: winter 9am–9pm; summer 9am–midnight; £E2, camera £E2, video £E5) – complete with Buddhas and a pagoda – five blocks east from Helwan metro station (turn left as you exit); ask for *Ganenit el-Arbaine Harami*. One hundred metres south of Ain Helwan metro station (one stop back up the line from Helwan station), a tacky but fun **Waxworks Museum** (*methaf sham*; daily 9am–3pm; £E2) portrays such moments in Egyptian history as the death of Cleopatra, and Salah al-Din's meeting with Richard the Lionheart. The sulphurous **Ain Helwan Baths** (daily 24hr; free) are less than 100m northwest of Ain Helwan station.

Gezira and the west bank

Flowing northwards through Cairo, the Nile divides into channels around the two major islands of Roda and Gezira. **Gezira**, the larger island, is further from the centre than Roda and notably more spacious and verdant than the rest of Cairo.

Across the island, elevated highways bear cross-town traffic to diverse **districts on the west bank** of the Nile, collectively known as **Giza** and administered as a separate governorate from Cairo. Moving south through its neighbourhoods, **Imbaba** is a working-class district and former site of Cairo's main camel market – a world apart from the adjoining **Aguza**, with its Corniche nightlife, and even more from the Dallas-style pretensions of **Mohandiseen**. Further south and east is **Dokki**, whose wealthy enclaves give way to *baladi* market quarters, the green lungs of Cairo's zoo and scattered university faculties, before the dusty expanse of Giza city extends to the Pyramids. Giza's **transport** and utilities are functionally integrated with Cairo's.

Gezira and Zamalek

Gezira (literally "island") dominates the waterfront from Garden City to Bulaq, its three sets of bridges spanning the Nile. Nearly 4km long and 1km wide, the island is big enough to encompass two distinct zones. The southern

GEZIRA & THE WEST BANK

EMBASSIES SHOWN THUS: *Algeria*

ACCOMMODATION
Cairo Marriott	3
El-Gezira Sheraton	6
El-Nil Zamalek	2
Longchamps/ Horus House	1
Mayfair	5
Pension Zamalek	4

RESTAURANTS AND CAFÉS

Aguza & Dokki
Cafeteria Nema	3
Ciao	4
Flying Fish	

Mohandiseen
Abou Shakra	W
Al-Omdah	aa
Baskin Robbins	X
Bon Appetit	E, T

Cairo Jazz Club	S	La Poire	D
Fraghly Fruits	O	Prestige Pizza	Z
Okamoto	C	Tandoori	U
Peking	J	Le Tirol	Y

Zamalek & Gezira
Al Dente	A	Five Bells	A
Angus Brasserie	I	Hana Korean Restaurant	G
Chin Chin	V	Justine	V
Deals	M	L'Aubergine	K
Don Quichotte	N	La Piazza	B
La Poire	H	Maison Thomas	Q
Prestige Pizza	R	Pub 28	F
Tandoori	U	Simmonds	P
Le Tirol	Y	Coffee House	L
		Zamalek	V

Labels on map: TAHRIR BRIDGE, 6 OCTOBER BRIDGE, SHARIA EL-BORG, Hadiket en-Nahr, Hadiket Mesla, Andalusian Garden, Riyadi Garden, GEZIRA, Gezira Youth Club, Cairo Tower, Modern Art Museum, Opera House, OPERA/GEZIRA, Mukhtar Museum, Fountain, Dr Ragab's Papyrus Institute, GALAA BRIDGE, SHARIA TAHRIR, SHARIA EL-NIL (CORNICHE), Cairo Sheraton, SHARIA SAAD EL ALI, Tahrir Cinema, Syria, Jordan, Yemen, Mahmoud Khalil/ Museum, EL-GIZA, SHARIA, Vaccination Centre, SHARIA WAZARET EL-ZERAA, DOKKI, Agricultural Museum, EL-SAID, D O K K I, SHARIA TAHRIR, SHARIA NADI, Shooting Club, SHARIA MOHI EL-DIN ABU EZZ, SHARIA AL-SUDAN half, featuring the Opera House complex, parks, a viewing tower and famous sporting clubs, is Gezira proper. **Zamalek** (pronounced "Zah-*mah*-lek"), further north, is pure real estate – apartments, villas, offices and embassies – with a Westernized ambience and nightlife. Both seem so integral to Cairo that it's hard to envisage their absence, yet the island itself only coalesced in the early 1800s and remained unstable until the first Aswan Dam regulated the Nile's flood in the 1900s.

Almost a third of the island belongs to the **Gezira Sporting Club** (see p.259), laid out by the British Army on land given by Khedive Tewfiq. The club's main pursuits were horse racing and polo, imbued with an extraordinary mystique. "It is on the Gezira polo grounds that the officers of the Cavalry Brigade are tested for military efficiency and fitness for command", wrote C.S. Jarvis in the 1920s. Diplomats and selected upper-crust Egyptians also belonged to the club and, after Nasser decided against expropriation following the revolution, it soon acquired members from the new elite. The hefty membership fees still restrict access to its golf course, tennis courts, stables, gardens and pet cemetery; non-members are resolutely excluded.

Approaches to Gezira and Zamalek: the bridges

The **6th October Bridge**, high above the Sporting Club, is more of a direct link between Aguza and central Cairo than a viable approach to Gezira (though there are stairs down to both banks of the island). However, it does overlook the offices and former ground (now used only for training) of **Ahly FC**, one of Egypt's top football teams, whose name means "National".

It's the southern bit of **Gezira**, however, that's most accessible and worth seeing. Despite heavy traffic, it's enjoyable to walk across the **Tahrir Bridge** (200m from Midan Tahrir), catching the breeze and watching barges and feluccas on the river. Gaining the island, you can strike 200m northwards past the *El-Borg Hotel* and turn left down an avenue to reach the Cairo Tower (10min), or follow the traffic heading for Dokki, which brings you to the Cairo Opera House and several museums (5–10min). Taxis or *caleches* are happy to oblige if you'd rather ride, but they expect the "tourist minimum".

To get to **Zamalek**, it's best to save yourself a long walk from central Cairo and grab a taxi (which shouldn't cost more than £E3–5). Buses from Midan Tahrir to Zamalek will drop you on Sharia Gabalaya on the western side of the district. In principle, there's no lack of minibuses heading west along **26th July Street** from Midan Ataba and Midan Ramses, but at the time of writing the road was partly closed while construction of a new elevated section was under way, and all road transport was taking a lengthy (often gridlocked) diversion via 6th October Bridge. Having traversed the island, the highway crosses the **Zamalek Bridge** onto the west bank, where Midan Sphinx funnels traffic into Mohandiseen (see p.197). When the new Metro line opens there will be a station in the north of the island called, unsurprisingly, Zamalek.

Cairo Tower

Rising 187m above Gezira, the **Borg al-Qahira** or **Cairo Tower** offers a stupendous view of the seething immensity of Cairo (daily: winter 8am–11pm; summer 9am–1am; £E32, video permit £E15); the entrance is to the north of the tower in Sharia el-Borg. Built between 1957 and 1962 with Soviet help, the tower combines pharaonic and socialist realist motifs within a latticework shaft of poured concrete that blossoms into a lotus finial.

On the fourteenth floor is an overpriced "Egyptian-style" restaurant (set menu payable with tower ticket: £E60 for entry and meal) that occasionally

Cairo's best views

The Cairo Tower, with its usually non-revolving restaurant, is just one of several high points where you can take in a view over Cairo. The newer and more reliably revolving restaurant at the *Royal Meridien* hotel (see p.101) is high enough, and well enough placed, to offer what must rate as the very best Cairo view, encompassing the Pyramids, the Citadel, the Nile and most of downtown. The rooftop bar at the *Nile Hilton* (see p.101) is a close competitor, with great views of Tahrir Square that only the front rooms at the *Ismailia House* hotel can equal. The Citadel itself offers a view over Islamic Cairo that isn't at all bad, and some of Islamic Cairo's minarets give you a vista as far as the Pyramids on a clear day if they are open (the Qalaoun complex and the Blue Mosque are among the best, but both were closed at last check). Finally, for a vista over the chaos and mayhem that calls itself Midan Ramses, the terrace café of the *Hotel Everest* (see p.131) is the place. Alternatively, just be sure to get a window seat on your flight home.

revolves; above it is a similarly styled cafeteria serving tolerable tea, with the viewing room – complete with telescopes – upstairs from here. The real attraction, though, provided by the café, restaurant and a **viewing platform** at the top, is the **panoramic vista of Cairo**. East across the river, the blue-and-white *Nile Hilton* and the antenna-festooned Television Building delineate an arc of central Cairo. Beyond lies the medieval quarter, bristling with minarets below the Citadel and the serene Muqattam Hills. Roda Island and deluxe hotels dominate the view south (upriver); to the north are Zamalek, Shubra and the Nile Delta. Westwards, the city extends to meet the desert, with the Pyramids visible on the horizon on clear days. Come a while before sunset to witness Cairo transformed by nightfall, as a thousand muezzins call across the water. Below the tower is the *Legends* nightclub which has bellydancing every night.

The Opera House complex

Fans of postmodernist architecture should check out the **Cairo Opera House**, which is near Tahrir Bridge and directly connected to the Metro (the station is called "Opera", but is confusingly marked as "Gezira" on the Metromap). Outwardly Islamic in style, its interior melds pharaonic motifs with elements of the Baroque opera houses of the nineteenth century: an audacious blend of Oriental and Occidental by Japanese architect Koichiro Shikida. A US$30 million gift from Japan, it was built in 1988, belatedly replacing the old building on Midan Opera, which burned down in 1971. Off to the right as you walk towards the Opera House is the **Modern Art Museum** (currently closed but due to reopen Oct 2002; Mon–Sat 10am–1pm & 5–9pm; £E10, students £E5), which displays paintings, sculptures and graphics by Egyptian artists since 1908; there is always something new on show.

Following Sharia Tahrir towards the west bank, you'll pass the old Gezira Exhibition Grounds, whose dilapidated pavilions formerly housed the **Gezira Museum** (objets d'art collected by the royal family), the **Museum of Egyptian Civilization** (illustrating national history from pharaonic to modern times) and a **Planetarium**; all, however, are closed for long-term renovation, and don't look like reopening for some time to come, if ever. Across the road to the south, just before the Galaa Bridge, the **Mukhtar Museum** (also currently closed for restorations; ☎02/340 2519) honours the sculptor Mahmoud Mukhtar (1891–1934), who is buried in the basement. Working in bronze and marble, he created several patriotic sculptures, including the *Renaissance of Egypt* monument that welcomes drivers into Dokki.

The 27-storey **El-Gezirah Sheraton** at the southern tip of the island can be reached by slip roads from the Tahrir and Galaa bridgeheads. On public holidays, a **fountain** in the middle of the Nile between Gezira and Roda shoots an immense jet of water into the sky.

Zamalek

Originally a very British neighbourhood, despite its Continental grid of tree-lined boulevards, **Zamalek** still has bags of social cachet: renting a flat here is the Cairene equivalent of moving into Manhattan. Unlike most parts of Cairo, the quarter feels very private; residents withdraw into air-conditioned high-rises or 1930s apartment buildings, and with so many foreign companies and **embassies** in the area (see p.274), most of the streets are lifeless after dark.

Somewhat paradoxically, Zamalek also features some of the trendiest **nightspots** in Cairo. Near the Aguza side of the Gezira Sporting Club on Sharia Hassan Sabry, the *Four Corners* complex contains, among others, a deluxe French restaurant, *Justine* (see p.244); there are more bars and restaurants to be found in the *Marriott Hotel*. Other places congregate north of the 26th July fly-over. Gay men and British expats favour *Pub 28*, at the junction of Shagar al-Durr and Hassan Assim streets, and *Harry's Bar* at the *Marriott*. A younger crowd congregate at *Deals* bar and the neighbouring café on Sharia Sayed el-Bakry. For eating with live music, there's *Five Bells* on Sharia Ismail Mohammed.

Zamalek by day has less to offer, though children may enjoy the **aquarium grotto** in **Galabaya Park** (daily 8.30am–3pm; 50pt), entered from Sharia Galabaya. For more cultural pursuits, head for the other end of Sharia el-Gezira as it curves around the northeastern edge of the Sporting Club. Here, a graceful nineteenth-century villa now houses the Museum of Islamic Ceramics (see below); the **Mahmoud Khalil Museum** that was formerly housed here is now in Dokki (see p.200). The modern annexes of the adjacent **Cairo Marriott Hotel** screen what was originally a "madly sumptuous palace" built for Empress Eugénie, later sold to wealthy Copts in lieu of Ismail's debts and turned into a hotel. Non-residents can wander in and loll amidst khedival splendour for the price of a drink.

Museum of Islamic Ceramics

Housed in a white-domed villa close to the *Cairo Marriott*, the **Museum of Islamic Ceramics** (Sat–Thurs 9am–1pm & 5–9pm; £E25, students £E5) is one of Cairo's most agreeable museums. Built by Prince Amru Abrahim in the late nineteenth century, the structure itself is worth a look for its elaborate marble inlays and floors, while the collection inside contains pieces from Egypt, Persia, Syria, Turkey, Morocco, Iraq and even Andalusia (Spain), ranging from the seventh century to the present. The illustrated guidebook (£E25) explains each piece in English and also gives a thorough account of the history of Islamic ceramics. Downstairs there's a museum of fine art (same hours; free) that exhibits original paintings and sculptures as well as prints by modern Egyptian artists such as Asraf and Alzamzami. All the works exhibited are for sale.

Imbaba and the new Bil'esh Camel Market

From Midan KitKat, 300m north of Zamalek Bridge, Sharia al-Sudan arcs through the **Imbaba** district, whose overspill covers the site of the "**Battle of the Pyramids**" where Napoleon's army routed the Mamlukes on July 21, 1798, prior to taking Cairo. Unfortunately for Napoleon – who dreamed of "founding a religion, marching into Asia riding an elephant", bearing "the new

Koran that I would have composed to suit my needs" – his strategic ambition to disrupt British power in India was literally scuppered when Nelson sank his fleet at Abu Qir Bay. Within eighty years, the Suez Canal had cemented the link between naval power, control of Egypt and Britain's empire "East of Suez"; a bond later reinforced by aviation. Although flying boats on the famous Cape-to-Cairo run used the Nile, most Imperial Airways flights used **Imbaba Airport**, now a flying school.

Formerly in Imbaba, but now held way out to the north at **Bil'esh**, is Cairo's Friday **Camel Market**, a weekly feast of drama and cruelty. Beaten into defecating ranks, the hobbled camels are assessed by traders who disregard their emaciation – caused by a month-long trek from northwestern Sudan to Aswan, followed by an overnight truck ride to Cairo – and concentrate on other features.

Strength and speed are discernible in the legs, chest, eyes, ears and position of the hump, while teeth reflect age; the clearly knackered are evaluated for their meat and hide. During rutting season, signs of irritation (an inflated mouth sac, ferocious slobbering and gurgling) often herald a kick or bite from an enraged bull camel. Docile females are generally preferred as mounts. They're also exchanged for goats and other livestock, while Bishari herdsmen and Egyptian merchants gossip over tea, unperturbed by throat-slittings and disembowelments near the piles of saddlery and tack. In an adjacent compound is a furniture and bric-a-brac market, not unlike a car-boot or yard sale.

Lasting from dawn till early afternoon every Friday, the *Souk el-Gamal* (pronounced "Gah*mell*") is busiest between 6 and 8.30am. To get there by taxi will cost around £E20, but the market is also accessible by service taxi microbus from the old site at Imbaba, or from Warraq (a village halfway between Imbaba and Bil'esh). Both are served by microbus from Sharia Sabtiya, off Midan Ramses; you then have to take another microbus for the final leg. Alternatively, you can catch the #214 bus from the *Nile Hilton* terminal in Midan Tahrir to Manashi by the Nile Barrage at Panatir (45min) and take a service taxi microbus from there. Going back into town, you should be able to find direct service taxis to Midan Ramses.

Mohandiseen

Laid out during the 1960s to house Egypt's new technocrats, Medinat Mohandiseen ("Engineers' City"), as the suburb was initially called, responded to an influx of business and media folk during the Sadat era by shortening its name to just **Mohandiseen** and emulating America. Nowhere else in Cairo can you cruise down a boulevard glittering with boutiques and junk food outlets, squint and imagine that you're in LA. Even the palm trees seem to hail from Hollywood, rather than the Nile. But around midday on Fridays, the illusion is ruptured as herds of camels are driven through Mohandiseen en route to the slaughterhouse, bringing traffic to a standstill.

Sharia Orabi runs northwest for 1.5km (strictly speaking, this area is called Sahafeyeen), but except for the **International Language Institute** (ILI), two blocks from the Al-Sudan ring road, it has no more to offer than the continuation of 26th July Street. Most of the action occurs along Mohandiseen's main axis, **Arab League Street** (Sharia Gameat al-Dowal al-Arabiya), also known as "The Mall", which is bisected by palms and shrubbery for its three-kilometre length. Due to its orientation, you can look down it on a clear day (admittedly rare in Cairo) and see the Pyramids of Giza in the distance. During summer Cairene families picnic here – an indication of how few green spaces are available. The avenue's main landmark is the **Atlas Zamalek Hotel**, 500m past Midan Sphinx. Starting with a pharaonic-style *McDonald's* opposite the

Atlas, fast food proliferates along the way to Midan al-Nasr, the centre of a radial grid of streets harbouring a dozen **embassies**.

To **reach the quarter** from central Cairo, you can catch buses from Midan Falaki, Midan Tahrir, Midan Ataba or Midan Ramses that end up on Sharia al-Sudan near Midan Lubnan. Alternatively, to get to Midan al-Nasr on Arab League Street, you can take buses from Falaki or Tahrir (Arab League Building), Ramses or Ataba (see p.97 for bus numbers). When roadworks on 26th July Street are complete, a faster way will be to jump on a service taxi microbus at Ataba or anywhere along 26th July Street and get whisked across Zamalek to Midan Sphinx or Arab League Street (but make sure of the destination of the microbus).

Beyond the ring road

Beyond the Al-Sudan ring road lies **Bulaq al-Dakhrour**, an unplanned sprawl of ramshackle dwellings built by migrant *fellaheen* from Upper Egypt and the Delta. Devoid of any proper sewage network (like parts of Imbaba and Giza), the neighbourhood is a sanitary inspector's nightmare. While some houses have cesspits, many households empty their waste into the drainage canals whose water is used by others for washing or drinking. Installing sewers here is merely one of the challenges facing the Cairo Wastewater Organization (see box below).

Bulaq al-Dakhrour ends at the **Maryotteya Canal**, beyond which the village of **Kerdassa** (see p.220) precedes another canal before the strip of luxury hotels (*Mövenpick Jollie-Ville, Ramada Renaissance, Oasis*) along the Desert Road to Alexandria.

Aguza and Dokki

A 100-metre-wide channel separates Zamalek and Gezira from the west bank districts of **Aguza and Dokki**. Being mainly residential and devoid of major "sights", they're only worth considering as a quieter place to stay than central Cairo, or for their nightlife – although you might just have business with certain

---

The Cairo wastewater project

Designed by British engineers in 1910 to serve a population of one million, **Cairo's sewage system** reached breaking point in the late 1970s. Fractured pipes regularly flooded at 120 locations (in one incident, exposed power cables electrocuted a donkey cart driving through a puddle). Worse still, a quarter of Cairo's by then twelve million population lived in areas beyond the sewage network. Cases of what was termed "summer sickness" (in fact, cholera) occurred annually. Besides the risk of epidemics, the practice of flushing raw sewage into the Nile also threatened the ecology of Lake Manzala, the richest fishing grounds in the Delta. Action was urgently needed.

With US and British backing, the **Cairo Wastewater Project** (CWC) aims to remedy these problems over the first few years of this century. On the west bank, where many areas have no sewers at all, an entirely new system is being created. The densely populated east bank poses a greater challenge, requiring extensive "blind" tunnelling. Plans of the old system were lost long ago; urban myth has it that a group of sewer repairmen have passed down their secret underground geography from father to son. Existing sewers are being fed into a huge new tunnel running from Fustat to Cairo's northern outskirts, where a gigantic pumping station is under construction; eventually, the sewage will also be treated at another plant. Given additional investments, the wastewater and nutrient-rich sludge could be used to irrigate and fertilize barren land.

local institutions. Yet it's typical of Cairo that these prim-looking neighbourhoods have generated as much scandal as the Clot Bey and Abdin quarters once did.

Aguza

Wedged between Mohandiseen and the Nile, **Aguza** ("Old Woman") stretches its legs **along the Corniche**. At the northern end of Sharia el-Nil, near the Zamalek Bridge, are the **Balloon Theatre** – a regular venue for the National and Reda dance troupes – and Egypt's **National Circus** (see p.260). Further south at no.192 is the **British Council**, a fulcrum of expat life and a sought-after place of employment (see p.70 and p.275). Beyond the *Scherezade Hotel* and Aguza Hospital, couples seek privacy in nooks along the embankment, oblivious to cruising cars. A popular stopover for taxi drivers and nightclubbers is the 24-hour *Cafeteria Nema*, opposite the Police Hospital near the 6th October Bridge.

From here down to Dokki the riverside is colonized by "**casinos**". These are not places where roulette and blackjack are played, but family-oriented places for eating and listening to music, with no gambling involved, that really come alive on Thursday nights. Some are taken over by wedding parties with traditional musicians and a bellydancer. Should you be invited to join a bash, accept without hesitation – they're always fun (see p.256). Street urchins and passersby peer through the gates, shouting blessings or ribald comments. The downside to the casinos is that some have poor food, and all of them are swarming with mosquitoes.

Fifty years ago the Corniche was also a mooring place for houseboats – then a fashionable alternative to rented flats. It was here that the Nazi spy Eppler used a famous belly dancer, Hekmet Fathy, to inveigle secrets from Allied staff officers aboard her *dahabiya*. Also involved was a young Egyptian officer, Anwar Sadat, who attempted to convey messages to Rommel and was subsequently jailed by the British for treason. Post-revolutionary Egypt was austere by comparison, but hardly innocent. In 1988 the government tried to suppress the memoirs of Eitimad Khorshid, a *femme fatale* who cut a swathe through the Nasserite establishment of the 1950s, and promised to reveal all in what became an underground bestseller.

To reach any of the above locations, catch a taxi via the 6th October Bridge, an elevated extension of which pushes 500m inland towards the **Agricultural Museum** (daily 9am–2pm; 10pt) in the grounds of the Ministry of Agriculture; the entrance is on the south side of the estate. A group of six pavilions – some closed for renovation, others that could themselves almost be museum pieces – these solemnly dingy museums of yesteryear contain exhibits on ancient farming techniques, with stuffed animals and models of native village life. There are also quirky items such as prettily arranged displays of insects and a rather horrific demonstration of various animal diseases. One of the pavilions houses the **Cotton Museum** (closed Mon, Thurs & Fri), which gives the rundown on Egypt's main cash crop. For most visitors, however, it has to be said that the pleasant grounds are more of a draw than the dusty old museums. The Ministry of Agriculture marks the point where Aguza merges into Dokki.

Dokki

The social geography of **Dokki** (usually pronounced "Do'i", with a glottal stop in the middle) is more complex than Aguza's. Broadly speaking, the rich occupy the land nearest the river and the Dokki Sporting Club, with a phalanx of private hospitals, VD clinics and covert bordellos separating their villas and apartments from the poorer market quarter to the southwest.

Coming over the Galaa Bridge from Gezira Island, you'll see Mahmoud Mukhtar's **Renaissance of Egypt statue** and the twin towers of the **Cairo Sheraton**. The hotel forecourt is the departure terminal for **buses to Tel Aviv and Jerusalem** (see p.283). From here, Sharia al-Sad al-Ali itself continues on to meet Suleyman Gohar, Dokki's vibrant **market quarter**. For **cinemas** and **restaurants**, look along Sharia Tahrir and Sharia al-Misaha, radiating west and southwest from the Galaa Bridge.

Two main roads head south from the *Sheraton*. Running one block inland, **Sharia el-Giza** passes the **Russian Embassy** and the former residence of President Sadat, where his widow, Jihan, still lives in guarded seclusion (photography is prohibited in this area). Another once-famous resident of Dokki was Field Marshal Amr, a long-time friend and ally of Nasser's who committed suicide after being accused of plotting a coup against him, and was posthumously scapegoated for Egypt's defeat in the 1967 war.

The main feature of interest on Sharia el-Giza, however, is the **Mahmoud Khalil Museum** (Mon–Sat 10am–6pm; ☎02/336 2376; £E25, students £E12; wheelchair access), two blocks south of the *Sheraton*, housed in the refurbished mansion where Khalil, a pre-war politician and Agriculture Minister, lived with his French-born wife, Emeline Hector. Together they built up this magnificent collection of art and sculpture, mostly French Impressionist and post-Impressionist works by the likes of Monet, Renoir, Gauguin and Pissarro, but also featuring artists such as Van Gogh, Delacroix and Rodin. There are information sheets on the artists in various languages, but the computer screens that tell you about the Khalils and their home are, unfortunately, in Arabic only.

Running parallel to Sharia el-Giza is the Corniche, **Sharia el-Nil** (now officially Sharia Gamal Abdel Nasser). Three boats moored 200m south of the *Cairo Sheraton* house **Dr Ragab's Papyrus Institute** (daily 9am–7pm; free), where the ancient craft of papyrus-making (which died out in the tenth century AD but was revived in modern times by Dr Ragab) is demonstrated. Although more of a papyrus emporium than a museum (and pricey to boot), you are not harassed to buy.

Beyond the Papyrus Institute are Cairo's **Rowing Club** and **Yacht Club**, both citadels of privilege. A few blocks nearer Giza, the Nasr Building contains two excellent Swiss-owned **restaurants**: *Le Chalet* and *Le Château*.

Dokki is well served by buses (including #166, #186, #194, #791 and #812) from the Arab League Building on Midan Tahrir, but you'll have to check which route suits your objective. "Dokki" metro stop is on Sharia Tahrir, which is reasonably close to both the Mahmoud Khalil Museum and Dr Ragab's Papyrus Institute.

Giza

In pharaonic times **Giza** lay en route between Heliopolis and Memphis and probably also housed the skilled corps of pyramid-builders. As Memphis declined during the Christian era, so Giza flourished, thanks to its proximity to the Fortress of Babylon, across the river; Amr's reopening of the ancient Delta–Red Sea canal subsequently boosted its prosperity under Muslim rule. Giza's apogee coincided with the reign of Salah al-Din – the Moorish traveller Ibn Jubayr described it as a "large and important burgh with fine buildings" – when its Sunday market attracted vast crowds. But the area's vulnerability to floods caused stagnation, and it wasn't until Ismail laid the Pyramids Road, drained swamps and built a palace in the 1860s that Giza became fashionable again. By Nasser's time, however, expansion was proceeding virtually unchecked. As Giza's population topped a million, a tide of high-rise hovels, tacky nightclubs and roaring flyovers devoured crumbling villas, erstwhile farmland and desert, right to the Giza Plateau beneath the Pyramids.

The zoo and Midan Giza can be reached by **bus** from Tahrir (#355 and #357, minibuses #82 and #83), Ramses (#30 and #83, minibus #83) and Ataba (#6, #9, #106 and #109); also by **metro**; and from Ramses and Ataba by service taxi microbus.

Around Cairo Zoo and University

The extensive grounds which Deschamps laid out for Ismail's palace are now divided into Cairo's **Zoological Garden** – which is packed on Fridays and public holidays, but fun to visit at other times (see p.259) – and the smaller **El-Urman Garden**. Like the **Israeli Consulate** and the **floating restaurants** near the **El-Gama'a Bridge**, they're marked on the "Old Cairo and Roda Island" map (see p.192). The bridge is named after **Cairo University**, which was founded in 1908 as a counterweight to traditionalist Al-Azhar but has never been any the less political. Access to its scattered faculties is controlled by Central Security, so foreigners may need a letter of introduction (or at least their passports) to pass beyond its gates. Aside from making student friends, morbid curiosity might inspire a visit to the Agricultural Faculty, near the bottom of Sharia Gameat al-Qahira. Occupying a former palace of Mohammed Ali, its basement holds remnants of his torture chamber.

Midan Giza and Pyramids Road

West of the **El-Giza Bridge** and south of the university belt, Cairo's second largest **bus and taxi terminal** agitates **Midan Giza**. Its seething ranks include buses to the Pyramids; minibuses to Tahrir, Ramses and Heliopolis; and service taxis to Fayoum City, Beni Suef and the Red Sea Coast. A few minutes' walk south is **Giza Station**. More flyovers funnel traffic onto the **Pyramids Road** (Sharia al-Ahram), which runs the gauntlet of **nightclubs** and tourist bazaars for 8km. It was outside a hotel on this avenue that seventeen Greek tourists were shot dead by Islamic radicals, who mistook them for a group of Israelis, in spring 1996. A couple of kilometres before the Pyramids of Giza, Sharia al-Ahram crosses two canals in quick succession; the second one marks the turning (left) for Saqqara. See pp.209–236 for details of both sites.

The northern suburbs

During the last century, Cairo's **northern suburbs** swallowed up villages and farmland and expanded far into the desert to form a great arc of residential neighbourhoods stretching from the Nile to the Muqattam. **Heliopolis**, with its handsome boulevards and Art Deco villas, is still favoured above the satellite suburbs that have mushroomed in recent decades, and retains a sizeable foreign community. Otherwise, tourists usually only venture into **Abbassiya** for the Sinai Bus Terminal, or to visit the Coptic Patriarchate and Sakakini Palace; and you have to be fanatically keen to bother hunting down the Virgin's Tree in **Matariyya**, Sadat's tomb in **Medinet Nasr**, or Mamluke edifices in **Bulaq**. See the "Greater Cairo" map on p.90 for a guide to the location of these areas.

Bulaq, Shubra and Rod el-Farag

Bulaq and its neighbours **Shubra** and **Rod el-Farag** (northwest of central Cairo) are run-down and overcrowded, averaging 170,000 residents per square kilometre – ten times the density of Garden City – and have a predominantly *baladi* ambience. But though more or less bereft of "sights", these quarters might appeal to visitors fascinated by ordinary Cairene life. **Getting there**, bus #134 serves Shubra from Tahrir and Ramses. However, Shubra and Rod el-Farag are best reached by metro. Bulaq was less accessible at the time of writing, as roadworks on 26th July Street in Bulaq have meant that buses and service taxis must make a diversion, but the new elevated roadway should make the journey faster when completed.

Bulaq

Immediately east of the 6th October flyover (see the "Central Cairo" map on p.110) lies the oldest of the northern suburbs, **Bulaq**, whose name derives from the Coptic word for "marsh". During medieval times, the westward shift of the Nile turned a sandbank into an island, which merged with the east bank as the intervening channel silted up. As the Fatimid port of Al-Maks was left high and dry, Bulaq became the new anchorage in the 1350s, rapidly developing into an entrepôt after Sultan Barsbey re-routed the spice trade and encouraged manufacturing. When Mohammed Ali set about establishing a foundry, textiles factory and modern shipyards here in the 1820s, Bulaq was the obvious site. Unfortunately, the Ottomans permitted free trade, enabling British manufacturers to undersell local industries and force Egypt back into its dependency on cotton exports to the Lancashire mills.

Since then, small workshops and apartment buildings have taken over Bulaq, while world affairs are handled in two towering landmarks along the Corniche: the **Television Building** and the **Cairo Plaza**. Inland of the latter is a one-time hostel for members of the Rifai order, next to the **Mosque of Sinan Pasha**, a sixteenth-century hybrid of Mamluke and Ottoman styles, attached to a still-working **hammam**. More revered by locals for its namesake's *baraka* is the fifteenth-century **Mosque of Abu'l'Ila**, on 26th July Street just west of the Corniche. Nearby stand the former **royal stables of Mohammed Ali**. Plans to convert the stables into a museum seem to have fizzled out, although the entrance still bears a faded sign reading "Royal Carriage Museum".

Shubra

Two million Cairenes live in the sprawling beehive known as **Shubra**, the older part of which is called Shubra al-Balad to distinguish it from the newer outgrowth beyond the Ismailiya Canal, dubbed Shubra el-Kheima. Originally an island (its name, "Elephant", supposedly comes from a ship that ran aground), Shubra became attached to the mainland about the same time as Bulaq, but was given over to orchards and villages until the nineteenth century. In 1808, Mohammed Ali built a summer palace here that caused Europeans to snigger ("The taste, alas! of an English upholsterer"), where he later died insane. Other palaces were erected by Ismail, who also laid a carriage road to the original residence, planted with sycamore-fig and acacia trees, where Cairenes promenaded.

The 1891 edition of *Murray's Handbook* deemed **Sharia Shubra** "the most republican promenade in the world. No description of vehicle, nor manner of animal, biped or quadruped, is excluded, and the Khedive and his outriders are jostled and crossed in a most unseemly fashion by files of bare-boned and sore-covered mules and donkeys, whipped in by ragged urchins." Nowadays the avenue seems thoroughly proletarian, for Shubra has long since evolved from a garden suburb into densely packed quarters where educated Copts and Muslims rub shoulders with poor rural migrants.

Though self-help projects have improved some of the bleak low-rise estates in Shubra el-Kheima, dire poverty inclines a minority towards radical Islam, and reinforces the traditional superstitions that most Cairenes at least half-believe. *Baladi* folk turn instinctively to **magic**, whereas educated people will exhaust rational solutions before resorting to a *sheikh* or *sheikha*. What psychologists might regard as mental illnesses are treated as cases of demonic possession, possibly caused by deliberate cursing. (One method of hexing is to recite the 33rd *sura* of the Koran backwards.) While certain moulids feature public **exorcisms**, most are private, especially those with pagan elements. Joseph McPherson, Cairo's secret police chief in the 1920s, witnessed a *zaar* where celebrants whirled to ancient and Muslim incantations, cymbals clashed, and a ram, ganders, doves and rabbits were sacrificed, their blood being daubed on the participants, whose frenzy increased:

Sometimes they bent their bodies back, till they formed a writhing and vibrating bow, resting on the ground by the heels and back of the head, whilst the muscles of their bodies carried on the dance with unbelievable contortions.

When all concerned believe in the ritual's spiritual efficacy, the desired result is frequently achieved.

Rod el-Farag
During the 1950s, a slice of Shubra al-Balad was developed as a separate residential and commercial district, named "Farag's Orchard" after its previous role. The name remains appropriate, since **Rod el-Farag** hosts Cairo's largest **fruit and vegetable market**, Abu el-Farag. Like the others, it's the exclusive preserve of one or two cabals of wholesalers. In Rod el-Farag's case, they hail from the villages around the capital, whereas elsewhere *Saiyidis* from Upper Egypt may control trade. The modern **Port of Cairo** is another local source of wealth with a shady underside.

Abbassiya, Hada'iq al-Qubba and Medinet Nasr
In practice, the demarcation lines between these northeastern districts (which subdivide into other quarters) and Heliopolis are blurred by sheer density, overcrowding and interlocking transport networks.

Abbassiya
The sprawling **Abbassiya** district gets its name from a palace built by Mohammed Ali's grandson, Pasha Abbas I, who dreaded assassination during his brief reign (1848–54) and kept camels saddled there for rapid flight into the desert – to no avail, for he was murdered by his servants. Previously, the area was called Ridaniya and was the site of the last battle between the Mamlukes and the invading Ottoman Turks, who went on to take Cairo. Nearer the centre, the British established the Abbassiya Barracks (where the nationalist leader Orabi surrendered after his defeat at Tell el-Kebir), which vastly expanded during wartime. Like the Army GHQ (still located in Abbassiya), it was later seized by the Free Officers in a bloodless coup against Egypt's monarchy on the night

of 22 July, 1952. Cairenes awoke next day to learn of a "revolution" led by General Naguib – a nominal figurehead, since it was Nasser who had engineered it and secretly controlled affairs until his public emergence as leader.

Abbassiya's Janus profile juxtaposes spacious institutions and crowded slums, marshalling yards and hospitals. Its main thoroughfare, Sharia Ramses, divides the oil-depot zone of Al-Sharabiyya from Gamra and El-Sakakini, two residential market quarters. On Sharia Sakakini, near Ghamra metro station, the ornate Rococo **Sakakini Palace**, built in 1898 for an Italian nobleman, has unfortunately been left to rot, but is still worth a detour if you are in the area for its outrageously kitsch facade. At the end of Sharia Sakakini, on Midan al-Zahir, the thirteenth-century **Mosque of Beybars the Crossbowman**, built in 1268 and covering ten thousand square metres, is one of Cairo's biggest mosques, and the first to be built outside the city's walls. Ceasing to be used for prayer in the sixteenth century, it was subsequently used as a military storehouse by the Ottomans, a barracks by Napoleon and a slaughterhouse by the British. Restoration started in the early 1990s but soon petered out, and the eastern side is now again in use as a mosque. The rest of it can be visited by tourists in the meantime. Its sturdy walls enclose a vast open courtyard, surrounded by a rather heavy arcade. A more conspicuous edifice is the curvaceous **Coptic Cathedral of St Mark**, the seat of the Coptic Patriarchate since it was raised in the 1970s. Visitors interested in joining pilgrim excursions to the Red Sea Monasteries should contact officials in the adjacent Church of SS Peter and Paul (*Al-Batrussiya*), at 222 Sharia Ramses (☎02/582 1274).

Other landmarks include the **Misr Travel Tower**, housing the Ministry of Tourism, 500m from the **Sinai Bus Terminal** near the junction of Salah Salem and Al-'Urubah, and a similar distance from the Engineering Faculty of **Ain Shams University**. Round about are sited numerous clubs (*nady*) and training schools belonging to professional unions, the police and military.

To get to Abbassiya, buses (including #130, #330, #400, #400/, #500, #828, #955 and #998) and minibuses (including #1, #4, #10, #24, #27, #28, #35 and #35/) run from Tahrir's Abdel Mouneem Riyad terminal via Midan Ramses.

Hada'iq al-Qubba: Nasser's Tomb

Northeast of Abbassiya along Sharia al-Khalifa al-Ma'mun (a continuation of Sharia Abbassiya), a modern mosque stands beside a dusty shrine containing the **Tomb of Gamal Abdel Nasser**. When Nasser died in September 1969, a million Egyptians followed his bier through the streets of Cairo and the whole Arab world mourned. His cult was subsequently downplayed by Sadat (who feared comparisons) and in recent years most of the visitors to Nasser's shrine have been foreign admirers or gloating Israelis. Whatever Egyptians may think about Nasser's son, Khalid – who was finally acquitted of involvement in *Thawraat Masri* (Egypt's Revolution), a Libyan-backed group that attacked US and Israeli targets in the 1980s – his father's legend remains a potent one. Saddam Hussein's claim to be Nasser's "spiritual heir" was only the latest attempt by an Arab leader to metaphorically wrest the sword from the stone.

The tomb lies on the edge of **Hada'iq al-Qubba**, a district named after Ismail's **Qubba Palace**. Its four hundred rooms were inherited by Khedive Tewfik and later contained King Farouk's vast collection of rare stamps, coins and other treasures, ranging from medieval Korans to a Fabergé thermometer. Now a presidential residence used for state conferences, it was here that the Shah of Iran spent the last days of his exile, mortally stricken by cancer. The palace's walled grounds can be seen along the #420 bus route from Abbassiya;

it and Nasser's tomb are best reached by Metro (Saray el-Qubba station and Kubri el-Qubi station respectively).

Medinet Nasr and Sadat's Tomb

During the 1960s and 70s a whole new satellite-suburb was created on the site of the Abbassiya Rifle Ranges, and many government departments were relocated to this "Victory City". But unless you've got business with the Inland Revenue or Transport Ministry, there's little in **Medinet Nasr** worth noting. Travellers coming in from Suez will pass the Olympic-size **Cairo Stadium** at one end of Sharia al-Nasr, where Cairo football clubs Ahly and Zamalek play, and where international matches and cup finals are also held (see p.259).

Alongside the boulevard is a landscaped parade ground centred on a pyramid-shaped **Victory Memorial** to the 1973 October War (see p.800). In 1981, Islamic radicals infiltrated the 6th October anniversary parade and blasted the reviewing stand with machine guns and grenades, fatally wounding President Sadat (Mubarak, who stood beside him, was unharmed). **Sadat's Tomb** is beneath the Victory Memorial. Next door to Sadat's Tomb and the Victory Memorial, the huge **October War Panorama**, opened in 1989, stands surrounded by a display of military hardware. It was built on a suggestion made to Hosni Mubarak by Kim Il Sung of North Korea when the Egyptian president visited that country in 1983. Construction was supervised by North Korean technicians, and it shows: the building looks like a pavilion in some Communist theme park of the 1950s and is decorated with Maoist-style reliefs, but instead of East Asian peasants and workers striding purposefully forward, it's Egyptian soldiers in front of the Pyramids. Every day it holds five showings (daily except Tues 9.30am, 11am and 12.30pm, plus in winter 5pm and 6.30pm, summer 6pm and 7.30pm; £E8, camera £E2) that start with two rather silly dioramas illustrating the opening round of the October War, and culminate in a really quite impressive three-dimensional panorama of the war in Sinai, during which the audience is rotated around 360° to take it all in. The commentary (in Arabic, with an English version available via headphones) explains the action with such phrases as "the glorious minutes passed rapidly", and the whole thing is so over-the-top in its triumphalism that you might almost think the Egyptians had actually won the October War.

Medinet Nasr is connected to Midan Roxi in Heliopolis by bus #67 (starting from Tahrir). From Midan Ataba minibus #34 runs through Abbassiya to the quarter and past the tomb. Minibuses #32 and #35 from Midan Tahrir also run past the tomb, as do trams from Heliopolis.

Heliopolis (Masr el-Gadida)

By the end of the nineteenth century, the doubling of Cairo's population and the exponential growth of its foreign community had created a huge demand for new accommodation, which fired the imagination of a Belgian entrepreneur. Baron Empain proposed creating a garden city in the desert, linked to the downtown area by an overground metro: a commercial venture attractive to investors, since Empain's company would collect both rents and fares from commuting residents of **Heliopolis**. Laid out by Sir Reginald Oakes in radial grid patterns, the suburb's wide avenues were lined with apartment blocks ennobled by pale yellow Moorish facades and bisected by shrubbery. Named after the ancient City of the Sun near Matariyya (see p.206), Heliopolis soon acquired every facility from schools and churches to a racecourse and branch of *Groppi's*.

Ancient Heliopolis, the Ennead and the cult of Re

Although Anthony Trollope scoffed "Humbug!" when he saw what little remained in 1858, the site of **ancient Heliopolis**, near modern Matariyya, originally covered perhaps five square kilometres. The City of the Sun (called *On* by its founders, but better known by its Greek appellation) evolved in tandem with Memphis, the first capital of Dynastic Egypt (see p.232). As Memphis embodied the political unification of Upper and Lower Egypt, so Heliopolis incarnated its theological aspect, syncretizing diverse local cults into a hierarchical cosmogony that proved more influential than other creation myths of the Old Kingdom.

Cosmogony

In the **Heliopolitan cosmogony**, the world began as watery chaos (Nun) from which Atum the sun-god emerged onto a primal mound, spitting forth the twin deities Shu (air) and Tefnut (moisture). They engendered Geb (earth) and Nut (sky), whose own union produced Isis, Osiris, Seth and Nephthys. Later texts often regarded this divine **Ennead** (Nine) as a single entity, while the universe was conventionally represented by the figures

Shu, Nut and Geb

of Shu, Nut and Geb. Meanwhile (for reasons unknown), the primal deity Atum was subsumed by Re or Ra, a yet mightier aspect of the sun-god.

Re manifested himself in multiple forms: as hawk-headed Re-herakhte (Horus of the Horizon); the beetle Khepri (the rising sun); the disc Aten (the midday sun); and as Atum (the setting sun). The Egyptians believed that Re rose each morning in the east, traversed the sky in his solar barque and sank into the western land of the dead every evening, to voyage through the Duat (netherworld) during the night, emerging at sunrise. This journey inevitably linked Re to the Osirian myth, and from the V Dynasty onwards it became *de rigueur* for pharaohs to claim descent from Re by identifying themselves with Horus and Osiris. The **cult of Re** was exclusive, for only the pharaoh and priesthood had access to Re's sanctuary, whose daily rituals were adopted by other divine cults and soon became inextricably entangled with Osiris-worship (see "Karnak" and "Abydos", Chapter Two). Ordinary folk – whose participation was limited to public festivals – worshipped lesser, more approachable deities.

Re

Remains

Having been eclipsed by Karnak and Amun-worship during the New Kingdom, Heliopolis was devastated by the Persians in 525 BC. Once rebuilt, however, its intellectual reputation attracted visitors such as Plato, Eudoxus (who probably invented the sundial after studying Egyptian astronomy) and Herodotus. But as Alexandria became the new focus for science and religion, Heliopolis inexorably declined; Strabo found it nearly desolate and the Romans totally ignored it. Today, the only tangible reminders of its existence are **Senusert's obelisk** and the **Spring of the Sun**, where Atum supposedly washed himself at the dawn of creation.

Wealthy Egyptians settled here from the beginning; merely prosperous ones moved in as foreigners left in droves throughout the 1950s. Meanwhile, poorer quarters started growing up around Heliopolis, ending its privileged isolation from Greater Cairo. During the 1970s, air-conditioned towers began to replace spacious villas, the racecourse was turned into a fun park, and burger joints proliferated. Today, visitors come for the restaurants and nightlife, or to admire the stylish architecture along its central boulevards; many foreigners also rent apartments or work in Heliopolis, which is nowadays called "New Cairo" (*Masr el-Gadida*).

Transport: the Heliopolis metro

Depending on your starting point, choice of transport, and whether it's rush hour, Heliopolis is between fifteen- and thirty-minutes' ride from downtown Cairo. The fastest way is to hail **service taxis** heading there from Bab al-Luq, Midan Opera and Midan Tahrir, via Salah Salem, which charge fixed rates. To reach Midan Roxi in Heliopolis, it's almost as quick to use **buses** or **minibuses** (see pp.97–99).

During the rush hour, **buses** from Tahrir and Ramses are slower than the suburb's **original tram system**, known as the **Heliopolis metro**, which begins at Midan Ramses. From there, its three tram lines follow the same track through Abbassiya, diverging shortly before Midan Roxi. Each has its own colour-coded direction boards:

• The **Abd al-Aziz Fahmi line** (green) runs past Merryland and Heliopolis Hospital on Sharia al-Higaz, before heading off towards the Shams Club.

• More centrally, the **Nouzha line** (red) veers off Sharia Merghani near the Heliopolis Sporting Club, and follows Al-Ahram and Osman Ibn Affan up to Midan Triomphe.

• Initially running alongside the red line, the **Merghani line** (yellow) then follows the street of that name past the International Language Institute (ILI) to Midan Triomphe, and out towards the Armed Forces Hospital.

Sights and activities

Nouzha-line, red-coded trams run through the heart of Heliopolis, whose finest **architecture** lines the boulevards between Sharia Merghani and Abu Bakr al-Saddiq. Stay on board to review Sharia al-Ahram's parade of handsome arcades topped with Andalusian balconies and pantiles, or alight near the **Heliopolis Sporting Club** and walk around the corner of the **Urubah Palace** onto Sharia Ibrahim. Other side streets have more of a 1920s feel, with crisply graceful Art Deco apartments. But the most famous landmark lies off Sharia al-'Urubah, further southeast. Resembling a Hindu temple, **Baron Empain's Palace** originally boasted a revolving tower that enabled its owner to follow the sun throughout the day. The now derelict structure (dubbed "Le Baron" by locals) can be glimpsed from some of the airport-bound buses.

Not far away – and directly accessible by Merghani tram – the **International Language Institute** (ILI) offers Arabic classes and also employs many foreigners as teachers (see p.70 and p.275). Along the Merghani tram route, too, are the Heliopolis and Heliolido **sporting clubs**, with tennis and squash courts, swimming pools and gymnasiums. The Heliopolis Sporting Club only admits foreigners in the summer and seems snootier than the Heliolido. Northeast of the latter, **Merryland** contains a boating lake and funfair, a small zoo and an overpriced café – nothing to get excited about, but it's nice to be surrounded by greenery – and it's a safe place for children to play. Green-coded trams continue on past Merryland, up Al-Higaz towards Midan Heliopolis.

Matariyya and beyond

Northwest of Heliopolis, several former villages have evolved into ramshackle *baladi* suburbs. **El–Zeitun** (the Olives) merits a footnote in history as the site of Sultan Selim's defeat of the Mamlukes in 1517 and of conspiratorial gatherings of Free Officers during the early 1950s. The adjacent **Helmiya** quarter gets its name from yet another khedival palace built last century. But for actual sights you have to venture even further out, into Matariyya.

The modern suburb of **Matariyya** traces its antecedents way back to the Old Kingdom and claims later acquaintance with the infant Christ. As evidence of the former, the neighbourhood's Midan al-Misallah displays a 22-metre-high, pink granite **Obelisk of Senusert I**. One of a pair raised to celebrate the pharaoh's Jubilee Festival (c.1900 BC), it originally stood outside the Temple of Re, erected by Amenemhat I, Senusert's father, who founded the XII Dynasty. Another pair, belonging to the XVIII Dynasty ruler Tuthmosis III, were moved by the Romans to Alexandria, whence they ended up in New York's Central Park and on London's Embankment. However, the significance of this site and its cult of the sun-god are far older, dating back to the earliest dynasties.

Cairo's metro makes this sector of the northern suburbs readily accessible from the centre. Matariyya metro station is eleven stops from Tahrir, in the direction of El-Marg; the neighbourhood can also be reached by tram from Heliopolis.

The Spring of the Sun, Virgin's Tree and Ain Shams

Nowadays, the **Spring of the Sun** waters a famous Christian relic, the **Virgin's Tree**. Located 500m south of the obelisk, this gnarled sycamore-fig is supposedly descended from a tree whose branches shaded the Holy Family during their Egyptian exile. Tradition has it that they rested here between Bilbeis and Babylon-in-Egypt (see p.185), and Mary washed the clothes of the baby Jesus in the stone trough that still lies beside the tree. Early this century, "Christian souvenir-hunting was so bad that the owner of the sycamore tied a knife to the tree and put up a notice begging people not to hack at it any more with axes, and to leave some of it for others" (Aldridge). Now enclosed within a compound, it grows near the **Church of the Virgin**, a modern building on the site of far older churches.

The spring's Arabic name has attached itself to the **Ain Shams** quarter, one metro stop beyond Matariyya. Densely populated and solidly working-class, the neighbourhood is regarded by the police as a hotbed of Islamic fundamentalism.

The Lake of the Pilgrims

Still further out, beyond El-Marg, caravans once prayed beside the **Lake of the Pilgrims** (*Birket el-Hagg*) before embarking on their journey to Mecca. Today, alas, the "covered litters of the female pilgrims and the picturesque corps of mounted *Bashi-Bazouks*" no longer "moves slowly forward on its desert route". Instead, the barren wastes outside Cairo have for several decades harboured rocket ranges, chemical weapons factories and other **military installations**, rendering vast tracts off-limits. Ironically, much of this research was undertaken in collaboration with Iraq, Egypt's main Arab ally before the Gulf War, during which they fought on opposite sides.

The Pyramids

All things dread Time, but Time dreads the Pyramids.

Anonymous proverb

For millions of people **the Pyramids** epitomize ancient Egypt: no other monument is so instantly recognized the world over. Yet comparatively few foreigners realize that at least 97 pyramids are spread across seventy kilometres of desert, from the outskirts of Cairo to the edge of the Fayoum. The mass of **theories, claims and counter-claims** about how and why the Pyramids were built contributes to the sense of mystery that surrounds them. Some of the recent contributions to this debate include *The Orion Mystery* (1994), in which Robert Bauval asserts that the orientation of the Giza Pyramids corresponds to the three stars in Orion's Belt, and the "ventilation" shafts in the Geat Pyramid were aligned with Orion's Belt and Alpha Draconis. Graham Hancock took this a stage further in *Fingerprints of the Gods* (1995), arguing that the entire pyramid field corresponded to an astronomical map. In later books he says that the Sphinx and Pyramids are far older than reckoned, and recall a vanished ur-civilization that was destroyed in 12,000 BC, having left its stamp on Angkor Wat, the Maya and Easter Island. Egyptologists have since been lining up to refute these theories; meanwhile you can read up on the latest crop – including some that figure Martians into the equation – on the Internet through links at Ⓦparanormal.about.com/cs/ancientegypt.

Most visitors are content to see the great **Pyramids of Giza** and part of the sprawling necropolis of **Saqqara**, both easily accessible from Cairo (tours to Saqqara often include a visit to the ruins of the ancient city of **Memphis**). Only a minority ride across the sands to **Abu Sir**, or visit the **Dahshur** pyramid field (see the map on p.210 for the location of all these sites). Still further south, the dramatic "Collapsed Pyramid" of **Maidum** and the lesser Middle Kingdom pyramids of **Hawara**, **El-Lisht** and **Lahun** are easier to reach from the Fayoum, so for the sake of convenience we've covered them in Chapter Three (see p.505). The pyramid at **Abu Ruash**, to the west of Cairo, inaccessible and little more than a pile of sand, is only of interest to specialists, as are the remains of a previously unknown pyramid unearthed nearby (if you do want to find them, service taxis from Giza train station serve the nearby village of Abu Ruash).

If you are really determined, and very energetic, it is possible to visit the pyramid sites at Giza, Abu Sir, Saqqara and Dahshur all in one day starting very early (say 7.30am from town). To do this, you will need to find a taxi driver who will take you, wait at each, and finally bring you back. Make sure the driver understands exactly what you want, and negotiate hard. In principle, you should be able to do this for around £E75, but £E100 would not be an unreasonable rate, it being a whole day's work for the driver. Some hotels (the *Berlin*, for example) have their own drivers who are used to taking tourists on such excursions. Alternatively, Salah Mohammed's tours (see p.224) take in both Giza and Saqqara in one day.

The Pyramids in history

The derivation of the word "pyramid" is obscure. *Per-em-us*, an ancient Egyptian term meaning "straight up", seems likelier than the Greek *pyramis* – "wheaten cake", a facetious descriptive term for these novel monuments. Then

▲ Alexandria

ACCOMMODATION
Mena House Oberoi — D
Salma Camping — G

RESTAURANTS & NIGHTLIFE
Africana — E
China Restaurant — F
Felfela Café — B
Felfela Village — A
Pariziana — C
Pyramids Restaurant — F

0 Kilometres 5

THE PYRAMID FIELD

PYRAMIDS
Great Pyramid of Cheops (Khufu)	1	Sun Temple of Userkaf	8	Unas	16	Khendjer	23

Great Pyramid of Cheops (Khufu) 1
Chephren (Khafre) 2
Mycerinus (Menkaure) 3
Sphinx 4
Unfinished Pyramid 5
Layer Pyramid 6
Sun Temple of Nyuserre 7

Sun Temple of Userkaf 8
Sahure 9
Nyuserre 10
Neferirkare 11
Raneferef 12
Teti 13
Userkaf 14
Step Pyramid of Zoser 15

Unas 16
Unfinished Pyramid of Sekhemkhet 17
Pepi I 18
Merenre 19
Djedkare-Isesi 20
Pepi II 21
Mastabat al-Faraun 22

Khendjer 23
Unfinished XIII Dynasty Pyramid 24
Seostris III 25
Red Pyramid (Snofru) 26
Amenemhet II 27
Bent Pyramid (Snofru) 28
Black Pyramid of Amenemhet III 29

again, "obelisk" comes from *obeliskos*, the ancient Greek for "skewer" or "little spit".

Whatever, the Pyramids' sheer **antiquity** is staggering. When the Greek chronicler Herodotus visited them in 450 BC, as many centuries separated his lifetime from their creation as divide our own time from that of Herodotus, who regarded them as ancient even then. For the Pyramid Age was only an episode in three millennia of pharaonic civilization, reaching its zenith within two hundred years and followed by an inexorable decline, so that later dynasties regarded the works of their ancestors with awe. Fourteen centuries after the royal tombs of the Old Kingdom were first violated by robbers, the Sa'te (XXVI) Dynasty collected what remained, replaced missing bodies with surrogates, and reburied their forebears with archaic rituals they no longer comprehended.

The Pyramid Age began at Saqqara in the 27th century BC, when the III Dynasty royal architect Imhotep enlarged a *mastaba* tomb to create the first **step pyramid**. As techniques evolved, an attempt was made to convert another step pyramid at Maidum into a true pyramid by encasing its sides in a smooth shell, but it seems that the design was faulty and the pyramid collapsed at some time under its own weight (see p.506). According to one theory, this happened during construction of what became the Bent Pyramid at Dahshur, necessitating a hasty alteration to the angle of its sides (see p.236). The first sheer-sided **true pyramid**, apparently the next to be constructed, was the Red Pyramid at Dahshur (see p.235), followed by the Great Pyramid of Cheops at Giza, which marked the zenith of pyramid architecture. After two more perfect pyramids at Giza, fewer resources and less care were devoted to the pyramid fields of Abu Sir and South Saqqara, and the latterday pyramids near Fayoum Oasis, and no subsequent pyramid ever matched the standards of the Giza trio.

The pyramids' **enigma** has puzzled people ever since they were built. Whereas the ancient Greeks vaguely understood their function, the Romans were less certain; medieval Arabs believed them to be treasure houses with magical guardians; and early European observers reckoned them the Biblical granaries of Joseph. The nineteenth century was a golden era of discoveries by Belzoni, Vyse, Petrie, Mariette, Maspero and Lepsius, which all suggested that the pyramids were essentially containers for royal tombs and nothing else. It was also the heyday of Pyramidologists like Piazzi Smyth and David Davidson, who averred that their dimensions in "pyramid inches" proved the supremacy of Christianity and the Jewish origin of the pyramid-builders.

Archeologists now agree that the pyramids' **function** was to preserve the pharaoh's **ka**, or double: a vital force which emanated from the sun-god to his son, the king, who distributed it amongst his subjects and the land of Egypt itself. Mummification, funerary rituals, false doors for his **ba** (soul) to escape, model servants (*shabti* figures) and anniversary offerings – all were designed to ensure that his *ka* enjoyed an afterlife similar to its former existence. Thus was the social order perpetuated throughout eternity and the forces of primeval chaos held at bay, a theme emphasized in tomb reliefs at Saqqara. On another level of **symbolism**, the pyramid form evoked the primal mound at the dawn of creation, a recurrent theme in ancient Egyptian cosmogony, echoed in megalithic *benben* and obelisks whose pyramidal tips were sheathed in glittering electrum.

Although the limestone scarp at the edge of the Western Desert provided an inexhaustible source of building material, finer stone for casing the pyramids was quarried at Tura across the river, or came from Aswan in Upper Egypt.

Blocks were quarried using wooden wedges (which swelled when soaked, enlarging fissures) and copper chisels, then transported on rafts to the pyramid site, where the final shaping and polishing occurred. Shipments coincided with the inundation of the Nile (July–November), when its waters lapped the feet of the plateau and Egypt's workforce was released from agricultural tasks.

Herodotus relates that a hundred thousand slaves took a decade to build the causeway and earthen ramps, and a further twenty years to raise the Great Pyramid of Cheops. Archeologists now believe that, far from being slaves, most of the workforce were actually peasants who were paid in food for their three-month stint (papyri enumerate the quantities of lentils, onions and leeks), while a few thousand skilled craftsmen were employed full-time on its **construction**. One theory holds that a single ramp wound around the pyramid core, and was raised as it grew; when the capstone was in place, the casing was added from the top down and the ramp was reduced. Other ramps (recently found) led from the base of the pyramid to the quarry. Apparently, pulleys were only used to lift the plug blocks that sealed the corridors and entrance; all the other stones were moved with levers and rollers. It is estimated that during the most productive century of pyramid-building, some 25 million tons of material were quarried.

Whether or not the ancient Egyptians deemed this work a religious obligation, the massive levies certainly demanded an effective bureaucracy. Pyramid-building therefore helped consolidate the state. Its decline paralleled the Old Kingdom's, its cessation and resumption two anarchic eras (the First and Second Intermediate Periods) and the short-lived Middle Kingdom (XII Dynasty). By the time of the New Kingdom, other monumental symbols seemed appropriate. Remembering the plundered pyramids, the rulers of the New Kingdom opted for hidden tombs in the Valley of the Kings.

The Pyramids of Giza

Of the Seven Wonders of the ancient world, only the **Pyramids of Giza** have withstood the ravages of time. "From the summit of these monuments, forty centuries look upon you", cried Napoleon; "A practical joke played on History", retorted another visitor. The Great Pyramid of Cheops has inspired more learned and crackpot speculation than any monument on earth. For millions of people, the Giza Pyramids embody antiquity and mystery. Burdened with expectations, however, you may find the reality disappointing. Resembling small triangles from afar and corrugated mountains as you approach, their gigantic mass can seem oddly two-dimensional when viewed from below. Far from being isolated in the desert as carefully angled photos suggest, they rise just beyond the outskirts of Giza City. During daytime, hordes of touts and tourists dispel any lingering mystique, as do the Sound and Light shows after dark. Only at sunset, dawn and late at night does their brooding majesty return.

Visiting the Pyramids

The site is directly accessible from Cairo by the eleven-kilometre-long Sharia al-Ahram (Pyramids Road) built by Khedive Ismail for the Empress Eugénie. Though heavy traffic can prolong the journey, **getting there** is straightforward. Taxi drivers often quote upwards of £E20, but the proper fare is around £E15 for a one-way trip from town. A cheaper option is to take a/c bus #355 or #357 (£E2), or ordinary bus #900 (25pt), all from Midan Ramses or from behind the Egyptian Museum in Midan Tahrir; minibus #183 from Midan Ataba (50pt); or a microbus service taxi from Ramses or Ataba (75pt; drivers heading for the pyramids shout, "Al-Ahram, al-Ahram".). Bus #30 from Midan Ramses also runs more or less all the way to the site. An easier one-day, mini-mum-effort way to visit the Giza Pyramids, while also taking in Saqqara, is to go on one of Salah Mohammed's tours (see p.224).

Opposite the *Mena House* is a **tourist office** (daily 8.30am–5pm; ☎02/383 8823). To visit the site during **opening hours** (daily: winter 8am–4pm; sum-mer 8am–5pm) you must buy a ticket (£E20, students £E10) covering the site, the Sphinx and Chephren's Valley Temple – though tickets aren't rigorously checked. Extra **tickets** are required for entry to the Great Pyramid of Cheops (£E40), the Solar Boat Museum (£E20), Chephren's Pyramid (£E10) and the Pyramid of Mycerinus (currently closed). Visiting after hours will probably cost

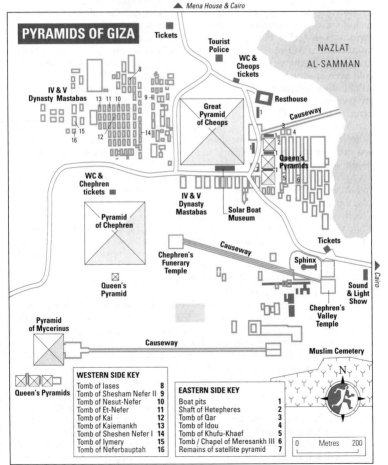

▲ Mena House & Cairo

PYRAMIDS OF GIZA

Tickets

Tourist Police

WC & Cheops tickets

NAZLAT AL-SAMMAN

Resthouse

IV & V Dynasty Mastabas

Great Pyramid of Cheops

Causeway

Queen's Pyramids

WC & Chephren tickets

IV & V Dynasty Mastabas

Solar Boat Museum

Pyramid of Chephren

Tickets

Chephren's Funerary Temple

Causeway

Sphinx

Queen's Pyramid

Sound & Light Show

Chephren's Valley Temple

Pyramid of Mycerinus

Causeway

Muslim Cemetery

▲ Cairo

Queen's Pyramids

N

WESTERN SIDE KEY

Tomb of Iases	8
Tomb of Shesham Nefer II	9
Tomb of Nesut-Nefer	10
Tomb of Et-Nefer	11
Tomb of Kai	12
Tomb of Kaiemankh	13
Tomb of Sheshen Nefer I	14
Tomb of Iymery	15
Tomb of Neferbauptah	16

EASTERN SIDE KEY

Boat pits	1
Shaft of Hetepheres	2
Tomb of Qar	3
Tomb of Idou	4
Tomb of Khufu-Khaef	5
Tomb / Chapel of Meresankh III	6
Remains of satellite pyramid	7

0   Metres   200

▼ Abu Sir & Saqqara

more, depending on your evasion and/or negotiation skills. Beware of con men posing as ticket collectors or "special guides", who offer commentary along the lines of "Cheops Pyramid very old" – ignore them, or threaten to call the tourist police if necessary. Also ignore horse and camel touts on the way in who try to tell you that their stables are "government". Such nuisances are supposedly set to disappear under the "Giza Plateau Conservation Project" (due to open sometime in the future, *insha'Allah*). The project will include an Imax cinema, cultural centres and more sites open to the public and, with the plateau effectively cut off from Nazlat al-Samman village, will exclude cars and touts.

Plan on spending half a day at the Pyramids, which are best entered early in the morning before the heat and crowds become unbearable (tour buses start arriving from 10.30am), or in the late afternoon – by 5pm most tour groups have left and people have yet to arrive for the nightly **Sound and Light Show**. These consist of two one-hour shows in different languages. For schedules, which vary seasonally, call ☎02/385 7320, 385 2880 or 386 3469, or check *Egypt Today*, *Cairo's* or the Internet at ⓦwww.sound-light.egypt.com/pyr.htm or ⓦwww.egypttourism.org/New%20Site/frm_info.htm). As the melodramatic commentary is rather crass, you might prefer one of the performances in Arabic. Hundreds of Egyptians enjoy a free show from vantage points such as past the Muslim cemetery, eschewing seats (£E44, video camera £E30), on the terrace facing the Sphinx. Bring a sweater, since nights are cold even in summer.

Behind the grandstand is a row of stables **renting horses and camels** that are generally in no better shape than the animals touted around the site by Nagama Bedouin. They usually demand £E50 for a brief camel ride, and you should beware of those offering rides at £E10 per hour – they have a tendency to lead you far out into the desert and then announce that the £E10 rate was only for the outward journey and it will be £E50 per hour to get back. As the site is small enough to cover on foot, riding is more of an experience than a timesaver, and haggling with these guys just might ruin your visit, but if you do want to ride a horse or camel, we suggest getting in touch with a reputable operator such as AA or KG (see p.257).

In Baedeker's day, it was *de rigueur* for visitors to climb the Great Pyramid: while two Bedouin seized an arm apiece and hauled from above, a third would push from below. **Climbing the pyramids** is now forbidden and it is undoubtedly very dangerous, although attempts are still made. Though **going inside** is quite safe, anyone suffering from claustrophobia or asthma should forget it. Clambering through all three shafts in the Great Pyramid will make your leg muscles ache the following day.

As site plans suggest, the pyramids' **orientation** is no accident. Their entrances are aligned with the Polar Star (or rather, its position 4500 years ago); the internal tomb chambers face west, the direction of the Land of the Dead; and the external funerary temples point eastwards towards the rising sun. It is also claimed that the trio of pyramids represents the three stars in Orion's belt. Less well preserved are the causeways leading to the so-called valley temples, and various subsidiary pyramids and *mastaba* tombs. The entire site is being renovated by the Supreme Council for Antiquities (SCA), and continues to yield surprises: notably the recent discovery of a possible secret chamber within the Great Pyramid, which some think will contain treasures as stunning as those from Tutankhamun's tomb; a previously unknown small pyramid by the southeastern corner of Cheops', with the oldest pyramidion (capstone) yet discovered; and tunnels under the seats in front of the Sphinx, whose age and purpose are so far unknown.

to buy **tickets** (£E40, students £E20, camera £E10, video £E100) as early as possible. Afternoon tickets go on sale from 1pm.

You enter the pyramid via an opening created by the treasure-hunting Khalif Ma'mun in 820, some distance below the original entrance on the north face (now blocked). After following this downwards at a crouch, you'll reach the junction of the ascending and descending corridors. The latter – leading to an unfinished chamber below the pyramid – is best ignored or left until last, and everyone heads up the 1.6-metre-high **ascending corridor**. According to medieval Arab chroniclers, intruders soon encountered an "idol of speckled granite" wreathed by a serpent which "seized upon and strangled whoever approached", but latterday visitors are merely impeded by the 1:2 gradient of the passage, which runs for 36m until it meets another junction.

To the right of this is a **shaft** that ancient writers believed to be a well connected to the Nile; it's now recognized as leading into the subterranean chamber and thought to have been an escape passage for the workmen. Straight ahead is a horizontal passage 35m long and 1.75m high, leading to a semi-finished limestone chamber with a pointed roof, which Arabs dubbed the "**Queen's Chamber**". Petrie reckoned this was the *serdab*, or repository for the pharaoh's statue, while the eccentric Davidson saw it as symbolizing the ultimate futility of Judaism. Either way, there's no evidence that a queen was ever buried here. In the northern and southern walls are two holes made in 1872 for the purpose of discovering the chamber's ventilation shafts; it was through one of these that the robot probe discovered the "secret chamber", at the end of a 65m passageway only twenty centimetres high and the same distance wide, which is aligned with the Dog Star, Sirius (representing the goddess Isis).

However, most people step up into the **Great Gallery**, the finest section of the pyramid. Built of Muqattam limestone, so perfectly cut that a knife blade can't be inserted between its joints, the 47-metre-long shaft narrows to a corbelled roof 8.5m high. (Davidson believed that its length in "pyramid inches" corresponded to the number of years between the Crucifixion and the outbreak of World War I.) The incisions in its walls probably held beams that were used to raise the sarcophagus or granite plug blocks up the steep incline (nowadays overlaid with wooden steps). Though no longer infested by giant bats, as nineteenth-century travellers reported, the Great Gallery is sufficiently hot and airless to constitute something of an ordeal, and you'll be glad to reach the horizontal antechamber at the top, which is slotted for the insertion of plug blocks designed to thwart entry to the putative burial chamber.

The **King's Chamber** lies 95m beneath the apex of the pyramid and half that distance from its outer walls. Built of red granite blocks, the rectangular chamber is large enough to accommodate a double-decker bus. Its dimensions (5.2 by 10.8 by 5.8 metres) have inspired many abstruse calculations and whacky prophecies: Hitler ordered a replica built beneath the Nuremberg Stadium, where he communed with himself before Nazi rallies. To one side of the chamber lies a huge, lidless **sarcophagus** of Aswan granite, bearing the marks of diamond-tipped saws and drills. On the northern and southern walls, at knee height, you'll notice two air shafts leading to the outer world, aligned with the stars of Orion's Belt and Alpha Draconis (representing Osiris and the hippo goddess Rer respectively).

Unseen above the ceiling, five **relieving chambers** distribute the weight of the pyramid away from the burial chamber; each consists of 43 granite monoliths weighing 40 to 70 tons apiece. These chambers can only be reached by a ladder from the Great Gallery, and then a passage where Colonel Vyse found

Khufu's name inscribed in red (the only inscription within the Giza Pyramids), but the flow of people normally rules this out.

On your way back down, consider investigating the 100-metre-long **descending corridor**, which leads to a crudely hewn **unfinished chamber** beneath the pyramid. There's nothing to see, but the nerve-wracking descent is worthy of Indiana Jones.

Subsidiary tombs

East of the Great Pyramid, it's just possible to discern the foundations of Khufu's funerary temple and a few blocks of the causeway that once connected it to his valley temple (now buried beneath the village of Nazlat al-Samman). Nearby stand three ruined **Queens' Pyramids**, each with a small chapel attached. The northern and southern pyramids belonged to Merites and Hensutsen, Khufu's principal wife (and sister), and the putative mother of Chephren, respectively; the middle one may have belonged to the mother of Redjedef, the third ruler of the dynasty. Between that and the Great Pyramid, the remains of a fourth satellite pyramid have recently been discovered, including its capstone, the oldest yet found, but the pyramid's purpose is so far unknown.

Just northeast of Queen Merites' pyramid is a **shaft** where III Dynasty pharaoh Snofru's wife Queen Hetepheres' sarcophagus was found, having been stashed here following lootings at its original home in Dahshur. To the east of it are the tombs of Qar and his son Idou, which contain life-size statues of the deceased and various reliefs. To the east of Queen Hensutsen's pyramid are the tombs of Cheops' son Khufu-Khaef, and Chephren's wife (also Hetepheres' daughter) Meres-ankh, the best preserved of all the tombs on the Giza plateau, complete with statues in the niches and reliefs showing scenes of daily life, with much of the paintwork intact. To get into these tombs, ask at the custodian's hut beside Hetepheres' shaft; naturally, the custodian will appreciate a tip for opening up.

To the west of the Great Pyramid lie dozens of **IV and V Dynasty mastabas**, where archeologists have uncovered a 4600-year-old mummified princess, whose body had been hollowed out and encased in a thin layer of plaster – a hitherto unknown method of mummification. Here are more **tombs** that until 1995 had been closed to the public since their discovery in the nineteenth century. In general, these are less interesting than those on the eastern side of the Great Pyramid, but that of Neferbauptah – almost parallel with the west side of Chephren's pyramid – has a dinosaur fossil preserved in the fifth block from the right of the second row up on its north side. Should you want to enter any of these tombs, ask at the Inspectorate office to the north. Beware of deep shafts with no fences around them.

The Solar Boat Museum

Perched to the south of the Great Pyramid, across the road from another cluster of *mastabas*, is a humidity-controlled pavilion (daily: winter 9am–4pm; summer 9am–5pm; £E20, students £E10, cameras £E10, video camera £E100) containing a 43-metre-long **boat** from one of the five boat pits sunk around Khufu's Pyramid. (Another boat has been located by X-rays and video cameras, but for the present remains unexcavated.)

When the pit's limestone roofing blocks were removed in 1954, a faint odour of cedarwood arose. Restorer Hagg Ahmed Yussef subsequently spent fourteen years rebuilding a graceful craft from 1200 pieces of wood, originally held together by sycamore pegs and halfa-grass ropes. Archeologists term these vessels "solar boats" (or barques), but their purpose remains uncertain – carrying the pharaoh through the underworld (as shown in XVII–IX Dynasty tombs at Thebes) or accompanying the sun-god on his daily journey across the heavens are two of the many hypotheses.

❶ The Pyramid of Chephren (Khafre)

Sited on higher ground, with an intact summit and steeper sides, the middle or **Second Pyramid** seems taller than Khufu's. Built by his son **Khafre** (known to posterity as Chephren), its base originally covered 214.8 square metres and its weight is estimated at 4,883,000 tons. As with Khufu's Pyramid, the original rock-hewn burial chamber was never finished and an upper chamber was subsequently constructed. Classical writers such as Pliny believed that the pyramid had no entrance, but when Belzoni located and blasted open the sealed portal on its north face in 1818, he found that Arab tomb robbers had somehow gained access nearly a thousand years earlier, undeterred by legends of an idol "with fierce and sparkling eyes", bent on slaying intruders. In March 1993, several tourists were injured by an explosion inside Chephren's Pyramid, probably caused by a bomb.

Chephren

Inside the pyramid (£E10, students E£5, camera £E10, video £E100; no current limit on numbers), you can follow one of the two entry corridors downwards, and then upwards, into a long horizontal passage leading to Chephren's **burial chamber**, where Belzoni celebrated his discovery by writing his name in black letters. This ebullient circus strongman-turned-explorer went on to find Seti I's tomb in the Valley of the Kings, and died searching for the source of the River Niger. Set into the chamber's granite floor is the sarcophagus of Khafre, who reigned c.2558–2533 BC. The square cavity near the southern wall may have marked the position of a canopic chest containing the pharaoh's viscera.

Chephren's Funerary Complex and the Sphinx

The funerary complex of Chephren's Pyramid is the best-preserved example of this typically Old Kingdom arrangement. When a pharaoh died, his body was ferried across the Nile to a riverside valley temple where it was embalmed by priests. After the process was complete, mourners gathered here to purify themselves before escorting his mummy up the causeway to a funerary (or mortuary) temple, where further rites preceded its interment within the pyramid. Thereafter, the priests ensured his *ka*'s afterlife by making offerings of food and incense in the funerary temple on specific anniversaries.

Chephren's **funerary temple** consists of a pillared hall, central court, niched storerooms and a sanctuary, but most of the outer granite casing has been plundered over centuries and the interior may not be accessible. Amongst the remaining blocks is a 13.4-metre-long monster weighing 163,000 kilos. Flanking the temple are what appear to be boat pits, although excavations have yielded nothing but pottery fragments. From here you can trace the foundations of a **causeway** that runs 400m downhill to his valley temple, near the Sphinx.

The **valley temple** lay buried under sand until its discovery by Mariette in 1852, which accounts for its reasonable state of preservation. Built of limestone and faced with polished Aswan granite, the temple faces east and used to open onto a quay. Beyond a narrow antechamber you'll find a T-shaped hall whose gigantic architraves are supported by square pillars, in front of which stood diorite statues of Chephren. Contrary to the widely accepted theory, a few scholars believe that mummification occurred at Memphis or Chephren's mortuary temple, this edifice being reserved for the "Opening of Mouth" ceremony, whereby the *ka* entered the deceased's body.

The Sphinx

This legendary monument, whose enclosure is entered through the Valley Temple, is carved from an outcrop of soft limestone that was supposedly left standing after the harder surrounding stone was quarried for the Great Pyramid; however, since the base stone was too soft to work on directly, it was clad in harder stone before finishing. Conventional archeology credits Chephren with the idea of shaping it into a figure with a lion's body and a human head, which is often identified as his own (complete with royal beard and *uraeus*, see p.294), though it may represent a guardian deity. Some thousand years later, the future Tuthmosis IV is said to have dreamt that if he cleared the sand that engulfed the **Sphinx** it would make him ruler; a prophecy fulfilled, as recorded on a stele that he placed between its paws. All these notions went unchallenged until 1991, when two American geologists argued that the Sphinx was at least 2600 years older than had been imagined: its bedrock was heavily weathered and eroded by water, probably during the Nabtian Pluvial era (3000–1200 BC). This argument is dismissed by Supreme Council of Antiquities director Zawi Hawas, who cites an analysis of the Sphinx's bedrock by the Getty Institute, which concludes that the erosion was caused by the action of mineral salts within the plateau and/or the wind. The controversy delighted the maverick Egyptologist John West, who has long claimed that Egyptian civilization was the inheritor of a more ancient, lost culture – the mythical Atlantis. The name "Sphinx" was actually bestowed by the ancient Greeks, after the legendary creature that put riddles to passers-by and slew those who answered wrongly; the Arabs called it *Abu el-Hol* (the Awesome or terrible one).

Used for target practice by Mamluke and Napoleonic troops, the Sphinx lost much of its beard to the British Museum and was sandbagged for protection during World War II. Early modern repairs did more harm than good, since its porous limestone "breathes", unlike the cement that was used to fill its cracks. There is also the problem of chemical pollutants from sewage and fires in the neighbouring settlement of Nazlat al-Samman. A more recent long-term **restoration project** (1989–1998) involved hand-cutting ten thousand limestone blocks, to refit the paws, legs and haunches of the beast; the missing nose and beard have not been replaced, deliberately.

Three **tunnels** exist inside the Sphinx, one behind its head, one in its tail and one in its north side. Their function is unknown, but none of them go anywhere. Other tunnels have been unearthed in the vicinity of the Sphinx; again, we don't know who built them or what they were for, but one suggestion is that they were created by later ancient Egyptians looking for buried treasure.

During Sound and Light shows, the Sphinx is given the role of narrator.

The Pyramid of Mycerinus (Menkaure)

Sited on a gradual slope into undulating desert, the smallest of the Giza Pyramids speaks of waning power and commitment. Though started by Chephren's successor, **Menkaure** (called Mycerinus by the Greeks), it was finished with unseemly haste by his son Shepseskaf, who seemingly enjoyed less power than his predecessors and depended on the priesthood. Herodotus records the legend that an oracle gave Mycerinus only six years to live, so to cheat fate he made merry round the clock, doubling his annual quantum of experience. Another story has it that the pyramid was actually built by Rhodophis, a Thracian courtesan who charged each client the price of a building block (the structure is estimated to contain 200,000 blocks).

Mycerinus

Because its lower half was sheathed in Aswan granite, this is sometimes called the Red Pyramid (a name also applied to one of Snofru's pyramids at Dahshur). Its relative lack of casing stones is due to a twelfth-century sultan whose courtiers persuaded him to attempt the pyramid's demolition, a project he wisely gave up after eight months. Medieval Arab chroniclers frequently ascribed the Giza Pyramids to a single ruler, who supposedly boasted: "I, Surid the king, have built these pyramids in sixty-one years. Let him who comes after me attempt to destroy them in six hundred. To destroy is easier than to build. I have clothed them in silk; let him try to cover them in mats." The **interior** (closed to the public until 2004) is unusual for having its unfinished chamber in the superstructure and the final burial chamber underground. Here Vyse discovered a basalt sarcophagus later lost at sea en route to Britain, plus human remains that he assumed were Menkaure's, but which are now reckoned to be a XXVI Dynasty replacement and rest in the British Museum.

The complex also features three subsidiary pyramids, a relatively intact funerary temple, and a causeway to the now-buried valley temple. Northwest of the latter lies the sarcophagus-shaped **Tomb of Queen Khentkawes**, an intriguing figure who appears to have bridged the transition between the IV and V dynasties. Apparently married to Shepseskaf, the last IV Dynasty ruler, she may have wed a priest of the sun-god after his demise and gone on to bear several kings who were buried at Saqqara or Abu Sir (where she also built a pyramid).

Kerdassa and Harranitta

These two villages have no connection with the pyramids, but tour groups often pay one or both of them a visit. **KERDASSA**, roughly due west of Imbaba (but accessible by minibus from Midan Giza), is where most of the scarves, *galabiyyas* and shirts in Cairo are made, plus carpets, which are sold by the metre. Although no longer a place for bargains, it's still frequented by collectors of ethnic textiles, particularly Bedouin robes and veils (the best-quality ones retail for hundreds of dollars). In times past, Kerdassa was also the starting point of the camel trail across the Western Desert to Libya.

Folks on Salah's tours (see p.224) are inevitably taken to **HARRANIYYA**, the site of the famous **Wissa Wassef Art Centre** (daily 10am–6pm; ☏02/385 0403, ✉taya@link.net). Founded fifty years ago by Ramses Wissa Wassef, an architect who wanted to preserve village crafts and alleviate rural unemployment, the centre teaches children to design and weave carpets, and has branched out into batik work and pottery. Superintended by his widow and the original generation of students, pupils produce beautiful tapestries, which now sell for thousands of dollars and are imitated throughout Egypt. You can see them at work between 10am and 5pm (except at lunchtime and on Fridays), and admire a superb collection in the museum designed by Hassan Fathy, a masterpiece of mud-brick architecture. To reach the Art Centre under your own steam, catch a taxi or minibus 4km south along the Saqqara road (Maryotteya Canal, west bank) from Pyramids Road, and follow the signs to *Salma* (or *Salome*) campsite, next door.

The Pyramids of Zawiyat al-Aryan

The **Zawiyat al-Aryan pyramid field** lies roughly midway between Giza and North Saqqara and about 3.5km from the Sun Temples of Abu Ghurab at Abu Sir (see below). Both its pyramids are sanded over and scarcely worth a detour, but Egyptologists still ponder their place in the evolution of pyramid-building.

The northerly **Unfinished Pyramid** makes extensive use of granite, suggesting that it might hail from the IV Dynasty, but never got beyond its foundations and enclosure wall – unfinished blocks and stone chippings are scattered all around. To the southeast lies a **Layer Pyramid** built of small stone blocks, which seems to have been intended as a step pyramid and thus presumably belongs to the III Dynasty.

Should you have a special urge to see these pyramids, your best bet is either to stop off here on a horse- or camel-ride from the Pyramids of Giza, or else take a service taxi microbus from Maryotteya Canal at Pyramids Road to the nearby village of Shabramant and walk from there.

The Pyramids of Abu Sir

This necropolis of V Dynasty (c.2494–2345 BC) pharaohs covers an arc of desert beyond the village of **ABU SIR**. The mortuary complexes here are smaller than the Giza Pyramids of the previous dynasty, suggesting a decline in royal power; their ruinous state and the effort required to reach them also mean that few tourists come here. Those who do often feel that Abu Sir's splendid isolation compensates for its monumental shortcomings. However, the site is bound to lose some of its enchantment, having opened as an official tourist site in 1999, complete with visitors' centre (daily: winter 8am–5pm; summer 8am–4pm), entry charge (£E10, students £E5) and a steadily increasing stream of tour buses along the new asphalt road.

Getting there

The Pyramids of Abu Sir are a ten-minute walk from the village of the same name, which can be reached by service taxi microbus from Maryotteya Canal at Pyramids Road or by taxi from Saqqara (£E5–8). The boldest option, however, is to visit them **en route between Giza and Saqqara** by horse or camel, spending three hours in the saddle. Making a round trip **from North Saqqara** (see below) is less demanding, but still requires commitment. With the Pyramids clearly visible 6km away, you can either walk (1hr 30min–2hr) or conserve energy by renting a horse or camel from near the refreshments tent (£E15–20 one-way).

The pyramid complexes

The four pyramid complexes are ranged in an arc that ignores chronological order. At the southern end of the pyramid field a low mound marks the core of the unfinished **Pyramid of Neferefre**, whose brief reign preceded Nyuserre's. As the core is composed of locally quarried limestone and was never encased in finer Tura masonry, no causeway was ever built. However, the desert may yet disgorge other structures: during the 1980s, Czechoslovak archeologists uncovered another pyramid complex, thought to belong to Queen Khentkawes, the mother of Sahure.

Dominating the view north is the much larger **Pyramid of Neferirkare**, the third ruler of the V Dynasty, who strove to outdo his predecessor, Sahure. If finished, it would have been 70m high – taller than the third pyramid at Giza – but Neferirkare's premature demise forced his successor to hastily complete a modified version using perishable mud-brick. Although too dangerous to climb, its summit commands a view of the entire pyramid field, from the three at Giza and the four at Saqqara to the Red and Bent pyramids at Dahshur, and even the Collapsed Pyramid of Maidum on the distant horizon. The valley temple and grand causeway of Neferirkare's Pyramid were later usurped to serve the **Pyramid of Nyuserre**, further north. A battered mortuary temple with papyriform columns mocks the original name of this dilapidated pyramid, "The Places of Nyuserre are Enduring"; the pharaohs who followed him preferred burial at Saqqara. A cluster of *mastabas* to the northwest includes the **Tomb of Ptahshepses**. Currently entered via a rickety ladder, the tomb's most curious feature is the double room off the courtyard, which may have held solar boats. If so, the only other known example of this in a private tomb is that of Kagemni in North Saqqara. Ptahshepses was Chief of Works to Sahure, the first of the V Dynasty kings to be buried at Abu Sir.

The **Pyramid of Sahure** is badly damaged, but its associated temples have fared better than others in this group. A 235-metre-long causeway links the ruined valley temple to Sahure's mortuary temple on the eastern side of the pyramid. Though most of its reliefs (which were the first to show the king smiting his enemies, later a standard motif) have gone to various museums, enough remains to make the temple worth exploring. It's also possible to crawl through a dusty, cobwebbed passage to reach the burial chamber within the pyramid (whose original name was "The Soul of Sahure Gleams"). Just to the north of the causeway, a series of fascinating reliefs shows scenes from the building of a pyramid, notably of workers dragging a pyramidion (capstone) covered with white gold, while dancers celebrate the pyramid's completion.

The Sun Temples of Abu Ghurab

Just northeast of Abu Sir is the site known as **Abu Ghurab** (if you are riding between Giza and Saqqara, you could ask the guide to stop here). Its twin temples were designed for worship of Re, the sun-god of Heliopolis, but their Jubilee reliefs and proximity to a pyramid field suggest a similar function to Zoser's *heb-sed* court at Saqqara.

Unlike the ruinous **Sun Temple of Userkaf**, 400m from Sahure's Pyramid, the more distant **Sun Temple of Nyuserre** repays a visit. At its western end stood a colossal *benben* or megalith as tall as a pyramid, symbolizing the primordial mound – of which only the base remains. Approached from its valley temple by a causeway, the great courtyard is centred on an alabaster altar where cattle were sacrificed. From the courtyard's vestibule, corridors run north to storerooms and south to the king's chapel. The "Chamber of Seasons" beyond the chapel once contained beautiful reliefs; to the south you can find the remnants of a brick model of a solar boat.

North Saqqara

While Memphis (see p.232) was the capital of the Old Kingdom, Egypt's royalty and nobility were buried at **Saqqara**, the limestone scarp that flanks the Nile Valley to the west – the traditional direction of the Land of the Dead.

Although superseded by the Theban necropolis during the New Kingdom, Saqqara remained in use for burying sacred animals and birds, especially in Ptolemaic times, when these cults enjoyed a revival. Over three thousand years it grew to cover seven kilometres of desert – not including the associated necropolises of Abu Sir and Dahshur, or the Giza Pyramids. As such, it is today the largest archeological site in Egypt. Its name – pronounced "sa' 'ah-rah" –

probably derives from Sokar, the Memphite god of the dead, though Egyptians may tell you that it comes from *saq*, the Arabic word for a hawk or falcon, the sacred bird of Horus.

Besides the pyramids and *mastabas* seen by visitors, Saqqara has an incalculable wealth of monuments and artefacts still hidden beneath the windblown sands. In 1986, the **tomb of Maya**, Tutankhamun's treasurer, was discovered, stuffed with precious objects (it won't be open to the public for some time). Yet aside from Zoser's Pyramid, the site was virtually ignored by archeologists until Auguste Mariette found the Serapeum in 1851.

The Saqqara necropolis divides into two main sections: **North Saqqara** – the more interesting area (covered here) – and **South Saqqara** (see p.233). North Saqqara boasts a score of sights, so anyone with limited time should be selective. The **highlights** are Zoser's funerary complex, the Serapeum, and two outstanding *mastabas*; if time allows, add other tombs to your itinerary. To take in the whole site you would need several days.

Getting there and other practicalities

North Saqqara lies 21km south of the Giza Pyramids as the camel trundles, or 32km from Cairo by road, being roughly opposite Helwan on the east bank of the Nile. Getting there **by public transport** is awkward and time-consuming. The quickest method takes about an hour: go by bus to Pyramids Road, get off at Maryotteya Canal (about 1km before the Pyramids) and take a service taxi microbus from there to Saqqara – be sure not to take one going to Abu Sir village, as you'll then have to walk all the way across the site to get to the ticket office. You can also take bus #987 from Midan Ramses, or behind the Egyptian Museum in Midan Tahrir, to El-Badrasheen, and then a minibus to Saqqara, by way of Memphis. Alternatively, take the metro to Helwan station (30min; 90pt), then a minibus to Tibiin, near the Marazi Bridge (20min; 50pt); another *servees* across to El-Badrasheen on the west bank (15min; 50pt); and finally one to Saqqara, again via Memphis (35pt). One disadvantage of all these methods is that they leave you in Saqqara village, still over a kilometre from the site entrance. Getting back to Cairo, it is wise not to leave too late, or you may not find transport in Saqqara village, and will have to either pay well over the odds for a taxi, or walk another 5km to El-Badrasheen (or at least to the Maryotteya Canal) to pick up a bus or microbus back to Cairo.

To save time and energy for the site, it's best to avail yourself of **tours** run by the affable Salah Mohammed Abdel Hafiez. You can contact him by phone (☎02/298 0650, mobile 012/313 8446), or send an email (ⓔsamo@link.net). Leaving around 8am, you'll be driven in an a/c minibus to Memphis, North Saqqara, the Wissa Wassef tapestry school at Harraniyya and the Pyramids of Giza – all accompanied by an English-speaking Egyptologist – before returning to Cairo at about 5pm. Be sure to ask to see the Mastaba of Ti during your trip. The price of the tour (£E40, £E5 discount to *Rough Guide* readers who book direct) doesn't include admission tickets. Thomas Cook, Misr Travel and American Express also run tours to Saqqara for upwards of £E50 per person. Another option is to rent a **private taxi** for the day (£E60–80 for just Giza and Saqqara, £E75–100 if you add on Abu Sir and Dahshur), splitting the cost between however many people you can assemble. Be sure to specify which sites are included and how long you expect to stay when you negotiate with the driver.

Lastly, you could plump for riding **across the desert from the Pyramids of Giza by horse or camel** (3hr). Although touts swear that the route takes you through the desert, past Zawiyet al-Aryan, the Sun Temples of Abu Ghurab and the Pyramids of Abu Sir, they often guide you along a more direct village track on the edge of the cultivated area, supposedly due to military restrictions. Either way, the journey will leave you stiff for days afterwards (see p.51 for the rudiments of camel-handling). Most people opt for a one-way ride (£E50–60 for a horse, £E40–50 for a camel); return trips cost twice that, plus a negotiable sum for waiting time (say £E120–150 in all). Be warned that some guides threaten to abandon travellers in the middle of nowhere unless they receive hefty *baksheesh*; it's usually safe to call their bluff.

Even if you don't emulate Lawrence of Arabia, bear in mind **conditions** at Saqqara. Over winter, the site can be swept by chill winds and clouds of grit; during the hottest months walking around is exhausting. Beware of deep pits, which aren't always fenced off. Bring at least one litre of water apiece, as vendors at Memphis and the refreshments tent at North Saqqara are grossly overpriced, like every restaurant along the Saqqara road; a packed lunch is also a good idea. Should you need a break after visiting the site, the *Sakkara Palm Club*, 500m from the site entrance, has a **pool**, coffee shop and restaurant, open daily 9am–9pm for a day membership fee of £E35.

Though **opening hours** are daily 8am to 4pm in winter, 8am to 5pm in summer, guards start locking up the tombs at least half an hour early. A kiosk on the approach road sells **tickets** (£E20, students £E10), while another just up from the car park has video camera (£E25) permits; camera permits (£E5) are only necessary if you intend to use your camera inside the pyramids or tombs. It's a good idea to check at the kiosk which tombs are open – especially those further afield – as they often close due to restoration work. Some guards encourage unauthorized snapping in the expectation of *baksheesh*, but aside from this you're not obliged to give anything unless they help with lighting or provide a guided tour. If you don't want a running commentary, make this clear at the outset.

To reduce foot-slogging around the site, consider **renting a camel** (£E30–35 per hour), **horse** (£E30–40 per hour) **or donkey** (£E20 per hour) from outside the refreshments tent near the Serapeum.

Zoser's funerary complex

The funerary complex of King Zoser (or Djoser) is the largest in Saqqara, and its **Step Pyramid** heralded the start of the Pyramid Age. When Imhotep, Zoser's chief architect, raised the pyramid in the 27th century BC, it was the largest structure ever built in stone – the "beginning of architecture", according to one historian. Imhotep's achievement was to break from the tradition of earthbound *mastabas*, raising level upon level of stones to create a four-step, and then a six-step pyramid, which was clad in dazzling white limestone. None of the blocks was very large, for Zoser's builders still thought in terms of mud-brick rather than megaliths, but the concept, techniques and logistics all pointed towards the true pyramid, finally attained at Giza.

Before it was stripped of its casing stones and rounded off by the elements, Zoser's Pyramid stood 62m high and measured 140m by 118m along its base. The original entrance on the northern side is blocked, but with permission and keys from the site's Antiquities Inspectorate you can enter via a gallery on the opposite side, dug in the XXVI Dynasty. Dark passageways and vertical ladders descend 28m into the bedrock, where a granite plug failed to prevent robbers from plundering the burial chamber of this III Dynasty monarch (c.2667–2648 BC).

Surrounding the pyramid is an extensive **funerary complex**, originally enclosed by a finely cut limestone wall, 544m long and 277m wide, now largely ruined or buried by sand. False doors occur at intervals for the convenience of the pharaoh's *ka*, but visitors can only enter at the southeastern corner, which has largely been rebuilt. Beyond a vestibule with simulated double doors (detailed down to their hinge pins and sockets) lies a narrow colonnaded corridor, whose forty "bundle" columns are ribbed in imitation of palm stems, which culminates in a broader **Hypostyle Hall**.

From here you emerge onto the **Great South Court**, where a rebuilt section of wall (marked ★ on our site plan) bears a **frieze of cobras**. Worshipped in the Delta as a fire-spitting goddess of destruction called Wadjet or Edjo, the cobra was adopted as the emblem of royalty and always appeared on pharaonic headdresses – a figure known as the *uraeus*. Nearby, a deep shaft plummets into Zoser's **Southern Tomb**, decorated with blue faïence tiles and a relief of the king running the *heb-sed* race. During the Jubilee festival marking the thirtieth year of a pharaoh's reign, he had to sprint between two altars representing Upper and Lower Egypt and re-enact his coronation, seated first on one throne, then upon another, symbolically reuniting the Two Lands. Besides demonstrating his vitality, the five-day festival confirmed the renewal of his *ka* and the obedience of provincial dignitaries.

Although the festival was held at Memphis, a pair of altars, thrones and shrines were incorporated in Zoser's funerary complex to perpetuate its efficacy on a cosmic timescale. The B-shaped structures near the centre of the Great Court are the bases of these altars; the twin thrones probably stood on the platform at the southern end of the adjacent **Heb-Sed Court**. Both shrines were essentially facades, since the actual buildings were filled with rubble. This phoney quality is apparent if you view them from the east: the curvaceous roof line and delicate false columns wouldn't look amiss on a yuppie waterfront development. Notice the four **stone feet** beneath a shelter near the northern end of the court.

Beyond this lies the partially ruined **House of the South**, whose chapel is fronted by proto-Doric columns with lotus capitals, and a spearhead motif above the lintel. Inside you'll find several examples of XVIII–IXX Dynasty tourist graffiti, expressing admiration for Zoser or the equivalent of "Ramses was here" – banalities which one scornful ancient graffitist likens to "the work of a woman who has no mind". Continuing northwards, you'll pass a relatively intact row of casing stones along the eastern side of Zoser's Pyramid. The **House of the North** has fluted columns with papyrus capitals; the lotus and the papyrus were the heraldic emblems of Upper and Lower Egypt.

On the northern side of the pyramid, a tilted masonry box or **serdab** ("cellar" in Arabic) contains a life-size statue of Zoser gazing blindly towards the North and circumpolar stars, which the ancients associated with immortality; seated thus, his *ka* was assured of eternal life. Zoser's statue is a replica, however, the original having been removed to Cairo's Antiquities Museum. The ruined mortuary temple to the right of the *serdab* is unusual for being sited to the north rather than the east of its pyramid, and for the underground tunnel which originally led to Zoser's burial chamber.

South of the complex

South of Zoser's funerary complex are several tombs and other ruins, dating from various dynasties. During the Old Kingdom, nobles were buried in subterranean tombs covered by large mud-brick superstructures; the name *mastaba* (Arabic for "bench") was bestowed upon them by native workmen during excavations last century. Three such edifices stand outside the southern wall of

Zoser's complex, although two of them are currently closed. The open one, the **Mastaba of Idut**, has interesting reliefs in five of its ten rooms. Among the fishing and farming scenes, notice the crocodile eyeing a newborn hippo, and a calf being dragged through the water so that cows will ford a river. The chapel contains a false door painted in imitation of granite, scenes of bulls and buffaloes being sacrificed, and Idut herself. Idut was the daughter of Pharaoh Unas, whose pyramid stands just beyond the **Mastaba of Nebet**, his queen. If accessible, its reliefs are also worth seeing: in one scene, Nebet smells a lotus blossom.

The Pyramid of Unas

Although its frontal aspect resembles a mound of rubble, the **Pyramid of Unas** retains many casing stones around the back, some carved with hieroglyphs. A low passageway on the northern side leads into its **burial chamber**, whose alabaster walls are covered with inscriptions listing the rituals and prayers for liberating the pharaoh's *ba*, and the articles for his *ka* to use in the afterlife. These **Pyramid Texts** are the earliest known example of decorative writing within a pharaonic tomb chamber, and formed the basis of the New Kingdom *Book of the Dead*. They speak of the pharaoh becoming a star and travelling to Sirius and other constellations. Painted stars adorn the ceiling, while the sarcophagus area is surrounded by striped, checked and zigzag patterns. Thomas Cook & Sons sponsored the excavation of the tomb by Gaston Maspero in 1881.

Unas

Unas was the last pharaoh of the V Dynasty, so his pyramid follows those of Abu Sir, which evince a marked decline from the great pyramids of Giza. Given the duration of pharaonic civilization, it's sobering to realize that only 350 years separated the creation of the Step Pyramid from this sad reminder of past glories. Originally, it was approached by a one-kilometre-long **causeway** enclosed by a roof and walls. Reliefs inside the short reconstructed section depict the transport of granite from Aswan, archers, prisoners of war, and a famine caused by the Nile failing to rise. The ruins of a valley temple face the ticket office below the plateau.

To the south of the causeway are two gaping, brick-lined **boat pits** that may have contained solar barques like the one at Giza, or merely symbolized them, since nothing was found when the pits were excavated.

Other tombs and ruins

A stone hut to the south of the Unas Pyramid gives access to a spiral staircase that descends 25m underground, to where three low corridors lead into the vaulted **Persian Tombs**. Chief physician Psamtik, Admiral Djenhebu and Psamtik's son Pediese were all officials of the XXVII Dynasty of Persian kings founded in 525 BC, yet the hieroglyphs in their tombs invoke the same spells as those written two thousand years earlier. The dizzying descent and claustrophobic atmosphere make this an exciting tomb to explore. Though often locked, it's not "forbidden" as guards sometimes pretend, hoping to wangle excessive *baksheesh*.

Further to the southeast lies the recently rediscovered **Tomb of Horemheb**. Built when he was a general, it became redundant after Horemheb seized power from Pharaoh Ay in 1348 BC and ordered a new tomb to be dug in the Valley of the Kings, the royal necropolis of the New Kingdom. Many of the finely carved blocks from his original tomb are now in museums around the world. Another set of paving stones and truncated columns marks the nearby

Tomb of Tia, sister of Ramses II. The **Tomb of Maya**, Tutankhamun's treasurer, was found nearby in 1986 and is still under excavation. Due east lie the sanded-over mud-brick ruins of the **Monastery of St Jeremiah**, which the Arabs destroyed in 960, four hundred years after its foundation. Practically all of the monastery's carvings and paintings have been removed to the Coptic Museum in Old Cairo. Just to its north, on the causeway of Unas, are four *mastabas* belonging to nobles.

It's indicative of how much might still be hidden beneath the sands at Saqqara that the **unfinished Pyramid of Sekhemkhet** was only discovered in 1950. Beyond his monuments, nothing is known of Sekhemkhet, whose step pyramid and funerary complex were presumably intended to mimic those of his predecessor, Zoser, and may also have been built by Imhotep. The alabaster sarcophagus inside the pyramid (which is unsafe to enter) was apparently never used, but the body of a child was found inside an auxiliary tomb.

From Sekhemkhet's pyramid and the monastery it's roughly 700m to the nearest part of South Saqqara.

Around the Pyramids of Userkaf and Teti

While neither of these pyramids amounts to much, the *mastabas* near Teti's edifice contain some fantastic reliefs. If you're starting from Zoser's complex, it's only a short walk to the pulverized **Pyramid of Userkaf**, the founder of the V Dynasty, whose successors were buried at Abu Sir (see p.221). From here, a track runs northwards to the **Pyramid of Teti**, which overlooks the valley from the edge of the plateau. Excavated by Mariette in the 1850s, it has since been engulfed by sand and may be closed; in one of the funeral chambers (accessible by a sloping shaft and low passageway), the star-patterned blocks of its vaulted roof have slipped inwards.

Teti

Although most of the VI Dynasty kings who followed Teti chose to be buried at South Saqqara, several of their courtiers were interred in a **"street of tombs"** beside his pyramid, which was linked to the Serapeum by an Avenue of Sphinxes (now sanded over). To do justice to their superbly detailed reliefs takes well over an hour, but it's rare to find all of them open.

The Mastaba of Mereruka

The largest tomb in the street belongs to **Mereruka**, Teti's vizier and son-in-law, whose 32-room complex includes separate funerary suites for his wife Watet-khet-hor, priestess of Hathor, and their son Meri-Teti. In the entry passage, Mereruka is shown playing a board game and painting at an easel; the chamber beyond depicts him hunting in the marshes with Watet-khet-hor (the frogs, birds, hippos and grasshoppers are beautifully rendered), along with the usual farming scenes. Goldsmiths, jewellers and other artisans are inspected by the couple in a room beyond the rear door, which leads into another chamber showing taxation and the punishment of defaulters. A pillared hall to the right portrays them watching sinuous dancers; a room to the left depicts offerings, sacrifices and birds being fed, with a *serdab* at the far end.

Beyond the transverse hall, with its tomb shaft, false door and reliefs of grape-treading and harvesting, lies the main offerings hall, dominated by a statue of Mereruka emerging from a false door. The opposite wall shows his funeral procession; around the corner are boats under full sail, with monkeys playing in their rigging. To the left of the statue, Mereruka is supported by his sons and litter-bearers, accompanied by dwarves and dogs; on the other side, children frolic while dancers sway above the doorway into Meri-Teti's undecorated funerary suite.

To reach **Watet-khet-hor's suite**, return to the first room in the *mastaba* and take the other door. After similar scenes to those in her husband's tomb, Watet-khet-hor is carried to her false door in a lion chair.

The Mastabas of Kagemni and Ankh-ma-hor

East of Mereruka's tomb and left around the corner, the smaller **Mastaba of Kagemni** features delicate reliefs in worse shape. The pillared hall beyond the entrance corridor shows dancers and acrobats, the judgement of prisoners, a hippo hunt and agricultural work, all rich in naturalistic detail. Notice the boys feeding a puppy and trussed cows being milked. The door in this wall leads to another chamber where Kagemni inspects his fowl pens while servants trap marsh birds with clap-nets; on the pylon beyond this he relaxes on a palanquin as they tend to his pet dogs and monkeys. As usual in the offerings hall, scenes of butchery appear opposite the false door. On the roof of the *mastaba* (reached by stairs from the entrance corridor) are two boat pits. As vizier, Kagemni was responsible for overseeing prophets and the estate of Teti's pyramid complex.

The **Mastaba of Ankh-ma-hor** is also known as the "Doctor's Tomb" after its reliefs showing circumcision, toe surgery and suchlike, as practised during the VI Dynasty. If the tomb is open it's definitely worth a look, unlike the sand-choked **I Dynasty tombs** that straggle along the edge of the scarp beyond the **Antiquities Inspectorate**.

Two outstanding mastabas

If your time is limited, these are the tombs to visit: the **Double Mastaba of Akhti- and Ptah-Hotep** lies 200m off the road to the refreshments tent, while the **Mastaba of Ti** is 500m in the other direction and easiest to get to from the Serapeum (see below). Outside the **refreshments tent** (£E4 minimum charge) you'll be importuned to rent a horse or camel.

The Mastaba of Akhti-Hotep and Ptah-Hotep

This *mastaba* belonged to **Ptah-Hotep**, a priest of Maat during the reign of Unas's predecessor, Djedkare, and his son **Akhti-Hotep**, who served as vizier, judge and overseer of the granaries and treasury. Though smaller than Ti's *mastaba*, its reliefs are interesting for being at various stages of completion, showing how a finished product was achieved. After the preliminary drawings had been corrected in red by a master artist, the background was chiselled away to leave a silhouette, before details were marked in and cut. The agricultural scenes in the entrance corridor show this process clearly, although with the exception of Ptah-Hotep's chapel, none of these reliefs was ever painted.

Off the pillared hall of Akhti-Hotep is a T-shaped chapel whose inside wall shows workers making papyrus boats and jousting with poles. More impressive is the chapel of his father, covered with exquisitely detailed reliefs. Between the two door-shaped steles representing the entrance to the tomb, Ptah-Hotep enjoys a banquet of offerings, garbed in the panther-skin of a high priest. Similar scenes occur on the facing wall, whose upper registers show animals being slaughtered and women bringing offerings from his estates. The left-hand wall swarms with activity, as boys wrestle and play *Khaki la wizza* (a leapfrog game still popular in Nubia); wild animals mate or flee from hunting dogs, while others are caged. A faded mural above the entrance shows the priest being manicured and pedicured at a time when Europe was in the Stone Age.

The Mastaba of Ti

Discovered by Mariette in 1865, this V Dynasty tomb has been a rich source of information about life in the Old Kingdom. A royal hairdresser who made an advantageous marriage, **Ti** acquired stewardship over several mortuary temples and pyramids, and his children bore the title "royal descendant".

Ti makes his first appearances on either side of the doorway, receiving offerings and asking visitors to respect his tomb **[a]**. The reliefs in the courtyard have been damaged by exposure, but it's possible to discern men butchering an ox **[b]**, Ti on his palanquin accompanied by dogs and dwarves **[c]**, servants feeding cranes and geese **[d]**, and Ti examining accounts and cargo **[e]**. His unadorned tomb (reached by a shaft from the courtyard) contrasts with the richly decorated interior of the *mastaba*.

Near his son's false door, variously garbed figures of Ti **[f]** appear above the portal of a corridor where bearers bring food and animals for the sustenance of his *ka* **[g]**. Beyond a doorway **[h]** over which Ti enjoys the marshes with his wife, funerary statues are dragged on sledges above scenes of butchery, and his Delta fleets are arrayed **[i]**.

Potters, bakers, brewers and scribes occupy the rear wall of a storage room **[j]**, while dancers shimmy above the doorway to Ti's chapel.

In the harvesting scene, notice the man twisting a donkey's ear to make it behave **[k]**. Further along, Ti inspects shipwrights shaping tree trunks, and sawing and hammering boards **[l]**. Goldsmiths, sculptors, carpenters, tanners and market life are minutely detailed **[m]**, like the

Feeding cranes

musicians who entertain Ti at his offerings table **[n]**. Peer through one of the apertures and you'll see a cast of his statue inside its *serdab*. The original is in the Egyptian Museum in Cairo.

Reliefs on the northern wall depict fishing and trapping in the Delta **[o]**; Ti sailing through the marshes while his servants spear hippopotami **[p]**; harvesting papyrus for boat-building, and ploughing and seeding fields **[q]**. The scene of hunting in the marshes is also allegorical, pitting Ti against the forces of chaos (represented by fish and birds) and evil (hippos were hated and feared).

The Serapeum

Saqqara's weirdest monument lies underground near a derelict building downhill from the refreshments tent. Discovered by Mariette in 1851, the rock-cut galleries of the **Serapeum** held the mummified corpses of the Apis bulls, which the Memphites regarded as manifestations of Ptah's "blessed soul" and identified with Osiris after death.

Having been embalmed on alabaster slabs at Memphis, the bulls were interred in sarcophagi weighing up to seventy tons apiece. Meanwhile, the priests began searching for Ptah's reincarnation amongst the sacred herd. Once a new bull had been chosen, it spent forty days at Nilopolis (across the river from Memphis), where women were allowed to approach it *only* to expose their vulvas (a practice believed to ensure fertility). After the full moon the bull was taken to its future residence in Memphis, where it had its own priestly attendants and a harem of cows.

The **cult of the Apis bulls** was assailed by Egypt's Persian conqueror, Cambyses, who stabbed one to disprove its divinity, whilst Artaxerxes I avenged his nickname "the donkey" by having a namesake beast buried here with full honours. But the Ptolemies encouraged native cults and even synthesized their own. "Serapeum" derives from the fusion of the Egyptian Osarapis (Osiris in his Apis form) and the Greeks' Dionysos into the cult of *Serapis*, whose temple stood in Alexandria.

Now that the lighting has been improved, the Serapeum galleries are much less spooky than when Mariette broke in. Although tomb robbers had plundered them centuries before, he found a single tomb miraculously undisturbed for four thousand years. The finger mark and footprints of the ancient workman who sealed the tomb were still visible, and Mariette also found a mummified bull and the coffin of Khamenwaset, son of Ramses II and high priest of Ptah. Sadly, none of the mummified bulls remains *in situ*.

The oldest of the galleries dates from that era, and is now inaccessible; the second is from the Saite period, and the main one from Ptolemaic times. Enormous granite or basalt **sarcophagi** are ranged either side of the Ptolemaic gallery, at the end of which is a narrow shaft whereby robbers penetrated the Serapeum. The finest sarcophagus squats on the right, while another one lies abandoned near the entrance to the Ramessid gallery.

Other curiosities

En route to the Serapeum you'll notice a concrete slab sheltering broken statues of Plato, Heraclitus, Thales, Protagoras, Homer, Hesiod, Demetrius of Phalerum and Pindar – the **Philosopher's Circle**. The statues formerly stood near a temple that overlaid the Serapeum, proof that the Ptolemies juxtaposed Hellenistic philosophy and ancient Egyptian religion with no sense of incongruity.

A cluster of **III Dynasty tombs** to the east of Ti's *mastaba* is now reckoned a likely site for the tomb of Imhotep, as yet undiscovered. The architect of Zoser's Step Pyramid was revered throughout pharaonic history and eventually became a demigod, credited with powers of healing; the Ptolemies associated him with Asclepius, the Greek god of medicine. Further northeast lie the **Ibis and Baboon Galleries** sacred to Thoth, which Flaubert visited in the 1840s: "We go down into a hole and then crawl along a passageway almost on our stomachs, inching over fine sand and fragments of pottery; at the far end the jars containing ibises are stacked like blocks of sugar at a grocer's, head to foot".

Memphis

Most tour excursions to Saqqara include a flying visit to the scant **remains of Memphis** in the village of **MIT RAHINA**. Sadly, these hardly stir one's imagination to resurrect the ancient city effaced over centuries by Nilotic silt, which now lies metres below rustling palm groves and oxen-ploughed fields. Although something of its glory is evident in the great necropolises ranged across the desert, and the countless objects in Cairo's Antiquities Museum, to appreciate the significance of Memphis you have to recall its history.

The city's foundation is attributed to Menes, the quasi-mythical ruler (known also as Narmer – and possibly a conflation of several rulers) who was said to have unified Upper and Lower Egypt and launched the I Dynasty around 3100 BC. At that time, Memphis was sited at the apex of the Delta and thus controlled overland and river communications. If not the earliest city on earth, it was certainly the first imperial one. Memphis was Egypt's capital throughout the Old Kingdom, regained its role after the anarchic Intermediate Period, and was never overshadowed by the parvenu seat of the XII Dynasty. Even after Thebes became capital of the New Kingdom, Memphis still held sway over Lower Egypt and remained the nation's second city until well into the Ptolemaic era, only being deserted in early Muslim times after four thousand years of continuous occupation.

Alas for posterity, most of this garden city was built of mud-brick, which returned to the Nile silt whence it came, and everyone from the Romans onwards plundered its stone temples for fine masonry.

The cults of Ptah and Sokar

In pre-Dynastic times, **Ptah** was the Great Craftsman or Divine Artificer, who invented metallurgy and engineering. However, the people of Memphis esteemed him as the Great Creator who, with a word, brought the universe into being – a concept that never really appealed to most Egyptians. Like most creator gods, he was subsequently linked with death cults and is shown dressed in the shroud of a mummy. The Greeks equated him with Hephaestus, their god of fire and the arts.

Another deity closely associated with Memphis is **Sokar**, originally the god of darkness but subsequently of death, with special responsibility for necropolises. He is often shown, with a falcon's head, seated in the company of Isis and Osiris. Although his major festival occurred at Memphis towards the end of the inundation season, Sokar also rated a shrine at Abydos, where all the Egyptian death gods were represented.

Ptah

Nowadays, leftover statues and steles share a garden (daily: winter 8am–4pm; summer 8am–5pm; £E14, students £E7, camera £E5, video £E25) with souvenir kiosks. The star attraction, found in 1820, is a limestone **Colossus of Ramses II**, similar to the one on Midan Ramses, but laid supine within a concrete shelter. A giant **alabaster sphinx** weighing eighty tons is also mightily impressive. Both these figures probably stood outside the vast Temple of Ptah, the city's patron deity.

By leaving the garden and walking back along the road, you'll notice (on the right) several alabaster **embalming slabs**, where the holy Apis bulls were mummified before burial in the Serapeum at Saqqara. In a pit across the road are excavated chambers from Ptah's temple complex; climb the ridge beyond them and you can gaze across the cultivated valley floor to the Step Pyramid of Saqqara.

South Saqqara

Like their predecessors at Abu Sir, the pharaohs of the VI Dynasty (c.2345–2181 BC) established another necropolis – nowadays called **South Saqqara** – which started 700m beyond Sekhemkhet's unfinished pyramid and extended for over three kilometres. Unfortunately for sightseers, the most interesting monuments are those furthest away across the site; renting a donkey, horse or camel (£E30–50 for the round trip) will minimize slogging over soft sand. It is also possible to walk from Saqqara village: just keep heading west until you emerge from the palm trees. If you stop to ask directions, bear in mind that, whatever you say (even if you say it in Arabic), the villagers will almost certainly assume you are looking for the Step Pyramid, and direct you accordingly.

Once you reach the site, two tracks run either side of several pyramids before meeting at the Mastabat al-Faraun. The western one is more direct than the route that goes via Saqqara village, set amidst lush palm groves 2km from North Saqqara's ticket office. There is no official entrance fee to the site, and you probably won't see another tourist. Apart from the tranquillity, however, what you get here, with the pyramids of North Saqqara clearly visible to your north, and those of Dahshur to your south, is the feeling of being in the midst of a massive pyramid field, somewhere very ancient and vast.

The site

Heading south along either track, you'll pass a low mound of rubble identified as the **Pyramid of Pepi I**. The name "Memphis", which Classical authors bestowed upon Egypt's ancient capital and its environs, was actually derived from one of this pyramid's titles. To the southwest, another insignificant heap indicates the **Pyramid of Merenre**, who succeeded Pepi. French archeologists are excavating the latter's pyramid, but neither site is really worth a detour.

Due west of Saqqara village, sand drifts over the outlying temples of the **Pyramid of Djedkare-Isesi**. Known in Arabic as the "Pyramid of the Sentinel", it stands 25m high and can be entered via a tunnel on the north side. Although a shattered basalt sarcophagus and mummified remains were found here during the 1800s, it wasn't until 1946 that Abdel Hussein identified them as those of Djedkare, the penultimate king of the V Dynasty. Far from being the first ruler to be entombed in South Saqqara, Djedkare was merely emulating the last pharaoh of the previous dynasty, whose own mortuary complex is uniquely different, and the oldest in this necropolis.

Built of limestone blocks, Shepseskaf's mortuary complex resembles a gigantic sarcophagus with a rounded lid; another simile gave rise to its local name, **Mastabat al-Faraun** – the Pharaoh's Bench. If you can find a guard, it's possible to venture through descending and horizontal corridors to reach the burial chamber and various storerooms. The monument was almost certainly commissioned by Shepseskaf, who evidently felt the need to distance himself from the pyramid of his father, Mycerinus. However, the archeologist Jequier doubted that the complex was ever used for any actual burial and Shepseskaf's final resting place remains uncertain.

Northwest of here lies the most complete example of a VI Dynasty mortuary complex, albeit missing casing stones and other masonry that was plundered in medieval times. The usual valley temple and causeway culminate in a mortuary temple whose vestibule and sanctuary retain fragments of their original reliefs. Beyond this rises the **Pyramid of Pepi II**, whose reign supposedly lasted 94 years, after which the VI Dynasty expired. A descending passage leads to his rock-cut burial chamber, whose ceiling and walls are inscribed with stars and Pyramid Texts. These also appear within the subsidiary pyramids of Pepi's queens, Apuit and Neith, which imitate his mortuary complex on a smaller scale. Various nobles and officials are buried roundabouts.

Dahshur

The **Dahshur pyramid field** (daily: winter 8am–5pm; summer 8am–6pm; last ticket sold an hour before closing; £E10, students £E5, camera £E5, video £E25) contains some of the most impressive of all the pyramids, and some of the most significant in the history of pyramid-building. **Getting to Dahshur** may prove problematic, and the easiest way to reach the site is by taxi. Otherwise, you should be able to get service taxi microbuses to Dahshur village from El-Badrasheen (see p.224 for advice on how to get there) or Giza train station (accessible by metro and a short walk from Midan Giza), and on Thursdays and Fridays direct from Midan Ramses. The village is 2km from the site entrance, to which it is connected by infrequent service taxis from the village, but most people will find it easier to take a private taxi (£E1–2) or walk (straight on from the bridge over the canal). **Getting back to Cairo** should not be left too late or you may find yourself stranded with the nearest public transport 10km away in El-Badrasheen – transport from Dahshur tends to dry up at around 5pm.

The pyramids are in two groups. To the east are three **Middle Kingdom complexes**, dating from the revival of pyramid-building (c.1991–1790 BC) that culminated near the Fayoum. Though the pyramids proved unrewarding to nineteenth-century excavators, their subsidiary tombs yielded some magnificent jewellery (now in the Antiquities Museum). To the north, the pyramids of XII Dynasty pharaohs Seostris III and Amenenkhet II are little more than piles of rubble, but the southernmost of the three, the **Black Pyramid** of Amenemhet III (Joseph's pharoah in the Old Testament, according to some), is at least an interesting shape: though its limestone casing has long gone, a black mud-brick core is still standing (its black basalt capstone is in the Antiquities Museum). More intriguing, however, are the two **Old Kingdom pyramids** further into the desert, which have long tantalized archeologists with a riddle. Both of them are credited to **Snofru** (c.2613–2588 BC), father of Cheops and founder of the IV Dynasty, whose monuments constitute an evolutionary link between the stepped creations of the previous dynasty at North Saqqara and the true pyramids of Giza.

The Red Pyramid

The first pyramid you come to if you follow the road past the ticket office is Snofru's northern **Red Pyramid**, which is named after the colour of the limestone it was built from. Despite its lower angle (43.5°) and height (101m), Snofru's Red Pyramid clearly prefigures Cheops's edifice, which is also the only pyramid that exceeds it in size, Snofru's Red Pyramid being larger than Chephren's Pyramid at Giza. It was probably Snofru's third attempt (see below) at pyramid building, but he was not laid to rest in any of the three burial chambers here – all were unused.

The Red Pyramid's **interior** is now open to the public, and you can climb up and descend into it to check out its three rather musty chambers. Electric lighting has been installed to illuminate them, but it sometimes fails, so it's a good idea to bring a torch or flashlight if you have one. The first two chambers are roughly parallel to each other, but the third is on a higher level and perpendicular to the other two. One definite advantage of visiting the interior of this pyramid rather than those at Giza is that you will very probably be alone to absorb the rather eerie, if fetid, atmosphere. What you will not find in any of the chambers is a sarcophagus. That is because Snofru was not buried in this pyramid.

The Bent Pyramid

From the Red Pyramid, a track leads south to the pyramid where Snofru was in fact buried, the **Bent Pyramid**, which is not only the most intriguing of all the pyramids, but, because of its state of preservation, also the most breathtaking. What makes Snofru's final resting place different from all the other pyramids is its change of angle towards the top: it rises more steeply (54.3°) than the Red Pyramid or Giza pyramids for three-quarters of its height, before abruptly tapering at a gentler slope – hence its name. The explanation for its shape, and why Snofru should have built two pyramids only a kilometre apart, is a longstanding conundrum of Egyptology.

Mindful of the truism that a pharaoh required but one sanctuary for his *ka*, many reasoned that the Bent Pyramid resulted from a change of plan prompted by fears for its stability, and when these persisted, a second, safer pyramid was built to guarantee Snofru's afterlife. But for this theory to hold water, it's necessary to dismiss Snofru's claim to have built a *third* pyramid at Maidum as mere usurpation of an earlier structure; and the possibility that its sudden collapse might have caused the modification of the Bent Pyramid must likewise be rejected on the grounds that he needed only one secure monument.

Snofru

In 1977, a professor of physics at Oxford University reopened the whole debate. Arguing that Snofru did, indeed, build the "Collapsed Pyramid" at Maidum, whose fall resulted in changes to Dahshur's Bent Pyramid, Kurt Mendelssohn overcame the "one pharaoh–one *ka*–one pyramid" objection by postulating a pyramid production line. As one pyramid neared completion, surplus resources were deployed to start another, despite the satisfaction of the reigning king's requirements. The reason for continuous production was that building a single pyramid required gigantic efforts over ten to thirty years; inevitably, some pharaohs lacked the time and resources. A stockpile of half-constructed, perhaps even finished, pyramids was an insurance policy on the afterlife.

Egyptologists greeted Mendelssohn's theory with delight or derision, but unlike the Great Pyramids, or the lives of Hatshepsut, Nefertiti and Akhenaten, the enigma of Snofru's pyramids has never excited much public interest. Nevertheless, of all the pyramids, the Bent Pyramid probably scores the most highly on the "ooohs" and "aaahs". The reason it seems so impressive lies in the fact that, although its corners have fallen away at the base, the pyramid's limestone casing is still largely intact, giving a clear impression of what it once looked like – smooth and white, it was visually stunning. All the Old Kingdom pyramids were originally clad in limestone, their surfaces smooth like this one, but they have almost all been stripped, the stone burned for lime. The Bent Pyramid escaped that fate because its narrower angle made it harder to remove the facing, though this has disappeared from much of the base.

In fact, the removal of the lowest courses of limestone cladding enables you to see not only how closely the blocks were slotted together, but something else too. On the ground at the northwest corner of the pyramid, pits and grooves have been carved into the bedrock. These were used to dress the pyramid, and presumably were carved before the pyramid was begun, indicating that construction began with the marking out of a base on the cleared bedrock. This is even clearer on the small satellite pyramid immediately to its south.

The Bent Pyramid is unusual in one final respect: it has two entrances, one on its west side as well as the more conventional one in its north face. The reason for this is unknown. To its south is a subsidiary queen's pyramid, possibly belonging to Snofru's wife Hetepheres (though some say Snofru himself was buried here). If it did belong to her, she didn't stay there too long: after robbers had entered both of Snofru's pyramids at Dahshur, Hetepheres' sarcophagus was moved to Giza for safekeeping, and hidden down a shaft next to the Great Pyramid of her son Cheops. The interior of the Bent Pyramid is unlikely to be open to the public in the near future, but you can see inside it on the Guardian's Egypt website at ⓦ www.guardians.net/egypt.

Consumers' Cairo

As befits its size, Cairo has the most varied culinary scene, shopping and nightlife in North Africa. Much of it is new, having developed in the Sadat era after decades of Nasserite austerity, and for those who can afford it, conspicuous consumption is very much the order of the day. As a visitor, you're well catered for, whether you're into sailing on the Nile, watching a belly dancer, or absorbing a whole world of popular culture at Cairo's religious festivals. All of this is fun to discover but more mundane practicalities can involve hassles and bureaucracy, mysteries and intricacies which we've tried to unravel beginning with "Money" on p.270.

Eating and drinking

The culinary scene in Cairo has diversified enormously since the 1970s, making it possible to eat anything from *sukiyaki* to Kentucky Fried Chicken. Don't fall into the trap of eating only in tourist restaurants, however, or thinking that Egyptian food doesn't rise beyond *kofta* and kebab. You can satisfy most tastes if you know where to look. The options range from Arab cafés offering a few simple dishes to extravagant "food weeks" at deluxe hotels (advertised in *Egypt Today*). Though few natives would agree with them, foreigners are generally pleasantly surprised by the cost of eating out in Cairo. Nearly all the downtown coffee houses, restaurants, cafés and bars are keyed to the map on p.238; for places in Zamalek and on the west bank, see the map on p.192. Drinking, though somewhat limited, is also quite affordable – see p.247.

Coffee houses, patisseries and juice bars

Cairene males have socialized in **coffee houses** or **tearooms** (*'ahwa*) ever since the beverage was introduced from Yemen in the early Middle Ages (for a rundown on coffee and tea drinking and preparation, see p.57). Although professional *qasas* (storytellers) have largely been supplanted by broadcast or taped music, other traditional diversions such as backgammon and dominoes are still popular, and smokers remain loyal to their waterpipes. Most *'ahwas* are shabby hole-in-the-wall places, with chairs overlooking the street, while a few – such as *Fishawi's* and *Al-Shataranj* – are large and more sophisticated, often with high ceilings and tall mirrors (these often also sell pastries, see below). Certain *'ahwas* are the haunt of hobbyists – chess players at *Al-Shataranj* in Saiyida Zeinab, literati at the *Ali Baba* on Midan Tahrir (where Mahfouz used to take coffee) or rural migrants (oasis folk frequent *Al-Wahia* on Sharia Qadry, off Sharia Bur Said), but most have an eclectic clientele. **All-night** *'ahwas* can be found around Bab al-Luq, Midan Ramses and Sharia Qalaa; those around the Saiyida Zeinab end of Sharia Mohammed Farid and Sharia el-Nasireya show videos (sometimes in English) throughout the night. There are also modern all-night coffee shops in the *Intercontinental*, *Meridien* and other deluxe hotels.

For daytime snacks, the upmarket coffee houses and tearooms (more akin to Western cafés than traditional *'ahwas*) serve selections of pastries, rice pudding, crème caramel and suchlike – the most famous are the branches of *Groppi's* (see below). As well as being great places to stop off during the day, they also

CENTRAL CAIRO: EATING & DRINKING

DRINKING

Barrel Lounge	4
Café Riche	34
Honololo	20
El-Horea	39
Jamaika	31
King's	30
Miamy	17
Palmyra	17
Scheharazade	5
Al-Shemi	8

RESTAURANTS & CHEAP EATS

Abou Tarek	25
Akher Saa	3
Alfi Bey	6
Arabesque	32
El-Dahan	2
Estoril	36
Fatatri Pizza el-Tahrir	43
Al-Gazaz	33
El-Guesh	9, 18
Al-Haty	41
Felfela	37
Fu-Shing	27
Gad	12
Greek Club	29
Kowloon	35
La Bistro	38
La Chesa	22
Lux	16, 40
Paprika	19
Peking	7
Scarabee	44
El-Tabei	1
El-Tahrir	24, 42
Valley of the Kings	11

COFFEE HOUSES & PATISSERIES

El Abd	14, 27
Brazilian Coffee Shop	20
Groppi	13, 15, 22, 28
El Shems Café	10
Simonds Coffee Shop	25

provide a welcome alternative to the monotony of standard hotel **breakfasts** (rolls and jam and/or cheese spread). Another option is to try one of the breakfast **buffets** offered by a range of deluxe hotels and open to non-residents (see listings overleaf). One of the best places for **rice pudding**, topped if you like with *basbousa* (a cake-like confection made with nuts and syrup), is *Foontana* on Sharia Handusa opposite the north side of Qasr el-Aini Hospital (see map p.176 – sign in Arabic only, but look for the honey pots in the window).

To take away or consume on the spot, however, it's cheaper to buy at **patisseries** like *El Abd* at 25 Talaat Harb and on the corner of 26 July with Sherif, *El-Sarkia* on Sharia Alfy Bey, or branches of the city-wide chain **La Poire**, where pastries are normally sold by weight with the price per kilo posted. The original and most central branch, at 1 Sharia Amerika Latina (near the British Embassy in Garden City), offers home-made *baklava* (£E30 per kilo) and eclairs (£E3); other branches are in Mohandiseen (opposite the *Atlas Hotel*), Giza (Sharia el-Nil, 100m south of the Gama'a Bridge), Heliopolis (92 Sharia al-Higaz, near Midan Heliopolis) and elsewhere.

Every main street has a couple of tiled stand-up **juice bars** (usually open 8am–10pm), recognizable by their displays of fruit, where you can pick up a glass of freshly squeezed juice – a great way to get the appetite going before breakfast. The ones near the *Café Riche* and *Felfela* charge more than most, but they're never expensive. The best one in Cairo is *Fraghly Fruits*, 71 Arab League Street, in Mohandiseen. Normally, you order and pay at the cash desk before exchanging a plastic token for your drink at the counter (where customers leave a 5–15pt tip). You'll also see a number of **nut shops** (*ma'la*) on the main thoroughfares, offering all kinds of peanuts (*fuul sudani*), edible seeds, and often

△ Enjoying tea and *Sheesha*

Groppi's coffee house

Synonymous with Cairo's erstwhile European "café society", the classic **Groppi** chain now has five locations. The coffee itself is terrible in all of them, but the pastries are great. The once-palatial branch on Midan Talaat Harb has lost much of its charm since renovation, but the pastries are just as tasty, and its a/c salon restful (daily 7am–midnight). The panelled interior of *Garden Groppi's* on Sharia Adly (daily 7am–midnight; minimum charge £E5) hasn't changed much since World War II – when soldiers in the lower ranks weren't allowed in – but its patio is a letdown. There's a far nicer terrace attached to *Groppi's in Heliopolis*, at 21 Sharia al-Ahram (daily 7am–midnight). Lacking the style of the others are two with the same name, *Groppi's Al'Americaine* at 44 Sharia Emad el-Din (daily 9.30am–midnight) and Sharia Talaat Harb (daily 7am–11pm), both on the corner of 26th July Street. Most branches double as delicatessens.

candies and mineral water, too. See Basics for more on the various types of juices and nuts.

Ice cream in Cairo is usually not very good, though you may find interesting flavours like guava and mango. A cut above the rest is *Rigoletto* in Zamalek, with delicious ice cream at £E2.50 a scoop, while *Baskin Robbins* (£E3.50 a scoop) have an outlet downtown at the *Café Paris* in the Al Bustan Centre on Sharia el-Bustan, plus branches in Mohandiseen, Heliopolis and Pyramids Road.

Coffee houses and buffet breakfasts

As *'ahwas* are numerous, pretty standard, and do not sell food, the listings below concentrate on more Western-style coffee houses and tearooms.

Downtown

Brazilian Coffee Shop 36 Talaat Harb. Café au lait, espresso and cappuccino, plus greasy burgers and grills; seats upstairs. Daily 6am–midnight.

Ibis Café on the ground floor of the *Nile Hilton*. Breakfast buffet is open daily 5–11am (£E55); there's also an unlimited all-day salad bar (£E36). Daily 24hr.

El Shems (New Sun) Café in the passage by 4 Sharia Tawfiqia. A *shai* and *sheesha* bar only really notable for its incredibly kitsch decor and high prices by *'ahwa* standards, but film-extra recruiting agents come here looking for Westerners most mornings around 10am. Daily 24hr.

Simonds Coffee Shop (4) 29 Sharia Sherif. A branch of the French-style café in Zamalek (see below) with a vintage *Gaggia* espresso machine and pastries, though the ceiling leaks and it looks as if it's fallen on hard times recently. Daily 9am–7pm.

Everest Hotel (see map p.131) 15th Floor, Midan Ramses, south side. The terrace café of an otherwise unremarkable cheap hotel, whose coffee isn't the best in town, but you can take a tea or fruit juice and enjoy a view over Midan Ramses and as far as the Citadel and the Muqattam Hills. Daily 24hr.

Roda Island

Fontana Coffee Shop in the *Meridien Hotel*. Continental (£E43) or buffet (£E70) breakfast daily 4–11am; also sumptuous buffet lunches and suppers. Daily 24hr.

Islamic Cairo and Saiyida Zeinab

Al-Shataranj 26 Midan Saiyida Zeinab. A meeting place for chess players; the top ones move on to *El-Horea* on Midan Falaki (see "Drinking").

Naguib Mahfouz Coffee Shop 5 Sikket al-Badestan. Upmarket a/c tourist café in the heart of the bazaar, serving snacks, coffee, mint tea and orange juice. Part of the *Cafeteria Khan el-Khalili* (see p.244). Daily 10am–2am.

Fishawi's behind the *El-Hussein Hotel* in Khan el-Khalili. Cairo's oldest tea house has been managed by the same family – and remained perpetually open – since 1773. Cracked mirrors, battered furniture, haughty staff and wandering vendors; imbibe the atmosphere with a pot of mint tea and a *sheesha*. Daily 24hr.

Zamalek

Simonds Coffee Shop 112 26th July St, near the Hassan Sabry intersection. Cappuccino, hot chocolate, lemonade, fresh croissants and *ramequins* (cheese puffs). Daily 7am–10pm.

Rigoletto Yamaha Centre, 3 Sharia Taha Hussein. Espresso, cappuccino, cheesecake and delicious ice cream (£E2.50 a scoop). £E5 minimum charge to eat in. Daily 9am–11pm.

No Big Deal Sharia Sayed el-Bakri. Small, Californian-style coffee shop, with infusions (and not just *yansoon* and *karkaday*), home-made cakes, and such exotic beverages as Earl Grey tea. Pleasant, but somehow not very Egyptian. Daily 9am–2am.

Heliopolis

Al-Sokkareya 61 Sharia Abdul Hamid Bedawi, near the *Al-Salam Hyatt* (bus #50, #128 or #330 from downtown). An upmarket garden café featur-

ing singers, musicians and sideshows only open during Ramadan (10pm–3am); the admission charge (around £E15) includes one soft drink and a *sheesha*. Call the *Hyatt* (☎02/245 5155) to confirm shows.

Pyramids of Giza

Khan el-Khalili Coffee Shop in the *Mena House*. Luxurious a/c cafeteria near the Pyramids. Skip the paltry Continental breakfast and have the £E29 "special". The "Oberoi" version includes fruit juice, pancakes and croissants; the "Egyptian" one yoghurt with honey and *fuul* with eggs. Also snacks and main meals. Daily 24hr. Breakfast served 3am–11am.

Restaurants, cafés and street food

Restaurants, cafés and street food comprise a culinary spectrum rather than distinctly separate categories. **Restaurants** run the gamut from *nouvelle cuisine* salons to backstreet kebab houses, while **cafés** range from air-conditioned bourgeois havens to open-fronted tiled diners. The ones devoted to *kushari* (£E2–4 a bowl) or *fuul* and *taamiya* (£E1.50 with salad and pickles) provide the cheapest nutritious meals going. A third type of outlet purveys *fatir*, or Egyptian pizzas, which are tastier and cheaper (£E6–10 depending on size and ingredients) than most Western-style pizzas in Cairo.

Despite the blurred line between hole-in-the-wall eateries and outright **street food**, running water remains a crucial factor – anywhere without it is risky. Markets and terminals offer the best outlets; a number of places off Ramses, Orabi, Ataba, Falaki, Lazoghli and Giza squares, and midway down Sharia Qalaa function **all night**.

At the other end of the gastro-cultural spectrum, every hotel rated three stars or above has at least one restaurant and coffee shop (maybe 24hr) that's accessible to non-residents (see above). If familiar food and no hassle are top priority, **hotel dining** is usually a safe bet. For those who need them, *McDonald's*, *Pizza Hut* and *KFC* have also arrived. All of them have several outlets around the centre as well as in Mohandiseen and Heliopolis. Perhaps surprisingly to Westerners, these chains are considered posh eating places by Cairenes, who may even dress up to go to them.

Between these extremes there's a huge variation in **standards** of cleanliness and presentation, and whether somewhere seems okay or grotty depends partly on your own values. We've tried to present a cross section of what's available in various parts of the city. The majority of places listed have **menus** in English or French and staff who understand both, but others deal only in Arabic; fortunately, many of them display what's on offer, so you only have to point (for information on tipping, see p.55). **Vegetarians** should have no trouble feeding themselves, but there is also one Western-style vegetarian place alongside the *felafel* and *kushari* joints: *L'Aubergine* in Zamalek.

In the following listings, we've given the following guide to cost: **inexpensive** means that you can get a full meal (starter, main course and soft drink) for £E20 or less, **moderate** means that a full meal costs £E20–40, and **expensive** will set you back over £E40 for a full meal. Many restaurants sell seafood and *kofta* and kebab by weight: a quarter of a kilo is one portion; a full kilo is usually enough for three to four people. Note that telephone numbers have been included for all restaurants where **reservations** are a good idea. At others, there's no need to bother – even assuming you could get through and make yourself understood.

Downtown Cairo

Aside from Egyptian restaurants, which range from very upmarket establishments to cheaper *kushari* diners (see "Really cheap downtown options" below), downtown Cairo has a fair number of different international cuisines to choose from, with several French, Levantine (Syrian/Lebanese), Italian, Chinese and Korean eating places, and others offering a variety of Western dishes.

Al-Haty 3 Sharia Halim, off 26th July St, behind the *Windsor Hotel*. Vintage decor, with mirrors and fans. The fare is inexpensive and traditional: kebab, fish, *mezze*, stuffed vine leaves (*dolma*), roast lamb (*moza*). No alcohol. Daily 2pm–2am (Ramadan 2–10pm). There is another, older branch in the passage off no.8, on the other side of 26th July St, open daily 11am to midnight (Ramadan 11am–2am).

Alfi Bey 3 Sharia Alfi Bey. Another vintage restaurant run by strict Muslims. Some of the staff claim to have been here since the 1940s; the panelling and chandeliers certainly have. Best for lamb dishes, chicken, macaroni, or pigeon stuffed with liver; good value and moderate prices. Daily noon–midnight.

Arabesque 6 Sharia Qasr el-Nil ☎ 02/574 8677. French and Levantine cuisine, strong on soups and meat dishes, but chiefly remarkable for its oriental decor and contemporary art gallery rather than the quality of the food. Wine and beer are served. Moderate. Daily noon–4pm & 7pm–midnight (Ramadan 5pm–midnight).

La Bistro 8 Sharia Hoda Shaarawi ☎ 02/392 7694. A bright, clean little place serving delicious French food, though the blue-and-white decor is a little jarring and the muzak excruciating. Moderate. Daily noon–midnight.

La Chesa 21 Sharia Adly ☎ 02/393 9360. Salubrious, Swiss-managed café serving good Western food, scrumptious pastries and great coffee. Expensive but worth it. Daily 7am–midnight.

El-Guesh 32 Midan Falaki, on the corner of Tahrir and Falaki streets. A family place serving *kofta* and kebab, or more exotic offerings such as kidney and testicles; inexpensive. Daily 11am–11pm.

Estoril 12 Sharia Talaat Harb – in the passage ☎ 02/574-3102. Good Franco-Levantine food in quiet surroundings. Its vintage bar deserves a Bogart. Moderate. Daily noon–midnight; closed Aug.

Felfela 15 Sharia Hoda Shaarawi. A tourist favourite, offering inexpensive, diverse veggie and meaty Egyptian dishes in a long, funkily decorated hall. Sells beer. Service can be a little snooty if you're scruffily dressed, and there's nothing you can get here that wouldn't be cheaper elsewhere. Daily 8am–midnight. *Felfela's* takeaway, around the corner on Talaat Harb, with another branch opposite the High Court on 26th July St (daily 6am–1.30am), does *shawarmas* and *taamiya* sandwiches, though again you'd pay less elsewhere.

Fu-Shing 28 Talaat Harb – in the passage. Founded by ethnic Muslim refugees from China, this moderately priced restaurant serves filling Chinese meals in a relaxed ambience. The spring rolls make a great snack. Sells beer. Daily noon–9pm.

Gad 13 26th July St. A modern and very popular takeaway downstairs, always crowded, but you can slip upstairs for a sit-down meal. The menu is in Arabic only, but includes – alongside the usual *taamiya*, *fuul*, *shawarma* and burgers – delicious specialities such as *kibda skanderani* (Alexandrian-style liver with chilli) and wonderful baked-on-the-premises Syrian-style pitta bread (*'aish shaami*). If you can make yourself understood on the phone, they also deliver (☎ 02/576 3353 or 3583). Branches at Midan Lazoghli and in Mohandiseen. Daily 24hr.

Greek Club above *Groppi's* on Midan Talaat Harb – entrance on Sharia Bassiouni. The cuisine is not particularly Greek, but the food isn't bad, and the summer terrace is pleasant. Moderate prices but you have to pay a temporary membership fee (£E5) to eat here. Serves alcohol. Evenings only, 6pm–1.30am.

Kowloon Restaurant entered via the *Hotel Cleopatra* on the corner of Midan Tahrir and Sharia el-Bustan. Expensive, but superb, Korean and Chinese food cooked by Korean chefs. The menu includes several pork dishes and the place is popular with East Asian expats. Mon–Sat 11am–11pm.

Paprika 1129 Corniche el-Nil, just south of the TV Building ☎ 02/578 9447. Based on a mix of Hungarian and Egyptian food, this place does tasty paprika-based dishes and *mezze*. Frequented by media folk (including Omar Sharif) and footballers, it's especially busy at weekends. Expensive. Daily noon–1am.

Peking Restaurant 14 Sharia Saray el-Azbakiya, off 26th July, near the *Windsor Hotel* ☎ 02/591 2381, ⌨ www.peking-restaurants.com. The poshest Chinese in town, though not prohibitively expensive. It's nowhere near as authentic as the *Fu-Shing* or the *Kowloon*, but they do takeouts and delivery, and boast branches in Zamalek, Mohandiseen and Heliopolis, and a floating restaurant (see p.247). Moderate. Daily noon–midnight.

Valley of the Kings on the 1st floor of the *Grand Hotel*. Complete with elegant fountain and stained-glass windows overlooking 26th July St. Moderate prices with good Franco-Levantine cuisine and special meal-deals for £E25.50 or £E32. Seldom crowded. Daily noon–5pm & 7pm–midnight.

Really cheap downtown options

There are hundreds of *kushari* diners in downtown Cairo, and opinion is divided as to which is the best, but basically it boils down to one of three: *Abou Tarek*, *Lux* or *El-Tahrir*. Most other really cheap eats are concentrated around Midan Orabi (especially along the first block of Sharia el-Azbakiya, the small street between the two patisseries) and Midan Falaki (especially on Sharia Mansur, outside Bab al-Luq market). They are not listed individually here, but worth a peruse. All of the following fall into the lower end of the inexpensive price band; you can fill up for well under £E10.

Abou Tarek 40 Sharia Champollion, at the corner of Sharia Maarouf ⌨ www.aboutarek.com. New, clean and a/c diner serving excellent *kushari* on two floors, with rice pudding for afters. You can't miss it as it's lit up like a Christmas tree. Daily 7am–12.30am.

Akher Saa 8 Sharia Alfi Bey, next to the Nile Christian Bookshop. A very popular 24hr *fuul* and takeaway with a sit-down restaurant attached. Not a bad place for breakfast either – *fuul*, omelette, bread and *tahina* for £E5.

Fatatri Pizza el-Tahrir Sharia Tahrir, one block east of Midan Tahrir (look for the marble facade on the right-hand side). *Fatirs* (with meat and egg) and crustier versions topped with hot sauce, cheese and olives make a delicious meal for around £E6–10. Also pancake-*fatirs* filled with apple jam and icing sugar. Daily 24hr.

Al-Gazaz 38 Sharia Abo Alaam. Clean, inexpensive 24hr diner, just off Midan Talaat Harb. Tasty *shawarma*, *taamiya* and other fried food, served in a tiny a/c dining room upstairs. You'd be hard-pressed to spend more than £E10.

Lux 26th July St, near the corner of Sharia Qasr al-Aini. Traditional in style and the original holder of the Cairo *kushari* title, with two offshoots at 68 Sharia Qasr al-Aini in the Garden City and on the south side of Midan Falaki. All open daily 7am–2am.

El-Tabei 31 Sharia Orabi, north of Midan Orabi. Delicious pick'n'mix *mezze* and a very passable moussaka head the list of Middle Eastern dishes served in this excellent-value souped-up *fuul* and *taamiya* diner. The takeaway sandwiches, though, are less good. Now has a branch at the bottom of a shopping mall on Talaat Harb with Abdel Hamid Said – you may not fancy eating there, but you can buy salads to go. If you can make yourself understood on the phone, they also deliver (☎ 02/304 1123–4). Daily 7am–1am.

El-Tahrir Sharia Tahrir between Midan Tahrir and Midan Falaki. An old established place, always good, but now revamped and even better, with a second branch at 19 Sharia Abdel Khaliq Sarwat, just off Sharia Talaat Harb. Connoisseurs say it knocks spots off even *Abou Tarek* – although the service is sometimes slow. Daily 5am–2am.

Garden City

Just south of the Downtown area, the Garden City has a floating restaurant (see p.247) and *fuul*, *fatir* and *kushari* joints (east side of Qasr al-Aini before the hospital, including *Lux* at no.68), plus pastry and pudding shops such as *La Poire* and *Foontana* (see p.239). Its most famous establishment, however, is **Abou Shakra** at 69 Sharia Qasr al-Aini, opposite the hospital (☎ 02/531 6111; see map p.176). Decorated in marble and alabaster, this famous, strictly Muslim establishment specializes in *kofta* and kebab sold by weight (around £E45 per kilo), to eat in or take out. It's open daily 1pm–1am (7pm–1am during Ramadan).

Islamic Cairo and Saiyida Zeinab

Although every main street and square in **Islamic Cairo** features poky eating places serving cheap grub, most tourists stick to the four places in Khan el-Khalili detailed below. But for those inured to flies and roaches, there are discoveries to be made, like the hole-in-the-wall near the market on Sharia Qalaa, which does freshly grilled shrimp sandwiches. If you are prepared to wander into **Saiyida Zeinab**, you can find some excellent, and low-priced, traditional Egyptian food, especially at night; a couple of places are listed here.

Cafeteria Khan el-Khalili 5 Sikket al-Badestan. Expensive, a/c "oriental" café/restaurant managed by the *Mena House Oberoi*, near the old gate 40m west of El-Hussein's Mosque (see map p.137). Western and Egyptian snacks (£E13) and meals (£E40–58) are served in the dining room (evening minimum charge £E15, plus £E1.20 "entertainment tax"; also see p.251) as well as ice cream (£E13). Daily 10am–2am.

El-Dahan On the Muski, beneath the *El-Hussein Hotel* (see map p.137). An excellent kebab house, where a quarter kilo of mixed kebab with salad and *tahina* costs £E18. There's also roast goat, but no alcohol. Has a branch on 26th July St in Bulaq, too. Daily 9am–1am.

Egyptian Pancake House Between Midan el-Hussein and Al-Azhar. Made-to-order *fatirs* filled with meat, egg, cheese, coconut, raisins, jam or honey (or any combination thereof). Soft drinks only. Inexpensive. Daily 24hr.

El-Gahsh A block along Sharia Abdel Meguid from Midan Saiyida Zeinab, on the way to Ibn Tulun Mosque (look for the mule's-head sign). It may not look much, but it is generally held to do the best *fuul* in Cairo (*fuul* sandwich 50pt). Daily 24hr.

Haram Zeinab On the corner of Sharia Abdel Meguid and Midan Saiyida Zeinab (next to *Al-Shataranj*, the chess players' coffee house). Serves excellent *fatirs* at slightly lower prices than you'd pay downtown. Daily 24hr.

El-Hussein On the roof of the *El-Hussein Hotel* (see map p.137). Fantastic views over Islamic Cairo; food inexpensive but grotty. Used for wedding parties at least two nights a week. *Loud music*. Daily 7am–1am.

Rifai 37 Midan Zeinab, opposite Saiyida Zeinab Mosque (hidden up an alley by the Sabil Kuttab of Sultan Mustapha). A renowned nighttime *kofta* and kebab joint – people are known to drive from Heliopolis for a takeout. Inexpensive at about £E55 a kilo for either. Open 9.30pm–5am.

Zamalek

As befits a high-rent, cosmopolitan neighbourhood, Zamalek boasts several upmarket restaurants devoted to foreign cuisine, plus **trendy nightspots** like *Matchpoint* and *Pub 28* (see "Drinking" below). Most of them are within ten minutes' walk of 26th July Street. All are keyed on the map on p.192.

Al Dente (Didos) 26 Sharia Bahgat Ali ☎02/735 9117. Quite justified in its claim to do the best pasta in town (choice of spaghetti, fettuccine, penne or fusilli with a range of sauces, £E5.50–18.50), this little place also does excellent salads and specialities such as Portuguese-style fish, but it could do with larger premises. Daily noon–1.30am.

Angus Brasserie 34 Sharia Yehia Ibrahim, inside the *New Star Hotel* ☎02/735 1865. Steaks, plus European veal, fish and squid dishes. Lunch menu £E24. Daily 7am–2pm & 5pm–1am.

Don Quichotte 9a Sharia Ahmed Heshmat ☎02/735 6415. Tiny, elegant restaurant sampling great cuisines of the world. The speciality of the house is *coquille bonne femme* (seafood in white wine sauce). Very expensive. Reservations advisable. Daily 12.30–4pm & 7pm–12.30am.

Five Bells corner of Adil Abu Bakr and Ismail Mohammed, north of the Zamalek Bridge ☎02/735 8970. It's worth dressing up for this swish Italianate joint, complete with garden and fountain. Expensive, and there's a £E3.50 cover charge. Daily noon–2am.

Hana Korean Restaurant Sharia Mohammed Mazar, next to the *El-Nil Zamalek Hotel* ☎02/738 2972. Small, friendly place offering various Asian dishes. A huge portion of *sukiyaki* (do-it-yourself stir-fry soup) costs £E30. Also does deliveries. Daily noon–11pm.

Justine 4 Hassan Sabry, in the Four Corners complex 2 blocks south of Galabaya Park ☎02/737 2119. Probably the finest and one of the most expensive restaurants in Cairo. *Nouvelle cuisine*, soft lighting, music and formal dress. Daily 12.30pm–4pm & 7.30–11pm. On the same floor (same phone number also) are: La Piazza, a stylish, much cheaper Italian restaurant (pasta dishes £E24–37), which is open daily noon–12.30am; the moderate–expensive Chin Chin Chinese restaurant (daily 7.30–11.30pm); and the Matchpoint video snack bar.

L'Aubergine 5 Sharia Sayed el-Bakri. Cairo's only specifically vegetarian restaurant, moderately priced with an adventurous-looking menu, changed weekly, featuring dishes like artichoke strudel and halloumi-stuffed eggplant. Unfortunately the cooking doesn't quite live up to the promise, but if you've been on a diet of *fuul* and *kushari* for a week, it's got to be worth a try. Daily 10am–11pm. Breakfast served 10am–2pm.

Maison Thomas 157 26th July St opposite the *Marriott Hotel* ☎02/735 7057. Deli-diner-takeout-delivery place serving freshly made baguettes and pizzas (both around £E14–24) as well as light meals (£E25–30). They make their own pork sausages and mozzarella, as well as doing bacon-and-egg breakfasts (8am–12.30pm; £E20). They will deliver to anywhere in central Cairo – even beer at £E5 a bottle. Daily 24hr.

Zamalek Restaurant 118 26th July St, near the intersection with Sharia al-Aziz Osman. Sit-down joint for *taamiya*, *fuul* and *tahina* (meals £E4–6). Soft drinks only. Daily 6am–2am.

Mohandiseen

The 1980s saw a proliferation of fast-food outlets and chic restaurants, mostly situated along or just off Arab League Street (Sharia Gameat al-Dowal al-Arabiya, also nicknamed "The Mall") and Sharia Batal Ahmed Abdel Aziz. Among more recent additions are a pharaonic-style *McDonald's* opposite the *Atlas Zamalek Hotel*, and the local branch of an Indian-ish city-wide chain called *Chicken Tikka* at 47 Sharia Batal Ahmed Abdel Aziz (☎02/346 0393). There are also two branches of *Peking*, the popular downtown Chinese restaurant (26 Sharia al-Atebba ☎02/749 9086; 9 Sharia al-Kawthar ☎02/749 9860); a branch of downtown fast-Egyptian-food-favourite *Gad* (47a Arab League St ☎02/335 7237); and a second outlet of the famous Garden City kebab and *kofta* restaurant *Abou Shakra* (17 Arab League St ☎02/344 2299). All of these restaurants will deliver within Mohandiseen/Dokki/Zamalek. All are keyed on the map on p.192.

Bon Appetit 21 Sharia Wadi el-Nil ☎02/346 4937. Elegant decor and *haute cuisine* variations on native light meals such as fish kebab and shrimp *kofta*. Better known for appetizers, pastries and desserts (try the mousse), takeout club sandwiches and fantastic espresso coffee. Moderate. Daily 9am–2am.

Al-Omdah 6 Sharia al-Gaza'ir, around the corner from the *Atlas*. An island – albeit a/c and priced over the odds for pukka Egyptian food (*kushari* £E3–5; *kofta* and kebab £E65 per kilo) – in a sea of plastic fast food. Daily 10am–2am, with take-out downstairs.

Okamoto 7 Sharia Ahmed Orabi, off Midan Sphinx ☎02/346 5264. Excellent Japanese food, well worth the high prices; serves *sake*. Daily noon–3pm & 6–10.30pm, closed Wed. Last orders 30min before closing.

Prestige Pizza 43 Gazirit al-Arab, just east of Sharia Wadi el-Nil ☎02/347 0383. A smart Italian restaurant with a more casual pizzeria attached for a choice of ambience – and price. Moderate–expensive; minimum charge £E7 plus service charge. Daily noon–2am.

Tandoori 11 Sharia Shehab, 2 blocks west of Arab League St ☎02/748 6301. Run by an ex-employee of the *Mogul Room*, this place has fine service and Indian cuisine. Try the tandoori chicken, curried lamb (*kema*) or prawns (*jhinga*). Moderately priced though takeouts and deliveries cost less. Also has some European and Egyptian dishes. No alcohol. Daily noon–midnight.

Le Tirol 38 Sharia Gazirit al-Arab, just west off Sharia Wadi el-Nil ☎02/344 9725. Swiss-chalet decor and tasty Central European cuisine at European prices. An Italian menu (*La Toscana*) is also available. Serves alcohol. Daily 9am–1am.

Aguza, Dokki and Giza

The rest of the west bank is less tempting than Mohandiseen, but hardly bereft of options. Cheap eating places abound in market quarters like Suleyman Gohar (Dokki) and Midan Giza, while overpriced kebab restaurants and hotel dining loom large along the Pyramids Road. Visitors with children should enjoy the **outdoor family restaurants** – such as *La Rose* or *Felfela Village* – beside the Maryotteya Canal (bring mosquito repellent), or the floating restaurants near the El-Gama'a Bridge (see the next section).

Aguza and Dokki

Cafeteria Nema 172 Corniche el-Nil, Aguza (see map p.192). The best takeaway *fuul* and *taamiya* sandwiches in Cairo – so taxi drivers swear. Hamburgers and *shawarma* rolls £E2. Daily 24hr.

Ciao 10 Midan al-Misaha, Dokki ☎02/352 2482 (see map p.192). Genuine wood-oven pizzas, albeit with beef instead of ham and pepperoni, are the main attraction at Dokki's leading Italian restaurant. Moderate, with pizzas £E12–24. Daily noon–midnight.

Flying Fish 166 Corniche el-Nil ☎02/749 3234 (see map p.192). Excellent and very classy seafood restaurant with specialities such as stuffed fish, squid (£E36 a kilo) and lobster (£E105 a kilo). Another Omar Sharif hang-out. Daily noon–1.30am.

Giza

Le Chalet in the Nasr Building (see map on p.176). Swiss-run, clean and pleasant, with fine views of the Nile. Offers salads and pasta, hot meat or fish platters and delectable pastries and ice creams; also a children's menu. Moderate. Daily 8.30am–11.30pm. The plush **Le Chateau** restaurant upstairs offers rich – and expensive – main courses and scrumptious desserts; expect a lot of corporate diners. Daily noon–12.30am. Reservations advisable for both ☎02/761 0165 or 748 5321.

El-Mashrabiah 4 Sharia Ahmed Nessim, opposite the El-Urman Garden ☎02/348 2801 (see map p.176). Elegant Moorish decor and excellent Middle Eastern and Egyptian food. Fairly expensive salads, lamb, *kofta* and turkey dishes. No alcohol. Daily 12.30pm–1.30am (Ramadan till 3.30am).

Pyramids area

China Restaurant 7 Sharia Abu el-Hol ☎02/385 2023. A highly rated Chinese-run restaurant in the street leading to the Sphinx. Inexpensive–moderate. Daily 10am–9pm.

Felfela Café 27 Alexandria Desert Road, 300m from junction on Pyramids Road between the turn-off for the Sphinx and the Pyramids site entrance ☎02/383 0234. An offshoot of *Felfela's*, whackily adorned with fake birds and trees, with a similar menu and prices to the downtown branch. Has an a/c dining room upstairs. Daily 9am–1am (nightly entertainment during Ramadan).

Felfela Village Maryotteya Canal ☎02/384 1515 or 1616. On a canal that crosses Pyramids Road, 1km north on the east bank, this rambling outdoor complex features a zoo and playground and a show with camel rides, acrobats, puppets and belly dancers – even dancing horses. The show (1–7.30pm) is presented during summer, Fri and Sun only. Restaurant open daily 10am–7pm.

The Moghul Room in the *Mena House*. Cairo's top Indian restaurant with a choice of set menu or à la carte. All curries are normally served in mild versions, including the vindaloo, so remember to tell them if you want them hot. Expensive. Daily 12.30–2.45pm & 7.30–11.45pm.

Pyramids Restaurant 9 Sharia Abu el-Hol, two doors down from the *China*. A plain honest-to-goodness chicken and kebab house with normal *baladi* prices (quarter-kilo *kofta* and kebab £E9, chicken £E10, salad and *tahina* cost extra), in spite of the plethora of tourists. Daily 10am–2am.

Heliopolis

The deluxe hotels in Heliopolis offer a variety of restaurants, coffee shops, nightclubs and snack bars. In the way of offshoots from popular downtown places, *Peking* have a branch at 115 Sharia Osman Ibn Affan (☎02/418 5612), and *Abou Shakra* have one at 82 Sharia Merghani (☎02/418 8891).

Amphitrion 18 Sharia Ibrahim al-Laqqani, on the corner of Sharia al-Ahram ☎02/258 1379. A restaurant with bar and snack bar/takeout attached, serving Middle Eastern and Western dishes, tea and coffee. Pleasant terrace. Moderate. Daily 8.30am–2am.

Mashawina 3 Sharia Abdel Moneim Hafez, off Sharia Sawra, 2km east of Midan Roxi ☎02/415 8442. Tasty, authentic Lebanese cooking in a relaxed environment. Moderate. Daily 8.30am–2am.

Petit Palmyra 27 Sharia al-Ahram ☎02/415 6836. Looks quite posh but prices of Egyptian dishes are low (pigeon stuffed with rice and nuts for £E14.50), though European dishes are significantly more expensive ("Seafood Symphony" for £E43). Daily 1pm–1am.

El-Tekia 105 Sharia al-Higaz ☎02/248 4343. Jazzed-up Arab food, including couscous with duck, fried rabbit with rice and mixed grills. Inexpensive. No alcohol. Daily noon–2am.

Floating restaurants

Floating restaurants can be an agreeable way to enjoy the Nile, but business has been badly hit by the slump in tourism. As cruise schedules change, it is wise to phone and check, and, with trade now recovering somewhat, make a booking, too. The price quoted is per person.

Nile Maxim ☎ 02/735 8888. Docked in front of and managed by the *Marriott* (see map p.192), runs lunch (2.30–4.30pm) and dinner (7.30–9.30pm & 10.30pm–12.30am) cruises on Fridays and some Saturdays, with live Egyptian music; dinner show features bellydancing.

Nile Peking ☎ 02/531 6388 or mobile 010/216912, ⓔ peking@intouch.com. Moored opposite the Nilometer, 200m west of Mari Girgis metro station, this is the floating branch of the citywide *Peking* chain of Chinese restaurants (see p.243). It sails daily 7pm–9pm, plus Fri & Sun 2–4pm, and Wed 10pm–midnight. The Wednesday late cruise features a bellydancing show. Food is à la carte when moored (minimum charge £E50), with a choice of twelve set menus (£E50–85) when sailing. There is also an on-deck café serving afternoon tea (daily noon–12.30pm; £E35) and a Mongolian barbecue restaurant, also on deck. Alcohol is served, except during Ramadan, and there's a bar with DJs.

The Nile Pharaoh & Golden Pharaoh ☎ 02/570 1000. Pair of mock-pharaonic barges complete with scarab friezes, picture windows, and golden lotus flowers or figures of Horus mounted on the stern and prow. Moored 1km south of the El-Gama'a Bridge (see map p.176) and operated by *Oberoi Hotels*, they cruise for lunch (2.30–4.30pm; £E70.50), sunset (Fri only 6–8pm; £E110.50) and dinner (7.45–9.45pm, 8.45–10.45pm, 10.30pm–12.30am & 11.30pm–1.30am; £E110.50). You should check in half an hour before sailing. The dinner cruises feature music and a belly dancer, while the lunch cruises have live "oriental" (ie Middle Eastern) music. There's also a Friday buffet brunch (11.30am–4.30pm, sailing 2.30–3.30pm; £E49).

Scarabee (34) ☎ 02/794 3444. Docked on the Corniche near *Helnan Shepheard's Hotel*. Offers two dinner cruises nightly (7.30–9.30pm & 10pm–midnight; £E90) with an "oriental" floor show, belly dancer and a dance band, plus Friday buffet lunch cruises (2.30–4.30pm; £E65) with a band and magician; other days, the boat remains docked for lunch (2.30–4pm; à la carte).

Drinking

As throughout Egypt, the sale of alcohol in Cairo is banned during Ramadan and other major Muslim festivals, and drinking is limited to indoor locations at all times. Besides restaurants and hotels, there are various **bars** to choose between. The cheapest of these are rather rough male-only hard-drinking dens. Others are chiefly meeting places for men and prostitutes (the only Egyptian women found there). The more upmarket bars often have a minimum charge, often unadvertised (usually around £E10–20).

Inevitably, there's also some overlap between bars and nightclubs (covered under "Nightlife and entertainment" on p.248).

Downtown

Spit-and-sawdust dens, usually open until around midnight – definitely not recommended for women on their own – include the *Stella Cafeteria* on the corner of Sharia Talaat Harb and Sharia Hoda Shaarawi, by *Felfela's* takeout; the *Cap d'Or Cafeteria* at 31 Sharia Abdel Khaliq Sarwat; the *Cafeteria Port Tawfik* in Midan Orabi on the corner of Sharia Orabi; the *Mourias* at 4 Sharia Adly; and a couple by the Forex bureau on Sharia Alfi Bey. Beer (Stella is £E5–6 in most of these) is usually served with free nibbles and lots of drunken bon-homie. Of the following bars, probably only the *Barrel Lounge*, *Café Riche* and *Taverne du Champs de Mars* offer hassle-free drinking for women.

Barrel Lounge On the first floor of the *Windsor Hotel*, Sharia Alfi Bey. Faded Anglo-Egyptian decor and charming ambience. Foreigners can buy alcohol during Ramadan. Native rum or brandy with Coke is the cheapest drink, followed by Stella and *zibiba*. Daily 10am–1am.

Café Riche 17 Sharia Talaat Harb. Once a hangout for artists and intellectuals, practically every Arab revolutionary of the last century has visited at least once – including Saddam Hussein – and although now strictly for tourists, it still oozes history. Have a chat with the owner, who can give you the full story; he was a pilot during the wars with Israel. Daily 8am–midnight.

El-Horea Midan Falaki. A mirrored, very 1930s, café that's hardly changed since then. Chess players meet here in the evening and people gather to watch them play – though drinking isn't allowed round the boards. Daily 8am–11pm.

Hard Rock Café in the *Royal Meridian*. The Cairo branch of the international chain, popular with bright young things, and rather pricey by local standards (£E50 minimum charge), but mostly notable for having Gamal Abdel Nasser's 1957 Ford suspended above the tables amidst the usual pop paraphernalia. Daily 8pm–3am.

Honololo Opposite the *Pensione Roma* on Sharia Mohammed Farid. A "cafeteria restaurant" where only *sheesha*, Stella (£E10), Heineken (£E22) and bar girls are in evidence – music after midnight. Not recommended for women. Daily 11am–4am.

Jamaika Sharia el-Bank el-Ahly, a small street off Sheria Sharif. Named after the island of Jamaica (the owner's sister went there once), this cosy little dive has £E5.50 Stella, *sheesha* and no bar girls. Daily 24hr.

King's Restaurant Sharia Ibrahim el-Kabari (off Sharia Qasr el-Nil, 20m east of Midan Talaat Harb). This pick-up joint serves kebab as well as beer and whisky. Not recommended for women. Daily 11am–6am.

Odeon Palace Hotel 6 Sharia Abdel Hamid Said. The 24-hour bar here is a popular and very pleasant location for a bit of after-hours rooftop drinking.

Al-Shemi Opposite the *Grand Hotel*, in a passage off Sharia Talaat Harb and 26th July St. Bar girls, beer and *sheeshas* – well sleazy, but fun if you're in the right mood. Not recommended for women. Daily noon–2am.

Taverne du Champs de Mars in the *Nile Hilton*. Come evening this splendidly ornate *fin-de-siècle* Brussels tavern – its interior brought over from Belgium and reconstructed here – becomes a predominantly gay pick-up joint. Draught Stella beer is £E18 a pint, and they also serve Meister and Carlsberg (£E20 a pint) plus Belgian snacks. Daily noon–12.30am.

Zamalek

Deals Sharia Sayed el-Bakri. One of Cairo's most congenial drinking spots, and one of the few with any kind of atmosphere, small, homely and popular with expats and Egyptians alike, with pop videos (not necessarily of the music that's playing), a range of cold beers, tasty and well-presented bar snacks, and no hassling of women. Happy hour 4–7pm, when all beers are £E7. Now has branches in Mohandiseen (2 Sharia Gol Gamal, cozy and intimate) and Heliopolis (40 Sharia Baghdad). Daily 4pm–2am.

Harry's Bar and **Eugene's Bar** in the *Marriott Hotel*. Both are extremely popular with expats (*Harry's* with gay men in particular of late). *Eugene's* is exquisitely decorated in the khedival

Arabesque style. Both daily 11am–2am. Harry's has a happy hour 6–7pm.

Matchpoint in the Four Corners complex, 4 Sharia Hassan Sabry. A pseudo-American video snack bar, frequented by rich young Cairenes attending the AUC. It's easy to exceed the minimum charge. Daily 1pm–1am; minimum charge £E15 (£E25 on Thurs). Couples only – though if you're smartly dressed and behave respectably there shouldn't be a problem.

Pub 28 28 Shagar al-Durr. The bar section – modelled on a British pub – is popular with expats and gay men but noted for its peremptory evictions. There's also an inexpensive restaurant serving *mezze*. Daily noon–2am.

Nightlife and entertainment

For current information about **what's on** at cinemas, concert halls and nightclubs, get hold of the daily *Egyptian Gazette* (on Saturday, the *Egyptian Mail*); the monthly *Cairo's* (£E5) or *Egypt Today* (£E10); the weekly *Middle East Times* (£E4); or the Thursday (English) edition of *Al-Ahram* newspaper (75pt).

Music

Aside from discos and the Opera House, you're unlikely to hear much Western music outside of tourist restaurants – Egyptians prefer music from the Arab world. For contemporary music, by far the liveliest **time of year** is after the school and university exams, from late June to November; you'll need an Arabic-speaking friend to tell you what's happening as none of it is advertised in the foreign press. Note that Egyptians make a clear distinction between a **disco**, where you dance to records, and a **nightclub**, where you have dinner and watch a floorshow; should you wish to go "clubbing", it's a disco, not a nightclub, that you want.

Contemporary and dance music
Contemporary Egyptian music can be categorized as either *Shaabi*, the urban folk music of *baladi* Cairo, blending traditional *mawals* (laments) with raunchy, satirical lyrics; or *Al-Jeel,* a fusion of Nubian, Libyan and Bedouin rhythms with a disco beat, reflecting the tastes of upwardly mobile Cairene youth.

Though both sounds are played everywhere, live acts are more elusive. *Shaabi* stars now perform at nightclubs along Pyramids Road, at rich weddings and private parties. Hotel nightclubs, open-air concerts at the Gezira and Heliopolis clubs or Cairo University (usually during summer vacation) are likelier venues for *Al-Jeel* stars. Up-and-coming performers might appear at downtown nightclubs.

The music accompanying these dancers is so-called **oriental dance music**, whose golden age was the 1940s and 1950s. Purists distinguish between classical *raqs sharqi* and music influenced by Umm Kalthoum or Western jazz – the torrid sounds associated with bellydancing and pre-revolutionary Cairo. Oriental dance music is also played at weddings.

Folk, classical Arab and religious music
During the Nasser era, numerous troupes were established to preserve Egyptian folk music and dance in the face of urbanization. Traditional rural numbers like *The Gypsy Dance* or *The Mamluke* are performed at the **Balloon Theatre** (☎02/347 1718) on Aguza's Corniche by the **National Troupe** and the **Reda Troupe**. However, none of this music commands a wide following today. There's also a dinner show with a folkloric dance troupe (Sun, Wed & Thurs 8pm–2am, show 10–11.30pm; US$35) at the *Felafel Restaurant* in the *Ramses Hilton* (☎02/575 8000).

All the moulids listed on p.254 feature **religious music** (the reading or chanting of the Koran), while few everyday sounds are more evocative than the call to prayer. Outstanding muezzins inspire local pride and professional jealousy. (In a celebrated court case it was ruled that no copyright existed on any expression of the Koran, since Allah created it.) The duets between the Rifai and Sultan Hassan mosques, and the muezzin near the *Pension Roma*, are superb.

Bellydancing and nightclubs

A Marxist critique of **bellydancing** would point the finger at imperialism, and with good reason. The European appetite for exotica did much to create the art form as it is known today: a sequinned fusion of classical *raqs sharqi* (oriental dance), stylized harem eroticism and the frank sexuality of the *ghawazee* (public dancers, many of whom moonlighted as prostitutes during the nineteenth century). The association with prostitution has stuck ever since, notwithstanding the fact that most dancers today are dedicated professionals, and the top stars wealthy businesswomen. When Fifi Abdou (see below) bought an apartment in the deluxe Giza Towers, other tenants, such as the Saudi royal family, protested that she lowered the tone of the place.

The homegrown tradition is now under threat from competition by Russian dancers and the increasing social stigma that deters Egyptian women from entering the profession. The Sheikh of Al-Azhar has decreed that pilgrimages to Mecca undertaken by dancers and actresses are invalid unless they renounce their jobs. "They should give up their sins and return to God," he said.

Despite all the scandalous perceptions, customers are not allowed to touch the dancers, no matter how much they pay in tips.

Five-star venues

If you want to see top acts, the place to go is the nightclub of one of the **five-star hotels**. All of these provide a delicious four-course meal to tide you through the warm-up acts until the star comes on sometime between midnight and 3am. There's usually a minimum rate or flat charge (£E100–250) for the whole deal. Reservations and smart dress are required. The top venue at present is the *Semiramis Intercontinental*, especially on Thursdays when Dina (see below) performs here. The nightclub is open daily 11pm–4am, with a £E235 minimum charge including dinner. Don't expect to see the main act until at least 1am.

Other five-star venues with high-class nightclubs featuring bellydancers are the *Meridian Heliopolis* (☎02/290-5055), *Helnan Shepheard* (Thurs only; ☎02/792 1000) and *Nile Maxim* (☎02/735 8888; see p.101). The *Royal Meridien's* nightclub (☎02/362 1717) has been out of action during the hotel's move into its new wing, but should be back on very soon. The *Cairo Sheraton* in Dokki (☎02/336 9700 or 9800) doesn't have a nightclub, but does have bellydancers performing (daily 10pm–midnight) in its Lebanese restaurant. In addition to the *Nile Maxim*, most of the other floating restaurants listed on p.247 also have bellydancers performing on some or all of their dinner cruises.

Among **performers** at these five-star venues, the number one dancer in the last couple of decades was **Fifi Abdou,** who exemplified the *bint balad*, or streetwise village girl in the big city. Her act included circus tricks, vulgar posturing and rapping. Now in her sixties – and despite trips to the US for plastic surgery – Fifi has pretty much retired. The big name nowadays is **Dina**, who performs at the *Semiramis Intercontinental Hotel* on Thursdays and sometimes Tuesdays. Other names to look out for are **Montaha** and two foreigners: Argentinian **Asmahan**, who soon got a big name in Cairo for her looks and for moves that were somewhat more risqué than Egyptians were used to, and **Yasmina**, from Britain, known to perform with a chandelier on her head, but off on maternity leave at last check. Another well-known name, **Lucy**, has more or less gone into retirement, but has been known to put in an impromptu performance at the *Pariziana* club, which she runs with her husband.

Cheaper venues

A step down from this are the somewhat sleazy, rip-off nightclubs **along Pyramids Road**, where the entertainments are varied and sometimes good, but the food is usually poor. **Cheaper places**, with no food to speak of, lurk downtown. Most of these are far from pleasant and, if you intend to check them out, you need to be aware of how they operate.

Most open their doors at around 10pm, but none of them really get going until at least midnight. Most have an entry fee or minimum charge, sometimes both, but be warned that many will also endeavour to rip you off with **hidden charges and sharp practices**. Napkins, for example, may be placed on your table and then charged on your bill. Waitresses may pour your drinks and add a charge for this, or demand *baksheesh*. Nibbles are placed on your table unordered, but they are far from free, and will cost you dear unless you are quick to refuse them. You need to be on your toes and stay relatively sober to keep refusing these extras, as the clubs count on customers getting too drunk to notice them. They may also add spurious taxes, or simply refuse to give change – even for a £E50 note. Such practices have driven most Egyptian customers away, and a lot of these clubs are now pretty much dead, certainly midweek, only livening up, if at all, on Thursday nights and public holidays. The dancers who perform any time before the small hours of the morning are almost uniformly awful; if it's late enough and you're lucky, you might catch one who has a little rhythm. Women are unlikely to enjoy themselves at most of these places as the atmosphere is generally sleazy, drunken, lecherous and male. The two big **exceptions** in the list which follows are the *Palmyra* and the *Fontana*, which are the only ones where women might go, in a group or accompanied by men, and have a good time, although the other places listed do have their redeeming features.

Fontana Hotel Off Midan Ramses ☏ 02/592 2321. Attached to the hotel of the same name, this is a lower-priced version of the nightclubs in the five-star hotels, and as such a lot more reputable than most cheap Cairo nightclubs. It operates on two days of the week only, and starts a lot earlier than most venues, but it's sufficiently upmarket to be a safe and respectable option and one where women can feel comfortable if accompanied. Sun & Thurs 8pm–4am. Minimum charge £E35.

Miamy In the passage at 16 26th July St. A small and spectacularly seedy venue, where the usual tricks are practised, though not to excess – just keep refusing the snacks and the napkins. The musicians are not bad as these places go. The *New Miamy* (*Goe's*), in the same passage, is similar. Daily 11pm–4am. Entry £E5. Stella £E10. No minimum charge.

Palmyra In the passage at 16 26th July St, next door to the *Miamy*. One of the few cheap venues that does not try to rip off its customers with spurious charges, a good-natured place where you can feel safe for a night out without having to keep your wits about you, and where the dancers actually make a bit of an effort, and interact with the audience. They even occasionally have other variety acts such as acrobats. Daily 10pm–4am. Entry £E5. Stella £E11. No minimum charge.

Pariziana Pyramids Road, north side, just east of Maryotteya Canal. Run by bellydancer Lucy and her husband, this is just about the only halfway decent nightclub on Pyramids Road, though somewhat more upmarket than places in town. Music and dancing start around midnight, and continue till 4am or beyond, but dinner is served as early as 9pm. Minimum charge £E120.

Scheharazade 1 Sharia Alfi Bey. The venue itself is a marvellous old vaudeville-style music hall, but unfortunately the establishment that runs it is as sleazy as they come. The usual tricks with nibbles and change refusal are played, and waiters may even try to insist that snacks (lowest price £E20) are compulsory with every beer. The *Arizona* opposite is to be avoided at all costs.

Discos

Cairo has a fair number of **discos** (the term "nightclub" is only used in its old-fashioned sense of a sit-down venue with a meal and floorshow) but nowhere to rave about. The music is usually last year's hits back home or current Egyptian stuff; light shows are unsophisticated. But dance floor manners are good, boozy boors are at a minimum and casual dress is acceptable at all but the ritziest places. More problematical is the trend towards a **couples-only policy**. Though you might imagine this is to prevent women from being swamped, locals say that it's to stop discos from becoming gay haunts (see below) or pick-up joints for prostitutes (see "Drinking", p.247, for some of

251

these). In practice, women can usually get into discos without escorts, but men without women have little chance. Call first to avoid disappointment.

There are no **gay** discos as such in Cairo, and the city's gay community remains in shock following the 2001 arrests at the *Queen Boat* (see p.77). Gay men do gather at some **bars** (try *Pub 28* or *Harry's Bar* in Zamalek, or the *Taverne du Champs de Mars* in the *Nile Hilton*), and *Jackie's* at the *Nile Hilton* used to have quite a gay contingent on Wednesday nights but has been operating a (heterosexual) couples-only policy of late. You may also find the odd single-sex couple on the dancefloor of the *Hard Rock Café*, though this doesn't necessarily indicate that they are gay. There are absolutely no venues for **lesbians** in Cairo, though the odd woman-only couple has on occasion been spotted at *Jackie's*. Further information on gay meeting places in Cairo can be found on line at Ⓦ www.gayegypt.com/centralcairo.html.

Unless otherwise specified, all of the venues below are open nightly.

Hotel venues

Most of the **hotel discos** cater to rich foreigners and Westernized Egyptians. Other places maintain their cachet by high prices and standards of dress, among them *Le Disco* in the *El-Gezirah Sheraton* (11.30pm–5am; minimum charge £E100) and *The Saddle* in the *Mena House* (10pm–3am; no minimum charge except £E60 on Thurs). *Jackie's* in the *Nile Hilton* (8.30pm–4am) admits **couples** and hotel guests only, certainly at weekends. However, **singles** are admitted to *The Castle* in the *Helnan Shepheard* (daily 11pm–4am, also Thurs & Fri 6–11pm "matinee" session; minimum charge £E50), though a couples-only policy operates from Thursday to Sunday.

Cheaper venues

Less fastidious, **cheaper venues** include the *Fontana Hotel* disco (daily except Sun & Thurs when there is bellydancing instead, 8pm–2 or 3am; minimum charge £E25). *Legends* at the base of the Cairo Tower (daily 10pm–6am) currently has no minimum charge, which may change the clientele it attracts, hitherto mainly young and well-off.

One of the city's most popular discos is the **Western-style** *Crazy House Disco* (daily midnight–6am; £E25, Thurs £E50), in the enormous Cairo Land entertainment complex at 1 Sharia Salah Salem, near the Southern Cemetery. Entry price includes two drinks, and there's a strict over-21s policy. For something a little more interesting, seek out *Africana*, about halfway along Pyramids Road in Giza (daily 11pm–4am; £E40 entry including a beer), which has a largely African crowd and plays mostly **African and reggae music**; it is rather seedy, however, and frequented by prostitutes, and it doesn't really get going until at least 1am.

The city's best music venue must surely be *Cairo Jazz Club* at 197 26th July St in Mohandiseen (daily 7pm–2am; ☎02/345 9939; minimum charge £E40), which often has live musicians, and also serves food. The lighting is soft, the seating comfortable and the crowd friendly. As its name suggests, it is mainly dedicated to **jazz music**, but not exclusively: Thursday in particular is jazz night, with Wednesdays dedicated to rai.

A couple of **bars** also have dance floors, including the *Hard Rock Café* in the *Royal Meridian Hotel* (see p.248; daily 8pm–3am; minimum charge £E50), the *Bull's Eye* at 32 Sharia Jeddah in Mohandiseen (daily 6pm–2am; minimum charge £E30), and *El Yotti* at 44 Sharia Mohi el-Din Abdel Izz in Mohandiseen (daily 1pm–4am), which is also a restaurant.

Cinemas

Most of the older **cinemas** in downtown Cairo are Art Deco relics of the 1930s and 40s, purpose-built for foreigners and trashed by rioters on "Black Saturday" in 1952 (see p.128). Never properly refurbished and now distinctly seedy, they still attract huge, virtually all-male audiences, who cat-call at anything remotely risqué. Lurid hoardings portray grotesquer versions of Hollywood mega-heroes, or the stock characters beloved of *baladi* films (indomitable matriarch, broken patriarch, star-crossed lovers, the hussy and the villain).

Though **foreign movies** are shown throughout the year, there's most choice during winter and Ramadan; see listings in the *Egyptian Gazette* or *Middle East Times*. Because they're subtitled in Arabic, audiences chatter and vendors hawk snacks, drowning out the soundtrack – you have to sit near the front to hear anything. However, the last few years have seen an explosion of expensive new cinemas, most in shopping centres: Al-Tahrir Cinema on Sharia Tahrir, in Dokki (☎02/335 4726; £E15–20); MGM on the top floor of the Maadi Grand Mall (☎02/519 5388; £E15); and Ramses Hilton Centre, opposite the hotel (☎02/574 7435; £E20–25). All have plush seats, stereo sound, a/c (turned to arctic setting), and prohibit chattering and smoking. At these cinemas it's advisable to book in advance, but elsewhere it's usually okay to buy tickets (£E2.50–10) an hour or so beforehand, except during Ramadan, when extra evening showings draw full houses and the Metro Cinema on Talaat Harb screens a different movie every night (no reserved seats), as does the Al-Tahrir.

To a greater or lesser extent, all films suffer from **censorship**, which sometimes leaves the plot in shreds. The only chance to view uncensored foreign movies comes during the **Cairo International Film Festival**, usually held during autumn or in December. Check the *Egyptian Gazette* or the tourist office for details.

Opera, ballet and theatre

The **Cairo Opera House** on Gezira (☎02/739 8132 or 739 8144, ⓦwww .aidepyramids.com) is the chief centre for performing arts. Its main hall hosts performances by prestigious foreign acts (anything from Kabuki theatre to Broadway musicals) and the **Cairo Ballet Company** (Sept–June). The smaller hall is used by the **Cairo Symphony Orchestra**, which gives concerts there every Saturday from September to mid-June. During July and August all events move to the marble-clad open-air theatre where a programme of youth concerts includes everything from Nubian folk-dancing to Egyptian pop to jazz. Programme listings appear in *Egypt Today* and the *Al-Ahram* weekly, and are available in more detail from the ticket office. Tickets to all concerts (£E5–25) should be booked several days beforehand (daily 10am–3pm & 4–9pm). A jacket and tie are compulsory for men attending events in the main hall.

Another venue for Western-style performing arts is the **AUC Theatre** at the Falaki Academic Centre on Sharia Falaki (between Sharia Mohammed Mahmoud and Sharia Rihan), whose plays, most of them in English, are open to the public and are usually advertised on campus. You might also hear about productions by two theatre groups run by Cairo's expat community, the **Cairo Players** (☎02/736 3488) and the **Ma'adi Community Players** (☎02/358 3577, ⓦwww.angelfire.com/ca/maadiplayers), both open to anyone who's interested; while for those who understand Arabic, the range encompasses everything from **comedy** at the **Thalia Theatre** (☎02/593 7948) on Midan Ataba to **political satire** at the **Miami Theatre** on Talaat Harb (☎02/574 5651; closed Mon).

Religious festivals and weddings

Though few foreign visitors frequent them, Cairo's **religious festivals** are quite accessible to outsiders – and a lot of fun. Many begin with a *zaffa* (parade) of Sufis carrying banners, drums and tambourines, who later perform marathon *zikrs*, chanting and swaying themselves into the trance-like state known as *jazb*. Meanwhile, the crowd is entertained by acrobats, stick dancers, dancing horses, fortune-tellers and other side shows.

Whereas most festivals are specifically Muslim (see the box below) or Christian (see below), people of both faiths attend the birthday or name-day celebrations of holy persons with *baraka* (the power of blessing) – known as

Muslim festivals

Note that since the Muslim calendar moves back approximately eleven days a year against the Western (Gregorian) calendar, the equivalent Gregorian months given will only be valid for the next few years.

MOHARRAM (Jan/Feb to Feb/March). New Year begins on **Ras el-Sana el-Hegira**, the first day of *Moharram* (see p.64 for dates). The initial ten days of this first month are blessed, especially the eve of the tenth day (*Leylat Ashura*), which commemorates the martyrdom of Hussein at Karbala. Until this century, it witnessed passionate displays by Cairo's Shia minority – the men would lash themselves with chains. Nowadays, Sunni Muslims observe the next day (*Yom Ashura*) with prayers and charity; the wealthy often feed poor families, serving them personally to demonstrate humility. But aside from *zikrs* outside Hussein's Mosque, there's little to see.

SAFAR AND RABI AL-AWWAL (March/April to May/June). In olden days the **return of the pilgrims** from Mecca (*Nezlet el-Hagg*) occasioned great festivities at the Bab al-Futuh towards the end of *Safar*, the second month. Nowadays, celebrations are localized, as pilgrims are feasted on the evening of their return, their homes festooned with red-and-white bunting and painted with *Hadj* scenes. However, it's still customary to congregate below the Citadel a week later and render thanksgiving *zikrs* in the evening. Previously, these gatherings blended into the **Prophet's birthday** (*Moulid al-Nabi*) celebrations during the next month, *Rabi al-Awwal*, which run from the third day to the night of the twelfth, the last being its great day (see p.64 for dates). The eve of the twelfth – known as the Blessed Night (*Leylat Mubarak*) – witnesses spectacular processions and fireworks, with *munshids* (singers of poetry) invoking spiritual aid while crowds chant *"Allahu Hei! Ya Daim!"* (God is Living! O Everlasting!). Midan el-Hussein, the Rifai Mosque and Ezbekiya Gardens are the best vantage points.

RABI EL-TANI (May/June to June/July). During the fourth month, *Rabi el-Tani*, the **Moulid of El-Hussein** gathers pace over a fortnight, its big day usually a Tuesday, its *leyla kebira* on Wednesday night. Hussein's Mosque in Khan el-Khalili is surrounded by crowds chanting *"Allah Mowlana!"* (God is our Lord!), dozens of *zikrs* and amplified *munshids*, plus all the usual side shows. Also in this month is the smaller **Moulid of Saiyida Sukayna** – at her mosque on Sharia el-Khalifa (see map on p.166).

GUMAD EL-TANI (Aug/Sept to Sept/Oct). On a Thursday or Friday in the middle of the sixth month, *Gumad el-Tani*, Sufis of the Rifai order attend the **Moulid of Al-Rifai** at his mosque below the Citadel. Those carrying black flags belong to the mainstream Rifaiyah; subsects include the Awlad Ilwan (once famous for thrusting nails into their eyes and swallowing hot coals) and the Sa'adiya (snake charmers, who used to allow their sheikh to ride over them on horseback). Dervishes are less evident moulids. Aside from the crowds (don't bring valuables, or come alone if you're a woman), the only problem is ascertaining festival **dates**. Different events are related to the Islamic, Coptic or secular calendars, and sometimes to a particular day rather than a certain date, so details below should be double-checked with Egyptian friends or the tourist office. As a rule, all the longer moulids climax in a *leyla kebira* (literally "big night") on the last evening or the eve of the last day – the most spectacular and crowded phase.

Coptic festivals

It should be emphasized that **Coptic festivals** are primarily religious, with fewer diversions than Muslim ones. Unless you're into church services, the

at the **Moulid of Saiyida Nafisa** (on a Wed or Thurs mid-month, or a Tues towards the end of the month), but the event is equally colourful.

RAGAB (Sept/Oct–Oct/Nov). The seventh month is dominated by the great **Moulid of Saiyida Zeinab**, Cairo's "patron saint", which lasts for fifteen days and attracts up to a million people on its big day and *leyla kebira* (a Tues & Wed in the middle of the month). A much smaller, "local" event is the **Moulid of Sheikh al-Dashuti** on the 26th day of *Ragab*, at his mosque near the junction of Faggala and Bur Said streets, 1km northwest of the Bab al-Futuh. The eve of the 27th is observed by all Muslims as the *Leylat el-Mirag* or **Night of Ascension**, with *zikrs* outside the Abdin Palace and principal mosques.

SHA'BAN (Oct/Nov to Nov/Dec). During the eighth month, *Sha'ban*, the week-long **Moulid of Imam al-Shafi'i** enlivens his mausoleum in the Southern Cemetery (see p.171) from one Wednesday to the next. The eve of the 15th is believed to be the time when Allah determines the fate of every human over the ensuing year, so the faithful hope to gain *baraka*.

RAMADAN (Nov/Dec to Dec/Jan) **AND EID AL-FITR**. The sighting of the new moon on the *Leylat er-Ruyeh* (Night of Observation) marks the onset of **Ramadan**, a month of fasting from sunrise to sunset, with festivities every night (see p.63 for more, and p.64 for dates). *Zikrs* and Koranic recitations draw crowds to El-Gumhorriya and El-Hussein squares, while secular delights are concentrated around Ezbekiya and other areas. The *Leylat el-Qadr* (Night of Power) on the eve of the 27th of the month was traditionally marked by Whirling and Howling Dervishes at Mohammed Ali's Mosque at the Citadel. The end of Ramadan heralds the three-day **Eid al-Fitr** or "Little Feast" (see p.64 for dates), when people buy new clothes, visit friends, mosques, shrines and family graves. In the past, this was followed by the procession of the *kisweh* (the brocaded cloth which covers the sacred Ka'ba at Mecca), a prelude to the departure of the pilgrims around the 23rd day of *Shawwal*. Given modern transport, however, most pilgrims now depart in the following month, *Zoul Qiddah*, with local send-offs that counterpoint the *Nezlet al-Hagg*.

ZOUL HAGGA (Dec/Jan to Jan/Feb). The twelfth month, *Zoul Hagga*, is notable for the "Feast of Sacrifice" or **Eid al-Adha** (the "Great Feast", **Corban Bairam**), which involves the mass slaughter of sheep and other livestock on the 10th, commemorating Ibrahim's willingness to sacrifice Isma'il to Allah (the Muslim version of the story of Abraham and Isaac).

MOULID OF SIDI ALI AL-BAYOUMI. Last but not least, there's another colourful parade of Dervishes at the **Moulid of Sidi Ali al-Bayoumi**, the Rifai sects proceeding from El-Hussein's Mosque to the Bab al-Futuh and thence into the Husseiniya quarter. Unlike most Muslim festivals, this is unrelated to the Islamic calendar, happening in early **October**.

"moveable" feasts centred around Easter (which follows the Coptic calendar rather than the Western one), Christmas (January 7), Epiphany (January 19) and the Feast of Annunciation (March 21) have little to offer.

However, there's more to enjoy at two festivals in Old Cairo: the **Moulid of Mari Girgis** at the round Church of St George (April 23, St George's Day) and the **Moulid of the Holy Family** at the Church of St Sergius (June 1). Moreover, all Egyptians observe the ancient pharaonic-Coptic spring festival known as **Sham el-Nessim** (literally "Sniffing the Breeze"), when families picnic on salted fish, onions and coloured eggs in gardens and cemeteries.

Weddings

There's nothing bashful about Cairo **weddings** or the curiosity of spectators. On Thursday nights the city resounds with convoys of honking cars conveying guests to Nile-side hotels and casinos; and with ululations, drums and tambourines welcoming the newlyweds (often preceded by a bellydancer), whom relatives shower with rose petals. In poorer quarters all the bridal furniture and wedding guests are first displayed to admiring neighbours.

At the reception itself, the couple sit receiving congratulations ("*Alf mabrouk*" is the formal salutation) while relatives and friends perform impromptu dances. Guests may be segregated, allowing both sexes to let their hair down: women can dance and smoke, men indulge in spirits (or hashish, in private homes). Although it's not uncommon for foreign onlookers to be invited into middle-class or *baladi* wedding parties, rich ones are predictably exclusive, but good for a brief show.

Whirling dervishes

The *Mowlawiyya* are Egyptian adherents of a Sufi sect founded in Konya, Turkey, during the mid-thirteenth century, and known to Westerners as the **Whirling Dervishes**. Their Turkish name, *Mevlevi*, refers to their original Master, who extolled music and dancing as a way of shedding earthly ties and abandoning oneself to God's love. The Sufi ideal of attaining union with God has often been regarded by orthodox Muslims as blasphemous, and only during Mamluke and Ottoman times did the Whirling Dervishes flourish without persecution.

In modern Egypt the sect is minuscule compared to other Sufi orders, and rarely appears at moulids, but a tourist version of the famous whirling ceremony is currently staged at the Citadel while the permanent venue, Ghuriya cultural centre in Al-Ghuri's Mausoleum, undergoes restoration. If the *Mowlawiyya* are in Cairo, **performances** are held on Wednesdays and Saturdays starting at 7.30pm in summer, 6.30pm in winter; arrive early to get a good seat, although this may entail getting cooked by the heat. You are supposed to arrive at least half an hour before the performance in any case. The performances are free, sponsored by the government, and last for about an hour. Photos are permitted but not videos – if you bring a video camera along you'll have to leave the battery at the desk.

Each element of the **whirling ceremony** (*samaa*) has symbolic significance. The music symbolizes that of the spheres, and the turning of the dervishes that of the heavenly bodies. The gesture of extending the right arm towards heaven and the left towards the floor denotes that grace is being received from God and distributed to humanity without anything being retained by the dervishes. Their camelhair hats represent tombstones; their black cloaks the tomb itself; their white skirts shrouds. During the *samaa* the cloaks are discarded.

Activities and kids' stuff

The two classic tourist activities are riding in the desert near the Pyramids and sailing on the Nile in a felucca. Other more or less adventurous trips are covered at the end of this chapter under "Excursions from Cairo" (see).

Riding in the desert

Despite the pitfalls mentioned under "The Pyramids of Giza", **riding in the desert** is a fantastic experience. Unless you relish haggling, authorized stables are a safer bet than footloose Bedouin operators; in either case, check to see that your horse is in good condition and well looked-after. Stables behind the Sound and Light grandstand near the Sphinx include AA (☏02/385 0531), which is good for children, and KG Stables round the corner (☏02/385 1065). Beware of imposters. Children and adults can take riding lessons (£E10 for 30min) at Heliopolis Racing Club (9am–5pm; ☏02/245 4090).

Felucca sailing

Something as restful as **sailing on the Nile in a felucca** can hardly be termed an activity. Since the boatman does all the work, the only effort involved is negotiating rental rates. Most of the feluccas moored along the river bank opposite the *Helnan Shepheard* and the northern tip of Roda can seat eight people and charge £E40 per hour. Bring a picnic and lots of mosquito repellent. For rather less cost, you can join one of the boats just south of Maspero Dock, which do round trips to the Nile Barrages at Qanatir (£E5). Shorter jaunts are available on boats from the quay just north of Tahrir Bridge on Gezira Island (£E2 for 30min). For an even cheaper no-frills ride on the Nile, catch a river-taxi (£E1) from the Maspero Dock to Giza or Old Cairo or, on Fridays and Sundays, up to Qanatir (£E2).

Parks

Cairo is incredibly densely populated, with green spaces few and far between. Even in prosperous Mohandiseen, local residents are forced to make use of the central reservations of the main boulevards for sitting out or picnicking. In **Gezira**, however, a number of small gardens are open to the public, with small entry fees. They include the **Andalusian Garden** just south of Sharia el-Borg (daily: winter 9am–9pm; summer 9am–midnight; £E2), and the **Riyadi Garden** next door, by the river (daily: winter 9am–9pm; summer 9am–11pm; £E2), complete with Cleopatra's Needle-style obelisk. Between them and the 6th October Bridge is another garden, the **Hadiket el–Mesla** (daily 9am–4pm; £E1) and, to its north, the **Hadiket el–Nahr** (daily 9am–7pm; same ticket). On the other side of the island, Gezira Youth Club is used by locals and residents as a park. The adjoining Gezira Sporting Club has a massive green space – the largest in Cairo – but keeps its fees high and its doors resolutely closed to non-members (day membership is possible and costs £E20, or £E30 on Fridays and public holidays, and does not allow use of the pool). However, **Saiyida Park**, in Saiyida Zeinab (on Sharia Qadry, one block off Sharia Bur Said; daily 8am–10pm), is a public landscaped garden in traditional Arabic style not far from the Ibn Tulun Mosque, a very welcome green lung in one of the most crowded parts of town, and an excellent place for a breather after a day's sightseeing in Islamic Cairo.

Further afield, the grounds of the **Agriculture Museum** in **Aguza** (daily 9am–2pm; 10pt; see p.199) are rather more enticing than the museum itself, and there is also the **Japanese Garden** in **Helwan** (daily: winter 9am–9pm;

summer 9am–midnight; £E2; see p.191). The **El-Urman Gardens** on Sharia Abdel Salam Aref near the zoo in **Giza** (daily: winter 8.30am–3.30pm; summer 8.30am–5pm; 30pt, camera 50pt, video £E20; see map p.176) is a stately remnant of the Khedival Gardens laid out by the French. Other options are Galabaya Park in Zamalek, the zoo in Giza, and Merryland in Heliopolis, all dealt with under "Chiefly for children", below.

Swimming pools

Swimming pools take on an extra allure in Cairo, whose only "public" pool is the spa at Ain Helwan (daily 8am–5pm; £E2.50; see p.191). The Heliolido (☎02/258 0070) off Midan Roxi costs £E20 a day, or offers monthly memberships for £E250. The nearby Heliopolis Sporting Club (☎02/417 0061, 0062 or 0063) on Sharia Merghani has a larger pool and admits foreigners over the summer (bring your passport), but the entrance fee (£E20) doesn't include use of the other facilities (eg additional £E5 to use the pool). The Olympic-size pool at the Ahli Club by the Opera House on Sharia Om Kalthoum is for more serious swimmers and also has women-only sessions – monthly membership costs US$50.

Hotel pools are more accessible, the best being the *Semiramis Intercontinental* (£E84), *Cairo Marriott* (£E65) and the *Atlas Zamalek* on Arab League Street in Mohandiseen (Mon–Thurs £E25, Fri–Sun £E30, including meal). The rooftop pool of the *Fontana Hotel*, off Midan Ramses, is cheaper for dipping (£E15) but hardly big enough for a swim.

Hammams

A totally different experience is available at traditional **hammams** (bathhouses), whose nondescript facades conceal gloomy warrens of sweatrooms and tubs. Some baths serve men in the morning and women in the afternoon; others assign them separate days, or only admit one sex. With no mixed bathing, Egyptian women can ignore taboos and talk frankly; foreigners may be adopted into their circle, which usually includes children being scrubbed. For men, baths are something of a centre for gay prostitution, and have been since Ottoman times, so many avoid them for that reason, although you can generally go there just for a bathe without being hassled. Egyptians pay £E3–5, but foreigners are likely to be charged £E10–20. Ask **around Islamic Cairo** – most of the baths are located on maps in that section. The oldest is the Hammam al-Sultan, four doors north of Barquq's complex on Sharia al-Muizz (currently closed for restoration).

Nearer to the Northern Walls are the eighteenth-century Hammam al-Malatili at 40 Sharia Amir al-Gyushi (daily 7am–7pm) and the harder-to-find Hammam al-Tanbali (near the El-Geish end of Bayn al-Haret, 1km east of Ramses). Around the Bab Zwayla are the As-Sukayna and Al-Muayyad baths – both Mamluke (see map p.149) – and the rather grubby Ottoman Hammam al-Sukkariyya. A medieval facade halfway down Sharia es-Silah (see map p.156) screens the modernized Hammam Bashtak (daily: women 10am–5pm; men 6pm–8am).

For a cleaner, more expensive and less traditional venue, around £E45 buys a **sauna** at the *El-Gezirah Sheraton*, a sauna *and* Turkish bath at the *Nile Hilton*, or both plus Jacuzzi at the *Ramses Hilton*.

Sports: participatory and spectator

Keeping fit in Cairo is difficult but not impossible. The expat Hash House Harriers (☎02/350 5577) is one of several clubs organizing **street running**, best done on Gezira, Roda or the west bank Corniche, before 8am or after 10pm to avoid heavy traffic and air pollution. Alternatively, by paying £E6 to enter the Youth Club under the Giza side of the 6th October Bridge (daily 6am–9pm), you can "stray" into the Gezira Sporting Club – just keep away from the built-up area near the running track, where guards check for tickets.

Although the Gezira Sporting Club's extensive facilities are only available to members and guests (see above), anyone can use the **gymnasiums** in the *Ramses Hilton* (£E25), *Nile Hilton* (£E54) and *Atlas Zamalek* (though currently closed) hotels; or call the Community Services Association, 4 Road #21, Ma'adi (℡02/358 5284), which runs a fitness centre with a weight room.

Of the city's spectator sports, **football** (soccer) is the most exciting. During the season (Sept–May), premier league teams Ahly and Zamalek take on challengers like Ismailiya, Mahalla and Masri at the Cairo Stadium in Medinet Nasr (Fri: usually 3pm in winter; 7pm in summer; £E3–15). The most exciting fixture of the season is the local derby between Ahly and Zamalek, when rivalry runs high and tickets sell out well in advance. Riot police with machine guns are regularly in attendance at matches since football riots, though infrequent, can be extremely bloody.

The Saturday *Egyptian Gazette* gives details of **horse racing** at both the Heliopolis Hippodrome Course and the Gezira race track, from mid-October to mid-May. Races start at 1.30pm every other Saturday and Sunday; the international ones and the local derby are both enjoyable. From November to April, Cairo's bridges provide a fine view of **rowing** races every Friday.

Chiefly for children

Besides the following places, children (and adults) should enjoy felucca and camel rides, the Sound and Light show, and theme restaurants like *Felfela Village* on Maryotteya Canal at Giza (see p.246). Because of Cairo's density, most of the parks and pleasure grounds are on the islands or the west bank (see above).

The Aquarium and zoo

The **Aquarium Grotto** in Galabaya Park in Zamalek (daily 8.30am–5pm; 25pt) displays 195 kinds of tropical fish amidst a labyrinth of passageways and stairs that children will love to explore. The entrance is on Sharia Galabaya, on the western side of the park.

For a larger park and more to see, check out **Cairo Zoo** in Giza (daily 9am–5pm; 30pt, camera 25pt, also 25pt to walk across the hippo pond), which can easily be reached from downtown by bus (#355 and #357 from Tahrir, #30 and #83 from Ramses, #6, #9, #106 and #109 from Ataba). As zoos go, Cairo's is reasonably humane, with quite large enclosures for most animals – the main exception is the lion house. You are greeted on entry by an impressive display of flamingoes, and children will enjoy helping to feed the camels or the elephants if they arrive at the right time. Try to avoid Fridays and public holidays, when the zoo is packed with picnicking families, and don't bother with the small museum of stuffed reptiles (25pt).

Dr Ragab's Pharaonic Village

Reached by half-hourly boats from the Corniche 2km south of the Giza Bridge, **Dr Ragab's Pharaonic Village** (daily: winter 9am–5pm; summer 9am–9pm; £E59 at the gate, £E49 at the Papyrus Centre; ℡02/571 8675) is a kitsch simulation of ancient Egypt on Jacob Island, upriver from Roda in Dokki. During the two-hour tour, visitors survey the Canal of Mythology (flanked by statues of gods) and scores of costumed Egyptians performing tasks from their floating "time machines", before being shown around a replica temple and nobleman's villa.

The circus and the puppet theatre

Those who enjoy animals performing tricks, acrobats, clowns and trapeze artists should visit the **National Circus** (☎02/347 0612) in Aguza, next to the Balloon Theatre near the Zamalek Bridge. The box office is open from 11am to 10pm (tickets £E10–30); performances run from 8.30pm to 11pm daily. Another traditional diversion is the **Cairo Puppet Theatre** (Thurs & Fri 7.30pm; ☎02/591 0954) in Ezbekiya Gardens, which stages *Sinbad the Sailor*, *Ali Baba* and other favourites, or campy musicals during season (Oct–May).

Rides and games

Fun rides and games are on offer at the **Cookie Amusement Park** near the Giza Pyramids, 400m up Mansoreya Canal from Pyramids Road (daily 10am–11pm; E£1 before 6pm, £E2 after) and the larger **Sinbad Amusement Park** near Cairo Airport, which has bumper cars, a small roller coaster and lots of rides for tots (winter 9–11pm, opens 10am on Fri; summer 9pm–2am; £E5 entry plus £E3–5 per ride). **Merryland** on Sharia al-Higaz, off Midan Roxi in Heliopolis, is a safe environment to play, with a merry-go-round, pedalo lake and small zoo (daily: winter 8am–4.30pm; summer 8am–7pm; 50pt at weekends, £E1 Fri & public holidays).

Shopping: bazaars and markets

Shopping in Cairo is a time-consuming process, which suits most locals fine. Cairenes regard it as a social event involving salutations and dickering, affirmations of status and servility; smoothly impersonal transactions are not an ideal. Excluding government stores, there are basically three types of retail outlet. **Department stores** (generally open daily 10am–2pm & 6–10pm) have fixed prices and the tedious system where you select the goods and get a chit, pay the cashier and then claim your purchases from a third counter. **Smaller shops**, usually run by the owner, stay open till 9 or 10pm and tend to specialize in certain wares. Although most of them have fixed prices, tourists who don't understand Arabic price tags or Egyptian currency are liable to be overcharged in certain places (around the Khan el-Khalili bazaar and Talaat Harb, especially). If you know the correct price, attempts can be thwarted by handing over the exact sum (or as near as possible).

In **bazaars** and **markets** haggling prevails, so it's worth window-shopping around fixed-price stores before **bargaining** for lower rates in bazaar stalls. When asked for a quote, merchants often riposte: "What do you think?" Suggest an absurdly low sum to make them respond and don't be fazed by mockery – it's all part of the game. Buyers' tactics include stressing any flaws

---

Ramadan hours

During Ramadan (see p.63), shopping hours go haywire, as some places close all day and operate through the night, while others open later and close earlier. Given that people splurge after sundown, Cairo's boutiques and bazaars are as busy then as Western stores before Christmas.

Markets

Although the bazaars deal in more exotic goods, Cairo's **markets** provide an arresting spectacle, free of the touristy slickness that prevails around the Khan el-Khalili bazaar in Islamic Cairo. Watch how people bargain over the humblest items (often recycled from other products), a paradigm of free enterprise in the gutter. What isn't apparent are the customs, guilds and rackets that govern business, as exemplified by the vast wholesale market at Rod el-Farag (see p.203), whence **fruit and vegetables** are distributed throughout the city. Street markets in central Cairo can be found at Bab al-Luq, halfway up Sharia Orabi, at the eastern end of Sheikh al-Rihan, and along Sharia Qalaa – all of which do business through the night, accompanied by local coffee houses. With the kilo price displayed on stalls in Arabic numerals, you shouldn't have to bargain unless they try toovercharge.

Elsewhere haggling is *de rigueur*. Promising locations are listed below.

• Secondhand clothing can be found in the *canto* section of the **Imam al-Shafi'i Market**, which straggles for 1km along the road leading from Al-Basatin to the Imam's mausoleum in the El-Khalifa district. Other parts of this Friday morning market sell scrap, grain, poultry, sheep and cattle.

• The **Camel Market** at Bil'esh is described on p.197.

• Cairo's **Bird Markets** (10am–2.30pm) are named after the days on which they're held: *Souk al-Hadd* (Sun; Giza Station), *Souk al-Gom'a* (Fri; by the Salah Salem overpass, south of the Citadel, see map p.166) and *Souk Itnayn w Khamis* (Mon & Thurs; in the Abu Rish area of Saiyida Zeinab, see map p.176).

• On Sharia el-Geish near Midan Ataba there's a daily **Paper Market**, selling all types of paper, dyed leather and art materials.

• For **fabrics** (from hand-loomed silk to cheap offcuts), **tools** and much else, you can't beat the daily **Wikalat al-Bulah**, on Sharia Abu'l'Ila in the Bulaq district.

that might reduce the object's value; talking of lower quotes received elsewhere; feigning indifference or having a friend urge you to leave. Avoid being tricked into raising your bid twice in a row, or admitting your estimation of the object's worth (just reply that you've made an offer). Providing you don't make an offer they're willing to accept, it's okay to terminate a lengthy session without buying anything.

Souvenirs, antiques and film

Scores of shops in the Khan and central Cairo purvey **souvenirs**, mostly kitsch reproductions of pharaonic art – scarabs, statuettes of deities, busts of Nefertiti, eyes of Horus – which are cheaper to buy at source in Luxor or Aswan.

Sheets of **papyrus** painted with scenes from temples or tombs are equally ubiquitous. A lot of it used to be made from banana leaves, unlike which **genuine** papyrus will withstand crumpling without cracking (though the paint won't). Nowadays, however, so much papyrus is grown for the trade that it is no cheaper to use banana leaf anyway, and the real scam lies in selling printed papyrus as hand-painted. Most of the papyri on sale are printed or partly printed, even if they have a signature. Prices range from around £E2 to £E80 and beyond, depending on size, intricacy, the quantity of gold paint used and where you're buying: around the Pyramids, in big hotels and the Khan, papyrus is sure to be extremely overpriced and most unlikely to be hand-painted. If you've got the stomach to bargain them down, itinerant street vendors give better deals.

You can see **papyrus-making** demonstrated at Dr Ragab's Papyrus Institute (p.200), one of the few places where you can be sure of buying a genuine, hand-painted article.

Copies of **prints** by David Roberts and other nineteenth-century illustrators also make nice souvenirs. For cheap poster-size or postcard editions, check out Reader's Corner and Lehnert and Landrock (see p.269). Old Egyptian **stamps**, **coins** and **postcards** can also be found at 33 Sharia Abdel Khaliq Sarwat, among other places.

Selling fake *antikas* (with spurious certificates) is an old tradition. Genuine pharaonic, Coptic or Islamic **antiques** cannot be exported without a licence from the Department of Antiquities. Old reproductions and foreign-made antiques are a safer bet. Dealers in the Khan include Old Shop and Ahmed Dahba (both at 5 Sikket al-Badestan; see map p.137).

Film and processing

Outside of big hotels, you can buy **film** fairly cheaply. Photo Greenwich at 16 Sharia Adly (daily 9am–8pm; ☎02/360 6990) sells Kodachrome and Agfa film for £E13–15 and also offers **photo-processing** and **printing**. Other outlets where you can buy film and get it developed include: Kodak Shop at 20 Sharia Adly (daily 9am–9pm; ☎02/394 2263) and Best Foto/Misr 2000, 6 Sharia Alfi Bey (daily except Fri 9am–9pm; ☎02/574 3975). Developing is £E4 at the Kodak Shop, £E2.50 at Best Foto/Misr 2000; both charge 60pt per print (9x13cm), and £E2 extra to get them done in an hour. Don't risk your film at the Kodak kiosk on 26th July Street outside the *Grand Hotel*. For where to get passport photos, see p.273.

Brass and copper ware

Egyptian craftsmen have been turning out **brass and copper ware** for over a thousand years, and aside from the tourist trade there's still a big domestic market for everything from banqueting trays to minaret finials. Amongst the items favoured as souvenirs are candlesticks, waterpipes, gongs, coffee sets, embossed plates and inlaid or repoussé trays (the larger ones are often mounted on stands to serve as tables). All of these are manufactured and sold within the Khan, particularly along the stretch of Sharia al-Muizz just before Qalaoun's complex, known as the **Coppersmiths Bazaar** (*Souk al-Nahhasin*).

Although the Khan offers the best range of decorative pieces, it's cheaper to buy **Turkish coffeepots** and hookah pipes between the Ghuriya and the Bab Zwayla, along Ahmed Maher, or from workshops on Sharia Khulud and other streets around Ramses. Be sure that anything you intend to drink out of is lined with tin or silver, since brass and copper react with certain substances to form toxic compounds. Test **waterpipes** for leaky joints and remember to call them *sheeshas* or *narghiles* rather than *hubbly bubblies* (which signifies hashish-smoking). Shops on Sharia al-Muizz just north of the Barquq complex specialize in waterpipes, backgammon boards and other coffee house sundries; a passage on the left just before the Sabil-Kuttab of Abd al-Rahman is full of shops selling pipes. Prices vary from £E10 to £E80, depending on the size; the ones with stainless steel rather than brass fittings are better made and more durable.

Gold and silver jewellery

Most Egyptians still regard **jewellery** as safer than money in the bank; for women, in particular, it constitutes a safety net in case of divorce or bereavement. Pharaonic, Coptic and Islamic motifs, Bedouin, Nubian and oasis designs, work from Syria, Jordan, Yemen and Arabia – Cairo's jewellers stock them all, and can also make pieces to order.

Gold and silver are sold by the gram, with a percentage added on for workmanship. Bullion prices fluctuate but Egyptian wages remain low. The current ounce price of gold is printed in the daily *Egyptian Gazette*; one troy ounce equals about 31 grams. Barring antiques, all **gold** work is stamped with Arabic numerals indicating its purity: usually 21 carat for Bedouin, Nubian or *fellaheen* jewellery; 18 carat for Middle Eastern and European-style charms and chains. Sterling **silver** (80 or 92.5 percent) is likewise stamped, while a gold camel in the shop window indicates that the items are **gold-plated brass**.

The Goldsmiths Bazaar

Downtown jewellers are concentrated along Sharia Abdel Khaliq Sarawt and Sikket al-Manakh, near Midan Opera. In Islamic Cairo, the **Goldsmiths Bazaar** (*Souk es-Sagha*) covers Sharia al-Muizz between the Muski and Sultan Qalaoun's complex, and infiltrates the heart of the Khan via Sikkets al-Badestan and Khan el-Khalili. For gold-plated *fellaheen* designs, check out Sigal and Al-Gamal Jewellery on Sharia al-Muizz. Oasian gold can be found at Rizk in the Khan, and at Gundi Shenouda, off Sharia al-Muizz in a tiny alley called Bab al-Talat (one of the medieval lanes whose old gateways now denote addresses – Bab al-Talat means "Third Gate"); the latter also sells original *faraoni* necklaces from Upper Egypt. Adly Fam (72 Muski) specializes in 21-carat *fellaheen* jewellery. There are several good **silversmiths** in the Wikala al-Gawarhergia. All of these places are shown on the map on p.137.

The most popular souvenirs are gold or silver **cartouches**, with given names in hieroglyphics. The price depends on the quantity of metal used, and whether the characters are engraved or glued on. Thin gold cartouches with glued letters cost about £E60; thicker ones with soldered letters £E90–170; silver cartouches cost much less (£E10 upwards). The cheapest way to get these is to go directly to a workshop where they are made. There are several above the passage of waterpipe suppliers off Sharia al-Muizz, left just before the Sabil-Kuttab of Abd al-Rahman Katkhuda (see map p.142) if coming from the Muski – the stairs are towards the end of the passage on the left. As well as getting a better price, you'll be able to see your piece being made; the disadvantages are that you won't see a selection of items on display here, and you'll be lucky to find anyone who speaks English.

Carpets, tent-making, appliqué and basketwork

Pure wool kilims and knotted carpets are an expensive (and bulky) purchase in any country, so serious buyers are advised to read up on the subject before spending hundreds of pounds on one. As most Egyptian **kilims** (pile-less rugs) and **knotted carpets** have half as many knots (16 per centimetre) as their Turkish counterparts, they should be significantly cheaper – especially the ones made from native wool rather than the high-grade imported stuff used in finer kilims. Prices posted in downtown stores like Omar Effendi (11 Sharia Adly/42 Sharia Sherif) or Sednaoui (on Clot Bey by Midan Ataba) can give you an idea of what to aim for in the bazaar.

Tapestries and rugs

More affordable – and ubiquitous – are the **tapestries and rugs** woven from coarse wool and/or camel hair. These come in two basic styles. Bedouin rugs carry geometric patterns in shades of brown and beige and are usually loosely woven (often purely from camel hair). The other style, deriving from the famous Wissa Wassef School at Harraniyya (see p.220), features colourful images of birds, trees and village life. Beware of stitched-together seams and gaps in the weave (hold pieces up against the light), and unfast colours – if any colour wipes off on a damp cloth, the dyes will run when the rug is washed.

While the suburban village of Kerdassa (p.220) replicates every style imaginable, the only authorized outlet for genuine Wissa Wassef Harraniyya tapestries and batiks is **Senouhi**, on the fifth floor of 54 Sharia Abdel Khaliq Sarwat (Mon–Fri 10am–5pm, Sat 10am–1pm; ☎02/391 0955). Crammed with carpets, jewellery, Bedouin embroidery, modern paintings, and some very high quality bric-a-brac, this small store is a fascinating place to browse, and its delightful owner is happy to show you around. The best site in the bazaar is Haret al-Fahhamin (see "Spices and perfume", p.267), where you can compare Rashidi and Shahatta Talba Manna (both at no.11) with Hamid Ibrahim Abdel Aal (no.5). Unfortunately, none of them is recognizably signposted (or even numbered), so you'll have to ask for directions to the right shop, though their locations are shown on our map (p.149).

Tent-making and appliqué

The traditional Cairene crafts of tent-making and appliqué work are still practised in half a dozen tiny workshops inside the Qasaba, near the Bab Zwayla – hence its sobriquet, the **Tentmakers Bazaar** (*Souk al-Khiyamiyya*; see map p.149). Colourful **appliqué work** comes in various forms: some designs are pictorial, based on pharaonic motifs or romantic Arab imagery; others are abstract, delicate arabesques (which tend to be dearer). Prices vary according to size and intricacy. A zippered pillowcase or cushion cover costs £E15–25; larger pieces, to be used as hangings, go for upwards of £E100, with bedspread-size ones starting at roughly £E350. A much cheaper alternative is the riotously patterned **printed tent fabric** used for marquees at moulids, or to screen unsightly building work. This costs about £E8 per metre, cut from a bolt of cloth roughly 1.4m wide; offcuts are cheaper still.

Another cheap souvenir is palm-frond **basketwork**, mostly from the Fayoum and Upper Egypt. Fayoumi baskets (for sewing, shopping or laundry) are more practical, but it's hard to resist the woven platters from Luxor and Aswan, as vibrantly colourful as parrots. You may also find baskets from Siwa Oasis, trimmed with tassels.

Clothing, bellydancing costumes and leatherwork

As a cotton-growing country with a major textiles industry, Egypt is big on retail **clothing**. Smartly dressed Cairenes are forever window-shopping along Talaat Harb and 26th July Street (downtown), Sharia al-Ahram (Heliopolis) and Arab League Street (Mohandiseen), to name only the main clusters of **boutiques** (open till 9/10pm). Staider threads can be had in **department stores** like Chemla and Cicurel on the downtown section of 26th July Street, or Omar Effendi at 2 Talaat Harb and 11 Sharia Adly/42 Sharia Sherif (daily 10am–2pm & 6–10pm). The cheapest outlets for clothes are **street vendors** along the Muski.

Egyptian clothes

Although few tourists can wear them outdoors without looking silly, many take home a caftan or *galabiyya* for lounging attire. Women's **caftans** are made of cotton, silk or wool, generally A-line, with long, wide sleeves and a round or mandarin collar (often braided). Men's **galabiyyas** come in three basic styles. *Ifrangi* (foreign) resembles a floor-length tailored shirt with collar and cuffs; the *Saudi* style is more form-fitting, with a high-buttoned neck and no collar; *baladi galabiyyas* have very wide sleeves and a low, rounded neckline. The fixed prices in downtown shops should be beatable by hard bargaining **in the Khan**, where there are also two fixed-price stores. Auf (pronounced "oaf"), on the north side of Sharia al-Azhar by the pedestrian bridge (see map p.139), stocks a wide assortment of ready-mades at reasonable prices, including black dresses with Bedouin-style embroidery. Atlas, on Sikket al-Badestan, does made-to-order garments in handwoven fabrics with intricate braidwork (allow several weeks; keep all receipts). Their cheapest caftans and *galabiyyas* are dearer than most garments in other shops.

Another fetching item is the heavy, woven, fringed or tassled black **shawls** worn by *baladi* women, which are sold along the Muski for upwards of £E10, depending on their size and composition (nylon or silk); check for any snags or tears in the weave. If you want to go the whole hog, invest in a *melaya*, the flowing black ankle-length wraps that *baladi* women wear over their house dresses when they go outdoors.

Bellydancing costumes

Cairo is the cheapest place in the world to buy bellydancing costumes, and many foreign dancers come here just to buy all the gear. Forget the rubbish sold to tourists, and look for one of the tiny specialist emporiums in Khan el-Khalili. The best one is Al-Wikalah at 73 Sharia Gawhar al-Qayid off Sharia Sanadiqia (see map p.137). There's a woman to help fit the costumes; anything they don't have in stock they can make in a few days. Lavishly beaded and sequinned bras and hipbands, with a skirt and veil, cost £E150–300; the more you buy, the lower the price. If you're really serious, go to Amira el-Khattan, 27 Sharia Basra, Mohandiseen (℡02/749 0322), where a full tailor-made costume will set you back about £E1800. For bellydancing tapes and videos of the great artistes, pay a visit to Es-Sawy, on the left of the passage just before you reach *Fishawi's*. If you're interested in lessons, Miss Raqia Hassan (℡02/748 2338) in Dokki comes recommended by several dancers who are now professional.

Leatherwork

Egyptian **leatherwork** is nice and colourful, if not up to the standards of its Turkish rival. You can get an idea of the range of products from several shops along Sikket Khan el-Khalili. Leather jackets cost upwards of £E100. Cheaper wallets, handbags and pouffes (tuffets) are sold throughout the Khan and central Cairo, whilst camel saddles in a variety of colours and sizes (£E100) are still produced in the **Saddlemakers Bazaar** (*Souk es-Surugiyyah*), south of the Qasaba (see map p.156).

Glass, ceramics and precious stones

Primitive factories on Haret al-Birkedar just outside the Northern Gates still produce **Muski glass**, a form of hand-blown glassware popular in medieval times, which is nowadays made from recycled bottles. Recognizable by its air bubbles and extreme fragility, Muski glass comes in five main colours (navy blue, turquoise, aquamarine, green and purple) and is fashioned into inexpensive glasses, plates, vases, candle holders and ashtrays – sometimes painted with arabesque designs in imitation of enamelled Mamluke glassware. In the bazaar, the main stockist is Saiyid Abd al-Raouf (8 Sikket Khan el-Khalili; see map p.137), but it's better to go to the factory, where you can see the glass being blown, and also get a better price. The main one is called Al-Daour, and can be found by leaving the walled city through Bab al-Futuh, crossing the main road (Sharia Galal) and finding Haret al-Birkedar about 50m to your right behind the first row of shops; the factory is more or less at the end of it (see map p.142).

A very different kind of glassware is the elegant handmade **perfume bottles** sold in the bazaars. The cheaper ones are made of glass and are as delicate as they look (£E2–10). Pricier versions (costing about four times more) are made of Pyrex and are a little sturdier (they should also be noticeably heavier). A reasonable and hassle-free place to buy them in the bazaar is Perfumes Secret just off the Muski in the lane opposite the *Radwan Hotel* (see map p.137).

Pottery and alabaster

Robust **household pottery** is sold outdoors near the Mosque of Amr in Old Cairo, along Sharia al-Ahram in Giza and the Corniche between Cairo and Ma'adi. For more refined **ceramics**, check out Senouhi (see p.264), and Ma'adi galleries such as Al-Patio (6 Road # 77c) and Haddouta (Sharia Amira, New Ma'adi). Vases and sculptures made from **alabaster** are ubiquitous in Cairo's tourist marts, but you can get better deals at source, in Luxor.

Precious stones

Although nothing can substitute for experience, it's worth relating a few tips about **precious stones**, which Egypt imports from all over, having exhausted its own supply through centuries of mining. Most emeralds in Egypt are of poor quality (good ones are clear, dark green); very large or transparent rubies (from India and Burma) are almost certainly fake; and real sapphires should be opaque. True amber will float when put in salt water. Pearls (from the Gulf Emirates and Japan) should feel like glass if tapped against your teeth; German onyx should be opaque and make a sharp sound if dropped onto glass; and genuine turquoise (from Sinai, Iran or the USA) should contain streaks and impurities. To test the authenticity of Brazilian topaz, amethyst or aquamarine, place them on a sheet of white paper – genuine ones should have only two shades within the stone.

Mashrabiya and inlay work

With little demand for the huge latticed screens that once covered nearly every window in Cairo, modern **mashrabiya work** is usually confined to decorative screens and table stands (see "Brass and copper ware", above). Generally made of imported red birch or oak, they consist of scores or hundreds of turned wooden beads, joined by dowels and glue, without nails. The technique is also applied to Koran stands (which make splendid magazine racks), the fancier ones being embellished with mother-of-pearl, bone and other inlays.

Inlaid **boxes** come in all sizes, from cigar holders to multi-drawer jewellery caskets. Small boxes cost upwards of £E7; prices increase with size and quality of workmanship. Senhoui (see p.264) has some higher-quality inlaid boxes than those you'll find in the bazaar. **Backgammon boards** (*thowla* – pronounced "dow-la") come in two broad varieties: very simple, with minimal (often poor-quality or plastic) inlay, for around £E35; and larger sets made of hardwoods, intricately inlaid with mother-of-pearl, bone or ivory. A multiple box set can cost £E140 or more.

Many backgammon sets have chessboards on the back; **chesspieces** in style and material are widely available, but good backgammon counters hard to find. Now that Egypt has stopped legal imports, fresh supplies of (whose sale is not illegal) are smuggled in from Sudan and Kenya, where poachers are decimating elephant herds. If that's not sufficient reason to boycott ivory products, almost all Western countries prohibit their importation. Inlaid or carved **bone** makes an acceptable, cheaper substitute.

Spices and perfume

As the world's main spice entrepôt from Fatimid times until the eighteenth century, Cairo remains the largest market for perfumes and spices in the Arab world, with some of its business still conducted in bazaars.

Spices and herbs

The Muski end of the **Spice Bazaar** is generally disappointing, with tourist tat impinging on old shops like Donia al-Henaur (incense, spices, candles) and Khedar al-Attar (herbal cures), between the Madrassa of Barsbey and Sharia al-Azhar. However, at the other end of the *Souk al-Attarin*, a narrow lane behind the Mosque-Madrassa of Al-Ghuri (see map p.149) – the **Haret al-Fahhamin** – is a welter of vivid colours and aromas, mingling with the dirt and stench of ages. Here, piled high and named in Arabic, *'irfa* (cinnamon) and *simsim* (sesame) are still evocative of distant lands. What is sold as saffron (*za'faraan*) is in fact safflower, which is why it seems ridiculously cheap compared with what you'd pay for the real thing back home – real saffron consists of fine red strands only, with no orange or yellow in it at all.

Some shop owners are also **herbalists** (*etara*), whose traditional remedies for every ailment from impotence to constipation are widely used. There are several *etara* on Al-Fahhamin and outside Barsbey's madrassa, but the most famous establishment is Abdul Latif Mahmoud Harraz (39 Sharia Ahmed Maher), opposite a *sabil* 200m west of Bab Zwayla in the Bab el-Khalq quarter, which has been run by the same family since 1885.

Incense and perfume

Just as herbal medicine blends into folk magic (many stalls purvey amulets), both make use of **incense**. The Spice and Perfume bazaars offer the widest range of musks and resins, but you can also find Sudanese vendors squatting beside aromatic cones and medicinal roots in the Ezbekiya Gardens.

Alongside the northern half of the *Souk al-Attarin* lies a warren of covered alleys that forms the **Perfume Bazaar**. Egypt produces many of the **essences** used by French perfumiers, which are sold by the ounce to be diluted 1:9 in alcohol for perfume, 1:20 for eau de toilette and 1:30 for eau de cologne. Local shops will duplicate famous perfumes for you, or you can buy brand imitations (sometimes unwittingly – always scrutinize labels). Almost all the perfume shops overcharge and cheat – around Talaat Harb especially, but also in the Khan. Boasting that their "pure" essence is undiluted by alcohol, crooked salesmen will omit to mention that oil has been used instead, which is why they rub it into your wrist to remove the sheen. In fact, if you know what you want and you know its name in Arabic, you can buy it from source: the shop the perfume sellers all get their supplies from is Karama Perfumes at the corner of Sharia al-Muizz with the Muski, or better still, the shop of the same name two doors up al-Muizz. They will still try to overcharge tourists, so you'll need to bargain hard, but a hundred grams of jasmine oil here, for example, should cost less than £E20, and most other essential oils should be cheaper still, around 15pt a gram.

Musical instruments and recordings

Cairo is a good place to buy **traditional musical instruments** such as the *kanoon* (dulcimer), *oud* (lute), *nai* (flute), *rabab* (viol), *mismare baladi* (oboe), *tabla* (drum), *riq* and *duf* (both tambourines; the latter is played by Sufis). All of them are made and sold by half a dozen shops on the right-hand side of **Sharia Qalaa** (walking from Midan Ataba towards the Islamic Art Museum; see map p.110 [Central Cairo]), which also deal in Western instruments and cheaper imitations from China.

Traditional instruments are also sold by itinerant vendors, especially during moulids, when a favourite buy is a hand-held dummy that claps its cymbals together when squeezed (known as a *Shoukoukou* after the famous comic monologist).

As the centre of the Arab music world and a melting pot for every tradition (see "Music" pp.814–818), Cairo is a superb place to buy recordings. You won't find anything on vinyl in Cairo, but authorized **cassettes**, and pirated versions of them, are sold from kiosks where it's quite acceptable (indeed, advisable) to listen before buying. Given that non-Arabic labelling is minimal, it helps to recognize labels like *Sout el-Beirut* (a green cedar-pine logo; Gulf and Levantine music), *SLAM!* (mostly *Al-Jeel* music) and the *Shaabi* imprint *Fel Fel Phone* (which has a retail outlet on Sharia Khulud, near Midan Ramses). The kiosks on Ezbekiya chiefly stock religious and folk cassettes (often cheap, inferior copies). For quality recordings of Umm Kalthoum, Abdel Wahaab and orchestral music, visit Sono Cairo on Sikket Ali Labib Gabr, between Qasr el-Nil and Talaat Harb (opposite the Radio Cinema). Cairo's main distributor, Abdullah, has a shop in the alley behind the *Café al'Americaine* at the top of Sharia Talaat Harb, with vast stocks and an even bigger mail-order catalogue of new wave Arab music. Western music is also available in many kiosks on tape. **CDs** are still not widely available, but one place that has a good selection of Arabic music on CD is Deals Music Store next to *Deals* bar on Sharia Sayed el-Bakri in Zamalek, which is open daily from noon to midnight, and also sells a small selection of Western music on CD.

Books and newspapers

Egypt is the world's largest publisher of Arabic books and newspapers, so those who know the language can find almost any type of **Arab literature** in Cairo. Aside from magazine and paperback stalls along the downtown thoroughfares, good sources include Dar al-Kitab al-Masri wal-Loubnani (on the first floor of 33 Sharia Qasr el-Nil) and Dar al-Maaref (27 Sharia Abdel Khaliq Sarwat); for Islamic heritage books, try Dar el-Tarath (22 Sharia Gumhorriya) and Ezbekiya Gardens.

Unlike most other places in Egypt, Cairo also has plenty of **books in foreign languages** (chiefly English, French and German). Generally, bookshops charge the original cover price for imported editions – usually at an unfavourable rate. For a huge range of material on all things Egyptian, plus novels, travel guides and dictionaries, visit the American University in Cairo Bookshop at the back of the main campus (Sat–Thurs 8.30am–5pm; use the entrance on Sharia Mohammed Mahmoud – you'll need to bring ID). There's another branch of the AUC bookshop in Zamalek at 16 Sharia Mohammed Ibn Thakib (Sat–Mon 10am–5pm, Tues–Thurs 10am–6pm). Another good place for fiction, Egyptology and local literature is Shorouk (1 Midan Talaat Harb), who also sell books on line (ⓦwww.e-kotob.com). Other good downtown bookshops are Lehnert & Landrock (44 Sharia Sherif) and the Anglo-Egyptian Bookshop (169 Sharia Mohammed Farid), which specializes in Arab politics, history and culture, but has an excellent all-round collection. Al-Ahram (165 Sharia Mohammed Farid) and Reader's Corner (33 Abdel Khaliq Sarwat) also sell books in English. Most of these **downtown bookshops** are closed on Sunday. In Zamalek, there are a couple of bookshops worth checking on Sharia Shagar al-Durr: the Zamalek bookshop opposite *Pub 28*, and Romancia on the corner of Sharia Ismail Mohammed, which has a better selection, especially of maps.

The best place for **second-hand books** is the book market in the northeast corner of Ezbekiya Gardens by Midan Ataba, many of whose titles are in English. Other places selling second-hand books in English include the newsstand opposite the AUC entrance on Sharia Mohammed Mahmoud (fair selection), one outside *Groppi's* on Sharia Qasr el-Nil (meagre and a bit pricey), one on Sharia Champollion by Midan Tahrir (small selection), and one outside the Algerian embassy on Sharia Brazil in Zamalek (mostly pulps). You may also find the odd English title among the books scattered on the sidewalk on Sharia Ramses between 26th July and Tawfiqia.

Newspapers and magazines

Foreign newspapers and magazines can be found in the bookshops of the five-star hotels or downtown at the stall on Qasr el-Nil, outside *Groppi's*. The best downtown newsstand is on Sharia Mohammed Mahmoud opposite the AUC entrance and by *McDonald's*, which sometimes even carries the *New York Times* and also a few foreign-language novels. The two bookshops on Sharia Shagar al-Durr in Zamalek also stock British papers. Purchasers of weekend editions of British papers should note that colour supplements are sold separately. You'll be hard-pressed to find a newspaper less than a few days old, so if you need the latest news you'd be better off paying £E5 at an Internet café and accessing the website of your favourite daily. You can sit and read English-language Indian newspapers for free at the Indian embassy visa office, 2nd floor, 37 Sharia Talaat Harb.

Booze and cigarettes

For those who enjoy tippling in their room or want a cache for consumption in "dry" parts of Egypt, there are several places which sell alcohol.

Downtown **liquor stores**, run by Greek or Maronite Christians, maintain a low profile; furtive Muslim customers are served at once, with hardly a word exchanged. The biggest concentration of stores is around the junction of Sharia Talaat Harb with 26th July Street. Outlets include: Orphanides, at 4 Sharia Emad el-Din, and opposite the High Court on 26th July Street; Corinthos (sign in Arabic only) on 26th July, 20m west of Sharia Talaat Harb; Nicolakis, on the corner of Sharia Talaat Harb and Sharia Suq al-Tawfiqia; Gianacus, below the *Hotel Claridge* at 41 Sharia Talaat Harb; Charalambos at 24 Sharia Bassiouni. All stock Egyptian beer, wine, *zibib*, *raki*, brandy and dubious lookalike brands such as *Johnny Wadie Whisky* (Red and Black labels) and *Gardan's Gin*: checking out the windows can be fun, but you wouldn't want to drink these lookalike brands. Most liquor stores are **open** from mid-afternoon till 8pm, Monday to Friday, and close down entirely during Ramadan and other major Muslim festivals.

Liquor regulations entitle foreigners to buy up to four litres of imported spirits (or three bottles of spirits plus a two-dozen-can carton of beer) at **duty-free prices** within 24 hours of arrival in Egypt if you buy them at the airport. You can buy a further three litres (or two plus the box of beer) within 48 hours of arrival, at the airport or, for about a dollar a bottle more, at the well-stocked Diplomatic Section of the Egypt Free Store, 500m beyond the *Atlas-Zamalek Hotel* on Arab League Street in Mohandiseen (daily 10am–3pm), or at the *Sheraton* in Dokki. To take advantage of this, you'll need your passport, as you'll get a stamp in it saying what you've bought.

There is a black market for duty-free booze (Johnny Walker Black Label is the most sought-after brand) if you have – or can be bothered to seek out – a buyer. However, **beware** of Egyptians who accost you in the street asking if you'll buy them some duty-free booze "for my sister's wedding". Buying alcohol for someone else is fine, but under no circumstances should you allow a stranger to be involved in the actual transaction inside the store. The paperwork for any duty-free purchase is filled out in Arabic, and some travellers have discovered on leaving Egypt that a TV or video has been bought duty-free with their passport. Being unable to produce the item for customs officials, they've had to pay duty on it, just as if they'd purchased and then sold it while in Egypt.

With **cigarettes** available on every corner, only smokers addicted to certain foreign brands need hunt down specialist outlets. Try Carvellis Frères (32 Sharia Talaat Harb), which also sells pipe tobacco, rolling tobacco and cigarette papers, and never overcharges. Just across the street, Babik, in the passage by 39 Sharia Talaat Harb, also stocks a range of smokers' requisites. Refilling stalls all over the city can recharge your lighter (even if it's "non-refillable") for 30–50pt, or change flints for 25pt.

Money

Though rates of exchange vary slightly, **banks** are chiefly distinguished by their opening hours and relative (in)efficiency. All the main banks are well represented in Cairo, and most of them open Sunday through Thursday, 8.30am to 2pm. Some also open 3 to 5pm in winter, 4 to 6pm in summer.

Aside from Thomas Cook or American Express (see below), it's usually quickest to **exchange money** or **travellers' cheques** at the **24-hour** Bank Misr exchange bureaux in the *Nile Hilton* and the *Ramses Hilton*, and outside the *Helnan Shepheard*; or at branches in other major hotels and off Midan Ramses, which are open daily till 8pm. However, none of the banks will change New Zealand dollars, or Scottish and Northern Irish sterling banknotes, and most will not change Israeli shekels (Bank Misr at the *Nile Hilton* is an exception). **Visa** or **MasterCard** holders can obtain cash advances in Egyptian pounds from the Bank of America (106 Sharia Qasr al-Aini, a couple of blocks south of Midan Tahrir), and from larger branches of Bank Misr.

An increasing number of **ATMs** (Bank Misr, National Bank of Egypt, NSGB, HSBC and others) now accept cashcards and credit cards, especially on Sharia Talaat Harb and the streets around in the downtown area, but also in Zamalek, Mohandiseen, and along Sharia Tahrir in Dokki. Malls and five-star hotels also have them. Most ATMs will take Visa, MasterCard, Cirrus, Electron and Plus, but it's a good idea to use machines in tourist areas as these are less likely to reject or swallow foreign cards, and it will be easier to explain what has happened if they do.

Forex

Private exchange bureaux – known as **Forex** – are usually open daily. They are faster and give a better rate for cash than banks and, unlike banks, will usually change Cyprus pounds, Jordanian and Libyan dinars – though not Sudanese pounds, New Zealand dollars, nor Scottish and Northern Irish sterling banknotes, and usually not Israeli shekels either. Some will accept travellers' cheques, but at a worse rate than banks, and they may demand to see receipts. Downtown Forex bureaux include the Horus in Sharia Alfi Bey and others at 6 Sharia el-Bustan, 14 Sharia el-Bustan, 29 Sharia Emad el-Din by the *New Cicil Hotel*, and on the corner of Sharia Qasr el-Nil and Sharia Sherif. There is also one in Midan Ataba at the top of Sharia Abdel Aziz, and one on Midan Hussein, up a flight of stairs opposite *Fishawi's*.

American Express

Aside from its overpriced tours and travel services, **American Express** (Amex for short) can be useful to travellers. Their main office at 15 Sharia Qasr el-Nil (Sat–Thurs 8.30am–5pm; during Ramadan 9am–3pm; ☎02/574 7991 or 7992, ℻574 7997) is the best place to send money or letters, although this mail service (closed Fri) is only available to holders of Amex travellers' cheques or cards. As a rule, it's quicker to change foreign currency or Amex cheques here than in commercial banks. Refunds for lost or stolen cards or travellers' cheques can take weeks, though they claim it's the next day. Amex is acutely suspicious of fraud, which is widespread in Cairo.

Other Amex branches can be found in the *Nile Hilton* (☎02/578 5001), at 21 Sharia Giza in Giza (☎02/567 2216), and 11 Sharia Almaza in Heliopolis (☎02/418 2144). Most of them will allow cardholders to draw out emergency cash on a personal cheque. They will also pay out US$ for Amex travellers' cheques and MoneyGram transfers (see below) for a 1-percent commission.

Thomas Cook

The modern-day descendant of the world's first tourist company, **Thomas Cook** can change foreign currency and most brands of travellers' cheques into Egyptian money. Their central branch at 17 Sharia Bassiouni (daily 8am–5pm; ☎02/574 3955, ℻576 2750) also sells travellers' cheques in return for dollars or sterling, with no nonsense about cardholders. It will also exchange one hard currency for another in the form of travellers' cheques. However, they have a bad reputation when it comes to lost or stolen travellers' cheques; you may have to kick up a fuss – or even demonstrate outside – to get a full refund.

There are **other branches** of Thomas Cook in the *Semiramis Intercontinental* (☎02/795 8544, ℻795 7061); at the airport (terminal 1, ☎02/265 3147, ℻290 4856); in Bulaq (World Trade Centre, 1191 Corniche el-Nil ☎02/578 0808, ℻578 0809); in Heliopolis (7 Sharia Baghdad ☎02/417 3511 or 3512, ℻418 5406; and 33 Sharia Nabil el Wakkad ☎02/419 4082, ℻414 8601); Mohandiseen (☎02/346 7187, ℻303 4530); and Ma'adi (88 Street 9, Station Square ☎02/359 1419, ℻358 2651).

Money transfers

There are several ways of **transferring money from abroad**. Transfers using MoneyGram (see p.44) can be picked up at any office of Thomas Cook or American Express, either in Egyptian pounds or, with a 1-percent commission charge, in US dollars. Western Union transfers (see p.44) can be picked up at branches of Misr America Bank (8 Sharia Ibrahim Naguib, Garden City ☎02/795 7071 or 7073; 12 Sharia Nadi el-Seid, Dokki ☎02/761 6623–7; or

6 Sharia Boutros Ghali, Heliopolis ☎02/258 8646; all open Mon–Thurs & Sun 8.30am–1.30pm), or at branches of Intel Business Associates (1079 Corniche el-Nil, Garden City ☎02/797 1385–6; 24 Sharia Suriya, Mohandiseen ☎02/331 3533; 27a Sharia el-Hegaz, Heliopolis ☎02/451 4544; 31 Sharia Golf, Ma'adi ☎02/359 6070; plus branches in Shubra and Nasr City, all open daily except Fri 9am–9pm). Thomas Cook will also accept transfers from any of their offices abroad (see p.44).

If for some reason you still prefer to send money by bank transfer, you will probably have to open an account with a bank in Cairo first. Banks with good international connections include: Barclays, opposite the AUC on Sharia Qasr al-Aini (☎02/354 2195, ℱ355 2746); Bank of America, 106 Sharia Qasr al-Aini (☎02/354 7788, ℱ355-5023), with a good reputation for transfers from the US; Citibank, 4 Sharia Ahmed Pasha, Garden Cit (☎02/355 1877, ℱ355 7743).

If you wish to use money received at banks to **buy travellers' cheques** at Thomas Cook or Amex, you must produce a Certificate of Transaction (which you have to request at the issuing bank) rather than an ordinary exchange receipt, proving that your Egyptian currency was legally acquired.

Bureaucracy

Most foreigners are no longer required to register with the authorities when entering Egypt; however, any **bureaucratic matters** involving visa extensions, travel permits and the like are almost certain to induce frustration. There's little choice but to relax and go with the flow – we've included some guidelines here to help ease your way through the ordeal.

Visa extensions at the Mugamma

Extending your visa entails visiting the **Mugamma**, that bureaucratic behemoth on Midan Tahrir (daily except Fri 8am–2pm). Display patience and good humour when dealing with the Mugamma; only stage a tantrum or nervous breakdown as a last resort. To avoid the crush, arrive first thing in the morning or during the evening shift. Unless you're certain which numbered "window" is currently appropriate (details below may become outmoded), check with the **information** desk upstairs on the first floor, before going through the door on your left.

For a six-month **tourist visa extension**, go to window #38 – accessed via entrance 4 on the same floor – and pick up a form (£E8.20). You need to provide a photocopy of the page in your passport with your photo on and also the page which carries your original visa – there are copying facilities on the ground floor. Take your form to window #47 to get a stamp (£E3.10), and then back to window #38 where your new visa will be issued. Windows #37–39 issue **tourist residence visas**; **re-entry visas** are handled by #1–4. In case of lost or stolen passports (see below), replacement entry stamps are obtainable from rooms #1 and #2; however, these may not pass muster with the Libyan, Syrian or Sudanese consulates.

Travel permits for restricted areas

Permits to travel in restricted areas (off-*piste* in the deep desert; on minor Delta and Sinai roads; between Mersa Alam and the Sudanese border) are usually issued by Military Intelligence (Mukaharabat 26), whose office is in Sharia

Manshia el-Bakry in Heliopolis. Rather than apply to them directly, however, your first approach should be to the Tourist Police at 5 Sharia Adly. You will need to show that you have a good reason for wanting to be in the area in question. Applications will require two photos and photocopies of the identifying pages of your passport and your Egyptian entry visa, plus justification for your journey. Processing takes anywhere between four and fourteen days. You should not need any special permit to travel directly from Mersa Matrouh to the Libyan border, for example if taking a bus or service taxi to Benghazi or Tripoli, but this does sometimes change so it is wise to check first.

Student cards

ISIC student cards are obtainable at Egyptian Student Travel Services, 23 Sharia el-Manial on Roda Island (☏02/531 0330; Mon–Thurs, Sat & Sun 8am–8pm, Fri 9am–6pm). You can get there by walking from El-Malek el-Suleh metro. The card costs £E50, and you'll need one passport photo as well as proof of student status – a letter or ID card from your own university is best. ISIC cards can also be obtained unofficially through some of Cairo's budget hotels. You can find out which ones by asking around, but there's no guarantee that you won't be sold a fake card, and the tourist police may not be amused if you try to use less-than-kosher cards at certain archeological sites.

Passport photos, photocopying and translations

Passport photos can be obtained from the studio in room #99 on the ground floor of the Mugamma (four colour photos for £E13.50, b/w £E11), or from photo booths in places like the *Nile Hilton* and even some metro stations. The best deal is offered by Mitry Colour, 3rd floor, 127 Sharia Ramses, at the corner of Sharia Khan el-Khouly (daily 10am–10pm), which charges only £E10 for eight photos delivered while you wait, or £E4 for a dozen photos plus one large print if you are prepared to wait until the next day to collect them. Another good deal is at the Kodak Shop, 20 Sharia Adly (see "Film and processing", p.262); they have a digital camera system and charge £E15 for twenty photos ready in five minutes – and you can have as many poses as you want.

Several shops along 26th July Street and Sharia Mahmoud (near the AUC Library) advertise **photocopying** services. For **translations**, contact Fouad Nemah, 2nd floor, 37 Sharia Qasr el-Nil (☏02/392 2124), or 14a Sharia Sherif, Heliopolis (☏02/454 5550; both offices open Mon–Thurs & Sun 8.30am–2.30pm).

Embassies, foreign visas and missing passports

Cairo is a major centre for acquiring visas, and travellers embarking on trans-African or Middle Eastern journeys, or long-distance flights, would do well to sort things out here. Most embassies and consulates are in Garden City, Zamalek, Dokki or Mohandiseen. Since everyday business is handled by consulates rather than embassies, we've listed the former only if there are two separate addresses.

For those applying for **foreign visas**, some countries require you to provide a **letter of recommendation** – which basically approves your visa application – from your own embassy. For some nationalities they're free, while others have to pay through the nose for them. Americans should note that their embassy is unlikely to issue letters of recommendation for its citizens to visit countries whose governments are considered hostile to the US; in particular, they will not issue one, nor do anything to help you, if you are applying for a visa to visit Sudan, let alone Libya (which it is illegal under US law for US citizens to visit).

Lost or stolen passports should be reported to the police as soon as possible. You'll receive a slip of paper indicating the police file number; take this and two photos plus any personal ID to your consulate to apply for a new passport. Then bring this and the police report to the Mugamma for verification of entry (see above). You'll also need to obtain a new Egyptian visa.

Algeria 14 Sharia Brazil, Zamalek ☎ 02/736 8527, ℱ 736 4158 (see map p.192). You need 4 photos, 4 photocopies of the page of your passport with your personal details, a letter of recommendation and a fee (currently £E136) to get a visa. Sun & Tues 9.30am–1pm, Mon & Thurs noon–1pm.

Australia 11th floor, World Trade Centre, 1191 Corniche el-Nil, Bulaq; 200m north of the 26th July Bridge ☎ 02/575 0444, ℱ 578 1638, ℮ austremb@dfat.gov.au, out-of-hours emergency number ☎ 012/213 7232. Letters of recommendation £E30. Mon–Wed & Sun 8.30am–noon & 1.30–4pm, Thurs 8.30am–1.30pm.

Canada 26 Sharia Kamel el-Shenawi, Garden City ☎ 02/794 3110, ℱ 796 3548, ⓦ www.canada-eg .com (see map p.110). Letters of recommendation £E125. Mon–Thurs & Sun 9am–2pm.

Congo (DRC) 5 Sharia Mansur Mohammed, Zamalek ☎ 02/735 3662, ℱ 735 4342 (see map p.192). Visas cost £E1000. Two photos and a letter of recommendation required. Mon–Fri 10am–3pm.

Cyprus 23a Sharia Ismail Mohammed, Zamalek ☎ 02/736 1288, ℱ 735 5170 (see map p.192). Office hours Mon–Fri 9am–3pm; visas dealt with Mon & Thurs 9–11am only, but most nationalities don't need them.

Denmark 6th floor, 12 Sharia Hassan Sabri, Zamalek ☎ 02/735 2502, ℱ 735 1780 (see map p.192). Letters of recommendation £E85. Mon–Thurs & Sun 8am–3pm.

Eritrea 6 Sharia el-Fellah, Mohandiseen ☎ 02/303 3504, ℱ 303 0516 (see map p.192).

Ethiopia 6 Sharia Rahman Hussein, Dokki ☎ 02/335 3696, ℱ 335 3699 (see map p.192). One photo, but no letter of recommendation required. Visas (US$63 single-entry for most nationalities, though US citizens get a US$70 multiple-entry visa) are issued in 24hr. Mon–Thurs & Sat 8.30am–4.30pm.

India 2nd floor, 37 Talaat Harb ☎ 02/393 9152, ℱ 393 6702 (see map p.111). Fifteen-day transit visas cost $10 or the equivalent in Egyptian pounds, six-month multiple-entry visas $40, one-year visas $65, free for South Africans, Americans pay $20 extra. Two photos required, and letters of recommendation currently required by Irish, Australians and New Zealanders, but not by

British, Americans or Canadians. Visas issued within 2–3 days. Special permits for places like Sikkim not issued. Mon–Thurs & Sun 8–11am.

Ireland 7th floor, Abu el-Feda Tower, just north of the Zamalek Bridge, Zamalek ☎ 02/735 8264, ℱ 736 2863 (see map p.192). Free letters of recommendation. Mon–Thurs & Sun 9am–noon.

Israel 6 Sharia Ibn Malek, Giza, near the El-Gama'a Bridge ☎ 02/761 0458, ℱ 761 0414 (see map p.176). Look for the security guards at the entrance or the Israeli flag flying aloft. Most foreigners can, in fact, obtain tourist visas at the border. Mon–Thurs & Sun 10.30am–12.30pm.

Jordan 6 Sharia Gohini, Dokki, 2 blocks west of the *Sheraton* ☎ 02/748 5566, ℱ 760 1027 (see map p.193). One photo and $88, but no letter of recommendation required. Open Mon–Thurs & Sun: applications taken 9am–noon; visas issued same day 1.30–2.30pm.

Kenya 29 Sharia el-Quds el-Sharif, Mohandiseen ☎ 02/345 3628, ℱ 302 6979 (see map p.192). Two photos and £E193, but no letter of recommendation required. Visas issued in 24hr. Mon–Thurs & Sun 9am–2pm.

Lebanon 22 Sharia Mansour Mohammed, Zamalek ☎ 02/738 2823–6, ℱ 738 2818 (see map p.192). One photo and a photocopy of your passport details required, plus £E150, but no letter of recommendation; takes one day. Daily except Fri 9.30am–noon.

Libya 7 Sharia Saleh el-Ayoub, Zamalek ☎ 02/735 1269, ℱ 735 0072 (see map p.192). Visas generally only issued to Egyptian residents, but they may be open to persuasion if you have an invitation from someone in Libya. Americans are forbidden to visit Libya by the US State Department. Two photos, a letter of recommendation and a stamp in your passport giving its details in Arabic are required; most embassies supply one free, except Britain (£E300; see p.273 for cheaper translations). Daily except Fri 9am–2pm.

Netherlands 18 Sharia Hassan Sabry, Zamalek ☎ 02/739 5500, ℱ 735 5249 (see map p.192). Letters of recommendation not issued. Mon–Thurs & Sun 8am–3.30pm.

New Zealand c/o Emeco Travel Services, 4th floor, 2 Sharia Talaat Harb ☎ 02/574 4062 (see map p.110). Cannot issue letters of recommendation – get them from the British embassy. Mon–Thurs & Sun 9am–3pm.

Norway 8 Sharia al-Gezira, Zamalek ☎02/735 3340, ⓕ737 0709, ⓦwww.norway.org.eg. Letters of recommendation free. Mon–Thurs & Sun 10am–noon.

Palestine 33 Sharia el-Nadha, Dokki ☎02/760 2997 or 2998, ⓕ760 2996.

Saudi Arabia 2 Sharia Ahmed Nessim, Giza ☎02/ⓕ760 4560, ⓕ760 4590 (see map p.176).

South Africa 18th floor, 21–23 Sharia Giza ☎02/571 7238–9, ⓕ571 7241. Mon–Thurs & Sun 9am–noon. Letter of recommendation free.

Sudan 1 Sharia Mohammed Fahmi el-Sayed, Garden City (see map p.110) ☎02/794 9661, ⓕ794 2693. Four photos, $56 (in US dollars only) and a letter of recommendation needed (the US embassy is unlikely to issue this for travel to Sudan); one-month visas usually take between 4 and 7 days. Mon–Thurs & Sun 9am–1pm.

Sweden 13 Sharia Mohammed Mazhar, Zamalek ☎02/736 4132 or 1132, ⓕ735 4357, ⓔsveamcai @link.net (see map p.192). Letters of recommendation E£50. Mon–Thurs & Sun 9am–2pm.

Syria 18 Sharia Abdel Raheem Sabry, Dokki ☎02/749 5210, ⓕ335 8232 (see map p.192). Prices and requirements for visitors vary, though everyone needs to bring two photos. British and Irish need E£265 plus a letter of recommendation; Americans E£310 but no letter; Canadians E£285 no letter; Australians E£155 plus letter; New Zealanders E£305 no letter. Visas take 1–3 days to issue. Daily except Fri 9am–12.45pm.

Tunisia 26 Sharia Gezira, Zamalek ☎02/341 8962, ⓕ341 2479 (see map p.192). Two passport photocopies, 2 photos and a letter of recommendation required: visas (E£29) take 2–15 days. Daily except Fri 9.30am–1pm.

Turkey 25 Sharia Falaki, Bab al-Luq ☎02/796 3318, ⓕ795 8110 (see map p.110). Most Western nationals who need visas can obtain them routinely on arrival. Mon–Fri 9–11am.

Uganda 48 Sharia al-'Urubah, Heliopolis ☎02/291 5953, ⓕ760 8601. Two photos and E£135, but no letter of recommendation required. Visas take 24hr to issue. Mon–Fri 8.30am–2.30pm.

UK 7 Sharia Ahmed Ragheb, Garden City ☎02/794 0852, ⓕ794 0859, ⓦwww.britishembassy.org.eg (see map p.110). Letters of recommendation E£84. Mon–Thurs & Sun 9am–1pm.

USA 5 Sharia Amerika Latina, Garden City ☎02/797 2301, ⓕ797 3602, emergencies ☎797 3300, ⓦwww.usembassy.egnet.net/consular.htm (see map p.110). Lost or stolen passports replaced overnight for E£300; limited passports issued for travel to Israel on request. Letters of recommendation are free, but the embassy may refuse to issue them for travel to countries it considers unsafe, in particular those with regimes opposed by the US government. Mon–Thurs & Sun 8am–noon (open for phone enquiries 8am–4.30pm).

Yemen 28 Sharia Amin Bey al-Rafi'i, off Midan al-Misaha, Dokki ☎02/761 4224, 4225 or 4226, ⓕ760 4815 (see map p.192). Tourist visas (E£190) not currently issued for individual travel. Tues, Wed & Sun 9am–1pm.

Cultural centres, clubs and language courses

Cultural centres are good for catching up on home news and making contacts; longer-staying visitors can join their libraries and sign up for **language courses**. Other courses are on offer at AUC Public Service Division, 28 Sharia Falaki (☎02/797 6872 or 6873, ⓔhamgiagi@aucegypt.edu), and the International Language Institute (ILI), 2 Sharia Mohammed Bayoumi, off Sharia Merghani, Heliopolis (☎02/418 9212 or 291 9295, ⓔili@ritsec3.com .eg), and another ILI (same name but different firm) at 3 Mahmoud Azmi, Sahafayeen (☎02/746 3087 or 302 8358, ⓕ303 5624, ⓔili@starnet.com.eg); see map p.192. **Private tutors** advertise in all these places. To find out about public lectures at the AUC, contact Mona Zaki (Oct–May; ☎02/357 5021, ⓔmonazaki@aucegypt.edu).

Institutes

American Research Center in Egypt 1st floor, 2 Midan Simon Bolivar, Garden City ☎02/794 8239. Organizes lectures and day-trips.

British Council 192 Corniche el-Nil, Aguza, near the Circus ☎02/303 1514, ⓦwww.britcoun.org.eg. Large library (annual membership E£60), including videos and cassettes. Also sponsors visiting cultural acts. Daily except Fri 8am–8.30pm.

Canadian Research Center 32 Road 103, Ma'adi ☎ 02/358 7214. Monthly lectures. Oct–April Mon–Thurs & Sun 8.30am–4pm.

Egyptian Centre for International Cultural Cooperation (ECIC) 11 Sharia Shagar al-Durr, Zamalek ☎ 02/736 5419. Organizes Arabic classes, exhibitions, recitals and occasionally tours. Daily except Fri 10am–noon & 5–7pm (but exhibitions open 10am–3pm & 4–9pm).

Goethe Institute 5 Sharia Abdel Salam Arif ☎ 02/575 9877. Public reading room; library membership and borrowing rights with ID. Mon–Thurs & Sun 1–7pm.

Israeli Academic Centre in Cairo 92 Sharia el-Nil, Dokki ☎ 02/749 6232. Lectures. Mon–Thurs & Sun 9am–3pm.

Netherlands Flemish-Institute 1 Sharia Mahmoud Azmi, Zamalek ☎ 02/738 2521–2, ✉ nvic@rite.com. English lectures about Egypt on Thurs at 5.30pm (Sept–June). Mon–Fri 9am–2pm.

Health care

For minor complaints, simply consult the nearest **pharmacy**: pharmacists can prescribe a wide range of drugs, including antibiotics. There are a number of 24-hour pharmacies, including: Talaat Harb Pharmacy, 33 Sharia Talaat Harb ☎ 02/392 5341; Al-Esa'af, 27 26th July St ☎ 02/574 3369; Al-Ataba, Midan Ataba ☎ 02/591 0831; and Al-Zamalek, 3 Shagar al-Durr, Zamalek ☎ 02/736 1338.

There are English- or French-speaking **private doctors** all over Cairo. A consultation normally costs £E40–50, excluding drugs. Some practices that are used to foreign patients include: Dr Naguib Badir at the Anglo-American Hospital, next to the Cairo Tower on Gezira Island (general practice; ☎ 02/735 6162 or 4); Dr Doss or Dr Emad Rushdi, *Nile Hilton Hotel* clinic (☎ 02/578 0444); Dr Zoheir Farid, 16 Abdel Khaliq Sarwat (tropical medicine; ☎ 02/392 5023.

Hospitals require a cash deposit of at least £E150 (it can go as high as £E1000) to cover the cost of treatment; medical insurance is not always accepted (though you can reclaim expenses later). The following are well equipped and used to foreigners: Anglo-American Hospital by Cairo Tower, Gezira ☎ 02/735 6162 or 6164; Al-Salam International Hospital, on the Corniche in Ma'adi ☎ 02/524 0077; Cairo Medical Centre, on Sharia Higaz, by the *Andalus* restaurant, just off Midan Roxi, Heliopolis ☎ 02/450 4903 or 4904. For any of these hospitals, take a taxi if you can; otherwise use the private **Al-Salam ambulance service** (same phone numbers as the hospital). **Public ambulances** offer free transport to whichever hospital is the nearest: call ☎ 123.

There are two places that provide **vaccinations** against cholera, yellow fever and other diseases. The Egyptian Organization for Biological Products and Vaccines, at 51 Sharia Wazart el-Zaraa (☎ 02/761 1111; daily 24hr), 100m north of the 6th October Bridge/Agricultural Museum intersection – take the first right inside the gate, then go round the side of the building on the left and up the stairs. It has English-speaking doctors and vaccines against cholera (£E8.50), yellow fever (£E50) and meningitis (£E29). The Public Health Vaccination Centre (daily except Fri 10am–1pm & 3–6pm), at the rear of the lobby of the largely disused *Hotel Continental-Savoy* on Midan Opera, is highly efficient, with no red tape or fuss. They do yellow fever jabs for E£1, but no others. If you need a **dentist**, try Dr Emad Zaghloul (☎ 02/345 5429), whose practice is in Mohandiseen.

Post and telecommunications

The **central post office** on Midan Ataba (daily except Fri 8am–7pm, during Ramadan 9am–4pm) and other main branches (daily except Fri 8.30am–3pm, during Ramadan 9am–3pm) are often extremely crowded. Mail can be sent to Ataba's **poste restante** or general delivery office (daily except Fri 8am–6pm, Ramadan 8am–4pm; Poste Restante, Post Office Ataba, 11511 Cairo). The entrance for the poste restante counter is in Sharia el-Bedak, round the corner from the main entrance, to the right of the building as you look at it – go to the last door, signposted "Private boxes", and it's inside at counter #10. They hold mail for a month, with no charge to collect – just be sure to bring your passport. They are prone to file letters under the wrong name, but it helps if your surname is underlined and highlighted on anything sent to you. Problems are less likely to occur if you have mail sent **c/o American Express** on Sharia Qasr el-Nil (see p.44); however, this service is only for holders of Amex cards or Amex travellers' cheques.

Although letters posted in the lobby of the *Nile Hilton* are said to arrive faster than those dropped in ordinary mailboxes (painted blue for overseas mail), **airmail letters** can still take two weeks to reach the British Isles, and three weeks to the US. However, Ataba's **express mail service** – opposite the Poste Restante – (daily except Fri 8am–7pm) promises worldwide delivery in two days; items under 500 grams cost £E57.10 to the British Isles, £E66 to North America, Australia or New Zealand. Any post office can send **registered letters**. It's quicker to buy **stamps** from hotel shops or cigarette kiosks, which charge about 5pt above normal rates (£E1.25 for a postcard/letter to anywhere in the world).

Parcels can only be mailed abroad from the Ramses Square post office. Your package should be taken in unsealed, submitted to customs for inspection, packaged up (this is done for you on the premises for E£2–3), and finally weighed and dispatched. Current air-mail prices for a 10kg package are: E£264.50 to the UK or Ireland, E£397.80 to the USA, E£394.50 to Canada, E£508.90 to Australia, E£588.10 to New Zealand. Surface mail is much slower (2–6 months), and saves you little money unless you intend to send something very heavy (in which case a shipping agent would be better). Anyone **receiving parcels** in Egypt should beware of **import duty** (for example, £E60 on a pair of contact lenses).

A faster and more reliable way of sending and receiving packages is by **courier**. International courier companies with offices in Cairo include DHL (El Mona Towers, 16 Sharia Lubnan, Mohandiseen ☎02/302 9801, ⓦwww.dhl .com/wrd/eg.html), FedEx (19 Sharia Khalid Ibn el-Walid ☎02/768 8888, ⓦwww.fedex.com; daily except Fri 11am–8pm) and UPS (7 Sharia Hussein Zohdy, Medinet Nasr ☎02/414 1456, ⓔeur1feb@europe.ups.com; 8 Road 78, Ma'adi ☎02/750 8555).

Phones

Cairo's telephone system keeps on being restructured, and the first three digits of Cairo phone numbers (indicating the local exchange) are particularly liable to change. Recent changes have affected the Downtown area and Garden City (where 35 at the beginning of a number has changed to 79), Zamalek (where 340 at the beginning of a number has changed to 735, 341 to 736, and 342 to 737), Mohandiseen (where 34 at the beginning of a number has changed to 74, and 36 to 76), Heliopolis (where 24 at the beginning of a number has changed to 63), and Ma'adi (where 350 at the beginning of a num-

The Nile Valley – most people's target after Cairo – is too distant for **day excursions** from the city. Elsewhere, however, you can choose between a jaunt to the seaside or remoter pyramids, a river trip or desert monasteries – and still be back in Cairo the same night. The notes below are an outline of possibilities and are intended (with the exception of the entries on the Nile Barrages and Muqattam Hills) to be used in conjunction with the full accounts in other chapters.

Those without the time to organize their own excursions might consider taking a set or tailor-made tour organized by a reputable travel agent or tour company (and there are plenty of disreputable ones about, so beware). Those worth trying include De Castro Tours (12 Sharia Talaat Harb ☎02/574 3213, Ⓔdecastrotours@link.net), Noga Tours (28 Sharia Quday Shubra ☎02/203 9310, ⓌWww.nogatours.com) and Eastmar Tours (in the passage of 13 Sharia Qasr el-Nil ☎02/574 5024).

The Nile Barrages at Qanatir

Roughly 20km downriver from Cairo, the Nile divides into two great branches which define the Delta, whose flow is controlled by the **Nile Barrages** at **Qanatir**. Decoratively arched and turreted, this splendid piece of Victorian civil engineering is surrounded by shady parks and lush islets – an ideal spot for a picnic.

Originally conceived by Mohammed Ali's French hydro-engineer, Mougel Bey, the Barrages were later realized as part of the nationwide hydrological system designed by Sir Colin Scott-Moncrieff. At the eastern end of the 438-metre-long Rosetta Barrage lies the *Istarahah al-Qanatir* or **Presidential Villa** that Islamic Jihad once considered attacking with an anti-aircraft cannon from the garden of one of their member's homes, across the river. Egypt's **State Yacht** (originally King Farouk's, on which he sailed into exile) is often moored at the quay.

Providing you don't come on Friday, when the area is ridiculously crowded, the Barrages make a pleasant excursion. Qanatir is accessible by bus #210 from the Abdel Mouneem Riyad terminal on Midan Tahrir, or by ferry from the Maspero Dock in front of the Television Building. Ferries leave hourly (6am–6pm; £E2) on Friday and Sunday and take two hours; or you can take a pleasure boat (daily round trips; £E5) to the south of Maspero Dock; the bus journey is less appealing. Travelling by felucca is very slow, since the mast has to be lowered at every bridge.

The Muqattam Hills and Wadi Digla

The **Muqattam Hills**, rising beyond Cairo, are seldom visited by tourists but readily accessible by #401 buses from Midan Ataba and Tahrir. Zigzagging up the hillside past caves and quarries, ruined shrines and guarded outposts, they terminate at **Medinet Muqattam**, an upmarket suburb whose avenues are flanked by villas and casinos. The Muqattam Corniche, circling the edge of the plateau, offers spectacular views across the Citadel and most of Cairo – an unforgettable vista at sunset.

People planning desert expeditions might consider a few training runs below the Muqattam. Victorian travellers used to engage a dragoman to lead them to the **Petrified Forests** – two expanses littered with broken, fossilized trunks, thought to date from the Miocene Period. The larger one (marked on our map of Greater Cairo) is really only accessible with a guide, but would-be explorers can easily find the "Little Forest" on the Jebel el-Khasab plateau, north of the Digla–Ain Sukhna road.

The **Digla–Ain Sukhna road** turns east off the Nile Valley expressway near a *zebaleen* village beyond Ma'adi. Roughly 25km from the turn-off, you'll pass the Jebel el-Khasab on the left; if you keep on, you'll notice various tracks leading off to the right, which eventually converge on a main desert track running east–west. By following it west, back towards Digla, you'll pass through several meandering wadis before the way is blocked by **Wadi Digla**. This miniature canyon is good for **rock-climbing** and **bird-watching**; bring water, food and shade.

The Fayoum

Fayoum Oasis, 100km southwest of Cairo, is another place to escape. Though Fayoum City holds little appeal, you can walk from its centre into lush countryside within half an hour. Irrigated by water wheels and canals, the Fayoum was a major centre during the Middle Kingdom, Ptolemaic and Roman times, as evinced by various ruins around its periphery. While some involve bumpy rides into the desert, others are reasonably accessible from Fayoum City by local bus or service taxi, with a pleasant walk to the site itself. The **ruins of Karanis** lie just off the Fayoum–Cairo road; the dramatic **"Collapsed Pyramid" of Maidum** a short ride from El-Wasta. Both sites are usually deserted, in blissful contrast to Giza and Saqqara. Either makes a good day excursion, but you should bring food and drink and be on your way by mid-morning. Service taxis from Midan Giza, or from Sharia Orabi by Ramses station, are the fastest way of reaching Fayoum City (2hr). See p.284 for details. The Maidum pyramid (see p.506) can be reached by service taxi from El-Wasta station, an easy train ride from Ramses.

Alexandria and the Monasteries of Wadi Natrun

A three-hour journey from Cairo, Egypt's second city and summer capital embraces the Mediterranean with its sweeping Corniche. **Alexandria** has little to show for its ancient glory (personified by Cleopatra) or former decadence (celebrated by Lawrence Durrell), but its fresh seafood and cool breezes are delightful. Aside from a quick spin through the Greco-Roman museum and a literary pilgrimage around the haunts of Durrell, E.M. Forster and the poet Constantine Cavafy, Alexandria's attractions include a Royal Jewellery Museum housed in a spectacularly over-the-top mansion, and the rather spooky Catacombs of Kom es-Shoqafa. With the discovery of Cleopatra's Palace on the ocean floor in Alex's Eastern Harbour (see p.601 for details), there may soon be even more to occupy visitors. Alex can be reached by bus from Aboud terminal (departures every 45min), train from Ramses station (2hr 10min on the *Turbino*), or service taxi from either of those (Aboud has more departures). For details, see p.283.

The Desert Road to Alex passes the turn-off for the fortified **Monasteries of Wadi Natrun**, which have long provided the Coptic Church's spiritual leadership. When not undergoing periodic fasts, the monks welcome pilgrims and other visitors. The most accessible of the monasteries are **Deir Anba Bishoi** and **Deir al-Suryani**, 10km from the rest stop on the highway (which can be reached by bus or service taxi from Cairo). To visit all four, it's best to rent a taxi or car for the day, either in Cairo or at the rest stop, which is roughly midway between Alexandria and Cairo. For more on Wadi Natrun and how to get there, see p.486.

Unless you start very early or have a car, it's not really feasible to visit both Alexandria and the monasteries in one day.

Ismailiya, Ain Sukhna and the Red Sea Monasteries

The canal city of **Ismailiya** is verdantly peaceful, with handsome promenades and colonial-era villas – a nice place to stroll or bicycle, also favoured by Egyptians as a honeymoon destination. Its museum and Garden of Stelae attest to ancient canals that once linked the Delta with the Red Sea; the House of Ferdinand de Lesseps commemorates the founder of the Suez Canal, one of the world's crucial waterways. Outside town you can watch boats slip between the desert on either side. Along the eastern embankment runs the Bar-Lev Line, a fortified Israeli barrier that was stormed on the first day of the 1973 war. Ismailiya itself can be reached by bus or service taxi from Turgoman Garage (2–3hr). For details, see Chapter Six (p.661).

Cairenes with transport visit **Ain Sukhna** on the Gulf of Suez for its **beaches** and offshore coral reefs. If you fancy swimming and **snorkelling**, it's worth renting a car

continues overleaf

from previous page

for the day rather than switching buses at Suez and having to hitch back. Bring food and drink (plus snorkel if required), since they're not obtainable there. Don't wander into areas ringed by barbed wire, which are still mined. Ain Sukhna is approachable via Suez (3hr) or by the Digla–Ain Sukhna desert road (see opposite). Further south and high inland are the **Red Sea Monasteries** of St Paul and St Anthony. With a car, you could combine a visit to St Anthony's with a swim at Ain Sukhna, but unless you leave at the crack of dawn it's impossible to get to both monasteries and return the same night. All three places are described in Chapter Eight (pp.745–748).

ber has changed to 358, 351 to 359, 352 to 702, 353 to 703, 36 to 76, 375 to 380, 376 to 768, and 377 to 706).

International calls can now be made using phonecards (see Basics p.60), and there are now Menatel cardphones at street corners citywide, Cairo's main **telephone and telegraph offices** (open 24hr), and other locations. There are four main offices: at 8 Sharia Adly; alongside the *Windsor Hotel* on Alfi Bey; on Sharia Ramses, opposite Sharia Tawfiqia; and 13 Midan Tahrir (the smallest). There are others in Midan Ataba and further afield, sometimes worth trying if you want to avoid queuing; for example, the one on Sharia Maglis al-Shad, by the National Assembly (ten minutes south of Midan Tahrir). Calls are booked and paid for in advance, and can either be taken in a booth or directed to an outside number such as a hotel. It remains slightly cheaper to make calls via a telephone office than on a street cardphone, and a lot cheaper in either of those than from a hotel. The cheapest way of all is with a PIN card (see p.60).

Telegrams, telexes and faxes

Telephone offices can also send **telegrams**, which you pay for by the word (including the address) – 60pt a word to the US, for example.

Faxes can be sent and received at the four downtown telephone offices (open 24hr); the EMS office by Ataba post office (daily except Fri 8am–7pm). The EMS office offers the lowest sending rates (British Isles or North America £E5 for the first minute, £E3.25 thereafter; Australia and New Zealand £E6 for the first minute, £E4.95 thereafter), but the phone offices do not charge much more (£E5.50 to the British Isles or North America; £E6.50 to Australia or New Zealand). To receive a fax costs around £E1 at any of these places, and is free for American Express clients at their office. EMS and the phone offices will inform you of its arrival if your name and phone number are at the top of the page. Fax numbers: Amex ⓕ02/574 7997; EMS ⓕ02/390 4250; downtown telephone offices at Sharia Adly ⓕ02/393 3909, Sharia Ramses ⓕ02/578 0977, Alfi Bey ⓕ02/589-7635, Midan Tahrir ⓕ02/578 0979.

Internet and email

Internet offices open and close with dazzling frequency, and the newest ones are likely to offer the lowest rates. You should have no trouble finding offices that charge £E5 an hour, and connections at all of them are reasonable, though few have fast broadband connections. Downtown, the most convenient offices are 4U at 8 Midan Talaat Harb (daily 9am–midnight), and Hany at 16 Abdel Khaliq Sarwat (daily 10am–10pm), both currently charging £E5 per hour. Onyx at 26 Sharia Bassiouny, downstairs from the *Hotel Dahab*, has similar rates, but its opening hours are sporadic. The *Berlin* and *Dahab* hotels also offer cheap Internet connections for their guests. For fast connections, 24-hour opening and comfortable surroundings at the same price, the best Internet office in town is the Internet Café at 25 Sharia Ismail Mohammed in Zamalek.

Travel details

Cairo is the linchpin of Egypt's transport network and its main link to the outside world. Many parts of the country are accessible from the capital by several forms of transport, while numerous airlines compete over flights to Europe, Africa and Asia.

Trains

All trains depart from **Ramses Station** (*Mahatat Ramses*), a cavernous beehive seemingly designed to bemuse. Almost all trains to points south halt at **Giza Station** 15min after leaving Ramses.

Ramses Station

Entering **Ramses Station** from Midan Ramses, you'll find the **tourist information office**, tourist police and sleeper booking offices on the left; to your right are platforms 1–4, serving Alexandria, the Delta and Canal Zone. Tickets for air-conditioned services to these destinations are sold at the far end of the main hall, directly opposite the main entrance from Midan Ramses, but if you want to use a slow, non-air-conditioned train, you'll find the ticket office outside, through the doorway to the left of the a/c ticket office.

To the right of the a/c ticket office is the doorway through to platforms 8–11, where southbound trains depart for Middle and Upper Egypt. All tickets for trains on this route, bar sleepers, are sold from offices alongside the furthest platform, #11, accessible via an underpass. Note that foreigners travelling to Upper Egypt are only allowed to use certain services (see below).

Opposite platform 4, a round **information kiosk** (☎02/575 3555) should be able to advise on departures, schedules and any problems you may have with ticket buying (although you may need to fall back on the tourist office if no one in the information booth can speak English). Card-carrying members of the Tourist Friends Association may also approach you, offering to help; they're quite sincere and don't expect *baksheesh*.

There is a **left luggage** (baggage deposit) office at one of the entrances from Midan Ramses (by platform 1). It charges £E1.50 per item per day, and is open 24/7.

Tickets

Buying tickets is rarely easy. In addition to there being separate offices for northbound services (by platform 4) and southbound services (by platform 11), each section has separate windows for 1st class/2nd class superior seating (which is reservable and has a/c) and ordinary 2nd class/3rd class (which isn't and doesn't), and these may change

locations. You have to find the right queue and get your requirements (it helps to have them written down in Arabic) across to clerks who may not give a damn. Tickets can be booked up to a week in advance and should be booked at least a day in advance; 1st and 2nd class superior seats sell out first. The peak seasons for travel are winter (for Upper Egypt) and summer (for Alexandria).

Card-carrying **students** are eligible for 30-percent reductions on all trains except sleepers, which must be booked at their own counters in the main hall. Prices given below are full adult fares.

Regular services and sleepers

At present, full train **timetables** are not available in leaflet or booklet form, but are posted up, in Arabic only, at various points around the station. Unless you can read Arabic, you will have to ask for help from the information office or from friendly passers-by. All services are individually numbered, and the number should be written on your ticket when you reserve a seat. Foreigners are not encouraged to buy ordinary 2nd or 3rd class tickets, and are not allowed to use ordinary services to Upper Egypt (see below).

There are two kinds of services to **Alexandria**: air-conditioned and not. Thirteen trains a day are air-conditioned, which also means fast with limited stops, and require reservations. These air-conditioned trains come in three varieties: Turbini, Spanish and French. The three daily non-stop Turbini trains are the best (currently departing at 8am, 2pm and 7pm; 2hr 10min), followed by the four daily Spanish trains – two non-stop (2hr 10min), and two stopping at Benha, Tanta and Damanhur only (2hr 30min). Slightly cheaper than the Spanish and Turbini services are the six daily French trains, which stop at Benha, Tanta and Damanhur, reaching Alexandria in two and a half hours. Lastly, there are some forty non-air-conditioned trains to Alexandria every day, composed of 2nd and 3rd class carriages only. These trains don't need reservations, cost a fraction of the price of the air-conditioned services, stop everywhere, and can take as long as four hours to reach Alexandria.

The only direct service to **Mersa Matrouh** is on the summer-only sleeper (see below), and failing this, it is far better to travel by bus from Cairo or Alex than to endure the interminable journey in ordinary 2nd or 3rd class from Alexandria.

Apart from the sleeper service (see below), there are nine daily departures for **Aswan** (14–17hr) and five more for **Luxor** (11–12hr). At present however, tourists are only authorized to use two of these trains (departing at 7.30am & 10pm) plus, in summer, the 12.30am "Phantom" service. Foreigners travel in special coaches guarded by armed plainclothes policemen, and are not allowed to buy tickets for any other train. Originally this was for protection from "terrorists", but it did tend to make the tourist trains potential targets for snipers, who occasionally took pot-shots at them on their way through Middle Egypt. Although the danger now seems to have passed, the rule still applies. Fares for ordinary seats (not sleeping berths) are £E67 in 1st class and £E40 in 2nd for Luxor, £E81 and £E47 for Aswan.

Sleeper services

In addition to regular services, there are daily **sleeper services** (8pm) to Upper Egypt, which include a bar and disco on the train. The cost per person for a double cabin is £E331.50 or US$71.30 one-way to Luxor or Aswan (you can stop over at Luxor and continue to Aswan on the same ticket). Solo travellers can reserve the entire cabin for £E495 or US$106.30, or consent to share it with a stranger of the same sex and pay the normal fare. From mid-June until mid-September, there are also six weekly sleeper trains to Mersa Matrouh (daily except Fridays 11pm, arriving 6am).

You can book at the sleeper office, next to the tourist office, until 6pm on the day of departure, but you are best off reserving a sleeper a few days in advance if possible. This can be done at the station, by phone or fax with Abela, who operate the sleeper trains (☎02/738 3682 or 3706, ℻738 3681), or on line at ⓦ www.sleepingtrains.com, where you can also check the latest fares and schedules. Tickets can also be booked through Hamis Travel, whose office is just outside the station, in the building by the third-class ticket office for Alexandria (☎02/574 9275, ℻574 9276). As well as taking Visa and MasterCard, they may also accept sterling or euros, though they prefer Egyptian pounds or US dollars, and they will also take bookings on line (ⓦ www.hamis.com.eg). Their staff tend to be somewhat more helpful than those in the station sleeper office. Bookings can also be made through De Castro Tours at 12 Sharia Talaat Harb, where they'll cost slightly more, or at the Carlson Wagon Lit office by the *Helnan Shepheard* hotel, where they cost more still.

Inter-city buses

Inter-city buses reach most parts of Egypt, making equal or better time than trains. Services depart from two main terminals: Turgoman Garage (services to the Canal Zone, Sinai, the Red Sea, Mersa Matrouh and the Oases, plus some services to Alex and the Delta, and all international departures) and Aboud (services to Alexandria, the Delta, the Fayoum, and Middle and Upper Egypt), neither of which will take bookings over the phone; tickets must be purchased in person. Tickets for East Delta buses to the Sinai can still be purchased at the old Sinai terminal in Abbassiya (which is where buses from the Sinai will probably leave you on arrival – see p.92), and tickets for Mansura and Damietta can still be purchased at Koulali Terminal off Midan Ramses, but the same tickets and buses can all be picked up at Turgoman Garage.

Unless stated otherwise, all services below run daily; however, schedules change, so you shouldn't rely on our timings. You can usually only get information on the spot, but wherever possible we've listed telephone numbers; whether you can get hold of someone who speaks English is of course another matter. As with most things in Egypt, persevere and you'll get there in the end.

Turgoman Garage

The new **Turgoman Garage** in Bulaq – 600m west of Ramses Station on Sharia Shanan – handles the majority of bus departures to destinations within Egypt and beyond. It is not really served by local public transport as yet, but it's an easy walk from Ramses station or from Sharia Ramses by Orabi metro. A taxi from Midan Tahrir should cost around £E3, and certainly not more than £E5. Most of the bus operators have ticket windows by the main entrance.

Two companies offer services to **Alexandria**: the smart A/C Superjet (first window on the left, ☎02/579 8181) buses leave every 30min (6am–11pm; 3hr; £E20), while West Delta Bus Co (fourth window from the left, ☎02/576 5582) services leave half-hourly (6am–1.30pm; 3hr; £E16–20). The West Delta Bus Co also has four daily departures to **Mersa Matrouh** (6hr; £E28–37).

Superjet also has services to **Hurghada** (3 daily; 5–6hr; £E45) and **Sharm el-Sheikh** (4 daily; 5hr; £E65). More frequent but slower services to Sharm (11 daily; 7hr 30min; £E55–65) are operated by East Delta Bus Co (sixth window from the left, ☎02/574 2814), who also run buses to **St Catherine's** (1 daily; 7hr 30min; £E37), **Dahab** (4 daily; 9hr; £E62–75), **Nuweiba** (3 daily; 9hr; £E53–58), **Taba** (3 daily; 10hr; £E74) and **El Arish** (2 daily; 5hr; £E20.50–21.25; tickets at the fifth window from the left). It is still possible to buy tickets for these East Delta buses and to board them at the old Sinai terminal in Abbassiya (☏02/483 9588), but Turgoman is likely to be far more convenient.

In the Canal Zone, East Delta have buses to **Port Said** (20 daily; 3hr; £E14–16), **Suez** (every 15min until 8pm; 2hr; £E7) and **Ismailiya** (every 20min until 7pm; 2hr; £E7). They also have services to the Delta, running to **Mansura** (hourly until 8pm; 2hr; £E8.50–9) and **Damietta** (16 daily; 3hr 30min; £E14–15). In fact, these latter two can be picked up in town at the old Koulali terminal on Sharia Orabi north of Sharia Ramses (☏02/576 6514; see map p.131), and both destinations are in any case better served from Aboud (see below). Also for the Delta, the Middle Delta Bus Co (tickets from an office by the departure quays) has buses to **Tanta** (16 daily; 1hr 30min) and **Mahalla** (16 daily; 2hr), but again there are more frequent departures to these places from Aboud.

The other company operating from Turgoman Garage is the Upper Egypt Bus Co (third window from the left, ☏02/576 0261), whose departures from here serve the Western Desert Oases (but not Siwa, which is reached from Mersa Matrouh or Alexandria). There is one daily departure to **Bahariya** (6hr; £E16), plus two to **Farafra** (8hr; £E30) and four to **Dakhla** (14–16hr; £E43). They have one overnight service to **Luxor** (9hr; £E60) and **Aswan** (12hr; £E70), but again there are more frequent services from Aboud, while the train is similarly priced and much more comfortable.

Aboud Bus Terminal

The **Aboud Bus Terminal**, 3km north of Ramses station, up Sharia Ahmed Helmi by the Sharia Shubra intersection, is now the main terminal for buses and service taxis to Alexandria and the Delta, and buses to Middle and Upper Egypt. It is most easily reached by service taxi microbus from Ramses station (50pt). A taxi will cost around £E2–3 from Ramses Station, £E5–6 from downtown.

The Delta is served by three companies, of which the West Delta Bus Co (☏02/431 6742) runs buses to **Alexandria** (every 45min 7.15am–11pm; 3hr; £E16) and **Damanhur** (every 45min 7.15am–11pm; 2hr; £E10), while Middle Delta Bus Co serves **Tanta** (half-hourly 6.30am–9pm; 1hr 30min; £E5), **Mahalla el-Kubra** (2hr 30min; hourly; £E8) and **Kafr el-Sheikh** (3hr; hourly; £E10). East Delta Bus Co covers **Benha**

(every 30min 6am–8pm; 1hr; £E2.50), **Zagazig** (every 20min 6.30am–9.30pm; 1hr 30min; £E5), **Faqus** (every 45min 7.45am–8.30pm; 2hr; £E8), **Mansura** (half-hourly 7am–7.30pm; 2hr £E10), **Damietta** (half-hourly 7am–7.30pm; 3hr 30min £E20) and, in summer (June–Sept), **Ras el-Bahr** (every 45min; 3hr; £E20).

For destinations southward up the Nile Valley, you will want a vehicle from the Upper Egypt Bus Co (☏02/431 6723). They have departures to **Fayoum** (every 15min 6am–8pm; 2hr; £E5.50–6), **Minya** (hourly 7.30am–1.30am; 4hr; £E11), **Mellawi** (hourly 7.30am–1.30am; 4hr 30min; £E15), **Assyut** (hourly 7am–1am; 6–7hrs; £E18–20), **Sohag** (hourly 7am–1am; 8–9hrs; £E23), **Qena** (hourly 7am–1am; 9–10hrs; £E30), **Luxor** (hourly 8am–10pm; 9hr; £E60) and **Aswan** (hourly 8am–10pm; 12hr; £E70). Passengers for the last two destinations in particular generally prefer the relative comfort of a train journey.

Other services

In addition to buses from Turgoman, there are five daily buses to **Hurghada**, departing from Adbel Mouneem Riyad bus terminal in front of the *Ramses Hilton* hotel. Tickets cost £E35 for just the five- to six-hour journey, or £E50 including drinks and snacks. Tickets can be bought from Egypt Star in Midan Falaki at the corner of Sharia Tahrir with Sharia Falaki, by *El-Guesh* restaurant (☏02/976 2660).

International buses

International buses are highly vulnerable to political upheavals, so none of the schedules and fares mentioned below can be taken for granted – double-check everything, including the availability of foreign visas (see p.274).

Of most interest to tourists, at any rate when the political situation is calm, are the services to **Tel Aviv** and **Jerusalem** – an 11–12hr journey via El-Arish and Rafah, skirting most of the Gaza Strip. Since the start of the second Palestinian *intifada* in 1999, these services have gradually been reduced and rerouted via Taba. At time of writing there are only three services a week, departing from the *Cairo Sheraton* in Dokki ($35 one-way, $50 return, plus border taxes). For tickets and information, contact Misr Travel at the *Cairo Sheraton*, ☏02/335 5470.

Less well known are the Superjet (aka Arab Union Bus Co; ☏02/579 8181) services from Turgoman Garage to Libya, Jordan and Syria. Buses to Jordan and Syria travel via the Nuweiba–Aqaba ferry, thus avoiding Israel.

Superjet have departures to **Benghazi** (1 daily; 17hr; US$68), **Tripoli** (1 daily; 36hr; US$130), **Amman** (2 weekly, currently Sun & Tues; 15hr; US$68 including ferry crossing) and **Damascus** (2 weekly, currently Sun & Tues; 30hr; US$92 including ferry crossing).

Inter-city service taxis

If you don't mind a slightly cramped and definitely hair-raising journey, **service taxis** (*servees*), whether Peugeots, microbuses or minibuses, are usually the fastest way to reach a host of destinations. Their biggest advantage is that they leave as soon as they're full; just turn up, and you'll probably be away in 15min (morning and late afternoon are prime times).

Drivers drum up custom by shouting out their destinations; anybody can point you towards the right vehicle for your destination. Fares generally work out 20–30 percent above the bus fare, though they are occasionally cheaper. Drivers are unlikely to overcharge you, but watch what Egyptians pay and you can hardly go wrong. If you're alighting halfway (for example, at Wadi Natrun, along the Desert Road to Alex), it's normal to pay the full fare.

For **Alexandria and the Delta**, the best place to pick up a *servees* is Aboud terminal, where you'll find vehicles to Alex, Benha, Damanhur, Damietta, Faqus, Mahalla, Mansura, Tanta and Zagazig, with very frequent departures and a direct route out of town. Vehicles to several of these destinations, in particular Alex and Tanta, can usually be picked up outside Ramses rail station too, especially during rush hours, but they may take a roundabout route getting out of town, and end up taking rather longer than taxis from Aboud.

Service taxis for **Suez** and **Ismailiya** leave from Sharia Orabi near Ramses station (see map p.131).

For **Fayoum**, the best place to pick up a *servees* is at Midan Giza (see p.201 for local bus connections), though you can also get them from Sharia Orabi near Ramses station (see map p.131). Midan Giza is also the terminal for service taxis to **Beni Suef**.

Destinations further afield are not generally reached in a single journey by service taxi, but at least one vehicle a day departs from the *Wahia Café*, 28 Sharia Qadry, in Saiyida Zeinab (see map p.166), bound for the desert oasis of **Bahariya** (£E15).

International service taxis

In addition to domestic runs, there are international service taxis to **Libya**. These are run by Wikala Suessi on Midan Opera (☎02/395 4480; see map p.110), and leave daily from there at around 8pm bound for Benghazi and Tripoli. It's wise to book your place a day or two ahead if possible.

Depending on the current political situation, it is also possible to get to **Palestine and Israel** by service taxi in stages. The most direct route, to the Gaza Strip, is inadvisable at time of writing due to the situation in Palestine, but should things settle down, you can take a *servees* from Sharia Orabi near Ramses station (see map p.131) to Suez, and another from there to the border at Rafah. On the other side of the border, you may have to take a "special" (ie. a private taxi) to Khan Yunis, where you will find service taxis to Gaza City and thence to the Israeli border at Erez. If you do this, you will need to set out early to avoid being stranded at Khan Yunis, where there is no accommodation. There is also transport from Rafah directly into Israel. Alternatively, there is a bus from Suez (currently departing at 3pm) to the Israeli border at Taba.

Domestic flights

Egyptair (for information ☎ 02/635 0260 or 0270) has flights to Abu Simbel (7 weekly; 2hr 35min; £E991 each way, return flight compulsory), Alexandria (8 weekly, weekdays only in winter, more flights in summer; 45min; £E248), Assyut (3 weekly; 1hr; £E364), Aswan (6–7 daily; 1hr 15min; £E759), Dakhla (1 weekly; 2hr 20min; £E619), Hurghada (2–6 daily; 1hr; £E573), Kharga (2 weekly; 1hr 15min; £E619), Luxor (5–7 daily; 1hr; £E554), and Sharm el-Sheikh (3–6 daily; 1hr; £E573). Egyptair's Cairo offices (generally open daily except Fri 8am–5pm) include: 6 Sharia Adly (☎02/392 7649); 9 Sharia Talaat Harb (☎02/393 2836); *Nile Hilton* (daily till 8pm; ☎02/579 3049); Opera Square, corner of Sharia Abdel Khaliq Sarwat (☎02/391 4501); *Cairo Sheraton*, Dokki (☎02/335 4863); Zamalek Club Fence, 26th July Street (☎02/347 2027); and 22 Sharia Ibrahim al-Lakani, Heliopolis (☎02/290 8453).

Tickets and terminals

During winter, Egyptair flights to the Nile Valley or Hurghada are often fully booked by groups – reserve as far in advance as possible, or hope to get a cancellation on stand-by. Tickets must be purchased in Egyptian currency backed by an exchange receipt, and return tickets cost double the one-way fare. Students may qualify for a reduction, but since Egyptair enjoys a monopoly it rarely offers big discounts.

Domestic flights leave from Terminal 1, the "old

airport" (*al-mataar al-qadima*), which can be reached by bus, minibus or taxi (£E30 is the going rate, though drivers may demand more). Both airport terminals are served by air-conditioned bus #356, minibus #27 and 24-hour bus #400, all from Abdel Mouneen Riyad terminal (in front of the *Ramses Hilton*) and Midan Ramses, and also by 24-hour bus #948 from Midan Ataba. During rush hour, and especially by bus, the journey can take well over an hour, so always allow plenty of time. It's safer of course to take a cab than to rely on bus services.

International flights

Many airlines make Cairo a stopover between the Near and Far East, or between Europe and sub-Saharan Africa, ensuring a competitive market in fares, student and youth discounts – but also heavy demand for flights. Don't leave buying tickets until the last moment. Especially during August, you should book weeks in advance on Eastern European airlines (which often have the cheapest flights to Western Europe, the British Isles and North America) or for popular long-haul destinations like Nairobi and Delhi.

All reservations should be reconfirmed 72 hours before departure. Also check which terminal you are flying from – most Western airlines use Terminal 2, the "new airport" (*al-mataar al-gadida*), while Egyptair and most East European airlines use Terminal 1, the "old airport" (*al-mataar al-qadima*). Both can be reached by bus (see above), or more reliably by taxi.

Agents and tickets

It's worth shopping around agents, who can often find seats when the airline itself swears that none exist, and may offer discounts. Places to try include De Castro Tours (12 Sharia Talaat Harb ☎02/574 3213, ©decastrotours@link.net), Spring Tours (11 Sharia Talaat Harb ☎02/392 2627), Norma Tours (10 Sharia Talaat Harb ☎02/576 0007), and Bon Voyage Egypt (16 Sharia Adly ☎02/390 8099 ⓦwww.bonvoyagegypt.com). Expect queuing and shoving in agencies and offices.

Although some agents and airlines may accept credit card payments for tickets, most don't – it's certainly not something to count on.

Student and youth discounts

To qualify for student discounts (20–50 percent) you must have a valid ISIC card and be under an age limit (24–31 years, depending on the airline or agency). Another age limit (24–26) determines eli-gibility for youth discounts, which don't require an ISIC card. There are rarely any student/youth discounts on flights to sub-Saharan Africa, India and the Far East.

Airline offices

Most of the airline offices are in central Cairo; some are represented by local travel agents.

Air Canada 26 Sharia Bassiouni ☎02/575 8939, ⓕ574 9129. Daily 9am–4pm (Ramadan 9.30am–4.30pm).

Air France 2 Midan Talaat Harb ☎02/575 8899, ⓕ02/577 1744, ⓦwww.airfrance.com/eg. Daily except Fri 8.30am–4.30pm.

Air India 1 Sharia Talaat Harb ☎02/393 4873 or 5. Mon–Thurs & Sat 8am–3pm.

Air Malta Room 34, 2nd floor, *Nile Hilton* arcade ☎02/380 4451.

Air Sinai *Nile Hilton* arcade ☎02/577 2949. Daily 8.30am–7.30pm.

Alitalia *Nile Hilton* arcade ☎02/578 5823–5, ⓕ577 9903, ©caiupaz@alitalia-egypt.com. Daily except Sat 9am–4pm.

Austrian Airlines 5th floor, 4D Sharia Gezira, Zamalek ☎02/735 2777, ⓕ738 2815, ⓦwww .aua.com.eg. Mon–Thurs & Sun 8.30am–4.30pm.

British Airways corner of Sharia Bustan and Midan Tahrir ☎02/578 0742–6, ⓕ574 7674. Daily 8am–4pm.

Balkan Airlines 17 Sharia Qasr el-Nil ☎02/393 1211, ⓕ393 9199. Daily except Fri 8.30am–5pm.

ČSA Czech Airlines 9 Talaat Harb ☎02/393 0416, ⓕ392 0463, ©cai@czechairlines.com. Mon–Thurs & Sun 8am–4pm, Fri 9am–noon.

Cyprus Airways c/o Apollo Tours, 10 Sharia Talaat Harb ☎02/579 7300 or 7400 or 7500, ⓕ575 3750, ©apollo@egynil.com. Daily 9am–4pm.

Delta 17 Sharia Ismail Mohammed, Zamalek ☎02/736 2039. Daily except Fri 8.30am–5pm.

Egyptair (see "Domestic flights" above).

El Al 1st floor, 5 Sharia el-Makrizi, just south of Zamalek Bridge, Zamalek ☎02/736 1795. Daily except Fri 8am–5pm.

Emirates 18 Sharia Elbatal Ahmed Abdelaziz, Mohandeseen ☎02/336 1555.

Ethiopian Airlines *Nile Hilton* arcade ☎02/574 0603, ⓕ574 0189. Daily 9am–4pm.

Iberia 15 Midan Tahrir ☎02/417 7297, ⓕ576 1988. Daily except Fri 8am–4pm.

Kenya Airways/KLM 11 Sharia Qasr el-Nil ☎02/580 5700, ⓕ580 5707, ⓦwww.klm.com.eg. Daily except Fri 8.30am–4.30pm.

Korean Air Room 26, 2nd floor, *Nile Hilton* arcade ☎02/576 8488, ⓕ576 4099. Daily except Fri 9am–4pm.

Lufthansa 6 Sharia Sheikh el-Marsafi, Zamalek ℡ 02/739 8339, ℻ 737 0475, ⓦ www.lufthansa.com.eg. Mon–Thur & Sun 8.30am–4.30pm. Also represents Air New Zealand, United and Thai.

Malaysia Airlines Room 38, 2nd floor, *Nile Hilton* arcade ℡ 02/579 9714–5. Daily except Fri 9am–4.30pm (Ramadan 9.30am–3pm).

Malev 3rd floor, 5 Sharia Talaat Harb ℡ 02/391 5083, ℻ 393 0107. Mon–Thurs, Sat & Sun 9am–4pm, Fri 11.30am–1pm.

Olympic Airways 23 Sharia Qasr el-Nil ℡ 02/393 1318, ℻ 391 0574. Daily 8.30am–4pm.

Royal Air Maroc 9 Sharia Talaat Harb (entrance in Sharia el-Bustan) ℡ 02/392 2956, ℻ 393 4574. Daily except Fri 9am–4pm.

Royal Jordanian 6 Sharia Qasr el-Nil ℡ 02/575 0875, ℻ 576 7005. Mon–Thurs, Sat & Sun 9am–4pm, Fri 9am–2.30pm.

Saudi Arabian Airlines 5 Sharia Qasr el-Nil ℡ 02/574 1200, ℻ 574 2804.

Singapore Airlines *Nile Hilton* arcade ℡ 02/575 0276, ℻ 574 7084. Daily 9am–4pm.

Sudan Airways 1 Sharia Abdel Salam Arif ℡ 02/578 7145, ℻ 575 9946. Daily 8am–7pm.

Swiss Air Lines 4 Mamar Behlar (between Talaat Harb and Qasr el-Nil) ℡ 02/392 1515. Mon–Thurs, Sat & Sun 8.30am–4.30pm.

Syrian Arab Airlines 25 Sharia Talaat Harb ℡ 02/392 8284, ℻ 391 0805.

TAROM 1st floor, 7 Sharia Qasr el-Nil ℡ 02/576 6655 or 6699. Mon–Thurs, Sat & Sun 9am–5pm, Fri 10am–3pm.

Turkish Airways Room 33, 2nd floor, *Nile Hilton* arcade ℡ 02/380 4451. Daily except Fri 9am–5pm.

Tunisair 14 Sharia Talaat Harb ℡ 02/575 3476, ℻ 574 0677. Daily except Fri 9am–5pm.

Nile cruises and boat services

Although luxury cruises operated by the *Hilton*, *Sheraton* and *Mena House Oberoi* remain prohibitively expensive, budget travellers may consider less ritzy boats run by agencies such as Eastmar Tours (in the passage of 13 Sharia Qasr el-Nil; ℡ 02/574 5024), which charges – depending on season – US$40–65 a night per person for a 4- to 7-night cruise. Be aware, however, that better deals could well be available from local agents in either Luxor or Aswan. For information on Nile cruises, see p.456, and for more on cruises and sailing on a felucca – a funkier and much cheaper experience – see p.454.

Tickets for the Hurghada–Sharm catamaran (see p.767) can be purchased from Amco Travel in Mohandiseen (46 Sharia Suriya ℡ 02/789 8921 or 7), or Downtown from De Castro Tours (12 Sharia Talaat Harb ℡ 02/574 3213, ⓔ decastrotours@link.net).

International lines

Several agencies can supply information and tickets for international lines, though, to be honest, the incentives for leaving Egypt by sea are minimal. The main service that you will want to use is from Nuweiba to the Jordanian port of Aqaba (see p.719 for details).

For details of the ferry service from Aswan to Wadi Halfa in Sudan, see p.458; for information on ferries from Suez to the Saudi port of Jeddah, see

The Nile Valley

CHAPTER 2 # Highlights

* **Valley of the Kings** The most famous of the magnificent burial complexes and mortuary temples that make up the Theban Necropolis. See p.388

* **Karnak Temple** It took 1300 years to construct this vast cult centre that's as large as ten great cathedrals. See p.366

* **Feluccas** A timeless way to view the Nile's scenery and temples, sailing downriver from Aswan to Edfu. See p.454

* **Abydos** The carvings in Seti I's mortuary temple are among the greatest produced by pharaonic civilization. See p.326

* **Shopping** All kinds of handicrafts, souvenirs and spices are sold in the wonderful bazaar at Aswan. See p.443

* **Nubian music and dancing** Exuberant and haunting by turns, they are best enjoyed on Sehel or Elephantine Island. See p.451

* **Philae** The island sanctuary of the goddess Isis was rescued from the rising waters of Lake Nasser by an international effort coordinated by UNESCO. See p.462

* **Abu Simbel** The monumental rock-cut temples of Ramses II and Nefertari are the highlights of Lake Nasser. See p.473

The Nile Valley

E gypt has been called the gift of the Nile, for without the river it could not exist as a fertile, populous country, let alone have sustained a great civilization five thousand years ago. Its character and history have been shaped by the stark contrast between the fecund **Nile Valley** and its Delta (covered in Chapter Five), and the arid wastes that surround them. To the ancient Egyptians, this was the homeland or *Kemet* – the Black Land of dark alluvium, where life and civilization flourished as the benign gods intended – as opposed to the desert that represented death and chaos, ruled by Seth, the bringer of storms and catastrophes.

Kemet's existence depended on an annual miracle of rebirth from aridity, as the Nile rose to spread its life-giving waters and fertilizing silt over the exhausted land during the season of inundation. Once the flood had subsided, the *fellaheen* (peasants) simply planted crops in the mud, waited for an abundant harvest, and then relaxed over summer. While empires rose and fell, this way of life persisted essentially unchanged for over 240 generations, until the Aswan Dam put an end to the inundation in 1967 – a breathtaking period of continuity considering that Jesus lived less than ninety generations ago.

This continuity and ancient history is literally underfoot. Almost every Nile town and village is built upon layers of previous **settlements** – pharaonic, Ptolemaic, Roman and Coptic – whose ancient names, modified and Arabized,

have often survived. When treasure-hunting "archeologists" first turned their attention to the ancient temples and tombs in the 1830s, they had to sift through metres of sand and debris before reaching their goal. Yet the centuries of burial preserved a panoply of ancient reliefs and carvings that would otherwise have been defaced by Coptic or Muslim iconoclasts, who hacked away at the pagan gods on the accessible friezes, pillars and ceilings, and plundered masonry for their own churches and mosques.

After a century and a half of excavation by just about every Western nation – and by the Egyptians since independence – the Nile's **monuments** constitute the greatest open-air museum in the world. Revealed along its banks are several thousand **tombs** (Thebes alone has more than 900) and scores of **temples**: so many, in fact, that most visitors feel satiated by just a fraction of this legacy.

To enjoy the Valley, it's best to be selective and mix sightseeing with felucca rides on the river, roaming around bazaars and camel markets, or attending the odd moulid. Most visitors succeed in this by heading straight for **Upper Egypt**, travelling by train or air to **Luxor** or **Aswan**, then making day-trips to the sights within easy range of either base – most notably the cult temple at **Edfu** – in addition to exploring the New Kingdom temples and tombs of **Karnak** and the **Theban Necropolis** from Luxor. Further north, **Middle Egypt** was shunned by tourists due to terrorist attacks by Islamic militants in the 1990s – with the exception of day-trips to the temples of **Dendara** and **Abydos** – but now adventure travel groups are again visiting the tombs of **Beni Hassan** and the ruins of Akhenaten's capital at **Tell el-Amarna**.

And lastly a word on the **terms from Egyptology** that fill this chapter: many may be unfamiliar and need a fuller explanation than a glossary allows (see p.843). Hence the boxes at intervals in the text: on statehood and symbolism on p.294; temple architecture under "Abydos" (p.220); funerary beliefs and practices under "The Valley of the Kings" (p.390); and gods and goddesses under their respective cult temples (see the main index for a list).

The river, its gods and pharaohs

The **Nile** is the world's longest river (6695km), originating in the highland lakes of Uganda and Ethiopia, which give rise to the White and Blue Niles. These join into a single river at Khartoum in Sudan, which flows northwards over a series of cataracts through the Nubian desert, before forming Egypt's Nile Valley and Delta, through which it travels 1545km to the Mediterranean Sea. The river's northward flow, coupled with a prevailing wind towards the south, made it a natural highway.

As the source of life, the Nile determined much of ancient Egyptian **society and mythology**. Creation myths of a primal mound emerging from the waters of chaos reflect how villages huddled on mounds till the flood subsided and they could plant their crops. Even more crucially, the need for large-scale irrigation works in the Valley and the consequent mobilization of labour may have engendered the region's system of centralized authority – in effect, the state.

Both the Valley and its Delta were divided into **nomes** or provinces, each with a nomarch or governor, and one or more **local deities**. As political power ebbed and flowed between regions and dynasties, certain of the deities assumed national significance and absorbed the attributes of lesser gods in a perpetual process of religious mergers and takeovers. Thus, for example, Re, the chief god of the Old Kingdom, ended up being assimilated with Amun, the prime divinity of Thebes during the New Kingdom. Yet for all its complexity, ancient Egyptian religion was essentially practical and intended to get results. Its preeminent concerns were to perpetuate the beneficent sun and river, maintain the righteous order personified by the goddess Maat, and achieve resurrection in the afterlife.

Abundant crops could normally be taken for granted, as prayers to Hapy the Nile-god were followed by a green wave of humus-rich water around June. However, if the Nile failed to rise for a succession of years there ensued the

❷ Travel restrictions and routes into the Nile Valley

Setting out from Cairo, you are faced with a variety of **approaches to the Valley,** but you need to bear in mind certain **travel restrictions**. Egypt is still trying to recover from the fall-out from the **terrorist attacks** on tourists that began in Middle Egypt in 1992 and climaxed with the massacre at Luxor five years later, which cast first the region and then the whole country as "hazardous" on the travel advisory sites of the US State Department and Britain's Foreign Office (see p.30). To win back tourists and reassure its allies, the government crushed the Islamist insurgency and struck a deal whereby Egypt would be re-classified as a **safe country** if they came up with a cohesive security system instead of *ad hoc* responses. The fact that no terrorist acts have occurred since the jailed leaders of Al-Jihad urged their followers to renounce violence in 1998 has not yet led to any relaxation in this regime, but the threat of violence has lifted.

The system relies on police checkpoints to filter traffic and ensure that tourists respect the **travel restrictions** listed below (note that these **don't apply** in other parts of Egypt). Officially, tourists can visit any place in the Valley providing they get there in a way that stays within the rules, but in reality it can be hard, if not impossible, to reach some places. Whereas tourists are unbothered by controls within the security "bubble" of Luxor and Aswan, in **Middle Egypt** the police insist on **escorting** them on excursions, or around town, and even confine them to their hotel after dark. While you have little choice but to comply and should certainly never get angry, the system is sufficiently inconsistent and fallible enough that you can sometimes persuade them to cut you some slack.

Bear in mind that you're a privileged visitor but also a nuisance to the **police**, who want you off their turf as soon as possible and preferably into another governorate's territory. Most of the cops are young conscripts, bored and starved of home comforts, so a little humour or a gift (not money) can make a big difference. Confusingly, each governorate fine-tunes the rules for their territory without reference to its neighbours – resulting in such **absurdities** as being allowed to travel on the road from Kharga Oasis to Luxor, but not in the opposite direction.

The following rules and exceptions **specifically apply to the Nile Valley**:

• **Trains** Travelling from Cairo's **Ramses Station to Luxor or Aswan**, tourists may only use three regular trains (guarded by plainclothes cops with Uzis) or the deluxe *wagons-lits* service (which has a restaurant and bar). Clerks will simply refuse to sell tickets for other trains. The journey is quite comfortable if you travel in 1st or a/c 2nd class on the three "tourist" trains, so a *wagon-lit* is something of an unnecessary extravagance. If you do want to try your chances on another train, you could try boarding and paying the conductor, but there's sure to be a fuss and the outcome is doubtful. The same restrictions apply to the return journey to Cairo, or onwards from Luxor. In **Middle Egypt**, however, you can usually buy a ticket for any train at the station kiosk with no difficulty, while travelling from Aswan to Luxor (but not the other way) you're allowed to use six trains, not just the three authorised for long-distance travel.

• In Upper Egypt, **tourist buses, hired taxis and cars driven by foreigners** must travel in **convoys** escorted by the police. There are three daily between Luxor and Aswan and Luxor and Hurghada; two from Aswan to Abu Simbel, and one from Luxor to Abydos. While local drivers know where and when the convoy departs, foreigners should always check with the tourist office, since schedules or muster "years of the hyena when men went hungry". Archeologists reckon that it was **famine** – caused by overworking of the land, as well as lack of the flood waters – that caused the collapse of the Old and Middle Kingdoms, and subsequent political anarchy. But each time some new **dynasty** arose to reunite the land and re-establish the old order. This remarkable conservatism persisted even

points can change. Arrive at least fifteen minutes early. There are **no scheduled convoys** through Middle Egypt; adventure tour groups make their own arrangements with each governorate, and individuals hoping to drive from Cairo should ask the Ministry of the Interior or the tourist office for advice.

• **Buses** leave from Cairo's **Aboud** and **Turgoman terminals**. There are several daily a/c services to Luxor and Aswan that are routed via the Red Sea Coast rather than Middle Egypt, thereby avoiding convoy restrictions, but though the journey time is roughly the same, they're a lot less comfortable than 1st- or 2nd-class trains. Non-a/c buses to Beni Suef, Minya, Assyut and Sohag in Middle Egypt do exist, but tourists are only supposed to use ones travelling in a scheduled convoy (which *don't* exist in this region; see above). If you do reach Middle Egypt (by train), then local cops may tolerate you using inter-city buses within the region or heading south to Luxor, from which point on you may use any bus – providing there aren't more than four tourists aboard the vehicle. Even this limit doesn't seem to apply to buses to Hurghada. Since few tourists are using buses at present, in practice you can probably rely on being able to catch any bus – though finding a seat may be another matter, as many arrive already full of Egyptians (standing is allowed).

• **Service taxis** leave from **Aboud**, bound for Minya or Assyut, from where there are connections further south – but at present, tourists aren't allowed to use service taxis anywhere along the Nile Valley and the police are quite vigilant about enforcing this. However, as the rule isn't always observed between Luxor and Aswan (though it is *in* Luxor and Aswan), and as this is potentially a great way of getting around, we've included some details of routes under town accounts, just in case the blanket restriction is lifted.

• **Planes** are the fastest, most expensive way to travel from one end of the Nile Valley to the other, and are not subject to any police restrictions. Depending on the level of tourism, there can be from two to a dozen flights a day to Luxor, Aswan and Abu Simbel, affording amazing views over the Valley's green belt of cultivated land. Tourists can also fly from Aswan to Abu Simbel, and Luxor to Sharm el-Sheikh in Sinai.

• **Package tours** may appeal to visitors with little time or inclination for independent travel, but first-timers often end up buying overpriced tours that turn out to involve substandard hotels and excursions. Many readers and hoteliers in Luxor and Aswan have complained of being misled by Amigo Tours, which has touts in many hotels and at the airport and station in Cairo; they also warn against using Hamis Travel. If you *do* want a tour, talk to Salah Mohammed at the *Luna Hotel* (see p.224) or Eastmar Travel (p.286) in Cairo – the latter also arranges cruises between Luxor and Aswan and the temples on Lake Nasser, and has branch offices in both Luxor and Aswan.

• With the slump in tourism, prices for **Nile cruises** have never been lower, whether you shop around on the Internet before you leave (see "Getting There" on p.11, p.15 and p.18), at travel agents in Cairo, Luxor and Aswan, or – cheapest of all – on the boats moored at Aswan, which is also the point of departure for **felucca** rides to Kom Ombo and Edfu (see the boxes on p.456 and p.454 for details).

For details of **ticket buying**, **prices**, **departure** and **journey times**, see "Travel Details" on p.281 at the end of the Cairo chapter.

under foreign rule: the Nubians, Persians, Ptolemies and Romans all continued building temples dedicated to the old gods, and styled themselves as pharaohs.

The people of the Nile Valley

Although the Nile Valley and its Delta represents a mere four percent of Egypt's surface area, it is home to 95 percent of the country's population. While Cairo and Alexandria account for about a quarter of this, the bulk of the people still

---

The two lands: Pharaonic symbols and cartouches

Much of the symbolism of ancient Egypt referred to the union of the **Two Lands**, the **Nile Valley** (Upper Egypt) and its **Delta** (Lower Egypt), whose establishment marked the onset of the Old Kingdom (c.3100 BC) – unless you buy the theory advanced by one Egyptologist that the Two Lands were actually the east and west banks of the Nile (which seems unlikely).

Each Land had its own deity – the Delta had **Wadjet**, the cobra goddess, while the Valley had **Nekhbet**, the vulture goddess. With union, however, their images were combined with the sun-disc of the

winged sun-disc

god Re to form the **winged sun-disc**, which often appeared on the lintels of temple doors. Another common image was that of the Nile-god, **Hapy**, binding together the heraldic plants of the Two Lands, the papyrus of the Delta and the lotus of the Valley.

Hapy binding the Two Lands

Much the same process can be observed in the evolution of **pharaonic crowns**. At state rituals, the pharaoh customarily wore first the **White Crown** of Upper Egypt and then the **Red Crown** of Lower Egypt, although by the time of the New Kingdom (c.1570 BC) these were often subsumed into the **Combined Crown**. Pharaonic crowns also featured the **uraeus** or fire-spitting cobra, an incarnation of Wadjet believed to be a guardian of the kings.

Another image that referred to the act of union (an act which had to be repeated at the onset of the Middle and New Kingdoms) was the **Djed column**, a symbol of steadfastness. Additional symbols of royal authority included the **crook** (or staff) and the **flail** (or scourge), which are often shown crossed over the chest – in the so-called Osiride position – on pharaonic statues. A ubiquitous motif was the **ankh**, symbolizing breath or life, which pharaohs are often depicted receiving from gods in tombs or funerary texts.

However, the archetypal symbol of kingship was the **cartouche**, an oval formed by a loop of rope, enclosing the hieroglyphs of the pharaoh's **nomen and prenomen**. Traditionally a pharaoh's title consisted of five names: four adopted on accession to the throne (Horus name, Nebty name, Golden Horus name and prenomen) and a birth name (nomen), roughly corresponding to a family name. The prenomen was introduced by a group of hieroglyphs meaning "He who belongs to the sedge and the bee" and was nearly always compounded with the name of Re, the sun-god. The nomen – the name by which pharaohs are known to posterity – was likewise introduced by an epithet, "Son of Re".

White Crown   Djed column   Red Crown   Crook   Combined Crown   Flail   Uraeus   Ankh

---

live in small towns and villages and, as in pharaonic times, the **fellaheen** or peasant farmers remain the bedrock of Egyptian society.

Most **villages** consist of flat-roofed mud-brick houses, with chickens, goats, cows and water buffalo roaming the unpaved streets, and elaborate multistorey pigeon coops (the birds are eaten and their droppings used as fertilizer). The plastered outside walls of the houses are often painted light blue (a colour believed to ward off the Evil Eye), and if the householder has made the pilgrimage to Mecca, they will be decorated with characteristic *Hadj* scenes (recalling the journey with images of ships and charter jets, lions and the sacred Kaaba). Children begin work at an early age: girls feed the animals, fetch water and make the dung patties which are used for fuel (though primus stoves are increasingly popular), while by the age of nine or ten, boys are learning how to farm the land that will one day be theirs.

Rural life might appear the same throughout the Nile Valley, but its character changes as you go further south. The northern part of the Valley is wider and greener, unconstrained by the desert hills; its people have a reputation for being quietly spoken and phlegmatic, notwithstanding a recent turn towards Islamic radicalism. By contrast, Egyptians characterize the **Saiyidis** of Upper Egypt as mercurial in character, alternating between hot-blooded passion and a state known as *kismet* – a kind of fatalistic stasis. To non-Saiyidis, they are also the butt of jokes mocking their stubbornness and stupidity. A further ethnic contingent of the southern reaches of the Valley are the black-skinned **Nubians**, whose traditional homeland stretching far into Sudan was submerged by Lake Nasser in the 1960s.

Nile wildlife

The exotic Nile wildlife depicted on ancient tomb reliefs – hippos, crocodiles, elephants and gazelles – is largely a thing of the past, though you might just see a croc near Aswan. However, the Valley has a rich diversity of **birds**. Amid the groves of palms (dates all along the Valley and dom palms south of Assyut), fruit and flame trees, sycamores and eucalyptus, and fields of *besoom* (Egyptian clover) and sugar cane, you can spot hoopoes, turtle- and laughing-doves, bulbuls, bluethroats, redstarts, wheatears and dark-backed stonechats; purple gallinules, egrets and all kinds of waders are to be seen in the river; while common birds of prey include a range of kestrels, hawks and falcons.

Middle Egypt

It was nineteenth-century archeologists who coined the term **Middle Egypt** for the stretch of river between Cairo and the Qena Bend; in native usage and current administration there's no such area, unlike Upper and Lower Egypt, which are ancient divisions. Nevertheless, it's a handy label for a region that's subtly distinct from Upper Egypt, further south (in this guide, the Middle Egypt account ends at Sohag; the sites to the south – at Abydos and Dendara – are dealt with in the Upper Egypt account as the best access to them is from Luxor). Owing little to tourism, the towns are solidly provincial, with social conservatism providing common ground for those wanting

Cairo

Lisht
Pyramid

Maidum
Pyramid

El-Wasta

*The
Fayoum*

Beni Suef

Sannur

River Nile

*Western
Desert*

Oxyrhynchus

Deir-al-Adhra

Samalut

Zawiyet el-Mayyiteen

Minya

Hermopolis

Tombs of
Beni Hassan

Antinopolis

Tuna al-Gabel

Mallawi

Deir Mawas

Tell el-Amarna

Meir Tombs

El-Qusiya

Burnt Monastery

Assyut

Dirunka

Abu Tig

*Eastern
Desert*

Gulf of
Suez

Ain Sukhna

Za'farana

Monastery of
St Anthony

Monastery of
St Paul

N

Akhmim

Sohag

Red & White
Monasteries

Girga

El-Balyana

Abydos

Nag Hammadi

Dishna

Qena

Dendara

0   kilometres   50

MIDDLE EGYPT

▼ *Kharga Oasis (230km)*

Luxor (67km) & Aswan (284km) ▼

Hurghada ►

Port Safaga (161km) ► & Hurghada (219km) ▼

to preserve peaceful relations between the Muslim majority and Middle Egypt's Coptic community (about 20 percent of the local population, roughly double the national average). During the 1990s this was badly strained by Islamic militants, whose attacks on Copts, the security forces and tourists made the region a no-go zone for foreigners. Though adventure tour groups are returning, few independent travellers have followed, and the restrictions intended to assure tourists' security can be off-putting even though the risk of danger has receded.

Even before this, most tourists rated Middle Egypt a low priority, as towns like **Minya** and **Sohag** lack the romance of Aswan or the stupendous monuments of Luxor, for all that the local antiquities have fascinated scholars. The rock tombs of **Beni Hassan** and the necropolis of **Tuna al-Gabel** are well-preserved relics of Middle Kingdom artistry and Ptolemaic cult-worship, while the desolate remains at **Tell el-Amarna** stand as an evocative reminder of the "heretic" Pharaoh Akhenaten. All these sites may now be safely visited again, and the mandatory police escort and travel restrictions (see p.292) are more about keeping Egypt's certification as a safe country than any genuine risk – but at the time of writing, only a few adventure tour groups and archeologists were going there.

Beni Suef

Beni Suef is one of Egypt's poorest governorates, with high unemployment due to a shortage of arable land. Many villagers actively welcome the siting of five **cement factories** on the east bank, despite the pollution they cause, as the only other work is quarrying for marble in the **Sannur Caves** – a job that has killed or crippled scores of men, and damaged alabaster formations, supposedly protected by law. Hopes for a better life rest on exploiting the **natural gas** fields beneath the Western Desert, with the new Kuraymat power station as the hub of a future grid of pipelines running to October 6th City, Assyut, Qena and Aswan. Another contributor to environmental pollution is the military air base that hosts Egypt's "Top Gun" **fighter pilots school**, whose students dogfight in the skies above the governorate.

There's no reason to visit the ramshackle capital of **BENI SUEF**, 120km from Cairo, except to switch transport for the Red Sea Coast, the Fayoum or the Pyramid of Maidum. Should this mean **staying** overnight, your best option is the two-star *Semiramis Hotel* (☎082/322-092, ⓕ326-017; ❷) behind the **telephone** and **post** offices, one block north of the **train station**. By carrying on till you come to a bridge and turning right, you'll find a **bank** on Shariya Sa'ad Zaghloul, while by crossing the canal and carrying for 200m before turning right, you'll reach the depot for **minibuses** and pick-ups to El-Wasta, from where a service can get you within range of the Pyramid of Maidum (see p.506). Frequent **buses** to Minya and the Fayoum, and one daily to Za'farana on the Red Sea – running past the turn-off for St Anthony's Monastery (see p.745) – leave from the bus station on Sharia Bur Said, 400m south of (and on the other side of the canal from) the train station. For **eating**, there's a choice between kebab or chicken at the *Semiramis*, or the *kushari*, *fuul* or *taamiya* outside the station.

Forgotten cities: Herakleopolis and Oxyrhynchus

Though nothing remains of them, two ancient cities once flourished along this stretch of the Nile Valley.

Herakleopolis is marked by a huge mound of rubble near the village of Ihnasya el-Medina, 15km west of Beni Suef. Founded early in the Old

Kingdom and long the capital of the twentieth nome, its rise coincided with the decline of the VIII Dynasty, which barely controlled the region around Memphis by 2160 BC. While anarchy reigned throughout the Two Lands, **Achthoes**, the nomarch of Herakleopolis, forged a new dynasty. Although his successors never achieved control of southern Egypt, their reassertion of centralized authority in the north paved the way for the XII Dynasty and the Middle Kingdom. The site is currently being excavated, yet again.

Of similarly academic interest, **Oxyrhynchus**, 9km northwest of Beni Mazar, was the capital of the nineteenth nome. It's noted for the discovery of numerous papyri – including third-century fragments of the gospels of Matthew and John; portions of plays by Sophocles, Euripides and Meander; and summaries of the lost books of Livy. More frivolously, it deserves to be remembered for revering the elephant-snout fish – perhaps the weirdest totemic creature on record.

Minya, Mallawi and surrounding sites

The best archeological sites in Middle Egypt are around **Minya**, 109km from Beni Suef, and **Mallawi**, 47km further south. This area was the epicentre of the conflict between Islamic militants and the security forces in the mid-1990s, when canefields were burned to deny the Islamists cover, and armoured cars patrolled the streets of Minya and Mallawi. Since the last militants were flushed out or ceased fighting in 1998 there have been no reported acts of violence, and locals point out that, even in the worst years, no tourists were attacked in Minya. Even so, the police and security forces are omnipresent and expect tourists to conform to security restrictions. This generally means **visiting the sites in private taxis**, with a police escort, rather than using local buses or service taxis – which makes trips more expensive – although for **inter-city travel** you may use any train up or down the Valley, and there's always a chance that you'll be able to pick up a bus or service taxi when the police aren't looking, or when they decide to turn a blind eye just to get you off their turf as fast as possible.

The main attractions are the rock tombs of **Beni Hassan**, roughly midway between the towns; these contain the finest surviving murals from the Middle Kingdom. Nearer to Mallawi are the ruins of **Hermopolis** and its partially subterranean necropolis, **Tuna al-Gabel**, while the Coptic **Monastery of the Virgin** lies across the river north of Minya. The major site of **Tell el-Amarna**, 12km south of Mallawi on the east bank, is covered separately on p.308; although the Burnt Monastery is closer to Mallawi, it is easier to travel there from Assyut (see p.321).

All **trains** between Cairo and Luxor stop at Minya en route. There are **buses** from Cairo's Aboud and Turgoman terminals (5hr) and **service taxis** (4hr) from the adjacent depot or Midan Giza. **Drivers** have a choice between the congested, scenic Agricultural Road that hugs the west bank of the Nile; the new Desert Road, further west, which mainly avoids the towns en route; or the older Desert Road along the east bank of the Nile, linked by a bridge to Minya.

Minya

Though **MINYA** is further from most of the sites, it is infinitely preferable to Mallawi as a base for excursions. The provincial capital, it derives considerable charm from the old villas built by Italian architects for Greek and Egyptian cotton magnates – now picturesquely decaying amidst their overgrown gardens –

and from its people, known in Egypt for their warmth and honesty – which have earned Minya the sobriquet, "Bride of Upper Egypt" (*Arous al-Sa'id*). Beneath the palm trees that shadow its squares, couples canoodle and vendors hawk sweet potatoes, and during Ramadan half the population seems to sleep outdoors. **Tourists** are usually permitted to wander freely about town, but the police will want to accompany you on any excursions to the surrounding sites.

▲ *Nefertiti & Aton (1km)*

MINYA

ACCOMMODATION
Akhenaten	4
Beach	3
Dahabiyya	1
Ibn Khassib	6
Lotus	2
Savoy	5
Seety	7

RESTAURANTS & CAFÉS
Cafeteria Ali Baba	A
Restaurant Afendina	B

River Nile

Governorate

CORNICHE

Cairo

Banque
du Caire

SHARIA ABDEL MOLEM

SHARIA BAGHER

SHARIA ADLI KRAM

SHARIA SALAH AL-DIN

National
Bank

CORNICHE

SHARIA GUMHORRIYA

Security
Department

MIDAN
TAHRIR

SHARIA AL-MUDIRIYYA

MIDAN
AL-
MAHATTA

Train
Station

SHARIA IBN KASEB

Service Taxis
to Samalut

Banque
Misr

MIDAN
SA'A

SHARIA EL-GEISH

Tourist
Office

SOUK

Service Taxi
Station

SHARIA SAAD ZAGHLOUL

Footbridge

Bus
Station

N

► *Zawiyet el-Mayyiteen*

0   Metres   100

Beni Hassan ▼ *(20km), Mallawi (47km) & Assyut (114km)*   ▼ *Assyut*

Outside the train station is a square reminiscent of some ex-colonial *ville* in North Africa. **Sharia Gumhorriya** leads past a row of cafés to reach **Midan Tahrir**, the hub of small-town life by day. Come evening, locals promenade along **Sharia Ibn Khasseb**, between Tahrir and **Midan Sa'a** (Clock Square), past shops and eating places replicated further up Gumhorriya, which terminates at the **Corniche** (aka Sharia el-Nil). Across the river rise the striated hills of the Eastern Desert. Thus constrained, Minya spreads alongside the riverbank and westwards across the **Ibrahimiya Canal**, encroaching on the agricultural plain beyond.

Practicalities

The main **tourist office** (daily except Fri 8am–8pm; ☎086/343-500) by the Nile and the branch in the train station (similar hours) are anxious to please but short on hard facts. They can even be wrong about whether sites like Beni Hassan and Hermopolis are open, so it's best to double-check vital information with the **tourist police** (☎086/364-527). Visitors are bound to come to the attention of the **security department**, which shares a building on the Corniche with the regular **police** (☎123).

There's a 24-hour **telephone office** beside the station, which sells Menatel cards for use in booths around town. The main **post office** (daily except Fri 8am–2pm), one block north of Sharia Abdel Moneim, has a **passport office** (daily except Fri 8.30am–2pm) on the floor above that can extend visas. Banque Misr on Midan Sa'a (daily except Fri 8.30am–2pm) does **cash advances** on Visa cards, and the National Bank of Egypt (daily except Fri 8.30am–2pm) at the Corniche end of Sharia Gumhorriya will change **travellers' cheques** and has an **ATM**. You can also change **money** at the Banque du Caire or Banque Misr, or transfer cash via Western Union (☎086/364-905), whose office is on the way between Midan al-Mahatta and Midan Tahrir. There's a **hospital** in the centre of town, between Sharia el-Geish and Sharia al-Mudiriyya. Minya's **souk** lies further south, and a Monday **market** that has been a fixture since Ottoman times takes place on the west bank of the Ibrahimiya Canal.

Accommodation

As elsewhere in Middle Egypt, the police prefer foreigners to stay in certain hotels and dissuade others from taking foreign guests – which generally tend to be the lowest-budget places. All of the following hotels are certain to take foreign guests, except for the last two, which are included for being so cheap, just in case the police relax their scrutiny.

Akhenaten on the Corniche ☎086/365-917, ☎365-918. Minya's most comfortable option if you can't afford the *Nefertiti & Aton*, this recently renovated hotel has rooms with a/c, satellite TV and fridges, and is used by Explore groups. ❹

Beach Sharia el-Gumhorriya ☎086/322-307. Around the block from the *Akhenaten*, this is a simpler hotel with clean rooms with shared or private bathrooms. ❷

Dahabiyya moored beside the Corniche ☎086/325-596. An atmospheric old houseboat owned by a Coptic couple, enjoying a fabulous view of the Nile and the Eastern Desert. Reservations are essential as there are only three cabins (with twin beds and washbasins); the single

bathroom is shared, but spotless, and hot water is abundant. They also do tasty meals. ❸

Ibn Khassib 5 Sharia Ragab ☎086/324-535. One of Minya's once-grand hotels, gone to pot. The gloomy rooms have high ceilings and antique furniture; some also have a/c and tiny bathrooms. A restaurant, bar and billiards table are bonuses. ❷

Lotus 1 Sharia Bur Said ☎086/364-541, ☎364-576. Located in a quiet part of town ten minutes' walk from the centre. Decent a/c rooms have showers and TV, and a top-floor restaurant, serving beer and wine, offers fine views. ❸

Nefertiti & Aton 1km north of Minya by the Nile ☎086/331-515, ☎326-467. Still known to locals as the *Etap*, this four-star retreat has been

spruced up in the hope of visitors, but only one of its three restaurants ever seems to be open. Go for one of the Nile-facing rooms rather than the garden bungalows. Its main attraction is the swimmming pool. ❼
   Savoy Midan al-Mahatta ☎086/363-270. Decrepit once-grand railway hotel, opposite the station, whose manager is presently reluctant to take foreign guests. Should he relent, rooms are cheap, with shared or private bathrooms. ❶
   Seety 71 Sharia Sa'ad Zaghloul ☎086/363-930. Two blocks south of the *Savoy*, the *Seety* looks equally run-down, but its small rooms are quite clean and comfy, with private bathrooms, and even cheaper than the *Savoy*. ❶

Eating

The *Akhenaten Hotel* is capable of laying on a splendid buffet for adventure tour groups and is one of Minya's better mid-range options for **eating**, together with the *Lotus Hotel*, which also has great views from its top-floor restaurant. For a simple chicken meal washed down with a Stella, you could also try the *Ibn Khassib* restaurant. The *Green House Coffee Bar* in the *Nefertiti & Aton* serves decent pasta, Continental and Egyptian dishes for £E20–40, but isn't really worth a special trip from town. Cheaper options include the *Cafeteria Ali Baba* near the Governorate building, dispensing *kofta* or kebab with salad, *tahina* and a soft drink for £E15 – which is also a good place for a croissant and coffee in the morning – and the *Restaurant Afendina* on Midan Tahrir, serving *shawarma*, roast chicken, *taamiyya* and *kushari*, accompanied by all the usual dips and salads.

Transport

Though *hantours* (horse-drawn buggies) are widely used for getting around, Minya is compact enough for walking, with its local and long-distance transport depots fairly close together. As in other towns further down the Valley, the police prefer you to use **trains** to reach Cairo, Assyut, Luxor or Aswan, and don't seem to mind which of the dozen or more daily services you catch. At present, they actively discourage foreigners from using inter-city **buses** to Assyut (hourly) or Cairo (every 2hr; 5hr), leaving from the bus station on Sharia Sa'ad Zaghloul, or **service taxis** to Samalut (from the "local" depot) or Mallawi (from the main service taxi station).

Across the river from Minya

Before describing the pharaonic sites, it's worth mentioning two places across the river: Minya's **City of the Dead**, and the **Monastery of the Virgin**. Thanks to the Minya Bridge, both can easily be reached by private taxi in a single excursion (£E20–30), and it would be feasible to use service taxis from the local depot were travel restrictions to be lifted in the future.

Minya's City of the Dead and the Church of Aba Hur

Beyond the east bank village of Al-Sawadah, 4km south of Minya, stretches an immense cemetery resembling Cairo's City of the Dead. Dubbed **Zawiyet el-Mayyiteen**, the "Corner of the Dead", it consists of thousands of mausolea: confessional enclaves interspersed with the homes of the living. A rash of mud-brick domes marks the Muslim quarters; a forest of crosses marks the Coptic burial grounds. Amongst one of the Muslim cemeteries lies the **Mausoleum of Hoda Shaarawi**, an early-twentieth-century feminist who campaigned for women's liberation and was the first woman to publicly remove her veil (in Cairo's Ramses Station). A caretaker can lead you to her mausoleum, a stately structure with *mashrabiyya* windows.
   Traditionally, locals visit their ancestral tombs during the Muslim months of *Shawwal*, *Ragab* and *Zoul-Hagga*, at the time of the full moon. On July 6, the

cemetery also serves as a camping ground for Coptic pilgrims attending the **Moulid of Aba Hur** at the subterranean rock church of **Deir Aba Hur**, a kilometre from Al-Sawadah. The church – entered via a narrow, stepped tunnel – contains finely inlaid *haikal* screens and a nineteenth-century icon of Aba Hur, a blacksmith's son whose faith under torture converted the Roman governor of Pelusium to Christianity.

Deir al-Adhra: the Monastery of the Virgin

Roughly 20km north of Minya, the east bank extrudes a cliff-like hill known as **Gabel et–Teir** (Bird Mountain), after the flocks said to haunt it on the birthday of a local saint – a name that's also applied to the Coptic monastery on its summit. The **Monastery of the Virgin**, properly called **Deir al-Adhra**, was inhabited until late last century, when Baedeker dismissed it as a "group of miserable huts, occupied not only by the monks but by laymen with their wives and children", whose reaction to passing tourist steamers had previously amused Gustave Flaubert: "You see these fellows, totally naked, rushing down their perpendicular cliffs and swimming towards you as fast as they can, shouting '*Baksheesh, baksheesh*'."

Nowadays a place of pilgrimage, the monastery's rude outbuildings screen a **rock–hewn church**, reputedly founded in 328 AD by Empress Helena, inside a cave where the Holy Family sheltered. One of its six columns has been hollowed out and serves for baptisms; the tales attached to it are only surpassed by the miraculous cures attributed to a picture of the Virgin that weeps holy oil. Forty days after the Coptic Easter, thousands of pilgrims come here for the week-long **Feast of the Assumption**; at other times the church is locked, but a caretaker can admit visitors.

Getting there by car, you can use the east bank Desert Road, which runs past both sites. This is faster than using public transport (even if the police allowed it), which would involve taking a service taxi or minibus (£E2–3) from Minya to **SAMALUT**, 30km north; then a pick-up (50pt) to the Nile and a car ferry (£E1) to the east bank. Once on the east bank, you cross a field to the rock-hewn stairway of 166 steps, ascending 130m to a hamlet beside the monastery – ask for the *kineesa* or church and somebody will fetch the keys. During the festival, minibuses run here directly from Minya.

Mallawi

MALLAWI has gone to the dogs ever since Minya supplanted it as the regional capital. Its littered streets stink of open drains; hovels are more prevalent than villas. To Egyptians, it is best known as the birthplace of Sadat's assassin, Khalid al-Islambouli, and his brother Shawky, who fought with the Afghan *mujahadin* and later formed his own terrorist group in Egypt. Mallawi bore the brunt of the state's counter-insurgency campaign in the mid-1990s, which crippled its ecomomy, and the town still feels sullen, with a heavy police presence. Needless to stay, the local cops want visitors to pass through town as quickly as possible, but the details below might prove useful if the situation ever improves – in which case, don't miss the derelict Hindu-Gothic-style **feudal palace**, 150m in from the main road. There's also a small **museum**, displaying artefacts from Hermopolis and Tuna al-Gabel (supposedly daily except Fri 9am–4pm; £E6).

Practicalities

Mallawi straggles along both sides of the Ibrahimiya Canal, with its **transport** terminals dispersed on either side. On the **east bank** are the train station and, further south, the depot for service taxis to all points south of Mallawi.

Northbound taxis leave from a depot 200m north of the canal bridge. On the other side of this is **Sharia Essim**, the main drag, along which buses and service taxis shuttle between Minya and Assyut. Also on Sharia Essim is a **restaurant** which serves meat and rice with salad and bread, soft drinks and tea, while on Sharia Bank al-Misr, across the bridge from the station, the *El-Horriya Restaurant* does hearty *kofta* **meals**. There are **no hotels** in town, and this is not a place where you would want to be stuck overnight even if the police would permit it. Mallawi's Banque Misr (Mon–Thurs & Sun 8am–2pm) can **exchange** currency and travellers' cheques. To reach the **post office** (daily except Fri 8.30am–3pm), follow the dirt road to the left of the bank and turn left after 100m.

The rock tombs of Beni Hassan

Roughly midway between Minya and Mallawi, a range of barren cliffs east of the Nile shelters the **rock tombs of Beni Hassan** (daily 7am–5pm; £E12, camera permit £E5), named after an Arab tribe that once settled hereabouts. The vivid murals in this necropolis shed light on the Middle Kingdom (2050–1800 BC), a period when provincial dignitaries showed their greater independence by having grand burials locally, rather than at Saqqara. Beni Hassan is also memorable for the stark contrast between the fertile banks of the Nile and the desert. A path links the tombs to the isolated temple of **Speos Artemidos**, 3km away. Neither site offers food or water.

At present, the only way of **getting there** is by **private taxi** from Minya, with a police escort. The taxi should cost £E30–50, depending on your bargaining skills and how long you stay. The taxi will take you to the ferry for Beni Hassan, and wait for your return. You need to buy **tickets** for the **ferry** (£E8 for individuals; £E6 for up to seven people; £E2 per person for eight or more) and the **site** itself before crossing the Nile. A guard will acccompany you up the steps to the tombs and unlock them for you; a tip of £E2–3 is expected. As at all the sites in the Nile Valley, there is a heavy police presence.

Previously, you could also get to Beni Hassan by catching a pick-up or service taxi (30–40min) from Minya or Mallawi to **ABU QIRKUS**, crossing the main canal bridge and grabbing another pick-up (£E1) at the end of the street for the 3km ride to the river bank.

The tombs

Although most of Beni Hassan's 39 tombs are unfinished, the four shown to visitors evince a **stylistic evolution** during the XI–XII Dynasties. Their variously shaped chambers represent a transitional stage between the lateral *mastaba* tombs of the Old Kingdom and the deep shafts in the Valley of the Kings, gradually acquiring porched vestibules and sunken corridors to heighten the impact of the funerary effigies at the back. The actual mummies were secreted at the bottom of shafts, accompanied by funerary texts derived from the royal burials of the Old Kingdom. Pharaonic iconography and contemporary reportage are blended in the **murals**, whose innovative wrestling scenes presaged the battle vistas of the New Kingdom. Though battered or effaced in parts, their details reward careful study; the following descriptions are keyed to the tomb plans on p.304.

Tomb of Baqet III (#15)

Taking the chambers in chronological order, you should begin with the **Tomb of Baqet III**. Like other tombs, its images are arranged in "registers" (rows), whose height above floor level reflects their spatial relationship. Thus, Nile

BENI HASSAN

River Nile

N

0   Metres   25

Tomb of
Amenemhet

Tomb of
Khnumhotep

Tomb of
Baqet III

Tomb of Kheti

▼ Speos Artemidos

TOMB OF AMENEMHET

a   b

c   d

f   e

TOMB OF KHNUMHOTEP

b   c

d

a

g   f   e

TOMB OF BAQET III

b

a

c

d

TOMB OF KHETI

b   c   d

a

e

i

i   h   g   f

scenes go below those involving the Valley, above which come desert vistas, the highest ones most distant. Mural **[a]** shows papyrus-gathering in the marshes; **[b]** a desert hunt (notice the copulating gazelles) above pictures of ball players, women spinning and fullers beating cloth. The rear wall **[c]** depicts nearly 200 wrestling positions, while the south wall **[d]** is covered with episodes from the life of this XI Dynasty nomarch; in one scene, his underlings count cattle and punish tax defaulters.

Tomb of Kheti (#17)

Baqet bequeathed the governorship of the Oryx nome to his son, who was buried in the nearby **Tomb of Kheti**, which retains two of its structurally inessential papyrus-bud columns. In the murals, hippopotami ignore the papyrus harvest **[a]**, as desert creatures are hunted **[b]** above registers of weavers, dancers, artists and *senet*-players (*senet* is a game a bit like draughts); metalsmiths labour, musicians entertain Kheti and his wife **[c]**, and minions bring offerings of gazelles and birds **[d]**.

On the rear wall, warriors storm a fortress below a compendium of wrestling positions **[e]**. Grape harvesting and wine-making **[f]**, herding cattle **[h]** and ploughing **[i]** are only some of the tasks overseen by Kheti, who appears beneath a sunshade attended by his dwarf and fan-bearers **[g]**, and elsewhere receives offerings. Notice Kheti's boats, and bulls locking horns, near the entrance **[j]**.

Tomb of Amenemhet (#2)

Columned porticos and a niche for statues (which replaced the Old Kingdom *serdab* or secret chamber) are hallmarks of the XII Dynasty tombs, 150m north. Proto-Doric columns uphold a vaulted ceiling painted with checkered reed-mat patterns in the **Tomb of Amenemhet**. This nomarch's campaign honours are listed beside the door near a text relating the death of Senusert I. Leather-workers, armourers, masons and weavers **[a]** precede the customary hunting scene **[b]**, beneath which Amenemhet collects tribute from his estates – a scene with scribes brow-beating defaulters at the bottom. Below the wrestling and siege tableaux, boats escort him towards Abydos **[c]**, while a niche **[d]** holds broken effigies of Amenemhet, his mother and his wife Heptet, who sits at her own table to receive offerings **[e]**. Fish are netted and spit-roasted above a false door flanked by scenes of music making, cattle fording and baking **[f]**. The destroyed statues in the shrine showed Amenemhet sitting between his wife and mother.

Tomb of Khnumhotep (#3)

Amenemhet's successor was also governor of the Eastern Desert, hence the imposing portal framed by proto-Doric columns outside the **Tomb of Khnumhotep**. Left of the *muwu* dancers accompanying his cortege **[a]**, servants weigh grain and scribes record its storage in granaries; while agricultural scenes surmount Khnumhotep's voyage to Abydos **[b]**. Beneath the desert hunt **[c]**, Semitic Amus from Syria pay their respects to him, their alien costumes, flocks and tribute all minutely detailed – the governor is shown accepting eye paint.

Remnants of his statue in the niche are eclipsed by vivid scenes of him netting birds, hunting with a throwing stick **[d]**, and spearing fish from a punt in the marshes **[e]**, above a hippo, crocodiles and fishermen. After the usual offerings **[f]**, he inspects boat-building timber from a litter and then sails to Abydos **[g]**. Higher and lower registers portray laundrymen, weavers and various other artisans.

Speos Artemidos

The cliffside path at Beni Hassan affords a fine view of the Nile and the abrupt transition from cultivation to desert. If the police let you, follow it for 2.5km past the Tomb of Kheti and turn 500m up a wadi to find the small rock-hewn **temple of Speos Artemidos**. Begun by Queen Hatshepsut, whose claims to have restored order after Hyksos misrule are inscribed above its door (but typically usurped by Seti I), the temple has only roughed-out Hathor-headed columns, and its sanctuary – dominated by a statue of the lion-goddess Pakht – is largely unfinished. However, scenes of Hatshepsut making offerings to the gods have been executed in the hall. Just before the site there's a small **grotto** (*speos*), whence comes the temple's Greek name. Further into the desert are early Christian **hermit cells**, after whom the wadi was called the Valley of the Anchorites.

Antinopolis

The ancient city of **Antinopolis**, 10km south of Beni Hassan, deserves a mention for its origins alone. Touring Egypt with his lover Antinous in 130 AD, the Roman emperor Hadrian was warned by an oracle to expect a grievous loss, whereupon Antinous drowned himself in the Nile to prevent a greater calamity befalling his master. In grief, Hadrian deified the youth and founded a city in his honour before continuing south to Thebes with his unloved wife Plotina. Today, little remains but some fine red-granite columns; most of the **ruins** were used to build the neighbouring village of Sheikh Abadah, or turned into cement in the nineteenth century.

Hermopolis and Tuna al-Gabel

Northwest of Mallawi are two sites whose vestigial remains are less dramatic than their mythical associations. According to one tradition, the Creation began on a primordial mound near **Hermopolis**, where two stone baboons recall the long-vanished Temple of Thoth. Rather more remains of the city's necropolis, **Tuna al-Gabel**, where thousands of sacred baboons and ibises were buried in underground galleries. Both sites have been shunned by tourists since two guards were shot dead at Hermopolis in 1995; nowadays, the area is safe, but the police insist that you hire a **private taxi** from Minya and provide an escort. Expect to pay £E20–30, depending on how long you spend at the site. Although Hermopolis and Tuna al-Gabel appear relatively close to Tell el-Amarna on a map, crossing the Nile and getting around are time-consuming, so you should reckon on six or seven hours for an excursion combining all three sites. Most importantly, **check first** at Minya's tourist office that the sites are actually open, to avoid a wasted journey. If travel restrictions are lifted in the future, it should be possible to reach Ashmunein from Mallawi by local minibus or service taxi.

The ruins of Hermopolis

The pulverized ruins of Hermopolis spread beyond the village of **ASH-MUNEIN**, 8km from Mallawi. An access road curving off to the west of Ashmunein brings you to a pair of **giant sandstone baboons** that once sported erect phalluses (hacked off by early Christians) and upheld the ceiling of the Temple of Thoth. Built by Ramses II using masonry from Tell el-Amarna, the temple stood within an enclosure covering 640 square metres, the spiritual heart of the city of the moon-god.

Hermopolis was a cult centre from early Dynastic times, venerated as the site of the primeval mound where the sun-god emerged from a cosmic egg. Like

Thoth and the Hermopolitan Ogdoad

In Egyptian mythology, **Thoth** was the divine scribe and reckoner of time, the inventor of writing and the patron god of scribes. His cult probably originated in the Delta, but achieved the greatest following in Middle Egypt; later, by association with Khonsu, he acquired the attributes of the moon-god and mastery over science and knowledge. Though usually depicted with a man's body and the head of an ibis (his sacred bird), Thoth also assumed the form of a great white baboon, invariably endowed with an outsize penis. Baboons habitually shriek just before dawn, and the Egyptians believed that a pair of them uttered the first greetings to the sun from the sand dunes at the edge of the world.

Thoth

Thoth's role is rather more complex in relation to the Hermopolitan cosmogony, which ordained that the chaos preceding the world's creation had four characteristics, each identified with a pair of gods and goddesses: primordial water (*Nun/Nanuet*), infinite space (*Heh/Hehet*), darkness (*Kek/Keket*) and invisibility (*Amun/Amunet*). From this chaos arose the primeval mound and the cosmic egg whence the sun-god was hatched and proceeded to organize the world. While stressing the role of this **Hermopolitan Ogdoad** (company of eight), Thoth's devotees credited him with laying the cosmic egg in the guise of the "Great Cackler", so it's difficult to know who got star billing in this Creation myth. By the New Kingdom it had generally succumbed to the version espoused at Heliopolis (see p.206), but Thoth's cult continued into Ptolemaic times.

Heliopolis (which made similar claims) its priesthood evolved an elaborate cosmogony, known as the Hermopolitan Ogdoad (see above). Though ancient Egyptians called the city *Khmunu*, history remembers it as **Hermopolis Magna**; its Ptolemaic title reflects the Greek association of Thoth with their own god Hermes. However, none of the mounds of earth and rubble that remain seems credible as the site of Creation, and there's little to see except 24 slender rose-granite **columns**, further south. Re-erected by archeologists who mistook the ruins for a Greek *agora*, they previously supported a Coptic basilica, but originally belonged to a Ptolemaic temple.

Tuna al-Gabel

From Ashmunein, a back road continues to the village of **TUNA EL-GABEL**, which lends its name to the ancient **necropolis** (daily 8am–5pm; £E12) 6km further on. Along the way, notice the boundary stele on a distant cliff, marking the edge of the agricultural land that was claimed by Tell el-Amarna, across the river (see section following). The necropolis itself is awash with sand, wind-rippled drifts casting its angular mausolea into high relief, but obscuring other features.

A path to the right of the entrance leads to the **catacombs** (*As-Saradeb*), which some believe stretch as far as Hermopolis. The accessible portion consists of several main corridors with blocked-off side passages, where the mummified baboons and ibises were stacked (a few bandages remain). A shrine near the ladder contains a baboon fetish and a pathetic-looking mummy; baboons were sacred to Thoth (see above). Beneath the main gallery lies the tomb of a temple priest.

Further along the main track is a miniature **City of the Dead**, with "streets" of mausolea that mostly reflect Hellenistic influences. The finest structure is the **Tomb of Petosiris**, High Priest of Thoth (whose coffin is in the Cairo Antiquities Museum), dating from around 300 BC. Its vestibule walls depict traditional activities such as brick-making, sewing and reaping (left), milking, husbandry and wine-making (right) – with all the figures wearing Greek costume. Inside the tomb are colourful scenes from the *Book of Gates* and the *Book of the Dead*. The most vivid scene shows nine baboons, twelve women and a dozen cobras, each set representing a temporal cycle. Notice the Nubians at the bottom of the opposite wall.

Behind this is another "house" whose upper room displays the **Mummy of Isadora**, a young woman from Antinopolis who drowned in the Nile around 120 BC. Victims of the life-giving river acquired posthumous sanctity, but the leathery state of Isadora's corpse owes to 2000 years of desert air rather than embalming techniques, which had by then degenerated. Beyond Isadora's tomb, and some **columns** from the Temple of Thoth that once dominated the site, lies the brick superstructure of *As-Saqiyya*, a **well** that once supplied the necropolis and its sacred aviary with fresh water, drawn up from 70m below the desert by a huge **water wheel**. The well is infested with bats.

Tell el-Amarna

TELL EL-AMARNA is the familiar name for the site where **Pharaoh Akhenaten** and **Queen Nefertiti** founded a city dedicated to a revolutionary idea of God, which later rulers assailed as heretical. During their brief reign, Egyptian art cast off its preoccupation with death and the afterlife to revel in human concerns; bellicose imperialism gave way to pacifistic retrenchment; and the old gods were toppled from their pedestals. The interplay between personalities, beliefs and art anticipates the Renaissance – and their story beats Shakespeare for sheer drama.

The interest of the **site** (see p.311 for access details) is chiefly romantic, for what remains is hardly comparable to the great temples further up the Nile. Only the faintest outline of the city is discernible, while the reliefs in its rock-cut tombs have been badly mutilated (initially by reactionaries, who defaced the images of Akhenaten and his deity). Nonetheless, it strikes some visitors as intensely evocative: a place of mystery whose enchantment grows the more one knows about it.

The story of Akhenaten and Nefertiti

Few figures from ancient history have inspired as much conjecture as Akhenaten and Nefertiti, as scholars dispute even fundamental aspects of their story – let alone the interpretation of the events.

The tale begins with Pharaoh **Amenophis III**, who flouted convention by making Tiy, his Nubian concubine, Great Wife, despite her lack of royal blood. **Queen Tiy** remained formidable long after Amenophis entered his dotage and their eldest son ascended the throne as **Amenophis IV**. Some believe this event followed his father's death, others that mother and son ruled jointly for twelve years. To square the former theory with the period of his reign (c.1379–1362 BC) and his demise around the age of thirty means accepting that Amenophis Jr embarked on his religious reformation between the ages of nine and thirteen. It seems an unusually early age, though a marriage at thirteen is quite likely.

The origins of Amenophis's wife, **Nefertiti**, are obscure. Her name – meaning "A Beautiful Woman Has Come" – suits the romantic legend that she was a Mesopotamian princess originally betrothed to Amenophis III. However, others identify her as Amenophis III's child by a secondary wife, or as the daughter of his vizier **Ay**, whose wife, **Tey**, was almost certainly Nefertiti's wet nurse. The pharaonic custom of sister–brother and father–daughter marriages allows plenty of scope for speculation, but the fair-skinned bust of Nefertiti in the Berlin Museum suggests that she wasn't Tiy's child, at any rate. (Amid all the fuss about Cleopatra being black, nobody seems to have noticed that Queen Tiy – and therefore her son, Amenophis IV – were indubitably so.)

Early in his reign, Amenophis IV began to espouse the **worship of Aten** (see p.310), whose ascendancy threatened the priesthoods of other cults. The bureaucracy was equally alarmed by his decree that the spoken language should be used in official documents, contrary to all tradition. To escape their influence and realize his vision of a city dedicated to Aten, the pharaoh founded a **new capital** upon an empty plain beside the Nile, halfway between Memphis and Thebes, which he named **Akhetaten**, the "Horizon of the Aten".

It was here that the royal couple settled in the fifth year of their reign and took Aten's name in honour of their faith. He discarded Amenophis IV for **Akhenaten** (Servant of the Aten) and vowed never to leave the city, while she took a forename meaning "Beautiful are the Beauties of the Aten", styling herself **Nefernefruaten–Nefertiti**. Her status surpassed that of any previous Great Wife, approaching that of Akhenaten himself. Bas-reliefs and stelae show her participating in state festivals and her own cartouche was coupled with Aten's – an unprecedented association. Tableaux from this period depict an idyllic royal family life, with the couple embracing their daughters and banqueting with Queen Tiy.

There's no sign that their happiness was marred by his decision to take a second wife, **Kiya**, for dynastic ends; nor of the degenerate condition that supposedly afflicted Akhenaten in later life. However, the great ceremony held at Akhetaten in their twelfth regnal year marked a turning point. Whether or not this was Akhenaten's true coronation (following his father's death), he subsequently launched a **purge against the old cults**. From Kom Ombo to Bubastis, the old temples were closed and their statues disfigured, causing widespread internal unrest. Although this was quelled by Akhenaten's chief of police, **Mahu**, his foreign minister apparently ignored pleas from foreign vassals menaced by the Hittites and Habiru, and the army was less than zealous in defending Egypt's frontiers. Akhenaten was consequently blamed for squandering the territorial gains of his forefathers.

What happened in the last years of Akhenaten and Nefertiti's reign is subject to various interpretations. The consensus is that Nefertiti and Akhenaten became estranged, and he took as co-regent **Smenkhkare**, a mysterious youth married to their eldest daughter, **Meritaten**. While Nefertiti withdrew to her Northern Palace, Akhenaten and his regent lived together at the other end of the city; the poses struck by them in mural scenes of the period have prompted suggestions of a homosexual relationship. Whatever the truth of this, it's known that Smenkhkare ruled alone for some time after the **death of Akhenaten** (c.1362 BC), before dying himself. Nefertiti's fate is less certain, but it's generally believed that she also died around the same time. To date, none of their mummies have been found (or, rather, definitely identified).

In the late 1970s, a novel solution to the puzzle of Smenkhkare's identity and the **fate of Nefertiti** was advanced by Julia Samson of the Petrie Museum in London. Samson argued that Smenkhkare *was* Nefertiti, who, far from being

Many scholars herald **Aten-worship** as a breakthrough in human spirituality and cultural evolution: the world's first monotheistic religion, and thus representing "a peak of clarity which rose above the lowlands of superstition".

Aten was originally just an aspect of the sun-god (the "Globe" or "Disc" of the mid-day sun), ranking low in the Theban pantheon until Amenophis III privately adopted it as a personal deity. Then Akhenaten publicly exalted Aten above other gods, subsuming all their attributes into this newly omnipotent being. Invocations to Maat (truth) were retained, but otherwise the whole cast of underworld and celestial deities was jettisoned. Morbid Osirian rites were also replaced by paeans to life in the joyous warmth of Aten's rays (which are usually shown ending in a hand clasping an *ankh*), as in this extract from the *Hymn to Aten*:

When you rise from the horizon the earth grows bright; you shine as the Aten in the sky and drive away the darkness; when your rays gleam forth, the whole of Egypt is festive. People wake and stand on their feet, for you have lifted them up … Then the whole of the land does its work; all the cattle enjoy their pastures, trees and plants grow green, birds fly up from their nests and raise their wings in praise of your spirit. Goats frisk on their feet and all the fluttering and flying things come alive.

Similarities between the *Hymn* and *The Song of Solomon* (supposedly written 500 years later) have encouraged speculation about the influence of Atenism on early Jewish monotheism. In *Moses and Monotheism*, Freud argued that Moses was an Egyptian nobleman and the Biblical Exodus a "pious fiction which a remote tradition has reworked in the service of its own biases". Conversely, a book by Ahmed Osman advances the theory that Akhenaten's deity derived from tales of the Jewish God related to him by his maternal grandfather Yuya, the Joseph of the Old Testament (see p.402).

Equally intriguing is the artwork of the Amarna period and the questions it raises about Akhenaten. **Amarna art** focused on nature and human life rather than the netherworld and resurrection. Royal portraiture, previously impersonally formalized, was suffused by naturalism (a process which began late in the reign of Amenophis III, as evinced by the stele depicting the obese king listlessly slumped beside Tiy). While marshes and wildlife remained a popular subject, they no longer implicitly associated birds and fish with the forces of chaos. The roofless Aten temples made new demands on sculptors and painters, who mixed sunk- and bas-relief carving to highlight features with shifting shadows and illumination.

Most striking is the rendering of **human figures**, especially Akhenaten's, whose attenuated cranium, curvaceous spine and belly, and matronly pelvis and buttocks (evident on the colossi in the Cairo Museum) have prompted speculation that the pharaoh may have suffered from Marfan's syndrome – a rare genetic disorder that leads to feel-

Nerfertiti and Akhenaten

ings of alienation and a slight oddness in physical appearance – or was possibly a hermaphrodite. Some argue that the Amarna style was essentially an acquiescence to Akhenaten's physiognomy, others that such distortions were simply a device that could be eschewed, as in the exquisite bust of Nefertiti. Advocates of the "Akhenaten was sick" theory point out that this was the only time when vomiting was ever represented in Egyptian art; however, Amarna art also uniquely depicted royalty eating, yet nobody asserts that other pharaohs never ate.

spurned by Akhenaten, finally achieved pharaonic status, adopting Smenkhkare as her "throne name". Since the faces on the stelae depicting Akhenaten and his co-regent have been obliterated, only their cartouches identify them; and previous hypotheses have never satisfactorily explained why Smenkhkare's should be coupled with "Nefernefruaten", Nefertiti's Aten-name. Conversely, the youth shown with a princess isn't identified as her husband, nor by name, but he does wear the royal *uraeus* (see p.294 for information on pharaonic symbols). Unfortunately, this figure looks too old to be the famous boy-king who succeeded Smenkhkare at the age of nine – known to posterity as **Tutankhamun**. Tut's own genealogy is obscure (some hold that his parents were Amenophis III and his half-sister Sitamun; others favour Ay and Tey, or Akhenaten and Kiya), but it's certain that he was originally raised to worship Aten, and named Tutankh*aten*. By renouncing this name for one honouring Amun, he heralded a return to Thebes and the old gods, fronting a **Theban counter-revolution** executed by Vizier Ay and General Horemheb.

Some think this was relatively benign while Tut and his successor Ay ruled Egypt, blaming **Horemheb** and Seti I for a later and ruthless extirpation of Atenism. Certainly, in time-honoured tradition, Seti plundered the abandoned city of Akhetaten for masonry to build new temples, ordered its site cursed by priests to deter reoccupation, and excised the cartouches of every ruler tainted with the "Amarna heresy" from their monuments and the List of Kings. So thorough was this cover-up that Akhenaten and Nefertiti remained unknown to history until the nineteenth century.

The site of Akhetaten

The **remains of Akhenaten's city** are spread across a desert plain girdled by an arc of cliffs. Except for a few palm groves beside the Nile, the site is utterly desolate, a tawny expanse of low mounds and narrow trenches littered with potshards. These fragments of pale terracotta, cream and duck-egg blue-glazed pottery seem more tangible links to the city's past than its vestigial remains. Because the city was created from scratch and deserted soon after Tut moved the court back to Thebes, its era of glory lasted only twelve years, and much of the building was never completed, so don't expect to find imposing ruins or statues, as everything of value has been removed to museums. However, a century of archeological research has identified the city's salient features, assisted by pictures found in contemporary tombs.

Visiting Tell el-Amarna

Tell el-Amarna (daily: Oct–May 7am–4pm, June–Sept 7am–5pm; £E12) lies on the east bank of the Nile, 12km southeast of Mallawi and roughly halfway between Minya and Assyut. While tour groups are coming again, independent travellers are still rare and presently only allowed to get there by **private taxi** from Minya or Assyut (£E30–50 return), accompanied by a police escort. However, if restrictions are relaxed it should be possible to get there **from Mallawi**, by taking a service taxi or covered pick-up from the depot south of the train station to the ferry crossing on the west bank. You have a choice of three ways to cross the Nile: by passenger launch (50pt), car ferry (50pt; last one at 6pm) or the blue tourist boat (£E4 return for one or two people; £E1 each for three or more) – tickets for the first two are sold on the west bank, tickets for the latter on the east bank.

Landing at **EL-TILL**, you'll be greeted by hordes of children touting colourful basketwork. Near the landing stage is a small office selling **tickets** for admission to the site and three different **bus tours**. A two-hour tour of the

Northern Tombs

El-Qusiya & Assyut ◀

▲ Mallawi (7 km)

N

Northern
Tombs

Ibrahimiya Canal

Northern
Palace

Tickets

El-Till

Great
Temple

State
Palace

Archives

Royal
Residence

Deir
el-Mawas

Sanctuary
of Aten

Wadi el-Melouk

River Nile

Workmen's
Village

El-Hagg
Qandil

ROYAL ROAD

Southern
Tombs

Al-Hawatah

Hatnub Quarries ▼

Northern Tombs and Palace costs £E8 (or £E3.75 for each person if there are more than three), plus which each individual has to pay £E12 (£E6 for students) on arrival at the tombs. A tour of the **Southern Tombs** costs £E23 (shared among one to eight people) or £E3.75 per person for groups of more than eight, while to visit the secluded **Royal Tomb** costs £E35 for the bus (up to eight people) or £E5 each if there are more than eight passengers. While there's no tour of the ruined city, you'll pass it en route to the Royal or Southern tombs, and could get off the bus on the return journey to explore the site before walking back to El-Till.

The City

The dirt track running south from El-Till follows the old **Royal Road** that formed ancient Akhetaten's main axis, and is known locally as the *Sikket es-Sultan*, the Road of the Sultan. Alongside is a Muslim cemetery, which overlies part of a vast rectangle stretching eastwards towards the ridge. This was once the **Great Temple of Aten**, whose northern wall incorporated the Hall of Foreign Tribute where emissaries proffered treasure (as depicted in tombs). Unlike traditional temples, which got darker as one approached the sanctuary, Aten's was roofless, admitting the rays of its namesake. It's thought that Horemheb ordered the temple's destruction after Akhenaten's death, and Ramses II quarried its foundations for his temples at Hermopolis, across the Nile.

TOMB OF HUYA (1)

TOMB OF MERY-RE I (2)

Royal Tomb •

TOMB OF AY (3)

0   kilometres   2

✳ Boundary Stele   **TELL EL-AMARNA**

Further south (and hard to distinguish beneath shifting sands) are the remnants of the Foreign Office **Archives**, where the **Amarna Letters** were discovered. Written in the Akkadian script used for diplomatic correspondence with Asiatic states, these clay tablets have revealed much about the period. Over 360 letters have been found, but more were undoubtedly lost, leaving an incomplete puzzle for archeologists to piece together and argue over. David Rohl believes that some refer to the Israelite monarchs Saul and David.

Next come three excavated rectangles that were once the **Royal Residence**. Their private apartments were separated from the stately reception halls that ran through the centre of the huge palace compound. When Flinders Petrie excavated Nefertiti's suite, he found wall tiles decorated with fruit and flowers, and a painted floor depicting fish, birds and insects (later smashed by a farmer who resented tourists walking across his fields). Across the Royal Road stood an even larger **State Palace**, with a dock for the royal barge. Both palaces were connected by a covered "flyover" spanning the road (part of one pylon remains), into which was set the **Window of Appearances**, whence Nefertiti and Akhenaten showered favoured courtiers with gold collars and other rewards.

To the south of their residence lay the **Sanctuary of Aten**, probably used for private worship by the royal family, and the home of the High Priest, Panehsi. Beyond spread the city's **residential quarters**; the richest homes beside the road, the poorest hovels backing onto desert. Also in this quarter was the workshop of the sculptor Tuthmosis, where the famous bust of Nefertiti was uncovered in 1912, before being smuggled to Berlin's Ägyptisches Museum.

Outlying palaces and stelae

The best-preserved outline of an Amarna building is Nefertiti's **Northern Palace** or summer residence, 1500m from El-Till. Low walls and hollows delineate rooms and courtyards grouped around a garden which once contained a pool that cooled the palace by evaporation. Like all Amarna residences, it was divided into public and private quarters, with north-facing doors to catch the prevailing wind. Rooms were plastered and painted, lit by oil lamps hung from pegs or set in niches, and warmed by braziers over winter. Fitted toilets and bathrooms also featured in the homes of the well-to-do. Although you can walk on bits of mosaic floor once trodden by Nefertiti, the finest section of painted flooring – depicting wildfowl and fish in the marshes – now lies in the Cairo Antiquities Museum. Unlike traditional marsh scenes, Amarna tableaux rarely feature hunting, suggesting that Akhenaten abjured the sport of kings.

In summer, Akhenaten and Nefertiti would ride in their electrum-plated chariot to the other end of the Royal Road, where another palace called Maru-Aten stood near the modern-day hamlet of Al-Hawatah. Alongside this **Southern Palace** lay a pleasure lake surrounded by trees and shrubs, which fed smaller pools within the palace. The walls of its columned hall were painted with flowers and inlaid with figures and Aten symbols. It was here that Petrie found hundreds of glazed pieces and flakes of paint adhering to blocks that bore Meritaten's cartouche superimposed over another, assumed to be that of Nefertiti – the rather shaky basis upon which archeologists devised the theory of Nefertiti's rejection in favour of Smenkhkare. In 1974, however, Professor John Harris re-examined the fragments and concluded that the hidden cartouches really belonged to Kiya, whose existence had been unknown to earlier scholars. From this point on, Samson developed her theory that Nefertiti and Smenkhkare were one and the same.

Akhetaten's periphery was defined by **boundary stelae** carved high up on the cliffs (marked ★ on our map); erected over successive years, their inscriptions and family portraits have enabled archeologists to deduce many events during Akhenaten's reign. Fine alabaster for the temples and public buildings was dragged from the **Hatnub Quarries**, 10km southeast of the city (only accessible by donkey or four-wheel-drive). On the way up the wadi are the remains of workmen's huts and pottery from diverse periods.

The Northern Tombs

Most visitors are content to see just the **Northern Tombs**, 4km from El-Till village. Although guards manipulate foil-covered boards to reflect sunlight into tombs without electric lighting, it's advisable to bring a torch to study the reliefs and paintings (now less clear than the exquisite copies made by Norman de Garis Davies, a century ago), and to spotlight uneven floors or deep shafts with flimsy railings. Note that, unless you insist, you won't be shown the most distant of the six **tombs** (#1 and #2). We have given plans for the two Northern Tombs which are the most rewarding to visit.

Tomb of Huya (#1)

As Steward to Queen Tiy and Superintendent of the Royal Harem, **Huya** is shown praying at the entrance, beside a *Hymn to Aten* **[a]** – see plan no. 1 on the map. In the following banqueting scene **[b]**, involving Tiy, the royal couple and two princesses, it may be significant that the dowager queen is merely drinking (which was acceptable by Theban standards of decorum), whereas the Amarna brood tuck in with gusto (an act never hitherto portrayed of royalty). Across the way they imbibe wine, *sans* princesses **[c]**, followed by a royal procession to the Hall of Tribute, where emissaries from Kush and Syria await Akhenaten and Nefertiti **[d]**.

On the rear wall, Akhenaten decorates Huya from the Window of Appearances (notice the sculptor's studio, lower down **[e]**), who displays his awards **[f]** on the other side of the portal, the lintel of which portrays three generations of the royal family, including Amenophis III. Along the east wall, Akhenaten leads Tiy to the temple built for his parents **[g]**. Huya's mummy was stashed in a burial shaft **[h]** below the transverse hall, beyond which is a shrine painted with offerings, containing an unfinished statue of Huya **[i]**.

Tomb of Mery-Re II (#2)
The last resting place of **Mery-Re II**, Overseer of the Two Treasuries, is similar in shape to Huya's tomb, but was constructed late in Akhenaten's reign, since his cartouches have been replaced by Smenkhkare's, and Nefertiti's by Meritaten's. Beyond the entrance (whose adoration scene and *Hymn to Aten* are largely destroyed), the inner walls portray Nefertiti straining a drink for the king, who is seated beneath a sunshade (to your left); and Mery-Re receiving a golden crown, followed by a warm welcome from his household (right). The rear wall bears an unfinished scene of Mery-Re being rewarded by Smenkhkare and Meritaten, drawn in black ink.

Tomb of Ahmose (#3)
This battered tomb is one of the four that visitors usually see. The entrance walls show **Ahmose**, Akhenaten's fan-bearer, praying to Aten, with a now-illegible inscription enjoining the deity to ensure "that there is sand on the shore, that fishes in the stream have scales, and cattle have hair. Let him sojourn here until the swan turns black and the raven white". Inside, you can just discern Ahmose carrying an axe and a fan, his official regalia. On the left-hand wall are reliefs of archers, shield-bearers and pikemen, crouched and moving, followed by an outsized horse and chariot outlined in red pigment (presumably intended to represent Akhenaten leading his army into battle, which never happened).

Tomb of Mery-Re I (#4)
High Priest **Mery-Re I** (father of Mery-Re II) rated a superior tomb (see plan no. 2 on the map), with a coloured cornice around its entrance **[a]** and columns of painted flowers at the rear of the vestibule **[b]**. Reliefs of Mery-Re and his wife, Tenro, at prayer flank the portal **[c]** into the main chamber, which retains two of its original papyrus-bud columns. Proceeding clockwise round the room, one sees Mery-Re's investiture with a golden collar **[d]**, the royal family leaving the palace **[e]**, and Akhenaten in a chariot (his face and the Aten symbol have been chiselled out, as usual). Scenes of offerings **[f]** and Aten-worship **[g]** flank the doorway into the unfinished rear chamber, which lacks any decoration. More interesting is the eastern wall **[h]**, depicting Akhenaten and the Great Temple (which has helped archeologists visualize the city's appearance). Notice the sensitive relief of blind beggars awaiting alms, low down in the corner **[i]**.

Tombs of Pentu (#5) and Panehsi (#6)

The third tomb in this cluster belongs to **Pentu**, the royal physician, whose statue in the endmost chamber has been disfigured. Its reliefs are in even worse shape, so there's no point wasting time here when you could be checking out the isolated tomb of High Priest **Panehsi**, 500m south along the cliff path. Unlike most of the others, its decorative facade has remained intact, but the interior has been modified by Copts who used it as a chapel. On the left of the entrance the royal family pray above their servants. The painted, apse-like recess in the main chamber is probably a Coptic addition. In one corner, steps spiral down into an underground sarcophagus chamber containing broken urns. Lower down the cliff are strata of rubble and potshards – vestiges of a medieval Coptic village.

Unas

The Royal Tomb

Secreted in a wild ravine 5.5km from the plain, reached by a rough track buffeted by tumbleweeds and sandstorms, the **Royal Tomb** is the first from the XVIII Dynasty to run directly from a corridor to a burial chamber. The burial scene and text were virtually obliterated by Amun's priests, and no mummies were ever found here. However, one of the side chambers off the main corridor contained fragments of a granite sarcophagus bearing Tiy's cartouche, suggesting this might have been a family vault. Almost certainly, it served for the burial of Meketaten, the royal couple's second-eldest daughter, for the walls bear scenes of her funeral and their grief. No one knows whether Akhenaten and Nefertiti were interred here (and perhaps dragged out to rot a few years later) or somewhere else. Some believe that the mysterious mummy found in Tomb #55 in the Valley of the Kings is Akhenaten's (see p.402).

The Southern Tombs

From El-Till, the bus takes half an hour to reach the **Southern Tombs**, 14km away, where visitors are allowed to linger as long as they wish. The tombs are scattered over seven low hills in two clusters: #7–15 and #16–25. Amarna notables buried here include Tutu, the foreign minister, and Ramose, Steward of Amenophis III; but the ones to look out for are Mahu and Ay.

Tomb of Mahu (#9)

Set amongst the northernmost group is the **Tomb of Mahu**, Akhenaten's chief of police and frontier security. The structure has a long, rough-cut corridor without decoration. On the right-hand entrance wall of the first chamber, Mahu appears before the vizier with two intruders whom he accuses of being "agitated by some foreign power". Further back are two more chambers at different levels, linked by a winding stairway and decorated with scenes of Mahu mixing with royalty.

Tomb of Ay (#25)

Ay's Tomb, the finest at Tell el-Amarna (see plan no. 3 on the map), lies some distance beyond the southern group and was never finished, since Ay built himself a new vault at Thebes after the court returned there under Tutankhamun. However, such paintings as were executed show the Amarna style at its apogee.

Both sides of the tomb's vestibule **[a]** are decorated. On the left, the king and queen, three princesses, Nefertiti's sister Mutnedjmet and her dwarves lead the court in the worship of Aten. Across the way is a superb relief of Ay and his wife Tey rendering homage and the most complete text of the famous *Hymn to Aten*. The really intriguing scenes, however, are in the main chamber. On the left side of the entrance wall, Ay and Tey are showered with decorations from the Window of Appearances, acclaimed by fan-bearers, scribes and guards **[b]**. Palace life is intimately observed: a concubine has her hair done, while girls play the harp and dance, cook and sweep; further along, Ay is congratulated by his friends, as servants carry the gifts away **[c]**. The top register shows doormen and peasants gossiping, whores and soldiers, and other streetlife. Along the rear wall are a ruined door-shaped stele **[d]** and a stairway leading to an unfinished burial shaft.

Ay and Tey are mysterious figures, honoured as "Divine Father and Mother", but never directly identified as being royal. Some reckon **Ay** was a son of Yuya and Thuya, Akhenaten's maternal grandparents; others that Tey was Nefertiti's wet-nurse, or that both conceived Tutankhamun. Certainly, Ay was vizier to Amenophis III, Akhenaten and Tutankhamun, and reigned briefly himself (1352–1348 BC). He was ultimately buried in the Western Valley of the Theban Necropolis (see p.402).

Assyut and around

Every country has at least one city which is universally loathed by all but those who live there. In Egypt, Assyut holds this honour.

Douglas Kennedy, *Beyond The Pyramids*

ASSYUT was the first part of Middle Egypt to become a virtual **no-go zone** for tourists, as locally based Islamic militants targeted foreigners as well as the security forces in their war against the state. The city endured nearly a decade of curfews and arrests as the conflict spread south before fizzling out, leaving Assyut with an overwhelming presence of police and security forces, and the mother of bad reputations. So it's not surprising that citizens – and the Christian population especially – should rejoice at the nightly **apparitions of the Virgin Mary** that occurred, or so people swear, in September 2000, in the form of a light above the tower of the Church of St Mark. Another cause for optimism since then is the upturn in the local economy, due to private and state investments in factories and businesses. Even so, tourism isn't likely to play much of a part in its economic revival, for Assyut has little going for it aside from the monasteries and tombs outside town, and few **visitors** feel comfortable being followed by a policeman wherever they go – even if it's supposedly for their own safety.

That said, anyone hoping **to reach Kharga Oasis** (see p.510) from the Nile Valley (or vice versa) might find it hard to avoid Assyut. The train from Luxor to Kharga only runs once a week and there's no public transport along the desert road between them (which tourists starting from Luxor aren't allowed to use, anyway), whereas there are regular service taxis and buses between Kharga and Assyut. And since the train, bus and service taxi stations are near each other in the centre of town, switching from one form of transport to another is easy. Be warned, however, that service taxis **arriving from Kharga** often terminate at a subsidiary depot beside the El-Mallah canal, so you'll have to catch a private taxi (£E5) to the bus or train station to continue your journey.

Information and accommodation

Assyut's low-key **tourist office** (daily except Fri 8.30am–2pm; ℡088/310-010), on the first floor of the Governorate building, is keen to help, but insists that tourists are escorted by police and will alert the cops if you haven't been noticed yet. Anyone hoping to visit Dirunka or El-Qusiya (see p.321) should seek their advice. Assyut's main **post office** faces the *Badr Hotel* behind the train station, while the 24–hour **telephone exchange** is further south. You can change **money** on Midan al-Bank, where the Bank of Alexandria and Banque Misr have ATMs; the latter does cash advances on Visa and MasterCard. The **police** (℡122) are on the Corniche and there's a **hospital** (℡088/322-016) attached to Assyut University; dial ℡123 for an ambulance.

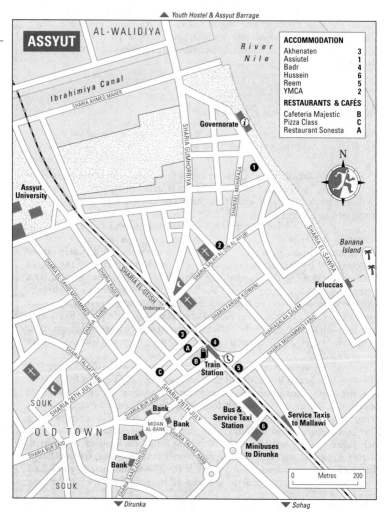

Assyut's militant tradition

In the late 1970s, **Assyut University** became a stronghold of **Islamic Societies** (*Gama'at Islamiya*) bent on turning Egypt into an Islamic republic. They managed to get music and co-ed drama banned, and cafeterias segregated by sex; violations of their standards were liable to be punished by club-wielding militants. The authorities turned a blind eye until 1981, when Sadat cracked down on religious extremism after years of tolerating it as a counterweight to the Left.

In response, members of the secret group **Al-Jihad** (Holy Struggle) assassinated Sadat in Cairo and stormed Assyut police headquarters the following day, hoping to launch a revolution. Two days of rioting ensued, causing 55 deaths. Among those later indicted at the mass "Trial of the Jihad 302" was the blind university theologian **Sheikh Omar Abd el-Rahman**, their "spiritual leader". Acquitted but exiled to the Fayoum, the Sheikh later moved to the US, where in 1995 he was sentenced to life imprisonment for conspiring to blow up the World Trade Center. By that time many of his followers had joined forces with al-Qaida (see p.809), whose own attack on the Twin Towers on September 11 was reputedly undertaken in Abd el-Rahman's name. In 2001 his son, Ahmed, was captured by US forces in Afghanistan, fighting with the Taliban.

The 1997 massacre at Hatshepsut's Temple (see p.403) was also related to the Sheikh and Assyut; the splinter-group responsible was recruited and led by Assyut-born Medhat Abd el-Rahman (no relation) and consisted of five students from Assyut University. A letter found on one of the terrorists claimed that they meant to seize hostages in a bid to bargain for Abd el-Rahman's release from prison.

Accommodation

It's best to hole up in a hotel near the station or the Governorate building on the Corniche. The police prefer that foreigners stay in upmarket hotels, and have told the managers of low-budget places not to accept foreign guests. Depending on how many comply, your options may be limited. The *Venus*, *Semiramis* and *Lotus* hotels are not recommended.

Akhenaten Sharia Mohammed Tewfik Khashaba ☎088/337-723, ⓕ331-600. This tower-block hotel on the edge of the commercial district has slighty gloomy but clean and comfy a/c rooms, with private baths and TV. ❸

Assiutel 146 Sharia el-Nil ☎088/312-121, ⓕ312-122. Agreeable three-star hotel overlooking the Nile, with a/c, satellite TV, fridges and baths in the rooms, and a bar and restaurant. ❺

Badr Sharia Nahda ☎088/329-811, ⓕ322-820. Right by the train station, and thus noisy, this hotel is palatial in a kitsch 1980s way; its padded, mirrored rooms come equipped with a video channel, mini-bar and a/c. Bar and restaurant. ❻

Hussein Sharia Mohammed Farid ☎088/338-437, ⓕ352-599. Small, comfortable hotel over-

looking the bus station; handy for transport connections but noisy. ❸

Reem Sharia el-Nahda ☎088/311-421, ⓕ311-424. A rather shabby three-star place beside the railway tracks; rooms at the back are quieter. ❸

YMCA Sharia Salah al-Din al-Ayubi ☎088/323-218. Sited in a quiet area, the old section has simple, clean doubles with fridges; the newer wing large carpeted rooms with a/c, TV and private bath for just over twice the price. ❷

Youth Hostel Lux Houses, 503 Sharia al-Walidiya ☎088/324-846. Shabby dorm beds, out near the Assyut Barrage; the entrance is on a side street. No HI membership required. Beds cost £E6 per person.

The City

A dusty metropolis seething with traffic, **Assyut** has largely erased its own history. Scores of rock tombs west of town are the only sign of pharaonic Sawty, a nome capital which the Greeks renamed Lycopolis (Wolftown) after the local god, **Wepwawet**, "Opener of the Ways". Represented as a wolf or jackal of the desert, he was an apt symbol for a city which later prospered from slavery, for it was here that survivors of the Forty Days Road (see p.549) emerged from the desert to be traded wholesale. Trafficking may have continued until 1883, although Amelia Edwards saw nothing amiss a decade earlier, when she enthused over the "quaint red vases" and "bird-shaped bottles" in Assyut's souks.

Nowadays the souks purvey nothing worse than flyblown meat at the seedy end of the sprawling commercial district that stretches from Sharia Talaat Harb into the **Old Town**. A shopper's mecca it's not, but **carpets** are a local speciality, and there's some pleasure to be had wandering the backstreets of decaying colonial mansions smothered in creepers, trying to locate a derelict **khan** that once stabled camels or the **Hammam al-Qadim** bathhouse, with its fine marble fountain.

On the other side of the tracks, Assyut's **riverside quarter** is freshened by breezes and greenery. Sharia Salah Salem leads directly to the Nile, where a felucca can be rented to reach **Banana Island** (*Gezira el-Mohz*), a lush picnic spot. Assyut's elite can be found in the Governorate building and private clubs en route to the British-built (1898–1903) **Assyut Barrage**, 2km downriver, which acts as a bridge across the Nile.

On the far bank lies the **Lillian Trasher Orphanage** (*Malga Trasher*), the largest and best-known institution of its kind in Egypt (there's another famous one in Tanta, funded by the pop star Mohammed Tharwat). It was founded in 1911 by an American missionary, Lillian Trasher (born in Jacksonville, Florida), who came to Egypt at the age of 23 and died in her adopted homeland in 1961. The orphanage is a source of pride for Assyut's Copts, and interested visitors are welcome (donations appreciated). Microbuses (50pt) from the centre of town stop nearby, or you can get a taxi (£E3).

Eating and drinking

All the larger hotels incorporate **restaurants**, and while none is anything special, you can get a decent pizza or escalope at the *Akhenaten* or a grill at the *Badr*, which serves wine as well as beer. You can also find beer and standard Egyptian meals at the *Cafeteria Majestic*, opposite the train station; while the *Restaurant Sonesta* on Sharia Nour serves roast chicken and mezzes, Egyptian-style pizzas can be enjoyed at *Pizza Class* on Sharia 26th July. For **cheaper eats**, the commercial district and the area around the train station abound in places selling *shawarma* sandwiches, *kushari*, *fuul* or *taamiya*.

Moving on from Assyut

The police prefer tourists to leave train, and so they don't restrict them to any particular service. About twenty **trains** a day run to Cairo (5–7hr), stopping at Mallawi (2hr), Minya (3hr) and Beni Suef (5hr) along the way, while a dozen services call at Sohag (2hr), Qena (4hr) and Luxor (6hr) en route to Aswan (12hr). If you're allowed to use **buses**, they run more or less hourly to Cairo (6–7hr), Qena or Sohag; every two hours to Minya; twice daily to Alexandria (7am & 7pm; 10hr); and once to Luxor and Aswan (at 8am). Additionally, there are seven buses daily to Kharga (4hr) between 7am and 10pm, one of which runs onto Dakhla Oasis (7–8hr), and there may also be two services daily to Hurghada (9am & 8pm) in the summer. While the police might allow you to catch a service to Kharga (4hr), the **service taxis** that run to every town along the Valley between Minya and Qena will probably be out of bounds.

Around Assyut

In the vicinity of Assyut are two **monasteries** that testify to the roots Christianity put down in this region in the fourth century. Copts believe that these and other sites were actually visited by the Holy Family during the four years that Mary, Joseph and the infant Jesus stayed in Egypt to escape King Herod's massacre of the first-born. Although the Bible says little about this period, details of their wanderings were revealed in a dream to Patriarch Theophilus in AD 500, and Copts have made much of this tradition ever since. Indeed, such tourism as exists in the Assyut region involves Copts from other parts of Egypt, making pilgrimages on holy days – athough Assyut's tourist office hopes to lure foreigners with the little-visited **Meir Tombs**.

Dirunka: the Convent of the Virgin

Copts believe that the Holy Family sought refuge in caves at **DIRUNKA**, 12km outside Assyut – as did later Christians. From such troglodyte origins, the present **Convent of the Virgin** (aka *Deir el-Adhra,* or Santa Maria) on the site has grown into what resembles a fortified campus – cynics might say a refuge for Assyut's Coptic population, should the worst ever occur.

The expansion is justified by the monastery having to accommodate 50,000 pilgrims for the **Moulid of the Virgin** (August 7–22). This occasions the parading of icons around the spacious cave church where they stand for most of the year. Coptic altars face east because it's from there that Jesus will return, but also because He is "the sun" of their religion. Pilgrims are photographed against a huge portrait of the Virgin, or the verdant plain overlooked by the convent's terrace, below which is a Coptic village where nuns operate a dispensary. About fifty nuns and monks live in the convent.

As the police will wish to escort visitors and are likely to frown on you travelling by minibus (25pt) from Assyut, a private taxi (£E10 round-trip) is the best way of **getting there**, and saves you a fifteen-minute uphill slog from the roadside. If you haven't retained a taxi, returning minibuses can be flagged down on the main road. It might be possible to **stay** at the convent rest-house outside the main gate, where a bed in a dormitory costs £E3, or one in a smaller room, £E5. Reception is open from 6am to 6pm daily, but there's **no food** available.

El-Qusiya: the Burnt Monastery and the Meir Tombs

Talk to the tourist office about the feasibility of this excursion. They want tourists to visit the Meir Tombs, but it's the police who decide whether foreigners can enter the area. If you get the go-ahead, you'll be obliged to hire a **private taxi** for you and your escort, which isn't a bad thing given the distances involved – but in the event that tourists are allowed to take service taxis, at least one if not both of the sites could be reached by public transport, using local pick-up trucks from El-Qusiya.

EL-QUSIYA, 42km north of Assyut, is an agricultural town of 40,000 people, three-quarters of them Copts. Its **notoriety** stems from two events that shocked Egypt. In 1998, security police investigating the murder of two Coptic youths tried to pin the blame on their families using torture to extract confessions and, after this failed, hauled in ever more relatives and associates – up to 1200 in a month – until Bishop Wissa alerted the world's media. Although arrests ceased after his intervention, Wissa was charged under the emergency laws with "endangering national unity", and no police officers were ever punished. While human rights activists stressed that police brutality and abuse of power were a problem throughout Egypt, for Muslims and Copts alike, this doesn't explain what happened a year later. On New Year's Eve, 1999, a fatal quarrel between a Coptic merchant and a Muslim customer was followed by a wave of shootings and arson that left twenty Copts and one Muslim dead and dozens injured, which the police did nothing to stop for two days. No convincing explanation for why and how it happened has emerged; one fatuous "solution" suggested – but not adopted – was to rename the town "Peace Village", since El-Qusiya can mean "Emnity" in classical Arabic.

Some 5km out of town, the **Burnt Monastery** (*Deir el-Muharraq*) stands near the desert's edge. Its tinderbox surroundings explain the name and protective walls; the crenellated inner rampart is still blackened from a conflagration that occurred during the **Moulid of the Virgin** (June 21–28) a decade ago. Except on fast days, visitors are shown around the thriving, modernized establishment. Many of the hundred students at its Theological College will become monks when they turn twenty-five. Within the compound are grouped the Abbot's residence, a fourth-century keep and two churches. Believers maintain that the **cave sanctuary** of the **Church of the Anointed** (*El-Azraq*) once hid the Holy Family for six months and ten days, and that the church was one of the first in the world, foretold in the Old Testament as "an altar to the Lord in the midst of the land of Egypt" (Isaiah 19:19–21). It's also said that what is now the altar stone was once used to block the cave's entrance. When an abbot ordered its replacement, the mason's hand was paralysed and a vision of Jesus appeared, intoning "Leave it alone." The icon of the *Virgin and Child* is said to be painted by St Luke; the apostles in the **Church of St George** come from Ethiopia. Remember to remove your shoes before entering the churches.

The **Meir Tombs** lie 15km north, near the village of Meir (or Mayr), reached by a secondary road. This necropolis belonged to the nomarchs of the fourteenth nome, whose capital Qis or Cusae was the ancestor of El-Qusiya. In 1999, nine of its seventeen tombs were opened to the public (daily 9am–5pm; £E16). Tombs #1 and #2 are inscribed with 720 deities, defaced by the Christian hermits that once resided there; while in tomb #4 you can see the original grid drawn on the wall to help the artists execute their designs. Best of all are the splendid desert hunting scene in the tomb of **Senbi-Sa-Ukh-hotep**, and the women's fashions of the XII Dynasty depicted in **Ukh-hotep**'s tomb.

Sohag

Set on a rich agricultural plain bounded by the hills of the Eastern and Western deserts, **SOHAG** (pronounced "So*haj*") is an industrious town of 75,000 with a large Christian community and a small university. Before the conflict in Middle Egypt, Sohag made a nice, relaxed stopover and a base for visits to the nearby **Red and White monasteries**, or Abydos Temple, further away (see p.326). Throughout the 1990s, tourists were afraid to come here, despite valiant efforts by the council to woo visitors by starting work on a new archeological museum, and promoting the colossal statue of an ancient Egyptian princess in **Akhmim**, across the river. Today, adventure tour operators have begun to feature Sohag on their itineraries again, but independent travellers have yet to follow. Anyone coming here should not only expect to be followed around by a policeman, but to be confined to their hotel after dark. This doesn't mean that Sohag is dangerous, just that the police are covering their backs.

Hopefully, the new **Sohag Museum** beside the Nile will be ready by 2004, to become a showcase for some five thousand artefacts found within the governorate, from the Middle Kingdom until Greco-Roman times. It's envisaged that the collection will grow as excavations in Akhmim unearth the temple of Ramses II and other New Kingdom structures. Meanwhile, Akhmim remains the centre of attention and Sohag's attractions are episodic. Its weekly *Souk el-Itnayn* (so-called because it occurs on Monday, 6am–noon) is a massive **animal market**, held just off the Girga road, while the whole town celebrates the **Moulid of Al-Aref** – Sohag's patron saint – a few weeks before the nation-wide feast of Eid al-Adha, outside the mosque that bears his name. Among other deeds, Al-Aref is remembered for hiding Murad Bey, the only Mamluke to escape the infamous massacre at the Citadel in Cairo, who fled to Upper Egypt.

Practicalities

The best **accommodation** is on the east bank of the Nile, where any Akhmim-bound service taxi can drop you near two hotels. The *Cazalovy*

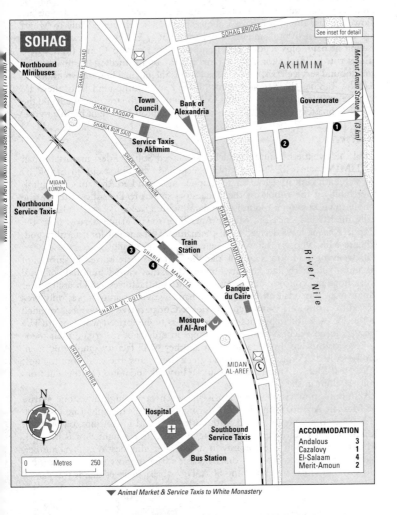

▼ *Animal Market & Service Taxis to White Monastery*

(☎093/601-185 or 601-170; ❸) is the best value, with a/c rooms and soap and towels provided for less than its three-star rival, the *Merit-Amoun* (☎093/601-985, ⓕ603-222; ❹). In Sohag itself the hotels are grungier and reluctant to accept foreigners, but if you have to choose between them, the *El-Salaam* (☎093/333-317; ❷) is cleaner than the *Andalous* (☎093/324-328; ❶). They are both on Sharia El-Mahatta.

Eating out is similar, insofar as the *Cazalovy*'s is the better of the two hotel restaurants, and other options boil down to a kebab and roast chicken place on Midan al-Aref, or the usual *kushari, fuul* and *tamiyya* outlets near the train station. You can make international calls from the **post and telephone office** on Sharia el-Gumhorriya (the Corniche); the 24-hour branch inside the train station is only for domestic calls. There are two **banks** along the Corniche. The **hospital** (☎093/332-007) is opposite the bus station, while the **police** (☎122) are by the mosque on the eastern side of the Nile bridge.

As in Assyut, the police prefer you to travel by **train** to Luxor (4hr), Cairo or anywhere else, and set no restriction on which service you take. If you are allowed to use them, you have a choice between seven **buses** daily to Minya and Cairo (5am–10pm), and one a day to Luxor (£E6.50) and Aswan (£E13), leaving at 6am, plus regular buses and **service taxis** to Qena, from where others run on to Luxor. Assyut (1hr 30min) is the furthest destination for northbound service taxis, while Qena (1hr) is the normal limit for southbound vehicles. Besides the depots for northbound and southbound taxis, there are separate ones for **local** service taxis to Akhmim (near the town council) and the White Monastery (west of the bus station), which tourists might be able to use.

Akhmim

Until the twentieth century, guidebooks ranked Sohag as less important than **AKHMIM**, across the Nile – a place reckoned "the oldest city in Egypt" by the sixteenth-century Moorish geographer-historian Leo Africanus. Akhmimis have built on the rubble of their ancestors since pre-Dynastic times, so the whole town rests on a mound of remains, with a maze-like street plan essentially unchanged since the Middle Ages. The town's name derives from the Coptic *Khmim*, itself derived from the name of an ancient local fertility god, Khente-Min, who was often represented by a giant phallus.

Its **weaving** tradition is equally old: the pharaohs were buried in shrouds of Akhmim silk. Early last century, imported textiles closed hundreds of local workshops and concentrated production into four factories, which used power looms from Rochdale in England. The hand-weaving tradition was only preserved by a missionary-inspired **Women's Cooperative** (*Rahabaat*), founded in the 1920s, whose tapestries are now sold as highly priced works of art. The weavers forgo celebrity and high earnings in order not to irritate their menfolk, so visitors are unwelcome – but another small factory, employing men, can be visited. It's the house with the green door across the road from the post office near Meryut Amun's statue. You can **buy** silk and cotton textiles cut from bolts of cloth in the factory shop.

Akhmim's most visible attraction is an eleven-metre-high limestone **statue of Meryut Amun**, found in 1981 during excavations to build a new school. Her statue is memorably vivid, with curled hair and rouged lips, but Meryut Amun herself is an enigma. History records her as a daughter of Ramses II, whom the pharaoh incestuously married after the death of her mother, Nefertari; and the cartouches on the statue's base support that identification. However, the former head of the SCA, Dr Gaballa, believes that it was carved during the earlier Amarna period and originally belonged to somebody else. In support of this theory, Gaballa evinces its almond-shaped eyes, protruberant belly and Amarna-style pleating, plus the fact that thirteen inscribed blocks from the Amarna era were unearthed beneath the statue. The answer may lie in future excavations beneath a nearby Islamic cemetery, where the roof of a temple of Ramses II pokes from the sand. Meryut Amun's statue is enclosed in a compound (daily 9am–5pm; £E10), but is so large that you can get a good view without buying a ticket.

Another reason for making the trip is that many of the service taxis that shuttle between Sohag and Akhmim (25pt) are lovely **vintage cars** from the 1930s and 1940s. These drop you at an intersection in Akhmim's centre known as "Setta Aziza"; from here, follow a road jinking north towards the market and the Al-Amri Mosque, to find Meryut Amun's statue a bit further on.

Monasteries near Sohag

The **Red and White monasteries** (daily 9am–8pm) to the south of Sohag are both small and dilapidated, yet their near-desolation seems more evocative of the early Christians who sought God in the desert than busier establishments like Dirunka. Only a handful of acolytes tend the chapels, timeworn stones and plastic medallions attesting to the thousands of Copts who visit them during Shenoudi's moulid in the first two weeks of July, when dozens of minibuses shuttle in the pilgrims.

At other times local service taxis (50pt) only run the 12km to the White Monastery, so to visit the Red Monastery (4km further on) and be sure of a lift back it's simpler to rent a **private taxi**. After hard bargaining (drivers only speak Arabic), the price for the round trip seems to be £E15–20. There's no admission charge for the monasteries, but *baksheesh* is appreciated.

The White Monastery

Across the plain from Sohag, near an arabesqued mosque, high limestone walls enclose the **White Monastery** (*Deir al-Abyad*). Named for the colour of its masonry (mostly taken from pharaonic or Roman buildings), the monastery had some two thousand monks during its heyday. Today it has only four residents, and its courtyard is flanked by ruined cloisters and cells, while discarded millstones and soot-blackened vaults show where the kitchen once stood. Remove your shoes before entering the **Church of St Shenoudi**, a lofty basilica admitting breezes and birdsong, observed by a stern-faced Christ Pantokrator. Note the monolithic granite pulpit halfway along the northern wall, Roman columns in the apses, and pharaonic hieroglyphics on the outer rear wall.

The monastery is also known as *Deir Anba Shenouda* after its fifth-century founder, who enforced the monastic rule with legendary beatings – on one occasion, fatally. Shenoudi condemned bathing as an upper-class luxury maintained by the sweat of the poor; early monks cleansed themselves by rolling naked in the sand. During **Shenoudi's moulid** (which reaches its climax on July 14), childless women roll down nearby hills in sacks, hoping to obtain divine intervention.

The Red Monastery

Down the road past walled Coptic and Muslim cemeteries, a straggling village conceals the **Red Monastery** (*Deir al-Ahmar*) in an unobtrusive cul-de-sac. Built of dark red brick, the monastery is attributed to St Bishoi, a penitent armed robber who became Shenoudi's disciple (retaining his club as a reminder); hence its other sobriquet, *Deir Anba Bishoi*.

The monastery's principal **church** is darker than Shenoudi's, its blackened tenth-century murals less remarkable than the finely carved tiers of niches. Whereas purloined Roman columns and the White Monastery's pharaonic-style corvetto cornice betray artistic debts, the intricate floral capitals inside the outer gate show that Coptic architecture soon transcended mere imitation. In the courtyard's far corner squats the smaller **Red Church**, whose inner sanctum is barred to women. Notice the intricate peg-locks on the doors.

Upper Egypt

In antiquity, **Upper Egypt** started at Memphis and ran as far south as Aswan on the border with Nubia. Nowadays, with the designation of Middle Egypt, borders are a little more hazy, though the **Qena Bend** is generally taken as the region's beginning and **Aswan** is still effectively the end of the line.

Within this stretch of the Nile is the world's most intensive concentration of ancient monuments – temples, tombs and palaces constructed from the onset of the Middle Kingdom (c.1990 BC) up until Roman and Byzantine times. The greatest of the buildings are the **cult temples** of **Abydos**, **Dendara**, **Karnak**, **Esna**, **Edfu**, **Kom Ombo**, **Philae** and **Abu Simbel**, each conceived as "homes" for their respective deities and an accretion of centuries of building. Scarcely less impressive are the multitude of tombs in the **Theban Necropolis**, most famously in the **Valley of the Kings**, across the river from **Luxor**, where Tutankhamun's resting place is merely a hole in the ground by comparison with those of such great pharaohs as Seti I and Ramses II.

Monuments aside, Upper Egypt marks a subtle shift of character, with the desert closing in on the river, and dom palms growing alongside barrel-roofed houses, designed to reflect the intense heat. One of the greatest pleasures to be had here – indeed one of the highlights of any Egyptian trip – is to absorb the riverscape slowly from the vantage point of a **felucca**. This is easily arranged in Aswan, whence you can sail downriver with no fear of being becalmed. Nile **cruise boats** provide a more luxurious experience, calling at the main sites between Luxor and Aswan. While cruises can be booked at short notice in either city, better deals are available in Aswan.

Abydos

As Muslims endeavour to visit Mecca once in their lifetimes and Hindus aspire to die at Benares, the ancient Egyptians devoutly wished to make a pilgrimage to **ABYDOS**, cult centre of the god Osiris. Those who failed to make it hoped to do so posthumously; relatives brought bodies for burial, or embellished distant tombs with scenes of the journey to Abydos (represented by a boat under sail, travelling upriver). Egyptians averred that the dead "went west", for the entrance to the underworld was believed to lie amidst the desert hills beyond Abydos. By bringing other deities into the Osirian fold, Abydos acquired a near monopoly on death cults, which persisted into Ptolemaic times. Its superbly carved **Temple of Seti I** has been a tourist attraction since the 1830s, and many rate its artwork as the finest in Egypt. Although the number of visitors dropped dramatically in the mid-to-late 1990s, the police guaranteed security for day-trippers with guarded convoys of coaches and taxis. This regime still applies, but may be relaxed as the troubles in Middle Egypt recede further into the past. Check the latest situation with the tourist office in Luxor.

Getting there from Luxor or El-Balyana

Assuming the rules have not yet changed, there's a shambolic daily **convoy** to Abydos and Dendara, leaving Luxor at 8am. Thomas Cook and other agencies offer **coach excursions** to one or both sites, but schedules are erratic and prices vary, so it's worth shopping around. Independent travellers are bound to save money by hiring a **private taxi** instead – especially if there are several people to split the cost. The official rates are £E95 for a five-seater taxi or £E155 for seven people, but it really depends on your bargaining skills; a taxi arranged through the *Oasis Hotel* costs £E190.

Alternatively, the police don't seem to mind people travelling outside the convoy if they use public transport to reach the town of **EL-BALYANA**, 10km from Abydos. The unoffical rule for **buses** is that there mustn't be more than four tourists aboard the vehicle, so it pays to be early for the 11am or 1.15pm bus; tickets are sold by the driver. Trains are less reliable for the outward journey, as not all of them stop at El-Balyana, but you can use any train that does to return to Luxor – indeed, the **police** in El-Balyana may insist you do so. Their aim is to get you to Abydos and then back to Luxor as quickly as possible, so anyone arriving by bus or train will be put in a local taxi and escorted to the temple and back for about £E5.

The **site of Abydos** (daily 9am–4pm; £E12) is reached by a well-surfaced road used by carts and camels bearing loads of sugar cane, which terminates on the main square of **AL-ARABA EL-MADFUNA** village, beside the ruins. While there are plenty of souvenir and soft-drink stalls, and even a kiosk for changing money that's sometimes open, there is sadly no way at present you can stay overnight. Both the *Osiris Park Camp* (☎093/812-200) in the village and the *Abydos Hotel* (☎093/812-102) 200m back towards El-Balyana have been forbidden to take foreign guests for many years, and nowadays just sell snacks and drinks – but the situation might change one day.

As for the temple, be sure to bring a **torch** to see its darkened reliefs properly. In the interests of "security", visitors are constantly followed by a custodian – even to the washroom!

The Temple of Seti I

While the temples of Karnak and Deir el-Bahri at Luxor are breathtaking conceptions executed on a colossal scale, it is the exquisite quality of its bas-reliefs that distinguishes the **Temple of Seti I** at Abydos. The reliefs are amongst the finest works of the New Kingdom, harking back to Old Kingdom forms in an artistic revival that mirrored Seti's political efforts to consolidate the XIX Dynasty and recover territories lost under Akhenaten. The official designation of Seti's reign (1318–1304 BC) was "the era of repeating births" – literally a renaissance.

It was in fact Seti's son, Ramses II (1304–1237 BC), who completed the reconquest of former colonies and the construction of his father's temple at Abydos. Strictly speaking, the building was neither a cult nor a funerary temple in the ordinary sense (see the box on p.330 for a general description of temple architecture), for its chapels contained shrines to a variety of deities concerned with death, resurrection and the netherworld, and one dedicated to Seti himself. Its purpose was

Seti I

essentially political: to identify the king with these cults and with his putative "ancestors", the previous rulers of Egypt, thus conferring legitimacy on the

ABYDOS: THE TEMPLE OF SETI I

Osireion

Inner Sanctuaries of Osiris

Isis
Seti
Horus

Seti   Ptah   Re-Herakhte   Amun   Osiris   Isis   Horus

j   i

k

m

h

g

l

Gallery of Kings

f   f

Inner Hypostyle Hall

e

Outer Hypostyle Hall

d

c   c

b

Forecourt

a

Pylon

0   Metres   20

N

▲ Temple of Senusert III

▲ Temple of Ramses II

▼ Village

Ramessid dynasty, whose ancestors had been mere Delta warriors a few generations earlier.

The temple's spell has endured through the ages, as New Age pilgrims follow in the footsteps of Dorothy Eady – known as **Umm Seti** (Mother of Seti) – who lived at Abydos for 35 years until she died in 1981, believing herself to be the reincarnation of a temple priestess and lover of Seti I. Her book *Abydos – The Holy City in Ancient Egypt* is on sale at the *Osiris Park Camp* shop, while her trances and prophetic gifts are related in Jonathan Cott's biography, *The Search for Omm Sety*.

The forecourt and Hypostyle Halls

The temple's original **pylon** and **forecourt** have almost been levelled but you can still discern the lower portion of a scene depicting Ramses II's dubious vic-

Ancient Egyptian temple architecture

From earliest times, two distinct types of temple evolved in Egypt: **cult temples**, dedicated to the principal god of the region, and **mortuary temples**, devoted to the worship of the dead king. Cult temples were regarded as the *pr-ntr* or "house of the god", whose effigy was cosseted with daily rituals and periodically taken to visit its divine spouse in another temple. Such centres were elaborate from the start, unlike mortuary temples, which began as two-roomed structures attached to the king's pyramid and joined to a valley temple by a causeway, only being divorced from their tombs and burgeoning into massive complexes during the New Kingdom.

Most of the great temples of the Nile Valley embody centuries of work by successive kings and dynasties, some of whom added major sections while others merely decorated a wall or carved their name on another pharaoh's statue. Built from stone, to last forever, their general form and layout hardly changed over millennia, and were still being imitated during Ptolemaic and Roman times.

Temple layout

Because each temple was envisaged as a progression from this world into the realm of divine mysteries, halls got darker and lower and doors narrowed as they approached the sanctuary. In accordance with this convention, additional halls or pylons had to increase in size as they grew more distant from the sanctuary. As a corollary of this, the architecture is generally older the further in you venture.

Temples were seldom accessible to commoners, being set within enclosures surrounded by lofty mud-brick walls. These **precincts** often contained priestly residences, workshops and storehouses, along with a **Sacred Lake** for ritual ablutions. In Ptolemaic and Roman times, they also usually featured a **Birth House** or *Mamissi*, which emphasized the king's divine antecedents. Entering the temple proper meant passing through a series of gated **pylons** whose towers bore giant reliefs of the pharaoh making offerings to the gods and smiting Egypt's enemies. A few also boasted graceful **obelisks** whose tips were sheathed in gold or electrum (an alloy of gold and silver). Between the pylons were open **courts**, often flanked with **colonnades** of Osiride pillars and guarded by **colossi** of a pharaoh or deity.

Another pylon (or a screen wall surmounted by open columns) divided the court from a **Hypostyle Hall**, whose forest of columns was intended to resemble a papyrus thicket, dimly illuminated by shafts of sunlight penetrating apertures in the roof. Beyond lay a series of **vestibules** or antechambers (often preceded by a smaller Hypostyle Hall), climaxing in the **sanctuary** where the deity's effigy and sacred boat reposed. Smaller rooms and **chapels** for storing valuables or worshipping subsidiary deities were grouped off the halls and behind the sanctuary. Some temples also had a **rooftop shrine** or kiosk for celebrating the resurrection of Osiris and revitalizing the divine effigy at New Year.

tory at Qadesh [a], women with finely plaited tresses [b], and Seti making offerings to Osiris (in a niche, nearby). From the damaged statues currently stored in the upper, second court, your eyes are drawn to the square-columned **facade**, where tiny birds inhabit fissures in the wall behind pillars covered with scenes of Ramses greeting Osiris, Isis and Horus [c]. Originally, the temple was entered by seven doors (corresponding to the shrines within), but Ramses ordered all except the middle one blocked up. The upper part of the facade has been crudely rebuilt in concrete.

The ponderous sunk-reliefs in the **outer Hypostyle Hall**, completed by Ramses after Seti's death, suggest that he used second-rate artists, having redeployed Seti's top craftsmen on his own (now destroyed) temple. The entrance wall portrays Ramses measuring the temple with the goddess Selket and presenting it to Horus on Seti's behalf, while on the wall to your right

Decoration

Virtually every temple wall is covered in **reliefs**, either carved proud (bas-reliefs, the most delicate and time-consuming method), recessed into the surface (sunk-reliefs) or simply incised (the quickest form to execute). They are arranged in rows called "registers", counted from the bottom of the wall upwards. Doorway lintels are always adorned with a winged sun-disc, symbolizing the Two Lands whose heraldic plants are a common motif. Some Ptolemaic temples also feature astronomical ceilings depicting heavenly bodies and creatures of the zodiac. Since reliefs were generally painted in bright colours, temples must once have looked far gaudier than their present state suggests.

Also striking are the variegated **columns**, which evolved from two basic types. Square-sectioned pillars were sometimes faced with a statue of the pharaoh as a god (usually Osiris – hence the term Osiride pillars) or crowned with the head of the goddess Hathor (perhaps surmounted by a sistrum, her sacred instrument). A wider variety derived from plant forms, with different permutations of shafts and capitals. The palm column had a plain shaft and leafy capital; the papyrus column chevron markings and a flowering or closed bud capital; while a cluster of rounded stems gave the lotus column its distinctive "bundle" appearance. By Ptolemaic times, capitals resembled Baroque bouquets and the established forms were mixed to create composite columns.

Chapels Sanctuary Rooftop shrine Vestibules Colonnaded court Winged sun-disc

Enclosure wall Sacred lake Hypostyle Hall Birth House Pylons

Ramses offers a falcon-headed box of papyrus to Isis, Horus and Osiris, and is led to the temple by Horus and Wepwawet (the jackal-headed god of Assyut) to be doused with holy water (represented by the interlinked signs for life and purity) **[d]**. On one of the roof-lintels is a cartouche which has come to achieve mythical status on the Internet; purportedly, it shows a helicopter and a submarine – though archeologists deride the "**Abydos helicopter**" as a simple case of palitation (the superimposition of one cartouche upon another, combining with erosion to produce an unusual shape), and the digitally enhanced image on the Web is far clearer than the murky original.

The deeper **inner Hypostyle Hall** was the last part of the temple decorated before Seti's death, and some sections were never finished, but others are exceptional. On the right-hand wall Seti stands before Osiris and Horus – who pour holy water from garlanded vases – and makes offerings before the shrine of Osiris, who is attended by Maat and Ronpet (the goddess of the year) in front, with Isis, Amentet (goddess of the west) and Nephthys behind **[e]**. Seti's profile is a stylized but close likeness to his mummy (in the Cairo Antiquities Museum). The east and west walls are of sandstone, the north and south of limestone. Two projecting piers **[f]** near the back of the hall depict Seti worshipping the *Djed* column while wearing the crown of Upper or Lower Egypt. The reliefs along the rear wall – showing him being anointed and crowned by the gods – are still brightly coloured. Best of all is a scene of Seti kneeling before Osiris and Horus, with the sacred persea tree in the background, which appears above head height on the wall between the sanctuaries of Ptah and Re-Herakhte **[g]**.

The sanctuaries

The finest **bas-reliefs** at Abydos are inside the sanctuaries dedicated to Seti and six deities. Though retaining much of their original colouring (showing how most temple reliefs once looked), their graceful lines and subtle moulding are best appreciated on the unpainted reliefs. Seti's classical revival eschewed both Amarna expressionism and the bombastic XVIII Dynasty imperial style, which his son embraced and raised to new heights of megalomania. The seven sanctuaries are roofed with false vaults carved from rectangular slabs, and culminate in false doors (except for Osiris's chamber, which leads into his inner sanctuaries).

To ancient Egyptians, these chambers constituted the abode of the gods, whom the king (or his priests) propitiated with daily rituals, shown on the walls. Having opened the shrine, the pharaoh offers the god sacrifices and washes and dresses its statue, which is then purified and presented with gifts. After further offerings before the god's barque, he scatters sand on the floor, sweeps away his footprints and withdraws, leaving the deity alone till next morning.

An exception to this rule is the **Sanctuary of Seti**, which emphasizes his recognition by the gods, who lead him into the temple and ceremonially unite the Two Lands along the northern wall. Below the barque near the back of the left-hand wall, Seti receives a list of offerings from Thoth and the High Priest Iunmutef, wearing the leopardskin and braided sidelock of his office. Finally, Seti leaves the temple, his palanquin borne by the souls of jackal-headed deities from the Upper Egyptian town of Nekhen and hawk-headed gods from the Delta capital of Pi-Ramses.

The fine unpainted reliefs of Seti and seated deities in Re-Herakhte's chamber make interesting comparison with similar painted scenes in the sanctuaries of Ptah, Amun, Osiris and Isis. On the side wall just outside the Sanctuary of

The cult of Osiris

Originally the corn-god of Busiris in the Delta, **Osiris** attained national significance early in the Old Kingdom, when he was co-opted into the Heliopolitan Ennead. According to legend, Re (or Geb) divided the world between Osiris and his brother Seth, who resented being given all the deserts and murdered Osiris to usurp his domain. Although the god's body was recovered by **Isis**, the sister-wife of Osiris, Seth recaptured and dismembered it, burying the pieces (and feeding the penis to a crocodile, in one version). Aided by her sister Nephthys, Isis collected the bits and bandaged them together to create the first mummy, which they briefly resurrected with the help of Thoth and Anubis. By transforming herself into a hawk, Isis managed to conceive a child with Osiris before he returned to the nether-world to rule as lord and judge of the dead. Secretly raised to manhood in the Delta, their child **Horus** later avenged his father and cast Seth back into the wilderness (see p.427).

Osiris

As the reputed burial place of the torso (or head) of Osiris, **Abydos** was the setting for two annual **festivals**. The "Great Going Forth" celebrated the search for and discovery of his remains, while the Osiris Festival re-enacted his myth in a series of Mystery Plays. In one scene, the god's barque was "attacked" by minions of Seth and "protected" by **Wepwawet**, the jackal-headed god of Assyut. This marked the final stage in a process of religious mergers, for it was Wepwawet who supplanted **Khentamenty**, the original death-god of Abydos, as the "Foremost of the Westerners", before his own assimilation into the cult of Osiris. The total identification of Abydos with **death cults** was completed by its association with **Anubis**, the jackal-headed god of embalming, always present in funerary scenes.

Horus, the pharaoh presents Maat to Osiris, Isis and Horus, a XIX Dynasty motif symbolizing righteous order and the restoration of royal legitimacy.

The **inner sanctuaries of Osiris** boast three side chapels whose colours were still fresh and shiny in the 1980s, but are now blackened by mould – a rapid rate of deterioration affecting many of the temples and tombs in the Nile Valley.

The southern wing

From the inner Hypostyle Hall you can enter the southern wing of Seti's temple. The portal nearest his sanctuary leads into the columned **Hall of Sokar and Nefertum**, two deities of the north representing the life-giving forces of the earth and the cycle of death and rebirth, who were integrated into the Osirian cult by Seti's time. The niches along the left-hand wall once contained Osiride statues. Reliefs across the way **[h]** depict Seti receiving a hawk-headed Sokar, and Nefertum in both his human and leonine forms (crowned with a lotus blossom). In the **Chapel of Sokar [i]**, Osiris appears in his bier and returns to life grasping his penis (near the back of the right-hand wall), while Isis hovers over him in the form of a hawk on the opposite wall. You'll need a torch to see inside the **Chapel of Nefertum**, next door **[j]**.

The other portal leads through into the **Gallery of Kings**, so called after the list of Seti's predecessors carved on the right-hand wall. For political reasons, the Hyksos pharaohs, Hatshepsut, Akhenaten and his heirs have all been omitted, and Seti has recorded his own name as *Menmare Osiris-Merneptah* (rather than *Menmare Seti-Merneptah*) to distance himself from his namesake

Seth, the killer of Osiris. Nonetheless, the list has proved immensely useful to archeologists, naming 34 kings (chiefly from the VI, VII, XII, XVIII and XIX Dynasties) in roughly chronological order. Seti and his son Ramses stand facing the list of their "ancestors", which begins with Menes (Zoser).

With the **Sanctuary of the Boats [k]** and the **Hall of Sacrifices [l]** off-limits, the best course beyond here is to follow the side corridor **[m]** past a vivid relief of Seti and Ramses harnessing a bull and running to greet Wepwawet, then go out through a rear door to the Osireion, behind the temple.

The Osireion and other remains

Recent discoveries at Abydos have reopened the debate over its role as a pharaonic cemetery, antedating the great Old Kingdom necropolis of Saqqara, outside Cairo. When Flinders Petrie excavated Abydos in the early twentieth century, he uncovered numerous *mastabas* which he believed to be royal tombs from the Old Kingdom, but which later Egyptologists held to be cenotaphs or Osirian burial places – dummy tombs, built to promote a closer association between the pharaoh's *ka* and Osiris, while his mummy reposed elsewhere, with Re. In 1991, however, a team from Pennsylvania University found a dozen royal **Solar Boats** buried at Giza beside the funerary enclosure of the II Dynasty pharaoh Khasekhemwy (c.2675 BC), which appear to be older than the boats at Giza, and may even date from the reign of the I Dynasty ruler Aha (c.2920–2770 BC). This raises the possibility that the early Dynastic burials attributed to Saqqara may have occurred at Abydos instead, and thus some of its presumed Osirian burial places were really once royal tombs. Don't get too excited, though – the Solar Boats aren't likely to be open to the public for years to come, and no one has found an intact royal tomb yet. However there's always the possibility that the team has moved to excavate the underground **tomb and temple of Senusert III** (c.1878–1841 BC) and a **town** of officials and priests; in 2001, the SCA discovered a **cemetery of mummified animals** dating from the Late Period, containing the gold-embellished coffins of rodents and falcons.

Abydos once covered a huge area, with various temple complexes, necropolises and sacred lakes, and a town centred upon the great Temple of Osiris. Nowadays, almost everything has been demolished or sanded over, and most of the ruins are only of interest to specialists and kept locked – with two exceptions.

The Gnostic Gospels

The **Nag Hammadi Codices** – better known as the **Gnostic Gospels** – were found near the town, below the caves of Jebel et-Tur, in 1945. The gospels are fourth-century Coptic translations of second-century Greek originals, although the Gospel of Thomas might date from 50–100 AD, and therefore be as early as – or even older than – the gospels of Matthew, Mark, Luke and John.

The Gnostics (from *Gnosis*, Greek for "knowledge") were early mystics who believed that God could only be known through self-understanding and that the world was illusory. Regarding self and the divine as one, they saw Jesus as a spiritual guide rather than the crucified son of God, pointing to his words in the Gospel of Thomas: *"If you bring forth what is within you, what you bring forth will save you. If you do not bring forth what is within you, what is within you will destroy you."* But the official church thought otherwise and condemned Gnosticism as a heresy; hence the burial of these codices (some of which can be seen today in Cairo's Coptic Museum).

Seti's Cenotaph, known as the **Osireion**, is the only Osirian burial place now visible, albeit half-buried and rendered partly inaccessible by stagnant water. Built of massive blocks, it once enclosed a room containing a mound surrounded by a moat (symbolizing the first land arising from the waters of Chaos at the dawn of Creation), where a pseudo-sarcophagus awaited resurrection. Less dramatically, there's also a **Temple of Ramses II** 300m to the west of Seti's temple. Though now much ruined and reduced in height, the temple was surely once magnificent, incorporating fine limestone, red and black granite and alabaster masonry. Fragments of scenes of the Battle of Qadesh and offerings can be discerned on the remnants of its enclosure walls and pillared courtyard.

Nag Hammadi and Dishna

At **NAG HAMMADI** (pronounced "Naja Ham*maadi*"), 40km south of El-Balyana, the Nile sweeps into the **"Qena Bend"**, and the main road and train tracks transfer from the west bank to the other side of the river. Nag Hammadi itself is an important agricultural centre with a large cement factory, otherwise only known for its past association with the Gnostic Gospels (see opposite). Travellers should beware that, **after dark**, road traffic to the east bank may be suspended for security reasons, due to the state of lawlessness in Dishna, across the river. **DISHNA** looks much like any other small town in the Valley, but is something of a bad joke amongst Egyptians. In the surrounding countryside, almost every male above the age of puberty carries a gun, owing to a generations-old vendetta between two neighbouring villages. The local police seldom leave their fortified post, and never get involved in fights. The gunmen come into their own at night, when it's not unknown for cars to be held up; in daytime, the road is perfectly safe and you'd never notice anything amiss. Dishna folk are actually renowned for their hospitality to guests; their hostility is reserved for their neighbours.

Dendara and Qena

The **Temple of Hathor** at **Dendara** lacks the sublime quality of Seti's edifice at Abydos, but its astronomical ceiling and rooftop sanctuaries offer a unique insight into the solar rituals at other cult sites where they have not survived. Dendara also shows how Egypt's Greek and Roman rulers identified themselves with the pharaohs and deities of ancient Egypt by copying their temples, rituals and iconography down to the last hieroglyphic – though they did tinker with a few details of reliefs and murals. Goddesses and queens became bustier, and the feet of royalty were shown with all their toes (instead of only the big toe, as the ancient Egyptians did).

Most tourists visit Dendara together with Abydos, travelling by coach or taxi in a convoy from Luxor. Under current restrictions it's a hassle to get there by public transport via **Qena** (8km away) and only justifiable for solo travellers unable to afford a private taxi – but if restrictions on using service taxis or staying at Dendara are lifted, Qena could be a useful base for excursions. Otherwise, it has little to offer visitors except transport connections to the Red Sea Coast.

Dendara – the Temple of Hathor

Across the Nile from Qena, fields of onions and clover recede towards the cliffs of the Western Desert and the Temple of Hathor near the village of

DENDARA. One of the few Egyptian temples whose rooftop remains intact – and accessible – it offers great views of the surrounding countryside. The **site** (daily 7am–6pm; £E12) deserves at least an hour and a half, and you'll need a **torch** to illuminate its darker recesses. Visitors who value atmosphere over comfort should **stay** at the *Happyland Camp* (❸) outside the temple's enclosure wall, whose basic rooms reopened a few years ago. If the cops relax further, you might also be able to camp there; but on the off-chance that restrictions are re-imposed, it's wise to enquire ahead through the *New Palace Hotel* in Qena. There is also a **café** at the site, serving soft drinks.

Getting to Dendara from Luxor

The daily **convoy** to Dendara and Abydos leaves Luxor at 8am, and returns in the afternoon. **Coach excursions** to one or both sites are offered by American Express and other agencies, but dates and prices vary, so ask around – and anyway, you're sure to save money by hiring a **private taxi** instead, especially if there are several people to share the cost. The official rates for a trip to Dendara and Abydos are £E95 for a five-seater taxi or £E155 for seven people, but it really depends on your bargaining skills; a taxi through the *Oasis Hotel* costs £E190. With tourism so down at present, there's little demand for **day cruises** from Luxor on the *Lotus Boat* or *Tiba Star* (bookable through the *Novotel* or travel agencies for £E170 per person, including lunch, tea and entrance fees), which may sail only once or twice a week – but it's worth asking if you're interested.

Although Dendara is also accessible **by public transport via Qena**, under current restrictions this is so awkward that it's hardly worth the effort – but if the ban on using intercity service taxis is lifted, this would be quick and inexpensive approach (see p.341 for details).

The Temple of Hathor

Although there have been shrines to Hathor, the goddess of joy, at Dendara since pre-Dynastic times, the existing **Temple of Hathor** is a Greco-Roman creation, built between 125 BC and 60 AD. Since the object of the exercise was to confer legitimacy on Egypt's foreign rulers, it emulates the pharaonic pattern of Hypostyle Halls and vestibules preceding a darkened sanctuary, "a progression from the light of the Egyptian sun to the mystery of the holy of holies" (T.G.H. James).

The temple **facade** is shaped like a pylon, with six Hathor-headed columns rising from a screen. Here and inside, Hathor appears in human form rather than her bovine aspect (see overpage). Because this section was built during the reign of Tiberius, its reliefs depict Roman emperors making offerings to the gods, namely Tiberius and Claudius before Horus, Hathor and their son Ihy **[a]**, and Tiberius as a sphinx before Hathor and Horus **[b]**. Nineteenth- century engravings show the temple buried in sand almost to the lintel of its portal, which explains why its upper sections bore the brunt of Coptic iconoclasm.

The Hypostyle Hall

Entering the **Hypostyle Hall** with its eighteen Hathor-headed columns, let your eyes grow accustomed to the gloom before examining its famous **astronomical ceiling**, which retains much of its original colouring. This is not a sky chart in the modern sense, but a symbolic representation of the heavenly bodies, the hours of the day and night, and the realms of the sun and moon. Although the Qena Bend dictates a north–south orientation rather than the customary east–west axis (since temples always faced the Nile), the ceiling

DENDARA: THE TEMPLE OF HATHOR

Iseum

Sacred Lake

Sanctuary

s t u v w

y y

x

r Hall of Ennead

q Hall of Offerings

o o

n

Hall of Appearances l

m j i k

Hypostyle Hall

f e d c e f

h s

a Facade b

Court

Sanatorium

Birth House of Nectanebo

Coptic Basilica

Roman Birth House

N

Toilets

Pro-Pylon

Ticket Office

0 Metres 25

Café

337

Uena (8km)

Happyland Camp ▼

The cult of Hathor

Worshipped from the earliest times as a cow goddess, **Hathor** acquired manifold attributes – body of the sky, living soul of trees, goddess of gold and turquoise, music and revelry – but remained essentially nurturing. Her greatest role was that of wet nurse and bedmate for **Horus**, and giver of milk to the living pharaoh. In her human aspect (with bovine ears and horns), the goddess paid an annual visit to Horus at his temple in Edfu. Escorted by priests and cheered by commoners, her barque proceeded upriver, where Horus sailed out to meet her on his own boat. After much pomp and ritual, the idols were left alone to reconsummate their union while the populace enjoyed a **Festival of Drunkenness**, which led the Greeks to identify Hathor with their own goddess of love and joy, Aphrodite. However, drunkenness at other times drew condemnation, as in this timeless rebuke to a lager lout: "You trail from street to street smelling of beer, you have been found performing acrobatics on a wall, people run from your blows. Look at you beating on your stomach, reeling and rolling about on the ground covered in your own filth!"

Hathor

maintains the traditional dichotomy between the northern and southern halves of the sky.

Above the central aisle, a row of flying vultures and winged discs separates the left-hand bays representing the southern heavens from those to the right, dedicated to the northern sky. Here, the first row **[c]** begins with the Eye of Re in its barque, above which appear the fourteen days of the waning moon. Beyond the full moon in the centre come the fourteen stages of the waxing moon (each with its own deity), culminating in the full disc worshipped by Thoth, and lastly the moon as Osiris, protected by Isis and Nephthys. Souls in the form of jackals and birds adore Re's barque as it journeys across the sun's register **[d]**.

Following these are two bands **[e]** showing the planets, the stars of the twelve hours of the night, and the signs of the zodiac (adopted from Babylonia). The end rows **[f]** are dominated by Nut, who gives birth to the sun at dawn and swallows it at dusk. On one side, the rising sun Khepri (the scarab beetle) is born **[g]**; on the other, the sun shines down on Hathor **[h]**.

The Hall of Appearances

The Ptolemaic section of the temple begins with the columned **Hall of Appearances**, where Hathor consorted with fellow deities before her voyage to Edfu (see below). With a torch, you can examine reliefs on the entrance wall depicting offerings **[i]**, and the foundation of the temple and its presentation to the gods **[j]**. Notice the "blank" cartouches, which attest to the high turnover of rulers in late Ptolemaic times, when stonemasons were loath to inscribe the names of Ptolemies who might not last for long – there were times when they wouldn't even know who actually reigned in Alexandria. Nonetheless, rituals continued at Dendara, where the priests kept holy objects of precious metal in the Treasury **[k]**, and drew water for purification ceremonies from a well reached by the so-called Nile Room **[l]**.

Corresponding chambers across the hall include the laboratory **[m]**, where perfumes, incense and unguents were mixed and stored (notice the reliefs showing recipes, and bearers bringing exotic materials from afar); and another room for storing valuables. A liturgical calendar listing festivals celebrated at the temple appears on the inner side of its doorway [n].

The Hall of Offerings and the Hall of Ennead

Beyond lies the **Hall of Offerings**, the entrance to the temple proper, with twin **stairways** to the roof (see below) up which sacrificial animals were led [o]. A list of offerings appears on the rear wall [p], across the way from a relief showing the king offering Hathor her favourite tipple [q].

Next comes the **Hall of the Ennead**, where statues of the gods and kings involved in ceremonies dedicated to Hathor once stood. Her wardrobe was stored in a room to your left, where reliefs show the priests carrying the chests that held the sacred garments. Just outside the sanctuary you can see the text of the Hymns of Awakening. The **Sanctuary** housed Hathor's statue and cere-monial barque, which priests carried to the riverside and placed upon a boat that worshippers towed upriver to Edfu for a conjugal reunion with Horus. Reliefs depict the daily rituals (described in the Abydos account – see p.332), and the king presenting Maat to Hathor, Horus and Harsomtus (rear wall).

Side chapels

Two corridors with side chapels run alongside (and meet behind) the sanctu-ary. Above the doorway into the Corridor of Mysteries, Hathor appears as a cow within a wooden kiosk mounted on a barque [r]. Past the chapels of Isis, Sokar and the Sacred Serpent, you'll find the "Castle of the Sistrum" (Hathor's musical instrument), where niches depict her standing on the sky, and the coro-nation of Ihy as god of music [s]. This is entered via the darkened *Per-Nu* chapel [t], whence Hathor embarked on her conjugal voyage to Edfu during the New Year festival (which fell on July 19 in ancient times).

The New Year procession began from the *Per-Ur* chapel [u], where nowadays a shaky ladder ascends to a small chamber containing reliefs of Hathor, Maat and Isis. In the *Per-Neser* chapel [v], one of the custodians will lift a hatch and guide you down into a low-ceilinged **crypt** carved with cobras and lotuses (*baksheesh* expected). The chapel itself shows Hathor in her terrible aspect as a lioness, for by Ptolemaic times she had assimilated the leonine goddess Sekhmet and the feline goddess Bastet. The temple's most valuable treasures were stored underneath the Chapel of Re [w].

If you haven't already stumbled upon it, return to the Hall of the Ennead, bear left through an antechamber and then right, to find the "Pure Place" [x] or **New Year Chapel**, whose ceiling is covered by a relief of Nut giving birth to the sun, which shines on Hathor's head. It was here that rituals were performed prior to Hathor's communion with the sun on the temple's roof. Check out the rooftop shrines (see below) before leaving the temple and walking round to the rear wall, where two defaced reliefs [y] of Cleopatra and her son Caesarion fea-ture in a procession of deities. The chubby face below the Hathor crown is so unlike the beautiful queen of legend that most people prefer to regard this as a stylized image rather than a lifelike **portrait of Cleopatra**.

Rooftop sanctuaries

From either side of the Hall of Offerings, a stairway ascends to the roof of the temple; the scenes on the walls depict the New Year procession, when Hathor's statue was carried up to an open kiosk on the rooftop to await the dawn. Touched by the rays of the sun, her father Hathor's *ba* (soul) was revitalized for the coming year. Besides the sun kiosk there are two suites of rooms dedicated to the death and resurrection of Osiris, behind the facade of the Hypostyle

Hall. Although such **rooftop sanctuaries** were a feature of most temples, those at Dendara are uniquely intact.

The one on the left (as you face south) is notable for the reliefs in its inner chamber, which show Osiris being mourned by Isis and Nephthys, passing through the gates of the netherworld, and finally bringing himself to erection to impregnate Isis, who appears as a hovering kite.

The other suite contains a plaster cast of the famous **Dendara Zodiac** ceiling filched by Lelorrain in 1820 and now in the Louvre. Upheld by four goddesses, the circular carving features a zodiac which only differs from our own by the substitution of a scarab for the scorpion, and the inclusion of the hippo goddess Tweri. The zodiac was introduced to Egypt (and other lands) by the Romans, who copied it from Babylonia. Mind your head on the low doorway.

Best of all is the magnificent **view** of the temple and the countryside from the rooftop. Also notice the **graffiti** left by French troops in 1799, including the name of their commander, Desaix.

Outlying buildings

Surrounding the temple are various other structures, now largely ruined. Ptolemaic temples were distinguished by the addition of *mamissi* or Birth Houses, which associated the pharaoh with Horus, the deified king. When the Romans surrounded the temple with an enclosure wall, it split in two the **Birth House of Nectanebo** (XXX Dynasty), compelling them to build a replacement. The **Roman Birth House** has some fine carvings on its south wall, and tiny figures of Bes and Tweri on the column capitals and architraves. Between the two *mamissi* lies a ruined, fifth-century **Coptic Basilica**, built with masonry from the adjacent structures; notice the incised Coptic crosses.

As a compassionate goddess, Hathor had a reputation for healing and her temple attracted pilgrimages from the sick. In the **Sanatorium** here patients were prescribed cures during dreams, probably induced by narcotics. Water for ritual ablutions was drawn from a **Sacred Lake** now drained of liquid and full of palm trees and birds.

Nearby stands a ruined **Iseum** used for the worship of Isis and Osiris, built by Cleopatra's mortal enemy, Octavian, after he became Emperor Augustus.

Qena

Despite being the provincial capital, **QENA** (pronounced "Gena") has long played second fiddle to Luxor in terms of tourism and investment, a grievance which might explain why it was the site of the first attack on tourists, in 1992. (The killers were traced to a nearby village, whose entire population was evicted, and their homes demolished, for "harbouring terrorists".) Yet its reputation as an Islamist stronghold sat oddly with its renown as a hotbed of vice in the mid-nineteenth century, when many of the professional singers whom Mohammed Ali exiled from Cairo for their "indecent" dances and prostitution settled here, and much of the fundamentalism seems to have evaporated since an energetic, honest Governor (sadly rare in Egypt) improved civic amenities. Nowadays, locals are proud of Qena's clean streets and leafy promenades, and the fact that people from Luxor come here to enjoy its decorous café society.

For foreigners, the main impression is of hundreds of portraits of Mubarak on the roads, as their convoy proceeds towards Dendara, or a view of the guarded government zone beside the Nile, where cruise boats dock. Further inland, once-graceful colonial villas give way to low-rise flats that resemble rejects from Eastern Europe, or maze-like souks that defy cartographers to produce an accurate map of the town. Fortunately, everything one needs to know about is easily found, using the two mosques on the main drag as landmarks. The older mosque (with one minaret) contains the tomb of a twelfth-century sheikh, who is honoured by the **Moulid of Abdel Rahim al-Qenawi**, on the 14th day of *Sha'ban*.

Due to the Qena Bend, the banks of the Nile lie north and south, rather than east and west of the river. The town is on the north bank, with a bridge to the other side, where Dendara is located.

Getting to Qena - and from Qena to Dendara

At present, independent travellers can only reach Qena by bus or train. There are eight **buses** a day from Luxor (£E3–5) which end up at the terminal outside the train station, and others originating elsewhere, that drop (and pick up) passengers at the bridge over the canal, 200m further west. **Trains** from Luxor are faster (40min), but you may be restricted to certain services and not all trains stop in Qena anyway.

Either way, you'd still have to get across town and out to the temple. Chances are the police will insist you do this by hiring a **private taxi** on the spot – but if they don't, you could use **local service taxis** (pick-ups) from the depot at a crossroads near the Nile, 2km away. Pick-ups for Dendara village (50pt) leave from the road to the Nile bridge, or you can take a service bound for Nag Hammadi, but get off soon after passing beneath a massive bridge that carries the new railway between Port Safaga and Kharga Oasis. The signposted side road to Dendara (1km) is 200m along, on the left.

If tourists were allowed to use **intercity service taxis**, they could easily catch one directly to this depot from Gezira, across the river from Luxor (see p.384), in only an hour, for just £E2.

Qena practicalities

Don't count on **staying** in Qena, where hotels have been told to remove signs in English to discourage foreigners. The seedy *New Palace* (☎096/322-509; ❷) behind the Mobil garage is the best of a bad lot, yet less appealing than sleeping at Dendara (see p.336). Standard Egyptian **meals** are available at *El-Prince* (which sometimes sells beer) and the *Hamdi Restaurant* on the main drag, where the usual *kushari, fuul* and *taamiya* stands are also located.

If needed, there are two **banks** (daily except Fri 8am–2pm) for changing cash and travellers' cheques. The **post office** (daily except Fri 8.30am–2pm) and the 24-hour **telephone exchange** are a short walk from the main intersection, while the **police** can be found in the train station.

Qena is a hub of **transport connections** for the Nile Valley and the Red Sea Coast. There are no restrictions on foreigners using a/c Superjets to Cairo (7am & 8pm; £E25), Hurghada (£18) and Suez (£E41), or the six ordinary buses to Hurghada and Suez (£E22–38) and others to Port Safaga (£E7) and El-Quseir (£E6) – but Nile Valley towns like Assyut, Sohag and Minya are better reached by train. Many of these destinations are also accessible by service taxis, leaving from different depots – but tourists can't use them at present.

Between Qena and Luxor

At present, the police make it difficult for tourists to visit any of the sites **between Qena and Luxor** which once attracted people as "undiscovered" locations. Private taxis are meant to stay with the convoy to Dendara, and even if you could find a service taxi willing to take you, you'd be turned back at the checkpoints around the Luxor security zone – which effectively rules out visiting Naqada or Garagos on the west bank. And while El-Madamud, Qus and Qift are accessible by bus from Luxor, most travellers are content to glimpse them en route to the Red Sea Coast.

Were restrictions to be lifted, however, service taxis from Luxor or Qena (£E2) run to most places mentioned below, and ferries cross the Nile between El-Ballas and Qift, and Naqada and Qus. There are no bridges until south of Luxor.

Along the east bank

Crowded with traffic for Luxor, the east bank marks the start of hairpin desert roads to El-Quseir and Port Safaga on the Red Sea Coast. The Valley comes closest to the coast near **QIFT**, ancient *Kebt* or *Koptos*: a mining depot which became a commercial entrepôt once a route to the coast was found. Nowadays well paved but lacking petrol stations, the 216-kilometre-long **road to El-Quseir** is described on p.775; don't be perturbed by the armoured car at the checkpoint on the bridge.

South towards Luxor, a new factory for converting *bagasse* (the waste product of sugar refining) into paper presages the large town of **QUS**, which was second only to Cairo during Fatimid and Mamluke times, when it served as a place of exile for deposed sultans. A relic of its former status is the eleventh-century **Al-Amri Mosque**, containing a fine arabesque *mihrab* and teak *minbar*.

Further south, near Khuzam, a side road leads to the Coptic community of **GARAGOS**, which produces artistic **ceramics** and **textiles**. As Garagos is

The primal alphabet

During ancient times there was a road between Abydos and Luxor through the Western Desert, which followed the **Wadi el-Hol**. In 1999 a team under John Darnell of Yale University identified two **rock inscriptions** there as the earliest known examples of a **phonetic alphabet**. The alphabet was previously thought to have been developed by Semitic-speaking people in ancient Palestine around 1600 BC, but the Wadi el-Hol inscriptions date from two or three centuries earlier. Darnell believes that Semitic merchants living in Egypt developed a "shorthand" based on Egyptian hieroglyphics. For example, "A" was the pictogram for a bull's head, turned upside down; the semitic for bull is *Aleph*, the first letter of the Hebrew alphabet, pronounced with the same "aah" sound as the Latin letter. It is possible that other symbols may be the precursors of the letters "L", "M", "T" and "R".

hard to reach by public transport, visitors previously arrived in hired taxis, which the Coptic staff in Luxor's tourist office would happily arrange. Nearing Luxor, you pass by **EL-MADAMUD**, which harbours a **ruined Temple of Mont** whose Ptolemaic–Roman avenue of sphinxes and monumental gateway belie its Old Kingdom origins. The site's overgrown desolation is all the more evocative for being totally undisturbed by tourists.

Along the west bank

EL-BALLAS, 23km from Qena, has manufactured white earthenware jars since antiquity; they are sold at Qena's **pottery** market alongside the town's own traditional wares – the porous water jars that women carry on their heads from childhood. South of here lay ancient Ombos, whose crocodile-worshipping residents never forgave the people of Dendara for eating one: a grudge reaffirmed at every Festival of Drunkenness (see box on p.338).

Further south, the predominantly Coptic village of **NAQADA** lends its name to two **pre-Dynastic cultures** that are reckoned to have existed between around 4000 and 3000 BC: Naqada I (early) and Naqada II (late). However, the reason to come here is to see the huge **Pigeon Palace**, built by a monk just over a century ago. Located in a field 200m west of the main road, the mud-brick *Qasr el-Hamam* enables ten thousand birds to recuperate from their flight over the Western Desert; food is provided – and in turn the keepers eat their resident charges. There are frequent service **taxis** (50pt) between Naqada and Gezira, across the Nile from Luxor.

Luxor

LUXOR has been a tourist mecca ever since Nile steamers began calling in the nineteenth century to view the remains of Thebes, ancient Egypt's New Kingdom capital, and its associated sites – the concentration of relics in this area is overwhelming. The town itself boasts **Luxor Temple**, a graceful ornament to its waterfront and "downtown" quarter, while just to the north is **Karnak Temple**, a stupendous complex built over 1300 years. Across the river are the amazing tombs and mortuary temples of the **Theban Necropolis**, and as if this wasn't enough, Luxor also serves as a base for trips to Esna, Edfu, Dendara and Abydos temples, up and down the Nile Valley.

In a town where **tourism** accounts for 85 percent of the economy, it's hardly surprising that you can't move without being importuned to step inside a shop, rent a *caleche*, or have your shoes shined. Hassled and overcharged at every turn, some tourists react with fury and come to detest Luxor. Keep your cool and sense of humour; it's possible to find genuine warmth here. Once you get to know a few characters and begin to understand the score, Luxor becomes a funky soap opera with a cast of thousands. Cool feluccca guys and bazaar hustlers, nervous rich tourists and piastre-pinching backpackers – their dealings and misunderstandings are almost as intriguing as the monuments. Read the box on p.346 for an idea of how things are.

Most foreigners come between October and February (especially Christmas and New Year), when the **climate** is cooler than you might imagine, with chilly nights and early mornings. Around the end of March the temperature shoots up 10°C, making April the nicest time of the year to visit, though the weather remains agreeable until May, after which the daytime heat is brutal till late October, when the temperature plummets. During the summer tourism is well down, and the locals have time to sleep by day and party at night.

▲ Airport & Qena

▲ Karnak Temple (2 km) & ❶ (4 km)

LUXOR

- - - Minibus routes
▨ Tourist bazaars

Metres: 0 ── 500

River Nile

Passport Office

SHARIA-IBN-KHALID-WALID

Olympic Pool

37

38

39

S

SHARIA EL-KARNAK

Service Taxi Station

2

Al-Amiri Hospital

Luxor Museum

Antiquities Office

Bank of Alexandria

SHARIA EL-BAHR

3 **4**

5

6

Banque Misr

City Council

7

Protestant Church

St Marks Hospital

Duty Free Shop

SHARIA AHMES

SHARIA AL-MONTAZAH

8

Catholic Church

C

SHARIA YUSSEF HASSAN

Police

10

11

Rainbow Internet

@

D

Bus Station

9

B

@

Brooke Animal Hospital

Avenue of Sphinxes

Mummification Museum

A

Cruise-Boat Moorings

Motorboats & Feluccas

River Nile

Local Ferry

Taxi Depot

G E Z I R A

ACCOMMODATION

Anglo	22	New Everest	17
Arabesque	14	New Radwan	21
Atlas	33	New Winter Palace	19
Club Med Bella Donna	37	Nile Hilton	1
Emilio	8	Novotel	29
Everest	27	Oasis	23
Fontana	35	Philippe	5
Gaddis	41	Princess Pension	30
Golden Palace	36	Pyramisa Isis	40
Grand	28	Ramoza	18
Happy Land	34	Saint Joseph	38
Horus	12	Saint Mark's	7
Little Garden	32	Saint Mina	13
Luxor	15	Shady	26
Luxor Sheraton Resort	43	Sherif	25
Mercure Coralia	6	Sonesta St George	39
Mercure Inn	16	Tutotel	24
Merryland	3	Venus	10
Mina Palace	9	Windsor	4
Moon Valley	31	Winter Palace	20
Movenpick Jolie Ville	42	Youth Hostel	2
Nefertiti	11		

EATING, DRINKING & NIGHTLIFE

Abou Ashraf	H
Abu Hameed nightclub	R
Abu Hassan el-Shazly	K
Al-Ahram Beverages	E
Aly Baba Café	G
Amoun & El-Hussein	D
Anubis	A
Bakkar	M
Barghouti store	O
Jamboree	B
Jem's	V
King's Head Pub	S
Marhaba	I
Micho's Grocery	F
Murphy's Irish Pub	T
New Karnak	J
New Royal Fish	N
Omar mini-market	Q
Pub 2000 & Esquire Restaurant	P
Saiyida Zeinab	L
Seven Days Seven Ways	W
Sinouhe disco	U
Venus Garden & Chez Omar	C

Awmia & 42

Banana Island

Train Station

Mosque of Abu el-Haggag

Luxor Temple

Motorboats & Feluccas

Thomas Cook

Egypt Air

Winter Palace Hotel

National Bank of Egypt

Tourist Office & Tourist Police

Pop 2000 Internet

Banque Misr

Television Tower

El-Gadid Hospital

Luxor International Hospital

Cruise Boat Moorings

Awmia

See inset for detail

0   Metres   250

345

A little history

The name Luxor derives from the Arabic *El-Uqsur* – meaning "the palaces" or "the castles" – a name which may have referred to a Roman *castrum* or the town's appearance in medieval times, when it squatted amidst the ruins of **Thebes**. This, in turn, was the Greek name for the city known to the ancient Egyptians as *Weset*, originally an obscure provincial town during the Old Kingdom, when Egypt was ruled from Memphis. After power ebbed to regional overlords in the First Intermediate Period, Weset/Thebes gained ascendancy in Upper Egypt under Mentuhotpe II (c.2100 BC), who reunited Egypt under the Middle Kingdom. Though this dissolved into anarchy, the town survived as a power base for local princes who eventually liberated Egypt from the Hyksos invaders, reunited the Two Lands and founded the XVIII Dynasty (c.1567 BC).

As the capital of the **New Kingdom**, whose empire stretched from Nubia to Palestine, Thebes' ascendancy was paralleled by that of **Amun**, whose cult temple at Karnak became the greatest in Egypt. At its zenith under the XVIII and XIX dynasties, Thebes may have had a population of around a million; Homer's *Iliad* describes it as a "city with a hundred gates". Excluding the brief **Amarna Period** (c.1379–1362 BC), when the "heretic" Akhenaten moved the capital northwards and forbade the worship of Amun, the dynasty's – and city's – supremacy lasted some five hundred years. Even after the end of the

The tourism scene

Since many visitors fly directly to Luxor, it's worth outlining some features of the local tourism scene. For starters, the number of visitors has slumped by forty percent since September 11, and although package tourists are gradually trickling back, the ongoing violence in Israel/Palestine has choked off the stream of overland travellers that used to be a major part of the tourist trade. As a consequence, hotels have been cutting back on maintenance and offering discounts, while *caleche* drivers are quoting fares they would have sneered at in the past.

Perhaps now more than ever it is important to consider financial transactions **from the locals' standpoint** rather than expecting to get the cheapest price as a matter of right. Hoteliers, felucca captains and salesmen earn good money one day, then little or nothing for ages – even in good times, and during high season. The hotel-touts who swear that your place of choice is closed or dirty know that most hotels in Luxor are half empty – so every guest counts. At **no-star hotels**, the price depends on how full they are, how many there are of you, and at what time you arrive – the cost per person is negotiable. Be fair and realistic, even if you're on a tight budget. To get a room with a private bath for £E7–10 per person is a good deal by any standards; trying to force them to go any lower is really taking advantage.

Where such hotels make their money is by surcharges on **taxi, caleche or donkey tours**. Although it's wise not to take the first deal offered, also bear in mind that the lowest price may not necessarily be a good deal: you could end up with someone who's so bad that they have to undercut better guides in order to get any work. The easiest way to spoil your day is to ask what someone else paid; if you're happy with what you've done and can afford it, why worry about what amounts to the price of a cup of tea or coffee back home?

It also helps to take a relaxed attitude towards **street hustlers** and react to such lines as "Hey – remember me?", "You've dropped your wallet", or "I know what you need" with a humorous rebuff (*Fil mish mish* – "In your dreams" – works well). You'll actually get hassled *less* once they recognize that you know the score – including the old ploy of asking you to translate a letter from abroad, as a way to lure you into conversation.

Ramessid line, when the capital returned to Memphis and thence moved to the Delta, Thebes remained the foremost city of Upper Egypt, enjoying a final fling as a royal seat under the **Nubian** rulers of the XXV Dynasty (c.747–645 BC).

Though Thebes persisted through **Ptolemaic** into **Roman** times, it retained but a shadow of its former glory, and might have been abandoned like Memphis were it not for Christian settlements. During Muslim times its only claim to fame was the tomb of Abu el-Haggag, a twelfth-century sheikh. However, Napoleon's expedition to Egypt awakened foreign interest in its **antiquities**, which were gradually cleared during the nineteenth century, and have drawn visitors ever since.

To be fair, not every visitor to Luxor has been unequivocally impressed by its ancient monuments: during the filming of *Death on the Nile*, Hollywood icon Bette Davis famously remarked that "In my day we'd have built all this at the studio – and better".

Arrival, orientation and information

Arriving in Luxor can be a stressful experience, especially at the **train station**, where you're mobbed by hotel-touts thrusting cards under your nose and bad-mouthing rival establishments. As most places are less than fifteen minutes'

That said, it's best to be forewarned about a few **scams**. Watch out for the hustlers on Sharia al-Souk who approach tourists offering to exchange euros or dollars, and rip them off by sleight of hand. The **black market** in duty-free booze – which tourists are asked to buy on the pretext that it's needed for "My brother's wedding" but is actually re-sold to bars or hotels – still goes on, though the practice has been curbed by the 24-hour limit on duty-free purchases. A bigger problem for tourists is that tour guides, touts, taxi and *caleche* drivers get **commission** on every transaction they facilitate – which is deftly added to your bill. Don't go shopping in the bazaar with a driver or a guide, or pay for a tour through middlemen, when you could deal directly with a tour operator.

Over the past decade, **sex tourism** has quietly become a way of life in Luxor, a "hidden" industry that turns many of the stereotypes of the sex trade inside out. Egyptian women and foreign heterosexual males are left on the sidelines as local men and boys get together with foreign women and gays in feluccas, bars and discos. Thousands of women have holiday romances in Luxor every year and word has got home, encouraging others to come. The exchange of sex for cash usually occurs under the guise of true love, with misled women spending money on their boyfriends or "husbands" until their savings run out and the relationship hits the rocks – but enough foreigners blithely rent toyboys and settle into the scene for locals to make the point that neither side is innocent. Morality aside, it isn't just their money that foreigners are risking or that Egyptians are bringing home to their families. HIV now exists on both sides of the river and **AIDS** could easily spread fast if nothing is done. Yet locals are in denial about the problem and tourists are hardly aware that it even exists.

Hissed invitations and whiffs of smoke by the Nile attest to a smoking subculture that's stronger in Luxor than anywhere else in Egypt except Dahab. **Bango** (marijuana) is easy to obtain if you know where to ask, and smoking shouldn't cause any problems if it's done discreetly; several low-budget hotels have a liberal atmosphere in this respect. A packet (*talga*) costs £E10–20. **Hashish** is costlier and often adulterated with henna. *Bango*, too, may be cut with *molukhiyya* (a vegetable), so it's better to buy whole buds, not broken stuff. *Caleche* drivers are likeliest to sell you rubbish.

walk away, it's fine to strike out towards your preferred option without further ado. Much the same goes if you arrive **by bus** at the depot on a side road just north of Luxor Temple, where you may prefer to catch a minibus, *caleche* or taxi if you are heading for the southern part of town around Television Street. Travellers who've come up **from Aswan by felucca** are dependent on private taxis from Edfu, whose drivers will rendezvous with hustlers at the checkpoint south of Luxor and steer you to their hotels. If you're not being met at **Luxor Airport**, a taxi into town should cost £E15–20, depending on the size of the car and your destination; a twelve-seater microbus costs £E30.

Orientation

Luxor spreads along the east bank of the Nile, its outskirts encroaching on villages and fields. For a general layout of the town along with Karnak and the Theban Necropolis, see the **map** on p.378; a detailed street plan appears on pp.344–345. **Orientation** in central Luxor is simplified by a relatively compact tourist zone defined by three main roads. **Sharia al-Mahatta** runs 500m from the train station towards Luxor Temple, where it meets **Sharia el-Karnak**, the main drag heading north to Karnak Temple (2.5km). Karnak is also accessible via the riverside **Corniche**, though tourists generally stick to the 1.5km stretch between Luxor Museum and the *Winter Palace Hotel*. The "circuit" is completed by a fourth street, known as **Sharia al-Souk** after its bazaar. In the last decade or so Luxor has expanded south towards the village of Awmia, with dozens of new hotels and other facilities along **Sharia Ibn Khalid Walid** (running 3km from the *Novotel* to the *Sheraton*) and **Television Street** (named after its TV tower), which now constitute extensions of the tourist zone.

Information

Once you've found somewhere to stay, it's a good idea to visit the **tourist office** (daily 8am–8pm; Ramadan 8am–sunset; ☎095/372-215 or 373-294) south of Luxor Temple to discover the latest official rates for taxis, *caleches*, feluccas or any other service you might be interested in. Confusingly, there are two offices next door to each other; you want to go into the one signposted "Egyptian Tourist Authority", not "Luxor City Information". There's also a branch at the airport (☎095/372-306), open 24 hours during winter and another at the train station (generally open daily 8am–8pm).

The **tourist police**'s "front" office lies across the way from the tourist office, while their headquarters is upstairs, around the back of the building (daily 24hr; ☎095/373-845 or 376-620). They also have a branch in the station (daily 8am–8pm). The regular **police** are based off Sharia el-Karnak, north of Luxor Temple, and supplemented on the streets by a host of plainclothes agents known as the "*galabiyya* police", plus uniformed Central Security troops – so you're never far from a cop of some kind if you need one. Whatever your problem, it's always best to go to the tourist police first. For *really* serious matters, contact Col. Hafiz Hussein – known as "Hafiz Bey" – in his office in the Corniche mall, near Luxor Temple (☎095/389-800 or 373-845).

Transport

Although you can easily explore central Luxor **on foot**, it takes some time to get used to the traffic (a balletic melee of bikes, cars, carts and minibuses) and being importuned at every step. **Caleches** are fun to ride and useful if you're burdened with luggage, but a bit pricey for regular use. Fares are set by the authorities but drivers charge whatever they can get. Expect an argument if you pay the official rate (£E5 for a ride within Luxor; £E10 for 1hr tour); rides to Karnak are a special case (see p.366). The Brooke Animal Hospital (see p.51) asks tourists to dissuade drivers from galloping their horses or taking more than four passengers. **Taxis** serve for trips to outlying hotels (£E5–9) or the airport, but are fairly superfluous around the centre (£E3–5) except for getting back from a disco. As with *caleches*, you'll have to haggle over the price (though see our note in the "Tourism Scene" box on p.346), which is bound to exceed the cost of public transport.

Surprisingly few visitors take advantage of the fleet of blue-and-white **minibuses** that shuttle between outlying points, constantly passing through the centre along Sharia el-Karnak. Northbound minibuses either turn off towards the taxi depot (*mogaf*), or run straight on to Karnak and the *Nile Hilton*. Heading in the opposite direction, they terminate at the public hospital (*moustashfa*) far down Television Street, or at Awmia, out near the *Sheraton*. The *moustafsha*-bound ones detour inland via the train station, while Awmia buses stick to Sharia Ibn Khalid Walid. The tactic is to wave down any minibus heading in the right direction, shout "*mogaf*", "*Hilton*", "*moustafsha*" (or whatever), and hop in if they're going there. There's a flat fare of 25pt on all routes.

While cycling in Luxor isn't advisable, many tourists rent **bicycles** to use on the west bank, for getting around the Theban Necropolis (see p.381). They can be carried on local ferries. Shops on Sharia al-Mahatta and Television Street, and many low-budget hotels, rent them from £E5–10 a day. Most bikes are one-speed only, if not defective in some respect (though bikes at *Happy Land* get daily maintenance), so it's always wise to check the machine and do a short test ride. A passport or other ID is generally required as security. You can also rent 150cc **motorbikes** from several places, including *Sinbad*, opposite the *Ramoza Hotel* on Sharia al-Mahatta, for about £E50 a day. The owner doesn't care whether you've got a licence or not, but the police will.

Accommodation

The cost and availability of **accommodation** varies with the time of year and fluctuations in tourism. Officially, there are just "high" (Nov–May) and "low" (June–Oct) **seasons**. In practice, however, hotel prices rise or fall depending on **demand**, which is affected both by the number of tourists and competition from cruise boats. When tourism is healthy, peak time coincides with the Egyptian school vacation (Dec 10–Jan 10), but in a depressed market, hotels will cut their prices even then, if necessary. Many low-budget places employ **hotel-touts**, who refer to netting tourists as "fishing", and happily poach them from rivals. If you've already decided on a hotel it's best to ignore offers to accompany you anywhere, as the touts' commission is usually quietly added to your bill.

As some places calculate prices on a per-person basis, and others by the room, the scope for **bargaining** varies. Three-star hotels may waive taxes, particularly newly opened places that haven't yet got many customers, or older ones threatened by better competitors. No-star hotels and *pensions* rarely charge tax anyway, and will often shave a few pounds off the price. As **breakfast** is pretty much the same everywhere, you needn't pay attention to lavish descriptions of what's on offer – though a **restaurant** with a good cook and a licence to sell **alcohol** are definite advantages.

Staff are crucial, too, as hotels that were good can become bad (or vice versa) just because the manager or receptionist changes – especially low-budget hotels leased on one-year contracts. Several **women travellers** have reported being drugged and sexually assaulted by staff in cheap, no-star hotels, but since nobody has laid charges with the tourist police the crimes haven't been investigated. Although the vast majority of hotels are safe, a few rate a **warning** and there's no certainty that the culprits might not get a job somewhere else in the future. Ultimately the only sure way to avoid worrying about spiked drinks is to stay at a hotel managed by its long-term owner, where the staff are strictly vetted, such as *Happy Land* or the *Fontana*.

The following hotels are all in **Luxor**; **places on the west bank** are detailed on p.386.

Low-budget hotels and pensions

Low-budget hotels and *pensions* range from cosy homes-from-home to utter fleapits, all varieties being represented on and off **Yussef Hassan**, **Al–Mahatta** and **Television** streets. The biggest selection lies around Television Street, no more than fifteen minutes' walk from Luxor Temple or the station. Despite its unpaved backstreets, this is an up-and-coming area that's safe to stay in and quieter than the centre of town, which offers few low-budget options. Unless stated otherwise, you should be sure of getting hot water and breakfast.

Anglo Sharia al-Mahatta ☏ & ☏ 095/381-679. Being so close to the train station is a big drawback, but the rooms are nice – with a/c, fan and TV – and the hotel has an alcohol licence. ❷

Atlas Off Sharia Ahmed Orabi ☏ 095/373-514. About five minutes' walk from the station, this 40-bed hotel is seldom full and has clean, simple rooms with fans or a/c and private baths. Guests can use the washing machine for a small fee. Charges only £E8 per person (breakfast not included), but their west bank tour is dearer than other hotels'. ❶

Everest Sharia Nozha, off Television St ☏ 095/373-260, ☏ everesthotel@hotmail.com. Large, clean rooms with fans or a/c, many with baths. Washing machine and shaded rooftop terrace. Useful noticeboard. Offers tours of the west bank and day excursions to Dendara. ❷

Fontana Sharia Radwan, off Television St ☏ 095/380-663. A longtime backpackers' favourite, the hotel is very clean and well furnished, with fans or a/c and private bathrooms, free use of the washing machine, an informative noticeboard, and a hands-on owner who speaks excellent English. However, quoted prices for rooms and west bank tours go up and down like a yo-yo, so be prepared to haggle or compare notes with other guests before agreeing to anything. ❶

Grand Off Sharia Mohammed Farid ☏ 095/382-905 or mobile 0105 285865. This quiet hotel is popular for its clean rooms with fans or a/c (£E3 extra), decent shared bathrooms and rooftop terrace. Also bikes for hire and a luggage room. ❶

Happy Land Sharia el-Kamrr, off Television St ☏ 095/371-828, ☏ 371-140, ☏ happylandluxor@hotmailcom. Another favourite, known for its cleanliness, honest staff and fixed prices. All rooms with fans, some a/c, most with private baths. There's also an a/c dorm with six beds (£E7.50); towels, toilet paper and mosquito-zappers provided. Breakfast includes cornflakes and fruit. A/c rooftop breakfast terrace with CNN news. Cheap Internet access, bike rental and west bank trips. ❶

Moon Valley Sharia Shamouz, off Televsion St mobile ☏ 0123 381797. Close to *Happy Land* but nowhere near as popular, this hotel has cleanish, basic rooms with fans or a/c and shared bathrooms, above a dingy reception. ❶

Nefertiti Sharia el-Karnak ☏ 095/372-386. Centrally located, with clean a/c rooms with bath, a pool table and Internet access. Its honest, friendly staff offer the usual tours without being pushy, and breakfast is above average, served on the roof terrace which overlooks the souk and Luxor Temple. Unrenovated rooms cost £E5–10 less. ❷

New Everest Off Sharia al-Mahatta ☏ 095/370-017 or mobile 0105 087945. Women should *definitely* avoid this place, although its rooms with fans and bathrooms aren't bad, and guests may use the kitchen and washing machine. Offers donkey or minibus trips on the west bank. ❶

Oasis Sharia Mohammed Farid mobile ☏ 0123 157107. Though its lobby looks better than upstairs does, the rooms are fairly spacious, with fans and shared facilities on two floors and a/c and private bathrooms on another. Its staff are keen to sell trips to the west bank, Abydos/Dendara or Edfu/Kom Ombo, and may turn nasty if you don't sign up. Room rates negotiable. ❶

Princess Pension Off Sharia Ahmed Orabi ☏ 095/373-997. Partly used as a billet by tourist policemen, the *Princess* is cheaper – and seedier – than anywhere else in Luxor, charging only £E4–6 for a bed. Women would be unwise to stay here, and men may have doubts, too. ❶

Saint Mina Sharia Cleopatra ℡095/375-409, ℻376-568. Friendly, clean hotel on a quiet backstreet in the Coptic quarter between Cleopatra and al-Asaita streets; the rooms have a/c, bedside lamps and en-suite facilities, or share a bathroom with two other rooms. ❷

Sherif Sharia Badr, off Television St ℡095/370-757. Women are strongly advised not to stay here, even if tempted by its shabby, basic rooms, and clean shared bathrooms. ❶

Venus Sharia Yussef Hassan ℡095/372-625, ℮venushotel@hotmail.com. While its faults were forgivable when the hotel was funky, it's harder to overlook the noise from the bazaar and the hustling on the premises now that the *Mars Bar* has lost its shine as a meeting place for travellers, and the rooms are so shabby. It remains to be seen if the newly renovated top floor (all rooms en-suite and a/c) heralds a return to past form. Room rates are negotiable, as are donkey, minibus and felucca trips. ❶

Mid-range hotels

Mostly rated with three stars, Luxor's mid-range hotels feature private bathrooms, a/c, phone and TV in the rooms, and a restaurant, bar and maybe also a pool on the premises. There the similarity may end, however, as each differs in its location, decor, atmosphere, clientele and rates. Although breakfast is included in the deal, don't expect anything more fancy than you'd get in a low-budget hotel.

Arabesque Sharia Mohammed Farid ℡095/371-299, ℻372-193. Sited on a busy road near Luxor Temple, with smallish, clean rooms (some overlooking the garden of the *Luxor*), a rooftop with a tiny pool and splendid views of the temple and the Nile, and Internet facilities. No alcohol is served. ❺

Golden Palace 600m down Television St ℡095/382-972, ℻382-974. Perhaps the best three-star option on the street, with facilities like the *Shady* but without its scene (see below) – although the *Abu Hameed* nightclub (see p.360) is just across the road. They will usually accept far less than the prices posted at reception. ❹

Horus Sharia el-Karnak ℡095/382-165, ℻380-965. The rooms are clean and the top two floors have a fine view of Luxor Temple, but the gloomy atmosphere and noisy location on a main road by the bazaar deter visitors. ❸

Little Garden Sharia Radwan, off Television St ℡095/381-746, ℮littlegardenlxregy@hotmail.com. A no-star hotel resembling a two-star one; spacious, clean and new, with comfy tiled rooms, a rooftop with sunbeds and showers, and a garden – all that's lacking is a pool. Free transfer from the airport or station for pre-booked guests. ❸

Luxor Sharia el-Karnak, near Luxor Temple ℡095/380-018, ℮hluxorhotel@hotmail.com. Still known to locals as the *Wena*, this once-grand Edwardian pile has gone way downhill during a legal dispute while somehow keeping its four-star status, but acknowledges reality by asking three-star prices and settling for less. Only one floor is habitable, but the high-ceilinged rooms, vast garden and pool, Arabesque arches and billiard room may outweigh the general shabbiness. Bargain hard. ❻

Merryland Sharia Nefertiti, between the temple and the museum ℡095/381-746 or 376-903. Although clean and quiet, with a fab view of the Nile from its rooftop, the claustrophobic rooms and lack of a pool make this place inferior to its nearby rivals, the *Windsor* and *Philippe*. ❸

Mina Palace On the Corniche near Luxor Temple ℡095/372-074, ℻382-194. Old-fashioned, but the rooms have fridges and overlook the Nile, while the "06" ones have an extra balcony facing the temple, which makes up for a lot. Its rooftop and terrace are cool drinking spots if you can endure the slow service. ❹

New Radwan Sharia al-Adasi ℡095/373-604, ℻380-060). Nice clean rooms and a small pool in the yard, but the location is extremely noisy, and for this price you can do better elsewhere. ❹

Philippe Sharia Labaib Habachi, near the Corniche ℡095/372-284, ℻380-050. Clean, carpeted rooms with fridges and a rooftop pool and sun terrace make this a favourite with adventure tour operators, but independent travellers may find the hotel rather impersonal, despite its good reputation. ❺

Ramoza Sharia al-Mahatta ℡095/372-270. Extremely dingy, and catering mainly to Egyptian tour groups, this place has clean rooms and hot water that works – but that's about all you can say for it. ❸

Saint Joseph Sharia Ibn Khalid Walid, near the *Sonesta St.George* ℡095/381-707, ℻381-727. Outclassed by its four-star neighbours, this three-star hotel has clean, slightly faded rooms with the usual amenities, and a pool on the roof. ❺

Saint Mark's Sharia el-Karnak ℡095/383-403. The small, depressing rooms are hard to sell, so they're willing to discount, but even the rooftop terrace with its tempting view of the *Mercure Coralia* pool makes you want to stay somewhere else. ③

Shady Television St ☎095/381-262, ⓕ374-859. The name (which is actually pronounced "Shardy") suits this hotel, for most of its guests are sex tourists, lounging around the pool with their toy-

boys. The rooms are okay, however. ④

Windsor Sharia Nefertiti, near the Corniche ☎095/375-547, ⓕ373-447, ⓔwindsor@click.com.eg. While its rooms are better than those at the *Philippe* and its roof terrace has a finer view, the pool is in a courtard, and tiny, so they charge less. ④

Upmarket hotels

The slump in tourism has hit Luxor's **upmarket hotels** especially hard, since tour groups are their mainstay. Though quoted prices for walk-in guests remain high, real bargains can be found on the Internet or through local travel agents. Many places charge premium rates for Nile-facing rooms; the prices below are for the least expensive (garden- or street-facing) rooms. Non-residents may use their restaurants, if not other facilities, too.

Club Med Bella Donna Sharia Ibn Khalid Walid, 700m beyond the *Novotel* ☎095/340-700, ⓕ380-879, ⓔlouvrec01@clubmed.com. Stylish, self-contained resort on the banks of the Nile, where all the guests and staff speak French. Accommodation on a B&B, half- or full-board basis, with discounts for children. ⑧

Emilio Sharia Yussef Hassan ☎095/376-666, ⓕ370-000. Centrally located and popular with European tour groups – reservations advisable. Comfy rooms with video channel, minibar and satellite TV; rooftop pool. ⑥

Gaddis Sharia Ibn Khalid Walid, 1km south of the *Novotel* ☎095/382-838, ⓕ382-837, ⓔgaddislxr@yahoo.com. Clean, stylish rooms with fridges; some suites have double beds. Smallish pool, plus a bar, disco and laundry service. Fifty-percent discount for *Rough Guide* readers. ⑦

Luxor Sheraton Resort Sharia Ibn Khalid Walid, 4km south of Luxor Temple ☎095/374-544, ⓕ374-941. Good facilities and service, but it's not worth paying premium rates for "Nile-view" rooms. Courtesy bus from outside the Luxor Museum seven times daily. ⑧

Mercure Coralia On the Corniche between Luxor Temple and the museum ☎095/380-944, ⓕ374-912. Still known to locals as the *Etap*, this anodyne four-star hotel has decent facilities and has traditionally been popular with British tour operators like Goldenjoy and First Choice – but anyone paying walk-in rates will get more for their money at the *Nile Hilton*. ⑧

Mercure Inn Near Luxor Temple ☎095/373-321, ⓕ370-051, ⓔh1933@accor-hotels.com. Cosy rooms with fridge and satellite TV, in large grounds with a decent-size pool. Used by Goldenjoy and Kuoni. Locals still call it the *Egotel*. ⑦

Mövenpick Jolie Ville Crocodile Island, 5km south of Luxor ☎095/374-855, ⓕ374-936, ⓔjolie.ville@movenpick-lxr.com.eg,

ⓦwww.movenpick-luxor.com. Comfy bungalows in extensive grounds, with tennis courts, a pool and a children's playground. Hourly courtesy bus to town (stops outside the *New Winter Palace*), and a motorboat three times daily. With higher occupancy rates than most other five-star hotels, it has no reason to offer discounts. ⑧

Nile Hilton 4km north of downtown Luxor and 1km from Karnak Temple ☎095/374-933, ⓕ376-571, ⓔhiltonluxorfo@lxr.com.eg. Club-class, Nile-view and garden-facing rooms in an enclave beside the river, with tennis courts, a giant chessboard and other diversions. Hourly courtesy bus from outside the *Mercure Inn* (see above). Often short of guests, so good for discounts. ⑧

Novotel Near the Nile 1km south of Luxor Temple ☎095/380-925, ⓕ380-972. Small as *Novotels* go, but with the usual atrium and facilities, a floating swimming pool, and great Nile views. ⑧

Pyramisa Isis Sharia Ibn Khalid Walid ☎095/372-750, ⓕ372-923, ⓔnazab@rite.com, ⓦwww.pyramisaegypt.com. Five-star complex set in lush grounds with wonderful views of the river. Owned by a relative of President Mubarak, who has a penthouse suite there. Italian and Chinese restaurants; large swimming pool; Internet. ⑧

Sonesta St. George Sharia Ibn Khalid Walid ☎095/382-575, ⓕ382-571, ⓔmanager@sonesta-hotel-luxor.com. The most lavishly decorated five-star hotel on the street, with Japanese and Italian restaurants, a Nile-side pool and a 24hr business centre. ⑧

Tutotel Sharia Salah al-Din ☎095/377-990, ⓕ372-671. A small four-star hotel with a rooftop pool and basement disco, that charges less than its larger rivals on Sharia Ibn Khalid Walid, though rates vary a lot according to demand. ⑥

Winter Palace On the Corniche south of Luxor Temple ☎095/380-422, ⓕ374-087, ⓔh1661@accor-hotels.com. The doyen of Luxor's hotels, founded in 1887, has played host to heads of state, Noël Coward and Agatha Christie (parts of *Death on the Nile* were written and filmed here). Combines old-fashioned elegance with modern facilities; rooms overlook the Nile or a huge garden with a pool. The adjacent *New Winter Palace* and *Pavilion Wing* cost less but lack character, though they share the same facilities; the *Pavilion Wing* is the better of the two. ❾

Hostelling or renting an apartment

With hotels around Television Street so cheap, you won't save any money by staying at the **Youth Hostel** (☎095/372-139, ℱ370-539), which is on a side-street near the Luxor Museum. Packed out with Egyptian teenagers in winter and closed over summer, the hostel has segregated dorms with bunks (£E13 per head) or "lux" rooms with three beds, for £E22 a head; HI membership is obligatory, but there's no age limit.

If you want to stay a long time in Luxor, it's easy to negotiate big discounts at hostels, especially over summer. For more privacy and independence, **renting an apartment** is appealing. A decent two-bedroom place in the centre costs £E400–500 a month, plus bills. Ask around and landlords will make themselves known.

Luxor Temple

Luxor Temple (daily: Oct–April 6am–9pm; May–Sept 6am–10pm; Ramadan 6am–6.30pm & 8–11pm; £E20) stands aloof in the heart of town, ennobling the view from the waterfront and tourist bazaar with its grand colonnades and pylons, which are spotlit at night. Though best explored by day – when its details can be thoroughly examined in a couple of hours – you should come back after dark to imbibe its atmosphere and drama with fewer people around. For a general guide to **temple architecture**, see p.330.

The temple's dedication and construction

Dedicated to the **Theban Triad** of Amun-Min, Mut and Khonsu (see p.367), Luxor Temple was the "Harem of the South" where Amun's consort Mut and their son Khonsu resided. Every spring a flotilla of barques escorted Amun's effigy from Karnak Temple to this site for a conjugal reunion with Mut in an *Optet* or fertility festival noted for its public debauchery.

Whereas Karnak is the work of many dynasties, most of Luxor Temple was built by two rulers during a period when New Kingdom art reached its apogee. The temple's founder was **Amenophis III** (1417–1379 BC) of the XVIII Dynasty, whose other monuments include the Third Pylon at Karnak and the Colossi of Memnon across the river. Work halted under his son Akhenaten (who erased his father's cartouches and built a sanctuary to Aten alongside the temple), but resumed under Tutankhamun and Horemheb, who decorated its court and colonnade with their own reliefs. To this, **Ramses II** (1304–1237 BC) of the XIX Dynasty added a double colonnaded court and a great pylon flanked by obelisks and colossi. Despite additions by later pharaohs and the rebuilding of its sanctuary under Alexander the Great, the temple has a coherence that reproaches Karnak's inchoate giganticism. When the French army first sighted it in 1799, the troops spontaneously presented arms.

The clarity of its **reliefs** owes to the temple having been half-buried by sand and silt, and overlaid by Luxor itself. Nineteenth-century visitors found a "labyrinthine maze of mud structures" nesting within its court; colonnades turned into granaries where dishonest merchants were hanged by their ears. "So stirs a mini-life amid the debris of a life that was far grander", wrote

Winter Palace Hotel

LUXOR TEMPLE

TEMPLE RELIEFS, ETC

Battle of Kadesh	a, b
Pharaoh Shabaka	c
Optet Festival	d
Sacrificial offerings	e
Amun's barque procession	f, g
Barque's return to Karnak	h
Roman altar	i
Roman paintings	j
Offerings scenes	k l
Birth of Amenophis II	m
Amun's barque shrine	n
Rimbaud	n

0 Metres 20

Park

Hypostyle Hall

Court of
Amenophis III

River

Nile

Colonnade

Court of
Ramses II

Mosque of
Abu el-Haggag

Remains of Roman Fort

Pylon

Obelisk

Colossi of
Ramses II

Tickets

Seraphis
Chapel

Avenue of
Sphinxes

Mummification Museum

Flaubert. When the French desired to remove an obelisk, and archeologists to excavate the temple, they had to pay compensation for the demolition of scores of homes.

Approaching the temple

The ticket office is on the Corniche side, where the gradual slope inside the entrance obscures the fact that the site lies several metres below street level – a measure of the debris that accumulated here over centuries. At the end of the ramp, to your left, is a restored **Chapel of Seraphis** dedicated by the Roman emperor Hadrian on his birthday in AD 126. Beyond this, the courtyard opens into an **Avenue of Sphinxes** with human faces that once led to Karnak Temple – a XXX Dynasty addition by Nectanebo I.

The temple gateway proper is flanked by massive pylons and enthroned colossi, with a single **Obelisk** soaring 25m high. Carved with reliefs and originally tipped with electrum, this was one of a pair until its mate was removed in 1835, taken to France and re-erected on the Place de la Concorde. The four dog-faced baboons at the base of each obelisk also sported erect phalluses until prudish Frenchmen hacked them off. Behind loom three of the six **colossi of Ramses II** that originally fronted the pylon (four seated, two standing). The enthroned pair have Schwarzenegger physiques and double crowns; reliefs of the Nile-god binding the Two Lands adorn their thrones.

The **Pylon** is 65m wide and once stood 24m high. It is notched for flagpoles and carved with scenes of Ramses' supposed victory over the Hittites at Qadesh. You can see Ramses consulting his commanders in the Egyptian camp **[a]**, before charging his foes and battling them until reinforcements arrive **[b]**. Centuries later, Nubian and Ethiopian kings left their mark: notice the relief of Pharaoh Shabaka running the *heb* race before Amun-Min, high up on the left as you walk through the pylon **[c]**.

Courts and colonnades

Beyond the pylon lies the **Court of Ramses II**, surrounded by a double row of papyrus-bud columns, once roofed over to form arcades. The courtyard is set askew to the temple's main axis, doubtless to incorporate the earlier **barque shrines** of Tuthmosis III, dedicated to Khonsu (to the right as you enter), Amun (centre) and Mut (nearest the river).

Incongruously perched atop the opposite colonnade (which is still bricked up to its capitals), the **Mosque of Abu el-Haggag** is a much-rebuilt Fatimid edifice bearing the name of Luxor's patron saint, whose demolition the townsfolk refused to countenance when the temple was excavated. To the right of the portal at the back of the court, you'll see the lower half of a frieze depicting Amun's procession approaching the temple during the Optet festival, when the god was presented with lettuces, symbolizing his fertility **[d]**. Here, Ramses makes offerings to Mut and Mont (the Theban war god), observed by his queen and seventeen of the hundred or so sons that he sired over ninety years. Notice the bullocks in the corner of the wall.

The portal itself is flanked by black granite statues of Ramses, their bases decorated with bound prisoners from Nubia and Asia. Beyond lies the older section of the temple, inaugurated by the lofty **Colonnade of Amenophis III**, with its processional avenue of giant papyrus columns whose calyx capitals still support massive architraves. Its scale is so vast that you can hardly take it in. On the walls are more damaged scenes from the Optet festival, intended to be "read" in an anticlockwise direction. After sacrifices to the boats at Karnak **[e]**, Amun's procession **[f]** arrives at Luxor Temple **[g]**, returning to Karnak 24 days later [h]. The pharaoh shown here is Tutankhamun, who had the colonnade decorated, but the cartouches honour his successor, Horemheb.

At the end of the colonnade lies the great **Court of Amenophis III**, surrounded on three sides by colonnades of papyrus-bundle columns with bud capitals – the most elegant form devised by the ancient Egyptians. Its decorations include artwork from the time of Alexander and Philip of Macedon, with some traces of colour still visible on the eastern colonnade. The southern one merges into a **Hypostyle Hall** with 32 papyrus columns, serving as a vestibule to the temple proper. Between the last two columns on the left of its central aisle [i] is a Roman altar dedicated to Emperor Constantine, before his conversion to Christianity. On either side of the hall's rear wall, Amenophis makes offerings to the gods.

The inner sanctums

Beyond the hall lies a columned **portico** or antechamber, whose central aisle was flanked by the barque shrines of Mut and Khonsu. Roman legionaries later plastered over the pharaonic reliefs and turned it into a chapel where local Christians were offered a choice between martyrdom or obeisance to the imperial cults. Paintings of Roman emperors are visible near the top of the walls, and around the niche on the south wall [j]; elsewhere the stucco has fallen away to reveal Amenophis offering sacrifices to Amun. In the smaller, four-columned **Hall of Offerings**, beyond, reliefs show the pharaoh leading sacrificial cows and presenting incense and sceptres [k].

More interesting reliefs occur in the **Birth Room** of Amenophis III, whose north wall [l] emphasizes his divine paternity, since he was not of direct royal descent. The ravaged lower register shows Amun, Hathor and Queen Mutemuia embracing; and Thoth leading Amun (disguised as Tuthmosis IV) into the queen's bedchamber, where the accompanying hieroglyphic caption states, "his dew filled her body". Examined from left to right, the middle register depicts Thoth foretelling Amenophis's birth; Mutemuia's pregnancy and confinement; Isis presenting the child to Amun; and the god cradling his son. Along the top register, Amenophis and his *ka* are nurtured by deities and presented to Amun; in the far right corner, Amenophis becomes pharaoh.

If the Birth Room is inaccessible from the Hall of Offerings you can reach it via the next hall, which Alexander the Great converted into the **Sanctuary of Amun's Barque** by removing four columns and installing a granite shrine [m]. Though its "doors of acacia inlaid with gold" are no more, some of the reliefs on the walls bear traces of their original colouring.

The remaining chambers to the south constituted the private apartments of the gods, reached by a transverse hall. However, this section of the temple is badly damaged and really only notable for the name *Rimbaud*, carved high up on the wall near the river [n]. Rimbaud spent the last sixteen years of his life roaming the Near and Far East; while living in Ethiopia he was feared dead, so Verlaine published his poems (all written by the age of 21), which took Paris by storm and inspired the Decadent movement.

Outside the walls, assorted pharaonic, Roman and Christian **stonework** is stored near the spot where, in 1989, workers uncovered a cache of 26 New Kingdom statues which are now on show in the Luxor Museum.

Luxor Museum

Luxor Museum (daily: winter 9am–1pm & 4–9pm; summer 9am–1pm & 5–10pm; Ramadan 10am–4pm; £E30; camera permit £E10, no flashes or tripods, camcorder £E20), on the northern end of the Corniche, complements the town's monumental assets, containing a small but choice collection of statues and funerary goods from local temples and the Theban Necropolis. The museum is well laid out with clear labelling in English, but bear in mind that some names may be rendered differently from those in this book (eg Amenhotep for Amenophis). An illustrated guidebook can be purchased at the information desk.

Works in stone include a large pink granite head of Amenophis III; a fine statue of Tuthmosis III in green-black schist; a jug-eared Senusert III (XII Dynasty); a human-bodied, crocodile-headed Sobek in alabaster; and two haunting busts of Amenophis IV (Akhenaten) from his temple at Karnak. There is also a wall from the same temple, consisting of small sandstone blocks known as *talatat*. These were later used as filler for the Ninth Pylon, wherein they were discovered in the 1960s. Now reassembled, the wall depicts Akhenaten, his wife Nefertiti and their court; figures have the strange physiognomy associated with Akhenaten's reign.

From **Tutankhamun's tomb** in the Valley of the Kings come a funerary bed, two model boats and a stunning gold-inlaid cow's head representing Merit Weri (an aspect of Hathor); the rest of the Tut finds are housed in Cairo. **Other highlights** include a dazzling mummy casing from the tomb of Lady Shepenkhonsu; canopic jars with animal- or human-headed lids; and a scowling statue of Amenhotep, Steward of Amenophis III, the probable architect of Luxor Temple.

The **New Hall** displays the cache of statues found in the temple. The most impressive ones are larger than life, amongst them Amenophis III, Tutankhamun, Ramses II, Queen Nefertari, Hathor and Horus. Archeologists disagree over whether the statues were cached at the start of the Roman occupation or nine hundred years earlier, when Egypt was invaded by the Assyrians, whose armies sacked Thebes in 664 BC.

Mummification Museum

In the mall beneath the Corniche near Luxor Temple, the **Mummification Museum** (daily: winter 9am–1pm & 4–9pm; summer 9am–1pm & 5–10pm; £E20, students £E10; camera permit £E10, camcorder £E100) explains the history and practice of mummification, and the beliefs surrounding it (see box on p.390). A host of reptile and bird mummies and a well-preserved XXI Dynasty official, Maserharti, are the star exhibits, but don't overlook the spoon and spatula that were used to remove the deceased's brain. This was discarded by the Egyptians as an unimportant organ, unlike the viscera, which were preserved in canopic jars. A statue of Anubis, the jackal god of mummification, watches over the exhibition.

Eating and drinking

Luxor's culinary scene is less diverse than in Cairo or Alexandria, but there's no shortage of places to eat. Upmarket **hotel restaurants** offer a/c, good service and cuisines such as Chinese (at the *Pyramisa Isis*), Japanese (at the *Sonesta St. George*), Italian or French (most places). Prices are usually steep, but there are some good deals, like the all-you-can-eat **salad bars** in the *New Winter Palace* and the *Mercure Coralia* coffee shop, or the rich spaghetti bolognese served at the *Gaddis*. Elsewhere you'll mainly find pizzas, kebabs, omelettes and other dishes palatable to tourists. Menus are written up outside and all the waiters know English, so it's easy to order. Providing you're ready for service charges and tax (up to 21 percent), the total cost shouldn't come as a shock.

All the usual **street food** can be found along El-Karnak, Ramses and Yussef Hassan streets, but it's hard for foreigners to avoid being overcharged, even if they know the proper price. The same is also true for tea, coffee and *sheeshas* at cafés, cigarettes, pastries and other items. One 24-hour **bakery** near the corner of Sharia al-Mahatta and the souk turns out pretzels and rolls, while *Twinky*, at the station end of Sharia al-Adasi, abounds in sticky confectionery. If you're into **self-catering**, lots of small **grocery shops** (*ba'al*s) sell canned goods, cheeses, olives, fruit yogurts and juices, which can be combined with fresh fruit and bread from the souk to make a wholesome meal – while the Omar mini-market on Sharia el-Medina el-Minawra and the Barghouti grocery store on Television Street stock a wider range of imported foodstuffs.

Most of the following **restaurants** are inexpensive by Western standards, and are open from mid-morning (or earlier) till 9–10pm (or later), though the range of meals diminishes as the evening wears on. Unless stated otherwise, they don't sell **alcohol**. We've only listed **cafés** that sell food, but there are scores of local coffee houses where you can sample exotic beverages – try *helba*, a bright yellow tea made from fenugreek. The poolside *gelateria* in the *Mövenpick Jolie Ville* serves the best **ice cream** in Luxor.

Additionally, there are some good places to eat on the **west bank**, near the ferry landing stage. See p.387 for details.

Abou Ashraf Sharia al-Mahatta. Brightly lit take-away and sit-down restaurant, serving roast chicken, *kofta, shwarma* and *kushari*, with a counter of sweet pastries for dessert. Inexpensive, but prone to creative accountancy. Open till midnight.

Abu Hassan el-Shazly Sharia al-Adasi. Kerbside *kofta* joint amid the spice and hardware souk, frequented by hustlers from the *Oasis Hotel*. Authentically *baladi* and maybe not for sensitive stomachs, but if you enjoy bazaar-watching and badinage, it's worth trying. *Abu Hagger*, next door, tends to deter foreigners with its Damien Hirst-like displays of cow haunches.

Aly Baba Café On the corner near the *Luxor*. The attraction is the view of Luxor Temple and the hotel gardens, which makes amends for the overpriced drinks and snacks. Waiters call "Hey you" to solicit custom.

Amoun In the tourist bazaar on Sharia el-Karnak. Touristy, yes, but the food is tasty and good value (regulars get bigger portions). The menu includes seafood, grills, pizzas and veggie options, and the service is friendly. There's a/c indoors, but most people sit outside to watch the street life. Superb fruit drinks. Open till midnight or later.

Anubis Beside the Mummification Museum. The spacious terrace overlooking the Nile is a winner, though the food doesn't match the setting or the cost (£E60–80, excluding drinks). Alternatively, you could just sink a beer or a non-alcoholic cocktail from the fancy juice bar, and shoot some pool in the corner.

Bakkar Sharia el-Kamrr, off Television St. Under the same management as the nearby *Happy Land Hotel*, this small, clean, a/c place offers fish, meat,

pizza and salads prepared by a chef from the *Mövenpick*, at lowish prices. Daily 10am–midnight.

Chez Omar In the garden on Sharia Yussef Hassan. Tasty Egyptian snacks and non-alcoholic drinks, served in a relaxed, shaded enclave near the souk, for surprisingly low prices. Popular with French tourists.

El-Hussein In the tourist bazaar on Sharia el-Karnak. Though its menu and prices are identical to the *Amoun*, next door, the food and service aren't as good and it gets far fewer customers.

Jamboree Sharia el-Montazah, near the Brooke Animal Hospital. Aimed at British tourists, its menu features jacket potatoes and Cajun chicken, seafood, and Egyptian dishes (£E25–35). The food is bland and the salad bar so dull it doesn't invite seconds, but their roof terrace, with a side-view of Luxor Temple, is quite appealing. Daily 10.30am–2.30pm & 6.30–11pm.

Jem's Sharia Ibn Khalid Walid, between the *Isis* and *Sheraton* hotels (☎ & ℱ 095/383-604, ℮ ahmed@jemsluxor.co.uk. It's worth reserving a table in this agreeably *faux*-grand restaurant, serving delicious seafood, pizzas, salads and other Euro-Oriental dishes. The *mezze* (£E25) are a meal in themselves, and even the beer and wine are inexpensive. Daily 9am–midnight (or later).

King's Head Pub Sharia Ibn Khalid Walid, near the passport office. Though the king in question is Akhenaten, this place looks and feels just like an English pub, offering toasted sandwiches, soups, chips and a Sunday lunch of roast beef and Yorkshire pud. Its beer and cocktails are as cheap as anywhere, and there's a billiards table and satellite TV. Open daily till 2am (later if there are customers).

Marhaba Above the tourist office. Its terrace overlooking Luxor Temple and the Theban Hills almost makes up for the uninspiring grills and *mezze*, providing the restaurant isn't full of tour groups. Serves alcohol.

Miyako *Sonesta St. George Hotel.* Worth a splurge for its Japanese food and upmarket surroundings, especially before 7pm, when there's a thirty-percent discount. Set meals of sashimi (£E86), lobster and shrimp (£E53) or meat (£E66), prepared by a Japanese chef. Smartish dress expected. Serves alcohol. Most credit cards accepted. Daily 5–11pm.

New Karnak Opposite the train station. Omelettes, soups, salads, curries and spaghetti with a smidgin of sauce, at lowish prices. A pit-stop for hustlers working the station, so you're likely to be accosted there.

New Royal Fish Off Television St. Quiet, clean and a/c, it serves tasty meals of Red Sea fish or *calamari* with rice, chips, salad and *tahina*, for £E10–30. It tends to move location every few years, but never strays from the area. Daily 8am–midnight.

Pink Panda *Pyramisa Isis Hotel.* One of Luxor's smartest restaurants, specializing in Szechuan cooking, which rivals the *Miyako* for excellence.

Appetizers cost £E9–27, main dishes £E33–50. Most credit cards accepted.

Pub 2000 and Esquire Restaurant Off Sharia Ibn Khalid Walid near the Law Courts. Not nearly as lively as the *King's Head*, and the restaurant downstairs is nearly always deserted, but you can save money on Stella (£E10) and other drinks during happy hour (8–9pm).

Saiyida Zeinab Television St. Rather shabby, but does great *kushari*: a filling meal or a snack, depending on which size portion you order (£E3–5). Open till 1am or later.

Seven Days Seven Ways Opposite *Jem's*. A haven for expat Brits run by two Johns from Leeds, serving British caff food and priding itself on its Sunday roast dinners (6pm, 7.30pm & 9pm; £E23). *The Royal Oak Pub* (4pm–2am) and *Showtime Lounge*, upstairs, are for boozing or watching sports and film channels on TV. Daily 9am–11pm.

Venus Garden Sharia Yussef Hassan. Right in front of *Chez Omar* (see above), this place offers cheap light meals and soft drinks, in a small shady garden overlooking a busy street – and also discreetly serves beer, from teapots.

Drinking and duty-free shops

If you don't mind paying about £E25, the classiest place to **drink** a cold Stella beer is the garden terrace of the *Winter Palace* or the Nile-side terrace of the *Sheraton*, both of which have fabulous views. However, the panorama is pretty good from the terrace of the *Anubis* restaurant, where beer costs £E12, or the shabbier terrace of the *Mina Palace Hotel* near Luxor Temple, where it's only £E10. For a livelier time in the evening, visit the *King's Head* or *Royal Oak* pubs, which charge £E10 for a Stella and £E12 for cocktails; both have satellite TV and are popular with expats – unlike the gloomier *Pub 2000*, which is really only tempting during happy hour (8–9pm), or the overpriced *Murphy's Irish Pub*, off Sharia Ibn Khalid Walid. Downtown, the *Mars Bar* in the *Venus Hotel* used to be the place for backpackers to meet and may be so again once the place is refurbished and the pool table is fixed – but in the meantime there's a lack of good bars in the centre.

Imported beer and spirits cost a fortune in hotels, but a modest sum at **duty-free shops**, which accept hard currency or £E. Tourists may only buy within 24 hours of arrival, but can do so twice: in the arrivals lounge at Luxor airport, and the duty-free shop on the street behind the *Emilio Hotel* (daily 10am–3pm & 7pm–midnight). You'll need your passport, in which the transaction(s) will be noted. Otherwise, fall back on Egyptian beer, wine or spirits (often labelled to resemble imported brands), sold at low-profile **outlets** like Baket on Sharia al-Souk, Al-Ahram Beverages on Sharia Ramses or Micho's Grocery on Sharia al-Mahatta. They tend to open from 10am to midnight, and as most are run by Christians, they close during Easter as well as Ramadan.

Nightlife

While the **Sound and Light Show at Karnak Temple** is the best in Egypt (see p.367), Luxor's nightlife is a paler shadow of Hurghada's, if only because most tourists are too tired out from sightseeing to fancy clubbing. With tourism at a low ebb many **discos** are almost empty, and even at the most popular ones Egyptian males far outnumber foreign females. *Sinouhe*, midway down Sharia Ibn Khalid Walid, has the best light show and plays a mixture of Arabic pop, Madonna and Kylie. Open till 5am every night, it rarely gets properly going before 2am, when revellers leave the *King's Head*. Beer costs £E12 and cocktails £E18, which is roughly what you'd pay in the basement disco in the *Tuthotel* on Sharia Salah al-Din, *Sinouhe*'s main rival. The *Lotus Boat* at the *Novotel* is the dearest of the three, while other hotel discos are so quiet that they're not worth a special journey unless there's something happening there. None of them charges for admission.

Most places feature a **belly dancer** who struts her stuff for half an hour or so. At some hotels this is just an interlude in the disco while at others it forms part of a floor show featuring **Sayidi music** and **folk dancing**. Among hotels which don't levy a cover charge, the *Pyramisa Isis* has a dancer in its disco (nightly 11.30pm) and bar (Sat 10.30pm), the *Nile Hilton* puts on more of a show every Tuesday night, and the less said about the *Lotus Boat*, the better. At the *Mercure Coralia*, there's a minimum charge of £E35 to see the dancer in the *Sabil* disco at 12.30am, while the *Mercure Inn* lays on *rababa* music and a buffet at its *Dawar al-Umda* outdoor restaurant, for £E45 per person (excluding drinks). The latter has no regular schedule and basically depends on the level of demand. If tourism picks up, other hotels may mount similar events.

The alternative is to visit a **real Egyptian nightclub**, where the decor is seedy and the clientele raucous (women are best off going with male companions); the music is brilliant and the belly dancers get sexier as the night wears on. You have to stay through till dawn to savour the build-up, as they tease gold-bedecked businessmen into throwing £E100 notes around, to shimmy alongside or toast themselves over the echo machine. The cash is collected in a box, which is dragged off at the end of each act and split equally among the dancer, the bandleader and the club. If the woman fails to arouse enthusiasm, the manager shoos her off and orders another on. Rich clients may demand a "White" (pale-skinned, blond) dancer, or come to blows over a woman, while poorer spectators sit in the shadows, quaffing booze and smoking *bango*. The only drinks sold are Johnny Walker (£E100 a bottle) and Stella (£E10); forget about food. Luxor currently has only one such club, *Abu Hameed*, opposite the *Golden Palace* hotel on Television Street. The dancing starts at 1am and runs through till 5am if enough patrons are still spending. It's best to go with an Egyptian friend, to get past the doorman who insists that there's a £E40 entry charge, or to argue if they add it to your bill – there isn't one, you should only pay for drinks.

For locals who can't afford such pleasures, the main diversions are playing backgammon (*thowla*) or dominoes in **coffe houses** like the one bearing a huge portrait of the singer Oum Kalsoum, near the Abu el-Haggag Mosque. Though café life is exclusively masculine, foreign women can usually feel comfortable there, even alone. Most places stay open as long as there are customers; Sharia Ramses has several all-nighters.

Festivals

If the whole year's programme of tourist events isn't cancelled – as happened in 2002 – wintertime visitors have a fair chance of witnessing the **International Rowing Festival** around December 18–22, or the **West Bank marathon** (starting and finishing at Deir el-Bahri) in February – the tourist office will have details if they happen. Additionally, there could be a revival of the

Gourna Festival of Saiyidi music, previously held on the west bank in February or March, where enthusiastic locals swayed in *zikrs* to musicians such as Sheikh Ahmed Berrin. For information, contact the French organizers or visit their website (Ⓔgourna@free.fr, Ⓦwww.gourna.free.fr).

Popular religious festivals, or **moulids**, are certain to occur each year, according to the Islamic calendar. Most are local affairs attended by a few thousand people, but there is also a huge carnival attracting half a million *fellaheen* from Upper Egypt. They generally occur during the two months of the Muslim calendar preceding Ramadan; locals can rarely tell you the exact date, but always know when one is due. Foreigners are welcome to attend; just beware of pickpockets.

The largest and most famous is the **Moulid of Abu el-Haggag** (pronounced "Hajjaj"), honouring Luxor's patron sheikh, whose mosque overlooks the temple. **Yussef Abu el-Haggag** (Father of the Pilgrimage) was born in Damascus (c.1150), moved to Mecca in his forties and finally settled in Egypt, where he founded a *zawiyah* in Luxor and met with other Sufi sheikhs such as Al-Mursi and Al-Shazli. Many of his descendants still live in the area, and the tradition of venerating local sheikhs is strong in villages around Luxor. During the festival, giant floats move through the densely packed streets, some dedicated to trades (the *caleche* drivers' bears a carriage), others to the sheikh himself. The parading of a large **boat** (or even three boats) is often compared to the solar barque processions of pharaonic times, though in Islamic symbolism boats represent the quest for spiritual enlightenment. Vast crowds attend the *zikrs* outside Abu el-Haggag's Mosque, and revel in traditional entertainments. There are **stick fights** (*tahtib*) to the music of drums and *mizmars* (a kind of oboe), and **horse races** (*mirmah*) where the riders gallop hell for leather, halting in a flurry of dust just before they plough into the crowd. Booze and *bango* are consumed quite openly. The festival runs from the 1st–14th of *Sha'ban*, ending two weeks before the start of Ramadan. During **Ramadan** itself, townsfolk compensate for its daytime rigours by gathering to hear *zikrs* and dance outside Abu el-Haggag's Mosque in the evenings.

Sheikh Ali Musa of Karnak was actually born in another village, and when he died the villagers demanded that his body be buried there instead. The Karnakis said, "Let the Sheikh decide", so his coffin was borne to the crossroads, whereupon it turned to face Karnak and was taken back in triumph. His moulid lasts a week, its *leyla kebir* (Big Night) falling on the 6th of *Rageb*. You can't miss the music, swings and lights around his tomb, near the entrance to Karnak village.

About the same time, on the other side of town, Awmia village honours its own **Sheikh Ahmed al-Adasi** – who is known for appearing in the dreams of Egyptians working in Italy and Morocco – with a week-long festival, whose curtain raiser is a day of stick fights, horse and **camel races** on a nearby wasteground. For the moulid itself, Awmia's main street is enclosed by a tent, where *munshids* sing at ear-splitting volume; further in are fairground rides and a tent of Sufis in a *zikr*. Following the *leyla kebir* on the 14th of *Rageb,* there's a final day of celebrations called *Ed-Dara*, when camels and horses are paraded through the streets and villagers throw candies at each other.

Other moulids occur across the Nile, at Gurna Ta'rif (p.389) and Riziq (p.421).

Shopping: bazaars and markets

The streets around Luxor Temple are infested with **tourist bazaars** whose salesmen use every trick in the book to lure you into their shops. Don't go shopping with a *caleche*- or taxi-driver, or you'll end up paying him commission on whatever you buy. Despite fierce competition you must bargain hard, as merchants rely upon fresh-off-the-plane tourists to pay way over the odds. Fixed-price shops are rare, but can provide a rough benchmark for bargaining at other places. **Gold and silver** are usually sold by weight and so prices should be roughly fixed; El Safa Bazar on Sharia Labaib Habachi is friendly and honest. **Crafts** include humble hand-made clay pots used for cooking, sold for as little as £E5 outside the police station; bowls hand-carved from lemon, orange or tamarisk wood in the village of Hegaza, on sale in the *Mövenpick*, and gorgeous handmade silks, linens and cottons averaging £E40–80 a metre, in the Winter Akhmeem Gallery in front of the *Winter Palace*. As a rule, it should be cheaper to buy **alabaster** or **papyrus** on the west bank. The Nefertari Papyrus Institute is one of the few fixed-price shops on that side of the Nile.

In Luxor, **curio and carpet shop**s have long been displacing the hardware, spices and clothing stalls from Sharia al-Souk to Sharia al-Adasi, but on Tuesdays there's still a **fruit and veg market** on Sharia al-Souk, and on Sharia el-Madina el-Minawra, near Television Street. Luxor's weekly **livestock market** is smaller and less camel-oriented than the *Souk el-Gamal* at Darow, near Aswan, or Cairo's market at Bil'esh, but just as rough on the nerves of animal lovers. The name of the route to the site – Sharia es-Salakhana, "Slaughterhouse Street" – says it all. The market is held every Tuesday (7–11am) in the village of El-Hebel, 4km outside Luxor. To reach El-Hebel by bicycle, follow Sharia Mustafa Kamel across the train tracks, turn right down Es-Salakhana and simply follow the stream of traffic.

Most non-tourist shops close for a **siesta** (2–5pm).

Activities

Sailing on the river in a **felucca** is a relaxing way to spend an afternoon, while a sunset cruise is the perfect way to end the day. Expect to pay at least £E30 an hour for a boat carrying two people, £E40 upwards for a craft seating six or seven. The favoured destination is **Banana Island** (*Gezira el-Mozh*), a lush peninsula 4km upriver, whose owner charges visitors £E5 each to land. It's enjoyable to wander through the cool, shady groves of mature banana trees, with their vaulting fronds and pendant flowers; the trail ends at a souvenir shop where you can get a drink. The round trip takes between two and three hours depending on the wind, or about half-an-hour each way by **motorboat** (*zobak*). You should be able to rent one for £E40 an hour by negotiating directly with boatmen. The best felucca and *zobak* captains are allocated berths below Luxor Temple and the *Winter Palace*; less skilled ones tie up nearer the *Mercure Coralia* and *Novotel*.

Although a new, Olympic-size pool now exists on Sharia Ibn Khalid Walid, only a few atheletes can use it, so you must still depend on hotels with **swimming pools** open to non-residents. The *Windsor, Philippe, Emilio, Shady* and *St Joseph* charge £E10 admission; the *Golden Palace* £E20 and the *Gaddis* £E25. At the *Mercure Inn*, the £E50 charge includes lunch, while at the *Mövenpick* one must rent a bungalow for the day – though the cost (£E120) can be split between several people. Non-residents are usually allowed to use the **tennis** courts at the *Winter Palace, Sheraton* and *Hilton*, while **horse-riding** on the west bank can be arranged through stables in Gezira that hire out Arabian thoroughbreds for £E20 an hour (see p.382). You can play **billiards** in the *King's Head Pub* (£E10), the *Nile Hilton* (£E20) or the *Luxor* (£E15). The *Luxor* has the nicest billiards room after the *Winter Palace*'s, which is not for use by non-residents but worth a look for its Edwardian splendour.

Finally, if money is no object, there's the luxury of drifting over the Necropolis in a **hot-air balloon**, which affords an awesome view of the temples, villages and mountains; to get the best photographic results use 200 or 250 ASA film. Cruising at 300 metres, you can smell the cooking fires and donkeys and overhear conversations below, in an eerie silence punctuated by the roar of the balloon's gas-burners. The course is determined by meteorological conditions and the skill of the pilot, so each flight is different – but you'll probably spend about an hour aloft. The three balloon companies operating in Luxor are fully insured and CAA-approved, and offer two or three flights daily in season (Oct–May), subject to cancellation at short notice. *Magic Horizon Balloons* (☎095/365-060 or mobile 0105 688439, ⓕ386-155, ⓔbooking@magic-horizon.com) has the largest balloon-basket and has taken a lot of trade away from its older rivals *Hod Hod Soliman* (☎ & ⓕ095/370-116) and *Balloons Over Egypt* (☎095/376-515). At the time of writing, a ride costs about US$138. Call the companies directly for a quote rather than pay a commission by booking through any of the hotels that advertise balloon trips. The deal should include an early-morning transfer from your hotel to the launch site, and refreshments.

THE NILE VALLEY | Luxor: Listings

Listings

American Express In the arcade outside the *Winter Palace*. Changes money and travellers' cheques, makes cash advances and transfers, sells cheques to Amex cardholders, and holds mail (daily 8am–8pm; ☎095/378-333, ⓕ372-862).

Banks and exchange Banque Misr, Sharia Labaib Habachi (daily 8.30am–9pm, Fri closed between 11.30am & 3pm), has a cash dispenser (Visa, MasterCard, Cirrus) outside. Other banks include National Bank of Egypt, 50m south of the *Winter Palace* (Mon–Thurs, Sat & Sun 8.30am–2pm & 5–9pm, Fri 8.30–11am & 5–9pm); Banque du Caire, Midan Salah al-Din, near Television St (winter daily except Fri 8.30am–2pm & 5–8pm; summer same days till 9pm). The Bank of Alexandria on the Corniche between the City Council and Luxor Museum exchanges cash, travellers' cheques and does Visa cash advances (Mon–Thurs & Sun 8.30am–2pm; Ramadan 10am–1.30pm). Many of the luxury hotels also do currency exchange.

Barbers Men can get a sharp haircut and shave plus the full facial exfoliation that Egyptians prefer at a barber shop near the *New Royal Fish* restaurant off Television St, for £E15–20.

Bookshops Aboudi and Gaddis in the bazaar near the tourist office, and Hachette, in the arcade of the *Etap*, stock loads of novels and books on Egyptology in foreign languages. A kiosk on the Corniche near the tourist office sells foreign newspapers. The best place for postcards is on the corner of Sharia al-Souk and Sharia Yussef Hassan.

British Consul (Honorary) Mr Ehab A.A. Gaddis can help British citizens in the event of trouble. Contact him at the "consulate" at the *Gaddis Hotel* on Sharia Ibn Khalid (Mon–Fri 10am–2pm;

☎095/382-838). See also "Legal advice", below.

Dentist Dr Moneer el-Shaoly, on Sharia al-Mahatta ☎095/373-710.

Doctors Dr Makrus Faoze, Sharia al-Adasi ☎095/382-614 or 0123 400729; dermatologist Dr Selim Fakhri ☎ 095/372-028; urologist Dr Samy Fakhri ☎095/374-964.

EgyptAir In the arcade outside the *Winter Palace* (daily 8am–8pm; ☎095/380-580 or 380-581).

Hospitals Inaugurated in 2001, Luxor International Hospital off Television St (☎095/387-192, -194 or -196) is the best in Upper Egypt, with consultants from Cairo and annual surgical visits by Sir Magdi Yacoub, but day-to-day care is rough and ready; and the hospital is hardly up to European standards. Even so, it's preferable to the older El-Gadid (☎095/382-698) on Television St, and the newer St Mark on Sharia el-Karnak opposite the hotel of the same name (☎095/370-465) – let alone the Al-Amiri on the Corniche near the Luxor Museum (☎095/372-025); all are open 24hr. Foreigners pay £E100 for an ambulance call-out; dial ☎123.

Internet cafés *Pop 2000* on the corner of Sharia al-Souk and Sharia al-Mahatta, the *Rainbow Internet Café* off Sharia Yussef Hassan and the nameless kiosk at the top end of Television St all charge £E10/hr for Internet use, with no minimum charge, as does *Happy Land Hotel*, while Aboudi, in the bookshop of the same name (see above) asks £E12/hr, and fancy hotels like the *Isis* or *Sheraton* £E20/hr. Rates should drop once Luxor's network is upgraded, in the near future.

Legal advice CBC Business Consultants, PO Box 92, New Hospital St (☎095/387-015, ⓔconsultants@computerized.net, ⓦwww

363

.consultants@computerized.net) can advise foreign women in property or child custody disputes, on a fee-paying basis. Contact André Chappot.

Mobile phones There are lots of retailers; for repairs, try Singer on Sharia Orabi, facing the *Abu Hassan el-Shazly* restaurant.

Passport office On Sharia Ibn Khalid Walid (Mon–Thurs & Sat 8am–2pm; ℡ 095/380-885). Visa extensions cost £E12 and require one photo. Some English spoken.

Pharmacies Exist all over town and have a rota for working nights, posted in Arabic. Many close for a siesta, and on Sundays. Hotels are generally aware of likely locations.

Post office At the temple end of Sharia al-Mahatta (Mon–Thurs & Sun 8am–2pm), with a branch in the station (daily 8am–8pm) and another next to the telephone exchange on Sharia el-Karnak (daily 8am–8pm). Street post boxes are only emptied when they're full, so it's better to post letters from a top-notch hotel. *Don't* use the poste restante; have letters sent c/o American Express or the *Winter Palace*. It's less hassle to send packages with DHL, on the Corniche next to the *Mina Palace Hotel* (daily 8am–6pm).

Telephone calls The cheapest way to call abroad is with a Menatel or Nile phonecard (£E15–30), sold at shops and kiosks and usable in booths all over town – though finding one in a quiet location can be a challenge. Alternatively, there are private telephone offices offering faster connections than the state-owned 24-hour office off Sharia el-Karnak, and hotels with a private line that get away with charging £E35 (minimum 3min) for international calls. Off-peak hours are 8pm–8am.

Thomas Cook Outside the *Winter Palace*. Changes currency and sells travellers' cheques. Also does tours and makes reservations (daily 8am–8pm; ℡ 095/372-402, ℻ 376-502).

Excursions from Luxor – and moving on

With Karnak Temple and the Theban Necropolis (see following sections) in the immediate vicinity, it'll be a while before you start considering **excursions** to other sites up and down the Nile Valley. However, the **temples of Esna, Edfu and Kom Ombo** are spaced along the way to Aswan, and bolder tourists may also hanker after **Abydos** and **Dendara**, around Qena. Any of these sites makes a feasible day excursion from Luxor.

Travel restrictions for foreigners are strictly enforced but rather illogical, insofar as some places are readily accessible by one form of transport but not by another, and certain journeys can be made in one direction but not the other way. All tourist coaches, taxis and private cars are obliged to travel in a **convoy** to **Aswan** (leaving Luxor at 7am, 11am and 5pm), which is scheduled to allow stops at Edfu and Kom Ombo (Esna is often omitted), while vehicles heading north towards **Dendara** and **Abydos** are restricted to a single convoy, leaving at 8am. There are also convoys to **Hurghada**, at 8am, 2pm and 6pm. However, almost all these places may also be reached by public buses that run at other times, so you needn't feel bound by convoy schedules. Another oddity is that tourists travelling to Aswan by train are supposedly limited to three services, but no such restriction applies to trains from Aswan to Luxor. And while tourists are forbidden to catch service taxis from Luxor or Aswan, they might possibly be able to pick them up in towns that lie along the way.

Many independent travellers club together to hire a **private taxi** for a day excursion to **Esna** and **Edfu** for about £E100 for a four-seater taxi or £E150 for a larger one, or opt for a longer trip that includes **Kom Ombo** and ends at Aswan (£E180–200 for four people, £E230–250 for seven). You'd find it hard to see all three sites in one day using public transport, and the more leisurely option of reaching them by felucca is really only feasible from Aswan (see box on p.454 for details), as captains dislike sailing between Luxor and Esna, where the Theban Hills block the wind from the north, leaving boats becalmed. Private taxis are also the easiest way to reach **Abydos** and **Dendara** (£E95 for a five-seater, £E155 for seven people), and much cheaper than Nile **cruises** aboard the *Lotus Boat* or *Tiba Star*, bookable through the *Novotel* or travel agencies for £E170 per person, including lunch, tea and entrance fees. When business is slack, the boats may sail only once or twice a week.

Moving on to other points in Egypt may be affected by seasonal factors such as Ramadan, or the level of tourism.

Buses

The inter-city **bus station** is just off Sharia el-Karnak, to the north of Luxor Temple. It's fairly easy to obtain information at the ticket kiosk, but tickets must usually be bought on the bus. There's an **unwritten rule** that no more than four tourists can travel on the same bus unless it goes in a convoy, but it doesn't seem to be strictly enforced – or at least, not on buses heading for the Red Sea. Services to **Aswan** (7.15am, 9.30am, 11.30am, 2.30pm & 8pm; 4hr; £E10) are only nominally a/c and often arrive full from Qena, so you're better off taking the train unless you want to get off along the way. Buses to **El-Balyana** (11am & 1pm; £E7) and **Qena** (6.30am, 8am, 10.30am, 11.30am, 2.30pm, 5pm, 7pm & 8pm; £E3–5) are equally uncomfortable, but run most of the way to Abydos or Dendara. The a/c bus to **Cairo** (7pm; 10–15hr; £E50) is a continuation of one of the services via **Safaga** (£E12–18; 4hr) and **Hurghada** (£E15–21; 5hr) on the Red Sea Coast to **Suez** (£E31–42), leaving at 6.30am, 8.15am, 10.30am, 11.30am, 2.30pm, 5pm and 7pm, while the 8pm bus runs on to **Port Said** (£E53). Avoid buses that travel the narrow desert road to Safaga after dark, as accidents are common. During wintertime, this includes the 5pm bus to **Sharm el-Sheikh** (£E85) and **Dahab** (£E95), which takes hours longer than advertised and stops at roadside cafeterias that charge a fortune.

Trains

For reasons of security, foreigners are only allowed to buy tickets for four trains to **Cairo** (12–14hr). On #981 (departing at 8.15am), #1903 (at 9.15pm) and #997 (at 11.10pm), a/c 1st (£E62-67, student £E40) and 2nd class (£E35–40, student £E27–32) seats are comfortable enough to sleep in, so there's no need to take the *wagon-lit* train #85 at 9.30pm (£E436/£E297 for a bed in a single /double compartment). The overnight services are more popular than the daytime one. A similar restriction applies to trains to **Aswan** (3hr; 1st class £E30–36, student £E18–23; 2nd class £E16–21/£E13–£E1417), but here the #996 (7.15am) and #1902 (9.30am) are preferred to the #980 (5.20pm). Additionally, there's a little-used weekly train to **Kharga Oasis** in the Western Desert (Thurs 7am; 6–10hr; £E10). Tickets should be bought the day before for morning departures, and as early as possible on the day for later services.

Service taxis

Currently, the **service taxi depot** off Sharia el-Karnak is of no use to foreigners, who are forbidden to take service taxis. However in the event that restrictions are lifted, they'll prove a quick and easy way of reaching most sites in Upper Egypt. The twelve-seater minivans wait beneath a sign in English for each destination, departing as soon as they're full. Journey times and per- person prices are: **Esna** (1hr; £E2), **Edfu** (1hr 30min; £E4), **Kom Ombo** (2hr 30min; £E8), **Aswan** (3hr 30min; £E8).

Flights

Flight schedules vary seasonally, so get the latest details from **EgyptAir** (daily 8am–8pm; ☏095/380-580). Destinations include **Cairo** (US$120 one-way), **Aswan** (US$56 one-way) and **Sharm el-Sheikh** (US$120 one-way); return tickets cost double, and student rates are about 25 percent lower. Book as far in advance as you can, or try for last-minute cancellations. There may also be a chance of **stand–by charter flights to Europe**, which can be extremely cheap. Ask at the airport, or approach tour reps at the big hotels.

Luxor Airport (☎095/374–655) is 6km east of town (£E15–20 by taxi).

Karnak

The temple complex of **Karnak** beats every other pharaonic monument but the Pyramids of Giza. Built on a leviathan scale to house the gods, it comprises three separate temple enclosures, the grandest being the **Precinct of Amun**, dedicated to the supreme god of the New Kingdom – a structure large enough to accommodate ten great cathedrals.

Karnak's magnitude and complexity owes to 1300 years of aggrandizement. From its XII Dynasty core, Amun's temple expanded along two axes – towards the river and the **Temple of Mut** – while its enclosure wall approached the **Precinct of Mont**. Though Pharaoh Akhenaten abjured Amun, defaced his images and erected an Aten Temple at Karnak, the status quo ante was soon restored at the behest of Amun's priesthood.

At the zenith of its supremacy Karnak's wealth was staggering. A list of its assets during the reign of Ramses III includes 65 villages, 433 gardens, 421,662 head of cattle, 2395 square kilometres of fields, 46 building sites, 83 ships, and 81,322 workers and slaves. The Egyptologist T.G.H. James likened it to an industrial giant "which generated a mass of business subsidiary to the practice of the cults and a huge army of officials and working people". Yet ordinary folk were barred from its precincts and none but the pharaoh or his representative could enter Amun's sanctuary. The whole area was known to the ancient Egyptians as *Ipet-Isut*, meaning the most perfect or esteemed of places.

Visiting Karnak

The **site** of Karnak covers over 100 acres, 2.5km north of central Luxor. The only part that's readily accessible is the Precinct of Amun (daily: winter 6am–5.30pm; summer 6am–6.30pm; £E20, students £E10; tripod camera £E20), which hosts nightly Sound and Light shows. This alone covers almost 62 acres, requiring at least two hours for a lookover, three or four hours for a closer examination. As there's little shade, it's best to wear a hat and bring water. Usually the temple is busy with tour groups in the morning, but almost deserted from mid-afternoon onwards, so if you can stand the heat, that's the best time to come. A café by the Sacred Lake sells tea and soft drinks, and toilets can be found near the grandstand and the open-air museum. A separate ticket (£E10), sold at the ticket kiosk outside Karnak, is required for the open-air museum.

There are two **approaches** from town: via the Corniche, which turns inland further north, or along Sharia el-Karnak, roughly following the **Avenue of Sphinxes** that once connected Luxor and Karnak temples, past the towering **Gateway of Euergetes II** and the precinct's **enclosure wall**. You could cycle or walk, but it's best to conserve your energy for the site. The cheapest way to get there (and back) is by minibus (25pt per person). The official rates for a one-way taxi (£E10) or *caleche* (£E10) ride provide a benchmark for haggling with drivers; if you rent them for the return journey (£E25 including two hours waiting time), be sure to agree on the deal first, and remember your *caleche* number.

Expect to pay a bit more for rides to the **Sound and Light Show** (£E33, students £25; sold at the Karnak ticket office). The first half consists of a four-stop tour through the temple, ineffably grander when gloomy and spotlit. Although the second half – when you view the ruins from a grandstand beyond the lake – drags on too long, the whole experience is unforgettable. *Caleches* cram in extra passengers for the homeward journey, and race back for a second load. There are three or four shows each night, at least one of them in English. Schedules are posted in the tourist office, and on Ⓦ www.sound-light.egypt.com.

The Temple of Amun

The great **Temple of Amun** seemingly recedes towards infinity in an overwhelming succession of pylons, courts and columned halls, obelisks and colossi.

Amun and the Theban Triad

Originally merely one of the deities in the Hermopolitan Ogdoad (see p.307), **Amun** gained ascendancy at Thebes shortly before the Middle Kingdom, presumably because his cult was adopted by powerful local rulers during the First Intermediate Period. After the expulsion of the Hyksos (c.1567 BC), the rulers of the XVIII Dynasty elevated Amun to a victorious national god, and set about making Karnak his principal cult centre in Egypt.

As the "Unseen One" (whose name in hieroglyphic script was accompanied by a blank space instead of the usual explicatory sign), Amun assimilated other deities into such incarnations as **Amun-Re** (the supreme Creator), **Amun-Min** (the "bull which serves the cows" with a perpetual erection) or ram-headed **Auf-Re** ("Re made Flesh"), who sailed through the underworld revitalizing the souls of the dead, emerging reborn as Khepri. However, Amun most commonly appears as a human wearing ram's horns and the twin-feathered *atef* crown.

His consort, **Mut**, was a local goddess in pre-Dynastic times, who became linked with Nekhbet, the vulture protectress of Upper Egypt. Early in the XVIII Dynasty she was "married" to Amun, assimilated his previous consort Amunet and became Mistress of Heaven. She is customarily depicted wearing a vulture headdress and *uraeus* and the Combined Crown of the Two Lands.

Amun and Mut's son **Khonsu**, "the Traveller", crossed the night sky as the moon-god, issued prophecies and assisted Thoth, the divine scribe. He was portrayed either with a hawk's head, or as a young boy with the sidelock of youth.

Karnak was the largest of several temples consecrated to this **Theban Triad** of deities.

Amun

Mut

Khonsu

Compared by T.G.H. James to "an archeological department store containing something for everyone", it bears the stamp of dozens of rulers, spanning some thirteen centuries of ancient history. Half-buried in silt for as long again, the ruins were subsequently squatted by *fellaheen*, before being cleared by archeologists in the mid-nineteenth century. The Karnak thus exposed was far more ruinous than today, with columns and colossi lying amidst piles of rubble and frogs croaking from the swampy enclosure. Since major repairs in the nineteenth century, the temple has been undergoing slow but systematic restoration.

Making sense of its convoluted layout is not easy, with the ruins themselves getting denser and more jumbled the further in you go. To simplify **orientation**, we've assumed that the temple's alignment towards the Nile corresponds with the cardinal points, so that its main axis runs east–west, and the subsidiary axis north–south.

It's worth following the main axis all the way back to the **Festival Hall**, and at least seeing the **Cachette Court** of the other wing. A break for refreshments by the lake is advisable if your itinerary includes the **open-air museum** or the **Temple of Khonsu**, off the main circuit.

Entering the temple

Walking towards the Precinct of Amun from the ticket office, and crossing over a dry moat, you'll pass the remains of an **ancient dock**, whence Amun sailed for Luxor Temple during the Optet festival. Before boarding a full-size boat, his sacred barque rested in the small **chapel** to the right, which was erected (and graffitied by mercenaries) during the brief XXIX Dynasty. Beyond lies a short **Processional Way** flanked by ram-headed sphinxes (after Amun's sacred animal) enfolding statues of Ramses II, which once joined the main avenue linking the two temples.

Ahead of this rises the gigantic **First Pylon**, whose yawning gateway exposes a vista of receding portals, dwarfing all who walk between them. Composed of regular courses of sandstone masonry, the 43-metre-high towers are often attributed to the Nubian and Ethiopian kings of the XXV Dynasty, but may have been erected as late as the XXX Dynasty (when Nectanebo I added the enclosure wall). Although the northern tower is unfinished and neither is decorated, their 130-metre width makes this the largest pylon in Egypt. High up on the right as you walk through the pylon, Napoleonic surveyors have inscribed Karnak's vital statistics and the distances to other temples in Upper Egypt.

The **Forecourt** is another late addition, enclosing three earlier structures. In the centre stands a single papyriform pillar from the **Kiosk of Taharqa** (an Ethiopian king of the XXV Dynasty), thought to have been a roofless pavilion where Amun's effigy was placed for its revivifying union with the sun at New Year. Off to the left stands the so-called **Shrine of Seti II**, actually a way station for the sacred barques of Amun, Mut and Khonsu, built of grey sandstone and rose granite.

The Temple of Ramses III to the Second Pylon

The first really impressive structure in the precinct is the columned **Temple of Ramses III**, which also held the Theban Triad barques during processions. Beyond its pylon, flanked by two colossi, is a festival hall with mummiform pillar statues, behind which are carvings of the annual festival of Amun-Min. A Hypostyle Hall precedes the darkened barque shrines of the temple, whose dedication reads in part: "I built it, sheathed it with sandstone, bringing great doors of fine gold; and I filled its treasuries with offerings that my hands had brought."

Though the pink granite **Colossus of Ramses II** beside the vestibule to the Second Pylon **[a]** is an immediate attention-grabber, it's worth detouring round the side of his temple to pass through the **Bubastite Portal**, named after the XXII Dynasty that hailed from Bubastis in the Delta. En route you'll pass some holes in the Second Pylon, where in 1820 Henri Crevier uncovered a host of statues and blocks from the demolished Aten Temple (including the colossi of Akhenaten in the Luxor and Cairo museums), which Horemheb used as in-fill for his pylon.

Pass through the Portal and turn left to find the **Shoshenk relief**, commemorating the triumphs of the XXII Dynasty Pharaoh Shoshenk. Traditionally, scholars have identified him as the Biblical Shishak (I Kings 14: 25–26) who plundered Jerusalem in 925 BC, thus establishing a crucial link between the chronologies of ancient Egypt and the Old Testament – an orthodoxy challenged by David Rohl's book, *A Test of Time* (see p.783). Although Shoshenk's figure is almost invisible, you can still see Amun, presiding over the slaughter of Rheoboamite prisoners in Palestine **[b]**. The scenes further along the wall are best seen after visiting the Great Hypostyle Hall.

To reach this, return to the forecourt and pass through the **Second Pylon**, one of several jerry-built structures begun by Horemheb, the last king of the XVIII Dynasty. The cartouches of Seti I (who completed the pylon) and Ramses I and II (Seti's father and son) appear just inside the doorway.

The Great Hypostyle Hall

The **Great Hypostyle Hall** is Karnak's glory, a forest of gigantic columns covering an area of 6000 square metres – large enough to contain both St Peter's Cathedral in Rome and St Paul's Cathedral in London. Its grandeur is best appreciated early in the morning or late in the afternoon, when diagonal shadows enhance the effect of the columns. In pharaonic times the hall was roofed with sandstone slabs, its gloom interspersed by sunbeams falling through windows above the central aisle.

The hall probably began as a processional avenue of twelve or fourteen **columns**, each 23m high and 15m round (requiring six people with outstretched arms to encircle their girth). To this, Seti I and Ramses II added 122 smaller columns in two flanking wings, plus walls and a roof. All the columns consist of semi-drums, fitted together without mortar. The central ones have calyx capitals that once supported a raised section of the roof incorporating clerestory windows (the stone grilles of several remain in place), elevated above the papyrus-bud capitals of the flanking columns. Some of the lintels are still painted, as in ancient times.

Their **carvings** show the king making offerings to Theban deities, most notably Amun, who frequently appears in a sexually aroused state. Some Egyptologists believe that the temple priestesses kept Amun happy by masturbating his idol, and that the pharaoh did his bit to ensure the fertility of Egypt by ejaculating into the Nile during the Optet festival. Similar cult scenes decorate the side and end walls of the hall, which manifest two styles of carving. While Seti adorned the northern wing with bas-reliefs, Ramses II favoured cheaper sunk-reliefs for the southern wing. You can compare the two styles on the Hypostyle Hall's entrance wall, which features nearly symmetrical scenes of Amun's barque procession.

In Seti's **northern wing**, the procession begins on the north wall with a depiction of Amun's barque, initially veiled, then revealed **[c]**. Thoth inscribes

KARNAK: THE PRECINCT OF AMUN

0   Metres   100

N

Chapels of the
Hearing Ear

Festival Hall

p   q

Precinct
of Mont

Temple of
Ptah

Central
Court

m

Sanctuary

6th Pylon
5th Pylon

Hatshepsut's
Obelisk

4th Pylon

Tuthmosid
Obelisks

j

3rd Pylon

f   a

Great
Hypostyle
Hall

e   c

2nd Pylon

a

STATUS, RELIEFS (*) ETC.

Colossus of Ramses II	a
Victory of Shosenq*	b
Amun's Barque*	c
Seti I with Thoth*	d
Seti I's Campaigns*	e
Battle of Qadesh*	f
Ramses II with Thoth & Horus*	g
Ramses II's Campaigns*	h
Ashkelon Wall*	i
Amun's Barque*	j
Wall of Records*	k
Heraldic Pillars	l
Hatshepsut's Wall*	m
Tuthmosis III's Jubilee	n
Table of Kings*	o
Botanical Garden*	p
Sanctuary of Alexander*	q
Chapel of Sokar	r
Tuthmosis III*	s
Epic of Pentaur*	t
Merneptah's Inscription & Israel Stele*	u
Usurped Doorway	v

Toilets

Open Air Museum

Forecast

Shrine of
Seti II

1st Pylon

Processional
Way

Grandstand

Nilometer

Sacred
Lake

Café

Osireion

Giant Scarab

Tip of Fallen
Obelisk

Jubilee Temple
of Amenophis II

Avenue of
Sphinxes

Cachette
Court

u

v

Seated
Colossi

9th Pylon

8th Pylon

7th Pylon

t

i

s

h

b

Bubastite
Portal

Temple of
Ramses III

Gateway of
Euergetes II

Temple of Khonsu

Temple of
Opet

Precinct of Mut

Luxor

Antiquities Office
(Karnak branch)

Ticket Office

the duration of Seti's reign on the leaves of a sacred persea tree **[d]** just beyond the doorway. By walking out through this door you'll come upon **Seti I's battle scenes**, whose weathered details are best observed in the early morning or late afternoon. One section **[e]** relates the capture of Qadesh from the Hittites in Syria (lower rows), and Seti's triumphs over the Libyans (above). Depicted elsewhere **[f]** are his campaigns against the Shasu of southern Palestine and the storming of Pa-Canaan, which the Egyptians "plundered with every evil".

Returning to the Hypostyle Hall, you can find similar reliefs commissioned by Ramses II in the **southern wing**, retaining traces of their original colours. Beyond the barque procession on the inner wall, Ramses is presented to Amun and enthroned between Wadjet and Nekhbet, while Thoth and Horus adjust his crowns **[g]**. On the outer wall are **Ramses II's battle scenes**, starting with the second Battle of Qadesh (c.1300 BC) **[h]**. Though scholars reckon it was probably a draw, Ramses claimed total victory over the Hittites. The text of their **peace treaty** (the earliest such document known) appears on the outer wall of the Cachette Court **[i]**.

This is known as the "**Ashkelon Wall**" after one of the four battle scenes flanking the treaty; another may depict a fight with the Israelites. Rohl argues that the enemy chariots in this scene contradict established chronology, since the Israelites didn't develop them until King Solomon's reign, but Ramses is conventionally supposed to have been the Pharaoh of the Oppression in the time of Moses, centuries earlier. Other clues from the Ashkelon Wall, Shoshenk's reliefs (see above) and the Israel Stele (see p.375) led Rohl to surmise that the Biblical Shishak was not Shoshenk, but Ramses II, and that the established synchronicity between Biblical and Egyptian history is three centuries out, due to an overestimation of the duration of the Third Intermediate Period (dynasties XXI–XXV). See p.783 in the Contexts section for more about Rohl's New Chronology hypothesis.

Pylons and obelisks

Beyond the XIX Dynasty Hypostyle Hall lies an extensive section of the precinct dating from the XVIII Dynasty. The **Third Pylon** that forms its back wall was originally intended by Amenophis III to be a monumental gateway to the temple. Like Horemheb forty years later, he demolished earlier structures to serve as core filler for his pylon. Removed by archeologists, these blocks are now displayed – partly reassembled – in the open-air museum. Two huge reliefs of Amun's barque appear on the far wall of the pylon **[j]**.

The narrow court between the Third and Fourth pylons once boasted four **Tuthmosid obelisks**. The stone bases near the Third Pylon held a pair erected by Tuthmosis III, chunks of which lie scattered around. Of the pink-granite pair erected by Tuthmosis II, one still stands 23m high, with an estimated weight of 143 tons. Once tipped with glittering electrum, the finely carved obelisk was later appropriated by Ramses IV and VI, who added their own cartouches.

At this stage it's best to carry on through the **Fourth Pylon** rather than get sidetracked into the Cachette Court on the temple's secondary axis (see p.375). Beyond the pylon are numerous columns which probably formed another hypostyle hall, dominated by the rose-granite **Obelisk of Hatshepsut**, the only woman to rule as pharaoh. To mark her sixteenth regnal year, Hatshepsut had two obelisks quarried in Aswan and erected at Karnak, a task completed in seven months. The standing obelisk is more than 27m high and weighs 320 tons, with a dedicatory inscription running its full height. Its fallen mate has broken into sections, now dispersed around the temple. After Hatshepsut's death, the long-frustrated Tuthmosis III took revenge, defacing her cartouches wherever they occurred and hiding the lower part of her obelisks behind walls – which inadvertently protected them from further vandalism during the Amarna Period.

The carved **tip** of Hatshepsut's fallen obelisk can be examined near the Osireion and Sacred Lake. On the way there, you'll pass a granite bas-relief of Amenophis II target-shooting from a moving chariot, protruding from the **Fifth Pylon**. Built of limestone, this pylon is attributed to Hatshepsut's father, Tuthmosis I. Beyond it lies a colonnaded courtyard with Osiride statues, built by one of the Tuthmosid pharaohs and possibly part of a large inner court surrounding the original Middle Kingdom temple of Amun.

Though the **Sixth Pylon** has largely disappeared, a portion either side of the granite doorway remains. Its outer face is known as the *Wall of Records* **[k]** after its list of peoples conquered by Tuthmosis III: Nubians to the right, Asiatics to the left. Beyond the latter is a text extolling the king's victory at Megiddo (Armageddon) in 1479 BC. By organizing tribute from his vanquished foes rather than simply destroying them, Tuthmosis III was arguably the world's first imperialist.

Around the Sanctuary

The section beyond the Sixth Pylon gets increasingly confusing, but a few features are unmistakable. Ahead stand a pair of square-sectioned **heraldic pillars**, their fronts carved with the lotus and papyrus of the Two Lands, their sides showing Amun embracing Tuthmosis III **[l]**. On the left are two **Colossi of Amun and Amunet**, dedicated by Tutankhamun (whose likeness appears with them) when orthodoxy was re-established after the Amarna Period. There's also a seated **statue of Amenophis II**.

Next comes a granite **Sanctuary** built by Philip Arrhidaeus, the cretinous half-brother of Alexander the Great, on the site of a Tuthmosid-era shrine which similarly held Amun's barque (whose pedestal is still *in situ*). The interior bas-reliefs show Philip making offerings to Amun in his various aspects, topped by a star-spangled ceiling. On the outside walls are sunk-reliefs depicting his coronation, Thoth's declaration of welcome, and Amunet suckling the young pharaoh, some still brightly coloured.

Around to the left of the Sanctuary and further back is a wall inscribed with Tuthmosis III's victories, which he built to hide a wall of reliefs by Queen Hatshepsut, now removed to another room **[m]**. **Hatshepsut's Wall** has reopened after lengthy restoration, as has the facing portion, where Tuthmosis replaced her image by offerings tables or bouquets, and substituted his father's and grandfather's names for her cartouches.

Beyond here lies an open space or **Central Court**, thought to mark the site of the original temple of Amun built in the XII Dynasty, whose weathered alabaster foundations poke from the pebbly ground.

The Jubilee Temple of Tuthmosis III

At the rear of this court rises the **Jubilee Temple of Tuthmosis III**, a personal cult shrine in Amun's back yard. As at Saqqara during the Old Kingdom, the Theban kings periodically renewed their temporal and spiritual authority with jubilee festivals. The original entrance **[n]** is flanked by reliefs and broken statues of Tuthmosis in *hed-seb* regalia. A left turn brings you into the **Festival Hall**, with its unusual tentpole-style columns, their capitals adorned with blue-and-white chevrons. The lintels – carved with falcons, owls, *ankhs* and other symbols – are likewise brightly coloured. During Christian times the hall was used as a church, hence the haloed saints on some of the pillars.

A chamber off the southwest corner **[o]** contains an eroded replica of the *Table of Kings* (the original is in the Louvre), depicting Tuthmosis making offerings to previous rulers – Hatshepsut is naturally omitted from the roll call. Behind the hall are further chambers, mostly ruinous. The so-called **Botanical Garden** is a roofless enclosure containing painted reliefs of plants and animals which Tuthmosis encountered on his campaigns in Syria **[p]**. Across the way is a roofed chamber decorated by Alexander the Great, who appears before Amun and other deities **[q]**. The **Chapel of Sokar** constitutes a miniature temple to the Memphite god of darkness **[r]**, juxtaposed against a (now inaccessible) shrine to the sun. A further suite of rooms is dedicated to Tuthmosis **[s]**.

Chapels of the Hearing Ear

Excluded from Amun's Precinct and lacking a direct line to the Theban Triad, the inhabitants of Thebes used intermediary deities to transmit their petitions. These lesser deities rated their own shrines, known as **Chapels of the Hearing Ear** (sometimes actually decorated with carved ears), which straddled the temple's enclosure wall, presenting one face to the outside world. At Karnak, however, they became steadily less approachable and were finally surrounded by the present enclosure wall.

Directly behind the Jubilee Temple is a series of chapels built by Tuthmosis III, centred upon a large alabaster statue of the king and Amun. On either side are the bases of another pair of obelisks erected by Hatshepsut, of which nothing else remains. Still further east lie the ruined halls and colonnades of a Temple of the Hearing Ear built by Ramses II. Behind this stands the pedestal of the tallest obelisk known (31m), which Emperor Constantine had shipped to Rome and erected in the Circus Maximus; it was later moved to Lateran Square, hence its name, the **Lateran Obelisk**. As the ancient Egyptians rarely erected single obelisks, it was probably intended to be accompanied by the Unfinished Obelisk that lies in a quarry outside Aswan, abandoned after the discovery of flaws in the rock.

Sekhmet

Sekhmet

Sekhmet – "the Powerful" – was the violent counterpart of the Delta goddess Bastet (see p.644). As the daughter of Re, she personified the sun's destructive force, making her a worthy consort for Ptah, the Memphite creator-god. In one myth, Re feared that humanity was plotting against him and unleashed his avenging Eye in the form of Sekhmet, who would have massacred all life had not Re relented and slaked her thirst with red beer, which the drunken goddess mistook for blood.

With the rise of Thebes and Amun's association with Ptah, a corresponding relationship was made between their consorts, Mut and Sekhmet. The New Kingdom pharaohs adopted Sekhmet as a symbol of their indomitable prowess in battle: the statues of the goddess at Karnak bear inscriptions such as "smiter of the Nubians". As "Lady of the Messengers of Death", Sekhmet could send – or prevent – plagues, so her priestesses also served as healers and veterinarians.

Around the Sacred Lake

A short walk from Hatshepsut's Obelisk or the Cachette Court brings you to Karnak's **Sacred Lake**, which looks about as holy as a municipal boating pond, with the grandstand for the Sound and Light Show at the far end. The main attraction is a shady (and pricey) **café** where you can take a break from touring the complex and imagine the scene in ancient times. At sunrise, Amun's priests would take a sacred goose from the fowl-yards which now lie beneath the mound to the south of the lake, and set it free on the waters. As at Hermopolis, the goose or Great Cackler was credited with laying a cosmic egg at the dawn of Creation; but at Karnak the Great Cackler was identified with Amun rather than Thoth. During the Late Period, Pharaoh Taharqa added a subterranean **Osireion**, linking the resurrection of Osiris with that of the sun. The **giant scarab beetle** nearby represents Khepri, the reborn sun at dawn.

The north–south axis

The temple's **north–south axis** is sparser and less variegated than the main section, so if time is limited there's little reason to go beyond the Eighth Pylon. The Gate of Ramses IX, at the southern end of the court between the Third and Fourth pylons, gives access to this wing of the temple, which starts with the Cachette Court.

The **Cachette Court** gets its title from the discovery of a buried hoard of statues early in the twentieth century. Nearly 17,000 bronze statues and votive tablets, and 800 figures in stone, seem to have been cached in a "clearance" of sacred knick-knacks during Ptolemaic times. The finest statues (dating from the Old Kingdom to the Late Period) are now in the Cairo Museum. The court's northwest corner incorporates a mass of hieroglyphics known as the *Epic of Pentaur* **[t]**, which recaps the battles of Ramses II depicted on the outside of the Great Hypostyle Hall. Diagonally across the court are an eighty-line inscription by Merneptah and a copy of the **Israel Stele [u]** that's in Cairo, which contains among a list of conquests the only known pharaonic reference to Israel: "Israel is crushed, it has no more seed". Rohl argues that the stele has been misread, and really relates the achievements of Merneptah's father and grandfather, Ramses II and Seti I.

More proof of the complexities of Egyptology is provided by the **Seventh Pylon**, which was built by Tuthmosis III, but decorated – and usurped – during the XIX Dynasty, a century or so later, when the cartouches on its door jambs **[v]** were altered to proclaim false ownership. It is fronted by seven statues of Middle Kingdom pharaohs, salvaged from pylon cores. On the far side are the lower portions of two **Colossi of Tuthmosis III**.

Although repair work has closed the **Eighth Pylon**, you might be able to walk around the edge for a distant view of its **four seated colossi**, or pay some *baksheesh* to be sneaked in for a closer look. The most complete figure is that of Amenophis I. Beyond a featureless court rises the **Ninth Pylon**, one of three erected by Horemheb and stuffed with masonry from the demolished Aten Temple, which is currently being rebuilt. Flanking the east wall of the final court is the ruinous **Jubilee Temple of Amenophis II**, which fulfilled a similar function to Tuthmosis III's temple in the main wing. The mud-brick houses of Karnak village are visible beyond the **Tenth Pylon**, from where an **Avenue of Sphinxes** once led to the Precinct of Mut.

The temples of Khonsu and Opet

Located in the southwest corner of Amun's Precinct are two smaller temples related to his cult. The **Temple of Khonsu** is dedicated to the son of Amun and Mut. Mostly built by Ramses III and IV, with additions by later kings, it is well preserved but crudely carved and dark inside. Many of the reliefs depict Herihor, first of Thebes' priest kings, who ruled Upper Egypt after the Ramessid pharaohs moved their capital to the Delta. This shift in power is also evident on the pylons, which show Pinundjem, another high priest, worshipping the gods as a king.

Alongside stands a smaller **Temple of Opet**, the hippopotamus-goddess traditionally believed to be the mother of Osiris. Its reliefs – dating from Ptolemaic and Roman times – are finer than Khonsu's, but it may not be possible to enter. The towering **Gateway of Euergetes I**, with its winged sun-disc cornice, was raised in Ptolemaic times and is now barred shut.

The open-air museum

The northern sector of Amun's Precinct contains an **open-air museum**, for which a separate ticket (£E10) must be bought before entering Karnak. Its prime attractions are two early barque shrines, reassembled from blocks found inside the Third Pylon. From the XII Dynasty comes a lovely **White Chapel**, carved all over with bas-reliefs. While most depict *Djed* columns, *ankhs* and other symbols, it's the scenes of Senusert I embracing a priapic Amun-Min that one remembers. The plainer **Alabaster Chapel** of Amenophis I contains more innocuous scenes of the pharaoh making offerings to Amun and his barque. Along the way you'll pass rows of blocks from Hatshepsut's **Red Chapel**, which archeologists have been unable to reconstruct since each block features a self-contained design rather than a segment of a large relief. This hasn't deterred Egyptologists from trying the same feat with the **Shrine of Tuthmosis III**, with more success. You'll also notice granite **statues of Sekhmet**, taken from a small **Temple of Ptah** alongside Karnak's enclosure wall, whose ruins aren't much reward for a 300-metre trek across broken ground.

Other temples at Karnak

Beyond the Precinct of Amun is a host of other ruins, intermingled with canals and villages. None of them is readily accessible or officially open to tourists, and sites under excavation are supposedly off-limits without permission from the **Antiquities Office** in Luxor (behind the museum) or Karnak (outside the precinct), whose Head and Deputy flit between offices, making it hard to catch them.

The Precinct of Mont

Dedicated to the falcon-headed Theban war-god of the Old Kingdom, who continued to be venerated after Amun gained primacy, the overgrown and ruinous **Precinct of Mont** is unusual for being oriented northwards rather than towards the river. Its main **Temple of Mont** (or Montu) dates from the XVIII–XIX Dynasty, while the **Temple of Amun** was added in the XXX Dynasty. Both are currently being excavated by the French Institute of Archeology in Cairo.

Also worth noting are the **chapels of Amenirdis**, daughter of the Nubian king Kashta (honoured by another chapel at Medinet Habu in the Theban Necropolis), and **Nitocris**, daughter of Psammetichus I, who is said to have avenged her brother's murder by constructing a sunken festival hall near the Nile, inviting the suspects to party, then opening hidden sluices and drowning them all – the basis of a short story by Henry James.

The Aten Temple

Likewise undergoing excavation, the **Aten Temple** 100m east of Amun's Precinct was demolished by Horemheb during the Theban counter-revolution that followed the brief Amarna Period. The temple was constructed early in Akhenaten's reign, before he quit Thebes for Tell el-Amarna, and, like the Aten shrine at Luxor Temple, constituted his opening move towards a revolutionary monotheism. Its reconstruction from the thousands of blocks scattered around the site or used as pylon-filling is based on a computer program devised by a retired US diplomat in 1965. The Canadian Egyptologist John Redford, who spent more than a decade excavating here, reckons that Akhenaten was an indolent paranoiac with an Oedipal complex, who compelled his acolytes to worship beneath the burning sun, rather than in shadowy temples.

The Precinct of Mut

As Amun's consort, the goddess Mut rated her own temple complex, linked to her husband's by an Avenue of Sphinxes. The **Precinct of Mut** covers roughly twice the area of Mont's enclosure, and centres around a kidney-shaped **lake**. Locals informed Flaubert that Karnak's priests submerged all the gold and silver ornaments here when the Persian emperor Cambyses sacked Thebes, but so far the site has merely yielded masonry. Near the enclosure entrance lies a headless granite colossus, which has been matched with a serene head and mighty forearm held by the British Museum (attributed to Amenophis III, Tuthmosis II or Ramses II). It was Amenophis III who commissioned the scores of grey diorite **statues of Sekhmet** that rise from the long grass, lie broken underfoot, or repose in museums. More than seven hundred exist, and there is a theory that they formed a calendar where each day was represented by two statues that received offerings every morning and evening.

The Theban Necropolis

Across the Nile from Luxor, the **Theban Necropolis** testifies to the same obsession with death and resurrection that produced the pyramids. Mindful of how these had failed to protect the mummies of the Old Kingdom pharaohs, later rulers opted for concealment, sinking their tombs in the arid Theban Hills while perpetuating their memory with gigantic mortuary temples on the plain below. The Necropolis straddled the border between the lands of the living and the dead: verdant flood plain giving way to boundless desert, echoing the path of the dead "going west" to meet Osiris as the sun set over the mountains and descended into the underworld.

Though stripped of its treasures over millennia, the Necropolis retains a peerless array of funerary monuments. The grandest of its tombs are in the **Valley of the Kings** and the **Valley of the Queens**, but there's also a wealth of vivid detail in the smaller **Tombs of the Nobles**. Equally amazing are the mortuary temples which enshrined the deceased pharaoh's cult: among these, **Deir el-Bahri** is timelessly magnificent and **Medinet Habu** rivals Karnak for grandeur, while the shattered **Ramesseum** and **Colossi of Memnon** mock the pretensions of their founders. On a humbler level, but still executed with great artistry, are the funerary monuments of the craftsmen who built the royal tombs, and the ruins of their homes at **Deir el-Medina**.

Beside its monuments, the west bank is interesting by way of contrast with Luxor: more rural than urban, and making fewer concessions to foreigners.

▲ *Valley of the Kings*

Western
Valley

Donkey Path

Valley of the
Kings

Deir
el-Bahri

Asasif
Tombs

Dra'Abul
Naga

ⓐ

❷   ❶

Tombs of
the Nobles   ⓑ

Deir el-Medina
(workers' village)

Gurna   ⓓ   ⓒ
ⓔ   ⓕ   Gurna Discovery
ⓖ
ⓗ   ⓙ

Donkey Path

German
House

❹

ⓘ
ⓚ
ⓛ
ⓜ

Ramesseum

Valley of the
Queens

Gurnat
Mura'i

Medinet
Habu

❺
❻   Temple of
Merneptah
❼

Sandy Path

❽   Tourist Police
❾   Ticket Office

Colossi of
Memnon

New
Gurna

Palace of
Culture

Monastery of
St Tawdros

ⓣ

❿   ⓫

Amun Temple   ⓬

Nefertari
Papyrus
Institute

Checkpoint

French House

Nag Lohlah

El-Kom

El-Tod

Malqata

Sugarcane Railway

Ezba

El-Fadiya Canal

▲ *Desert*

Lakalta
Foq

Sandy Path

TOMBS OF THE QUEENS
AND THE NOBLES

Amunhirkhepshef	k
Khaemhat	j
Khaemweset	m
Khoka Tombs	a
Khonsu, Userhet & Benia	c
Menna	b
Nakht	d
Nefertari	i
Ramose	g
Rekhmire	f
Sennofer	e
Titi	l
Userhat	h

Esna, Haggar Daba'iyya & ⓳ *(5 km)* ▼   ▼ *Armant*

LUXOR, KARNAK & THE THEBAN NECROPOLIS

ACCOMMODATION

Abou el-Kassem	3
Al-Moudira	19
Amenophes	12
Amoun el-Gazira	15
Gezira	16
Gezira Gardens	17
Habou	10
Marsam	6
Nile Valley	14
Nour el-Qurna	7
Osiris	1
Pharaoh's	9

EATING & DRINKING

Africa Restaurant	13
Donia Café	5
Hatshepsut Restaurant/No Galag	2
Maratonga Café	11
Mohammed Cafeteria	8
Ramesseum Resthouse	4
Tout Ankhamon Restaurant	18

Sun Temple

Qena

Stoppelaer House

Gurna Ta'rif

Carter's House

Checkpoint

Temple of Seti I

Clinic

El-Jebanah

Nile Hilton

El-Fadiya Canal

Sugarcane Railway

El-Fadiya Canal

River Nile

Temple of Mont

SHARIA EL-KARNAK

Temple of Amun

KARNAK

Temple of Mut

Arabian Horse Stable

Gezira

Pharaoh's Stables

Taxi Depot

Youth Hostel

SHARIA EL-KARNAK

Service Taxi Station

Cruise Boats

Luxor Museum

Motorboats

Local Ferry

LUXOR

Bus Station

Luxor Temple

Winter Palace Hotel

Train Station

Novotel

N

Qena

Airport

0   Kilometres   1

Luxor Bridge (7 km)

Livestock Market (4 km)

Many of the Egyptians that you'll meet in Luxor actually come from villages on the west bank, and a lot of the money made in Luxor is invested there. The symbiosis between the two communities is underscored by the fact that, when speaking English, locals invariably refer to the west bank as "**the other side**" (in Arabic, *min Gharb*) – yet people living there also jokingly liken it to "Palestine", living under the rule of "Israel", due to a land dispute between the villagers and Luxor City Council.

Visiting the Necropolis

Spread across wadis and hills beyond the edge of the cultivated plain, the Theban Necropolis is too diffuse and complex to take in on a single visit. Even limiting yourself to the Valley of the Kings, Deir el-Bahri and one or other of the major sites, you're likely to feel all tombed out by the end of the day. Most people favour a series of visits, taking into account the climate and crowds – both major factors in the enjoyment of a trip. In **winter**, mornings are pleasantly hot, afternoons baking but bearable, and most coach tours are scheduled accordingly, making the Valley of the Kings crowded between 9am and 2pm (other sites are less overrun). As lots of people come early "to beat the crowds", the royal tombs are actually emptiest in the late afternoon. In **summer**, it's simply too hot throughout the afternoon, and you should get here as early as possible.

The **opening hours** of the sites are liable to change with the season and security restrictions, but are currently from 7am to 5pm daily, though some of the lesser tombs may close two or three hours earlier over summer, and Nefertari's tomb keeps separate hours (see p.416). Making a full tour of the Necropolis is expensive – although a **student card** entitles you to a 50-percent discount. If you wanted to see all the sites in the necropolis, you'd end up spending around US$65 just on tickets (at the full rate) – but most people are satisfied to see far less than that.

Hotels and hustlers in Luxor strive to sell **tours** which come in all shapes and sizes (see p.382). Even if you like the idea, don't sign up for the first one offered – at least, not without an idea of what's available elsewhere, and the scope for **independent travel**. Virtually all tours include a visit to a papyrus or alabaster "factory" where your guide stands to earn a commission on **sales**; some agencies own the shops where they send their clients (for example, Seti I Travel and Sobek Papyrus). There's no point in getting indignant about this unless you spend more time there than at the sites, but bear in mind that the asking price will initially be determined by the company you're keeping, since a busload of middle-aged tourists is patently wealthier than a few backpackers on donkeys.

Useful **things to bring** include a torch, plenty of water and small change. If you're planning to cycle or donkey it, a hat and double rations of water are vital. A snack, too, is a good idea, as the choice of food and drink is limited, and prices are higher than in Luxor.

Crossing the Nile

There are several ways of crossing over **from Luxor** to the west bank. A shabby **local ferry** sails frequently during daytime and sporadically after midnight from the landing stage on the Corniche signposted "National Ferryboat". It then docks near **Gezira village** on the west bank. Locals pay 10pt for the ride, tourists £E1. Crowded with villagers, bicycles and baggage, the ferry psyches you up for the day ahead. Alternatively, dozens of **motorboats** and **feluccas** inveigle for custom by the water's edge, charging £E1 per person (£E5 minimum per boatload) after a brief haggle. Motorboats (called "lunches" in English or *zobak* in Arabic) are the fastest way to cross the river and may land or leave from anywhere along either riverbank, whereas crossing the Nile by felucca is more of a leisurely experience than a quick journey.

You should be able to take **bicycles** for free on all these vessels, but **motorbikes** can only be carried aboard the local ferry. Keep **safety** in mind: overcrowded boats or waterways at night are a recipe for disaster, as was proved during the festival of Abu el-Haggag in 2001, when some 35 passengers drowned after a ferry hit their motorboat in the dark. During winter, when the Nile is at its lowest, ferries sometimes get stranded on sandbanks for hours, and irate passengers have been known to rip up the seats in a Nilotic version of road rage. Stepping across rickety wharfs after dark is a more mundane but regular hazard.

Since the opening of **Luxor Bridge**, 7km south of town at Bogdadi, all coaches, minibuses and taxis from Luxor use this circuitous route, which can take an hour if traffic is heavy. Some operators get round this by sending the vehicle on ahead, to meet passengers taken across the Nile by motorboat – and crossing by boat remains by far the most pleasant option.

Getting around

Once across the Nile, how you choose to get around will depend on the time of year and what you plan to see, your budget and your sense of adventure. If you intend to visit the Necropolis more than once, try using various modes of transport. As most entail negotiating a price, it helps to know the ins and outs beforehand. Unless stated otherwise, none of the prices given below include the cost of admission tickets, which have to be bought at the west bank ticket office.

• One option that's often overlooked is exploring parts of the Necropolis **on foot**, having got there by public transport. From the taxi depot above the ferry landing stage in Gezira, covered **pick-ups** shuttle passengers to Old Gurna (known to drivers as *Gurna Foq*), bringing you within fifteen minutes' walk of Medinet Habu, the Valley of the Queens or the Ramesseum, for a mere 25pt. Some run on to Dra' Abu Naga, leaving you closer to the Tombs of the Nobles or Deir el-Bahri. The drawback with this strategy is that the Valley of the Kings remains out of reach unless you're up to hiking over the hills and back again. In summertime, it's only feasible to cover shorter distances, and then only in the morning.

• Assuming that you're reasonably fit, the cheapest way – after walking – to cover the Necropolis is by **cycling**. During winter, you'll feel cool when riding but start sweating once you stop. Guard against heatstroke and keep swigging water. A day's touring might involve cycling 30km: for example, 3km from the river bank to the ticket kiosk, 8km from there to the Valley of the Kings (mostly uphill – beware of traffic), and 3km from Deir el-Bahri to Medinet Habu. The main drawback is that you can't walk over the hills from the Valley of the Kings to Deir el-Bahri. Cycling during summer is a lot more demanding, so it's imperative to take the long uphill stretch to the Valley of the Kings early in the morning, allowing you to coast back downhill in the afternoon heat. Roads vary from smooth tarmac to stony *pistes*. Bicycles (*ajila*) can be rented in shops and hotels in Luxor (see p.349) for £E5–10 a day, or from two places in Gezira (£E10) which send boys down to the waterfront. Test your bike before hiring; many have no gears, which makes any uphill stretch against a headwind murder.

Alternatively, you could drive a **motorbike**. Several bike shops in Luxor rent them by the day; after much haggling, you can probably get one for £E50. Be especially careful of children and livestock when riding on the west bank.

There are workshops for bicycle **repairs** on the road between the ticket office and Medinet Habu, and in the village of El-Jebanah.

• Getting around by **private taxi** is economical for groups, and the least tiring way of visiting a lot of sites, besides enabling you to set your own itinerary. Taxis are usually hired for four to six hours; expect to pay anywhere between £E50 and £E100, depending on your haggling skills and the current state of tourism. It's best to hire a taxi at Gezira on the west bank, where the competition is fiercest; arranging a taxi through a hotel in Luxor will almost certainly mean paying more. For one-off journeys, you can also use pick-ups (see above) as private taxis; if the vehicle is empty or it's after 10pm they'll take you to almost any village on the west bank for £E5 (group rate).

• Many visitors prefer organized, **guided tours**, bookable through any hotel or travel agency in Luxor. Some will tag you onto existing groups, travelling in a/c buses; others lay on a minibus or taxi. Most low-budget hotels offer a **minibus** trip featuring the Colossi of Memnon, the valleys of the Kings and Queens and Deir el-Bahri. Prices and the standard of guiding vary, but *Happy Land Hotel*'s tour is as cheap as any (£E67; student £E45; admission tickets included). A veteran guide with a good knowledge of Egyptology is Abu El Naga Gabrail, whose group rate is between US$90–200 (£E400–1000) depending on the size of the group, which hotel the trip is booked from, or whether you negotiate with him directly (☎ & ☎ 095/374-594 or mobile 0123 772074, ✉ abuelnaga@yahoo.com). Coach tours from agencies like Misr Travel (☎ 095/373-551) cost from US$40 per person, but may reach sites, such as Medinet Habu or the Ramesseum, that minibus tours don't cover. Large tour groups get priority access to the royal tombs and a higher standard of commentary than is offered by unofficial guides, but lack atmosphere and spontaneity.

• If you want spontaneity, travelling by **donkey** offers the thrill of riding up the Theban Hills as mist cloaks the plain, skirting precipices and abandoned tombs before you descend into the Valley of the Kings, and returning via Deir el-Bahri and the Tombs of the Nobles – with fantastic views denied to other travellers. But it's a physically gruelling five-hour trip that's not for anyone with vertigo, nor children. Light relief is provided by the donkeys, who disobey commands of *Hoosh!* (stop) or *Hatla!* (faster) whenever they encounter another beast on heat, or anything edible. As "mountain" donkeys know the trail, mishaps are more comical than serious. Although few hotels offer donkey trips nowadays besides the *Venus* (£E35 per head, excluding tickets), they're popular with adventure holiday companies like Explore, which rent their donkeys from the Khalifa family in Gezira; contact Tayeb Khalifa if you're interested (☎ 095/310-747 or mobile 0123 592468, ✉ kingofluxor66@hotmail.com). A more laid-back donkey option is a **village tour** of Beirat, using farm trails and backroads, which can be lovely if it's not too hot.

And though a **horse** or **camel** aren't any use for exploring the Necropolis, they're great fun to ride in the desert beyond Medinet Habu. Either can be hired for £E20 an hour from Pharaoh's Stables (☎ 095/310-015 or mobile 0123 437116) or the Arabian Horse Stable (mobile ☎ 0105 048558) in Gezira. Both places are well run, with experienced guides and helmets available. Bakri and Nasser at Pharaoh's train the dancing horses that appear at local moulids, while Nobi at Arabian Stables will collect clients from Luxor on his motorboat, *Titanic*.

• A **hot–air balloon flight** gives a majestic view of the whole Necropolis. This amazing experience is worth a splurge if you can afford it, and the three companies involved have recently cut their prices. See p.363 for details.

Buying tickets for the Necropolis

It's best to decide which sites in the Necropolis you wish to visit beforehand, since you really only get one chance to buy **tickets**. You can't buy tickets at the individual sites, nor gain admission without them (though at the Tombs of the Nobles it may be possible to bribe your way in). The only exception is the ticket for Tutankhamun's tomb, which you may also buy from a kiosk at the Valley of the Kings itself. For all other sites, the main **ticket office** lies shortly beyond the Colossi of Memnon, and features separate hatches for students (who pay half the full-rate prices given below) and non-students. Should you decide at the last minute that you want to view more tombs than you have tickets for, it may be possible to have a guard go back to the main office to get tickets for you – for *baksheesh* of course.

Of the various **tomb tickets** available, most people start with a "Valley of the Kings" ticket, which is valid for three tombs in the Valley of the Kings, excluding Tut's. This is generally enough for most people. It's certainly unlikely that you'll use more than six or seven tickets in a day's outing. Tickets are only valid for the day of purchase (with no refunds for unused ones).

Tickets are numbered and **priced** as follows.

#1	Valley of the Kings (three tombs)	£E20
#2	Tomb of Tutankhamun	£E40
#3	Ay (Western Valley)	£E10
#4	Deir el-Bahri (Hatshepsut's temple)	£E12
#5	Medinet Habu (Temple of Ramses III)	£E12
#6	Ramesseum	£E12
#7	Asasif Tombs (Kheru-ef, Ankh-hor)	£E12
#8	Tombs of Nakht and Menna	£E12
#9	Tombs of Rekhmire and Sennofer	£E12
#10	Tombs of Ramose, Userhat and Khaemhat	£E12
#11	Deir el-Medina (two tombs)	£E12
#12	Tomb of Peshedu (Deir el-Medina)	£E10
#13	Valley of the Queens	£E12
#14	Temple of Seti I	£E12
#15	Tomb of Pabhasa	£E12
#16	Tombs of Khonsu, Userhet and Benia	£E12
#17	Khokha Tombs	£E12
#18	Tomb of Nefertari	£E100

Tickets for the Temple of Merneptah (see p.414) are also sold here, but not numbered or listed yet. Ask if you want one.

Dusk and early morning are the **best times** to capture the landscape and temples of the west bank. To photograph inside any of the tombs you'll require a **photo permit** for each tomb (£E10 per tomb; student £E5), sold at both ticket kiosks. There's a £E50 surcharge for using a tripod. Flashes are forbidden as they harm the paintings, so sensitive film is required. Illegal flash-photography may result in the film being confiscated. Video cameras are not allowed into the Valley of the Kings, but can be stashed at the entrance. Like tickets, photo permits are non-refundable and valid only on the day of issue. There are no student discounts.

Some suggested itineraries

If you're forced to cram the highlights into half a day, a **minimalist schedule** might run: **Valley of the Kings** (1hr 30min), **Deir el-Bahri** (20min), the **Tombs of the Nobles** (30min–1hr), **Medinet Habu** (30min), and/or the **Ramesseum** (30min).

If you're limited to a couple of days, two **itineraries** make sense:

Day one: catch a taxi to the **Valley of the Kings** before 9am, spend a couple of hours there and then walk over the hills to **Deir el-Bahri**, arranging to be met there for another ride to **Medinet Habu** or **Deir el-Medina** and the **Valley of the Queens**. Alternatively, you could spend time at the **Tombs of the Nobles** and the **Ramesseum** before returning to the landing stage.

Day two: this is basically devoted to whatever you missed the first time around.

For those who like to linger over every carving, the tombs and temples on the west bank could easily fill three or four days.

The west bank villages

The **west bank villages** are incidental to most tourists visiting the Theban Necropolis, but integral to the landscape and atmosphere. Their fields stretch from the river banks to the temples on the desert's edge; their goats root amidst the Tombs of the Nobles. Though land remains paramount, almost every family is involved in tourism, either renting out donkeys or making souvenirs on the west bank, commuting to hotel jobs in Luxor, or sailing motorboats or feluccas on the Nile. Family and village ties bind them together and help them exploit the stream of rich visitors that flows across their land. Crafty, warm-hearted and proud, they are worth getting to know. Richard Critchfield's *Shahhat* (sold in most Luxor bookshops) gives a fascinating glimpse into their lives a generation ago.

Your first encounter will be with **GEZIRA**, where ferries disgorge villagers returning from Luxor, and tourists arrive in motorboats. The depot for private and service **taxis** to villages on the west bank is up the slope; floodlit at night, it proclaims the urbanization of Gezira. In recent years, the government has laid claim to land beside the Nile, where villagers have built houses and hotels, which only escaped demolition after the matriarch of the Khalifa family lay down in front of the bulldozers. Traditionally, Gezira's role in tourism has been to ferry tourists about or guide them on donkeys through the Necropolis, but it now also has restaurants, Internet cafés and a dry-cleaners, besides **bike shops** and **stables**. The village straggles to the El-Fadiya Canal, where **EL-TOD** begins. Its inhabitants call the canal "the Nile", and those residing on one side of it regard themselves as superior to folks on the other, although they live similar lives and intermarriage is common. A police **checkpoint** ensures that no traffic goes up the road to the Necropolis before 6am.

Across the main road lies **NEW GURNA** (*Gurnat el-Jedid*), built in the 1940s with government funds to wean villagers away from old Gurna in the hills. Designed by Hassan Fathy, a leading advocate of creating architecture suited to local conditions, the settlement contains two superbly proportioned public buildings – the **mosque** and **Palace of Culture** – made of Fathy's favourite material, mud-brick. However, the village failed to attract many Gurnawis, and others moved in instead, to find that Fathy's houses were too small for their extended families, obliging them to add breeze-block extensions.

Beyond the Colossi of Memnon, the barren, windswept foothills are pockmarked with the Tombs of the Nobles and the ramshackle dwellings of old **GURNA** (often spelt "Qurna", but pronounced with a "G"). Besides a sentimental attachment to their ancestral homes (many of them painted with splendid *Hadj* scenes), the villagers are loath to lose a traditional source of income – **tomb-robbing**. Over nine hundred tombs are dug into the hills, and undisclosed finds are still made. Once again, the government wants the Gurnawis out, and is pressuring people to move into a new settlement in a flood-prone wadi. In 1998 they sent in bulldozers backed by police; the ensuing violence left four dead and more than twenty injured. Wary of more bad publicity, they now insist that people demolish their old houses in Gurna before being given the title deeds for their new homes. Several tombs have been damaged due to the haphazard use of bulldozers. The village's history is related in the local Gurna Discovery exhibition (see p.407).

Skirting Gurna, the road runs on to **DRA' ABUL NAGA**, whose blue-and-yellow houses contrast with the arid moonscape all around, which glitters with light reflected off mica and alabaster dust. The village manufactures the statues and ashtrays sold in tourist shops throughout Egypt. Its **alabaster workshops** vie for attention with garish murals and craftsmen shaping vases and bowls with hand-grinders outside each showroom.

At Dra' Abul Naga, a spur road turns off towards Hatshepsut's temple, while the main one carries on to a crossroads beside a cemetery, where the road to the Valley of the Kings begins. The mud-brick complex on the hilltop was **Howard Carter's house** during his search for Tutankhamun's tomb. There's talk of turning it into a museum, but nothing has happened yet. In the vicinity is another archeological residence called the **Stoppelaer House**, designed by Hassan Fathy. Japanese, French and German Egyptologists also have residences on the west bank.

The wasteland at the crossroads is the site for the annual **Moulid of Abu Qusman** on the 27th of *Sha'ban*. It commemorates a local holy man known for his miracles and outspokenness, who died in 1984. On one occasion Abu Qusman supposedly crossed the Nile on his handkerchief after the ferry refused to take him because he lambasted the tourists on board for immorality. His moulid used to last all night, but nowadays the police wind it up at midnight.

West Bank practicalities

Gezira's high street has two **Internet** dens (the Internet Business Centre is the cheaper at £E8/hr; daily 8.30am–midnight) and a **dry-cleaners** (£E3 per item). If you need medical treatment, go to Luxor; the **clinic** in El-Jebanah is awful. Although there are no currency exchanges on the west bank, most hotels will change **money** unofficially.

Generally, the **police** leave tourists alone, but the checkpoint at the El-Fadiya Canal won't allow traffic to pass up the road to the Necropolis before 6am – which spoils things for donkey-groups hoping to catch the sunrise, unless they sneak through the fields – and service taxi drivers at Gezira's depot have been told not to take foreigners beyond the west bank **security zone**, which ends at Haggar Daba'iyya (to the south) and Gurna Ta'rif (to the north) – and after dark, even travel to Haggar Daba'iyya is regarded with suspicion, as the village is reputedly a den of *bango* dealing. Apropos of which, it's worth bearing in mind that plainclothes cops often visit bars and restaurants in all the west bank villages, to enjoy free hospitality, collect a bribe and keep an eye on the clientele.

Staying on the west bank

Staying on the west bank is a good way to avoid the hassles of Luxor and to get closer to the sights, but it won't save you any money. Tourists staying here are deemed to be "living in Kuwait", and charged more for rooms and meals than they'd pay in Luxor. Still, the pleasure of living beside an ancient temple or fields alive with birds may outweigh the disadvantages. There's also a trade-off between the newer, better **hotels** further from the monuments, and the older basic ones, near temples – so consider the location (see the **map** on p.378), and phone ahead to check there are vacancies before crossing the Nile with your baggage. If not within walking distance of the ferry docks in Gezira village, they're accessible by pick-up (25pt) or private taxi (£E3–7) from the depot. A few hotels are unlicensed and barely signposted, but that doesn't mean that they're not okay.

It is also possible to rent **apartments** for between £E150–2000 per month, depending on the amenities, location and landlord. The family that owns the *Gezira* and *Gezira Gardens* has several flats for rent for £E700 per month, and you can find places in almost any village if you ask around. In fact, dozens of foreigners live on the west bank on a semi-permanent basis.

Abou el-Kassem East of Seti I's temple ☎095/312-671, ✉mohamed@abou-el-kassem.com. Sited beside the El-Kassem alabaster workshop, this neglected hotel has dusty, carpeted rooms with fans and showers. Bikes (£E5 per day), donkeys and meals available. It's quite a way from many of the sites; take El-Jebanah- or Gurna Ta'rif-bound pick-up. ❷

Al-Moudira Near Haggar Daba'iyya, 5km from Medinet Habu and 1km from Luxor Bridge ☎0123 251307, ☎0123 220528, ✉moudirahotel@yahoo.com, ⓌWww.moudira.com. Imagine an Ottoman palace at your disposal, with exquisite courtyards, gardens and pool. Its 54 individually styled suites feature antiques, mosquito nets, a/c, satellite TV and minibar; some even contain a fountain and a Turkish hammam. Built by a Lebanese woman, Zeina Aboukheir, the hotel's only drawback is that it's miles from anywhere, so guests must rely on taxis (£E10–15) if they don't have a car. Rates are higher at New Year. ❽

Amenophes (or Amenhotep) Nag Lohlah ☎095/311-228 or mobile 0122 123719, ☎095/311-228. Clean, friendly new hotel with tiled rooms with fans, proper bed linen, bathrooms and balconies. Only a few minutes' walk from Medinet Habu, but the view from the rooftop is marred by houses. ❺

Amoun el-Gezira Gezira, 300m from the ferry landing; turn off the main road at the El-Tayeb pharmacy ☎095/310-912 or mobile 0122 732754, ☎095/311-205. Very clean rooms with fans and bathrooms, with a shared terrace on each floor, a shady garden, and a rooftop view of the village. Serves meals and beer. Rents bikes (£E15 per day), camels, horses and donkeys. ❹

Gezira Gezira, 200m from the landing stage ☎095/310-034 or mobile 0123 617143, ☎095/310-034. Similar to the *Amoun el-Gezira*, but its rooms have balconies and are £E20 cheaper. The delightful terrace overlooks a canal that turns fetid in the summer, when mosquitoes are a big problem. Serves beer and meals. ❸

Gezira Gardens Gezira ☎095/312-505 or mobile 0123 617143, ☎095/310-034, ✉geziragardens@hotmail.com. Owned by the same family as the *Gezira*, this compound of spacious new two-bedroom a/c self-catering apartments with double and twin beds, balconies, kitchen and bathroom, has a restaurant, bar and shop in the grounds. Apartments rent for £E150 per night for four people, £E120 per night for two; reductions for longer stays. It's on the southwestern edge of the village. ❺

Habou Nag Lolah, directly opposite Medinet Habu temple ☎095/311-611. Immortalized in Critchfield's *Shahhat*, this seedy mud-brick labyrinth has stuffy barrel-vaulted rooms, but the shared bathrooms are clean and there's a fantastic view of the temple from the rooftop, if you can stand the mosquitoes. Usually empty, so prices are negotiable. ❸/❹

Marsam Off the main road to the Tombs of the Nobles ☎095/372-403, ✉marsam@africamail.com. Rambling split-level compound built for US archeologists and later owned by Sheikh Ali Abdul Rasoul, who helped discover the tomb of Seti I, this west bank institution is now managed by Czech-Australian Natasha. Its peaceful ambience, tasty lunches (£E16) and veggie dinners (£E10) compensate for the simple rooms with fans (four with bathrooms) and lack of alcohol – and there's even a decent library and the odd archeologist in residence. ❸

Nile Valley Gezira, 30m from the motorboat dock ☎095/311-477 or mobile 0106 509513, ✉karinkhalifa@hotmail.com. Pleasant rooms with fans and bathrooms, beneath a fab rooftop restaurant with a view of Luxor Temple across the river, and a promising garden. Cool ambience, with live music and a buffet on Sunday evenings. Breakfast includes a choice of cheese or Spanish omlette. Sells beer (£E8) and wine. ❸

Nour el-Qurna Across the road from the tourist police ☎095/311-430 or mobile 0101 295812. Secluded in a palm grove, with a garden, its eight stylish mud-brick rooms have fans, mosquito nets, palm-frond beds with duvets, and tiled baths – you need to reserve well ahead since it featured in a French lifestyle magazine. ❸

Osiris (or Osoris) Dra' Abul Naga ☎095/310-685. The rooms are clean, with fans or a/c and shared or private bathrooms, and the low price may outweigh their lack of mozzie screens and proximity to a mosque. ❷

Pharaoh's Nag Lohlah ☎095/310-702 or mobile 0105 288084, ✆pharaohshotel@hotmail.com. Cosy, clean a/c rooms with bathrooms; the roof features a few larger ones costing £E20 more, and a side view of the temple. Serves beer (£E7), ice cream and meals (£E10-15) on a shady patio, plagued by mozzies in the summer. ❸/❹

Eating and drinking on the west bank

Almost all **hotels** serve *kofta* or chicken with rice, vegetables and salad – the *Nile Valley* also has pizza and fish on the menu, and does a lavish oriental **buffet** (£E35) at 7pm on Sundays – and there are five other al fresco **restaurants** that do a tasty full meal for £E25-30. The 24-hour *Mohammed Cafeteria* near the **ticket office** serves the coldest Stella on the west bank, makes delicious goat's cheese and rates three cheers for its spotless toilets, a/c dining room and garden with a 600-year-old acacia tree. By the **temples**, the *Maratonga Café* does a mean *tajine* (not on the menu) and the *Ramesseum Resthouse* is like an Egyptian ranch, selling beer and wine. In **Gezira**, the *Africa Restaurant* near the taxi depot is good for fish and veggie dishes and has a nice patio, while the *Tout Ankhamon*, past the motorboats, is owned by Hagg Mahmoud, who used to cook for the *Mövenpick* in Europe. Customers are thrilled by his coconut curries, spicy lentil and vegetable stews (not strictly vegetarian) – served as a set meal, with pastries and watermelon for afters – but some are deterred by the crude hygiene and tables, right by the Nile. For light meals or **snacks**, there's a *kushari* joint on Gezira's high street which also sells pasta in bechamel sauce as a takeaway (£E10), or the *Donia Café* opposite the *Marsam Hotel*, which does *kofta* sandwiches and omelettes (£E5).

Although public **drinking** is taboo, most of the places mentioned above sell alcohol. The *Ramesseum Resthouse* is the cheapest (beer £E6, wine £E35), but the rooftop *Nile Valley* in Gezira and the Rasta-fied *No Galag* ("No Hassle") in Dra' Abul Naga are far livelier **at night**, with taped or improvised music and sometimes dancing. You can also play pool at the *Donia Café* (which also has satellite TV) or the high street pool-shack in Gezira.

The Colossi of Memnon

A kilometre or so beyond New Gurna the main road passes the **Colossi of Memnon**, looming nearly 18 metres above the fields to the right. This gigantic pair of enthroned statues originally fronted the mortuary temple of Amenophis III, once the largest complex on the west bank, and possibly even larger than Karnak – which later pharaohs plundered for masonry until nothing remained but the king's colossi. Both have lost their faces and crowns, and the northern one was cleaved to the waist by an earthquake in 27 BC. Subsequently, this colossus was heard to "sing" at dawn – a sound probably caused by particles breaking off as the stone expanded, or wind reverberating through the cracks. The phenomenon attracted many visitors during antiquity, including the Roman emperors Hadrian (130 AD) and Septimus Severus, who gave orders for the statue to be repaired (199 AD), after which it never sang again.

Previously, the sound had been attributed to the legendary Memnon, whom Achilles killed outside the walls of Troy, greeting his mother, Eos, the Dawn, with a sigh. The Greeks identified the colossi with Memnon in the belief that his father, Tithonus, had been an Egyptian king. Before this, the colossi had been identified with Amenhotep, Steward of Amenophis III, whom posterity honoured as a demigod long after his master was forgotten. This association had some grounds in truth, since it was Amenhotep who supervised the quarrying of the monoliths at Silsilah, and their erection on the west bank. He was also probably responsible for Amenophis III's section of Luxor Temple.

By standing beside the barrier rope you can appreciate what **details** remain, mostly on the thrones and legs of the sandstone colossi. On the sides of the nearer one, the Nile-gods of Upper and Lower Egypt bind the heraldic plants of the Two Lands together. The legs of each colossus are flanked by smaller statues of Queen Tiy (right) and the king's mother, Mutemuia (left). As high as one can reach, both are covered in graffiti, including Roman epigrams. There are plans to open a new archeological park behind the Colossi, to offer more than the brief photo opportunity that they provide at present.

The Valley of the Kings

Secluded amidst the bone-dry Theban Hills, removed from other parts of the Necropolis, the **Valley of the Kings** was intended as the ultimate insurance policy on life eternal. These secretive tombs of New Kingdom pharaohs were planned to preserve their mummies and funerary impedimenta for eternity. While most failed the test, their dramatic shafts and phantasmagorical murals are truly amazing. The descent into the underworld and the fear of robbers who braved the traps is still imaginable in the less crowded, darker tombs.

Royal burials in the "Place of Truth" date from the early XVIII to the late XX Dynasty. The first to be buried here was probably Tuthmosis I (1525–1512 BC). Until the time of Ramses I, queens and royal children were entombed here. **The tombs** were hewn and decorated by skilled craftsmen (known as "Servants at the Place of Truth") who dwelt at nearby Deir el-Medina. Work began early in a pharaoh's reign and never exceeded six years' duration; even so, some tombs were hastily pressed into service, or usurped by later kings. Broadly speaking, there are two types: the convoluted, split-level ones of early XVIII Dynasty rulers such as Tuthmosis I and Amenophis II, and the straighter, longer tombs of the XIX–XX dynasties.

Seal of the Valley of the Kings

The weaker rulers of the XX Dynasty were unable to prevent **tomb-robbing** on a massive scale. Both the vizier and police chief of Thebes were implicated in the disposal of treasure, while many of the robbers were the workmen who had built the tombs, embittered over arrears in pay. In desperation, the priests reburied many sarcophagi and objects in two **secret caches** that were only discovered in the late nineteenth century.

The exploration of the Valley began in earnest with a series of **excavations** sponsored by Theodore Davis in 1902–14, when more than thirty tombs and pits were cleared. In 1922, the discovery of Tutankhamun's tomb made headlines around the world, while as recently as 1995 a **mass tomb for the sons of Ramses II** was uncovered beneath tomb KV5, long regarded as empty. Using clues from a papyrus codex in Turin, Professor Kent Weeks found a complex of one hundred and fifty tomb chambers, some as large as four hundred square metres. Though inscriptions suggest that fifty of Ramses' one hundred or so sons were meant to be interred here, only the remains of four adults

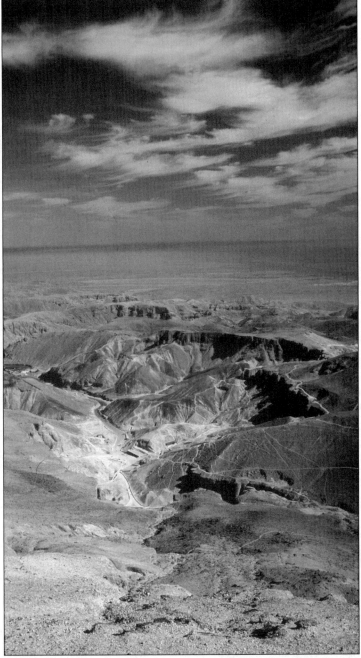

△ View of the Valley of the Kings from mountains

in their twenties have been found so far, to be X-rayed for comparison with Ramses' mummy in the Cairo Museum (DNA testing has been ruled out). For the latest news from the dig and views of many of the tombs, visit the Theban Mapping Project **website** (Ⓦ www.kv5.com) – or read Weeks's book *The Lost Tomb*.

Sadly, the Valley of the Kings is accutely susceptible to mass **tourism** and changes in the local **geology**. During the 1990s, cracks appeared in three tombs and the ceiling of a fourth collapsed. To prevent further damage to the **reliefs** and pigments, caused by friction, carbon dioxide and moisture (the

Mummification and the Underworld

The **funerary beliefs** manifest in the Valley of the Kings derive from two myths, concerning Re and Osiris. In that of **Re**, the sun-god descended into the underworld and voyaged through the hours of night, emerging at dawn to sail his barque across the heavens until sunset, when the cycle began anew. **Osiris**, king of the underworld, offered hope of survival in the afterlife through his death and resurrection.

Mummification and burial

To attain the afterlife, it was necessary that the deceased's name (*ren*) and body continued to exist, sustaining the **ka** or cosmic double that was born with every person and inhabited their mummy after death. **Mummification** techniques evolved over millennia, reaching their zenith by the New Kingdom, when embalmers offered three levels of mummification. The deluxe version entailed removing the brain (which was discarded) and the viscera (which were preserved in canopic jars); dehydrating the cadaver in natron salts for about forty days; packing it to reproduce lifelike contours, inserting artificial eyes and painting the face or entire body red (for men) or yellow (for women); then wrapping it in gum-coated linen bandages, and finally cocooning it in mummiform coffins. On the chest of the mummy and its coffin were placed heart scarabs, designed to prevent the deceased's heart from bearing witness against him during the judgement of Osiris.

Royal burials were elaborate affairs. Escorted by priests, mourners and musicians, the coffin was dragged on a sledge to the Valley of the Kings, where the sarcophagus was already occupied by a *sem* (death) priest, who performed the **Opening of the Mouth** ceremony, touching the lips of the mummy with an adze and reciting spells. As the mummy was lowered into its sarcophagus, priests slashed the forelegs of sacrificial animals, whose limbs were burned as the tomb was sealed. The tomb's contents (intended to satisfy the needs of the pharaoh's *ka* in the afterlife) included food, drink, clothing, furniture, weapons, and dozens of *shabti* figures to perform any task that the gods might require. Then the doors were walled up, plastered over and stamped with the royal seal and that of the Necropolis. To thwart robbers, royal tombs featured deadfalls and false burial chambers; however, none of these devices seem to have succeeded in protecting them.

The Journey of Re
From right to left: Sunset; Year; Eternity; Everlasting; Maat (justice); Re; Heka; Sunrise

average visitor leaves behind 2.8g of sweat), the SCA has installed glass screens or dehumidifers. A graver threat is posed by a sub-stratum of grey shale, which has expanded upwards beneath the limestone, rupturing several tombs from below. Some blame this on 25 years of leaks from a (now demolished) tourist rest-house, while others contend that the water table has risen due to the High Dam (see p.461).

The upshot is that tombs may be closed for years or reopened after ages under wraps. Remember that the artwork is **fragile**, so help preserve it by not touching the walls.

The journey through the underworld and judgement of Osiris

Funerary artwork dwelt on the journey through the underworld, whose pictorial representation inverted the normal order, so that each register was topped by sand instead of sky. The **descent** into the underworld, or *Duat*, echoed that of a sarcophagus into its tomb, involving ramps, ropes and gateways. Each of the twelve **gates** was personified as a goddess and guarded by ferocious deities (for example, the "Lady of Duration" and the "Flame-eyed" serpent at the fifth gate). In the darkness between them lay twelve **caverns** inhabited by beings such as the jackal-headed gods who fed on rottenness at the first cavern, or the wailing goddesses with bloody axes who waited at the tenth. Voyaging through the twelve **hours** of the night in his solar barque, Re had to overcome the serpent Apopis and other lesser denizens of **primeval chaos**, which threatened the **righteous order** personified by the goddess Maat.

It was Maat's Feather of Truth that was weighed against the deceased's heart (believed to be the seat of intelligence) during the **Judgement of Osiris**. With Anubis on the scales and Thoth waiting to record the verdict, the deceased had to recite the **negative confession** before a tribunal of 42 **assessor gods**, each attuned to a sin. While the hearts of the guilty were devoured by crocodile-headed Ammut, the righteous were pronounced "true of voice" and led into the presence of Osiris to begin their **resurrection**, which paralleled Re's passage through the underworld. Helped by Anubis, Isis and Nephthys (often shown as serpents), Aker the earth-god (whose back bore Re's barque) and Khepri the scarab beetle, Re achieves rebirth in the fifth hour, and is fully restored to life by the tenth. Here the two myths part company, for whereas Re emerges from the body of the sky-goddess Nut to travel the heavens again, the Osirian journey concludes in an afterlife that is sometimes identified as the **Fields of Yaru**.

Since many of the scenes were supplemented by papyri buried with the mummy, funerary **artwork** is categorized in literary terms. The *Book of the Dead* is the name now given to the compendium of Old and Middle Kingdom Pyramid Texts and Spells, known in the New Kingdom as the *Book of Coming Forth*. Other **texts** associated with the New Kingdom include the *Book of Gates*, *Book of Caverns*, *Book of Hours*, *Book of Day and Night* and *Book of Amduat* (That Which is in the Underworld).

The Judgement of Osiris
From left to right: Anubis escorts the deceased and weighs his heart before Ammut and Thoth;
then Horus leads him to Osiris, Isis and Nephthys

Visiting the tombs

The main **approach** to the valley (known as *Biban el-Melouk*, "Gates of the Kings" in Arabic) is via a serpentine road that follows the route of ancient funeral processions. Before the road, when donkeys were the only means of travel, its silence and emptiness were striking ("White earth; sun; one's rump sweats in the saddle", noted Flaubert). Nowadays, though, you'll only get this feeling on the trail across the hills from Deir el-Medina, the Workers' Village, which is still travelled by donkeys (see p.482). Minibuses and coaches park near a pricey **cafeteria**, from where you can walk or ride a *tuf-tuf* (£E1) to the site entrance, 500m away.

The valley is surrounded by limestone crags, the loftiest of which was the abode of Meretseger, snake-goddess of the Necropolis. This natural suntrap is hot even in winter, the heat permeating the deepest tombs, whose air is musty and humid (drink plenty of water). The **site** resembles a Nevada missile base on open day, sightseers wandering from one bunker-like entrance to another. It's hard to predict exactly which tombs will be open in the future, so we have left unchanged entries for tombs which may be closed during your visit.

Most people find three to five **tombs** enough for one visit; of the 64 tombs (numbered in order of discovery, not chronologically), less than a score are open at any one time – Luxor's tourist office knows which. A "Valley of the Kings" ticket is valid for three tombs only, and you can't buy them outside the site entrance, though the kiosk there does sell tickets for Tut's tomb. Video cameras must be deposited at the kiosk just inside the barrier.

The best **strategy** is to head for tombs on the periphery, such as Tuthmosis III, Amenophis II, Merneptah, Tawsert/Sethnakht, Seti II or Monthuhirkhopshef – while watching out for a chance to duck into other tombs if there's a break between groups. Although we've listed tombs in the order you'd encounter them in an anticlockwise circuit of the valley, it's better to select the most promising ones beforehand, and take whichever route makes sense.

Tomb of Ramses VII (#1)

Set apart near the entrance to the valley, the short tomb of **Ramses VII** lay wide open for millennia, and is now glassed over. Greek and Roman graffiti mars its sunk-reliefs and vivid colours (red, yellow and blue on white), whose freshness is obviously due to restoration (the tomb was reopened in 1995). Amid the standard imagery are odd details like the figures entombed in cartouches on the walls of the final corridor, while the hippo-goddess Tweri is prominent in the nocturnal pantheon on the ceiling of the burial chamber, whose sarcophagus is veined with blue imagery. The tomb isn't visited much, so you can wander round in peace. However, other Ramessid tombs are finer, so visitors limited to three tombs should look elsewhere.

Tomb of Ramses IV (#2)

The next tomb, that of **Ramses IV**, is more of a crowd pleaser. Its cheerful colours make amends for the inferior sunk-reliefs and abundant Greek and Coptic graffiti (notice the haloed saints on the right near the entrance). The ceiling of the burial chamber is adorned with twin figures of Nut. On the enormous pink-granite sarcophagus are magical texts and carvings of Isis and Nephthys, to protect the mummy from harm. When these seemed insufficient, the priests stashed Ramses in the tomb of Amenophis II, whence the now empty sarcophagus has been returned. Notice the Coptic graffiti in the end storage room beyond the burial chamber. As for Ramses himself, his mummy

VALLEY OF THE KINGS

TOMBS

1 **Ramses VII**
2 **Ramses IV**
3 Intended for Ramses III
4 Ramses XII
5 Sons of Ramses II
6 **Ramses IX**
7 Ramses II
8 **Merneptah**
9 **Ramses VI**
10 Amenmeses
11 **Ramses III**
12 No inscriptions
13 Intended for royal functionary
14 **Tawsert/Sethnakht**
15 Seti II
16 **Ramses I**
17 Seti I
18 Ramses X
19 **Monthuhirkhopshef**
20 Hatshepsut
21 Unfinished
22 Amenophis III
 (in the Western Valley)
23 **Ay** (in the Western Valley)

24-25 No inscription
 (in the Western Valley)
26-33 Unfinished
34 **Tuthmosis III**
35 **Amenophis II**
36 Maherpra,
 fan-bearer to Hatshepsut
37 No inscription
38 Tuthmosis I
39-41 No inscriptions
42 Possibly Tuthmosis II
43 Tuthmosis IV
44 No inscription
45 Private tomb
46 **Yuya and Thuya**
47 **Siptah**
48 Vizier Amenemopet
49-54 No inscriptions
55 **Tiy or Smenkhkare**
56 No inscriptions
57 **Horemheb**
58 Tutankhamun annex
59-61 No inscriptions
62 **Tutankhamun**

Bold text denotes an entry in the text

N

Ramses VII 1

Tickets

Ramses IV 2

Toilets

3

Yuya & Thuya 46

4

Merneptah 8

7

5

6 Ramses IX

Ramses VI 9

55 Tiy/ Smenkhare

62

Tutankhamun

12 Horemheb

57 58 56

Amenophis II 35

49-52 48

53

36

11 10

Ramses III

16 17 Seti I

18

54

45

44

28
27

21

61

13 29

Siptah 47

60

14

38

Tawsert/Sethnakht

40

26

20

19

Seti II 15

30

59

31

43

Monthuhirkhopshef

32 37

42

Donkey path

33 34 Tuthmosis III

39

| 0 | Metres | 100 |

▼ *Deir el-Medina*

in the Cairo Museum shows him to have been a short, bald man with a long nose. He became pharaoh in his forties after the failure of a conspiracy to usurp the throne (see p.419), and recorded the "testament" of his illustrious father, Ramses III, in the Great Harris Papyrus.

Tomb of Ramses IX (#6)

The tomb of **Ramses IX** belonged to one of the last rulers (1140–1123 BC) of the XX Dynasty, towards the end of the New Kingdom. It's indicative of waning majesty that the initial scenes in sunk-relief soon give way to flat paintings, akin to drawings. The walls of its stepped corridor (originally bisected by ramps, for moving the sarcophagus) depict Ramses before the gods, and symbolic extracts from the *Book of Caverns*. Notice the solar barques bearing crocodiles, heads and other oddities, on the left-hand wall. The burial chamber is memorable for its *Book of Night* in yellow upon a dark blue background. Two sky-goddesses stretch back-to-back across the ceiling, encompassing voids swirling with creatures, stars and heavenly barques. While the king's sarcophagus pit gapes empty, his resurrection is still heralded on the walls by Khepri, the scarab incarnation of the reborn sun at dawn.

Tomb of Tutankhamun (#62)

One of the world's most famous tombs, the tomb of **Tutankhamun** is neither large nor imposing by the standards of the Valley of the Kings, reflecting Tut's short reign (c.1361–1352 BC; see p.311) as an XVIII Dynasty boy-pharaoh. Its renown stems from its belated discovery and its amazing hoard of treasures (now mostly in the Cairo Museum). After archeologist **Howard Carter** had dug in vain for five seasons, his financial backer, **Lord Carnarvon**, was on the point of giving up when the tomb was found on November 4, 1922. Fears that it had been plundered were dispelled when they broke through the second sealed door – officially on November 26, though in fact Carter and Carnarvon secretly entered the previous night, stole several items and resealed the door. Otherwise, the tomb was cleared meticulously. Each of its 1700 objects was documented, drawn and photographed *in situ* before being removed to an improvised laboratory in the tomb of Seti II, for stabilizing and cleaning by Arthur Mace. Unpacking everything took nearly ten years, the whole process being recorded in more than 1800 superb photographs by Harry Burton, who converted an empty tomb into a darkroom.

Lord Carnarvon's death in Cairo from an infected mosquito bite in April 1923 focused world attention on a warning by the novelist Marie Corelli, that "dire punishment follows any intruder into the tomb". (At the moment of Carnarvon's death, all the lights in Cairo went out.) The **Curse of Tutankhamun** gained popular credence with this and each successive "mysterious" death. The US magnate Jay Gould died of pneumonia resulting from a cold contracted at the tomb; a famous Bey was shot by his wife in London after viewing the discovery; a French Egyptologist suffered a fatal fall; Carter's secretary died in unusual circumstances at the Bath Club in London; and his right-hand man Arthur Mace sickened and died before the tomb had been fully cleared. However, of the 22 who had witnessed the opening of Tut's sarcophagus, only two were dead ten years later. Howard Carter died in 1939 at the age of 64, while others closely involved lived into their eighties (not least Dr Derry, who performed the autopsy which suggested that Tut died from a blow to the head, aged about nineteen). Notwithstanding this, a new explanation for the "curse" was advanced by a scientist at Cairo University in 1991. Professor Thebat believes that Carnarvon and Mace were fatally weakened by radioactivity emanating from an unknown substance used as part of the mummification process, which had accumulated in the tomb over 3000 years; he also claims to have detected radioactivity in seventeen of the mummies in the Egyptian Museum.

As for the tomb itself, it is now glassed over to protect its paintings, and the number of visitors has been reduced by a steep admission charge. **Tickets** for Tut's tomb are available at the entrance to the Valley of the Kings, or the main ticket office – but at £E40 you might well decide that the tomb isn't worth it.

TOMB OF TUTANKHAMUN

In 1922, Carter found the door at the bottom of the stairway **[a]** walled up and sealed with Tut's cartouche and the seal of the Necropolis, but signs of repairs, the detritus in the corridor **[b]** and another resealed door at the end indicated that robbers had penetrated the antechamber **[c]** during the XX Dynasty.

Most of the funerary objects now in the Cairo Museum were crammed into the undecorated chambers **[c, d** (now walled up) and **e]**. Another wall (now replaced by a barrier) enclosed the burial chamber, which was almost filled by four golden shrines packed one inside another, containing Tut's stone sarcophagus and triple-layer mummiform coffin, of which the innermost, solid **gold coffin** – and **Tut's mummy** – remain.

The colourful murals run in an anticlockwise direction, starting with the funeral procession where nine friends and three officials drag Tut's coffin on a sledge **[f]**. Next, his successor Ay performs the Opening of the Mouth ceremony **[g]** and makes sacrifices to the sky-goddess Nut **[h]**. The deceased king embraces Osiris, followed by his *ka* (in the black wig) **[i]**. His solar boat and sun-worshipping baboons appear on the left wall **[j]**. On the hard-to-see entrance wall, Anubis and Isis escort Tutankhamun to receive life from Hathor **[k]**.

Tomb of Ramses VI (#9)

One reason why Tut's tomb stayed hidden for so long was that it lay beneath mounds of rubble from the tomb of **Ramses VI** (1156–1148 or 1151–1143 BC), which has been a tourist attraction since antiquity, when the Greeks called it the "Tomb of Memnon". The first two corridors have suffered from centuries of graffiti, but far worse occurred in 1992, when the ceiling fell down and had to be glued back on in nearly one thousand pieces. The tomb was **closed** at the time of writing.

It was begun by Ramses V but usurped and enlarged by his successor, whose offering of a lamp to Horus of the Horizon opens the *Book of Gates* **[a]**, which faces other sunk-reliefs from the *Book of Caverns* **[b]**. Like the astronomical ceiling, this continues through a series of corridors (note the winged sun-disc over the lintel and Ramses' cartouches on the door jambs **[c]**). Where the *Book*

TOMB OF RAMSES VI

t

s   u

Sarcophagus

r

p   q

n   o

l   m

j   k

h   i

f   g

d   e

c

a   b

0   10m

of *Gates* reaches the Hall of Osiris **[d]**, a flame-breathing snake and catfish-headed gods infest the *Book of Caverns* **[e]**. As Re's barque approaches the Seventh Gate, beyond which twelve gods hold a rope festooned with whips and heads **[f]**, the *Book of Caverns* depicts a procession of *ka* figures **[g]**. From here on, the astronomical ceiling features an attenuated sky-goddess and the *Book of Day and Night*.

The eighth and ninth divisions of the *Book of Gates* **[h]** and fifth division of the *Book of Caverns* **[i]** decorate the next chamber, originally a vestibule to the hall beyond, which marked the limits of Ramses V's tomb. This contains the concluding sections of the *Book of Gates* **[j]**, the seventh division of the *Book of Caverns* **[k]** and a summary of the world's creation **[l]**. The rear wall also features a scene of Ramses VI making offerings and libations to Osiris. On the pillars, he makes offerings to Khonsu, Amun-Re, Meretseger, Ptah-Sokar, Ptah and Re-Herakhte **[m]**.

The descent to the next corridor is guarded by winged serpents representing the goddesses Nekhbet and Neith (left), Meretseger and Selket (right). On the corridor walls appear the introductory **[n]** and middle sections **[o]** of the *Book of Amduat*; on the ceiling, extracts from the *Books of Re* and the *Book of Day and Night*. Scenes in the next corridor relate the fourth and fifth **[p]** and eighth to eleventh **[q]** chapters of the *Book of Amduat*. The small vestibule beyond contains texts from the *Book of Coming Forth by Day*, including the "negative confession" **[r]**. On the ceiling, Ramses sails the barques of Day and Night across the first register, while Osiris rises from his bier in the second.

Lovely back-to-back versions of the *Book of Day* and *Book of Night* adorn the ceiling of Ramses VI's burial chamber, where his image makes offerings at either end of one wall [s]. The rear [t] and right-hand walls carry portions of the *Book of Aker*, named after the earth-god of the underworld who fettered the coils of Apopis, safeguarding Re's passage. Incarnated as a ram-headed beetle, the sun-god is drawn across the heavens in his divine barque [u]. The king's black granite **sarcophagus** was smashed open by treasure hunters in antiquity, and his mummy left so badly damaged that the priests had to pin the body to a board to provide the remains with a decent burial in another tomb.

Tomb of Merneptah (#8)

Merneptah (1236–1223 BC), the fourteenth son of Ramses II, didn't become pharaoh until his fifties, having outlived thirteen brothers with prior claims on the throne. On the evidence of his mummy, he was afflicted by arthritis and hardening of the arteries, and underwent dental surgery in old age. On the strength of his "Israel Stele" at Karnak and the identification of his father as the Pharaoh of the Oppression, many scholars hold that Merneptah was the Pharaoh of the Exodus (although this is disputed by Rohl; see p.787).

TOMB OF MERNEPTAH

Sarcophagus

Like other tombs of the XIX Dynasty, his descends in corridors, with a total length of about 80m. Merneptah is welcomed by Re-Herakhte and Khepri [a], the *Litany of Re* [b] unfolds opposite the sixteen avatars of Osiris [c], Re's barque is pulled through the underworld [d], and Nekhebkau leads his soul towards Anubis [e]. Beyond a pit watched by Thoth and Anubis [f], another corridor decorated with the *Book of Amduat* [g] leads to an antechamber with images of Osiris and Nephthys [h], and Merneptah as Imutef [i].

The next hall is a false burial chamber (a trick that seldom fooled robbers) decorated with hymns to Osiris [j] and scenes from the *Book of Gates*. Notice the binding of the Serpents of Chaos [k], a tug-of-war over a "rope" of human souls [l], and the Osirian avatars above the lintel. The final corridors are largely bare, but you'll stumble upon the outer **lid** of Merneptah's sarcophagus – left there by thieves – and the faint image of a monkey [m].

In the real burial chamber, the gods voyage through the night across the ceiling, while murals show the metamorphosis of Khepri into Re, encircled by bird-men requesting the deceased's *ba* (soul) [n], and Khnum piloting a boat with the pharaoh's mummy floating above [o]. There is a carving of the sky-goddess Nut inside Merneptah's massive granite **sarcophagus**.

Tomb of Ramses III (#11)

The grandest of the Ramessid tombs open at present is that of **Ramses III**. His thirty-one-year reign (1198–1166 BC) marked the heyday of the XX

TOMB OF RAMSES III

Dynasty, whose power declined under the later Ramessids. Like his temple at Medinet Habu, the tomb harks back to the earlier glories of the New Kingdom. Uniquely for royal tombs, its colourful sunk-reliefs include scenes of everyday life. From another vignette derives its popular name, the Tomb of the Harpers.

Off the entrance corridors lie ten side chambers, originally used to store funerary objects. Within the first pair are fragmentary scenes of butchery, cooking and baking **[a]**, and ships setting sail, those with furled sails bound downriver **[b]**. Next, Hapy blesses grain-gods and propitiates snake-headed Napret, with her escort of aproned *uraei* **[c]**. The bull of Meri (right) and the cow of Hesi (left) coexist with armoury scenes **[d]**, while hermaphrodite deities bring offerings **[e]** to a treasury **[f]**. Ramses owns cattle and minerals **[g]**, and from his boat inspects peasants working in the Fields of Yaru **[h]**. In a famous scene, two harpists sing to Shu and Atum, while Harsomtus and Anhor greet the king; the lyrics of the song cover the entrance wall **[i]**. The twelve forms of Osiris **[j]** are possibly linked to the twelve *decans* (divisions or hours) of the night.

The dead-end tunnel **[k]** shows where diggers accidentally broke into a neighbouring tomb, at which point the original builder, Pharaoh Sethnakht, abandoned it and appropriated Tawsert's (see below). When construction resumed under Ramses, the tomb's axis was shifted west. The corridor has scenes from the fourth **[l]** and fifth **[m]** hours of the *Book of Amduat*. Part of the *Book of Gates* specifies four races of men: Egyptians, Asiatics, Negroes and Libyans (along the bottom) **[n]**. On the facing wall, the pinioned serpent Apopis is forced to disgorge the heads of his victims, in the fifth chapter of the *Book of Gates*. In the side room **[o]** are scenes from the *Book of Amduat*. The rest of the tomb has been barred since its ceiling fell down.

Tomb of Horemheb (#57)

General **Horemheb** was the power behind the throne of Tutankhamun and his aged successor Ay, and finally became pharaoh himself. His reign (1348–1320 BC) marked the height of the Theban counter-revolution against the Amarna heresy and the last gasp of the XVIII Dynasty, and was spent shoring up the crumbling empire bequeathed by his predecessors. He died without leaving an heir (though Rohl thinks that he gave his daughter as a bride to King Solomon) and was succeeded by a military deputy called Paramessu, who took the throne name Ramses and founded the Ramessid dynasty.

Due to be reopened "next year", the tomb's layout prefigures Seti's (see p.401), with a long, steep descent through undecorated corridors to a well room which depicts Horemheb with deities, highly detailed and coloured. Hathor, Isis, Osiris, Horus and Anubis reappear in the anteroom before the burial chamber, whose entrance is guarded by Maat. Its unfinished scenes range from stick-figure drawings to fully worked carvings; the *Book of the Dead* begins to your left and runs clockwise round the chamber, whose huge sarcophagus is carved with a relief of Nut. In the second room to the left, you can see Osiris before a *Djed* pillar.

Tomb of Amenophis II (#35)

One of the deepest tombs in the valley lies at the head of the wadi beyond Horemheb's tomb. Built for **Amenophis II** (1450–1425 or 1427–1400 BC) midway through the XVIII Dynasty, it gets hotter and stuffier with each lower level, having over ninety steps. When the tomb was discovered in 1898, the body of the king was still in its sarcophagus and nine other royal mummies were found stashed in another chamber. The tomb's defences included a deep pit (now bridged) and a false burial chamber to distract robbers from the lower levels (which would have been sealed up and disguised).

From a pillared vestibule, steps descend into the huge chamber. On its six square pillars, Amenophis is embraced and offered *ankhs* by various gods. Beneath a star-spangled ceiling, the walls are painted pale beige and inscribed with the entire *Book of Amduat*, like a continuous scroll of papyrus. Notice the preliminary pen sketches to the left of the left-hand niche. When found in his quartzite sarcophagus (still *in situ*), the king's mummy had a floral garland around its neck. The second chamber on the right served as a cache for the mummies of Tuthmosis IV, Merneptah, Seti II, Ramses V and VI (hacked to pieces) and Queen Tiy, after their original tombs proved insecure.

Tomb of Tawsert/Sethnakht (#14)

Located en route to Seti II's tomb, this one is unusual for having two burial chambers. It originally held the mummy of Seti's wife, Queen **Tawsert**, but was usurped by Pharaoh **Sethnakht** (c.1200–1085 BC) after his own tomb (now Ramses III's) ran into difficulties. In the first corridor one finds Sethnakht making offerings to Horus and Isis, and Osiris enshrined. Further on, a ram-headed god with a knife is followed by Anubis and Wepwawet. Texts from the *Book of the Dead* cover what was meant to be Tawsert's tomb chamber beyond which steps lead down towards Sethnakht's vault.

At the bottom of the stairs, the pharaoh's soul attains harmony with Maat, cherishing the Papyrus and Lotus of the Two Lands; while Anubis embalms his mummy in a side chamber further on. A hall of texts from the *Book of Caverns* and the Opening of the Mouth ceremony precede the burial chamber, whose pillars show the gods greeting Sethnakht, while the walls depict the resurrection of Osiris and Re's journey through the night.

Tomb of Siptah (#47)

Siptah (1194–1188 BC) was the only son of Seti II, born not of Queen Tawsert, but of a Syrian concubine, Sutailja. Since he was only a boy, with an atrophied leg, Tawsert ruled as regent in alliance with an official named Bay (also of Syrian origin). After Siptah came of age, Tawsert married him; some believe that his death six years later was orchestrated by Tawsert and Bay. His one recorded achievement was to have led a campaign in Nubia, but it is more likely that he had it sent in his name. To complete his run of bad luck, Siptah's tomb was usurped by a later pharaoh, its contents smashed up in antiquity, and his mummy ended up in the tomb of Amenophis II. There it was found in 1905, when it was determined that he probably had cerebral palsy or polio as an infant. However, his tomb looks impressive, with a finely dressed Siptah mingling with the gods in the *Litany of Ra*, and floating through scenes from the *Book of Amduat*.

Tomb of Seti II (#15)

At the end of the wadi lies the seldom-visited tomb of **Seti II** (1216–1210 BC), which Arthur Mace used as a storage and restoration area during the excavation of Tutankhamun's tomb. Its long, straight corridors are typical of the XIX Dynasty, decorated with colourful scenes. Due to Seti's abrupt demise, however, there was only time to carve sunk-reliefs near the entrance, and the rest was hastily filled in with paintings or outline drawings. The king's mummy was later hidden in tomb #35 and replaced by that of an anonymous dignitary, which was plundered by thieves, who left only the sarcophagus lid. His mummy indicates that he suffered from arthritis, but had good teeth, which was unusual for that time.

Tomb of Tuthmosis III (#34)

Likewise secreted in a separate wadi, high up in a cleft, the tomb of **Tuthmosis III** (1504–1450 or 1479–1425 BC) is one of the oldest in the valley. Its concealment and (futile) defences make this tomb especially interesting, though some are disappointed by its artwork. Having ascended a wooden stairway to the cleft, you descend through several levels, crossing a pit by footbridge to reach a vestibule. Its walls depict 741 deities as stick figures, in imitation of the format used on papyrus texts from the Middle Kingdom onwards, which was favoured for murals early in the New Kingdom. Reduced to their essentials, the ramps and shafts that led into the underworld, and

TOMB OF TUTHMOSIS III

Burial Chamber

Sarcophagus

Vestibule

Pit

N

0   5m

Khepri's role in pulling Re's barque, are clearly visible.

The unusual rounded burial chamber is also decorated with outline figures and symbols. Although the yellow background simulates aged papyrus, the texts were only painted after Tuthmosis had been laid to rest; there's a crossed-out mistake on the "instruction" fresco.

Elsewhere you'll notice double images (as at Abu Simbel), believed by some archeologists to have been meant to suggest motion, and others to be the result of overcarving. On one of the pillars, Tuthmosis's mother stands behind him in a barque; the register below shows three wives and a daughter, to the right of which a tree-goddess suckles the young king. By shining a torch inside the quartzite sarcophagus, you can admire a lovely carving of Nut, whose arms would have embraced his mummy before priests removed it to a safer hiding place near Deir el-Bahri.

Tomb of Seti I (#17)

Despite pledges it would reopen in 2001, after a decade spent restoring damage wrought by the rising water table and tourists, sadly the tomb of **Seti I**, the finest tomb in the valley, is still **closed**. Dehumidifiers have been installed, but it seems that the tomb is still too fragile to expose. Discovered in 1817, it is the longest in the valley (over 120m) and has superlative carvings and gilded paintings comparable to those in Seti's temple at Abydos. It was Seti I (1318–1304 BC) who consolidated the XIX Dynasty, regained the colonies lost under Akhenaten, and paved the way for his second son, Ramses II, to reach new heights of imperialism. His tomb fared badly at the hands of European collectors: some of its reliefs are now in the Louvre and the Turin Museum, while Seti's sarcophagus lies in the Sir John Soane Museum in London. There are now plans to create a life-size replica of Seti's tomb on the Giza Plateau outside Cairo.

Tomb of Ramses I (#16)

Buried next door to Seti is his father, **Ramses I**, founder of the XIX Dynasty, who was not of royal blood, but the son of a commander from Avaris. During his one-year reign (1320–1318 or 1295–1294 BC), Ramses campaigned in Asia, reopened the turquoise mines of Sinai, and married Sitre, the daughter of another soldier from the eastern Delta, siring an heir to continue the dynasty. His tomb has the shortest entrance corridor of any in the valley, leading to a small, finely painted burial chamber, the colours still bright against a blue-grey background. On the left wall are nine black sarcophagi in caverns, above twelve goddesses representing the hours of the night, from the *Book of Gates*. Elsewhere, Ramses appears with Maat, Anubis, Ptah, Osiris and other deities. The king's mummy has never been found, although it was recently claimed to be in the Niagrara Falls Museum, where it had lain, unidentified, since it was dubiously acquired in 1850.

Tomb of Monthuhirkhopshef (#19)

Sited high up a side-wadi, the seldom-visited tomb of **Monthuhirkhopshef** casts light on the life of princes – in this case, a son of Ramses IX, named "The Arm of Montu is Mighty". Monthuhirkhopshef died in his teens – before his father – for he wears the blue-and-gold sidelock of youth, offset by a finely-pleated linen skirt and elaborate makeup (used by both sexes in ancient Egypt), as he makes offerings to deities in the entrance corridor of his tomb.

Tomb of Queen Tiy/Smenkhkare (#55)

The undecorated tomb, designated **KV55,** has been a conundrum ever since its discoverer, Theodore Davis, failed to record its contents before removing the decrepit mummy in 1907, thus destroying crucial evidence. The mummy was initially attributed to **Queen Tiy** – the wife of Amenophis III – due to its pelvic shape and "feminine" position (left arm bound across the chest, right arm alongside the body), and a gilded panel that depicted her with Akhenaten. Later, however, the bones were identified as those of a man under 26 with signs of hydrocephalus, which seemed to fit Pharaoh Akhenaten instead. Yet another examination in 1933 found no signs of water on the brain (hydrocephalus), but diagnosed a platycephalic (abnormally flat) skull similar to Tutankhamun's – suggesting that this was the mummy of his mysterious predecessor, **Smenkhkare**.

Although new evidence has since been advanced for this being the mummy of Akhenaten, the Egyptian Museum remains unconvinced, and still attributes it to Smenkhkare.

Tomb of Yuya and Thuya (#46)

Another tomb with nothing to see (its contents are in the Cairo Museum) but a story attached is that of **Yuya and Thuya**, the parents of Queen Tiy. Though seemingly not of noble birth, Yuya was the highest official under Tuthmosis IV and Amenophis III. The latter's marriage to their daughter led to Thuya and Yuya becoming the grandparents of Pharaoh Akhenaten. In *Stranger in the Valley of the Kings*, Ahmed Osman argues that Yuya – whose mummy has a non-Egyptian appearance – was the Biblical Joseph (Genesis 41:39–40), whose talk of Yahweh subsequently inspired the monotheistic religion of Akhenaten (see Tell el-Amarna, p.310). However, others believe that Yuya and Thuya were of Nubian origin, as evinced by a famous bust of Tiy, whose face is indubitably African.

The Western Valley and the Sun Temple of Thoth

A neglected offshoot of the Valley of the Kings, the **Western Valley** (*Biban el-Gurud*) contains only four tombs (two of them royal), of which just one is open. The **Tomb of Ay** (#23) was built for Tutankhamun's successor, who had earlier been Akhenaten's vizier and prepared himself a tomb at Tell el-Amarna. His crypt in the Western Valley is notable for the blend of royal and noble imagery in the burial chamber, where the *Book of Amduat* is juxtaposed with a typical nobles' vignette of the deceased spearing fishes and birds. Unfortunately, given the distance by road off the main route to the Valley of the Kings (the Western Valley is clearly signposted), you can only get there by car or with a trail bike – check with the ticket office to avoid a wasted journey.

Locals call the valley "Wadi Monkey", after the caches of mummified baboons found there, probably connected with a remote **Sun Temple of Thoth** (to whom baboons were sacred). Uniquely for an Egyptian temple, this structure – which isn't open to tourists – is sited 400m above the Nile, on a spur of the Theban range that the ancients called the "Crown of Thebes". As Hungarian

This wonderfully scenic hike is easiest over winter, but feasible at other times so long as you guard against heatstroke. Though **the hike** can be done in thirty minutes, it's worth taking it slowly once you've shaken off the souvenir vendors who wait above the start of the trail, where the donkey guides rest up. If you're tempted to be rude, remember that the vendors only come here because they can't afford to bribe the police to let them work in the Valley of the Kings.

When the path forks, take the left-hand track running flat along the top of a rock "loaf", before crossing the ridge to behold the Nile Valley. Directly beneath the sheer cliff lies Hatshepsut's temple; to see it, walk right for a bit before peering *carefully* over the edge. To descend, follow the path alongside the trampled fence till you reach a crag where the trail divides. Ignore anyone who tries to lure you down the steepest trail, to render "help" for *baksheesh* – the slightly less precipitous left-hand path is the one to take. Hiking along **other trails** in the Theban Hills is likely to be firmly discouraged by the police.

Egyptologists recently discovered, the mud-brick temple built by Mentuhotpe II in the XI Dynasty overlays a stone temple from the Archaic Period – the oldest known one in Upper Egypt. The temple is distantly visible at the start of the road to the Valley of the Kings, but can only be reached on foot or by donkey (1hr 30min–2hr) by a steep 5km path starting from near Howard Carter's house.

Deir el-Bahri

Of all the sites on the west bank, none can match the breathtaking panache of **Deir el-Bahri**. Set amidst a vast natural amphitheatre in the Theban Hills, the temple rises in imposing terraces, the shadowed verticals of its colonnades drawing power from the massive crags overhead. Its great ramps and courts look modern in their stark simplicity, but in ancient times would have been softened and perfumed by gardens of fragrant trees. The reliefs that cover its colonnades and chapels bespeak of an extraordinary woman, and dynastic intrigues. *Deir el-Bahri* (Northern Monastery) is the Arabic name for the **Mortuary Temple of Hatshepsut**, the only woman ever to reign over Egypt as pharaoh (1503–1482 BC). A daughter of Tuthmosis I, married to his successor Tuthmosis II, Hatshepsut was widowed before she could bear a son. Rather than accept relegation in favour of a secondary wife who had produced an heir, Hatshepsut made herself co-regent to the young Tuthmosis III and soon assumed absolute power.

To legitimize her position, she was depicted in masculine form, wearing a pharaoh's kilt and beard; yet her authority ultimately depended on personal willpower and the devotion of her favourite courtier, Senenmut, who rose from humble birth to the stewardship of Amun's estates, before falling from grace for reasons unknown. When Tuthmosis came into his inheritance after her death, he defaced Hatshepsut's cartouches and images, consigning her memory to oblivion until her deeds were rediscovered by archeologists.

In 1995, the temple was used to stage Verdi's *Aïda*, which was a financial flop due to poor promotion and colossal expenditure, not least on building a road to the Nile so that VIPs could arrive by boat from Karnak, which has hardly been used since. However, dozens of coach parties arrive along the road from Dra' Abul Naga, making this one of the busiest sites in the Necropolis.

Tragically, in November 1997 it made headlines when 58 tourists and four guards were shot or stabbed to death by Islamist extremists, on the temple's Middle Terrace. The terrorists might have escaped in a hijacked coach if the driver hadn't deliberately crashed it near the Valley of the Queens, and if they hadn't been chased by villagers, for the police took an hour to reach the scene. The day is vividly remembered on the west bank, especially by the donkey guides who witnessed the **massacre** from the clifftop above. Ever since then, all the sites have been heavily guarded, and watchposts installed on the Theban Hills – a security regime that looks set to stay.

Hatshepsut's temple

Hatshepsut called her temple **Djeser Djeseru**, the "Splendour of Splendours". In ancient times an avenue of sphinxes probably ran from the Nile to its **Lower Terrace**, which was planted with myrrh trees and cooled by fountains (the stumps of a few 3500-year-old trees remain). At the top and bottom of the ramp to the next level stood pairs of stone lions (one of each pair is still *in situ*). Before ascending the ramp, check out its flanking **colonnades**, whose reliefs were defaced by Tuthmosis III, and later by Akhenaten. While Hatshepsut's image remains obliterated, those of Amun were restored after the Theban counter-revolu-

Hatshepsut

tion. Behind the northern colonnade (right of the ramp) are idealized scenes of rural life; reliefs in the southern (left) colonnade show the transport by river of two obelisks from Aswan – doubtless the pair that she erected at Karnak.

The **Middle Terrace** once also boasted myrrh trees, which Hatshepsut personally acquired from the Land of Punt in a famous expedition that's depicted along one of the square-pillared colonnades flanking the ramp to the uppermost level. Together with the Birth reliefs behind the other colonnade, and scenes in the chapels at either end, these are the highlights of her temple.

The Birth And Punt colonnades

To the right of the ramp is the so-called **Birth Colonnade**, whose reliefs assert Hatshepsut's divine parentage. Starting from the left, its rear walls show Amun (in the guise of Tuthmosis I) and her mother Queen Ahmosis (seated on a couch), their knees touching. Next, bizarre deities lead the queen into the birth chamber, where the god Khnum fashions Hatshepsut and her *ka* (both represented as boys) on his potter's wheel. Her birth is attended by Bes and the frog deity Heqet; goddesses nurse her, while Thoth records details of her reign. The sensitive expressions and delicate modelling convey a sincerity that transcends mere political expediency.

At the far end of the colonnade, steps lead back into a **Chapel of Anubis** with fluted columns and colourful murals. Tuthmosis III and a falcon-headed sun-god appear over the niche to the right; Hathor on the facing wall; offerings by Hatshepsut and Tuthmosis to Anubis on the other walls. As elsewhere, the images of Hatshepsut were defaced after her death by order of Tuthmosis.

On the other side of the ramp is the famous **Punt Colonnade**, relating Hatshepsut's journey to that land (thought to be modern-day Somalia). Though others had visited Punt to obtain precious myrrh for temple incense, Hatshepsut sought living trees to plant outside her temple. Despite the faintness of the reliefs, you can follow the story as it unfolds (left to right). Commissioned by Amun "to establish a Punt in his house", the Egyptian flotilla sails from the Red Sea Coast, to be welcomed by the king of Punt and his grotesquely fat wife (perhaps afflicted by elephantiasis). In exchange for metal axes and other goods, the Egyptians depart with myrrh trees and resin, ebony, ivory, cinnamon wood and panther skins; baboons play in the ships' rigging. Back home, the spoils are dedicated to Amun and the precious myrrh trees bedded in the temple gardens.

The Punt Colonnade leads into a larger **Chapel of Hathor**, whose face and sistrum (sacred rattle) form the capitals of the square pillars. In the first pillared chamber, the goddess appears in her bovine and human forms, and suckles Hatshepsut (whose image has not been defaced here) on the left-hand wall. The next chamber features delicate reliefs of festival processions (still quite freshly coloured) in a similar location. Peering into the gated sanctuary, you'll see another intact Hatshepsut worshipping the divine cow (left), and an alcove (right) containing a **portrait of Senenmut**, which would have been hidden when the doors were open. Apocryphally, it was this claim on the pharaoh's temple that caused his downfall. After fifteen years of closeness to Hatshepsut and her daughter Neferure (evinced by a statue in the Cairo Museum, which some regard as proof of paternity), Senenmut abruptly vanished from the records late in her reign. When archeologists excavated the sanctuary in the early twentieth century they found it stacked with baskets full of wooden penises, seemingly used in fertility rituals.

The Upper Terrace and sanctuaries

Reached by a ramp terminating in vultures' heads, the **Upper Terrace** has now emerged from decades of research and restoration work by Polish and Egyptian teams. Beyond its Osiride portico lies a courtyard flanked by colonnades and sanctuaries. In the **Sanctuary of Hatshepsut** (left) are stylish reliefs of priests and offerings bearers. On the other side is the **Sanctuary of the Sun**, an open court with a central altar.

The central **Sanctuary of Amun** is dug into the cliff, aligned so that it points towards Hatshepsut's tomb in the Valley of the Kings on the other side of the mountain. In Ptolemaic times the sanctuary was extended and dedicated to Imhotep and Amenhotep, the quasi-divine counsellors of Zoser and Amenophis III. Beneath it lies another burial chamber for Hatshepsut, presumably favoured over her pro forma tomb in the Valley of the Kings, since it was dug at a later date.

Other temples

From the heights of Hatshepsut's temple you can gaze southwards over the ruins of two similar edifices. The **Mortuary Temple of Tuthmosis III** was long ago destroyed by a landslide, but a painted relief excavated here can be seen in the Luxor Museum; more remains of the far older **Temple of Mentuhotpe II**, the first pharaoh to choose burial in Thebes (XI Dynasty). Unlike his XVIII Dynasty imitators, Mentuhotpe was actually buried in his mortuary temple; his funerary statue is now exhibited in the Cairo Museum.

Secret tombs and lavatory humour

Whereas Mentuhotpe's remains weren't discovered till modern times, many of the New Kingdom royal tombs were despoiled soon after their final burial in the Valley of the Kings. Towards the end of the XXI Dynasty, the priests hid forty mummies in a **secret cache** in the next hollow to the south above Mentuhotpe's temple, which the villagers of Gurna found in 1875 and quietly sold off for years until rumbled by the authorities, who forced them to reveal the cache's location. Amongst the mummies recovered were Amenophis I, Tuthmosis II and III, Seti I and Ramses II and III. Archeologists were baffled to find a XXII Dynasty coffin, beyond a passage blocked by royal mummies from an earlier period. As the steamer bore them downriver to Cairo, villagers lined the banks, wailing in sorrow or firing rifles in homage – a haunting scene in Shady Abdel Salem's film *The Mummy*, a classic of Egyptian cinema (1975).

Worth a look if you can persuade a guard at Deir el-Bahri to unlock it is the **Tomb of Senenmut**, just beyond the temple precincts. Its steep shaft descends past a bust of Senenmut into a chamber with a lovely astronomical ceiling; on its walls are extracts from the *Book of the Dead*. Why Senenmut should have built this tomb when he already had one at Gurna is uncertain; in any event, its unfinished burial chamber was never used.

Alas, the SCA is not willing to display a rare example of ancient Egyptian **lavatory humour** in a cave to the north of Hatshepsut's temple. Amongst the doodles and inscriptions is a drawing of a man buggering a figure wearing pharaonic headgear and women's underwear. Could this be Senenmut and Hatshepsut – or a fantasy of revenge by the juvenile Tuthmosis?

The Asasif Tombs

Midway between Deir el-Bahri and the Tombs of the Nobles lies a burial ground known as the **Asasif Tombs**, currently being studied by several archeological teams. While some of its 35 tomb chapels date from the XVIII Dynasty, the majority are from the Late Period (XXV–XXVI Dynasty), when Thebes was ruled by Nubian kings, and then from the Delta. Several of the tombs may be open to visitors (ask at the ticket office).

The most likely to be open is the **Tomb of Pabasa (#279)**, the steward to a Divine Votaress of Amun during the XXVI Dynasty. His tomb reflects the Saïte Dynasty obsession with the Old Kingdom, having a similar design to tombs at Saqqara. Its massive gateway leads into a pillared court with scenes of hunting, fishing and viticulture (note the bee-keeping scene on the central column). A funeral procession and the voyage to Abydos appear in the vestibule.

Also worth noting is the **Tomb of Kheru-ef (#192)**, a steward of Queen Tiy during the Amarna period. His scenes depict a Jubilee Festival, Tiy and Amenophis III, musicians, dancers and playful animals – as lyrical as those in Ramose's tomb (see p.408).

The Tombs of the Nobles

The **Tombs of the Nobles** are a study in contrasts to their royal counterparts. Whereas royalty favoured concealed tombs in secluded valleys, Theban nobles and high officials were ostentatiously interred in the limestone foothills overlooking the great funerary temples of their masters and the city across the river. The pharaohs' tombs were sealed and guarded; the nobles' were left open, for their descendants to make funerary offerings. Whereas royal tombs are filled with scenes of judgement and resurrection, the nobles' chosen artwork dwells on earthly life and its continuation in the hereafter. Given more freedom of expression, the artists excelled themselves with vivid **paintings** on stucco (the inferior limestone on this side of the hills militates against carved reliefs). One detail found in all these tombs is the blue lotus, which one Swedish Egyptologist reckons was a drug used for sexual rituals, containing bioflavonoid compounds similar to gingko extract.

The **tombs' layout** marks a further evolution in funerary architecture since the Middle Kingdom tombs of Beni Hassan. Most are entered via a courtyard, with a transverse hall preceding the burial shrine with its niche containing an effigy of the deceased (or statues of his entire family). Strictly speaking, they are tomb chapels rather than tombs, since the graves themselves lie at the bottom of a shaft (usually inaccessible).

Excluding the Asasif Tombs nearer Deir el-Bahri (see above), all the tombs open to visitors cluster around the ramshackle village of old Gurna, where they're divided into four groups (each requiring a separate ticket), namely: **Rekhmire and Sennofer**; **Ramose, Userhat and Khaemhat**; **Nakht and Menna**; and **Khonsu, Userhat and Benia**. The first two lie furthest west and back from the road; the next trio downhill towards the Ramesseum; and the last two sets of tombs to the northeast, closer to Deir el-Bahri. Though signposting has improved, the uneven, littered **site** is still confusing; with houses interposed between sunken tombs, enclosed by low walls – so you may welcome directions. The car park down the hill from Rekhmire's tomb is a good place to start.

As visiting all the tombs plus the museum would take two hours or so, most people limit themselves to a single group or the highlights from each (marked ★ in the accounts following). Unlike at the Valley of the Kings, the guards might hassle for *baksheesh* or even play tricks with the lighting, so having a flashlight definitely helps.

Gurna Discovery

En route to Rekhmire's tomb, the **Gurna Discovery** exhibition (daily except Tues 7am–noon & 2–5pm) relates how the village has changed over the centuries that it has been excavated by foreigners. Originally, the Gurnawis were Bedouin who moved up from the plain to dig for treasure; but as European scholars sought papyri, potshards and other items formerly discarded as worthless, tomb-robbing became a wholesale business. Conflict with the authorities deepened the Gurnawis' mistrust of outsiders; while the trade in antiquities was deplored by archeologists but covertly upheld by museums and collectors abroad. In modern times, the Gurnawis have been denied a basic civic amenity – piped water – lest it leak into the bedrock and damage the tombs; only the mosque and the German House are supplied, so women and girls carry pails uphill every day. Illustrated with photographs and copies of drawings by Robert Hay (the originals are in the British Library), the exhibition was organized by Caroline Simpson, a long-time resident, and people from Gurna, whose hopes and fears for the future of their village are expressed in the final section. There is no admission charge, but donations are appreciated; for information see ⓦ www.sepcom.demon.co.uk/Hay/main.html.

Tomb of Rekhmire (#100)*

The richly decorated tomb of **Rekhmire** casts light on statecraft and foreign policy under Tuthmosis III and Amenophis II, whom Rekhmire served as vizier. The badly damaged murals in its transverse hall show him collecting taxes from Upper **[a]** and Lower **[b]** Egypt, and inspecting temple workshops, charioteers and agricultural work **[c]**. Around the corner from his ancestors **[d]**, grapes are trod in large tubs and the juice is strained and stored in jars **[e]**.

TOMB OF REKHMIRE

N

0   2m

Along the rear wall are depicted a desert hunt **[f]** and a famous scene of Rekhmire receiving tributes from foreign lands **[g]**. Amongst the gifts shown are vases from Crete and the Aegean Islands (fourth row); a giraffe, monkeys and elephant tusks from Punt and Nubia (third row); and chariots and horses from Syria (second row).

Growing in height as it recedes towards the false door at the back, the long corridor is decorated with scenes of work and daily life. Slaves store grain in silos **[h]**, whence it was later disbursed as wages to armourers, carpenters, sculptors and other state-employed craftsmen **[i]**. An idealized banqueting scene with female musicians **[j]** merges into an afterworld with a lake and trees **[k]**. Also note Rekhmire's funeral procession and offerings to sustain him in the afterlife **[l]**.

Tomb of Sennofer (#96)

From Rekhmire's tomb, slog 50m uphill to the left to find another colourful tomb, in better condition. Entered by a low, twisting stairway, the tomb of **Sennofer** is known as the "Tomb of Vines" after the grapes and vines painted on the textured ceiling of the antechamber. As mayor of Thebes and overseer of Amun's estates under Amenophis II, Sennofer's responsibilities included local viticulture. The walls of the burial shrine depict his funeral procession (left), voyage to Abydos (back, right) and mummified sojourn with Anubis (right). Its square pillars bear images of Hathor, whose eyes follow you around the room; a small tree-goddess appears on the inner side of the rear left-hand pillar.

Tomb of Ramose (#55)*

Down a dirt road to the southeast lies the tomb of **Ramose**, who was vizier and governor of Thebes immediately before and after the Amarna revolution. His spacious tomb captures the moment of transition from Amun- to Aten-worship, featuring both classical and Amarna-style reliefs, the latter unfinished since Ramose followed Akhenaten to his new capital. Besides its superb reliefs, the tomb is notable for retaining its courtyard – originally a feature of all these tombs.

Along the entrance wall of its pillared hall are lovely carvings that reflect the mellowing of classicism during the reign of Amenophis III, Akhenaten's father. Predictable scenes of Ramose and his wife **[a]**, Amenophis III and Queen Tiy **[b]** making offerings come alive thanks to the exquisite rendering of the major figures, carried over to their feasting friends and relatives **[c]**. The sinuous sway-

TOMB OF RAMOSE

ing of mourners likewise imparts lyricism to the conventional, painted funerary scene **[d]**, where Ramose, wife and priests worship Osiris.

The onset of Aten-worship and the Amarna style is evident in the reliefs at the back, despite their battered condition. Those on the left **[e]** were carved before Amenophis IV changed his name to Akhenaten and espoused Aten-worship, so the pharaoh sits beneath a canopy with Maat, the goddess of truth, receiving flowers from Ramose. (At the far end, note the red grid and black outlined figures by which the artist transferred his design to the wall before relief-cutting took place.) However, the corresponding scene **[f]** depicts the pharaoh as Akhenaten, standing with Nefertiti at their palace window, bathed in the Aten's rays. Ramose is sketched in below, accepting their gift of a golden chain; his physiognomy is distinctly Amarnan, but rather less exaggerated than the royal couple's (see p.310).

By a quirk of Egyptian security, a low wall bars access to Ramose's inner shrine, but there is nothing at all to prevent one from venturing into a dark tunnel leading off the hall, which suddenly plummets into his grave, 15m below – beware.

Tomb of Userhat (#56)

Immediately south of Ramose's tomb lies that of **Userhat**, a royal scribe and tutor in the reign of Amenophis II. Although some of the figures were destroyed by early Christian hermits who occupied the shrine, what remains is freshly coloured, with unusual pink tones. The tomb is also interesting in that it's still illuminated by means of a mirror reflecting sunlight inside, just as it was when the artists decorated the tomb.

Along the entrance wall of the antechamber are scenes of wine-making, harvesting, herding and branding cattle, collecting grain for the royal

storehouse **[a]**, and the customary offerings scenes **[b]**. On the rear wall are reliefs of baking, assaying gold dust, and – lower down – a barber trimming customers beneath a tree **[c]**. The funerary feast scene **[d]** was extensively damaged by hermits, particularly the female figures. The inner hall contains paintings of Userhat hunting gazelles, hares and jackals from a chariot in the desert **[e]**; fowling and fishing amidst the reeds **[f]**; and funerary scenes **[g]**. In a niche at the end is a headless statue of the deceased's wife.

Tomb of Khaemhat (#57)

Next door is the tomb of **Khaemhat**, royal scribe and inspector of granaries under Amenophis III, which is reached via a forecourt off which two other tombs, now locked, once led. Flanking its doorway outside are battered reliefs of Khaemhat worshipping Re, and the complete set of instruments for the Opening of the Mouth ceremony (right). In the transverse antechamber with its red and black patterned ceiling, the best reliefs are on the left as you enter. Although Renenet the snake-headed harvest-goddess has almost vanished, a scene of grain boats docking at Thebes harbour is still visible nearer the niche containing statues of Khaemhat and Imhotep. In the bottom row to the left of the door into the corridor, Hathor breastfeeds a boy-king, surrounded by sacred cows.

Fishing, fowling and family scenes decorate the right-hand wall of the corridor, leading to a triple-niched chapel containing seated statues of Khaemhat and his family.

Tomb of Nakht (#52)*

Northeast of Ramose's tomb lies the burial place of **Nakht**, whose antechamber contains a small museum with drawings of the reliefs (which are covered in glass) and a replica of Nakht's funerary statue, which was lost at sea en route to America in 1917. Nakht was the overseer of Amun's vineyards and granaries under Tuthmosis IV, and the royal astronomer, but stargazing does not feature among the activities depicted in his tomb. The only decorated section is the transverse antechamber, whose ceiling is painted to resemble woven mats, with a *kherker* frieze running above the brilliantly coloured murals.

To one side, Nakht supervises the harvest in a scene replete with vivid details **[a]**. In the bottom register, one farmer fells a tree, while another swigs from a waterskin; of the two women gleaning in the row above, one is missing an arm. Beyond a stele relating Nakht's life **[b]** is the famous banqueting scene **[c]**, where sinuous dancers and a blind harpist entertain friends of the deceased, who sits beside his wife, Tawi, with a cat scoffing a fish beneath his chair; sadly, their figures have been erased.

The defacement of Nakht's image and Amun's name is usually ascribed to Amarna iconoclasm, but the gouging out of his eyes and throwing sticks in the hunting scene **[d]** suggests a personal animus. Happily, this has not extended to the images in the corner **[e]**, where peasants tread grapes in vats, and birds are caught in clap-nets and hung for curing (below). The plain inner chamber has a false door painted to resemble Aswan granite; and a deep shaft leading to the (inaccessible) burial chamber.

Tomb of Menna (#69)

More scenes of rural life decorate the nearby tomb of **Menna**, an XVIII Dynasty inspector of estates. Accompanied by his wife and daughter, Menna worships the sun in the entrance passage. In the left wing of the first chamber, he supervises field labour (notice the two girls pulling each other's hair, near the far end of the third row), feasts and makes offerings with his wife. Across the way they participate in ceremonies with Anubis, Osiris, Re and Hathor. Though chiefly decorated with mourning and burial scenes, the inner chamber also features a spot of hunting and fishing, vividly depicted on the right-hand wall. The niche at the end contains the legs of Menna's votive statue.

Notice the finely painted **Hadj scene** on the outside of the house near the tomb.

Tombs of Khonsu, Userhet and Benia

This trio of small tombs near those of Nakht and Menna was opened to the public in 1992. The themes are standard, with scenes of offerings, hunting, fishing and funerary rites. In the tomb of Userhet (not to be confused with the Userhat in tomb #56), the guard will produce a mummified head for *baksheesh*.

Khoka Tombs

Set apart from the others – accessible by a track leaving the main road opposite the El Sheikh Abd El Gurna alabaster workshop – the **Khoka** tombs were built for a trio of New Kingdom officials. Neferonpet (known as Kenro) was a treasury scribe; the tomb's inner chamber depicts him assessing deliveries of gold and food, and the work of sculptors and weavers. The golden-yellow, red and blue murals, the brightly patterned ceilings and the votive statues of the deceased and his wives (badly disfigured) are also characteristic of the tomb of Nefersekheru, next door. Here, the wives enjoy greater prominence, flanking Nefersekheru pictorially (to the right as you enter) and sculpturally (in niches), and known to posterity as Maatmou, Sekhemui and Nefertari. Their mummies were buried in a shaft off the rear corridor, which leads into the adjacent tomb of Dhutmosi (now inaccessible).

The Ramesseum

The **Ramesseum** or mortuary temple of Ramses II was built to awe the pharaoh's subjects, perpetuate his existence in the afterlife and forever link him to Amun-United-with-Eternity. Had it remained intact, the Ramesseum would doubtless match his great sun temple of Abu Simbel for monumental grandeur and unabashed self-glorification. But by siting it beside an earlier temple on land that was annually inundated, Ramses unwittingly ensured the ruination of his monument, whose toppled colossi would later mock his presumption, inspiring Shelley's sonnet *Ozymandias*:

Ramses II

I met a traveller from an antique land
Who said: Two vast and trunkless legs of stone
Stand in the desert ... Near them on the sand,
Half sunk, a shattered visage lies, whose frown,
And wrinkled lip, and sneer of cold command
Tell that its sculptor well those passions read
Which yet survive, stamped on these lifeless things,
The hand which mocked them, and the heart that fed.
On the pedestal these words appear:
'My name is Ozymandias, King of Kings:
Look upon my works ye Mighty, and despair!'
Nothing beside remains. Round the decay
Of that colossal wreck, boundless and bare
The lone and level sands stretch far away.

Nineteenth-century writers knew the ruins as the *Memnonium*. Their present name only caught on late in the nineteenth century, by which time the Ramesseum had been plundered for statuary – not least the seven-ton head of one of its fallen colossi, now in the British Museum. Yet its devastation lends romance to the conventional architecture, infusing it with the pathos that moved Harriet Martineau to muse how "violence inconceivable to us has been used to destroy what art inconceivable to us had erected". As bus parties seldom intrude, the Ramesseum seems peaceful, its tranquillity enhanced by a group of trees near the First Pylon, which offer a pleasant contrast to the desolation of other sites in the Necropolis. Half an hour suffices to see the famous colossi and the best reliefs, but you may care to linger. The nearby **Ramesseum Rest-house** sells cold drinks and hot meals, and has toilets.

Exploring the Ramesseum

Like other mortuary temples in the Theban Necropolis, the Ramesseum faces towards the Nile, and was originally entered via its **First Pylon**. Wrecked by the earthquake that felled the colossi, the pylon stands marooned in the scrub beyond a rubble-strewn depression that used to be the **First Court**. In 1983, Rohl found evidence for his "New Chronology" in an inscription on a block balanced atop the pylon, asserting that during the eighth year of his reign, Ramses plundered a city named "Shalem", which Rohl thinks was Jerusalem in the time of King Solomon (see p.783).

Visitors enter the temple via the northern flank of its **Second Court**, to be confronted by the awesome **fallen colossus of Ramses II**. This seated megalith once towered over the stairs from the first into the second court [a]; over 18m tall and weighing about 1000 tons, it was only surpassed by the Colossi of Memnon thanks to their pedestals. When it toppled some time after the first century AD, its upper half smashed through the Second Pylon into the court, where its head and torso lie today [b], measuring 7m across the shoulders; the cartouche on its bicep reads: "Ruler of Rulers". In the lower court are other fragments, notably feet and hands. As Dean Stanley wrote in 1852, "You sit on his breast and look at the Osiride statues which support the porticos of the temple, and they seem pygmies before him".

Behind the chunky Osirian pillars rises what's left of the **Second Pylon**, whose inner face bears scenes from the second Battle of Qadesh, surmounted by a register depicting the festival of the harvest-god Min [c]. At the far end of the second courtyard, where three stairways rise to meet a colonnaded portico, is a **smaller fallen colossus** of Ramses [d], more fragmented, though its face has suffered merely nasal damage. Originally there were two colossi, but the other – dubbed the "Young Memnon" – was acquired for Britain in 1816 by Belzoni. The name "Ozymandias" arose from the ancient Greeks' misreading of one of the king's many titles, *User-Maat-Re*.

Beyond here, the core of the Ramesseum is substantially intact. The first set of reliefs worth noting occurs on the front wall of the **portico**, between the central and left-hand doorways [e]. Above a bottom row depicting eleven of his sons, Ramses appears with Atum and Mont (who holds the hieroglyph for "life" to his nose), and kneels before the Theban Triad (right) while Thoth inscribes his name on a palm frond (centre). The top register shows him sacrificing to Ptah and making offerings to an ithyphallic Min.

The **Great Hypostyle Hall** had 48 columns, of which 29 are still standing. The taller ones flanking the central aisle have papyrus shafts and turquoise, yellow and white lotus capitals, supporting a raised section of roof; while the lower side columns have papyrus-bud capitals. On the wall as you come in, reliefs depict Egyptian troops storming the Hittite city of Dapur, using shields to protect themselves from arrows and stones [f]. At the back of the hall, incised reliefs [g] show lion-headed Sekhmet (far right) presenting Ramses to an enthroned Amun, who gives him the breath of eternal life from an *ankh*; along the bottom are depicted some of the king's hundred sons. Notice the names of

THE RAMESSEUM

Sanctuaries

Magazines

k

i   j

h

g

Great Hypostyle Hall

Temple
of Tuya

► *Deir el-Bahri*

f

e

Ramesseum
Resthouse

N

Second Court

d

b

c

Second Pylon

a

STATUES & RELIEFS (*)

Base of Ramses' Colossus	**a**
Head & torso of Colossus	**b**
Battle of Qadesh & Min festival *	**c**
Smaller fallen Colossus	**d**
Ramses before the gods *	**e**
Storming of Dapur *	**f**
Ramses receiving eternal life from Amun *	**g**
Belzoni & Salt	**h**
Amun's barque *	**i**
Barques of Mut and Khonsu *	**j**
Ramses with Sheshat, Atum & Thoth *	**k**

Royal
Palace

First Court

0	Metres	20

First Pylon

the treasure-hunter Belzoni and his patron, the British Consul Henry Salt, carved on the right-hand door jamb **[h]**.

Beyond this lie two **smaller Hypostyle Halls**. The first retains its astronomical ceiling, featuring the oldest known twelve-month calendar (whether lunar or solar months is debatable). Notice the barques of Amun, Mut and Khonsu (**[i]** & **[j]**), and the scene of Ramses beneath the persea tree with

Atum, Sheshat and Thoth **[k]**. "Pukler Muskau" is the oddest of the many names scrawled on the columns over millennia. The ruined **sanctuaries** were presumably dedicated to Amun, Ramses the god and his glorious ancestors, for the edifice stood alongside an earlier temple of Seti I, which itself contained shrines to Seti and his father, Ramses I, both of whom were linked to Amun. Its scant remains lie to the northeast of the portico and Hypostyle Hall.

The whole complex is surrounded by mud-brick **magazines** that once covered about three times the area of the temple and included workshops, storerooms and servants' quarters, that has survived far better than the **royal palace** and **Temple of Tuya** that once adjoined the temple, of which only stumps of walls and columns remain.

Other mortuary temples

In ancient times, the Ramesseum was one of half a dozen mortuary temples ranged along the edge of the flood plain with no regard for chronological order. The **Temple of Merneptah**, built by Ramses' thirteenth or fourteenth son, lies just south of the Ramesseum, intruding onto the edges of, and reusing masonry from, the vast complex of Amenophis III that once spread to the Colossi of Memnon. Recently opened to the public after thirty years' study and restoration by Swiss Egyptologists, the site consists of fragments and portions of the temple, placed in their original positions and supported by modern stonework. The entrance is reached by walking past the *Marsam Hotel*, and represents the original position of the first pylon. An informative **museum** exhibits stone-carvings from the site (forty percent of them originally belonging to Amenophis III's temple or Deir el-Bahri) and records its excavation (1971–2001). Further in to the left stands a copy of the famous **Israel Stele** also replicated at Karnak, which features the earliest reference to Israel outside of the Bible (see p.375). Guards can unlock another section, containing the remains of a monumental gateway from Amenophis III's temple, clearly reused to build Merneptah's edifice. This site is not yet listed at the west bank ticket office, but you can obtain a **ticket** (£E20, student £E10) there.

While nothing remains of the temples of Tuthmosis IV, Tuthmosis II, Ay and Horemheb that once extended towards Medinet Habu, there is a substantial **Temple of Seti I** near the village of Gurna Ta'rif (accessible by pick-ups from old Gurna or Gezira). The site is still being excavated by German Egyptologists, but you can enter the temple, with its crude reliefs dedicated to Amun, Seti and Ramses I. Again, you must buy a ticket in advance at the main ticket office.

Deir el-Medina: the Workers' Village

Deir el-Medina, the **Workers' Village**, housed the masons, painters and sculptors who created the royal tombs in the Valley of the Kings. Because many were literate and left records on papyrus or *ostracae*, we know such details as who feuded with whom, their sex lives and labour disputes. As state employees, they were supposed to receive fortnightly supplies of wheat, dried meat and fish, onions, pulses and beer, corresponding in value to the price of a bull. When these failed to arrive (as often happened during the ramshackle XX Dynasty), the workers downed tools, staged sit-ins at Medinet Habu, or demonstrated in Luxor.

Normally they worked an eight-hour day, sleeping in huts near the tombs during their ten-day shift before returning to their families at Deir el-Medina – a pattern followed over generations, as most occupations were hereditary. In

Sex in ancient Egypt

While the pharaohs are known to have married their sisters, had multiple wives and dozens of concubines, our knowledge of the sex lives of the lower classes largely depends on murals, *ostracae* and papyri found at Deir el-Medina in the 1900s. Hushed up by prudish scholars of the time, this evidence has been re-examined by Professor Lynn Kersell of Columbia University, and suggests that sexual mores were very different from today. Apparently, the ancient Egyptians had no concept of illegitimacy or virginity, and regarded fertility as so paramount that female servants would bear a child for the family if the wife proved infertile. There is also the recorded case of a serial adulterer who slept with many wives in Deir el-Medina, but went unpunished; nowadays, such behavior would incur death under the unofficial "honour code" of Upper Egypt. Yet even liberals would draw a line at some of the practices that Kersell believes were commonplace; one *ostraca* seems to show children assisting their parents in making love.

their spare time craftsmen worked for private clients or collaborated on their own tombs, built beneath man-size pyramids. Their own murals appropriated imagery from royal and noble tombs, which was parodied in the famous *Satirical Papyrus*, showing animals judging souls, collecting taxes and playing *senet,* and humans having sex (see box above).

Anyone taking the donkey trail to the Valley of the Kings can get a fine **overview** of the village from the hillside – but the real attraction is its tombs. Visitors should bear in mind that the "Deir el-Medina" **ticket** (#11) doesn't cover the tomb of Peshedu, which needs a separate ticket (#12) – both are available only from the main ticket office. You can easily walk to Deir el-Medina from the main road; it's also feasible to do so from the Valley of the Queens or Medinet Habu.

The nearest pyramid to the entrance marks the **Tomb of Sennedjem** (or Sennutem), whose vaulted burial chamber is reached by steep flights of steps and two antechambers. Its colourful murals feature ithyphallic baboons (right end wall), Osiris and the Fields of Yaru, and Anubis ministering to Sennedjem's mummy (facing wall, far left). The **Tomb of Ankherha** (#359) has a similar design, with an antechamber whose ceiling is decorated with intricate abstract patterns. On the left wall of the burial chamber, Ankherha appears with Wepwawet and Khepri; Anubis breathes life into his mummy; his wife adores Horus as a falcon; and his naked daughters make libations. In the **Tomb of Peshedu** (#3), one can see the deceased praying beneath the tree of regeneration, below which flow the waters of the *Amuntit*, the "Hidden Region" where souls were judged. Unusually for Deir el-Medina, the **Tomb of Iphy** (#217) eschews ceremonial scenes and deities for tableaux from everyday life.

Just north of the village stands a **Ptolemaic temple** dedicated to Maat and Hathor, whose head adorns the pillars between the outer court and naos. Each of its three shrines is decorated with scenes from the *Book of the Dead*; near the back of the left-hand shrine, a hyena-like "Devourer of Souls" awaits those who fail the Judgement of Osiris. Ancient Greek graffiti is scrawled around the temple's entrance. Early in the Christian era, the temple and the workers' village were occupied by monks – hence the site's Arabic name of *Deir el-Medina* (Monastery of the Town).

The Valley of the Queens

The **Valley of the Queens** is something of a misnomer, for it also contains the tombs of high officials (who were interred here long before the first queen was buried in this valley during the XIX Dynasty) and royal children. Polygamy and concubinage produced huge broods whose blood lines were further entangled by incestuous marriages between crown princes and their sisters, in emulation of Osiris and Isis. Princes were educated by priests and scribes, taught swimming, riding and shooting by officers, and finally apprenticed to military commands around the age of twelve. Less is known about the schooling of princesses, but several queens were evidently well versed in statecraft and architecture.

Originally named the "Place of Beauty", but now known in Arabic as *Biban el-Harem* (Gates of the Harem), the valley contains nearly eighty tombs, most of which are uninscribed and simple in plan. Although the finest murals rival those in the Valley of the Kings for artistry, many have been corroded by salt deposits, or badly vandalized.

Tomb of Queen Nefertari (#66)

Queen Nefertari was the principal wife of Ramses II, with whom she had achieved almost equal status by the end of his reign. Her ascendancy was signified by the appearance of her image beside the king's on the pylon of Luxor Temple; the dedication of a shrine within the Ramesseum to Nefertari and the Queen Mother, Tuya; and finally by a massive temple at Abu Simbel, which identifies her with the goddess Hathor. After Ramses' death, Nefertari may have retired to a palace near the Fayoum or died herself, for no more is heard of her.

Her **tomb**, the most illustrious in the valley, was found in 1904 by an Italian archeologist, Ernesto Schiaparelli. Its extreme fragility and the damage caused by its plaster dehydrating, and salt crystals forming beneath its paintings, kept the tomb closed for decades while a solution was debated; eventually the EAO and the Getty Conservation Institute began restoration in 1986. It took five years and US$6 million to clean the murals and re-adhere paint and stucco to the walls, without altering or adding any colours. To avoid the humidity that causes salt crystallization, only 150 visitors a day are allowed in ten at a time, for exactly ten minutes, for £E100 a head. Assuming you're willing to spend that much, **tickets** go on sale at 6.30am, at the ticket office beside the Gurna road. Buying a ticket is less chaotic than it used to be – when touts fought to buy all the tickets and re-sold them to travel agencies, or sometimes in the Valley of the Queens – as the tourist police are keeping tighter controls, but individual travellers still need to come early. The tomb is **open** from 7.30am in summer and 8.30am in winter until noon.

Descending a stairway and passing beneath a lintel bearing Nefertari's titles and a winged sun-disc flanked by Isis and Nephthys, you enter a hall ablaze with murals. On either side are extracts from the *Book of Gates*, and Nefertari before Osiris. Notice the picture of the queen playing a board game, above the offerings benches. Across the hall, two projecting sections feature Anubis and Neith, Osiris and Selket, while the sons of Horus appear over the portal of a corridor slanting off towards the burial chamber. At the entrance to the latter, Nefertari makes burnt offerings to Amun and Isis; inside she venerates the *Book of Gates* to ensure her safe passage through the underworld, by formulae depicted on the far wall. She wears a sheer white gown and a golden vulture headdress with feathered plumes. The predominant colours are scarlet, black and gold, with touches of dark green.

Tomb of Amunhirkhepshef (#55)

If you can't afford to see Nefertari's tomb, the next best one belongs to **Amunhirkhepshef**, a son of Ramses III who accompanied his father on campaigns and perhaps died in battle at the age of nine. He is shown wearing the royal sidelock of youth, in lustrous murals where Ramses conducts him through funerary rituals, past the Keepers of the Gates, to an unfinished burial chamber containing a granite sarcophagus. A glass case displays a mummified foetus that his mother aborted through grief at Amunhirkhepshef's death, and entombed with her son.

Tomb of Queen Titi (#52)

Sited along the well-trodden route to Amunhirkhepshef's tomb, this cruciform structure was commissioned by **Queen Titi**, wife of one of the Ramessid pharaohs of the XX Dynasty. A winged Maat kneels in the corridor (where Titi appears before Thoth, Ptah and the sons of Horus) and guards the entrance to the burial chamber with Neith (left) and Selket (right).

The burial chamber itself boasts jackal, lion and baboon guardians, plus three side chambers, the finest being the one to your right. Here, Hathor emerges from between the mountains of east and west in her bovine form, while the tree-goddess pours Nile water to rejuvenate Titi, who reposes on a cushion across the room. Sadly, most of these murals are faded or damaged.

Tomb of Prince Khaemweset (#44)

Relatively few people visit this colourfully painted tomb, which lies uphill. **Prince Khaemweset** was one of several sons of Ramses III who died in a small-pox epidemic, and the murals in his tomb give precedence to images of Ramses, making offerings in the entrance corridor and worshipping funerary deities in the side chambers. In the second corridor, decorated with the *Book of Gates*, Ramses leads Khaemweset past the fearsome guardians of the Netherworld to the Fields of Yaru; bearing witness for him before Osiris and Horus in the burial chamber. Notice the four sons of Horus on the lotus blossom.

Medinet Habu

Medinet Habu (Habu's Town) is the Arabic name for the gigantic **Mortuary Temple of Ramses III**, a structure second only to Karnak in size and complexity, and better preserved in its entirety. Modelled on the Ramesseum of his illustrious ancestor, Ramses II, this XX Dynasty extravaganza deserves more attention than it usually gets, being the last stop on most tourists' itineraries. The site itself was hallowed long before Ramses erected his "House of Millions of Years" and is still imbued with magical significance by the local *fellaheen*. Its massive brick enclosure walls sheltered the entire population of Thebes during the Libyan invasions of the late XX Dynasty and for centuries afterwards protected the Coptic town of

Ramses III

Djeme, built within the great temple. You can get a fine **overview** of Medinet Habu from the top of the mound of earth near the southeast corner, or by drifting low over the temple in a hot-air balloon (see p.363).

The temple precincts

The entire complex was originally surrounded by **enclosure walls**, sections of which rise at intervals from the plain. Its front facade is quite asymmetrical,

MEDINET HABU

Enclosure Wall

Sanctuaries

t

n   o
         p

        Chapels

m   Hypostyle
     Hall

k

     Second
j   Court

Second Pylon

     h   i

g   First
     Court

s   e   f

First Pylon

c   d

Nilometer

Chapels of the
Votaresses
          b

Migdol Gate   Small
& Harem   Temple   Sacred
                   a   Lake

Palace

Enclosure Wall

Enclosure Wall

r

q

l

Amun Temple

Mound

Ptolomaic
Pylon

N

Maratonga Café

Habou Hotel

Ticket office

with a jutting **Ptolemaic Pylon** whose winged sun-disc glows with colour since its recent restoration, overshadowing the entrance to the temple precincts. This **Migdol Gate** is named after the Syrian fortress that so impressed Ramses with its lofty gatehouse that he built one for his own temple, and often relaxed with his **harem** in a suite above the gate, decorated with reliefs of dancers in slinky lingerie. As social conditions worsened during the latter years of his reign, a secondary wife, Tiy, hatched a harem conspiracy to murder him during the Optet festival, so that her son, Pentwere, could inherit – but the conspirators were discovered and forced to commit suicide, and Ramses' chosen heir eventually succeeded him. The two statues of Sekhmet by the gate's entrance may have served to transmit the prayers of pilgrims to Amun, who "dwelt" within the temple.

North of here stands a **Small Temple**, reputedly sited where the primeval mound arose from the waters of Chaos, preceding the creator-god Re-Atum of the Hermopolitan Ogdoad. The existing structure was built and partly decorated by Hatshepsut, whose cartouches and images were erased by Tuthmosis III. Akhenaten did likewise to those of Amun, but Horemheb and Seti replaced them. Some defaced reliefs **[a]** show Tuthmosis presiding over the foundation ceremonies, "stretching the cord" before the goddess Seshat, "scattering the gypsum" and then "hacking the earth" before a priapic Min.

Wheras the Small Temple antedates Ramses' work by three centuries, the **Chapels of the Votaresses** are Late Period additions. Several date from the XXV Dynasty of Nubian kings, who appointed these high priestesses of Amun and de facto governors of Thebes. The best reliefs are in the forecourt **[b]** and shrine of Amenirdis, sister of King Shabaka, whose alabaster funerary statue is now in the Cairo Museum. Ironically, these chapels remained objects of veneration long after Ramses' temple had been abandoned.

In the right-hand corner of the enclosure are the remains of a **Sacred Lake** where childless local women came to bathe at night and pray to Isis for conception. Behind this lies a ruined **Nilometer**, once fed by a canal from the river. Originally, this whole area was a garden.

Entering the Mortuary Temple of Ramses III

Like Deir el-Bahri and the Ramesseum, this mortuary temple was a focus for the pharaoh's cult, linking him to Amun-United-with-Eternity. The effigies of Amun, Mut and Khonsu paid an annual visit during the Festival of the Valley, while other deities permanently resided in its shrines. Ramses himself often dwelt in the adjacent palace, his Libyan and Sardinian bodyguard billeted nearby. Aside from its lack of freestanding colossi, the sandstone temple gives a good idea of how the Ramesseum must have looked before it collapsed.

Had it not lost its cornice and one corner, the **First Pylon** would match Luxor Temple's in size. For *baksheesh*, a guard may unlock a stairway to the top, which offers a panoramic view of the temple, Theban Hills and Nile Valley. Reliefs on the outer walls (copied from the Ramesseum) show Ramses smiting Nubians **[c]** and Syrians **[d]**, though he never warred with either. Those on the inner wall relate genuine campaigns with Ramessid hyperbole. An outsized Ramses scatters hordes of Libyans in his chariot **[e]**. Afterwards, scribes tally the severed hands and genitals of dead foes (third row from the bottom) **[f]**.

Until the nineteenth century, the ruined houses of Coptic Djeme filled the **First Court**, now cleared to reveal its flanking columns. Those on the right bear chunky Osiride statues of the king, attended by knee-high queens. The other side of the court abuts the royal palace (now ruined and entered from outside). In the middle of this wall was a Window of Appearances **[g]** flanked by reliefs of prisoners' heads, whence the king rewarded loyal commanders with golden collars. Yet more scenes of triumph cover the outside of the **Second Pylon**, where Ramses leads six rows of prisoners to Amun and Mut **[h]** (those in the third row are Philistines) and a long inscription lauds his victories in Asia Minor **[i]**. The winged cobras and sun-discs on the ceiling of the pylon's gateway are still coloured.

Halls and sanctuaries

During Coptic times most of the Osiride pillars were removed to make room for a church, and a thick layer of mud was plastered over the reliefs in the **Second Court**. Now uncovered, these depict the annual festivals of Min **[j]** and Sokar **[k]**, with processions of priests and dancers accompanying the royal palanquin, the original colouring still intact. Elsewhere, the events of Ramses' fifth regnal year are related in a long text lower down the wall **[l]**.

The now-roofless **Hypostyle Hall**, beyond, once had a raised central aisle like the Great Hall at Karnak, and still has some brightly coloured pillars at the back. To the right lie five **chapels** dedicated to Ramses, his XIX Dynasty namesake, Ptah, Osiris and Sokar. On the opposite side are several (locked) treasure chambers whose reliefs show the weighing of myrrh, gold, lapis lazuli and other valuables bestowed upon the temple **[m]** – also visible on the outer walls.

Beyond this lie two **smaller halls** with rooms leading off. To the left of the first hall is the funerary chamber of Ramses III **[n]**, where Thoth inscribes his name on the sacred tree of Heliopolis. The other side – open to the sky – featured an altar to Re. On the lintels that once supported the roof **[o]**, Ramses and several baboons worship Re's barque. The central aisle of the next hall is flanked by statues of Ramses with Maat or Thoth. At the back are three **sanctuaries** dedicated to the Theban Triad of Mut (left), Amun (centre) and Khonsu (right). The false door behind the central one was for the use of Ramses' *ka*.

Along the outer walls

Some of the best reliefs at Medinet Habu are on the **outer walls** of the temple, involving a fair slog over broken ground. As most are quite faint, they're best viewed early or late in the day, when shadows reveal details obscured at midday. The famous **battle reliefs of Ramses II** run along the temple's northern wall, starting from the back. Although you'll encounter the last or middle scenes first, we've listed them in chronological order, as Ramses intended them to be seen. The first section **[p]** depicts the invasion of land-hungry Libyans, early in his reign. In the vanguard of the battle are Ramses, a lion, and the standard of Amun. Afterwards, scribes count limbs and genitals to assess each soldier's reward in gold or land. Yet despite this victory, Ramses was soon beleaguered on two fronts, as the Libyans joined with the Sea Peoples (Sardinians, Philistines and Cretans) in a concerted invasion of the Nile Delta. A giant Ramses fires arrows into a melee of grappling ships, in the only Egyptian relief of a sea battle **[q]**. A third invasion by the Libyans **[r]** was also thwarted, but their descendants would eventually triumph and rule Egypt as the XXIII and XXIV dynasties.

On the other side of the temple behind the First Pylon is a dramatic relief of Ramses hunting antelopes in the desert and impaling wild bulls in a marsh **[s]**, near a ruined **Palace** where he resided during visits. A calendar of festivals appears at the far end of the temple **[t]**, which is surrounded on three sides by mud-brick **storehouses**, eroded into worm-like shapes.

Other sites on the west bank

The village of **NAG LOHLAH** beside the temple will be familiar to readers of Richard Critchfield's *Shahhat* as the birthplace of its eponymous hero and the irascible Hagg Ali, owner of the *Habou Hotel* (which still exists, though the Hagg is deceased). Most families have one foot in tourism and the other in farming, so that one finances the other as fortune allows. While Medinet Habu brings customers to their doorsteps – the *Maratonga Café* is ideal for cooling off – few visitors realise there's also an **Amun Temple** in someone's backyard (no set hours; admission free). Though small and knocked about, its reliefs are colourful, particulary the white background that has faded in other temples.

If it's not too hot, the Monastery of St Tawdros in the desert beyond Medinet Habu makes an interesting excursion. You can walk there in about 20 minutes, or cycle; even better, go riding in time for sunset. Be sure to cover your head and bring plenty of water; the unpaved track from Medinet Habu to the French House is easy going, but has no shade at all.

Monastery of St Tawdros

Roughly 200m off the track, into the desert, the **Monastery of St Tawdros** is easily identified by its beehive domes. Pharaonic, Greek and Roman masonry is incorporated into the low-vaulted church, whose shrines are dedicated to the Coptic martyrs Tawdros, Elkladius and Foktor. Tawdros (295–306 AD) was a leader in the Roman army before his conversion to Christianity, hence the monastery's alternative name, *El Muharrib* (The Warrior). The day of his martyrdom (January 20) and Easter see crowds of Copts descending on the monastery, but at other times the nuns who live there receive few visitors and seem pleased if anyone rings the bell.

Malqata

Further on, the **French House** stands guard over the scant **remains of Malqata**. This legendary pleasure palace built by Amenophis III had an artificial harbour linked to the Nile, for the royal family to arrive on its barge, *Aten Gleams*. Today the only visible remains are a depression flanked by parallel mounds and low foundation walls, but archeologists from Waseda University have analyzed thousands of flakes of paint and stucco, to visually reconstruct the paintings on the walls and ceilings of the king's bedroom and harem chambers (see ⓦwww.waseda.ac.jp/projects/egypt).

Riziq

Travelling further afield is difficult, for police checkpoints seldom let tourists stray outside the security zone surrounding the Necropolis. However, many of the service taxis that carry pilgrims from Gezira to the **Moulid of St George** in the town of **RIZIQ** (also known as Razagat) – 15km south – travel by a desert track that avoids the checkpoints. Attended by Copts and Muslims alike, the moulid is certainly not for the squeamish, as the circumcision of infants and the slaughter of animals play a major role in events. Held in and around the town's **Monastery of St George** (*Mari Girgis*), it lasts for nearly a week, climaxing on November 11. Otherwise, the town is the start of the **road to Kharga Oasis** that was opened with much fanfare in the mid-1990s but has yet to realize its potential, as there's no water or petrol en route and tourists are forbidden to use it to reach Kharga (though they can use it to travel from Kharga to Luxor, if they get a permit first).

Esna

Small-town life and ancient stone are boldly juxtaposed at **ESNA**, where a huge pit in the centre of town exposes part of the **Temple of Khnum**. Some visitors are disappointed by what they find: the only part to have been excavated is the Hypostyle Hall, whose somewhat inferior reliefs detract from the forest of columns and lofty astronomical ceiling. That said, Esna is worth a stopover en route to the fabulous **temple at Edfu** if you can arrange it, but unless you care to visit the early Saturday morning **animal market**, there's no reason to linger after seeing the temple, which takes less than an hour.

Visible just north of Esna are two **barrages** that act as bridges over the Nile. The nearest was built by the British in 1906 as part of a grand scheme to tame the Nile, with barrages at four points along its length. In the 1990s, the river was further exploited by an Italian-built hydroelectric barrage, known to locals as the "Electricity Bridge". Both barrages have **locks** to allow vessels to pass through, while trucks and carts trundle across the top. Now that cruise boats no longer moor on the Esna's Corniche for passengers to visit the temple, salesmen throw their wares on to the decks for sunbathing tourists to inspect and hope that the cash doesn't fall in the water.

For overland travellers, Esna is the "border" between the Qena and Aswan governorates, whose respective **police** forces pass over the responsibility for escorting convoys here (hence the delay). Their reaction to independent travellers arriving in their midst or wanting to leave is hard to predict. It may depend on which direction you're travelling in, since Esna's cops are more concerned with foreigners on their own territory than tourists entering the Aswan governorate.

If they make you wait for a convoy, it's diverting to read Gustave Flaubert's account of the courtesan Kuchuk Hanem entertaining him at her home in Esna by dancing "The Bee" (see "Books" in Contexts).

Practicalities

Esna lies on the west bank of the Nile 54km south of Luxor and 155km north of Aswan. Alas for the local economy, nowadays tourism largely bypasses Esna, as **cruise boats** merely pass through the locks and travellers on **feluccas** from Aswan disembark 30km short of the town to catch taxis directly to Luxor. Such visitors as there are usually arrive in convoys from Luxor or Aswan, having clubbed together to hire a **private taxi** for a day excursion to Esna and Edfu for about £E100–150, or £E180–120 (£E230–250 in a larger vehicle) for a longer trip that includes **Kom Ombo** (see p.429).

Getting there by **train** is awkward, as the station is on the east bank of the Nile, far from the temple, and not all trains stop at Esna anyway. **Buses** are handier, with six a day from Luxor and Aswan (£E3), which drop you in the centre of town, just under 1km from the temple. You're unlikely to be able to reach Esna by **service taxi** from Luxor or Aswan, but people sometimes manage it from Edfu or Kom Ombo. The taxi depot is situated around the curve of the canal from the bus station, but passengers are often dropped off on the main thoroughfare into the centre, where *caleche* drivers wait for customers, asking £E5 each way for the ten-minute drive to the temple.

To reach the temple on foot, you can either follow the Corniche south past the empty cruiser berths, or surrender yourself to the flow of the crowd through the souk, until you reach the sandbagged **police** station. Backtrack one block and turn right down a side street, which should bring you out by the temple. Another advantage of the riverside route is that it takes you past some old *mashrabiya* houses, a **bank** (daily except Fri 8.30am–2pm; during Ramadan 10am–1.30pm) and a **post office** (daily except Fri 7am–2pm). The **tourist police** are near the temple ticket booth, further down the Corniche.

With Luxor so close, there's no reason to stay in Esna, even if you could tolerate the grimy *El-Haramin* (☏095/400-340; ❶), Esna's only **hotel**, 800m past a café near the cruise berths, and a humbler place on the corner by the temple, serving **meals**. Street food is sold in the souk.

The Temple of Khnum

When Amelia Edwards visited Esna, the **Temple of Khnum** (daily: Oct–May 6am–5.30pm; June–Sept 6am–6.30pm; £E12) was "buried to the chin in the accumulated rubbish of a score of centuries" and built over with houses. To minimize their destruction, only a portion was excavated in the 1860s. Now 10m below ground level, the temple resembles a pharaonic Fort Knox: its boxy mass fronted by six columns rising from a screen, the open space above them covered with wire mesh to discourage nesting birds. **Tickets** are sold at the riverside kiosk beyond the covered tourist bazaar, which runs between the temple and the river, five minutes' walk from the souk.

A Ptolemaic-Roman replacement for a much older structure dedicated to the ram-headed creator-god of ancient myth, the temple faced eastwards and probably rivalled Edfu's for size. Since what you see is merely the Roman section (dating from the first century AD), the **facade** bears the cartouches

of Claudius **[a]**, Titus **[b]** and Vespasian **[c]**, and the battered sun-disc above

---

Khnum and Hapy

In Upper Egypt, **Khnum** was originally the ram-headed creator-god who moulded man on a potter's wheel, and the guardian of the Nile's source (which myth assigned to the caves just beyond the First Cataract, although the ancient Egyptians must have known better).

Later, however, Khnum was demoted to an underling of Amun-Re and shared his role as river deity with **Hapy**, god of the Nile in flood, who was also believed to dwell in an island cavern near the First Cataract. Shown with a blue-green body and a female breast, wearing a crown of lotus or sedge (the heraldic plants of Upper and Lower Egypt), he should not be confused with Horus's son, Hapi, the ape-headed deity of canopic jars.

Hapy

the entrance is flanked by votive inscriptions to these emperors.

Entering the lofty **Hypostyle Hall**, your eyes are drawn upwards by a forest of columns that bud and flower in variegated capitals. Their shafts are covered with festival texts (now defaced) or hieroglyphs in the form of crocodiles **[d]** or rams **[e]**. One is a *Hymn of Creation* that acknowledges Khnum as the creator of all, even foreigners: "All are formed on his potter's wheel, their speech different in every region . . . but the lord of the wheel is their father too …"

The hall's **astronomical ceiling** rivals Dendara's for finesse and complexity, but gloom, soot and distemper render much indiscernible. However, the zodiac register **[f]** visibly crawls with two-headed snakes, winged dogs and other creatures. Notice the pregnant hippo-goddess Tweri (whom the Greeks called Thoeris), and the scorpion in the next aisle **[g]**. Registers on the walls below show Septimus Severus, Caracalla and Geta before the gods.

The last Roman emperor mentioned is Decius **[h]**, whose persecution of Christians (249–51) anticipated the "Era of Martyrs" under Diocletian. Further along **[i]** is the cartouche of Ptolemy VI Philometor (Mother Lover), whose father began the construction of Esna temple. To the right of the portal, Decius makes offerings to Khnum, including a potter's wheel **[j]**. The liveliest reliefs are near the foot of the northern wall **[k]**, where Khnum, Horus and Emperor Commodus net fish and malignant spirits. To the left of this tableau stands an ibis-headed Thoth; to the right, Sheshat, goddess of writing. Around the outer walls of the temple are texts dedicated to Marcus Aurelius **[l]** and stiffly executed scenes of Titus, Domitian and Trajan smiting Egypt's foes before the gods **[m and n]**. Several blocks from an early Christian church lie in front of the temple.

Edfu and around

The provincial town of **EDFU** boasts the best-preserved **cult temple** in Egypt, dedicated to the falcon-headed god **Horus** (see p.427). Though actually built in the Ptolemaic era, this mammoth edifice respects all the canons of pharaonic architecture, giving an excellent idea of how most temples once looked. In terms of sheer monumental grandeur, it ranks alongside Karnak and Deir el-Bahri as one of the finest sites in the Nile Valley. A "must see" for backpackers and package tourists alike – on every cruise boat or felucca itinerary – it has saved Edfu from the fate of Esna, even if tourism is well down on previous years.

The same can't be said of other sites, which had few visitors even before travel restrictions made getting there more difficult, but if deserted ruins are your thing, **El-Kab** fits the bill; **Silsilah** makes an interesting stopover on felucca journeys between Aswan and Edfu; and **Kom al-Ahmar** deserves a mention even if visits aren't permitted.

Edfu practicalities

Situated on the west bank of the Nile, roughly equidistant from Luxor (115km) and Aswan (105km) and 65km north of Kom Ombo, Edfu is most easily reached by **taxi** in a **convoy**. While foreigners remain barred from using service taxis, the only other way of getting there is by bus or train. Awkwardly, the **train** station is on the east bank of the Nile, 4km from the temple, and **buses** travelling between Aswan and Luxor either drop passengers there or on the highway, from where you'll need to catch a covered pick-up to the bridge and then another into town (each costs 25pt), or rent one for the entire journey to the main square, five minutes' walk from the temple.

Arriving by river is a different story, as **cruise boats** moor far from the temple, to be met by *caleches*. Since a branch of the Brooke Hospital was set up in Edfu, drivers have stopped whipping their horses to get there and back as fast as possible. The ride costs £E10-15, depending on your bargaining skills. **Feluccas** are also moored away from the centre, so their passengers may have to use *caleches* too.

Sharia al-Maglis, Edfu's main street, leads past a **police station** and a **bank** (Mon–Thurs & Sun 8.30am–2pm) to a circular junction named **Temple Square**. Further along, the temple lies off the tourist bazaar; the **tourist police** are based at the site entrance. Edfu's fruit and vegetable souk occupies an unpaved area of Tahrir and Gumhorriya streets, with the former continuing south into a textiles souk, while Gumhorriya carries on past the **post office** (daily except Fri 8am–2.30pm).

Don't plan on staying in Edfu, since the only **hotel** – the *El-Madina* (℡097/711-326; ❷) – is utterly filthy and grossly overpriced. The *Zahrat el-Medina* **restaurant** on Sharia al-Maglis serves basic chicken and vegetable dishes, or you can buy *fuul* and grilled fish in the fruit and vegetable market – ask the price first.

Leaving Edfu can be difficult, as the police don't like foreigners waiting for buses on the highway, nor catching trains. They might insist that you hang around drinking tea with them until the next convoy is due, before putting you on a bus.

The Temple of Horus

The **site** (daily: Oct–May 7am–4pm; June–Sept 7am–5pm; £E20) is a huge excavated compound overlooked by mud-brick houses and catcalling children. Ahead stretch the sandstone enclosure walls and towering pylon of the **Temple of Horus**, which lay buried to its lintels until the 1860s, when Auguste Mariette cleared the main building; a splendid drawing by David Roberts shows the courtyard full of sand and peasant houses built atop the Hypostyle Hall. Yet the mammoth task of excavation was nothing compared to the temple's construction, which outlasted six Ptolemies, the final touches being added by the twelfth ruler of that dynasty.

Modern-day visitors approach the temple from the rear and have to walk its full length in order to enter through a gate in the pylon, fronted by two giant black-granite **falcons**. The **Pylon** was erected by Ptolemy IX before he was ousted from power by his brother Alexander, who was later usurped by another ruler, for its exterior reliefs show Neos Dionysos smiting foes before Horus the Elder [a].

Entering the immense **Court of Offerings**, you can study the festival reliefs on the inner walls of the pylon, which continue around the court along the bottom of the wall. In the *Feast of the Beautiful Meeting*, Horus's barque tows Hathor's to the temple, where the deities retire to the sanctuary after suitable rituals **[b]**. Later they emerge from the temple, embark and drift downstream to the edge of the Edfu nome, where Horus takes his leave **[c]**. Beneath the western colonnade, Ptolemy IX makes offerings to Horus, Hathor and Ihy **[d]**; his successor appears before the Edfu Triad across the way **[e]**. However, most visitors are content to photograph the pair of **Horus statues** outside the

TEMPLE OF HORUS

n   o
p

Nilometer

Sanctuary
of
Horus

m   q

Stairs
to roof

k   Hall of Offerings

i

r   Festival
Hall

j

h   h

Hypostyle Hall

f   g

Horus Statues

d   Court of Offerings   e

c   b

Birth House

a   a

Pylon

Falcons

0   Metres   10

Hypostyle Hall **[f]**. One hawk stands higher than a man, the other lies legless in the dust.

The great **Hypostyle Hall** dates from the reign of Ptolemy VII (145–116 BC), known to his contemporaries as "Fatty". With a torch, you can examine two small rooms in the entrance wall: the Chamber of Consecrations, where the king or his priestly stand-in dressed for rituals **[f]**; and a Library of sacred texts adorned with a relief of Sheshat, the goddess of writing **[g]**. The reliefs showing the foundation of the temple and the deification of Horus **[h]** have been mutilated by iconoclasts. From here on you encounter the oldest section of the temple, begun by Ptolemy III in 237 BC and completed 25 years later by his son, who styled himself Philopator (Father Lover).

Try to imagine the shadowy halls during the annual festivals rhapsodized in temple texts, when the **Festival Hall** was decorated with faïence, strewn with flowers and herbs and perfumed by myrrh. Incense and unguents were blended according to recipes inscribed on the walls of the Laboratory **[i]**. Nonperishable offerings were stored in the room next door **[j]**, while libations,

The cult of Horus

Horus

Originally the sky-god of the Nile Valley, whose eyes were the sun and moon, the falcon deity **Horus** was soon assimilated into the Osirian myth as the child of Isis and Osiris (see p.465 and p.333). Raised in the swamps of the Delta by Isis and Hathor, Horus set out to avenge his father's murder by his uncle Seth. During their titanic struggle at Edfu, Horus lost an eye and Seth his testicles. Despite this, Seth almost prevailed until Isis intervened on her son's behalf and Osiris pronounced judgement upon them from the netherworld, exiling Seth back to the wilderness and awarding the throne to Horus. Thus good triumphed over evil and Osiris "lived" through his son.

All pharaohs claimed to be the incarnation of Horus the "living king" and reaffirmed their divine oneness in an annual **Festival of Coronation**. A live falcon was taken from the sacred aviary, crowned in the central court and then placed in an inner chamber where it "reigned" in the dark for a year as the symbol of the living king. Another event, sometimes called the **Festival of Triumph**, commemorated the Contendings of Seth and Horus in a series of Mystery Plays. At the equally lavish **Feast of the Beautiful Meeting**, his wet nurse and wife Hathor sailed from Dendara aboard the *Lady of the Lake* to be met near Edfu by his own barque, *The First Horus*. Public ceremonies preceded their conjugal encounters in the privacy of the temple's sanctuary. Besides these festivals, Horus also underwent a reunion with the sun-disc at New Year, similar to Hathor's at Dendara.

To complicate the cult of Horus still further, he was also associated with the Divine Ennead of Heliopolis and another variant of the Creation myth. Having distinguished the Osirian Horus from the Heliopolitan deity by terming the latter **Horus the Elder**, the Egyptians split him into archetypes such as **Herakhte** (often conjoined with Re), **Hariesis** (stressing his kinship to Isis) and **Haroeris** (see p.430). His priesthood asserted a place for Horus in the Creation myth by crediting him with building the first house amidst swamps at the dawn of the world, or even laying the Cosmic Egg whence the sun-god hatched. In rituals associated with the **Myth of the Great Cackler**, they launched a goose onto the sacred lake near Edfu temple, whose egg contained air and the potential for life – crucial elements in the world's creation.

fruit and sacrificial animals were brought in through a passageway connected to the outside world.

The sacred barques of Horus and Hathor appear in glorious detail on either side of the doorway into the **Hall of Offerings**. During the New Year Festival, Horus was carried up the ascending stairway [k] to the rooftop; after being revitalized by the sun-disc, his statue was returned to the sanctuary via the descending stairway [l]. The ritual is depicted on the walls of both stairways, but you'll need a torch, and locked gates may prevent you from going far. Otherwise, carry on to the **Sanctuary of Horus**, containing a shrine of polished black granite and an offerings table. Reliefs on the lower half of the right-hand wall show Philopator entering the sanctuary and worshipping Horus, Hathor and his deified parents.

There are several chambers worth noting off the corridor surrounding the sanctuary. The Linen Room [m] is flanked by chapels to Min and the Throne of the Gods, while a suite nominally dedicated to Osiris contains colourful scenes of Horus receiving offerings [n], a life-size replica of Horus's barque [o] and reliefs of his avatars [p]. Equally arresting is the **New Year Chapel**, with a blue-coloured relief of the sky-goddess Nut stretched across its ceiling [q].

Returning to the Festival Hall, you can gain access to an external corridor running between the inner and outer walls, where the priesthood tallied tithes assessed on the basis of readings from the temple's own **Nilometer**. On the other side are tableaux from the Triumph of Horus over Seth, depicting Mystery Plays in which Seth was cast as a hippopotamus, lurking beneath his brother's boat [r]. At the end of the play, the priests cut up and ate a hippo-shaped cake, to destroy Seth completely.

Don't miss the colonnaded **Birth House**, a focus for the annual Coronation Festival re-enacting the divine birth of Horus and the reigning pharaoh. Around the back of the building are reliefs of Horus being suckled by Isis, both as a baby (low down on the rear wall) and as a young man (on the inside of the columns).

Around Edfu: El-Kab, Kom al-Ahmar and Silsilah

Fifteen kilometres downriver from Edfu, the east bank road between Luxor and Kom Ombo passes the site known as **EL-KAB**, once the ancient city of *Nekheb*, dedicated to the vulture-goddess of Upper Egypt. Only opened to tourists in the late 1980s, the scattered ruins are meagre compared to other sites and you have to be pretty keen to bother. Tickets are sold from a kiosk by the highway, which bisects the site. Buses from Aswan or Luxor can drop you there on request.

The most conspicuous part of **the site** (daily 8am–6pm; £E10) lies towards the Nile, where the vast mud-brick **walls** that once enclosed the city stand, along with the conjoined **temples** of Nekhbet and Thoth, now reduced to stumps of painted columns and a series of **crypts** (notable for a scene of baboons dancing to the rituals of Mut). Across the road and up the slope from the ticket office, other ruins are scattered eastwards across the desert. You may not fancy hiking 3.5km to a small Chapel of Thoth and a Ptolemaic Temple of Nekhbet, but there are four **tombs** dug into the nearest ridge of hills. The best preserved is that of **Daheri**, royal scribe and tutor, and son of Tuthmosis I, which features ranks of lotus-sniffers and field workers. Next door are the lacklustre tombs of **Setau**, high priest of Nekhbet, and the commander **Aahmes**; superintendent **Renini** has a sprucer tomb, to the left.

On the far side of the Nile lies another site – **off-limits** to tourists – known as **Kom Al-Ahmar** (Red Mound), which the ancient Egyptians called *Nekhen* and the Greeks **Hierakonopolis** (City of the Falcon). As its names suggest, the city was closely associated with Horus and an earlier, local falcon-god, Nekheny. It flourished during the late Predynastic and Early Dynastic periods (c.4000–2686 BC) and may have been the first administrative capital of the Two Lands, judging by such famous artefacts as the Palette of Narmer and the Scorpion Macehead – though vital evidence was lost during the first, poorly recorded excavation, which later generations of archeologists have tried to recover from other digs. Recent finds include Egypt's earliest cult-temple (a timber-framed structure fronted by cedar-wood pillars) and brewery (beer was one of the "four libations" offered to the gods).

Travelling between Edfu and Kom Ombo by felucca, you'll pass a succession of ancient quarries, most notably at **Silsilah**, where the river is constricted by sheer cliffs and the bedrock changes from Egyptian limestone to Nubian sandstone. The site's ancient name, *Khenu* (Place of Rowing), suggests that rapids once existed here during the season of inundation. If your boatman is willing to stop, the most imposing **quarries** lie on the east bank, approached by a narrow defile down which cut stones were dragged to waiting barges. Workmen's graffiti covers the rocks, while two formal inscriptions record the cutting of stone for Aten's temple at Karnak, and the reopening of the quarry early last century to provide stone for the Esna Barrage. Across the Nile are 32 rock-hewn **shrines** dedicated to officials, priests, and pharaohs Merneptah and Horemheb.

Kom Ombo

Thirty kilometres before Aswan, the arid hills of the Eastern Desert recede from the river banks and bumper crops of sugar cane are harvested on reclaimed land. Here, too, around the town of **KOM OMBO**, many of the **Nubians** displaced by Lake Nasser have settled. In ancient times this town stood at the crossroads of the caravan route from Nubia and trails from the gold mines of the Eastern Desert; under Ptolemy VI (180–145 BC), it became the capital of the Ombos nome and a training depot for African war elephants, which the Ptolemies required to fight the pachyderms of the Seleucid empire.

While modern-day Kom Ombo is known to the *fellaheen* for its sugar refinery and felucca-building yards, tourists associate it with the Ptolemaic **Temple of Haroeris and Sobek**. Unlike other temples in the valley, this still stands beside the Nile, making the approach by river one of the highlights of a felucca journey or Nile cruise.

Practicalities

Kom Ombo lies along the east bank "highway" between Luxor (170km) and Aswan (45km), roughly 60km south of Edfu. Since the temple is 4km from town, it's preferable to arrive on a felucca or cruise boat that moors nearby, rather than face the hassle of **getting there** by other means. Tourist coaches and private taxis must travel in a **convoy**, and foreigners can't use service taxis from Luxor or Aswan, so independent travellers must rely on buses (4–5 daily) or trains between Luxor and Aswan, which call at Kom Ombo. Coming from Aswan, ask the driver to drop you at the signposted turn-off before town, from where you can walk or hitch 1.5km to the temple. Otherwise, covered pick-ups

(25pt) run from the town's service taxi depot to a ferry landing stage on the Nile, from where it's 800m walk to the temple, or you can get a private taxi directly to the site and back for around £E10.

The local **police** are not keen on tourists wandering around town, and try to confine boat passengers to the vicinity of the temple, so **staying** in Kom Ombo is out of the question, even if you could stomach the grungy *Radwan Hotel* on the main road (☎097/501-827; ❶). In town, the *Restaurant El-Noba*, south of the mosque, provides an alternative to **eating** at *fuul* and *taamiya* stands; meanwhile near the temple is an outdoor theme café called *Rural Home*, featuring a herb garden, *shaduf* irrigation, henna-tattooing and other diversions for boat-trippers. **Internet**, phone and fax are available in a kiosk near the Nile.

The Temple of Haroeris and Sobek

The **Temple of Haroeris and Sobek** stands on a low promontory near a bend in the river whose sandbanks were a basking place for crocodiles in ancient times. This proximity to the Nile has both preserved and damaged the **site** (daily 8am–4pm; £E10), covering the temple with sand which protected it from Coptic iconoclasts, but also washing away its pylon and forecourt, and undermining columns within the temple. What remains was aptly described by Amelia Edwards as a "magnificent torso"; truncated and roofless, it is still imposing, with traces of its original paint.

However, its main characteristic is its bisymmetry, with twin entrances and sanctuaries, and halls that are nominally divided down the middle. The left side is dedicated to the falcon-headed Haroeris, the "Good Doctor" (a form of Horus the Elder) and his consort Ta-Sent-Nefer, the "Good Sister" (an aspect of Hathor). The crocodile-god Sobek (here identified with the sun as Sobek-Re), his wife (another form of Hathor) and their son Khonsu-Hor are honoured on the right side of the temple.

Visitors approach the temple at right angles to its main axis, via an entrance by the **Gate of Neos Dionysos**. Only half of this gateway still stands and its provenance is obscure, as scholars disagree over the number, order and dates of the various Ptolemies, each of whom adopted a title such as Soter (Saviour), Euergetes (Benefactor) or Philometor (Mother Lover). Some identify Neos Dionysos as Ptolemy XII, others as Ptolemy XIII; however, there's general agreement that he fathered the great Cleopatra, had an interrupted reign (80–58 and 55–51 BC) and was nicknamed "The Bastard".

Before entering the temple you can pop into the **Chapel of Hathor** to see three **mummified crocodiles**, found nearby during roadworks in the 1970s.

The facade and Hypostyle Halls

With the forecourt (added by Trajan in 14 AD) reduced to low walls and stumps of pillars, your eyes are drawn to the **facade** of the Hypostyle Hall. Rising from a screen wall, its surviving columns burst in floral capitals beneath a chunk of cavetto cornice bearing a winged sun-disc and twin *uraei* above each portal. Bas-reliefs on the outer wall show Neos Dionysos being purified by Thoth and Horus [a], and yet again in the presence of Sobek, whose face has been chiselled away [b].

Wandering amidst the thicket of columns inside the **outer Hypostyle Hall**, notice the heraldic lily of Upper Egypt or the papyrus symbol of the Delta carved on their bases. On the inner wall of the facade are splendid carvings of Neos Dionysos's coronation before Haroeris, Sobek, Wadjet and Nekhbet (the goddesses of the north and south) [c], and his appearance before Isis, Horus

KOM OMBO: THE TEMPLE OF HAROERIS AND SOBEK

o p Outer Corridor

Inner Corridor

n

Inner Corridor

Sanctuary of Haroeris

Sanctuary of Sobek

Outer Corridor

m

j l k

h i

g

Inner Hypostyle Hall

f e

Outer Hypostyle Hall

d c

a b

Sacred Well

Cruise boats

Forecourt

Chapel of Hathor

Birth House of Ptolemy VII

Underground Corridor

Gate of Neos Dionysos

Entrance

Tourist Bazaar

0 Metres 10

Rural Home

River Nile

Cruise boats

the Elder and a lion-headed deity **[d]**. Neos Dionysos makes offerings to the same deities at the back of the hall, whose right side retains much of its roof, decorated with flying vultures.

Entering the older, **inner Hypostyle Hall**, you'll find a relief of Sobek in his reptilian form between the portals **[e]**. Ptolemy II receives the *hps* (sword of victory) from Haroeris (accompanied by his sister Cleopatra and his wife of the same name) in the southwest corner of the hall **[f]** and makes offerings to gods on the shafts of the pillars, while his elder brother does likewise to Haroeris at the back of the hall, where a list of temple deities and festivals appears between the doors **[g]**.

Vestibules and sanctuaries

Beyond lies the first of three, now roofless, **vestibules** (each of which sits a little higher than the preceding one) decorated by Ptolemy VI. Scenes at the back depict the foundation of the temple, with Sheshat, goddess of writing, measuring its dimensions **[h]**; and offerings and libations to Sobek **[i]**. To maintain the temple in a state of purity, these foundation rituals were periodically repeated. Only priests were admitted to the next vestibule, which served as the **Hall of Offerings**. The ruined chamber to the right once held vestments and sacred texts, as at Edfu and Dendara. Offerings to Haroeris **[j]**, a description of the temple and an address to Sobek **[k]** appear on the southern wall, which also features a tiny relief of a woman giving birth, at roughly chest height **[l]**. Notice the painted vultures on the ceiling, too.

A fine relief between the doors of the sanctuaries **[m]** shows Ptolemy and his sister-wife being presented with a palm stalk from which hangs a *heb-sed* sign representing the years of his reign. Khonsu does the honours, wearing a blue crescent and red disc, followed by Haroeris and Sobek (representing air and water, respectively); Ptolemy himself sports a Macedonian cloak. Because so little remains of the **sanctuaries**, you can espy a secret corridor between them, whence the priests would "speak" for the gods; accessible via an underground crypt in one of the **shrines** behind the inner corridor **[n]**.

The outer corridor and precincts

In the **outer corridor** between the Ptolemaic temple and its Roman enclosure wall, pilgrims scratched graffiti on the pavements to while away the time before their appointment with the Good Doctor, who was represented by a statue in the small niche behind the central chapel. The carved ears heard their pleas and the eyes symbolized the health they sought. Though these carvings have been gouged away by supplicant fingers, other reliefs are in better shape. One shows Marcus Aurelius offering a pectoral to Ta-Sent-Nefer, the Good Sister (aka Sennuphis) **[o]**. The other testifies to sophisticated surgery nearly 2000 years ago, depicting instruments such as scalpels, suction cups, dental tools and bone saws **[p]**.

Finally, you can wander around the temple grounds, where other rituals were once enacted. The most intriguing structure is a finely built **Sacred Well** with two stairways descending to its depths (now out of bounds), which drew its water from the Nile. The small **pool** nearby was used for raising sacred crocodiles. Another curiosity is the partially exposed **underground corridor** leading to the **Birth House of Ptolemy VII** – or what's left of it since half the ruins fell into the Nile in the nineteenth century. A few reliefs are faintly visible, notably the scene of Ptolemy IX and two gods in a papyrus thicket, observed by an ithyphallic Min-Amun-Re clutching lettuces (which symbolize fertility).

The last Forty Days Road

The camel trail from northern Sudan to Upper Egypt is one of the last great desert droving routes still active. The camels are reared in Sudan's Darfur and Kordofan provinces and herded 300–400km eastwards across the Libyan Desert to Dongola on the Nile, whence they follow the river into Egypt. Herdsmen call this month-long route the **Forty Days Road** (*Darb al-Arba'in*), perhaps from folk memory of the old slave trail from Kobbe to Assyut (see p.549), which was even longer and harder.

Now, as then, the drovers are usually Bishari or Rizayqat nomads, who sometimes appear at Egyptian markets in their traditional garb of flowing trousers, woollen cloak, dagger and sword. For what amounts to three months' work in atrocious conditions, each drover receives the equivalent of £100 sterling, the guide about £150. The camel owners are town-dwelling Sudanese merchants who fly up to supervise the sale, on which they can expect to make a profit of 500 percent.

Darow

Traditionally, **DAROW** (pronounced "De-*rau*") marks the point where Egypt begins to shade into Nubia: a distinction underlined by its **camel market**, attended by tribesmen from the northern deserts of the Sudan, and by a remarkable Nubian house called the **Hosh al-Kenzi**. Darow itself is a ramshackle sprawl of mud-brick compounds either side of the highway and railway line.

Although Darow is not a stopover for convoys or most taxi excursions, **getting there** from Aswan (37km) is straightforward, as lots of buses and all trains except sleepers call here. At present, you can't use service taxis from Aswan (40min; £E1) or Kom Ombo (10min; 50pt), but private taxis in Darow might agree to take you to Kom Ombo Temple and back for £E10–20.

Darow Camel Market

The **Camel Market** (*Souk el-Gamal*) happens every **Tuesday** throughout the year, and maybe also on Sundays or Mondays over winter. Although hours (7am–2pm) remain constant, with activities winding down after 11am, the location of the market changes seasonally. Over winter, it's often held in two dusty compounds on the eastern outskirts of Darow (fifteen minutes' walk from the main intersection; cross the bridge, walk on past the cane fields and turn right down a lane flanked by mud-brick walls). During summer, it may take place on the other side of town beyond the fruit, vegetable and poultry souk – just follow the crowds. The giveaway is truckloads of camels bumping hither and thither along a dusty lane.

At the end you'll find several hundred camels with their forelegs hobbled in the traditional manner, and scores of drovers and buyers drinking tea and smoking *sheeshas* beneath awnings. As the principal camel market between Dongola and Cairo, Darow is a good place to do business. The camels spend two days in quarantine before being sold to *fellaheen* who need a beast of burden, or merchants who plan to sell the camels for a profit at Cairo's Bilesh market. Many are destined to end up on the dinner tables of the poor, or in a knackers' yard. The *Souk el-Gamal* coincides with a **livestock market** where donkeys, sheep and cows jostle for space with people and trucks amidst trampled mud and dung. Over summer, the two markets are often held side by side.

Hosh al-Kenzi

A somewhat cooler attraction is the **Hosh al-Kenzi** – a fabulous house in the traditional Nubian style, built of mud-bricks and dom palms, with beehive domes, inner courtyards and spacious rooms divided by reed-lattice partitions, to allow air to circulate. Its rooms are furnished with Nubian artefacts and the exterior decorated with geometric patterns and ceramic plates. The house was built in 1912 by the grandfather of its present occupant so that his descendants would retain something of the ancestral village that was sacrificed to the first Aswan Dam. Its owner, Aid Mohammed Hassanein, is happy to show visitors around and talk about Nubian culture – indeed, he regrets that more tourists don't come. The house is beside the Gar Rasoul Mosque on Sharia al-Kunuz; turn right outside the train station, walk along the road and head left to find it.

Aswan and around

Egypt's southernmost city (population 150,000) and ancient frontier town has the loveliest setting on the Nile. At **ASWAN** the deserts close in on the river, confining its sparkling blue between smooth amber sand and rugged extrusions of granite bedrock. Lateen-sailed feluccas glide past the ancient ruins and gargantuan rocks of Elephantine Island, palms and tropical shrubs softening the islands and embankments till intense blue skies fade into soft-focus dusks. The city's **ambience** is palpably African; its Nubian inhabitants are lither and darker than the *Saiyidis*, with different tastes and customs. Although its own monuments are insignificant compared to Luxor's, Aswan is the base for **excursions** to the **temples of Philae and Kabasha**, near the great dams beyond the First Cataract, and the Sun Temple of Ramses II at **Abu Simbel**, far to the south. It can also serve for day trips to Darow Camel Market, Kom Ombo, Edfu and Esna – the main temples between here and Luxor. But the classic approach is to travel upriver by felucca, experiencing the Nile's moods and scenery as travellers have for millennia – or on a luxurious cruise, as tourists have since the nineteenth century. The ins-and-outs of **felucca journeys** and **Nile cruises** are described on p.454 and p.456. However, Aswan itself is so laid-back that one could easily spend a week here simply hanging out, never mind going anywhere. The **tourism** scene is much the same as in Luxor (see box on p.346).

Climate

The time of year is a major influence on people's level of activity. Situated near the Tropic of Cancer, Aswan is hot and dry nearly all the time, with average daily **temperatures** ranging from a delicious 23–30°C in the winter to a searing 38–54°C over summer. Late autumn and spring are perfect times to visit, being less crowded than the peak winter period, yet not so enervating as summer, when long siestas, cold showers and air conditioning commend themselves, and the number of tourists dwindles.

Aswan in history

Elephantine Island – opposite modern Aswan in the Nile – has been settled since remotest antiquity, and its fortress-town of *Yebu* (or *Abu*) became the border post between Egypt and Nubia early in the Old Kingdom. Local governors, known as the "Guardians of the Southern Gates", were responsible for border security and trade with Nubia, for huge quarries for fine red granite, and mining in the desert hinterland of amethysts, quartzite, copper, tin and malachite. Military outposts further south could summon help from the Yebu garrison by signal fires and an Egyptian fleet patrolled the river between the First and Second Cataracts.

Besides this, Yebu was an important cult centre, for the Egyptians believed that the Nile welled up from subterranean caverns at the **First Cataract**, just upriver (see p.457). Its local **deities** were Hapy and Satet, god of the Nile flood and goddess of its fertility, though the region's largest temple honoured Khnum, the provincial deity (see p.423).

During settled periods, the vast trade in ivory, slaves, gold, silver, incense, exotic animal skins and feathers spawned a **market town** on the east bank (slightly south of modern Aswan, its linear descendant), but the island remained paramount throughout classical times, when it was known by its Greek appellation, *Seyene*. In the Ptolemaic era, the Alexandrian geographer **Eratosthenes** (276–196 BC) heard of a local well into which the sun's rays fell perpendicularly at midday on the summer solstice, leaving no shadow; from this he deduced that Seyene lay on the Tropic of Cancer, concluded that the world was round and calculated its diameter with nearly modern accuracy – being only 80km out. (Since that time, the Tropic of Cancer has moved further south.)

The potency of the **cult of Isis** at nearby **Philae** (see p.462) made this one of the last parts of Egypt to be affected by **Christianity**, but once converted it became a stronghold of the faith. From their desert Monastery of St Simeon, monks made forays into Nubia, eventually converting the local Nobatae, who returned the favour by helping them to resist Islamic rule through Fatimid times, until finally subjugated by Salah al-Din. However, Bedouin raiders persisted through to 1517, when Sultan Selim garrisoned an entire army here, by which time the town's name had changed from Coptic *Sawan* to its present form, and the population had embraced **Islam**.

From the early nineteenth century onwards, Aswan was the base for the conquest of the Sudan and the defeat of the Mahadist Uprising (1881–98) by Anglo-Egyptian forces. As British influence grew, it also became the favourite **winter resort** of rich, ailing Europeans, who flocked to Aswan for its dry heat and therapeutic hot sands, luxurious hotels and stunning scenery, spiced with the thrill of being "at the edge of civilization". Its final transformation into the Aswan of today owes to the building of the **High Dam**, 15km upriver, which flooded Nubia, compelling its inhabitants to settle in new villages built around Kom Ombo and Aswan itself, which is now predominantly Nubian.

To assert its identity, the city has established an **Africa University** for the study of African science and culture, and a **Nubia Museum** tracing the Nubians' history. The relationship between the Egyptian and Sudanese governments has been somewhat fragile, however, and the weekly ferry between Aswan and Wadi Halfa was suspended for a time in the mid-1990s because of tensions – at the time of writing, however, the ferry is running and inter-state relations are stable (see box on p.458).

Arrival, information and transport

Most tourists travel directly to Aswan from Cairo (889km) or Luxor (215km), as detailed in the introduction to this chapter; a few arrive by bus or train from Esna, Edfu or Kom Ombo (see the respective entries for details).

From **Aswan airport**, 23km south of town, you can get a taxi for £E20 (agree the price first), or one of the El Gouna buses scheduled to coincide with EgyptAir flights (£E1, plus £E1 for luggage), which terminate not far from the **train station** in the northern part of town, five minutes' walk from the Corniche or the bazaar quarter. The intercity **bus station** is smack in the cen-

ASWAN

0   Metres   500

EATING & DRINKING

Aswan Moon	E
Aswan Panorama	I
Chef Khalil	A
El-Madina	C
El-Masry	D
El-Shatti	H
Emy	F
Mona Lisa	G
Nubian House	K
Nubian Restaurant	J
Zoom	B

N

Ferry to West Bank

SHARIA MOHOUS

SHARIA ABTAL EL-TAHIR

Governorate

CORNICHE EL-NIL

El Gouna Buses ★

Train Station

Bicycle Rental

St Simeon's Monastery

Tourist Police

SHARIA ABTAL AL-TAHIR

SHARIA AL-SOUK

SHARIA SAAD ZAGHLOUL

Camels

Bus Station

Local Service Taxis

Catholic Church

SHARIA ABBAS AL-AKKAD

Rowing Club

Palace of Culture

Police

Mausoleum of the Aga Khan

SHARIA ABU ZID

Banque Misr

SHARIA MAHMOUD AHMED YACOUB

Ferry to Oberoi

SHARIA SAYIDA NAFISA

Banque du Caire

Bank of Alexandria

CORNICHE EL-NIL

Amun Island

SHARIA SALAH AL-DIN

SHARIA AL-SOUK

SHARIA SAYIDA NAFISA

SHARIA SHEIK AL-BANDAR

Hotel Ferry

Ferry to Elephantine

Isis Island

National Bank of Egypt

SHARIA ABTAL AL-TAHIR

SHARIA ABBAS FARID

K

436

Thomas Cook

0   Metres   100

▼ Sehel Island

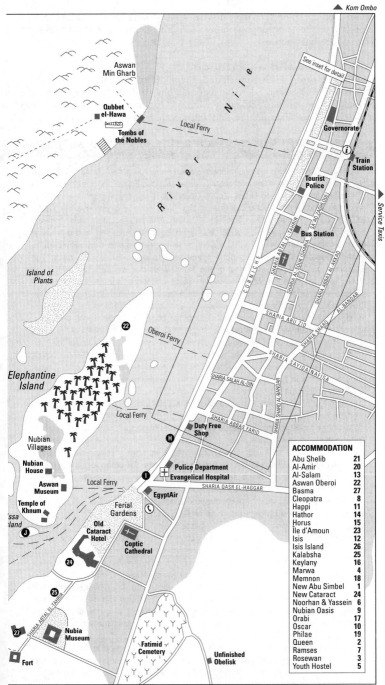

Kom Ombo

Aswan
Min Gharb

Qubbet
el-Hawa

Tombs of
the Nobles

Local Ferry

Governorate

Train
Station

Tourist
Police

Service Taxis

Bus Station

River Nile

Island of
Plants

Oberoi Ferry

Elephantine
Island

Local Ferry

Nubian
Villages

Nubian
House

Aswan
Museum

Temple of
Khnum

ssa
sland

Local Ferry

Duty Free
Shop

Police Department
Evangelical Hospital

EgyptAir

SHARIA QASR EL-HAGGAR

Ferial
Gardens

Old
Cataract
Hotel

Coptic
Cathedral

Nubia
Museum

Fatimid
Cemetery

Unfinished
Obelisk

Fort

SHARIA ABTAL EL-TAHRIR

CORNICHE

SHARIA ABTAL EL-TAHRIR
SHARIA SAAD ZAGHLOUL
SHARIA AL-SOUK (SHARIA)
SHARIA ABBAS AL-AKKAD

SHARIA ABU ZID

SHARIA SHARO
AL-BANDAR

SHARIA SAYIDA NAFISA

SHARIA SALAH AL-DIN

SHARIA SHARO AL-BANDAR

SHARIA ABBAS FARID

See inset for detail

ACCOMMODATION

Abu Shelib	21
Al-Amir	20
Al-Salam	13
Aswan Oberoi	22
Basma	27
Cleopatra	8
Happi	11
Hathor	14
Horus	15
Île d'Amoun	23
Isis	12
Isis Island	26
Kalabsha	25
Keylany	16
Marwa	4
Memnon	18
New Abu Simbel	1
New Cataract	24
Noorhan & Yassein	6
Nubian Oasis	9
Orabi	17
Oscar	10
Philae	19
Queen	2
Ramses	7
Rosewan	3
Youth Hostel	5

Aswan Dams & Sculpture Park ▼   ▼ Northern Quarries

tre on Sharia el-Tahrir, while **feluccas** tie up alongside the Corniche. The inter-city **service taxi** depot is more awkwardly located, across the tracks and south of the train station.

Information and assistance

The **tourist office** (daily 8am–2pm & 7–9pm; Ramadan 9am–2pm & 6-8pm; ☎ & ℱ 097/312-811) is housed in a domed Nubian-style building outside the station. The erudite and charming Shukri Sa'ad and Hakeem Hussein can answer just about any question, and will recommend good felucca captains, if

Nubia and the Nubians

Nubia and Egypt have been neighbours since time immemorial. Some believe that Nubia was the cradle of the civilization that emerged in Egypt, for there's evidence of settlements in northern Nubia 10,000 years ago and archeologists have discovered the **world's oldest solar calendar** of standing stones, dating from around 6000 BC, at **Nabta Playa**, 100km from Abu Simbel. The two cultures seem to have evolved in similar ways until 3500 BC, when Egypt's unification raised the Old Kingdom to a level from which it could exploit Nubia as a source of **mineral wealth**, exotic goods and **slaves** – a pattern that was to last nearly 5000 years. The Egyptians called it *Ta-Seti* (Land of the Bow), after the weapons for which the Nubians were renowned, while its modern name is thought to derive from *nbw*, the ancient word for gold, which was mined there until Greco-Roman times. Although the collapse of centralized authority allowed Nubia to reassert its independence during the First Intermediate Period, the onset of the Middle Kingdom saw the annexation of Lower Nubia – the land between the First and Second Cataracts of the Nile – and a chain of mud-brick **fortresses** built to safeguard trade; while under the New Kingdom, Nubia was divided into nomes and ruled by a viceroy entitled the King's Son of **Kush** (Kush being its southern province), aided by the priesthood of cult-**temples**. It was only in the Third Intermediate Period that Nubia got its own back, as the local rulers of **Napata** took advantage of Egypt's disunity to invade and establish their own **Kushite Dynasty** (747–656 BC) of pharaohs, who reigned as their Egyptian predecessors had done until the Assyrian invasion of Egypt in 671 BC.

Thereafter the **Kingdom of Meroe** between the Fourth and Fifth Cataracts alternated between war with foreign conquerors like the Persians, and amicable relations with most of the Ptolemies; some claim that Cleopatra (or *Kilu baba tarati* – "Beautiful Woman") was a Nubian born near Wadi Halfa. Relations with the Romans were stormy, as the Nubians supported the Egyptians' revolt against Emperor Augustus but then signed a treaty with Rome; towards the end of the first century AD another local principality, the **Blemmyes**, began raiding Egypt's southern border and occupied towns up until the reign of Diocletian – later breaking their peace treaty to ally themselves with the Nobatae tribes and revolt against Emperor Justinian (550 AD). The **Nobatae** were converted to **Christianity** by evangelical monks and became the chief bulwark against attacks by the Islamic rulers of Egypt during the twelfth and thirteenth centuries, until in 1315 the last Christian king was replaced by a Muslim one and most of the population accepted **Islam**.

Khalifs, sultans and Mamlukes made little attempt to control Nubia so long as it remained a "corridor to Africa" and supplied the ivory, slaves and exotica that they prized, until **Mohammed Ali** visited devastation on Nubia when he sent his son Ibrahim to enslave its male population as cannon fodder for his new army. Resentment smouldered through the reigns of khedives Abbas, Ismail and Tewfiq, drawing in the **British**, who began by supporting their forces and ended up underwriting an Anglo-Egyptian government in 1899, when the border between Egypt and Sudan was drawn 40km north of Wadi Halfa and Nubia was divided, yet again.

asked beforehand – they won't pass judgement if you've already made a deal. They also provide current private taxi rates. Shukri is worth talking to about anything, having read and travelled widely, whilst remaining close to his roots.

The **tourist police** (℡097/316-436) are based near the Corniche beside Misr Travel, with a branch in the train station; both are open round the clock. In serious cases, try to deal with Sayed Abu Hamed (℡097/303-436). The Aswan Governorate's **Police Department** occupies a grand modern tower on the Corniche, which also contains the passport office, and there's another, colonial-style police station on Sharia Abtal el-Tahrir.

Meanwhile, the **Nubians** remained true to their ancestral homeland, extending from the First Cataract to Khartoum. Traditional life centred around **villages** of extended families, each with its own compound of domed houses. The people made a livelihood farming the verges of the river, planting date palms, corn and *durra* melons, as well as fishing and transporting trade goods. Socially and spiritually, the Nile formed the basis of their existence. The whole village celebrated births, weddings and circumcision ceremonies with Nile rituals, and, despite converting first to Christianity and then to Islam, they retained a belief in water spirits, petitioning them for favours. They also brewed beer and date wine.

This way of life – which had existed pretty much unchanged for five millennia – was shattered by the **Aswan Dams**. The first dam, built in 1902 and successively raised, forced the Nubians to move onto higher, unfertile ground: unable to subsist on agriculture, many of the menfolk left for Cairo and the cities, sending back remittances to keep the villages going. With construction of the High Dam, the Nubians' traditional homeland was entirely submerged, displacing the entire 800,000-strong community. Around half of them moved north, settling around Aswan and Kom Ombo, where the government provided homes and assistance with agriculture and irrigation. The rest were repatriated to Sudan, where many ended up in the Kassala/New Halfa area, a thousand miles to the south. Meanwhile the **ancient monuments** of Nubia were moved to higher ground or foreign museums, under a huge program coordinated by UNESCO.

In Egypt, the **Nubian community** has done well. Many have taken advantage of higher education and business opportunities, making their mark in government, commerce and tourism (85 percent of Nubian males in Aswan earn their living from tourism). Others from the first wave of emigration continue to provide the backbone of Cairo's janitors and servants; Nubians as a whole have always been noted for their honesty and reliability. Remarkably, the community has maintained its cultural identity, with the resettled villages (which took their old names) acting as guardians of tradition.

A few Nubian phrases
In the list below, accents indicate stress.

Er raigráy? or *er-minnabóu?*	How are you? (to a man or woman)
Ai raigérry	I'm fine
Ekináira?	What's your name?
Aigi ...	My name is ... (followed by *-era*)
Er fárdiray?	Are you busy?
Tégus	Sit down
Er wenáyseso	I am honoured
Asálgi	Tomorrow
Kattaháiruk	Thank you
Ena fiadr	Goodbye

Transport

Unless you're burdened with luggage or bound for a distant hotel, there's no need to rent a **taxi** or **caleche** (£E4–5; agree the price first), since Aswan is compact enough to get around on foot. Although **bicycles** can be rented from a shop on the far side of the railway footbridge, for £E15 a day, they are virtually useless unless you want to cycle to the Unfinished Obelisk or the Sculpture Park; all the attractions close at hand are reached by river – mostly by felucca.

For better or worse, **feluccas** are inseparable from the Aswan experience. It's wonderfully relaxing to drift downstream while egrets swoop overhead, or tack between rocky islands, but on the downside, it's all too easy to get irked by boatmen who fritter away time before demanding *baksheesh* for an unfulfilled itinerary; or get wearied of the persistent touts along the Corniche. Despite **rates** being fixed by the authorities at £E15 an hour per boatload (1–4 people) with landfalls, or £E18 for an hour's non-stop sailing, market rules and haggling prevail. If big spenders abound, boatmen will sniff at official rates; if business is slack, they'll undercut each other. Unsurprisingly, prices are highest at the landing stage beneath the luxurious *Old Cataract Hotel*. (Longer felucca trips to Sehel Island, or downriver towards Luxor, are covered on p.457.)

Accommodation

As in Luxor, **accommodation** varies depending on the tourist trade and the season, and newly arrived tourists are importuned by **touts** (some board the train at Kom Ombo, to pre-empt their rivals). **Cruise boats** try to steal customers away from hotels by slashing their prices – and a week in a two- or three-star hotel can't compare with a week's cruise on the Nile. Though high season officially runs from October 1 to April 30, the squeeze is only felt (if at all) from mid-December to mid-January, when some hotels are booked up by Egyptian groups. The nadir of the low season (May 1–Sept 30) comes in the summer, when most places are empty and desperate for business. Many offer **reductions** of 15 to 50 percent at this time or will waive service charges and taxes after a bit of haggling.

In many mid-range and low-budget hotels guests may be subjected to **pressure** to sign up for taxi or felucca trips, whereby the hotel takes up to 50 percent of whatever you agree to pay the driver or boatman. Listen to their spiel, but don't let yourself be railroaded into a hasty decision.

Location counts for much in Aswan: hotels on the Corniche may have fabulous views, if not from the rooms, then from the rooftop. The poshest places are at the south end of the Corniche, or on private islands. Hotels in the bazaar tend to be cheaper, noisier, and often pitched at Egyptians rather than foreigners. The least attractive area is north of the train station, where the crumbling low-rise buildings are hardly what you'd want, though two of the hotels here are pretty good.

Of the mid-range places – aside from being sure of getting a private bathroom – **standards** vary depending on the age of the place and how well it's maintained. Hotels on the Corniche charge a higher rate for Nile-view rooms, which tend to be larger and better than rooms at the back. With temperatures in the 50s°C, **air conditioning** (or at least a fan) is an essential in summer.

All the accommodation listed below is keyed to the **map** on p.436. **Breakfast** is included unless otherwise stated.

Low-budget hotels

Abu Shelib Sharia Abbas Farid ℡ 097/303-051. Once popular with overland tour groups, its reputation rests on its cheap restaurant (no alcohol served) and friendly management, who are willing to negotiate about the price of its clean, dark rooms with fans or a/c, washbasins or bathrooms. The nearby mosque and bazaar make it noisy, however. ❶

Keylany Sharia Keylany ℡ 097/317-332, ℮ mohamed@aswanet.com.eg. An excellent low-budget hotel located in a side street off the southern end of the bazaar. It has clean, simple rooms with fans or a/c and spotless bathrooms, plus Aswan's best Internet café on the premises. ❷

Marwa Off Sharia Abtal el-Tahrir ℡ 097/308-532. This tiny place charges less for a bed (£E5) than the youth hostel across the road, and is aimed at hardcore budget travellers. Rooms are cramped, with three or four beds and a fan or a/c (£E2 extra), and the communal showers have hot water. Breakfast not included. ❶

New Abu Simbel Sharia Abtal el-Tahrir ℡ 097/306 -096. The nicest hotel in the northern part of town, 10 minutes' walk from the station. Spacious, carpeted a/c rooms with baths; some have Nile views and balconies, fridges, TV or double beds. Large, attractive garden and friendly management. ❷

Noorhan Off Sharia al-Souk ℡ 097/316-069. Look for the pink building on the corner, 5 minutes' walk from the station. This much-hustled place has gloomy, clean rooms with fans, a/c and bathrooms. Internet (£E15/hr), beer (£E6) and simple meals available; breakfast not included. Arranges tours, but not unduly pushy. ❶

Nubian Oasis Off Sharia al-Souk ℡ 097/312-123 or mobile 0124 089739, ℱ 097/312-124, ℮ nubianoasis@infinity.com.eg. Two blocks south of the *Noorhan*, this backpackers' favourite has shabby, clean rooms with fans, a/c and bathrooms. Internet (£E12 p/h), laundry service and café; tepid beer (£E6). Breakfast not included. Organizes trips, but not too pushy. ❷

Orabi Off Sharia al-Souk ℡ & ℱ 097/317-578. Not nearly as smart as its picture on the business cards, but its location, on a quiet side street in the heart of the souk, and the liberal atmosphere on its rooftop, kind of make up for the fairly basic rooms and (clean) communal bathrooms. Staff are keen to sell tours, but good fun, too. Breakfast not included. ❶

Oscar Sharia Abbas al-Akkad ℡ & ℱ 097/306-066. This quiet, clean hotel in the Coptic quarter behind the bazaar has spacious rooms with a/c and baths, and a seedy bar selling Stella, local brandy and *zibiba*. Its honest management doesn't try to push tours – or even arrange them. ❷

Queen Off Sharia Atlas ℡ 097/326-069. A pleasant new hotel that's close to the station but far enough away to escape the noise. Its clean rooms have tiny bathrooms, and fans; it's worth paying £E5 more for a Nile-facing a/c one. ❷

Rosewan Off Sharia Atlas ℡ 097/304-497. Around the corner from the *Queen*, this place remains popular despite its shabby, dark, cramped rooms and erratic hot water, perhaps due to its eccentric owner who makes things from papier mâché, or his engaging son who manages the hotel. No Internet, contrary to some reports. ❶

Yassein Off Sharia al-Souk ℡ 097/307-753, ℱ 317-109, ℮ yassenhotel@hotmail.com. Next to the *Noorhan*, its rooms are nicer but within earshot of the train tracks at the end of the street. Rooftop bar and restaurant; laundry service. Breakfast not included. ❶

Youth Hostel Sharia Abtal el-Tahrir ℡ & ℱ 097/302-235. Reached by a side entrance in the same block as a governorate-owned hostel that also calls itself a youth hostel, this place has clean dorms, showers and toilets, and is usually empty except during Egyptian university breaks. It makes a point of separating foreign and local guests. Vague curfew, around midnight. Dorm beds £E7.60 (£E8.60 for non-members).

Mid-range hotels

Al-Amir Sharia Abbas Farid ℡ 097/314-732. A street back from the Corniche, this small three-star hotel unjustly boasts of its Nile views and is mainly aimed at Gulf Arabs, who presumably don't mind being awoken by a mosque next door, nor that the restaurant doesn't serve alcohol. The rooms are clean and comfy, with a/c and phone, but overpriced. ❺

Al-Salam Midway along the Corniche ℡ 097/302-651, ℱ 303-649. Breezy a/c rooms with private baths, and maybe also balconies overlooking the Nile, make this a nicer option than the *Hathor* on the other side of the access passage (see below), not to mention the great view of the river from its restaurant and lounge. Used by Explore groups. ❸

Cleopatra Sharia al-Souk ℡ 097/314-001, ℱ 314-002. The smartest hotel near the bazaar, boasting comfy, clean a/c rooms with bath, phone, fridge and TV. Its best feature is the rooftop pool, overlooked by taller buildings. Bar, restaurant and Internet (£E20/hr). Faces stiff competition from cruise boats, so likely to give discounts if you haggle. ❻

Happi Just off the Corniche ☎ 097/314-115, ⓕ 307-572. Pleasant a/c rooms with spotless, elegant bathrooms; some also have TV, double beds, balconies and Nile views. Its restaurant, which faces Elephantine Island, sells beer. Guests enjoy free use of the *Cleopatra*'s pool. Used by Imaginative Traveller groups. ❸

Hathor Midway along the Corniche ☎ 097/314-223, ⓕ 303-468. Given the hotel's prime location and rooftop swimming pool, it's disappointing that its a/c Nile-facing rooms are cramped and shabby (albeit better than the ones with fans on the 2nd floor, which cost £E10 less), and the management shows little interest in its guests beyond selling them tours. ❸

Horus The Corniche ☎ 097/303-323, ⓕ 313-313. A choice between large, pleasant rooms with baths and a/c – some with Nile views – or tattier ones at the back, and a rooftop bar-restaurant with cool views make this hotel preferable to the *Hathor* up the road. Sadly, there's no swimming pool. ❸

Memnon Above the National Bank of Egypt on the Corniche; entrance via a back alley ☎ 097/300-483. Crassly decorated, clean and comfortable, with a/c, soft beds, and a small pool on the roof. Staff can be pushy about selling trips. ❸

Philae The Corniche ☎ 097/312-090. Don't bother staying here if you can get a Nile-view room at any of the other Corniche hotels listed above, since the *Philae* is inferior to all of them, but charges higher rates. ❸

Ramses Sharia Abtal el-Tahrir ☎ 097/304-000, ⓕ 315-701. Centrally located hotel covered in mock-pharaonic carvings. Small, clean rooms with a/c, fridge, phone, satellite TV and private baths. Some overlook the Tombs of the Nobles. Restaurant, bar and laundry service. Used by Nouvelles Frontières groups. ❸

Upmarket hotels

Aswan Oberoi Elephantine Island ☎ 097/314-667, ⓕ 313-538. While guests enjoy spacious rooms, spa, pool and lovely gardens with magnificent views, the rest of Aswan must suffer this five-star 1970s eyesore that looks like an airport control tower. It's served by a ferry done up like a pharaonic barge, which sails from the *Isis*. ❽

Basma On the hillside above the *Old Cataract* ☎ 097/310-901, ⓕ 310-907. This newer four-star complex has a large pool and a garden terrace with stunning views of the Aga Khan's mausoleum and the southern end of Elephantine, and manages to be less of an eyesore than the nearby *Kalabsha* or *New Cataract*. Hourly free bus from the *Isis*, in town. ❽

Île d'Amoun Amun Island, facing the *Old Cataract* ☎ 097/313-800, ⓕ 317-190. Small, chic Club Med resort of a/c bungalows set amid a lush garden with exotic birdlife. All the guests and staff speak French. Reservations advisable in high season. Reached by private ferry from the EgyptAir docks. ❾

Isis Midway along the Corniche ☎ 097/315-100, ⓕ 315-500. A mini-resort with cramped a/c bungalows in a small garden with a pool, it only gets away with charging such high prices due to its prime location facing Elephantine. ❽

Isis Island Upriver from Aswan ☎ 097/317-400, ⓕ 317-405. Owned by a relative of Mubarak, this five-star colossus was built beside a nature reserve containing the only primordial Nilotic vegetation left in Egypt, and is reached by a private launch from the docks near EgyptAir. ❽

Kalabsha Sharia Abtal el-Tahrir ☎ 097/302-666, ⓕ 305-974. Sited uphill from the southern end of the Corniche, this tower-block hotel is far cheaper than its four-star neighbours but nowhere near as classy, although guests may use the pool at the *New Cataract* for free, and some of the rooms enjoy a fantastic view of the First Cataract of the Nile. ❼

New Cataract By the Ferial Gardens ☎ 097/316-000, ⓕ 316-011. Charmless modern annexe to the *Old Cataract*, next door, containing a disco, bar, 24-hour café, restaurants and shops, with tennis courts and a large pool outside. ❽

Old Cataract By the Ferial Gardens ☎ 097/316-000, ⓕ 316-011. A splendid Edwardian-Moorish relic, tastefully refurbished and jealously guarded against interlopers. Its river-facing rooms have glorious views and the others overlook a fine garden, but some complain that the food and service don't match the high prices, ranging up to US$1215 to stay in the Agatha Christie or King Farouk suites. Shares all facilities with the *New Cataract*. ❽

The Town

Ignoring the residential and industrial suburbs (as every tourist does) greatly simplifies **orientation**. Although Aswan's sinuous **Corniche** follows the river bank for more than 4km, most things worth noting lie along the 1500-metre stretch between the Palace of Culture and **Ferial Gardens** (where the road swings inland), culminating in the *Old Cataract Hotel* facing the southern end of **Elephantine Island**. Otherwise, the main focus of interest is **Sharia al-Souk** (aka Sharia Sa'ad Zaghloul), which runs two to three blocks inland as it snakes down from the train station to Sharia Abbas Farid. For most of the way it is paralleled by another busy thoroughfare, **Sharia Abtal el-Tahrir**, which runs ever closer to the Corniche but never quite touches it, and finishes up as a narrow backstreet. (Note that not all the streets off the bazaar appear on our **map** of town, on p.436.)

The bazaar and Corniche

Aswan's **bazaar** is renowned as the best in Egypt outside Cairo, and is not yet entirely corrupted by tourism. Traditional wares such as spices, ebony, basket-work and rugs are still in evidence, but souvenir shops are gradually forcing humdrum vendors into the alleys off Sharia al-Souk. Nonetheless, it's a pleasure to wander around, with its smells and colours evoking the Sudan and camel caravans across the Sahara. Fresh produce is chiefly sold around the junction of Sharia Saiyida Nafisa and Sharia al-Souk, and at the station end of the latter. Shop in the morning, since quality drops as the temperature rises. Conversely, the spice, textiles and jewellery souks are barely active before 3pm, but thronged after sundown. The most attractive part is the stretch of tall wooden shopfronts to the north of Sharia Abdel Magid Abu Zid, mostly given over to souvenirs.

As in Luxor, going shopping with a guide or driver will mean paying a hidden commission. Popular buys include colourful **Nubian skullcaps** or long

△ Aswan bazaar

443

scarves, which go for about £E5; heavier, woven **shawls** from £E10 upwards; or **baskets and trays** in various sizes, some semi-antiques (£E50 for a medium-sized tray) and others new (£E10 for a small plate). **Galabiyyas** and embroidered Nubian robes can be bought off the peg or tailored to order; try the shop of Metry Tawdros Mansour on Sharia Saiyida Nafisa. Pyramids or baskets of **spices** and dyes are another eye-catching feature of the bazaar; dried hibiscus (used to make *karkaday*), indigo dye and what is labelled as "saffron" (actually saf-saf flower) are common tourist purchases, and Aswan is also famous for the quality of its peanuts and its henna powder, sold in different grades. Local people are also proud of their salted fish, which comes in jars, but is something of an acquired taste.

Aswan's **Corniche** is the finest in the country, less for its architecture (which is mostly modern and undistinguished) than for the superb vista of Elephantine Island, and feluccas gliding over the water like quill pens across papyrus, with the tawny wastes of the Western Desert on the far bank. Unfortunately, you can't walk along the esplanade without being pestered by boatmen or their juvenile sidekicks; stay on the other side of the street and they'll leave you alone. Sunset is best enjoyed from the rockbound **Ferial Gardens** or the terrace of the **Old Cataract Hotel** (featured in the movie *Death on the Nile*), which afford a sublime **view** of Elephantine's headland and the smaller islands beyond – although the *Old Cataract* now relegates non-residents to a lower terrace and levies a minimum charge of £E35 to discourage outsiders. If you're willing to walk further uphill past the Nubia Museum, the *Nubian House* restaurant (see p.450) commands an even finer vista of the First Cataract.

The Nubia Museum

Aswan's **Nubia Museum** (daily: Oct–May 9am–1pm & 5–9pm; June–Sept 9am–1pm & 6–10pm; £E20; camera permit £E10, camcorder £E20) has been widely acclaimed, delighting its sponsors, UNESCO, and posthumously crowning the career of its architect, the late Mohammed al-Hakim. Opened in 1998 after fifteen years on the drawing board, the museum is housed in an impressive modern building, loosely based on traditional Nubian architecture and faced in limestone, surrounded by landscaped grounds. It displays some 5000 artefacts, excellently organized and clearly labelled in English, making it a "must see" introduction to the history and culture of the Nubians.

At the entrance to the main hall, a scale model of the Nile Valley shows the magnitude of the Nilotic civilizations and their architectural achievements. The exhibits lead you from prehistory through the kingdoms of Kush and Meroe into Christian and Islamic eras, until the drowning of Nubia beneath Lake Nasser and the salvage of its ancient monuments by UNESCO. Among the highlights are a quartzite statue of a Kushite priest of Amun, an eight-metre-high Ramses II, horse-armour from the Ballana tombs and frescoes from the Coptic churches of Nubia. There are also life-size models of traditional Nubian houses and photographs of the mud-brick fortresses, churches and cemeteries that were abandoned to the rising waters of Lake Nasser as the temples were moved to higher ground.

In the grounds are further monuments and exhibits, including the mausoleum of 77 *wali* (Muslim sheikhs), a traditional Nubian house, and a cave containing prehistoric rock art removed from now inundated areas. An artificial watercourse runs through the corner of the grounds nearest the main road, attractively spotlit at night.

The museum is just uphill from Aswan's **Coptic Cathedral**, near the *Old Cataract* hotel. It's about thirty minutes' walk from the town centre, though most visitors take a taxi (£E10 return). If you've still got some energy after the museum, you can trek uphill past the *Basma Hotel* to find a derelict mud-brick **fort** with a watchtower, built in Mohammed Ali's time, which offers a great view of the First Cataract and the Eastern Desert, and the Fatimid Cemetery in the other direction. The *Nubian House* restaurant, nearby, amply rewards the effort (see p.450).

The **Fatimid Cemetery**, the **Unfinished Obelisk** and the **Sculpture Park** are covered under "Excursions from Aswan", on p.452.

Elephantine Island

Elephantine Island takes its name from the huge black rocks clustered around its southern end, which resemble a herd of pachyderms bathing in the river. Its spectacular beauty is marred only by the towering *Aswan Oberoi Hotel*, reached by its own private ferry and cut off from the rest of the island by a lofty fence. (An even larger hotel lies semi-constructed beyond the *Oberoi* and seems likely to remain unfinished as investors have backed out.)

South of this, three **Nubian villages** nestle amidst lush palm groves, their houses painted sky-blue, pink or yellow and often decorated with *Hadj* scenes. Chickens peck in the dust and goats chew garbage in mud-brick alleys twisting past walled gardens, where the only concession to tourism is a signposted **Nubian House** whose owner sells tea and handicrafts and arranges live music some evenings (see "Entertainments and activities" on p.451). This can be seen en route to, or after, the Aswan Museum and ruins at the end of the island, using the public **ferries** (every 15min 6am–10pm; 25pt) that sail to Elephantine from the landing stages near Thomas Cook and EgyptAir. Alternatively you could get there by felucca (negotiable rates), which dock just below the Aswan Museum.

The Aswan Musuem

The small **Aswan Museum** (daily: winter 8.30am–5pm; summer 8.30am–6pm; £E10, ticket also valid for the Nilometer and ruins further south) casts light on the island's past, when its southern end was occupied by the town of *Yebu* (meaning both "elephant" and "ivory" in the ancient Egyptian language). Most of the museum's best exhibits have been moved to the Nubia Museum, but a mummified gazelle and jewellery found at the island's Temple of Satet are worth a look, as is the new **Annex**, whose highlights include a life-size granite statue of a seated Tuthmosis III, a colobus monkey embracing a pillar, and a pre-nuptial agreement from the reign of Nectanebo II. The museum was originally the villa of Sir William Willcocks, who designed the first Aswan Dam, and is set amid fragrant subtropical **gardens**. Come back and enjoy them once you've visited the Nilometer and the ruins of Yebu.

The Nilometer

In ancient times the **Nilometer** at Aswan was the first to measure the river's rise, enabling priests to calculate the height of the inundation, crop yields over the next year and the rate of taxation (which peasants paid in kind). Ninety enclosed rock-hewn steps lead down to a square shaft by the riverside; the stair walls are graduated in Arabic, Roman and (extremely faint) pharaonic numerals, reflecting its usage in ancient times and during the late nineteenth century. To get there from the museum, follow the path southwards for 300m to find a sycamore tree (the pharaonic symbol of the tree-goddess, associated with Nut and Hathor), which shades the structure. Should you approach the Nilometer by river, notice the rock embankments to the south, which bear **inscriptions** from the reigns of Tuthmosis III, Amenophis III and the XXVII Dynasty ruler Psammetichus II.

The ruins of Yebu

The southern end of the island is littered with the **ruins** of the ancient town, which covered nearly two square kilometres by Ptolemaic times. To the south-west of the Nilometer, a massive platform and foundation blocks mark the site of the **Temple of Khnum**, god of the Aswan nome, founded in the Old Kingdom (when it accounted for two-thirds of the town's area) but entirely rebuilt during the XXX Dynasty. On its north side are the remains of pillars painted by the Romans, and Greek inscriptions; to the west stands the imposing gateway added by Alexander II, shown here worshipping Khnum.

Immediately to the north lies a Greco-Roman **Necropolis of Sacred Rams**, unearthed in 1906, while further northwest stands the small **Temple of Hekayib**, a VI Dynasty nomarch buried in the Tombs of the Nobles (see p.448) who was later deified; the stelae and inscriptions found here by Labib Habachi in 1946 revealed much about Aswan during the Middle Kingdom.

Due east lies a **Temple of Satet** where excavations continue to produce discoveries. Built by Queen Hatshepsut around 1490 BC, it was the last of more than thirty such temples on this site, dating back four millennia, dedicated to the goddess who incarnated the fertile aspect of the inundation. Beneath the temples, German archeologists have found a shaft leading 19m into the granite bedrock, where a natural **whirl hole** is thought to have amplified the sounds of the rising water table (the first indication of the life-giving annual flood) and was revered as the "Voice of the Nile". Although the High Dam has since silenced its voice, a half-buried statue near the temple still draws new brides and barren women longing for the gift of fertility.

To the southwest of Khnum's temple, the layered **remains of ancient houses** have yielded Aramaic papyri attesting to a sizeable **Jewish colony** on Elephantine in the sixth century BC. A military order by Darius II permitting the Yebu garrison to observe Passover in 419 BC suggests that they defended the southernmost border of the Persian empire. Although nothing remains of their temple to Yahweh, the Germans used leftover blocks from Kalabsha (see p.468) to reconstruct a **Ptolemaic sanctuary** with decorations added by the Nubian Pharaoh Arkamani in the third century BC, at the southern tip of the island.

The rocky passage between Elephantine and Amun islands looks its best from a felucca. If you're not already waterborne, the surrounding coves are frequented by lads who'll happily sail you across to the Island of Plants or the west bank, but drive a hard bargain. **Amun Island** itself features a reclusive *Club Med*, reached by private ferry from a landing stage near the telephone office. Further south you'll see a newer, grander hotel complex on **Isis Island**, likewise accessible by private ferry.

The Island of Plants

Almost hidden from town by the bulk of Elephantine, the smaller, lusher **Island of Plants** (*Geziret an-Nabatat*) is still commonly referred to by tourists as "Kitchener's Island". Presented with the island in gratitude for his military exploits in the Sudan, Consul-General Kitchener here indulged his passion for exotic flora, importing shrubs and seeds from as far afield as India and Malaysia. This beautiful island-wide **botanical garden** (daily 7am–sunset, until 5/6pm in summer; £E5) is an ideal place to spend the afternoon, having seen the other sites, with colourful **birdlife** flitting through the trees.

The island is accessible by rowing boat or felucca (£E1.50 per person) from the west bank or Elephantine Island.

The west bank

The main attractions on the **west bank** of the river are the **Mausoleum of the Aga Khan** (which is closed to the public) and the desert **Monastery of St Simeon**. When negotiating a price for a felucca, be sure to establish how long you plan to spend on the west bank. Unless you're prepared to hike for more than 2km across the hills, the more northerly **Tombs of the Nobles** are best visited as a separate excursion.

The Aga Khan's Mausoleum

Just uphill from the embankment is a walled estate comprising a private villa and riverside garden, and a stairway ascending the barren hillside to the **Mausoleum of the Aga Khan**. Outwardly modelled on the Fatimid tombs of Cairo, its open court culminates in a Carrara-marble *mihrab* and sarcophagus, enshrining Aga Khan III, the 48th Imam of the Isma'ili sect of Shi'ite Muslims, who was weighed in jewels for his diamond jubilee in 1945. After his death in 1957, his tomb attracted hordes of pilgrims, whose camps posed a health hazard until the government banned mass pilgrimages.

The Aga Khan was initially drawn to Aswan by its climate and hot sands, which relieved his rheumatism; subsequently he fell in love with its beauty, built a villa and spent every winter here. Until she died, his widow, the Begum, ensured that a fresh red rose was placed on his sarcophagus every day; legend has it that when none was available in Egypt, a rose was flown in by private plane from Paris on six successive days. Since the Begum's death in 2000 the whole compound has been closed and nobody knows if the Isma'ilis will ever reopen it as a shrine. Still, it's an impressive sight on the hillside.

The Monastery of St Simeon

Unless you walk across the desert from the Tombs of the Nobles (see below), the ruined **Monastery of St Simeon** (daily 7am–5pm; £E12) must be approached from the valley below. You can either slog uphill through soft sand (30min) or rent a camel from the pack near the landing stage (£E25 round-trip with half an hour's waiting time; a camel seats two); the latter is more fun and less effort, but whichever way you approach, it's a good idea to bring water.

Founded in the seventh century and rebuilt in the tenth, *Deir Anba Samaan* crowns the head of a desert valley, which used to be cultivated down to the river's edge. Built like a fortress, it was originally dedicated to Anba Hadra, a local saint of the fourth century who encountered a funeral procession the day after his wedding and decided to renounce the world for a hermit's cave before the marriage was consummated. From here, monks made evangelical forays into Nubia, where they converted the Nobatae to Christianity. After the Muslim conquest, the Nobatae used the monastery as a base during their own incursions into Egypt, until Salah al-Din had it wrecked in 1173.

One of the custodians will show you around the split-level complex, whose lower storeys are made of stone, the upper ones of mud-brick. The now-roofless **Basilica** bears traces of frescoes of the Apostles, their faces scratched out by Muslim iconoclasts. In a nearby chamber with a font, you're shown the place where St Simeon (about whom little is known) used to stand sleeplessly reading the Bible, with his beard tied to the ceiling so as to deliver a painful tug if he nodded off. The central **Keep** has room for three hundred monks sleeping five to a cell, a tunnel-like refectory, bathhouse, ovens and bakeries (notice the millstones). Beware of sheer drops when exploring. At sunset the surrounding desert turns madder-red and violet; foxes emerge to hunt and hawks soar aloft.

The Tombs of the Nobles

Relatively few tourists bother with the **Tombs of the Nobles** (daily 7am–5pm; £E12; camera permits £E10 per tomb), which are hewn into the hillside further up the west bank and whose artwork has an immediacy and concern for everyday life that makes a refreshing change from royal art. If you're curious, **local ferries** ply between the station end of the Corniche and the landing stage of the west bank village of **ASWAN MIN GHARB** (every 30min 6am–10pm). The fare is 25pt, but they'll try to charge £E1 (preferably each way). At the site kiosk, beware of being palmed off with used **tickets**. As there are no slides of these tombs available commercially, consider buying a couple of photo permits; the custodian might let you photograph additional tombs without extra permits, for *baksheesh*. In order to combine a visit with the monastery and mausoleum, start early with the tombs, then ascend to the domed hilltop Muslim shrine known as **Qubbet el-Hawa** (Tomb of the Wind), and walk across the desert to St Simeon's (45min; bring plenty of water). Alternatively you could do the route in reverse, being dropped off below the monastery from which point you can hire a camel to do the leg-work between the sites for you (£E45 for two people on one camel).

The Tombs of the Nobles lie at different heights (**Old and Middle Kingdom** ones uppermost, **Roman** tombs nearest the waterline), and are numbered in ascending order from south to north. Taking the path up from the ticket kiosk you reach the high-numbered ones first.

Tomb of Sirenput I (#36)

Turn right at the top of the steps and follow the path downhill around the cliff-side to find the tomb of **Sirenput I**, overseer of the priests of Khnum and Satet and Guardian of the South during the XII Dynasty. The six pillars of its vestibule bear portraits and biographical texts. On the left-hand wall he watches bulls fighting, and spears fish from a papyrus raft, accompanied by his sandal-bearer, sons and dog. On the opposite wall he's portrayed with his mutt and bow-carrier, and also sitting above them in a garden with his mother, wife and daughters, being entertained by singers; the lower register shows three men gambling. Amongst the badly damaged murals in the hall beyond, you can just discern fowlers with a net (on the lower right wall), a hieroglyphic biography (left), and a marsh-hunting scene (centre). Beyond lies a chapel with a false door set into the rear niche; the corridor to the left leads to the burial chamber.

Tombs of Pepi-Nakht (#35) and Harkhuf

To reach the other tombs from Sirenput I's, return to the top of the steps and follow the path southwards. Among a cluster of tombs to the left of the steps are two rooms ascribed to Hekayib (whose cult temple stands on Elephantine), called here by his other name, **Pepi-Nakht**. As overseer of foreign troops during the long reign of Pepi II (VI Dynasty), he led colonial campaigns in Asia and Nubia, which are related on either side of the door of the left-hand room.

A bit further south lies the (unnumbered) tomb of **Harkhuf**, who held the same position under Pepi I, Merenre and Pepi II. A badly eroded hieroglyphic biography just inside the entrance mentions his gifts to the young Pepi II, which included incense, leopard skins and ebony, and a "dancing dwarf from the land of spirits" (thought to be a pygmy from Equatorial Africa).

Tombs of Sirenput II (#31)

The largest and best-preserved tomb belongs to **Sirenput II**, who held the same offices as his father under Amenemhat II, during the apogee of the Middle Kingdom. Beyond its vestibule (with an offerings slab between the second and third pillars on the right) lies a corridor with six niches containing Osiride statues of Sirenput, still brightly coloured like his portraits on the four pillars of the chapel, where the artist's grid lines are visible in places. Best of all is the recess at the back, where Sirenput appears with his wife and son (left), attends his seated mother in a garden (right), and receives flowers from his son (centre). Notice the elephant in the upper left corner of this tableau.

Tombs of Mekhu (#25) and Sabni (#26)

At the top of the double ramps ascending the hillside (up which sarcophagi were dragged) are the adjacent tombs of a father and son, which are interesting for their monumentality – a large vestibule with three rows of rough-hewn pillars, flanked by niches and burial chambers – and for their story. After his father **Mekhu** was killed in Nubia, **Sabni** mounted a punitive expedition that recovered the body. As a sign of respect, Pepi II sent his own embalmers to mummify the corpse; Sabni travelled to Memphis to personally express his thanks with gifts, as related by an inscription at the entrance to his tomb. Both tombs are crudely constructed and decorated, with small obelisks at their entrances, and twin vestibules that form a single rectangular room. Sabni's chapel has columns painted with fishing and fowling scenes.

Eating and drinking

Eating out in Aswan offers the pleasures of fresh fish and Nubian dishes such as okra in spicy tomato sauce, in riverside **restaurants** that are great on balmy nights but empty when it's cold. You won't find any Chinese food, and Italian or French cuisine is limited to a few big hotels. The bazaar is good for **street food**, with *fuul* and liver sandwiches sold near the station end of the street, and fruit and nuts on every corner. There are simple **cafés** for chicken and fish meals or *kushari*, and the usual array of juice bars and coffee houses. All the Corniche places are **open** till around midnight (or later if there is custom); the cafés in the bazaar may close an hour or two earlier. Phone numbers are given where **reservations** are advisable.

Restaurants

Aswan Moon The Corniche near the *Horus Hotel*. Distinguished by its castle gate and a floating extension hung with colourful fabric. Cool by day, loud and lively at night; a place to meet felucca captains and hear Nubian music. Fish, chicken, vegetable dishes, pizzas and pasta main dishes go for £E5–15, plus tax. Serves beer and wine.

Aswan Panorama The Corniche opposite Duty Free. Entrées cooked in clay pots, so-called vegetarian dishes, iced drinks and herbal teas. Try the rice pudding with nuts and rosewater. Similar prices to the *Aswan Moon*. Beer is served.

Chef Khalil Sharia al-Souk, near the station. Small fish restaurant with a kitsch fountain. Delicious lobster, prawns, sea bass and other fish from Lake Nasser and the Red Sea, sold by weight and accompanied by salad, chips and *tahina*. A mixed seafood platter costs £E35. No alcohol.

El-Madina Sharia al-Souk, near the *Cleopatra Hotel*. Clean, share-a-table diner with set meals (£E6–16) of liver, chicken or fish with salad, *tahina*, vegetable stew, rice, bread and Coke. No alcohol.

El-Masry Sharia Abu Zid. Friendly, clean, a/c restaurant decorated in arabesque tiles, serving tasty set meals (£E23) based around fish, kebab, pigeon or stuffed courgettes. Popular with Egyptian families and tourists alike. No alcohol.

Emy On a boat beside the *Aswan Moon*. Shabbier and less popular than the *Moon*, but with better views, a nice breeze, and billiards. Meals are slightly cheaper, but not so good; the fruit cocktails are great, however. Sells alcohol.

Nubian House On a hill behind the *Basma Hotel* ℡ 097/326-226. Worth the journey for its amazing views over Elephantine Island and the First Cataract as well as its Nubian meals (£E8–25), this small restaurant is deservedly popular. Not to be confused with the *Nubian House* on Elephantine, which is more of a venue for music (see p.451).

Nubian Restaurant Issa Island, south of Elephantine ℡ 097/302-465. Good for an evening's entertainment, with a Nubian buffet (£E55) and a folkloric show after dinner. Beer and wine are expensive. Phone to ask when the show starts. Free boat from the dock opposite EgyptAir.

Zoom Sharia al-Souk, just north of the *El-Madina*. No-frills sit-down patisserie with ice cream and sticky cakes; cheap – mostly under £E2.

Drinking places

El-Shatti On the riverside, near Thomas Cook. Has several terraces, okay for drinking beer but not much else.

Mona Lisa The Corniche, near the *Aswan Moon*. A sweatbox during the summer, this shabby haunt of courting couples and solitary drinkers serves the cheapest beer in town and features worn-out music tapes and handpainted Cairo bazaar scenes.

Entertainments and activities

Traditional Aswani diversions include **promenading** along the Corniche and bazaar, meeting friends in riverside **restaurants**, and listening to Nubian **music**. Most tourists spend their days sightseeing or shopping, and when not attending the **Sound and Light Show at Philae** (see p.464), usually opt for an early night – which is why the **nightclubs** in the *Oberoi* and *New Cataract* and the **disco** in the *Isis* (except Mon 11pm–3am) are so empty.

Nubian music and weddings

Nubian music found a global audience in the 1990s, as the septuagenarian **Ali Hassan Kuban** hit the charts with *From Nubia to Cairo* and *Walk Like a Nubian*, and other musicians and vocalists teamed up to cut a series of CDs under the name **Samalat** (all on the Piranha label; ⓦ www.pirhana.de). Kuban grew up playing at weddings and parties and once earned his living as a tillerman; many other Nubian stars have similar backgrounds. His soulful vocals and rhythmic backing-section are quite unlike the style of **Sayyed Gayer** (now retired), who sang poems and love songs to the simple accompaniment of a *douff* (drum), or the semi-classical compositions for the *oud* (lute) written by **Hamza ad-Din**, a Nubian composer born in Wadi Halfa in 1929, whose Sufi beliefs are expressed in such haunting compositions as *Escalay* (The Waterwheel).

While top stars rarely perform in Aswan you can hear their music playing in bazaars and cafés and performed by other musicians. If you like the sound, buy cassettes or CDs in Aswan's souk – salesmen will let you listen to a selection – as they're not widely available elsewhere (particularly in Cairo and Alex, which scorn the music of the south). Impromptu performances may occur at the *Aswan Moon* or Ferial Gardens, but live bands mainly appear at weddings, during the summer months.

Nubian weddings are celebrated on a lavish scale, with guest musicians who charge as much as £E5000. The bridegroom recoups the expense by inviting hundreds of his friends and charging them £E10 each, which makes summer – the wedding season – an expensive time for locals. The wedding ceremony is followed by a week of celebrations, culminating in "pigeon nights" when guests devour quantities of pigeon to increase their sexual potency. (King

Farouk was said to consume the juice of six birds a day.) As guests from foreign lands are held to be auspicious, tourists are often invited (but should never presume) to attend weddings in the villages around Aswan. However, beware of crooks inveigling you to their village with a phoney invitation in the hope of getting you drunk or stoned, to rob or molest you later.

Over winter, locals flock to see the **Nubian Folk Troupe** perform stories of village life, wedding and harvest routines and the famous Nubian stick dance, which pantomimes a sword fight. Two-hour performances at Aswan's Soviet-inspired **Palace of Culture** (℡097/313-391) usually take place every night (8.30–10pm) except Friday from November to March; tickets (£E10) are sold on a first-come, first-served basis. Alternatively, you can enjoy a **show with a meal** at the *Nubian House* on Elephantine (£E35 for dinner and music), the *Nubian Restaurant* on Issa Island (£E55; see p.450), or two delightful **houses** on Sehel Island (see p.457). The Kenzi House is run by Mohammed Hassan (℡097/301-577), a cousin of the owner of the Hosh al-Kenzi in Darow (see p.434), while the other residence belongs to Omar Abdel Aziz (℡097/301-514), who can often be found at the felucca dock opposite EgyptAir. If enough people are interested, either can arrange food and entertainment for about £E30 per person, including transport to the island by motorboat.

Elaborate **designs in henna** on the hands and feet of brides are another feature of Nubian culture, and one that belongs to its women. If foreign tourists are interested, several shops and hotels in the bazaar advertise "tattooing" and act as intermediaries for the women who do the designs.

Festivals

On **Aswan Day** (January 15), the Corniche witnesses a good-natured parade of civic and military hardware; fire engines and ambulances following jeeploads of perspiring frogmen and rubber-suited decontamination troops. To appreciate the joke, catch the farcical orgy of drilling and polishing that transpires outside the Police Department and the Governorate Building the day before. Otherwise, the only events are an international **rowing festival** which may or may not happen in December, and the month-long international **Sculpture Symposium** sometime in the spring, when you can see sculptors at work on the terrace of the *Basma Hotel*, before their artworks are packed off to the Sculpture Park (see "Excursions from Aswan", p.453).

Listings

Airlines EgyptAir on the Corniche (daily 8am–8pm; ℡097/315-000) and at the airport (℡097/480-568) near the High Dam, 23km south of town (£E20 by taxi; £E1 by El Gouna bus).

Airport police ℡097/480-509.

American Express The Corniche (daily 9.30am–5pm; ℡097/306-983, ℻302-909). Will exchange currency and travellers' cheques, hold client mail and organize travel.

Banks There are ATMs (Visa/MasterCard/Plus/Cirrus) outside the Banque Misr (Mon–Thurs & Sun 8.30am–9pm) and the National Bank of Egypt (Mon–Thurs & Sun 8.30am–2pm) on the Corniche, where you can also change money or travellers' cheques at the Banque du Caire (Mon–Thurs & Sun 8.30am–2pm & 3–10pm) or Bank of Alexandria (Mon–Thurs & Sun 8am–2pm).

MasterCard and Visa cash advances are available from the Banque Misr.

Dry-cleaners On the ground floor of the *Nubian Oasis Hotel* (£E1.50–3 per item).

Duty Free Southern end of the Corniche (daily 10am–3pm & 7pm–midnight). Poorly stocked and fusty, selling alcohol and cigarettes upstairs. You can only buy imported booze within 24 hours of arrival in Egypt; domestic wine and spirits cost more than in Luxor, and this appears to be the only retail outlet in Aswan.

Foreign newspapers and books You'll find the *Egyptian Gazette*, *Al-Ahram Weekly* and the odd foreign paper on the Corniche near the *Horus* and *Philae* hotels. An expensive shop in the *New Cataract* offers the widest range of Egyptology books and novels; the Islamic Bookshop near the local taxi station and the Dar Al-Maaref in the arcade beside the tourist police stock a smattering of each at reasonable prices.

Internet Local provider Aswanet offers the fastest connections and lowest prices (£E10/hr) at its café in the *Keylany Hotel* (daily 9am–midnight). *Tareek Internet* is a no-frills outlet (£E12/hr) at the same end of the bazaar, while the Rowing Club on the Corniche has more of a café (£E20/hr); both keep the same hours. If the manager is around, guests can go online at the *Nubian Oasis* (£E12/hr), while the *Cleopatra* has a terminal in its lobby that anyone can use for £E20 an hour.

Medical emergencies The Evangelical Mission Hospital off the Corniche (⊕097/317-176) charges £E100 for a consultation (Mon–Sat 7am–noon & 4–6pm), but for serious problems you're better off at the Mubarak Military Hospital out towards the airport (⊕097/317-985 or 314-739; ambulance ⊕123. The tourist office can recommend doctors.

Passport office On the 2nd floor of the Police Department (Mon–Thurs & Sun 8.30am–1pm & 6-8pm; ⊕097/317-006). Registration all day; visa extensions mornings only.

Pharmacies El-Nile, next to the Banque du Caire on the Corniche (daily 8am–1am, closed 1–5pm on Fridays; ⊕097/302-674); Galal, next to the *Happi Hotel* (daily 7am–3pm & 6pm–midnight; ⊕097/303-011). Others are dotted all over town – ask at your hotel for the nearest.

Photo developing Photo Sabry on the Corniche near EgyptAir (Mon–Thurs, Sat & Sun 9am–2pm & 6.30–11.30pm, Fri 7–11pm; ⊕097/306-452). Sells film.

Post office Main GPO (daily except Fri 8am–2pm) near the Rowing Club; the section for poste restante (same hours) is on Sharia Abtal el-Tahrir, one block inland behind the Bank of Alexandria. Outward-bound mail arrives quicker if posted from a major hotel.

Swimming Non-residents may use the pools at the *Cleopatra* (£E10) and *Isis* (£E25), but foreigners aren't admitted to the municipal baths on the Corniche. Though local boys happily bathe in the Nile, tourists seldom do so for fear of bilharzia, which is a problem near the riverbanks and islands that impede the water's fast flow. If you're still keen, there are some lovely bathing spots out at the First Cataract.

Telephone calls International calls can be made from the 24-hour telephone office near EgyptAir, or Menatel card booths all over town. It costs less to send a fax at the telephone office than at the BC Business Centre one block south of the Police Department, or in major hotels. Off-peak rates 8pm–8am.

Thomas Cook On the Corniche near the Police Department (daily 8am–2pm & 5-8pm; ⊕097/304-011, ℱ306-839). Changes money, sells cheques and arranges tours to Abu Simbel.

Excursions from Aswan

Aswan is a base for **excursions** to numerous sites, some of which can only be reached from here, while others are also accessible from Luxor. Providing you start early enough, it's possible to fit two or more sites into a **full day's itinerary**, albeit one that doesn't allow you to linger at each place for long. Much depends on whether you engage a private taxi or rely on public transport, which is more time-consuming. Some tourists try to cram the highlights into two long day trips: south to Abu Simbel and Philae; and north to Kom Ombo, Edfu and Esna.

The classic half-day excursion is to **Philae Island** with its lovely Temple of Isis, situated in the lake between the **Aswan Dams**. Typically, groups of tourists rent a private taxi to take them to the Philae launch dock, then the dams and back to Aswan, briefly visiting the **Unfinished Obelisk** and the **Fatimid Cemetery** on the outskirts of town (another short trip from town is to **Sehel Island**). For a four-hour tour (which suffices), four-seater taxis should accept £E30–40; larger Peugeot 504s, seating seven or eight, roughly £E65. For £E70–80, you can probably persuade them to extend the tour to include **Kalabsha Temple**, which otherwise entails a separate trip.

As far as **Abu Simbel** goes (and it *is* far), most tourists get there on a minibus or coach excursion in a convoy from Aswan. Thomas Cook and other agencies ask about £E450 for a ten-seater minibus, while budget hotels like the *Nubian Oasis* and *Orabi* charge £E35 per head for a more cramped vehicle. It's also possible to get there by bus, but you won't save any money; it does, however, allow you to travel outside of convoy hours and stay overnight if you wish.

Alternatively – and much more expensively – you can reach Abu Simbel by **flying**, or a four-day **cruise on Lake Nasser**, departing from the High Dam (see box on p.462 for details).

The other main circuit takes in one or more of the **temples between Aswan and Luxor**. Relying on public transport, you could feasibly combine **Kom Ombo** with **Edfu**, but to see **Esna** as well really calls for a private taxi. Expect to pay between £E180–200 for a four-seater taxi, or £E230–250 for a larger vehicle to take you to each site for an hour and then on to Luxor. Taxis are obliged to travel in a **convoy** from Aswan; the one leaving at 8am is for sightseeing, while the 1pm convoy travels directly to Luxor without any stopovers. Alternatively, you could visit Kom Ombo and Edfu by felucca or a cruise boat.

The sites nearer town are described below; for accounts of the Aswan Dams, Philae, Kalabsha Temple and Abu Simbel, see the subsequent sections; for information on moving on from Aswan and felucca trips see below.

The Fatimid Cemetery, the Unfinished Obelisk and the Sculpture Park

Some 500m from the grounds of the Nubia Museum, you'll see a green metal fence surrounding hundreds of mud-brick tombs ranging from simple enclosures to complex domed cubes. This veritable lexicon of Islamic funerary architecture is known as the **Fatimid Cemetery**, though the majority of tombs actually date from Tulunid times. Some of the domes are built on a drum with the corners protruding like horns, a design unique to Upper Egypt. Most tombs had marble inscriptions attached until a freak rainstorm washed them off, and they were taken to Cairo in 1887 without any record of their original locations, leaving the tombs starkly unadorned. While not as grand as the mausolea in Cairo's Cities of the Dead – or inhabited by squatters – they're an eerie sight, which might tempt you to explore the cemetery (open 24 hours; no admission charge). Its main gate is ten minutes' walk from the roundabout where the road to the airport forks off the Corniche. By aiming for the three-storey building on the far side of the cemetery, you can emerge from the necropolis to join the road to the Unfinished Obelisk and Northern Quarries 1km further on.

The **Northern Quarries** (daily 7am–5pm; £E12) are the best-known of the many quarrying sites in the hills south of Aswan, which supplied the ancient Egyptians with fine red granite for their temples and colossi. Its fame derives from a gigantic **Unfinished Obelisk**, roughly dressed and nearly cut free from the bedrock, before being abandoned after a flaw in the stone was discovered. Had it been finished, the obelisk would have weighed 1168 tons and stood nearly 42 metres high. It's reckoned that this was the intended mate for the so-called Lateran Obelisk in Rome, which originally stood before the temple of Tuthmosis III at Karnak and is still credited as being the largest obelisk in the world. From chisel marks and discarded tools, archeologists have been able to deduce pharaonic quarrying techniques, such as soaking wooden wedges to split fissures, and using quartz sand slurry as an abrasive. A new **Visitors Centre** displays tools and fragments of statues and columns found when a rubbish dump on the site was cleared, and there are plans to establish a tourist-trail through the quarries.

While it's just about feasible to walk to the Northern Quarries, you definitely need wheels to reach the **Sculpture Park** near the **Southern Quarries** out towards the Old Dam. The park displays work by artists attending Aswan's International Sculpture Symposium, who spend a month on the terrace of the *Basma Hotel* creating works that are either judged fit to grace the streets of Aswan (the "Tottering Skyscraper" on the roundabout near the Coptic

The Nile's timeless scenery is best appreciated on longer **felucca** journeys between Aswan and Luxor. While cruise boats are more comfortable and predictable, feluccas offer an unforgettable, uniquely Egyptian experience, which many travellers rate as the highlight of their trip – though tales of misery aren't uncommon either. Whether your felucca trip is blissful or boring, tragicomic or simply unpleasant, depends on a host of factors and your own expectations.

Firstly, bear in mind the time of year and **conditions on the river**. Feluccas are dependent on the wind, which nearly always blows south. Travelling downstream (towards Luxor) therefore involves constant tacking, unless you simply drift with the sluggish current, but there's no chance of being becalmed, unlike sailing upriver, where the cliffs between Esna, Edfu and Kom Ombo block the wind – which is why most tourists start from Aswan. The usual trips on offer are to Kom Ombo (two days, one night), or Kom Ombo and Edfu (three days, two nights); during winter, when daylight hours are short, it's likely that **schedules** will slip and you might not reach Edfu in less than three nights. As feluccas are prohibited from sailing after 8pm, most stop at sunset for an evening round a campfire, enlivened by Nubian singing and drumming. Each day will be different from the last: stow your watch and take things as they come.

Another factor is the **water level**. Between October and May, so little is allowed through the High Dam that feluccas must be careful near shore, and inexperienced pilots have come to grief on sandbanks in the Nile. While it's obviously vital to choose an experienced captain, some tourists urge pilots to go faster than is wise, and it's hard for them to disagree.

The point at which the **journey ends** often causes friction, as tourists who think they're going to **Edfu** find themselves 30km short of town, in the villages of Hammam, Faris or Al-Ramady, where minivans are on hand to drive them to the temple and then on to Luxor and whichever hotel the captain has a deal with, for £E10 per person. Establish the drop-off point before you go, and refuse to hand over the rest of the cash if they cut the trip short while there's still sailing time left. But if nightfall is approaching and you've still got far to go, the crew's wish to finish the job is understandable and you might feel the same about the trip. Though in theory one could sail all the way to Luxor, nobody is likely to agree to go beyond Edfu.

Arranging a felucca trip

Assembling a group of six to eight people is easily done by asking around in Corniche restaurants or responding to messages posted in the tourist office. Since you'll be spending many hours in close proximity, the character and habits of your fellow travellers are a prime consideration (vid. Sartre, "Hell is other people"). Women will benefit from teaming up with a couple of men for the duration: an all-female group is likely to have problems. Agree on the number of passengers before you go and don't be talked into accepting others later on, downriver, or food supplies and space will be more limited than you'd expected.

The **tourist office** can recommend good captains and where to find them, but won't deliver a verdict on guys with whom you've already started negotiations. Arranging things through a hotel will probably work out costlier than finding your own captain, and in the event of a dispute it will be harder to recover any cash, since the hotel will have taken a hefty commission. On the other hand, hotels usually vet their captains, minimizing the risk of you ending up with a baddie. Try socializing with a few before **choosing a captain** and opening negotiations. Would-be voyagers are entitled to a free cruise around Aswan "bay" to check out the boat and its crew in action. Typically, a large vessel has an English-speaking Nubian captain and carries up to eight passengers who sleep either ashore after the boat has tied up, or on mattresses aboard. Nights are chilly (and maybe damp) for much of the year, so a sleeping bag is essential, as the blankets supplied are insufficient. Ensure that the **boat** has a canvas awning to protect you from the sun (which doubles as a tent at night), adequate mattresses, a jerry can for water, a kerosene stove and lamp, proper cutlery and a padlocked luggage hold. It is unwise to travel on a felucca lacking any of these items. Some captains have been guilty of taking tourists for a jaunt on a smart boat, and then substituting an inferior vessel (or crew) on the day of departure. If this happens, refuse to set sail and report it to the tourist office, who'll act as an intermediary between you and the tourist police.

Payment and registration

Rates are calculated on the basis of six to eight passengers, according to the duration of the journey, but also vary with fluctuating demand. The tourist office quotes £E25 per person for a trip to Kom Ombo and £E45 for Edfu, which doesn't include the cost of food for the trip, nor registration. Though most captains will accept less in the summer, travellers who push the price too low risk being robbed by a crew bent on getting proper remuneration. Don't pay the whole amount until you reach your destination, lest the boat "break down" and curtail the trip prematurely, and be sure that all members of the group know what has been negotiated, to ensure solidarity in the event of a dispute with the crew.

Don't hand over your passport; captains or middlemen like to collect them as proof that they've got some passengers in the bag while they go hunting for more. A **photocopy** of the page(s) with your personal details and photograph suffices for **registration** with the River Police, which is mandatory for all travellers. This can be arranged by felucca captains or local travel agencies – all of which charge £E5 per person for the effort, though there is no official fee.

Food and hygiene

Meals, prepared on a campfire or primus stove, consist of *fuul*, rice, bread, feta cheese and salad, washed down with tea. The ingredients are easily found in the souk, along with crisps, biscuits, jam and other "luxuries". Some groups prefer to agree on a price without food and take the responsibility for their own **shopping**; others strike a deal that includes food, in which case it's wise for somebody to accompany the captain when he goes provisioning, to see what you're getting. Be sure to buy plenty of bottled water, or the crew may dip into the Nile for drinking or cooking purposes. There's a real risk of getting sick on a felucca journey if **hygiene** precautions aren't observed. Bring extra-strong sterilizing tablets to purify the jerry can of Nile water used for washing up (one tab per 25 litres); also purchase carbolic soap and be sure that everyone uses it (food is mostly eaten with fingers); burn rubbish and bury excrement (the Nile's banks are badly littered) – few captains will bother with any health precautions unless pressed. Also strongly **recommended** are a hat and sunscreen (the river feels cool but reflects sunlight with great intensity) and bug repellent (the shallows swarm with mosquitoes).

Recommended feluccas

Recommending good felucca captains is tricky, for once they appear in guidebooks they soon marry foreigners and move to Europe or Australia, leaving younger, inexperienced cousins to run the boats in their name – as has happened with the famous Jamaica family on Elephantine – or you get other captains pretending to be them. Shukri and Hakeem at the tourist office keep an eye on the situation and recommend boats rather than individuals by name: ask for the *Washington*, *Lucky*, *Elizabeth* or *Sheraton*. Given that sexual harassment can be a problem and a few felucca men have drugged passengers, it pays to be careful; travellers can help by reporting offenders to the tourist police.

Cathedral), or join the others in the park. Besides the sheer variety and imaginativeness of the sculptures, the park enjoys a wonderful **view**, especially at sunset. Be sure to get a taxi whose driver knows what you mean by "*El Mathaf el-Maftoua*" and a rough idea of the route (about 30 minutes' journey). Take the road for the Old Dam, but turn off onto an uphill road rather than towards the Shellal docks (for ferries to Philae). Continue until you reach the top; the sculptures are on the right, the quarries to the left.

While **taxi tours** to Philae often briefly stop at the obelisk and the cemetery on the way back to Aswan, they ignore the park since few tourists ask to visit it. If your fellow passengers agree, it shouldn't be hard to persuade the driver to make the brief detour for £E10 extra. Otherwise, hire a taxi in Aswan for a few hours to visit all three sites in one trip (£E20–30).

Nile cruises

No visitor to Aswan or Luxor can fail to notice the dozens of cruise boats moored along their Corniches. Though mainly used by prepaid package tourists, there's nothing to stop independent travellers from striking a deal and enjoying a cruise – and prices are so low that they compare favourably with staying in hotels. There are basically two kinds of **cruises**: seven nights there and back (always starting in Luxor) or a briefer cruise commencing at either end. Starting at Luxor will mean two nights' sailing time, with stopovers at the temples of Edfu and Kom Ombo, while from Aswan it's a one-night, two-day cruise only stopping at Kom Ombo or Edfu; in both cases, there's an indeterminate **wait** to pass through the locks at Esna, which makes it unwise to rely on getting back to Luxor or Cairo in time for a scheduled flight home.

You'll be told that all the **boats** rate five stars, which the Ministry of Tourism has indeed awarded them, though standards vary from bog-average three-star up to the truly palatial. Distinctions are best assessed in person; put on clean clothes, leave your luggage behind and go hopping from one boat to another, as far along the Corniche as you can walk. The boats are moored two to four abreast, and their lobbies give a fair idea of what the cabins are like. Even the average vessel will have decent cabins with en-suite facilities, a restaurant, bar, sun deck and swimming pool, but the superior boats have cabins with double beds, large bathrooms, patio doors and even balconies. The cruise schedule for each boat will be posted in the lobby.

Try to **deal** with the boat manager (*not* the captain, who'll be an old river-pilot speaking little English), who's likelier to quote a lower rate than travel agencies, whose commission is factored into the price. This is especially true if the boat is near its sailing time and only half full, or you have a bottle of Johnny Walker Black Label (the real thing, not the Egyptian rip-off) to throw into negotiations, which are invariably in US dollars (beware of being screwed on the exchange rate if you're using other currencies). **Prices** can go as low as $US30 per person per night, including all meals per 24-hour period, but not **drinks**, which cost from £E6 for a bottle of water, £E15 for a beer and £E25 for a cocktail, to £E65 for a bottle of wine; Black Label costs £E37 a shot. Many travellers smuggle booze aboard to stash in their cabin fridge, despite the ban on doing so on some boats. The **meals** provided range from mediocre catering food to sumptuous buffets, but snacks are rarely available.

Boats profit by charging passengers ludicrous sums for extra **offshore excursions**, such as £E100 to visit Karnak Temple from the nearby mooring berths in Luxor. While the management won't object if you find a cheaper way of doing things, they will *not* be happy if you let other passengers know about it, nor what you've paid for the cruise – which could well be a fraction of what they've shelled out. British tourists who'd rather book a cruise from home can find **flight-inclusive deals** on Sky Television's TV Travel Shop (channels 630-632, available online at Ⓦwww.tvtravelshop.co.uk).

Sehel Island and the First Cataract

Travellers enamoured of felucca journeys should visit **Sehel Island**, 4km upriver from Aswan. With a strong wind behind you, it can be reached in an hour or so; on calmer days, allow longer. The recommended rate for a three-hour felucca trip is £E50. Bring water and a hat, and come well shod: although the river is cool, the rocks and sand are scorchingly hot. Landing on the east side of the island, you'll be mobbed by kids wanting to take you to the **Nubian village** to the west, for *baksheesh*. Hospitality and handicrafts pervade the charming **Kenzi House** modelled on the Hosh al-Kenzi in Darow, and another house in the village, both of which offer **music** and **meals** in the evening (see "Entertainments and activities", p.451).

Village kids are also keen to lead you to the "ruins", two hills of jumbled boulders that dominate the island. Here are over 250 **inscriptions** from the Middle Kingdom until Ptolemaic times, "bruised" rather than carved into the weathered granite. Most record Egyptian expeditions beyond the First Cataract or prayers of gratitude for their safe return, but atop the eastern hill you'll find a Ptolemaic **Famine Stele** (#81). Backdated to the reign of Zoser, it relates how he ended a seven-year famine during the III Dynasty by placating Khnum, god of the cataract, with a new temple on Sehel and the return of lands confiscated from his cult centre at Esna, which had provoked Khnum to withhold the inundation.

The summit provides a superb view of the **First Cataract**, a lush, cliff-bound stretch of river divided into channels by outcrops of granite. Before the Aswan Dams, the waters foamed and boiled, making the cataract a fearsome obstacle to upriver travel. Until early last century, it was necessary to offload cargo and transport it overland while the lightened boats risked rowing against the rapids. Amelia Edwards described "the leap – the dead fall – the staggering rush forward", waves and spray flooding the boat and the oars audibly scraping the rocks on either side.

In ancient times the cataract was credited as being the source of the Nile (which was believed to flow south into Nubia as well as north through Egypt) and the abode of the deity who controlled the inundation (either Hapy or Khnum, or perhaps both working in tandem). The foaming waters were thought to well up from a subterranean cavern where the Nile-god dwelt. Offerings continued to be made at Sehel even after its putative location shifted to Biga Island during the Late Period or Ptolemaic times (see "Philae", p.462).

Moving on from Aswan

For foreigners, **travel restrictions** are an important consideration for onward travel, and rules in force at time of writing are subject to change. Aswan's tourist office is up to date with the current regulations.

Private and service taxis

The convoy rule definitely applies to **private taxis** to Kom Ombo and other points north of Aswan, so if you're renting a special taxi for an excursion, be prepared to start with the 8am convoy even if you quit it later. A second convoy leaves at 1pm, but this runs directly to Luxor without any stopovers. At the time of writing, foreigners were banned from using **service taxis**, which are the fastest way to get anywhere. The main service taxi depot beyond the train tracks serves **Darow** and **Kom Ombo** (£E1.50), **Edfu** (£E3.50), **Esna** (£E6), **Luxor** (£E8) and other points north. **Aswan environs**, **Hazan/the Old Dam** (£E1) and points south, plus Kom Ombo, are served by a "local" depot around the corner from the *Abu Simbel Hotel*.

Buses

The unwritten **rule** is that tourists may only travel in buses outside of a convoy if there are no more than four tourists aboard the vehicle. This isn't likely to cause any difficulties when tourism is at a low ebb, but could make problems if more foreigners start wanting to travel, as places are allocated on a first-come, first-served basis, and the Upper Egypt Bus Co. doesn't sell tickets in advance. The company runs four buses daily **between Aswan and Luxor** (4hr; £E10), which stop at each town en route, and three direct a/c buses to **Cairo** (13hr), leaving at 8am, 3.30pm (£E55) and 4.30pm (£E48). Travellers bound for the Red Sea Coast or Sinai can use one of the three daily buses which go to **Hurghada** (7hr; £E25–35) and on to **Suez** (12hr; £E30-40). They also have four buses a day to **Abu Simbel** (£E12), but it's better to use a private operator, **El Gouna** (whose terminus is behind the Governorate), which lets you book in advance or buy return tickets on its two daily services (9am & 6pm; £E15).

Trains

Trains are best used for long hauls. Tourists may catch six daily services to **Luxor** (4hr; 1st class £E30, a/c 2nd class £21), stopping at Darow, Kom Ombo, Edfu and Esna en route. However, they can only buy tickets to **Cairo** (15hr; 1st class £E69, a/c 2nd class £E38; students £E45/£E29) on trains #981 (5am), #1903 (6pm) and #997 (8pm), plus the deluxe *wagons-lits* sleeper #85 (£E365 for a bed in a double cabin), leaving at 6.15pm. Most tourists economize by travelling on a regular train, as both 1st and a/c 2nd class have comfortable seating that makes an overnight journey quite tolerable.

Flights

For those with sufficient money, EgyptAir does flights to **Luxor** (45min; US$56), **Cairo** (90min; US$169) and **Abu Simbel** (30min; US$69). The prices quoted are one-way fares – except for Abu Simbel, which is usually visited on a day-return ticket that includes transfers between the temple and the airport. Abu Simbel may also be served by local charter companies like Luxor Air, Orca, Pharaoh and Scarabee, but flights are subject to demand and, as such, are less reliable than EgyptAir.

By ferry to Sudan

For the truly adventurous there's a weekly **ferry from Aswan to Wadi Halfa**, in Sudan. The boat leaves from the High Dam Dock in Lake Nasser on Monday afternoon and takes 24 hours to reach Wadi Halfa; the return trip from Wadi Halfa departs Wednesday. One-way **tickets** (1st class £E195, 2nd class £E120) are sold at the Nile River Valley Transport Corporation (daily except Fri 8am–2pm) in the crumbling shopping arcade behind Aswan's tourist police station, where just enough English is spoken to seal the transaction. The price includes an obligatory departure card, meals and drinks – bring extra food for the journey. All foreigners need a **Sudanese visa**, which can *not* be obtained on arrival in Wadi Halfa, but only from the Sudanese Consulate in Cairo, which requires up to a month's wait and a mass of forms and photographs (see p.275 for details). As the decades-old civil war between the Islamist regime in the north and Christian or Anamist tribes in the south seems to be inching towards a peace treaty, there's hope for a better future for the country of which it is said, "Allah didn't know whether to laugh or cry when he made it".

The Aswan Dams

Under a good administration the Nile gains on the desert; under a bad one the desert gains on the Nile.

Napoleon

The **Aswan Dams** attest that Egypt's fundamental dilemma is more intractable than suggested by John Gunther's pithy diagnosis:"Make more land. Make fewer people. Either solution would alleviate the problem, but neither is easy". Although each dam has brought large areas under cultivation, boosted agricultural productivity and provided hydroelectricity for industry, the gains have been eroded by a population explosion that again threatens to outstrip resources – impelling Egypt to undertake yet more ambitious irrigation projects.

Ever conscious of the dams' significance, Egyptians are inclined to view them as a tourist attraction, whereas most foreigners simply regard the edifices as a route to the temples of Abu Simbel, Philae and Kalabsha, which were reassembled on higher ground following the construction of the High Dam. Views from the top of the dams are spectacular, though, so don't begrudge tours' obligatory stopovers.

The Old Dam

Just upriver from the First Cataract stands the old **Aswan Dam**, built by the British (1898–1902) and subsequently twice raised to increase its capacity. Once the largest dam in the world, it stands 50m tall, 2km long, 30m thick at the base and 11m at the top. Driving across, you'll notice the 180 sluice gates that used to be opened during the inundation and then gradually closed as the river level dropped, preserving a semi-natural flood cycle. Now that its storage and irrigation functions have been taken over by the High Dam, it chiefly serves to generate hydroelectricity for the nearby Kima factory, producing chemical fertilizers. **Philae** (see p.462) is visible amongst the islands to the south of the dam.

Near the eastern end of the dam lies a former Reservoir Colony, now called **HAZAN**, where colonial villas nestle amidst verdant gardens. Service taxis and pick-ups run here from Aswan, but won't carry foreigners at the time of writing.

The High Dam (Al-Sadd al-Ali)

By 1952 it was apparent that the Aswan Dam could no longer satisfy Egypt's needs nor guarantee security from famine. Nasser pledged to build a new **High Dam**, 6km upstream, that would secure Egypt's future, power new industries and bring electricity to every village. When the World Bank reneged on its promised loan under pressure from the US, Nasser nationalized the Suez Canal to generate revenue for the project and turned to the USSR for assistance. The dam's construction (1960–71) outlasted his lifetime, as well as the era of Soviet–Egyptian collaboration. When Egypt decided to install more powerful turbine generators in the late 1980s, they bought them from America. Nowadays, Norwegians, British and French engineers are involved in an ambitious new project at Toshka, backed by Gulf and European investors.

Lake Nasser and the environmental consequences

The most visible consequence of the High Dam is **Lake Nasser**, which backs up for nearly 500km, well into Sudan. Over 180m deep in places, with a surface area of 6000 square kilometres, the lake is the world's largest reservoir, and seems more like an inland sea. During the decade of drought that saw the Nile

ASWAN ENVIRONS & LAKE NASSER

fall to its lowest level in 350 years, it saved Egypt from the famine that wracked Ethiopia and Sudan. When heavy rainfall caused the Nile to flood in 1988, the High Dam prevented Aswan from being inundated like Khartoum. Since a dam burst would wash most of Egypt's population into the Mediterranean, its security is paramount. The surrounding hills bristle with radar installations and anti-aircraft missiles; threats to bomb the dam made by Israel during the 1967 and 1973 wars, and by Gaddafi in 1984, have not been forgotten.

Although its human, cultural and environmental costs are still being evaluated, the dam has delivered most of its promised **benefits**. Egypt has been able to convert 700,000 *feddans* (a measurement of land roughly equal to one acre) of cultivated land from the ancient basin system of irrigation to perennial irrigation – doubling or tripling the number of harvests – and to reclaim more than one million *feddans* of desert. The dam's turbines have powered a 30 percent expansion of industrial capacity, too; humming pylons carry megavolts to Aswan's chemical and cement factories, the Helwan Iron and Steel Mill, and the refineries of Suez. Fishing and tourism on Lake Nasser have developed into profitable industries, and the new Toshka pumping station and the Sheikh Zayed Canal are set to turn more desert into farmland as the **Toshka Project** progresses (see box on p.477).

While the main losers have been the **Nubians**, whose homeland was submerged by the lake (see p.439), other **environmental consequences** are still being assessed. Evaporation from the lake has caused haze, clouds and even rainfall over previously arid regions, and the water table beneath the Sahara has risen as far away as Algeria. Because the dam traps the silt that once renewed Egypt's fields, farmers now rely on *Nitrokima* fertilizers, which have entered the food chain. The soil salinity caused by perennial irrigation can only be prevented by extensive drainage projects, which create breeding grounds for mosquitoes and bilharzia-carrying snails. Ancient monuments have been affected by damp and salt-encrustation, blamed on the rising water table and greater humidity. Some even think that this has made Egypt more vulnerable to earthquakes. And with no silty deposits to replenish it, the Delta coastline is rapidly being eroded by the Mediterranean.

It's estimated that the lake itself will be filled by silt within five hundred years. But whereas some reckon that the Nubian desert may have reverted to its prehistoric lushness by then, others fear international conflicts over water resources within the first century of the new millennium. Civil wars have hitherto prevented Ethiopia and Sudan from harnessing the White Nile and the watery Sudd for their own needs, but Egypt has already expressed its objections, citing a vested interest in the Nile's headwaters. Former UN Secretary-General Boutros-Boutros Ghali prophesied that Egypt may go to war over the Nile during the twenty-first century.

Visiting the High Dam

The High Dam is 13km from Aswan, and can be crossed anytime between 7am and 5pm. All vehicle passengers are charged a £E5 **toll** and may have to show their passports. Along the western approach stands the **Soviet-Egyptian Memorial**, a giant lotus-blossom tower built to symbolize their collaboration and the dam's benefits, as depicted in heroic, Socialist Realist bas-reliefs; its observation deck, reached by elevator, is sometimes open. Off the road at the east end of the dam is a **visitors' pavilion** (daily 7am–5pm), which the curator will unlock for *baksheesh*. Exhibits include a fifteen-metre-high model of the dam, plans for its construction (in Russian and Arabic), and a photo narrative of the relocation of Abu Simbel.

Cruises and fishing trips on Lake Nasser

To appreciate the vastness of Lake Nasser and see the otherwise inaccessible sites known as **Wadi el-Seboua**, **Amada** and **Qasr Ibrim** (described on p.470), you really have to take a cruise. **Cruise boats** began operating on the lake in 1993 on the initative of Mustafa al-Guindi, a Cairo-born Nubian who was responsible for the first two vessels, the *Eugénie* (modelled on an early twentieth-century hunting lodge) and the *Qasr Ibrim* (in 1930s Art Deco style), both operated by Belle Epoque Travel in Cairo (℡02/516-9654, ℻516-9546).

There are now four other boats on the lake: *Prince Abbas* (℡097/314-660 or mobile 0122 206747), *Queen Abu Simbel* (℡097/306-512), the *Nubian Sea* (mobile ℡0123 222065) and the *Tania* (℡097/316-393) – all rated 5-stars, except for the 4-star *Tania*. Each follows a similar **schedule**, departing on a four-day cruise from the High Dam or a three-day voyage from Abu Simbel, taking in the three sites mentioned above plus Abu Simbel and Kalabsha. Most passengers are package tourists who've pre-booked in their own country, but trips can be arranged through Belle Epoque in Cairo, or agents on the Corniche in Aswan such as Eastmar Travel (the *Nubian Sea*) or Travco (the *Tania*). Prices start from US$90 per person per day, including meals and admission to the sites; the *Nubian Sea* wins the prize for the finest food. As on Nile cruises, drinks are expensive, and some travellers choose to smuggle a supply aboard.

Additionally, two other companies offer weekly **fishing trips** from September to December and February to June. The *African Angler* (℡097/316-052) is run by former Kenyan safari guide Tim Bailey, in conjunction with Abercrombie & Kent in Cairo (℡02/394-7735), while *Wild Nuba* (℡ & ℻097/309-191, ✉wildnuba@yahoo.com) is operated by Pascal Artieda, a former manager of the *Eugénie*. Both offer fishing enthusiasts the chance of breaking their own personal records by reeling in a Nile perch – the largest yet caught weighed nearly 100kg – and boasting of how they evaded the crocodiles that roam the lake's murky depths and shallows. Fishing trips cost more than regular cruises, and should be booked up to six months ahead.

However, unless you ask to visit the tower (*burg*) or "model" (*mekat*), taxis will only **stop midway across the dam** for a brief look. From this vantage point the dam's height (111m) is masked by the cantilever, but its length (3830m) and width at the top (40m) and base (980m) are impressive. From the southern side of the dam you can gaze across Lake Nasser to Kalabsha Temple. The **view** northwards includes the huge 2100-megawatt power station on the east bank and the channels through which water is routed into the Nile, rushing out amidst clouds of mist, sometimes crowned by a rainbow. **Philae** lies amongst the cluster of islands further downriver.

As foreigners may not use service taxis from Aswan, the only public transport to the High Dam is a 3rd-class train (hourly 6am–4pm; £E1) which terminates at **Sadd al-Ali Station**, 5km south of the eastern end of the dam, near the **docks** for the **ferry to Wadi Halfa** and Lake Nasser **cruise boats** (see the boxes on p.458 and above). However, tourists disembarking there are allowed to catch a service taxi from outside the station, into Aswan (£E1).

Philae

The island of **PHILAE** and its **Temple of Isis** have bewitched visitors since Ptolemaic times, when most of the complex was constructed. The devout and curious were drawn here by a cult that flourished throughout the Roman empire well into the Christian era. Although the first Europeans to "rediscover" Philae in the eighteenth century could only marvel at it from a distance after their attempts to land were "met with howls, threats and eventually the spears of the natives living in the ruins", subsequent visitors revelled in this mirage from antiquity. "If a procession of white-robed priests bearing aloft the veiled ark of the God were to come sweeping round between the palms," mused Amelia Edwards, "we would not think it strange".

After the building of the first Aswan Dam, rising waters lapped and surged about the temple, submerging it for half the year, when tourists would admire its shadowy presence beneath the translucent water. However, once it became apparent that the new High Dam would submerge Philae forever, UNESCO and the EAO organized a massive operation (1972–80) to **relocate its temples** on nearby **Aglika Island**, which was landscaped to match the original site. The new Philae is magnificently set amidst volcanic outcrops, like a jewel in the royal blue lake, but no longer faces Biga Island, sacred to Osiris, whence its holiness derived.

Getting there

Most people visit Philae on **taxi tours from Aswan** (see p.452), which is the only easy way of getting there and back. Taxis drop you at the **Shallal** motorboat dock, 2km from the eastern end of the Old Dam, where you buy site **tickets** (daily 7am–5pm; Ramadan 7am–4pm; £E20). Having agreed on a price for a motorboat to the island (officially £E20 return per boat-load or £E2.50 each for more than eight people), you shouldn't pay anything until you're back on shore, obliging the boatman to wait while you explore; if you linger more than an hour, *baksheesh* is in order. There's nowhere to buy food or drink on the island.

Sound and Light Show

Some reckon that Philae's **Sound and Light Show** is even better than the one at Karnak, due to its island setting. There are two or three performances nightly; check the schedules at the tourist office. As at Karnak, the show consists of an hour-long tour through the ruins, whose floodlit forms are more impressive than the melodramatic soundtrack. By manoeuvring yourself into the front row, you can enjoy a panoramic view of the entire complex without having to swivel your head during the second act. **Tickets** (£E33; no student reductions) are sold at the dockside just before the first show begins. You'll need to rent a **taxi** from Aswan to take you there and back; expect to pay £E20 for a four-seater cab (including waiting time), plus £E22 for the motorboat ride there and back.

The Temple of Isis

Philae's cult status dates back to the New Kingdom, when Biga Island was identified as one of the burial places of Osiris – and the first piece of land to emerge from the primordial waters of Chaos. Since Biga was forbidden to all but the priesthood, however, public festivities centred upon neighbouring **Philae**, which was known originally as the "Island from the Time of Re".

Excluding a few remains from the Late Period, the existing **Temple of Isis** was constructed over some eight hundred years by Ptolemaic and Roman rulers who sought to identify themselves with the Osirian myth and the cult of Isis (see above). An exquisite fusion of ancient Egyptian and Greco-Roman architecture, the temple complex harmonizes perfectly with its setting, sculpted pillars and pylons gleaming white or mellow gold against Mediterranean-blue water and black Nilotic rock.

Approaching the temple

Motorboats land near an ancient quay at the southern end of the island. In ancient times, on the original Philae, visitors ascended a double stairway to the **Vestibule of Nectanebo** at the entrance to the temple precincts. Erected by a XXX Dynasty pharaoh in honour of his "Mother Isis", this was the prototype

The cult of Isis

Of all the cults of ancient Egypt, none endured longer or spread further than the worship of the goddess **Isis**. As the consort of Osiris, she civilized the world by instituting marriage and teaching women the domestic arts. As an enchantress, she collected the dismembered fragments of his body and briefly revived him to conceive a son, Horus, using her magic to help him defeat the evil Seth and restore the divine order. As pharaohs identified themselves with Horus, the living king, so Isis was their divine mother; a role which inevitably associated her with Hathor, the two goddesses being conflated in the Late Period. By this time Isis was the Great Mother of All Gods and Nature, Goddess of Ten Thousand Names, of women, purity and sexuality.

Isis

By a process of identification with other goddesses around the Mediterranean, **Isis-worship** eventually spread throughout the Roman empire (the westernmost *Iseum* or cult temple extant is in Hungary). The nurturing, forgiving, loving Isis was Christianity's chief rival between the third and fifth centuries. Many scholars believe that the cult of the Virgin Mary was Christianity's attempt to wean converts away from Isis; early Coptic art identifies one with the other, Horus with Jesus, and the Christian cross with the pharaonic *ankh*.

for the graceful kiosks of the Ptolemaic and Roman era. Notice the double capitals on the remaining columns: traditional flower shapes topped with sistrum –Hathor squares that supported the architrave. The screens that once formed the walls are crowned with cavetto cornices and rows of *uraeus* serpents, a motif dating back to Zoser's complex at Saqqara, nearly three thousand years earlier.

Beyond the vestibule stretches an elongated trapezoidal courtyard flanked by colonnades. The **West Colonnade** is the better preserved, with finely carved capitals, each slightly different. The windows in the wall behind once faced Biga, the island of Osiris; the one opposite the first two columns is topped by a relief of Nero offering two eyes to Horus and Isis. The plainer, unfinished **East Colonnade** abuts a succession of ruined structures. Past the foundations of the **Temple of Arensnupis** (worshipped as the "Good Companion of Isis" in the Late Period) lies a ruined **Chapel of Mandulis**, the Nubian god of Kalabsha. Near the First Pylon, an unfinished **Temple of Imhotep** honours the philosopher-physician who designed Zoser's Step Pyramid and was later deified as a god of healing. Its forecourt walls show Khnum, Satis, Anukis, Isis and Osiris, and Ptolemy IV before Imhotep.

The Pylons and Forecourt

The lofty **First Pylon** was built by Neos Dionysos, who smites enemies in the approved fashion at either corner, watched by Isis, Horus and Hathor. Set at right angles to the pylon, the Gate of Ptolemy II **[a]** is probably a remnant of an earlier temple. The pylon's main portal **[b]** is still older (dating from the reign of Nectanebo II) and was formerly flanked by two granite obelisks; now only two **stone lions** remain. Inside the portal are inscriptions by Napoleon's troops, commemorating their victory over the Mamlukes in 1799. The smaller door in the western section of the pylon leads through to the Birth House and was used for *mamissi* rituals; the entrance depicts the personified deities of Nubia and the usual Egyptian pantheon **[c]**. On the back of the pylon are scenes of priests carrying Isis's barque.

Emerging into the **Forecourt**, most visitors make a beeline for the Birth House (see below) or the Second Pylon, overlooking the colonnade to the east. Here, reliefs behind the stylish plant columns show the king performing rituals such as dragging the barque of Sokar **[d]**. A series of doors lead into six rooms which probably had a service function; one of them, dubbed the Library **[e]**, features Thoth in his ibis and baboon forms, Maat, lion-headed Tefnut and Sheshat, the goddess of writing. At the northern end stands a ruined chapel **[f]**, which the Romans erected in front of a granite outcrop that was smoothed into a stele under Ptolemy IV and related his gift of lands to the temple.

Set at an angle to its forerunner, the **Second Pylon** changes the axis of the temple. A large relief on the right tower shows Neos Dionysos placing sacrifices before Horus and Hathor; in a smaller scene above he presents a wreath to Horus and Nephthys, offers incense and anoints an altar before Osiris, Isis and Horus. Similar scenes on the other tower have been defaced by early Christians, who executed the paintings in the upper right-hand corner of the pylon passageway, leading into the temple proper.

The Birth House

The western side of the forecourt is dominated by the colonnaded **Birth House** of Ptolemy IV, which linked his ancestry to Horus and Osiris. Most of the exterior reliefs were added in Roman times, which explains why the Emperor Augustus shadows Buto, goddess of the north, as she plays a harp before the young, naked Horus and his mother at one end of the central register, behind the Hathor-headed colonnade **[g]**. Further south and higher up, the Roman reliefs overlie inscriptions in hieroglyphs and demotic characters that partly duplicate those on the Rosetta Stone **[h]**. Inside the *mamissi*, a columned forecourt and two vestibules precede the sanctuary, which contains the finest scenes **[i]**. Although iconoclasts have defaced the goddess suckling the child-pharaoh on the left-hand wall, you can see Isis giving birth to Horus in the marshes at the bottom of the rear wall. Around the back of the sanctuary behind the northern colonnade is a corresponding scene of Isis nursing Horus in the swamp **[j]**.

Inside the Temple of Isis

Immediately behind the Second Pylon lies a small open court that was originally separated from the **Hypostyle Hall** by a screen wall, now destroyed. A lovely drawing by David Roberts shows this "Grand Portico" in its rich original colours: the flowering capitals in shades of green with yellow flowers and blue buds; crimson and golden winged sun-discs flying down the central aisle of the ceiling, which elsewhere bears astronomical reliefs. The unpainted walls and column shafts show the hall's builder, Ptolemy VII Euergetes II, sacrificing to various deities. After the emperor Justinian forbade the celebration of Isis rituals at Philae in 550 AD, Copts used the hall for services and chiselled crosses into the walls. On the left-hand jamb of the portal **[k]** into the vestibule beyond, a piece of Roman graffiti asserts *B Mure stultus est* ("B Mure is stupid").

As at other temples, the **vestibules** get lower and darker as you approach the sanctuary. By a doorway **[l]** to the right of the first vestibule, a Greek inscription records the "cleansing" of this pagan structure under Bishop Theodorus, during the reign of Justinian. On the other side of the vestibule is a room giving access to the **stairs** to the roof (see below). The next vestibule has an interesting scene flanking the portal at the back **[m]**, where the king offers a sistrum (left) and wine (right) to Isis and Harpocrates. On the left-hand door jamb, he leaves offerings to Min, a basket to Sekhmet and wine to Osiris, with the sacred bull and seven cows in the background. In the partially ruined transverse vestibule, the king offers necklaces, wine and eye paint to Osiris, Isis, Hathor and Nephthys, outside the sanctuary **[n]**.

Dimly lit by two apertures in the roof, the **sanctuary** contains a stone pedestal dedicated by Ptolemy III and his wife Berenice, which once supported the goddess's barque. On the left wall, the pharaoh faces Isis, whose wings protectively enfold Osiris. Across the room, an enthroned Isis suckles the infant Horus (above) and stands to suckle a young pharaoh (below, and now defaced). The other rooms, used for rites or storage, contain reliefs of goddesses with Nubian features.

The Osirian Shrine

Try to persuade a guard to unlock the stairway to the roof, where a series of sunken rooms dwells on the resurrection of Osiris. After scenes of lamentation in the vestibule of this **Osirian Shrine**, you can see Isis gathering up his limbs, and the slain god lying naked and tumescent upon a bier (as always, the phallus has been vandalized). Mourned by Isis and Nephthys, Osiris revives to impregnate his sister-wife, while Selket and Douait reconstruct his body for its solar rebirth. Cast as the hawk-headed Sokar, Osiris is borne away to a papyrus swamp by the four sons of Horus, to be anointed with holy water with Anubis in attendance.

Hadrian's Gate

By leaving the temple through the western door of the first vestibule you'll emerge near **Hadrian's Gate**, set into the girdle wall that once encircled the island. Flanking your approach are two walls from a bygone vestibule, decorated with notable reliefs. The right-hand wall **[o]** depicts the origin of the Nile, whose twin streams are poured forth by Hapy the Nile-god from his cave beneath Biga Island, atop which perches a falcon. To the right of this, Isis, Nephthys and others adore the young falcon as he rises from a marsh.

Above the door in the opposite wall **[p]**, Isis and Nephthys present the dual crowns to Horus, whose name is inscribed on a palm stalk by Sheshat (right) and Thoth (left). Below, Isis watches a crocodile drag the corpse of Osiris to a rocky promontory (presumably Biga). Around the gate itself, Hadrian appears before the gods (above the lintel) and the door jambs bear the fetishes of Abydos (left) and Osiris (right). At the top of the wall, Marcus Aurelius stands before Isis and Osiris; below he offers Isis grapes and flowers.

North of the gateway lie the foundations of the **Temple of Harendotes** (an aspect of Horus), built by the emperor Claudius.

The Temple of Hathor and Trajan's Kiosk

To complete the cast of deities involved in the Osirian myth, a small **Temple of Hathor** was erected to the east of the main complex. Aside from two Hathor-headed columns *in situ* and fragmented capitals out back, the ruined temple is only notable for a relief of musicians, amongst whom the god Bes plays a harp. More eye-catching and virtually the symbol of Philae is the graceful open-topped **Kiosk of Trajan**, nicknamed the "Pharaoh's Bedstead". Removed from its watery grave by a team of British navy divers, the reconstructed kiosk juxtaposes variegated floral columns with a severely classical superstructure; only two of the screen wall panels bear reliefs.

Last in order of priority come the ruined **Temple of Augustus** and the **Gate of Diocletian**, which shared the northern end of old Philae with a mud-brick Roman village that was so eroded by repeated soakings that it was left to be submerged by the lake. The **toilets** lie in this direction.

Kalabsha

The hulking **Temple of Kalabsha** broods beside Lake Nasser near the western end of the High Dam, marooned on an island or strung out on a promontory, depending on the water level. Between the site and the dam lies a graveyard of boats and fishy remains, enhancing its mood of desolation. The main temple originally came from Talmis (later known as Kalabsha), 50km to the south of Aswan; in a German-financed operation, it was cut into 13,000 blocks and reassembled here in 1970, together with other monuments from Nubia. Strictly speaking, "Kalabsha" refers to the original site rather than the temple itself, which is named after the god Mandulis, and has no historic connection with two smaller monuments in the vicinity, relocated here from other sites in Nubia.

Getting there

Taxis are the best way of getting to Kalabsha and back. Official rates for a round trip from Aswan are £E25–30 for a four-seater taxi, £E45 for a seven-seater Peugeot. Better still, include Kalabsha in a half-day taxi tour taking in Philae, the dams and the Unfinished Obelisk (see p.452). Either is preferable to the penny-pinching alternative of taking a **train** to Sadd al-Ali Station (see p.462), then walking or hitching up to the dam and across to the other side of the lake (almost 10km in all).

In recent years it has been necessary to reach Kalabsha **by boat**. Motorboats will take you there and back for £E25 (for the whole boat; 6–8 people) with an hour at **the site** (daily 7am–5pm; £E12), which is sufficient; tickets are sold at the temple itself.

The Temple of Mandulis

The **Temple of Mandulis** is a Ptolemaic-Roman version of an earlier XVIII Dynasty edifice dedicated to the Nubian fertility god Marul, whom the Greeks called Mandulis.

By Ptolemaic times, Egypt's Nubian empire was a token one, dependent on the goodwill of the powerful Nabatean empire ruled from Merowe near the Fourth Cataract, about 400km south of Abu Simbel. Having briefly restored old-style imperialism, the Romans abandoned most of Nubia during the reign of Diocletian, falling back on deals with local rulers to safeguard Egypt's southern border. As the linchpin of the last imperial town south of Aswan, the temple bears witness to this patronage and the kingdoms that succeeded the Nabatean empire, which disintegrated under the onslaught of marauding Blemmye (c.550 AD), a group of nomadic tribes who were perhaps the ancestors of the modern Beja.

The causeway, court and facade

Approaching the sandstone temple from behind, you miss the dramatic effect of the great stone **causeway** from the water's edge, used by pilgrims in the days when Kalabsha was a healing temple, like Edfu and Dendara. For reasons unknown, its chunky **pylon** is skewed at a slight angle to the temple, a blemish rectified by having a trapezoidal **courtyard** whose pillars are set closer together along the shorter, southern side.

The first batch of reliefs worth a mention occurs on the **facade** of the Hypostyle Hall at the back of the court. While Horus and Thoth anoint the king with holy water in a conventional scene to the left of the portal, the right-hand wall bears a decree excluding swineherds and their pigs from the temple (issued in 249 AD); a large relief of a horseman in Roman dress receiving a wreath from the winged Victory; and a text in poor Greek lauding Siklo, the Christian king of the Nabatae, for repulsing the Blemmye.

The Hypostyle Hall and Sanctuary

The now roofless **Hypostyle Hall** is distinguished by columns with ornate flowered capitals, and some interesting reliefs along the rear wall. Left of the portal, a Ptolemaic king offers crowns to Horus and Mandulis, while Amenhotep II (founder of the XVIII Dynasty temple) presents a libation to Mandulis and Min. Across the way, a nameless king slays a foe before Horus, Shu and Tefnet.

Within the **vestibules** beyond, look for figures personifying the Egyptian nomes, below a scene of the king offering wine to Osiris and a field to Isis and Mandulis (near the stairs off the pronaos or outer vestibule); and a rare appearance by the deified Imhotep (low down on the left-hand wall of the naos or inner vestibule).

The **Sanctuary** is similar in size to the vestibules and, like them, once had two columns. Along its back wall you can identify (from left to right) the emperor offering lotuses to Isis and the young Horus, and milk to Mandulis and Wadjet; then incense to the former duo and lotuses to the latter. Although the god's cult statue has vanished, Mandulis still appears at either end of the scene covering the temple's **rear wall**: in his royal form, with a pharaonic crown, sceptre and *ankh* sign (right); and as a god whose ram's-horn crown is surmounted by a solar disc, *uraeus* and ostrich plumes (left).

From the temple's pronaos, you may be able to ascend a stairway to the **roof**, which features an abbreviated version of the Osirian shrines found at other complexes. The **view** of Lake Nasser and the High Dam, over the temple courtyards, is amazing. A passageway between the temple and its enclosure wall leads to a well-preserved **Nilometer**.

The Kiosk of Qertassi and Beit al-Wali

Re-erected near the lakeside at the same time as Kalabsha Temple, the **Kiosk of Qertassi** resembles a knocked-about copy of the "Pharaoh's Bedstead" at Philae, but actually came from another ancient settlement, 40km south of Aswan. Aside from its fine views of Lake Nasser, this Ptolemaic-Roman edifice is chiefly notable for two surviving Hathor-headed columns, which make the goddess look more feline than bovine. In the forecourt, notice the women pleading for mercy as Ramses seizes their menfolk, and the Nubians paying tribute in the form of gold, ivory, leopard skins, feathers, and even an ostrich.

The oldest monumental relic from Nile-inundated Nubia is a temple dug into the hillside behind Kalabsha Temple. Originally hewn under Ramses II, who left his mark throughout Nubia, this cruciform rock-cut structure is known by its Arabic name, **Beit al-Wali** (House of the Holy Man). The weathered reliefs flanking its narrow court depict the pharaoh's victories over Nubians and Ethiopians (left), Libyans and Asiatics (right). By contrast, scenes in the transverse hall are well preserved and brightly coloured. Here, Ramses makes offerings before Isis, Horus and the Aswan Triad (Hapy, Satet and Khnum), and is suckled by goddesses inside the sanctuary, whose niche contains a mutilated cult statue of three deities.

Wadi el-Seboua, Amada and Qasr Ibrim

As Lake Nasser rose behind the High Dam, flooding ancient Nubia, mud-brick fortresses and burial grounds were excavated and photographed before being abandoned to the rising waters, and half a dozen temples and tombs were salvaged, to be reassembled on higher ground or in foreign museums. At the time of writing, the three reconstructed sites known as **Wadi el-Seboua**, **Amada** and **Qasr Ibrim** can only be seen while **cruising on Lake Nasser** (detailed in the box on p.462), but spur roads to Wadi el-Seboua and Amada have already been built and airports for charter flights are on the cards, so access may improve in the next few years if security restrictions are eased. Meanwhile, cruise boats provide their passengers with motorboat rides to Wadi el-Seboua and Amada, moor tantalizingly close to Qasr Ibrim (where you can't land), and end or start their tours at Abu Simbel or Kalabsha.

Wadi el-Seboua

Cruise boats departing from the High Dam must sail nearly half the length of Lake Nasser before they reach **Wadi el-Seboua**. They usually moor there after dark for passengers to enjoy an awesome floodlit vista of three temples, joined by what appears to be a long processional avenue, which is revealed next morning to be a track across a desert of tan-coloured sand and grey rocks. The landscape is dotted with a few swathes of grass and a half-submerged crane that was used to transport the main temple from its original location, 4km away. **Admission** to the site costs £E30 (no student reductions).

    Wadi el-Seboua means "Valley of the Lions" in Arabic and refers to the **avenue of sphinxes** leading to the **temple** of that name. It was built during the reign of Ramses II by his viceroy of Kush, Setau, using Libyan prisoners of war, who also worked on Abu Simbel. Like Abu Simbel, it was dedicated to Amun-Re, Re-Herakhte and the deified pharaoh, whose role as a conqueror is emphasized by images of Libyan and Asiatic captives carved on the pedestals of the statues of the king that flank its gateway. In the second court, the human-headed sphinxes give way to falcon-headed ones, representing the four forms of Horus, and archeologists have discerned a subtle attempt to "rehabilitate" Seth – the reviled murderer of Osiris – by using red sandstone for the steps and base of the temple proper. (Red was the colour associated with Seth, who was the patron deity of the Delta city of Avaris, whence the Ramessid dynasty originated.)

    Beyond the temple **pylon** is an **open court** with columns fronted by Osiride statues of Ramses, notable for their thick legs. Scholars disagree whether this reflected his physique or was merely to make him look stronger, but this feature occurs on all statues of Ramses, whose virility is further attested to by images of his numerous progeny (53 princes and 54 princesses) below the offering scenes on the walls. The remainder of the temple is cut from rock and once served as a Christian church; its **reliefs** retain much of their scarlet, white and yellow paint due to being covered by plaster for centuries. The best-preserved ones are in the transverse vestibule, including an unusual portrayal of Hathor with a woman's body and a cow's head. You can also see Ramses making offerings to his own sphinx, above and behind the doorway into the sanctuary, where a votive niche contains remnants of the Christian murals that once covered the walls, resulting in a surreal tableau of Ramses offering flowers to St Peter.

Temple of Dakka

From Wadi el-Seboua, passengers can walk or ride a camel (£E30) 1.5km across the desert to the hilltop **Temple of Dakka** that once stood 40km north of its present site. Its most striking feature is an elegant freestanding **pylon**, which is over 12m tall; visitors are sometimes allowed to climb it, which affords them a fantastic view of the area. You may also see **hawks**, hovering on thermals above the pylon. There isn't much carving on the walls but the gateway is crowned by a winged sun-disc, and on its left-hand side is graffiti in Meroitic script thought to have been left by Nubian soldiers, retreating from Aswan in 23 AD.

The temple itself was started by **Arkamani**, one of the rulers (218–200 BC) of the Kingdom of Meroe – which at that time controlled Lower Nubia – and was added to by his contemporary, **Ptolemy IV**, and decorated by later Ptolemies. You can see the Hellenistic influence in the composite capitals (combining Greek and Egyptian forms) and scenes in the pronaos, where Isis sports big breasts in the Greek style. Also notice the four sacred cobras, carved in the corners of the entrance wall. On many of the reliefs in the temple the king performing the rituals is simply identified by a cartouche reading "Pharaoh", as the masons didn't know who was in power at the time in Alexandria, or didn't want to inscribe the name of a Ptolemy who wouldn't be on the throne for long – though this wasn't the case for Ptolemy IV and his sister-wife Arsinoe, who are shown offering a Maat (truth) figure to Thoth and Wepset on the lintel of the doorway into the vestibule.

At the back of the vestibule is a passageway and stairs leading to the **roof**, which affords a stunning view, while beyond lies the **Chapel of Arkamani** that originally served as the temple's sanctuary. Here, Arkamani makes offerings to the gods beneath a frieze of his cartouche interspersed with falcons and ibises, while on the rear wall is an interesting relief of Thoth as an ape adoring Tefnut, who is shown as a lioness. The temple was dedicated to a local form of Thoth called Thoth of Pnubs (literally, "sycamore-fig tree"), his consort Tefnut and their "offspring" Arensnupis, a Nubian god of the Meroitic era whom the Egyptians called "The Good Companion of Isis". A baboon worshipping a lion can also be seen in the side-passage leading off the chapel, while another ape consorts with a cow beneath a persea tree low down in the near right-hand corner of the sanctuary, which was built and decorated under the Roman emperors Augustus and Tiberius. Upon leaving the temple, walk around the east wall to see a **waterspout** in the shape of a lion's head, which shows that there must have been the occasional rainfall in ancient times.

Temple of Maharraqa

A short way downhill back towards the shore stands the small **Temple of Maharraqa**, taken from a site 50km north of its present location, which was the southern frontier of Egypt in Greco-Roman times. Its floral capitals and reliefs were left unfinished – in some places only roughly sketched in reddish-brown paint – and the temple's most interesting feature is the **spiral staircase** up to the roof, the only spiral staircase known in an ancient Egyptian building. The temple was probably dedicated to Seraphis.

Amada

Beyond Wadi el-Seboua, Lake Nasser describes an S-shaped curve that takes it past another set of temples in one of the loveliest parts of Nubia, where the rocky desert shoreline is fringed with acacia scrub. As at Wadi el-Seboua, cruise passengers are ferried to **Amada** by motorboat, and all three monuments are covered by one **ticket** (£E30; no student reductions). Bring a **torch** for examining the reliefs inside the temples.

Temple of Amada

The site is named after the **Temple of Amada**, which is the oldest surviving structure on Lake Nasser and contains some of the finest relief-carving to be seen on any of the Nubian monuments. It was built by the XVIII Dynasty pharaohs Tuthmosis III, Amenophis II and Tuthmosis IV, and restored and decorated during the XIX Dynasty. Like most of the Nubian temples, it was dedicated to Amun-Re and Re-Herakhte, who appear with various pharaohs in the usual offerings scenes. For archeologists, the temple is particularly interesting for two historic **inscriptions**: the first, carved on a stele on the left side of the entrance, describes the Libyan invasion of Egypt in the fourth year (1232 BC) of Merneptah's reign; while the other, on the back wall of the sanctuary, dates from the second year (1423 BC) of Amenophis II's reign, and relates how he dealt with seven leaders of a revolt in Syria, whose heads and limbs were hung on the gates of Thebes as a warning to other would-be rebels.

When Amelia Edwards visited Amada in 1873 she found the temple "half-choked" with sand, so that she had to crawl into the sanctuary on all fours; judging by the **camels** drawn by Bedouin and pilgrims on the cornice of the facade, it was buried so in medieval times. The inner part of the temple consists of a vestibule and sanctuary with a small cult-chamber on either side, whose **reliefs** are as lapidary as any produced during the XVIII Dynasty. The ones in the right-hand room depict the foundation and consecration of the temple; Tuthmosis III and Amenophis II make offerings to the gods in the other chamber. Amada Temple originally stood 2.6km from its present site, and was moved there on flatcars by French engineers in a race against the rising waters of the lake.

Temple of Derr

A few minutes' walk from Amada is the smaller **Temple of Derr**, once located on the east bank of the Nile (the only one in Nubia on that side of the river). With its gateway gone and its pillared forehall reduced to stumps, the temple now confronts visitors with a rugged portico featuring four square pillars and statues of Ramses II only roughed-out up to waist-level. The interior of the temple was entirely hewn from rock, with few straight lines or right angles, and its sunk-reliefs finished in stucco with painted details. On the side walls of the pillared hall, Re-Herakhte's sacred barque is carried in a procession on the shoulders of priests, as Ramses walks alongside wearing a leopard-skin cloak; the white background and the yellow of the barque and cloak are still visible. More colours survive on the walls of the sanctuary, where Ramses burns incense and pours a libation to the barque before annointing Re-Herakhte with his little finger (right). At the back, the four cult-statues that originally represented Ramses, Amun-Re, Re-Herakhte and Ptah were hacked away by Christian iconoclasts.

Tomb of Pennut

Leaving Derr temple it's worth hurrying on ahead to get to the **Tomb of Pennut**, as it's only large enough to hold a few people. Pennut (or Penne) was a high official in Lower Nubia during the reign of Ramses VI, whose tomb was originally dug into a hillside at Aniba, 40km south of its present site. Sunk-reliefs in the rectangular offerings chamber show Pennut and his wife before the gods, mourners at his funeral, and Pennut worshipping the cow-goddess Hathor in the Western Mountains. Upon leaving the tomb, its custodian delves into a bucket to extract a baby **crocodile**, which he offers to tourists for a photo opportunity. The shallows of Lake Nasser are home to many crocodiles (some reportedly up to 5m long) and monitor lizards, but they avoid the spots frequented by tourists and are mainly only seen by the 5000 fishermen who spend up to six months at a time in small rowing boats, collectively harvesting up to 50,000 tonnes of fish a year from the lake.

Qasr Ibrim

Qasr Ibrim – the last stop on the cruise before Abu Simbel – is unique for being the only one of the Nubian sites to remain *in situ*, albeit nowadays on an island rather than the summit of a hill, since the lake rose 70m. This continuity has allowed the Egypt Exploration Society to carry out **excavations** every two years since 1961 and establish that Qasr Ibrim was occupied throughout successive periods from the late New Kingdom until the early nineteenth century, when it was inhabited by Bosnian mercenaries of the Ottoman empire, who married into the local Nubian community. Before their arrival in the sixteenth century, Qasr Ibrim was one of the last redoubts of Christianity in Lower Nubia, as it had previously been the last area to forsake paganism, abandoning the worship of Isis 200 years after the rest of Egypt. Its ruined sandstone **cathedral** dates back to the eighth century and overlies a temple of Isis built by the Nubian XXV Dynasty pharaoh Taharka; as many as six temples once have existed here. The cathedral's broken vaults rise amidst a muddle of dry-stone and cut-masonry walls, riddled with portals, niches and cavities, attesting to the age and complexity of the site. Due to its fragility and the ongoing excavations, tourists are not allowed to land here, but boats moor so close to the shore that the ruins can easily be seen, or closely examined with **binoculars**. Qasr Ibrim's unusual name is derived from the ancient *Pedme*, which became *Primis* in Greek, *Phrim* in Coptic and finally *Ibrim* in Arabic (which has no sound for "p").

Abu Simbel

The great **Sun Temple** of **Abu Simbel** epitomizes the monumentalism of the New Kingdom during its imperial heyday, when Ramses II (1304–1237 BC) waged colonial wars from the Beka'a Valley in Lebanon to the Fourth Cataract. To impress his power and majesty on the Nubians, Ramses had four gigantic statues of himself hewn from the mountainside, whence his unblinking stare confronted travellers as they entered Egypt from Africa. The temple he built here was precisely oriented so that the sun's rays reached deep into the mountain to illuminate its sanctuary on his birthday and the anniversary of his coronation. The deified pharaoh physically overshadows the sun-god **Re-Herakhte**, to whom the temple is nominally dedicated, just as his queen, **Nefertari**, sidelines **Hathor** in a neighbouring edifice, also hewn into the mountain.

The first European to see Abu Simbel since antiquity was the Swiss explorer Burckhardt, who found the temples almost completely buried by sand drifts in 1813. Although Belzoni later managed to clear an entrance, lack of treasure discouraged further efforts and the site was soon reburied in sand so fine "that every particle would go through an hourglass"; a process repeated throughout the nineteenth century. After Robert Hay took a cast of the face of the northern colossus, leaving it disfigured by lumps of plaster, Amelia Edwards ordered her sailors to remove the residue and tint the white stains with coffee, dismaying the vessel's cook, who had never "been called upon to provide for a guest whose mouth measured three feet and a half in width". Finally cleared, the temple became the scenic highlight of Thomas Cook's Nile cruises.

It was the prospect of losing Abu Simbel to Lake Nasser that impelled UNESCO to organize the salvage of Nubian monuments in the 1960s. Behind the temporary protection of a coffer dam, Abu Simbel's brittle sandstone was stabilized by injections of synthetic resin and then hand-sawn into 1041 blocks weighing up to thirty tons apiece. Precision was mandatory; the cuts had to be no more than 6mm wide. Two years after the first block was cut, Abu Simbel was reassembled 210m behind (and 61m above) its original site, a false mountain being constructed to match the former setting. The whole operation (from 1964 to 1968) cost US$40 million and is still being paid for; the cost of Egyptian tourist visas supposedly goes towards repayments.

Visiting Abu Simbel

Abu Simbel lies on the west bank of Lake Nasser, 280km south of Aswan and 40km north of the Sudanese border. A road runs there from Aswan, used by tourist vehicles travelling in a convoy, and public buses at other times. The site can also be reached by air or water – notably on the **luxury cruises** (p.462) that also visit other sites on Lake Nasser (see Wadi el-Seboua, Amada and Qasr Ibrim, on p.470). Although most tourists visit Abu Simbel on a **day trip** from Aswan, it's quite feasible to spend a night there.

Getting there

From Aswan, Thomas Cook, Misr Travel and other agencies offer daily **excursions** by a/c coach for groups of ten (£E450), while low-budget hotels like the *Nubian Oasis, Noorhan* and *Orabi* offer trips in cramped minibuses for £E35 per head. Both travel in a **convoy** of tourist vehicles which leaves town at 4.30am, arrives at Abu Simbel three and a half hours later, and starts the return journey at 10am. This might seem a weird schedule, but it makes sense given the heat of the desert. If you're not fazed by the temperature and want to stay longer at Abu Simbel, there are regular public **buses** from Aswan, which tourists can use providing there aren't more than four of them aboard the vehicle. Upper Egypt Bus Co. services (£E12) depart at 8am, 11.30am, 3pm and 5pm, while El Gouna buses (£E15) leave at 9am and 6pm. El Gouna lets passengers book seats in advance, and return journeys too.

For those with more cash, **flying** saves time and provides a unique view of Lake Nasser and Abu Simbel. EgyptAir flights from Aswan are scheduled according to demand, with a dozen flights a day in boom years, or between two

Photographing Abu Simbel

Abu Simbel is an awkward subject for **photography**. The immense facade should be snapped in the morning before it's cast into shadow, and needs a wide-angle lens to do it justice; details, however, are best captured with a telephoto lens (it also helps to underexpose the shot by 1–1.5 stops). To photograph Abu Simbel from the air, sit on the left side of the plane and use a telephoto (at least 200mm) lens with a haze filter. Depending on how many tour groups are visiting, it may be difficult to photograph the interior of the temples. There is **no charge** for cameras or camcorders, but flash photography is forbidden.

and six when tourism is low. In today's depressed market most of the charter airlines born in the late 1990s have cut schedules to the bone or suspended flights entirely, but if business recovers you may find that Luxor Air (mobile ☎0123 170464), Orca (mobile ☎0122 185257), Pharaoh (mobile ☎0123 169947) or Scarabee (mobile ☎0123 220104) are competitive with EgyptAir, which currently charges US$69 for a same-day return flight, including transfers. Most travel agencies will know which charter airlines are running, and can tell you if the two Russian-built **hydrofoils** that once ran to Abu Simbel are back in service. Both were mothballed for financial reasons when last heard, but a return trip used to cost US$70 and take four hours. For those with more time and money, a luxury **cruise** to Abu Simbel is the best way to appreciate Lake Nasser and see the temples as the pharaohs did (see p.462 for details).

Abu Simbel town practicalities – and the Sound and Light Show

Roughly 2km from the temple site, the new town of **ABU SIMBEL** (meaning "Father of the Ear of Corn" in Arabic) looks a desolate place as you roll in past the airport, but once beyond the main square it becomes quite picturesque as it straggles around rocky headlands dotted with beehive-domed houses and crimson oleander bushes. From the junction with its row of **cafés**, you can turn left and follow the main road as it curves around towards the temple, 1km away. This takes you past a **telephone office**, a **pharmacy** and three **banks** (none with ATMs; all closed Fri), followed by a **post office** with the **tourist police** around the corner, before you pass the town council and reach the stone-faced souvenir arcade that precedes the visitors centre and ticket office for the temples – about fifteen minutes' walk in all.

Should you decide to stay, the only cheapish option is the *Abu Simbel Village* (☎097/400-092; ❸), a small, pink complex of a/c rooms with TV, fridges and bathrooms, 200m from the main intersection in the opposite direction from the temples, past the derelict *Noblah Ramses Hotel*. Two dearer places are out towards the temple: the *Seti Abu Simbel* (☎097/400-720, ℉400-829, ℰreservation@setifirst.com, ✆www.setifirst.com; ❽), near the three banks, has a/c rooms with fridge, TV and large bathrooms, in a lush garden with three pools, overlooking Lake Nasser; and the *Nefertari* (☎097/400-508, ℉400-510; ❾), reached by a turn-off between the town council and the tourist arcade, which is older and shabbier but otherwise similar. Both officially charge the same year-round, but discounts can often be obtained through Eastmar Travel in Aswan (on the Corniche near Thomas Cook) or Cairo (13 Sharia Qasr el-Nil) in the summer.

If needed, there's a small **hospital** en route to the *Abu Simbel Village*, which probably exists because President Sadat had a holiday villa built at Abu Simbel (it's seldom used by Mubarak). Tourists on cruise boats may feel like VIPs themselves, insofar as it's hard to go far from the boats (which moor nearby, but just out of sight of, the temples) without an armed escort.

Cruise-boat passengers provide most of the audience at the nightly **Sound and Light Show** (£E44; no student discounts), starting at 8pm between April 28 and September 28, and at 7pm, 7.45pm and 8.30pm the rest of the year. Don't worry about which language the show is in, as they provide headphones for simultaneous translation and, in any case, the images projected onto the temple facades are more arresting than the soundtrack. Tickets are sold at the temple ticket office.

The Sun Temple of Ramses II

Having checked out the **Visitors Centre**, which relates how the temples were moved to their present location, visitors walk around the hill to be confronted by the great **Sun Temple** (daily 6am–5pm, later if planes land in the evening; £E36, student £E19), seemingly hewn from the cliffs overlooking Lake Nasser. Having been depicted on everything from T-shirts to £E1 notes, its impact is perhaps a little diminished by familiarity: the technicolour contrast between red rockscape and aquamarine water is more startling than the clean-swept facade, which looks less dramatic than the sand-choked Abu Simbel of nineteenth-century engravings. For all the meticulous reconstruction and landscaping, too, it's hard not to sense its artificiality … but gradually the temple's presence asserts itself and your mind boggles at its audacious conception, the logistics of constructing and moving it, and the unabashed megalomania of its founder.

Although Re-Herakhte, Amun-Re and Ptah are also billed as patron deities, they're clearly secondary to Ramses, the pharaoh-god whom courtiers feared as "a powerful lion with claws extended and a terrible roar". He ruled for 67 years, dying at the age of 96, having sired scores of sons, most of whom predeceased him.

The colossi and facade

The temple facade is dominated by four enthroned **Colossi of Ramses II**, whose twenty-metre height surpasses the Colossi of Memnon at Thebes (though one lost its upper half following an earthquake in 27 BC). Their feet and legs are crudely executed but the torsos and heads are finely carved, and the face of the left-hand figure is quite beautiful. Between them stand figures of the royal family, dwarfed by Ramses' knees. To the left of the headless colossus is the pharaoh's mother, Muttuy; Queen Nefertari stands on the right of the colossus; Prince Amunhirkhepshef between its legs. On the right leg of this same figure, an inscription records that Greek mercenaries participated in the Nubian campaign of the Saïte king Psammetichus II (c.590 BC).

Cross-section of the Sun Temple

The **facade** is otherwise embellished with a niche-bound statue of **Re-Herakhte**, holding a *was* sceptre and a figure of Maat. This composition is a pictorial play of words on Ramses' prenomen, *User-Maat-Re*, so the flanking sunk-reliefs of the king presenting the god with images of Maat actually signify Ramses honouring his deified self. Crowning the facade is a corvetto cornice surmounted by baboons worshipping the rising sun. On the sides of the colossal thrones flanking the temple entrance, twin Nile-gods entwine the heraldic papyrus and sedge around the hieroglyph "to unite". The rows of captives depicted beneath them are divided between north and south, so that Asiatics feature on the northern (right-hand) throne, Nubians on its southern (left-hand) counterpart.

The Hypostyle Hall and Sanctuary

This schematic division reappears in the lofty rock-cut **Hypostyle Hall**, flanked on either side by four pillars fronted by ten-metre-high statues of

Ramses in the Osiris position, carrying the crook and flail (the best is the end figure on the right). Beneath a ceiling painted with flying vultures, the walls crawl with scenes from his campaigns, from Syria to Nubia. On the entrance walls, Ramses slaughters Hittite and Nubian captives before Amun-Re (left) and Re-Herakhte (right), accompanied by his eight sons or nine daughters, and his *ka*. But the most dramatic **reliefs** are found on the side walls (all directions as if you're facing the back of the temple).

The right-hand wall depicts the **Battle of Qadesh** on the River Orontes (1300 BC), starting from the back of the hall. Here you see Ramses' army marching on Qadesh, followed by their encampment, ringed by shields. Acting on disinformation tortured out of enemy spies, Ramses prepares to attack the city and summons his reserve divisions down from the heights. The waiting Hittites ford the river, charge one division and scatter another to surround the king, who single-handedly cuts his way out of the trap. The final scene claims an unqualified Egyptian triumph, even though Ramses failed to take the city. Notwithstanding this, the opposite wall portrays him storming a Syrian fortress in his chariot (note the double arm, which some regard as an attempt at animation), lancing a Libyan and returning with fettered Nubians. Along the rear wall, he presents them to Amun, Mut and himself (left), and the captured Hittites to Re-Herakhte, lion-headed Wert-Hekew and his own deified personage (right).

The eight **lateral chambers** off the hall were probably used to store cult objects and tribute from Nubia, and are decorated with offering scenes. Reliefs in the smaller **pillared hall** show Ramses and Nefertari offering incense before the shrine and barque of Amun (left) and Re-Re-Herakhte (right). Walk through one of the doors at the back, cross the transverse vestibule and head for the central **Sanctuary**. Originally encased in gold, its four (now mutilated) cult statues wait to be touched by the sun's rays at dawn on February 22 and October 22. February 21 was Ramses' birthday and October 21 his coronation date, but the relocation of Abu Simbel has changed the timing of these **solar events** by one day. Perhaps significantly, the figure of Ptah "the Hidden One" is situated so that it alone remains in darkness when the sun illuminates Amun-Re, Re-Herakhte and Ramses the god. Before them is a stone block where the sacred barque once rested.

The Toshka and East Oweinat irrigation projects

Inaugurated by President Mubarak in 1997, the **Toshka Project** is a huge-scale venture whose goal is to cultivate 500,000 acres of desert northwest of Abu Simbel, and settle millions of people there. The alluvial soil is potentially fertile and experimental farms have already successfully grown cotton, cucumbers, tomatoes, watermelon, bananas, grapes and wheat. To irrigate the land, the Egyptians are building the world's largest **pumping station** to extract 177 billion cubic feet of water from Lake Nasser annually, and the **Sheikh Zayed Canal**, with a projected length of 550km. The government plans to deliver water to the edge of each property, leaving the owner with the responsibility for its distribution across their land. One such investor is Saudi Prince Alwaleed Bin Talal, whose KADCO farm is visible on the way to Abu Simbel. At the time of writing the pumping station was nearly operational, 100km of canal had been dug, and new roads were being constructed to link Toshka to another irrigation project at **East Oweinat**, using aquifer water. Some fear that these projects are too ambitious and may turn out to be white elephants; however, the same was said of the High Dam, without which Egypt could not sustain itself.

The Hathor Temple of Queen Nefertari

A little further north of the Sun Temple stands the smaller rock-hewn **Temple of Queen Nefertari**, identified here with the goddess Hathor, who was wife to the sun-god during his day's passage and mother to his rebirth at dawn. As with Ramses' temple, the rock-hewn facade imitates a receding pylon (whose corvetto cornice has fallen), its plane accentuated by a series of rising buttresses separating six **colossal statues of Ramses and Nefertari** (each more than 9m tall), which seem to emerge from the rock. Each is accompanied by two smaller figures of their children, who stand knee-high in the shadows. A frieze of cobras protects the door into the temple, which is simpler in plan than Ramses', having but one columned hall and vestibule, and only two lateral chambers; it runs 24m into the hillside.

The best **reliefs** are in the hall with square, Hathor-headed pillars whose sides show the royal couple mingling with deities. On the entrance wall Nefertari watches Ramses slay Egypt's enemies; on the side walls she participates in rituals as his equal, appearing before Anuket (left) and Hathor (right). In the transverse vestibule beyond, the portal of the sanctuary is flanked by scenes of the royal couple offering wine and flowers to Amun-Re and Horus (left), Re-Herakhte, Khnum, Satet and Anuket (right). The **Sanctuary** niche contains a ruined cow-statue of Hathor, above which vultures guard Nefertari's cartouches. On the side walls, she offers incense to Mut and Hathor (left), while Ramses worships his own image and that of Nefertari (right). The predominance of yellow in the paintings may allude to Hathor's title, "The Golden One".

Birdwatching at Abu Simbel

Due to its location on a large body of water surrounded by desert, near the Tropic of Cancer, Abu Simbel sustains both indigenous African and migrant species of birds. Among the rarities are pink-backed pelicans, yellow-billed storks, long-tailed cormorants, African Skimmers and pied wagtails, and pink-headed doves. While serious twitchers will haunt the coves with binoculars, casual birdspotters can see quite a few dazzling birds in the grounds of the visitors centre or the *Nefertari* and *Seti Abu Simbel* hotels.

The Western Desert Oases

CHAPTER 3 **Highlights**

* **White Desert** A surreal landscape of wind-eroded *yardangs* shaped like falcons, camels, lions and mushrooms, in Farafra Oasis. See p.523

* **Al-Qasr** This fantastic labyrinth of mud-brick dwellings dating back to the tenth century is one of several once-fortified *qasr* villages in Dakhla Oasis. See p.536

* **Siwa Oasis** Its citadel, palm groves, rock tombs and salt lakes make Siwa a must for travellers. See p.561

* **Hot springs** Found in all the oases, the coolest bathing spot is Bir Wahed in the outer dunes of the Great Sand Sea, near Siwa Oasis. See p.573

* **Dunes** Knife-edged *seif* dunes can run for over 140km, reform as crescents when they fall over an escarpment, or pile up as mountainous whalebacks. See p.560

* **Prehistoric rock art** *The English Patient* cast a spotlight on the Cave of the Swimmers in the remote Gilf Kebir, and there are many other sites at Jebel Uwaynat. See pp.555 & 557

* **Jeep or camel safaris** Whether you spend a night in the White Desert, or two weeks in the Great Sand Sea and the Gilf Kebir, you'll never forget the experience. See pp.487 & 520

* **Bird-watching** Flamingoes, Senegal coucals and grey herons are only some of the species found at Lake Qaroun and Wadi Rayan. See p.500 & 502

The Western Desert

Oases

For the ancient Egyptians civilization began and ended with the Nile Valley and the Delta, known as the "Black Land" for the colour of its rich alluvial deposits. Beyond lay the "Red Land" or desert, whose significance was either practical or mystical. East of the Nile it held mineral wealth and routes to the Red Sea Coast; west of the river lay the Kingdom of Osiris, Lord of the Dead – the deceased were said to "go west" to meet him. But once it was realized that human settlements existed out there, Egypt's rulers had to reckon with the **Western Desert Oases** as sources of exotic commodities and potential staging posts for invaders. Though linked to the civilization of the Nile Valley since antiquity, they have always been different – and remain so.

Siwa Oasis, far out near the Libyan border (and covered last in this chapter as it is furthest away), is the most striking example: its people speak another language and have customs unknown in the rest of Egypt. Its ruined citadels, lush palm groves, limpid pools and golden sand dunes epitomize the allure of the oases.

The four "inner" oases of **Bahariya**, **Farafra**, **Dakhla** and **Kharga** lie on the "**Great Desert Circuit**" that begins in Cairo or Assyut – a Long March through the New Valley Governorate, where modernization has affected each oasis to a greater or lesser extent. While Bahariya and Farafra remain basically desert villages, living off their traditional crops of dates and olives, Dakhla and Kharga have full-blown modern towns. The appeal of the latter two is stronger in the journeying – across hundreds of miles of awesome barrenness, most of it gravel pans rather than pure "sand desert".

Much nearer to Cairo (and suitable for day excursions) are two quasi-oases: the Fayoum and Wadi Natrun. The **Fayoum** is more akin to the Nile Valley than the Western Desert, with many ancient ruins to prove its importance since the Middle Kingdom. Though a popular holiday spot for Cairenes, it doesn't attract many foreign tourists except for hunters and ornithologists. **Wadi Natrun** is significant mainly for its Coptic monasteries, which draw hordes of Egyptian pilgrims but comparatively few foreigners.

The desert

Much of the fascination of this region lies in the desert itself. It's no accident that Islam, Judaism and Christianity were forged in deserts whose vast scarps and depressions displayed the hand of God writ large, with life-giving springs and oases as manifestations of divine mercy in a pitiless landscape. Although much of this landscape was once savannah, it was reduced to its current state millennia ago by geological processes and overgrazing by Stone Age pastoralists.

The **Western Desert**, which covers 681,000 square kilometres (over two-thirds of Egypt's total area), is merely one part of the Sahara belt across northern Africa. Its anomalous name was bestowed by British cartographers who viewed it from the perspective of the Nile – and, to complicate matters further, designated its southern reaches and parts of northwestern Sudan as the "Libyan Desert". Aside from the oases, its most striking features are the **Qattara Depression**, the lowest point in Africa, and the **Great Sand Sea** along the Libyan border, an awesome ocean of dunes that once swallowed up a whole army. Further south, the **Gilf Kebir** and **Jebel Uwaynat** feature some of the most magnificent prehistoric rock art in Egypt and were the setting for the events in the book and film *The English Patient*.

All the **practicalities** of visiting the oases (including the best times to go) are detailed under the respective entries in this chapter. The most comprehensive source of historical, ethnographic and geographical **information** is Cassandra Vivian's *The Western Desert of Egypt: An Explorer's Handbook* (last updated in 2000), which includes many useful maps and GPS (satellite navigation) way-points, and is available from good bookshops in Cairo.

Wadi Natrun

The quasi-oasis of **Wadi Natrun**, just off the Desert Road between Cairo and Alexandria, takes its name – and oasis stature – from deposits of natron salts, the main ingredient in ancient mummifications. Wadi Natrun's most enduring legacy, however, is its **monasteries**, which date back to the dawn of Christian monasticism, and have provided spiritual leadership for Egypt's Copts for the last 1500 years. Their fortified exteriors, necessary in centuries past to resist Bedouin raiders, cloak what are today very forward-looking, purposeful monastic establishments. Coptic monasticism experienced a revival during the 1980s, twenty years after an English writer dismissed the monasteries as "of little interest except to the specialist".

The area surrounding Wadi Natrun is known as **Liberation Province** (*Mudiriyat el-Tahrir*). In the 1950s, model villages, olive groves and vineyards were planted here to reclaim 25,000 hectares of land from the desert, a project initially financed by the sale of King Farouk's stamp collection and other valuables. The soil is potentially fertile, but lacks water; hitherto, the main springs and lakes in Wadi Natrun have been saline. Now, after decades of patient **land reclamation**, palms, flowers or hothouse vegetables grow beside the **Desert Road** to Alex, with ranks of saplings receding up to the horizon. To the east of the highway, a whole new conurbation, **MEDINET SADAT** (Sadat City), represents Egypt's aspirations for the 21st century: a dormitory suburb, science park and film studio rolled into one. On the other side of the highway, motels have sprung up around the turn-off for Wadi Natrun, which runs via the ramshackle township of **BIR HOOKER** (named after Mr Hooker, an early manager of the Egyptian Salt & Soda Co.) into the Natrun Valley.

Visiting the monasteries

Wadi Natrun makes a memorable **day excursion** from Alex or Cairo, but a few caveats are in order. Getting within striking distance requires little effort, time or cash, but reaching more than one or two of the monasteries can be difficult without using rented vehicles – see below for transport details.

Visiting hours vary from monastery to monastery, as does the extent to which each closes during the five seasons of **fasting**: 43 days before the Nativity, 3 days in commemoration of Jonah in the Whale, 55 days preceding Lent, the fast of the Holy Apostles (from Pentecost to July 12), and 15 days marking the Assumption of the Virgin Mary (Aug 7–22). Deir Anba Bishoi

Desert driving

An increasing number of visitors are driving themselves, even to sites beyond the inhabited oases of the Western Desert. The following advice should be borne in mind even if you're going to stick to main roads; for motorists considering more ambitious trips, it's only the bare outline of what you need to know. (For detailed handbooks, see "Books" in Contexts chapter.)

Permits

Motorists may now drive anywhere in the Western Desert without permission, with the following exceptions. Travel along the road **between Siwa and Bahariya** needs a permit from Military Intelligence in Siwa or the Desert Police in Bahariya, which is readily granted at short notice. To reach **Ain Della** also requires a permit, which can be issued in Cairo (and perhaps also in Siwa) but not in Farafra or Bahariya, the nearest oases – but even in Cairo you'll have to satisfy the branch of Military Intelligence responsible for the surveillance of foreigners (Section 26, Sharia Manshia el-Bakry, Heliopolis). Applications can be made through Misr Travel in Cairo (1 Sharia Talaat Harb ☎02/393 0010, ⓕ392 4440, ⓔmisrtrav@link.com.eg), at least two weeks before your intended departure date. You'll need to submit the names and passport numbers of everyone travelling, two photocopies of the main page and Egyptian visa in their passports, and the route and dates of travel. This rule also applies to everywhere south of Dakhla or Kharga oases – specifically the **Gilf Kebir** and **Jebel Uwaynat** – where all expeditions must be **accompanied** by an Egyptian army officer; applications should be submitted at least one month in advance (two to be on the safe side).

Vehicles

The desert is a potentially lethal environment, so it's crucial to get the right vehicle. Many local safari operators swear by Libyan army-surplus Toyotas or Ford trucks, which are robust and easy to fix, and handle well in the desert – but don't have a/c or other extras that tourists expect, which are standard on the 4WD Landcruisers used by Cairo-based firms (or available for rental in Cairo). Mechanical reliability, high ground clearance and four-wheel-drive are absolutely vital; non-automatic gears, a water-cooled engine and an electrical fuel pump are strongly advised. Desert travel is extremely hard on tyres, so even if the car isn't fitted with the best Michelins (£E650 apiece), they must be in good condition and have inner tubes; always carry two spare wheels, a tyre pump and pressure gauge, levers and a jack. A fire extinguisher, vital spares and a full tool/repair kit are also essential.

Ideally, your vehicle should also have the following **modifications**: steel plates welded below the sump and fuel tank to prevent them being holed; fireproof lagging around the fuel lines where they pass the exhaust manifold; crossover seat belts; fabric-covered seats; an extra, false roof above the cab (painted gloss white for maximum cooling effect); and a mileometer for navigational calculations – but it's rare that you'll encounter a car with all of these.

If you're renting a car, weigh the pros and cons of **diesel or petrol** engines. Diesel fuel costs £E8 for 20 litres, as opposed to £E1 per litre of petrol – a significant difference if you're planning an expedition that requires hundreds of litres of fuel; but diesel pumps and ignition systems are far harder to repair if there's a breakdown, so you'll need to carry replacements for all the critical parts.

Equipment

You can never carry too much **water** (in metal or heavy-duty polythene jerry cans, securely fixed to brackets) or **fuel** – travelling off-track can reduce a car's normal mileage by half. Even staying within the limits of an oasis depression, it's vital to be able to orient yourself. A vehicle-mounted **compass** must be adjusted to the car's magnetic field, which will also distort readings on hand-held compasses if you stand too close (as do ferrous rocks in Bahariya Oasis).

An increasing number of expeditions rely on **GPS** (Global Positioning System) for **navigation**. GPS sets can be hand-held or mounted on a dashboard to give your exact position in latitude and longitude, your compass-bearing, and record "Waypoints" so that routes can be retraced. While GPS ensures that you know *where* you are and can plot a course to any given point, it doesn't take any account of obstacles that might prove insurmountable – so choosing the best route still depends on knowing the terrain, whether it's the lie of dune "lanes" or the fragility of saltpans.

For details of the best relevant **maps** for exploring the oases, see p.31.

Desert driving

Decide from the start whether you plan to travel on paved roads, unpaved tracks, or through trackless open desert. It's safe to travel alone by road, as the checkpoints at either end (and at intervals along major routes) will raise the alarm if you fail to arrive. Always **travel in pairs** of vehicles if you're going off-road (though locals often drive alone on familiar territory). Never set off – or keep going – during **sandstorms**; should you get caught in one, shelter in the lee of cliffs or palm trees and turn the car's rear end towards the wind, lest it sand-blast the front windscreen and head-lights into opacity.

Driving at **night** is likewise taboo: potholes are vicious and it's easy to crash or get lost. The **best times for driving** are early morning and late afternoon, when there's less risk of overheating or misjudging the terrain. During the middle of the day, the details of the landscape are lost in the glare, making it harder to judge **distances and scale**. Both are distorted by the desert, where drivers often perceive near-vertical slopes as level ground, or discarded jerry cans as villages. These kind of optical illusions are commoner than **mirages** of shimmering "lakes".

If you are driving cross-country, stay alert for **changes in the desert's surface**, often indicated by a shift in colour or texture. Wheel ruts left by other vehicles can also yield clues: a sudden deepening and widening usually means softer sand (another sign of which is vegetation around the edges of dunes). Generally speak-ing, gravel plains provide a firm surface, while salt flats and dunes are the most unstable. Deflating one's **tyres** increases their traction on soft sand, but also their surface temperature and the car's fuel consumption, so keep a conservative speed.

Dunes

There's no substitute for experience of **dunes**, but a few points need making. Never crest a dune at high speed, in case the far side has collapsed, leaving a slipface. If you *do* go over, accelerate hard (which tends to lower the rear of the vehicle), charge down the slope and hope to butch it out. Braking or slewing sideways seems the natural reaction, but it's likely to somersault or roll the car over the edge. It's far safer to make a controlled descent in second gear and speed up as you reach the bottom.

When deflating tyres for better traction, do this just before you drive onto sand, and pump them up again before gaining firm ground. Shifting into a lower gear should likewise be done in advance. If stuck in soft sand, revving the engine will only dig you in deeper. Stop at once, change into low gear and try driving out slowly. If this fails, deflate the tyres as far as possible (or put traction mats, brushwood, rocks, etc beneath the rear wheels) and try again.

Health care and emergencies

Dehydration, heatstroke and sunburn are the main **health** hazards. You can monitor your own water-level by watching your urine; so long as you're "pissing clear" every-thing's okay (as the army adage has it). Wear loose, light clothing and keep your

continues overleaf

head covered (a Bedouin *keffiyah* works far better than a baseball cap, and can be used to veil your face against dust or grit). Use sun block and skin cream, particularly if you're travelling to the super-arid Gilf Kebir. Some travellers find air conditioning a mixed blessing, since alternating between a chilled interior and a furnace-hot environment causes passengers to catch colds.

While the odds that you'll be sleeping out when a sandstorm strikes are thankfully remote (if so, hunker down behind your rucksack), getting stuck, breaking down or crashing in the desert can be fatal if you compound the misfortune by acting wrongly. Assuming you're driving solo, *never leave your own vehicle* unless you're within 5km of a plainly visible settlement or major highway. Otherwise, stay put, keep cool (literally) and try to attract attention. By day you can burn oil-soaked sand or bits of rubber to produce thick black smoke; at night, make a fire. A vehicle, smoke or fire are hard enough for search parties to locate; a person on their own is virtually impossible.

Other **emergencies** arise simply through drivers getting lost. The moment you suspect this, stop and try to get oriented using a compass or the sun; take your time calculating how much water and fuel remain, then deciding on a course of action. The worst thing to do is simply drive on by instinct – it's a sure way of wandering even further in the wrong direction.

Although proper spares are obviously preferable, **improvised materials** can serve for vital **repairs**: nylon tights make a substitute fan belt and chewing gum can plug holes in fuel tanks or radiators.

---

alone is open every day of the year; Deir al-Suryani and Deir el-Baramus have regular opening times but close during most of the feasts; while Deir Abu Maqar will only admit those with a letter of introduction from the **Coptic Patriarchate** in Cairo (next to the Cathedral of St Mark, 222 Sharia Ramses, Abbassiya ☎02/282 5374 or 284 3159) or Alexandria (in the Cathedral of St Mark on Rue d'Iglise du Copte; ☎03/483 5522). The Patriarchate can verify the opening dates of specific monasteries. Fridays, Sundays and public holidays are best avoided when visiting any of the monasteries as they are often swarmed by Coptic pilgrims from all over Egypt.

Male tourists interested in **staying the night** in a monastery must get written permission from the appropriate "residence" in Cairo: Deir Anba Bishoi (☎02/591 4448); Deir al-Suryani (☎02/592 9658); Deir el-Baramus (☎02/592 2775); Deir Abu Maqar (☎02/577 0614). As other guests are devout pilgrims, you should make at least a token effort to attend prayers, and leave a donation in return for the tea and bread that's provided. Women are not allowed to sleep in any of the monasteries. Otherwise, there are several swanky motels (❺–❻) along the Desert Road, near the turn-off for Wadi Natrun.

Getting there

Unless you rent a car, or take a taxi (£E150–200 depending on how many monasteries you visit), reaching the monasteries is a two-stage process. The best way of **getting there** from Cairo is by the West Delta buses that leave from the Turgoman terminal (hourly 6.30am–6.30pm; £E3). Tickets are bought on the bus, which terminates at Bir Hooker, where you should be able to catch a pick-up (£E1) to Deir Anba Bishoi, or negotiate hiring a taxi to tour the monasteries for about £E20. Otherwise, you can get a service taxi from Cairo (Aboud terminal) or Alex (Sidi Gaber) to the **Wadi Natrun Resthouse** on the Desert Road – a bunch of motels, gas stations and cafés where non-express inter-city buses also stop. From here, you can negotiate a private taxi ride to

Desert safaris

Easier than driving yourself is to take an **organized desert safari**, through **local operators** in the oases (detailed under each in the text) or companies based in **Cairo** or **abroad**. Sadly, a lot of them care little for the desert, leaving rubbish behind and even encouraging tourists to take flint arrowheads or spray water on prehistoric rock paintings so that they look clearer in photos. The following outfits are experienced and respect the environment. In the case of foreign firms, and operators that offer trips to the Gilf Kebir or Jebel Uwaynat, they may only organize one or two expeditions a year, so you have to book more than six months ahead to be sure of getting a place (see p.550 for details).

Amr Aladin Shannon ☎ mobile 0121 778188 or 0123 417496, ⓔ ashannon@internetegypt .com. An artist who has guided small groups into the desert for twenty years, and is known in Egypt for his *Desert Stories* TV programmes, Amr speaks English, Italian and Arabic. His tours feature the remote Roman forts of Kharga Oasis.

Ancient World Tours ☎ 07071/222-950, ⓕ 01483/237-398, ⓔ mra@dial.pipex.com, ⓦ www.ancient.co.uk. A British firm specializing in archeological and desert travel, that runs two trips a year to the Gilf Kebir and or Jebel Uwaynat, starting from Britain.

El-Badawiya Safari 63 Midan Kit Kat, Dokki ☎ & ⓕ 02/345 8524, mobile 0122 148343, ⓔ badawya@link.net. The Cairo sales office for an outfit based in Farafra Oasis, that does 4WD, camel and walking treks in the Western Desert.

Fliegel Jerzerniczky Expeditions ⓦ www.fjexpeditions.com. A Hungarian company run by Sahara enthusiast András Zboráy, which mounts twice-yearly 10–14-day expeditions to the Gilf Kebir and Uwaynat, and is the only operator visiting Ain Doua on the Libyan side of Uwaynat. András speaks English and German.

Lama Tours ☎ 0049-69/944 7897. Run by Samir Lama, the greatest living explorer of the Western Desert, and his German wife and co-explorer Waltraud (Wally), this Frankfurt/Main-based firm does six or seven tours a year to the far southwest of Egypt and into Sudan, lasting 15–21 days. He and his wife speak English, German, French and Arabic.

Pan Arab Tours 5 Saudi Egyptian Bldg, Sharia el-Nozha, Heliopolis ☎ 02/418 4409, ⓕ 291 3506, ⓔ pat@moussa.net. A Cairo-based agency offering numerous tours and tailor-made safaris all over the Western Desert.

Zarzora Expedition c/o Minerva Travel & Tours, 5b Sharia Mamalik Baharia, Manial ☎ 02/736 0350, ⓕ 02/735 0360, ⓔ info@ zarzora.com, ⓦ www.zarzora.com. Cairene desert experts Wael Abed and ex-brigadier Ahmed Mestekawy run 16- and 18-day tours in the footsteps of Rohlfs and Almássy, and a 21-day Uwaynat grand safari that includes Ain Della and the Great Sand Sea.

the nearest monastery (£E5 one-way), or hope to be offered a lift by one of the busloads of Coptic pilgrims that come this way.

Returning to Cairo or Alex by bus or service taxi from the Resthouse, you'll probably have to pay the full inter-city rate. There are hourly buses to Cairo until 7pm; departures for Alex are fewer and further between, with perhaps only two buses in the afternoon, when people are most likely to be leaving having visited the monasteries.

The monasteries of Wadi Natrun

Christian monasticism was born in Egypt's Eastern Desert, where the first Christian hermits sought to emulate St Anthony, forming rude communities; however, it was at Wadi Natrun that their rules and power were forged. Peter Levi's study of monasticism, *The Frontiers of Paradise*, notes how this coincided with the persecution of Christians in urban areas, especially under Diocletian.

Certainly, several thousand **monks** and hermits were living here by the middle of the fourth century, harbouring bitter grudges against paganism, scores which they settled after Christianity was made the state religion in 330 by sacking the temples and library and murdering scholars in Alexandria. E.M. Forster judged them "averse to culture and incapable of thought. Their heroes were St Ammon, who deserted his wife on their wedding eve, and St Anthony, who thought bathing was sinful and was consequently carried across the canals of the Delta by an angel". The Muslim conquest and Bedouin raids encouraged a siege mentality amongst the monks, who often lapsed into idle dependence on monastic serfs. Nineteenth-century foreign visitors unanimously described them as slothful, dirty, bigoted and ignorant – the antithesis of the monks here today.

The **four Wadi Natrun monasteries** have all been totally ruined and rebuilt at least once since their foundation during the fourth century; most of what you see dates from the eighth century onwards. Each has a high wall surrounding one or more churches, a central keep entered via a drawbridge, containing a bakery, storerooms and wells, enabling the monks to withstand siege, and diverse associated chapels. Their low doorways compel visitors to humbly stoop upon entry (don't forget to remove your shoes outside).

The monastic rule and working day

All Egyptian monasteries are cenobitic, meaning that the monks share food and possessions and unconditional submission to the rule of their abbot (a word that derives from the Arabic *abd*, "father").

The **monastic day** begins at 3am with an hour of silent prayer in individual *laura* (cells), before two hours of collective worship in the chapel, followed by unrelenting labour until the main meal of the day at noon. Afterwards, the monks work until 5pm, assemble for prayers and then return to their tasks until sheer exhaustion forces them to bed.

Work and prayer are seen as equal holy obligations, and many of the younger monks and novices are qualified engineers or scientists. High-tech coexists with spiritualism, which is clearly apparent during liturgies. Black garments symbolize their death to the world of bodily desires; their hoods (possibly representing the "helmet of salvation" in Ephesians 6) are embroidered with twelve crosses, after Christ's disciples.

Their **churches** – like all Coptic chapels – are divided into three sections. The *haikal* (sanctuary) containing the altar lies behind the iconostasis, an inlaid or curtained screen, which you can peer through with your escort's consent. In front of this is the choir, reserved for Coptic Christians, and then the nave, consisting of two parts. *Catechumens* (those preparing to convert) stand nearest the choir, while sinners (known as "weepers") were formerly relegated to the back.

Deir Anba Bishoi

The most accessible monastery is **Deir Anba Bishoi**, 10km from the highway, with a signpost of sorts on the paved road. Over one hundred and fifty monks and novices live here, and the monastery of St Bishoi receives a stream of Coptic pilgrims (daily: winter 7am–6pm; summer 7am–8pm). Foreigners are usually shown around by the English-speaking Father Shedrak.

The legend of **Bishoi** suggests he was one of the earliest monks at Wadi Natrun. An angel told the saint's mother that he was chosen to do God's work even before his birth in 320; two decades later he moved here to study under St Bemoi alongside John "the Short". Adopting a rather imaginative chronology, the legend also recalls that Bishoi later met Christ as an old man, carried him to church, washed his feet and was allowed to drink the water as a reward. Whatever the truth, since Bishoi's death in 417 his body has reportedly remained uncorrupted within its casket, which is carried in procession around the church every year on July 17. Next to him lies Paul of Tammuh, who was revered for committing suicide seven times.

St Bishoi's is the oldest of the five **churches** in the monastery, and features three *haikals* dating from the fourth, ninth and tenth centuries. The **keep**, built three to four hundred years later, has chapels at ground level (around the back) and on the second storey, one floor above its drawbridge. There's also a fifth-century **well** where Berber tribesmen washed their swords after massacring the 49 Martyrs of the Monastery of St Makarius.

The multi-domed building furthest away from the entrance is the **residence of Pope Shenouda III**, the current Coptic pope. He uses it normally as an occasional retreat, though he was exiled here for some years by Sadat. Most of the Coptic popes have been chosen from the monks of Wadi Natrun, and Deir Anba Bishoi in particular.

Deir al-Suryani

A sixth-century dispute over the theological importance of the Virgin led dissenting monks to found another monastery, 500m from St Bishoi's. After they returned to the fold it was purchased for a group of Syrian monks, hence its name, **Deir al-Suryani** (winter Mon–Fri & Sun 9am–6pm, Sat 9am–3pm; summer Mon–Fri & Sun 9am–7pm, Sat 9am–5pm). It was here that Robert Curzon came searching for ancient manuscripts (the ostensible reason for his tour of Balkan and Levantine monasteries in the 1830s), and found them lying on the floor or serving as covers for jars, all "well begrimed with dirt". The keep's oil cellar held a "mass of loose vellum pages", while the consistory of Abyssinian monks contained a library of Aramaic texts, hanging from pegs in individual leather satchels. Nowadays, the monastery's antique volumes are lovingly maintained in a modern **library**, and they have recently discovered a cache of manuscripts up to 1500 years old. The monastery also boasts the remains of some twelve saints and a lock of hair from Mary Magdalene.

Deir al-Suryani's principal **Church of the Virgin** (*al-Adhra*), built around 980, contains a *haikal* with stucco ornamentation, and a superb ebony "**Door**

of Prophecies", inlaid with ivory panels depicting the disciples and the seven epochs of the Christian era, culminating in the split with the Orthodox Church and the Coming of Islam. Some **murals** dating back to the church's foundation were recently discovered beneath the plaster, and can be seen through small apertures. A dark passageway at the back of the church leads to the **cave** where Bishoi tied his hair to a chain hanging from the ceiling to prevent himself sleeping for four days, until a vision of Christ appeared. The marble basin (*lakan*) in the nave is used by the abbot to wash the feet of twelve monks on Maundy Thursday, emulating Christ's act during Passion week.

The large **tamarind tree** in the grounds is said to have grown from the staff of St Emphram, who, as a monk, thrust it into the earth after his fellows criticized it as a worldly affectation. As Coptic pope, he established cordial relations with the Fatimid khalif in 997.

Deir el-Baramus

If you're keen on seeing one of the more remote monasteries, **Deir el-Baramus** fits the bill (daily: winter 9am–5pm; summer 9am–6pm). A road running 4km north from the vicinity of St Bishoi's Monastery has reduced its isolation amidst barren sands, but it still feels far from the madding crowd. Visitors are greeted outside by a picture of St Moses the Black, a Nubian robber who became a monk under the influence of St Isidore. The monastery itself was founded by St Makarius (see below) in 340, making it the oldest of the four that remain in Wadi Natrun. Its name, "Monastery of the Romans", honours Maximus and Domidus, two sons of the Roman Emperor Valentinus who died from excessive fasting; the younger one was only nineteen years old.

Their bodies are reputedly buried in a crypt below the **Church of the Virgin**, whose principal altar is only used once a day, since Mary's womb begot but one child. An adjacent altar, normally curtained off, serves the "Immaterial Fathers", the spirits of bygone saints and abbots who occasionally leave droplets of water sprinkled there. The relics of Moses and Isidore are encased in glass; pilgrims drop petitions into the bier. Notice the photo of a T-shirt bearing a bloody cross, the relic of an exorcism performed at the monastery in the 1980s, where the departing *afrit* (spirit) left a lurid sign as it was expelled from the body of the possessed victim.

Restoration work has revealed layers of medieval **frescoes** in the nave, the western end of which incorporates a fourth-century **pillar** with Syriac inscriptions. It was behind here that St Arsanious prayed with a pebble in his mouth, grudging every word that he spoke (including a statement to that effect).

The ninth-century church (whose belfries of unequal height symbolize the respective ages of Maximus and Domidus) shares a vine-laden courtyard with a **keep** and four other churches. Deir el-Baramus has eighty monks and novices, one of whom will show you around.

Cellia and birdlife

The monks may also tell you about **Cellia** (or El-Muna), the name given to the **ruins** of some five hundred **hermitages**, spread over a wide area 30km north of Deir el-Baramus. Cellia was founded by St Anthony, who is said to have told monks at Wadi Natrun who wished to live as hermits, "Let us take food at the ninth hour and then go forth and pass through the desert and consider the place". It's thought that Cellia maintained links with the pilgrim city of Abu Mina (see p.620) until their freshwater springs dried up. In 1995

American archeologists unearthed the Monastery of St John, plus traces of five subterranean monasteries that had been "lost" since their discovery by Prince Tousoum in 1930.

This remote part of Wadi Natrun has a melancholy beauty, its numerous **saline lakes** rimmed by crusts of **natron**, a mixture of sodium carbonate and sodium bicarbonate, which the ancient Egyptians used for dehydrating bodies and making glass. Ducks, waterhens, jacksnipes and sandpipers are typical of the **birdlife** around these lakes, which also harbour Egypt's last surviving wild **papyrus**. Due to the salinity, it is a dwarf subspecies of the plant that once flourished throughout the Nile Valley, but gradually became extinct; the last large papyrus (which could reach 6m) was found by a Prussian soldier in the Delta in the mid-nineteenth century. Today it exists only on small plantations, thanks to Dr Rageb, who rediscovered the lost technique of making papyrus paper and began to manufacture souvenirs from the stuff.

You'll need a **car** to explore the area.

Deir Abu Maqar

The oldest and furthest of the monasteries, **Deir Abu Maqar** lies 18km southwest of St Bishoi and can also be reached by an eight-kilometre spur off the Desert Road, midway between the main turn-off and Sadat City. It is not open to casual visitors, but will admit those with a letter of authorization from the Patriarchate (see p.486).

Enclosed by a circular wall ten metres high, the monastery requires visitors to pull a bell rope; in times past, two giant millstones stood ready to be rolled across to buttress the door against Bedouin raiders. Its founder, **St Makarius**, died in 390 "after sixty years of austerities in various deserts", the last twenty of which were spent in a hermit's cell at Wadi Natrun. He's said to have been so remorseful over killing a gnat that he withdrew for six months to the marshes, getting stung all over until "his body was so much disfigured that his brethren on his return only knew him from the sound of his voice". A rigorous faster, his only indulgence was a raw cabbage leaf for Sunday lunch.

Despite repeated sackings, Abu Maqar has hung onto the bodies of the numerous Coptic popes that have been buried here, plus the 49 Martyrs whom the Berbers killed in 444. In 1978, monks discovered what they believed to be the head of John the Baptist; however, this is also claimed to be held in Venice, Aleppo and Damascus. Since its nadir in 1969, when only six monks lived here, the monastery has acquired a hundred brethren, a modern printing press and a farm employing six hundred workers. The monks have mastered pinpoint irrigation systems and bovine embryo transplant technology in an effort to meet their abbot's goal of feeding a thousand laypersons per monk, revitalizing a landscape which "might be supposed to boast of nothing but the salt and natron for which it is indebted to its barrenness and its name" (*Murray's Handbook*, 1891).

The Fayoum

Likened in Egyptian tradition to a bud on the stem of the Nile and an "earthly paradise" in the desert, the **Fayoum** depends on river water – not springs or wells, like a true oasis. The water is distributed around the depression by a system of canals going back to ancient times, creating a lush rural enclave of palm trees dividing cotton and clover fields, orchards, and carefully tended crops of tomatoes and medicinal plants in the sandier outlying regions. Pigeons nest in mud-brick coops shaped like giant Victorian trifles, blindfolded cattle turn threshing machines and water buffalo plod home for milking. Along one shore of Lake Qaroun are fishing communities, while on the periphery are encampments of semi-nomadic Bedouin. About two million people live here, in half a dozen towns and 158 villages.

Visiting the Fayoum

Given easy access from Cairo, there have to be good reasons why foreign tourists are so thin on the ground. Number one is the Governorate capital, **Fayoum City**, which has all of Cairo's **drawbacks** and few of its advantages. Avaricious drivers bedevil day excursions to the distant **antiquities**, whilst *baksheesh*-hungry locals pester visitors to **Lake Qaroun**, where wealthy tourists are bussed in for shooting holidays. It is possible to get into the diverse **birdlife**, local **moulids** or **desert expeditions**, but you have to be committed. If you're only lukewarm, a brief day-trip will probably discourage further contact.

As for the **best time to go**, the Fayoum's winters are warmer and drier than Cairo's, its summers milder than in Upper Egypt; however, cold winds in spring – known as the *khamseen*, coat everything with dust. At other times, the clarity of the air causes the sun's rays to burn more strongly than you'd expect.

Getting there

The **road from Cairo** to the Fayoum starts near the Pyramids of Giza, whose silhouette sinks below the horizon as the road gains a barren plateau dotted with army bases, then (76km later) reaches the edge of the Fayoum depression. Once here, the Ptolemaic-Roman site of Kom Oshim is passed (on the left) before you sight Lake Qaroun and cruise down through Sinnuris into Fayoum City, driving past the Obelisk of Senuset I. **Buses** (£E4) from Cairo's Ahmed Helmi and Giza terminals (every 30min between 7am and 7pm) do the 100km journey in two hours; advance bookings are usually only necessary from midday Thursday till late on Saturday, or during Ramadan, Fayoumi moulids and public holidays. An alternative is to go to Midan Ramses or Midan Giza and grab a **service taxi**. These seven-seater Peugeots or pack-'em-in minibuses run practically non-stop from early morning to late at night, charging £E5 for a stomach-churning high-speed ride past the wrecks of previous crashes, reaching Fayoum City in just over an hour – *inshallah*. The four daily **trains** from Cairo's Ramses and Giza stations (3rd class; £E2) take a leisurely three or four hours to reach Fayoum City's central train station.

Coming from the Nile Valley, catch one of the half-hourly buses or service taxis **from Beni Suef**, which reach Fayoum City in an hour. The road runs through a cultivated strip beside the Bahr Yussef, so there's little sense of entering an oasis; en route it passes the start of tracks to the Lahun and Hawara pyramids. Buses and service taxis coming from this direction terminate at the Hawatim depot in the southwest of town.

Fayoum City

A kind of pocket-size version of Cairo, with the Bahr Yussef canal in the role of the Nile, **FAYOUM CITY**★ makes a grab at the wallets of middle-class Egyptians who come to bask beside Lake Qaroun during summertime, and any foreigners that come to hand. Most of the latter are whisked through in buses and remain immured in luxury hotels, so independent travellers bear the brunt of local hustlers – and obnoxious teenagers, if you're a woman. Another major drawback is that mosquitoes swarm from every nook and waterway, making evenings a misery. Add makeshift buildings, weaving traffic and malodorous canals and you've got half a dozen reasons not to linger.

On the plus side, the city has the cheapest accommodation in the area and serves as the jumping-off point for almost everywhere you might consider visiting in the oasis. It also musters a pleasant **souk**, a couple of venerable **mosques** and some colourful **moulids** – the biggest of which is that of *Ali er-Rubi* (see p.497) in the middle of the month of *Sha'ban*.

Arrival and information

Trains from Cairo terminate at the **station** in the centre of town, while buses and service taxis end up at the **Kubri al-Misalla** depot beneath the bridge past the Gamal Abdel Nasser Mosque. Coming from Beni Suef you arrive at the **Hawatim** depot south of the old town, which is too far from town to walk – a taxi or horse-drawn cab (*hantour*) shouldn't cost over £E5. If you're feeling adventurous and can read Arabic numerals, green-and-white minibuses (25pt) shuttle between outlying transport depots or suburbs and the centre of town (*wust al balad*), while motorbike taxis (£E1–3) weave around the downtown area. Minibuses #7 and #8 run from the Hawatim depot to the train station.

Once downtown, most things worth seeing can be reached on foot, with the Bahr Yussef canal facilitating **orientation** as an obvious landmark. Alas, the Fayoum's **tourist office** has little to offer but an outdated brochure and a confusing map of town, and its staff speak little English, whether you try the tourist hut (daily except Fri 9am–2pm) near the four water wheels, or the main office (daily except Fri 8am–2pm; ☎084/342-313) at the rear of the Governorate building, 2km north of the centre (accessible by #5 minibus from in front of the Banque Misr). Even less English is spoken by the **tourist police** (☎084/347-298), who are usually near the four water wheels, and will send a cop to any hotel that reports having foreign guests, to explain the restrictions on travel within the oasis (see p.497).

You can **change money** at any of the four banks along the Bahr Yussef – the Banque du Caire and Banque Misr both have **ATMs** – but only the Bank of Alexandria on the north bank of the canal takes travellers' cheques or gives Visa cash advances (Mon–Thurs & Sun 8.30am–2pm; during Ramadan 10am–1.30pm). The main **post office** (daily except Fri 8am–2pm) on Sharia

---

★The city is officially **Medinet el-Fayoum**, but known as **El-Fayoum** or **Fayoum** in colloquial usage (not *El-Medina*, as some guidebooks say). The word "Fayoum" probably derives from *Phiom*, the Coptic word for "sea", although folklore attributes it to the pharaoh's praise of the Bahr Yussef: "This is the work of a thousand days" (*alf youm*).

FAYOUM CITY

N

▲ Hawara   ▲ El-Wasta

◀ Cairo (100 km)

◀ Governorate (100 m)

◀ Seven Waterwheels (3 km)

◀ Ain es-Silyin (9 km) & Lake Qaroun (20 km)

◀ Kiman Faris

▲ Lake Qaroun

▼ Medinet Madi (35 km)

▼ Beni Suef (40 km)

Obelisk of Senusert I

Zoo

Buses & Service Taxis to Cairo

Gamal Abdel Nasser Mosque

KUBRI AL-MISALLA

SHARIA SA'AD ABDEL NASSER

SHARIA SA'AD ZAGHLOUL

SHARIA EL-HADAKA

SHARIA GUMHORRIYA

SHARIA HORRIYA

HADAKA

Police

Palace of Culture

@

SHARIA EL-BOSTA

Four Waterwheels

Bahr Tanhale

Bahr Sinnuris

SHARIA TAWFIQIYYA

MUNSHA'AT LOTFALLAH

Stadium

SHARIA AL-SADD AL-ALI

SHARIA MOHAMMADIYA

Catholic Church

SHARIA GUMHORRIYA

SH. EL-BAMZA

Anglican Church

SHARIA 26TH JULY

SHARIA MUSTAFA KAMIL

SHARIA BATAL AL-SALAM

Hanging Mosque

Bahr Yussef

SOUK AL-QANTARA

SHARIA ES-SAGA

Church of the Virgin

Hawatim Service Taxi Station

Local Buses & Service Taxis

HAWATIM

Pottery Market

Buses & Service Taxis to Ibshaway

Qaitbey's Mosque

Mosque of Ali er-Rubi

SHARIA GUMHORRIYA

SHARIA HORRIYA

Service Taxis to Ain es-Siliyin & Lake Qaroun

0   500 m

ACCOMMODATION
Honeyday	3
Mecca	5
Montazah	2
Palace	4
Queen	1
Youth Hostel	6

EATING & DRINKING
Governorate Club	A
Haidar Restaurant	D
Kebabgi	B
Nagaf	C
Said Kushari	E
Sherif	F

el-Bosta has EMS and poste restante, and a photo shop can be found nearby, while for international calls you should head west along the canal to the 24-hour **telephone** exchange. Patients must pay cash up front at the **hospital** (⑦084/342-249) on Sharia Sa'ad Zaghloul, 1km north of the centre, and would do better seeking treatment in Cairo.

Accommodation

Outside of *Er-Rubi*'s festival, there shouldn't be any difficulty **finding a room** in town, where there are five hotels, plus a hostel. Other options exist at Ain es-Siliyin, Lake Qaroun, Wadi Rayan and Kom Oshim (see sections following).

Honeyday 105 Sharia Gamal Abdel Nasser ⑦084/340-105, ⑥341-205. Ten minutes' walk from the centre, off the road to Senusert's obelisk, this clean and friendly two-star hotel has a/c rooms with TV and fridge. Breakfast included; 25-percent discount for groups. ❹

Mecca Sharia Mohammadiya ⑦084/311-223. Under the same management as the *Palace* (see below), it has simple rooms with fans and shared bathrooms. ❶

Montazah Sharia Ismail al-Medany ⑦084/324-633. Near the Bahr Sinnuris canal in the quiet residential area of Munsha'at Lotfallah, this hotel isn't as comfy as the nearby *Queen*, but some rooms are a/c. Rents bikes and motorbikes. ❷

Palace Sharia Horriya ⑦084/351-222. Overlooking the Bahr Yussef in the centre of town, it has fairly decent rooms with optional baths and a/c. The manager speaks good English and rents bicycles, motorbikes and cars. ❷

Queen Sharia Ata-Allah Hassan ⑦084/337-828 or 326-819. The best place in Munsha'at Lotfallah, with spotless rooms with private bathrooms (a/c and TV £E20 extra), a peaceful courtyard and a nice restaurant. Breakfast included. ❷

Youth Hostel Lux Housing, Block #7, flat #7 ⑦084/323-682. Located on a nameless street in the Hadaka district, 2km from the centre, the *Beit es-Shabab* is a last resort, with a communal kitchen and 46 beds in slightly dingy dorms for £E8 per person. IYHF membership not required. ❶

The city

Groaning away behind the tourist kiosk are four large wooden **water wheels**, symbolic of Fayoumi agriculture. Because Nile water is introduced into the sloping depression at its highest point, gravity does half the work of distribution. Sluices at El-Lahun regulate the current, which is strong enough to power water wheels for lifting irrigation water where needed – except during January, when the whole system is allowed to dry out for cleaning and maintenance.

Coptic and Muslim folklore ascribes the **Bahr Yussef** (River of Joseph) to its Biblical namesake, who's believed to have been the pharaoh's vizier and minister for public works. Originally a natural waterway branching off the Nile near Beni Suef, it was regulated from the XII Dynasty onwards, and since the building of the Ibrahimiya Canal in the nineteenth century, has drawn water from the Nile at Dairut, nearly 300km further south.

Walking west alongside the canal and crossing the fourth bridge from the tourist kiosk, you can follow a street with a wooden roof into the **Souk al-Qantara**, a labyrinth of alleys with stalls selling copperware and spices, grain and pulses, clothing and other goods – all without a hint of tourism. **Sharia es-Sagha**, the Street of Goldsmiths, is crammed with jewellers shops, mostly owned by Christians. Like Beni Suef, Fayoum City has a substantial Christian minority – mainly Copts, but also Anglicans and Catholics – whose churches are ranged along Sharia 26th July. The oldest is the **Church of the Virgin**, dating from the 1830s, which contains an altar dedicated to the local saint Anba Abram (1829–1912), Bishop of Fayoum and Giza, who was reputedly able to transport himself across distances in a miraculous fashion.

Near the souk you'll also find three historic mosques. The **Mosque of Ali er–Rubi** is dedicated to a local sheikh whose renown among the Fayoumis eclipses even Anba Abram's. His mausoleum, down some steps from the mosque's courtyard, is surrounded by an enormous *darih* or carved box-frame, and people muttering or shouting supplications to the saint. Further west beside the canal, the **Mosque of Qaitbey** is the oldest in the Fayoum, built (or perhaps restored) by the Circassian Mamluke sultan Qaitbey (see p.172). Ancient columns from Kiman Faris (see box on p.499) uphold its dome, while the stone carving around the doorway, and the ebony *minbar* inlaid with Somalian ivory, are distinctly Mamluke. Qaitbey was also responsible for building the twin-arched **bridge** nearby, which was once named after his favourite concubine, Khwand Asl Bey (as was the mosque), but is now known as Bridge of the Gate of Farewells because it leads to a cemetery.

Crossing the bridge you can head along the riverside to find the **Hanging Mosque**, so called because its north frontage is upheld by five arches, once occupied by artisans' workshops; or delve into the backstreets near the cemetery to visit the weekly **pottery market** off Sharia el-Mudaris (Tues only). Most of the red, pink or unglazed pots are made at the village of Nazla, south of Ibshaway.

The **Palace of Culture** is Fayoum City's newest landmark, a modernistic structure like an inverted pyramid, that houses a cinema, theatre and library. Behind it stands the **Gamal Abdel Nasser Mosque,** one of many that Nasser had built in provincial towns in the 1960s, and which bear his name. Another, earlier, hero of Egyptian nationalism is commemorated by Sharia Sa'ad Zaghloul, running out past the hospital and a modest **zoo** (daily 8am–5pm; £E1.50) to the Governorate building, containing a small **museum** of local history and fauna, only labelled in Arabic (daily except Fri 8am–2pm; free).

The Seven Water Wheels and the Obelisk of Senusert I

For a pleasant half-hour's walk in the morning or evening, follow the right bank of the Bahr Sinnuris northwards out of town for 3km to reach the **Seven Water Wheels** (not to be confused with the four by the tourist kiosk). First comes a single wheel near a farm; slightly further on, a quartet revolves against a backdrop of mango trees and palms; the final pair is a little way on, near a crude bridge. The Fayoum has about two hundred such water wheels (introduced by Ptolemaic engineers in the third century BC), which have a working life of ten years if properly tarred and maintained. They act as pumps rather than powering machinery, using the flow of the stream to lift the water to a higher level, for irrigation.

Entering or leaving town by the Cairo road, you'll see the thirteen-metre-high red-granite **Obelisk of Senusert I**, the only obelisk in Egypt to have a rounded tip. Senusert was the second king of the XII Dynasty, who displayed a special fondness for the Fayoum and was the first to regard it as more than just a hunting ground, building the Lahun and Hawara pyramids, Medinet Madi and Qasr es-Sagha. Following the XII Dynasty (1991–1786 BC), interest in the Fayoum declined, and didn't properly revive until the advent of the Ptolemies, fourteen centuries later.

Eating and drinking

Eating out in the city is cheap, but don't expect to find any foreign cuisine or fancy **restaurants**. Perhaps the best choice, in fact, is the *Queen Hotel's* restaurant, which is nicely decorated, with a longish menu – try the *shish tawouk* or *escalope panée*. For those with money, a splurge at the *Auberge du Lac-Fayoum* on

Lake Qaroun is recommended (see p.500). Otherwise, there are half a dozen places to eat in the centre of town, together with numerous teahouses and the odd juice bar.

Governorate Club Opposite the stadium. Accessible by *hantour* or #9 minibus, the restaurant in the grounds of the *Nady al-Muhafza* (£E3 admission) does cheap, filling meals of kebab, chicken or steak; spaghetti with salad and *tahina* hits the spot for vegetarians. The club has a nice garden out back where you can watch waterbirds on the Bahr Sinnuris, and is open till 1am.

Haidar Restaurant Sharia Mustafa Kamil. One of the few cafés near the Bahr Yussef that's sign-posted in English, it serves stewed lamb, grilled chicken and salad, and is good value for money.

Kebabgi Sharia Mustafa Kamil. Another cheap eatery, usually offering a choice of kebab, *kofta*, chicken and rice, with side orders of spinach, zucchini, white beans or potatoes.

Nagaf Sharia Mustafa Kamil. Up the road from the above, this sit-down and takeway place sells *fuul* and *taamiya*, macaroni, fried liver, lamb *tajine*, salads, sandwiches, and a kind of rice pudding called *ma'ammar*.

Said Kushari Bahr Sinnuris. An oddly shaped *kushari* diner beside the sluice. You could almost imagine you're eating on a boat.

Sherif Sharia Mustafa Kamil. Across the road from *Kebabgi*, this is the place for ice cream, cakes and other sweets. On cold winter nights they offer *bilela*, a dish of hot wheat and milk topped with raisins, nuts and sugar.

Festivals

It's worth visiting Fayoum City purely for its **festivals**, as lots of *fellaheen* do. Hotels overflow during **Ali er-Rubi's moulid** in *Sha'ban*, when the alleys around his mosque are crammed with stalls purveying sugar dolls and horsemen, and all kinds of amusements, while the devout perform *zikrs* in the courtyard.

The other big occasion is the "viewing" (*Er-Ruyeh*) of the new moon that heralds **Ramadan**. This calls for a huge procession from the Gamal Abdel Nasser Mosque. Headed by the security forces, followed by imams and sheikhs, a parade of carnival floats "mimes" the work of different professions and bombards spectators with "lucky" prayer leaflets.

During the month of Ramadan, there's a small moulid at the domed white tomb of **Sheikha Mariam** (between the sluice of the Bahr Sinnuris and the four water wheels). The **Great Feast** (starting on the tenth of *Zoul Hagga*) is a more private occasion, with most eateries closed, so avoid coming then.

On the Monday after the movable **Coptic Easter**, locals and day-trippers from Cairo picnic along the canalsides in the popular festival of "Smelling the Breeze" (*Sham el-Nessim*); many others celebrate it on the shore of Lake Qaroun.

Around Fayoum Oasis

The oasis's other populous centres – Sinnuris, Ibshaway, Itsa and Tamiya – hold little interest. However, there are enjoyable scenic spots easily accessible from Fayoum City in the form of the springs of **Ain es-Siliyin** and **Lake Qaroun**. Reaching the waterfalls of **Wadi Rayan** or the seldom-visited **ancient sites** on the periphery of the oasis is more tricky, so don't undertake a jaunt lightly nor set off without adequate water and food for the day – you can't rely on finding either in the remoter places.

As in the Nile Valley, foreign visitors may find their freedom of movement impeded by the local **tourist police**, who may require that you use a private car or taxi to go any farther than Lake Qaroun. However, they don't keep a

THE FAYOUM

▲ Widan al-Faras   ▲ Cairo

Qasr es-Sagha

Jebel Qatrani

Dimah es-Siba

Kom Oshim

Auberge du Lac-Fayoum

Oasis Motel

Tamiya

Lake Qaroun

Shakshuk

Ain as-Siliyin

Sanhur   Sinnuris

Qasr Qaroun

Tunis   Ibshaway

Maidum Pyramid

Fayoum

Nazla

Hawara Pyramid

Lahun Pyramid

Abu Ghandir

Wadi Rayan

Itsa   Deir al-Azab   El-Lahun

Medinet Madi

Al-Mudawara   Qalamshah   Deir al-Malak Ghobriel

Beni Suef

River Nile

0   10 km   Farmland

▼ Assyut

◄ Valley of the Whales

► El-Lisht Pyramids

► Cairo

strict watch on **public transport** terminals, so it's semi-feasible to get around by covered pick-ups (with fixed fares and routes) or local buses. There's no denying, though, that having your own transport makes life a lot easier; the *Palace Hotel* can arrange a **car** (with or without driver) and also rents **motorbikes**, like the *Montazah Hotel*. **Bicycles** (£E10-15 per day) can be rented from both these hotels and the sports centre opposite the Governorate Club, and are a nice way of getting around the oasis if you're not travelling too far.

Aside from being alert for tractors, children and livestock, **drivers** should take care when visiting the remoter sites. You'll need a car with high ground clearance, if not 4WD; adequate water (for humans and radiators); and shovels and traction mats or boards (for digging cars out of soft sand). Always travel with at least one other car and heed local advice about the weather; and never travel during the *khamseen*.

Ain es-Siliyin

Fayoumis rate **Ain es-Siliyin** as a major beauty spot – and perhaps it was so in the days before the cafeterias, football pitch, pool and chalets were built in the hollow where the Siliyin **springs** bubbled forth. Nowadays they spurt from pipes, and hordes of picnickers (Fridays are busiest) have trampled the surrounding vegetation. The pool itself (25pt admission) is perennially packed with children and, whatever Egyptians say, it's *not* a good idea to drink the spring water, which is rich in titanium and supposedly good for low blood pressure. The road to the springs is lined with restaurants serving kebab and pigeon, and vendors selling seasonal fruit (mangos, guavas, plums, apricots and prickly pears).

Sobek and Crocodilopolis

Sobek

Kiman Faris (Horseman's Mounds) is the local name for a site on the northern outskirts of Fayoum City, rapidly disappearing beneath new colleges. Although nothing exists to justify a visit, it deserves a mention as the **site of Crocodilopolis** (later renamed *Arsinoë* after Ptolemy II's sister-wife), the Fayoum's ancient capital and centre of the **crocodile cult**. This supposedly began with Pharaoh Menes, the legendary unifier of Upper and Lower Egypt, whose life was saved by a croc while he was hunting in the Fayoum marshes. Crocodiles infested the lake beyond Kiman Faris (which was much larger in ancient times), so an urge to propitiate the creatures is understandable.

The crocodile deity, **Sobek**, was particularly favoured by Middle Kingdom rulers but assumed national prominence after he became identified with Re (as Sobek-Re) and Horus. He was variously depicted as a hawk-headed crocodile or in reptilian form with Amun's crown of feathers and ram's horns. At the Sacred Lake of Crocodilopolis, reptiles were fed and worshipped, and even adorned with jewellery, by the priests of Sobek.

To reach the springs, which are sited 9km north of town just before the village of the same name, ask for directions to the taxi and pick-up depot serving Sanhur, Shakshuk and other points north. This is currently located just off the railway tracks several blocks west of Bahr Sinnuris. Public **transport** is cheap: to the springs or Sanhur by pick-up costs about 50pt; don't be fooled into renting a private taxi instead of a service taxi. Should you want **to stay**, the *Ain as-Siliyin Hotel* (☎084/500-062; ❷) has seedy, fanless chalets.

Lake Qaroun

To reach **Lake Qaroun**, ride on to Sanhur and catch a pick-up heading for "*El-Birka*" (The Pond), as it's familiarly known. Some pick-ups join the lakeside road 3km east of the *Auberge du Lac-Fayoum* hotel and then run west along the shore towards Shakshuk; others head directly for Shakshuk and then continue eastwards past the hotels. West of Shakshuk, the holiday villas of wealthy Cairenes spread out along the road that ultimately leads to **Qasr Qaroun** and **Wadi Rayan** (see below). If you've got a car, keep going, since local women and children pester you remorselessly for *baksheesh*.

The lake

Short of tankers gliding between the sandbanks of the Suez Canal, Egypt has no weirder juxtaposition of water and desert than **Birket Qaroun** (Lake of Horns), where fishing boats bob against a backdrop of arid hills and the immensity of the Western Desert. While the Orientalist Lane reckoned that the lake's name derived from the horn (*qorn*)-shaped peak on an island in the middle, Fayoumis believe that it is named after a character in the Koran, who was swallowed up by the earth as a punishment for being "exultant in his riches". Folklore also has it that he was a sorcerer who turned the land barren, or a Jew whose treasure still lies at the bottom of the lake. Although "glassy and brooding, surrounded by beaches encrusted with salts, the recipient of all the drainage canals in the region" (as one nineteenth-century guidebook described it), Cairenes favour the lake as a **bathing resort**, undeterred by the beach of broken shells and saline gunk (keen swimmers may be glad to note that, though foul-tasting, the water is at least free of bilharzia). The "season" runs year-round, but from January to April it's too cold to swim.

The view can be enjoyed at various establishments beside the shore, including the jutting *La Promenade Café* of the **Auberge du Lac-Fayoum**, a hotel that was once King Farouk's hunting lodge, where Allied and Arab leaders met after World War II to carve up the Middle East. If you ask nicely, they might let you see the suite used by Farouk, now faded and uncared-for. With a pair of binoculars, you can observe the lake's prolific **birdlife**: 88 species, including flamingoes, which have a colony on **Horn Island** (*Geziret el-Qorn*). If the ubiquitous tourist police raise no objections, you can rent **rowing boats** at the *Auberge* and, 3km away, the *Oasis Motel*, and there are boatmen willing to row you out to the island or the far shore of the lake for a negotiable sum.

The lake itself covers 214 square kilometres, at 45m below sea level, a fraction of its size when the Nile first broke into the wind-eroded Fayoum depression seventy thousand years ago, forming a lake 40m above the current level. Egyptian mythology identified this with *Nun*, the waters of chaos and primeval life; from the Stone Age onwards people lived around the lake, which had shrunk considerably by Dynastic times.

Although the Middle Kingdom emerged at nearby Herakleopolis, it wasn't until Pharaoh Amenemhat I moved his capital from Upper Egypt to Lisht that the Fayoum became important. He had canals dug and the channel to the Nile deepened, draining parts for agriculture and submerging a greater area with what the ancients called **Lake Moeris**. It was this that the Ptolemies lowered to reclaim land for their settlements, whose decline by the end of the Roman period matched the lake's drop to 36m below sea level. Increasing salinity was a problem by medieval times, and after the lake came into equilibrium with the water sheet 40m beneath the Western Desert in 1890, it became too salty for its freshwater fish; since the 1970s, ten new marine species have been introduced, including eel, mullet, sole and shrimp. In recent years the water table has risen again, flooding houses, hotels and fields beside the lake.

Practicalities

For those with kids, the best **eating** options are the *Café Gabal el-Zinah*, 2km west of the *Auberge*, which has children's play areas and serves fish, like the less expensive *Qaroun Beach Café*; or *Café Louloua*, 3km in the other direction, which does pizzas and other Western dishes. The *Auberge* is known for its wildfowl dishes, but they don't live up to expectations or the price, though you might feel that the surroundings are worth it.

The same goes for **accommodation**, as the *Auberge du Lac-Fayoum* (☏084/572-002, ☏572-003, ✆wassefraafat@hotmail.com; ❸) is comfy rather than luxurious, with a/c rooms, tennis and squash courts, two pools, four restaurants and a disco (closed over winter) – sadly, the view from the rooms is spoilt by the chalets in the garden beside the lake. The *Oasis Motel* (☏ & ☏084/830-666, ✆oasis666@hotmail.com; ❺), 3km down the road, is more affordable and has satellite TV, but its a/c is wheezy and a speaker plays music through the night. However, its manager is friendly and speaks good English, and visitors can rent **jet skis** in the winter. The *Auberge* has various sporting facilities, and hires guns to those who enjoy **shooting ducks**, as does the *Panorama Hotel*, beyond the *Oasis*.

Qasr Qaroun and Tunis

Qasr Qaroun, the best-preserved of the Fayoum's **Ptolemaic temples** (daily 8am–4pm; £E16), lies on the northwestern rim of the oasis, 45km from Fayoum City. If the police don't insist that you travel by private taxi, it's possible to **get there** by taking a service taxi from the depot across the canal from Qaitbey's Mosque to Ibshaway (1hr; 75pt), and then another one from there towards the village of Qaroun (1hr; £E1.50); the temple is close to the road, just before its namesake.

Not a palace as its Arabic name suggests, Qasr Qaroun is an outwardly plain but inwardly labyrinthine temple. You'll need a torch to explore its warren of chambers, stairs and passageways at different levels; beware of scorpions, bats, snakes and lizards – the last resemble miniature crocodiles, as befits a temple dedicated to Sobek. Round about are the **ruins of Dionysias**, a Ptolemaic-Roman town believed to have been abandoned in the fourth century AD when the lake shrank (it's now 45 minutes' walk away), leaving desiccated stalks of vegetation. Early European travellers undertook nine-hour horse rides to this site, believing that it was the famous Labyrinth described by Herodotus and Strabo (see "Hawara", p.505). West of the temple is an even more ruinous **fortress**, constructed during the reign of Diocletian against the Blemmye (an indication of how far north these Nubian raiders went).

En route to or from Qasr Qaroun you'll pass through **Tunis**, a farming village turned **artists' colony** of houses built in the vernacular style, using local materials. Among the first residents were Ahmed Abu Zed – one of Egypt's leading potters – and the Swiss couple Evelyne Porret and Michel Pastore, who set up a **pottery** school for local children to learn the craft. Phone to make an appointment to view the products of Ahmed's studio (☎084/820-357) or the school (☎084/820-405).

Wadi Rayan and the Valley of Whales

Wadi Rayan is a separate depression 15km outside the oasis, which has become a wildlife haven and beauty spot thanks to human ingenuity. The idea of piping excess water from the Fayoum into the wadi was first mooted by the British, but only put into practice in 1966. Since then, two lakes and a waterfall have formed, vegetation has flourished and the area has become a major nesting ground for birds. The lakes have been stocked with fish and a small fishing industry established, while the tourist board is now promoting Wadi Rayan as a major attraction, which doesn't always sit happily with its status as a **nature reserve**, harbouring the world's only known population of slender-horned gazelles (*gazella leptoceros*), eight other species of mammals, 13 species of resident birds and 26 migrant and vagrant ones – not to mention unique fossils in the **Valley of the Whales**. Hopefully, in the face of protests from Egypt's Environmental Affairs Agency, they won't repeat the mistake of routing the 2000 Paris–Dakkar–Cairo rally through Wadi Rayan, which disrupted the wildlife and littered the locality.

As no public transport goes anywhere nearby, you can only **get there** by car; bargain hard for a taxi from Fayoum City (about £E100) or Lake Qaroun (£E40-60). Now that the access road is finished the route is easy: leave the lakeside road at a signposted turning 28km west of the *Panorama Hotel*, and follow it 8.5km to the entrance gate, where passengers are charged an **admission fee** of £E5 each plus £E5 for the vehicle. The open desert beyond gets sandier and lovelier the closer you get to the azure **lakes**, where a track leads down to the **waterfalls** (*shallalat*). The only ones in Egypt, they've appeared in countless videos and films despite being only a couple of metres high and shrinking as the level of the lower lake rises. Hordes of visitors descend here on Fridays and holidays, overwhelming its **visitors centre**, cafeterias and **mosque** built of reeds, to sunbathe and play ghettoblasters on the beach around the falls.

Come at any other time to enjoy swimming, sunbathing and **bird-watching**. Besides the ubiquitous cattle egrets and grey herons, there are hard-to-spot wagtails, skylarks, kestrels, kites and coucals from Senegal. The reed beds developing here are being colonized by wetland species such as the little bittern, adding to the diversity of the habitat. As you continue south from the waterfalls turn-off, the beauty of the lower lake is offset by golden dunes (which sometimes encroach on the road), and you can hike up to the hill known as **al-Mudawara** (The Lookout) for a spectacular **view** of the reed-fringed lake and the desert scarp beyond. At another point, 12.5km on, there's a signposted turning to a bird-watching site by the shore, followed 4km later by magnificent *seif* **dunes** 30m high. These parallel an inlet fringed by tamarisks, with three sulphur **springs** nearby. Thereafter, the road crosses a boring stretch of desert to return to the oasis. All of this route can be done in a 2WD car.

The Valley of the Whales

At the time of writing, **access** to the Valley of the Whales had just been restored by the park authorities following the deployment of more rangers in order to protect the fossils from further plundering but check at the Wadi Rayan visitors centre or the *Paradise Safari Camp* (see below) to find out what the current situation is. In any case, the route is quite difficult and it is safer to have two cars; the guys from the camp will either take you as a passenger, or you can bring your own 4WD and they will lead you in theirs.

The **Valley of the Whales** (*Wadi al-Hitan*) is extraordinary not only for its fossils, but for its surreal **boulders** like giant toasted marshmallows oozing syrup. Geologically, they belong to the Qasr es-Sagha Formation created by the ancient Tethys Sea, whose **fossils** consist of land mammals deposited by the swirling waters and sea creatures stranded when the sea receded during the Eocene era, 45 million years ago. The site was surveyed in 1877 by the geologist George Schweinfurth, who found 200 fossilized skeletons of what he thought was a reptile named Basilosaurus, that was later reclassified as a mammal with a slender body 20m long and small but fully developed hind feet. It's thought that this Zeuglodon was an evolutionary dead-end in the evolution of whales that began when some land mammals migrated into the sea; another, smaller whale found here, called Dorudon, may prove to be the ancestor of modern whales. At Wadi al-Hitan, one Zeuglodon lies prone beneath a promontory of fossilized coral, as if it had sought shelter as the waters shrank. Sadly, the pathos and scientific value of the site hasn't deterred visitors from removing vertebrae and other souvenirs. Look, photograph, but please don't touch.

Accommodation and safaris

To get the most from Wadi Rayan you should **stay the night**, and venture further into the desert. Within walking distance of the falls, the *Paradise Safari Camp* has large **tents** with beds with clean sheets, lit by candles, and a lovely outdoor restaurant serving meals of chicken or fish, where Bedouin parties are sometimes held. Beds (£E20 per person) can be reserved through Marzouk Desert Cruises, 1 Midan Ibn Sandar, Hammamat al-Qubba in Cairo (☎ & ℱ 02/258 8083), owned by the hospitable Mohammed Marzouk who runs the camp. His company specializes in 4WD **safaris** to the Valley of the Whales and camel treks to Bahariya Oasis via the *Darb al-Rayan*.

Medinet Madi

Medinet Madi (City of the Past) is another temple site in the desert, roughly 35km southwest of Fayoum City. **Getting there** entails catching the El-Qasmiya bus from the Hawatim depot and riding on through Itsa, El-Minia and Abu Gandir. Ask to be dropped off at Menshat Sef, roughly one hour later. From this bridge it's about an hour's walk to the temple. Turn right, follow the canal to the next bridge, cross over and take a narrower canal path past a small village on your left, aiming for a stone hut on the rise ahead, beyond which lies the site.

Squatting in a sandy hollow where excavations are revealing an avenue of sphinxes and lions (one of them ruffed and bearded like a Renaissance grandee), the **Temple of Medinet Madi** was built for the XII Dynasty pharaohs Amenemhat III and IV, and dedicated to twin deities. Sobek appears in relief on the outside of the rear wall, while Renenutet the serpent-goddess (also associated with harvests) can be seen in the left-hand room of the limestone edifice. Ptolemaic additions include two female winged sphinxes, and the **ruined town** of mud- and fired bricks to the southeast. Although legend attributes its destruction to a tribe of eleventh-century Nejd warriors enraged by the town's refusal of hospitality, the real cause of its blight was probably the shrinking of the lake. What looks like an embankment north of the temple was actually the storm beach of the lake in ancient times, 68m above its present level.

To return to Fayoum City, catch the bus from Menshat Sef (going in the same direction, as the route is circular).

Kom Oshim: ancient Karanis

The most accessible of the ancient sites in the Fayoum is **Kom Oshim** (daily 8am–4pm), 30km north of Fayoum City, where the Cairo road descends into the depression. Ask a bus or taxi driver to drop you at *Mat'haf Kom Oshim*, the small **museum** by the road, where **admission tickets** are sold (£E6 for the museum; £E16 for the site). Its curator speaks good English and is keen to explain details. Pottery and glassware, terracotta figures used for modelling hairstyles and a lifelike "Fayoum portrait" (see p.505) convey the wealth and sophistication of the ancient frontier town whose ruins lie behind the museum.

The **ruins of Karanis** clearly show the layout of this Ptolemaic-Roman town, founded by Greek mercenaries and their camp followers during the third century BC, which had a population of three thousand or so until the fifth century AD. Although the mud-brick houses have been reduced to low walls, two stone **temples** are better preserved – no thanks to the nineteenth-century Antiquities Department, which allowed contractors to destroy Roman buildings for their bricks. The larger one was built towards the end of the first century BC and dedicated to two local crocodile gods, Petesouchos and Pnepheros.

Professor Scott Woodward of Bringham University believes that the population of Fayoum Oasis was the most genetically diverse in ancient times, and is reflected in the genetic make-up of Egyptians today. He reckons that over one million corpses are buried around the edges of the oasis, and at Karanis in particular, where eighty-five percent of the upper strata are blond-haired (northern Mediterraneans), and couples are genetically dissimilar; the lower layers, however, contain evidence of many brother-sister marriages. Scott attributes the change to the advent of Christianity (with its taboo on incest) in the Fayoum, which seems to have happened in the first century AD, two hundred years earlier than was previously thought.

To return to Fayoum or Cairo, flag down any passing bus or service taxi. During opening hours the museum can usually provide a **guide** for excursions to Qasr es-Sagha and Dimeh es-Siba (see below). The *Karanis Tourist Restaurant* serves simple **meals** in a shady garden, and you can pitch a **tent** in the grounds of the museum for £E5.

Qasr es-Sagha, Dimeh es-Siba and Widan al-Faras

For those with a 4WD and a hankering to explore the desert, there are several satisfyingly remote sites to the **north of Lake Qaroun**. Though you don't need permission to visit them (they're unguarded), it's strongly advisable to take a guide from the Karanis museum, as the track to Qasr es-Sagha (40km) is not always apparent, and may have difficult patches of soft sand, though the initial stretch is clear enough, and busy with trucks coming from a nearby quarry.

The small Middle Kingdom temple known as **Qasr es-Sagha** (Palace of the Jewellers) nestles inconspicuously halfway up an outlying scarp of the Jebel Qatrani. Although lacking any friezes or inscriptions, it's remarkable for its masonry, which is unlike that of any other Egyptian temple. The blocks are irregularly shaped, with odd angles and corners fitting together like a jigsaw; the overall effect is of an Inca edifice transplanted from the Andes. Notice the enigmatic dead-end **passage** built into the front wall of the temple. Lake Qaroun, which once lapped at the temple's base, now lies 11km away, beyond the ruins of Dimeh es-Siba, a Ptolemaic town that pegged out as the lake shrank.

To reach this you drive 9km south past hundreds of giant egg-shaped **boulders** that have fractured into halves or slices due to the baking heat. It's hard to imagine that a town of well-fed Greek soldiers and courtesans once flourished here. Starkly visible against the desert, the ruins of **Dimeh es-Siba** (Dimeh of the Lions) are ringed by a mud-brick wall up to 10m high and 5m thick. In the centre is a rough-hewn, ruined stone temple that was dedicated to Soknopaios, a form of Sobek (see p.499); the hill on which it stands was originally an island in the crocodile-infested lake. Approaching from that direction – a 2.5km walk – you'll come first to a 400-metre-long road (flanked by stone lions as late as the nineteenth century), running past ruined houses into the temple enclosure. The ruins are frequented by **owls**, and occasionally **jackals**.

Gung-ho 4WD types can also follow an ancient road (8km) from Qasr es-Sagha to the Old Kingdom **quarries** of **Widan al-Faras**. Here, the basalt used to make pots and statues simply fell off the hillside, to be loaded onto sledges and dragged down the escarpment to barges at Qasr. The quarry road, known as the *Rali Al-Farainah*, is perhaps the **world's oldest paved road**, made 4000 years ago from stones and chunks of fossilized wood (akin to the Petrified Forest in the Muqattam Hills outside Cairo). It has been used by scientists to measure the erosion of the desert, for where they once stood level, the road is now almost 1m above the desert's surface, meaning that the wind strips away 3cm per century. Widan al-Faras itself is a mountain extruded from the **Jebel Qatrani** range, whose fossil-rich sandstone and clay beds from the Eocene era are capped with a thick layer of black basalt. Guides who really know their stuff can navigate across the trackless desert from the Cairo–Bahariya highway about 70km from Bawiti (the capital of Bahariya Oasis), and descend the escarpment into the Fayoum.

Pyramids around the Fayoum

The Fayoum is associated with four separate **pyramid sites**, two of them beyond its limits, the other pair more conveniently sited off the Beni Suef road. The latter, at **Lahun** and **Hawara**, both date from the XII Dynasty, which governed Egypt – and ordered the waterworks that transformed the Fayoum – from its capital *Itj-tway* (Seizer of the Two Lands). This lay 30km to the northeast, near **El-Lisht**, where the dynasty's founder Amenemhat I built his own pyramid.

The fourth site, **Maidum**, is unconnected with the others (which it predates by seven centuries), but its dramatic-looking "Collapsed Pyramid" marks an evolutionary step between the pyramids at Saqqara and Giza.

Hawara Pyramid

Hawara (Great Mansion) may have stood on the shores of Lake Qaroun when it was built during the XII Dynasty, and later became the finishing point of a 100-kilometre **desert endurance race** instituted by Pharaoh Taharqa (690 BC) to train his troops (this was revived as an annual event in 2001). Aside from the race, held every November, Hawara gets few visitors, for its 54-metre-high **Pyramid of Amenemhat III** (daily 8am–4pm; £E16) has degenerated into a mud-brick mound since its limestone casing was removed in antiquity. Unlike most pyramids, its entrance was on the south side: one of many ruses devised to foil tomb-

Amenemhat III

robbers. Alas, due to rising ground water, you can't go inside to examine such features as the stone portcullises that sealed the corridor or the roof block that was lowered into place once the sarcophagus was in the burial chamber, both operated by sand. None of them saved the body of the pharaoh (1842–1797 or 1855–1808 BC) from being looted and burned centuries before Petrie rediscovered his sarcophagus alongside that of his daughter, Nefru-Ptah, which was stored here while her own tomb was being constructed. It was found intact with her treasures in 1956. East of the pyramid (the direction from which visitors approach) lies a bone- and bandage-littered necropolis, with deep shafts to ensnare the unwary.

To the south, towards and beyond the canal, a few column stumps and masses of limestone chippings mark the **site of the Labyrinth**. All that's known about this fabled building comes from Strabo, Herodotus and Pliny. Herodotus wrote that it contained over three thousand chambers hewn from a single rock, surpassing all the "great works of the Greeks . . . put together", while Strabo maintained that it had as many rooms as there were provinces, so that each could be represented by officials at ceremonies. Most archeologists think that it was Amenemhat III's mortuary temple, although Rohl argues that it may have been an eternal representation of the bureaucracy and waterworks that Joseph devised to prepare Egypt for the seven years of famine foretold by the pharaoh's dream (Genesis 41:1–4).

During the early excavations at Hawara in the nineteenth century, Petrie unearthed 146 brilliantly naturalistic **"Fayoum Portraits"** (100–250 AD) in the Roman cemetery to the north of the pyramid. Executed in beeswax-based paint while their sitters were alive, they were cut to size and stuck on to the bandaged cadavers, whose mummification was perfunctory compared to the embalming of Dynastic times. One such portrait graces the Karanis museum (see p.303); others can be admired in Cairo's Egyptian Antiquities Museum.

Getting to the pyramid involves a ten-kilometre service taxi ride from Fayoum City's Hawatim depot to the village of Hawara, where you cross the Bahr Yussef by a bridge, turn right at the T-junction beyond the village and walk on for about 3km until the pyramid appears. From its summit (easily reached by climbing the southwest corner) you should be able to see the Lahun Pyramid on the southeastern horizon.

Lahun Pyramid

Ten kilometres beyond Hawara, the incoming Nile waters pass through El-Lahun, where modern sluices stand just north of the **Qantara of Sultan Qaitbey**, the thirteenth-century equivalent of the regulators installed by Amenemhat III. (Photographing these installations is forbidden.) Lahun gets its name from the ancient Egyptian *Le-hone* (Mouth of the Lake), and gives it to the Pyramid of Senusert II sited 5km away. Most of the service taxis from the Hawatim depot to El-Lahun stop where the track leaves the main road; it's well over an hour's walk to the pyramids from there. Part of the route follows a massive **embankment** thought to have

Senusert II

been part of Amenemhat I's original barrage to divert water into the Fayoum. It ends at the desert's edge, where visitors buy an **admission ticket** for the site (daily 8am–4pm; £E20) and pick up a police escort to walk the final kilometre to the pyramid.

Built seven or eight centuries after the pyramids at Giza, the **Pyramid of Senusert II** employed a new and different technique, devised by the architect Anupy. The core consists of a rock knoll on which limestone pillars were based, providing the framework for the mud-brick overlay, which was finally encased in stone. Mindful of flooding, Anupy surrounded the base with a trench full of sand and rolled flints, to act as a "sponge".

The subsequent removal of its casing stones left the mud-brick pyramid exposed to the elements, which eroded it into its present mess. When Petrie entered the pyramid and found Senusert's sarcophagus it had been looted long ago; however, Brunton discovered the jewellery of Princess Sat-hathor, which is now divided between Cairo's museum and the Metropolitan Museum of Art in New York.

Senusert II (1897–1878 or 1880–1874 BC), Amenemhat III's grandfather, ordered eight rock-cut *mastabas* for his family to the north of his pyramid; east of them is the shapeless so-called **Queen's Pyramid**, apparently lacking any tomb.

Maidum Pyramid

Although technically outside the limits of the Fayoum, the **"Collapsed Pyramid" of Maidum** (daily 8am–4pm; £E18) can be reached from there (or from Beni Suef in the Nile Valley). Take an early morning train from Fayoum to El-Wasta (1hr), and then a service taxi to the village of Maidum (10–15min). From the far end of the village it's a short walk across the fields and two canals into the desert; beware of potholes and skulls underfoot. The pyramid is visible from the Nile Valley road, and during the last stage of the train journey. Tickets include admission to two *mastabas* and a ruined mortuary temple. Ask to see them or you won't get into either.

Standing isolated and truncated amidst the sands "with much of its outer layers collapsed into piles of rubble, it looks more like the keep of a medieval castle than a proper pyramid", as T.G.H. James observed. It rises in sheer-walled tiers above mounds of debris: a vision almost as dramatic as the act of getting inside used to be, when "visitors had to hang by their hands from the ledge above and drop into the entry guided by a guard". Nowadays you climb a 30m stairway on the north side, descend 75m to the bedrock by a steep passageway and then ascend to the airless **burial chamber** (bring a torch). Two new chambers were recently found using an endoscope; they have not been entered yet, but may have served to relieve the weight on the burial chamber. Round about the pyramid are unfinished *mastabas*, reduced to ruinous lumps, where the exquisite "Maidum Geese" frieze and the famous statue of Prince Ra-Hotpe and his wife Nofret were found (both can now be seen in the Cairo Egyptian Museum).

Archeologists ascribe the pyramid to **Snofru** (see p.235), the first king of the IV Dynasty (c.2613–2494 BC), or to **Huni**, the last ruler of the preceding dynasty. Partisans of Huni argue that Snofru is recognized as having built the Red and Bent pyramids at Dahshur, and would therefore not have needed a third repository for his *ka*. Mendelssohn's *The Riddle of the Pyramids* advances the contrary theory that Maidum was started by Snofru as a step pyramid (like Zoser's at Saqqara), and then later given an outer shell to make it a "true" pyramid. But the design was faulty, distributing stresses outwards rather than inwards, so that its own mass blew the pyramid apart. Mendelssohn argues that Snofru had already embarked on another pyramid at Dahshur, whose angle was hastily reduced (hence the Bent Pyramid), and that the Red Pyramid was a final attempt to get things right. Crucial to his argument is the idea that pyramids were built in production-line fashion, whether there were pharaohs to be buried in them or not; thus, kings who died before the completion of their own pyramid could be allotted one from the "stockpile".

El-Lisht Pyramids

The **Pyramids of El-Lisht** are the most inaccessible and ruined of the Fayoum collection, with little claim to anyone's attention. The larger of them, the **Pyramid of Amenemhat I** (1991–1962 BC), commemorates the founder of the XII Dynasty, whose capital, *Itj-tway*, was somewhere in the vicinity. Slightly to the south and harder to reach is the **Pyramid of Senusert I**, Amenemhat's son.

Fayoumi monasteries

Tradition has it that St Anthony personally inspired the first hermits in the Fayoum during the fourth century, and within two hundred years the depression held 35 monastic communities. As elsewhere in Egypt, Coptic monasticism gradually declined after the Muslim conquest, and only started to revive during last century. But the habit of pilgrimage never faded, and still ensures visitors to monasteries that are virtually deserted except on holy days.

Deir al-Azab, the nearest monastery to Fayoum City, is reached by heading 5km out along the Beni Suef road, and turning left at a fork; the monastery is on the right after just over a kilometre. Founded during the twelfth century and recently rebuilt *sans* style, the "Bachelor's Monastery" no longer houses monks, but draws many Coptic visitors on Fridays and Sundays, and also holds the **Moulid of the Virgin** (Aug 15–22). It's the burial place of St Abram, the revered Bishop of Fayoum and Giza between 1882 and 1914, whose portrait is said to reach out and shake hands with blessed visitors.

The remoter, more picturesque **Deir al-Malak Ghobriel** (Monastery of the Archangel Gabriel) squats on a desert hillside overlooking the cultivated lowlands. Pilgrim buses may turn up for the **Moulid of Archangel Gabriel** (Dec 18), but otherwise it's very quiet. Wolves have been known to make their dens in the hillside caves; from the ridge you can see the Lahun gap, and sometimes the Lahun and Hawara pyramids. Service taxis for Qalamshah run past a yellow stone barn in the village of Qalhana, whence a dirt track leads to the monastery (5km; 1hr walk). Its **church** dates from the tenth or eleventh century and contains some superb medieval **frescoes** found during restoration work in 1991, plus the naturally mummified "**Naqlun Martyrs**" – unknown monks, women and children murdered at some time in the distant past. Their corpses aren't on show, but the monastery's shop sells gory photos.

The Great Desert Circuit

Only feasible for tourists since the 1980s, the **Great Desert Circuit** is one of the finest journeys Egypt has to offer. Starting from Cairo, Luxor or Assyut, it runs for over 1000km through a desert landscape pockmarked by dunes and lofty escarpments. En route, amid wind-eroded depressions, **four oases** are sustained: Bahariya, Farafra, Dakhla and Kharga. Unlike Siwa, these "inner oases" have been almost continuously under the control of the Nile Valley since the Middle Kingdom, ruled by the pharaohs, Persians, Romans, Mamlukes, Turks and British, who have left their mark in the form of temples, tombs, forts, mosques or roads.

Although each has a central focus, the differences between them are as marked as their similarities. **Bahariya** and **Farafra** both score highly on their hot springs and palm groves, but Bahariya is influenced by Cairene ways and a major centre for **desert safaris**, whereas Farafra is more rural and traditional. In **Dakhla** and **Kharga** the modern centres are less appealing than the ancient ruins and villages on their peripheries, redolent of historic links with the Nile Valley or caravan routes from Sudan. Staying overnight in the haunting **White Desert** between Bahariya and Farafra is a must; while for those with more time and money there are safaris to remoter sites like the **El-Qaf** stalactite cave, or the uninhabited oases along the desolate road to **Siwa Oasis**, which allows die-hard travellers to visit all of the Western Desert oases in a mega-circuit of over 1400km. If you haven't got a car, this journey is only really possible in the other direction, starting from Siwa.

For those limited to **public transport**, travelling the whole circuit from Bahariya to Kharga will take at least a week. As the nearest oasis to Cairo, Bahariya attracts many who fancy a few days in the desert but aren't committed to doing more. If you're short on **time**, it may seem enough; carrying on to Farafra via the White Desert will add two or three days to your schedule, while once past Farafra there's little point in turning back.

Visiting the oases

Though **conditions** are getting easier, you shouldn't expect comforts in the oases. Accommodation is generally basic; there's little choice of things to eat, seldom any alcohol, and no bright lights. Passengers might have to stand during long bus journeys, while motorists must reckon on potholed roads and very few petrol pumps, hundreds of kilometres apart. Keep your passport handy to show at checkpoints. There are **banks** in the "capitals" of Bahariya, Dakhla and Kharga oases, and all the oases now have **telephone** (if not Internet) links with the outer world.

Broadly speaking, the oases share the **climate** of Nile Valley towns on the same latitude – Bahariya is like Minya, and Kharga like Luxor – but the air is fresher (although the dust sometimes causes swollen sinuses). Winter is mild by day and near freezing at night (bring a sleeping bag); during summertime temperatures can soar to 50°C at midday and hover in the 20°s after dark. From October to April, each oasis can usually muster half a dozen visitors, making it easy to assemble a group for excursions to hot springs and other sites – unlike over summer, when tourism evaporates. Spring and autumn are the **best times** to visit the oases, with the orchards in bloom or being harvested, and enough fellow travellers around to make sharing costs easy.

Tourism is in the hands of local officials and entrepreneurs whose competence and honesty varies. Hustling is big in Bahariya but nonexistent in Kharga; Farafra and Dakhla fall somewhere in between. Tourist officials claim to be able to arrange trips at lower prices than the private operators charge. In some places this may be true, in others not. The only way to be sure is to sound out different sources and compare what they're offering. But don't let over-suspicion sour things, since you really need local help to get the best from the oases and will have to strike a deal with somebody in the end – preferably one that both sides feel happy with, as disgruntled guides or tourists can spoil even the most magical spot.

Visitors should respect local values by dressing modestly and observing the conventions on bathing in **outdoor springs** (mostly concrete tanks, fed by a pipe or water percolating up from below). The ones nearest town are always

The New Valley

The four "Great Desert Circuit" oases are situated along a dead, prehistoric branch of the Nile, and depend on springs and wells tapping the great aquifer beneath the Libyan Desert. In 1958 Nasser's government unveiled plans to exploit this, irrigate the desert, and relocate landless peasants from the overcrowded Nile Valley and Delta to the **"New Valley"** (*El-Wadi el-Jedid*). This was vital for social reasons, but also intended to forestall landless *fellaheen* from emigrating to Syria, which was at that time joined with Egypt in the United Arab Republic, and relatively underpopulated. Nasser set up a Desert Authority which found the oases to be isolated, with no roads or modern facilities, and many of their ancient wells and canals blocked. From this emerged a five-year plan and a New Valley Governorate to run Kharga, Dakhla and Farafra oases, in collaboration with the Giza Governorate, which administers Bahariya Oasis.

Since work began in the 1970s, the project has been through ups and downs, as investments proved costlier than expected, and doubts surfaced about the subterranean water table. Previously it was thought to be replenished by underground seepage from Lake Chad and Equatorial Africa, whereas now it's believed to be a finite geological legacy, sufficient for between one and seven hundred years. For a while, the oases were caught in mid-stride, partly modernized but unsure of their long-term viability – but now the government is once again forging ahead with **new projects** to bring Nile water to Kharga Oasis via the **Sheikh Zayed Canal** and exploit the groundwater beneath the desert at **East Oweinat**. So hopes of prosperity and fears of decline still turn on the caprices of hydrology and the wits of the oasis people, as they have since ancient times.

used by local men; if women bathe there, it is only after dark, never when males are present, and only fully covered by a *galabiyya*. Tourists can avoid these restrictions by bathing in more isolated spots, but most **women** cover up anyway to discourage lechery from guides and hangers-on. Women on their own should beware of entering palm groves or gardens – regarded here as an invitation to sex – or accepting rides from drivers who haven't been cleared with the tourist office.

Transport from Cairo or the Nile Valley

Starting from **Cairo**, book seats a day beforehand at the Turgoman bus terminal. **Buses** to Bahariya (6hr; £E14) leave every day at 7am, 8am, 3pm and 6pm. The 8am and 6pm buses continue on to Farafra (8–10hr; £E27) and Dakhla (13–14hr; £E30). Direct buses from Cairo to Dakhla or Kharga oases are routed via the Nile Valley and Assyut–Kharga road; some enter Assyut, while others bypass the city. There are daily services to Kharga (8hr; £E30–32) at 9am and 7pm; the 7pm service continues to Dakhla (11hr; £E38). The journey times given here are only estimates; it can take longer if the bus has a wheezy engine or bursts a tyre. All Upper Egypt and Superjet buses running these routes are a/c – whether it works is another matter.

There are EgyptAir **flights** between Cairo and Kharga (1hr; US$131) on Wednesday and Sunday. These used to fly on to Dakhla before returning to Cairo, but don't at present. The Sunday morning flight is routed via Assyut to Kharga and then back to Cairo, and there are plans to build an airport at Bahariya. The view of the desert from the air is awesome.

As tourists are currently barred from using the direct road from Luxor to Kharga (though they can use it travelling the other way), visitors **coming from the Nile Valley** can either take the weekly **train from Luxor** (Thurs 7am; 7–12hr; £E10) to Kharga Oasis, or get there from **Assyut**. The bus to Kharga takes four to five hours (£E7–8), and one bus continues on to Dakhla (8hr; £E10–12). Service taxis cost £E8–9 to Kharga, from where you can pick up another service to Dakhla.

For details of the journeys to (and between) each oasis, see the relevant sections.

Bahariya Oasis

Bahariya Oasis is the smallest of the four depressions, only 94km long and 42km wide; its desert floor and lower escarpments formed of Cretaceous sandstone, overlaid by limestone and basalt from the Eocene period. Despite having the highest elevation above sea level of the four oases, its water table is nearer the surface, making agriculture easier here. It is known to have been under pharaonic control by the Middle Kingdom, when *Zezes* (as the oasis was known) exported wine to the Nile Valley. During the Late Period Bahariya thrived as an artery between Egypt and Libya, while throughout Islamic times, Arab armies, merchants and pilgrims passed through. Today, it is tourists who come here to enjoy the hot springs and palm groves, or undertake safaris into the dunes and rock formations of the Western Desert.

As in most of the oases, people, springs and palm groves are scattered around a large depression. Although Bahariya's covers 1200 square kilometres, less than one percent is actually cultivated, with date palms, olive and fruit trees, vegetables, rice and corn. Since a dramatic slump half a century ago when 32 springs dried up, 63,900 palm trees died, and thousands emigrated to Cairo, the population has risen again to 30,000, including over 1000 settlers from the Fayoum.

The **journey from Cairo** (360km) takes 4–5 hours; it can take an hour merely to reach Giza, where the Pyramids are visible as you enter the Western Desert. Not long afterwards you'll pass **6th October City**, one of the new satellite cities meant to reduce Cairo's congestion. To relieve the tedium of traversing flat, featureless desert, vehicles stop at a filthy halfway **resthouse** (with biscuits, *fuul*, soft drinks and toilets). Running alongside is a **railway** for transporting ore to the steel mills at Helwan, supplied by a vast open-cast iron **mine** that imparts a ferrous hue to the surrounding desert. Soon after entering Bahariya Oasis the road passes a gravel track to the outlying settlement of El-Harra, and subsequently side roads to the villages of Mandisha and Agouz. Don't get off if the bus calls at any of these places – wait for the end of the line at the oasis "capital", **Bawiti**.

Due to its proximity to Cairo the oasis comes under the Giza Governorate, which means that if you're **phoning from Cairo** you don't need to use the prefix ☎02. Some subscribers still have six-digit numbers instead of the more common seven digits.

Bawiti

BAWITI harbours a picturesque nucleus of old houses on a ridge overlooking luxuriant palm groves, but that's not what you see on arrival. The lower ground beside the Cairo–Farafra road is littered with half-finished New Valley projects, disrupting donkey traffic but not the ramshackle shops and cafés that enliven Bawiti's "strip". Almost everything of note from a practical standpoint can be found here, and buses from Cairo or Farafra drop you right in the centre. You'll immediately be accosted by guys from **rival outfits** who'll try to get you to stay at their place or sign up for trips. Animosity seethes in Bawiti's tourist trade; over-the-top tales of misdeeds, corruption and hotel closures have amused travellers for years.

Arrival and information

Before terminating at the bus ticket kiosk, buses from Cairo are boarded by a tourist cop who asks foreigners where they're going to be staying in the oasis – just give the name of any hotel or campground and he'll be satisfied. It's an enquiry that not only mystifies newcomers, but also Mohammed Abd el-Qader at the low-key **tourist office** (daily except Fri 8.30am–2pm and sometimes also 5–8pm; ☎02/847 3039, @mohamed_kader26@hotmail.com) on the ground floor of the government building on the main drag. He claims to be able to arrange local tours and longer desert safaris for less than the price asked by all the other operators (see p.520), most of whom will make themselves known to anyone who hangs around for a few days. All of them are useful **contacts** to some extent, and mindful of competition from others when negotiating the price of an excursion. Just be aware that you're entering a minefield of grudges; most of the players cut their teeth working at the *Alpenblick Hotel* or *Ahmed Safari Camp*, while the tourist office once closed all of the hotels and campgrounds in Bahariya just so that the Government Resthouse would get a few visitors. It's also worth knowing that the tourist office and the **tourist police** (☎02/847 3900) are separated by more than just 1km of road, for Abd el-Qader is a local guy while the cops are all from outside of the oasis. He says that none of them speak English, but in fact, Captain Ibrahim does.

You can change **money** (but not travellers' cheques) at the National Bank for Development (Mon–Thurs & Sun 8am–2pm) behind the **post office** (daily

Ain-al-Muftillah (2 km)
Siwa Oasis (420 km)
Ahmed Safari Camp (3 km)
▼ Farafra Oasis (180 km)

A L QASR

AL QASR

Ain Bishmu
Tomb of Sheikh al-Bishmu
Tombs of Zad-Amun ef-Ankh & Bannentiu
Bank
Bus tickets
BAZAAR
Police

except Fri 8am–2pm) on the main drag, while there's a **telephone** office (daily 8am–midnight) near the *Alpenblick Hotel* and an **Internet** (£E12/hr) kiosk in the bazaar. There are two **pharmacies** (open from morning till late evening) and a **hospital** (☎02/847 2390), but you'd be better off travelling to Cairo if there's a serious problem.

Accommodation

Hotels and campgrounds cater for every taste and budget and are rarely full, so it's a buyers' market. Decide whether you want desert seclusion or to have the "facilities" of Bawiti close at hand, and what kind of scene you fancy in the evenings. While locals make music and party on some of the campgrounds, the hotels are devoid of nightlife, and while most campgrounds provide free transport out from town, and usually into town too, for some of the hotels you might have to rely on taxis or borrow a bicycle.

The term **campground** here doesn't specifically refer to a place where you pitch a tent (though you can), but to a place that rents palm-thatch or mud-brick huts with sleeping platforms and mattresses – or proper rooms with beds and baths on the fancier sites. Most can rustle up a meal even if they lack a restaurant. All the rates below include **breakfast**, unless stated otherwise.

Hotels

Alpenblick Bawiti ☎02/802-184. The first hotel in the oasis, known to thousands of travellers, it now suffers from age and poor maintenance. Dusty rooms with fans and sinks; don't pay extra for a private bathroom (the shared facilities are cleaner), and avoid the cell-like "budget" rooms. The nice garden and convenient location are its only redeeming features. ❷

El Beshmo Lodge Bawiti ☎02/847 3500. Overlooking palm groves and the desert beyond, it is both central and scenic, with clean rooms with

fans and private or shared facilities, a restaurant and laundry service. It's used by the SCA team excavating the Golden Mummies, so you might even catch sight of Egypt's best-known archeologist, Dr Hawass. The only drawback is the noisy generator nearby. Rooms cost 20 percent less over summer. ❺

International Hot Spring On the edge of Bawiti, before the Black Mountain ☎ & ℻02/847 2322, mobile 0123 212179, ✉whitedesert@link.net, ₩www.whitedeserttours.com. Comfortable,

Oasis
Heritage
Museum

Tourist Police

Arch

Antiquities
Inspectorate

ACCOMMODATION		EATING & DRINKING	
Alpenblick Hotel	6	Grilled Chicken place	A
Desert Home	4	Hillal Coffee shop	E
El-Beshmo Lodge	2	Popular Restaurant	B
International Hot Spring Hotel	3	Rashid Restaurant	D
New Oasis Hotel	1	Titanic Café	C
Paradise Hotel	5		

German-managed spa hotel with 27 rooms and eight chalets built around a thermal pool, with a gym, sauna and restaurant – plus a palm tree growing out of a deep hole in the ground. Beside the room rate guests must pay for half-board (children under 5 free, 50 percent off for under-12s). Sells beer and wine. ⑥

New Oasis Bawiti ☎02/847 3030. Similar to the *El Beshmo Lodge* across the ravine, but all of its rooms have baths, and it also has a swimming pool. ❸

Oasis Panorama 2km outside town, halfway up the Black Mountain ☎02/847 3354, ☏847 3896, mobile 0127 313908, ✉oasispanorama@hotmail.com, ⊛www.oasispanorama.com. An eyesore that locals call "The Hospital", this place feels like a beach hotel whose sea has receded, leaving it

stranded. Its rooms are cool and clean, with baths, fans and mosquito-zappers, but despite being well-managed, the hotel feels rather soulless. ❺

Palm Valley On the side road between Agouz and Zabu, 5km from town ☎02/849 6271, ☏849 6272. Superior to the *Oasis Panorama* in its architecture, location and view of the Black Mountain, it also has larger, comfier rooms. Half- or full-board options available. Reductions between May and Sept. ⑥

Paradise Bawiti ☎02/802-600. A brazen misnomer for six basic rooms and a grimy shower, near a truck stop on the main road in the centre of town. A bed costs only £E5 (without breakfast), but even at that price you'd do better on a campground. ❶

Campgrounds

Ahmed Safari 4km south of Bawiti ☎02/847 3399, mobile 0124 925563, ☏847 9090, ✉ahmed_safari@hotmail.com. The doyen of Bahariya's campgrounds has long since become a hotel in all but name, but kept a few huts for old times' sake (£E5 per person). It has lots of cosy rooms with fans and baths (£E50) around a lovely garden, plus nine larger a/c ones costing twice as much. They sell beer and meals, and promise free transport into town; the site is close to Alexander's Temple but otherwise remote, and if overland safari groups don't turn up, it can feel rather lonely. ❸

Bedouin Village Agouz, 2km from Bawiti ☎02/848 6331, ✉as_sadiq@hotmail.com.

Located just beyond the local school, 200m from the highway, the campground is small and bleak, but has friendly staff, clean rooms (with baths) and a large tent for Bedouin parties with a liberal atmosphere. They charge £E20 per person, not including breakfast. ❷

Bir el-Ghaba Bir el-Ghaba, 11km from town (no phone, contact through the *Alpenblick Hotel*). A primitive *kraal* of straw and mud huts, across the road from a hot spring that's okay to use at night. Overland tour groups often stop by for a beer and party in the dunes. The site is terrible for mosquitoes and has no electricity or fridge, so guests should bring candles and food (a few snacks are sold); getting a ride back into town may be hard if there are no visitors. A mattress in a hut costs ££10. ❶

Desert Home On the edge of Bawiti ☎02/847 2276, mobile 0127 313908, ⓔ khozamteego3@hotmail.com. Semi-finished at the time of writing, this place has largish rooms with en-suite facilities and a proper restaurant, but no garden to speak of. ❷

Eden Valley Ain Gufar, 10km from town ☎02/847 3727, mobile 0127 311876, ⓔ edengarden3@hot-mail.com. Friendly, well-run site in a mini-oasis with a hot spring, cold pool, cosy huts (££10 per person), two a/c rooms with baths (££50) and an outdoor lounge where you can sleep for £3 (breakfast not included). Perfect for chilling out or partying, depending on how many people are

around, but the "road" to the highway is so bad that you don't travel into town lightly. ❶

Government Resthouse Bir al-Mattar, 7km from town ☎02/847 3652. A "health resort" that never got off the ground due to embezzlement, it has grotty rooms and no facilities whatsoever except a nearby hot spring (used by farmhands), nor is transport provided. Even at £5 a night there don't seem to be any takers.

New Star En route to Bir al-Mattar ☎02/847 3652. Closer to town, this new campground has huts with mattresses, a kitchen with a fridge and a lounge for guests, but as the site is shadeless, windswept and near a noisy diesel-pump, they charge only £5 a night, "with breakfast", so they promise. ❶

The town

On Bawiti's **main street**, battered 4WDs weave between tractors and veiled women, past a typical array of coffee houses, hardware and grocery stores, culminating in a mosque. Raucous, dusty and making few concessions to tourists, it's worth a stroll if the sun isn't too hot. Indeed, most tourists seem content to focus on a few museums and sites that are peripheral to the locals – except for those with a financial interest in taking you there.

Oasis Heritage Museum

Bawiti's most visible "sight" is the **Oasis Heritage Museum** created by Mohammed Eed, a 29-year-old self-taught artist, who was inspired by Badr in Farafra (see p.525). Some feel that his fired-clay statues are more expressive than Badr's but he has yet to enjoy the same success abroad. Both artists portray a way of life that's almost disappeared in the oases, for the men at least, whose job it once was to hunt gazelles and weave mats; clothes and bread were made at home (women's roles haven't changed so much). A supine Bedouin drinking *arak* and a barber-doctor operating on a squirming patient are reminders that life wasn't so bucolic; old jewellery and robes hanging on the walls lend further authenticity. You can't miss the museum, as two nearly life-size camels stand outside, flanked by women carrying water jars. Admission is free but donations are welcome. Mohammed has now embarked on a **new museum** which lies 1km beyond the town limits; a large stockade with a pigeon tower and beehive domes houses more statues, including one of a man shooting from a hide and another undergoing a traditional rheumatism cure with hot sticks, plus a 3D panorama of old Bawiti. If you want to visit, Mohammed can be found in the old museum or contacted by phone (☎02/847 3666). Otherwise, it's plainly visible beside the highway, near the turn-off for Agouz.

Antiquities Inspectorate

The unobtrusive **Antiquities Inspectorate** near the hospital displays four **mummies** from the huge cache found outside Bawiti. Three are encased in gilded and painted *cartonage* (linen pasteboard) and have sculpted stucco masks – two of them gilded – hence their sobriquet "The Golden Mummies". Poignantly, the boy and girl were buried with their parents, and their mother's mummy had its head inclined towards her husband's. Notice the "chest plates"

All the **antiquities** officially open to the public (the tombs of Zad-Amun ef-Ankh, Bannentiu and Amunhotep Huy; the Temple of Alexander; the chapels of Ain al-Muftillah) are covered by a single **ticket** (£E30) and **photo permit** (£E25) sold at a kiosk downhill from the Antiquities Inspectorate in the centre of town. This also includes admission to the Inspectorate's makeshift museum, displaying five of the famous "Golden Mummies". However, as several of the sites are outside Bawiti, you'll need transport to realize the full value of the ticket – at least to reach Ain al-Muftillah and Alexander's Temple – and return to town.

on the adult females, one sculpted with tiny triangular breasts and the other with articulated cones that wobbled – a funerary fashion in Greco-Roman times. In this era mummification was often perfunctory, as you can see from the sad, natron-soaked bundle that was once a child. All the mummies so far removed have rapidly deteriorated.

The tombs

From the Antiquities office you can walk downhill and cross the road to reach **Qarat Qasr Salim**, a dusty ridge harbouring two tombs that were opened to the public a few years ago. Both belonged to local merchants of the XXVI Dynasty, whose wealth enabled them to construct **tombs** of a kind previously reserved for high officials. **Zad-Amun ef-Ankh**'s is sunk in a steep-sided pit; its hall has rounded pillars (unusual for Bahariya) and is decorated with deities (notice the people bringing gifts, to the left), painted in ochre, brown and black upon a white background. Nearby is the tomb of his son, **Bannentiu**, at the bottom of a 10m shaft – mind your head on the steel grating and the low entrance to its votive hall. Here the pillars are square and the murals are in brick red, golden yellow, pale blue and black upon white, and some of the deities have only been sketched in, but there's a fine solar barque at the back, and the embalming process is shown on the right-hand wall.

Strange as it sounds, several tombs found by Fakhry in the 1930s were later lost, choked by sand and built over by villagers. The tomb of **Zad-Khonsu ef-Ankh** was only rediscovered in 2000, beneath ten houses on Qarat al-Subi. It belonged to Bahariya's governor in the reign of the XXVI Dynasty pharaoh Amasis, who was buried in an alabaster sarcophagus enclosed within a limestone one, which Dr Hawass thinks were quarried near Tell el-Amarna and Giza, shipped along the Nile and then dragged 200km overland to Bawiti. While Zad-Khonsu's tomb won't be accessible for some time yet, the SCA has reopened another, belonging to his XVIII or XIX Dynasty counterpart, **Amunhotep Huy**. This lies on a ridge called **Qarat Hilwa**, 3km from town to the northwest of the Farafra road, which is hard to find without a guide and not really worth the effort.

The old quarter, Ain Bishmu and Al-Qasr

Bawiti's **old quarter** is in the centre of town, a huddle of mud-brick homes and mausolea flanking a main street where elders sit and gossip on *mastabas*. To appreciate its commanding position, follow the alley winding off to **Ain Bishmu**, a craggy fissure in the bedrock where a spring was hewn in Roman times, gushing hot water (30°C) into a natural basin, to flow into the **palm groves** below. Sadly, the ravine is now disfigured by rubbish and a pumping station, although the two hotels that have been built here try not to mar the breathtaking view of the palm groves. Mostly owned by the Dawawida family, the gardens look especially lovely when spangled with apricot blossom in spring. Nearby is the dovecote-shaped **Tomb of Sheikh al-Bishmu** which local children will happily lead you into.

The old quarter's main street runs into **Al-Qasr**, an older village built directly over the capital of the oasis in pharaonic times and continuously inhabited since then – though many of the houses are now abandoned or used as live-stock pens. Narrow alleys snake past secretive courtyards and walled gardens, abruptly ending or joining up with other lanes – making it easy to go astray. Some of the houses incorporate stones from a bygone XXVI Dynasty temple, and a Roman triumphal arch that survived until the mid-nineteenth century.

Ain Al-Muftillah and the Temple of Alexander

The ancient town once extended 3km to **Ain al-Muftillah**, a spring that's nowadays almost lost on the outskirts of the desert. It's feasible to cycle but better to get there by car, as the route is not signposted or easy to explain. Look out for a barbed wire enclosure containing four **ruined chapels** excavated by Steindorff and Fakhry. Built during the XXVI Dynasty, they don't conform to the canons of temple architecture and are built of local sandstone, streaked with ochre and sienna, which makes them look unusually colourful but is liable to flake. One of the temples was dedicated to Bes, the patron deity of musicians and dancers, but all that remains of his image is a foot and a tail (though Bawiti's museum has a fine statue). By crossing the rise and a dune beyond, you can enjoy a **panoramic view** of Al-Qasr, Bawiti, and the springs and mountains described below.

Further out in the locality of Tibniya, ask at *Ahmed Safari Camp* for directions to the **Temple of Alexander**, 400m away via a sandy track. Built of the same stone as the chapels, its reliefs have suffered even worse from being sandblasted by the wind for centuries, and nothing remains of the face and cartouche of Alexander the Great that archeologists recorded in the 1930s – though you can still discern Amun, receiving offerings from the pharaoh. This is (or was) the only temple in Egypt to bear Alexander's figure and cartouche, and Fakhry's belief that it was founded by Alexander when he passed through the oasis en route from Siwa to Memphis is shared by Hawass★, who frequents Bahariya to supervise the excavation of the Valley of the Golden Mummies, 500m from the temple.

Valley of the Golden Mummies

In May 1996, a donkey owned by one of the guards at Alexander's Temple stumbled into a hole in the desert, and by alerting its master, led him to what turned out to be the **largest cache** of mummies ever found in Egypt. Surveys have since shown that the necropolis covers six square kilometres and may contain 10,000 mummies, stacked in family vaults. Whereas some were simply wrapped in linen, others were in terracotta coffins adorned with human faces, their bodies covered in gilded *cartonage* and their faces with stucco masks. The **Golden Mummies** caught the imagination of the public, and TV networks bid US$3 million to film the opening of the main burial chamber in 1999. Coins and other artefacts buried with the mummies show that they date from Greco-Roman times, when the oasis was a thriv-

★ Dr Hawass's richly illustrated book on the Golden Mummies remains the last word on the subject and describes what it's like to excavate a site that reeks of mummified cadavers. You can take a look for free at Ⓦ www.egyptrevealed.com.

ing exporter of wine and wheat, ruled by an expatriate elite. Hopes that DNA testing would reveal their ethnicity have been called into question by Dr Iskander – the first forensic examiner, later sacked – who claims that body parts were mixed up and double-counted, and that the cadavers were so poorly mummified that they have deteriorated into mere skeletons and organic dust, which is almost worthless from a scientific standpoint. More alarmingly, it seems that they start decomposing once removed from their graves, which has halted excavations.

The main **excavation** site at "Kilo Setta" is officially **off limits** to tourists, though for a time some hotels were able to "fix" visits for guests for £E30 per person – there's no guarantee this will continue, however.

Eating

Eating out in Bawiti is unexciting, as in most of the oases. Grilled chicken, salad and rice can be had at several of the hotels and campgrounds, but most visitors gravitate to Bawiti's *Popular Restaurant*, which cooks one set meal a day of soup, vegetable stew, lamb, rice and salad (£E20), sells beer, and acts as the nerve centre of gossip and tourism in the oasis. The nearby *Titanic Café* serves only soft drinks, and the *Rashid Restaurant* is better for its desserts and *shishas* than its meals, so the only alternative is a nameless grilled-chicken place in the bazaar at the western end of the main street, where there are several more tea and *shisha* dens, including the *Hillal Coffeeshop* that doubles as a bus stop (see p.521). Besides the *Popular Restaurant*, you can buy **beer** at the *Oasis Panorama*, *International Hot Spring* and *Palm Valley* hotels (which also have wine and spirits) and *Ahmed Safari*, *Bir el-Ghaba* and *Eden Valley* campgrounds.

Around the oasis

Several operators run **half-day tours** of the oasis, visiting the Black Mountain, Jebel el-Dist and Bir el-Ghaba to the northeast of town. Usually priced per jeepload (four or five passengers), they range from £E80 at the *Alpenblick Hotel* or £E100 at *Eden Valley Camp* to £E130 at the *El Beshmo Lodge* (whose tour also includes Ain al-Muftillah); a **night trip** to the hot springs costs £E40–50. Alternatively, you could rent a **bike** for £E10 a day from New Newasha Handicrafts near the *Titanic Café*, and cycle out to Bir el-Ghaba – about 25km round-trip – or settle for exploring the palm groves and springs within walking distance of town.

Northeast of Bawiti

The hottest (45°C) and nearest spring to Bawiti is **Bir Ramla**, a nice 2km walk from Bawiti past palm and fruit orchards, but quite exposed. Males can bathe here in shorts; women only at night, in full-length opaque clothing. Similar rules apply to **Bir al-Mattar**, a concrete tank of warm (25°C), faintly sulphurous water, 7km northeast of Bawiti. This "Well of the Airport" gets its name from an abandoned wartime airstrip, visible en route. Skirting palm groves, the road becomes a track leading on to **Bir el-Ghaba** (Well of the Forest), a hot and a cold spring in a eucalyptus grove. While kids or farmhands often bathe here by day, tourists can enjoy it at night (women should wear a long T-shirt), and groups sometimes party at the campground across the road (see p.513).

Visiting Bir el-Ghaba by day affords a view of mountains and hills that can be excursions in themselves. **Jebel el-Dist** (Mountain of the Pot) is more accurately described by locals in the tourist trade as "Pyramid Mountain", and the ever-changing play of light across it has inspired another name, "Magic Mountain". Alas, tours don't stop for long enough for you to reach the mountain, let alone go looking for **dinosaur remains** on the far side (see box opposite), but the fields and acacia groves nearer Bir el-Ghaba abound in **camels**, insects and **birdlife** – most noticeably wheatears, which semaphore to each other with their black-and-white tails, while birds of prey stay aloft, soaring on thermals.

En route to all these sites lies the aptly named **Black Mountain**, whose dolomite and volcanic basalt mass is crowned by a ruined look-out post used by Captain Williams to monitor the Senussi in 1916, for which it is nicknamed *Jebel el-Ingleez*, the "English Mountain". Most of the inhabited parts of the oasis are visible from its summit, whose rocks have an oddly sticky texture and smell faintly of biscuits. Cars usually halt in a wadi not far below the summit. There are several hotels and campgrounds in the locality of the Black Mountain (see pp.512–514).

Villages around Bawiti

Most tourists pay little heed to the **villages** outside Bawiti, whose people are friendly and hospitable. It's feasible to walk to **AGOUZ** (Old One), only 2km

The Dinosaurs of Bahariya

In June 2001 a team from the University of Pennsylvania announced the discovery of a previously unknown type of dinosaur in Bahariya Oasis which, from the length of its forearm (1.69m), was the second-largest known to science (only surpassed by Argentinosaurus): 26–34m long and weighing 60–70 tonnes. This long-necked plant-eater lived 94 million years ago during the Late Cretaecous era when the local environment resembled the Florida Everglades, with mangrove swamps and tidal creeks – hence the title bestowed on it, **Paralititan** (Tidal Giant). Its full name, *Paralititan stromeri*, honours the Bavarian paleontologist **Ernst Stromer** (1870–1952), who first discovered dinosaur remains in Egypt between 1911 and 1915. He identified a giant herbivore, **Aegyptosaurus**, and three predators called **Spinosaurus** (Spine Lizard), **Carcharodontosaurus** (Shark-toothed Lizard) and **Bahariasaurus** – whose bones ended up in a Munich museum, where they were destroyed by an Allied air raid in 1944. When searching for Stromer's dinosaur beds, the Pennsylvania team only knew that they were somewhere near **Jebel el-Dist**; they wrote down the wrong GPS coordinates and got lost in the oasis, where by chance they found another site near **Jebel el-Fagga**, yielding the skeleton of Paralititan – with a tooth from a Carcharodontosaurus stuck in its pelvis – fossilized fish, turtles and ferns. The bones are now on show at the Geological Museum in Cairo; an impression of the creature appears on the **Bahariya Dinosaur Project website**, Ⓦ www.egyptdinos.org.

from town, off the Cairo highway. Agouz is reputedly inhabited by the descendants of families banished from Siwa Oasis for the loose morals of their womenfolk, but they would rather forget this slur on their ancestors. There's a campground in the village, and a hotel on the link road to **MANDISHA**, which lends its name to a field of **dunes** called Ghard Mandisha, that threatens neighbouring **ZABU**, where houses and palm groves have been drowned in sand. Behind the gardens at the back of the village, facing towards the escarpment, you can follow a track into a canebrake to find **Qasr el-Zabu** – a giant sandstone boulder where Libyan nomads and other travellers have carved **inscriptions** since the twelfth century. Besides petroglyphs and sun symbols, you can see horses, a charioteer, a woman with her arms akimbo, and the name of the explorer Hyde.

South of Bawiti

The southern part of the oasis is generally seen by tourists bound for the White Desert on 4WD safaris. While some make a cursory detour off-road into the **Black Desert** (*Sahara Suda*) of charred outcrops and table-top rocks, others swing around the far side of **Jebel Gala Siwa** to see a lovely **dune** that has formed in the lee of the escarpment – which you can "ski" down – and may stop for lunch at **Heiz el-Bahri**, a grove of palms and tamarisks around a cold spring, which is one of several fertile enclaves in the locality called "El-Heiz". Unfortunately they seldom visit **Ain al-Ris**, to the south of the highway, where Roman and Christian ruins attest to its settlement in ancient times (Fakhry reckons that this was the "fourth oasis" described by texts in the temple at Edfu). This might be because the SCA made such a hash of "restoring" the **Church of St George** that they'd rather nobody saw the result; Copts believe that one of Christ's apostles, St Bartholomew, visited Bahariya before his martyrdom, and perhaps even died there. Ain al-Ris also harbours a mudbrick **Roman fortress** and remnants of an ancient **date-wine brewery**. Sticking to the highway, instead, you may notice a white **tomb** in the desert roughly 30km from Bawiti: a monument to Swiss man René Michel, a pioneer of tourism to Bahariya, who died here from heatstroke in 1986.

Desert safaris

Bawiti is the main **departure point for safaris in the Western Desert**, ranging from forays into Farafra's White Desert (see p.523) to long-range expeditions to the remote Gilf Kebir and Jebel Uwaynat (p.550). While local outfits and freelancers vie for business, you shouldn't consider the price as the only factor, for the farther you go into the desert the more vital their competence becomes. Anyone offering **4WD** trips should provide at least one jeep as logistical support for the car carrying tourists (trips are usually priced on the basis of four passengers; more than that requires another car). In the case of **camel treks**, the supply-car stays out of sight and only appears to set up camp when needed, as trekkers alternate between riding and walking. While even local boys can handle the White Desert by 4WD (so they boast), trips to Siwa or Dakhla – never mind the Gilf or Uwaynat – require guides that know the route and how to travel off-road by 4WD or camel. Although **GPS** (satellite navigation) is invaluable, really expert guides don't need it, having memorized tracks and landmarks from experience.

Besides the operators listed below, there are other **freelancers** such as Ayman Aiadei (☏02/847-2232), Adel Sadiq Elbdramany (@aa_sadiq@hotmail.com) or Karim El-Abed, alias "Chocolate" or the "Desert Lion" (@kareim69@yahoo.com), who run overnight excursions to the White Desert for about £E100 per person.

Contact details for guides operating through **hotels** or campgrounds appear under Bawiti's "Accommodation" listings on pp.512–514.

The Bahariya and Farafra depressions are separated by a limestone **escarpment** where gigantic drifts of sand flank the road as it traverses the **Naqb es-Sillum** (Pass of the Stairs), and two microwave masts relay signals between the oases (there's a first aid post with an ambulance by the mast nearest Bahariya). From here on, many safari groups head off-road to reach Agabat and the White Desert, as described under "Farafra Oasis".

Magdy Deyab *Oasis Panorama Hotel.* This guy has been organizing safaris for ages and still participates, despite his girth. Though mostly semi-off-road to the White Desert in 4WD (£E160 per day per person), he can also arrange camel trekking to Dakhla or Siwa oases for £E300 per person per day if enough people are interested. **Yehiya Kandil** ☏02/847 2835, mobile 0123 216790, @yahiakandil@yahoo.de or leberli@yahoo.de. A long-time freelancer who offers a night in the White Desert and on to Farafra for £E550 (group rate), or one day and one night, including the Black Desert and Agabat, ending in Farafra or returning to Bahariya, for £E580. Also El-Qaf and on to the Fayoum for US$50 per person per day. Yehiya has a GPS, and is gearing up for trips to the Giff Kebir.
Khaled and Rose-Maria Khalifa With well over a decade of experience, *Khalifa Expeditions* (mobile ☏0123 215445, @khalifa_exp@link.net, @www.khalifaexp.com) covers the whole of the Western Desert by 4WD, including the Gilf Kebir and Jebel Uwaynat (9–14 days at US$135 per person per day), using GPS. They specialize in camel trekking, with an 8-day trek to Siwa via

Nuweisima, Bahrein and Areg oases for US$1100 per person, and also do "meditation" tours.
Mohammed Abdel Latif ☏02/847 2636. A great driver, musician and all-round entertainer – known as "Bodadi" – who usually works for others. His own trips are sure to be fun but probably not the most organized, nor fit to venture far beyond the White Desert. He can also be contacted through Guus Kruis in Holland (@gkruis@omni-trade.nl).
Talaat Mola *Eden Garden Camp.* Mainly off-road tours as far south as Dakhla Oasis, for £E125–150 per day per person. He hires guys like "Bodadi" or "Chocolate" to generate a buzz, but makes sure that the logistics run like clockwork and clients enjoy themselves. Talaat also runs camel treks for £E150 per person per day.
Ahmed Abdel Rahim *Ahmed Safari Camp.* Ahmed has been organizing safaris for decades but doesn't play an active role any more. His eight-day tour of the oases from Bahariya to Luxor is more on- than off-road (US$40 per person per day; minimum five), but he can also arrange camel trekking or walking tours.

Reda Abd al-Razzoul is a local geography and history teacher who styles himself the "Desert Fox" and has led safaris as far as Luxor or Assyut for twenty years. A fine guide and a fantastic storyteller, he can be found at school or the *Bedouin Village Camp* in Agouz, or at his handicrafts shop at the far end of Bawiti's main street.

Lotfi Abd el-Sayed *El Beshmo Lodge*. Lotfi was the first guy in the oasis to do safaris and his experience outweighs his limited English or lack of a GPS. His rates contain a differential between travel-

ling by day (US$25–40 per person) or night (US$40–75 per night), whether it's to the Black and White Deserts, El-Qaf, or Wadi Rayan. He can also send a car load of passengers to Siwa for £E1000.

Peter Wirth *International Hot Spring Hotel*. A guide for self-drive and tailor-made 4WD safaris all over the Western Desert. He's certainly not the cheapest (ask for a quote), but took the GPS readings for Cassandra Vivian when she was updating her *Explorer's Handbook*. Peter speaks English and German, and his wife, Miharu, Japanese.

Moving on from Bahariya

If you've had enough of the desert, four buses daily run to **Cairo** (4–5 hr; £E14): you can book seats on the 7am and 3pm services departing from the ticket kiosk (9am–1pm & 7–11pm) near the post office, but not on the buses from Farafra and Dakhla, which pass through Bawiti around noon and midnight, collecting passengers at the *Hillal Coffeeshop* down the road.

Although there is a direct **road to Siwa Oasis** (420km), local drivers charge at least £600–700 for the journey, and you may be hard pressed to find enough fellow travellers to bring the cost down to an affordable level. People with their own car (preferably 4WD) may use it, but should exercise caution; the road is in very bad condition with no facilities whatsoever, and only the odd checkpoint. The drive takes at least seven hours, more if there's a lot of sand on the road. Currently, you simply have to register your passport and driving licence with the Desert Police in Bawiti, but you should enquire at the tourist office in case the rules have changed. See p.576 for a description of the oases along the way.

Tourists not returning to Cairo invariably carry on to **Farafra Oasis**, maybe stopping for a night in the **White Desert** en route. While most people visit the White Desert on safaris (see p.523), it is possible to get there by **bus**, using the service that leaves between noon and 1pm. **Hitching** a lift from Bahariya to Farafra is possible, but you should be sure that it's going all the way; quiz drivers at the military checkpoint. The 180-kilometre journey takes about three hours, so motorists hoping to reach the White Desert before sunset should allow a bit longer, to select a campsite. Fill up on **fuel** in town as there are no pumps until Farafra. The journey requires about 100 litres, of which 20 litres are consumed by the off-road stuff between Crystal Mountain, Agabat and the White Desert.

Farafra Oasis

Farafra Oasis is the least populous, most isolated of the four oases on the circuit. When camels were the only means of travel, the Farafonis had less contact with Bahariya (a journey of four days) than with Dakhla, which was tenuously connected to the Forty Days Road. Fakhry relates how the villagers once lost track of time and could only ascertain the right day for Friday prayers by sending a rider to Dakhla. Before the paved road was built in 1978 it took 4WD and a winch truck a whole day to climb the Bahariya escarpment. Yet the oasis had dealings with the Nile Valley as early as the V Dynasty, when it was called *Ta-ihw*, the "Land of the Cow". Even today, Farafra's cows are of the same breed

Siwa Oasis   Bahariya Oasis   Bahariya Oasis

FARAFRA OASIS   N

0   25 km

Microwave masts

Naqb el-Sillum

Crystal Mountain   Agabat
Twin Peaks

Wadi al-Ubayyid

Ain Dalla   Infidel Rock   *White*   Ain al-Wadi

Desert

Ain Sewal

Bir Setta   Bir Regwa

Quss Abu Said Plateau   Qasr al-Farafra

Ain Besai   Bir Qarawein

Iron Pyrites   Ain Sheikh Mazouk   Bir Dikkur

Abu Minqar

Valley of Shells

El-Qaf

Dakhla Oasis   Al-Qasr (Dakhla Oasis)

as those depicted in ancient tombs and temples (though no pharaonic monuments have been found in the oasis), and are so valued that they are smuggled to Bahariya, using trails that avoid police checkpoints.

Qasr al-Farafra was the only village in the oasis before the New Valley scheme seeded a dozen new hamlets across the depression, and most of its 4000 inhabitants belong to four extended families. This tightknit community is noted for its piety, apparent during Ramadan, when the mosque overflows with robed imams and sheikhs. **Tourism** has been kept at a distance and largely remains the preserve of the Ali family, whose hegemony was recently secured by the election of Atif Ali as mayor, ensuring that his brothers Sa'ad and Hamdy need fear little from outsiders who've tried to move onto their turf. This lack of competition is not so good for visitors, as the cost of excursions is way above what you'd pay in Bahariya Oasis (even though the distances involved are far less), while Atif's desire for respectability coupled with a crackdown on *bango* has ended the nocturnal parties that used to be a feature of Farafra's tourist scene, which now seems staid compared to Bahariya's.

Crystal Mountain, Agabat and the White Desert

Coming from Bahariya, you'll enjoy a succession of fantastic views as you enter the Farafra depression. Many safaris stop at *Jebel al-Izaz* or the **Crystal Mountain**, sited beside the highway shortly before the Naqb es-Sillum starts its descent into the oasis. This ridge is entirely composed of quartz crystal and has a man-high natural arch through the middle, which is why locals call it

Hagar al-Makhrum, the "Rock with a Hole". Small crystals lie all around, and there are lumps the size of footballs farther from the road. At this point, 4WDs may turn off onto tracks leading to Agabat, or continue along the highway, past the landmark **Twin Peaks** at the end of the range of hills on the left.

Agabat, "the Difficult" in Arabic, is the name given to scores of rock sugar-loaves surrounded by soft sand and powdered chalk. The sand can easily entrap vehicles that try to reach it from the direction of the highway, so it's easier to approach it off-road from the Crystal Mountain, whence a steep, dramatic descent into Agabat is possible.

This spectacularly rugged terrain merges into the famous **White Desert** (*Sahara el-Beida*) that stretches on either side of the highway. Here, the wind has eroded chalk monoliths into surreal forms resembling skulls, ostriches, hawks, camels, mushrooms and leopards – to mention but a few of the names given to them – which loom above a dusty pan littered with shells, crystals and iron pyrites shaped like sea urchins, twigs or turds. The chalk *yardangs* glint pale gold in the midday sun, turn violet and pink around sunset, and resemble icebergs or snowdrifts by moonlight – while **gazelles** may be glimpsed at daybreak as they forage for a few hours. Safari operators distinguish between the "Old" and "New" White Deserts to the east of the highway and the larger inselbergs near the western escarpment – but you're sure to be entranced whatever the local-ity. It can be hard to find a spot to camp out of sight of other groups at Christmas or Easter, when many people travel down from Cairo. Try to pre-serve this wonderful landscape by ensuring that no rubbish is left behind.

Although the White Desert is in Farafra Oasis, it's cheaper to arrange **excursions** from Bahariya (see p.520 for a list of guides). Most tourists want to camp **overnight**, so safaris usually leave in the morning, to visit the Black Desert and Crystal Mountain before reaching the White Desert in time to set up camp by nightfall. For this, Yehiya Kandil charges £E550 (group rate), or £E580 for a longer trip via Agabat, while others such as Talaat Mola (£E125–150) or Magdy Deyab (£E160) charge on a per person per day basis – rates that com-pare favourably with El-Badawiya Safari in Farafra, which demands US$60 per person per day. In each case, the deal should include transport, meals and bed-ding, with Bedouin music and dancing for good measure. If this is beyond your means, the alternative is to take a **bus** from Bahariya to Farafra (or vice versa) and ask to be dropped off in the White Desert, catching another bus out next day (bring plenty of water, a sleeping bag, food and firewood); or to hire a **taxi** or pick-up in Farafra to drive you there and back for about £E50 (which only allows a brief look by day). It's worth noting that most of the White Desert is accessible by **2WD** vehicles, providing that the driver can distinguish between soft sand and firmer ground – but anyone travelling without a guide should be aware that **mobile phones** only work close to Qasr al-Farafra, unless you climb up on top of a *yardang* to get a stronger signal.

Qasr al-Farafra

As in Bawiti, the low ground in **QASR AL-FARAFRA** has been colonized by New Valley infrastructure, which obscures your view of the hilltop village, backing onto palm groves. Its traditional mud houses have an austere beauty, their low windowless facades topped by flowing pediments or crenellations. Facing the street are broad *mastabas* where mothers chat and elders ruminate. Everyone knows each other and their lineage; many are of Libyan ancestry and bear the surname Senussi. Farafra's population has long been minuscule (only 542 according to the first census in 1892) and agriculture limited to the nearby palm groves and a few outlying springs, keeping the oasis poor – a poverty reflected in Farafra's lack of traditional jewellery, unlike the other oases. Even today its shops and market are meagre by comparison and frugality is the order of the day, despite a few wealthy locals who've built villas on the edge of town.

Arrival and information

While a triumphal arch welcomes traffic from Dakhla, **buses from Bahariya** pass the *El-Badawiya Hotel* on the outskirts before dropping passengers at the fuel station and the shops down the road.

The **post office** (daily except Fri 8am–2pm) and **telephone exchange** (24hr) are behind the Town Council, and international calls can also be placed at the private **Internet** (£E25/hr) and fax place up the hill from the **pharmacy**. Farafonis are proud of their new **hospital,** where once a year doctors from Cairo come here for a week and treat locals free of charge. In the absence of a bank, you may be able to change small amounts of **cash** with locals. There's an office advertising **car rental**, which seldom seems to be open but might be worth investigating.

Aqua Sun Hotel & Bir Setta ▲ (6 km)   Hospital, El-Badawiya Hotel (300 m) & Bahariya Oasis (180 km) ▲

Villas ▶

Badr's Museum

N

Town Council

Fortress   Car rental

Men's Bathhouse

Al-Tamawy Restaurant

Hussein Restaurant

Kiosk

Bir Qarawein (62 km) ▶

Shops & Bakery

Samir Restaurant

@   Pharmacy

QASR AL-FARAFRA   0 ———— 50 m

Dakhla Oasis (310 km) ▼

Tourism and the **Ali family** are virtually synonymous, as Atif manages the *El-Badawiya Hotel*, Sa'ad and Hamdy run El-Badawiya Safari trips, and their artist brother Badr sells work to visitors. They're happy to impart **information** in the hope of you signing up for a trip or buying a sculpture, and they know all there is to know about Farafra. "Mr Socks", who sells home-made camel-hair woollies in their hotel, is another local character. The other two **safari operators** are out-of-towners who know less about the oasis: AquaSun Desert Safaris (Ⓔsafari@eg-westerndesert.com, Ⓦwww.eg-westerndesert.com), based at the *AquaSun Hotel*, and Mohsen from Kharga (see p.542), who can sometimes be found at his uncle Mohammed's gold shop near Badr's museum. As these guys constitute the only game in town and the number of tourists is tiny, how good a time you have boils down to personal chemistry.

Acccommodation

The *El-Badawiya* (Ⓣ092/510-060, Ⓕ510-400, Ⓔbadawya@link.net; ❺) is the only **accommodation** in town and most people's choice: a tidy holiday village whose classiest rooms are split-level, with a lounge and a raised bed with mosquito net (£E100); regular ones come with or without bathrooms (£E50), and there are also a few tents with camp-beds (£E5 per person). For those with more cash and a desire for solitude, the new *AquaSun Hotel* (no Ⓣ at time of writing; ❻) is a fancier *qasr*-style place with a/c rooms (US$60), satellite TV and a warm pool, fed by a hot spring outside the grounds, located at **Bir Setta**, 6km from town; pick-ups (£E1–2) from the fuel station run within 200m of the hotel.

The village

Behind the school you'll find **Badr's Museum**, the creation of a self-taught artist who has successfully exhibited in Germany, France and Britain, but stayed in the oasis, about which he feels passionately. Badr detests the urban-style buildings of New Valley, believing that Farafra can be developed in harmony with its traditional character. His museum resembles a *qasr*, with reliefs of camels and farmers decorating its walls, and an antique wooden lock on the door. Its dozen-odd rooms exhibit Badr's rustic sculptures and surreal paintings; stuffed wildlife, weird fossils and pyrites. The Farafonis find his desert garden incomprehensible, but relish his portraits of local people. The museum opens when Badr wishes; there's no admission charge, but donations are appreciated.

Previously, he painted *Hadj* **murals** of snarling lions and flying eagles on local houses. Sadly they have all vanished due to salt corrosion and only two more have been painted since – one for Atif and one for their parents. Badr's "Fourth Dream" (as he puts it) is a studio-house embodying his ideas about architecture and creativity – if you're invited to visit, accept the offer. The brothers' **villas** are on the edge of the windblown desert, their high walls decorated with camels' heads and other symbols.

Otherwise, you can investigate the mud-brick **fortress** (*qasr*) that gives the village its name (though the full appellation is rarely used in everyday speech). Until early in the twentieth century, the Farafonis would retreat inside when invaders came; each family had a designated room, where, during normal times, provisions were stored and guarded by a watchman. Damaged by heavy rainfall, it began to crumble in the 1950s; the less damaged parts are now home to a few families, and blend into the surrounding houses.

You can also wander around the **palm groves** behind the village, which look especially lovely an hour before sunset. They are divided into walled gardens planted with olive and fruit trees as well as date palms (whose branches are used to fence the land). You can walk the paths freely, but shouldn't enter the gardens uninvited; for single women to do so is regarded as provocative. Likewise, avert your eyes from the **men's bathhouse** on the edge of the village, where youths splash around in a concrete tank fed by a pipe gushing warm water. Foreigners are expected to bathe at other springs.

Come nightfall, there's little to do but hang out in teahouses or maybe wallow in the hot spring at Bir Setta (see below), unless you happen to chance upon a *zikr* in somebody's home. **Zikrs** are a Sufi ritual where the participants seek to attain oneness with God by rhythmic swaying and chanting, which play an important role in the religious and social life of Farafra. The host throws his house open to male visitors; foreigners of both sexes are welcome, providing they respect that they are guests at a religious ritual, not spectators at a tourist attraction – which means modest dress and behaviour.

Excursions

There are many other beauty spots besides the White Desert, which can be seen as part of an extended safari from Qasr al-Farafra or Bahariya Oasis. Depending on how much you want to see, they can take two or three days to cover, or longer if you carry on to Dakhla or El-Qaf. As with the White Desert, it's cheaper to arrange safaris in Bahariya than Farafra, though in both cases they are usually priced on a per person per day basis, assuming a minimum of four passengers. Accounts start on p.527.

There seems to be little demand for trips to springs within Farafra Oasis, such as **Bir Setta** (Well Six), which is a concrete tank of sulphurous hot water that's good for wallowing but stains clothes brown (the *AquaSun Hotel* is nearby; see p.525); **Ain Besai**, a cold freshwater pool beside the rock tombs and chapels of a settlement abandoned in Christian times; the small, uninhabited oasis of **Ain el-Tanien**; or **Ain Sheikh Mazouk**, a hot sulphur spring feeding a tank where local men bathe. While Bir Setta is accessible by local pick-ups from town, and Ain Sheikh Mazouk is close enough to the highway to be reached by bus, the others require private transport. This is also true of two sites of geological interest, namely an area of desert strewn with flower-shaped **iron pyrites**, and the **Valley of Shells** (*Wadi el-Khawaka*) out beyond Abu Minqar.

Eating and drinking

It doesn't take long to sample the culinary delights of Farafra. *El-Badawiya* serves decent spaghetti bolognese, *kofta*, kebab and salad, at higher prices than the humbler *Al-Tamawy*, *Hussein* and *Samir* **restaurants** in town, which do omelettes, *fuul*, grilled chicken, salad, rice or soup, but often run out of food by 5pm, and only sell soft drinks thereafter. For *sheeshas* and tea or Turkish coffee, there's a single teahouse (which also serves as a bus stop) among the shops on the main street, where you'll also find a **bakery**. At the time of writing, nowhere in Farafra sold **alcohol**, but imported and domestic brands of non-alcoholic beer were available from the kiosk near the *Hussein Restaurant*.

Moving on from Farafra

If you're doing the circuit in reverse, **buses to Bahariya** (2–3hr; £E14) and **Cairo** (8–10hr; £E27) leave at around 10am and 10pm daily. You buy tickets on board and there's usually no problem getting a seat, but be sure to arrive in good time, as the bus may leave before its scheduled departure time. Otherwise, there's a faint chance of **service taxis** to Bahariya, or lifts from cars that have just deposited tourists after a night in the White Desert. Expect to pay about £E15 per person for a full taxiload.

Buses to Dakhla Oasis (4hr; £E15) leave between 1pm and 2pm and 1am and 2am. Service taxis also cover the route, maybe once or twice a day. In a fully loaded vehicle passengers pay £E15 each; fewer individuals pay more. If you're planning to do this, spread the word so drivers know that you're interested. Buses both ways can be flagged down outside the *El-Badawiya* and also stop at the teahouse among the shops in town for a few minutes. **Hitchhiking** from the military checkpoint outside town is also feasible, but be sure your ride is going all the way.

Between Agabat and Bir Regwa

There are endless ways of combining Agabat and the White Desert with springs and wadis to the east of the highway. One follows a track from Agabat to **Bir Regwa** (aka Bir al-Akhbar), a hot spring beside the highway, 33km from Qasr al-Farafra. Starting from Agabat, you pass through the desolate **Wadi Hinnis** (Valley of John) to enter a small depression called **Ain al-Wadi**, whose golden sand is dotted with shrubs and palms and has recently been used to grow watermelons. For geologists, the wadi is significant for containing the oldest exposed bedrock in the Farafra depression, dating from the Danian era. From there you travel to the ancient watering hole of **Ain Hadra**, recognizable by a single palm tree rising from a clump of fronds on a sandy hillock, surrounded by potsherds from Roman, Coptic and medieval times. Beware of camping here, as there are not only mosquitoes but **horned vipers**, which usually sleep in the winter but will wake up if disturbed. A short way beyond lies **Wadi Sunt**, otherwise known as "Acacia" after the venerable tree that shades the spot, whence the trail carries on past picturesque *yardangs* nicknamed the **Tents**, the **Ice Cream Cones** and the **Mushrooms**.

El-Qaf

A few operators run trips to the remote **cave** called **El-Qaf** (or Gara), 100km east of Farafra, shortly before the great sand barrier of the Ghard Abu Muharik that blocks any approach from the Nile Valley. Though doubtless known to Bedouin long before it was "discovered" by Rohlfs in 1873, its whereabouts were forgotten until it was rediscovered by Carlo Bergmann in 1991. Entered via a fissure in the ground that becomes a narrow corridor, the cave has one large chamber and two small ones, full of white **stalactites**. Beware of the crack in the floor, harbouring snakes and scorpions. While Rohlfs found El-Qaf while wandering off the caravan route to Assyut, it is nowadays reached by a track that leaves the highway near the southern microwave mast at Naqb es-Sillum. The cave can be reached in seven hours, but as the desert is flat and boring for most of the way safaris include detours to Agabat or the White Desert that extend the excursion over two or three days.

Ain Della

Only 120km from Farafra by road, yet tantalizingly inaccessible, **Ain Della** (Spring of the Shade) has played an epic part in the history of the Westen Desert as the last waterhole before the Great Sand Sea, used by raiders and smugglers since antiquity, motorized explorers in the 1920s and 1930s, and the Long Range Desert Group in World War II. It now has a small Egyptian army garrison that chases smugglers using 4WD instead of camels, as in the days of the Frontier Camel Corps, which once pursued a caravan of hashish all the way across the desert to Giza. Visiting Ain Della requires special **permission** from

The Lost Army of Cambyses

One of the most famous tales in the *Histories* of Herodotus is of the Persian conqueror **Cambyses** (525–522 BC), son of Cyrus the Great, who sent an army across the desert to destroy the Siwan Oracle – which vanished in a sand storm. According to Herodotus, the 50,000-strong **army** marched from Thebes (Luxor) for seven days to an "oasis", and thence towards Siwa – which leaves room for doubt as to whether the oasis was Kharga or Farafra. Depending on which story you favour, their last watering hole was Ain Amur or Ain Della, beyond which the army ran out of water and perished in the Great Sand Sea after a sand storm blew up from the south, scattering and burying the weakened troops. Some ascribe this to the Persians' inability to calculate longitude, which lead them to believe that Siwa was on a bearing of 289° from Kharga, instead of 310°; others to their ignorance of the environment. The mystery of where the army disappeared tantalized explorers such as Almásy (see p.554), who claimed to have found the site but never disclosed its location.

In 2000 Dr Ali Barakat, a geologist from Helwan University, caused a sensation when he announced the **discovery** of bronze arrowheads and human skeletons north of Wadi al-Ubayyid. As later research by Tom Bown and Gaille McKinnon proved inconclusive, an SCA expedition foundered in the sands, and the results of forensic tests have yet to be published, all that can be theorized is that the army numbered far less than 50,000 (Persian sources routinely over-estimated the size of armies, and Bown estimates that 50,000 troops would have needed 3000 tonnes of water and fodder), and may have been no larger than 5000 soldiers. Human bodies have been preserved by the desert for 5000 years, but no indubitably Persian corpse has been found yet – though Bown reckons that they exist in the lee of rock buttes, where the army might have camped or taken shelter.

Whatever the fate of his "Lost Army", Cambyses seems to have been a disastrously incompetent general, for while the Siwan expedition was marching towards its death, he was personally leading another army up the Nile to Ethiopia, which ran out of food in the Nubian Desert and had to resort to cannibalism to survive. News of these two disasters caused disaffected nobles in Persia to unite behind his son and stage a revolt, and it was en route to recover his throne that Cambyses accidentally stabbed himself in the thigh with his own dagger and died of gangrene in Syria. As an invader who had wantonly desecrated the Serapeum and sought to destroy the Oracle of Amun (said to control desert storms), these misfortunes must have seemed divine punishment for his arrogance.

Cairo – which is rarely granted – but it's possible to get there from Siwa Oasis with a permit from Military Intelligence there. One of the routes through the Great Sand Sea runs via **Wadi al–Ubayyid**, where Italian archeologists are investigating a **prehistoric village** dubbed the "Hidden Valley" and a cave containing **rock art**. Should restrictions on travel from Farafra be lifted, the road starts at a checkpoint in the White Desert, and has great rock formations for most of the way. At 53km into the journey to Ain Della one passes the so-called **Infidel Rock** or "Church of the Spirits of the Lost Persian Army", an anthropomorphic rock formation on a hillock, that locals believe marks the last known location of the fabled Lost Army of Cambyses (see box above).

The road to Dakhla

Relatively few vehicles follow the 310-kilometre road **between Farafra and Dakhla Oasis**, where the only fuel en route is reserved for road gangs and military outposts. Once past Ain Sheikh Mazouk, the desert shifts from white stone to gravel and sand until you reach **Abu Minqar** (Father of the Beak). A green smudge in the wilderness, where wells have been sunk and houses built in an effort to attract settlers, it is the westernmost point on the Great Desert Circuit, and an obligatory tea-stop. Beyond lie more gravel pans, where golden orioles flit across the highway as it veers towards the escarpment that delineates **Dakhla Oasis**, where you'll pass through Al-Qasr and Mut Talatta before reaching Mut, Dakhla's main centre.

Off-road to Dakhla Oasis

Travelling off-road to Dakhla (173km) is an exciting journey. A paved road starting in Qasr al-Farafra runs out to **Bir Qarawein**, whose ancient well has now been supplemented by boreholes, allowing watermelons to be grown here (and *bango*, until the plantation was spotted by chance by an army helicopter). By turning off the road halfway to Qarawein, you can follow a track to the sweetwater spring of **Bir Dikkur**, marked by two palms and a camel's skeleton, and into the **dune lanes** that run parallel in a southeasterly direction. Some have trees protruding from their crests, where the dunes have buried whole palm groves on their relentless march towards Dakhla. Further on lie the **Black Valley**, whose floor is covered in iron pyrites, and the **Marble Labyrinth**, whose sharp stones are equally hard on tyres. Mobile phones don't work beyond Bir Dikkur, so a breakdown means serious trouble for cars travelling alone. The route ends at Al-Qasr (see p.536) in Dakhla.

Dakhla Oasis

Verdant cultivated areas and a great wall of rose-hued rock across the northern horizon make a feast for the eyes in **Dakhla Oasis**. Partitioned by dunes into more or less irrigated, fertile enclaves, the oasis supports 75,000 people living in fourteen settlements strung out along the Farafra and Kharga roads. Although it's the outlying sites that hold most attraction, the majority of travellers base themselves in **Mut** (pronounced "moot"), Dakhla's "capital", which has better facilities. Buses and pick-ups between Mut and the villages enable you to see how the Dakhlans have reclaimed land, planted new crops, and generally made the best of New Valley developments. Water is relatively abundant in the oasis, which has over 520 wells in its 410 square kilometres.

Most **villages** have spread down from their original hilltop maze of medieval houses and covered streets, into a roadside straggle of breeze-block houses, schools and other public buildings. Besides this exotic architecture, Dakhla has pharaonic, Roman and Coptic antiquities, dunes, palm groves and hot springs to explore. It was in this region that the *Breitling Orbiter 3*, the first balloon to circumnavigate the globe, touched down in 1999.

Mut

Dakhla's capital, **MUT**, was branded a miserable-looking place by travellers early in the nineteenth century, but it has come on apace since the 1950s, as the Dakhlans have subverted or embraced planned "modernity" according to their needs and tastes. The architect of Mut's already crumbling low-rise flats is unlikely to have foreseen their balconies being converted into extra rooms or pigeon coops, and the four-lane Sharia al-Wadi that snakes through town rarely carries anything heavier than cyclists. Yet the locals welcome the hospital and schools, and big capital investments like the Fish Pond wastewater project.

Arrival and information

Arriving by bus you can get off at Midan Tahrir or Midan Gam'a, as buses run into the centre before winding up at the new bus station near the hospital. Entering town from the west, you'll pass the **tourist office** (daily 8am–2pm, and maybe 6–9pm; ☎092/821-686), 250m west of Midan Tahrir, where energetic, conscientious Omar Ahmed is usually at his desk, and also swears that you can contact him at home (☎092/820-782) at other times. Well-informed and

El-Hindaw (6 km)

Balat (35 km), Bashendi (42 km) & Kharga Oasis (193 km)

Pick-ups for Balat & Bashendi

MUT

New Bus Station

Mut Talatta (3 km), Bedouin Camp (7 km), Al-Qasr (32 km) & Farafra Oasis (310 km)

Service Taxi Station

Police

SHARIA 10TH RAMADAN

SHARIA ES SALAM

City Council

SHARIA ES-SAWRA AL-KHADRA

MIDAN TAHRIR

EgyptAir

Pick-ups for Al-Qasr

State Information Office

Banque Misr

SHARIA AL WADI

Ethnographic Museum

ACCOMMODATION

Anwar	3
El-Forsan	5
El-Mebarez	2
El-Negoom	1
Gardens	4

EATING & DRINKING

Abu Mohammed Restaurant	C
Ahmed Hamdy Restaurant	A
Al-Dakhla Cafeteria	I
Al-Wadi Fiteer	B
Bakery	F
Fuul & Taamiya	D&G
Stella Shop	E
Qalamuni Cafeteria	H

SHARIA BASATEEN

MIDAN SA'AF

Pharmacy

OLD TOWN

Old Mosque

Ruins

N

Unfinished Tourist Village

SHARIA AL WADI

Bus Station

MIDAN GAM'A

New Mosque

SHARIA 23RD JULY

SHARIA EL GUMHORRIYA

Mut el-Khorab

King Farouk Resthouse

0   250 m

Khamis Camp (1 km)

Khamis Camp (2 km), Airport (8 km) & Jebel Uwaynat

helpful, he is the best man to see about excursions. Besides Omar there are unofficial **fixers** like Nasser (who owns the *Nasser Hotel* in Sheikh Wali and whose brothers own the *Ahmed Hamdy*, *Hamdy* and *Abu Mohammed* restaurants) or the gofers of the *Anwar Hotel*, who often approach visitors. And while staying at the *Bedouin Camp* in El-Douhous, you're sure to meet Hagg Abd el-Hameed and Yosef Zeydan, who lead safaris. All of them are useful sources of information, as long as you bear in mind that they'll badmouth their rivals and try to persuade you to sign up for an excursion (see below). Mut also has a conspicuous **State Information Office**, which offers no help but is often mistaken for the tourist office.

Mut's Banque Misr (daily except Fri 8am–2pm) can change **money** or travellers' cheques and give advances on Visa, and the tourist office also exchanges cash. Menatel card-phones all over town can be used for international calls if you can't be bothered to queue at the **telephone exchange** (24hr) or balk at paying premium rates at private exchanges or the *El-Mebarez Hotel*. There are **post office**s on New Mosque Square and beside the telephone exchange (daily except Fri 8am–2pm).

Mut's **hospital** (☎092/821-555; ambulance ☎123) is well equipped by the standards of the Western Desert, and most of the villages in the oasis have a medical post. You'll pass the **police station** (☎092/821-500) en route to the hospital, and tyre-repair shops and a **fuel station** along the road to Mut Talatta.

Accommodation

As oases go, Dakhla offers a fair range of **accommodation**: in Mut; at Mut Talatta springs (3km north); or out in the villages of Sheikh Wali (5km; see p.537), El-Douhous (7km; see p.534) and Al-Qasr (32km; see p.536). All these places can easily be reached by pick-up truck.

Mut

Anwar Sharia Basateen ☎092/820-070, mobile 0123 577749. Though staff are pushy about selling tours, this is otherwise a decent low-budget hotel, with a restaurant next door. Rooms have fans and shared bathrooms; a/c and private baths for £E20 extra. Sells beer. ❷

El-Forsan Sharia al-Wadi ☎092/821-343, ✉elforsan1@yahoo.com. This central hotel has decent rooms with fans (some with baths, a/c and fridges), and a hilltop garden with a kids' playground and a coffee shop with a view. Breakfast not included. ❶

El-Mebarez Sharia es-Sawra al Khadra ☎ & ℻092/821-524. Clean, carpeted a/c rooms with soft beds; fridge and private bathroom optional. Has a pool (not always full) and views of palms at the back, plus a restaurant and international phone line. Sells beer. Used by Explore tour groups. ❸

El-Negoom A few blocks behind the tourist office ☎ & ℻092/823-084. A bit hard to find, but the location is quiet, and the hotel is extremely clean, with a shady garden and patio. Most rooms have balconies, a/c, phones and private baths, or share a bathroom and a TV lounge with two other rooms. ❸

Gardens Near the *Anwar* ☎092/821-577. A step down from its neighbour, this shabby, friendly hotel has mosquito-screened rooms with fans, lumpy beds and grungy shared bathrooms; a palm garden and washing machine. ❶

Khamis Camp Off the airport road, 2km south of Mut ☎092/822-435. Very quiet, remote site, surrounded by dunes, with a hot spring nearby. Under the same management as the *Gardens Hotel*, this campground is still under construction, but its mud-brick and thatched huts are available for £E15 per person, or you can pitch a tent for £E5. Hot water is unreliable, meals are unlikely and you'll need a bike to get into town. There's a short cut across the fields from King Farouk's Resthouse. ❷

Mut Talatta

Sol y Mar ☎092/821-530. Six small, immaculate rooms with fans and baths, around a large hot spring; there's also a villa that can sleep thirty people (mostly used by tour groups). It's a nice place but way overpriced, as are meals and drinks. ❻

Sheikh Wali

Nasser ☏ 092/822-727, mobile 0106 826467. Homely, ramshackle campground of adobe rooms with fans and clean shared bathrooms, beside a lukewarm pool overhung with oleanders. A menagerie of cats, dogs, goats and babies ensures that it's never dull. Nasser charges £E15 per person, or £E10 to pitch a tent in the yard. ➋

El-Douhous

Bedouin Camp Near El-Douhous, 300m off the road ☏ 092/850-480, mobile 0126 221359. The most popular campground in the oasis, run by friendly Bedouin, it sits on a hill overlooking dunes and fields. Guests pay £E20 per person to sleep in cool thatched huts with mattresses on platforms and mosquito nets, or clapboard huts with wooden beds and no nets. Meals are served or you can bring your own food and cook. ➋

Al-Qasr

Al-Qasr Inn ☏ 092/876-802. Sited in the new town, across the road from and 200m past the old settlement, this small nondescript hotel has five rooms with baths, but is often locked; phone ahead to avoid a wasted journey. ➏

Al-Qasr Resthouse ☏ 092/876-013. A better option, this friendly place has simple triples with clean shared bathrooms, tasty meals, satellite TV and tabletennis. Guests pay £E10 per person, or £E2 to sleep on the roof, which has a fantastic view of the medieval settlement. ➊

The town

With its low-rise blocks and whitewashed trees, the **New Town** presumably once looked good on a drawing board but has little appeal for visitors, and while locals are friendly, you can get tired of kids' incessant pleas for **pens**. Reputedly, this craze in Egypt originated in Mut back in the 1970s, when the first tourists to visit the oasis caused a sensation by not only wearing shorts, but handing out novelty "striptease" pens; tourists ever since have paid for their folly. It's also ironic that **Hassan Fathy**'s pioneering design for a **tourist village** in Mut remains unfinished, but later inspired similar complexes all over Egypt; whereas his social housing at Gurna and Baris Gedida proved a failure (see p.384 and p.548).

Behind the ridge where his buildings and the Islamic cemetery are located lies the **Old Town**, which is still inhabited by about 2000 people. Mut originated as a hilltop *qasr* or citadel of windowless facades and twisting passages, its interior divided into quarters separated by gates that were locked at night; and was still a fortified town when Harding-King saw it in 1909. Though the summit is in ruins, the lanes below are still bustling with life, and worth exploring. You can enter from the north and exit on to Midan Gam'a (aka New Mosque Square), using the Old and New **mosques** as landmarks. **Midan Gam'a** used to be the hub of social life, but is pretty sleepy nowadays.

Off to the south you can glimpse the remains of **Mut el-Khorab** (Mut the Ruined), an ancient city dedicated to the Theban goddess Mut. Fennec foxes dwell in burrows in the sides of pits left by treasure-hunters, emerging to hunt at dusk, and can be seen on the way back from enjoying the sunset over the **dunes** that rise beyond the fields. This is the most accessible dune field in Dakhla, but not the finest. A bit further down the road to the airport is a modest colonial-style villa that was once **King Farouk's Resthouse**, which is now used to lodge visiting VIPs.

By arrangement with Omar at the tourist office, you can also visit Mut's **Ethnographic Museum** (£E2). Arranged like a family dwelling with household objects on the walls and a complex wooden lock on the palm-log door, its seven rooms contain clay figures posed in scenes from village life, by the

Khargan artist Mabrouk. Notice the gazelle-hide receptacle for carrying fat on long camel journeys, and the spiked basket that Dakhlans hid beneath the sand to ensnare gazelles. Preparing the bride and celebrating the pilgrim's return from Mecca are two scenes that remain part of oasis life today.

Eating and drinking

Most **restaurants** in Mut offer similar menus of soup, pasta, vegetable stew, chicken or *kofta*, with a few starters or desserts for around £E8–12 all in. They don't always have everything listed, but you can certainly fill your stomach. Besides the *Anwar*, *Gardens* or *El-Mebarez* hotels, you can eat in or outdoors at the *Abu Mohammed*, *Hamdy* or, best of all, *Ahmed Hamdy*. The *Qalamuni Cafeteria* on New Mosque Square does a few dishes, too, unlike the *Al-Dakhla*, which just serves soft drinks. Otherwise, you can buy *fuul* and *taamiya* off Midan Tahrir and on Sharia al-Wadi; hot rolls from the **bakery** on Midan Sa'af; fruit at the **market** on Tahrir; or sticky desserts at *Al-Wadi Fiteer* on Sharia es-Sawra al-Khadra. **Beer** is available at the *Abu Mohammed*, *El-Mebarez*, *El-Megourn* and *Anwar*, around the corner from which is a shop selling Stella for £E7 (everywhere else charges £E10).

Transport within the oasis

Transport around Dakhla is hit and miss, depending on your destination. **Taxis** are the priciest option, with hard bargaining required should you wish the driver to wait at sites and then return to Mut, but Omar at the tourist office can fix one for a decent rate, with no hassle; also a **minibus** or **4WD** vehicle, with driver.

Most Dakhlans get around by covered **pick-ups**, which speed out towards both ends of the oasis from depots in the northern part of town. Pick-ups to Al-Qasr and other western destinations cluster just off Midan Tahrir, while vehicles for points east of Mut leave from a depot near the bus station. They can be flagged down at any point and charge a flat(ish) fare of £E1. Some **minibuses** also cover the same routes; those leaving from beside the hospital are for the eastern villages beyond Balat, which is the terminus for pick-ups from the eastbound depot. Both kinds of vehicle are faster than local buses, and most active in the morning. Beware that drivers may be tempted to charge "special" rates if you request somewhere like Mut Talatta late at night; or if there are no other Egyptians on board.

Cranky **local buses** from Midan Gam'a stop at villages en route to Al-Qasr or Teneida (£E1). They run to no specific timetable so aren't worth waiting for; some may be routed via Gedida rather than Budkhulu. You can also use long-distance buses to reach outlying villages. In both cases, simply buy tickets on board.

Out of town it's always worth **hitching** if you're stuck somewhere. Although payment at pick-up rates is customary, you might get a free lift. If you're into cycling – feasible in wintertime – **bicycles** can be rented from the *Abu Mohammed Restaurant* (£E5) or the *Gardens Hotel* (£E7). You need to be fit, though, since visiting outlying villages will involve a round trip of at least 60km.

Excursions and safaris

As some places are hard to reach, and it takes local knowledge of natural beauty spots to get the best from Dakhla, organized **excursions** kill two birds with one stone. Omar can arrange half-day trips either to the east or the west (£E50 for the car) or a full day-trip to both (£E80–100), while the others combine Al-Qasr and Muzawaka with the Magic Spring and some dunes. Nasser charges £E200 (group rate) for a 4WD tour, the *Anwar Hotel* £E100 per person, and Bedouins £E150 per person by jeep or camel. All three also do **overnight** excursions into the escarpment north of the oasis, or the dunes to the southwest, that can be extended over days. Nasser prices his on the basis of four people per jeep (£E350 per night group rate; £E320 after five nights); the *Anwar* charges £E200 per person by jeep or £E250 by camel; and the Bedouins' camel treks cost £E300 per night (minimum five people). Although the first two are fine for **Bir Dikkur** or the **White Desert**, they're not up for an expedition to the **Gilf Kebir**, unlike the Bedouins, whose eight-day safari costs £E800 per person per day, plus £E100 per day for the guide.

Moving on from Mut

Upper Egypt **buses** leave Mut for **Kharga** (3hr; £E7–8) daily at 6am, 8.30am, 1pm, 5pm and 10pm; all but the 1pm run on to **Assyut** (8hr; £E14–15). For **Farafra** (4hr; £E12), **Bahariya** (6hr; £E20) and **Cairo** (13hr; £E30) the bus departs at 6am and 6pm. Superjet run two buses a day to Cairo (13hr; £E35–£E40); both run via Kharga (3hr; £E8). Tickets to Cairo should be purchased the day before. All buses leave from the new bus station; they also pick up passengers from the ticketing office in New Mosque Square. **Minibuses and service taxis** also run to the other New Valley oases and charge similar rates to the buses providing they are full; it's best to try and leave early to ensure this is the case – the depot is just off Midan Tahrir. If enough tourists are interested, the *Anwar Hotel* can arrange a private minibus to **Luxor** (10hr) for £E70 per person. Before leaving Mut, **motorists** should fill up at the fuel station, as there's no more petrol until Kharga or Farafra. Since the weekly flight from Dakhla to Cairo was scrapped after September 11, the **EgyptAir** office in the old city council building has been closed.

West of Mut

Most visitors are initially drawn to the western part of the oasis by the village of **Al-Qasr**, which is deservedly renowned for its old town, an abandoned enclave of medieval mud-brick architecture, and easily reached by public transport. Should they ever reopen, the colourful **Muzawaka Tombs** are also within striking distance, as is the recently restored Roman temple of **Deir al-Hagar**, which lies further from the main road. To cover more ground than this requires days to spare or private transport. Compare what Omar and the various safari operators in Mut have to say about trips to other villages, or **springs** and **dunes** you can reach by camel at sunset (staying overnight if desired) – then take the better deal.

The routes to Al Qasr

There are two **routes** to Al-Qasr via different villages, so, if you can, it's worth following one out and the other one back. Most traffic leaves Mut by the main road (and shorter route; 32km), with buses and pick-ups stopping at the villages of Rashda and Budkhulu; while along the secondary loop road (45km) they call at Qalamoun, Gedida and Mushiya. On the way you'll pass the **hot springs** and resort at **Mut Talatta** (3km) – which are open 24 hours, free of charge – and the drainage lake for irrigation water known as the **Fish Pond** – a great spot for **bird-watching** (avocet, stilt and coot). With private transport, try a brief initial **detour** along the desert road via **Huwana**, to see the domed and coffin-shaped tombs of an **Islamic cemetery** between Huwana and the Bedouin village of **EL-DOUHOUS**, where the desert road joins the

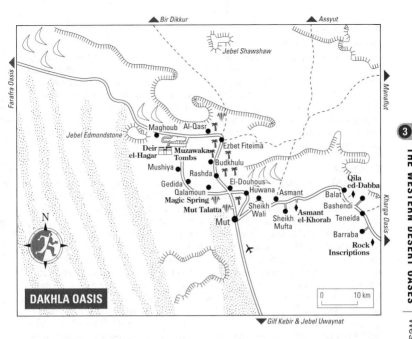

highway and the loop road begins. There are dunes in the distance, and the family that runs the **campground** (see p.532) does 4WD and camel **safaris** all over the oasis and as far away as the Gilf Kebir.

The main road

On the main road beyond El-Douhous, olive groves and orchards presage the clifftop village of **Rashda**, set far back from the highway. The local custom that when he marries, a man must build a new house for his bride, accounts for Rashda's modern appearance. A nicer stopover is **BUDKHULU**, where new buildings flank an **old quarter** of covered streets and houses with carved lintels, surrounding a ruined **Ayyubid mosque** with a pepperpot minaret and a palm-frond pulpit. Visible on a hill as you approach the old quarter is a **Turkish cemetery** with scores of tombs shaped like bathtubs or grave markers in the form of ziggurats, plus a dozen *qubbas*: the freshly painted one belongs to a revered local sheikh, Tawfiq Abdel Aziz. During the Islamic era, Budkhulu was a customs post on the caravan routes between Kharga, Assyut and Farafra.

The loop road

Since the spring at Bir el-Gabel, near the escarpment, was trashed by thoughtless users, tourists have been taken to bathe at the so-called **Magic Spring**, a warm, deep pool in a pit fringed by palms, just off the **loop road** to Al-Qasr, that links three villages interspersed by stagnant pools and desert. **Qalamoun** dates back to pharaonic times, and many families are descended from Mamluke and Turkish officials once stationed here, whereas the next village is only 200 years old – hence its name, **GEDIDA** (New). Mut's tourist office can arrange a visit to the **mashrabiya factory**, a new source of employment in a village whose men have traditionally worked in Cairo, taking it in turns to share the same job with a friend back home. Shortly before reaching **Mushiya**, the road

535

passes **Bir Mushiya**, a keyhole-shaped tank fed by a tepid spring, where tourists are also taken to bathe.

The side road joins the highway between Al-Qasr and the turn-off for the Muzawaka Tombs, opposite a golden **dune field**. Originating on the plateau above the escarpment, the dunes cascade down the cliff and reform below, to continue their way southwards. Tourists are brought here by jeep or camel to enjoy rolling down the dunes, and to take in the view at sunset. The dunes have occasionally been heard to "sing" in a slow rhythm that locals have traditionally attributed to spirits, and scientists explain as the friction of one layer of sand slipping over another.

Al-Qasr

AL-QASR (or *'Asr*, as locals say) is a must – an amazing Islamic settlement built upon Roman foundations, that may be the longest continually inhabited site in the oasis and was indubitably Dakhla's medieval capital. The SCA and Dutch specialists have taken pains to safeguard its fabric without destroying its integrity. The **old town** crowns a ridge above palm groves and a salt lake with wading birds, set back from sprawling New Qasr beside the highway. Aim for the white mosque marking the start of the tourist trail through the now abandoned city, where a guide will appear to offer a tour for a negotiable sum. Though you could probably find your way by following the Arabic signs, he holds the key to the finest buildings, which are kept locked. Many houses have acacia-wood lintels whose cursive or kufic inscriptions name the builders or occupants (the oldest dates from 1518). The **Beit Omda** (mayor's house) is built on a Ptolemaic temple and incorporates pharaonic door posts and trapezoidal niches for books. Low passageways upheld by palm trunks, with gates to be locked at night, punctuate the maze of alleys perpetually shadowed by high walls; notice the rooftop air-scoop (*mala'af*). The tenth-century **madrassa** (school and court) features painted *liwans*, niches for legal texts, cells for felons, and a beam above the door for whippings; while the twelfth-century **Nasr el-Din Mosque** has a 21-metre-high **minaret** with a "pepperpot" finial, typical of Ayyubid architecture.

An antique **water wheel** (*saqqiya*) and donkey-powered **grain mill** show how they once processed foodstuffs, and the ancient craft of **pottery** still thrives near the base of the hill, where you can watch potters at work on treadle-wheels. Other facets of the old way of life are covered in an **Ethnographic Museum** founded by the anthropologist Aliya Hussein, containing artefacts and photos from all of the oases in the Western Desert. It's located in an old house off to the left, behind the white mosque at the start of the trail; knock to be admitted (£E5).

If you fancy **staying** there's a cheap and cheerful resthouse beside the main road, and a fancier inn on the opposite side, further west (see p.532).

The Muzawaka Tombs

Five kilometres west along the highway from Al-Qasr, a signpost indicates the track to the **Muzawaka Tombs**, a twenty-minute walk or a slow drive through the silent desert, past rock buttes gouged with empty tombs. Of the three hundred or so recorded by Fakhry in 1972, two deserve his exclamation "Muza!" (Decorations), from which their name derives. Sadly, both have been **closed** for years as restoring them has proved far harder than was anticipated due to their clay composition – but tour groups often come anyway to see the eerie-looking site, and the curator is ready to produce a pair of **mummies** from another tomb for a photo opportunity (*baksheesh* expected).

The **Tomb of Petosiris** is vividly painted with Roman-nosed blonds in pharaonic poses, curly-haired angels and a zodiac with a bearded Janus figure on the ceiling. In the back right-hand corner is a man standing on a turtle, holding a snake and fish aloft – a curious amalgam of Egyptian and Greco-Roman symbolism. Better-preserved, cruder murals in the **Tomb of Sadosiris** show Anubis (weighing the deceased's heart in one scene), Osiris judging on the rear wall, and another Janus – looking back on life and forward into the hereafter – just inside the entrance. Heading back, you can try hitching towards Al-Qasr, or cut across the desert towards the village. There's little risk of getting lost, since by climbing a table plateau you can always get oriented – and the views are splendid.

Deir al-Hagar

Unless you've rented a taxi, getting to **Deir al-Hagar** (daily 8am–5pm; £E20) demands commitment. The trail begins 2km further west along the highway, where an unmarked road runs south past some Roman ruins to a small, colourfully painted village (1km); beyond here a track crosses a ridge, whereupon the temple becomes visible on the right. Notwithstanding its Arabic name, "Stone Monastery", Deir al-Hagar is actually a Roman temple dedicated to the Theban Triad and the god of the oasis, Seth, and was originally called *Est Ah* (Land of the Moon). Its sandstone Hypostyle Hall, sanctuary and brick enclosure wall were built in the first century AD, under emperors Nero, Vespasian, Titus and Domitian (whose cartouches can be seen) and later served as a Coptic monastery (notice the mural of Christ, the lion and the lamb, in a niche to the left of the pylon), until a huge dune consumed it, collapsing the roof and leaving only the tops of the columns visible. One is inscribed with the names of almost every explorer who visited Dakhla in the nineteenth century, including Edmondstone, Drovetti, Cailliaud, and the entire Rohlfs expedition. It was they who named Dakhla's only mountain, **Jebel Edmondstone**, after the first European to reach the oasis since ancient times; Sir Archibald Edmondstone beat his French rival, Drovetti, by ten days, in February 1819, to "discover" it in the name of England. Such notions were incomprehensible to the oasis people, who attributed other motives to explorers; legend has it that Rohlfs sacrificed a servant to the spirits guarding the temple's treasury, in order to rob it. Trumpeting finches and other **birds** frequent the locality.

East of Mut

Villages on the east side of the oasis are more or less accessible from Mut by pick-ups (which rarely venture far beyond Balat) or Teneida-bound buses. Unfortunately, most places of interest lie some way from the main road, so visiting more than one or two could be hard without transport. Bring food and water.

Heading out from town, you'll see where irrigation canals have enabled wheat, rice and peanuts to be grown on once barren land. **SHEIKH WALI** is on the verge of becoming a suburb of Mut, yet backs onto desert, with olive groves and goat-pens surrounding a Biblical **water wheel**, while **dunes** swell in the distance. **Asmant**, 6km on, has the usual sprawl of modern buildings by the roadside and a high-walled **old village** on the hill further back. There's accommodation in Sheikh Wali (see p.532).

Asmant el-Khorab

Asmant lends its name to an ancient site 9km further east and 1km off the highway. **Asmant el-Khorab** (Asmant the Ruined) is the local name for the

ruins of Kellis, a Roman and Coptic town inhabited for seven centuries, whose two cult temples and three churches mark the shift from pagan Rome to Byzantine Christianity. Though accessible by a track 4km past the spur road to Sheikh Mufta, the site is **off limits** while excavations continue.

Fragmentary paintings appear in the larger, eastern temple, while the churches are mud-brick with plastered walls. The partially excavated site includes the remains of aqueducts, farmhouses and tombs, where archeologists have found 34 mummies and wooden codices, casting light on religion and daily life in the third century AD.

Balat and Qila ed-Dabba

After the swathe of desert beyond Asmant one welcomes the casuarina-tree-lined road through **BALAT**, whose teahouse is a *de facto* bus stop. Cross the road to explore the wonderful old village beyond the TV mast, with its maze of twisting **covered streets** that protect the villagers from sun and sandstorms and once prevented invaders from entering on horseback. Its mud-brick **houses** are stained oxblood, salmon or terracotta, with carved lintels and wooden peg-locks, only slightly less impressive than the ones in Al-Qasr – but still inhabited. Although the oldest dates from Mamluke times, Balat was a town and a governors' seat (its name means "Palace of the Lord") way back in the Old Kingdom, when it prospered through trade with Kush (ancient Nubia).

There's proof of this in Balat's ancient necropolis, known to the locals as **Qila ed-Dabba** (or "Ed-Dabba"), where five mud-brick *mastabas* once clad in limestone but long ago reduced to lumps, mark the **tombs of VI Dynasty governors**. In 1977, French archeologists discovered an intact one from the reign of Pepi II (2292–2203 BC) by excavating a deep pit resembling an inverted step pyramid, to expose the burial chamber (daily 8am–5pm; £E20). Its painted reliefs are faint, but you can see the governor, Khentika, his wife and son; people ploughing, driving cattle and sailing boats; and Wadjet eyes. It took

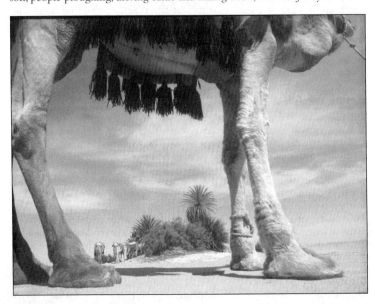

forty workers 763 days to construct the tomb. The ticket is also valid for the ruins at **Ain Asil** (Spring of the Origin), 1.5km east of the necropolis, where a fortress and farming community called "Our Root is Lasting in the Oasis" existed from the Old Kingdom until Ptolemaic times. Both sites are reached by a track 100m east of Balat's teahouse, and from Ain Asil a back road continues to Bashendi – about 5km in all.

Bashendi

Pick-ups can drop you at the turn-off for **BASHENDI**, 2km off the main road, whose sugary pink mosque with three white domes resembles a marquee from afar. The name Bashendi derives from "Pasha Hindi", a medieval sheikh who is buried in the local cemetery, which dates back to Roman times. Tombs form the foundations of many of the houses, which are painted pale blue or buttercup yellow with floral friezes and *Hadj* scenes, merging into the ground in graceful curves.

The cemetery is at the back, where the desert begins. Some empty sarcophagi separate the domed tomb of Pasha Hindi (where locals pray for the recovery of lost items) from the square **Tomb of Kitnes**. While both structures are of Roman origin, the latter still retains its original funerary reliefs, depicting Kitnes meeting the desert-gods Min, Seth and Shu. Its key is held by a villager who can be fetched, but since admission costs £E16, you might settle for viewing its pharaonic lintels.

There is also a **carpet-weaving** factory, established with the help of Helwan University of Fine Arts, to train youths in making rugs and kelims. Ask at Mut's tourist office to arrange a visit (£E1.50 entrance fee).

Teneida and beyond

TENEIDA, on the eastern edge of the oasis, is a modern affair centred on a leafy square, whose only "sight" is a **cemetery** on the outskirts with weird tombstones resembling tiny houses. In desert lore, Teneida is known for the three Zwayah tribesmen who staggered out of the desert in 1931, alerting the authorities to a tragedy that was already weeks old. Bombed from their homes at Kufra Oasis in Libya by the Italians, five hundred Zwayah nomads had trekked 320km south over waterless desert to Jebel Uwaynat, where they found springs but no grazing. Faced with starvation, half the tribe struck out towards Dakhla without knowing the way, while the others remained to await their end. Thanks to the men's 21-day, 670km march (a feat of endurance with few parallels), search parties managed to rescue almost three hundred stragglers from the wilderness.

With a car you can press on to see some curious **rock inscriptions** just off the highway 10km past Teneida. Among the sandstone outcrops south of the road is a large one in the form of a seated camel, whose base is covered in prehistoric and Bedouin drawings of giraffes, camels and hunters, plus the name of Jarvis (British governor of Dakhla and Kharga in the 1930s) and many other visitors. In olden times, this marked the intersection of two caravan routes, the *Darb al-Ghabari* (Dust Road) between Dakhla and Kharga, and another track that linked Teneida to the Forty Days Road.

The road to Kharga

Beyond Teneida's last flourish of greenery, wind-sculpted rocks soon give way to dun table-tops and gravelly sand, persisting for most of the way from Dakhla to Kharga (193km). Following the ancient Darb el-Ghabari, the modern road skirts the phosphate-rich Abu Tartur Plateau that separates the two depressions.

The appearance of a phosphates factory and railroad 45km outside Kharga alerts you for a treat to follow. Golden **dunes** march across the depression, burying lines of telegraph poles and encroaching on the highway. Villagers faced with their advance have been known to add an extra storey to their house, live there while the dune consumes the ground floor, and move back downstairs once it has passed on. These dunes are outstretched fingers of the **Ghard Abu Muharik** (Dune with an Engine) range, of the type known as "whalebacked". Folk wisdom asserts that the less common *barchan* or crescent-shaped dunes are always separate from whalebacks; you'll see a cluster of baby ones in the desert to the left, nearer town.

Kharga Oasis

Despite being the nearest of the oases to Luxor and the capital of the New Valley, **Kharga Oasis** gets far fewer tourists than the others. Because tourists aren't allowed to use the direct road from Luxor under current restrictions, and the train service from Luxor is so infrequent, Assyut remains its main link to the Nile Valley. **El-Kharga** city is a modern metropolis of 50,000 people that has adequate facilities and a decent museum, but is otherwise a byword for tedium. And although the oasis contains many interesting sites – and the ascent of the scarp wall en route to Assyut or Luxor is one of the most dramatic journeys Egypt can offer – many sites are only accessible by 4WD, with a guide, which can be found at only two places in El-Kharga and may be too expensive for those travelling alone. Don't expect any help from the tourist office, either; the local museum is a better bet.

Submerged by the sea aeons ago, leaving fossils on the high plateau, the Kharga depression is hemmed in by great cliffs and broken up by massifs, with belts of dunes advancing across the oasis. It's thought that there were no dunes in Kharga during Roman times; myth has it that they erected a brass cow on the escarpment, which swallowed up the sand. Historically, Kharga's importance owes to the desert trade routes that converged on the oasis, notably the **Forty Days Road** (see p.549). Deserted Roman forts and entire villages that claim descent from Mamluke soldiers attest to centuries of firm control by Egypt's rulers, who have used Kharga as a place of exile since the fourth century. In modern times, the founder of the popular daily newspaper *Al-Akhbar* was banished here by Nasser, and since 1994, Islamists have been incarcerated in the maximum-security **Kharga Prison**, known as "The Scorpion" (visible from the highway as one enters the oasis from the north).

Kharga is also seen by some as a portent that the New Valley spells ruin for the oases. The influx of *fellaheen* from the Nile Valley has changed agricultural practices; **rice** cultivation has proved more water-intensive than expected, depleting aquifers and turning land saline. Social **life** has also changed; people stay indoors and watch TV more than socialize nowadays, and the once strong community spirit is disappearing.

It's indicative of the mixed antecedents of its citizens that the **name** Kharga may be pronounced "Harga" or "Harjah", depending on who's talking. Both the oasis and its capital are called Kharga; we've used the prefix "El-" to denote the city.

El-Kharga

As the capital of the New Valley Governorate (comprising Kharga, Dakhla and Farafra oases), **EL-KHARGA** has grown into a sprawl of mid-rise buildings and highways that belies romantic stereotypes of an oasis town, unless you go searching around the souk. Hotels, banks and offices line the main drag, **Sharia Gamel Abdel Nasser**, which is too long and monotonous for pleasant walking, despite its ornamental obelisks, shrubs and jaunty green-and-white-striped kerbs. But **getting around** is easy, with covered pick-ups shuttling non-stop between Midan Showla and the Mabrouk Fountain, at either end of town.

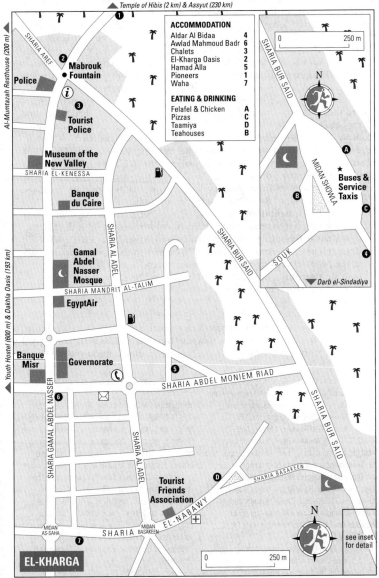

ACCOMMODATION

Aldar Al Bidaa	4
Awlad Mahmoud Badr	6
Chalets	3
El-Kharga Oasis	2
Hamad Alla	5
Pioneers	1
Waha	7

EATING & DRINKING

Felafel & Chicken	A
Pizzas	C
Taamiya	D
Teahouses	B

Temple of Hibis (2 km) & Assyut (230 km)

SHARIA AREF

Al-Mumtazah Resthouse (200 m)

Police

Mabrouk Fountain

Tourist Police

Museum of the New Valley

SHARIA EL-KENESSA

Banque du Caire

Youth Hostel (600 m) & Dakhla Oasis (193 km)

Gamal Abdel Nasser Mosque

SHARIA AL ADEL

SHARIA MANDRIT AL-TALIM

EgyptAir

Banque Misr

Governorate

SHARIA GAMAL ABDEL NASSER

SHARIA ABDEL MONIEM RIAD

SHARIA AL ADEL

SHARIA BUR SAID

SHARIA BUR SAID

SHARIA BUR SAID

Buses & Service Taxis

MIDAN SHOWLA

SOUK

Darb el-Sindadiya

Tourist Friends Association

EL-NABAWY

SHARIA BASAKEEN

MIDAN AS-SAHA

MIDAN BASAKEEN

SHARIA BASAKEEN

see inset for detail

0   250 m

0   250 m

N

N

EL-KHARGA

Pottery & Carpet Factory (50 m), Train Station (5 km) & Baris (90 km)

Midan as–Saha, near the *Waha Hotel*, marks the "fare stage", being a 10pt ride from each terminus; the full journey costs 20pt. Ring the bell on the roof to let the driver know when you want to get off.

Arrival and information

Arriving by bus it makes sense to decide on a hotel before and get dropped off at the nearest point on Sharia Gamal Abdel Nasser, rather than riding on to the terminus on Midan Showla (unless you're going to stay at the *Aldar Al Bidaa*). Stashing your luggage and having some refreshments will be your first priorities after the long and tiring journey. Don't rest any hopes on Kharga's **tourist office** (Mon–Thurs & Sun 8am–2pm and maybe 5–10pm; ⊕ & ℱ 092/921–205), as its boss speaks little English and is unsure of even basic facts, while his PR assistant, Mohsen Abd Al Moneam – who speaks far better English and seems well informed – is chiefly interested in promoting his own **tours** from an office out back (⊕092/921-026, mobile 0101 806127, ℯmohsen_di@yahoo.com). He charges £E350 (group rate) for a day excursion to the main sites around the oasis (excluding Ain Umm Dabadib). Rather, it's far better to ask the Museum of the New Valley's Inspector of Antiquities, Mansoor Osman (⊕092/920-874), who'll send one of his curators as a guide, or even go himself if he's not busy. The museum has its own 4WD, and Mansoor owns a dirt bike. The **tourist police** (⊕092/921-673; 24hr) are next door and the regular **police** (⊕122; 24hr) across the road.

You can change **money** and travellers' cheques at the Banque du Caire (Mon–Thurs & Sun 8am–2pm) and Banque Misr (Mon–Thurs & Sun 8am–2pm). The **hospital** (⊕092/920-777) is on Sharia Basateen, where there are also several **pharmacies**; while Sharia Abdel Moneim Riad is the place to find the **post office** (daily except Fri 9am–2pm) – which has EMS post – and 24-hour **telephone** exchange – though it's easier to make international calls using the Menatel card-phones on the main streets.

There are **petrol** stations on Sharia Bur Said and Sharia al-Adel, and a tyre-repair place off Sharia el-Nabawy.

Accommodation

Buses entering town can drop you off at a hotel if they pass by en route to Midan Showla; otherwise, catch a pick-up. By oasis standards there's a good choice of **accommodation** spread over the town. Book ahead if you're fussy about where you stay.

Aldar Al Bidaa Off Midan Showla ⊕092/921-717. Handy for the souk and bus station but rather noisy, this hotel has clean doubles, triples and quads, some with fans and bathrooms. ❷

Al-Mumtazah Resthouse Off Sharia Aref ⊕092/920-820. Weird 1960s Soviet beach-resort hotel gone to seed. Its vast rooms have picture windows, carpets and grotty bathrooms, fans or a/c. Opposite a mosque. No English spoken. ❶

Awlad Mahmoud Badr Sharia Gamal Abdel Nasser ⊕092/922-689. Breezy, friendly budget hotel with simple rooms with fans and shabby shared bathrooms; one room has private facilities. Breakfast not included. ❷

Chalets (or *Villa*). Spacious carpeted chalets holding up to nine people with TV, bath, phone, fan or a/c. Behind the tourist office, which handles reser-

vations. Probably the best deal in town at £E25 per person. ❷

El-Kharga Oasis Sharia Aref ⊕092/921-500, ℱ921-615. Large a/c rooms with soft beds, bathrooms, and balconies overlooking a palm garden – it sounds great, but the hotel is always empty, as if waiting for a convention or tour party that never arrives. It's possible to pitch a tent in their nice but mosquito-ridden garden for £E7 per person. The restaurant serves Stella. ❹

Hamad Alla ⊕092/920-638, ℱ925-017. Sited on a quiet backstreet a few blocks off the main drag, this small hotel has clean a/c rooms with soft beds; some have bathrooms, fridges, TV, heaters and balconies. Friendly staff. Restaurant. Sells beer. ❸

Pioneers ⊕092/929-751, ℱ927-983. Out

towards the Temple of Hibis, Kharga's fanciest hotel has stylish carpeted rooms with a/c, fridge and satellite TV, built around a pool and a garden with a *qasr*-style coffe shop, restaurant and bar attached. Half-board obligatory. ❻

Waha Off Midan as-Saha ☎092/920-393. Simple rooms with grungy shared bathrooms; it's worth paying £E8 more for a "lux" room with private facilities and a fan. ❶

Youth Hostel 600m west of Sharia Gamal Abdel Nasser ☎092/922-640. The unsignposted red, white and blue *Beit es-Shebab* has beds (£E6) in clean dorms, each with their own bathroom, but is inconveniently located on the edge of town. ❶

The town

Prominently located on Sharia Gamal Abdel Nasser, the **Museum of the New Valley** (daily 8am–3pm; £E20) is housed in a modern building modelled on the tombs at Bagawat, and contains artefacts from sites scattered across three oases. Of the exhibits on the ground floor (labelled in English), the most impressive are Greco-Roman: painted sarcophagi from Maks al-Qibli and Dakhla; death masks from Qasr el-Labeka; and mummified rams, eagles and ibises from the Muzawaka Tombs. The Old Kingdom is represented by an offerings tablet, scarabs and headrests from the tombs of the VI Dynasty governors in Balat. Look out for the *ba* birds, representing the soul of the deceased, unearthed by the French Mission at Dush. Upstairs you'll find Coptic textiles and pottery, and floral friezes from the Fatimid and Ottoman eras, mostly unlabelled.

While in the vicinity, check out the (dry) **Mabrouk Fountain**, just up the road at the main junction, created by a local artist in three days. Its lusty figures symbolize Mother Egypt dragging her unwilling child (the oases) towards its destiny. Aside from the **Gamal Abdel Nasser Mosque** (one of dozens that Nasser built in provincial towns in the 1960s), and a **Coptic Church** discreetly located off the high road, there's nothing else to see until you reach the lower part of town (it's best to take a pick-up, unless you fancy the 2–3km walk).

Here, dusty **Midan Showla** is abuzz with people and traffic, a lively **souk** running off into an old quarter of mud houses painted apricot or azure and daubed with the Hand of Fatima. Turn left shortly after entering the souk and you should find yourself in the **Darb el-Sindadiya**, a dark, twisting street roofed with palm trunks, which once extended over 4km; its oldest part dates from the tenth century. Only the initial stretch is inhabited nowadays and most of the passageways are used as barns. Foreigners aren't discouraged from entering, but it's wise not to venture too far in without a guide.

The tourist office can arrange visits to El-Kharga's **pottery and carpet factory**, or the **date factory** (both daily except Fri 8am–2pm; free) down the road. And to chill out by day, you can use the **pool** at the *Pioneers Hotel* for £E10 minimum charge; this doesn't cover the cost of a beer.

Eating

Eating out is mediocre. Simple meals of chicken, beans, rice and salad are all you can hope for in the nameless cafés by the *Waha Hotel* and on Midan Showla, where you can also buy pizzas and *felafel* sandwiches. The restaurants in the *Hamad Alla* and *El-Kharga Oasis* hotels offer much the same fare (at a higher price), plus mutton stew. Ask if they do *firik*, roasted green wheat served like rice or used as stuffing for chicken. **Beer** is sold at the *Pioneers*, *El-Kharga Oasis* and *Hamad Alla* hotels for £E10 while the *Pioneers* also runs to wines and spirits.

Moving on from El-Kharga

If you've got the money, EgyptAir **flights** from El-Kharga's New Valley Airport can get you to Cairo in two hours. Departures are on Wednesday and Sunday mornings, and a one-way ticket costs US$131; book through their office

(☎092/920-838) on the main street. The airport turn-off is 3km north along the Assyut road, then 2km southeast; a taxi costs £E10–15.

There are daily **buses** to Cairo at 6am (by the Valley Road; £E32) and 9pm (by the Desert Road; £E39), which take 7–8 hours; five services daily to Assyut (4–5 hr; £E8), and one bus a day to Dakhla at 7am (£E8). It's worth travelling by day and getting seats on the left to see the magnificent rock escarpment en route to Assyut, one of the most dramatic vistas Egypt has to offer. All buses, minibuses and **service taxis** leave from Midan Showla. Minibuses and service taxis run to all the previously listed destinations and, providing they are full, cost a little more than the buses, and are usually slightly quicker.

A **train** leaves every Friday at 7am for Luxor, from the ornate train station 5km out along the road to Baris. The carriages are third-class only and passengers are sometimes required to help shovel sand from the tracks, which can make the journey longer than the seven hours advertised. Bring food and drink for the duration.

There is also a **direct road to Luxor** (275km), which quits the oasis at Jaja. There are no buses, however, so you really need your own vehicle; and a **travel permit** from Cairo is obligatory. The road is excellent, enabling one to reach the Nile Valley in only two hours, with two first aid stations with water, but no petrol supplies, en route. The road meets the Nile Valley at Riziq, 15km south of Luxor, where you may have to wait for a police escort.

North of El-Kharga

Compensating for the paucity of sights in El-Kharga, two of the finest ancient monuments in the oasis are just a few miles from the town. The **Temple of Hibis** is the best-preserved temple in the Western Desert, but is currently being dismantled to move it to higher ground. However, you won't be disappointed by the nearby **Bagawat Necropolis** – one of the oldest Christian cemeteries in Egypt – backed by an imposing ruined monastery, **Deir el-Kashef**. Further north, the depression is pockmarked with ruins of ancient towns and forts, with tunnels and other feats of Roman engineering waiting to be explored – but only accessible by 4WD with a guide who knows the way. Talk to Mohsen if you're serious about visiting **Ed-Deir**, **Qasr el-Labeka** or **Ain Umm Dabadib** (the most difficult site to reach); if not, forget 'em.

The Temple of Hibis

Although you can get there by catching a pick-up from Midan Showla bound for El-Munira and asking to be dropped at *el-ma'abad* (the temple), it's fun, if you're feeling energetic, to walk from the Mabrouk Fountain (2km). En route, you'll catch sight of the ruined Ptolemaic **Temple of Nadura** atop a low hill in the desert to your right, whose eroded sandstone wall and pronaos aren't worth the trudge, though the view is.

The **Temple of Hibis** stands just up the road amidst the palm groves on the left, a short walk away by tarmac path beyond the swamp. Besides reminding sightseers that most pharaonic sites originally looked verdant, the lush vegetation around it covers the site of ancient Hibis, an XVIII Dynasty settlement that prospered under the Saïtes, Persians and Ptolemies. Unfortunately, rising ground water is endangering the sixth-century BC temple dedicated to Amun-Re. Thus one of the few Persian monuments left in Egypt is now swathed in scaffolding and being dismantled to be reassembled on higher ground near the Bagawat Necropolis. Depending on how close you can get, you may be able to see graffiti by Francis Catherwood, later famous for discovering Mayan temples in Central America.

The Bagawat Necropolis

Blocks from the temple are stacked beside the path that leads to the **Bagawat Necropolis** (daily: summer 8am–6pm; winter 8am–5pm; £E20). The 263 mud-brick chapels were used for Christian burials between the third and seventh centuries, and display diverse forms of mud-brick vaulting or Roman-influenced portals, but are best known for their Coptic murals. A guard should appear to unlock the **Chapel of Peace**, whose dome is decorated with images of Adam and Eve, the Ark, Abraham and Isaac, sadly defaced by Greek inscriptions. Flowery motifs and doves of peace can be seen inside **Tomb #25**, one of three adjacent family vaults on the ridge, where the guard usually asks *Shouf bebe?* If you reply affirmatively he'll produce a hideous mummified child, expecting male tourists to react with sang-froid and women tourists with dismay; not to mention *baksheesh* worthy of his efforts. Give him his due, but not until you've seen the frescoes in the **Chapel of the Exodus**. Crudely executed yet vivid, they depict Roman-looking pharaonic troops pursuing the Jews, led by Moses, out of Egypt, and other Biblical scenes.

Deir el-Kashef

From the Bagawat ticket office, a track curves around behind the hill on which the necropolis is built, past the ugly resthouse of the archeologist Fakhry and a series of rock-cut tombs, to reach the dramatic ruins of **Deir el-Kashef**, the Monastery of the Tax Collector. Named after a Mamluke governor, Mustafa, the five-storey monastery once accommodated hermits and travellers in its vaulted cells, nowadays choked by sand, and still commands a view of the point where the *Darb al-Ghabari* from Dakhla crossed the Forty Days Road. In the valley below you can see the ruins of a small **church** or hermitage, with Greek texts on the walls of the nave and the tiny cells where the monks slept. Beyond, four mighty crescent **dunes** to the north have spawned two infants downwind, either side of the Assyut road, near a crowd of whalebacks. Though disproving the notion that *barchan* and *seif* dunes don't mix, its physical causes are still explicable in terms of formulae devised by the explorer Bagnold, whose classic book *The Physics of Blown Sand and Desert Dunes* (1939) later helped NASA to interpret data from its Martian space probes. The book was written after five years' experimentation with a home-made wind tunnel and builder's sand; after his desert journeys of the 1920s, Bagnold felt "it was really just exploring in another form".

Other sights

For those with a **4WD car** (or dirt bikes) and a local guide, there are many other sites to explore. The most rewarding area lies west of the Assyut road, where a track from Bagawat skirts the foothills of the bat- and snake-infested **Jebel el-Teir** (Bird Mountain), whose wadis contain prehistoric, ancient and Coptic **inscriptions**. It then diverges into two trails leading to the finest **Roman fortresses** in the oasis. Invariably built near springs, such structures once guarded, taxed and sheltered caravans on the road to Assyut. As a single caravan contained thousands of people and animals, they probably settled for the night in several forts; the bustle is unimaginable in the desolate ruins today.

Qasr el-Labeka is secluded in a wadi at the base of the northern escarpment, its twelve-metre walls enclosing sand-filled chambers. On an outcrop further north stands a ruined mud-brick temple, where one of the lintels still bears a painted vulture; another temple was dedicated to Hercules. Between the two buildings lies the spring that sustained the fort – a subterranean aqueduct (now silted up) of the kind found on a grander scale at **Ain Umm Dabadib**. Though it's only 18km from Qasr el-Labeka, Ain Umm Dabadib is approached by an extremely rough track; getting there from the south means locating a corridor through the dune fields. The site covers 60,000 acres, including a ruined fortress, churches and tombs, plus a remarkable **underground aqueduct** that worked by liberating ground water, like the *qanats* of ancient Persia (Fakhry suggests that the system originated under Persian rule). Known as *manafis* in the oasis, this one runs for 15km with access holes every few metres, and part has recently been cleared by a local farmer and used to irrigate a patch of land to the southeast of the temple.

Further west of Ain Umm Dabadib, out beyond the limits of the Kharga depression, lies the totally isolated, windblown spring of **Ain Amur** (The

Lovely One), situated 200m up the northwestern cliffs of the Abu Tartur Plateau. At 525m above sea level, this is the highest **spring** in the Western Desert and, like Ain Tafnis (see p.548), is fed by surface water trapped in the escarpment rather than water below the floor of the depression. Near the spring are the **ruins** of a Roman fortress with Coptic graffiti, one of which relates how an early Christian traveller was "faint from thirst" when the spring saved him. Some believe that Ain Amur was the last watering hole of the legendary Lost Army of Cambyses (see box on p.528). Travel to Ain Amur is **forbidden** without permission and a guide from the Museum of the New Valley in El-Kharga.

Far across the oasis near the eastern scarp wall, **Ed-Deir** once guarded the shortest camel route to the Nile, which climbs out of the depression at the Abu Sighawal (Father of Underwear) Pass. The fort lies 1km beyond the end of a track starting near Munira (the checkpoint on the road as you enter Kharga Oasis from the north), which later turns into decrepit asphalt, so you could risk it in a regular car, walking over the dunes at the end. Its twelve rounded towers are connected by a gallery, surrounding a well, and the surviving rooms covered in **graffiti** drawn by generations of soldiers: Turks in fezzes, tanks, airplanes, and obscenities. The **abandoned railway** in the distance was built by the British in 1906–08 and once carried special carriages with double roofs and wide eaves to protect passengers from the heat. Trips to Ed-Deir do not require permission.

South towards Baris

Exploring the **southern spur of the oasis** means flitting between sites off a highway, which isn't a prospect to relish if you're reliant on buses (hitching is not advised). On the positive side, access roads have been improved to the point that the temples can be reached by 2WD car, so it's possible to negotiate with pick-up or **taxi** drivers on Midan Showla, who may agree to take you to the temples of Qasr el-Ghweita, Qasr al-Zayn and Dush for between £E150–250. **Buses** bound for Baris (90km; 2hr; £E3) leave El-Kharga at 7am and 2pm, making it essential to start early if you want to visit at least one site and not be stranded, as they start the return journey at 10am and 5pm. Travellers used to be able to sleep in three government **resthouses** – at Nasser, Bulaq and Baris – but of these only Baris's survives and as a private venture – so check with the tourist office in El-Kharga before planning to stay there.

Five kilometres south of town you'll pass Kharga's **train station**, an Islamic-style edifice whose marble interior aspires to a grander role than the terminus of the once-a-week train from Luxor, which is ultimately planned to run down to Baris. Since a "tourist train" made its inaugural journey from Port Safaga in 1998, with celebrities like Michael Palin aboard, the reality has been a third-class train that hardly anybody uses, whose 477km journey to Luxor is supposed to take seven hours but often takes twelve, if passengers have to clear sand-drifts from the tracks. It was moving sand dunes that scuppered the British-built railway from the Nile Valley (see above), and as the Ghard Abu Muharrik forges southwards, the new line is also in jeopardy.

Qasr el-Ghweita and Qasr al-Zayn

Eighteen kilometres south of town a 2km spur road leads to the fortified temple of **Qasr el-Ghweita** (Fortress of the Small Garden), crowning a hilltop (daily 8am–5pm; £E16). The climb lets you appreciate its commanding view of the area, which was intensively farmed in ancient times. Ten-metre-high walls enclose a sandstone temple dedicated to the Theban Triad, built by Darius I on the site of an older shrine, and modified by the Ptolemies. Its Hypostyle Hall contains scenes of Hapy the Nile-god holding symbols of the nomes of Upper and Lower Egypt. Nearby you can see the adobe remnants of a Ptolemaic settlement.

The spur road continues 5km south to **Qasr al–Zayn** (daily 8am–5pm; £E16), a Ptolemaic-Roman temple that lends its name to a village built over the ancient town of *Tkhonemyris*. This proximity to daily life helps you imagine it as a bustling settlement in antiquity. As at Qasr el-Ghweita, the temple is enclosed within a mud-brick fortress, together with living quarters for the garrison, a cistern and a bakery. Its portal bears the cartouches of Antonius Pius, who restored the temple in 138 AD. The plain hereabouts is 18m below sea level, the lowest point in Kharga Oasis.

As you return to the highway, the first large settlement, **Bulaq** ("to watch"), is divided into a picturesque old village to the west, and a larger modern one to the east. Its **hot springs** are visible immediately before you enter town, on the right. Leaving Bulaq, you pass the whitewashed tomb of Sheikh Khalid shortly before the microwave tower that presages a string of New Valley settlements founded in the 1980s, named Kuwait, Palestine and Aden in a gesture of Arab solidarity. **Jaja** is of ancient lineage, but it looks as modern as the others; it's here that the **road to Luxor** (275km) begins (permit required).

Baris and beyond

BARIS is the second largest settlement in the oasis after El-Kharga; a sign at the entrance welcomes you to "Paris", but don't expect to find anything grand. There are some shops and a place dispensing *fuul* and *felafel* and you can **stay** at the laidback *Amrit Baris Resthouse* (T092/963-015; ❷). Two kilometres before this, you'll pass the abandoned village of **Baris Gedida** (New Baris), begun in the early 1960s, which the architect Hassan Fathy based on the principles of traditional oasis architecture, including wind shafts to cool the marketplace. Alas for his idealism, work was halted by the Six Day War of 1967 and never resumed, so the initial settlers soon drifted away. Today, old Baris is set to develop further once the **Sheikh Zayed Canal** – drawing water from Lake Nasser (see p.477) – reaches Kharga, entering the depression at Baris.

If you arrive by bus, everyone knows you need a local **pick–up** to reach the Temple of Dush, 23km away, and that the only bus back to El-Kharga leaves at 5pm – so drivers ask over £E30 for the return journey, including waiting time. With a **4WD**, however, you can make a scenic detour using a track that leaves the highway to the east of Baris Gedida, leading to **Ain Tafnis** (14km). Tafnis is one of two springs in the oasis that's nearly 200m above the floor of the depression, located on the slope of a mountain protruding from the escarpment. Greek, Coptic and Arabic **inscriptions** can be found in caves nearby, and the area is strewn with potsherds. En route to the escarpment the track passes a cluster of *yardangs*.

Further south are two villages divided by a sand ridge and linked by history. For over five centuries, **MAKS BAHRI** (Customs North) and **MAKS QIBLI** (Customs South) lived off the caravans that passed along the infamous *Darb al-Arba'in* or **Forty Days Road** (see box opposite), taxing each slave that entered the oasis, selling supplies and pandering to the slavemasters. Today, there's no evidence of their slave-trafficking past in either village, though in Maks Qibli you can still see a small mud-brick fort, the **Tabid el-Darawish**, built by the British after the Dervish invasion of 1893. Nowadays, the Forty Days Road has been paved as far south as Bir Tafarwi, to link up with the new

The Forty Days Road

Of all the trade routes between North Africa and the tropical south, the **Forty Days Road** (*Darb al-Arba'in*) was the one most involved in **slavery** – the only business profitable enough to justify the risks and rigours of the thousand-mile journey. The slaves, purchased at the Dongola slave market or kidnapped by the fierce desert tribes, were assembled at **Kobbé**, a town (no longer existing) 60km northwest of El-Fasher, the capital of Sudan's Darfur Province, once an independent kingdom.

After a few days' march from Kobbé, the slaves were unchained from their yokes, for there was no way to escape. With no permanent water source until Bir Natrun, 530km away, they could only survive on the ox skins of water that burdened the camels. From **Bir Natrun**, caravans trekked 260km northeast across waterless, open sands, vulnerable to attack by bandits from the Arab Kababish and Bedayatt tribes, or the black Gor'an from Nukheila Oasis. The next stop, **Laqiya al-Arba'in**, had water but scant grazing for camels, and with their reserves of fodder exhausted they could easily weaken and stumble along the rocky 280-kilometre journey to **Selima Oasis**. While human losses were erased by the sands, the road gained definition from its Bactrian casualties; a 1946 survey of northwestern Sudan noted "a track about one mile wide marked with white camel bones".

W.G. Browne, the first European to complete the route, estimated the slave caravan's value at £115,000 sterling – a huge sum for the time (1762). Egyptian customs posts taxed caravans arriving in **Kharga Oasis**, the last stage before their ultimate destination, Assyut. As the caravans approached, small boys were hidden in empty water skins to evade tax, but officials would beat them to thwart this ploy. The most valuable slaves were young Nubian women – prized as concubines because their skin remained cool whatever the heat. Having sold their chattels at **Assyut**, traders bought "fabrics, jewellery, weaponry and kohl" for the return journey.

Traffic along the Forty Days Road effectively ended in 1884, after the rise of the Dervish empire closed the Egyptian–Sudanese border. When it reopened slavery had been prohibited, so the caravans ceased. As the illiterate slave-drivers died off, memories of the *Darb al-Arba'in* faded, as Michael Asher discovered when he tried to retrace the route from Darfur in the 1980s. Yet its name lives on, as geographers have designated the region through which it once ran as the **Darb al-Arba'in Desert**.

agricultural project at East Oweinat, but cars can't go beyond the checkpoint 5km south of Maks Qibli without a permit from Cairo.

In ancient times, another route led to Esna and Edfu in the Nile Valley, with a Roman fortress to protect trade and the community of **Kysis**, straddling the *Darb al-Dush*. Today, a spur road off the highway south of Maks Bahri leads to the ruins of Kysis and its hilltop **fortress**, whose walls are six metres high, with four or five storeys below ground. Abutting this is the **Temple of Dush** (daily 8am–5pm; £E16), built by Domitian and enlarged by Hadrian and Trajan, who built a monumental gateway. Reputedly once partly sheathed in gold, it is covered in dedications to the last two emperors, and the gateway in graffiti by Cailliaud and other nineteenth-century travellers. The discovery of an elaborate system of clay pipes and a Christian church suggests that the town was abandoned when its wells dried up, some time after the fourth century AD. "Dush" is believed to derive from *Kush*, the name of the ancient Nubian kingdom with which the Egyptians traded along the Nile.

The Gilf Kebir and Jebel Uwaynat

Egypt's final frontier is the vast wilderness to the southwest of Kharga and Dakhla oases, where the Great Sand Sea gives way to the **Uwaynat Desert**. Unlike the flat sand-sheet of the Darb al-Arba'in Desert, this region is pock-marked with craters and outcrops and dominated by the huge plateau of the **Gilf Kebir**. Riven by wadis draining into lakes that dried out thousands of years ago, with colossal dunes leapfrogging each other to climb the 1000-foot-high escarpment, the Gilf is the closest environment on earth to the surface of Mars and has been studied by NASA since the 1970s. More recently, this obscure corner of Egypt has been thrust into the limelight by the book and film *The English Patient*, dwelling on the exploits of the explorer Almásy and his discovery of the **Cave of the Swimmers** at **Wadi Sura**. This magnificent example of **prehistoric rock art** is only one of thousands of engravings, drawings or paintings in the wadis of the Gilf Kebir and **Jebel Uwaynat**, a massif straddling the borders of Egypt, Libya and Sudan. In ancient times Jebel Uwaynat was inhabited by cattle pastoralist cultures who left equally amazing rock art at **Karkur Talh** and Ain Doua. Their depictions of giraffes, ostriches, lions and cattle – and people hunting and swimming – suggests what the environment was like before the decisive shift from savannah to desert occurred at the end of the Holocene wet period, around 5000 BC.

Since then, the Uwaynat Desert has become the **driest desert on earth**, with an aridity index of 200 (meaning that the solar energy received could evaporate 200 times the amount of precipitation received). Rainfall is less than a millimetre a year, and may fall only once a decade at Uwaynat and every twenty years on the Gilf. Barring a fluke rainfall such as allegedly saved Rohlfs in the Great Sand Sea, the nearest **water** supply is at least 500km away at Bir Tarfawi, where an experimental farm called East Oweinat draws on fossil water and the road to civilization begins. Beyond Bir Tarfawi there are only tracks or trackless desert; no fuel, food nor means of communication with the outside world (unless you bring a satphone); nor any people except a few survey or **safari expeditions**. The **experience** of deep desert travel is fantastic – but not for everyone. The cost alone may be prohibitive, and if it isn't, you need to **reserve** at least six months ahead to be sure of getting a place; expeditions only run from February to March and September to November, when the tempera-ture is tolerable. Even so, **discomfort** is inevitable: sand gets into every crevice of your body, there's no water to spare for washing, and you start to stink – like everybody else in the vehicle. Unless you're willing to rough it and muck in when needed there's no point in coming at all. But if you do, you're sure to remember it for the rest of your life.

Getting there

Safaris to the Uwaynat Desert are a major logistical effort, involving tangles of red tape, tonnes of supplies, high-tech communications and navigation gear. Don't even think of going with less than three 4WD vehicles, or without a GPS set and satellite phone. Also essential is a **guide** who's done the trip enough times before to be confident; few of them use maps or compass bearings to chart the route, depending on their memory of landmarks, handed down from guide to guide. To prevent foolhardy ventures the authorities require all expeditions to have a permit from Military Intelligence in Cairo (see p.484), and since a 4WD ran over a landmine in 1999, have insisted that safaris are also **accompanied by an army officer** who knows where mines have been laid. They know lots about the desert, too, and often go into the safari business once their army careers are over; former brigadier Mestekawy of Zarzora Expedition being the prime example.

Most of the safari outfits below are willing to take people in their own 4WDs providing they're able to handle the **driving**, which needs experience, skill and nerve. If you have doubts on any of these scores then you should come as a **passenger** and let the safari team handle all the practicalities; just sit back and enjoy the awesome natural beauty and isolation. Some safaris start from Cairo, others from Dakhla or Baharia oases; several firms are based in Europe and may organize package deals. Check that your travel **insurance** covers deepdesert journeys, and what (if any) back-up exists in case of **emergencies**; some outfits have contracts with an air-ambulance service whose light aircraft can land in the desert. Though the operator will supply meals, tents and bedding, you need to **bring** such personal essentials as sun block and skin cream and any luxuries like alcohol or cigarettes (the nearest supply is in Kharga or Dakhla oases). Binoculars are a must, too.

Safari operators

Ancient World Tours ☏ 07071/222-950, ℻ 01483/237-398, ✉ mra@dial.pipex.com, ✇ www.ancient.co.uk. Twice-yearly tours to Wadi Sura and/or Karkur Talh; flights from Britain and luxury accommodation in Cairo are included in the 13-day package deal (£1995).
Hagg Abdel Hameed (mobile ☏ 0106 445154) and **Yosef Zeydan** (mobile ☏ 0106 221359) of the *Bedouin Camp* (☏ & ℻ 092/850-480) in Dakhla Oasis do an eight-day safari costing £E800 per person per day, plus £E100 a day for the guide.
Fliegel Jerzerniczky Expeditions ✇ www .fjexpeditions.com. Twice-yearly expeditions (10–14 days) in the footsteps of Almássy, starting from Cairo. Flights to Egypt can be included; land-only costs about US$1500 per person. They also run a tour to the Libyan side of Uwaynat, starting from Libya.
Khalifa Expeditions mobile ☏ 0123 215445, ✉ khalifa_exp@link.net, ✇ www.khalifaexp.com.

Nine- to fourteen-day safaris out of Baharia Oasis, for US$135 per person per day.
Lama Tours ☏ 0049-69/944 7897. Fifteen- to 21-day safaris ranging into Sudan; prices depend on the scope and the number of people involved.
Pan Arab Tours ☏ 02/418 4409, ℻ 291 3506, ✉ pat@moussa.net. Tailor-made safaris to the Gilf and Uwaynat, run by real pros.
White Desert Tours ☏ &℻ 02/847 2322, mobile ☏ 0123 212179, ✉ whitedesert@link.net, ✇ www.whitedesertours.com. Another Baharia-based outfit, doing tailor-made safaris; Peter Wirth will also act as a guide for self-drivers.
Zarzora Expedition ☏ 02/736 0350, ℻ 02/735 0360, ✉ info@zarzora.com, ✇ www.zarzora.com. Sixteen - and eighteen-day trips in the footsteps of Rohlfs and Almássy, and a 21-day safari including Ain Della and the Great Sand Sea.

The approaches

There are two classic **approaches** to this corner of Egypt. One takes the *Darb el-Tarfawi* south from Dakhla Oasis and then a track to **Abu Ballas**, en route to the Gilf and then Uwaynat. The other assumes a more easterly starting point, from Kharga Oasis or even Aswan or Abu Simbel, and uses the *Darb al-Arba'in* – recently paved as far south as Bir Kiseba – to reach **Bir Tarfawi**, from where the first motorized explorers approached Uwaynat in the mid-1920s, finding the desert easier to cross than they'd expected. Approaching the Gilf from the north was – and is – more difficult due to the Great Sand Sea, but some safaris do it, in which case Regenfeld is a mandatory stopover (see p.559).

From Dakhla

Abu Ballas (Father of Pots) is 240km from Dakhla, before the southeastern tip of the Great Sand Sea. Named by Prince Kemal el-Din in 1916, this hill is an ancient water cache strategically located between caravan trails and springs. Once there were hundreds of **pots**, each able to hold about 30 litres of water, probably stashed by Tebu tribesmen to sustain their raids on Dakhla. Men from the oasis are said to have found their cache and smashed the pots; archeologists, explorers and tourists have removed most of the fragments, though a fewremain photogenically posed. Ball suggested that the "lost oasis" of Zerzura might actually be Abu Ballas and refer to a *zir* or water jug rather than the Arabic name for a small black starling found in the Western Desert. There is **rock art**, too, halfway up the southeast face: a cow suckling its calf, a bearded hunter and his dog chasing an antelope with a bow and arrows, and a man's profile. An hour's drive beyond Abu Ballas is a field of mud *yardangs* resembling basking sea lions, dubbed the **Mud-Lions**. Thereafter, dunes impede the way to the Gilf..

From Kharga

Depending on how far south you follow the *Darb al-Arba'in* and which roads you use, you may pass the ancient spring of **Bir Tarfawi**, in a depression surrounded by palms, acacias and tamarisks, that was once filled by two lakes, ringed by Neolithic settlements. In 1981, radar imaging from the Space Shuttle revealed ancient riverbeds that convinced Farouk al-Baz that fossil water lay beneath the desert. His hypothesis proved to be correct, for the government has dug wells and established experimental **farms** at **Bir Sahara** and **El Ain**. Collectively named **East Oweinat** (the spelling differentiates it from Jebel Uwaynat, far away and unrelated to the project), they consist of circular fields irrigated by giant sprinklers, where high-value crops are grown for export to France from an airstrip. As the area is linked by road to Abu Simbel and Toshka and there are plans to extend the Sheikh Zayed Canal to Kharga Oasis, one can envisage a time when the middle of the Darb al-Arba'in Desert turns green – but not for a decade, perhaps.

The Gilf Kebir

For a hundred miles the great cliff went on. It seemed like the frontier of some "lost world" ... unbroken except where the mouths of deep unlit gorges appeared as black slits, from the bottom of which an ancient debris of boulders spilled out fanwise for miles into the plain. It was tempting to go and explore one of those gorges. What might there not be far inland up the valleys which they drained? ... But it was impossible to get close to the foot of the cliff without risking the cars.

Ralph Bagnold, *Libyan Sands: Travel in a Dead World*

Named the **Gilf Kebir** (Great Barrier) by the first European to sight it, this 7770-square-kilometre limestone and sandstone plateau roughly the size of Switzerland rises 300m from the desert floor, an even more formidable obstacle than the Great Sand Sea. Early explorers only skirted its edges and it wasn't until the 1930s that they entered its valleys and found that the Gilf consists of two landmasses joined by an isthmus, almost cut through by a pass called Aqaba. Aeons ago in the late Tertiary age, the Gilf was a watershed draining water in all directions; its wadis were eroded by water and then by wind and sand over 100,000 years. The sheer cliffs on the south and southwest sides are the highest, while the northeasterly ones have been worn down by the Sand Sea: an unstoppable force meeting an unmovable object – and winning. **Dunes** have filled up the valleys and are climbing one on top of another to reach the plateau at Lama Pass; trillions of tonnes of sand on the march, white by the Sand Sea, or red around the middle of the plateau and its southern landmass. Despite being the "heart of aridity", the top of the plateau gets just enough rainfall for hardy **flora and fauna** to survive. While its Barbary sheep have been hunted to the verge of extinction by Libyan poachers, nobody is endangering the foxes and lizards seen by Misonne in 1969, nor the whittiers, butterflies and Rose of Jericho flowers that Samir Lama and Cassandra Vivian saw in 1998. And then there are the acacia trees that early explorers found, which were shrivelled when last seen but likely to survive until the next shower. Visitors may also find other surprises, too, like the wreck of an RAF Blenheim bomber that turned up on the plateau in 2001 (thought to be one of five planes that took off from Kufra Oasis in 1941).

For many visitors the Gilf's allure has more to do with its fantastic **prehistoric rock art** – at Wadi Sura, Wadi Abd el-Malik and other sites – or the romance attached to the **explorers** who "discovered" it (though Tebu and Gor'an nomads were fully aware of it all along, since it was their ancestors who created it). Almássy gets all the limelight, naturally, but Michael Ondaatje's novel also mentions other explorers of the 1920s and 1930s, such as the Egyptian Prince Kemal el-Din, the Englishmen Ralph Bagnold, Douglas Newbold and Kennedy Shaw, and the Irishman Patrick Clayton. During World War II, they set up the Long Range Desert Group (LRDG) that wreaked havoc behind Italian and German lines, while their former comrade Almássy served on the other side with the Afrika Korps. Since the 1960s the tradition of exploration has been revived by British, Belgian-Libyan, US, French and American-Egyptian expeditions, and by tourists from Germany, Italy, France, Hungary, Spain and Britain – a hundred or so of whom visit the Gilf Kebir every year.

The "Zerzura" wadis

When Almássy and Lord Clayton took three cars and a plane to the Gilf in February 1932, the aim of their **Zerzura Expedition** was to find the legendary lost oasis of that name, which had obsessed Western explorers for generations (see p.559). Almássy was away visiting the Italians in Kufra when Clayton and Penderel flew over the northern Gilf and glimpsed "an acacia-dotted wadi" that they were unable to pinpoint on a map. After Almássy's return with a dozen bottles of Chianti, they made further flights and spotted two such wadis from the air, but couldn't locate them on foot. Both Almássy and Clayton believed that these were two of the three valleys mentioned by Wilkinson in his 1835 list of unknown sites that set the European search for Zerzura rolling. But fate intervened in their plans, for Clayton died of polio on a visit to England, followed within a month by the expedition's sponsor, Prince Kemal el-Din, leaving Almássy to seek new sponsors and Clayton's widow to continue her husband's quest independently (see box overleaf).

Returning next spring in cars with balloon tyres, Almássy's party explored **Wadi Abd el-Malik** (Valley of the Servant of the King), the longest of the deep fissures in the northern Gilf. They found lots of acacia trees and sites of Tebu encampments and a large cave with **drawings** of longhorn cattle, men, and a prehistoric dwelling. (Another grotto was later found by Peel and Bagnold, containing **paintings** of cattle and a dog.) It was a Tebu caravan guide who told Almássy the name of the wadi and its side-valley, **Wadi Talh** (Acacia Valley), and spoke of a third valley called Wadi Hamra. When asked if he knew of Zerzura, he replied: "Oh, those silly Arab people, they do not know anything; they call these three wadis in the Gilf, Zerzura, but we local people know their real names". Almássy was sure that they had found Zerzura.

Today, expeditions are drawn to **Wadi Hamra** (Red Valley) by its gorgeous **red dunes**, drifting down a black mountainside – a Martian landscape found nowhere else in Egypt. The wadi's sandstone rocks bear **engravings** of giraffes, oryx, ostriches, gazelles and Barbary sheep – the prey that hunter-gatherers killed with dogs, lassos, bows and arrows during the Early Holocene epoch (8000–6000/5000 BC). This rock art is centuries if not thousands of years older than the images in the Cave of Swimmers. Wadi Hamra was found in 1931 by Patrick Clayton, who noted plenty of trees and Barbary sheep, while Almássy discovered that it led up to the Gilf plateau. During the war, he reputedly tried to persuade Rommel to land glider-troops on top of the Gilf and bring them down into Wadi Hamra.

László Almássy – the real "English Patient"

While Michael Ondaatje's book The English Patient and the subsequent Oscar-winning film rescued Almássy's name from obscurity, both texts took liberties with the truth to cast "Count Ladislaus de Almasy" as a romantic hero whose love for another man's wife sealed their fates and left him dying of burns in an Italian villa. The real story is rather different.

Born in 1895, in Borostyánkő, Hungary (now Bernstein, Austria), **László Ede Almássy** learned to fly while at boarding school in England. During World War I he was a fighter ace and then an aide to the last Hapsburg monarch (who once mistakenly called him "Count" – a title that stuck), serving as his driver during two farcical attempts to regain the throne in 1921. Almássy then became a salesman for the off-road-car manufacturers Steyr, for whom he won many races, and in 1926 took Steyrs into the desert on the first of his numerous Sahara expeditions, about which he wrote several books.

In February 1932 he initiated the **Zerzura Expedition** to the Gilf Kebir, the first to combine cars with light aircraft. His co-explorers were **Lord Robert** and **Lady Dorothy Clayton East Clayton** (the fictional Geoffrey and Katherine Clifton), the Irish desert surveyor **Patrick Clayton** (no relation) and Squadron Leader Penderel. Unlike in fiction, Lord Clayton died of a sudden illness back home in England, and although his widow returned to the desert to continue searching for Zerzura, she didn't meet Almássy again or share his discovery of the Cave of Swimmers – nor did she perish there in 1939, but rather in a fall from her plane in England six years earlier. Thus the "motive" for Almássy's collaboration with the Germans in The English Patient is pure invention.

As a reserve officer in the Hungarian air force, Almássy could hardly refuse being posted to Rommel's **Afrika Korps**, which used his expertise as a spotter and his photos for their official handbook – to the fury of his old companions in Egypt, many of whom were now in the LRDG. Thanks to the codebreakers of Bletchley Park, the British knew of Almássy's infiltration of two German spies into Egypt, whom he guided through the Gilf to Kharga Oasis in 1941. He later made amends by visiting Patrick Clayton in an Italian POW camp and getting him moved to a better one. Almássy himself wound up in a Soviet camp where he lost his teeth from scurvy, before a Peoples' Court cleared him of being a Nazi sympathizer after testimony that he had sheltered Jewish neighbours in his flat in Budapest. His **final years** were spent in Africa, where he flew gliders and ran safaris. After catching dysentery in Egypt, he died in a clinic in Salzburg in 1951.

Wadi Sura - the Cave of the Swimmers

Although *The English Patient* transposes the Cave of the Swimmers to Ain Doua at Jebel Uwaynat, it actually lies in **Wadi Sura** (Picture Valley), where Almásy found it in October 1933, with the Frobenius expedition that was searching for rock art at Uwaynat and in the western valleys of the Gilf that had been explored by Patrick Clayton two years earlier. Clayton's son believes that his father found the wadi and its other caves first, but it was Almásy's privilege to discover the Cave of the Swimmers and name the valley. There are five caves (or hollows) in all, two outside and three inside the wadi; the largest and most impressive are within 50m of the other cliff face.

The **Cave of the Archers**, on the south side of the wadi, contains dark red and white figures of naked men clutching bows, some of them shooting at cattle – whose presence assigns these pictures to the Cattle Period (5000–2500 BC) of North African rock art. Hans Winkler of the 1938 Mond expedition termed the style of the male figures "balanced exaggeration", for they all have wide shoulders and hips, tiny waists and tapering limbs; feet and hands are rarely shown, and heads often omitted too – unlike the spear-carrying hunters depicted in Karkur Talh at Jebel Uwaynat, which are otherwise similar in style.

Twenty metres to the north, the **Cave of the Swimmers** harbours well over a hundred figures in diverse styles. The famous swimmers are 10cm long and painted in red; with small rounded heads on stalks, tadpole-shaped bodies and spidery arms and legs. Some are diving, implying that a lake once existed here (for which there's geological evidence). A second group of figures are depicted standing, with clumsy limbs, thick torsos and pea-shaped heads; hands only appear on the larger figures. Most are dark red, with bands of white around their ankles, wrists or waists, similar to the hunters at Karkur Talh. Still more intriguing are two yellow figures that seem to be stretching out their arms to welcome a third, smaller, red one, that may be a child and its parents. Cattle, giraffes, ostriches and dogs are also depicted on the walls.

The cliff-face resembles a row of giants with outlying sentinels guarding the mouth of the wadi, where there are two caves (or hollows) on its southern lip and a third cave outside. Sadly, some cretin from London has hacked his name into the rock nearby.

On the sandy plain beyond the wadi a huge fallen rock covers the **Giraffe Cave**, found by Clayton in 1931. Stooping to enter, one sees giraffes, cattle and dogs painted in black or white.

Other wadis

The southern part of the Gilf is riddled with wadis, some easy to enter, others nearly impossible. **Wadi Mashi** (Walking Valley) gets its name because the mountains vanish and reappear as you approach, but has yet to yield any finds, unlike **Wadi Dayyiq** (Narrow Valley), where a large area is covered by stone-chippings left by prehistoric people manufacturing knives, blades and arrow-heads from hard rocks; or **Wadi al-Bakht**, where four **prehistoric settlements** have been found. Besides ostrich eggs, grinding stones and bones there's heaps of pottery dating back to 6930 BC, that's as old as the pottery at Nabta (see p.784) but different in style and colour. It's thought that people lived here for centuries, hunting ostriches and raising cattle around the shores of a lake until it disappeared by 5200 BC.

Nor is it just prehistory that has been preserved, for in 1991 a World War II ammunition truck was found in the desert to the east of Wadi Dayyiq. After being refuelled it started, and is now in the war museum at El-Alamein. There are **relics of the Long Range Desert Group** (see box) all over the region,

The Long Range Desert Group (LRDG)

Founded by Ralph Bagnold in June 1940, to reconnoitre Axis forces and engage in "piracy on the high desert", the **Long Range Desert Group**'s motto was "Not by Strength, but Guile". Led by Bagnold and other pre-war explorers such as Patrick Clayton, Kennedy Shaw and Douglas Newbold, it consisted mainly of New Zealanders, who soon learnt the arts of desert warfare. As with Special Forces ever since, the emphasis was on self-reliance and mobility. Each patrol took all it needed for a cross-desert journey of 1500 miles (which could be doubled by establishing a forward supply dump), in stripped-down Chevy trucks fitted with sand mats and channels (doubling as air markers for supply drops) and a sun compass invented by Bagnold. Patrols operated for up to eleven weeks (without washing) as they espied convoys or delivered SAS commandos to attack airfields; destroying over 400 planes in ten months (more than the RAF). British Foreign Secretary Anthony Eden called them "my mosquito army", while the Italians dubbed them the Ghost Army. After Axis forces in North Africa surrendered in 1943, the LRDG were sent to the Balkans. They spoke a weird argot composed of English, Arabic, Hindi, German and Italian, and wore a mixture of uniforms, with a unit badge of a scorpion within a wheel, made by jewellers in Khan el-Khalili.

You can **read** about the LRDG's exploits in Bagnold's *Sand, Wind and War: Memoirs of a Desert Explorer*, Peter Clayton's *Desert Explorer* (about his father, Patrick), or on the LRDG Preservation Society's website ⑩ www.lrdg.org.

from a Ford lorry and a GM stake-bed truck 10km southeast of the Gilf's southern tip, to hundreds of metal petrol cans with the Shell logo, laid out to form route markers. An evocative example is the **abandoned aerodrome** with a landing strip marked by concentric rings of petrol cans, near the wadi known as **Eight Bells**. This cluster of hills and depressions is the result of a vast prehistoric drainage system from around 5000 BC, that carried water south into an even larger one that fed a super-lake stretching from Lake Chad to within 600km of the Gilf Kebir.

Circumventing the southern Gilf, cars pass through **Wadi Wassa** (Wide Valley), another ancient drainage valley with dozens of side wadis, islands, and a wrecked Chevy used by the LRDG. On the *col* that divides Wadi Wassa from **Wadi Faragh** (Empty Valley), Shaw found a cave containing engravings of cows and more ancient giraffes; it was thereafter shown on maps as **Shaw's Cave**, despite being known to caravan guides as the Cave of the Arch (*Magarat el-Qantara*). It's here that a military escort is most appreciated, for there are **mines** on the plain where two tracks cross about 5km west of the mouth of Wadi Faragh – which wrecked a tourist 4WD in 1983 – and others are rumoured to have been laid at other strategic points. Only the Egyptian army knows which are mined and which are bluffs. Wadi Faragh is also distinguished by a **Monument to Prince Kemal el-Din**, erected by Almássy to commemorate his patron's expeditions to Uwaynat, the Gilf and Merga Oasis, using Citröen caterpillar-tracks in the 1920s.

The Clayton Craters and Jebels Peter and Paul

The two main tracks towards Jebel Uwaynat pass the **Clayton Craters**, discovered by Patrick Clayton on the second Bagnold expedition in 1931. Measuring up to 1km across, the twenty craters have sandstone rims rising about 30m from the desert floor, enclosing domes of greenish igneous rock or cork-shaped basalt formations, with dry stream-beds. While the baked and fused sandstone suggests a volcanic origin, the geologist Rushdi Said argues that springs caused the ground to collapse, forming the craters. Elsewhere in the Libyan Desert, remote sensing satellites have identified craters formed by meteor strikes, near Kufra Oasis in Libya and in the Great Sand Sea.

The meteorite that created the four-kilometre-wide al-Baz Crater (named after its Egyptian-American discoverer, Farouk al-Baz, a pioneer in using satellites to search for water in arid regions) may also have produced the mysterious silica glass found in the Great Sand Sea, from which the scarab on Pharaoh Tutankhamun's pectoral cross was carved, raising the possibility that the ancient Egyptians knew of the Sand Sea and its silica glass and perhaps even of its extraterrestrial origins.

Otherwise, the chief landmarks are the twin mountains called **Jebels Peter and Paul**, steep-sided quartz trachyte plugs in the Precambrian bedrock, like the northern part of Uwaynat. Safari groups give them a wide berth, as **mines** have reputedly been laid roundabouts.

Jebel Uwaynat

On a map of North Africa, the ruler-straight borders of Libya, Egypt and Sudan intersect at **Jebel Uwaynat**, the highest point in the Libyan Desert. Surrounded by sand-sheets, it rises through a "vertical battlement" to 1898m above the desert floor and 600m above sea level, just high enough to attract a little rainfall, which percolates down to eight small pools or "springs" at its base (after which Uwaynat is named). The valleys there are fertile if watered, sustaining communities from prehistoric times until the early 1930s. Yet Uwaynat's location remained a mystery to the outside world until 1923, when it was reached by Hassanein Bey by camel from Kufra Oasis in Libya. With its co-ordinates established the next challenge was to find a route from Egypt, which was accomplished in 1925 by Prince Kemal al-Din and John Ball who followed a half-track from Bir Tarfawi. They were followed by Shaw, Almássy, Bagnold *et al*, whose exploration of the Gilf was initally motivated by the desire to find a route to Uwaynat from the north.

After the Italians occupied Kufra and placed an outpost at Uwaynat, the possibility that it could be an unguarded back door into Egypt during wartime occurred to both Bagnold and the Italian commander Lorenzini – but not to the HQ staff-wallahs who turned down Bagnold's proposal for car patrols along the frontier. It wasn't until Italy declared war in June 1940 that the newly appointed General Wavell summoned him and learned that cars could easily drive from Uwaynat to Aswan in two days. The risk of a surprise attack that would cut links to Sudan and make all of Egypt hostage to a threat to blow up the Aswan Dam was too terrible to ignore, so Bagnold was authorized to set up long-range patrols to monitor any activity. In the event, the Italians never tried anything so bold, but Almássy later slipped through from Kufra via Uwaynat and the Gilf, to guide two German spies as far as Kharga Oasis, before returning to Libya.

Karkur Talh and other sites

Jebel Uwaynat covers 1500 square kilometres and consists of granite, sandstone and quartz trachyte formations. As in the Gilf, the northern slopes have borne the brunt of wind erosion and bizarre rock forms abound, while the wadis all around the base (called *karkurs*) contain engravings, drawings and paintings spanning thousands of years. One of the richest sites is **Karkur Talh** (Acacia Valley), where Hassanein Bey found images of lions, giraffes, ostriches, gazelles and cows engraved on the rocks at ground level – plus paintings of camels from a later epoch (camels reached Egypt in 525 BC). Higher up the valley, Shaw discovered ninety human figures drawn on the roof of a sandstone cave 1m high, whose figures were lither than the hunters in the Cave of the Archers at Wadi Sura but otherwise similar, leading Winkler to conclude that both were the work of the ancient Tebu (Rock People) who once ranged across the Sahara from their mountainous homeland of Tibesti, in Chad. Besides the rock art in the main valley there are 200 paintings and engravings in a lateral wadi, and over 1000 other locations in the areas that the Belgian expedition of 1968 called **Wadi Talh I** and **II**.

All the other rock-art sites lie over the heavily mined border in Sudan or Libya and are currently **inaccessible** (except on Fleigel Jerzerniczky Expeditions tours, via Libya). These include **Karkur Murr**, where Clayton found starving refugees from Kufra in 1931, and the massif's largest "spring", **Ain Doua**, which was the fictional location of the Cave of the Swimmers in *The English Patient* – though the rock art here was actually discovered by Almásy's driver.

The Great Sand Sea and the "Lost Oasis"

Between the Gilf Kebir and Siwa Oasis lie 72,000 square kilometres of dune fields that the explorer Gerhard Rohlfs named the **Great Sand Sea**. Though maps still define parts as beyond the "limits of reliable relief information", its overall configuration is known. From thick "whalebacks" and a mass of transverse dunes near Siwa, it washes south in parallel *seif* dunes (oriented north–south, with a slight northwest–southeast incline) as far as the eye can see.

Although its general existence was known at the time of Herodotus, the extent to which it stretched southwards wasn't realized until the Rohlfs expedition of 1874 headed west from Dakhla, bound for Kufra Oasis in Libya. With seventeen camels bearing water and supplies, they soon met the *erg*'s outermost ranges: "an ocean" of sand-waves over 100m high, ranked 2–4km apart. Rohlfs estimated that their camels could scale six dunes and advance 20km westwards on the first and second days, but that their endurance would rapidly diminish thereafter, so with no prospect of water or an end to the dunes they were forced to turn north-northwest and follow the dune lanes towards Siwa. Their isolation was intense:

If one stayed behind a moment and let the caravan out of one's sight, a loneliness could be felt in the boundless expanse such as brought fear even in the stoutest heart ... Nothing but sand and sky! At sea the surface of the water is moved, unless there is a dead calm. Here in the sand ocean there is nothing to remind one of the great common life of the earth but the stiffened ripples of the last wind-storm; all else is dead.

By the eighteenth day the expedition could no longer water every camel and the animals began dying. Then, according to the English version of his adventures, there was torrential rainfall in a spot where barely a drop falls for years, saving their lives and replenishing their water supply. Rohlfs called the spot **Regenfeld** (Rainfield) and marked it with a cairn before he left, wondering "Will ever man's foot tread this place again?". However, in the German edition of his book, *Drei Monate in der libyschen Wüste*, he described a smaller expedition with no hint of supply problems – and whether or not a miraculous rainfall really saved their lives, Regenfeld has since been visited by scores of explorers and tourists. The message that he left in a bottle was removed by Hassanein Bey in 1923, who substituted a message of his own, followed decades later by Samir Lama and Jacques Monod. Now, all the messages, wine bottles and empty water tanks left by previous explorers have been taken by souvenir hunters.

Rohlfs' feat of trekking for 36 days over 675km (480km across the dunes) wasn't repeated until 1921–24, when Colonel de Lancey Forth entered the Sand Sea twice by camel from Dakhla and Siwa. Beneath a layer of sand he found campfires, charred ostrich eggs, flint knives and grinders from Neolithic times, when the desert was lush savannah.

Meanwhile, Ball and Moore had managed to round the Sand Sea's southeastern tip (near latitude 24) by car in 1917, while in 1923 Hassanein Bey circumvented its western edge as part of an extraordinary 3550-kilometre camel journey from Sollum on the Mediterranean to El-Fasher in Sudan's Darfur Province. He also confirmed the existence of the hitherto legendary Jebel Uwaynat, whose water source encouraged motorized explorers to seek new routes to the southwest. For Prince Kemal el-Din in his fleet of caterpillar-tracked Citröens, and Bagnold and co. – who found customized Model-T Fords more effective – the next obstacle was the Gilf Kebir, which barred the way to remoter Libyan oases.

Zerzura: the "Lost Oasis"

With the "discovery" by motorized explorers of Selima, Merga and the Forty Day Road's water holes, the number of unlocated oases diminished until only the **"Lost Oasis" of Zerzura** remained. First mentioned in 1246 as an abandoned village in the desert southwest of the Fayoum, it reappeared as a fabulous city in the fifteenth-century treasure-hunters' *Book of Hidden Pearls*:

This city is white like a pigeon, and on the door of it is carved a bird. Enter, and there you will find great riches, also the king and queen sleeping in their castle. Do not approach them, but take the treasure.

Citing native sources in 1835, Wilkinson placed the oasis "five days west of the road from El-Hayiz to Farafra", or "two or three days due west from Dakhleh". *Murray's Handbook* (1891) reported an "Oasis of the Blacks . . . also called Wady Zerzura" to the west of Farafra, and described it quite matter-of-factly. But Zerzura was still unlocated, and the stories placing it west of Dakhla gained credibility after Europeans "discovered" Kufra Oasis in Libya, which the same tales had mentioned. However, both the Rohlfs and Harding-King expeditions heard accounts of black men who periodically raided Dakhla from an oasis seven or eight days' journey to the southwest.

Having weighed the evidence for various speculative locations in the last chapter of *Libyan Sands*, Bagnold demarcated three zones. The "northern" one – encompassing the whole Sand Sea, but rating the areas west of Dakhla and Farafra as likeliest – was propounded by de Lancey Forth, citing the story of a

Sand seas and dunes

The true life of the desert is not made up of the marches of tribes in search of pasture, but of the game that goes endlessly on. What a difference in substance between the sands of submission and the sands of unruliness! The dunes, the salines, change their nature ... as the code changes by which they are governed.

Antoine de Saint-Exupéry, *Wind, Sand and Stars*

Though gravel plains, limestone pans and scarps account for 90 percent of the Sahara Desert, it's the **sand seas** or *ergs* that captivate the imagination. Covering hundreds of thousands of square kilometres of Algeria, Libya and Egypt, these dune fields are awesomely lifeless, yet shift and reproduce. Formed by wind and particles, vortices and accretion, their shapes, hues and textures are defined by light and shadow, a mutable reality. Venturers into this unearthly world must accept its whims and logic – this is elemental, not mortal terrain. Its sandstorms have buried armies and scoured paint from cars; soft spots and slip faces can trap the unwary, break limbs or axles; getting lost and dying of heat and thirst are real possibilities here.

While prevailing winds are the dominant factor, local geology and whatever precipitation or vegetation exists also determine the shape of **dunes**. Where sand is relatively scarce and small obstructions are common, windblown particles tend to form **crescent-shaped** *barchan* dunes, which advance horns first, moving over obstacles without altering their height. Baby dunes are formed downwind of the horns, which produces parallel lines of *barchans* with flat corridors between them, advancing up to 19m each year. *Barchans* can grow as high as 94m, extend for 375m, and weigh up to 450 million kilos. However, their mass is nothing compared to **parallel straight** dunes, or *seif* dunes (from the Arabic word for "sword"); some in the Great Sand Sea are over 140km long. Formed by a unidirectional wind, they have slipfaces on both sides and a wavy, knife-edged crest along the top. When *seif* dunes fall over an escarpment they reform at the bottom as crescent dunes, which is why *barchans* are the prevailing form in Dakhla and Kharga. Occasionally, they pile one on top of another to create mountainous **whalebacks** or mega-*barchans*. When the wind direction alters constantly, it can even form **star-shaped** (*rhord*) dunes. These are rare in Egypt, but one has been recorded at Wadi al-Bakht in the Gilf Kebir. Another type of formation is the flat, hard-packed **sand-sheet**, found in the Darb al-Arba'in Desert.

town with iron gates, seven days' camel journey to the south, in the *Siwan Manuscript*; plus tales of Bedouin chancing upon unknown oases while pursuing missing camels. Unfortunately, similar yarns also pointed towards the far south – that vast wilderness between Dakhla and the Selima and Merga oases in Sudan. Dr Ball and Newbold favoured this area, largely free of dunes and often low enough to approach the subterranean water table; in addition, Newbold thought he glimpsed an oasis during a flight over the desert.

The third, "central" zone extended southwest from Dakhla as far as Jebel Uwaynat and was championed by Harding-King, who cited native accounts of incursions by "strange cows", Tebu raiders and a "black giantess". When Ball discovered a cache of Tebu water jars at Abu Ballas, southwest of Dakhla, it supported the stories but argued against an oasis; for if a water source existed, why bother to maintain a depot in the middle of nowhere? Then came Almásy and Lord Clayton, who were sure that three wadis in the northern Gilf Kebir were the legendary Zerzura – but they failed to convince others.

Accepting Ball's theory of a consistent water level beneath the Libyan Desert, Bagnold argued that Zerzura could only exist in low-lying areas or deep, wind-eroded hollows. As the desert was surveyed, the possibility of such sites escaping notice diminished, and Bagnold doubted that an undiscovered oasis existed. Perhaps Zerzura might once have been a water hole or an area favoured with periodic rainfall, but the fabled oasis of palms and ruins must be a figment of wishful thinking: a Bedouin Shangri-la that tantalized foreign explorers.

Siwa Oasis

Isolated by hundreds of kilometres of desert, **Siwa Oasis** remained virtually independent from Egypt until the late nineteenth century, sustaining a unique culture. Yet despite – or because of – its isolation, outsiders have been drawn here since antiquity. The legendary Army of Cambyses was heading this way when it disappeared into a sandstorm; Alexander the Great journeyed here to consult the famous Oracle of Amun; and Arabic tales of *Santariyah* (as the oasis was known) were common currency into the nineteenth century. In modern times, Siwa has received visits from kings and presidents, anthropologists and generals. Tourism only really began in the mid-1980s but has gathered steam in recent years, as Siwa has become a firm favourite with independent travellers and adventure tour groups. Though welcoming its economic benefits, the Siwans want to keep tourism within bounds, and hope that direct charter flights into Siwa will never materialize.

The oasis offers all you could ask for in the way of desert **beauty spots**: thick palm groves clustered around freshwater springs and salt lakes; rugged massifs and enormous dunes. Equally impressive are the **ruins** of Shali and Aghurmi, labyrinthine mud-built towns that once protected the Siwans from desert raiders. Scattered around the oasis are ruined **temples** that attest to Siwa's fame and prosperity during Greco-Roman times; some claim that the tomb of Alexander the Great lies here. Visitors are also fascinated by **Siwan culture**, and how it is reacting to outside influences like TV, schooling and tourism. Nowadays, it is mostly only older women who wear the traditional costume, silver jewellery and complex hair-braids; younger wives and unmarried women dress much the same as their counterparts in the Nile Valley. But the Siwans still observe their own festivals and wedding customs; and among themselves they speak *Siwi*, a Berber tongue. Though things are changing, the Siwans remain sure of their identity and are determined to maintain it.

A little history

Beyond the fact that it supported hunter-gatherers in Paleolithic times, little is known about Siwa Oasis before the XXVI Dynasty (525–404 BC), when the reputation of its **Oracle** spread throughout the Mediterranean world. Siwa's population seems to have been at risk from predatory desert tribes, so their first settlement was a fortified acropolis, about which Classical accounts reveal little about this beyond its name, **Aghurmi**, and its position as a major caravan stop between Cyrenaica and Sudan. The Siwans were related to the Berbers of Algeria, Tunisia and Morocco, and their language is just a variant of the Berber tongues, so their society may have originally been matriarchal. Their later history is detailed in the *Siwan Manuscript* (its whereabouts are a closely guarded secret), a century-old compilation of oral histories that relates how Siwa's rulers considered poisoning the springs with mummies in order to thwart the Muslim conquest (date uncertain), and how Bedouin and Berber raids had reduced Aghurmi's population to a mere two hundred by the twelfth century AD.

Shali and Siwan society

Round about 1203, seven families quit Aghurmi to found a new settlement called **Shali** (the Town). Their menfolk are still honoured as the "forty ancestors", and these pioneering families were probably the most vigorous of the surviving Siwans. Later, newcomers from Libya settled in the oasis, giving rise to the enduring distinction between the "Westerners" and the original, more numerous "Easterners", whose historic feud began after they disagreed over the route of a causeway that both had undertaken to build across the salt lake of Birket Siwa. Nonetheless, both coexisted within a single town built of *kharsif*: a salt-impregnated mud which dries cement-hard, but melts during downpours – fortunately, it only rains heavily here every fifty years or so. Fearful of raiders, Shali's *agwad* (elders) forbade families to live outside the walls, so as the population increased the town could only expand upwards. Siwan households added an extra floor with each generation, while the *agwad* regulated the width of alleys to one donkey's-breadth in an effort to ensure some light and air within the labyrinth.

Siwan bachelors aged between twenty and forty were obliged to sleep in caves outside town, guarding the fields – hence their nickname, the "club-bearers". Noted for their love of palm liquor, song and dance, these *zaggalah* shocked outsiders with their open **homosexuality**. Homosexual marriages were forbidden by King Fouad in 1928, but continued in secret until the late 1940s. Today, Siwans emphatically assert that homosexuality no longer exists in the oasis – whatever may be said on the (police-monitored) website Ⓦ www.gayegypt.com. And palm liquor has now been superceded by *arak* made from dates.

Another feature of Shali was the tradition of violent **feuds** between the Westerners and Easterners, in which all able-bodied males were expected to participate. Originally ritualized, with parallel lines of combatants exchanging blows between sunrise and sunset while their womenfolk threw stones at cowards and shouted encouragement, feuds became far deadlier with the advent of firearms, occasioning gun battles "on the slightest grounds". (Even now, Siwans know which clan they're descended from, and the town council is sited midway between the two neighbourhoods.) Yet they immediately closed ranks against outsiders – Bedouin raiders, khedival taxmen or European explorers.

Egyptian and British control

Visitors of the eighteenth and nineteenth centuries regularly experienced Siwan **xenophobia**. "Whenever I quitted my apartment, it was to be assailed with stones and a torrent of abusive language", Browne wrote in 1762. Having poked around the antiquities in Muslim guise, Frederick Hornemann was pursued into the desert, where "the braying of three hundred donkeys announced the arrival of the Siwan army", and only escaped thanks to his assistant's recitation of Koranic verses. Frederic Cailliaud was permitted to visit the gardens and ruins in 1819, but the town remained barred to strangers until six hundred troops sent by Mohammed Ali compelled the oasis to recognize **Egyptian authority** in 1820.

Although the Siwans subsequently revolted against their governor and defaulted on taxes (payable in dates) half a dozen times over the next sixty years, the oasis began to change. With the desert tribes suppressed, and Shali rendered unsafe by heavy rains, the *agwad* permitted families to settle outside

Siwi

Siwi is an unwritten Berber dialect that is the mother tongue of all native Siwans; children only start to learn Arabic from the age of six, in school. However, as Arabic is used in public life, visitors needn't deal with Siwi unless they want to. A few phrases can get you started.

yes	*mashi*	Give me ...	*ooshi ...*
no	*oola*	donkey(s)	*yeizite (zitan)*
How are you?	*Tanta elhalenik?*	horse	*agmare*
What's your name?	*Bit in insmitinik?*	camel(s)	*alghum*
Where are you going?	*Imani tehab?*	dates	*tenii*
What do you want?	*Tanta ekhsitta'?*	olives	*azumour*
I want ...	*ehk sehk ...*	water	*aman*
What's this?	*Tanta wook?*		

the walls. From the 1850s onwards the great reformist preacher Mohammed Ibn Ali al-Senussi cast a spell over the desert peoples from Jaghbub Oasis just over the border, and Siwa – the site of his first *zawiya* – supported **Senussi** resistance to the Italian conquest of Libya (1912–30), until it became clear that their Senussi "liberators" would not restore Siwan independence. Thus in 1917, British forces were "welcomed by the cheering Siwans, who declared their loyalty as they always did with every new victorious conqueror" (Fakhry).

Anglo-Egyptian control of Siwa was maintained by the Frontier Camel Corps and Light Car Patrols. Agricultural advisors, a school and an orthodox imam were introduced following King Fouad's visit to the oasis in 1928. When the British withdrew as the Italians advanced across North Africa in 1942, the Siwans accepted Axis **occupation** with equal resignation. Unlike Rommel, who made a favourable impression during his flying visit, King Farouk dismayed the Siwans by wearing shorts, and asking if they "still practised a certain vice" when he visited the oasis in 1945.

More recently ...

Paradoxical as it sounds, Siwa's biggest problem is an excess of fresh water, which gushes from springs and drains into salt lakes, increasing their volume and salinity. As the explorer Bagnold put it: "the air, hot and breathless, has a characteristic oasis smell, slightly sweet, of rank grass faintly charred, decaying through increasing saltiness". Smelly, mosquito-infested ponds all over town attest that the **water table** lies only twenty centimetres underground. **Land reclamation** projects have tried to tackle the problem since 1907, but creating drainage catchment areas in an oasis lying 18m below sea level has always proved hugely expensive.

While Egyptian military bases exist here on sufferance, the Siwans have welcomed developments in health care, education and communications. Two hospitals (one for women and children) treat patients who once had to travel to Mersa Matrouh. Over thirty Siwans have graduated from university, and returned to live in the oasis. The road to Matrouh (completed in 1984) has encouraged exports of dates and olives, and tourism to the oasis, and during the 1990s the local economy was boosted by new factories producing olive oil, mineral water and carpets.

Visiting Siwa

Visitors to Siwa Oasis no longer require **military permission**, unless they wish to travel to the remoter oases of Qara, Areg, Bahrein or Sitra; permission for these trips can be obtained from Military Intelligence in Siwa itself. Aside from lacking a **bank** (bring enough cash for your stay), Siwa has all the basic facilities – though **petrol** might be unavailable until the delivery truck shows up.

The **best time** to come is during spring or autumn, when the Siwans hold festivals and the days are pleasantly warm. During winter, windless days can also be nice, but nights – and gales – are chilling. From May onwards, rising temperatures keep people indoors between 11am and 7pm, and the nights are sultry and mosquito-ridden. Even when the **climate** is mild you'll probably feel like taking a midday siesta or a swim.

Siwa is well known for its conservatism in matters of **dress** and **behaviour**. The tourist office requests visitors to refrain from public displays of affection or drinking alcohol (which is not sold here), and women to keep their arms and legs covered – especially when bathing in pools. Women should also avoid wandering alone in places with few people around. Local people are generally more reserved than the Egyptians, and invitations home are less common. Siwan households are segregated, with the women's quarters on the ground floor; foreign women who get invited upstairs have reason to be suspicious.

Besides the official ban on **photographing** military installations (including the airport, and sandbagged dugouts in unexpected locations), visitors should respect Siwan feelings on the issue. As a rule, local women are taboo subjects, whereas Siwan males – particularly the younger ones – don't mind being snapped (but always ask them first). Discreet long shots are easier than close-ups. For streetlife and visual clarity, take your pictures before 9am, or during the hour or so before sunset; people stay indoors when the sun is high, and its glare bleaches colours and textures from photographs.

Getting there: the routes

Unless you sign up with a desert safari – which might reach Siwa via the Qattara Depression – there are only two possible **approaches**. One is via the dire road from Bahariya Oasis (see p.576); the other is from Alexandria or Mersa Matrouh – the route favoured by most visitors.

There is one a/c **bus** daily from Sidi Gaber in Alexandria to Siwa (11am; 9hr; £E27), which calls briefly at Moharrem Bey. It takes on extra passengers at Mersa Matrouh, three to four hours later. Matrouh is also the starting point for a further three buses a day to Siwa (4–5hr; £E12–15), leaving at 7.30am, 1.30pm and 3.30pm. You may also be able to catch a service taxi or **minivan** from Matrouh to Siwa; the fare is £E10 per person.

The 300km **journey** from Matrouh to Siwa takes four hours by car or bus. If you're driving, the Siwa road turns off the highway 20km west of Matrouh, at a checkpoint. There are minefields to the left for 50km into the desert, marked by triangular signs. About 100km further there is a tiny **resthouse** entitled the "*Desert Rose Hotel*" but better known as **Bir Nous** (Halfway Well), selling tea, soup and soft drinks. Its toilets are the nearest one gets to the horrors of this route before the road was built. Until the nineteenth century there was only a camel trail (eight days from Matrouh) across this flat desert and the few landmarks might be obscured by dust clouds or sandstorms. The sharp limestone ridges and hollows beneath the powdery surface of this *shabak* (net) desert also made the route hazardous for early motorists, who followed the line of telegraph poles. Nowadays the monotonous vistas – interspersed with army camps – keep going until the last 40km, when rock outcrops presage the appearance of the oasis.

Siwa Town

Most visitors rate **SIWA TOWN** and the pools, rocks and ruins around as the oasis's main attractions, and not many bother to visit the outlying villages. Siwa Town has grown as its population has risen to 20,000 (at least 1000 of them from outside the oasis, and many from two villages near Minya), and people

Hill of the Dead (1 km), White Mountain Eco Lodge (16 km) & Mersa Matrouh (300 km)

SIWA TOWN

N

Bus Station

Mother & Child Hospital

Hassan's Handicrafts and English Bookshop

Police

Pharmacy

Traditional Siwan House

Mosque of Sidi Suleyman

Town Council

RUINS OF SHALI

Covered passage

Oil press

Market

Pharmacy

Siwa Net

EATING & DRINKING

Abdou's	D
Alexander Restaurant	B
Dunes Restaurant	E
East–West Restaurant	C
New Sun Restaurant	A

ACCOMMODATION

Alexander Hotel	2
Arous al-Waha Hotel	1
Cleopatra Hotel	8
Palm Trees Hotel	6
Shali Lodge (& Kenouz Restaurant)	5
Shally Hotel	7
Siwa Inn	9
Siwa Safari Paradise Hotel	3
Youssef Hotel	4

Military Intelligence

Carpet Factory

Olympic Stadium & Pool

Military Intelligence

MILITARY ZONE

Radio masts

MILITARY ZONE

Fatnis Island (6 km)

Aghurmi (3.8 km) & Cleopatra Bath (5 km)

Jebel Dakhrour (6 km)

0   100 m

Desert Rose Hotel (3 km) & Bir Wahed (15 km)

have moved into breeze-block houses or low-rise flats, forsaking their traditional mud-brick dwellings – just as their ancestors had previously abandoned the fortified hilltop city of **Shali**, whose ruins overlook the modern town. A triumphal arch and broad roads debouch onto a central market area, but the town slips away into a maze of alleyways, and loses itself amidst the encircling palms. Boys driving donkey carts transport fodder and decorously wrapped Siwan women, and the braying of donkeys resounds from every quarter of town. After dark, a thousand stars emerge and Siwa's isolation from the world beyond the Great Sand Sea becomes almost palpable.

Arrival and information

Entering town from the north, Siwa's tourist office (daily except Fri 9am–2pm; in summer also Fri 6–8pm; ℡ & ℻046/460 2338, mobile 0105 461992, ℮mahdi_hweiti@yahoo.com) is directly opposite the flesh-pink Mother and Child Hospital, and close to the bus station. The office is personified by Mahdi Hweiti, a native Siwan and English-speaking sociology graduate of Alexandria University. He knows everything about the oasis and can arrange trips to outlying villages. Should you have any trouble in Siwa, go to him rather than the police. The Siwans rely on nine tribal sheikhs to resolve their disputes; nobody wants the law involved. In the afternoon, Mahdi can be found at Hassan's Handicrafts and English Bookshop (which sells copies of Fakhry's classic *Siwa Oasis*) or at home (℡046/460 2130).

Mahdi can arrange **tours** to Maraki, and advise on prices for other excursions, run by a diverse bunch of **safari operators**, such as Salah at the *Palm Trees Hotel*, Tiger Safari at the *Alexander Hotel*, Abu Bakr at the *East West Restaurant* or Abdullah Baghi at the Siwa Original Handicrafts shop. As tours are much the same but prices vary, it pays to shop around. More details are given under specific destinations, on pp.573–577.

Aside from a bank, Siwa has all the basic facilities. There are two **pharmacies** in the centre and a fairly grungy **hospital** on the outskirts. The police (℡046/460 2008) share a building with the **post office** (daily except Fri 8am–2pm), which is quite reliable, and both public (24hr) and private (9am–11.30pm) **telephone exchanges** can make international and local calls, though connections are slow. This also applies to **Internet** access at Siwa Net (℡046/460 2049) beside the *Palm Trees Hotel*, whose owner advises composing on a word processor (£E8/hr) before going online (£E1.50 for three minutes), and also has a **digital camera** for rent. Siwa Net is usually open mid-morning and in the evening.

Siwa's **fuel station** is the only one in the oasis, and the last until Mersa Matrouh or Bahariya Oasis.

Accommodation

Siwa has both low-budget and upmarket **hotels**, including a lakeside "ecolodge" 16km from town. While it's worth reserving ahead if you're fussy about where you stay, the only time it's essential to do so is during Siwan festivals, when tour groups block-book hotels. On the whole, though, it's safe to assume that you'll find a bed. People wanting to stay for a long time can rent furnished **apartments** for £E300 a month, through Mahdi at the tourist office.

Providing you inform the tourist office first, **camping** is allowed throughout the oasis, but since any land that's cultivated or near a water source is sure to belong to somebody, you should ask their permission. Perhaps the best place to camp is Bir Wahed (see p.573) – which has two tents for visitors' use (£E5 per person) – or, if you just want a roof over your head, there are some mud-brick shelters by Jebel Dakhrour. Bring a sleeping bag and bug repellent.

Unless stated otherwise, **breakfast** is not included at hotels. Places out of town are marked on the **map** of Siwa Oasis on p.572.

Alexander 200m from the tourist office ℡046/460 0512, mobile 0124 627553, Ⓕ460 0006. Friendly, simple hotel with clean rooms and fans; get one with a private bath, as the shared ones are tiny. Guests can use the washing machine. ❷

Amun Jebel Dakhrour, 6km outside town (no phone). Grungy rooms and squat toilets; no showers, shops or cafés. Run by a crazy old man and strictly for hermits, but it does have a wonderful view of the oasis. £E5 per person, £E25 with sand bath (burial in baking sand is a noted therapy for rheumatism and arthritis). ❶

Arous al-Waha Opposite the tourist office ℡046/460 2100. A government hotel whose name means "Bride of the Oasis", it has slightly shabby but clean, semi-carpeted rooms with fans, baths and bedside lamps, plus two four-bed suites (£E120). Breakfast is included and there's a pleasant garden. ❸

Cleopatra 200m past the market ℡ & Ⓕ046/460 2148. Range of clean, simple rooms, some with toilet, balcony and fan; those in the quieter "chalet" block have all three (£E45). There's also an a/c suite with TV and fridge (£E113). Bad for mosquitoes. ❷

Desert Rose 3km south of town ℡046/460 1550). This small hotel on the way to Bir Wahed has its own pool and is free of mosquitoes, but you should phone ahead to avoid a wasted journey. It takes an hour to walk there, past the stadium and into the fields; look out for the building with prancing horses on its roof, off to the left. ❷

Palm Trees Just off the main square ℡046/460 2304. Popular for its central location and lovely palm garden, this place has basic rooms with fans and cleanish shared facilities (a few have bathrooms). The manager, Salah, speaks excellent English, and it's a good place to meet other travellers. They rent bikes, and there's an Internet place next door. ❶

Shali Lodge 100m off the main square ℡046/460 2399, Ⓕ460 1799, Ⓔinfo@eqi.com.eg. This lovely small hotel is built of kharsif and palm-logs in the traditional oasis style, with rooms surrounding a stone pool that keeps them naturally cool; its rooftop features a palm tree growing out from the middle, and the "gastronomic" Kenouz Restaurant. Easily the

nicest place in town, it was a prototype for the ecolodge (see below). ❻

Shally Below the ruins of Shali ℡046/460 2203. Small, friendly, clean low-budget place; all the rooms have fans, and some have baths, and balconies overlooking Shali – the view from the roof is also superb. Discounts for long stays. ❶

Siwa Inn Beyond the radio masts ℡ & Ⓕ046/460 2285. A rustic-style place run by an Alexandrian couple, 25 minutes' walk from the centre of town. The ten cosy rooms have fans and baths, and overlook a shadeless garden with a bathing spring; there's also satellite TV and a restaurant serving tasty food, including croissants and free-range eggs. ❻

Siwa Safari Paradise 200m off the main square ℡046/460 2289, Ⓕ460 2286. Touristic village of fifty a/c rooms with fridge, bathroom and satellite TV (double £E290), and twenty bungalows with fan, heater, bathroom and TV (£E250) around a large cold spring pool for swimming. Restaurant with traditional Siwan feast once a week. Rates include half-board and are fifteen percent cheaper from mid-May to mid-Sept. ❻

Taghaghen Touristic Island (aka Safety Land) Birket Siwa, 8km from town ℡046/460 0455, mobile 0122 155596, Ⓔh_boshra@hotmail.com. A Bahariya-style campground of thatched chalets on a small island in the salt lake, reached by a causeway. You can get most of the way there by pick-up, but getting back into town could be difficult. ❷

White Mountain (better known as the ecolodge), 16km west of town (reservations through Cairo: ℡02/736 7879, Ⓕ735 5487, Ⓔinfo@eqi.com.eg). An amazing kharsif-built complex at the foot of a mountain, with stunning views over the lake to the edge of the oasis and the Sand Sea beyond, and no phones, TV or electricity to mar its splendid isolation. The simple but lovely rooms are kept naturally cool and lit by candles, and there are several restaurants serving organic food, a 24-hour bar, a large pool and palm garden, and horses to ride – all included in the daily rate of US$200 per person. See p.574 for more about the place. ❾

Youssef On the main square ℡046/460 2162. Noiser than the Palm Trees and without a garden, this budget place has tiny, clean rooms with fans, some with bathrooms and/or balconies, and a fantastic view of town from its rooftop. ❶

The town

The **ruins of Shali**, looming above the centre and floodlit in the evening, are a constant invitation to explore. Until late last century this hermetic labyrinth attained a height of over sixty metres, with many levels of chambers, passages and granaries. Its surreal remains cover the entire saddle of rock below a **mosque**, which is said to have been the last one in Egypt where the muezzin still shouted out the call to prayer without the benefit of a loudspeaker. Down behind the hill around the back of Shali is a donkey-driven **oil-press** that dates back centuries (only used in Dec & Jan). From vantage points in Shali, you can see the whole modern town, its palm groves, the salt lakes and table-top rocks beyond; and providing you don't peer too obviously into the houses below, it's possible to glimpse the Siwans at home. Downstairs, women busy themselves with cooking (cockerels and goats roam the alleys) and childcare; a few mats and painted chests, used for storing the family valuables, constitute the only furniture.

You can get a closer look at home life at the sanitized **Traditional Siwan House** (Mon–Wed & Sun 10am–noon; £E1.50; opened out of hours by arrangement with the tourist office for a minimum of four people). Set up with funds raised by the wife of the Canadian Ambassador, who feared that few such mud-brick dwellings would survive another deluge and the trend towards breeze-block housing, it serves as a museum of traditional dress, jewellery and toys, resembling a handicrafts shop. There are several handicrafts shops in the vicinity of the **market** on the main square, which is busiest on Fridays, when villagers come in to buy and sell. The other focus of life is the **Mosque of Sidi Suleyman**, built by King Fouad next to the whitewashed **tomb** of Siwa's patron sheikh (see box on p.570).

By following the Matrouh road out of town and then bearing right, you'll reach the unmistakable Jebel al-Mawta, or **Hill of the Dead**, also known as the Ridge of the Mummified. Amongst scores of XXVI Dynasty and Ptolemaic tombs reused by the Romans, who cut *loculi* for their own burials, four locked ones still retain murals or inscriptions. A custodian who lives nearby will unlock them if you make your presence known (daily 9am–2pm; admission free but *baksheesh* expected).

In the **Tomb of Si-Amun**, murals depict with great artistry a bearded, Greek-looking merchant and his family worshipping Egyptian deities; unfortunately, they were vandalized by Allied soldiers after the tomb's discovery in 1940, when the Siwans dug into the necropolis to escape air raids and also found the **Tomb of Mesu-Isis**. Another third-century BC creation, this was used for two burials although the decorators never got far beyond the entrance.

Whereas Si-Amun's tomb bespeaks of Cyrenaic influence, the **Tomb of the Crocodile** reflects Siwa's longstanding ties to the Fayoum, where the crocodile cult flourished – with a dash of Hellenistic style in the painting of gazelles nibbling at a tree.

The battered XXVI Dynasty **Tomb of Niperpathot** has a ruined court, side rooms, and a tiny burial chamber covered with red inscriptions, including praise of Niperpathot as "the straightforward one". Here, you can see two Greek **mummies** found at the Hill of the Dead a few years ago, and a once-mummified skull, complete with hair.

Lastly, there's Siwa's new, incongruously pink and empty **Olympic stadium and pool**, built within an army base to the south of town. With seating for 20,000, it could accommodate the entire population of the oasis, but is currently only used by a few army officers, as it awaits its place in Egypt's bid to host the Olympic Games some time in the future. You'll pass it if you take the road out towards the *Desert Rose Hotel* or Bir Wahed.

Crafts

Traditional **crafts** still flourish in the oasis, particularly pottery and basket-making. Embroidery had been declining, but has now revived owing to tourists' liking for dresses, shawls and waistcoats. Most of the work is done at home by women and marketed through informal co-operatives in handicrafts shops. Many women now earn significant sums for this work, belying the stereotype of passive, dependent Siwan womanhood. Other products made mostly by the women include black **robes** with orange or red piping, and embroidered **wedding dresses** embellished with antique coins, shells or beads (for £E250–400); and all kinds of **baskets** woven from palm-fronds. The largest is the *tghara*, used for storing bread, which costs £E100–250 depending on its size. Smaller kinds include the red and green tasselled *nedibash* (from £E10), or platters like the *tarkamt*, traditionally used for serving sweets (£E5–50). Women also mould **pottery** and fire it at home in bread-ovens: robust cooking and storage pots, delicate oil lamps, and a kind of baptismal crucible called the *shamadan en sebaa*. Popular buys include the *adjra*, used for washing hands, and *timjamait*, or incense burners; the smaller ones cost about £E5.

Unlike the gold-loving Egyptians, the Siwans have traditionally preferred **silver jewellery**, which likewise served as bullion assets for a people mistrustful of banks and paper money. The designs are uniquely Siwan, influenced by Berber rather than Egyptian jewellery. Local silversmiths once produced most of it, but in modern times it has largely come from Khan el-Khalili. Today, almost all the antique silver has ended up abroad and locals now prefer to buy gold jewellery from Alexandria, but Siwa Original Handicrafts, next to *Abdou's*, retains a few pieces (which you can't buy), and is one of several places selling modern replicas of traditional designs for £E50–150. Broad silver bracelets and oval rings wrought with geometric designs are the most popular items with visitors, while *Al-Salhat*, with its six pendants hung from silver and coral beads, is the easiest type of necklace to identify. You'll also recognize the *tiyalaqan*, a mass of chains tipped with bells, suspended from huge crescents; and an ornament for the head, consisting of silver hoops and bells suspended from matching chunks of bullion, called a *qasas*. Finally, there's the *aghraw*, a silver collar from which girls used to hang a decorative disc or *adrim*, that was removed on their wedding day – a custom that's no longer practised.

Eating

As the oases go, Siwa is good for eating, with several nice **restaurants** in the palm groves. *Kenouz*, on the rooftop of the *Shali Lodge*, has the fanciest menu, with spicy and sweet-and-sour dishes as well as Egyptian staples, a range of desserts and fruit cocktails; expect a full meal to cost £E25–30. Cheaper al-fresco alternatives include the *New Star*, which does a good beefsteak, and *Dunes*, whose chicken biryani is recommended (though their couscous isn't). At all of these places you can recline on cushions and smoke a *sheesha*. If you don't mind doing without a garden, *Abdou's* is the place for soup, omelettes, *shish tarwook* (chicken marinaded in yogurt and spices) and people-watching. The *East West* (named after the rival clans of Shali) is also okay for breakfast, or you can try *Alexander* for a change of scene. Providing there are customers, all are open till around midnight. Local **shops** are well supplied with canned goods, sweets, juices and bottled water, while fresh bread is available from a hole-in-the-wall bakery. If you're serious about self-catering, the **market** stocks seasonal vegetables, dates and olives galore (which you're allowed to sample to find the recipe you like best).

Siwan festivals and weddings

Siwan festivals represent the most public side of a largely private culture, so it's worth making an effort to attend one. Since many Egyptians enjoy going to them, it is wise to reserve a room well in advance, and get there several days early, as buses to the oasis fill up nearer the time.

The largest and most famous is the **Siayha**, or **Tourism Festival**, which, despite its name, is a genuine event with a long tradition. Some 10,000 Siwans assemble at Jebel Dakhrour for three days of feasting, dancing and relaxation – acting as tourists in their own oasis. A sheikh from Sidi Barrani comes in to bless the feast, and local kids enjoy a school holiday and a truckload of ice cream, sweets and sugar cane. Many non-Siwans and foreigners come too, and are made welcome. *Siayha* always occurs during the period of the full moon in October.

Two other festivals are celebrated by Muslims everywhere: the **Lesser Bairam**, at the end of Ramadan, occasioning festivities similar to those elsewhere in Egypt; and the **Corban Bairam** (Great Feast), which starts earlier in Siwa. The gathering of fuel and salt over the preceding nine days is reckoned to be as much a part of the event as the mass slaughter of sheep after festival prayers on the tenth day of *Zoul Hagga*. The sheep's hide is stewed together with its offal in an earthenware pot; its head and stomach are eaten the next day, when cuts of meat are distributed amongst relatives (new brides especially); and finally, any leftovers are preserved.

The **Moulid of Sidi Suleyman** used to involve Dervishes performing *zikrs* outside his tomb beside the mosque, but is barely observed nowadays. However the Siwans still tell tales about this local saint, whose miraculous powers were manifest even before he was born, for when his pregnant mother craved fish, a pigeon dropped a fully cooked one at her feet. He is also said to have once conjured up a sandstorm to bury an army of Tebu raiders.

Ashura, on the tenth of *Moharram*, was once Siwa's principal feast, and fervently Shi'ite; the Fatimid Shia reached Egypt via the North African oases. Nowadays it's chiefly an event for children, who decorate their homes with palm stalks soaked in olive oil, and fire them at sunset, singing while the town is illuminated by torchlight. Afterwards the children go from house to house exchanging presents.

Weddings

Although you might be invited to join the tea-drinking crowd outside the bride-groom's family house, foreigners rarely witness the intricate ritual of **Siwan weddings**, which used to last a week but now take two or three days. Preceded by reciprocal visits of kinsfolk, and a ritual bath where the removal of an item of jewellery symbolizes her abandonment of maidenhood, the bride is "kidnapped" by her spouse's family, returned, and then delivered wrapped in a sheet. The wedding dress of embroidered shawls and skirts is as flamboyant as the outdoor garb of married women is drab. Nowadays, unmarried girls wear Egyptian fashions rather than Siwan costume, and the usual age of marriage has risen from fourteen to sixteen years (the national average) since the mid-1980s.

Traditionally, a Siwan widow commanded the same *mahr* (dowry) as a virgin since both were "daughters of the forty ancestors", but could only remarry after one year of bereavement. Cruelly, the Siwans regarded newly bereaved widows as "devourers of the soul" (*ghulah*), and forced them to spend forty days in solitary confinement before they were "cleansed" – a taboo now largely lapsed.

Moving on from Siwa

Buses leave from a depot near the tourist office, where you should buy tickets the night before to be sure of getting a seat on the morning services (although standing passengers are seldom turned away). There are two daily to **Alexandria** (9hr; £E27), leaving at 7am and 10am. Both call at **Mersa Matrouh** (4–5hr; £E12), while a third bus, leaving Siwa at 1pm, terminates there. Additionally, there is usually a **minivan** to Matrouh in the afternoon, leaving from Sidi Suleyman's mosque.

The **road to Bahariya Oasis** (420km) gives fabulous views of dunes and scarps and allows travellers to reach the four oases on the Great Desert Circuit directly from Siwa, without having to return to Cairo first – but far fewer people use it than you'd imagine. The road is bad all the way, with no facilities, only army checkpoints. If nothing goes amiss, a jeep can make the journey in eight or nine hours. Crossing in a regular car may be possible, but is not advisable as the road is very bumpy and frequently covered in sand. Traffic is very rare, so a breakdown can leave you stranded for days. While motorists might still be game, tourists without a car are often deterred by the **price**; around £E700 by jeep. Finding other travellers to split the cost involves a trade-off; more passengers means greater discomfort but less expense.

Getting a group together could take a few days, depending on how many foreigners are in Siwa. Check with Mahdi at the tourist office that the following procedure still applies: take a photocopy of your passport to the nearer of the two Military Intelligence offices in the morning, pay £E10.50 per person, and collect your permit later the same day. For those with their own 4WD, the **formalities** are simple: just register your passport and licence number with the police in Siwa before you leave. The turn-off for Bahariya is 6km north of town on the right-hand side of the Mersa Matrouh road.

With your own 4WD you can visit four uninhabited **oases** along the way, which are described on p.576.

Around Siwa Oasis

Although the **Siwa Oasis** depression is some 82km long and up to 28km wide, cultivated areas amount to less than 2000 acres and the total population is only 20,000; in some areas both population and cultivation have diminished since salination turned ancient gardens into barren *karshif*. Nearer town, dense **palm groves** and wiry olive trees are carefully tended in mud- and palm-leaf-walled gardens: dates and olives are the chief crops. Siwa has as many as 80,000 olive trees and over 310,000 palm trees, of which around 23,000 are male palms, valued only for the white heart at the top of the tree, a local delicacy.

Palms form the backdrop to most places that you're likely to go, especially the **pools** or **baths**, which for many visitors are the highlight of the oasis. The nearer sites can be reached by bicycle, donkey *caretta* or on foot; just time your visit to avoid travelling in the hottest part of day. **Bicycles** can be rented from Hassan's Handcrafts or places near the *Youssef* and *Palm Trees* hotels, for £E5 a day. *East West Restaurant* offers bikes for the same price, or £E25 with a guide for the day. Test bikes out before embarking on a long ride.

Should you be invited to visit **private springs and gardens**, it's wise to consider your would-be host's motives before accepting. Financial designs aren't necessarily a deterrent – it's quite acceptable to pay for a good time –

but lecherous intentions are something else: women without male escorts should definitely be wary.

Aghurmi and Jebel Dakhrour

For this excursion it's best to hire a *caretta* for the return journey to Dakhrour (£E15), as it's too tiring to walk that far in the heat, and having a guide means there's no risk of getting lost – not that you can go far astray on the road that begins at Siwa's main square and runs through the palm groves for 4km (a nice hour's walk if you're not going much further). Keep going straight on past the crossroads and the modern village of **AGHURMI** appears shortly before the hill where the ancient Siwans built their first fortified settlement. Raised 12m above the plain and entered by a single gateway, Aghurmi had its own deep well (to the left, inside), making it impervious to sieges. The ruins are signposted as the "Alexander Crowning Hall", for it was here that the **Siwan Oracle** reposed in antiquity. Though some German architects have been criticized for crudely restoring the **temple** with concrete, it's no longer in danger of collapse and you can go inside again. There's a fabulous **view**, encompassing two salt lakes, Dakhrour and Siwa Town in the distance, and a great mass of palms.

Fakhry dates the existing temple to the reign of Amasis the Drunkard (570–526 BC) but reckons it evolved from a seventh- or eighth-century BC site dedicated to Amun-Re. Though others have attributed the primal shrine to the ram-headed Libyan god Ammon, experts agree that the **Oracle of Amun** was renowned from the XXVI Dynasty onwards.

Its history is subsequently much documented: a Persian army sent to destroy it was obliterated by the desert; emissaries sent by Cimon of Athens were told of his death as it happened; assured of success by the oracle, Eubotas of Cyrenaica took his own victory statue to the 93rd Olympiad; and Lysander tried bribery to win the oracle's endorsement of his claim to the Spartan throne.

But the most famous petitioner was **Alexander the Great**. Having liberated Egypt from its hated Persian rulers and ordered the creation of a city on the Mediterranean, Alexander hurried to Siwa in the spring of 331 BC. It's thought that he sought confirmation that he was the son of Zeus (whom the Greeks identified with Amun), but the oracle's reply – whispered by a priest through an aperture in the wall of the sanctuary – is unrecorded. Alexander kept it secret unto his death in Asia eight years later. Despite his personal wish to be buried near the oracle, he was probably interred in Alexandria, the capital he never saw – though two Greeks do claim to have found his tomb in Siwa (see p.574).

On to Jebel Dakhrour

From the ruins of Aghurmi you can gaze across thickets of palms to a cream-coloured pillar – part of a **ruined Temple of Amun** viewed side-on. To get there, continue along the road and take the signed turn to "Umm Ubayda". A painted bas-reliefed wall and giant blocks of rubble are all that remain of this once-substantial XXX Dynasty creation after it was dynamited by a treasure-hunting governor in 1897. Locally known as *Umm Ubaydah*, it was probably founded by Nectanebo II (360–343 BC), who also rebuilt the Temple of Hibis at Kharga Oasis.

Follow the path on to reach Ain Juba, known to tourists as the **Cleopatra Bath**, a deep pool of gently bubbling spring water, where local men bathe. Being fully visible to anyone passing along the trail, it is not often a place where women can comfortably swim, although Siwan brides used to do so before ritual ablutions were moved to the **Tamusi Bath**, secluded 150m back along the path. Nowadays, the nuptial couple arrive by car, drive around the pool and away, without bathing at all. There is also a café and toilet near the spring.

Heading on from the Cleopatra Bath, bear left at the fork and take the first path on the right. A ten-minute walk through clover fields and groves of palms will bring you out in the desert near **Jebel Dakhrour**. This rugged massif is the site for the *Siyaha* **festival** in October, and affords stunning **views** from its summit. In contrast to the verdant oasis and the silvery salt lake, the southern horizon presents a desolate vista of crescent dunes and blackened mesas: the edge of the Great Sand Sea. The **hot sand** at Dakhrour is efficacious for rheumatic conditions, so sufferers come here to be buried up to their necks during the summer months, and there is talk of building a clinic.

To get back from Dakhrour, follow the first dirt road you come to, which enters the centre of town by the *Palm Trees Hotel*. It's about half an hour's walk.

Bir Wahed

One of the best excursions Siwa can offer is a trip into the outer dunes of the Great Sand Sea, to **Bir Wahed** (Well One). Despite its prosaic name it's a magical spot: a **hot pool** the size of a large Jacuzzi, into which sulphurous water gushes; the run-off irrigates a garden around the pool. To soak up to your chest, puffing a *sheesha*, while the sun sets over the dunes and mesas all around, is a fantastic experience. Only its custodian and the odd jeep driver are present, so women may wear one-piece bathing costumes without causing a stir. You can climb outcrops or hunt for **fossils** in the vicinity, while on the way there or back you can plunge into a deep, jade-green **cold pool**, or sand-surf or roll down the sides of huge knife-edged **dunes**. Bir Wahed is roughly 12km southwest of town, so most visitors get there on 4WD **excursions** organized by the *Palm Trees* or *Alexander* hotels or the guys that hang out at *Abdou's*, for £E40–60 per person (£E85 for an **overnight** trip). However, if it's not too hot and you carry at least four litres of water, it's possible to **walk** there from town in four hours, following the road out past the Olympic stadium and the *Desert Rose Hotel*, and then the jeep tracks into the dunes. You can sleep in a **tent** (£E5) and buy water, *fuul* and feta cheese at Bir Wahed, but anyone considering staying more than one night should bring supplies from town.

Fatnis Island, Birket Siwa and the ecolodge

The most popular excursion is to "Fantasy" or **Fatnis Island**, on the salt lake of Birket Siwa, 6km west of town. An easy bike ride, it can also be reached by *caretta* (£E10 in time for sunset; £E15 for a longer stay) or on foot (1hr). Take the road out past the town council and take the left-hand road at the first fork; there's a signpost at the next intersection that might cause confusion. En route you'll pass the Abu Alif Bath, where farmhands wash; beyond the palm groves, follow a causeway across salt-encrusted pans onto Fatnis Island, where palms surround a large, circular, tiled **pool**, fed by fresh water welling up from clefts in the rock 15m below. There's a small café selling tea and *sheeshas*, and chairs for sitting and watching the sunset, at which time tourists are joined by off-duty soldiers. Women are advised to bathe earlier and wear a long T-shirt.

It's not hard to envisage a time when Fatnis will no longer be an island, for the **Birket Siwa** is receding as it becomes ever more saline, forming a thick crust that blackens the surrounding vegetation. Yet despite its faintly acrid smell the lake is extremely beautiful, with sculpted table-tops on the western horizon. The largest is **Jebel Beida** – the White Mountain – which the Siwans call in their own language *Adrar al-Milal*, and the Egyptians know as Sidi Jaffar.

On the far side of the mountain is the extraordinary **ecolodge** (see p.567 for booking details), a vast, fantasy *qasr*-style hotel entirely built of *kharsif*, palm logs and translucent salt slabs (used instead of glass). The brainchild of environmental engineer Mounir Nematalla, the ecolodge uses local materials wherever possible, down to olive wood and palm fibres for the furniture; and is designed to save energy and water, and recycle waste products on its organic farm. Since it often has no guests at all, they don't mind the occasional visitor looking around, providing you get permission from the *Shali Lodge* in town first. The ecolodge is reached by a spur road off the lakeside route to Maraki, which turns off the Matrouh highway 1km north of town. It's rather far to cycle (16km) so you'll need to take a car (£E10–20 return). You could probably include it as a stopover on excursions to Balad el-Rum (see below).

Maraki and "Alexander's Tomb"

MARAKI is the collective name for several **villages** at the western end of the depression, separated from the main oasis by a rocky desert riddled with caves and tombs. The area was populous and intensively cultivated from Roman times until the fifteenth century, but is now mostly used for grazing by the **Bedouin** Al-Shihaybat tribe, which has settled at Bahaj al-Din. Most buildings are quite new as the old settlements were destroyed by the deluge of 1982, which forced residents to shelter in caves at Balad el-Rum.

In 1991, Maraki made news when Liana and Manos Souvaltzi announced their discovery of the "**Tomb of Alexander the Great**" beneath a ruined **Doric temple** near the village of **BALAD EL-RUM** (Town of the Romans). The Antiquities Council endorsed their claim, but backed off after the Souvaltzis failed to refute criticism that they had misread vital inscriptions. They now claim that the tomb belonged to a Macedonian VIP and *may* shed light on the whereabouts of Alexander's tomb, which they still believe is in Siwa Oasis. Most scholars agree, however, that he was buried somewhere in Alexandria, though exactly where, and whether his body was destroyed by the Romans, is still debated.

The temple is guarded while excavations continue, and casual visitors are excluded – not that there's much to see above ground except for the lower courses of the walls and some blocks carved with rosettes. If you're interested in the excavations, talk to Mahdi at the Siwa Town tourist office, who knows when work is in progress and can arrange a visit to the site. An **excursion** to the tomb and surrounding villages costs £E30 (group rate). You could also get there by pick-up from outside the tourist office (£E2). The temple is easy to reach, being at the far end of the village, on the left side of the road before the water tower. If you're **driving** from Siwa, turn left off the Matrouh road 1km north of town and keep going.

At Bahaj al-Din a track runs off to **Girba Oasis**, occupied by the Bedouin settlement of **Shiatta** and a detachment of soldiers. In olden times this was the *Masrab el-Ikhwan* (Road of the Brotherhood) from Jaghbub Oasis in Libya, whereby Senussi preachers reached the Western Desert oases. (*Masrab* is the Siwan word for a camel route, called a *darb* in other oases.) Today the soldiers try to catch **smugglers** of hashish, videos, petrol or cloth; the punishment for capture is summary execution. Another hazard is the **minefields** along the Libyan border, sown by the British and Italians soon after they defined it in 1938, and by the Egyptians and Libyans since the 1970s. All this area is **off limits** to foreigners.

Around Birket Zeitun

The largest salt lake in the oasis, **Birket Zeitun** is visible from Aghurmi and Jebel Dakhrour. Only the far shore is inhabited, with villages that flourished in Roman times before centuries of slow decline set in. The lake's increasing salinity is both the cause and result of depopulation: as fewer irrigation works are maintained, more of the fresh water from the **Ain Qurayshat** spring flows unused into the lake, crystallizing mineral salts as it evaporates. The source is enclosed by a pool where you can bathe.

Near the spring are two ancient **ruins**, roughly 100m apart: a heap of rubble, which still constituted a temple during Steindorff's visit in 1900; and the remains of a brick building attributed as "the abode of King Ghashsham" by the *Siwan Manuscript*. Though Siwans still dig round about, in the hope of finding loot, Ain Qurayshat is better for bathing than antiquities.

The best of the **bathing** is around 35km southwest of Siwa Town at **ABU SHUROUF**, where there's a large, deep, clear pool with bug-eyed fishes swimming about, opposite the Hayat mineral water bottling plant. Just before this you'll see the ruins of a small stone **temple**; the village, beyond the pool, is remarkable for harbouring all the female **donkeys** in the oasis, which are kept and mated here. In Siwan parlance, "Have you been to Abu Shurouf?" is a euphemism for "Have you had sex?"

Further south along the lake, the village of **AL-ZEITUN** was once a model Senussi community tending the richest gardens in the oasis, until it was abandoned following an Italian bombing raid in 1940. At the heart of the ruins is an ancient kiosk-**temple**, where the locals sheltered from the bombs. Two kilometres further on, the hillside is pockmarked with the eerie **Roman tombs** of **Abu Awaf**, overlooking the last **checkpoint** in the oasis before the *Darb Siwa* to Bahariya Oasis enters the deep desert (see below).

Qara Oasis and the Qattara Depression

If you have the means and are seriously into desert travel, **Qara Oasis** has a compelling fascination. The smallest and poorest of the inhabited oases, it has been described as "Siwa yesterday". Visitors are so rare that the villagers turn out to welcome them and serve a meal in their honour. Until flooding rendered it unsafe in 1982, the Qarawis occupied a Shali-like labyrinth atop "a solitary white mushroom of rock", edged by a "high smooth wall, impregnable to

Checkpoint Charlies

Travelling from Siwa to Bahariya or on other roads across the most desolate tracts of the Western Desert, spare a thought for the luckless **soldiers** at the **checkpoints**, marooned there for forty days at a stretch, with only each other and a pet cat or dog for company. Young conscripts, far from home and unused to the rigors of desert life, they are utterly bored and welcome any diversion that passing travellers can offer. They're not seeking *baksheesh*, but certainly appreciate Arabic newspapers or magazines (available in Cairo, Alex or Matrouh but not in Siwa or Bahariya), fresh fruit or candy – and such **gifts** will smooth your way through the inevitable licence- and permit-checks. Remember, these guys are here to ensure that if a car breaks down in the desert its passengers will be missed and a search launched – so it's only fair to look out for them, too.

raiders, with one black tunnel for a street". Now, most families live in new houses on the plain. According to legend, the Qarawis once made a pact (or were cursed) that their population would never exceed 317; whenever a child was born an older person would die in the night. It's thought that Alexander the Great paused here on his return journey from Siwa to Memphis.

The shortest **route** from Siwa to Qara is via the *Masrab Khidda* (125km), but its rough terrain and featureless mud flats make it essential to have someone who knows the way. Alternatively, you can head north towards Matrouh and turn off at the checkpoint just before the Bir Nous resthouse, on to a dirt road to Qara. Though not a regular destination for **safaris**, Fathy at the *Alexander Hotel* will take you there and back for £E300–400 (group rate).

Northeast of Qara the land plummets into the **Qattara Depression**, which is seven times the size of all the Western Desert oases combined and may be the largest depression in the world. At 60–134 metres below sea level, it is one of the lowest places on earth, and the lowest point in Africa. Ever since Dr Ball first proposed it in the 1920s, Egyptian planners have dreamed of piping water 38km from the Mediterranean to the depression, utilizing the fall in height to generate hydroelectricity, and run desalination plants and irrigation systems. But all attempts have foundered through lack of capital, and nothing seems likely to happen in the future. There is, however, exploration for **oil** at many points in the desert between Qattara and Mersa Matrouh, which explains the upgraded tracks that crisscross the wilderness. With a permit, even 2WDs can use the **El-Alamein–Bahariya desert road** (273km) that dips into the depression at **Naqb Abu Dweis** (**mined** on both sides of the wadi; don't leave the road), and carries on past a series of checkpoints and turn-offs to drilling facilities, before joining the Cairo–Bahariya highway. While crossing the depression, it passes the uninhabited **Maghra Oasis**, where Jurassic **fossils** of mastadons, reptiles, fish and mammals have been found; petrified wood lies around, and there's a salt lake.

From Siwa to Bahariya: Areg, Bahrein, Nuwamisa and Sitra oases

The ancient *Darb Siwa* caravan route from Siwa to Bahariya hardly merits the name of a **road**, since the asphalt is so degraded and often covered by sand drifts in the aftermath of storms. Traffic may be limited to one or two vehicles every few days in the winter and nothing at all for weeks during the summer, so you would be mad to ask to be dropped off somewhere in the hope of hitching a ride the rest of the way. Six **checkpoints** en route provide assurance that vehicles which break down will be missed, but otherwise there are no sources of water, nor any fuel for 420km.

While safari operators in Siwa and Bahariya charge £E700–900 for a 4WD-load of passengers to travel from one to the other, it's important to stress that they all pass by the uninhabited oases off the road, stopping at which would redeem an otherwise dull and uncomfortable journey. The trip takes at least seven hours if you don't stop, while detours to the oases can make it last nine hours even if you don't camp overnight. Their beauty is best appreciated on camel treks out of Bahariya (see p.520), but anyone with a 4WD at their disposal can see something of each oasis. Tiger Safari in Siwa runs an overnight excursion to Bahrein (returning to Siwa) for £E100 per person.

Areg Oasis lies 1km off the road, about 175km from Siwa, girdled by an escarpment which 4WDs should only descend with caution and in pairs, though it's easy to scramble down on foot, providing you avoid the brittle overhangs of the cliffs that ring the depression. The eroded floor resembles shredded cloth, surrounded by striated buff and white chalk buttes looking like giant brioches that have sat in the oven for too long. The oasis was regarded as a haunt of bandits by nineteenth-century travellers and its cliffs are riddled with **tombs**, but no trace of a settlement has ever been found, raising the question of why the ancients should have gone to the trouble of burying their dead in such a remote location.

Bahrein Oasis lurks off the other side of the road, down a track from the third checkpoint. Just as you're wondering why you bothered to cross this dull stretch of desert, the oasis appears in all its glory. Named after its two azure salt lakes, Bahrein is awash with custard-coloured sand, hemmed in by giant crois-sant-like buttes, riddled with **tombs** whose *loculi* date them from Greco-Roman times, where you can still find bones. Seductive as they look, the **salt lakes** are surrounded by mushy sand and salt crusts that can trap unwary vehicles, and if safari groups camp here, they usually do so in the palm groves on the far side, away from the mosquitoes and protected from sandstorms.

Nuwamisa Oasis is equally lovely, with a salt lake rimmed by palms and crescent cliffs – but its name, Oasis of the Mosquitoes, is all too true. Literally millions of **mosquitoes** swarm as soon as the sun goes down, making camping a nightmare, even if you're all zipped up in your tent. For that reason, trav-ellers often hasten on to **Sitra Oasis**, which isn't so badly infested and used to be a watering hole for Bedouin smugglers bringing hashish into Egypt. During the last 45km of the journey to Bahariya the road skirts the **Ghard Kebir** (Great Dunes), whose sandy crests were likened by Bagnold to "unclipped horses' manes". The dunes are slowly making their way south from the Qattara Depression, destined to arrive in Bahariya in a few hundred years.

Alexandria and the Mediterranean coast

Highlights

✳ **Fresh seafood** Alexandria is famous for its seafood restaurants, where customers select their meal from a mound of fish and crustaceans. See p.609

✳ **Coffee houses and patisseries** *The Trianon*, *Athineos* and *Pastroudis* have an old-world charm and many literary associations. See p.609

✳ **Diving** Explore the underwater remains of Cleopatra's Palace, Roman galleys and French warships. See p.613

✳ **Catacombs of Kom es-Shoqafa** This eerie subterranean Roman necropolis is full of bizarre carvings, with a dining room for mourners. See p.603

✳ **Bibliotheca Alexandrina** The city's new Library is a stunning example of contemporary architecture, aimed at reviving the legendary "Mother Library" of antiquity. See p.601

✳ **El-Alamein** The war museum and cemeteries are stark reminders of the decisive battle in 1942, and the hinterland harbours wrecked tanks and an abandoned field hospital. See p.621

✳ **Agiiba Beach** The loveliest and easiest to reach of the beaches around Mersa Matrouh. See p.629

4

Alexandria and the Mediterranean coast

For ancient Egyptians, the **Mediterranean coast** marked the edge of the "Great Green", the measureless sea that formed the limits of the known world. Life and civilization meant the Nile Valley and the Delta – an outlook that still seems to linger in the country's subconscious. For, despite the white beaches, craggy headlands and turquoise sea that stretch for some five hundred kilometres, much of the Egyptian Med is eerily vacant and underpopulated.

Anywhere on the European side of the sea, mass tourism would have taken hold years ago. Here, though, in part due to a lack of freshwater sources, towns are few and generally small, and far outnumbered by military bases. Such tourism as exists is largely domestic and overwhelmingly male; there is virtually no alcohol on sale and standards of dress verge on the puritanical. Foreign women, especially, could well find that the hassles far outweigh any pleasure to be gained here – in contrast to the much more relaxed beaches in the Sinai. The best resorts are **Mersa Matrouh** (a jumping-off point for Siwa Oasis) and **Sidi Abd el-Rahman**, while historical interest focuses chiefly on the World War II battlefield of **El-Alamein**.

Alexandria, however, is an entirely different animal. Egypt's second city feels as Mediterranean and cosmopolitan as Athens or Marseille, its nineteenth-century architecture redolent of the colonial days immortalized by E.M. Forster, the poet Cavafy and, most famously, Lawrence Durrell. But its sights belong to an earlier age, when it was the capital of Greco-Roman Egypt, and the seat of Cleopatra, the last of the Ptolemies.

Finally, a word about the **weather**: Egypt's Med coast gets hotter and drier the further west you travel, but Alexandria can be cold and windy in the winter, with torrential downpours and waves crashing over the Corniche for days on end. And should you happen to be there over New Year, beware of the blizzard of crockery that Alexandrians throw out of their windows at midnight.

Alexandria (El-Iskandariya)

Alexandria, princess and whore. The royal city and the anus mundi.

Lawrence Durrell, *The Alexandria Quartet*

ALEXANDRIA turns its back on the rest of Egypt and faces the Mediterranean, as if contemplating its glorious past; a hybrid city characterized by Durrell as the "Capital of Memory". One of the great cities of antiquity, Alex slumbered for 1300 years until it was revived by Mohammed Ali and transformed by Europeans, who gave the city its present shape and made it synonymous with cosmopolitanism and decadence. This era came to an end in the 1950s with the mass flight of non-Egyptians and a dose of revolutionary puritanism, but Alexandria's beaches, restaurants and breezy climate still attract hordes of Cairenes during the summer, while its jaded historical and literary mystique remains appealing to foreigners.

Alexandria in history

When **Alexander the Great** wrested Egypt from the Persian empire in 332 BC at the age of twenty-five, he decided against Memphis, the ancient capital, in favour of building a new city linked by sea to his Macedonian homeland. Choosing a site near the fishing village of **Rhakotis**, where two limestone spurs formed a natural harbour, he gave orders to his architect, Deinocrates, before travelling on to Siwa and thence to Asia, where he died eight years later. His corpse was subsequently returned to Egypt, where the priests refused burial at Memphis; its final resting place remains a mystery, although most archeologists believe it lies somewhere beneath Alexandria.

Thereafter Alexander's empire was divided amongst his Macedonian generals, one of whom took Egypt and adopted the title **Ptolemy I Soter**, founding a dynasty (323–30 BC). Avid promoters of Hellenistic culture, the **Ptolemies** made Alexandria an intellectual powerhouse: among its scholars were Euclid, the "father of geometry", and Eratosthenes, who accurately determined the circumference and diameter of the earth. Alexandria's great lighthouse, the

Pharos, was literally and metaphorically a beacon, rivalled in fame only by the city's library – the **Bibliotheca Alexandrina** – the foremost centre of learning in the ancient world.

While the first three Ptolemies were energetic and enlightened, the latter members of the dynasty are remembered as decadent and dissolute – perhaps due to their brother-sister marriages, in emulation of the pharaohs and gods of ancient Egypt – and relied on Rome to maintain their position. Even the bold **Cleopatra VII** (51–30 BC) came unstuck after her lover, Julius Caesar, was murdered, and his successor in Rome (and her bed), Mark Antony, was defeated by Octavian. The latter hated her and so detested Cleopatra's capital at Alexandria that he banned Roman citizens from entering Egypt on the pretext that its religious orgies were morally corrupting.

Roman rule and Arab conquest

Whereas Alexandria's Egyptians and Greeks had previously respected one another's deities and even syncretized them into a common cult (the worship of Serapis), religious conflicts developed under **Roman rule** (30 BC–313 AD). The empire regarded Christianity, which was supposedly introduced by St Mark in 45 AD, as subversive, and the persecution of Christians from 250 AD onwards reached a bloody apogee under Emperor Diocletian, when the Copts maintain that 144,000 believers were martyred. (The Coptic Church dates its chronology from 284 AD, the "Era of Martyrs", rather than Christ's birth.)

After the emperor Constantine made **Christianity** the state religion, a new controversy arose over the nature of Christ, the theological subtleties of which essentially masked a political rebellion by Egyptian **Copts** against Byzantine (ie Greek) authority. In Alexandria, the Coptic patriarch became supreme and his monks waged war against paganism, sacking the Serapis Temple and library in 391 AD, and murdering the female scholar Hypatia in 415.

Local hatred of Byzantium disposed the Alexandrians to welcome the **Arab conquest** (641 AD), whose commander, Amr, described the city as containing "4000 palaces, 4000 baths, 400 theatres, 1200 greengrocers and 40,000 Jews". But while the Arabs incorporated elements of Alexandrian learning into their own civilization, they cared little for a city which "seemed to them idolatrous and foolish", preferring to found a new capital at Fustat (now part of Cairo).

Owing to neglect and the silting up of the waterways that connected it to the Nile, Alexandria inexorably declined over the next millennium, so that when Napoleon's expeditionary force arrived in 1798, they found a mere fishing village with four thousand inhabitants.

Mohammed Ali and colonial rule

Alexandria's **revival** sprang from the sultan Mohammed Ali's desire to make Egypt a commercial and maritime power, which necessitated a seaport. The Mahmudiya Canal, finished in 1820, once again linked Alexandria to the Nile, while a harbour, docks and arsenal were created with French assistance. European merchants erected mansions and warehouses, building outwards from the Place des Consuls (modern-day Midan Tahrir), and the city's population soared to 230,000.

Nationalist resentment of foreign influence fired the **Orabi revolt** of 1882, in retaliation for which British warships shelled the city, whose devastation was completed by arsonists and looters. Yet such was Alexandria's vitality and commercial importance that it quickly recovered.

Having survived bombing during World War II, Alexandria experienced new turmoil in the post war era, as anti-British riots expressed rising **nationalism**. The **revolution** that forced King Farouk to sail into exile from Alexandria in 1952 didn't seriously affect the "foreign" community (many of whom had lived here for generations) until the Anglo-French-Israeli assault on Egypt during the Suez Crisis of 1956. The following year, however, Nasser expelled all French and British citizens and nationalized foreign businesses, forcing a hundred thousand non-Egyptians to emigrate. Jewish residents also suffered after the discovery of an Israeli-controlled sabotage unit in the city, so that by the year's end only a few thousand Alexandrian Greeks and Jews remained. Foreign institutions, street names and suchlike were Egyptianized, and the custom of moving the seat of government to Alexandria during the hot summer months was ended.

Contemporary Alex – and the city in literature

Though "old" Alexandrians undoubtedly regret the **changes** since Suez, Durrell's complaint that they produced "leaden uniformity" and rendered Alexandria "depressing beyond endurance" seems jaundiced and unjustified. Egypt's second city (pop. 5,000,000) has become more Egyptian and less patrician, but it doesn't lack contrasts and vitality (except by comparison with Cairo). The difference is that middle-class Egyptians set the tone, not Greeks, Levantines and European expats. If Cavafy, *arak* and child-brothels represented the old days, McDonald's, Coke and Nike symbolize a new and brasher kind of cosmopolitanism. Overcrowding, pollution and traffic have all worsened, but – unlike pressure-cooker Cairo – the Med still keeps Alex cool.

With few monuments to show for its ancient lineage and much of its modern heritage rejected, one seeks Alexandria's past in institutions like the *Pastroudis* café; minutiae such as old nameplates; the reminiscences of aged Arabs, Greeks and Jews; and in the **literary dimension**. E.M. Forster's *Alexandria: A History and a Guide* (1922) remains the classic source book, but Forster reckoned that the best thing he did was to publicize the work of Alexandrian-born Constantine Cavafy. Nostalgia, excess, loss and futility – the leitmotifs of Cavafy's poems – also pervade Lawrence Durrell's *The Alexandria Quartet*: indeed, Durrell used Cavafy as the basis for his character Balthazar. Generally, though, Durrell had little time for Egyptians, and his novels are not well-regarded in Egypt. Bearing in mind the ancient adage that "a big book is a big nuisance", you might prefer Naguib Mahfouz's *Miramar*, a concise evocation of post-revolutionary Alex from an Egyptian standpoint. For foreign views of Alex, check out Charlie Pye-Smith's *The Other Nile*, Douglas Kennedy's *Beyond the Pyramids*, and Paul William Roberts' *River in the Desert*.

Though travel writers have ignored Alex since the mid-1990s, books on the city's **archeology** and cultural heritage continue to be published. The French archeologist Jean-Yves Empereur of the Centre d'Etudes Alexandrines (Ⓦwww.cea.com.eg) has written two excellent guides to the city's sites and history, *Alexandria Revealed* and *Alexandria Rediscovered*, plus guidebooks to the Greco-Roman Museum and the Catacombs; while the Hungarian Egyptologist Győző Vörös touches on the city's maritime history in his book *Taposiris Magna: Port of Isis*. All these books are available in local bookshops (see p.614) or can be consulted in the library of the Archeological Society of Alexandria, 6 Sharia Mahmoud Mokhtar (Mon–Wed & Sun 4.30–7.30pm; ☏03/486 0650).

Approaches to Alex

Alex is easily reached **from Cairo**, with a choice of train, bus, service taxi or plane. Buses and service taxis offer two routes to Alex, travelling by the verdant Desert Road past the turn-off for Wadi Natrun (whose monasteries are covered in Chapter Three), or by the hazardous, congested Delta Road, which is much slower though the distance is roughly similar (about 225km). Remember that transport can get booked up during "the season" (mid-June to late Sept), so reserve seats unless you're prepared to use service taxis.

The best **buses**, which do the journey in three hours, are operated by the Superjet company from the Turgoman Terminal; you can also buy tickets and board the bus at Abdel Mouneem Riyad beyond the flyover off Midan Tahrir. The fastest **trains**, a/c Spanish and Turbini services, both leave three times daily and take just over two hours. There is also the so-called French service that has nine daily departures, takes forty minutes longer and costs thirty percent less. Service taxis do the run in about three hours, their advantage being that they leave all through the day, as soon as they're full; in Cairo both car- and minibus-taxis cluster outside Ramses Station and at the Aboud Terminal, their drivers bawling "*Iskandariya! Iskandariya!*". For details of bus, train and taxi schedules and terminals, see "Travel Details" at the end of Chapter One (p.281).

Flying from Cairo is expensive and won't save you time either, once you take getting to and from the airports into account. There are also safety concerns about Alex's airports, used by BA, Lufthansa, Air France and Olympic flights **from Europe** (see below).

Getting to Alex **from other parts of Egypt**, buses and/or service taxis are your best bet. Transport from the Delta and the Canal Zone is fairly regular; from the Nile Valley, daily buses run from Beni Suef. See the relevant chapters for details.

Arrival, orientation and information

West Delta and Superjet **buses** drop passengers at the **15th May Station**, in Sidi Gaber, west of downtown; you can reach the centre by bus #1, tram #2 or #4 (25pt), or taxi (£E3–5). Trains from Cairo usually stop at Sidi Gaber Station (north of the bus terminal) before terminating at **Masr Station,** about 1km south of downtown Midan Sa'ad Zaghloul, which you can reach by walking up Sharia Nabi Daniel (10–15min). **Service taxis** are likely to wind up on **Midan el-Gumhorriya**, outside Masr Station, but might terminate at the outlying **Moharrem Bey** depot; from there, catch a minibus to Midan el-Gumhorriya (25pt) or a taxi into the centre (£E5).

Alexandria is currently served by two **airports**, neither of which live up to their "International" status. **Nozha**, 5km south of the city, has such decrepit runways and air-traffic control that some airlines have switched to an ex-military airfield at **Burg al-Arab**, 60km west of Alex, till Nozha is refurbished. Neither has any exchange facilities, ATMs or duty-free shops, so passengers arriving from abroad need to purchase some Egyptian currency beforehand, to pay for getting into town. However, if you're planning to get a **visa** on arrival, this can only be bought with US dollars, pounds sterling or euros. Public **transport** into town is erratic, namely bus #555 from Burg al-Arab to Midan Sa'ad Zaghloul, or minibus #703 from Nozha to Midan Ramleh; a taxi to Alex from Burg al-Arab costs £E50–60; from Nozha £E20–25.

Orientation, maps and street names

Alexandria runs along the Mediterranean for 20km without ever venturing more than 5km inland – a true waterfront city. Its great **Corniche** sweeps around the **Eastern Harbour** and along the coast past a string of city **beaches** to **Montazah** and **Ma'amoura**, burning out before the final beach at **Abu Qir**. (The beaches to the west of Alex are dealt with in the "Mediterranean Coast" account; see p.617.) Away from the beach, visitors hang around the downtown quarter of **El-Manshiya**, where most of the restaurants, hotels and nightclubs are within a few blocks either side, or inland, of **Midan Sa'ad Zaghloul**.

The Corniche (and breezes blowing inland) make basic orientation quite simple, but the finer points can still be awkward. Unlike Cairo, downtown Alex has yet to be properly mapped. The standard Lehnert & Landrock *Map of Alexandria* omits whole streets and blocks, and our **maps** aren't faultless either. **Street names** are also problematic, for signs don't always square with the latest official designation or popular usage (usually one change behind). Other street names have simply been Arabicized: Rue or Place to Sharia or Midan; "Alexandre le Grand" to "Iskander el-Akbar". In the downtown area, most of the nameplates are in French and Arabic, and people may use either variant when giving directions. For areas away from downtown there's a useful map inside *Alexandria Night and Day*, which also shows the locations of the beaches. Bookshops sell a historical map of *Archeological Sites of Alexandria*, published by the Alexandria Preservation Trust.

Information

The main **tourist office** off the southwest corner of Midan Sa'ad Zaghloul (daily 8.30am–6pm, mid-July to mid-Aug to 8pm; Ramadan 9am–4pm; ☎03/485 1556), is staffed by very helpful English-speakers, can provide a free information booklet, *Alexandria Night and Day*, and answer most questions. It has branches at Nozha airport (daily 8am–8pm; ☎03/425 0528), Masr Station (daily 8am–8pm; ☎03/392 5985), Sidi Gaber Station (daily 8.30am–3pm; ☎03/426 3953) and the Maritime Station (daily 8.30am–3pm; ☎03/480 3494). The university and foreign cultural centres are obvious sources of **contacts**; on Thursday nights you'll find half the expat community in the Portuguese Club in Roushdi (see p.611). Of the **websites** related to Alex, ⓦwww.alexandriatour.com has a wide range of practical information and links, and ⓦwww.houseofptolemy.org covers the city's ancient and modern history.

City transport

Downtown is compact enough to walk around, and along the Corniche to Fort Qaitbey makes a healthy constitutional (35–50min). However, you really need transport to reach other outlying areas. The main downtown terminals are **Ramleh**; the square outside Masr Station, **Midan el-Gumhorriya**; and **Midan Khartoum**, to the east of the Greco-Roman Museum. Minibuses running along the Corniche can be boarded from the seafront side of both Midan Orabi and Sa'ad Zaghloul.

Trams, buses and minibuses

Trams are integral to Alex life, conveying all classes at a snail's pace and rattling past the houses of rich and poor alike. Services run from 5.30am to midnight (1am in summer), with fares between 20pt and 25pt. Destinations and route numbers are in Arabic only, but you can get an idea from the vehicle's livery where it's heading, as all trams running east from Ramleh are painted blue, while those going west are yellow and red. More arcane clues lie in the colour of the background to the numeral(s) on the signboard, which identify routes #1 (blue), #2 (red), #3 (blue on yellow), #4 (white on blue), #5 (black on white) and #14 (blue). On trams with three carriages, the middle one is **reserved for women**. Some have double-decker carriages, with a fab view from the top floor. Standing downstairs, you may have difficulty seeing the names of the tram stops, which are written in English on certain routes. All eastbound trams stop at the Sporting Club except for #4, which terminates at Sidi Gaber.

   Buses (keeping similar schedules and likewise numbered in Arabic; 25–50pt) are dirtier and faster, with passengers boarding on the run between Sa'ad Zaghloul, Tahrir and El-Gumhorriya squares – the major terminals. They are often very crowded, and made worse by gropers and pickpockets. Whenever possible, it's best to use another form of transport. Fortunately, **minibuses** offer the chance of a reasonably comfortable ride and cover many of the same routes. Those run by the municipality are blue and white, while privately operated minibuses are blue. Both charge the same fares (50pt–£E2.25) and run similar hours to trams and buses.

Trams

#1 and #2	Ramleh to Victoria, via the Sporting Club and Roushdi
#8	Ramleh to San Stefano, via the Sporting Club
#14	Ramleh to Sharia Moharrem Bey (near the Fine Arts Museum), via Anfushi and Ras el-Tin
#15	Ramleh to Ras el-Tin, via El-Gomruk and El-Anfushi (near Fort Qaitbey)
#16	Midan St Katerina to Bitash
#25	Ras el-Tin to Sidi Gaber, via Ramleh

Buses

#1	Midan Sa'ad Zaghloul to the 15th May bus station/Sidi Gaber train station
#2	Ramleh to Hannoville, via Bitash
#3	Mandara to Hannoville, via Masr Station
#260	Ramleh to Abu Qir, via Sharia Iskandar el-Akhbar and the Corniche
#309 and #709	Ramleh to Pompey's Pillar
#460	Midan Khartoum to Hannoville, via the Corniche

Minibuses

#703	Ramleh to Nozha airport
#735	Ramleh to Montazah, via the Corniche
#736	Ras el-Tin to Ma'amoura, via the Corniche
#728 and #729	Masr Station to Abu Qir
#736	Ramleh to Ma'amoura, via the Corniche
#750	Midan Khartoum to El-Agami (Bitash), via the Corniche
#755	Masr Station to El-Agami (Bitash)
#760	Midan Khartoum to El-Agami (Hannoville), via the Corniche
#765	Masr Station to El-Agami (Hannoville)

Taxis, caleches and car rental

Regular black-and-orange (or yellow) **taxis** seldom use meters and will charge whatever they can get away with (especially going to Masr Station or some other point of departure). You should pay about £E3 for a ride across downtown (say, to Shatby), £E15–20 for a trip to Hannoville or Montazah. The larger, blue Peugeots are a lot pricier than regular taxis, so don't take one by mistake.

Leather-hooded, brass-trimmed **horse-drawn carriages** solicit passengers with cries of "*caleche, caleche*" outside Masr Station and along the Corniche. Providing you don't get stuck in traffic jams or feel self-consciously "colonial", they can be a good way of touring the quieter parts of Alex and enjoying the sea breezes. You'll have to negotiate a price – reckon on roughly £E8–10 an hour.

If you want to **rent a car**, try Avis in the *Hotel Cecil* (daily 8am–8pm; ☏03/485 7400), which offers Toyota Corollas for US$50 per day and 4WD Cherokees for $90. You must be over 25 years old and have an international licence held for at least one year. They can also supply English-speaking drivers at US$15 per (10hr) day. Alternatively, Alex Limousine, 25 Sharia Talaat Harb (☏03/482 5253), rents luxury cars with drivers.

Accommodation

Alexandria's **hotels** run the gamut from old *pensions* to glitzy citadels of *Sheraton*-style internationalism, with something for every visitor's taste and budget. A sea view is a big plus, and hotels charge accordingly – though in cheap hotels these rooms are freezing in wintertime. Two drawbacks that only later become apparent are **tram noise** and giant orange **cockroaches** – the twin banes of hotels near the waterfront. Basically, you either learn to live with them or move further inland. Bear in mind that the choice and availability of rooms is limited during high season (June 15–Sept 15), when **reservations** are advisable. **Price codes** quoted below are for the high season and refer to rooms without a sea view. You can count on hot water, and breakfast being included, unless stated otherwise. The downtown hotels are all keyed to the map on p.592.

Alexandria's **youth hostel** (☏03/592 5459, ℉591 4759) is on a main road opposite St Mark's College in Shatby, 1km east of the downtown area. Take tram #1 or #2 from Ramleh to the College and turn towards the Corniche; the hostel is at 32 Sharia Bur Said, next to some Greco-Roman tombs. It has clean dorms (£E13 per bed) and double and triple rooms, some with fridges. Breakfast is included.

If you're intending to stay a while in Alex, **renting a flat** makes sense. Most expats stay in the Roushdi district, a few kilometres east of the downtown area, where a two-bedroom flat costs £E1200–2000 a month. If you don't mind a longer journey into town, apartments in Hannoville (see p.618) cost about £E500 a month.

Downtown hotels

Acropole 27 Sharia Gamil el-Din Yassin ☎03/480 5980. Highly central and within earshot of trams, this old-fashioned hotel has dusty rooms with sinks, balconies and brass beds; none overlooks the harbour directly, but some have views of Midan Sa'ad Zaghloul. Hot water in only one of the bathrooms, which aren't clean. ②

Cecil 16 Midan Sa'ad Zaghloul ☎03/480 7055, ⓕ485 6555. Dead central, with great views of the Eastern Harbour, the *Cecil* is an Alexandrian institution. Durrell, Churchill, Noël Coward and Somerset Maugham head the list of former guests, but modernization has dispelled the old ambience. Regular rooms are cosy and a/c but nothing special; the corner suites are grander. French and Chinese restaurants, nightclub, *Monty's Bar*, Avis desk and a bank. Same rates year-round. ⑧

Hyde Park 21 Sharia Amin Fikhry, 8th floor ☎03/483 5666. A gone-to-seed *pension* whose business card promises "water inside the room", "beans services 24 hours" and "to lament to inside the Repubic" (whatever that means), but fails to mention the glassed-in balconies that are its only redeeming feature. ①

Leroy 25 Sharia Talaat Harb, 8th floor ☎03/486 9224. Huge, shabby, gloomy Art Deco warren with a few nice rooms on the 9th floor, and distant views of the Eastern Harbour. The bathrooms are clean but lack hot water. No breakfast. ②

Marhaba 10 Midan Orabi ☎ & ⓕ03/480 0957. Louis XIV-style lounges and fancy wallpaper mark this out as the former summer residence of King Idris of Libya. Cosy, clean, carpeted rooms with fans and showers, soap and towels provided. Bar, restaurant, coffee shop, pool table. ③

Metropole 52 Sharia Sa'ad Zaghloul ☎03/486 1465, ⓕ406 2040, ⓔresamet@paradiseinnegypt .com. Centrally located on the corner of Midan Ramleh, this wonderfully ornate 1900s hotel has been refurbished to four-star standards. All rooms a/c with fancy bathrooms; the suites are furnished with antiques and have Jacuzzis. French restaurant. ⑧

New Hotel Welcome House 28 Sharia Gamil el-Din Yassin, 5th floor ☎03/480 6402. Across the road from the *Acropole*, this aged budget place is marginally better than its sister hotel the **Victoria** on the same floor, and definitely preferable to the **Normandie** (☎03/480 6830) or **Gamil** (☎03/481 5458) on the floor below. Try to get one of the three double rooms facing the harbour, which have their own shower and toilet. The lift may not work. No breakfast. ①

Picadilly 11 Sharia Horriya, 6th floor ☎03/393 4802. This tatty old hotel on the corner of Sharia Nabi Daniel has large, airy rooms, clean sheets, and hot water; a private bathroom costs £E6 extra. No breakfast. The lift may not work. ②

Sea Star 24 Sharia Amin Fikhry ☎03/480 5343, ⓕ487 2388. Far superior to the *Ailema* on the same street, it has clean, carpeted rooms with baths; some have double beds. Restaurant and international phone line. Same rates all year. ③

Triomphe 26 Sharia Gamil el-Din Yassin, 5th floor ☎03/480 7585. Slightly nicer than the *New Hotel Welcome House* next door, this is one of the better budget options on the street, but standards have risen and fallen over the years, so it's worth comparing several places before choosing. No breakfast. ①

Union 164 Sharia 26 Yulyu, 5th floor ☎03/480 7312, ⓕ480 7350. Three blocks along the Corniche from Midan Sa'ad Zaghloul. Bright, clean Art Deco place with friendly staff and a cool lounge facing the Eastern Harbour. Spacious, carpeted rooms with private baths, TV and balconies; the best ones are on the 6th floor. ③

Windsor Palace 17 Sharia ash-Shohada ☎03/480 88700, ⓕ480 8439, ⓔresawin@ paradiseinegypt.com. Two blocks west of the *Union*, this delightfully kitsch Edwardian hotel has been refitted by the chain that owns the *Metropole*. Its facilities are only three-star, but its ambience is nice and many of the rooms have great views of the harbour. ⑧

Upmarket hotels at Montazah

If you don't mind being miles from the centre, there are several **upmarket hotels** at **Montazah** (a locality described on p.607).

El Salamlek Palace Montazah Gardens ☎03/547 7999, ⓕ547 3585, ⓔsalamlek@san-giovanni.com, ⓦwww.sangiovanni.com. This grandiose pseudo-Alpine chalet was once the residence of the Austrian mistress of Khedive Abbas and is lavishly decorated in period style. Amenities include a private beach, the only casino in Alex (open to non-residents with passports; 9pm–5am), French and Italian restaurants (smart dress required). ❽

Helnan Palestine Near Montazah Beach and Palace ☎03/547 4033, ℉547 3378, ℮resph @helnan.com. Originally built to house Arab leaders attempting to solve the Palestinian problem in 1964, it has been refurbished as a five-star venue for conferences and bridge tournaments. Spacious rooms overlook the palace or a lagoon. Water sports and a small cinema during the summer. Costs around 30 percent less off-season. ❽

Montazah Sheraton Near Montazah Palace ☎03/548 0550, ℉540 1331, ℮smontaza@hot-mail.com. Five-star tower overlooking a busy intersection outside the grounds of the palace. Nightclub, disco, heated pool and tennis court. All rooms with twin or double beds, a/c, minibar and satellite TV. Same rates year-round. ❾

Renaissance Alexandria 544 Tariq el-Geish ☎03/549 0935, ℉549 7690, ℮alexandria@ren-aissance-htl.com.eg. Another five-star tower facing Sidi Bishr beach, 14km from the centre. Swimming pool, cocktail bar, disco, Chinese and Italian restaurants. Check your room for traffic noise. ❽

The city

> I loved the shabbiness of the streets and cafés, the melancholy which hung over the city late of an evening, the slow decay (not destruction, mind you) of what the Europeans had left behind when they fled.
>
> Charlie Pye-Smith, *The Other Nile*

Alex encourages nostalgia trips and random exploration, if only because "the sights" are limited and chance incidents often more revealing. Don't be afraid of following your nose and deviating from the usual itineraries, which could be completed in a day if done at the trot. While the Roman Theatre and the Catacombs of Kom es-Shoqafa are the monumental **highlights** of Alex – whose classical heritage is enshrined in the Greco-Roman Museum – it's the ambience of the former European and "native" quarters that sticks in your mind.

For convenience, these accounts start with the downtown area and work outwards, interweaving the ancient, remembered and existing cities. The **historical map** published by the Alexandria Preservation Trust helps make sense of the ancient city as you walk around, while anyone interested in **archeology** should check out the links on ⓦwww.houseofptolemy.org.

Midan Sa'ad Zaghloul to the Greco-Roman Museum – and back to Ramleh

Since E.M. Forster wrote his guide to Alexandria in 1922, the city's centre has shifted eastwards from the former Place Mohammed Ali (now Midan Tahrir) to the seafront **Midan Sa'ad Zaghloul**, a square named after the nationalist leader (1860–1927) whose **statue** gazes towards the Mediterranean. His deportation by the British to Malta provoked nationwide rioting (1919) and guaranteed Zaghloul a hero's return, though the national independence he sought was denied for another generation. Zaghloul is referred to as "the Pasha" in Naguib Mahfouz's novel, *Miramar*.

With no trace of the Caesareum that stood here in ancient times (see below), the square today looks post-colonial. Decrepit edifices that could have been lifted from Naples or Athens overshadow the **tourist office**. The dominant building is the pseudo-Moorish **Hotel Cecil**, where British Intelligence hatched the El-Alamein deception plan from a suite on the first floor. No longer the decadent and moribund establishment of *The Alexandria Quartet*, it now belongs to the *Sofitel* chain.

A similar mystique used to attend Alexandrian **patisseries**, of which there are three nearby. *Délices*, beneath a red awning, has followed the famous old *Trianon*, on the corner, in installing air conditioning and a doorman. *Athineos*, by Ramleh tram station, used to be the grandest but now has gaping holes in its Art Nouveau decor. All three levy £E3–8 minimum charge per person (plus service tax), so you'll feel that you've been ripped off if you just order coffee (see p.609 for full reviews of these and other patisseries).

The *Trianon* stands just behind the former site of **Cleopatra's Needles**, two giant obelisks that once marked the entrance to the Caesareum (see below). Nineteenth-century visitors enjoyed sketching and photographing the one still standing and its fallen companion (toppled by an earthquake in 1301) until both were removed in the 1870s, to be re-erected on London's Embankment and in New York's Central Park. Their popular name is a misnomer, for they originated at Heliopolis fourteen centuries earlier, and were moved to Alexandria fifteen years after the queen's death by suicide.

Sharia Nabi Daniel: the Synagogue and Coptic Cathedral

Starting as an inconspicuous backstreet beside the tourist office, **Sharia Nabi Daniel** grows wider as it runs south along the route of the ancient **Street of the Soma**. Paved in marble and flanked by marble colonnades, this dazzled the Arabs in 641, even though its finest buildings had already vanished. Before its destruction by feuding Christians in the fourth century, the north end of the street was crowned by the **Caesareum**, a temple begun by Cleopatra for Antony, which Octavian completed and dedicated to himself. Full of "choice paintings and statues", the complex was entered by a gateway fronted by two huge obelisks ("Cleopatra's Needles"; see above) that he took from Heliopolis.

A short way down Nabi Daniel, high wrought-iron gates front the **Eliyahu Ha-Navi Synagogue**, entered via an alley to the north (Mon–Fri 10.30am–1pm; bring your passport). Built in 1885 by Baron Jacques de Menasce, its splendid Italianate interior features stained-glass windows, giant *menorahs* and a collection of Torah scrolls from bygone neighbourhood synagogues that once served a Jewish community of 100,000, tracing its ancestry back to the city's foundation. Nowadays only about fifty elderly Jews remain, watched over by the Communauté Israélite Grand Rabbinat office, whose head, Joe Harari, is pleased to show visitors around and tell them all about the Alexandrine Jews.

Across the road, another set of gates marked by crosses betrays the **Coptic Cathedral of St Mark**, in a compound enclosed by taller buildings, entered from Sharia al-Kineesa al-Kobtiyya (aka Rue de l'Eglise Copte), which joins Nabi Daniel further south. The cathedral is named after the Apostle martyred by pagans in 67 AD; kidnapped while giving Mass, he was dragged by horses through the streets of Alexandria, where his remains were held by a local church until 828, when the Venetians smuggled the body out of Muslim-ruled Alexandria in a barrel of salt pork, to reinter it at the Basilica di San Marco; the head was transferred to the custody of the Church of Mari Girgis in Cairo. In 1997, Pope John Paul II returned one of St Mark's fingers to Pope Shenouda III as a gesture of ecumenical reconciliation. The cathedral itself is an early twentieth-century Byzantine pastiche, whose interior was unfairly described by Forster as "fatuously ugly". Remains of some of the first 47 patriarchs of the Alexandrian See are buried in a chapel to the left of the iconostasis. Daily services are held from 6 to 8pm and 8 to 10pm.

This part of town is classic Durrell territory: Darley and Pombal shared a flat

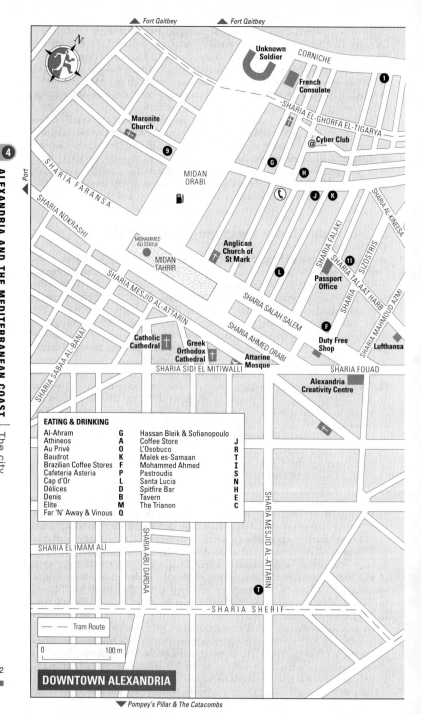

Port ◀

Fort Qaitbey ▲   Fort Qaitbey ▲

CORNICHE

Unknown
Soldier

French
Consulate

1

SHARIA EL-GHORFA EL-TIGARYA

Maronite
Church

@ Cyber Club

9

G

H

MIDAN
ORABI

SHARIA FARANSA

SHARIA AL-KINEESA

J   **K**

SHARIA NOKRASHI

SHARIA FALAKI

MOHAMMED
ALI STATUE

Anglican
Church of
St Mark

SHARIA TALAAT HARB

SIZOSTRIS

11

MIDAN
TAHRIR

L

Passport
Office

SHARIA MESJID AL-ATTARIN

SHARIA SALAH SALEM

SHARIA MAHMOUD AZMI

SHARIA SABAA AL-BANAT

SHARIA AHMED ORABI

F

Duty Free
Shop

Lufthansa

Catholic
Cathedral

Greek
Orthodox
Cathedral

Attarine
Mosque

SHARIA SIDI EL MITIWALLI

SHARIA FOUAD

Alexandria
Creativity Centre

EATING & DRINKING

Al-Ahram	**G**	Hassan Bleik & Sofianopoulo	
Athineos	**A**	Coffee Store	**J**
Au Privé	**O**	L'Osobuco	**R**
Baudrot	**K**	Malek es-Samaan	**T**
Brazilian Coffee Stores	**F**	Mohammed Ahmed	**I**
Cafeteria Asteria	**P**	Pastroudis	**S**
Cap d'Or	**L**	Santa Lucia	**N**
Délices	**D**	Spitfire Bar	**H**
Denis	**B**	Tavern	**E**
Elite	**M**	The Trianon	**C**
Far 'N' Away & Vinous	**Q**		

SHARIA EL IMAM ALI

SHARIA ABU DARDAA

SHARIA MESJID AL-ATTARIN

T

SHARIA SHERIF

--- Tram Route

0   100 m

DOWNTOWN ALEXANDRIA

Pompey's Pillar & The Catacombs ▼

MEDITERRANEAN SEA

CORNICHE

Buses to
Sidi Gaber &
Nozha Airport

British
Airways

Abdel
Wahab
Theatre

MIDAN SA'AD
ZAGHLOUL

EgyptAir &
Olympic

SHARIA SAAD ZAGHLOUL

MIDAN
Ramleh
Tram Station

SHARIA ISKANDAR EL-AKHBAR

RAMLEH

SHARIA SA'AD ZAGHLOUL

SHARIA SAFIYA ZAGHLOUL

SHARIA MOHAMMED RAFAT

SHARIA AMIN FIKHRY

SHARIA KOLLIET EL-TIBBA

ACCOMMODATION	
Acropole	6
Cecil	2
Hyde Park	8
Leroy	11
Marhaba	9
Metropole	7
New Hotel Welcome House	4
Picadilly	12
Sea Star	10
Triomphe	5
Union	3
Windsor Palace	1

Coptic Cathedral
of St Mark

Eliyah Ha-Navi
Synagogue

Zawiya
Internet Café

Coptic
Patriarchate

MIDAN
KHARTOUM

SHARIA SULTAN HUSSEIN

SHARIA AL SHAHID SALAH

AL-KOBTIYYA

SHARIA NABI DANIEL

Cavafy
Museum

Rialto Cinema

Church of
St Saba

Said Darwish Theatre

Renaissance
Royal Cinema

Metro
Cinema

Greco-Roman
Museum

British Council

Goethe Institute

Russian Centre

SHARIA PHARAANA

American
Center

SHARIA HORRIYA

TARIQ GAMAL ABDEL NASSER

French
Centre

Amir
Cinema

Globalnet

Mosque of
Nabi Daniel

KOM
EL-DIKKA

Villa of
the Birds

Old Walls

Roman
Theatre

SHARIA YUSSEF

SHARIA SULIMAN YOUSRI

Stadium

MIDAN

EL-GUMHORRIYA

Local buses &
minibuses

Masr Station

SHARIA MAHMOUD BEY

Service Taxis
for Cairo

Minibuses
for Abu Qir

SHARIA MOHARREM BEY

Fine Arts
Museum

Durrell's House

on Nabi Daniel, while Clea, Justine and Nessim had their residences on Rue Fuad Premier (now Sharia Fouad/Sharia Horriya).

Cavafy in the backstreets

A tangible relic of Alexandria's literary heritage can be found in a backstreet just off Nabi Daniel, formerly called Rue Lepsius but now named Sharm el-Sheikh; to find it, turn off onto Sultan Hussein and follow the alley running off between a luggage store and a lighting shop. At no.4, near the far end, a tiny sign in Greek identifies the **Cavafy Museum** (Tues, Wed, Fri & Sat 10am–3pm, Thurs & Sun 10am–5pm; £E8), which recreates the second-floor flat where **Constantine Cavafy** (1863–1933) lived at the zenith of his poetic talent, above a bordello around the corner from the Greek Orthodox Church of St Saba. "Where could I live better?" he asked, "Below, the brothel caters for the flesh. And there is the church which forgives sin. And there is the hospital where we die". He died there indeed, and was buried in the Greek Cemetery at Shatby.

His belongings were later used to create a small exhibition in the Greek Consulate, which bought Cavafy's former flat and established the present museum in 1992. Its custodian relates how "Cavafis" (as he is known) had nine brothers, loved candlelight, and died of throat cancer from drinking – but draws a veil over his homosexuality ("He never married"). Visitors can see his brass bed, icons, books and death mask, and the modest desk where he wrote *The Barbarians*, *Ithaca*, and his elegiac *The City*:

You won't find a new country, won't find another shore.
This city will always pursue you.
You'll walk the same streets, grow old
in the same neighbourhoods, turn grey in the same houses.
You'll always end up in this city. Don't hope for things elsewhere:
there's no ship for you, there's no road.
Now that you've wasted your life here, in this small corner,
you've destroyed it everywhere in the world.

There is also a room devoted to **Stratis Tsirkas**, a student of Cavafy's who wrote the trilogy *Drifting Cities*, about Greek underground politics in wartime Jerusalem, Cairo and Alexandria.

Across the road stands the Greek Orthodox **Church of St Saba** (daily 7.30am–12.30pm & 3.30–6pm), built over an ancient temple of Apollo. The seventeenth-century church contains a marble columnar tablet on which St Catherine is said to have been beheaded, a giant bronze bell and some fine paintings. Though Alexandria's Greek population has shrunk from 300,000 (pre-1957) to about 1000 today, the city is still the seat of a Patriarchate encompassing all Africa (ⓦ www.greece.org/gopatalex). When it moved to new premises, excavations on the old site beside St Saba revealed channels and cisterns from the ancient city's water supply.

On to Midan el-Gumhorriya

Ancient Alexandria's crossroads lay near the modern-day intersection of Nabi Daniel, Fouad and Horriya streets. The last used to be the **Canopic Way**, lined by marble colonnades extending all the way from the Gate of the Sun, where visitors entered the city. Many scholars believe that this junction was the site of the **Mouseion** (Shrine of the Muses), an institution from which our word "museum" derives. Founded by Ptolemy I Soter (323–282 BC), it incorporated lecture halls, laboratories, observatories, and the legendary "Mother" Library (see p.602). Across the way stood the **Soma**, a temple where Alexander the Great was originally entombed, as were several Ptolemies. Here the victorious Octavian is supposed to have paid his respects to Alexandria's founder but disdained his heirs: "I wished to see a king, I did not wish to see corpses".

Part of the site is occupied by the nineteenth-century **Mosque of Nabi Daniel**, whose modern entrance is set back from the street. The mosque's crypt is popularly believed to hold the remains of the Prophet Daniel (in reality, it contains those of Mohammed Danyal al-Maridi, a Sufi sheikh, and one Lukman the Wise). Legends that Alexander's tomb lay deeper underground impelled the Egyptian Antiquities Organization to excavate in the early 1990s, but nothing was found; two Greeks later claimed to have found it near Siwa Oasis (see p.574); while Professor Fakharani of Alexandria University believes that the Romans reburied him outside the Royal Quarter, where the Christian cemeteries are today.

Sharia Nabi Daniel ends at **Midan el-Gumhorriya**, a seething mass of bus and taxi ranks outside the neo-Baroque **Masr Station**, designed by a Greek and an Italian in 1927. You can beat a retreat into the Roman Theatre off Sharia Yussef.

The Roman Theatre and the Villa of Birds

Since 1959 Polish archeologists and staff from the Greco-Roman Museum have removed the Turkish fort and slums on *Kom el-Dikka* (Mound of Rubble), revealing a substratum of **Roman remains** beneath a Muslim cemetery (daily 9am–4pm; Ramadan 9am–3pm; £E6; cameras free, camcorders £E150). During Ptolemaic times this was the Park of Pan, a hilly pleasure garden with a limestone summit carved into the shape of a pine cone, onto which Roman villas, baths and an amphitheatre later encroached. The elegant **Roman Theatre** has marble seating for seven to eight hundred, cruder galleries for the plebs, and a forecourt with two patches of mosaic flooring. In Byzantine times, gladiatorial games were superceded by chariot races, with teams based on the Blues and Greens of Constantinople's hippodrome; some of the seats in the theatre bear graffiti supporting one of the teams (which were closely associated with political factions).

A separate ticket, sold at the main entrance, entitles you to enter the newly opened **Villa of Birds** (£E5; camera £E10, camcorder £E150) – so called because of its mosaic floors, depicting nine different species of birds (and a panther). En route to the villa you'll pass a laboratory for cleaning antiques, with assorted masonry recently dredged from the sea bed laid outside.

Further north within the compound they're excavating a **residential quarter** (closed to visitors) whose jumbled arches and walls resolve into streets, shops and houses at close quarters. Many of the buildings are constructed from alternating courses of brick and stone, a technique called *opus mixtum* (mixed work). Five centuries later, the Arabs used the same method to build a wall around the shrunken city, which was reinforced by the Turks. A multi-layered section of the **old walls** remains behind some houses in an alley off Sharia Horriya, which can be seen on the way to the Greco-Roman Museum, while the **east gate** of the Arab city is embedded in the Stadium behind Masr Station.

The Fine Arts Museum and Sharia Safiya Zaghloul

Since Alexandria's **Fine Arts Museum** (daily 9am–1pm & 5–8pm; free) handed over its paintings to the Modern Art Museum in San Stefano (see p.606), it has become a venue for **temporary exhibitions** and book fairs, often closed between events. Ask at the tourist office if anything is happening there, to avoid a wasted journey from Masr Station, following Sharia Mahmoud Bey (parallel to, and south of the tracks) for 150m before turning right; the museum lies ahead, at 18 Sharia Menasce.

Alternatively, you can turn the corner of the archeological site and head northwards up **Sharia Safiya Zaghloul**. In Cavafy's day this was called the Rue Missala and known for its billiard halls and rent-boys; today the street is noted for its cinemas and restaurants. By turning off just beyond the Metro Cinema, you'll be on course for the Greco-Roman Museum – its classical facade is visible from the far end of the street.

The Greco-Roman Museum

The **Greco-Roman Museum** contains Egypt's best collection of antiquities from the Classical era (Mon–Thurs, Sat & Sun 9am–5pm, Fri 9–11.30am & 1.30–5pm; £E16, camera permit £E10, video permit £E150). Though artefacts are mostly labelled in English, anyone seeking a fuller explanation should buy Jean-Yves Empereur's *Guide to the Greco-Roman Museum*.

Turning left off the entrance vestibule into Room 6, you encounter **relics of the Serapis cult** promoted by Ptolemy I. A fusion of Osiris and Dionysos, Serapis was represented as a bearded, avuncular fellow, and by a giant granite bull carved during the reign of Hadrian (who's commemorated by a bust). Besides maintaining the old cults, the Romans added flourishes like the **death masks** they hung indoors as *memento mori*.

The Ptolemies also adopted the Fayoumi cult of Sobek (see p.499), hence the **mummified crocodile**, fragmentary chapel and funerary accoutrements in Room 9. The most remarkable of the human **mummies** bears a superbly life-like portrait of the deceased, executed in the Fayoum c.100–250 AD, when naturalism was taking hold. Although a life-size Marcus Aurelius dominates the other **statues** in Room 12, it can't distract you from Ptolemy X (who mortgaged Egypt to Rome), whose resemblance to the actor Donald Pleasence is quite remarkable.

Amongst the **busts of Roman emperors** in Room 14 are Julius Caesar, a cold-faced Augustus (Octavian) and a bearded Hadrian, and there's more evidence of sculptural talent in rooms 16–17, beyond the chunk of wall decorated with a **Ptolemaic mural** of an ox turning a water wheel. The colossal headless red porphyry statue has been identified variously as Christ Pantokrator (Christ in Majesty) or the rabidly anti-Christian Diocletian.

Pharos-shaped lamps can be seen in Room 18, whose annexe showcases delicate **tanagra figures**, buried with young women and children. Notice the hideous effigy of Bes (Room 20) and the finely carved schist head of a young man (Room 23), which precede a huge collection of **antique coins**.

Finally, you can catch a breath of air with **rock-cut tombs** and a giant head of Mark Antony in the garden, before going in search of the mummy with a cross on its neck, amongst the **Christian antiquities** (rooms 1–5). Here too are some splendid textiles (the ancient Copts were great weavers) and objects related to the Monastery of St Mina (see p.620).

While in the neighbourhood, you can investigate the **foreign cultural centres** on Sharia Phara'ana and Sharia Batalsa (aka Rue de Ptolomeés), which are detailed on p.614. This pleasant quarter marks the onset of the Bab Sharq district, covered on p.604. To return to the downtown area, make your way back to Sharia Safiya Zaghloul and continue north, or take either of the two main streets before it; all will bring you out near **Ramleh tram station**, east of Midan Sa'ad Zaghloul.

Around Midan Orabi and Midan Tahrir

The old heart of "European" Alexandria lies nine blocks west of Midan Sa'ad Zaghloul. To get there, you can catch a tram along Sharia el-Ghorfa el-Tigarya, or walk along **Sharia Sa'ad Zaghloul**, which starts as a busy shopping street aglow with neon, and ends as a shadowy alley. Along the way you may meet local **characters** like the stationer whose family escaped the Armenian genocide, arrived here penniless, got rich by founding a piano factory and then lost everything in 1957; a father-and-daughter team of acrobats; or a seedy old guy who pimped for British soldiers in his youth, and will regale you with sordid tales for the price of a drink in one of the backstreet **bars** (see p.611).

Emerging onto **Midan Orabi**, you'll see a Neoclassical **Monument of the Unknown Soldier** towards the seafront. No trace remains of the French Gardens where expatriates once strolled amongst the acacia trees and shrubs, but a derelict synagogue on the corner of Sa'ad Zaghloul and a **Maronite Church** off the square attest to the area's social complexion a century ago.

Midan Tahrir

South of the French Gardens lay "Frank Square", the European city's social hub; "There is nothing in Alexandria but the Frank Square and the huts of the Alexandrians", wrote Florence Nightingale in 1849. Originally the Place des Consuls, it was renamed in honour of **Mohammed Ali**, whose equestrian **statue** at the far end now barely stands out against the scabrous facades in the background. After the Orabi Revolt of 1882, rebels were tied to the acacias,

△ Friday prayers in the street

shot and buried there by British forces. Not surprisingly, its name was changed to Liberation Square – **Midan Tahrir** – following the Revolution.

Midan Tahrir also witnessed two crucial events of the Nasser era. In October 1954, a member of the Muslim Brotherhood fired on Nasser during a public speech; the botched assassination gave Nasser an excuse to ban the Brotherhood and supplant General Naguib (who was falsely implicated in the conspiracy) as Egypt's acknowledged leader. Two years later, on the fourth anniversary of King Farouk's abdication, Nasser delivered a three-hour speech broadcast live from here on national radio, climaxing in the announcement that Egypt had taken possession of the Suez Canal; the repetition of the name "Lesseps" earlier in his peroration was actually the codeword for the operation to begin.

To the Attarine Mosque and beyond

A few streets around Midan Tahrir deserve a mention, if not a ramble. Leading off to the southeast, the erstwhile Bond Street of Alexandria, Rue Chérif Pacha, was Cavafy's birthplace; on the corner stood the Cotton Exchange that once echoed with the cries of European merchants. Renamed **Sharia Salah Salem** after a colleague of Nasser's, the street is less chic but still the place to find **antiques** and **jewellery**, much of it once owned by "foreigners" dispossessed by Nasser. Its main landmark is the Moorish-Gothic **Anglican Church of St Mark**, whose congregation includes many Sudanese. Six blocks further down at no.30 stands a copy of the Palazzo Farnese in Rome, built for an Italian bank and now housing the **Banque Masr**, whose lavish interior is worth seeing. In 1942, Durrell worked around the corner in a propaganda bureau at 1 Sharia Mahmoud Azmi. A plaque at no.2 marks the first trading company established by the **Al-Fayeds** – two poor lads born in Alex's Sharbangi Alley who became international business moguls. Mohammed Al-Fayed is best known for his ownership of Harrods in London, and the relationship between his son Dodi and Princess Diana. Al-Fayed's belief that they were killed by MI6 is widely shared in Egypt.

Jewellers also crop up in the backstreets north of Salah Salem, and along two thoroughfares further south: Ahmed Orabi and Mesjid al-Attarin. The latter gets its name from the **Attarine Mosque**, which occupies the site of the Church of St Athanasius, named after the rector who argued the "dual nature" of Christ against his theological opponent, Arius the Monophysite. The mosque has a lacey, multi-tiered minaret, reminiscent of Al-Nasir Mohammed's mosque in Cairo, and likewise dates from the fourteenth century. It was from here that Napoleon's forces removed a seven-ton sarcophagus, thought to be Alexander's, and later surrendered it to the British Museum, which attributed it to Nectanebo I.

Further west are two reminders of the city's multi-sectarian legacy. The **Greek Orthodox Cathedral** underpins a small Hellenistic enclave, while a huge **Catholic Cathedral** stands aloof from the bustling junction of Mesjid al-Attarin and Abu Dardaa streets. Northwest of Midan Tahrir, grandiose European architecture gives way to smaller-scale buildings that segue into the city's **souks**. Here, the main arteries are **Sharia Nokrashi** – heaving with fruit and vegetable stalls, butchers, bakeries and hardware stores – and **Sharia Faransa** (French Street), full of shops selling clothes, cloth and dressmaking materials. The network of alleys between the two thoroughfares is known as **Zinqat as-Sittat**, "The Women's Squeeze". Before the revolution, Nokrashi was notorious for its child bordellos. In *The Alexandria Quartet*, Justine sought her kidnapped daughter here, Mountolive was mauled by child prostitutes, and Scobie killed his neighbours with moonshine whisky.

Anfushi, Fort Qaitbey and the Pharos

Although the **Eastern Harbour** is no longer the busy port of ancient times, its graceful curve is definitely appealing. As it sweeps around towards Qaitbey's Fort, bureaucratic monoliths from the last decades of the twentieth century give way to stately palms and weathered colonial mansions, likened by Michael Palin to "Cannes with acne". Nearer the fort, fishermen cast rods and mend nets while the fresh catch is marketed and shipwrights work on hulls in a boatyard. Walking at least some of the way along the Corniche is highly recommended, but you may wish to use minibuses or trams over longer distances.

In ancient times, a seven-league dike – the **Heptastadion** – connected Alexandria with Pharos, then an island. Allowed to silt up after the Arab conquest, the Heptastadion gradually turned into a peninsula that the newcomers built over, creating the **Anfushi quarter**. Its Ottoman mosques and some old *mashrabiya*-ed houses are the only "sights" as such, but the variety of streetlife makes this an interesting area to explore. The best strategy is to hop on tram #14 or #15, running one block inland from the Corniche, which travel past most places of interest.

The **Terbana Mosque**, 700m along, is chiefly remarkable for its antique columns – no one knows where they came from. A huge pair with Corinthian capitals supports the minaret. Lesser columns are ranged eight to an arcade within and painted gloss white; there's also some fine tiling quietly going to pot – the mosque has been subject to slapdash "improvements" ever since it was built in 1685. The black-and-red-painted brickwork on the facade is a common Delta style.

The city's foremost religious building, the **Mosque of Abu al-Abbas al-Mursi** is located the same distance again further north. It honours the patron saint of Alexandria's fishermen and sailors, a thirteenth-century Andalusian sheikh. Although the present building was erected as recently as 1943 – in gratitude for Al-Mursi's supernatural defence of the quarter against Luftwaffe bombers, so legend has it – it looks as old as the sixteenth-century original. Bold keel-arched panels, elaborately carved domes and cornices make a visually satisfying pastiche. Women are only allowed into a room at the back of the mosque.

After a visit, have a drink in the arcade across the street and watch life go by. If you're feeling adventurous, you can investigate the maze of old houses behind the mosque; otherwise, press on to Qaitbey's fort.

Fort Qaitbey and the Pharos

One tram stop after Al-Mursi's mosque and a short walk past the fishing port and boat yard will bring you to the promontory bearing Sultan Qaitbey's fort. The **Aquarium** and **Institute of Oceanography** en route are not worth the time of day: the first is cramped and miserable, and the second musters a weird collection of lacquered sea creatures. You'll also pass the **Alexandra Yacht Club**, which holds an annual regatta in October.

Fort Qaitbey (daily 9am–4pm; £E6; camera permit £E10) is an Alexandrian landmark, a Toytown citadel buffeted by wind-borne spray, its flag forever rippling. Built during the 1480s and later beefed up by Mohammed Ali, it commands great views of the city and the spume-flecked Mediterranean. Within the keep there's a mosque whose minaret was blown away by the British in 1882; upstairs, relics of Roman and Napoleonic sea battles comprise a small **Naval Museum** (same hours; £E12).

The fort occupies the site of the **Pharos**, Alexandria's great lighthouse, one of the Seven Wonders of the ancient world. A combination of aesthetic beauty and technological ambition, it transcended its practical role as a navigational aid and early-warning system, becoming synonymous with the city itself. Possibly conceived by Alexander himself, it was built during Ptolemy II's reign (c.279 BC) under the direction of an Asiatic Greek, Sostratus, and exceeded 125m – perhaps even 150m – in height, including the statue of Poseidon at its summit.

Its square base contained three hundred rooms* and possibly hydraulic machinery for hauling the fuel up the second, octagonal storey; otherwise, this would have been accomplished by a procession of pack mules climbing a spiral ramp. The cylindrical third storey housed the lantern, whose light is thought to have been visible 56km away. Some chroniclers also mention a "mirror" that enabled the lighthouse keepers to observe ships far out at sea; a form of lens (whose secret was lost) has been postulated.

Around 700 AD the lantern collapsed, or was demolished by a treasure-hunting Khalif; the base survived unscathed and Ibn Tulun restored the second level, until an earthquake in 1303 reduced the whole structure to rubble. The northwest section of the fort's enclosure walls incorporates some huge red-granite pillars that might have been part of the Pharos. Since the 1990s, divers from the CEA have located over 2500 stone objects **underwater** at depths of 6–8m. These include the head of a colossus of Ptolemy as pharaoh and the base of an obelisk inscribed to Seti I, which have been brought to the surface, and several monoliths, weighing 50–70 tonnes apiece, that can only have belonged to the lighthouse. Five hundred metres offshore they've found wrecks of Greek and Roman trading vessels laden with amphorae of wine and fish sauce, and over fifty anchors of all eras – more pieces in the mosaic picture of ancient Alexandria that's emerging from surveys of the Eastern Harbour (see below).

The Anfushi Tombs, Ras el-Tin and the Western Harbour

Trams run on to the Ras el-Tin quarter, where you can alight at Sharia Ras el-Tin to find the rock-cut **Anfushi Tombs**, uncovered in 1901. Sited in pairs around a staircase leading to an open court, the four tombs are painted to simulate costly alabaster or marble and belonged to third-century BC Greek Alexandrians who adopted ancient Egyptian funerary practices. The right-hand set has pictures of Egyptian gods, warships and feluccas; a Greek workman has also immortalized his mate's virtues in graffiti. Both the left-hand tombs have vestibules with benches for the deceased's relatives to eat and drink in their memory. Hang around and a keeper should appear to unlock the tombs (daily 9am–4.30pm; £E12).

It's possible that the necropolis extends beneath the gardens of **Ras el-Tin Palace**, overlooking the Western Harbour. In the days when Pharos was an island, a Temple of Neptune stood here. Now strictly off limits as Admiralty Headquarters, the "Cape of Figs" palace was built for Mohammed Ali, its audience hall sited so that he could watch his new fleet at anchor while reclining on his divan. Rebuilt and turned into the summer seat of government under Fouad I, it witnessed **King Farouk's abdication** on July 26, 1952. "What you have done to me I was getting ready to do to you", the king informed General Naguib, adding "Your task will be difficult. It is not easy to govern Egypt". Wearing an admiral's uniform, Farouk departed on the royal yacht to a 21-gun

---

*Legend has it that these rooms once housed the seventy rabbis who translated the Hebrew scriptures into Greek for Ptolemy Philadelphus (c.200 BC), producing identical texts despite having worked alone. In reality, this Septuagint version of the Bible wasn't completed until 130 BC, and the rabbis lived in huts on the island.

salute; with him went the royal family, an English nursemaid, three Albanian bodyguards, a dog trainer and 244 trunks.

Egypt's main port and naval base since the mid-nineteenth century, the **Western Harbour** is not for sightseeing. Inland, blocks of warehouses with their foreign names still faintly visible are given over to the **cotton industry**, "greasy fluff" and rags littering the streets as in Forster's day. Another major industry is smuggling, for which the **port** is notorious; its 62 quays handle over 5000 ships every year, carrying about 75 percent of Egypt's import and export trade.

On the way back you could enjoy lunch at one of the many **fish restaurants** on Sharia Safar Pasha, between Ras el-Tin and Anfushi, or *Kadoura* along the Corniche back towards the centre (see p.610).

Silsileh and the ancient Royal Quarters

The opposite jaw of the Eastern Harbour is formed by a narrow promontory called **Silsileh** ("the Chain"), that's occupied by the navy and out of bounds. Aside from being the site of Naguib Mahfouz's fictional *Pension Miramar*, its interest lies in the **underwater discoveries** made since 1996 by Franck Goddio and other members of the National French Centre for Studies, whose survey of the sea bed has revealed an extensive area of submerged ruins including red granite columns, statues, sphinxes, pavements, ceramics and a pier from the ancient Royal Quarters of Alexandria. In October 1998 they hauled up a sample of the treasures to show the world: the largest and most striking objects were a metre-tall, black-granite figure of the goddess Isis holding a canopic jar, and an intact 380kg diorite sphinx with the face of what is thought to be Ptolemy XII, Cleopatra's father. Both have since been returned to the sea bed, but can be viewed on Goddio's **website**, Ⓦ www.underwaterdiscovery.org.

Goddio was quick to claim that they had found the site of **Cleopatra's palace** on the island of Antirrhodos (where she committed suicide), which had been plunged into the sea by a series of earthquakes and tidal waves some 1600 years ago. The Egyptians enthused about the idea of creating the world's first underwater museum – with Plexiglass tunnels that would allow visitors to stroll around five metres below the surface. However, many archeologists felt that the site of the palace and the provenance of the ruins had only been tentatively established, since several palaces existed there over a timespan of centuries. As a marine treasure-hunter rather than an archeologist by profession, Goddio was also criticized as a gadfly who dashed from one project to another without completing any – yet still he kept turning up finds, not just in the Eastern Harbour, but also at Abu Qir (see p.608). His secret weapon is a nuclear resonance magnometer that can detect likely antiquities by measuring the relative density of submerged objects against the earth's magnetic field, and plots them on a digital map synchronized to GPS satellites. But as Goddio goes from triumph to triumph, the idea of an underwater museum has been quietly shelved after it was realized that the murkiness of the harbour made the whole scheme impractical. **Diving**, however, remains a possibility (see p.613 for details).

The Bibliotheca Alexandrina

On the mainland, another wonder of antiquity has been resurrected in a new form. The **Bibliotheca Alexandrina** (Mon–Thurs & Sun 9am–7pm) resembles a giant discus embedded in the ground at an angle, representing a second sun rising beside the Mediterranean. Pictograms, hieroglyphs and letters from every known alphabet are carved on its sweeping exterior, evoking the diversity of knowledge embodied in the ancient library and the aspirations of the new one. Designed by a Norwegian-Austrian team of architects, the complex includes a planetarium (the spheroid structure on the plaza facing the sea), exhibition spaces and the library itself, whose vast reading area is a stunning cascade of levels upheld by stainless-steel pillars suggestive of the columns in ancient Egyptian temples. You don't have to be a bibliophile to be impressed by the design, nor the inclusion of a high-tech facility for the blind, named after Taha Hussein, the blind poet and novelist. It's possible to wander in from Sharia Bur Said (opposite the Commerce Faculty of Alexandria University, inland) during opening hours, but you can only get access to the lower levels on **guided tours**. The library hosts an **international book fair** (July), exhibitions, lectures and other events, listed on its **website** Ⓦ www.bibalex.gov.eg.

The project to create a new Bibliotheca Alexandrina was approved by UNESCO in 1987 and cost US$172 million, met by Saudi Arabia, the Arab Emirates and Iraq (before the Gulf War), with the Egyptian government donating a further US$182 million. Its opening date was repeatedly set back and the belated inauguration ceremony in April 2002 lacked the bevy of foreign VIPs that had been expected. The library hopes to put these false starts behind it, while acknowledging that its staff will be cataloguing the estimated four- to eight million volumes – in every language from Polynesian dialects to Mandarin Chinese – for years to come.

Meanwhile, scholars are pursuing a project to uncover the secrets of the **ancient library**. Founded shortly after Alexandria itself, on the advice of Ptolemy I's counselor Demetrius of Phalerum, it stood beside the Mouseion in the heart of the city (see p.594). Dedicated to "the writings of all nations", it welcomed scholars and philosophers and supported research and debates. By law, all ships docking at Alexandria were obliged to allow any scrolls on board to be copied, if they were of interest. By the mid-first century BC it held 532,800 manuscripts (all catalogued by the Head Librarian, Callimachus), and later spawned a subsidiary attached to the Temple of Serapis; the two were known as the "Mother" and "Daughter" libraries, and together contained perhaps 700,000 scrolls (equivalent to about 100–125,000 printed books today). As many as 40,000 (or even 400,000) were burned during Julius Caesar's assault on the city in 48 BC, when he supported Cleopatra against her brother Ptolemy XIII; as compensation, Mark Antony gave her the entire contents of the Pergamum Library in Greece (200,000 scrolls). It was Christian mobs that destroyed this vast storehouse of "pagan" knowledge, torching the Mother Library in 293 and the Daughter Library in 391, though medieval Europe later mythologized its **destruction** as proof of Arab barbarism. An apocryphal tale had the Muslim leader Amr pronouncing: "If these writings of the Greeks agree with the Koran they are useless, and need not be preserved; if they disagree, they are pernicious, and ought to be destroyed".

Pompey's Pillar and the Catacombs of Kom es-Shoqafa

The poor **Karmous quarter** in the southwest of the city contains two of Alex's best-known ancient monuments. **Pompey's Pillar** can be reached by taxi (£E5) or bus #309 or #709 from Ramleh. From Pompey's Pillar you can easily walk to the **Catacombs of Kom es-Shoqafa**. If you've just arrived in Egypt, the poverty of the slums that lie between the two might seem shocking.

Pompey's Pillar

"An imposing but ungraceful object", **Pompey's Pillar** towers 25m above a limestone ridge and garden, surrounded by the fruits and pits of excavations.

Despite its name, the red-granite column was actually raised to honour Diocletian, who threatened to massacre the dissenting populace "until their blood reached his horse's knees", but desisted when his mount slipped and bloodied itself prematurely. The column came from the ruined Temple of Serapis, which once rivalled the Soma and Caesareum in magnificence, and contained a "Daughter Library" of religious texts. Both were destroyed by Christians during their final assault on Alexandria's pagan intellectuals in 293.

Three subterranean galleries where the sacred Apis bulls were interred (see "Saqqara", p.231) are all that remain: you'll find them west of the ridge, which also features a Nilometer, three sphinxes (originally from Heliopolis) and some underground cisterns. Overall, however, the **site** (daily 9am–5pm, Ramadan 9am–3pm; £E6) is pretty disappointing considering what used to exist here.

The Catacombs of Kom es-Shoqafa

One of Alexandria's most memorable monuments, the **Catacombs of Kom es-Shoqafa** (daily 9am–5pm, Ramadan 9am–3pm; £E12; camera permit £E10) combine spookiness and kitsch, never mind their prosaic Arabic name, "Mound of Shards". To reach them, turn right around the corner after leaving Pompey's Pillar and follow the road uphill and straight on for about 500m; the entrance to the catacombs is on the left beyond a small square.

This triple-level funerary complex descends some 35m underground, and is reached via a spiral stairway, past the shaft down which bodies were lowered. From the vestibule with its well and scalloped niches, you can squeeze through a fissure (right) into a lofty **Caracalla** riddled with *loculi*, or family burial niches, each once sealed with a stone slab on which were painted the names and ages of the deceased. Even more arresting is the **Triclinium** (left), where relatives toasted the dead from stone couches. When the first archeologists entered the chamber they found wine jars and tableware; and recently murals, only visible under ultraviolet light. But the main attraction is the **Central Tomb** downstairs, whose vestibule is guarded by reliefs of bearded serpents with Medusa-headed shields. Inside are comically muscle-bound statues of Sobek and Anubis wearing Roman armour, dating from the second century AD when "the old faiths began to merge and melt" (Forster). Water has flooded the **Goddess Nemesis Hall** (still accessible) and submerged the lowest level, hastening the catacombs' decay. For more information, buy Jean-Yves Empereur's excellently illustrated *A Short Guide to the Catacombs of Kom es-Shoqafa*.

Moharrem Bey, Bab Sharq and Smouha

East of Karmous lies **Moharrem Bey**, a once-affluent suburb of mansions and villas, now derelict and slummy. The district grew up in the mid-nineteenth century as a result of the **Mahmudiya Canal** (dug at the cost of 20,000 lives), which revitalized commerce and created a mercantile elite who built palatial residences along its banks, described by *Murray's Handbook* as the "fashionable afternoon promenade". Its charm endured for a century, the final decades of which were embellished by the presence of residents like Cavafy (before he moved to the Rue Lepsius) and Durrell. In 1943 **Durrell** rented the top floor of a turreted **house** at 19 Sharia al-Ma'amoun, where he met his second wife, the Alexandrian Eve Cohen, who became the model for Justine. Subsequently leased to the painter and sculptor Effat Nagui and her husband and fellow artist Sa'ad el-Khadem, the house has been threatened with demolition for several years. To see if it's still standing, catch tram #14 to Sharia Nabil al-Wakad, walk up the street and turn right onto Sharia al-Ma'amoun, or walk there from Masr Station down Sharia Moharrem Bey (about 3km).

Bab Sharq

Separated from Moharrem Bey by the train tracks converging on Masr Station, the **Bab Sharq** district can be as easily approached via the backstreets behind the Greco-Roman Museum (see p.596) or en route to the Corniche beaches (see below). Starting from Moharrem Bey, catch any bus or minibus heading north up the Suez Canal Road, which meets the Corniche near the Bibliotheca Alexandrina. Halfway, it crosses the main east–west thoroughfare, named Tariq (or Sharia) Gamal Abdel Nasser at this point, and Sharia Horriya further to the west.

The junction is flanked on two sides by the hilly **Shallalat Gardens**, which blaze with scarlet flame trees over summer. Their nineteenth-century French designer utilized remnants of the **Arab city walls** and the Farkha Canal to create rockeries and ornamental ponds; if any trace of it remained, the ancient "Gate of the Sun" would have doubtless been accorded pride of place. There is a boating lake and a restaurant where you can sometimes hear live music.

Across the road lies a sprawling necropolis of high-walled **cemeteries** consecrated to diverse faiths. Though most of the tombs date from the nineteenth or twentieth centuries, burials have occurred here since ancient times. Professor Fakharani thinks that a marble chamber found beneath the Catholic cemetery near the crossroads may belong to a royal tomb, perhaps even that of Alexander himself. Like the Catholic compound, the Coptic, Greek Orthodox, Armenian, Maronite, Uniate, Protestant and Jewish cemeteries are full of lavish mausolea and sculptures, from the heyday of European supremacy. The necropolis extends nearly as far as St Mark's College in Shatby, in relation to which the Jewish cemetery is nearest.

During summer, affluent citizens hang out at the **Alexandria Sporting Club**, 1km east along Tariq Gamal Abdel Nasser. Its pool and tennis courts are the best in the city; polo and golf matches, or billiards and movies at night, are just some of the entertainments. Non-members pay £E25 to use the facilities. All eastbound trams stop at the Sporting Club except for the #4.

Smouha

Thanks to the **Zahran Mall** and **Smouha Shopping Centre**, with their multiplex cinemas and Internet cafés, the **Smouha** district has become a magnet for young Egyptians with a little disposable income. It's about 1km south of the Sporting Club; to get there, catch bus #1 from outside the *Cecil Hotel* on Midan Sa'ad Zaghloul to the 15th May bus station in Sidi Gaber. Head south away from the train station till you hit a main road and take a right; 200m later you'll reach a roundabout where you take the second left. Alternatively, you can get a taxi for £E3–5.

The district is named after the Baghdad-born Jewish architect Joseph Smouha, who moved to Egypt in the 1920s. His Smouha City (as it was originally called) was the local equivalent of Cairo's Heliopolis, a modern suburb for the upper-middle classes. Though all the "foreigners" were dispossessed by Nasser, their legacies – and names – survive in present-day Alexandria. The **Zoological Gardens** (daily: winter 9am–sunset; summer 9am–9pm; 25pt) were opened in 1907 and cover 26 acres; among the many species of birds are macaws that swear like troopers, tutored by long-departed British soldiers. Outside, Sharia Smouha serves as an improvised horse-racing track on Sundays (see p.614). Next door, diverse trees planted by Khedive Ismail have grown to maturity in the **Nouzha Gardens** (same hours; 50pt), where military bands once played. Here, E.M. Forster had his first date with Mohammed el-Adl, a tram conductor whom he met at Ramleh in the winter of 1916–17. Before

Mohammed, Forster's sexual passions had never been reciprocated. The racial, class and sexual barriers that their relationship challenged underlie the finale of *A Passage to India*, which Forster was struggling with when he learned of Mohammed's death in Egypt.

Just south of Nouzha are the tranquil **Antoniaidis Gardens** (same hours; 50pt). Embellished with classical statuary, they were once the private grounds of a wealthy Greek family. In ancient times, the Nouzha area was a residential suburb inhabited by the likes of Callimachus (310–240 BC), the Head Librarian of the Bibliotheca Alexandrina. It was around here, too, that Amr's Muslim forces camped before entering the city in 641 AD.

Corniche beaches

Alexandria's beaches are an overworked asset. Hardly a square metre of sand goes unclaimed during high season, when literally millions of Egyptians descend on the city. Before June the beaches furthest out are relatively uncrowded, with predominantly local users; however, Alexandrians alone can number hundreds on Fridays, Saturdays and public holidays – days to be avoided.

The popularity of the beaches doesn't imply Western-style beach culture. On most of the beaches you will rarely see any woman past the age of puberty wearing a swimsuit – they wander into the sea fully clad. For Western women who want to swim without the hindrance of a *galabiyya*, or a lot of attention, the only place where even a modest one-piece seems OK is the Westernized enclave of **Ma'amoura**. As far as facilities go, most beaches have parasols and chairs for rent, and sometimes public showers, while fish restaurants, soft-drink and snack vendors are ubiquitous. Since 1991, the civic authorities have solved the image problem posed by the 47 sewage outlets that used to pollute the seaside from the centre of town to Montazah by pumping sewage into Lake Mariout instead, whence it finds its way into the Med more discreetly.

If that deters you, there are still three indisputable attractions: the **Royal Jewellery Museum** in Glym, the **Modern Art Museum** in San Stefano and the extensive grounds of the **Montazah Palace**, further along the coast. Many visitors go to **Abu Qir** for its seafood – though you can eat just as well in nicer surroundings in central Alexandria.

East to Montazah and Abu Qir

Travelling eastwards past the Corniche beaches looks simple on the map, but isn't so easy in practice. For the initial stretch as far as Cleopatra beach, minibuses (#719, #728, #729, #735 and #736) run a block inland, and tram #2 three to five blocks in, leaving you with only the stops – mostly named after beaches – to go on. As most of the **city beaches** amount to an arc of sand with a few hotels and a casino (for food, drink and light music, not gambling), they're hard to differentiate without a landmark in the vicinity. The following account includes some places a fair way inland.

Shatby to Glym

The district known as **Shatby** (or Chatby) is overshadowed by **St Mark's College**, a massive red-brick neo-Baroque edifice whose dome is visible from afar. Founded to educate the city's Christian elite, it now forms part of Alexandria University. On the far side of Sharia Bur Said is the grandly named **Shatby Necropolis** (daily 9am–4.30pm, Ramadan 9am–3pm; £E6), a small pit exposing some rock-cut ossuaries and sarcophagi from the third century BC, which can be viewed for free by peering over the wall of the nearby youth hostel. Shatby **beach** looks fit to spawn the "Swamp Thing", and subsequently mutates into **Ibrahimiya**. An Egyptian-Greek archeological team has recently found huge underground cisterns between Ibrahimiya and Sidi Gaber.

Shortly before Cleopatra beach, tram #2 turns further inland, visiting **Sidi Gaber Station** and passing through the **Bacos** quarter where Gamal Abdel Nasser was born on January 15, 1918. He was eleven years old when he attended his first nationalist demonstration, got truncheoned and was jailed overnight. Tram #1 runs closer to **Cleopatra** beach, which has no connection with the lady herself, although the nearby **Roushdi** district was the site of Nikopolis, which Octavian (or Augustus Caesar, as he then styled himself) founded because he hated living in Alexandria. The British also built barracks and houses there, in the districts they named Stanley, Glym and San Stefano. Today, Roushdi is the centre of expat life in Alex, and many foreigners rent flats here – but a vestige of its origins remains in the form of the **Mustafa Kamel Necropolis** (daily 9am–4pm; £E12, camera £E5). Discovered in 1933, the four tombs date from the second century BC; two are upheld by Doric columns and one contains a mural of a horseman. To get there, catch tram #2 from Ramleh to Roushdi tram station and walk towards the Corniche along Sharia al-Mo'asker al-Romani.

The Royal Jewellery Museum

The **Royal Jewellery Museum** (daily 9am–5pm, Ramadan Mon–Thurs, Sat & Sun 9am–3pm, Fri 9–11.30am & 1.30–4pm; £E20, camera £E10, video £E150) is midway between Glym and San Stefano, three blocks in from the Corniche. It's a short walk from the El-Fenoun el-Gamilia or Qasr el-Safa stop on the #2 tram line to the mansion at 27 Sharia Ahmed Yehia, whose decor is as splendidly vulgar as the treasures on display. All the exhibits are labelled, so you'll have no trouble identifying Mohammed Ali's diamond-inlaid snuffbox, King Farouk's gold chess set or the platinum crown with 2159 diamonds. Don't miss the diamond-studded gardening tools. The main gallery downstairs is lined with stained-glass cameos of courtly love in eighteenth-century France, while Provencal farmers, milkmaids and food decorate the service corridors. Upstairs you'll find the wildest his 'n' hers bathrooms; hers with tiled murals of nymphs bathing in a waterfall, his with scenes of Côte d'Azur fishermen. The mansion was built for Mohammed Ali's granddaughter Princess Fatima el-Zaharaa (1903–83) and her husband Ali Heider.

The Modern Art Museum

Aside from the Library, Alexandria's latest cultural attraction is the **Modern Art Museum** (daily 10am–6pm; £E10), in a two-storey villa once owned by Mahmoud Said (1897–1964). A judge who painted as a hobby, Said was the first Egyptian artist to receive a state prize, yet disliked official commissions such as the wall-sized *Inaugural Ceremony of the Suez Canal* that greets visitors to the museum, preferring to paint pensive, sensual women – *The Siren of Alexandria, Egyptian Country-Woman* and *Nabawiya with a flowered dress* – or landscapes of Alexandria, Lebanon and Stockholm. Upstairs, six rooms are devoted to the brothers Seif (1906–1979) and Adham (1908–1959) Wanly, who founded the first Egyptian artists' studio in 1942 and taught Fine Arts at Alexandria University after the revolution. Seif was an Expressionist who depicted such bourgeois delights as casinos, nightclubs and horse racing, whose prolific output included 3000 oil paintings, more than 80,000 sketches, and theatre and opera sets; while Adham was into Cubism, abstraction and Socialist Realism, producing such polemical works as *Hunger, Peace* and *Palestine*. There are also two rooms showcasing the work of contemporary local artists like Myriam Abdel Alim,

Magda Sa'd el-Din and Abdel Hadfi al-Gazzar, where you might also find the odd abstract by Farouk Hosni, Egypt's Minister of Culture since 1987. To get there, take tram #2 to San Stefano (the stop after the Jewellery Museum), cross the tracks, head up the steps to the raised road and turn right; the museum is on Sharia Mahmoud Said Pasha, a little way along to the left.

San Stefano and Sidi Bishr
San Stefano – named after a famous resort hotel of the 1930s (featuring a small private beach; £E8 including chair and umbrella) – used to entertain promenaders with an orchestra. As in Forster's day, the tram lines converge here, inland of San Stefano's promontory, terminating at Victoria (now Nasser) College.

Minibuses carry on to **Sidi Bishr**, 14km east of the centre, where Sidi Bishr's mosque stands between two beaches with the same name. Below the Automobile Club, east of the mosque, are the **"Spouting Rocks"** of Bir Mas'ud, where the ancient Alexandrians placed water-powered horns and mills, delighting in gadgetry. It was here, too, that the geometrician Hero invented the world's first hurdy-gurdy and coin-operated vending machine (dispensing holy water) in the first century AD.

Beyond Sidi Bishr, the **Miami Casino** gives way to two more sandy inlets, **Asafra** and **Mandara**.

Montazah
Eighteen kilometres east of downtown Alex you reach **Montazah**, the city's walled pleasure grounds. You can enter the grounds (daily 7am–midnight; £E4, £E5 Fri and holidays) by the gates opposite the *Sheraton*. The 400 acres are well laid-out and tended, with brass lamps, diverse palms and flowers, plus a *Wimpy*, *Pizza Hut* and *Tikka Grill* that might have pleased the gluttonous King Farouk.

Farouk's ancestor Khedive Abbas II ordered the fabulous **Montazah Palace**, a Turko-Florentine hybrid whose central tower mimics the Palazzo Vecchio in Florence. During World War I it was a Red Cross hospital, where E.M. Forster worked as a nurse. It was from Montazah that King Farouk fled to Ras el-Tin before abdicating. Sadat spent £E7 million on restoring the building, which is now a presidential residence and guesthouse, closed to the public. There are two luxury **hotels** within the grounds and a third just outside the entrance (see p.589).

Montazah's sandy **beach** (£E9.50 admission) is separated from Ma'amoura by a promontory with a picturesque "Turkish" **belvedere**; gaps in the fence may enable one to reach Ma'amoura directly, rather than via the distant fee-paying entrance.

Ma'amoura and Canopus
East of the palace grounds, **Ma'amoura** has developed into a private enclave of holiday flats and villas, charging visitors £E3.25 admission before they've even glimpsed the **beach**, access to which costs a further £E5. Its sands are cleaner than most, and women can get away with wearing one-piece costumes. The main beach entrance is off a roundabout on the Abu Qir road, about 1km east of the *Sheraton*. A #736 minibus will deliver you to the residential *Ma'amoura Palace Hotel*, within the enclave, which has its own private beach (£E25 admission).

Past Ma'amoura, the road runs inland of a swathe of military and naval bases, occupying the ancient site of **Canopus**. Not that anything significant remains of this once-great Delta city, which flourished when a branch of the Nile reached the sea by the nearby "Canopic Mouth", but declined as this dried up and Alexandria arose. Classical mythology has it that Canopus was founded by a Greek navigator returning from the Trojan war, whom the locals later worshipped in the form of a jar with a human head. Nineteenth-century archeologists bestowed the title **Canopic jars** on similar receptacles used to preserve mummies' viscera. Each organ had its own protective deity (a minor son of Horus) whose visage adorned the stopper (human heads went out of fashion late in the XVIII Dynasty). Even after XXI Dynasty embalmers began replacing organs in the mummies, the practice of leaving Canopic jars in tombs continued.

Abu Qir

When a straggle of jerry-built houses appears beyond the naval bases, you know you're entering **Abu Qir** (pronounced *Abu Ear*). This small fishing town can be reached by service taxi, or minibus #728 or #729 (from Masr Station); if you're coming from Montazah, the minibus stop is under the bridge and left around the corner of the palace walls from the *Sheraton* – look for knots of people waiting near the butchers. Abu Qir is garbage-strewn and ugly, and the raw sewage flowing down its **beach** should deter anyone from bathing; the only things going for it are itinerant vendors peddling everything from dolls to candelabras, and its **seafood restaurants**. While the once renowned *Zephyrion* (Greek for "sea breeze") has gone downhill since its old owner died, the *Bella Vista* next door is an enjoyable place to eat squid and drink *zbiba*.

Abu Qir was once famous for two historic **battles**. Admiral Nelson's defeat of the French fleet at Abu Qir Bay (1798) effectively scuppered Napoleon's dream of an eastern empire and went down in British history as the Battle of the Nile, inspiring Mrs Hemans to write, "The boy stood on the burning deck …".

Though evenly matched in numbers, Admiral Bruey had his ships cabled together in shallow water when Nelson's fleet charged them amidships, inflicting carnage at close quarters. The French lost eleven ships and 17,000 men, the English two ships and 218 sailors. In 1998–99, Goddio's divers found the **wrecks** of the French flagship *L'Orient*, the *Sérieuse* and *Artémise* at a depth of 11m, 8km offshore.

But Bonaparte had his revenge, for in 1799 he personally led ten thousand cavalry against fifteen thousand Turks landed by the Royal Navy, pushing them back into the sea. Fittingly, Abu Qir is now the site of Egypt's **Naval Academy**. During summer, it's possible to take a motorboat to **Nelson's Island** (45min; £E50 for three people); ask for El Mu'allim Desouki, on the beach at the end of Sharia el-Bahr el-Mayyit.

In 2001 Goddio's team announced the discovery of **Herakleion**, the fabled ancient entrepôt to Egypt that fell into the sea 1300 years ago. Buried by sediment for centuries in Abu Qir Bay, its identity was confirmed by a stele inscribed with the city's name, erected by Nectanebo I, and the pink-granite naos believed to belong to the temple of Heracles-Khonsu seen by Herodotus when he visited Herakleion in the fifth century BC. Divers also found three colossal statues of the Nile-god Hapy; in ancient times, the city stood at the mouth of a branch of the river.

Eating and drinking

Alexandria can't match Cairo for culinary variety, but it beats the capital when it comes to **seafood and Greek restaurants** – and when these pall you can always fall back on Egyptian favourites like *shawarmas*, pizzas, *fuul* and *felafel*, or seek refuge in a few Oriental-ish places. **Coffee houses**, too, are an Alex speciality, and there are some good **bars** if you know where to look.

Alongside all this, Western **fast-food outlets** are springing up all over town. *McDonald's* (daily 10am–11pm) is near the top of Sharia Safiya Zaghloul, around the corner from *Kentucky Fried Chicken* and *Baskin-Robbins* (both daily 10am–2am) on Ramleh. *KFC* has another branch on the Corniche in Roushdi, near *Pizza Hut* (which also has an outlet in Montazah) and *Wimpy* (whose franchise by the *Fish Market* complex is run by deaf people).

Coffee houses and patisseries

Coffee houses and **patisseries** like *Athineos* and the *Trianon* have accumulated a heavy load of mystique, and even if you couldn't give a toss about Cavafy or Durrell, their opulent interiors and cakes should not be missed. All of them are shown on the map on p.592. For nocturnal types, there are expensive **24-hour coffee shops** in the *Cecil, Montazah Sheraton* and *Renaissance Alexandria* hotels.

Traditional **Arab cafés** (*ahwas*) are another world from the European patisseries, and a male preserve not recommended for women on their own. If you're into sipping tea or *karkaday* surrounded by guys slapping down backgammon counters or dominoes between lung-charring tokes on *sheeshas*, there are loads of places around Midan el-Gumhorriya. You can always locate them by the sound of coughing, audible above Koranic recitals or Umm Kalthoum sobbing from the radio.

Athineos Midan Ramleh. Decorated with classical motifs and mirrors and frequented by eccentrics; beware of the pushy waitress, eager to boost your bill. Check out the gilded friezes and columns in the restaurant upstairs – the entrance is around the corner. Daily 8am–midnight.

Baudrot 23 Sharia Sa'ad Zaghloul. Don't be deterred by the shabby rooms off the street; its spacious, vine-trellised courtyard is an ideal retreat from the heat, serving inexpensive cakes, coffee, chicken or fish meals and beer. Daily 7am–midnight.

Brazilian Coffee Stores Corner of Nabi Daniel and Sa'ad Zaghloul, near the tourist office. This popular stand-up breakfast spot features antique coffee mills, a glass map of Brazil and other period furnishings. Great coffee – espresso costs just £E1.50 – and greasy pastries. There's also a sit-down branch on Sharia Talaat Harb. Both daily 7am–11pm.

Délices Between Midan and Sharia Sa'ad Zaghloul. Less inviting since they smartened it up, junked the teak bar and installed air conditioning, but the tables outside have a nice view. Sells cakes, savouries, soft drinks and beer. Daily 7am–11pm.

Pastroudis 39 Sharia Horriya. Established in 1923, this dark-panelled café features in *The*

Alexandria Quartet, and was another haunt of Cavafy, but is now a sad parody of itself. The pavement tables on the south side overlook an outdoor antiques market; alcohol-drinkers must sit at the back indoors. Minimum charge £E5. Daily 9am–midnight.

Sofianopoulo Coffee Store 18 Sharia Sa'ad Zaghloul. Another vintage coffee shop with silver grinders and sacks of beans. From Mon–Sat they sell excellent cappuccino (£E2) and croissants (£E1.25); on Sun you can only buy coffee beans. If you feel hungry, the *Hassan Bleik Restaurant* is next door (see below). Daily 9am–11pm.

The Trianon Corner of Sa'ad Zaghloul and Ramleh. Redecorated and air-conditioned, the swankiest of Alexandria's patisseries boasts gilt columns and a splendidly ornate restaurant, not in use. The menu includes a three-course French breakfast with coffee (£E12), moussaka (£E13), beer, creamy cakes, beverages (£E6 minimum charge) and wine (Egyptian £E70, French £E180, champagne £E450!). Try the flambé dishes. Cavafy used to work upstairs. Daily 7am–1am.

Vinous Corner of Nabi Daniel and Horriya. A faded Art Deco salon, serving cakes and coffee. Daily 7am–midnight.

Restaurants and cafés

The following **restaurants and cafés** more or less represent the culinary and budgetary spectrum. Most of them are downtown, in the area delineated by Ramleh, Safiya Zaghloul, Nabi Daniel and Horriya streets (see map on

pp.592–593), but there are also some recommendations far along the Corniche (marked on the city plan on pp.582–583). Phone numbers are only given where reservations are advisable.

(side margin text)

Abu Ashraf 28 Sharia Safar Pasha, Anfushi. Accessible from downtown by tram #14 or #15, this street is full of good-value fish or kebab restaurants, tempting passers-by with their out-door charcoal grills. *Abu Ashraf* is devoted to fish and seafood, which is sold by weight (red mullet £E30 per kilo; king prawns £E120) and cooked in front of your eyes. Daily 24hr.

Au Privé Sharia Verdi ☎ 03/484 1881. Down an alley off the junction of Sharia Horriya and Nabi Daniel, this trendy bar/restaurant serves salads, seafood, burgers and dips at the bar (£E10–40), and richly sauced poultry, game and seafood dish-es in the restaurant. Daily noon–2am.

Bella Vista Abu Qir beach. Since the *Zephyrion* (see below) hit the rocks, this is the best place in Abu Qir to eat freshly caught seafood and enjoy the sea view and cool breezes over a beer or a *zibiba*. Daily noon–1am.

Cafeteria Asteria 40 Sharia Safiya Zaghloul. Sandwiches, macaroni, pizzas, ice cream and hot drinks at reasonable prices. Walk through the outer room to find a nice glass-roofed annexe, popular with lovers. Friendly, English-speaking Greek pro-prietor. Daily 8am–11pm.

China House *Hotel Cecil*, Midan Sa'ad Zaghloul ☎ 03/487 7173. The best of Alex's Chinese restau-rants affords splendid views of the harbour. Try the delicious spring rolls, chicken dumplings, sweet-and-sour-shrimp, or grilled beef with garlic sauce – but leave room for the fried bananas with maple syrup and vanilla ice cream. Daily 11am–11.30pm.

Denis 1 Sharia Ibn Basaam, off Ramleh. 1930s-style Greek fish bar where you select your *samak* or *calamari* from the freezer. Fish with chips, salad, *tahina* and beer costs around £E40. Sells wine too. Daily 10am–midnight.

Elite 43 Sharia Safiya Zaghloul. Old-fashioned bohemian place decorated with Chagall and Picasso prints; owner Madame Christina enjoys reminiscing about the artists and writers she has known. Simple Greco-Levantine dishes: choose from the long menu on the wall rather than the short one given to tourists. Serves beer and *zibiba*. Moderate prices. Daily 8am–midnight.

Fish Market Anfushi. 2nd floor of a waterfront complex that includes the *Tikka Grill* (see below) and a *Wimpy* ☎ 03/480 5119. Spacious and snazzy, with a great view of the harbour, and serv-ice verging on the obsequious. No menus; you choose from a mound of fish (£E45–80 per kilo) and crustaceans (£E105–160). The salad platter is

a meal in itself. Wine and beer. Daily 1pm–1am.

Hassan Bleik 18 Sharia Sa'ad Zaghloul. Long-established, inexpensive Lebanese restaurant behind a patisserie beside the *Sofianopoulo Coffee Store*. Authentic dishes such as *kibbeh* (meat-filled cracked-wheat croquettes), *fatta* (chickpeas, lamb and liver on a bed of rice and bread in a garlicky sauce) and quail and brain with rice make up for the grubby tablecloths. Daily noon–10.30pm.

Kadoura 33 Sharia Bairam al-Tonsi, off the Corniche in Anfushi ☎ 03/480 0405. Widely rated the best fish restaurant in Alex, *Kadoura* (pro-nounced '*Adoura*') is quite unpretentious, with no menu. Diners choose from an ice-packed array of sea bass, red and grey mullet, bluefish, squid, shrimp and crab (some still moving), to be eaten upstairs, overlooking the Corniche. All orders come with a selection of *mezze*. Seafood prices vary seasonally. Daily noon–midnight.

Malek es-Samaan Off Sharia Attarine. Look for the sign with a picture of a bird to find this humble open-air eatery in a yard that hosts a clothes mar-ket by day. Delicious spit-roast quail is all they serve (£E6 per bird). Daily 8pm–1am (or later).

Mohammed Ahmed 17 Sharia Shakor Pasha, off Sa'ad Zaghloul. One of the cheapest places for a takeaway or a quick meal downtown, it serves tasty *fuul*, *felafel*, and other Egyptian eats. Daily 6am–1am.

Mohammed Hosni 48 Sharia Safar Pasha, Anfushi. This semi-outdoor restaurant in a court-yard on the same street as *Abu Ashraf* (see above) serves seafood, kebabs and quail; two courses cost £E16–25. Daily till midnight or later.

L'Osobuco 14 Sharia al-Horriya ☎ 03/487 2506. Run by the same firm as *L'Aubergine* in Cairo, this candlelit restaurant has an excellent menu that spans three continents and includes plenty of vegetarian dishes (£E30–50 for two courses), plus a bar featuring live jazz some evenings. Daily 11am–3am.

Samakmak 42 Qasr Ras el-Tin, Anfushi ☎ 03/481 1560. Fancier than *Kadoura* or *Abu Ashraf*, this fish restaurant is renowned for its crab *tajine*, crayfish, and spaghetti with clams, and belongs to a retired belly-dancer, Zizi Salem. In the summer you can eat outdoors in a large tent. Expect to pay £E80 for a full meal, excluding drinks.

Santa Lucia 40 Sharia Safiya Zaghloul ☎ 03/486 0332. One of Alex's most venerable restaurants, still popular with the older *haute bourgeoisie*, it serves seafood, rabbit and poultry cooked to

ALEXANDRIA AND THE MEDITERRANEAN COAST | Eating and drinking

French recipes (£E50–60 for two dishes), with a pianist and dancing in the evenings. Accepts Visa. Daily noon–1am.

Tavern Opposite Ramleh tram terminal. Popular chain restaurant with a *shawarma* and kebab takeaway downstairs. Does tasty Egyptian and Western-style pizzas (£E10–18), seafood and soup, and there's a salad bar (£E2.50). Plus a takeaway-only branch in Montazah Gardens. Both daily 8am–3am (2am in winter).

Tikka Grill Anfushi. Underneath the *Fish Market* ☎03/480 5114. Plush surroundings and great service, though the chicken tikka is nothing special. Serves alcohol. Daily 1pm–1am. Has an outlet in the Montazah Gardens.

Zephyrion Abu Qir beach. Once the best seafood place at Abu Qir, it has gone downhill since the previous owner's son took over, but its breezy terrace is still alluring, even if the *Bella Vista* (see above) does better food. Daily noon–midnight.

Drinking

Although Alex is the centre of Egypt's wine and spirits industry (the vineyards are at Giancolis, near Lake Mariout), **bars** have a fairly low profile. *Monty's Bar* (daily 4pm–2am) in the *Hotel Cecil* is an anodyne place to sip beer or cocktails, but the roof garden has a great view of town. If you're going to pay five-star prices, the *Fouad Bar* (daily 11am–2am) in the *El Salamlek Palace Hotel* at Montazah is plusher, with piano music in the evenings (smart dress required). But foreign residents and local drinkers prefer other watering holes, with lower prices and more character. Until a few years ago it was customary to do a Thursday night pub crawl, starting at the *Spitfire Bar* and ending up at the *Havana Bistro*, but nowadays few expats come downtown to drink, preferring to socialize in Roushdi – and the wonderful *Havana* has closed down. If you just want to buy booze, there's a Stella shop on the corner of Sharia Gamil el-Din Yassin and Sharia el-Ghorfa el-Tigarya and several stores selling local spirits further along the main road, while imported brands are sold at the **duty-free shop**, 31 Sharia Salah Salem (daily 11am–9pm, Ramadan 10.30am–2.30pm & 8–11pm), which only takes US dollars, Visa or MasterCard. All of the following are keyed to the map on p.592 unless stated otherwise.

Al-Ahram Off Sharia Sa'ad Zaghloul. Split-level bar and coffee shop refuge for middle-aged sports fans, where foreigners are seldom seen. Upstairs, a beer will cost you £E7 and you can watch satellite TV while you eat – though it's often tuned to German stations. Not a place for women to feel relaxed. Closed Fri.

Cap d'Or Sharia Adib, off Sharia Sa'ad Zaghloul. Art Nouveau gilded mouldings, carved teak and engraved mirrors. Dubbed "The Trapdoor" by expats, but mostly frequented by Egyptians. Sells shrimps and other snacks (check the price first); a pint of Stella is £E10. Daily noon–3am.

Elite 43 Sharia Safiya Zaghloul. Simple blue-painted extension to the restaurant of the same name. Frequented by tourists, writers and odd-balls; a place to talk and meet people. Sells beer, *zibiba* and brandy. Usually open till midnight.

Far 'n' Away 14 Sharia Horriya. The closest Alex gets to a preppy American-style bar, with hard-wood floors, cocktails, burgers and Tex-Mex food, and a DJ spinning diverse US sounds on Thursday and Friday nights. Takes Visa. Daily 1pm–1am.

Portuguese Club 42 Sharia Abd el-Qader Ragab, Roushdi ☎03/542 7599. A cultural centre by day, the *Centro de Portugal* is the hub of social life for expat residents of Roushdi, with a seafood restaurant, garden, pool tables, satellite TV, and dancing if people are in the mood. The £E50 admission fee for non-members is redeemable in food and drink. Phone to check that they're not closed for some Portuguese holiday unknown to the rest of the world. Located in a side road behind the BMW showroom on Tariq Gamal Abdel Nasser, 3km from the centre (£3–5 by taxi); see the map on p.583. Daily 1pm–2am.

Spitfire Bar Off Sharia Sa'ad Zaghloul. Small, friendly hangout covered in stickers from oil companies, warships and overland travel groups (the kind of foreigners that frequent the place), where little coteries of Egyptian and Greek intellectuals argue under the benign gaze of the five brothers who own the bar. You can get imported as well as domestic liquor. Mon–Sat noon–midnight.

Nightlife and entertainment

Thursday and Friday are the big nights out in Alex, but there's something happening all week. Several hotel **nightclubs** offer a programme of dinner with a slightly risqué "Russian Show" and a belly dancer. The best ones are in the *Helnan Palestine* (June–Sept daily 11pm–4am; £E45 minimum charge) and the *Montazah Sheraton* (Thurs 11pm–4am; £E105 minimum charge; June–Sept daily pool-side belly dancing 11pm–2am; £E35); the show in the *Hotel Cecil* (£E66 minimum charge) is not up to much. Foreigners who turn up at the *Crazy Horse* inside *Athineos* on Midan Ramleh are discouraged from entering the nightclub, which is full of prostitutes (10pm–5am; minimum charge £E75). You're better off heading to the Latin-American Show on the terrace of the *El-Salamlek* (June–Sept daily 7–11pm; minimum charge £E75), an all-singing, all-dancing affair that also features a DJ.

On Thursdays and Fridays, resident expats and Westernized Egyptians go **dancing** at the *Portuguese Club* or *Far 'n' Away* (see "Drinking") – where rock oldies, reggae and last year's chart hits are the order of the day – while *baladi* youths prefer the kind of discos that exude sweat and Arabic pop from the upper floors of seedy buildings. Unfortunately, they open and close so often that it's hard to be specific about venues – listen out and you might locate one. Punters who aren't in mixed-sex couples may be refused admission to the pricier, Westernized discos in the top hotels, such as *Black Gold* in the *Renaissance Alexandria* (daily 10pm–5am; minimum charge £E30) or *Aquarius* in the *Montazah Sheraton* (daily July–Sept, Thurs–Tues the rest of the year; £E35 minimum charge, £E45 on Thurs).

Arts and festivals

While Cairo has enjoyed a state-of-the-art opera house for twenty years, Alexandria can only dream of modernizing its own nineteenth-century one, which is so decrepit that it looks derelict – symptomatic of a general underfunding of the arts, cultured Alexandrines lament. Although the new Library may become a major venue for performing arts in the future, the current line-up of venues and festivals has hardly altered in years.

The most promising venue is the newly refurbished **Alexandria Creativity Centre** on Sharia Fouad (☎03/492 4533), which hosts chamber concerts of **classical music** – Arabic as well as European, with guest musicians from Egypt and abroad. Larger orchestral works, **ballet** and **plays** still have to be staged in the former opera house, a once grand Beaux Arts edifice that used to be the Theatre Mohammed Ali – he would turn in his grave to see its rotting boxes, uncarpeted auditorium and staff asleep on the floor. It is now named the **Said Darwish Theatre** (☎03/486 5602), after the father of modern Arabic drama. It lurks in a cul-de-sac off 22 Sharia Horriya, about 200m east of the Creativity Centre, followed by the **Conservatoire de Musique d'Alexandrie** at no.90 (☎03/483 5086). None has regular programmes; events are advertised at foreign cultural centres and the *Elite* restaurant.

In August you can see **bellydancing and folk dances** by the Rida Troupe (*Fir'et Rida*) or the National Troupe (*El-Fir'a el-Qawmiyya*) at the outdoor **Abdel Wahab Theatre** (☎03/482 3637), on the Corniche east of Midan Ramleh. Nightly shows start at 10.30pm; tickets cost £E5–20, and are best reserved two days before; avoid the box seats. During summer there's also a **circus**, which sets up either at Azarita near the Abdel Wahab Theatre, or at St Marks College, near the youth hostel. Performances start at 9pm, or 5pm on Fridays and Sundays; tickets cost £E8–31.

Come September, the biennial **Alexandria World Festival** of drama and music alternates with an **International Film Festival**, which gives Egyptians a rare opportunity to see foreign movies in an uncensored state; every cinema in town screens a few. Film-going is popular throughout the year, with extra showings at all **cinemas** during Ramadan. Downtown, the refurbished Royal Renaissance (mobile ☎0122 275493) by the Said Darwish Theatre and the Amir (☎03/491 7972) on the corner of Sharia Horriya and Safiya Zaghloul devote two of their three screens to English-language films you might have seen last year. These are trumped by first-releases at the scruffy old Rialto (☎03/486 4694) on Safiya Zaghloul, which far outclass the awful B-movies at the lovely Art Deco Metro (☎03/487 0432) down the road. Out in Smouha, the Renaissance (☎03/424 0844) in the Zahran Mall is Alex's newest multiplex, with four screens showing first-release Hollywood blockbusters. The Osman Group Cinema (☎03/424 5897) in the Smouha shopping centre next door is similar. Tickets cost from £E15–25.

Other events include the **Alexandria Biennial**, an exhibition of art from Mediterranean countries staged every other November under the auspices of the Fine Arts Museum; and an annual **International Yachting Regatta** in October, sponsored by the *Helnan Palestine Hotel*, which sometimes hosts exclusive **bridge tournaments**, attended by Omar Sharif.

During Ramadan, the Egyptian, Islamic side of Alex revels in five **moulids** over five consecutive weeks, starting with *zikrs* outside the Mosque of Al-Mursi. The day after its "big night", the action shifts to Sidi Gaber's mosque, then Sidi Bishr's; these are followed by the moulids of Sidi Kamal and Sidi Mohammed al-Rahhal.

Sport and activities

For those qualified to go **diving**, there are many **ancient ruins and wrecks** in the waters around Alex (5–11m). Alas, the Eastern Harbour is so murky that it's hard to see the weed-encrusted remnants of the Royal Quarter or a German fighter plane shot down during the war unless you're practically touching them. Visibility may be better outside the harbour, where blocks from the Pharos litter the sea bed near Qaitbey's fort and Roman trading vessels lie 500m offshore – but here divers may face strong waves or undertows. If you're still interested, visit Alexandra Dive (☎03/480-0363, ✉alxdiv@dataxprs.com.eg, ⓦwww.alexandra-dive.com) beside the *Tikka Grill* on the Corniche, which will take a minimum of three people to dive at two different sites for US$90 each (including lunch and the fee to Underwater Archeology Department; diving gear costs US$30 extra). They run PADI, CMAS or SSI open-water (US$350), dive master (US$800) and specialist diving (US$90–150) **courses** and offer **windsurfing** (£E80/hr), **jet skiing** (£E150/hr), **water skiing** (£E200/hr) and **parasailing** (£E150). If you can muster enough participants, they can also arrange half-day **fishing trips** for a minimum of four (US$50 each) and longer **boat safaris** for groups of ten, to Abu Qir and Nelson's Island (1 day; £E100 per person); El Alamein or Marina Beach (2 days; £E75 each); or Ras el-Hikma, Ubayyad, Agiiba, Cleopatra and Alam el-Rum beaches near Mersa Matrouh (£E325 each).

Other activities can be pursued at the **Sporting Club** (☎03/543 3627), where one-day membership (£E25) entitles you to use the **swimming pools**, tennis and squash courts, go horse riding or even play golf on the 18-hole course (£E10). If you can't gain access to the club, non-residents are sometimes allowed to use the pools at the *Renaissance Alexandria* (☎03/549 0935) or *Montazah Sheraton* (☎03/540-1331). Phone to check before turning up. If you'd rather watch **football**, check out who's playing at the Municipal Stadium, the home ground of **Al Ittihad**. Founded by students from Ras el-Tin in the 1920s, the club has won the Egyptian cup six times and is currently ranked eleventh in the league. Alternatively, you might want to watch a uniquely Alexandrian form of **horse racing** at Smouha, where *baladi* folk race horses with every kind of carriage attached, on the wide road beside the Zoo. The event is on Sunday, starting at 1.30pm from November to May and at 6pm in the summer (75pt admission).

You can play **pool** at any number of places. *Free Ball*, on the second floor of the southwest corner of Midan Ramleh, is a friendly den with reasonable hourly rates (billiards £E15; snooker £E20), but if you want to drink alcohol, head for the pool table in the *Marhaba Hotel* on Midan Orabi (£E10/hr; nightly 10pm–2am).

Listings

Airlines EgyptAir (2–3 daily flights to Cairo; ☎03/486 5701), BA (2–3 flights weekly to London; ☎486 1565) and Olympic (twice weekly to Athens; ☎03/486 1014) are on Midan Ramleh; Air France (☎03/483 8901) at 22 Sharia Salah Salem; Lufthansa (3 weekly flights to Frankfurt; ☎03/486 2607) at 9 Sharia Talaat Harb. Most are closed Fri and Sun. Foreign airlines without an office are represented by local travel agents, mostly open daily except Fri 9am–4pm.

Arabic language courses The British Council (see Cultural centres, below) schedules six-week courses every two months from September to July, and an intensive three-week course in August; each costs £E800 for 36 hours' tuition.

Banks Bank of Alexandria, 59 Sharia Sa'ad Zaghloul, 23 Sharia Talaat Harb and 26 Sharia Salah Salem (Mon–Thurs & Sun 8.30am–2pm, Ramadan 10.30am–1pm); the National Bank of Egypt in the *Montazah Sheraton* (daily 10am–2pm; ATM accepts MasterCard) or the *Hotel Cecil* (Mon–Thurs & Sun 8.30am–8pm, Fri & Sat 9am–noon & 4–7pm); or Thomas Cook (see below). The HSBC has ATMs (accepting Visa, Cirrus, Electron, Plus and MasterCard) at its branch at 47 Sharia Sultan Hussein and the *El Salamlek Palace Hotel*; and there's another ATM accepting Visa, MasterCard, Cirrus and Plus at the Banque Misr, 1 Sharia Talaat Harb.

Bookshops There's some evidence of Alex's old literary cosmopolitanism at the Dar el-Mostakpal bookshop at 32 Sharia Safiya Zaghloul; the Al-Ahram bookshop at 10 Sharia Horriya – stocking a good range of books on Egypt as well as English-language classics – and El-Ma'aref (between Midan and Sharia Sa'ad Zaghloul, next to *Délices*), which offers foreign novels and textbooks. You can rummage through second-hand novels (abridged for students of English) on the pavement opposite the French Centre on Sharia Nabi Daniel. Foreign newspapers are sold outside the Ramleh telephone exchange.

Consulates Britain, 3 Sharia Mena, Roushdi (Mon–Thurs & Sun 8am–1pm; ☎03/546 7001); Germany, 5 Sharia Mena (Mon–Thurs & Sun 10am–noon; ☎03/545 7050); France, 2 Midan Orabi (Mon–Thurs & Sun 9am–1pm; ☎03/483 5513); Ireland, 236 Sharia Kafr Abdou, Kafr Abdou (Mon–Thurs & Sun 8am–1pm; ☎03/546 0081); Israel, 15 Sharia Mena, Loran (Mon–Thurs & Sun 9.30am–3.30pm; ☎03/544 9501); Italy, Midan Sa'ad Zaghloul (Mon–Thurs 9am–12.30pm; ☎03/483 0095); Spain, 101 Sharia el-Horreya, el-Shallalat (Mon–Thurs & Sun 9.30am–12.30pm; ☎03/493 9185). Australia, New Zealand, the US and Canada have no consular representation; other consulates are listed in *Alexandria Night and Day*.

Cultural centres American Center, 3 Sharia Phara'ana (Mon–Wed & Sun 10am–6pm, Thurs 10am–4pm, Ramadan Mon–Thurs & Sun 10am–3pm; ☎03/486 1009, ✉AmericanCenterAlexandria@yahoo.com); British Council, 9 Sharia Batalsa (Mon–Wed & Sun 10am–8pm, Sat & Thurs 10am–3pm; Ramadan daily except Fri 9.30am–3.30pm; ☎03/486 0199, ✉british.council@britishcouncil.org.eg); French Centre, 30 Sharia Nabi Daniel (Mon–Thurs & Sun 9am–1pm & 4–8pm; ☎03/492 0804); Goethe

Institute, 10 Sharia al-Batalssa (Mon–Thurs & Sun 10am–1pm & 4–7pm; ℡483 9870); Russian Centre, 5 Sharia Batalsa (Mon–Thurs & Sun 10am–1pm & 5–8pm; ℡03/486 5645).

Film processing Kodak film is sold and developed opposite the Rialto Cinema on Safiya Zaghloul; other places can be found on Sharia Sa'ad Zaghloul.

Hospitals The private Al-Madina al-Tibaia, Sharia Ahmed Shawky, Roushdi (℡03/543 2150), Al-Markaz al-Tiby, 14th May Road, Smouha (℡03/427 2652), and the Armed Forces Hospital on the Corniche in Sidi Gaber (℡03/544 8858) are used to dealing with foreigners. For non-emergencies, ask your consulate or hotel to recommend a doctor.

International calls There are Menatel booths all over town. The 24hr exchange on Midan Ramleh has direct-dial phones and sells phonecards; the exchanges on Midan el-Gumhorriya and Sharia Sa'ad Zaghloul (both daily 8am–11pm) work on the pre-booking system. Speedy connections can be obtained at any of the top hotels, which charge 50–70 percent above the normal rate.

Internet The American Center (see above) offers free Internet access to anyone doing "research", and doesn't seem to mind if they just read their email. Otherwise, *Cyber Club*, near the *Spitfire Bar*, and *Zawiya Internet Café*, off Sharia Safiya Zaghloul, are highly central and signposted in English (both Mon–Thurs, Sat & Sun noon–4am, Fri 4pm–4am; £E5/hr); *Globalnet*, on the 6th floor of 29 Sharia Nabi Daniel, is only signposted in Arabic (daily 24hr; £E5/hr). Trendy local teenagers and resident expats favour two places in the shopping centre beside the Zahran Mall in Smouha: *Click-It Internet* (daily 10.30am–1am; £E8/hr) on

the ground floor, and *Access Cybercafe* on the floor above (daily 9am–midnight; £E5/hr).

Passport office To renew your visa, go to the office at 25 Sharia Talaat Harb (Mon–Thurs, Sat & Sun 8am–3pm; ℡03/484 7873). You'll need one photo and a photocopy of the relevant pages from your passport.

Pharmacies Khalil, on Sharia el-Ghorfa el-Tigarya, off Midan Sa'ad Zaghloul (Mon–Thurs, Sat & Sun 9am–midnight; ℡03/480 6710); Strand, by the intersection of Safiya and Sa'ad Zaghloul streets (daily 9am–1am; ℡03/486 5136). There are others on Safiya Zaghloul and Nabi Daniel streets.

Post offices Midan Ramleh (daily 8am–3pm), Sharia el-Ghorfa el-Tigarya (same hours) and Masr Station (daily 8am–5pm). The poste restante service is unreliable, so ask if you can have mail sent c/o the *Hotel Cecil*. Express Mail Service is open till 2pm at all the main post offices.

Teaching English Holders of RSA or Trinity TEFL certificates may be able to find work in private schools, though wages might barely cover the cost of renting a flat. The British Council (see above) pays the best rates (£E4000 per month). Make enquiries there and at the American Center or ask around the expat community.

Thomas Cook 15 Midan Sa'ad Zaghloul ℡03/484 7830, ℻487 4073, ✉tcalex@attmail.com. Can change money and travellers' cheques, give cash advances on Visa and MasterCard, and deal with stolen ones. Daily 8am–5pm.

Tourist police Above the tourist office (℡03/487 3378; in the Maritime Station ℡R03/480 4633; at the entrance to Montazah gardens ℡03/547 3814; in the Greco-Roman Museum ℡03/484 5594. All except the last are open 24 hours.

Moving on from Alexandria

Most of the places covered in the remainder of this chapter can be reached from Alexandria by public transport. Using the quickest available method it's also feasible to make **day excursions** to Rosetta and Tanta in the Delta (see Chapter Five) or the Monasteries of Wadi Natrun (see Chapter Three). Moving on from the city, there are also direct services to Port Said in the Canal Zone.

Buses

The **15th May Terminal** behind Sidi Gaber Station (accessible by tram #2) is the city's main bus station. Hourly a/c services to **Cairo** (£E20) are operated by the West Delta (5.30am–10.30pm; ℡03/427 0916) and Superjet (5.30am–10.30pm; ℡03/428 9092) companies; bookings should be made at the appropriate kiosk. There is also a 1am Superjet that runs directly to Cairo airport (£E31). Hourly West Delta express buses to **Mersa Matrouh**

(£E15–23) run all year, supplemented by slightly comfier Superjet services (daily 7.15am & 4pm; £E24) over the summer. The 11am and 2pm West Delta buses run on to **Siwa Oasis** (£E27). Other destinations include **Port Said** (Superjet 6.45am; £E22; West Delta 6am, 8am, 3.30pm & 4.30pm; £E17–22); **Hurghada** (Superjet 8pm; £E80; West Delta 6.30pm; £E60); **Tanta** (West Delta 6.45am, noon & 1.15pm; £E6) and **Zagazig** (West Delta 8am, 10am, 2pm, 3pm & 4pm; £E13–15). Tickets for West Delta buses can also be bought at their office (☎03/480 9685) on the corner of Midan Sa'ad Zaghloul and Sharia el-Ghorfa el-Tigarya – if their computer isn't down.

Trains

Train services between Alex and Cairo are detailed on p.281. At **Masr Station**, tickets for 1st and 2nd class a/c trains are sold from the office beside the tourist information booth on platform one, while ordinary 2nd class and 3rd class tickets are sold in the front hall. Services to Tanta and Cairo can also be boarded at **Sidi Gaber Station**. Unless you travel in 1st or a/c 2nd class, trains are generally less comfortable than buses or service taxis.

Service taxis

The **Moharrem Bey Terminal** (known as *El-Mogaf Gedida*, the "New Terminal") on the city's outskirts can be reached by minibus from the western side of Midan el-Gumhorriya (25pt) or by taxi (£E5). Its ranks of Peugeots, Toyota minibuses and minivans run to almost everywhere that's worth mentioning within 200km of Alexandria, including **Cairo** (£E10), **Abu Sir** (£E2), the **Monastery of Abu Mina** (£E2), **El-Alamein** (£E3.50), **Mersa Matrouh** (£E12), **Port Said** (£E10), **Tanta** (£E4) and **Zagazig** (£E10). Listen for the drivers shouting out destinations, or ask for directions to the right clump of service taxis. If you don't mind a hair-raising trip with a few strangers, service taxis are the quickest way to get anywhere.

The Mediterranean coast

Egypt's 500-kilometre-long **Mediterranean coast** has beautiful beaches and sparkling sea all the way to Libya. However, many stretches are still mined from World War II (see below) or off limits due to military bases, or simply hard to reach – while all the most accessible sites have been colonized by holiday villages. Unlike in Sinai and Hurghada, these cater exclusively to Egyptians, whose beach culture is significantly different from Westerners'.

Most foreign travellers heading this way are aiming for Siwa Oasis (see p.564) rather than the disappointing resort town of **Mersa Matrouh**. Aside from the **beaches** near Matrouh, other coastal sites are awkward to reach (or leave) without private transport, though you may consider it worth making the effort to get to the famous World War II battlefield of **El-Alamein**, or the swanky resort at **Sidi Abd el-Rahman**. In general, though, even the sea can seem reclusive here, hidden from sight of the "coastal" highway by **holiday villages** or barren ridges, while the B-road and railway along which many of the region's villages are located run still further inland.

Between Alexandria and El-Alamein

The "sights" **between Alexandria and El-Alamein** are relatively neglected by tourists, in some cases deservedly so. Getting there can involve much toing and froing around unsignposted crossroads miles from anywhere and, without your own transport, none of the places below is easy to reach as stops en route to El-Alamein or Mersa Matrouh. If you're using public transport, it's better to consider them as day excursions from Alex.

There are many new **holiday villages** along the highway to Matrouh. Some are reserved for elite sections of Egyptian society such as the army, navy and diplomatic corps, while others cater to anyone wealthy enough to afford an apartment there. If you have a car and loads of money, their gorgeous beaches and middling to luxurious facilities could be worth investigating. Otherwise, they're simply blights on the landscape that induce a numbing fatalism, as one succeeds another, for mile after mile.

El-Agami

Some 20km west of downtown Alex is the ever-growing resort of **EL-AGAMI**, whose white sands were first appreciated by rich, villa-building Egyptians in the 1950s. Confusingly, it comprises two resorts: **Bitash** (or "El-Agami"), consisting of villas and upmarket hotels, and **Hannoville**, 1km further west, where flats and cheaper hotels predominate. Each is approached by a separate road turning off the highway to Mersa Matrouh – Sharia Bitash and Sharia Hannoville – which runs towards their respective **beaches**. Both are somewhat less crowded than the Corniche beaches in Alex, but suffer from the same drawbacks, namely litter and sexual harassment. You might encounter foreign expats living here, who commute to work in Alex; a two-room **flat** costs £E500 per month.

The easiest way of **getting there** from Alex is by minibus from Midan Khartoum (#750 to Bitash, #760 to Hannoville) or Masr Station (#755 to Bitash, #765 to Hannoville). Although #460 buses from Midan Khartoum run to both resorts (first Bitash, then Hannoville), they're incredibly crowded and far slower than minibuses. In Bitash, minibuses drop you across the road from the *Summer Moon Hotel*; in Hannoville, at the *Costa Blanca Hotel*.

Bitash

By Egyptian standards Bitash has a fairly liberal atmosphere, with the odd bikini to be seen on the semi-private **Fardous Beach**, reached by turning left by the telephone office on Sharia Bitash and carrying on to the end of Sharia Hanafiyya. The best places to stay are the beach-front *Agami Palace* (☎03/433 0230, ☏433 3503; ❸) and *Summer Moon* (☎ & ☏03/433 0367; ❼) **hotels**, which have pools, discos and other amenities; their rates include breakfast. There are two other **discos** nearby, at *Felfela* (which also has a swimming pool and billiard room), and the expensive open-air French restaurant, *Michael's*.

Siwa Oasis

Places to eat proliferate along Sharia Bitash. *Abu Hussein* and *Mu'min* are cheap and cheerful sandwich bars; *Gino's* does tasty pizzas and pasta; *Saber* serves up sugary desserts. A right turn at the end of the street will bring you to *La Poire* on Sharia Shahr al-Asal, offering excellent *shawarmas* and chicken sandwiches, next to which are *Pizza Hut, Kentucky Fried Chicken* and *Baskin-Robbins*.

There are two private **hospitals** on Sharia Bitash: Al-Wafaa (☏03/433 8318) at no.54 and Ibrahim Farouk (☏03/433 2925) at no.62. You'll also find a **pharmacy** (daily 9.30am–midnight) at no.79, a **bank** (Mon–Thurs & Sun 8.30am–2pm) at no.84, an **Internet café** and a **telephone office** (daily 8am–midnight).

Hannoville

With fewer places to eat and a dirtier beach, **Hannoville**'s main attraction is its cheaper **accommodation**. Two hundred metres before the beach, you pass the clean and friendly *Costa Blanca Hotel* (☏03/430 3112; ❷). Don't bother with the overpriced four-star places on the beach – if you're going to pay that kind of money it's better to stay at Bitash. Inexpensive and outstanding **meals** are available at the *Gad Restaurant*, across the road from the *Costa Blanca*. There's a **bank** (Mon–Thurs & Sun 8.30am–2pm) on the same street.

Abu Sir and Burg al-Arab

Thirty kilometres beyond El-Agami the coastal highway passes the site called **Abu Sir**, better known to archeologists by its Roman name, **Taposiris Magna**. Here, the limestone ridge to the south of the road bears the ruins of an ancient **port city** that the Egyptians called *Per Usiri* (Dwelling of Osiris) and the Greeks, *Busiris*. There were actually two ports: one on the Mediterranean and the other on Lake Maryut, to the south, which was linked to the Nile until the twelfth century AD. Egypt's agricultural wealth was shipped by barge to Maryut and transferred to seagoing vessels, while imported luxuries travelled the other way; customs posts levied duties on both. In Roman times, the Maryut region produced as much grain as the Fayoum and the Nile Valley, which went to appease the potentially riotous plebs in the imperial capital.

Vital to this commerce was a chain of lighthouses from Alexandria to Cyrenacia (Libya), which warned mariners of the abrupt change from sea to sand, along a low-lying coastline largely devoid of landmarks but plagued by reefs and shoals. While Alexandria's Pharos has disappeared, you can get an idea of its shape from the sole surviving **lighthouse** in the chain, at Abu Sir. Most Egyptologists believe that this was a one-tenth scale replica of the Pharos, although Győző Vörös (excavator of the sun temple on Thoth Hill; see p.402) thinks it was the prototype for the Pharos, rather than a scaled-down copy. The triple-tiered structure rises above several natural caves amidst an ancient cemetery where both humans and sacred animals were buried. The latter were probably related to a ruined **temple of Osiris**, surrounded by fourth-century BC enclosure walls; its gutted interior was used as a Christian church at the end of the fourth century, and later as a fortress by the Arabs, a hideout by Bedouin caravan-robbers, and a coastguard station by the British.

On the slopes to the south of the temple lies the partially excavated **ruined city**, including a winery and a public bathhouse from the time of Justinian. Lower downhill was once a busy harbour on Lake Maryut, where pilgrims bound for the Osiris temple disembarked, followed centuries later by Christians on their way to Abu Mina (see p.620), and then by Muslims travelling to Mecca. The lake became ever more saline as the Canopic branch of the Nile silted up and the British dug canals to flood it with sea water, to create a defensive barrier to the west of Alexandria. Nowadays, parts often dry out entirely in summer and others are used as drainage basins for industrial effluents or excess water from Alex – but the **view** from the ridge is still beautiful.

Unfortunately, **getting there** offers lots of scope for getting lost, as the drivers of minibuses from the Moharrem Bey terminal in Alex (£E2) either confuse Abu Sir with Abu Qir (see p.608) or with Burg al-Arab, 4km inland from Abu Sir. It's better to hire a taxi (£E100–150), but be sure that the driver understands exactly which site you have in mind.

Confusion arises because the lighthouse is often referred to as the **Burg al-Arab** (Arab's Tower), the name given to a coastal watchtower destroyed by the British in 1882, which was later bestowed on a model village designed by Wilfred Jennings-Bramly in 1915, on the opposite side of the lake from Abu Sir. Burg al-Arab served as RAF headquarters during the battle of El-Alamein and was later graced with a villa where President Sadat planned the October War of 1973. It still occupies a guarded enclave on the edge of the sprawling community.

To confuse things further, there's also the five-star **Burg al-Arab Hilton** (☎03/990-730, ⓕ990-760, ⓔhiltonborg@hotmail.com; ⓪) on the coast, whose amenities include a private beach, a large pool and a children's splash pool, a gym and sauna, entertainments, and the *Stingers* disco over summer. Rates are heavily discounted in winter, when foreign tour operators charge as little as US$50 for a double room, including breakfast. Package tourists fly straight into **Burg al-Arab airport**, an ex-military airfield that currently serves as Alexandria's international terminal.

The Monastery of Abu Mina

If you're hiring a car to visit Abu Sir, consider a side-trip to the Coptic **Monastery of Abu Mina**, 15km inland. It can also be reached from Alexandria by minibus from the Moharrem Bey terminal (£E2), and there are enough pilgrim coaches heading for the site to make hitch-hiking feasible – though not the best strategy to adopt at the outset.

Deir Mari Mina (as it's known locally) honours **St Menas**, an Egyptian-born Roman legionary who was martyred in Asia Minor in 296 after refusing to renounce Christ. His ashes were buried here when the camel that was taking them home refused to go any further. Miraculous events on the spot persuaded others to exhume Menas in 350 and build a church over his grave, later enclosed within a huge basilica. A pilgrim city grew up as camel trains spread his fame (Menas is depicted between two camels), and "holy" water from local springs was exported throughout Christendom. But when these dried up in the twelfth century, the city and its vineyards were abandoned and soon buried by sand, only a small community of monks remaining.

While its belfry towers are visible from far away, high walls enclose the concrete buildings of the modern monastery, erected in 1959, which is outwardly graceless and luridly decorated within, like all modern Coptic architecture. Not that monks and believers would agree, or even think it relevant; what counts is the spirit of devotion, most evident on November 11, when pilgrims celebrate **St Menas's Day**. (A Coptic encyclical of 1943 asserted that it was Menas, the "wonder-worker of Egypt", who ensured the Allies' victory at El-Alamein.)

In addition to Menas, the crypt houses the body of Pope Kyrillos VI (1959–71), whom Copts regard as a saint, writing petitions on his marble grave. With permission from the monks, you may be allowed to explore the nearby **ruins** of the ancient monastery and pilgrim town. Fragments of marble paving, granite and basalt columns and mosaics of semi-precious stones give some idea of how large and lavishly decorated the basilica of St Menas was, at a time when Christian churches in Europe were primitive structures, if they existed at all. Until its water dried up, the pilgrim town even featured a hospice with hot and cold baths. Artefacts found here can be seen in Alexandria's Greco-Roman Museum.

Beach resorts near El-Alamein

The coastal road to El-Alamein is flanked by wall-to-wall **holiday villages** built during the 1990s. These gigantic eyesores were reputedly to blame for the devaluation of the Egyptian currency. Speculators borrowed billions of pounds to construct resorts whose projected value was pledged as security for the loans but turned out to be grossly overestimated, leaving banks with a massive liquidity crisis. Worse, over 80km of unspoilt beaches and wildlife habitats disappeared under shoddy apartments and construction debris, ruining the coastline forever. Each resort is presaged by billboards long before you pass its ostentatious entrance, guarded by armed security men. Mostly moribund over winter, they come alive as BMW-borne families move in for the summer. At some, apartments can be rented on a short-term basis and their beaches and pools are open to non-residents for a charge. Their **beach scene** is more Western than elsewhere on the coast; bikinis and cocktails are taken for granted among the Egyptian smart set.

One top-class place that's open all year is the *Aida Beach Hotel* (☎03/499 0851, ⓕ499 0867; ◐), 30km from El-Alamein. It has two rates for day-visitors that fluctuate with the season: the lower (£E15–30) rate includes snacks, while the higher one (£E30–100, minimum two people) gets you lunch and the use of a beach cabin. Rent a double room or a six-person villa and you'll also get breakfast and dinner. Bookings can be made in Alexandria at 18 Sharia Kolliet el-Tibba (☎ & ⓕ03/438 5882).

Barely 16km before El-Alamein, the sprawling low-rise *Atic Hotel* (☎03/410 6183, ⓕ410 6182; ◐) has a beautiful beach. Its day-rate (£E50) includes lunch and the use of two pools and a children's playground; other facilities cost extra. At the even larger condominium spread of the *Marina Beach Club*, 4km on, visitors can use an equally lovely beach (but not the pool) for £E20; an overnight stay with use of the beach and pool by day costs £E200, and villas can be rented for £E4500 a month. If you're going to swim here, beware of the strong currents. Billboards for the resort have barely ceased when the roadside erupts in signs alerting you to the imminence of El-Alamein.

El-Alamein

Before Alamein we never had a victory. After Alamein we never had a defeat.

Winston Churchill, *The Hinge of Fate*

EL-ALAMEIN ("Two Worlds") is an apt name for a place that witnessed the turning point of the North African campaign, determining the fate of Egypt and Britain's empire. When the Afrika Korps came within 100km of Alexandria on July 1, 1942, the city and the capital experienced "The Flap": documents were burned, civilians mobbed railway stations, and Egyptian nationalists prepared to welcome their Nazi "liberators". Control of Egypt, Middle Eastern oil and the Canal route to India seemed about to be wrested from the Allied powers by Germany and Italy. Instead, at El-Alamein, the Allied Eighth Army held, and then drove the Axis forces back, to ultimate defeat in Tunisia. Some 11,000 soldiers were killed and 70,000 wounded at El-Alamein alone; total casualties for the North African campaign (September 1940–March 1943) exceeded 100,000.

Travellers who wish to pay their respects to the dead or have an interest in military history should find the **cemeteries** and the **war museum** worth the effort of getting there. Commemorative **services** are held at El-Alamein each October; contact the British, Italian or German embassies in Cairo for details.

Getting there – and leaving

The utterly misnamed "City" of El-Alamein squats on a dusty plain 106km west of Alexandria, situated along a spur road that turns inland from the coastal highway. Anyone driving past could blink and see nothing except construction debris until they pass the Italian War Cemetery 9km down the highway. If you can afford it, the easiest way of visiting El-Alamein is by **rented car**. Renting through Avis in Alex, you should expect the round trip to cost about £E180. Thomas Cook will do a car with driver for £E350. Depending on your bargaining skills, it should also be possible to rent a **taxi** for the day in Alex, for about £E150. Though comparatively expensive, a car enables you to reach the far cemeteries and leave El-Alamein without difficulty – a major advantage over public transport.

West Delta **buses** from Alex to Mersa Matrouh can drop you at the police checkpoint by the turn-off for the Allied War Cemetery, or 1km further west along the highway, closer to the War Museum (see below); you'll pay £E6–7 for the journey. The other way is to catch a **minibus** (£E3.50) from the Moharrem Bey terminal in Alex. While getting there is straightforward enough, leaving can be harder. Basically, you walk back to the highway and flag down any bus or minibus heading in the right direction – but be sure they're going all the way to your destination (whether it's Alex or Mersa Matrouh), otherwise you risk being stranded if they turn off the highway to settlements such as Bahig or Ras al-Hikma, from which there may be no onward transport unless you fork out for a private taxi (£E60 or more). **Staying** in El-Alamein is not recommended, as the *Al-Amana Hotel* (☎03/493 8324; ❷), opposite the museum, is pretty grotty – though for something more comfortable, there's the *Hotel Atic* (see above), about 15km east on the Alex road.

The Battle and its legacy

Rather than the dramatic, single clash of forces that people generally imagine, the **Battle of El-Alamein** alternated between vicious fighting and relative lulls over four months (July–November) in 1942. The **Afrika Korps'** initial advance on El-Alamein was stymied by lack of fuel and munitions and stiff Allied resistance organized by Auchinleck. Once resupplied, however, Field Marshal Erwin **Rommel** was able to press the advantage with 88mm cannons that outranged the Allies' guns, as well as faster, better-armoured tanks.

At this time General Bernard **Montgomery** ("Monty") took over the Allied **Eighth Army**, and his first command was that it would retreat no further. He negated his army's weaknesses by digging his tanks into pits with only the gun turrets poking out above ground, protecting them until the German Panzers came within range. Aware that the Allies were being quickly re-supplied, Rommel now launched a huge offensive, attacking Alam Halfa ridge with ten divisions. Suffering heavy losses (August 31 to September 6) and desperately short of fuel, the Afrika Korps withdrew behind a field of 500,000 landmines; however, Monty patiently reorganized his forces, resisting pressure from his superiors to attack until he had amassed 1000 tanks.

Having cracked the "Enigma" code, the Allies were now able to exploit a huge tactical advantage – Rommel was absent sick in Italy, and the Allies knew it. When they punched a corridor through the minefields of the central front on October 23, the Germans, who had expected the main assault on their southern flank, were taken unawares. Rommel managed to return two days later, but was obliged to concentrate his mobile units further north, stranding four Italian divisions in the south. The Allies had established a commanding position at Kidney Hill, from which point Monty launched the decisive strike on November 2, using air power and artillery and leaving Rommel with only 35 operational tanks by the end of the day. The Eighth Army broke out on November 5 and surged west, and the Afrika Korps fought rearguard actions back through Libya until its inevitable surrender six months later.

The War Museum and cemeteries

All the Allied memorials lie beside a spur road off the highway, which begins just after the turn-off for the Qattara Depression (see below). First comes the **Greek Memorial**, followed 400m later by the **South African Memorial**, and then the **Allied War Cemetery** (daily except Fri 7am–2.30pm; free) secluded on the reverse slope of a hill. Planted with trees and flowers, it is a tranquil site for the graves of 7367 Allied soldiers (815 of them nameless, only "known unto God"), with memorial cloisters listing the names of 11,945 others whose bodies were never found. Though over half were Britons, the dead include Australians, New Zealanders, Indians, Malays, Melanesians, Africans, Canadians, French, Greeks and Poles. If you want to find a particular headstone, the Commonwealth War Graves Commission in London can tell you exactly where to look. Walking down to the cemetery, you'll pass the **Australian Memorial**, honouring the 9th Australian Division that stormed Point 29 and Thompson's Post during the penultimate phase of the battle.

If you're coming by bus or service taxi, you're likely to be dropped further west along the highway, where a Sherman tank (not of World War II vintage, but captured from the Israelis) near a gas station marks the start of an uphill turn-off leading to the museum ("*El Mathaf*", in Arabic). Follow this to a T-junction and turn left; the museum is 200m ahead, past a telephone exchange. The **War Museum** (daily: summer 8am–6pm; winter & Ramadan 9am–3pm; £E5; camera £E5, camcorder £E20) is small but well presented, with photos and models conveying the harsh conditions in the field. Due weight is given to the experience of both sides, and Egypt's role in the Allied struggle is deservedly credited. Notice the section on the explorer Almássy (of *The English Patient*) and his role in guiding two German spies through the desert. Outside are two dozen tanks, cannons and trucks, including a lorry belonging to the Long Range Desert Group that was found in the desert in 1991 (see p.555). There's also a restored **Command Bunker** that was used by Monty during the battle, which you'll have to ask a guide to unlock.

On the highway west of El-Alamein is a **plaque** marking the furthest point of the Axis advance, which asserts: *Manco la Fortuna, Non Il Valore* (Lacking Fortune, Not Valour), *1.7.1942, Alessandria 111km*. Further out you'll glimpse the **German Cemetery**, which overlooks the sea from a peninsula to the north: a squat octagonal building that houses the remains of 4280 German soldiers. An elegant white tower marks the **Italian Cemetery**, 3km further along the highway, which contains a small museum, and a chapel with the dedication: "To 4800 Italian soldiers, sailors and airmen. The desert and sea did not give back 38,000 who are missing". Do not wander around between these cemeteries; while the grounds themselves have been cleared, the intervening strips of land are still mined.

The battlefield

The battlefield itself is generally far too dangerous to explore, due to the **minefields** laid by both sides. A staggering 17.2 million landmines are estimated to remain in the Western Desert, which still kill and maim local Bedouin to this day. Casualties were highest in the 1950s, when a foreign scrap-metal dealer taught locals to make bombs from unexploded shells and blow derelict tanks into portable chunks. So far, the former combatants have ignored Egyptian and Libyan demands that they fund de-mining programs. Though a few Bedouin with 4WDs are prepared to take people to such strategic strong-points as **Kidney Ridge** and **Tell el-Issa**, you would be foolish to rely on assurances that they know safe routes through the minefields.

However, at least two relics of the struggle can be seen without any risk from the road to the Qattara Depression that starts near the Greek Memorial. To the east of the road, **El-Alamein Station** looks much as it did in 1942, albeit no longer thronged with Allied troops (who dubbed the station "Heaven") and supplies; while 24km further south, the ridge on the western side is honey-combed with trenches and tunnels belonging to the **Italian Field Hospital** and defensive positions that were stormed by the Allied 30th Corps in "Operation Lightfoot". This road is well surfaced and eventually dips down into the Qattara Depression to meet up with the Cairo–Bahariya highway (see p.576) but you do need a **permit** to use it – and whatever you do, don't stray off the tarmac road, as the verges and surrounding areas are heavily mined.

Sidi Abd el-Rahman

Nine kilometres past the last of the battlefield memorials, a spurt of new hous-ing anounces **SIDI ABD EL-RAHMAN**, which is used as a pit-stop by buses going to Matrouh and Siwa. There's no point in lingering here unless you're going to use the stunning white **beach** at the *El-Alamein Hotel* (☎03/468 0140, ℗468 0341; ❼), a fancy resort where the day-charge for a cabin and lunch for two is £E350, and the rooms and villas are often reserved up to a year in advance. It lies about 3km past a township established to settle Awlad Ali **Bedouin** who moved in from Libya onto the lands of the weaker Morabiteen tribe a couple of centuries ago. Many have abandoned their tradi-tional goat's-hair tents for stone houses, but they still maintain flocks, which they graze on scrubland or pen behind their now-immobile homes. Ten kilo-metres into the desert behind them lies a **graveyard of Panzers**, destroyed in the final rout of the Afrika Korps from the battlefield; it was here that Von Thoma, the commander of the nearly obliterated 15th and 21st Panzer divi-sions, surrendered. Earlier in the campaign, the Afrika Korps' heaquarters and tank repair depot were located at Sidi Abd el-Rahman, behind a belt of mine-fields and gun emplacements 8km in depth.

Mersa Matrouh

Although **MERSA MATROUH** has grown phenomenally and sees itself as a sophisticated resort, it remains a hick town at heart, which in summer is clogged with Egyptian and Libyan holidaymakers. All the local **beaches** have been ruined, leaving only the magnificent cove at Agiiba and neighbouring Ubbayad beach, both far from town. Whatever Egyptians might say, by no stretch of the imagination does Matrouh fit the tourist board's promise of a hedonist's playground. The only people likely to think so are the Libyans who've started coming here since the border was reopened; Egyptians go the other way, seeking work in Libya, while Western visitors are generally more interested in reaching Siwa Oasis (see p.561).

MERSA MATROUH

MEDITERRANEAN SEA

Rommel's Beach

Port

Rommel Museum

Lido Beach

Governorate

Corniche

Military Hospital

National Bank of Egypt

EgyptAir

Pick-ups to Aqiba

Pick-ups to Bus Station

Passport Office

Train Station

SHARIA ASH-SHATTA

SHARIA GALAA

SHARIA TAHRIR

SHARIA ALAM RUM

SHARIA AHMED AL-ROTAB

SHARIA AL-QADI

SHARIA ZAHER GALAL

SHARIA BUR SAID

SHARIA CLEOPATRA

SHARIA ISKANDARIYA

SHARIA OMAR MUKHTAR

SHARIA LIBYA

SHARIA SHOKRI AL-QUWATI

SHARIA IBRAM ABU TAMAM

SHARIA AL-MATHAF

SHARIA GALAA

SHARIA IBRAM ABU TARAM

N

500 m

0

▼ Bus & Service Taxi Station (1.5 km) & Alexandria (209 km)

Sidi Barrani & Sollum ▲ Cleopatra's ▲ Beach ▲ Beach of Lovers
(7 km) & Aqiba (24 km)

ACCOMMODATION

Arafat	10
Arous el-Bahr	4
Beau Site	1
Ghazala	11
Hamada	9
Lido	7
Negrescu	2
Reem	3
Riviera Palace	6
Rommel House	8
Youth Hostel	5

EATING & DRINKING

Abu Aly Pizza	A
Abu Rabie	D
Abdu Kofta & Hammo al-Temsah Fish	B
Panyotis Greek Restaurant	C

4

ALEXANDRIA AND THE MEDITERRANEAN COAST | Mersa Matrouh

625

A grid of mould-poured low-rise blocks housing eighty thousand people, the **town** spreads up from the coast towards a ridge festooned with radar dishes. As Matrouh has gone from being a quiet fishing port to the booming capital of the Mediterranean Governorate, immigrants have poured in from other parts of Egypt, inspiring mixed feelings amongst the locals.

Despite appearances, Mersa Matrouh ("Sheltered Anchorage") has a long **history**. Founded by Alexander the Great on his way to Siwa, it was here that Mark Antony and Cleopatra sought solace after their defeat at Actium, and that her fleet put out to sea for its final battle against Octavian. During the Islamic era, Matrouh was a busy trading port with a sideline in smuggling; its other main industry (dating back to Roman times) was harvesting sponges. Divers came from as far away as the Cyclades – up to two thousand of them per year in the early part of last century. To pluck the sponges from the sea bed 60–90m below, they used a stone to make themselves sink faster, which they jettisoned at the bottom. Sponge-harvesting ceased in the early 1980s.

Getting there

The 209km journey **from Alex** is best accomplished **by bus**. There are hourly West Delta services (£E15–23) throughout the year, augmented from June to September by comfier Superjets (7.15am & 4pm; £E24) that likewise depart from the Sidi Gaber terminal and take about three hours. Both are faster and a lot less scary than **service taxis** from the Moharrem Bey depot (£E12; 3hr 30min). The only **trains** from Alex are filthy 3rd class services, used by conscripts en route to or from their postings in Mersa Matrouh, which take between six and nine hours (£E3.50).

Matrouh can be reached directly **from Cairo** in about six hours by Superjet buses from the Turgoman Terminal (4 daily; £E28–37). Book seats a day or two beforehand. Mornings are the best time to catch sporadic **service taxis** (£E20) from Ahmed Helmi and Koulali squares, near Ramses Station, which take about seven hours; an alternative is to ride to Alex and pick up another service there. From mid-June to September there are sleeper **trains** from Ramses Station (daily except Fri; US$62) to Matrouh, leaving at 11pm and arriving at 6am next morning, and EgyptAir **flights** (Thurs, Fri & Sun; 1hr; US$55 one-way).

Tourists intent on **travelling to Siwa Oasis without staying in Matrouh** should catch either one of the direct services from Alex, or an early morning bus from Cairo to Matrouh, and then the afternoon bus on to Siwa. Since Matrouh's bus station is far from the centre of town, you won't have that much time to look around and have lunch before returning to board the bus, between 3.30pm and 4pm. Advice on travelling on to Siwa appears at the end of this chapter.

Arrival and information

On **arrival**, you can catch a pick-up (25pt) or taxi (£E2–3) into the centre of town from Mersa Matrouh's bus and service taxi station, train station or airport. Donkey *carettas* or blue-and-white taxis are the mainstay of **transport** around town (£E1–3) and to the nearer beaches, but the donkeys are so abused that few tourists can bear to use them. The best way to get around is to rent a bike from one of the stands along Sharia Iskandariya (£E2 per hour, £E10 per day).

The municipal **tourist office** (daily: winter 9am–7pm; summer 9am-8pm; ☏ & ℻046/493 1841) near the Corniche has friendly, English-speaking staff who can answer most questions but can't supply a map of town – the only one available is included in the brochure *Alexandria Night and Day*, available in Alex or from a few of the more upmarket hotels in Mersa Matrouh.

The **tourist police** (☎046/493 5575) are next to the tourist office on the Corniche, while the regular **police** (☎046/493 3015) are just inland on Sharia ash-Shatta; both are open 24 hours. Little English is spoken at either, so if you have a problem, try to get one of the women at the tourist office to act as interpreter. On the same street are the **post office** (daily except Fri 8.30am–2pm) and 24-hour **telephone exchange**, but the latter is so crowded and unreliable for international calls that it's worth paying extra for a direct line at the *Rivira Palace*. Alternatively, use the Menatel card-phones along Sharia Iskandariya. Non-residents may use the **Internet** (£E5/hr) at the *Beau Site Hotel*.

The National Bank of Egypt (daily 8.30am–5pm & 6–9pm) on Sharia Galaa can **change money** and travellers' cheques and has an ATM, like the Banque Masr, five blocks east on the corner of Sharia Zaher Galal, which also gives cash advances on MasterCard and Visa. Should you need to extend your visa, the **passport office** (daily except Fri 9am–3pm) lies in the vicinity of the train station.

For medical emergencies, try the military **hospital** (☎046/493 5286; closed Fri) on Sharia Galaa rather than the public one (☎046/493 3355), or go to Cairo if possible. For less serious ailments, there's the Al-Farghaly **pharmacy** (daily: summer 8am–2am; winter 8am–9pm; ☎046/493 9393), on the corner of Sharia Iskandariya and Sharia Alam Rum.

Accommodation

Matrouh's **tourist season** runs from June to early October, peaking in July and August. It's wise to make **reservations** if you're fussy about where you stay. Generally speaking, hotels are overpriced but have little problem filling their rooms over summer; some of them close down (or slash their prices) over winter. The **youth hostel** (☎046/493 2331; £E9, non-members £E10), in a dingy locality 600m west of Sharia Iskandariya, has dinky shared rooms with bunk beds (unsuitable for women) and a kitchen, and is only open from May to October. Although you can pitch a tent on beaches within the town limits for free, you *must* inform the tourist office (who'll notify the tourist police) exactly where you're **camping**. Unauthorized campers risk being taken for smugglers and shot by police patrols.

Where distances are given below, they refer to the distance from Sharia Iskandariya. **Rates** are for low/high season as applicable. Unless stated otherwise, breakfast is included.

Arafat Sharia Tahrir ☎046/493 3606. Dusty rooms with clean bathrooms just off Sharia Iskandariya, beside the *Hani el-Omda Restaurant*; follow the red arrow to the right. Open all year. ❷

Arous el-Bahr Corniche ☎046/493 4420, ℱ493 4419. Opposite the Med, which makes up for a lot, the "Bride of the Sea" has plain, clean rooms with baths; some have balconies. Closed out of season. ❸

Beau Site 1.5km west along the Corniche ☎046/ 493 2066, ℱ493 3319, ℰ beausite@hiba.com, ℗www.beausite.masr.com. Matrouh's best hotel, it has a/c rooms with satellite TV, overlooking a private beach and blue lagoon. Open all year, its rates include a buffet breakfast, plus dinner or lunch during high season. ❻/❽

Ghazala Sharia Alam Rum ☎046/493 3519. Spartan double, trible and quad-share rooms with sinks but no locks; guests pay £E10 per person, £E15 if they want a room to themselves. The hot water in the shared shower-toilets may be turned off over summer. No breakfast. Helpful management. ❶

Hamada (aka *Mersa Matrouh*) Sharia Iskandariya ☎03/493 3300. Strictly for misers, this place has poky rooms with shared cold-water facilities, above a noisy café. No breakfast. Open all year. ❶

Lido Sharia Galaa ☎046/493 2248. Rooms are small but clean, with fans, TV, balconies, and soap and towels in the bathroom. Breakfast not included. Open all year. ❷/❸

Negrescu 600m west along the Corniche ☎046/493 4491, ℱ493 3960. Spotless rooms with a/c, TV and fridge; the family suites have camp-beds with mattresses for the kids. Open all year. ❻

Reem Corniche ☎046/493 3605, ⓕ493 3608. A 1970s' slab of simple rooms with baths and balconies, some overlooking the sea. Open year-round, but cold in winter. ❸

Riviera Palace Sharia Iskandariya ☎ & ⓕ046/493 3045. Central three-star hotel with a good restaurant (no alcohol) and pleasant, carpeted rooms with fridges. Open all year. Often block-booked from June to September. ❼

Rommel House 300m east along Sharia Galaa ☎046/493 5466, ⓕ347 1496. Clean, spacious but slightly gloomy rooms with fans, TV and fridges. From Oct–May half-board is obligatory but not included in the rates. ❸/❺

Beaches

Beaches are Matrouh's saving grace, so it's a real shame that women can't enjoy them. As in Alex, Egyptian women sunbathe and swim fully clothed, accompanied by male relations; a foreigner acting differently can be subject to persistent eyeballing and pestering, if not an encounter with exhibitionist wankers. An exception is the *Beau Site's* **private beach**, which admits non-residents who have to rent a beach umbrella (£E15 per day) and deck chair (£E4); security guards ensure that women don't get hassled.

The nearer beaches are accessible by *caretta* (£E5) or rented bicycle; **transport** to the western beaches varies with the season. From June onwards you should be able to catch a microbus or a pick-up truck from the stand on the corner of Sharia Galaa (£E2–3 to Agiiba), or an open-sided *tuf-tuf* bus (£E2–3) that shuttles back and forth along the Corniche every hour or so from 9.30am to sunset, to Cleopatra and Agiiba beaches.

Beaches close to town

The three beaches around Matrouh's crescent-shaped bay are separated by a litter-strewn swathe and a small port further east. Beyond this, a spit of land curves around to face the town, rimmed on the landward side by **Rommel's Beach**. The Desert Fox supposedly bathed here in between plotting the Alam Halfa offensive from a nearby cave, now turned into a small **Rommel Museum** (summer daily 9am–2pm; £E5). His maps, desk and greatcoat (donated by his grandson, Manfred) are among the exhibits, which carry amusing captions like: "Rommel was the professor of contemporary military leaders to the extent that he was in every place at the same time". Rommel's beach is a popular sunbathing spot for Egyptians. With diving gear, you can investigate the **sunken u-Boat** that lies offshore, 25m beyond a red buoy. One of a pack of u-Boats that slipped into the Mediterranean in December 1941, U-568 was sunk by an Allied aircraft after an audacious raid on Matrouh's harbour, before the town fell to the Germans in May 1942.

Having ruined **Lido Beach**, curving west around the bay, litterbugs are doing the same to the **Beach of Lovers** (*Shahata al-Gharam*) on its western horn. Further west (roughly 7km from town) lies the cleaner, windier **Cleopatra Beach**, which drops away sharply a metre offshore. Across the dunes on its far right-hand side is **Cleopatra's Bath**, a hollow rock whirlpool bath where she and Mark Antony reputedly frolicked. Outside of the bath, heavy surf and sharp, slippery rocks make this a bad place to swim. The road to these beaches is a continuation of the Corniche, which turns south at the end of Lido Beach and then winds its way westwards.

Ubayyad and Agiiba beaches

Ubayyad Beach, 14km from town, is a vast expanse of silvery sand where the sea is calm and shallow up to 200m out. As you'd expect, it has not gone uncolonized: besides the Badr Tourist Village (open to the public) there is a private resort for army officers. Five kilometres further on, near the village of Umm Abraham, the sands have disgorged a tiny **ruined temple-fort** dedicated to Ramses II by his general Nebre, which marked ancient Egypt's westernmost port. **Zawiyat Umm al-Rukham** (its local name) isn't signposted from the coastal road, and is currently off limits while excavations continue.

From the next headland, 24km from town, a path slopes down to **Agiiba Beach**. Agiiba ("Miraculous") is an apt name for this stunningly beautiful cove, but "beach" is rather a misnomer. To swim in the calm, crystal-clear turquoise water, you can dive off rocky shelves protruding into the sea or wade in off a tiny beach gunked up with algae. From July onwards it's necessary to walk around the headlands and along the shore to find uncrowded sites. Bring food and drink as there's no guarantee of stalls operating on the cliff top, which overhangs some caves.

Eating

Matrouh's high street overflows with grocery stores and bakeries, and a fruit and veg **market** on nearby Sharia Omar Mukhtar – though many places are open year-round there's more cooking and places stay open longer in summertime. While the *Beau Site* and the *Riviera Palace* are swanky by local standards, other hotel **restaurants** have less to offer than the places listed below. The opening hours given are for summertime; over winter, most places close before midnight, though coffee houses on the main drag and around the market stay open till the small hours.

Abdu Kofta Corner of Sharia Tahrir and Zaher Galal. Simple, clean place to consume grilled chicken, *kofta* or kebab, accompanied by *babaghanoug*, rice and salad. You can also enjoy grilled fish from *Hammo al-Temsah Fish* next door (see below). Try the *molukhiyya* soup. Daily 10am–2am.

Abu Aly Pizza Sharia Iskandariya. This two-storey diner three blocks from the Corniche offers fresh pizza (£E11–20), *shawarma*, sandwiches, soups and desserts, in a brightly lit, clean setting. Open daily 9am–2am, 9am–3am in summer.

Abu Rabie Sharia Iskandariya. Sitdown and take-away diner offering *fuul*, *taamiya*, shrimp

(*gambari*) or *calamari* sandwiches for about £E1.50, or any of those served with rice and salad as a sit-down meal, for under £E10. Open till midnight year-round.

Hammo al-Temsah Fish Sharia Tahrir. Select your fish or prawns, order grilled or fried, watch them being dusted with spices and slapped on a grill; then go next door to *Abdu Kofta*, order the trimmings, and sit back to await a delicious meal.

Panyotis Greek Restaurant Sharia Iskandariya. Established in 1922, by one of the two families of Greek descent still living in Matrouh, it serves tasty fried fish or *calamari* with salad in the summer, but only alcohol out of season. Daily 8am–midnight.

Drinking, nightlife and entertainment

Matrouh is not exactly a metropolis, but it has a fair spread of restaurants and a few entertainments – over summer, at least. The **Governorate Festival** (Aug 24) catches the season in full swing, with a folkloric parade of dancers, horses and camels down the main street and along the Corniche, and films and dramas in the evening. In July and August, there's also **live music** in the pleasure gardens en route to the *Beau Site Hotel*, which has a **disco** on the premises and opens up a **bowling** alley across the road over the summer. Out of season, there's little to do but watch TV in coffee houses, or drown your boredom by **drinking**. The bar at the *Beau Site* is nice but pricey and a long walk from the centre, whereas the *Panyotis Greek Restaurant* is right on the main drag and inexpensive. You can drink beer downstairs, but *zibiba* or brandy must be consumed upstairs or taken away wrapped.

Moving on

Matrouh's **EgyptAir** office (Tues–Sun 9am–2pm & 6–9pm; ☎493 4398) is only open from June to September, when there are flights to Cairo (Wed, Fri & Sun).

To Siwa

As said earlier, you don't have to stay in Matrouh in order to reach **Siwa Oasis** – actually, there's more call to do so on the way back, if only to break the nine-hour journey from Siwa to Alex.

In any event, there are three a/c **buses** a day from Matrouh to Siwa, leaving at 7.30am, 1.30pm and between 3.30pm and 4pm (£E15) – and possibly an extra one at 7pm in the winter. Allow half an hour to reach the bus station from the centre of town (by pick-up truck from the junction of Omar Mukhtar and Cleopatra streets). There shouldn't be any problem getting a seat except around major Muslim or Siwan festivals, and tickets can normally be bought on the bus. There may also be the odd **minibus** (£E10 per person for a full load) from the depot across the way, but this should be used only as a last resort, not in preference to the bus. Bring plenty of food and water for the six-hour journey.

Motorists should avoid travelling in the midday heat and fill up before leaving Matrouh, as there are no petrol stations along the 300km route. The Siwa road is reached by following the Corniche west out of town, turning inland and passing the airport turn-off, and then heading south at the next junction, 20km from Matrouh. There's a police checkpoint, so you can't miss it. Don't stray far from the road if you stop for a leak; there are minefields on either side for miles into the desert.

Remember to **change money** before you set out, as Siwa has no bank.

West of Matrouh: the road to Libya

The **road to Libya** reflects relations between the Arab Republic of Egypt and the Libyan *Jamahiriyah* (State of the Masses). During the 1960s, when Gaddafi regarded Nasser's Egypt as the vanguard of revolutionary Arab nationalism, people and goods flowed both ways, encouraging the Libyan leader to propose that the two countries unite in 1973 – an ambition that came to nought as President Sadat cultivated the Western powers and finally signed a peace treaty with Israel. In response, Libya severed relations, closed the border and began agitating for the overthrow of the Egyptian government; a cold war ensued, with sporadic incursions by Libyan warplanes and saboteurs during the 1980s.

It wasn't until the end of the decade that relations were restored and the border was reopened. Despite an upturn in civilian traffic, there's still an overwhelming military presence along the 120km to **Sidi Barrani** – a small port named after the Senussi missionary Sidi Mohammed el-Barrani, which was bitterly contested during the Western Desert campaign, but is now just a gas-stop on the road to Sollum (60km). **SOLLUM** (pronounced "Sa-loom") is more arresting, overlooking the sea from a 180-metre cliff with a harbour at the bottom. A small **Allied War Cemetery** at the eastern entrance to town recalls the toll exacted at "Hell Fire Pass" (Halfaya), where five waves of British tanks were destroyed by German guns dug into the ridge. Otherwise, the town has a **bank**, a telephone office, a few grubby eateries and an ultra-basic **hotel** (☎046/480 0148; ❷).

The **border** crossing beyond the Halfaya Pass is officially open 24 hours, but its lethargic customs officials and sweltering queues of vehicles suggest otherwise. While Egyptians and Libyans cross over regularly, foreign tourists are only just beginning to visit Libya, which hardly encourages impulse visits. Libyan **visas** must be obtained beforehand in Cairo (see p.274), and in all honesty it's far easier to travel directly to Benghazi or Tripoli on a Superjet from the capital (see p.283), than catch the daily **bus** from Matrouh to Sollum (leaving at 7am; £E10; 4hr) and then a service taxi to the border crossing (£E2). On the Libyan side of the border, local service taxis run to Al-Burdi, whence buses go to Tobruk and Benghazi. If you're planning to **drive** your own vehicle along the coast and into Libya, be sure to have your passport and car papers ready to show at the innumerable checkpoints along the way.

The Delta

Map labels: MEDITERRANEAN SEA, ISRAEL, JORDAN, SAUDI ARABIA, RED SEA, LIBYA, SUDAN, N

Highlights

* **Moulid of Saiyid Ahmed el-Bedawi** The city of Tanta becomes a seething mass of chanting Sufis, musicians, vendors, circus acts and spectators in the Delta's biggest festival of the year, held in October. See p.641

* **Rosetta's Delta Style Architecture** The little town of Rosetta has been busy restoring its legacy of highly distinctive eighteenth- and nineteenth-century man-sions, making it a very worthwhile stopover en route from Alexandria into the Delta. See p.638

* **Tanis** The most interesting archeological site in a region admittedly not known for its antiquities. See p.646

* **Lake Manzala** One of Egypt's top sites for birdwatching, where herons, spoonbills, pelicans and flamingoes wade the shallows in search of fish. See p.650

5

The Delta

While the Nile Valley's place in ancient Egypt remains writ large in extraordinary monuments, the **Nile Delta**'s role has largely been effaced by time and other factors. Although several pharaonic dynasties arose and ruled from this region – Lower Egypt – little of their twenty provincial capitals remains beyond mounds of debris known as *tell* or *kom*. The pharaohs themselves set the precedent of plundering older sites of their sculptures and masonry – hard stone had to be brought to the Delta from distant quarries, so it was easier to recycle existing stocks – and nature performed the rest. With a yearly rainfall of nearly 20cm (the highest in Egypt, most of it during winter) and an annual inundation by the Nile that coated the land in silt, mud–brick structures were soon eroded or swept away. More recently, farmers have furthered the cycle of destruction by digging the mounds for a nitrate-enriched soil called *sebakh*, used for fertilizer; several sites catalogued by nineteenth-century archeologists have all but vanished since then.

Of the Delta's show of ancient monuments, the ruins of **Tanis**, **Avaris** and **Bubastis** are certainly worth knowing about, if not visiting. As for Islamic architecture, there's a sprinkling of "Delta Style" mansions and medieval mosques in the coastal towns of **Rosetta** and **Damietta**. Practically everywhere else on the map is an industrialized beehive or a teeming village, only worth visiting for **moulids** or popular festivals, of which the region has dozens. Combining piety, fun and commerce, the largest events draw crowds of over a million, with companies of *mawladiya* (moulid people) running stalls and rides, while the Sufi *tariqas* perform their *zikrs*. People camp outdoors and music blares into the small hours. Smaller, rural moulids tend to be heavier on the practical devotion, with people bringing their children or livestock for blessing, or the sick to be cured.

The great **Moulid of Saiyid el-Bedawi**, held at **Tanta** just after the cotton harvest in October, starts a cycle of **Muslim** festivals lasting well into November. At one- to two-week intervals, pilgrims and revellers congregate for week-long bashes at **Basyouni**, **Dasuq**, **Mahmudiya**, **Fuwa** and **Rosetta**. The Muslim month of *Shawwal* (following Ramadan) also occasions moulids at **Bilbeis** and **Zagazig**. During May, the remote **Monastery of St Damyanah** witnesses one of Egypt's largest **Christian moulids** and, come August, another event transpires at the village of **Mit Damsis**. In January a unique **Jewish moulid** takes place at **Damanhur**.

The Delta's other possible attraction is its flat, intensely green **landscape**, riven by waterways where feluccas glide past mud-brick villages and wallowing buffalo. The northern **lakes** are a wintering ground for herons, storks, great crested grebes and other water birds, while doves and pigeons – reared for human consumption in cotes shaped like Khmer temples – join other **birdlife** pecking around the cotton-, rice- and cornfields. In ancient times, wealthy Egyptians enjoyed going fowling in the reeds, using throwing sticks and hunting cats; their modern-day counterparts employ shotguns. The Delta is also still a habitat for wildcats and pygmy white-toothed shrews, but boars have been driven out and the last hippopotamus was shot in 1815.

More sombrely for the ecology, the Delta is one of the world regions most vulnerable to the effects of **global warming**. Oceanographers predict that a one-metre rise in the sea level would swamp Alexandria and submerge the Delta as far inland as Damanhur, destroying six percent of Egypt's cultivable land and displacing 3.3 million people. The freshwater Delta lagoons, which provide much of the nation's fish catch, would also be ruined. A more immediate threat is **erosion** by the Mediterranean. Now that the Delta is no longer renewed by silt from the Nile, its coastline is being worn away.

Visiting the Delta

As few visitors have time for more than one moulid or site, we've dealt with the region in less detail than other parts of Egypt. Depending on where you're aiming for, it might be better to start from Alex, Cairo or the Canal Zone: Rosetta and Damanhur are easiest to reach from Alex; Tanta from Cairo; and Zagazig from Ismailiya.

From Cairo, buses and service taxis to all parts of the Delta leave from Aboud terminal in Shubra (see p.283). There are direct buses from Cairo to the Delta resorts over summer. In some cases, a shortage of local **accommodation** makes day trips more feasible than overnight stays. Trains are OK for reaching major towns, but service taxis and buses are the best way of **getting around**. Renting a car isn't necessarily a good idea: it's easy to have accidents on the Delta roads, and the unsurfaced ones are legally off limits to foreign drivers – a hangover from 1960s spy-phobia. Should the police decide to make a fuss, you could conceivably spend a night in jail.

Rosetta, Damanhur and the Western Delta

The broader Rosetta branch of the Nile delineates one edge of the **Western Delta**, whose other flank fades into desert. Its cottonfields and mill towns are visible enough from the Delta Road or the Cairo–Alexandria railway, and few places merit closer inspection. **Rosetta** makes a nice day excursion from Alex (there's no tourist accommodation), and **Damanhur** hosts two remarkable moulids, but you have to be pretty keen on archeology to bother with the *koms* off the Tanta road.

Rosetta (Rashid)

The coastal town of **ROSETTA** has waxed and waned in counterpoint to the fortunes of Alexandria, 65km away. When Alex was moribund, Rosetta burgeoned as a port, entering its heyday after the Ottoman conquest of Egypt in the sixteenth century, only to decline after Alexandria's revival. The modern-day town is still "surrounded by groves of orange and lemon trees", as Eliza Fay wrote home in 1817, but its "appearance of cleanliness ... so gratifying to the English eye" has dissipated, and these days few tourists come to wander through its run-down, littered streets in search of once-elegant Ottoman mansions. It's certainly a far cry from the early nineteenth century, when E.D. Clarke saw "English ladies from the fleet and the army" wearing "long white dresses", riding "the asses of the country".

This earlier European fascination owed to the discovery of the **Rosetta Stone** by French soldiers in 1799. Their officer realized the significance of this second-century BC basalt slab inscribed with ancient hieroglyphs, demotic Egyptian and Greek script, which was forwarded to Napoleon's savants in Cairo. Although their archeological booty had to be surrendered in 1801 – which is how the Stone, "Alexander's Sarcophagus" and many other objects wound up in the British Museum – it was a French professor, Jean-François Champollion (1790–1832), who finally deciphered the hieroglyphs by comparison with the Greek text, and unlocked the secret of the ancient Egyptian tongue.

Getting there

The quickest way to reach the town is by **service taxi** (1hr; £E4) from Alexandria's Midan el-Gumhorriya. There is also one **train** a day from Alex, which takes two hours. From Cairo, there is no direct transport, and the best way to get here is by train or service taxi to Damanhur, from where you can take a taxi (E£1) across town to pick up a *servees* to Rosetta; the journey from Damanhur takes 1hr 15min and costs E£1.75. There are no longer any train services between Rosetta and Dasuq, Damanhur, Tanta or Cairo.

The Town

Rosetta's main appeal lies in its **"Delta Style" architecture**, much of it currently undergoing restoration with the aim of attracting tourism. The Delta hallmarks are pointed brickwork (usually emphasized by white or red paint), inset beams and carved lintels, and a profusion of *mashrabiya*-work. Some of the mansions also incorporate ancient columns. A couple of examples can be seen almost opposite the *servees* station: one next to the mosque, still under restoration at the time of writing, and another – **Ramadan House** – just two doors on. Ramadan House can be visited (daily 9am–4pm; E£12, students E£6, ticket includes Hammam Azouz), but you have to buy your ticket at present from the tourist office opposite the museum (see below).

Further examples of Rosetta's Delta Style architecture lie on, or just off, Sharia Sheikh Qanadili, which runs north, parallel to the river, and is the second turning on your left past Ramadan House. The first house worth investigating along this street is **Al-Qanadili House**, on the left after 200m. It is currently undergoing restoration, but you may be able to pop in for a quick look, although the outside is more impressive. **Thabel House**, 50m farther on the left, was built in 1709, which makes it about a century older than most of the other prominent Delta Style houses. Just around the corner, at the end of the next turning on the left (Haret al-Hag Youssef) is **Al-Manadili** House.

For a better idea of how the Ottomans lived, visit the **Beit al-Amasyali**, 50m further on along Sheikh Qanadili, straddling a corner. A superb wooden ceiling and mother-of-pearl-inlaid *mashrabiyas* ennoble the reception room upstairs. Next door you'll find the **Abu Shahim Mill**, with its huge wooden grinders and delicately pointed keyhole arches. Both were built around 1808 for the Turkish Agha, Ali al-Topgi, who bequeathed them to his servant Al-Amasyali. Both are being restored but should be open to the public shortly.

From here, a left turn after 50m takes you onto Sharia el-Guesh, with its small church. A left just before the church leads to the rail station, where one morning train to Alex and an afternoon train to Mamoura are the only departures. Continuing on El-Guesh past the church and roughly straight ahead, you come to **Beit Kili** off Midan al-Hurriya, an eighteenth-century house containing a small **museum**. The museum is currently closed for restoration, but its only notable exhibit in the past was a diorama showing British soldiers being trounced by the locals (it should reopen daily 9am–4pm, with tickets probably costing E£20, students E£10, camera E£10). Opposite, in a small park, is the **tourist office** (claims to be open 24hr), where you can buy tickets to visit the buildings in town that are currently open to the public: Ramadan House (see above), and **Hammam Azouz**, a nineteenth-century bathhouse (daily 9am–4pm; E£12, students E£6, ticket includes Ramadan House). To find Hammam Azouz, take the street parallel to the river one block inland, and turn right after half a kilometre. The marble interior, with its marble floors and fountains, has been lovingly restored, enabling you to see a fine example of a traditional bathhouse. Near the tourist office, three cheap hotels offer **accommodation**, should you wish to stay in town.

To make a day of it, consider an excursion to the **Fort of Qaitbey** (daily 9am–4pm, Ramadan 9am–3pm; £E20, students E£10), 7km from town. Built in 1479 to guard the mouth of the Nile, it served as the first line of defence against the Crusaders and was later reinforced by the French, whose use of masonry imported from Upper Egypt led to the discovery of the Rosetta Stone. The fort can be reached from town by green-and-white taxi (£E8–12, £E15–20 round-trip) or fishing boat (£E30 after bargaining). Alternatively, you can visit the tranquil old **Mosque of Abu Mandar**, 5km upriver from

△ Tinware

Rosetta; taxi-boats leave from the docks near Midan al-Horriya – expect to pay £E10–15 after haggling.

Around mid-November, the chain of festivals that started in Tanta the previous month should reach Rosetta. Don't despair if you come a few weeks earlier, since similar **moulids** occur at Fuwa, Mahmudiya and Dasuq, further inland. Salted fish (*fisikh*) and hummus are the traditional snacks at these events.

Damanhur and around

Most of the land between Alex and Tanta is given over to **cotton**, Egypt's major cash crop, whose intensive cultivation began under Mohammed Ali. His French hydroengineer's scheme to regulate the flood waters by means of barrages across the Rosetta and Damietta branches of the Nile was ultimately realized by Sir Colin Scott-Moncrieff in 1880–90. The shift from flood to perennial irrigation enabled three or four cotton crops a year to be grown in the Delta, as is still the case.

Hardly surprising, then, that local towns are heavily into textiles; particularly the Beheira Governorate capital, **DAMANHUR**, once *Tmn-Hor*, the City of Horus. This is also the main **transport** hub for the Western Delta, with regular trains to Cairo and Alex, plus service taxis to the same places or to Tanta from Kubra Helu station, and to Rosetta, Dasuq or Kafr el-Sheikh from Kubra el-Felah station. A £E1 taxi ride will get you from either of the two *servees* stations to the other or to the train station.

Although much of Damanhur is drably functional, this city of 170,000 people gains a dash of colour from green-shuttered houses and bougainvillea-laden archways, and blossoms during its festival, **Moulid of Sheikh Abu Rish**, when turbaned Sufis perform *zikrs* and *munshids* to enthusiastic crowds. This occurs in late October or early November, a week after the festival at Dasuq, across the river. With venues so close together, the *mawladiya* (moulid people) can easily move on to the next event: barbers, circumcisers and all.

Egypt's only **Jewish moulid**, held over two days in January, is a very different scene. The shrine of **Abu Khatzeira** (Father of the Mat), a nineteenth-century mystic, is cordoned off by security police who rigorously exclude non-Jewish Egyptians, fearing a terrorist attack. Within the cordon a few thousand mostly French or Israeli visitors bring sick relatives or bottled water to be blessed, and "bid" for the key to Abu Khatzeira's shrine; the money raised supports its upkeep.

Two moulids: Dasuq and Fuwa

A week or so after Tanta's festival (see below), the agricultural town of **DASUQ** (the "q" usually pronounced as a glottal stop) holds the **Moulid of Ibrahim al-Dasuqi** (in mid- to late October), drawing almost as many people. Al-Dasuqi (1246–88) was the only native-born Egyptian to found a major Sufi order, the Burhamiya (whose chosen colour is green): the other brotherhoods originated abroad, or were started here by foreigners.

Should you decide to attend the eight-day event, Dasuq is probably easiest to reach from Damanhur by bus or service taxi. You can also get to it by *servees* from Kafr el-Sheikh and Rosetta, and there are two very slow daily trains from Cairo via Damanhur. Service taxis from Dasuq also serve **FUWA**, 13km northwest, where another **festival** occurs in late October or early November.

Between Damanhur and Tanta

A couple of **ancient sites** reduced to *kom* lie off the road **between Damanhur and Tanta** (64km). Roughly 23km out of Damanhur, a track leads three kilometres left off the main road to the village of El-Nibeirah, near two low mounds marking the site of **Naucratis**. During the XXVI Dynasty, when Egypt was ruled from the Delta, King Amasis (570–26 BC) granted this Greek colony a monopoly of trade between Egypt and Greece. Excavating the site for the British Museum in the nineteenth century, Flinders Petrie found it littered with shards of Greek pottery, and imagined that he was "wandering in the smashings of the Museum's vase-room".

At Itai El-Baroud, the last town before crossing the Rosetta branch of the Nile, another turn-off runs fourteen kilometres south to El-Tud, by the "Mound of the Fort", *Kom el-Hisn*. This used to be **Imaou**, which became the capital of the Third Nome (an administrative district) during the New Kingdom, and was turned into a necropolis by the Hyksos pharaohs. A temple enclosure and numerous tombs are still evident.

Tanta and the Central Delta

Tanta, Egypt's fifth largest city, hosts the country's greatest moulid, which is worth experiencing for at least a day. The city also serves as a jumping-off point for practically everywhere else in the **Central Delta**. Depending on your bent, there are several other moulids and a host of ancient sites scattered around the region. With regular trains and service taxis to Alex (roughly a 2hr journey) and Cairo (1hr 30min) running from early morning till nigh on midnight, you don't have to stay in Tanta; indeed, you'd be lucky to find a vacant room while the moulid's on. Elsewhere, tourist accommodation is virtually nonexistent anyway. Because the northwestern corner of this part of the Delta is easier to reach from Damietta or El-Mansura, we've allocated sites there to the "Eastern Delta" section (see p.643).

Tanta

A bustling industrial city with strong rural ties, **TANTA** marks the end of the cotton harvest in October with Egypt's largest festival, the **Moulid of Saiyid Ahmed el-Bedawi**. Tanta's population jumps from 230,000 to nearly three million as visitors pour in from the Delta villages, other parts of Egypt and the Arab world. Streets and squares fill with tents and stalls; Sufis prepare for *zikrs*, while musicians test their amps ("Allah, two, three"). Thousands camp out amidst heaps of blankets and cooking pots, though sleep seems impossible. With music and chanting, vendors and devotees, a circus with lions and tigers and a levitation act, Tanta becomes a seething cacophony. If you plan to attend the week-long festival, it is best to leave all your valuables somewhere safe. Pickpocketing is rife and injuries may result from crushing or fist-fights in the dense crowd.

The moulid honours the founder of one of Egypt's largest Sufi brotherhoods. Born in Fès in Morocco in 1199, **Saiyid Ahmed el-Bedawi** was sent to Tanta in 1234 by the Iraqi Rifaiyah order, and later established his own *tariqa* (brotherhood), the Ahmediya. His name is invoked to ward off calamity – "*Ya saiyid, ya Bedawi!*" – but his moulid is anything but angst-ridden. "Although a religious festival, pleasure is the chief object of the pilgrims, and a few *fatahs* at the tomb of the saint are sufficient to satisfy every pious requirement", noted *Murray's Handbook* in 1891. The climax to the eight-day festival occurs on a Friday, when the Ahmediya – whose banners and turbans are red – parade with drums behind their mounted sheikh. Events focus on the triple-domed,

Ottoman-style **mosque** wherein Bedawi and a lesser sheikh, Abd el-Al, are buried.

Tanta is known for its roasted chickpeas or garbanzo beans (*hummus* in Arabic, where it does not necessarily mean that they are mashed with olive oil and tahini). They can be bought at any shop or street stall selling nuts and the like.

Practicalities

Should you wish **to stay** in the vicinity during the moulid (or other festivals – see below), book a room as far in advance as possible. The *Green House Hotel* on Sharia el-Borsa, off Midan el-Gomhurriya, some 500m east of the station (☎040/333 0761 or 0762, ℉333 0320; ❺), has comfortable, homely rooms with a/c, TV and minibar, and friendly staff who can organize most things for you. If that is not sufficiently deluxe, the *New Arafa Hotel* (☎040/340 5040–7, ℉335 7080, ⓦwww.arafahotel.com; ❻), outside the train station, has larger rooms with the same facilities. One **bank** that cashes travellers' cheques is the Delta Bank, diagonally opposite the *Green House*; there's an ATM for Visa and MasterCard outside the Banque Misr across the road.

As the **transport** hub of the Delta region, Tanta is well served, with regular buses to Cairo's Aboud terminal (half-hourly 6am–9pm; 1hr 30min). These serve the **Gomla bus station**, 2km north of the city centre (£E1–2 by taxi), where you will also find buses to Damanhur and Alexandria (every 45min till 6.15pm), and to Mansura and Port Said (4 daily, all in the morning), plus service taxis to Cairo (1hr 15min), Damanhur (1hr) and Alex (2hr 15min). Buses to Mahalla el-Kubra leave every fifteen minutes from **Mura Shaha station**, which is connected with Gomla by minibus (25pt), and where you will also find service taxis to Mahalla (1hr), Mansura (1hr 30min), Ismailiya (2hr) and Zagazig (1hr 30min). From the handsome railway station in the city centre, there are eight air-conditioned **train** services a day to Benha, Cairo, Damanhur and Alexandria, plus innumerable slow ones to those destinations, as well as sixteen to Mansura (1hr 30min), nine to Damietta (2hr) and five to Zagazig (1hr 30min).

Sites around Tanta

Some of the places below are directly accessible from Tanta; to reach others you might need to change once or twice. For the committed, renting a private **taxi** gives the greatest scope for excursions.

As a footnote to bygone rulers, it's worth mentioning (but not visiting) the village of **Mit Abu el-Kom**, near the small town of Quweisna to the south of Tanta, as the **birthplace of Anwar Sadat**. Born in 1908, he escaped rural life by joining the army, became a nationalist and conspired with like-minded officers to overthrow King Farouk. As Nasser's heir, President Sadat waged war against, and then signed a peace treaty with, Israel; opened Egypt to Western capitalism – generating a consumer boom and massive corruption; and was ultimately assassinated by Islamic militants in 1981.

Buto and Xois

Only those with private transport and a consuming passion for **ancient sites** will bother trying to reach **Tell al-Faraoun** (Mound of the Pharaoh), on the edge of some marshes north of Ibtu village, itself 5km north off the Dasuq–Kafr el-Sheikh road. The site appears on maps as **Buto**, the Greek name for a dual city known to the ancient Egyptians as *Pr-Wadjet*. **Wadjet**, the cobra-goddess of Lower Egypt (and whom the Greeks called Buto) was worshipped in the half of the city known as Dep. The other city, known as Pe, was dedicated to Djbut, the heron-god, who was later supplanted by Horus. Nothwithstanding all this, the 180-acre site had been obliterated down to its paving stones by the time Petrie excavated it.

Should you carry on to **KAFR EL-SHEIKH** and follow the Tanta road south, you'll pass the village of Sakha, occupying the site of **Xois**, ancient capital of the Sixth Nome.

Saïs

Nothing but a few pits filled with stagnant water remains of the once great city of **Saïs**, near the modern village of **Sa el-Hagar**, beside the Rosetta branch of the Nile. Founded at the dawn of Egyptian history, it was always associated with the goddess of war and hunting, **Neith**, whose cult emblem appeared on pre-Dynastic objects. In Egyptian cosmology, she was also the protectress of embalmed bodies; the Greeks identified her with Athena.

The city became Egypt's capital during the **Saïte Period**, when the XXVI Dynasty (664–525 BC) looked back to the Old Kingdom for inspiration, refurbishing the pyramid tombs and reviving archaic funerary rituals. In 525 BC the Dynasty was overthrown by the Persian emperor Cambyses, who's said to have had the body of the penultimate Saïte king, Amasis "the Drunkard", removed from its tomb, whipped and burnt.

El-Mahalla el-Kubra and Sammanud

EL-MAHALLA EL-KUBRA, 24km northeast of Tanta, is Egypt's fourth largest city and a taxi staging-post for journeys to the riverside town – almost a suburb, these days – of **SAMMANUD**. Should you wish to stay in El-Mahalla, the town's top **hotel** is the *Omar Khayyam* on Midan 23rd July (☎040/223 4299, 🖷223 6050; ❸).

Immediately west of the Sammanud taxi depot, near the hospital, a large mound and a scattering of red and black granite blocks mark the site of the Temple of Onuris-Shu, rebuilt by Nectanebo II to grace **Tjeboutjes**, the capital of the Twelfth Nome. Another city, **Busiris**, occupied a bluff overlooking the river further south, along the road out of Sammanud. However, part of a XXVI Dynasty basalt statue and fragments of a monumental gateway are all that remain of this reputed birthplace of Osiris.

The H8 road, which runs northeast from Sammanud to Talkha, takes you past the site of ancient *Pr-Hebeit*, 10km to the west, better known by its Roman name, **Iseum**. Here, the great **Temple of Isis** which Nectanebo began and Ptolemy II completed has been reduced to an enclosure wall, some carved granite blocks and Hathor-headed capitals. From Talkha, you can easily cross the river to El-Mansura (see p. 000).

The Eastern Delta and the Delta resorts

The **Eastern Delta** scores on several counts. **Tanis**, **Avaris** and **Bubastis** are the best **pharaonic ruins** that Lower Egypt can offer; there are **moulids** aplenty, both Christian and Muslim; and if you include the places on the Central Delta coast, which are easier to reach from here, the region can also claim three low-key **beach resorts** and some fine **bird-watching**.

For some of these destinations it might be simpler to approach the Eastern Delta from Port Said or Ismailiya, rather than from Alex.

Bastet

The feline goddess **Bastet** was originally depicted as a lioness, her head surmounted by a solar disc and *uraeus* serpent. As the daughter of Re, she was associated with the destructive force of the sun-god's eye. This aggressive side of Bastet can be seen in texts and reliefs describing the pharaoh in battle. Her epithet, "Lady of Asheru", also linked her to the goddess Mut at Karnak, where temple reliefs show the pharaoh running ritual races in front of Bastet.

After about 1000 BC, however, this aspect of Bastet became subsumed by Sekhmet (see p.374), and the goddess herself was portrayed more commonly as a cat, often with a brood of kittens, and carrying a sacred rattle. The *Coffin Texts* of the Middle Kingdom frequently invoke her protection as the first-born daughter of Atum (another aspect of the sun-god). In return, the Egyptians venerated cats and mummified them at several sites, including Bubastis and Memphis.

The Greeks later identified Bastet with Artemis, the Virgin

Bastet

Hunter, who was believed to be able to transform herself into a cat. The Egyptian association with cats remained strong even after the arrival of Christianity, and it was from Egypt that cats are thought to have arrived in Europe during or before the fourth century AD.

Zagazig and the ruins of Bubastis

The charmingly named **ZAGAZIG** (pronounced "Za'a'zi") is less appealing in reality, blighted by fumes from a soap factory. Only founded in 1830, it boasts of being the home town of Colonel **Ahmed Orabi** (1839–1911), leader of the 1882 revolt against British rule, whose statue stands outside the station. As a provincial capital with a thriving university, Zagazig is reticent about being the source of most of the **papyruses** sold in tourist shops throughout Egypt, which are manufactured in sweatshops and sold to dealers for as little as £E3–4 apiece. From a tourist's standpoint, its attractions are the **Moulid of Abu Khalil**, held outside the main mosque sometime during the month of *Shawwal*, and the paltry ruins of Bubastis, to the southeast of town.

Whatever its shortcomings, Zagazig has the merit of being readily accessible. You can travel the 80km from Cairo by **bus** (every 20min; 1hr 30min; £E5) or **service taxi** (1hr 15min; £E3.50) from the Aboud terminal; coming back, service taxis for Cairo leave from just by the railway station. To find the bus station, cross the tracks via the pedestrian underpass, then turn left, and it's 300m ahead on the right. Buses from here also serve Benha (half-hourly; 45min), Alexandria (3 daily; 3hr 30min), Ismailiya (2 daily; 2hr) and Port Said (1 daily; 4hr). To find service taxis for Ismailiya and Port Said, you'll have to go the Ismailiya *servees* station, 5km from the town centre, reached by microbuses (50pt) from outside the train station. Buses and service taxis for Tanta, Mansura and Faqus leave from the Mansura bus station, which you can also get to by microbus from in front of the station. **Trains** from Zagazig serve Cairo (13 daily; 1hr 30min), Benha (13 daily; 40min), Faqus (4 daily; 1hr), Ismailiya (12 daily; 1hr 15min) and Port Said (7 daily; 2hr 30min).

Should you need to stay in Zagazig, there are two cheap **hotels** opposite the train station. The better of the two by far is the *Opera* (☎055/230 3718; ❷), which is not immediately obvious as its entrance is tucked away down a side alley and its sign is in Arabic only. The alternative is the *El Eraky* just next door

(☎055/230 2853; ❷), which is not only a good deal less clean but also costs more.

Bubastis

To reach the site of **Bubastis** (daily 8am–4pm; £E10, camera £E10, no student reductions), take the underpass to the back side of the station and continue straight ahead (southeast) along Sharia Farouq for just under a kilometre, either on foot, or by microbus from the beginning of Farouq (15pt), or by taxi (£E1). The site is about 100m to your right at the end of the street. You are likely to get a thorough grilling on entry from the guards, who are not really used to foreign visitors, and may even follow you around the site, and there's little to see beyond the few displayed artefacts but scattered blocks and gaping pits. Nonetheless, archeologists have found here Old and New Kingdom cemeteries and vaulted catacombs full of feline mummies. The city was known to the ancient Egyptians as *Pr-Bastet* (House of Bastet), after the cat-goddess whom they honoured with licentious festivals. Pilgrims sailed here in high spirits, saluting riverside towns with music, abuse and exposed loins. In the fifth century BC, Herodotus noted that 700,000 revellers consumed more wine than "during the whole of the rest of the year", and described how the city lay on raised ground encircling a canal-girt temple, "the most pleasing to look at" in all of Egypt. Begun by the VI Dynasty pyramid-builders, Bubastis was enlarged and embellished for over 1700 years, attaining its apogee after its rulers established the XXII Dynasty, though the capital in this period was probably still Tanis (see p.646).

Bilbeis and Benha

To the south and southwest of Zagazig a couple of minor towns are worth a passing mention. **BILBEIS**, 10km away by road or rail, hosts a couple of festivals during *Shawwal*: its **moulids** of Abu Isa and Abu Alwan predate Abu Khalil's in Zagazig. Further west, beside the Damietta branch of the Nile, **BENHA**, on the Cairo–Alex train line, is near another ancient site. To the northeast of town, 150m off the road, *Kom el-Atrib* is what remains of **Athribis**, once the capital of the Tenth Nome. This was the birthplace of Psammetichus I (664–610 BC), who restored pharaonic authority over Upper and Lower Egypt, replacing the so-called *Dodekarchy* with centralized government by the Saïte dynasty. Benha is served by eight air-conditioned fast trains a day, plus numerous slow ones, and there are buses every twenty minutes from 6am to 9pm from Cairo's Aboud terminal, plus service taxis from Aboud and also – but slower – from in front of Ramses station.

Tanis, Avaris and the "Land of Goshen"

Early archeologists were drawn to the eastern marches of the Delta in search of clues to the Israelites' Biblical sojourn, but what they found proved more important to knowledge of ancient Egypt. Fragmented statues and stelae, papyrus texts and layers of debris have shed light on dynastic chronologies and religious cults, the movement of Delta waterways and imperial borders, invasions and famines. Fresh discoveries are still being made – particularly at Avaris, a site associated with the Hyksos "Shepherd Kings" who seized control of the Delta after the collapse of the Middle Kingdom, and which may also have been inhabited by the Israelites during their sojourn in Egypt. The following accounts simplify a mass of contradictory evidence and theories thrown up by archeologists.

Tanis

One of the oldest-known sites is a huge *kom* near the village of **San el-Hagar** (San of the Stones), 167km northeast of Zagazig. Barring a stint by Petrie, the excavation has mostly been in French hands since the 1860s. Although best known by its Greek name, **TANIS**, the city was called *Zoan* in the Bible and known to the ancient Egyptians as *Djanet*. It originally stood beside the Tanite branch of the Nile, which has long since dried up. In the film *Raiders of the Lost Ark*, it is here that Indiana Jones uncovers the Ark of the Covenant.

The **age and identity** of Tanis have been much debated, as scholars have frequently conflated it with Avaris, the capital of the Hyksos, or the much later city of Pi-Ramses, supposedly the "City of Bondage" from which the Israelites fled. In recent decades, however, both have been firmly identified with other sites (see below), and Tanis is now thought to have come into existence long afterwards, during the Third Intermediate Period. Some theorize that the XXI Dynasty founded Tanis as their capital at the same time as they abandoned the traditional cult of Seth in favour of the Theban Triad.

The desolate **site** looks as if the huge Ramessid **Temple of Amun** was shattered by a giant's hammer, scattering chunks of masonry and fragments of statues everywhere. Confusingly for scholars, the founders of Tanis plundered masonry from cities all over the Delta (some predating the Hyksos, who had earlier usurped it). In 1939, Pierre Montet discovered the **tombs of Psusennes II and Osorkon II**, containing the "Treasure of Tanis", which is now in the Cairo Museum. Perplexingly, it was soon noted that the tomb of the XXI Dynasty ruler Psusennes seems to have been built *after* that of Osorkon, who is supposed to have lived well over a century later, during the XXII Dynasty. Rohl argues that the two dynasties were actually contemporary, and that by assuming that they were sequential, archeologists have overestimated the duration of the Third Intermediate Period by at least 140 years – thus distorting the whole chronological basis of Egyptology. Rohl's views, which are hotly debated, are outlined in detail in his book *A Test of Time* (see p.783). Criticism of them can be found on a number of websites, best accessed through the Waste of Time homepage at ⓦmembers.aol.com /lan%20/Wade/Waste/Index.htm.

While the site at Tanis can be wandered at will, **getting there** is awkward. The best jumping-off point is **FAQUS**, 37km to the south, which can be reached by service taxi from Ismailiya, Cairo or Zagazig, by bus from Zagazig or from Cairo's Aboud terminal (every 45min 7am–8.30pm; 2hr), or even by train (4 daily) from Cairo and Zagazig. From Faqus, you can catch a local bus or service taxi to San el-Hagar, or rent a private taxi for the round trip.

Avaris

Since 1966, excavations by Manfred Bietak at **Tell ed-Daba** (Mound of the Hyeena) have yielded many discoveries that have confirmed it as the site of **AVARIS**, the long-vanished **Hyksos** capital. The most sensational find, in 1991, were **Minoan-style frescoes** in a Hyksos-era palace on the western edge of the site, evincing strong links with the Minoan civilization on Crete, 500 miles away, even if not disproving the idea that the Hyksos originated in Palestine or Syria. (The term Hyksos derives from *hekau-khasut*, "princes of foreign lands".) Painted as Cretan civilization reached its zenith, the murals feature Cretan mountain landscapes and acrobats vaulting over bulls, as in the Minoan frescoes at Knossos. Both the Minoans and the Hyksos are thought to have associated bulls with the worship of storm gods.

However, the Hyksos finds are only half the story, for Avaris existed long before their invasion, and may hold the key to early Biblical history. Before finding the frescoes, Bietak's team excavated what had been a hilly residential quarter, uncovering grave goods that suggested that the bulk of the population originated from Palestine and Syria. This lay above a stratum of evidence for an older, more sophisticated community of non-Egyptians, where 65 percent of the burials were of children below the age of two. Rohl argues that this represents the **Israelites** during their sojourn in Egypt and the culling of their male newborn by the "pharaoh who did not know Joseph", which places the events of Exodus in the reign of Djudmose of the XIII Dynasty, c.1447 BC – two or three centuries earlier than is commonly accepted. The plagues that struck Egypt, followed by the Exodus, left the Delta exposed to invasion by the warlike nomads later known as the Hyksos. Having been taken over by these newcomers, Avaris remained the Hyksos capital until its destruction by Ahmosis I, the founder of the New Kingdom.

Tell ed-Daba is only 7km from Faqus, and although the site is not yet officially open to tourists, those with a special interest can get permission to visit from the Supreme Council of Antiquities in Cairo.

The "Land of Goshen"

Many archeologists have striven to uncover the **"Land of Goshen"** where the Israelites toiled for the pharaoh before Moses led them out of Egypt – though some shrewdly plugged the Biblical connection to raise money for digs with other aims (notably Petrie at Tanis). Public opinion was fixated on the Biblical "store cities of Pithom and Raamses", speculatively assigned to many locations between Avaris and the Bitter Lakes (the area through which the Suez Canal runs). "Raamses" has usually been identified as Pi-Ramses, the royal city of the XIX Dynasty pharaoh Ramses II – which is why his successor, Merneptah, regularly gets fingered as the pharaoh of the Exodus. Conversely, Rohl argues that the Bible was really referring to Avaris, but using the name of the Ramessid city that existed at a later date, which would have been familiar due to Ramses II's wars in Palestine.

It is more certain that **Pi-Ramses** was centred on the modern-day village of **Qantir**, 3km northeast of Tell ed-Daba, but extended far enough to cover most of Avaris, which had been laid to waste centuries earlier. A mud-brick palace dating to the earliest phase of the city was discovered in 1929, and Bietak's excavations have revealed barracks and workshops, also from the Ramessid era. Unfortunately for those who believe that this was the "City of Bondage", no evidence of a foreign population was found in any of the strata associated with the New Kingdom – whereas at Tell ed-Daba, there are extensive traces from the Middle Kingdom, and even mass graves that fit the Biblical account of a calamity. Rather, Pi-Ramses was a parvenu city founded by Seti I and turned into a royal capital by Ramses II, which had dwindled in significance by the end of the New Kingdom. Much of its stonework was later taken to Tanis or Bubastis during the XXI and XXII dynasties; the most notable bits still *in situ* are the feet and one arm of a colossus of Ramses II, lying 50m apart in a field.

If the Israelites did flee from Avaris, what of the other cities mentioned in the book of Exodus – Pithom and Succoth? Here, the evidence is less conclusive, but they could well have been somewhere around **Tell el-Maskhuta**, an enormous *kom* off the road between Zagazig and Ismailiya. If Tell el-Maskhuta was really Pithom, then another *kom* a few kilometres to the west may have been Succoth.

To reach Sinai, the Israelites presumably went through Wadi Tumaylat, nowadays the route for traffic between Zagazig and Ismailiya (hourly buses). Before Tell el-Maskhuta, it passes **Tell el-Kebir**, where Orabi's rebellion was finally defeated by the British in September 1882. In the 1920s, the government sponsored a reforesting project in what was then virgin desert, and now supports plantations and orchards all the way to Ismailiya.

Mit Damsis and El-Mansura

Trains and inter-city buses take the shortest route **between Zagazig and El-Mansura**, and for most of the year that's a sensible option. In August, however, you might consider the alternative Mit Ghamr–Aga road in order to visit **Mit Damsis** village near the Damietta branch of the Nile, site of the Coptic **Moulid of St George**. Buses and service taxis **from Cairo** to El-Mansura, Zagazig and Faqus go mainly from the Aboud terminal; some minibus service taxis depart from outside Ramses train station, but these leave town by a more roundabout route and end up taking longer.

Mit Damsis

The **Moulid of St George** (August 2–28) is notable primarily for its **exorcisms**. Copts attribute demonic possession to improper baptism or deliberate curses, and specially trained priests bully and coax the *afrit* (demon) to leave through its victim's fingers or toes rather than via the eyes, which is believed to cause blindness.

Egyptian Muslims likewise believe in possession, but don't always regard it as malign; in some cases they try to harmonize the relationship between the spirit and its human host rather than terminate it. Egyptians of both faiths take precautions against the Evil Eye. Christians put store in pictures of St George and the Virgin, while Muslims display the Hand of Fatima – literally hand-printed on the walls of dwellings – and perhaps the legend "*B'ismallah, masha' Allah*" ("In the name of God, whatever God wills").

Because the **moulid** is well attended there's a fair chance of lifts along the seven-kilometre track that turns west off the main road, 15km south of Aga. Mit Damsis rarely appears on maps; don't confuse it with Damas, which does.

El-Mansura

EL-MANSURA was founded as the camp of Sultan al-Kamil's army during the 1218–21 siege of Damietta, though its name ("The Victorious") was a premature boast, since the Crusaders reoccupied Damietta in 1247. Weakened by cancer and tuberculosis, Sultan Ayyub was unable to dislodge them, and died here in 1249 – a fact concealed by his widow, Shagar al-Durr, who issued orders in Ayyub's name, buying time until his heir could return from Iraq. Encouraged by the Mamlukes' withdrawal, Louis IX led a sortie against the enemy camp, slaying their general in his bath. But with victory in sight, the Crusaders fell sick after eating corpse-fed fish, just before a devastating counterattack launched by Beybars the Crossbowman. Louis was captured and ransomed for Damietta's return, and later met a similar fate on his Tunisian crusade.

The medieval house where Louis was imprisoned, **Beit Luqman**, still stands near the Mwafi Mosque (20m north of the train station), but much of the rest of today's El-Mansura is modern, with tree-lined avenues, a university, and a central mosque whose twin minarets are visible from far away. For outsiders, the town's most interesting feature is delicious buffalo-milk ice cream.

Buses to Cairo (half-hourly 6am–9pm; 2hr) and Zagazig (every 15min; 1hr 30min), as well as **service taxis** to the same destinations, run from the international bus station, which is 300m east of the train station down Sharia Gamal el-Din el-Afghani at the junction with Sharia el-Guesh. Buses from here also serve Sinai and the Canal Zone, with five a day to Sharm el-Sheikh (7hr). For

Tanta, Mahalla el-Kubra and Alexandria, buses and service taxis run from Talkha station across the river. **Trains** from Mansura are all pretty slow, and serve Cairo (4 daily; 3hr), Zagazig (9 daily; 2hr–2hr 30min), Damietta (9 daily; 2hr), Tanta (16 daily; 1hr 30min) and Mahalla el-Kubra (16 daily; 40min).

El-Mansura has several **hotels** to choose from: worth a try are the *Marshal el-Gezirah*, 2km west of the town centre on the Corniche (℡ & ℻050/221 3000–3; ❻); the *Cleopatra*, a kilometre west of the train station at 13 Souk el-Toggar el-Gharby (℡050/223 6789 or 224 6789, ℻224 1234; ❸); the *Marshal Hotel* opposite the station on Midan Umm Kathoum (℡050/233 3920 or 2 or 3, ℻233 3921; ❸); or the *Abou Shama Hotel*, 300m west of the station on Sharia Bank Misr (℡050/225 5810, ℻225 5811; ❷).

The Monastery and Moulid of St Damyanah

Normally difficult to reach without private transport, the **Monastery of St Damyanah** becomes accessible during its namesake's **moulid** (May 15–20), when service taxis and private buses convey pilgrims across to the small town of Bilqas Qisim Awwal, whence it's 3km by track to Deir Sitt Damyanah.

The monastery – whose four churches date from the nineteenth and twentieth centuries – is, in fact, rather less interesting than **Damyanah's story** and her **festival**, which is one of the largest Christian moulids in Egypt. The daughter of a Roman governor under Diocletian, Damyanah refused to marry and insisted that her father build a palace into which she and forty other virgins could retire. All refused to worship Roman gods, and their example eventually converted her father – enraging Diocletian, who had the lot of them executed.

As with the Church of St George at Mit Damsis, Copts ascribe the building of Damyanah's shrine to St Helena, the mother of the Roman emperor Constantine. Pilgrims bring sick relatives (or livestock) to be blessed, and believe that Damyanah manifests herself at night as a pigeon, which can be distinguished from other birds by the trajectory of its flight. Icons and special pottery (inscribed "Happy returns, Damyanah") are popular buys at the fair, where Muslim tattooists do a brisk trade in St George, Christ on the cross, snakes, birds and other motifs, which punters select from display boards.

Damietta (Dumyat)

Sited near the mouth of the eastern branch of the Nile, the port city of **DAMIETTA** became prosperous in medieval times, through its trade in coffee, linen, dates and oil. However, it was always wide open to seaborne invasions and was seized by the Crusaders in 1167–68 and 1218–21, on the latter occasion accompanied by St Francis of Assisi – who ignorantly imagined that the Sultan al-Kamil knew nothing of Christianity, although he numbered Copts amongst his advisors. The main function of the Crusaders in Egypt, however, was pillage, and Damietta suffered heavily during its occupations. When Louis "the Pious" returned with a further crew in 1247, the inhabitants fled or deliberately sold the Crusaders contaminated fish – one cause of their defeat at El-Mansura (see above). Unfortunately, Damietta suffered a far worse attack under the Mamlukes, who razed the town and rendered its river impassable as a punishment for suspected disloyalty and a precaution against future invasions.

It was the Ottomans who revived the town and built **"Delta Style" mansions** of the kind found in Rosetta; their last pasha surrendered to the Beys here just before the rise of Mohammed Ali. With the opening of the Suez

Canal, Damietta had to reorient its trade towards Port Said, some 70km away. Nowadays it's a thriving port city of 120,000 inhabitants, with the status of a provincial capital.

Having said that, there's little call to come here unless you're mad on Delta architecture, or into bird-watching or beachcombing. There are several modest **hotels** on the Nile-side Corniche, plus the *El-Manshy* (☎057/323-308; ❷) on Sharia el-Nokrashy. As for **transport**, Damietta is linked by rail to Tanta, Zagazig, Alex and Cairo, and by hourly buses (6am–5pm) or service taxis to Cairo. Closer at hand are Port Said (30min drive along the causeway between Lake Manzala and the Med) and the beach resorts of the Central Delta.

Lake Manzala

East of Damietta lies **Lake Manzala**, a great place for **bird-watching** if you can find a boatman to take you through the reeds. Nineteenth-century European visitors tended to be more interested in shooting wildfowl than observing it. "Their compact mass formed living islands upon the water; and when the wind took me to these, a whole island rose up with a loud and thrilling din to become a feathered cloud in the air", wrote one hunter.

Winter is the best time to see herons (*balashon* to locals), spoonbills (*midwas*), pelicans (*begga*) and flamingoes (*basharus*). Along the Nile, these last are called "water camels" (*gamal el-bahr*).

Three Delta resorts

Ranged along the coast of the Central Delta are three beach resorts popular with middle-class Egyptians: **Ras el-Bahr**, **Gamasa** and **Baltim**. During summer, they can be reached by service taxis or special a/c buses from Cairo's Aboud terminal, near Midan Ramses. Buses and taxis from Damietta are another option, at least to Ras el-Bahr or Gamasa; Baltim is accessible by service taxi from El-Mansura. Out of season many of the resorts' hotels and summerhouses are boarded up.

Ras el-Bahr, where the eastern branch of the Nile flows into the Med north of Damietta, is a pleasant beach resort with several restaurants and **hotels**. Try *Abu Tabl* at 4 17th St (☎057/528-166; ❾), *El-Mobasher* at 1 56th St (☎057/527-097; ❷) or *El-Salam* at 6 44th St (☎057/528-156; ❷). Across the river lies the busy fishing port of **Ezbet el-Bourg** (unmarked on most maps), named after an abandoned nineteenth-century **coastal fort** that's fun to explore. Hidden beneath a section of the walls is the **command bunker** (code-named Centre #10) containing seven small rooms in which Sadat's generals directed the October War of 1973.

During summer (June–Sept), Ras el-Bahr is readily accessible from Cairo by service or private **taxi** from Aboud terminal, whence there are also **buses** (every 45min; 3hr 30min). Between 8am and 3pm, there are also hourly buses to **GAMASA**, further along the coast, which has two cabin-type **hotels**, *Beau Rivage* (☎057/760-268 or 9; ❷) and *Hanoville* (☎057/760-750; ❷), plus the slightly fancier *Amun* (☎057/761-709; ☏761-710; ❷), near the market.

The third resort, **BALTIM**, is actually halfway to Rosetta, but only accessible from there by a long detour inland. It has a couple of simple **hotels**, the *Baltim Beach* (☎047/501-451; ❶) and *Cleopatra* (no phone; ❶).

The Canal Zone

Highlights

❋ The Canal The Suez Canal endures as a symbol of the triumph of Victorian engineering; a number of museums chart its history and strategic military role. **See p.664**

❋ Ship-watching International ferries are among the many giant ships that ply the Canal, still a crucial trade link between the West and the East. **See p.671**

❋ Garden City A European-style Ismailiya constructed for the builders of the Canal. **See p.681**

❋ Umm el Khaloul A local speciality shellfish, popular in Suez and Ismailiya. **See p.665**

❋ Mediterranean air The fresh sea breeze, shopping and pleasant street cafés are a particular attraction of Port Said. **See p.667**

❋ Limbo Festival A doll-burning festival held annually in Ismailiya a week after Easter. **See p.666**

❋ Birds of prey Migrating vultures and eagles fly over Suez in spring. **See p.660**

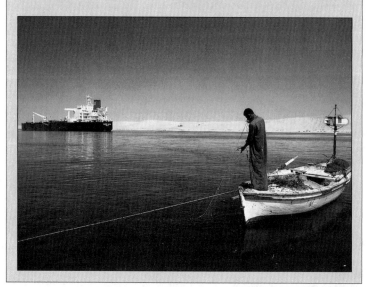

6

The Canal Zone

N o longer feted as a triumph of nineteenth-century engineering, nor regarded as the linchpin of Britain's empire, the **Suez Canal** seems as Joseph Conrad described it: "a dismal but profitable ditch", connecting the Red Sea and the Mediterranean. Except around the harbour mouths or where ships are glimpsed between sandbanks, it's a pretty dull waterway, too, relieved only by the Canal cities of Port Said and Ismailiya.

With its evocative waterfront, prosaic beaches and duty-free shopping, **Port Said** feels like Alexandria minus its cultural baggage – and a place that's somehow more authentic as a maritime city. By contrast, the Canal scarcely impinges on the leafy, villa-lined streets of **Ismailiya**, once the residence of the Suez Canal Company's European staff and now a popular honeymoon destination. Foreigners generally overlook both cities, prejudging them on the basis of **Suez**, a neglected city but a vital transport nexus between Cairo, Sinai and the Red Sea Coast.

Heading to south Sinai, bus passengers (or car drivers) cross the Suez Canal at either the **Ahmed Hamdi Tunnel** (12km north of Suez City) or the **car ferry** 7km north of Ismailiya. Destinations in **north Sinai** are served by a passenger ferry, at **Qantara**, and the new **Ferdan Suspension Bridge** nearby, both to East Qantara. Built in cooperation with Japan, and opened in October 2001, the 4.1km bridge, also known as the Salaam or Peace-Mubarak Bridge, is intended to accommodate the expected increase in traffic caused by several major development projects on the north coast. A couple of kilometres to the south is the Ferdan Railway Bridge, built on the site of an old track hastily built to transport army troops to Gaza during World War I, but dismantled by the Israelis in 1968. The largest retractable bridge in the world, it was planned during a period of optimism in the Middle East, when a rail network running the Orient Express was planned, linking Egypt to Turkey and Europe via Palestine, Israel and Lebanon. This has been put on hold, but you can still see the bridge – which sits parallel along the canal when not in use – closing daily at 9am until 11am and again from 9pm to 1am, a process which takes twenty minutes, to allow trains and cars to cross the canal. Buses and service taxis run direct from Ismailiya to El-Arish in Sinai. Drivers should be aware that stretches of the canal are **off limits** and should stick to main routes to avoid questioning by the military.

The canal's history

The **first attempts** to link the Red Sea and the Mediterranean by means of a canal are usually attributed to Necho II (610–595 BC) of the XXVI Dynasty. Herodotus claims that 120,000 workers had died before the project was abandoned after an oracle predicted that only Egypt's foes would benefit from it. Sure enough, it was the Persian emperor **Darius**, around 500 BC, who completed the first canal in the region, linking the Red Sea and the Great Bitter Lake, whence an older waterway created by Ramses II connected with Bubastis on the Nile and thence to the Mediterranean.

Refined by the Ptolemies and Trajan (who added an extension leading to Babylon-in-Egypt), this system of waterways was restored by **Amr** following the Muslim conquest and was used for shipping corn to Arabia until the eighth century, when it was deliberately abandoned to starve out rebels in Medina. Although the Venetians, Crusaders and Ottomans all considered renewing the old system, the idea of a canal running direct between the Red Sea and the Mediterranean was first mooted – and then vetoed – by Napoleon's engineers, who miscalculated a difference of ten metres between the two sea levels.

The discovery of their error, in the 1840s, encouraged a junior French consul, **Ferdinand de Lesseps**, to present his own plan to Said Pasha, who approved it despite British objections. ("It cannot be made, it shall not be made; but if it were made there would be a war between England and France for the possession of Egypt", Palmerston asserted.)

Work began at the Mediterranean end in 1859 and continued throughout the reign of Said's successor, Ismail (hence the names of Port Said and Ismailiya). Of the twenty thousand Egyptians employed in the **construction of the Suez Canal**, a great many died from accidents or cholera, while Ismail himself went bankrupt attempting to finance his one-third share of the £19 million sterling investment, most of which went on bankers' charges.

In 1875, Ismail was forced to sell his shares to Britain for a mere £4 million sterling and the Suez Canal effectively became an imperial concession. By appealing to the Rothschilds for a loan over dinner, Prime Minister Disraeli bought Ismail's shares before France could make an offer, and reported to Queen Victoria: "You have it, Madam". When the Canal finally opened in 1888, its vast profits went abroad with the **Suez Canal Company**, which acted as a state within a state, while two world wars saw the **Canal Zone** transformed into the largest military base on earth.

Following the end of World War II nationalist protests against the British presence grew, and guerrilla attacks in the Zone led to the British assault on Ismailiya's police barracks that sparked "Black Saturday" in Cairo (see p.661). After the 1952 Revolution, Egypt's new leaders demanded the withdrawal of British forces and a greater share of the Canal's revenue, and when the West refused to make loans to finance the Aswan High Dam, Nasser announced the Canal's **nationalization** (July 26, 1956). Britain and France tried to hamper this process, smearing Nasser as an "Arab Hitler". Israel's advance into Sinai that October became the agreed pretext for them to "safeguard" the Canal by bombarding and invading its cities. But by standing firm and appealing to outraged world opinion, Nasser emerged victorious from the **Suez Crisis**.

The battered Canal cities had hardly recovered when the **1967 War** with Israel caused further damage and blocked the Canal with sunken vessels. The Canal was closed and Suez was evacuated during the "War of Attrition" that dragged on until 1969, while Israel fortified the **Bar-Lev Line** along the east bank, which the Egyptians stormed during the **October War** of 1973 (known as the *10th Ramadan* or *Yom Kippur* war, respectively, to Arabs and Israelis). Although the Canal was reopened to shipping in 1975, both sides remained dug in on opposite banks until 1982, when Israel withdrew from Sinai. While the Canal was closed, supertankers were built to travel around Africa – and were too large to pass through Suez once it reopened.

Despite this, the Canal today handles up to ninety ships a day, carrying fourteen percent of the world's trade; the direction of traffic is alternated, with an average transit time of fifteen hours. At 167km long, it's the third longest canal in the world and the longest without locks; current plans to deepen the Canal and double its width render further statistics pointless.

Suez (El-Suweis) and Port Tewfiq (Bur Tewfiq)

Since its devastation by Israeli bombardments, and the evacuation of almost the entire population between 1967 and 1973, **SUEZ** has risen from the rubble to reclaim its inheritance. Unlike Port Said and Ismailiya, the city's history long predates the Canal, going back to Ptolemaic *Klysma*. As Arabic *Qulzum*, the port prospered from the spice trade and pilgrimages to Mecca throughout medieval times, remaining a walled city until the eighteenth century, when Eliza Fay described it as "the Paradise of Thieves". The Canal brought modernization and assured revenues, later augmented by the discovery of oil in the Gulf of Suez. All this was lost during the wars with Israel, requiring a massive reconstruction programme financed by the Gulf states. While noxious petro-chemical refineries, cement and fertilizer plants ring the outskirts, most of the city's 300,000 inhabitants have been rehoused in prefabricated estates or the patched-up remnants of older quarters.

What Suez lacks in looks is made up for to some degree by the friendliness of the local people. For the foreign visitor, however, it's best to dress for the city wherever you are, saving your shorts and skimpy tops for the beaches of Sinai. The paucity of things to do in Suez is perhaps most keenly felt by the city's young people, many of whom spend their evenings hanging out and smoking

SUEZ AND PORT TEWFIQ

Israeli Tanks

Yacht Club

Canal Shipping Co.

Bank ●1

Suez Canal

SHARIA EL-GEISH

El Salam Maritime Transport Co. ●7

●6

Misr Travel

SUEZ CANAL STREET

Menatours

Passenger Boat Terminal

Docks

(i)

Tourist Police

Saudi Consulate

ACCOMMODATION

Arafat	7
Green House	2
Red Sea	1
Sina	5
Star	4
Summer Palace	6
White House	3

EATING & DRINKING

Abu Ali	B
Dolphin	F
Misr and Sudan	C
Social Club	E
Sweet Spot	D
The Telegraph	A

joints – the monotony broken only by their home team playing football in the city's stadium. Despite its important contribution to the Egyptian economy, Suez has yet to see significant investment in its infrastructure. Its residents seem to feel they have been largely forgotten by their government.

Arrival – and moving on

Like the other Canal cities, Suez has regular connections with **Cairo** by bus (half-hourly 6am–6.30pm; £E7-8) and service taxi (£E5), from either Turgoman station (see map p.90) or the Al-Mazah terminal in Heliopolis. Both cover the 134km in just over two hours. Don't bother with the hot and uncomfortable trains from Cairo (6 daily), which run on to Ismailiya (6–7hr). Arriving by bus or service taxi, you're bound to be dropped at Suez's new bus terminal on the outskirts of town on the Cairo–Suez road. From here you can take a taxi (£E5) or a microbus (50pt) into the town centre. The train station – which you are unlikely to need – is 1.5km west of the city centre's Arba'in market (50pt by minibus).

For the benefit of people arriving by ship, the **tourist office** (Mon–Thurs & Sat–Sun 8am–3pm, Fri 9am–2pm; ☎062/331-141) and **tourist police** (24hr) are way out on the edge of Port Tewfiq, on Suez Canal Street; you can catch a minibus out along Sharia el-Geish as far as the Passenger Terminal. The tourist office can supply a decent map of the city, but little else in the way of useful information.

Overland connections

Suez is mainly seen by travellers as an **interchange between Cairo, Sinai and Hurghada**. Travelling overland from Hurghada, you can reach Suez rapidly and cheaply by service taxi, and then get other transport on to Sinai, but you should aim to reach Suez by noon to be sure of getting a bus to your destination – otherwise you may have to stay overnight. For **El-Arish** you will need to get to Ismailiya, then pick up a bus or taxi. The new bus station has three ticket kiosks: one for **Cairo**, one for East Delta buses to **Sinai**, **Alexandria** and **the Delta**, and one for Upper Egypt buses to **Hurghada**, **Luxor** and **Aswan**. Each kiosk has a timetable, but schedules change often so be prepared to hang around for a connection. You will also find service taxis here that go to all major destinations. Fares vary widely, according to demand.

•**Sinai** Most of the buses from Suez to the Sinai start their journey in Cairo or Ismailiya. In the past this meant you couldn't always find a seat by the time the bus arrived in Suez. However, direct Superjet buses between Cairo and Sharm el-Sheikh – that don't stop in Suez – are proving popular, lessening demand on the East Delta buses that do, so seat availability has improved. There are six buses daily from Suez to **Sharm el-Sheikh** (8.30am, 11am, 1.30pm, 3pm, 5pm & 6pm; 4hr; £E27), one of which (3pm) goes on to **Nuweiba** (5hr 30min; £E32) and **Taba** (6hr 30min; £E32); and one (11am) to **Dahab** (9hr; £E32). There is one bus daily to **St Catherine's Monastery** (2pm; 6hr; £E27). Service taxis are often quicker but will be packed with bodies and there's no a/c – expect to pay around £E35 to Dahab, £E25 to St Catherine's, £E27 to Nuweiba and £E27 to Sharm el-Sheikh.

•**Ismailiya** Buses run every 30min (6am–4.30pm; 45min–1hr; £E4.50), and service taxis just as frequently (45min; £E5). There are also five buses daily to **Port Said** (7am, 9am, 11am, 12pm & 3.30pm; 2hr; £E10); a service taxi will cost £E10 (1hr 50min). There are frequent service taxis to **Qantara** (see p.667).

•**Alexandria** Four buses daily (7am, 9am, 2.30pm & 5pm; 6hr; £E25). Service taxis charge £E20 and may be a little quicker (5–6hr).

• **Cairo** Buses leave every 30min (1hr 30min–2hr; £E7–8) throughout the day.

• **Hurghada** Nine buses daily (6am–10pm; 6–8hr; £E21–26), most of which also stop at the nearer Red Sea resort of **Ain Sukhna** (1hr; £E5). Service taxis (4–5hr; £E25).

• **Upper Egypt** Buses leave for Luxor (5am, 8am, 10.30am, 2pm, 5pm & 8pm; 6hr; £E35–38) and Aswan (5am, noon & 5pm; 8hr; £E36–48). You can also get buses to Assyut (7am & 7pm; 7hr; £E25–27) and Qena (hourly 6am–11pm; 8hr; £E30–35).

International ferries

Suez is the point of departure for passenger **boats to Saudi Arabia and Sudan**; the former are used by migrant workers or pilgrims, the latter by a few determined travellers. Ferries to the Saudi port of **Jeddah** sail every day, and there are additional sailings during the *Hadj* season (six weeks either side of the Muslim month of *Zoul Hagga*). Boats leave around 2pm and arrive in Jeddah around 10am three days later. Prices start at £E180 for deck space and £E320 per person in a four-berth second class cabin (first class is £E350–370). Providing there's not a storm, sleeping on deck represents no real hardship. Whether boats carry on to **Port Sudan** is hard to predict as schedules change from month to month. Optimists should call operators Telstar in Cairo (☎02/794 4600) for up-to-date details or enquire at El Salam Maritime Transport Co. (☎062/326-251 or 326-252) or Menatours (☎062/228-821), both in Port Tewfiq.

Be warned that they won't sell you a **ticket** unless you already have the right visa(s). The Saudi consulate in Port Tewfiq has sections for work and *Hadj* **visas** but tourist visas can be harder to obtain, so it might be a better idea to get a transit visa in Cairo, where you can also obtain a Sudanese visa – *inshallah*. Should you succeed, the ferry takes a week to get to Port Sudan, so take enough food and drink for the journey.

Accommodation

Outside of the *Hadj* season, **finding a room** in Suez should be easy. Except where indicated, breakfast is not included in the rates given below.

Arafat Hotel off Sharia el-Geish in Port Tewfiq ☎062/338-355. Clean, small rooms with balconies and fans, some with bathrooms. The only budget option if you need to stay in the Port area. Manager has information about passenger ships for Saudi Arabia etc. ❷

Green House Hotel corner Sharia el-Geish and El Nabi Mousa St ☎062/331-553, ℻331-554. Smarter sister of the *White House* (see below) though still a little run down. Clean a/c rooms with Gulf views. Swimming pool. No bar, but serves Stella (£E8). Popular with foreign engineers based in the area. ❼

Red Sea Port Tewfiq ☎062/334-302, ℻334-301. Clean and comfortable a/c rooms with bath, phone, balcony and satellite TV – the smartest hotel in Suez. Sixth-floor *Mermaid Restaurant* has great views of the canal. Breakfast included. ❼

Sina 21 Sharia Banque Misr ☎062/334-181.

Small rooms with fans, TV and clean shared bathrooms, with a fridge on each floor. A good, central, low-budget option. ❷

Star 17 Sharia Banque Misr ☎062/228-737. A mixture of large and small rooms with fans and balconies; some have baths. Another good budget option, a little cheaper than the *Sina*. ❸

Summer Palace Port Tewfiq ☎062/224-475, ℻321-944. Run-to-seed three-star hotel, chiefly notable for its Gulf views and freshwater pool. Overpriced, but worth a visit to its alfresco café to enjoy the views. ❼

White House 322 Sharia el-Geish ☎062/331-550. Has dropped its rating by one star (now down to only two) to reduce the price of rooms. Clean, slightly shabby rooms with a/c, TV and bathroom. The bar is gone, but they still serve local beer. Restaurant and international phone; breakfast included. ❹

The City

Should you decide to stay (or simply pass a few hours between buses), Suez City is readily accessible by microbus from the bus terminal (50pt) or taxi (£E5). The main street, **Sharia el-Geish** (Army Street), is a two-kilometre-long swathe where cruising minibuses drop and collect passengers along the way to Port Tewfiq. Dusty palms and decrepit colonial-era buildings (including several churches) are followed by a strip of hotels, restaurants and currency exchanges. The stadium, on Tariq el-Horriya in the south of the city, is home to Suez FC, enthusiastically supported by the local residents.

The backstreets to the south of El-Geish harbour cheap cafés, while **Sharia Sa'ad Zaghloul** runs past consulates and a fun park towards the Governorate. North of El-Geish, a tawdry souk overflows **Sharia Haleem**, presaging a quarter of workshops and chandlers, crumbling century-old apartments with wooden balconies interspersed by modern government-built low-rises. There's a better **bazaar** to the northwest in Arba'in.

Along El-Geish itself, you'll find the **Convent of the Good Chapel Sisters**, an imposing colonial-style building given to the international sisterhood in 1872 by the Suez Canal Company after one of its directors recovered from a mystery illness while in their care. A decline in their numbers (from 45 down to around five) led the nuns to give their chapel over to the Coptic church, but they still run a primary school and a dispensary for the poor and provide a home for around fifteen underprivileged children. The convent's most notable feature, however, is its **Statue of Our Lady**, which draws pilgrims from all over Egypt and beyond, particularly cancer patients and women with fertility problems. The statue's miraculous properties date back to its discovery by a group of fishermen in the Gulf of Suez in 1882; the men took it back to their village and presented it to the most respected family, but by morning it had disappeared. The fishermen searched the village to no avail; only when they returned to sea did they find the statue in exactly the same place they first saw it. They decided it should be kept somewhere more holy and took it to the sisters who have looked after it ever since.

Should you happen to be by the Canal in spring, migratory **birds of prey** provide a more arresting sight. Griffon vultures and Imperial and Steppe eagles overfly Suez to avoid crossing the Red Sea, which lacks the rising thermals on which they depend for flight. A more permanent resident is the Indian House crow – recognizable by its ear-splitting *caaarrrr* – which is thought to have arrived from India on ships during the course of the nineteenth century.

Eating, drinking and other practicalities

Eating out in Suez is limited but adequate. Your best bet for seafood is the *Dolphin* restaurant on Tariq El-Horiya, opposite the Social Club (which also does seafood), or *Abu Ali* on Sharia el-Geish, near the *White House*. For good value *shawarma*, sandwiches or baked macaroni, check out the *Sweet Spot*, also on Sharia el-Geish, west of the *White House*, or *Misr and Sudan* near Arba'in market. For *kushari* there's *Al Tabareh Restaurant* on Sharia Banque Misr near the *Star Hotel*.

Drinking is even more limited, with only one bar, the *Saint George* (next to *Sweet Spot*), where you can be sure of finding Suez's expat community gathered in the evening. For non-alcoholic beverages, try *The Telegraph* coffee shop on Sharia 23rd July; you'll also find an **Internet café** further down the street.

You can **change money** at the Bank of Alexandria on Sharia el-Geish (daily: summer 9am–2pm & 5–8pm; winter 8am–2pm & 6–9pm), or the National

Bank of Egypt on Sharia Sa'ad Zaghloul (Mon–Thurs & Sun 8.30am–2pm & 5–8pm), private exchanges in the souk, or the Banque du Caire in Port Tewfiq (Mon–Thurs & Sun 8.30am–2pm & 5–8pm). Also in Port Tewfiq is Menatours (☎069/228-821), the agents for **American Express** (beside the tourist police) and a branch of the **post office** – the main one is on Sharia Hoda Sharawi, in the centre of town (both daily except Fri 8am–3pm). You can make international calls from the **telephone exchange** (daily 8am–midnight) on the corner of Sa'ad Zaghloul and El-Shahada, or extend your visa at the **passport office** (daily except Fri 8am–2pm) inside **police** headquarters on Sharia Horriya; as always, arrive early with your passport and photo, a pen, something to read and a sense of humour.

Ismailiya

ISMAILIYA's schizoid character is defined by the rail line that cuts across the city. South of the tracks lies the European-style **garden city** built for foreign employees of the Suez Canal Company, extending to the verdant banks of the Sweetwater Canal. Following careful restoration, its leafy boulevards and placid streets of colonial villas look almost as they must have done in the 1930s, with

The Muslim Brotherhood and the Battle of Ismailiya

Ismailiya – one of the most Europeanized of Egyptian towns – was the birthplace of the **Muslim Brotherhood** and its founder, **Hassan el-Banna**. As a child, El-Banna nailed up leaflets calling upon Muslims to renounce gold and silks, and awoke his neighbours before dawn prayers. When older he campaigned against female emancipation, delivering fiery sermons in rented cafés. He founded the *Ikhwan el-Muslimeen* in 1928 and within fifteen years the Brotherhood had spread throughout Egypt and spawned offshoots across the Middle East, articulating an Islamic response to modernization on Western terms.

From campaigning for moral renewal it went on to organize paramilitary training and terrorist cells, and was outlawed by King Farouk (whose agents assassinated El-Banna) in 1949. Despite this, the Brotherhood mounted attacks against the British and an economic boycott in the Canal Zone. The British suspected that they received arms from sympathizers in the Egyptian police and tried to disarm the main barracks outside Ismailiya, whose garrison was ordered to resist by their superiors and only surrendered after fifty of them had been killed. The **Battle of Ismailiya** (January 25, 1952) outraged Egyptians and provoked an orgy of rioting in Cairo next day – **"Black Saturday"** – when the police stood by as Brotherhood activists sped around in jeeps, torching foreign properties.

Legalized after the 1952 Revolution, the Brotherhood was soon suppressed again for trying to kill Nasser in Alexandria. Hundreds of Brothers spent years in concentration camps, until amnestied by President Sadat, who sought to co-opt them as a counterweight to the left. Eventually, their growing influence and criticism of his policies led Sadat to jail them *en masse*, whereupon his assassination by *Al-Jihad* proved that other groups had grown up in the Brotherhood's shadow and surpassed it in radicalism. To isolate these new militants, Mubarak, too, wooed the Brotherhood with all kinds of concessions short of legalization. In **recent years** he has followed a less clear policy. While he has ordered the arrest of scores of Brothers and the closure of their headquarters in Cairo, associates or sympathizers of the Brotherhood currently form the second largest bloc in the National Assembly after the NDP, and the government appears to view them as a moderating influence within the Islamist movement.

ISMAILIYA

0 ——————— 250 m
Central area only

ACCOMMODATION

Crocodile Inn	5
El-Bourg	2
Isis	1
Mercure Forsan Island	6
Nefertari	3
Traveller's Hotel	4
Youth Hostel	7

RESTAURANTS

El-Gandool	G
Fabiola's	C
George's	F
Groppi's	D
King Edward	B
Pizza Inn	A
Nefertiti's	E

Suez Canal University

CIRCULAR ROAD

EL ESHREEN   Bus Station & Service Taxis   EL ESHREEN

RIDA

Approx 2 km

EL-TOGARI

Approx 1 km

★ Service Taxis   Train Station

SHARIA EL-HORRIYA   MIDAN ORABI   SHARIA EL-HORRIYA

SHARIA TAHRIR   Bank   SHARIA TAHRIR

SHARIA TALATINI   SHARIA AHMED ORABI   SHARIA SAAD ZAGHLOUL   MIDAN GUMHORRIYA   SHARIA F. HASSAN NADH   SHARIA   SAAD ZAGHLOUL   MIDAN M. KAMIL

SHARIA SULTAN HUSSEIN

SHARIA EL-GEISH   Passport Office   SHARIA EL-GEISH   Ismailiya Museum

De Lessops House   Police   Garden Of Steles

MOHAMMED ALI QUAY   SHARIA SALAH SALEM

Sweetwater Canal   Mallaha Park

NEFERTARI ROAD / NO.6 ROAD

SHARIA AL-MONTANISHAT

Customs   Suez Canal Authority

Lake Timsah

G 7 & Beach

bilingual street signs nourishing the illusion that the British empire has just popped indoors for cocktails.

North of the train tracks you move into another world of hastily constructed flats grafted onto long-standing **slums**, and a quarter financed by the Gulf Emirates that provides a *cordon sanitaire* for the wealthy suburb of **Nemrah Setta** (Number Six). This Janus-profile reflects the city's twentieth-century **history**, when two disparate sons of Ismailiya had a lasting effect on Egyptian society. **Hassan el-Banna** created the Muslim Brotherhood that was the bane of the British, and has vexed Egypt's rulers since independence (see box on previous page). Two generations later, Ismailiya became synonymous with **Osman Ahmed Osman**, a self-made millionaire contractor whom Sadat appointed as Minister of Housing and Reconstruction in 1975. As Gulf investments poured into the Canal Zone, billboard-size pictures of Osman began to outnumber those of his patron, who finally agreed to opposition demands for an audit. By the time it was discovered that millions had been stashed in Swiss banks, Osman had fled the country. Subsequent investigations into his political connections proved inconclusive and he is now back in business.

Arrival, information and accommodation

Although Ismailiya can be reached by train (6 daily; 3–5hr), buses or taxis are a quicker way of **getting there from Cairo**. Buses (every 30min 6.30am–6.30pm; £E7) and service taxis (£E6.50) both leave from the Turgoman Garage, in Bulaq, stopping at the Al-Mazah terminal in Heliopolis thirty minutes later, and take two to three hours. The 120-kilometre desert road runs through two places worth noting. **Khanka** contains Egypt's main asylum for the criminally insane, which has made its name a popular synonym for "totally crazy". Further out, a spate of country clubs presages **Medinet Ashara Ramadan** (10th of Ramadan City), a satellite city for the new breed of Cairene commuters, complete with quasi-American suburban homes and steak houses.

All buses and service taxis wind up at the new **bus station** on the ring road outside Ismailiya, opposite the massive Suez Canal University building. From here take a taxi (£E3) or microbus (50pt) into the town centre.

The old town's grid-plan and clearly named streets make **orientation** a doddle. The **tourist office** is inside the new Governorate Building on El-Togari Street, in the north of the city 2km from downtown (daily except Fri 9am–2pm; ☎064/321-072 or 321-076); it's an inconvenient location and does little other than supply a booklet with some information and a map. Hotel staff are likely to prove more informative and helpful.

Accommodation

Apart from a couple of smart hotels, most of Ismailiya's accommodation has seen better days. However, the majority of the hotels are safe, reasonably clean and cheap, and Ismailiya only really gets busy during festivals and the summer season – May to September – when it's a popular honeymoon destination for Egyptian couples. Finding accommodation at other times should be easy, with some hotels likely to be empty – a fact reflected by a general lack of atmosphere in town. Breakfast is included in rates given below unless indicated otherwise.

Crocodile Inn 172 Sharia Sa'ad Zaghloul ☎064/331-555, ℻ 331-666. The only reasonably smart hotel in the town centre, with a restaurant and 24-hr coffee shop. Nice a/c rooms with balconies, and breakfast included, but overpriced. ❻

El-Bourg (or *New Palace*), Midan Orabi ☎064/326-327, ℻ 327-761. A wonderfully pretentious nineteenth-century pile with a/c rooms, satellite TV and private baths. Popular with honeymooners, so often full. A good-value option, especially for those travelling on their own, with single rooms just £E50 including breakfast. ❹

Isis Midan Orabi ☎064/357-821. A range of rooms with fans. Friendly, helpful staff. Reductions for long-staying guests. A low-budget option. No breakfast. ❷

Mercure Forsan Island 2km from town ☎064/338-040, ℻ 338-043. Leafy four-star resort set in fifty acres of grounds. a/c rooms and

villas with satellite TV, minibar and international phone. Swimming pool and watersports. Operates on a half-board basis. ❼

Nefetari 41 Sharia Sultan Hussein ☎064/322-822, ℻ 321-108. A good choice with agreeable rooms, some with a/c and private baths. No breakfast. ❷

Traveller's Hotel Sharia Ahmed Orabi ☎064/358-304. Also called *Hotel des Voyageurs*. Colonial-style hotel that's stronger on atmosphere than creature comforts. Nice rooms with balconies, but no restaurant, breakfast or anything much else. Fans on request. ❶

Youth hostel at Sharia Imhara Siyahi, 1km from the centre and £E2 by taxi ☎ & ℻ 064/322-850. Overlooks Lake Timsah and has its own beach. It has 26 double, triple or six-person rooms with private baths. Double £E44 with breakfast; dorm bed £E23. Non-members pay £E1 extra. ❷

The town and around

Shaded by pollarded trees, Ismailiya's carefully restored old town is a pleasure to walk or bike around. Most of the sights can be reached on foot within ten minutes, although a couple of places outside town warrant renting a bicycle in the backstreets off Mohammed Ali Quay, or catching a service taxi from the turn-off near Mallaha Park.

Starting on Mohammed Ali Quay, first on the trail is the large, vaguely Swiss-looking **House of Ferdinand de Lesseps**, who lived here during the Canal's construction. Disappointingly, you can only visit the interior if you're some kind of VIP, since the house now serves as a private hotel for guests of the Suez Canal Authority. In De Lesseps's study, books and photographs are scattered around his desk and bed as if the Frenchman had been reviewing his life's work, while his carriage stands outdoors, encased in glass. Lone visitors might chance a peek inside if the rear gate is open; otherwise, you could try presenting yourself at the Suez Canal Authority and bluffing the press officer into fixing a visit – though this could well prove a waste of time.

A pleasant fifteen minutes' walk down the street from the De Lesseps House, the **Ismailiya Museum** (Mon–Thurs & Sat–Sun 9am–4pm, Fri and during Ramadan 9.30am–noon & 1.15–4pm; £E6, students £E3, video cameras £E100) leans towards ancient history, devoting a section to the waterways of Ramses and Darius. The highlights of its collection of four thousand Greco-Roman and pharaonic artefacts is a lovely mosaic from the fourth century AD, depicting Phaedra, Dionysos, Eros and Hercules. Other sections cover the canal in modern history, the Battle of Ismailiya and the "Crossing" of October 1973.

With permission from the museum, one can also visit some plaques and obelisks from Ramses II's time, in the **Garden of Steles** down the road, past the guarded residence of the head of the Canal Authority. It's nicer to wander amid the 500 acres of exotic shrubs and trees of **Mallaha Park**, or stroll alongside the shady **Sweetwater Canal** that was dug to provide fresh water for labourers building the Suez Canal. Previously, supplies had to be brought across the desert by camels, or shipped across Lake Manzala to Port Said.

Lake Timsah

Notwithstanding its name, "Crocodile Lake", there are several nice **beaches** around **Lake Timsah**, which you can reach by taking a taxi or walking 1km out along Sharia Talatini. You can dine outside near picturesque fishing boats, or pay £E5–10 to use the manicured lawns and beaches of the private resorts and clubs (which may include snacks and drinks in the deal), but you might find many of these places are closed outside of high season. Wealthier citizens patronize the *Mercure Forsan Island* with its **waterskiing**, **windsurfing** and **tennis** facilities; you can use the beach and swimming pool for £E15, or £E25 on Fridays and holidays.

The Bar-Lev Line and other excursions

Service taxis turning off near Mallaha Park are usually bound for "Ferri Setta" (50pt), outside town, where locals use a **ferry crossing** to the east bank of the canal. Here, a vast sand rampart breached by deep cuts marks the former **Bar-Lev Line**, named after the Israeli general who designed it. Intended to stall any attack on Sinai for 48 hours, this 25-metre-high embankment was defended by forty mined strongpoints. In the event, they were totally surprised by Egypt's assault on **October 6, 1973**. As hidden artillery opened up at 2pm, eight thousand commandos dragged launches to the water's edge, roared across the 180-

metre-wide canal and scaled the ramparts with ladders. Within hours, high-pressure hoses ordered from Bavaria "for the Cairo Fire Department" were blasting gaps for the Egyptian armour massing behind pontoon bridge layers.

However, although "The Crossing" was an Egyptian triumph (still remembered with pride), the war subsequently turned against them. An Israeli force under Ariel Sharon counterattacked across the canal between Lake Timsah and the Great Bitter Lake, wheeled inland to cut the Cairo–Suez road, and had virtually encircled the Egyptian army in Sinai by the time the superpowers imposed a ceasefire. Disengagement on the ground began with UN-sponsored talks at **Kilometre 101** – the nearest Israeli tanks came to Cairo.

A more scenic but distant view of the Canal can be had from **Nemrah Setta**, an exclusive suburb of French colonial-style villas on a hilltop outside town, where, in 1969, an Israeli shell killed the Egyptian Chief of Staff, General Abdul-Monaim Riad. To get there costs £E2–3 by private taxi, or take a service taxi from Midan Orabi to "Ferri Setta" (50pt) and walk up the hill.

The surrounding countryside also has its charms. By taking a service taxi (£E2) from Sharia Talatini (just past the rail line) to **El-Mahsama**, and alighting at Dr Hassan's Hospital, you can walk along the Nile tributary past fields irrigated by archaic water-pumps and old men on donkeys – a scene redolent of the Biblical land of Goshen.

Eating, nightlife and other practicalities

Ismailiya is good for **eating out**. When the weather's fine, citizens dine alfresco near the fishing port on Lake Timsah; it's worth the cost of a taxi (£E2–3) out along Sharia Talatini to eat fish straight from the lake. You might even risk the local speciality, *Umm el-Khaloul* – a kind of shellfish that's best avoided during hot weather when there's a greater risk of it going off. Otherwise, there are several decent restaurants in the centre. The most popular **drinking** spots are *King Edward* (see listings below) and the bar at the *Mercure Forsan Island*, both of which attract an interesting crowd as the night wears on. Alternatively, most of the evening streetlife can be found around Sharia Talatini, Sharia Sa'ad Zaghloul and Sharia el-Geish, where shops, cafés and juice bars are open late into the night.

You can't miss the **post office** (daily except Fri 9am–4pm) and 24-hour **telephone exchange** on Midan Orabi, nor the **passport office** (daily except Fri 8am–2pm). You can **change money** at the Bank of Alexandria or National Bank of Egypt (both Mon–Thurs & Sat–Sun 8.30am–2pm, 5–8pm, Fri 8.30am–12pm; the latter takes Visa and MasterCard) just off Midan Orabi, but you might get a slightly better rate for cash at the exchange at 22 Ahmed Orabi, near the *Traveller's Hotel*. There are several **pharmacies**, including one near the *Isis* on Sharia el-Horriya and another on Sharia Sa'ad Zaghoul. To buy or develop **film**, try either Kodak or Fuji, both near *Groppi's*. Fuji sells slide and Advantix film. For **Internet** access, try the Internet café on Sharia Tahrir, near Midan Gummhorriya (£E4 per hr).

Restaurants

El-Gandool past Fayrouz Beach, a £E2–3 taxi ride from town. Being refurbished at the time of writing, this renowned fish restaurant on Lake Timsah is due to reopen soon.

Fabiola's off Sharia Sa'ad Zaghloul. Inexpensive pizza joint, but don't bother if it's empty as this could mean a long wait for mediocre food. Daily 11am–11pm.

George's Sharia Sultan Hussein. Quiet, a/c Greek restaurant specializing in seafood and kebabs. Has a well-stocked bar, the only one in town. £E14–38 for a full meal. Daily 11am–1am.

Groppi's Sharia Sultan Hussein. Branch of the Cairo patisserie chain. Open 9.30am–9.30pm; closed Sun and during the first half of Ramadan.

King Edward 171 Sharia Tahrir ☎ 064/325-451. a/c haunt of expats and affluent natives, offering tasty Continental and Egyptian food (main dishes £E10–30), wine and beer. DJ plays Western and Middle Eastern music, but don't expect it to get going till after 11pm.

Pizza Inn 41 Sharia Talatini. Busy takeout and sit-down eatery for burgers (from £E4) and pizzas (from £E6). Free delivery. Daily 10am–2am.

Nefertiti's Sharia Sultan Hussein ☎ 064/220-494. Specializes in fish (£E15–20) and shrimps (£E36), but does meat dishes, too. Sells beer and wine. Daily noon–midnight.

Festivals

Should you happen to be here around Easter, Ismailiya is a good place to witness the spring festival of **Shams el-Nessim**, when families picnic in the park between the Sweetwater Canal and Lake Timsah, and a **Flower Festival** adds colour to the occasion.

Even better is the "**Doll-Burning**" or **Limbo Festival**, held a week later. Its curious title refers to a hated nineteenth-century local governor – Limbo Bey – effigies of whom were torched by the citizenry. Ever since then, it has been customary to burn dolls resembling one's pet hate: footballers are popular targets whenever Ismailiya's soccer club does poorly. The dolls are burned on the streets after dark.

Moving on

To get anywhere from Ismailiya, it's back to the bus station on the ring road opposite the new Suez Canal University building. Private taxis (£E2–3) or service taxis (50pt) to the bus station leave from the rank on Sharia Talatini just north of the railway tracks.

● **North Sinai** Buses leave eight times a day for **El-Arish** (8.30am, 9am, 10am, noon, 1pm, 2pm, 3.30pm & 5pm; 3hr; £E8.50); service taxis cost £E6. There are also service taxis to **Rafah** (£E8).

● **South Sinai** Buses leave throughout the day and night to **Sharm el-Sheikh** (6.30am–midnight; 6hr; £E33), two of which carry on to **Dahab** (2.30pm & 12.30am; 7–8hr; £E40). A service taxi to Sharm el-Sheikh costs £E25–30. There's also a nightly bus to **Nuweiba** (9pm; 7–8hr; £E48).

● **Canal cities** Buses travel regularly via Ismailiya between **Port Said** (half-hourly 6.45am–6.45pm; 1hr; £E5.50) and **Suez** (hourly 6.30am–6pm; 1hr; £E4.50) while service taxis are a bit cheaper (Port Said £E5; Suez £E4). A service taxi to **Qantara** is £E1.25.

● **Lower Egypt** There are two buses daily to **Alexandria** (7am & 2.30pm; 4hr; £E22) and frequent departures for **Cairo** (every 45min 6.30am–7pm; 2hr; £E7). Outside of these hours you can still get to Cairo by service taxi (£E5) or to the Delta town of **El-Mansura** (£E6).

North of Ismailiya – canal crossings

Seven kilometres north of Ismailiya, a **car ferry** crosses the canal more or less non-stop during daylight hours. Together with the Ahmed Hamdi Tunnel outside Suez, it used to carry almost all the traffic between mainland Egypt and Sinai until the opening of the Salaam (or Ferdan) Suspension Bridge in October 2001. The bridge is now the most direct route from Cairo to Israel, so, assuming the situation in Palestine improves and tourist traffic between the two countries resumes, the car ferry is likely to be less busy with **international and tour buses**.

The New Kingdom war machine

Recent excavations in the Eastern Delta and Northern Sinai have cast light on the revolution in Egyptian warfare during the New Kingdom. The Hyksos invasion forced the Egyptians to adopt the weapons of their enemy - horses, chariots, composite bows, edged swords and bronze armour – and master cavalry tactics, hitherto unknown. **Chariots** became the key to their success, allowing rapid movement on the battlefield and over long distances. Light enough to be lifted over obstacles by their crew, they were kept on the road by mobile repair units and stables at the rear; one for 400 horses has been found at Tell ed-Daba in the Delta. Twelve **fortresses** along the **Great Horus military route** across Northern Sinai (depicted on Seti I's reliefs in the columned court at Karnak) provided defence in depth and stores for major campaigns; one at Tell Habouh, near Qantara, covers 12,000 square metres. Armies were supplied by donkeys or by galleys in coastal waters. Such logistics enabled Tuthmosis III to move 20,000 troops 400km in nine days – without being detected – while Ramses II extended Egypt's strategic reach to 2000km by pioneering the use of oxen (the mainstay of military logistics for the next thousand years). This formidable war machine made imperialism inevitable, and was fed by the spoils of war: 894 chariots, 2000 horses and 25,000 pack animals were taken at the battle of Meggido alone.

The fortresses lie within what is still a sensitive military area, not yet open to tourists. Anyone with a serious interest should contact the **Centre for Sinai Studies** at the Archeological Institute in West Qantara (☎064/342-713 or 333-718).

The only other crossing point is at **QANTARA**, 44km from Ismailiya and 80km from Port Said. As its name ("Bridge") suggests, this was the route used by pilgrims and armies to cross the marshy Isthmus of Suez before the canal was built. Since then, it has been spanned by pontoon bridges in wartime, but is now negotiated by a small passenger ferry, carrying locals, bikes and donkeys from one side of Qantara to the other. Most of the town is on the west bank, whose unpaved main drag has a busy souk and lines of service taxis going to Cairo and the Canal cities; the battered, poorly rebuilt houses are a reminder that armies clashed here as recently as 1973. On the east bank of the canal there's a cafeteria and service taxis for El-Arish (2hr 30min; £E5), but it's easier to take one direct from Ismailiya.

Port Said (Bur Said)

Founded at the start of the canal excavations, **PORT SAID** was long synonymous with smuggling and vice, boasting an "even larger stock of improper photos than Brussels or Buenos Aires". The adventurer De Monfreid was amused by the Arab cafés where "native policemen as well as coolies" smoked hashish in back rooms, supplied by primly respectable Greeks. "If anyone had even had the bad taste to pronounce the forbidden word, I believe that they would have all turned into pillars of salt. All the same, every single one of them got his living from trafficking in hashish, either as a retail seller, or as a small-scale smuggler who haunted the liners".

Nowadays, this bustling city of 400,000 people earns its living as a free port and beach resort, yet a faintly raffish atmosphere lingers around its old streets of timber-porched houses, vaguely resembling the French Quarter of New Orleans. Prior to the current downturn in tourism caused by the unrest in Israel and the Occupied Territories, which has rather halted development in

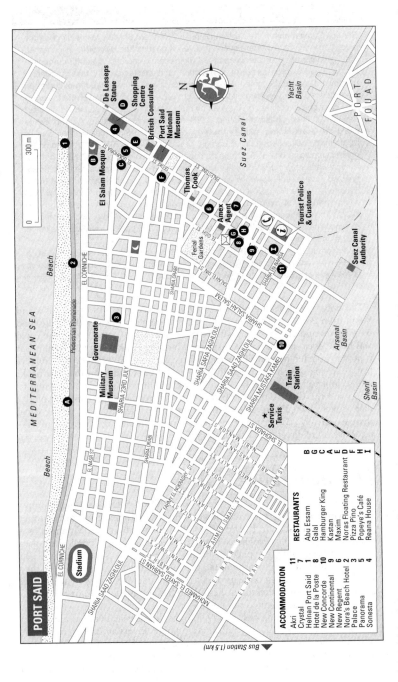

PORT SAID

MEDITERRANEAN SEA

Beach

Stadium

Beach

Pedestrian Promenade

EL CORNICHE

EL CORNICHE

El Salam Mosque

De Lesseps Statue

Shopping Centre

British Consulate

Port Said National Museum

Thomas Cook

Amex Agent

Tourist Police & Customs

Suez Canal

Suez Canal Authority

Ferial Gardens

Military Museum

Governorate

SHARIA 23RD JULY

SHARIA ORABI

SHARIA ORABI

EL NASR ST

NABIL MANSOR

SHARIA SAAD ZAGHLOUL

EL CORNICHE

MOHAMED EL SAYED SABHAN ST

SHARIA SAFIA ZAGHLOUL

SHARIA SAAD ZAGHLOUL

SHARIA MUSTAFA KAMEL

EL SHOHADA ST

SHARIA SALAH SALEM

SHARIA EL NAHDA

SALAH E DIN ST

EL GISH ST

PALESTINE ST

SECRET ST

Train Station

Service Taxis

Arsenal Basin

Sherif Basin

Yacht Basin

PORT FOUAD

N

300 m

0

Bus Station (1.5 km)

ACCOMMODATION

Akri	11
Crystal	7
Helnan Port Said	1
Hotel de la Poste	8
New Concorde	10
New Continental	9
New Regent	6
Nora's Beach Hotel	2
Palace	3
Panorama	5
Sonesta	4

RESTAURANTS

Abu Essam	B
Galal	G
Hamburger King	C
Kastan	A
Maxim	E
Nora's Floating Restaurant	D
Pizza Pino	F
Popeye's Café	H
Reana House	I

6

the region, *Bur Said* had been attempting to lure tourists away from Alexandria by promising better shops and less crowded beaches, cheap hotels and good restaurants. Aside from day-trippers off cruise liners, foreign tourists seldom visit the city and hustlers are rare, making it an agreeable place to relax for a day or two if you don't mind the lack of "sights" and diversions and are content to hang out on the beach or one of the European-style street cafés.

Arrival, information and accommodation

Trains **from Cairo** (six daily) take at least four and a half hours to reach Port Said via Ismailiya, and are grimy to boot, making it more appealing to do the 220km journey by bus (3hr). Regular a/c East Delta buses depart from Cairo's Turgoman Garage (every hr 6.30am–10pm; 4hrs; £E13–16). In the absence of direct trains **from Alexandria**, seats on buses (4 daily; 6hr; £E18–22) should be reserved the day before, at the East Delta kiosk on Midan Sa'ad Zaghoul. All buses, including those from Suez (4 daily; 2hr 30min; £E9.50), Ismailiya (hourly 6am–7pm; 1hr 30 min; £E5.50) and Luxor (1 daily; 7–8hr; £E37), terminate at Port Said's new bus station at the entrance to the city. Service taxis provide the fastest transport **from Suez and Ismailiya** and augment buses **from the Delta**, where Damietta and El-Mansura have the best connections. Coming **from El-Arish** in north Sinai, you can catch a service taxi (£E9–10) direct to the city.

Because Port Said is a **duty-free port**, visitors are supposed to pass through **customs** upon entering and leaving the city. You may not have to, but if you do pass through customs, it is advisable to declare any cameras or other gadgets, which they might think you bought at a discount here, or you may be subject to a twelve percent levy as you go out (ships' passengers are exempt). Simply request a paper (£E1) and fill it in with details of your belongings, keeping it to show when you leave. The main **point of arrival** is the new bus station, which is on the outskirts of Port Said just off the main road from Ismailiya, from where you can catch a taxi (£E2) downtown (along and around Sharia el-Gumhorriya). **Orientation** is straightforward, as most things of interest or use to tourists can be found on three thoroughfares: the waterfront Sharia Filastin (Palestine Street); Sharia el-Gumhorriya (Street of the Republic), two blocks inland; or Sharia 23rd July.

The **tourist office** (daily 9am–1.30pm & occasionally also 4–8pm; ☎066/235-289) on Sharia Filastin can supply a useful map of the town with listings of hotels and services and some historical background, while the **tourist police** (☎066/228-570) are at the back of the main customs building, and have another office in the train station (both open 24hr).

Accommodation

Sharia el-Gumhorriya offers the widest range of **hotels**, from modern tower blocks to old-style *pensions*. If one is full or seems uncongenial, there's always another within easy walking distance. Be aware, however, that accommodation can be hard to find on Thursday and Friday nights, when many Egyptians come here to do weekend duty-free shopping. The **youth hostel** on Sharia al-Amin (☎066/228-702, ℱ 226-433; £E18.50), near the stadium, has clean but gloomy dormitory rooms; it admits non-members (£E1 extra). Rates given below include breakfast unless stated otherwise.

Akri 24 Sharia el-Gumhorriya ☎066/221-013. Run-down, atmospheric Greek *pension* near the harbour. Basic, clean rooms and sporadic hot water in shared bathrooms; ask for a balcony.

Rooftop restaurant, breakfast not included. ❶
Crystal Hotel 12 Sharia el-Gumhorriya ☎066/222-747. A big complex which resembles a youth hostel, with large en suite a/c rooms. ❹

Helnan Port Said El Corniche St ℡ 066/320-890, ℻ 323-762, ℮ reshps@helnan.com. Retains its five-star rating chiefly because of its location on the beach. Has a pool, gym and sauna. **❼**

Hotel de la Poste 46 Sharia el-Gumhorriya ℡ 066/229-655, ℻ 228-898. Rambling 1940s-style place offering high-ceilinged rooms with fans and baths; TVs and fridges cost extra. Prices vary according to room; breakfast not included. **❻**

New Concorde Sharia Mustafa Kamel ℡ 066/235-342, ℻ 235-930. Carpeted rooms with baths, fans and TV, near the train station. Some of the rooms on the upper floors have views of the canal. **❺**

New Continental 30 Sharia el-Gumhorriya ℡ 066/225-024, ℻ 333-088. Pleasant enough, though a bit shabby; a/c rooms with satellite TV, international phone and balconies. **❹**

New Regent off Sharia el-Gumhorriya ℡ 066/223-802, ℻ 224-891. Small but comfortable hotel offering a/c rooms, all with TV and fridge. **❻**

Nora's Beach Hotel El Corniche St ℡ 066/329-834, ℻ 329-841. Huge beachside complex with 200 apartments and suites – a bit frayed at the edges but still comfortable – with a/c, private bathroom, satellite TV, minibar, balcony or terrace. With its three swimming pools and a health club, it's popular with Egyptian families. **❺**

Palace 19 Sharia Ghandi, opposite the Governorate building, near the beach ℡ 066/239-450, ℻ 239-464. Pleasantly furnished rooms with a/c and private bathrooms. **❺**

Panorama Hotel Shari el-Gumhorriya ℡ 066/325-101, ℻ 325-103. A/C rooms with satellite TV, private bathrooms and big balconies. Great views especially from the billiard room on the eleventh floor. A bit worn, but clean and comfortable. **❺**

Sonesta Sharia Sultan Hussein ℡ 066/325-511, ℻ 324-825, ℮ reservations@sonestaportsaid.com. a/c rooms have private bathrooms, satellite TV and a minibar, and overlook the canal entrance and fishing harbour. There's also a nice pool, but no beach. Breakfast costs extra. **❼–❽**

The City

Sharia el-Gumhorriya reflects Port Said's metamorphosis from a salty entrepôt to a slick commercial centre, plate-glass facades superseding early twentieth-century balconies as the street progresses from the Arsenal Basin to Sharia 23rd July.

The adjacent **bazaar** quarter is a microcosm of Egyptian consumer aspirations, ranging from humble stalls on Sharia el-Togary to the smart boutiques on Sharia en-Nahda. These have been joined by designer shops such as Hugo Boss and sports stores like Nike and Reebok at the junction of Sharia el-Gumhorriya with Sharia 23rd July. There is even a Clark's shoe shop downtown and an M&S in the shopping centre opposite the *Sonesta*.

The **Military Museum** (Mon–Thurs & Sat–Sun 9am–2pm, also Fri in summer 6–10pm; £E2) gives a strong sense of the Canal's embattled history. The 1956 Anglo-French-Israeli invasion is commemorated by lurid paintings and dioramas, while another room is dedicated to the October War of 1973. This gives pride of place to the storming of the Bar-Lev Line (see p.624), a heroic feat of arms ultimately wasted by the high command's failure to exploit Egypt's breakthrough in Sinai. Curiously absent from the large display of weaponry are the Soviet-made *Strella* and *Molutka* rockets that enabled Egyptian infantrymen to destroy Israeli jets and armour, rated by strategists as a minor revolution in modern warfare. It's about 15–20 minutes' walk from here to the National Museum.

Opened in 1987, the **Port Said National Museum** (Mon–Thurs, Sat & Sun 9am–5pm, Fri 9am–noon & 2–5pm; £E12, students £E6, camera £E10) runs the gamut of Egyptian history. Highlights of the well-displayed collection include two mummies, an exquisitely worked faïence shroud and painted coffin, Ptolemaic funerary masks, Islamic tiles and *mashrabiyas*, Coptic textiles (especially a tunic adorned with images of the Apostles) and the coach of Khedive Ismail, used during the Canal's inauguration ceremonies. Cool and uncrowded, the museum makes a pleasant retreat from the heat and hubbub around this part of the waterfront.

Come evening, townsfolk and holidaymakers **promenade** along the Corniche, or near the National Museum, watching dozens of vessels at anchor, their bulky hulls dwindling to lights bobbing far offshore. At the far end of the quay is a massive sandstone plinth that used to bear a huge **statue of De Lesseps**, before it was torn down following the 1952 Revolution. For an idea of the Canal's workings, take a cruise on the *Noras* floating restaurant or catch the free **ferry** (every 15min) across to Port Fouad (see below).

You can rent chairs and parasols for £E5 on Port Said's shell-strewn **beach**, which has public showers at 100m intervals. For calmer water and more relaxed sunbathing, consider paying £E20 to use the **pool** at the *Sonesta* hotel. The pool at the *Helnan* costs a hefty £E50 but this includes use of the gym and sauna.

Port Fouad

Founded as a suburb for Canal bureaucrats in 1927, **PORT FOUAD** is quieter than its sister city. Residents boast of commuting between Asia and Africa – an enjoyable ride in a battered ferry reeking of everything but inter-Continental status. The suburb's decrepit but stylish **1930s architecture** can be appreciated by making a tour of Port Fouad's Art Deco flats, colonial villas and well-tended gardens. Travellers hoping to work their passage to the Med or the Indian Ocean could ask around at the **yacht basin**, although success is far from assured.

Eating and drinking

Eating out in Port Said is enjoyable, as fresh seafood abounds and most places have tables outdoors, allowing you to savour the bustling streetlife. If you fancy cruising the Suez Canal while you eat, make a reservation at the *Noras* **floating restaurant** on the waterfront near the National Museum. The *Noras* sails at least twice daily (2.30pm and 8.30pm) but schedules change, so check times at the *Noras Beach Hotel* where you can also reserve tickets. The 90-minute cruise costs £E10 if you settle for a soft drink, or £E36–60 including lunch or dinner. Besides the places listed below, there are lots of patisseries and coffee houses on Sharia el-Gumhorriya. The spit-and-sawdust *Cecil Bar* beneath the *Reama* restaurant is where to go **drinking** if you want to imbibe an atmosphere redolent of the olden days, in the company of aged Greeks. The bar is open till midnight or later. There is also the standard duo of *KFC* and *Pizza Hut* on 23rd July if you're feeling homesick.

Abu Essam El-Corniche St, diagonally opposite the *Helnan*. Excellent fish restaurant with moderate prices. A full meal costs £E20–30.

Galal on the corner of Gaberti and El-Gumhorriya. A nice place to sit outside, drink beer and eat *kofta* sandwiches or seafood (£E15–20). They also do *shawarma* takeaways. Daily 7am–1am; closed during Ramadan.

Hamburger King corner of Sharia el-Gomhorriya and Sharia Tarh el-Bahr ☏066/224-877. Burger bar popular with young Egyptians. Hamburgers, (£E2) sandwiches, *shawarma* (£E2–6) and pizza (£E10–20). Also serves fresh fruit juice (£E3) and does home delivery.

Kastan El-Corniche St, towards the stadium. Large and very busy 24-hr seafood and fish restaurant on the beach. Around £E30 for a full meal. Recommended.

Maxim in the shopping centre on the corner of El-Gumhorriya and El-Corniche. Port Said's most expensive fish restaurant, with splendid views of ships entering the Canal. A full meal costs £E40–60.

Pizza Pino on the corner of El-Gumhorriya and 23rd July streets. Popular joint with slick decor and a seductive range of Italian dishes and ice cream.

Popeye's Café Sharia el-Gumhorriya, opposite the *Hotel de la Poste*. A pleasant Mediterranean-style street café serving a wide selection of food, including huge banana splits. Daily 8am–midnight.

Reana House 5 Sharia el-Gumhorriya, diagonally across from the *Akri Hotel*. Tasty Korean and Chinese food including vegetarian dishes, at reasonable prices. Serves alcohol. Open till midnight or later.

Listings

Consulates British (☎066/231-155), French (☎066/322-875) and Belgian (☎066/223-314) consulates are located in the commercial centre just beyond the National Museum, while Denmark and Norway are represented at the Norwegian Seaman's Service (☎066/336-730) on the 4th floor of 30 Sharia Sultan Hussein, one block north along the waterfront from the tourist office.

Currency exchange Numerous private exchanges around Sharia en-Nahda and the shopping malls at the northern end of Sharia el-Gumhorriya can change money with less hassle than banks and sometimes at a slightly better rate. Travellers' cheques can be cashed at Thomas Cook, at 43 Sharia el-Gumhorriya (daily 8am–5pm; ☎066/227-559, ☎ 236-111). Menatours, at no. 18 (☎066/225-742), still claims to be the local agent for American Express, but its role has been usurped to some degree by the arrival of American Express Bank (daily except Fri 8am–3pm) on

Sharia el-Gomhorriya near the British Consulate. Several of the banks along Sharia el-Gumhorriya now have ATMs which accept Visa and MasterCard.

Hospitals The best equipped and newest hospital is Al-Soliman near the sports stadium (☎066/331-533). Emergencies can also be treated at the Al-Mabarrah (☎066/220-560) or El-Tadaman (☎066/231-790) hospitals.

Passport office In the Governorate building on Sharia 23rd July (Thurs & Sat 8am–2pm).

Pharmacy The 24-hr Hussein Pharmacy on Sharia el-Gumhorriya (☎066/339-888) is diagonally opposite the *Hotel de la Poste*.

Post office The main branch (daily except Fri 9am–2pm) is near the southeast corner of Ferial Gardens.

Telephone exchange Just along from the tourist office on Sharia Filastin (24hr).

Moving on

East Delta **buses to Cairo or Alexandria,** Superjet a/c services to Cairo and **buses to Ismailiya or the Delta** all leave from the main bus station at the edge of town on the road to Ismailiya. The buses and **service taxis** must stop at the customs station outside the city.

To get to **Limassol by ferry**, the *Princess Marissa* departs around 7.30pm every Tuesday and Saturday in the summer (Tues & Fri in the winter), arriving in Limassol the next morning around 10am. At time of writing the onward journey to Haifa had been suspended. The fare to Limassol is US$120 per person one-way for a cabin (4 persons max). Tickets are available from Nasco Tours on Sharia Filastin, north of the tourist office (☎066/329-500, ☎ 238-850).

Sinai

CHAPTER 7 # Highlights

* **Na'ama Bay** By night, the bars and clubs of Egypt's premier resort are teeming with revellers. See p.693

* **Ras Mohammed** This national park at the tip of the Sinai peninsula offers some world-class diving. See p.690

* **Reefs and wrecks** Check out the infamous blue hole, or wreck-diving the Thistlegorm. See p.685

* **Desert safaris** Camel or jeep safaris are possible to secluded palm-fringed wadis with Bedouin hosts. See p.725

* **Nabq** This national park holds spectacular scenery and the most northerly mangroves in the world. See p.707

* **Mt Sinai** Climb the mountain where Moses received the Ten Commandments and see dawn break over the Sinai desert. See p.730

* **St. Catherine's monastery** Built by Byzantine Empress Helena to commemorate the sight of the burning bush at the foot of Mount Sinai. See p.726

* **Bedouin culture** Moulids and weddings are held at full moon in the desert. See p.718

* **Dahab** Chill out in Asilah, renowned for its diving, laid-back beach cafés and cheap accommodation. See p.707

* **Sandy beaches** Between Nuweiba and Taba stretch miles of beautiful beaches, peppered with budget-priced camps for travellers. See p.720

7

Sinai

The **Sinai** peninsula has been the gateway between Africa and Asia since time immemorial and a battleground for millennia. Prized for its strategic position and mineral wealth, Sinai is also revered by disparate cultures as the site of God's revelation to Moses, the wanderings of Exodus and the flight of the Holy Family. As Burton Bernstein wrote, "it has been touched, in one way or another by most of Western and Near Eastern history, both actual and mythic", being the supposed route (there's no archeological proof) by which the Israelites reached the Promised Land and Islam entered North Africa, then a theatre for Crusader-Muslim and Arab-Israeli conflicts, and finally transformed into an internationally monitored demilitarized zone.

Though mostly wilderness, Sinai looks far too dramatic – and too beautiful – to be dismissed as "24,000 square miles of nothing". The interior of southern Sinai is an arid moonscape of jagged ranges harbouring **Mount Sinai** and **St Catherine's Monastery**, where pilgrims climb the Steps of Repentance from the site of the Burning Bush to the summit where God delivered the Ten Commandments. Further north, the vast **Wilderness of the Wanderings** resembles a Jackson Pollock canvas streaked with colour and imprinted with tank tracks. The Sinai is also home to a remarkably high number of plants and wildlife; over sixty percent of Egypt's plant life thrives in this area, and thirty-three species are unique to the Sinai. Among a number of mammals that inhabit the region are the hyena, ibex and the rabbit-like hyrax. Venture into this "desert" on a **camel trek** or **jeep safari** and you will also find remote springs and lush oases, providing some insights into **Bedouin culture**.

Above all, however, the south has the lure of exquisite coral reefs and tropical fish in the **Gulf of Aqaba**, one of the finest **diving** and **snorkelling** grounds in the world. The beach resorts at **Sharm el-Sheikh** (which includes **Na'ama Bay**), **Dahab** and **Nuweiba** cater to every taste and budget. From Sharm el-Sheikh you can also make expeditions to Egypt's deepest reefs and most diverse aquatic life at **Ras Mohammed**, a mini-peninsula at the southern tip of Sinai, and the **Tiran Strait**, scattered with the wrecks of ships that have floundered on the reefs of this narrow passageway connecting the Red Sea to the Gulf of Aqaba. Northwest of here, the **Gulf of Suez** pales by comparison with its eastern counterpart – though year-round winds make it a great destination for diehard windsurfers, there are no reefs and few sites to interest the general visitor.

Northern Sinai is visited by almost no Western tourists, although in summer it fills up with Egyptian holidaymakers. With a barren coastline, which you scarcely glimpse from the road, it has a single town and focus in **El-Arish**, a

DIVE SITES

Blue Hole & The Canyon	7
Dunraven	18
El-Gharkana	10
El-Muqeibila	3
Fjord	1
Maagana Beach	4
Near, Middle & Far Gardens	15
Ras Abu Galum	6
Ras al-Shaitun	4
Ras Atantur	9
Ras el-Mamleh	6
Ras Mohammed National Park	19
Ras Nasrani, Jackson	14
& Gordon Reefs	17
Ras Umm Sidd	13
Shark Bay	8
Southern Oasis	11
Sun Pool	14
Thistlegorm	
Tiran Island Protected Area	14
The Tower, Amphoras	
& Turtle Bay	17

TREK SITES

Ain el-Furtaga	F
Ain Khudra Oasis	H
Ain Umm Ahmed	D
Arched Canyon	A
Bir es-Sawa	C
Blue Valley	B
Coloured Canyon	J
El-Haduda	G
Forest of Pillars	I
Nuwamis	K
Sheikh Hamid	E
Wadi Huweiyit	N
Wadi Kid	O
Wadi Mandar	L
Wadi Naseb	M

laid-back if conservative place with a palm-fringed beach and a weekly Bedouin market.

Some history

Fifty million years ago the Arabian Plate began shearing away from the African landmass, tearing the Sinai peninsula from the mainland while the Red Sea inundated the gap. Hot springs on the sea bed indicate that the tectonic forces which created Sinai are still active – the Gulf of Suez is widening by three inches each year. In **prehistoric times** the climate was less arid and Sinai supported herds of gazelles which Stone Age people trapped and slaughtered in stone enclosures.

Bronze Age Semites from Mesopotamia were the first to exploit Sinai's lodes of copper ore and turquoise, foreshadowing the peninsula's colonization by the III Dynasty pharaohs, who enslaved its Semitic population to work the mines, and build roads and fortresses. According to Egyptian mythology, it was in Sinai that Isis sought the dismembered body of Osiris; and Hathor, also associated with the region, was called "Our Lady of Sinai". **Pharaonic rule** continued until the invasion of the Hyksos "Shepherd Kings", whose occupation of northern Egypt lasted well over a century, till Ahmosis I drove them out and finally destroyed their last bastion in Gaza. This was subsequently the route by which Tuthmosis III and Ramses II invaded Palestine and Syria.

The Exodus

Enshrined in the Old Testament and by centuries of tradition, the **Exodus of the Israelites** is a historical conundrum, as no archeological evidence of their journey through Sinai has ever been found – though excavations at Avaris in the Delta (see p.646) suggest that this was the "City of Bondage" from which they fled. This is generally thought to have happened during the reign of the XIX Dynasty pharaoh, Merneptah (1236–1223 BC), although Egyptologist David Rohl argues that it occurred two centuries earlier (c.1447 BC), under Dudimose of the XIII Dynasty (see p.787).

To identify their route and various crucial sites, scholars have compared Biblical descriptions with physical features and tried to reconcile myths with realities. The **"Red Sea"** found in the King James Bible is a mistranslation of the Hebrew *Yam-suf*, or **Sea of Reeds**, which fits the salt lakes and marshes to the north of Suez, known today as the Bitter Lakes. From there, the Israelites proceeded down the coast to **Ain Musa** and followed **Wadi Feiran** inland towards **Mount Sinai**; although a contrary theory has them trekking across northern Sinai and receiving the Ten Commandments at **Jebel Halal**. Either way, the subsequent forty years in the wilderness are only explicable in terms of a lengthy stay at "Kadesh Barnea", identified as the oasis of **Ain Kedirat**, where there are extensive ruins.

Christianity and Islam

Over the next millennium or so, Sinai was invaded by Assyrians, Hittites and Babylonians, recaptured by Egypt, and conquered in turn by the Persians and Greeks. While the Ptolemies built ports along the Mediterranean coast, Semitic tribes from Petra established themselves between Aqaba and Gaza, both ultimately succumbing to the **Romans**. Whether or not the **Holy Family** had previously crossed Sinai to escape Herod's massacre, the region had begun to attract hermits even before Emperor Constantine legalized **Christianity**, which rooted itself in cathedrals and **monasteries** under Justinian's patronage.

In 639–40 the **Arabs** swept into Sinai, fired with the zeal of **Islam**. The new faith suited local tribes, which turned to plundering the desert monasteries while the Arabs sacked the cathedral cities. Northern Sinai eventually became a pawn in the **Crusades**, the area between Aqaba and Rafah belonging to the Frankish Kingdom until its collapse at Acre.

After the Crusades, the victorious Mamlukes reopened Sinai's trade routes but the peninsula remained Egypt's Achilles heel, as the Ottoman Turks and Mohammed Ali demonstrated with their conquests of 1517 and 1831.

Twentieth-century Sinai

Sinai's strategic importance increased with the completion of the **Suez Canal**, and in 1892 Britain compelled Turkey to cede it as a buffer zone. Backed by Germany, the Turks retook it in 1914, laying roads and water pipelines along the northern coast and across the interior. Anglo-Egyptian forces only dislodged them – and went on to take Jerusalem – after a prolonged campaign.

During World War II Sinai witnessed little fighting, but the **creation of Israel** brought the territory right back into the front line. In 1948 the Israelis repulsed Arab attacks from all sides and took the **Gaza Strip** and **El-Arish** before an armistice was signed, only withdrawing under British pressure. By closing the Gulf of Aqaba to Israeli shipping and nationalizing the Suez Canal, however, Nasser brought together British and Israeli interests. It was Israel's advance into Sinai in October 1956 that was the agreed pretext for Anglo-French intervention in the **Suez Crisis**; though militarily successful, the three states were compelled to quit by international opposition, UN peacekeeping forces establishing a buffer zone in Gaza and guaranteeing free passage through the Gulf of Aqaba.

But further **Arab-Israeli wars** were inevitable. When Egypt ordered the UN to leave and resumed its blockade in **1967**, Israel launched a pre-emptive strike and captured the entire peninsula, which it retained after the **Six Day War** and fortified with the Bar-Lev Line along the east bank of the Suez Canal. In the **October War of 1973**, Egypt broke through into Sinai but then suffered a devastating counterattack across the canal.

US-sponsored peace negotiations culminated in President Sadat's historic visit to Jerusalem, the **Camp David Accords** and a peace treaty signed in 1979, which led to Egypt's decade-long expulsion from the Arab League. Under its terms Israel evacuated all settlements founded during the occupation of Sinai and the territory reverted to Egypt; a phased transition completed in 1982, except for the disputed enclave of Taba, finally resolved in 1989. The Multinational Force and Observers (**MFO**) based at Na'ama Bay monitors Sinai's "banded" demilitarized zones from orange-flagged outposts around the peninsula.

Introduced to Sinai by the Israelis, **tourism** initially suffered from the hand-over, as the Camp David Accords forbade any development for five years. Since 1988, however, its recovery has shifted into overdrive: where the Aqaba coast once had just five hotels it now has more than 150, with at least a further fifty under construction. While the areas of Ras Mohammed, Abu Galum and Nabeq are protected by their status as nature reserves, the entire coastline north of Nuweiba, and from Sharm el-Sheikh to Nabeq National Park, are highly developed. With plans to extend hotel development further into the desert, and ever more charter flights arriving from Europe to the newly upgraded airport at Sharm el-Sheikh, by the end of the twentieth century Sinai's days as a wilderness looked set to be numbered. That is, of course, until **September 11, 2001**, and subsequent events in Israel. Although the Sharm el-Sheikh resorts remain busy, the short-term outlook of other Sinai destinations, especially

Most of Sinai's population are **Bedouin** who claim descent from the tribes of the Hejaz on the Arabian Peninsula, and thus rate themselves amongst the purest Arab genealogies. Only the Jebeliya tribe is anomalous, tracing its origins to the Caucasus.

Traditionally, each tribe roamed its own territory in search of grazing and settled around local oases. The Mizayna claimed the land between El-Tor and Nuweiba; the Tarabeen a swathe from Nuweiba to El-Arish; the Jebeliya the St Catherine's region, and so on.* Tribal and family honour were paramount, raids and camel-rustling a perpetual cause for blood feuds that might persist for generations. Agriculture or fishing was a hand-to-mouth activity, secondary to herding goats and camels – the latter being the measure of a tribe's wealth, with racing camels esteemed above all. Though devout Muslims, the Bedouin retained pagan superstitions and practices from the "time of darkness", with their own common law ('urf) instead of regular Islamic jurisprudence.

Unsurprisingly, the Bedouin took advantage of discarded weaponry to resist outside authority, attempts to settle the nomads having little success until the 1970s, when Israel constructed water tanks, schools and clinics at various sites. By providing employment and exposing the Bedouin to Western comforts, the coastal resorts had an equally profound effect on traditional lifestyles. Nowadays, many earn their living through tourism, taxi driving or construction work, and stone huts with corrugated iron roofs and TV antennae are more common than black tents. Although relations between the Bedouin and Egyptians are generally peaceful, grievances do arise; they are usually focussed on administrators and entrepreneurs from mainland Egypt whom many Bedouin regard as here on sufferance, but who are steadily growing in numbers.

For more on traditional Bedouin culture see p.735.

*The number of **tribes** in Sinai is uncertain, ranging from 14 to 27 depending on which of their subdivisions are counted. Other tribes include the Sawalha, Alekat, Walad Shaheen and Tiyahah. Collectively, they are known as the Tawarah ("Arabs of Tor"), after the ancient name of the peninsula, or simply as Al-Arab.

those around Taba and Nuweiba, is, at the time of writing, uncertain. Here the dearth of Israeli visitors means that attempts to create one vast tourist zone around the Gulf of Aqaba – rebranding Taba, Eilat in Israel and Aqaba in Jordan as the "Red Sea Riviera" – have been, for the time being, scuppered; the airport at Taba is rarely used nowadays, and the tourist camps along the coast around Nuweiba are now mostly empty. The Bedouin camps at Tarabeen in particular have been particularly hard hit and are almost completely devoid of life.

Visiting Sinai

The differences between Sinai and mainland Egypt can induce culture shock. For those accustomed to Egyptian towns and beaches, Sinai will seem amazingly uncrowded, laid-back and hassle-free – especially so for women. If you arrive from Israel or Jordan, of course, spending some days on a Sinai beach and then heading on to Cairo, you experience the reverse. Native Bedouin and recent settlers from the mainland both assert Sinai's distinctive character and disparage Egyptian government, often comparing it unfavourably with the period of Israeli rule. Even the customary salutation is different: "Kif halak" ("How is your health/situation?") instead of "Izzayak".

For the purposes of this guide, the peninsula divides into three zones – the **gulf coasts of Suez and Aqaba**, the **interior**, and **northern Sinai**. Communications between the resorts along the coastal strip of the Gulf of Aqaba and the interior around St Catherine's are well established (these two areas make up the administrative region of **South Sinai**), but northern Sinai is effectively sundered from both, despite the upgrading of a route between El-Arish and Nekhl, inland. Transport to each zone **from mainland Egypt** is described at the start of each section, while the **approaches from Israel and Jordan** are covered in Basics – see p.23.

Unlike elsewhere in Egypt, you can visit part of the peninsula on a free **Sinai-only visa**, valid for two weeks, which can be obtained at Taba (on the border with Israel), the port of Nuweiba (where boats arrive from Jordan), or Sharm el-Sheikh airport, 10km north of Na'ama Bay, where charter flights from Europe land. This is *only* valid for the Aqaba coast down to Sharm el-Sheikh and the immediate vicinity of St Catherine's Monastery (effectively it's a visa for South Sinai); if you wish to visit Ras Mohammed, other parts of Sinai's interior or or mainland Egypt, you'll need a **regular Egyptian visa**, which *cannot* be issued at Nuweiba or the Taba border crossing, but can be obtained upon arrival at Sharm el-Sheikh airport (US$15). It is possible to pay in sterling, but the exchange rate will not be favourable so use dollars if you can.

Climate, activities and maps

Sinai's **climate** is extreme. On the coast, daytime temperatures can reach 50°C (120°F) during summer, while nights are sultry or temperate depending on the prevailing wind. In the mountains, which receive occasional snowfall over winter and the odd rainstorm during spring, nights are cooler – if not chilly or freezing. Outside of winter, you should wear a hat, use high-factor sunscreen and drink four to six litres of water a day (more if you're trekking) to avoid sunburn and heatstroke.

The climate is obviously a factor affecting tourist **activities** in Sinai. During summer, the heat is likely to make you spend less time on the beach and more time in the water, and to forgo trekking or camel riding entirely. Happily, **diving** or **snorkelling** can comfortably be done at any time of the year, and constitute Sinai's greatest attraction. If you're new to either or simply unfamiliar with how and where it's done here, the account on pp.683–688 should give an idea of what's on offer. Details of dive centres, courses and trips are given under each resort as appropriate. We've done the same with **camel** and **jeep safaris**, giving a general rundown on p.725 and specifics under the localities where trips are arranged or occur. As a rule, sites near the coast can be visited at any time of the year by jeep, and between October and April by camel, while **trekking** in the High Mountain Region (see p.724) is unfeasible in winter owing to snow, and only possible in summer if you're fit enough to stand the heat.

While the **map** at the start of this chapter indicates the main diving and safari sites, serious divers or trekkers should acquire the 1:250,000 *Sinai Map of Attractions*, an English-language tourist map based on Israeli army surveys, which is sold at the Taba border and most resorts. At a pinch, divers could make do with one of the maps produced by dive centres or travel agents, which outline the chief dive sites and Ras Mohammed National Park. For local information you can pick up a copy of *The Peninsula*, a free quarterly **listings magazine** or pay £E5 for the more compact *Sinai Today*; both are widely available in Sharm el-Sheikh, but harder to locate in Nuweiba and Dahab.

Transport, accommodation and costs

All the main tourist spots are accessible by well-paved roads and some form of public transport. Most travellers find it easy to get around, as **buses** are frequent and cheap, and **service taxis** run to and from every resort. The sole exception is the **border at Taba**, which has only a couple of buses a day waiting to take people further south – as well as a few service taxis, whose drivers are notorious for taking financial advantage of the shortage of buses. Foreign **motorists** are restricted to main roads; given the baking heat and huge distances, **hitchhiking** is a dubious proposition unless your destination is nearby or you're certain of a ride all the way (or at least to somewhere with shade and buses). Women should *never* hitch alone. MFO personnel are forbidden to give lifts.

The type of **accommodation** varies from place to place, ranging from costly holiday villages at Na'ama Bay to cheap "campgrounds" at Dahab – not campgrounds in the usual sense, these consist of huts of stone, concrete, bamboo or palm leaves, and may or may not have electricity and bathrooms. Although tourism is a year-round business, there are definite peak periods when hotels charge higher prices and are liable to be full. To some extent this depends on the resort: Sharm el-Sheikh receives a surge of European package tourists over spring, autumn and Christmas. Before the political situation between Israel and the Palestinians deteriorated, the Bedouin-run camps between Taba and Dahab, especially those at Tarabeen and to the north, were flooded with Israelis during Jewish holidays. Also bear in mind **Egyptian holidays** – December 22–February 2, March 1–May 3 and July 19–October 31 – when you should try to book in advance.

Aside from accommodation, the **cost** of everyday items, meals and transport is higher in Sinai than anywhere else in Egypt, but still cheaper than in Israel or Europe. The tap water is not drinkable in Sinai, so you'll need to buy bottled water – a considerable expense if you're on a budget, particularly if you buy it from hotels. There are **banks** in all the main resorts, while US dollars can be exchanged in many shops. Many dive centres and hotels will also take payments in euros now, while Israeli shekels (NIS) are common currency in Dahab and Nuweiba, with an unofficial exchange rate of 1:1 on the £E.

The gulf coasts

Sinai rises and tapers as the peninsula runs towards its southern apex, red rock meeting golden sand and deep blue water along two gulf coasts. Even the **Gulf of Suez**, as E.M. Forster noted, looks enticing from offshore – "an exquisite corridor of tinted mountains and radiant water" – though it's nowadays transformed after dark into a vision of Hades by the flaming plumes of oil rigs.

For most travellers, however, Suez is merely an interlude before the **Gulf of Aqaba**, whose amazing coral reefs and tropical fish have given rise to a number of popular resorts. The beach scene here is the best Egypt can offer and should aquatic pursuits pall – if such a thing is possible – there are opportunities for making trips into the wild **interior** by jeep or camel. Even from the beach, the view of the mountains of Sinai and Saudi Arabia is magnificent.

Approaches to the gulf coasts

Aside from those arriving from Israel or Jordan, most travellers approach the gulf coasts from **Cairo**, **Suez** or **Hurghada**. Note, however, that most services to Taba and Nuweiba travel across the interior of the peninsula, avoiding both gulf coastlines for much of the way.

• Most people come **from Cairo** by **bus** from the **Sinai Terminal** (*Mahattat Seena*) in the Abbassiya district, or from **Turgoman Garage** behind the *Ramses Hilton* in downtown Cairo – the latter has an overnight (11pm) Superjet bus to Sharm el-Sheikh. Check schedules and reserve seats the day before (earlier during Ramadan). Eight East Delta buses run daily to **Sharm el-Sheikh** (7–8hr; £E55–65); four to **Dahab** (9hr; £E55–70); four to **Nuweiba** (8–10hr; £E55–70), three of which carry on to **Taba** (9hr; £E65) and one to **St Catherine's Monastery** (8hr; £E55). All services are a/c, offer on-board snacks and halt at one or two resthouses en route; refreshments are expensive.

Rapid access to Sinai and great views of the peninsula might entice those with plenty of cash onto EgyptAir **flights**. There are at least three daily from Cairo to Sharm el-Sheikh airport (US$138 one-way; 1hr).

• **Suez City** is the interchange for numerous buses coming from Hurghada, Cairo or northern Sinai. **Buses** leave from the new bus terminal on the Ismailiya Road, going to **Sharm el-Sheikh** (5 daily; 5–6hr; £E25), **Dahab** (daily at noon; 7–8hr; £E30), **Nuweiba** (daily at noon & 3pm; 6–7 hr; £E30), **St Catherine's** (daily at 2pm; 6hr; £E25) and **Taba** (daily at 3pm; 7–8 hr; £E30). **Service taxis** also leave from the bus terminal for Dahab (£E35), St Catherine's (£E20), Nuweiba (£E25) and Sharm el-Sheikh (£E25).

• The third option is to travel directly **from Hurghada** to **Sharm el-Sheikh** by **air** (Mon 3.30am, Sat 6am, Sun 11.30pm; one-way US$96) or **sea** (see p.767 for details), or charter a seven-seater **taxi** for the 750km drive (£E700 shared among passengers).

• There are also thrice-weekly EgyptAir **flights** to **Sharm el-Sheikh from Luxor** (Tues 9.30pm, Thurs & Sat 9.15pm; one-way US$115) and two a week **from Alexandria** (Mon & Fri 8.45am; one-way US$185).

Diving and snorkelling

The Red Sea offers some of the finest **diving** and **snorkelling** in the world, accessible to most travellers at a fraction of the cost of getting to the Seychelles or the Great Barrier Reef. Much of the diving here is easy to reach and relatively sheltered from harsh winds and currents, making it a popular destination for those who have little or no experience.

It's a cheap place to **learn open-water diving** and gain a PADI, BSAC or CMAS certificate, entitling you to dive anywhere in the world (NAUII, SSI or MDEA are less widely accepted); indeed, many people visit Sinai simply to acquire their certificates on one of the scores of diving **courses** available. The initial step is a five-day **open-water** (OW) course, costing US$280–350 (plus US$30–35 for the certificate). Most centres offer a supervised introductory dive (US$40–60) for those uncertain about shelling out for a full course. Qualified divers can progress through **advanced open-water**, **dive master** and **instructor** certification, and take **specialized courses** in underwater rescue, night or wreck diving (to name but a few that are available).

When **choosing a dive centre**, the main considerations should be the quality of the instructors and the state of the equipment. Linguistic misunderstandings can be dangerous, so you need an instructor who speaks your **language** well. Ask to see a card proving that he or she is qualified to teach the course (PADI, BSAC or whatever), and not merely a dive master. Amazingly, dive centres in Egypt were virtually unregulated until 1996, and there is still some question over how well the new laws are being enforced. Though centres associated with big hotels are safer bets than outfits on their own, smart premises are less important than the **equipment**. If left lying about, chances are it'll also be poorly maintained. Also notice the location of the compressor, used to fill the tanks; if it's near a road or other source of pollution, you'll be breathing it in underwater. Ask around and then stick to the dive centres that have been there the longest and have proper links with organizations like PADI. Remember that with diving, there is no substitute for a good training and safety record.

Broadly speaking, most dive centres in Sharm el-Sheikh and Nuweiba are very good. In Dahab, however, regulations are less likely to be adhered to and competition between dive centres is cut-throat, encouraging some divers to simply go for the cheapest option. One famous Dahab dive site, the **Blue Hole**, is entirely unsuitable for inexperienced divers – having claimed the lives of several people in recent years.

Note that if you're certified but haven't logged a dive in the past three months, you will have to take a "check dive" as a refresher before you can go on a sea trip.

Dive centres are detailed under each resort, while **dive sites** are summarized below. The type of diving and the degree of experience required are mainly determined by underwater topography and currents. Around Sharm el-Sheikh the chief activity is **boat diving** (you enter the water offshore) at sites ranging from novice-friendly to demanding. Up the coast past Dahab and Nuweiba this gives way to **shore diving**, where you wade or swim out to the reefs. Some slope gently out to sea while others drop off sharply; the deeper the drop-off the richer the variety of corals and fish. **Liveaboards** (also called safari boats) are vessels that allow you to spend days or weeks at sea, cruising the dive sites and shipwrecks of the north Red Sea around Ras Mohammed and the Tiran Strait or the more southerly reefs beyond Hurghada. During quiet periods, bookings can be arranged at short notice either directly on the boat at the marina or through a dive centre, but to be sure of what you're get-

Protecting the reefs

As far as the **environment** goes, the position of divers is ambiguous. While the sport enables millions of people to witness the marvel of tropical coral reefs and learn about the fragile ecosystem that maintains them – Egypt's marine national parks alone attract two million tourists each year – divers also pose one of their most serious **threats** to their existence. Boat diving is now so popular in Sharm el-Sheikh that many sites are now considered to be "over-dived". Meanwhile, hundreds of divers happily stay in hotels built directly overlooking the sea that through construction pollution and badly managed beach policies have irreversibly damaged the reefs below. Perhaps it is understandable that the most environmentally aware resort in the Sinai – Basata (see p.721) – doesn't welcome divers.

Always **remember** that reefs are very fragile, so the fundamental rule is: **look but don't touch**. In areas protected by law, you are forbidden to feed the fish, or remove anything from the sea. Don't buy **aquatic souvenirs**, the export of which is illegal. Tourists can help by boycotting stores selling them, and telling the shopkeepers why. Even shells from the beach shouldn't be collected as souvenirs; they will be confiscated at the airport or border when you leave Egypt, with a US$1000 **fine**.

ting it's best to book in advance through an agent (see Basics for details). Some operators offer a discount if you book by email or telephone.

Snorkelling is also great fun and costs much less. If you're planning to do a lot, it's cheaper to buy your own gear in Cairo or Israel than to rent it from dive shops in Sinai (you might be able to sell it when you leave). Coral reefs and spiny urchins can rip unprotected feet to shreds; in all events you should only walk in designated "corridors" to protect the corals – if the water is too shallow to allow you to float above them. However cool the water may feel, the sun's rays can still burn exposed flesh (water magnifies the effects of ultra-violet), so always wear a T-shirt and use waterproof sunscreen.

Sinai dive sites

The following sites are all marked on the map on p.676.

Amphoras Between Ras Um Sidd and Na'ama Bay. Named after a Turkish galleon laden with amphoras of mercury that lies on the reef – the site is also known as "Mercury".

Blue Hole 8km north of Dahab. The challenge of this 80-metre-deep hole in the reef is to swim through a passage 60m down and come up the other side – which is highly risky even for expert divers. You can safely snorkel around the rim of the hole, however.

Canyon Near the Blue Hole. A narrow reef crack, 50m deep, which is only for experienced divers.

Dunraven En route from Bombay to Newcastle, the *Dunraven* steered onto a reef in fine weather on April 25, 1873 and sank 25m. Though its 25 crew escaped, the captain was found negligent (he fatuously remarked, "Twenty-five is my lucky number!").

El-Gharkana A luxuriant reef, offshore from mangroves and lagoons with rare waterfowl and flora. Part of the Nabeq protected area.

El-Muqeibila 25km south of Taba. A lovely diving beach stretching 15km from Mersa el-Muqeibila to Ras el-Burqa, often within walking distance of the main road.

Fjord 10km south of Taba. A picturesque cleft with underwater reefs.

Gordon Reef Off the coast of Ras Nasrani, in the shipwreck-littered Tiran Strait. Sharks and strong currents. Popular with experienced divers; not for beginners.

Jackson Reef A large reef between Tiran Island and the mainland, with a 70-metre drop-off, sharks and pelagic fish, and the shipwreck *Lara*. Strong currents; dangerous for beginners.

Maagana Beach 5–10km north of Nuweiba. The reef falls sheer around the "Devil's Head" to the north, getting shallower and less impressive further south.

Near, Middle and Far gardens 1–5km north of Na'ama Bay. A series of lovely coral reefs, good for easy diving and snorkelling. The Near Gardens are within walking distance of Na'ama.

Pharaoh's Island Near Taba. Superb underwater scenery and strong currents; a diving guide is recommended. Israelis call it "Coral Island". Easy access by boat.

Ras Abu Galum 50km south of Nuweiba. A protected area with a deep virgin reef wall and great fish. Access by 4WD or boat.

Ras Atantur Between Dahab and Nabeq. Colourful, abundant reef, with a shipwreck – the *Maria Schroeder* – 10km further south. Access by 4WD.

Ras el-Mamleh 20km south of Nuweiba. Another slab of virgin reef wall on the northern edge of the Ras Abu Galum protected area. Access by 4WD or boat.

Ras Mohammed National Park 25km southwest of Sharm el-Sheikh. Wonderful corals, mangrove lagoons, anemone gardens and crevice pools, with shark reefs offshore. Also site of the *Yolanda* shipwreck (see below).

Ras Nasrani Sheer reef wall riddled with shark caves; the Light and the Point are notable spots. Beware of sharks and strong currents. Not for inexperienced divers.

Ras Um Sidd Within walking distance of Sharm el-Sheikh. Exquisite fan corals and fish. Up the coast towards Na'ama are other popular sites like Turtle Bay, Amphoras and The Tower.

Shark Bay Colourful reef just off the beach of a small resort, 10km north of Na'ama Bay. Good for novices and experienced divers alike; snorkellers too.

Southern Oasis Gently sloping reef to the south of Dahab. Easy diving and snorkelling.

Sun Pool 10–15km south of Taba. A gorgeous diving beach extending as far north as the Fjord.

Thistlegorm Near El Tor in the Gulf of Suez. Sunk by German bombers in 1941, this British ship, discovered by Jacques Cousteau, was laden with rifles, uniforms, trucks and jeeps. It was also packed full of ammunition, which exploded, ripping the ship apart and killing most of the crew. Tubeworms grow out of the bathtub in the captain's cabin. A popular dive from Sharm el-Sheikh.

Tiran Island Protected Area An archipelago with over 20 dive sites, all amazing. Sharks and strong currents; only for experienced divers unless explicitly stated otherwise.

The Tower South of Na'ama Bay. Sheer reef pillar dropping 60m. Easy access from the beach and mild currents; good for novice divers.

Turtle Bay Between Ras Um Sidd and Amphoras. Shallow bay with turtles, easy to enjoy. Access by boat.

Yolanda Off Ras Mohammed. A Cypriot freighter that struck a reef during a storm in 1981; its cargo includes a BMW and scores of porcelain lavatories.

Coral reefs and tropical fish

Created by the same tectonic stresses that formed the Dead Sea and East African Rift Valley, the **Red Sea basin** is more than three kilometres deep in places, yet effectively separated from the Indian Ocean by an underwater "sill" at Bab el-Mandab, roughly 100m below the surface. Circulation between the Red Sea and the Gulf of Aqaba is similarly limited by the 200-metre-deep Tiran Strait, although the gulf itself attains depths of 1830m. As neither is fed by rivers and their rate of evaporation far exceeds any rainfall, both are exceptionally warm and salty – providing an ideal environment for tropical fish and coral reefs.

It's the warmth of the Red Sea water that is responsible for the Sinai's particular brilliance of coral – a revelation if you have previously snorkelled in such places as Hawaii or the Caribbean, whose reefs will ever after seem dull by comparison.

Coral reefs

The **coral reefs** that fringe the Sinai coastline from El-Tor to Taba have been created by generations of minuscule polyps extracting calcium from the sea water and depositing limestone exoskeletons on the remains of their ancestors. Fossilized reefs form the bedrock for living ones, which can grow 4–5cm a year, but are easily bruised or killed; if snapped off, coral loses its colour within hours of being removed from the sea.

Reefs come in all shapes and sizes, some more encrusted with coral growths than others, but the idealized representation given on below should give you an idea of where different species might be found. Some corals live 300 metres down, but you'll find most corals within 20–30 metres of the surface. The presence of sharks is usually a sign of a reef's good health.

Just below the shoreline, the warm water and eroded, sand- and rubble-covered bottom of the **lagoon** attract starfish, sea slugs and stinging anemones. Clams and sea urchins hide in crevices, while small yellow anemone fish and schools of viridian and carmine damselfish flit about. Other species include azure and opal blennies, tentacled clown fish and multitudes of butterfly fish.

Beyond lies the **reef flat**, a barren, fossilized shelf curving up towards the **reef**

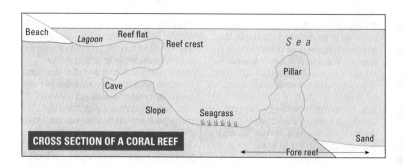

CROSS SECTION OF A CORAL REEF

Beach — Lagoon — Reef flat — Reef crest — Sea — Pillar — Cave — Slope — Seagrass — Sand — Fore reef

crest, overgrown with organ-pipe corals and anemones. Damselfish, angelfish, snappers and parrotfish are ubiquitous, while sea worms and eels emerge from deep **caves** below the crest. Mountain and stag-horn corals encrust the upper **slope**, whose lower section merges into bare terraces or sandy shelves overgrown with **sea grass**, the habitat of sea horses and pipefish.

Close to the surface further out are **pillars**; their own richly developed coral formations attract damselfish, basslets, wrasses and grunts, to name but a few. The **forereef** tends to draw larger fish, octopuses and squids, with stingrays and mantas (whose wingspans can reach nearly 5m) gliding along the sea bed.

Tropical fish and other creatures

The Red Sea's flora and fauna are related to tropical Indo-Pacific species, with no observable migration from the Mediterranean, although blue-speckled parrotfish have travelled the other way. The following are the most basic notes for identification – and avoiding the odd dangerous species.

Wherever soft, stinging anemones cling to the reef you're likely to see yellow **anemone fish**, recognizable by their twin vertical stripes. Equally commonplace are **angelfish**, with their long dorsal fins diminishing to filaments. Crescent angelfish are blue at the front, with a yellow vertical stripe and black hindquarters, while Emperor angelfish are horizontally pinstriped in blue and yellow, and the larger Arabian angelfish (up to 50cm long) is blue all over but for a yellow splotch. The same colour scheme in reverse appears on **butterfly fish**, which favour sunny slopes and forereefs; around lagoons, pillars and crests you'll also see racoon butterfly fish, striped in yellow and black, with a black and white eye patch.

Slopes and forereefs are the habitat of small **goatfish** (red mullet) with horizontal stripes of blue and yellow (or yellow and black in the case of Forsskal's goatfish). Diverse types of **parrotfish** and **snappers** frequent deeper water alongside crests and pillars. Parrotfish are easily recognizable by their beaky mouths and vibrant colours; snappers are similarly sized, with silvery scales striped and spotted in red, green or electric blue. Likewise bulky and diversely hued are **wrasses**, related to the bigger **Napoleon fish**, which can dwarf a person. Dugongs or **sea cows** are equally large and harmless, unlike small, sharp-toothed and armoured **triggerfish**, **filefish** and **porcupine fish**, more commonly found in deeper water.

Dangers of the deep

Considering all the **dangerous creatures**, it's remarkable that most visitors get nothing worse than the odd cut from sharp coral. Poisonous species include spiny **scorpion fish**, wildly coloured **turkeyfish** and **dragonfish**, and the oddly finned **lionfish**. By not touching anything remotely fitting their description you should avoid danger from these sources.

The lethal **stonefish**, camouflaged as a gnarled rock, is harder to spot but fortunately rare. You're more likely to be at risk from stinging **purple anemones** and burning **fire coral**, or **black sea urchins** with needle-like spines, which nestle in crevices. Dark caves sometimes harbour razor-toothed **moray eels**, which may bite if they feel threatened. **Stingrays** can deliver a painful dose of venom, and at certain times of the year **jellyfish** arrive in hordes, contact with which can cause mild irritation.

Although makos, hammerheads and other **sharks** frequent the deep waters around Ras Mohammed and the Tiran Strait, they're seldom found near the coast. However, blood in the water can attract them from afar, so never enter the sea with an open wound. Hammerheads and white-tip reef sharks have been known to attack with little provocation, though some divers consider **barracuda** more aggressive. Sighting either predator near shore, climb out quickly but calmly and spread the word; if you're diving in deeper water, keep still and you'll almost certainly be ignored.

Between Suez and Sharm el-Sheikh

The 338km journey between **Suez** and **Sharm el-Sheikh** takes only a few hours by bus or service taxi, and there's little point in stopping unless you've got private transport or you are an avid windsurfer. Such attractions as exist along (or off) the route are otherwise awkward to reach (or leave), so most travellers pass them by. Beyond **El-Tor**, the area's administrative capital, there's little of interest until you reach the diving grounds of **Ras Mohammed**.

Although the resort of **Ras Sudr** is essentially an oil town, its proximity to Cairo means it is becoming increasingly popular with Cairenes as a weekend get-away, while its year-round wind draws windsurfers from further afield. Further south, and inland, the pharaonic ruins at **Serabit el-Khadim** are also starting to attract larger numbers of visitors, most of them arriving from Sharm el-Sheikh or Dahab by jeep. For simplicity's sake, we've covered them here rather than later.

If you're not already booked on a through-service to Sinai, Suez is the place to catch a bus or service taxi. Most traffic uses the **Ahmed Hamdi Tunnel** – named after an Egyptian general killed in the October War – 17km north of Suez. Though there has long been a ferry at **Qantara,** access to **north Sinai** has been improved with the construction of a 4km-long suspension bridge at **Ferdan,** 49km south of Port Said near Qantara.

South along the Gulf of Suez

As you head south by road, the **Gulf of Suez** is sensed before it appears as a glint on the horizon, beyond the sands that rim the west for much of the way. Roughly 50km past the Ahmed Hamdi Tunnel, a dirt road turns off towards the coast to **AIN MUSA**, the **"Springs of Moses"**. According to scholastic conjecture and local legend, it was here that the Israelites halted after crossing the Red Sea, and Moses threw a tree into the bitter spring of Marah, which miraculously became drinkable (Exodus 15). Ain Musa is recognizable from the highway by the deposits of calcium and magnesium salts that surround the oasis, where only one of the twelve springs mentioned in Exodus remains, yielding water that has a strong chemical odour and acts as a powerful laxative. Many of the palm trees in the oasis were decapitated during various Sinai conflicts; an Israeli battery stationed here shelled Suez and Port Tewfiq during the War of Attrition, until Egypt recaptured Ain Musa in 1973. Camping is possible, although limited by the lack of food and water, and transport out. Ask at the village if you're interested, and you may find a willing Bedouin guide. Alternatively, overnight trips (£E50 per person including dinner and guide, minimum of five people) can be arranged at *Marah Beach* hotel in Ras Sudr (see below).

Ras Sudr and Hammam Faraoun

Famed for the variety of seashells washed up on its beach, the resort of **RAS SUDR** is marred by a reeking oil refinery that doesn't seem to bother the middle-class Cairenes who patronize its holiday villages and **hotels**. One of the oldest, *Sudr Beach Inn* (☎069/400-402, ⓕ400-885; ❹) is a bit worn, but has clean a/c rooms with baths, TVs and terraces looking onto a pretty beach. Next door, *Marah Beach* (☎069/400-166; ❸) looks in serious need of refurbishment, but they also have tents on the beach (£E30) or you can pitch your own.

This part of the coast is so windy it is often overlooked by travellers who seek the calmer reef-fringed shores of Sharm el-Sheikh, but the year-round and day-long cross-shore gusts make it a paradise for **windsurfers** who head for *Moon Beach*, 40km south of Ras Sudr (☎069/401-501, mobile 0105 810088, ⓕ069/401-503, ⓔgybemasters@btinternet.com; ❼), which costs US$90 half-board. Booking in advance through the British-run Gybemasters Windsurfing Company UK office (mobile ☎0158 0753824, ⓔgybemasters@btinternet .com, ⓦwww.gybemasters.co.uk) gets you a week for £295. This small and friendly British-run windsurfing operation offers lessons for beginners includ-ing boards and rigs (£E80 per hour) and rental of kit for intermediate and advanced surfers (£E60 per hour or £120 per week if booked in the UK). To get to *Moon Beach* from Cairo or Sharm el-Sheikh, you will need to alight at Ras Sudr and take a taxi (around £E40). Alternatively, from Cairo you can hop on the direct bus that leaves Al Maza, close to Heliopolis, three times a week (Thurs, Fri & Sat 8am, returning 5pm; 3hr; £E15).

Unless you are a serious windsurfer, there is little to choose between the **holi-day villages** which pepper the coast road to the north of Ras Sudr; if you're stuck for somewhere to stay, try *Banana Beach Village* (☎069/380-697; ❹), *Helnan Royal Beach* (☎069/400-102, ⓕ400-108; ❼) or *Mesalla Beach* (☎069/ 380-428; ❻) – all offer half-board.

The coast improves 55km further south, where a turn-off leads to **HAM-MAM FARAOUN** (Pharaoh's Bath), several near-boiling **hot springs** which Arab folklore attributes to the pharaoh's struggles to extricate himself from the waves that engulfed his army as he chased Moses and the Israelites. Local Bedouin use the springs for curing rheumatism, and it is possible to bathe; a cave in the hill beside the shore leads into "the sauna", a warren of chambers awash with hot water, but it's more comfortable to bathe where the springs flow into the sea. Plans are afoot to build a health resort nearby, but in the meantime the only option if you want to stay is to **camp**. You must inform the soldiers posted nearby, who enforce a ban on visiting the beach after 6pm.

Serabit el-Khadim and the turquoise mines

Built upon a 755-metre-high summit reached by a tortuous path, the **rock-hewn temple** known as **Serabit el-Khadim** ("Heights of the Slave" in Arabic) is the only pharaonic temple in Sinai, surrounded by some of the region's grandest scenery. Erected during the XII Dynasty, when turquoise mining in the area was at its peak, it is an enduring symbol of pharaonic power over the nameless thousands who toiled in the mines of Sinai. Though Bedouin still glean some local turquoise by low-tech methods, the amount that remains isn't worth the cost of industrial extraction.

The temple itself consists of open courts and sanctuaries dedicated to the goddess Hathor in her aspect as "Mistress of Turquoise", and the god Soped, "Guardian of the Desert Ways". Both deities are invoked on rock-cut and free-standing stelae relating to mining expeditions. These were only possible for half of the year due to the heat and scarcity of water, and thus a permanent colony was never established. The temple (whose precincts were segregated from the mining area by a crude stone wall) was abandoned during the reign of Ramses

VII. Known to the Bedouin for centuries, it was first "discovered" by Reinhold Niebuhr in 1792, but not excavated until early in the nineteenth century.

Serabit el-Khadim is becoming a popular stop on **jeep safaris**. From Sharm el-Sheikh, they approach Serabit from the south, via a track leading off the road from St Catherine's into **Wadi Mukattab** – the Valley of Inscriptions. Here you can find dozens of hieroglyphic texts carved into the rocks, alongside Proto-Sinaitic **inscriptions** that continue into Wadi Maraghah, where ancient mine workings and stelae were damaged when the turquoise mines were revived by the British and before going bust in 1901. Said Kader in Dahab (mobile ℡0101 888906, ℮said@desert-divers.com) and Ahmed (mobile ℡0124 630281) based in Sharm el-Sheikh can arrange jeep or camel safaris for about US$50 per person per day.

El-Tor

There's little to see along the coastal highway – which often veers inland, giving a wide berth to airstrips and oil terminals – besides a scattering of holiday resorts all the way to **EL-TOR**, the administrative capital of South Sinai. Originally, the Egyptian government based its administrators at Abu Rudeis, near the fledgling oilfields that were their prime concern – not realizing that this lay outside the territory of the main Bedouin tribal confederation and thus limited their influence over the tribes. After capturing South Sinai in 1967, the Israelis used ethnographic data to devise a system that exploited tribal allegiances, under a military governor in Sharm el-Sheikh, then called Ofira. The Egyptians took note and, once they had recovered the region, established their own South Sinai Governorate at El-Tor, just within the territory of the powerful Mizayna tribe.

The town consists of a scattering of government buildings and a mass of housing, offering no inducement to visit – though it is possible to get a **visa extension** from the governorate office here (Mon–Thurs & Sun 8am–2pm; ℡069/661-622), rather than having to travel to Cairo. Visitors without a car risk being stranded (there are surprisingly few local buses or service taxis to Sharm el-Sheikh, 108km away) with an unenviable choice of **hotels**. The *Moses Bay* (℡069/770-315, ℉774-345, ℮mosesbayresort@yahoo.com; ❻), 2km north of the city centre on the coast, is the most attractive hotel in the area with a/c rooms with baths, satellite TV and a large sandy beach. Otherwise the *Delmoun*, at the edge of town just back from the coast (℡ & ℉069/771-060; ❹), has a/c rooms with bath; *Tur Sinai* (℡069/770-059; ❸) is conveniently located next to the bus station.

If you do happen to get stuck in El-Tor, it is well worth visiting the **hot springs** of **HAMMAM MUSA**. You can find them under the shadow of the looming hill named after the springs, a couple of kilometres north up the coast from *Moses Bay*. Plans to build a health resort are now well underway with bungalows, huts and a restaurant under construction. Entry to the baths is US$5. A path leading half-way up the hill affords spectacular views.

All in all, however, it's better to settle back in your seat and dream of the reefs that fringe the Gulf coast from El-Tor onwards; the account on pp.683–688 should provide some food for thought.

Ras Mohammed

RAS MOHAMMED is a small peninsula, fringed with lagoons and reefs, that was declared a nature reserve in 1983 and became Egypt's first marine **National Park** in 1989. All of the thousand-odd species of fish that occur in

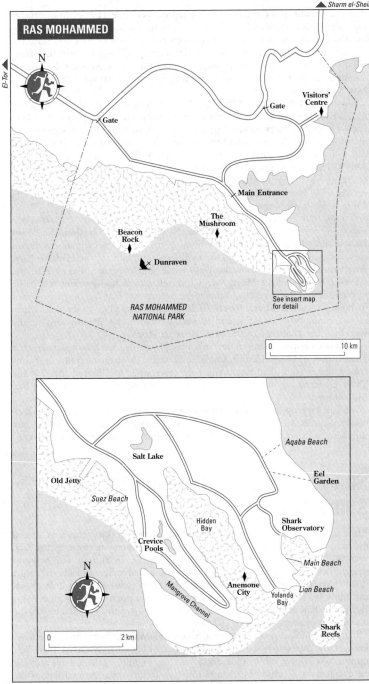

the Red Sea and 150 types of corals are represented here. The age of this amazing ecosystem is evinced by marine fossils in the bedrock dating back twenty million years; on the shoreline are newcomers only 75,000 years old. Since the section entitled "Coral reefs and tropical fish" on pp.683–688 covers in general what you'll see, suffice it to say that Ras Mohammed should not be missed. Though chiefly for **divers**, there are enough calmer reefs for **snorkellers** to have a great time as well.

You can **visit** the National Park any day from sunrise to sunset, providing you have a full Egyptian **visa** and not just a Sinai-only one (they check). The US$5 entry charge is usually included in the cost of excursions by jeep or boat from Sharm el-Sheikh (bear in mind that as the number of dive boats allowed each day is limited, you can't be certain of a place on a boat at short notice). Alternatively, if you just plan to snorkel you could rent a taxi (about £E100) or car (US$45–85) for the day. There are two perimeter gates on the road between El-Tor and Sharm el-Sheikh, leading to a main entrance whence it's 24km to the nearest reefs.

Various trails – accessible by regular car – are marked by colour-coded arrows. The blue one leads to **Aqaba Beach**, the **Eel Garden**, the **Main Beach** and a **Shark Observatory** 50m up the cliffside, which affords distant views of the odd fin. Purple and then red shows the route to the **Hidden Bay**, **Anemone City** and **Yolanda Bay**, while green signifies the way to the **Crevice Pools** and the **Mangrove Channel**, where children can safely bathe in warm, sandy shallows. Divers prefer the deeper sites that can only be reached by boat, such as the **Shark Reefs** off Yolanda Bay (the place to see sharks, barracuda, giant Napoleon fish and manta rays); and **The Mushroom** or the **wreck** of the *Dunraven*, out towards **Beacon Rock**.

A **visitor centre** (10am–sunset) off the road between the Sharm gate and the main entrance shows videos in English and Arabic on alternate hours, and contains a library, shop and restaurant. Free **telescopes** are located there, at the Shark Observatory, and at Suez Beach. You can't rent diving equipment at Ras Mohammed.

You can pick up a form for a **camping** permit (US$5 per person per night; children under 12 free) at the entrance to the park. There is no shop to buy supplies; the nearest is in Sharm el-Sheikh, about thirty minutes away by car.

Sharm el-Sheikh, Na'ama Bay and Shark Bay

Although technically one destination, **Sharm el-Sheikh** comprises several different areas – and constant development means there are more added each year. You will often hear Sharm el-Sheikh referred to as **Sharm**. This is not as straightforward as it may seem. Basically, if you are anywhere outside the resort (Dahab, say, or Cairo, or the UK) that appellation refers to the whole resort, including Na'ama Bay, while if you are anywhere in the resort itself (in Na'ama Bay, say, or Ras Nasrani) the term Sharm refers only to the area that covers the downtown precinct of Sharm el-Maya.

Sharm el-Sheikh's downtown area, **Sharm el-Maya**, is home to a large market area, the port and marina. It can be a cheaper base than **Na'ama Bay**, 7km up the coast, where most of the best hotels and nightlife are based. Na'ama has an excellent wide sandy beach and top-class facilities; the general feel of the place is much like any Mediterranean coastal resort, while Sharm el-Maya retains a *baladi* ambience reminiscent of Suez or Cairo, which can come as a shock to package tourists leaving their hotels for the first time. Whereas beachwear is de rigueur at Na'ama, tourists staying in Sharm el-Maya would do well to **dress** modestly off the beach to avoid unwelcome attention.

Southeast of Sharm el-Maya bay, a string of hotels and villas have sprouted along the coast. This stretch, which extends from the Ras Um Sidd dive site north to The Tower dive site, is known as **Ras Umm Sidd**. With the swankiest resorts perched close to the coast, cheaper hotels favoured by British tour operators fill up the land behind. It's a pretty bleak area, with poor beaches, and guests have to rely on shuttle buses to get them to the better amenities of Na'ama Bay.

The cliff above Sharm el-Maya bay is home to a prosperous residential area called **Hadaba**; further north, roughly half-way between Sharm el-Maya and Na'ama Bay, you come to another largely residential area, **Hay el-Nur,** which is home to the main bus station, a hospital and a well-stocked supermarket.

Hotel development has not stopped at Na'ama Bay and tourist villages, some up to a million square meters in size, now line the coast up **to Ras Nasrani** and even beyond to the borders of the **Nabeq** protected area. The once-beautiful and isolated retreat of **Shark Bay**, 8km north of Na'ama, is now swamped by large resorts – it still boasts a fine beach, however, and a view of Tiran Island.

Divers are no longer allowed to explore the reefs near Na'ama and Sharm el-Sheikh independently; all diving must now be done with a guide, which in practical terms means sticking with trips run by the dive operators.

Getting to Sharm and Na'ama

East Delta **buses from Cairo and Suez** terminate at the Hay el-Nur bus station behind the Mobil station, while Superjet buses end their journey in Sharm el-Maya on the main road to Na'ama Bay. The **port** where the catamaran arrives from Hurghada is 600m south of Sharm el-Maya.

Sharm el-Sheikh **airport**, 10km north of Na'ama, is busy with charter flights from Europe, whose passengers are driven off to their holiday villages by bus; arriving on your own you'll be dependent on costly taxis to get anywhere.

Transport between Sharm el-Maya and Na'ama is frequently available from the **minibuses** that carry local workers between the two resorts (£E1 per person, possibly more if you have luggage); you can pick these up by flagging them down at any point along the road. But bear in mind you won't be sharing space with cosmopolitan Egyptian holidaymakers, so it's advisable to be modestly dressed. Private **taxis** demand £E15–20 per carload.

Sharm el-Sheikh

A hunk of sterile buildings on a plateau commanding docks and other installations, **SHARM EL-SHEIKH** was developed by the Israelis after their capture of it in the 1967 war. Their main purpose was to thwart Egypt's blockade of the Tiran Strait and to control overland communications between the Aqaba and Suez coasts. Tourism was an afterthought – though an important one, helping to finance the Israeli occupation and settlements, which Egypt inherited between 1979 and 1982. Since then, Sharm's infrastructure seems to have expanded in fits and starts, without enhancing its appeal much. Despite some plush hotels and reams of propaganda about it being a slick resort, Sharm el-Sheikh is basically a **dormitory town** for the Egyptian workers who service Na'ama Bay. Aside from package tourists conned by brochures, the only

SINAI | Sharm el-Sheikh

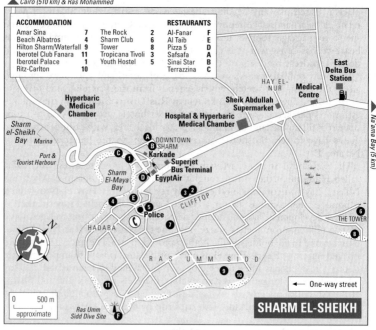

Cairo (510 km) & Ras Mohammed

ACCOMMODATION				RESTAURANTS	
Amar Sina	7	The Rock	2	Al-Fanar	F
Beach Albatros	4	Sharm Club	6	Al Taib	E
Hilton Sharm/Waterfall	9	Tower	8	Pizza 5	D
Iberotel Club Fanara	11	Tropicana Tivoli	3	Safsafa	A
Iberotel Palace	1	Youth Hostel	5	Sinai Star	B
Ritz-Carlton	10			Terrazzina	C

East Delta Bus Station

Hyperbaric Medical Chamber

HAY EL-NUR Medical Centre

Sheik Abdullah Supermarket

Hospital & Hyperbaric Medical Chamber

Sharm el-Sheikh Bay   Marina

Na'ama Bay (5 km)

Port & Tourist Harbour

A DOWNTOWN
B SHARM
Karkade
Superjet
Bus Terminal

Sharm El-Maya Bay

EgyptAir

CLIFFTOP

Police

THE TOWER

HADABA

R A S   U M M   S I D D

← One-way street

0   500 m
approximate

Ras Umm Sidd Dive Site

SHARM EL-SHEIKH

SINAI | Sharm el-Sheikh

foreigners here are divers – drawn by the proximity of **Ras Um Sidd** and other **reefs** – and a few backpackers who take advantage of its cheapish accommodation and commute into Na'ama Bay. Sharm has a beach, but its small bay doesn't match that of Na'ama and the (illegal) daily burning of garbage nearby also detracts from the hotels' "luxury" pretensions. But in its defence, **Sharm el-Maya** is the cheapest place in the area to go shopping for food and has some good restaurants, snack bars and souvenir shops.

Arrival and information

While there is a **bank** at *Iberotel Palace*, other facilities are concentrated on the Hadaba clifftop where an arcade contains three banks (daily 8am–2pm & 6–8pm) that change travellers' cheques; a **post office** (daily except Fri 8am–3pm; you can also buy stamps in shops and post letters in hotels) and a **pharmacy** (daily 9am–3pm & 6–11pm). Further inland is a 24-hour **telephone** exchange that sells international phonecards for £E20 (3min). The **police** and **tourist police** (both open 24hr) share a building beyond the mosque at the top of the cliff overlooking Sharm el-Maya.

Accommodation

Most **accommodation** is either deluxe and costly or simple and relatively inexpensive. The former enables package tourists to ignore Sharm's general lack of charm, while the latter serves as a fallback if the *Pigeon House* in Na'ama or *Shark's Bay Camp* at Shark Bay are full. Otherwise the windswept **clifftop** area, away from the beach, is the best place to look for mid-priced options. You can **camp** at Ras Mohammed (see p.692) if you have your own transport.

694

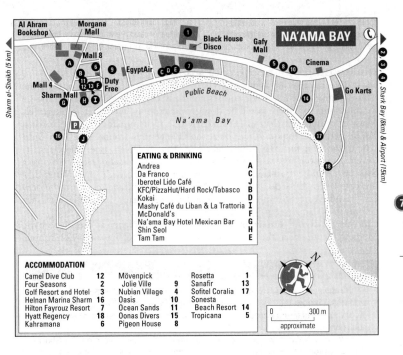

NA'AMA BAY

EATING & DRINKING

Andrea	A
Da Franco	C
Iberotel Lido Café	J
KFC/PizzaHut/Hard Rock/Tabasco	B
Kokai	D
Mashy Café du Liban & La Trattoria	I
McDonald's	F
Na'ama Bay Hotel Mexican Bar	G
Shin Seol	H
Tam Tam	E

ACCOMMODATION

Camel Dive Club	12	Mövenpick		Rosetta	1
Four Seasons	2	Jolie Ville	9	Sanafir	13
Golf Resort and Hotel	3	Nubian Village	3	Sofitel Coralia	17
Helnan Marina Sharm	16	Oasis	10	Sonesta	
Hilton Fayrouz Resort	7	Ocean Sands	11	Beach Resort	14
Hyatt Regency	18	Oonas Divers	15	Tropicana	5
Kahramana	6	Pigeon House	8		

If you are booking a package from the UK, you are best off picking a hotel in Na'ama Bay (see p.698).

Amar Sina Clifftop area ☎069/662-222, ⓕ662-233. Eclectic, good-looking hotel, full of domes and arches, designed by its owner-in-residence. More than 85 a/c rooms with satellite TV. They've also created a "traditional" Egyptian farm and veterinary clinic around the back. ❻

Beach Albatros On the cliff overlooking Sharm el-Maya, access to the beach below by a very long staircase or lift ☎069/663-924, ⓕ663-925. Construction of the beach here involved in-filling a stretch at the back of the reef, causing the latter's death. This hotel now has the best beach in this part of town, as well as a great view of the mountains and Ras Mohammed from the pool. ❻

Hilton Sharm Waterfall Resort On the beach at Ras Um Sidd ☎069/663-232, ⓕ663-200. *Hilton's* latest addition to Sharm has 117 a/c rooms with all the trimmings, including an impressive waterfall feature and a small cable car to an even smaller beach. ❼

Iberotel Club Fanara On the beach at Ras Um Sidd, next to the lighthouse ☎069/663-966, ⓕ663-819. Well-designed all-inclusive on one of the few good beaches in the area, especially for snorkeling. a/c rooms with satellite TV and terrace, pools and the latest in resort facilities. ❽

Iberotel Palace Sharm el-Maya ☎069/661-111, ⓕ661-293. Over 240 rooms and luxury facilities, with a large section of beach. Lots of restaurants and sports facilities, bicycle rental, bank. ❽

Ritz-Carlton By the beach at Ras Um Sidd ☎069/661-919, ⓕ661-920, ⓔritzcarltonssh@sinainet.com.eg. Trumpeted as the first *Ritz* in Africa, this hotel has Internet access via the TV in each of the huge a/c rooms, a fitness center, beauty salon and a spa. There is a beach with direct access to a reef (meaning it is good for snorkelling and diving but bad for swimming) and two pools with a "river" and waterfall. ❾

The Rock Clifftop area ☎069/661-765, ⓕ660-203, ⓔtherock@sinainet.com.eg. A/c rooms with TV and bath. Pool and shuttle bus. Also rents apartments for four or six people. ❻

Tropicana Tivoli Clifftop area ☎069/661-381, ⓕ661-380. Rooms with a/c and kitchenette, sited around a large pool. Also runs a shuttle bus to its sister hotel in Na'ama Bay and the beach at Ras Um Sidd. ❻

Youth hostel Clifftop area ☎ & ⓕ 069/600-317. Cramped a/c dorms with bunks, and cleanish bathrooms; a new building is under construction so things might improve. May be full of young Egyptians or otherwise virtually empty. Non-members admitted (£E1 extra). Breakfast included. ❶

Diving courses and excursions

Most **dive centres** are firmly attached to hotels, but the majority of them are happy to take non-guests for courses and daily boat diving. Before signing up for anything, ask where you'll be doing your training; the water in Sharm el-Maya is less pleasant than in Na'ama Bay due to its proximity to the marina. You're better off looking there or at the dive centres around **Ras Um Sidd** where you will find the long-established African Divers (see below), Rasta Divers and more recent arrivals Waterland at *Royal Paradise Hotel*. Colona, a five-star PADI centre based at *Amar Sina* is good value with Open Water diving courses for US$330, while Dive Africa at *Beach Albatros* claims to be very eco-friendly. Prices for most dive trips and courses mirror those offered by dive centres in Na'ama (see p.701 for details).

In case of **diving emergencies**, contact Dr. Adel Taher at the Hyperbaric Medical Centre near the Sharm el-Sheikh marina (☎069/660-922, mobile

---

Sharm el-Sheikh dive centres

All the **dive centres** are **open** daily (mostly 8.30am–6pm). Dive boats set off (at around 9am) from the marina in Sharm el-Maya; most centres will collect you and drop you off again if necessary. (This is crucial if you're marooned at one of the hotels on the cliff in Ras Um Sidd.)

Sharm and Na'ama Bay's major dive centres have recently formed the **Sharm Diving Union** (☎ & ⓕ069/660-418, ⓔsharm_diving_union@sinainet.com.eg). Among other things they organize regular clean-ups of the sea.

For a list of dive centres based in **Na'ama Bay** and **Shark Bay**, see p.701 and p.706.

African Divers Ras Um Sidd ☎ & ⓕ069/600-307, ⓔafrican@sinainet.com.eg. PADI, CMAS, NAUI, SSI.

Colona Dive Club *Amar Sina* ☎069/663-670, ⓕ662-233, ⓔcolona@sinainet.com.eg. PADI Gold Palm 5-Star IDC Centre, SSI, Nitrox. Also offers liveaboard trips.

Dive Africa *Beach Albatros* ☎069/663-122, ⓕ663-398, ⓔdiveafrica@sinainet.com.eg. Liveaboards available. PADI and SSI.

New Waves *Tropicana Tivoli* ☎069/663-399, ⓕ662-211, ⓔinfo@duvebewwaves.com.

PADI 5-Star Gold Palm Resort. Five-day packages and liveaboards available. SSI, BSAC, NAUI.

Rasta Divers Ras Um Sidd ☎069/663-086, mobile 0122 133881, ⓔrasta@sinainet.com.eg. Somewhat exclusive, catering mostly to private groups. Liveaboards available. PADI, CMAS, SSI.

Waterland *Royal Paradise* Ras Um Sidd ☎069/663-613, ⓕ661-503, ⓔwaterland@sinainet.com.eg. PADI, SSI.

Liveaboards

We've indicated those dive centres in Sharm and Na'ama that offer **liveaboards**; you can also contact the operators and boats listed below directly. They operate out of offices in Hadaba, and set off from the marina in Sharm el-Maya.

Blue Bubbles ☎069/600-1360, mobile 0123 103755, ⓕ069/663-458, ⓔmoharram@sinainet.com.eg. Liveaboards on a number of boats of varying standards; from $90–120 per person per day.

King Snefro Boats Mobile ☎0123 150612, ⓕ069-661-201, ⓔboats@kingsnefro.com. Four boats and sixteen years' experience in

the Red Sea, specializing in the waters from Abu Nuhas to the Tiran Strait. The cost, US$91–113 per person per day, includes transfers and full board. Children under seven go free.

Sea Queen I, II and III Mobile ☎0122 186669, ⓔseaqueen@link.com.eg. Managed by Karim Fayed, this is liveaboard in style.

0122 124292); there is also a new decompression facility at the pyramid-shaped International Hospital in Hay el-Nur (☎069/660-272).

Eating, drinking and nightlife

Aside from **eating and drinking** in hotels, Sharm el-Maya offers a wide range of restaurants, coffee shops and *fuul* and *taamiya* stalls. **Seafood** is especially good; *Al Taib* (mobile ☎0101 557686), set in the gardens on the hill leading up to Hadaba from Sharm el-Maya serves excellent and good-value fish, shrimps and *calamari*. They also offer takeaway and home delivery. Popular with tour groups, the *Sinai Star* and the more expensive but intimate *Safsafa* are two other seafood restaurants in the main market area, where a meal will cost you £E25–50. *Terrazzina* is a beach restaurant next to the *Iberotel Palace*, popular with local residents, where you can eat the catch of the day in a relaxed atmosphere. The stunningly located *Al-Fanar* at Ras Um Sidd lighthouse serves excellent Italian food and has a vast sea view taking in Ras Mohammed.

7

Moving on from Sharm el-Sheikh

Sharm el-Sheikh is the transport hub of South Sinai, with overland services to Cairo, the Canal Zone and most points in the peninsula, boats to Hurghada, and flights to domestic and international airports.

The direct a/c Superjet nightbus leaves for **Cairo** at 11pm (£E55) from the Superjet terminal (☎069/601-622) next to EgyptAir. You will need to buy your ticket in advance to be sure of getting a seat, but this bus makes fewer stops and tends to be quieter than the East Delta buses to Cairo that leave from the bus station in Hay el-Nur (8 daily; £E55; also evening buses at 10pm, 11pm & midnight; £E65). You have to reserve seats in person at the bus station (or the office next to the Superjet terminal).

Leaving from the main bus station in Hay el-Nur, it's worth turning up early for the 9.30am bus to **St Catherine's Monastery** (£E15; note that this bus won't get you there in time to see the monastery, which closes at midday). The 9am service to **Taba** (£E25) also stops at **Dahab** which can also be reached by direct buses at 6.30am, 8am, 2.30pm, 5pm, 8pm, 9pm and 12.30am (£E11). Services to **Nuweiba** (9am, 2pm & 5pm; £E20) can be crowded. Buses also run to the Canal cities of **Suez** (7am, 9am [a/c], 10am, 2pm, 4pm, 6pm & 7pm; £E25) and **Ismailiya** (7 daily; £E35); as well as to **Luxor** (6am; £E65) and **Alexandria** (7.30am; £E45).

In the absence of a bus you'll be thrown back on **service taxis**, whose rates are negotiable. The usual destinations on offer are Suez, Dahab and St Catherine's, though others can be agreed if the price is right. The larger the group, the less each person pays.

Voyaging across the Red Sea or the Gulf of Aqaba has been transformed by the **catamaran**, a high-speed service between Sharm and **Hurghada**. Tickets for the ninety-minute journey across the Gulf of Suez (6pm Mon, Thurs & Sat; US$40/€45/£E200, cars from £E150); can be bought at Travco in the *Iberotel Palace*, or in Na'ama Bay through Thomas Cook in the Gafy Mall next to *Pigeon House* (daily 9am–2pm & 6–10pm; ☎069/601-808) or at the port one hour before departure.

The EgyptAir office in Sharm el-Sheikh (daily 9am–2pm & 6–9pm; ☎069/661-056, ℉661-057) can sell tickets for **flights** to other cities in Egypt and Tel Aviv. There are regular flights from Sharm el-Sheikh airport, 10km north of Na'ama, to **Alexandria** (Mon & Fri 11.45am), **Cairo** (daily except Fri), **Hurghada** (Sun 11.30pm, Mon 3.30am, Sat 6am) and **Luxor** (Thurs & Sat 7.50am). For **flights to Europe**, check with the representatives of UK tour operators such as Explorers (☎069/601-406) and Goldenjoy (☎069/601-600).

The cheapest **snacks** are egg or *taamiya* sandwiches, sold in the main market area. *Yara*, next to Al Shaikh bakery, sells sandwiches and a good selection of typical Egyptian desserts like *rozz y laban* (rice pudding) and *Om Ali* (a kind of bread pudding). There are also a couple of pizza joints; *Pizza 5* (☎069/663-436) next to *Safety Land* at the foot of the cliff also does delivery.

For picnics, the best **supermarket** in Sharm el-Maya is Sharm Express. However the supermarket with the most choice – at least until the much-heralded Metro supermarket opens in Hadaba – is Sheikh Abdullah's, a minibus ride away in Hay el-Nur. **Fruit** and **vegetables** are best bought from the stalls in the main market, rather than in the supermarkets who charge far more. **Beer** is available from a shop beside the *Sinai Star* (a bottle of Stella costs £E5).

Nightlife is somewhat limited. Ras Um Sidd can offer *Alf Leila Wa Leila* (☎ & ⓕ069/663-110), an Oriental fantasy show with belly dancers and a "sound and light show" that started life in Hurghada. The English-language version (Mon 9.30pm; US$15 or US$30 with dinner) is followed by a disco that lasts till the early hours.

The reefs between Sharm and Na'ama

The fabulous array of **dive spots** around Sharm and Na'ama is the chief attraction of both resorts, offering endless scope for boat or shore diving. The most accessible site is **RAS UMM SIDD**. The area is basically all coral reef without any natural sandy beaches – what sand there is has been imported by the hotels to create their own beaches. The endless construction has inevitably increased the debris many divers now encounter underwater in this area.

From Ras Umm Sidd, a paved road lined with holiday villages and hotels runs to **THE TOWER**, a fine diving beach colonized by the *Tower* (☎069/600-231, ⓕ600-230; ❽) and *Sharm Club* (☎069/600-260, ⓕ600-733; ❽) **hotels**. The *Tower's* beach café is a good place for people-watching but the real lure is a huge **coral pillar** just offshore, which drops 60m into the depths.

It's easy to get to The Tower by taxi from either Sharm or Na'ama, but it is no longer possible to access most of the reefs between Ras Umm Sidd and the Tower from land, as hotels along this stretch of coast now effectively block public access to the sea. Diving these reefs by boat, in order of appearance after Ras Um Sidd, you come to Fiasco, Paradise, Turtle Bay, Pinky's Wall and Amphoras. **Turtle Bay** has warm sun-dappled water that's lovely to swim in, even if there are fewer **green turtles** (*Chelonia myades*) than you'd wish for. **Amphoras** gets its name from the cargo of clay jars aboard an Ottoman ship that sunk on the reef; as the jars contain mercury, it's lucky that they remain sealed. Diving down to the **wreck** is safe enough for novices.

Na'ama Bay

With its fine beach and upmarket facilities, **NA'AMA BAY** has transformed itself so rapidly even the residents have trouble keeping up. In a few short years the bay has grown from a few huts on the beach and one lone hotel to what looks like a mini-city, especially at night when the electric lights blaze in the desert sky. The **diving** and **snorkelling** are still the main draws, with dive centres, hotels and malls being the only points of reference along the beachfront strip. The **beach** is divided into hotel-owned plots that are supposedly open to anyone providing they don't use the parasols or chairs – but hippy-looking types may be hassled and topless bathing is not only illegal, it is highly unadvisable. There are two public beaches (£E5), though they can be hard to find, squeezed in next to the *Novotel* and the *Hilton*.

Accommodation

Luxurious **holiday villages** featuring acres of marble floors and lush land-scaped gardens are the norm here, so independent travellers on a **tight budget** either stay in downtown Sharm and commute by microbus, or roost at the *Pigeon House*, the best cheapish hotel in Na'ama. (The *Oasis* next door has similar accommodation but is definitely lacking in atmosphere.) Bargains can be had if hotels are booked as a **package** from the UK, but be warned: what looks to be a very good deal often means that you are actually booking into one of the luxury beach hotel "extensions", which offer a lower standard of accommodation and an awkward highway crossing to get to the sea.

Alternatively, a few of the **diving colleges** rent out rooms to divers on their courses. The *Red Sea Diving College* (☎069/600-145, ⓕ600-144, ⓔoperations @sinai-services.co.com; ⓺) is central and on the beach with clean, en-suite a/c rooms. They also have dorm beds with a/c and breakfast included for US$10 per person; *Oonas Divers* (☎069/600-581, ⓕ600-582, ⓔoonas@sinainet.com.eg; ⓺), at the northern end of the bay, also has a/c rooms, all with balconies and views, and guests are allowed to use the beach and pool at the nearby *Sonesta*. Attached to one of the best dive centres, *Camel Dive Club Hotel* (☎069/600-700, ⓕ600-601, ⓔreservations@cameldive.com; ⓻) is a small, well-designed hotel right in the heart of Na'ama, on the main strip one block from the beach. A/c rooms have satellite TV, and the rooftop *Camel Bar* is popular with divers.

If you have your own transport, you might consider **camping** at Ras Mohammed (see p.692).

Four Seasons 9km north of Na'ama ☎069/603-555, ⓕ603-550. New, glitzy hotel. Expect six-star treatment and facilities. ⓽

Golf Resort and Hotel 7km north of Na'ama ☎069/603-200, ⓕ603-225, ⓔgmgolfsharm@hotmail.com. 270 luxurious a/c rooms, high-quality gym and health club, the best swimming pool in the area and of course, an 18-hole championship golf course. The beach, however, is disappointing. ⓽

Helnan Marina Sharm At the southern end of Na'ama Bay, on the main strip ☎069/600-751, ⓕ600-712, ⓔgmhms@hotmail.com. Na'ama's first (Israeli-built) hotel. Some disabled-friendly rooms. Notable mainly for having one of the better beaches in Na'ama. ⓻

Hilton Fayrouz Resort On the beach ☎069/600-140, ⓕ660-040, ⓔgm_fayrouz-vil@hilton.com. Comfortable and spacious a/c chalets set in pretty landscaped gardens. One of the largest beaches in Na'ama Bay and home to one of the locals' favourite pubs, *Pirates Bar*. Children under twelve stay free. ⓼

Hyatt Regency Just north of Na'ama Bay ☎069/601-234, ⓕ603-600. Expensively bedecked hotel ovelooking the coral gardens – this means a poor beach, but beautiful landscaping, along with good management, disabled rooms, non-allergenic sheets and towels, and an excellent if pricey Thai restaurant. ⓽

Kahramana Hotel Three blocks back from the beach ☎069/601-071, ⓕ601-176, ⓔkahramana@sinainet.com.eg. Centrally located four-star complex built around a pool with a nice bar and pool table. Worth considering if booking a package from the UK. ⓺

Mövenpick Jolie Ville In the middle of Na'ama ☎069/600-100, ⓕ600-111. This hotel is so large that it has a shuttle bus from one end to the other. Popular beach bar and nightly cabaret entertainment. Also home to the first casino in the area and the *Cactus Disco*. Its five-star amenities are guarded against interlopers. ⓼

Oasis On the edge of the desert, 400m from the beach ☎ & ⓕ069/601-602. Next to the better *Pigeon House* (see below) and only worth considering if the latter is full. Similar prices and accommodation, but no atmosphere. ⓸–⓹

Ocean Sands Two blocks back from the beach T & ⓕ069/600-805. Opposite *Hard Rock Café*, so not the quietest of places, but conveniently located for nightlife and popular with divers on packages from the UK. ⓺

Pigeon House At the north end of Na'ama Bay, 400m from the beach ☎069/600-996, ⓕ600-995, ⓔpigeon@access.com.eg. This Bedouin-owned and -run hotel is the most popular budget option in Na'ama, with a choice between rooms with fans and shared bathrooms or en-suite and a/c. Good for solo travellers. Arranges safari trips, and guests get a ten percent discount at the on-site Anemone Dive Centre. Breakfast included. ⓸–⓹

Rosetta Opposite the *Hilton*, on the other side of the highway ☎069/601-888, ⓕ601-999. Large a/c rooms with satellite TV; there are two pools, a nice outdoor Egyptian restaurant, and the *Black House* disco. It's the base for Emperor Divers. ➐

Sanafir One block back from the beach on the main strip ☎069/600-197, Ⓕ600-196, Ⓔsanafir@access.com.eg. One of the first hotels in Na'ama, its huts have long gone, replaced by a much-imitated white-domed compound of a/c rooms. There's a pool, and several restaurants and bars, which make it one of Na'ama's most popular evening venues. It's especially lively after midnight when *The Bus Stop*, Na'ama's coolest club, gets going. Good buffet breakfast included but be warned, it can get noisy here. ➏

Sofitel Coralia On the north hill overlooking Na'ama Bay ☎069/600-081, Ⓕ600-085, Ⓔsofitel@sinainet.com.eg. Impressive-looking

resort with 300 a/c rooms with terraces. One of the largest pools in Sharm, with a beach normally not too unfriendly to (female) interlopers from the *Pigeon House*. On-site stables for horseriding expeditions to the desert. ➑

Sonesta Beach Resort At the northern end of Na'ama on the beach ☎069/600-725, Ⓕ600-733. Beautifully designed hotel which manages to make you feel as if it were the only hotel on the beach. Fabulous facilities, recently expanded, include a water-gym and a Kids' Club. ➑

Tropicana Hotel Next to the *Pigeon House* ☎069/600-652, Ⓕ600-649. Small complex of a/c rooms away from the beach, but with a pool. Guests can use the public beach next to the *Hilton*. Welcoming to disabled guests; used by British tour operators. ➏

Diving courses and excursions

Much of Na'ama's appeal lies in its plethora of **dive centres** (see box opposite), which offer an extensive range of courses, trips and equipment rental. Though generally good, their prices and operating styles vary, so it's worth shopping around.

Total novices can make a supervised **introductory dive**; most places charge US$45–60 including equipment. Five-day open-water **diving courses** progress from classroom theory to your first dives in the hotel swimming pool or from the shore at Na'ama Bay or Shark Bay, finishing with a few boat-dives at the end. Anemone offers one of the cheapest **open-water PADI** courses in Na'ama (US$280, plus US$30 for the certificate) while Emperor and Colona both charge US$300 (plus US$30 for certificate). At the other end of the skill spectrum, you can be trained as an instructor or pursue **specialized courses** like night diving or underwater navigation (US$200–400).

Nearly all diving, except on the courses, is done from a boat, with dive centres offering a variety of daily **boat trips** to the sites. One day's diving at "local" sites like **Ras Nasrani** costs US$50–60, which includes two dives, tanks and weights, while trips further afield to the **Gordon** and **Jackson reefs** in the Tiran Strait (see p.685) or **Ras Mohammed** (p.690) will set you back US$55–65. (Remember that entry to Ras Mohammed costs US$5 extra and requires a full Egyptian visa, so visitors with Sinai-only visas are not permitted to dive there.) A one-day **Thistlegorm** trip (see p.685) with two dives costs US$80 with Camel, US$100 with Colona. Emperor offers a two-day trip with full board and five dives for US$185 (including equipment). Space permitting, **snorkellers** can join any boat for US$25–30.

If you want to do lots of boat diving, **dive packages** can be a good deal: Oonas charges US$230 for a five-day package (ten dives), which is discounted if booked in advance. Rates do not include lunch on the boat (£E25) or **equipment rental**, which costs US$20–25 per day at most centres.

For many divers, **liveaboards** are the best way to get the most out of the Red Sea; giving them the opportunity to get to less-visited sites out of "peak hours" and to make up to five dives a day rather than the two dives offered by daily boats. They can also work out cheaper than staying in a hotel and buying a dive package seperately, particularly since prices have actually gone down in the last couple of years, averaging around US$100 per person per day for a boat with 4–8 a/c cabins. Although this price should include full board, airport transfers

All the dive centres are open daily (mostly 8.30am–6pm). Dive boats start (at around 9am) from the marina in **Sharm el-Maya**, so reckon on a minibus journey there and back. Most dive centres will collect you and drop you off again.

Sharm and Na'ama Bay's major dive centres have recently formed the **Sharm Diving Union** (T & F069/660-418, Esharm_diving_union@sinainet.com.eg). Among other things they organize regular clean-ups of the sea.

For a list of dive centres based in **Sharm el-Sheikh** and **Shark Bay**, see p.696 and p.706. And for more **liveaboards**, see p.696.

Anemone Dive Centre *Pigeon House* T & F069/600-999, Eanemone@sinainet.com .eg. Laid-back and good value, offering discounts for those staying at *Pigeon House* and for anyone carrying a *Rough Guide*. PADI, NAUI, SSI. Recommended.
Aqua Active *Ghazala Hotel* mobile T0121 223931, Ereservation@aquaactive.com. Free shuttle bus for clients in other hotels. Fifteen percent discount on diving, except courses, if pre-booked by email. PADI, SSI.
Camel Dive Club Next to the *Sanafir* T069/600-700, F600-601, Ereservations@cameldive.com. Good facilities and lots of daily dive trips. All affiliations. Recommended.
Colona Dive Club *Oasis* T069/663-670, F662-233, Ecolona@sinainet.com.eg. Liveaboards available. PADI Gold Palm 5-Star IDC Centre, SSI, Nitrox.
Divers International Near Gafy Mall T069/601-939. PADI, NAUI, SSI.

Emperor Divers & Red Sea Scuba Schools *Rosetta* T069/601-734, F601-735, Eemperor.divers@sinainet.com.eg. Liveaboards available. PADI.
Ocean College *Ocean Sands* T069/600-802, Eocean@sinainet.com.eg. PADI, BSAC.
Oonas Divers Near the *Sonesta* T069/600-581, F600-582, Ecaroline@oonasdiveclub.com. Five-star PADI dive centre. Recommended.
Red Sea Diving College Na'ama beach T069/600-145, F600-144, Eoperations@sinai-services.com. Fine facilities and tuition, and liveaboards available. PADI; sells PADI books. Recommended.
Sinai Dive Club *Hilton Fayrouz Resort* T069/600-136, F601-040, Einfo@dive-club.com. Liveaboards available. PADI, CMAS, SSI and NRC Nitrox courses.
Sinai Divers *Ghazala Hotel* T069/600-697, F600-158, Einfo@sinaidivers.com. Efficient and experienced. Liveaboards available. PADI, CMAS, SSI. Recommended.

and tanks and weights, diving equipment and alcohol are usually an extra that you will need to arrange in advance.

In case of **diving emergencies**, contact Dr. Adel Taher at the Hyperbaric Medical Centre in Sharm el-Sheikh (T069/660-922, mobile 0122 124292). The International Hospital in Hay el-Nur (T069/660-272) has a decompression facility.

Snorkelling and watersports

While diving is the main pursuit, Na'ama is also great for **snorkelling** – a less demanding but equally pleasurable activity. If you've never snorkelled before and find breathing through a tube unsettling, start with the baby reefs just off the beach, where the sea is only waist deep. By the time you've circled a reef and seen its profusion of rainbow-hued fish, snorkelling should feel like fun and you'll be ready to move on to bigger things. Unfortunately, unless you're going to join a dive boat to get to further-flung sites (which is a very relaxing way of doing things; see p.696), visiting the local reefs involves some walking: drinking water, a hat and proper footwear are essential. It's wise to start early as the sea is usually calmest in the morning, an important factor when you've got to swim over serrated reefs.

The best **reefs** – aptly known as coral gardens – run for several miles **north** of **Na'ama Bay**. They don't get many divers (being deemed inferior to The Tower or Shark Bay) but are ideal for snorkelling. Just look for a safe descent from the rocks and the shortest, smoothest reef flat, with dark water beyond its edge. Bear in mind that these reefs are regularly visited by glass-bottom boats, so you will need to take care while you're in the water. The **Near Gardens** can be reached on foot by following the coast beyond Oonas Dive Centre. Plummeting to unseen depths beyond its crest, the reef has spawned offshore pillars and fantastic encrustations, swarming with angelfish, parrotfish and blue snappers. From here you can swim to the equally amazing **Middle and Far gardens**, further up the coast.

If you're willing to pay to reach **other sites**, several agencies run overland snorkelling trips to the mangrove forests of **Nabeq** for around US$35 (see below), or boat trips to the less demanding reefs at **Ras Mohammed**, **Ras Nasrani** or **Shark Bay**. Sun'n'Fun, which has branches in many hotels in Na'ama and beach kiosks by the *Hilton* (℡069/601-623, ✉sunnfun@sinainet .com.eg), offers a full-day boat trip to Ras Mohammed or Tiran for US$36 (plus US$5 entry fee), while Fanous Moto Safari (℡069/603-059) runs snorkelling trips to the Near and Far gardens and White Knights. A full-day overland trip to Nabeq, including Shark Bay and Dahab, costs US$70.

Apart from snorkelling, there's a wide variety of **watersports** on offer from most beachfront hotels, including sailing, windsurfing (instructors for both are available), water skiing, parasailing and pedalos. Thankfully, swimmers are spared having to dodge jetskiers, banned in Na'ama Bay since 1998, when two Italian tourists crashed into each other and were killed. There are, of course, **glass-bottom boats** if you don't want to get wet at all. Sun'n'Fun has boats leaving every two hours throughout the day (1hr 30min; £E55, children £E30).

Overland trips and safaris

Should the wonders of the deep pall, safari and travel agencies (see box opposite) can arrange tours by jeep, camel, motorbike or quads.

Some of the most popular **day excursions** by jeep are a mangrove-and-snorkelling visit to **Nabeq** (Sun'n'Fun does a half-day trip for US$35); a 4WD trip to the **Coloured Canyon** followed by a swim with the **dolphin** in **Nuweiba** (most places charge around US$60, but the dolphin is not guaranteed to make an appearance); or **St Catherine's Monastery** (overnight trip including climbing **Mount Sinai** for US$50). Nearer to Na'ama lies **Wadi Mandar**, visited on sunset trips by jeep (US$30) or camel (US$20 with tea, US$35 with dinner). If you see trips advertised for less, they probably involve travelling by bus rather than jeep. A bit further up the road is **Wadi Ain Kid**, a long fertile canyon culminating in an oasis of palm trees, a well and Bedouin farm; overnight excursions with Hussein from the *Pigeon House* cost US$50 including a Bedouin dinner. Several companies also offer excursions to **Serabit el-Khadim** (see p.689) and **Hammam Faraoun** (p.689). If a **longer** time in the wild appeals, Hussein at the *Pigeon House* can organize tailor-made jeep safaris for around US$50 per person per day; Khaled Liston can arrange desert or diving safaris for around US$100 per person per day for up to a fortnight; and Madian Adventure offers jeep safaris and mountain trekking from US$80 per person per day (for details of all these, see box below). Note that most of these sites, except for Nabeq, Wadi Mandar and Wadi Ain Kid are covered elsewhere in this chapter, and are cheaper to reach from Nuweiba or Dahab.

Horse-riding in the desert can be arranged at the *Sofitel* Equestrian Centre (℡069/600-081); where desert trips cost US$27 per hour or overnight trips start from US$100. The norm for **camel rides** is US$20 with a stop for

Travel agents

Abu Noub Morgana Mall ℡069/600-066, ℱ600-855. Established, reliable agent.
Nass Tours Mall 8 ℡ & ℱ601-258, ℰnasstours@sinainet.com.eg. Can help with booking trips to Petra.

Thomas Cook Gafy Mall ℡069/601-808. Friendly agent that can help with most general travel arrangements for the rest of Egypt, including selling tickets for the catamaran to Hurghada (see p.697).

Safari operators

Desert Blues Safaris ℡ & ℱ069/600-999, mobile 0101 436127, ℰbarbara@sinainet.com.eg. Very experienced Bedouin guide; charges from US$70 per person per day.
Hussein Abu Ahmed mobile ℡0101 135967, ℱ069/600-995, ℰpigeon@access.com.eg. Long-standing, excellent-value Bedouin guide based at *Pigeon House*. Around US$50 per person per day.

Khaled Liston ℡069/662-068, ℰkhaledliston@hotmail.com. Desert and diving safaris for US$100–120 per person per day.
Madian Adventure ℡069/660-593, ℱ600-594, ℰpeninsula@menanet.net. One of the first guides in the area, and very experienced; charges US$80 per person per day.

Bedouin tea, or US$35 with dinner, though it will cost you less and be less artificial if you arrange it with Bedouin guides at the *Pigeon House*.

"Quads" or **quadrunners**, also known as ATVs (All-Terrain Vehicles) are another popular way of charging into the desert. Canyon Safari at the *Pigeon House* (℡069/600-997, mobile 0123 158121) rents quads (double US$28 per hour, single US$18), and also runs a popular guided sunset trip (double US$35, single US$25) which takes two hours with a stop for Bedouin tea. Other quad excursions include a six-hour trip to Nabeq with lunch (US$110 double, US$90 single) and a Bedouin dinner trip (US$50 double, US$35 single).

If you fancy venturing out on your own **by car**, a Jeep Cherokee can be rented for US$90 a day from Avis in Morgana Mall (℡069/602-400) and at the *Sonesta* (℡069/600-979). Prices for a smaller car such as a Ford Fiesta start from US$35 a day; try Shark Limousine (℡069/603-200) at the *Golf*, or Hertz at the *Sanafir* (℡069/600-459). Of the other major companies, you'll find Budget in the *Marriott* (℡069/600-190), in the centre of Na'ama Bay, and Thrifty at the *Mövenpick* (℡069/600-100).

Keep in mind that it is illegal for unaccompanied foreigners to go **off-road**; there are still many unexploded landmines in Sinai and you won't know where they are.

Other activities

Thrill-seekers can try **go-kart racing** at the state-of-the-art *Ghibili Raceway* (℡069/603-737, ℱ602-323, ℰspeed@ghibiliraceway.com) on the Airport Road just before the entrance to the *Hyatt Regency*. For US$12–15 during the day or US$20–25 at night (until 1am), you will get 10–15 minutes of racing round one of four circuits, including one for children over seven. All first-timers have to undergo a training session. Or perhaps the **bungee rocket** in front of the *Helnan Marina* (℡010/669-6968; £E75 per person), a bungee adapted to carry two people in a large ball that drops violently from a great height. A slightly quieter time can be had on the nearby **trampolines** (£E20 per person for five minutes).

SINAI | Na'ama Bay

7

Shopping

A number of **malls** and recreated "**souks**" compete to attract the attention of tourists, but there's little here you can't find in Cairo or Luxor – at lower prices. However there are a few interesting shops: Aladdin at the *Camel Dive Club Hotel* (which has another branch at the *Falcon El-Diar* further down the street on the opposite side), and Bashayer, in Sharm Mall behind Red Sea Diving College, are worth taking a look at for arts and crafts, mostly from Upper Egypt; nearby, Karkade (☎069/602-885) has a good selection of oils, spices and herbs, plus an interesting collection of antiques. They have another, larger shop in Sharm el-Maya.

Eating, drinking and nightlife

There are no really cheap places to eat or drink in Na'ama, so what passes for inexpensive is relative. On the plus side, the quality of the **food** is high if you like hotel-style cuisine which ranges from Egyptian, Italian and seafood to Japanese and Thai; prices tend to be higher along the **beach promenade** where every hotel offers at least one beachside restaurant, and along the inland strip outside the *Sanafir* and *Camel Dive Club* hotels – both these stretches offer excellent people-watching opportunities.

If you fancy **eating on the beach**, try the *Hilton's* Italian restaurant, or venture up to the fish restaurant at *Shark's Bay Camp* (see p.706).

Andrea In the mall opposite *Hard Rock Café*. Mostly chicken-based dishes, but also good-value Egyptian food; from £E10–15 for a meal.

Da Franco *Hotel Ghazala*, on the promenade between the *Mövenpick* and *Hilton*. Excellent pizza and pasta restaurant; reasonably priced main dishes (£E15–25).

Hard Rock Café Just around the corner from the main strip. Serves hamburgers with all the trimmings; hugely popular nightspot. Daily 12.30pm–2am (till 3am Sat).

Kokai *Hotel Ghazala* next to *Da Franco*. Japanese restaurant, slightly cheaper than *Kona Kai* at the *Marriott*.

Mashy Café du Liban *Sanafir*. Al fresco Lebanese cuisine. Good value, especially if you're a meat lover. Open daily for lunch and dinner; dishes £E20–45.

Safsafa Next to *Hard Rock Café* ☎069/603-313. Good quality seafood restaurant.

Shin Seol Sharm Mall. Reasonable Chinese restaurant with roof garden. About £E25 for a three-course meal.

Tabasco On the roof of the *Hard Rock Café*. A new branch of the famous Cairo Oriental pub serving excellent international food.

Tam Tam *Ghazala* ☎069/600-150. Tasty Egyptian food near the beach with rooftop seating and live music. Excellent *karkade*, lentil soup and Egyptian sweets. Does takeaway. Daily until 1am.

La Trattoria *Sanafir*. Good, basic Italian restaurant, run by Italians. Pasta from £E15.

Viva Next to Red Sea Diving College. Reasonably priced seafood restaurant near the beach. Good pasta too.

Sinai Wildlife Clinic

Sinai Wildlife Clinic (☎069/601-610 ext 241, ✉wildlifeclinic@sinainet.com.eg) is a non-profit organization that works with the National Parks to care for local wildlife in the Sinai, as well as the Bedouin and their herds. Some of its most important work takes place during autumn, when 32 different species of raptors and cranes and 82 percent of the world's population of white storks pass through the area on their journey south. Each week more than 500 sick and injured birds are treated in the animal hospital at *Coral Bay Hotel*, 6km north of Na'ama Bay, where there is also a wildlife visitor centre (daily 9am–4pm).

Periodically **volunteers** are taken on to work on the clinic's various projects; those with veterinary and nursing skills are especially welcome. Contact Heike at the centre for more information.

Nightlife

Alcoholic drinks are widely available at European prices, perhaps more so than anywhere else in Egypt; the **duty-free shop** in front of the *Kahramana* (daily 11am–2pm & 6–11pm) sells cheap booze, though at the time of writing you can only buy duty-free within the first 24 hours of arrival in Egypt, an attempt by the government to stop Egyptians and hotels using foreigners' passports to buy drink. The bar at the *Pigeon House* is a good place to start your evening as it often has special promotions, as does Sinai Divers. The favourite for divers is *Camel Dive Bar* – also known as *Chris's Place* – at Camel Dive Club, but you will find more locals at the nautically themed *Pirates Bar* in the *Hilton* (happy hour 5.30–7.30pm), which also serves food. *The Mexican Bar* (1pm–midnight) at the *Na'ama Bay Hotel* under the cliff at the end of the main strip is a relative newcomer and is popular with British holidaymakers who come for the beer and resident DJ, while the café at the *Iberotel Lido* is a good spot for watching the sun set over Na'ama Bay.

Na'ama's premier nightspot however is the **Sanafir**, where you'll find a range of nightlife. From 9.30pm there is an Oriental show featuring – mainly Russian – belly dancers. There is a cover charge of £E25 unless you eat at one of their restaurants. If you prefer something a bit more low-key, their rooftop bar *Star Talks* is a favourite hideaway for holiday romancers. The *Bus Stop* (£E25, includes one drink), Na'ama's hippest club, doesn't get going until past midnight and goes on to 3am. On Thursday it is host to *House Nation* (£E60) a club night that often has guest DJs from Europe, the UK and Russia. If it's a really big event, the club moves to the *Sanafir's* venue in the desert, *The Echo Temple* (details from ⓦ http://sharmevents.com). Its main competition, notably popular with Italians, is the **Hard Rock Café**, just round the corner from the main strip (disco daily 8pm–2am, until 3am Sat; ☎069/602-665).

Other **discos** include the *Black House Disco* at the *Rosetta*, *Cactus* at the *Mövenpick* – both of which are popular with hotel staff – and the Latin-themed *La Luna* at the *Golf*; none is likely to be very lively before midnight. There are **pool tables** in many of the hotel bars, including the *Kahramana* and the *Sanafir*. For a more Egyptian-style evening, the main strip outside the *Sanafir* is now lined with countless coffee shops offering *sheeshas*, Oriental drinks and people-watching.

And then there are always the **casinos**. Na'ama Bay now has several that open late into the night including the *Casino Royale* at the *Mövenpick*. You will need to show your passport before entering – proof of your ability to part with your money.

The *Safir* hotel, on the edge of town on the Airport Road, just up from the *Pigeon House*, has a **cinema**, where you can watch relatively new Hollywood films for £E10.

Listings

Banks and exchange Most hotels in Na'ama have banks which are open daily (8.30am–2pm & 6–9pm). The National Bank of Egypt has branches in the *Ghazala*, *Mövenpick* and *Hilton*. You can get cash advances on Visa and MasterCard at Banque Misr (9am–1.30pm & 5–8pm) in the Sharm Mall. Several banks now have ATMs; one that usually works is at the HSBC Bank next to *McDonald's*. For changing money, Swiss Exchange in Morgana Mall (daily 9am–midnight) may offer slightly better rates than the banks (cash only).

Books and newspapers Most of the four- and five-star hotels have small bookshops and provide newspapers according to the nationality of their guests. Several have a "library" where you can pick up books left behind by past guests, though English-language books can be hard to find.
Dentist Dr Mohammed el-Hadidy, at the Morgana Mall (☎069/601-111, mobile 0101 535372).
Doctor Dr Wael Habib, at the Mount Sinai Clinic in the *Mövenpick* (☎069/600-100, 24hr mobile 0122 189889). For **diving emergencies**, Dr Adel Taher at

the Hyperbaric Medical Centre in Sharm el-Sheikh (☎069/660-922, emergency mobile 0122 124292). **Hospitals** The nearest hospitals are in Sharm El-Sheikh, in Hay el-Nur: Sharm International Hospital (☎069/661-624) Sharm Medical Centre (☎069/661-744).

Internet cafés Nearly all the hotels and several bars offer Internet access. Try Cyber Disco at the *Hilton Fayrouz* (☎069/600-136; £E20 per hour) or Camel Cyber at *Camel Dive Club* (☎069/600-700, ⓔinfo@cameldive.com; £E20 per hour). Sinainet has Internet cafés at the *Ghazala* and *Ghazala Gardens* (on either side of the main highway between the *Hilton* and *Mövenpick*), the *Mövenpick* and the *Kahramana*, all charging £E20 per hour. There's also GlobalLink in Mall 8 (daily 10am–midnight; ☎069/601-819, ⓔeam@globallink.8m.com; £E10 for 30min).

Supermarkets Cherry, Sharm Mall (daily 9am–midnight); Shamandoura, next to the *Sanafir* (daily 9am–midnight). However, Sheikh Abdullah's in Hay el-Nur (see p.693) is the cheapest and offers the most variety.

Pharmacy Towa, in the Sharm Mall (daily 10am–1am; ☎069/600-779), offers free home delivery if you're too sick to go there in person. Also, Na'ama Bay Pharmacy (☎069/660-338) and Na'ama El Khaligy (☎069/600-974). The best-stocked pharmacy is next to the hospital in Hay el-Nur in Sharm el-Sheikh.

Telephone exchanges Sharm No. 2 is opposite the entrance to the *Sheraton*, about 1km north of Na'ama Bay (daily 10am–10pm).

Thomas Cook Gafy Mall (daily 9am–2pm & 6–10pm). Usual range of travel services as well as Visa cash advances. Sells tickets for the catamaran to Hurghada (which leaves from the marina in Sharm el-Maya; see p.697).

Travel agents See p.703.

Western Union At the DHL office in the *Rosetta* (Mon–Thurs & Sun 9am–9pm; ☎069/602-222, ⓕ602-223).

Shark Bay

Ten kilometres up the coast from Na'ama, the once tranquil and secluded resort of **SHARK BAY** is now overlooked and overwhelmed by large holiday villages, and the sandy track that used to lead there has been replaced by a variety of tarmacked roads servicing the hotels. But that hasn't deterred its many visitors, particularly the scores of day-visitors from Na'ama. Despite the bay's forbidding name (*Beit el-Irsh*, "House of the Shark" in Arabic), all the sharks have been scared away by divers, leaving a benign array of tropical fish and coral gardens just offshore, with deeper reefs and bigger fish further out. There's a £E10 charge to use the beach which includes the use of showers and a soft drink.

If you want to **stay**, Sheikh Embarak's **Shark's Bay Camp** (☎069/600-942, ⓕ600-941, ⓔsharksbay@sinainet.com.eg) is a pleasant mix of bungalows (❹) and beach huts (❶) with its own dive centre and jetty – it shares the beach with the nearby *Pyramisa Hotel*. The *Camp*'s **dive centre** (ⓔumbi@sinainet.com.eg) runs boat trips to the Tiran Strait (day-dive US$45; liveaboard US$95 a day) while Bedouins who hang out there can arrange jeep safaris into the interior. Its restaurant and Bedouin café are quiet nightspots that close around midnight; guests wanting more action generally club together for a taxi into Na'ama.

The Tiran Strait and Nabeq

The headland of Ras Nasrani beyond Shark Bay marks the onset of the **Tiran Strait**, where the waters of the Gulf of Suez flow into the deeper Gulf of Aqaba, swirling around islands and reefs. In 1992, the Tiran archipelago was declared a protected area, and it may one day become a fully fledged national park. Meanwhile, there's no admission charge or facilities and the only access is by boat from Sharm el-Maya or Shark Bay. This is *not* an excursion for novice divers, as the sea can be extremely rough and chilling (bring high-calorie drinks and snacks to boost your energy).

Sharks, manta rays, barracuda and Napoleon fish are typical of the deepwater sites around the **islands of Tiran** and **Sanafir**, though there are also shallow reefs like the Small Lagoon and Hushasha. The multitude of **shipwrecks** in the Gulf is due to treacherous reefs and currents, insurance fraud, and Egypt's blockade of the Strait in the 1960s. The **Jackson Reef** has a spectacular 70m drop-off and the wreck of the *Lara* to investigate, while the **Gordon Reef** boasts the hulk of the *Lucila*. Two notable sites at **Ras Nasrani** are the **Light**, with a 40m drop-off and pelagic fish; and the **Point**, with a dazzling array of reef fish.

Nabeq

Beyond the mouth of the Gulf of Aqaba, a 90km swathe of the coast as far north as Dahab City has been designated another protected area, named after the small oasis and **Bedouin village** of **NABEQ**. As few dive boats come here from Na'ama, the **reefs** are quieter than at Tiran or Ras Mohammed. Most visitors are on half-day trips to see Nabeq's mangrove forests – the most northerly in the world. **Mangroves** can filter salt from sea water and thus survive in tropical coastal areas. As sediment traps, they reduce erosion and provide a habitat for mating fish and migratory birds (in summer and autumn), acting as the ecological interface between the coast and the interior, whose flood-prone wadis sustain ibex, hyrax, foxes and other **wildlife**.

All approaches to Nabeq are best made by someone who knows the way; wander off the track and you might inadvertently encounter **mines** left over from Israeli-Egyptian wars, which killed a jeepload of tourists in 1995. Admission to the protected area costs US$5; the only facilities are a **cafeteria** and visitors centre.

Anyone considering **staying** in the Nabeq area should bear in mind that it is much windier here than in Na'ama, transport connections are limited to shuttle buses and the beaches can be poor. However, the *Nubian Village* 25km north of Na'ama (mobile ☎0101 149000, ℱ069/215-6364; ❻), is a very beautiful hotel designed to resemble a Nubian village, offering full board only.

Dahab and Asilah

Jagged mountains ranged inland of Na'ama Bay accompany the road 95km northwards, providing a magnificent backdrop for **Dahab**'s tawny beaches, from which its Arabic name – "gold" – derives. The resort divides into two localities: a cluster of holiday villages catering for affluent visitors, and the Bedouin settlement of **Asilah** 2.5km up the coast, where younger travellers hang out in a kind of "Goa by the Red Sea" – though as Asilah moves upmarket, the distinction between them is blurring. A third area is developing to the north of Asilah, near the dive sites of the Canyon and Blue Hole, but most construction was unfinished at time of writing.

Dahab City

Don't be discouraged by **DAHAB CITY**, the colony of municipal housing and government offices next to the holiday villages. The only reason to go there is to use its facilities: a **post office** (daily except Fri 8.30am–3pm) and 24-hour **telephone exchange** (international calls with phonecards); a **bank** which accepts travellers' cheques and Visa (winter Mon–Thurs, Sat & Sun

▲ *Canyon Dive Resort (10 km)*

DAHAB & ASILAH

ACCOMMODATION

DAHAB BAY
Ganet Sinai	19
Hilton Dahab	22
Helnan Dehab	21
Swiss Inn Golden Palace	20

ASILAH
Bamboo House	7
Bedouin Lodge	2
Blue Beach Club	3
Christina Residence	15
Crazy Camel	6
Daniela Village	1
Diver's House	13
Fighting Kangaroo	5
Gulf Paradise	17
Inmo Divers' Home	16
Jasmine Pension	14
Lagona Village	18
Mirage Village	4
Mohammed Aly Camp	8
Nesima	9
New Sphinx	10
Sphinx House	12
Venus	11

Reef 2000 Diving Centre

Desert Divers

One Stop Business Centre & W. Union Money Transfer

Casablanca Travel

National Bank of Egypt

Camels for rental

MASBAT

DAHAB CITY

East Delta Bus Station

Bank

Supermarket

ASILAH

MASHRABA

Banque de Caire

Dahab Bay

Lagoon

N

RESTAURANTS
Crazy House	E
Dolphin Café	D
Friends	B
Jays	A
Pizzeria Trattoria	F
Spaghetteria	G
Tota	C

NOT TO SCALE

8.30am–2pm & 5–8pm, Fri 8.30–11am & 5–8pm; summer Mon–Thurs, Sat & Sun 9am–12.30pm & 6.30–8.30pm, Fri 10–11.30am & 6.30–8.30pm), and a **supermarket** (daily 8am–10pm). The **tourist police** is conveniently located opposite the *Novotel*, while the nearest **hospital** is in Sharm el-Sheikh (see p.697).

Most tourists are heading straight for Asilah; every bus is met by **taxis** and **pick-ups** that charge £E1–2 per person for the journey, £E5 for solo travellers. Most places aren't more than ten minutes' walk from the taxi drop-off point.

The **holiday villages** around Dahab Bay are self-contained, with private beaches and access to a coral reef on the headland. Their guests might have little in common with the crowd drawn to Asilah, but they, and day-trippers from Sharm el-Sheikh and Na'ama, come to Asilah to shop, eat and drink. And the travellers of Asilah can also be found at the ultra-modern *Zanzibar* disco at the *Helnan* (June–Oct; £E10).

The **Ganet Sinai Hotel** (☎069/640-440, ⓕ640-441; ❼) has a/c rooms with TVs and sea views, a private beach without coral (£E15 for non-guests, which includes a soft drink) and a windsurfing centre. Buffet breakfast is included in the price. Next door is the **Swiss Inn Golden Palace Resort** (☎069/640-471, ⓕ640-470; ❽). The newest of the Dahab resorts, the opulent **Hilton Dahab** (☎069/640-310, ⓕ640-424; ❾) is about as far away as you can get from hippy huts and if you transgress its boundaries, they'll want a wopping US$20 to use the beach. The **Novotel Coralia Dahab** (☎069/640-301, ⓕ640-305; ⓔrsrv.novotel.dhb@sinainet.com.eg; ❻–❼) is a four-star complex with some charm that monopolizes a windswept bay enclosed by a sandbar. It's a fabulous spot if you want to learn how to windsurf. Further round the bay, the somewhat isolated **Helnan Dahab Hotel** (☎069/640-425, ⓕ640-428; ❼–❽) offers five-star facilities along with a good beach.

Note that hotels north of the lagoon are covered under Asilah, though some of them are actually closer to Dahab Bay.

Asilah

If lazing on the beach, stoned, is your idea of heaven, **ASILAH** is the place to be – though the arrival of the diving scene has changed this somewhat, so that many people now laze on the beach and talk about the Blue Hole, instead. Asilah's pre-eminence in Egypt as *the* place for hippy travellers started in the 1960s, when Israeli troops started coming here for a bit of R & R, introducing the Bedouin to another way of life. Nowadays, the Bedouin village of tin shacks and scrawny goats has changed beyond recognition: concrete buildings stretch back behind scores of restaurants and campgrounds, while local children wander beneath the palm trees selling Bedouin trousers (made in China), friendship bracelets and camel rides. Most of the palm huts were long ago replaced by hotels (some of which are very smart) while a section of the beach has recently been paved to create a "corniche" – yet Dahab manages to live on as a travellers' ghetto offering time-out from all that cultural immersion. Such is the lure that visitors often stay longer than they'd expected, getting stuck in a daily routine of café life, or if they are more active, working at one of the dive centres (mostly in return for food, accommodation and some diving).

Given Asilah's reputation, it's important to stress the limitations on pure hedonism. Women can generally sunbathe here without any hassle, but **going topless** violates Egyptian law, and there are periodic crackdowns on **dope**: if you consume it, it's at the risk of the police deciding they need to make up numbers on their arrest forms (see box on p.710). While stories abound of duplicitous locals, beware also of being ripped off by resident **con-artists** from Israel or Europe, who exploit the naive, and unpleasant, travellers' belief that it's only natives who "can't be trusted". Stick to bottled water to avoid the risk of **hepatitis** from contaminated cisterns; a dozen or so cases of infection occur every year.

Arrival and information

People **arriving** in Asilah are usually dropped at the bottom end of **Masbat**, the local name for the strip of beachfront cafés and shops running north beyond the lighthouse on a headland. To the south of the *Mohammed Aly* campground lies a succession of campgrounds and hotels extending towards the holiday villages: this area is known as **Mashraba**.

There are several **Internet cafés** dotted along Mashraba, including the *Lagoon* at *Christina Residence* (£E20 per hour, £E3 to send one email) and *White Hawk* (£E1 for three minutes). Most have **telephone, fax** and photocopying facilities too; *Lagoon* charges £E7 per minute to call abroad. If you have a phonecard there is a callbox at Baraka supermarket near *Friends* restaurant. There's a National Bank of Egypt next door and a Banque de Caire opposite *Star of Dahab* (daily 9am–12.30pm & 6–9pm) with a smaller branch at *Sabry Palace*. The One Stop Business Center at *Bamboo House* has safety deposit boxes (£E20 per week or £E3 per day, £E10 key deposit); a Western Union money transfer service and you can also make international calls and find **second-hand books** here.

Accommodation

While we've listed and reviewed Asilah's hotels below, most visitors stay in **campgrounds**, walled compounds of concrete or palm huts, of which there at least fifty. The main reason for their popularity is quite simply that they're cheap, enabling guests to spend their money on food, drugs or diving instead – which is how the campgrounds earn a profit. At the low end you've got basic concrete cells, usually with padlocks and electricity, with showers, sinks and toilets in the yard, while the more upmarket versions have en-suite facilities, sea views and a/c. Everywhere charges the same **rates**: £E10–20 per person

---

Drug smuggling and cultivation in Sinai

The Sinai Bedouin have a long tradition of **smuggling** hashish into Egypt. During colonial times the route followed the Mediterranean coast, until the militarization of El-Arish and the Canal Zone compelled smugglers to seek new routes across the interior. When this also became militarized due to war with Israel, they switched their attention to the mountains of South Sinai and the Aqaba coast. Under Israeli rule their activities were tolerated so long as the dope was bound for Egypt, but the emergence of an Israeli market caused a clampdown in the 1970s, at a time when hash supplies from Lebanon were drying up.

Meanwhile, however, foreign hippies were flocking to Sinai and asking the Bedouin for grass (using the Indian term *ganja*, from which *bango*, the Egyptian word for marijuana, derives). Thus was planted the seed of a local **cultivation** industry, which really got going once Sinai was returned to Egypt and its police chief took a hand in the business for a decade. Today, Sinai is one of Egypt's main sources of *bango*, as cultivators can't be prosecuted owing to a loophole in the Camp David Accords – unlike dealers, who risk long-term imprisonment or even hanging, and rely on bribery to get off the hook. But the police must make *some* arrests, so it's rather like an auction where the lowest bidders are cast as scapegoats. This applies equally to **foreigners** – especially those who bring heroin or ecstasy to sell in Dahab.

depending on the quality, though you can get a room for less if business is slow or you plan on spending a few weeks or more. Double rooms with a private shower cost upwards of £E30–90. Aside from the sleeping arrangements, factors to consider when choosing a site are: whether, and when, they have hot showers, how they're rigged up to deal with mosquitoes, and noise levels (watch out for anywhere near the main strip at Masbat). Several camps have added extra storeys and become quasi-hotels – a process furthest advanced at the *Mohammed Aly Camp*. Apart from those listed below, other camps worth mentioning are *Venus*, *Fighting Kangaroo*, *Dolphin*, *El Dorado* and *Seven Heaven*.

If Asilah's unceasing commercialization leaves you cold, you might prefer to seek out the limited, rather primitive accommodation at **Ras Abu Galum**, the protected area between Dahab and Nuweiba (see p.714).

Bamboo House Hotel Masbat ☏ 069/640-263. A proper hotel with a/c rooms and a Western Union money transfer service. ⑤

Bedouin Lodge aka **Auski** Pleasant rooms with good sea views. *Auski* is the older and cheaper section. ③

Blue Beach Club 300m north of the lighthouse ☏ 069/640-413. Relatively new Swiss-managed place, with 18 rooms with fans, fridges and balconies with sea views. It's a very windy spot. ⑤

Canyon Dive Resort 11km north of Masbat. Attractive two-star place next to the Canyon dive site. Worth considering if all you want to do is dive, but otherwise a bit far from town. ⑤

Christina Residence Mashraba ☏ 069/640-390, ℻ 640-406, ✉ christina_residence@yahoo.com. Smart, clean, Greek-inspired hotel one block back from the beach; currently adding a beachfront extension. Only 10 rooms with a/c or fans but no breakfast. Has a small Internet café. ③–④

Club Red North end of Mashraba, next to *Mohammed Aly Camp* ☏ & ℻ 069/640-380, ✉ clubred@intouch.com. This dive centre also offers dorm beds (£E30) and rooms with fans or a/c and sea views. Discounts with dive packages. ③

Crazy Camel Masbat ☏ 069/640-662, ✉ info@crazy-camel.de. Ten rooms, three with a/c, set in a garden courtyard. Also has apartments for rent and bamboo huts on the roof. ③

Daniela Village 3km north of Dahab on the way to Canyon dive site ☏ 02/348-2671, ℻ 360-7750. Comfortable place with 40 large a/c rooms with sea views, a laundry, shop and bar. ⑦

Diver's House Tucked away in the south of Mashraba ☏ & ℻ 069/640-451. Small English-run hotel, nicely designed and very clean. Preference given to divers. ④

Inmo Divers' Home Mashraba ☏ 069/640-370, ℻ 640-372, ✉ inmo@inmodivers.com. Stylish lodgings around a dive centre. All rooms have double beds and bathrooms; discount for longer stays, divers and advance bookings. ⑥

Jasmine Pension On the beach next to *Diver's House* ☏ 069/640-370, ℻ 640-372. Good food and some nice rooms with balconies. ③

Lagona Village South of Mashraba, on the way to Dahab Bay ☏ 069/640-350, ℻ 640-351. Comfortable rooms facing a private beach. Neat and clean, but a bit isolated. ⑤

Mirage Village Near the lighthouse ☏ 069/640-341. Tucked away behind a walled compound; pleasant rooms, clean bathrooms and the added bonus of being mosquito-free thanks to its windy disposition. ③

Mohammed Aly Camp On the beach where Masbat meets Mashraba ☏ 069/640-268. Although it is very central and offers 115 rooms, only a few of them have much appeal. The best overlook the sea, and have fans and their own bathrooms. The camp toilets are not that pleasant. ②–③

Nesima Mashraba ☏ 069/640-320, ℻ 640-321, ✉ nesima@menanet.net. Possibly the most beautiful hotel in Asilah, with a great pool setting. Used by British dive operators Regal and Crusader Travel. Discounts on rooms with fans in quiet periods. ⑥

New Sphinx Mashraba ☏ & ℻ 069/640-032, ✉ sphinx_d@intouch.com. Forty rooms with bath, a/c and satellite TV, plus a pool. ⑥

Sphinx House Mashraba ☏ & ℻ 069/640-032, ✉ sphinx_d@intouch.com. Older than its sister hotel, *Sphinx House* has 54 rooms with a/c or fans, private or shared baths. The popular bar has free pool tables. ④–⑤

Eating, drinking and nightlife

A score of **restaurants** by the beach vie for custom. House, trance and chill-out music fill the air; floor cushions and posters reflect the amalgam of Bedouin and hippie influences. Everywhere serves soft drinks (though not all places have alcohol licences) and you can sit around for hours without being required to eat (dishes take a long time to prepare, in any case). With menus displayed outside, it's easy to compare prices. Ask other visitors where they've eaten (and not got sick) – everyone has their favourite place.

Pancakes with bananas, apples, ice cream or honey are popular for **breakfast** or late-night munchies, while main **meals** consist of pizzas, pasta or fish. *Jays*, run by an English woman, is popular with resident divers for its safe food (only open in the evenings); *Friends*, nearby, is another favourite. *Crazy House* is one of the few places with tables and chairs; their food is good but pricey by local standards and they serve beer. *Tota* (recognizable by its ship facade) serves delicious lasagne and a range of pizzas, as does *Pizzeria Trattoria* (from £E8), while the Italian restaurant *Spaghetteria*, north of *Sphinx House*, serves good pasta and coffee. *Dolphin Café*, just up from the police station, offers reasonable Indian vegetarian baltis and noodles. Many places display a tempting heap of fresh **fish** and crustaceans outside; just check the price before ordering.

Unless you splash out on lobster, you can eat quite well in Asilah for £E20–35 a meal, including drinks and dessert. If you want to spend a little more, then *Lakhbatita* south of *Sphinx House* offers a Levantine and Egyptian menu. Most places are open until midnight (or later), though the choice of food diminishes after 9pm. There are also numerous **supermarkets** (daily 7.30am–midnight), **fruit stalls** and *taamiya* stands.

At the time of writing **nightlife** was still based in the hotels and restaurants that sell alcohol. There are three main **drinking** hangouts: the bars at *Nesima* (happy hour 7–9pm), which stay open until 3am or later and are popular with the diving set, especially on Fridays; the bar at the *Sphinx House* (happy hour 7–9pm) which has free pool tables and is a bit more low-life; and *Tota*, which has satellite TV and has created a large, attractive beer garden in the back. Those who prefer quieter entertainment can enjoy yoga and meditation at *Club Red*, *Blue Beach* or *Nesima*, or borrow a book from the library at the Arabesque Bazaar on the beachfront near the lighthouse.

Diving, snorkelling and windsurfing

In recent years aquatic pursuits have begun to be taken as seriously in Dahab as in Na'ama. Here, however, **shore diving** is the norm, with the reefs reached by pick-ups. The nicest reefs to the north of Dahab Bay just past the lagoon; at Asilah the reefs are meagre, except for the area around the lighthouse, and much of the sea bed is covered in rubbish. Most divers head 7–8km up the coast where you can find the Eel Garden, Canyon and Blue Hole dive sites. Daily trips to these sites are arranged by most dive centres (see box opposite). You can also contact *Casablanca Travel* near the bank in Asilah (£E10 per person) or get there by taxi (£E40 per carload). Masks and fins can be rented (US$35–40) at any dive centre.

The **Canyon** is a dark, narrow fissure that you reach from the shore by swimming along the reef and then diving to the edge of a coral wall. It can be frightening for inexperienced divers, as it sinks to a depth of 50m, but there's plenty to see at the top of the reef. Further north lies the notorious **Blue Hole**, which claims several lives every year. This spectacular shaft in the reef plunges to 80m; the challenge involves descending 60m and swimming through a transverse passage to come up the other side. Divers who ascend too fast risk getting "bent"; inexperienced divers should not attempt this dive under any circumstances. Fortunately, the Hole can be enjoyed in safety by staying closer to the surface and working your way round to a dip in the reef known as the Bridge, which swarms with colourful fish and can even be viewed using snorkelling gear.

Asilah dive centres

Adventure Dive Club At the Lighthouse ⓣ & ⓕ 069/640-161. PADI.
Canyon Dive Club Masbat, and at The Canyon ⓣ 069/640-043. PADI.
Club Red *Mohammed Aly Camp* ⓣ 069/640-380. PADI.
Dive Zone Masbat ⓔ divezonedahab@ yahoo.com. PADI.
Fantasea Dive Club At the Lighthouse ⓣ & ⓕ 069/640-043. PADI, SSI.
INMO Mashraba ⓣ 069/640-370, ⓕ 640-372. PADI.

Lagona Dive Centre *Lagona Village Hotel* ⓣ 069/640-356, ⓕ 640-355. CMAS, SSI, PDIC.
Nesima Dive Centre *Nesima Hotel* ⓣ & ⓕ 069/640-321. PADI, BSAC.
Sinai Dive Club *Novotel Holiday Village* ⓣ 069/640-302, ⓕ 640-303. PADI.
Sub Sinai Khaled Amin, *Bedouin Lodge* ⓣ & ⓕ 069/640-317, ⓔ info@subsinai.com. PADI.

The main destination for day-long **dive safaris** is the Ras Abu Galum protected area, a 30km stretch of coast with three diving beaches, accessible by jeep or camel. **Naqb Shahin** – closest to Dahab – has fantastic coral and gold fish but the sea is very turbulent, so many divers prefer **Ras Abu Galum** or **Ras el-Mamleh**, further north. All three sites have deep virgin reefs with a rich variety of corals and fish. Club Red does a one-day, two-dive trip by camel to Ras Abu Galum for US$68 including tanks and weights (US$88 with all diving equipment), while Fantasea does a two-dive trip for US$65, including tanks, weights and lunch. Trips to the *Thistlegorm* (see p.685) are also available from Club Red, US$110 including transport, food and three dives. A quirkier aquatic option is to go **lobster hunting** at night, when the creatures are at their liveliest; excursions culminate in a lobster feast on the beach. For details, contact Hamid the "Lobster Man" at the *Crazy Camel Camp* (ⓣ & ⓕ 069/640-662, mobile 0122 708230, ⓔ info@crazy-camel.de).

Diving courses

While **renting equipment** is actually costlier here than in Na'ama, **diving courses** are generally cheaper. Competition means cut-price deals, especially when business is quiet, but you should keep a sense of perspective – the rock-bottom outlets are not necessarily going to be rigorous about your safety. Stick to the long-established centres like Club Red (OW course US$250 plus US$30 certification), Nesima (OW US$254 plus US$30 for certification), INMO or Lagona (which has good facilities for disabled divers) or big names like Divers International.

Windsurfing

The wind blows at least two hundred days each year at Dahab, making this area a haven for windsurfers. Fantasea and the **windsurfing** centre at the *Novotel* both rent boards for US$20 an hour; an introductory lesson costs US$35, and a three-day beginner's course is US$180.

Jeep and camel safaris

If you fancy **riding on the beach** at Asilah, look out for the boys who rent out horses (£E50 for one hour) or camels (£E10–15 per hour); they hang out by the restaurants on the beach near the palm trees in Masbat. A more exciting option is to sign up for trips into the rugged interior, which can be organized by most campgrounds, through safari agencies, or by negotiating directly with guides.

Desert and diving safaris

Desert Divers mobile ☎ 0101 888906, ℮ said@desert-divers.com, ⓦ www .desert-divers.com. Tailor-made desert and diving safaris that can be combined with activities like yoga and windsurfing. **Embah Safari** Masbat, next to *Tota* restaurant ☎ & ℱ 069/640-447,

℮ embah@intouch.com. Desert and diving day trips, excursions to St. Catherine's and the Coloured Canyon. **Hamid** *Crazy Camel* ☎ & ℱ 069/640-662, ℮ info@crazy-camel.de. Camel and jeep desert safaris, lobster-fishing and diving safaris by jeep.

The most popular **day excursions** are by jeep to the **Coloured Canyon** (see p.718), which costs £E55 per person for a group of six; by camel to **Wadi Gnay**, a Bedouin hamlet with palms and a brackish spring (£E25 per person); or by camel to the mangrove forest of **Nabeq** (£E40–55). Try to find Hajj Amr in the camel area at Masbat, or Hamed Abu Suliman in Asilah (☎ 069/640-149).

If you want to spend more time in the desert, Hamid, "The Lobster Man" at *Crazy Camel*, arranges camel and jeep safaris from US$50-60 per person per day, while Said Kader at *Desert Divers* can arrange camel and jeep safaris with either diving, windsurfing or yoga themes. *Embah Safari* offers diving, camel or jeep safaris from US$60 per person per day. For contact details, see the box above.

Ras Abu Galum

The coast between Dahab and Nuweiba are hidden from view as the road veers inland, but this remote area, the **Ras Abu Galum** Protectorate, harbours some of the richest wildlife in the Sinai. One of the Bedouin villages there has begun to provide **accommodation** for the visiting divers in a protected bay. Access is limited to a coastal track (walking or camel only) from Dahab or an unpaved road (4WD) that branches off from the main road 20km short of Nuweiba. There are huts on the beach (£E10 per person), and a couple of small supermarkets and restaurants, but it is wise to bring extra food if you plan on staying a while. It is possible to walk from Dahab (Ras Abu Galum is approximately two hours from the Blue Hole) or you can rent a pick-up truck (£E10–20).

A number of dive operators offer **safaris** to Ras Abu Galum; see above.

Moving on from Asilah and Dahab

Buses leave from Dahab City outside the East Delta ticket office. Of the buses to **Sharm** (9 daily; 1hr 30min; £E11), seven continue on to **El-Tor** (3hr; £E40); there are four buses daily to **Cairo** (7–8hr; £E55; £E70 for 10pm bus), and the 8am Cairo bus also stops at **Suez** (4–5hr; £E30). Two buses daily go to **Zagazig** (6–7hr; £E40) and **Ismailiya** (8am, 10am; 6–7hr; £E40). There are two daily buses to **Nuweiba** (10.30am and 6.30pm; 1hr; £E10), with the earlier one continuing on to **Taba** (3hr; £E20). The bus to **St Catherine's** (1hr; £E15) leaves around 9.30am, but you will miss the monastery if you take this bus, so unless you want to stay overnight it's best to go on an organized trip (see below).

If you would rather take a **shared taxi** to your destination, you can book a place in advance at any of the safari agencies and at most camps; it's worth asking around, as prices can vary for the same trip. Casablanca Tours, near the lighthouse in Masbat, offers a good-value overnight trip to St. Catherine's Monastery and Mount Sinai (£E40 per person) with a guide in a comfortable minibus. They also offer a **microbus** service to Cairo (8am £E45; 11pm £E55).

Nuweiba and Tarabeen

NUWEIBA is another resort on the Gulf of Aqaba, consisting of a **port** with nearby tourist complexes, followed 4km up the coast by **Nuweiba "City"**, an administrative and commercial centre grafted on to a former Israeli *moshav* (co-operative village). During the late 1970s, thousands of Israeli and Western back-packers flocked here to party and sleep on the beach; nowadays, the resort attracts a staider crowd of moderately affluent Egyptians and package tourists, for whom it constitutes a kind of cut-price Na'ama Bay. For others, however, Nuweiba is simply a stepping stone to Taba on the border with Israel – though at the time of writing traffic between Egypt and Israel was seriously diminished – or the place to catch ferries to Aqaba in Jordan.

Like Dahab, Nuweiba is also home to a neighbouring Bedouin settlement, which draws younger, low-budget travellers. Named after the local Bedouin tribe, **TARABEEN** is – or was – much like Asilah used to be. Before relations with Israel soured, there were more than twenty campgrounds and a few hotels on its wide and sandy beach, buzzing with restaurants and tourist bazaars; now the place is eerily empty, with only a few camps still working, waiting for the situation to improve and tourists to come back to the place.

If you yearn for the "old days" of Sinai when you could see only the stars and hear the waves, undisturbed by bright lights or loud music, head to the **DUNAS**, just south of Nuweiba City, or further north to the campgrounds and cafés around **RAS AL-SHEITAN** and **BIR SWAIR**. Like Dahab these places used to be very popular with Israelis especially because of their proximity to the border.

Arrival and information

The main **bus stop** is at the port and although the buses also stop at the *Helnan* hotel in Nuweiba City, it is never for long and they are easy to miss. Taxis charge £E15–20 for the journey from the port to Tarabeen, £E10 from Nuweiba City to Tarabeen. You can walk from the *Helnan* to Tarabeen in twenty minutes, via the beach; it takes slightly longer by road. Package tourists fly into **Sharm el-Sheikh airport**, whence shuttle buses convey them to the *Coral Hilton* or *Helnan* hotels.

Accommodation

Accommodation is concentrated in three main locations: near the port, in Nuweiba City and in the Bedouin village of Tarabeen, though there is also

---

The dolphin

One of Nuweiba's main attractions is a female **dolphin** named Olin, who lives off-shore from the Bedouin fishing village of Sayadeen, in Maagana bay. The story goes that having lost her mate in 1992, the dolphin made friends with **Abdullah**, a deaf fisherman, and has hung around ever since. Abdullah claims that swimming with her has improved his hearing. Scientists have suggested that Olin stays in the bay because she is disturbed and her communication problems prevent her from living normally with other dolphins. In any case she soon became a major tourist attrac-tion in Sinai – tour operators in Sharm el-Sheikh and Na'ama offer day-trip excur-sions – and village entrepreneurs, headed by Abdullah, charge visitors £E10 to "swim" with her. At the time of writing her attendance has been sporadic, however, so check first to see if she is in the area.

NUWEIBA CITY, PORT & TARABEEN

Taba (70km)

1 ▲ El-Salaam Tourist Village (1km)

2

3

TARABEEN 4

A

5

6

Focus Photo Express

Pharmacy

B   C

Bus Stop

✚ ✉ ☎

NUWEIBA

Bus Stop ★ 7 Tourist Police

D

8

9

10 11 12 13

Recycling Centre

Sand Dunes

14

15

Duty Free Shop

Banks

Bus Station

16

17

Gulf

of

Aqaba

N

0   2 km

ACCOMMODATION

Amun-Yahro Camp	9
Big Duna Camp	10
Café & Camp Sinai	17
City Beach Village	5
Coral Hilton Resort	16
El-Khan	6
El-Salam Tourist Village	1
Habiba	8
Helnan Nuweiba Hotel	7
Nakhil Inn	2
Sababa	3
La Sirene	14
Small Duna Camp	11
Sun Beach Camp	13
Swelm Camp	4
Tropicana Nuweiba	15
Zula Camp	12

RESTAURANTS

Blue Bus	A
Dr Shishkabab	B
El Suezi	C
Han Kang	D

Dahab (70km)

some basic accommodation available at *Café & Camp Sinai* (℡069/520-188, ⓔeid-sinai@sinainet.com.eg; ❶) in the Bedouin village of **Sayadeen**, where Olin the dolphin hangs out.

Tarabeen is the place to find cheap **campgrounds** (❶–❷) à la Dahab, though these tend to come and go, and eventually many of them evolve into hotels. At the time of writing, few were still open, so you may find your choice rather more limited than the list below suggests. If you really want to get away from it all, head south of Nuweiba City to the sand dunes of **Dunas**, where a couple of camps (no electricity) can give you complete peace and quiet. Most camps do not include breakfast in the price and prices can (or rather, they used to) rise dramatically during Israeli holidays.

Amon-Yahro Camp Nuweiba City, the last camp before Dunas ℡069/500-555, ⓕ500-244. Clean camp with raised huts with electricity. ❶–❷
City Beach Village Between Nuweiba City and Tarabeen ℡069/500-307, ⓕ500-146. Basic huts or attractive stone-built rooms with baths and a/c or fans. Restaurant, pool table and beer available. Safe for valuables. ❸–❺
Coral Hilton Resort East of the port ℡069/520-320, ⓕ520-327. Luxury holiday village with two heated pools and lots of sports facilities. Sells catamaran tickets to Aqaba in Jordan. Non-guests can use the beach for £E20. ❽
El-Khan East of the road between Nuweiba City and Tarabeen ℡069/500-319. Bungalows and rooms. Good restaurant, Bedouin handicrafts exhibition and shop. You can arrange camel and jeep safaris here. ❸
El-Salam Tourist Village By the beach north of Tarabeen, reached by a signposted track (1km) from the main road ℡ & ⓕ069/500-440. Nice a/c rooms with baths. Bar, restaurants, two swimming pools and a private beach with a reef. ❻
Habiba Nuweiba City ℡069/500-770, ⓔhabiba@nuweiba.net. Comfortable a/c bungalows and huts. Very good restaurant. Breakfast included. ❺

Helnan Nuweiba Hotel Nuweiba City ℡069/500-402, ⓕ500-407. A/c bungalows with TV, as well as a disco, dive centre and private beach. An adjacent compound (*Red Rocks*) has beach huts sleeping three (❸), with electric lighting but no other facilities. Rents bicycles. ❼
Nakhil Inn North Tarabeen ℡069/500-879, ⓕ500-878, ⓔsurf@sinainet.com.eg. Newish rooms, all with a/c, satellite TV, bath and international telephone. Children under 12 stay free. On-site dive centre. ❻
Sababa Central Tarabeen. One of the nicest camps in the area. ❶–❷
La Sirene Between Nuweiba City and the port ℡069/500-701, ⓕ500-702. Attractive a/c bungalows dotted along a beautiful stretch of beach, with an on-site dive centre. ❻
Small Duna South of Nuweiba City ℡069/500-198. Run by Mgbul Abdalla from the Mzeina tribe. Basic huts and fish restaurant. ❶
Sun Beach Camp South of Nuweiba City ℡069/500-163. Similar setup to *Small Duna* with huts on the beach. ❶
Tropicana Nuweiba Between Nuweiba City and the port ℡069/500-056, ⓕ500-022. Comfortable four-star branch of *Tropicana* chain. ❼

Diving, snorkelling and inland safaris

Aside from the **dolphin** (see box on p.715), Nuweiba has fewer water-related activities to offer than other resorts. There are several shallow **reefs** offshore, the best of which is the **Stone House**, beyond the southern promontory; though fine for **snorkelling**, they're not so great for **diving** unless you're still a novice, so the divers that come here usually travel to Ras Abu Galum (p.714)

Nuweiba dive centres

Dive Point *Coral Hilton Resort* ℡069/520-320, ⓕ520-327. PADI.
Diving Camp Nuweiba *Helnan Nuweiba Hotel* ℡069/500-403, ⓕ500-260, ⓔdcn@sinainet.com.eg. PADI, CMAS.

Emperor Divers *Nakhil Inn* & *Tropicana Nuweiba* ℡069/500-056, ⓕ500-022, ⓔinfo@emperordivers.com. PADI.
Scuba Divers *La Sirene* ℡069/500-701, ⓕ500-702, ⓔscuba@gega.net. SSI.

or sites north of Nuweiba (see p.720). These trips can be arranged by any of the four **dive centres** in Nuweiba: Dive Point has a jeep dive trip to Ras Mamleh for US$60, and a two-day trip to Ras Mamleh and Ras Abu Galum for US$195 including food and four dives. Diving Camp Nuweiba charges US$650 per person for a six-day camel, jeep and boat-diving package and they also rent out surfboards, pedaloes and canoes.

Jeep and camel safaris

Local Bedouin guides offer a wide range of **camel or jeep safaris** into the interior. Their duration depends on your destination and mode of transport; it usually takes two or three times as long by camel as it does by jeep. Most guides charge £E60–100 per person per day (camel journeys are more expensive than jeep), which should include meals and the cost of registering the trip with the police. Drinking water may cost extra and be more expensive the further you get from shops, so it's wise to buy plenty to take along.

The nearest destinations are the palmy oasis of **Ain el-Furtaga** (which can be reached by regular car) and the colourful sandstone canyon of **Wadi Huweiyit** (by camel or 4WD). Slightly further north lies **Moyat el-Wishwashi**, a large rainwater catchment cistern hidden in a canyon between imposing boulders. All these sites can be reached by camel in a day. The most popular day excursion by jeep is to the **Coloured Canyon** (about £E50 per person) via a trail from Ain el-Furtaga. Its name comes from the vivid striations on the steep walls of the canyon, which is sheltered from the wind and eerily silent. Having got there by 4WD, you can hike through the canyon in either direction. Other destinations include **Wadi Ghazala**, with its dunes and acacia groves where gazelles may be glimpsed; **Ain Umm Ahmed**, whose deep torrent fed by snow on the highest peaks of the Sinai shrinks to a stream as the seasons advance; and the oasis of **Ain Khudra**, supposedly the Biblical Hazeroth, where Miriam was stricken with leprosy for criticizing Moses.

A **recommended guide** is Anis Anisan at *El Khan Camp* (T & F 069/500-319), who can arrange trips for small or large groups and will try to include a trip to a Bedouin wedding, camel race or a full moon *zwara* (traditional Bedouin meeting). The all-night **Bedouin weddings** are worth seeing as they provide a rare opportunity for young Bedouin men and women to mingle; the women wear beautiful wedding shawls decorated with sequins that catch the light of the full moon while the men perform dances to impress them. Also recommended is Hassan Hamid at *Sun Beach Camp* (T 069/500-889), who takes groups of up to six people by jeep to Ain Khudra, Ain el-Furtag and the Coloured Canyon (£E50 per person excluding food), and also offers the same itinerary by camel (£E80 per person including food). At *Nakhil Inn* camel trips are available at the same rate, but jeep safaris cost a little less (£E40 per person for 6–8 people). Suliman Hamid (T 069/500-084), Farraj Suliman and Sallah also organize trips from *Zula* camp in Dunas. Other **guides** can be contacted at a kiosk near the highway at Ras al-Shaitun, 10km up the coast, which is the starting point for many excursions (see p.720).

Eating and nightlife

Although Tarabeen has a number of passable beachside cafés and restaurants, Nuweiba City offers the widest choice of **places to eat**. The mall in the bazaar area contains an excellent 24-hour **bakery** and a **supermarket** (daily 8am–4pm & 6–10.30pm), and there are a couple of stalls selling fresh fruit near *Dr Shishkabab*. **Nightlife** boils down to a disco in the *Helnan* (£E15 admission) in Nuweiba City, or playing guitars, drums or backgammon and getting stoned at Tarabeen. There are no **bars** as such; if you want a beer, you'll have to venture to the *Helnan*.

Restaurants

Blue Bus Tarabeen. Camp and restaurant serving reasonable fish, pasta and pizza. Nice position on the beach.

Dr Shishkabab Nuweiba City. Sandwiches (£E5–8) and meat and vegetarian (£E8) dishes in the bazaar area. A favourite with budget travellers. Daily 7am–1am.

El Suezi Near *Dr Shishkabab*, Nuweiba City. Mostly seafood, with dishes from £E810–20.

Habiba Nuweiba City. Well-prepared food at this camp's beachfront buffet restaurant, which gets very busy at lunchtimes serving tourists on day trips from Sharm el-Sheikh and Na'ama. Daily 11am–midnight.

Han Kang Nuweiba City, opposite *Helnan*. Excellent Chinese-Korean restaurant. Daily 11am–2pm & 6–10pm.

Listings

Banks and exchange There's a bank in the *Helnan* (daily except Fri 9am–1pm & 6–9pm). Further afield there are banks in the port area and at the *Hilton*.

Bicycle rental From the *Helnan*.

Doctor There is a doctor on call at the *Helnan*. (The hospital in Nuweiba is poorly equipped, so head for Sharm el-Sheikh if you're seriously ill; see p.697.)

Film and processing Fuji Focus Photo Express in the bazaar area near the bakery (daily 10am–10pm). Sells slide and Advantix film.

Internet Café *Habiba* camp (daily 10am–10pm; £E60 per hour).

Pharmacy Gasser, near *Dr Shishkabab* (daily 10am–10pm; ☎069/500-605).

Police Near the Town Council ☎069/500-242; the tourist police office is beside the parking lot outside the *Helnan*; both are open 24 hours.

Post office North of the mall (daily except Fri 8am–3pm); has EMS.

Telephone office North of the mall (open 24 hours), has international phones which take phonecards. For local calls there is a stall with phones near *Dr Shishkabab* that also sells international newspapers.

Moving on

Although the bus makes a stop outside the *Helnan* in **Nuweiba City**, the main bus stop is in front of the port. **Buses**, with schedules that change from winter to summer and can run late or early, go to Dahab (1hr; £E10), Na'ama Bay (3hr; £E20) and Sharm el-Sheikh (3hr; £E15), leaving daily at 6.30am and 3.30pm; services to Taba depart at 5.30am and 11.30am (1hr; £E10). Of the two buses to **Cairo**, the 10am service (7hr; £E55) runs via St Catherine's Monastery, while the 2.30pm service (£E60) travels further north across the interior of the peninsula via Nekhl. There is sometimes a 5pm Cairo bus, which has a better chance of having seats. There are other, less comfortable buses to Cairo that leave directly from Nuweiba Port; these have no fixed schedule and leave when they're full.

You might find **service taxis** hanging around Tarabeen if business picks up, bound for Taba, Dahab, Sharm el-Sheikh or St Catherine's. Prices are negotiable, so bargain hard.

Boats to Aqaba in Jordan

From Nuweiba's port (☎069/520-216) you can catch a **boat to Aqaba** in Jordan; either an ordinary ferry or the high-speed catamaran. Whichever one you opt for, it's advisable to turn up at the port two hours before the scheduled departure time.

The **ferry** leaves daily at noon (an extra trip is put on in the afternoon during busy periods such as the *Hadj* season) and takes 3–5 hours, depending on the weather. Foreigners must buy a first-class **ticket** (US$38 one-way), and can *only* pay in US dollars. During Ramadan or the *Hadj* season, it's a definite advantage to have access to the first-class lounge, as the boat is crowded with Egyptian workers returning home, or pilgrims bound for Mecca. The ferry also carries **vehicles** (US$100). Tickets are sold inside the port's entrance; you'll need to show your passport to go through the gates, and once inside you're not allowed to leave. Foreigners are assigned an official to guide them through customs and immigration and onto the boat. Don't be surprised if it leaves much later than scheduled. On boarding you'll be asked to hand over your passport, which will be returned at Aqaba customs or, if you go searching for it, on the boat.

The **catamaran** also operates daily, departing at 3pm and taking about an hour. **Tickets** (US$45 one-way) are sold at the *Coral Hilton Resort*, east of the port. The vessel is far more comfortable than the ferry, but it doesn't carry cars. Formalities at Nuweiba's port are identical to those for the ferry.

Jordanian visas (valid for one month) are issued on board the ferry and catamaran, or immediately after disembarkation. Things go more quickly if you've already obtained one in Cairo, but British, Canadian, US, Australian and New Zealand citizens shouldn't have any trouble getting one on the spot. Visa charges vary according to nationality: for Australians it's free, British citizens pay US$35, New Zealanders US$20, US citizens US$48, and Canadians have to cough up US$60. If there are five or more of you travelling, you can ask for a **group visa**, which is free of charge for a minimum four-night stay. It is no longer a problem if your passport shows **evidence of a visit to Israel**, though this will still preclude entry to Syria.

If you just want to visit Petra and return, you can book trips through *Habiba* camp (☎069/500-770, ⓦ www.sinai4you.com).

Between Nuweiba and Taba

The 70km of coastline **between Nuweiba and Taba** (the border crossing into Israel) was for a long while relatively untouched, scattered with just a few appealing low-key resorts. They're still there, but have since been joined by plenty of new holiday villages and a massive new tourist development called **Taba Heights**. Occupancy of these resorts is variable; since September 11, 2001, many have been virtually empty due to the dearth of Israeli visitors and some hotels and camps have closed completely. If the situation in Israel improves they may well pick up again, but in the meantime independent travellers who venture up here will get long stretches of beautiful beaches more or less to themselves. The nicer places are signposted from the highway and may be visible depending on the terrain. **Buses** can drop you at any point along the way if you ask the driver. Just bear in mind that there are no **banks** until Taba, nor anywhere to buy **food** except the resorts' restaurants, which are usually quite pricey.

The first spot worth noting is **MAAGANA BEACH**, whose southern end – called **Lami Beach** – begins 8km from Tarabeen. Though its reefs are quite shallow and unimpressive, the beach itself is nice, with public showers and toilets and striking rock formations. There's a **campground** with huts (❷) and a cafeteria frequented by Bedouin who run **camel and jeep trips** to Wadi Huweiyit (see p.725) and other sites. Two kilometres further on lies the picturesque headland of **RAS AL-SHAITUN** (Devil's Head), where the **reef** drops off sharply to the north, making it ideal for shore diving and snorkelling.

Castle Beach resort (mobile ☎0123 174754; ❸) has **beach bungalows** with verandahs, a good restaurant, and a shop selling souvenirs. There is a "house" reef for divers, and you can **rent camels** and guides for excursions to Moyat el-Wishwashi (see p.718). There are several other camps nearby with a variety of accommodation. *Meditation*, run by Said at the north end is recommended, as is Ayash's camp, simply called *Ras Satan*. Note that **fishing** is forbidden at both sites.

If you are interested in **exploring the desert** in this area, ask Said at *Meditation* about Sallah. He organizes three- to four-day camel trips to places such as Ain Hudra and Wadi Ghazala for £E70 per person per day. Another of Said's friends, Sheikh Mohamed Hoder, can take you to his village near Gebel Gunna in the St Catherine's Protectorate. Otherwise, guides hang out on the beach and at a kiosk beside the highway.

Another 8km up the coast is the more upmarket beach resort of **Bawaki** (☎069/500-470, ℉500-471; ❻-❼), boasting a/c rooms with hot showers and a few triple-bed huts (❺). It has a restaurant, bar and pool, and may soon have a dive centre; **horse-riding** costs £E40 an hour. Breakfast is included in the price of accommodation, but other meals are expensive.

Just beyond Bawaki, there are several more camps at **MAHASH**, which occupies a particularly fine stretch of white sandy beach with a cool breeze even on the hottest summer days. Camps that are still open include *Yasmina* (☎069/500-108), *Ma'ayan* and *Eden*, which has a small supermarket (all around ❶-❷ per person). A bit further north you will find *Ananda* (mobile ☎0122 560462, ✉anandasinai@hotmail.com; ❸-❺) a more upmarket camp with very comfortable, spacious huts, beautiful domed rooms, and a good restaurant. It attracts groups on yoga, Tai Chi, Qi Gong and meditation holidays from Europe.

Basata

The trendiest resort in these parts is **Basata** (Arabic for "Simplicity"), which lies by the headland of Ras el-Burqa. Created by the German-educated Sherif el-Ghamrawy, it is Egypt's most eco-friendly resort, with its own greenhouse, generator, bakery and desalination plant. Organic waste is fed to Basata's donkeys, goats, pigeons and ducks, or used to fertilize the fruit and vegetables. The huts are made entirely from natural materials; empty Baraka bottles are shredded and sent back to the company for recycling, and children can earn treats by collecting cigarette butts from the beach. Alcohol, drugs, television and loud music are forbidden lest they spoil the ambience, which is family-oriented with a New Age ethos. There's a communal vegetarian or fish dinner each night, and guests may help themselves in the kitchen and bakery: write down what you've taken and pay when you leave. You can store your own food in the fridge.

Such is Basata's popularity that it's advisable to **reserve ahead** (☎ & ℉069/500-481; ❹). There are sixteen huts, some of them mud-brick, or you can pitch a tent on the beach. Guests can sign up for **inland safaris** (£E70 per person per day by jeep, £E90 by camel) or rent **snorkelling** gear (£E20), but divers aren't really welcome. You'll either feel at home with Basata's New Agers, or find them unbearably cliquey.

Bir Swair and on to Taba

Five kilometres beyond Basata comes *Aquasun* (☎069/530-391, ℉530-390; ❹), a less eco-conscious mixture of rooms with or without a/c and bathrooms. Though you might be allowed to camp here, it's not encouraged. The quiet sandy beach has a lovely **reef**, and is a very pleasant place to do a PADI open

SINAI | Between Nuweiba and Taba

water course (US$330) with the resident **dive centre**. Guests can also make **jeep or camel trips** to Wadi Quseib and other destinations. A mile or so further on is **Sallyland** (℡069/530-380, ℻530-381; ❺), an a/c two-star hotel of little note except that it has one of the few bars in the area. Others can be found at the newish hotels that are popping up along the coastal road, such as the *Steigenberger, Safari Beach* and *Dolphin Beach Resort*.

Next to *Sallyland* is **BIR SWAIR**, a Bedouin settlement that has spawned a new wave of beach camps. Several camps have closed due to lack of visitors from Israel, but at the time of writing, four were still open; *Antica, Bir Swir, Alexandria* and *Aquarium*. They all have basic but comfortable huts on one of Sinai's nicest beaches, as well as friendly staff and atmosphere (❶–❷). If you stay here, you can visit the Bedouin village behind the camps in the mountains; you will be graciously received with tea and hospitality, but it is recommended you give them a few Egyptian pounds in return and, as ever, always ask before taking photographs.

Travellers with their own car and scuba gear can explore several wonderful **reefs** within walking distance of the highway, notably **El-Muqeibila**, 25km before Taba. Ten kilometres north is another great spot for beach-diving called the **Sun Pool**, which begins with a gentle slope and then plunges as it nears the **Fjord**, a beautiful inlet in the hills by the shore. It's here that one finds *Salima* (mobile ℡0123 704303; ❹), a few rooms with communal showers, behind a nice café overlooking the Fjord.

Pharaoh's Island

Seven kilometres before Taba you'll sight **Pharaoh's Island** (*Gezirat Faraun*), known to Israelis as "Coral Island". Its barren rocks are crowned by the renovated ruins of a **Crusader fort** built in 1115 to levy taxes on Arab merchants while ostensibly protecting pilgrims travelling between Jerusalem and St Catherine's Monastery. The fort was subsequently captured by Salah al-Din but abandoned by the Arabs in 1183. Being only 250m offshore, it can be admired just as well from the mainland if you'd rather not pay £E10 for the boat ride (leaves from the *Salah al-Din* hotel; see below) and another £E10 to tour the fort, which retains several towers and passageways along with a large cistern. There's also an expensive cafeteria that only opens when there are lots of tourists around. Actually, the main reason to come is to dive or snorkel in the maze of **reefs** off the northeastern tip of the island, which used to draw boatloads of visitors from Eilat and Aqaba. As the currents are strong and the reefs labyrinthine, it's best to be accompanied by a guide. This can be arranged at the *Salah al-Din* **hotel** (℡069/530-340, ℻530-343, ✉mstc@ritsec3.com.eg; ❻) by the road on the mainland opposite the island (children under twelve stay free). The price includes breakfast.

Taba – and the border

Right on the border, **TABA** is in the throes of development, with cafés, travel agencies and shops springing up on the Egyptian side. It is still dominated by the deluxe *Hilton Taba Hotel* (℡069/530-140, ℻02/578-7044; ❽) which, despite the problems in Israel, continues to pull in plenty of Israeli visitors, thanks to its casino. It took ten years of bitter negotiations before international arbitration finally returned this disputed border enclave to Egypt in 1989. Hitherto, Israel had claimed that Taba lay outside the jurisdiction of the Camp David Accords, and then demanded US$60 million compensation for its return to Egypt.

A new development just south of Taba covering 4.5 million square metres of land and with 5km of beach, **Taba Heights** has ambitions to change the topography of the Sinai. This huge resort complex is based around a "village", which features a casino, watersports and dive centre, restaurants, bars, cafés, shops, bazaars and a medical clinic. However, the political situation over the border in Israel has scuppered the success of the venture to date, including the use of Taba airport as an alternative to Sharm el-Sheikh and Eilat airports for package tourists from Europe. Only time will tell if the "Red Sea Riviera" will ever take off, but meanwhile among the places already open – which are much cheaper if booked as part of a package in the UK – are the following:

Hyatt Regency Acacia ☎02/402-7178, ℱ401-2833. Huge five-star hotel with 426 rooms with balconies, a/c, disabled rooms, six restaurants and bars, shops, three pools, private beach, kids' club, health centre, tennis courts, shuttle bus and car rental. ❺

Intercontinental ☎02/366-1041, ℱ366-1043. 480 a/c rooms with satellite TV, four restaurants and bars, shops, laundry, health club, tennis and squash, four pools and an aqua-centre. ❽

Sea Star Resort Taba ☎02/582-8141, ℱ581-9977, ℮seastar@link.com.eg. Some 171 rooms a/c rooms with satellite TV, overlooking the Gulf of Aqaba. Plus children's facilities, travel agency and shopping arcade. ❻

7

SINAI | Taba – and the border

Buses from Taba run daily to **Nuweiba** (6.30am, 9am, 2pm & 3pm; £E10), **Dahab** and **Sharm el-Sheikh** (3pm; £E10–15), **Cairo** (8am, 10am & 2pm; £E65–70) and **Suez** (7am; £E30). You can also get an a/c minibus operated by Europcar from the *Hilton* to Nuweiba (£E35) and Dahab (£E70) at 6.30am, 9.30am, 11.30am, 1pm and 5pm, but this is taking business away from local Bedouin taxi drivers who operate **service taxis** (try and aim for per person rates of: Tarabeen £E30, Nuweiba £E30, Dahab £E50, Sharm £E75).

Crossing the border

Despite recent political troubles between Israel and the Palestinians, to date, the **border with Israel** is still open 24 hours, year-round except for during Yom Kippur and Eid el-Adha. (And as almost all transport and businesses in Israel shut down over *shabbat*, you'd be foolish to cross after mid-morning on Friday or any time on Saturday.) The whole process can be very quick – unless you get caught behind a large group. There's an **exit tax** of £E2 payable on leaving Egypt. The Israelis issue free three-month **visas** to EU, US, Australian and New Zealand citizens. Travellers must walk across a no-man's land between the Egyptian and Israeli checkpoints; from the Israeli checkpoint you catch a shared taxi or a #15 bus into Eilat.

Coming from Israel there is an NIS70 exit tax and a £E18 entry tax into Egypt. Visas can be obtained from the Egyptian Embassy in Basel Street, Tel Aviv, or the Eilat consulate on Efroni St (both Mon–Thurs & Sun 9–11am, allowing you to pick up the visa the same day after 2pm). Visas for UK nationals cost NIS75. If you are planning only to go to Nuweiba, Dahab, St Catherine's or Sharm el-Sheikh, you can opt for the fourteen-day **Sinai-only visa** (see p.26), issued for free at the border. Don't listen to any taxi drivers who tell you that you need to take a taxi to the bus stop – it is less than five minutes' walk.

If you need to **change money**, the exchange rate on the Egyptian side, at Bank Misr, is better than the Israeli bank where you pay your exit tax. If this is closed there is another branch nearby at the Taba *Hilton*.

The interior

The **interior of Sinai** is a baking wilderness of jagged rocks, drifting sand and wind-scoured gravel pans, awesome in its desolation. Yet life flourishes around its isolated springs and water holes, or whenever rain falls, renewing the vegetation across vast tracts of semi-desert. Hinterland settlements bestride medieval pilgrimage routes, which the Turks transformed from camel tracks into dirt roads, then the Egyptians and Israelis improved and fought over. Both sides also built and bombed the airstrips which the MFO now use to monitor the Sinai's demilitarized zones.

As a result, the only readily accessible part of the interior is **St Catherine's Monastery**, **Mount Sinai** and **Feiran Oasis**, although some other, smaller oases can be reached by jeep or camel from the Aqaba coast or St Catherine's (see below). That said, most buses from Cairo to Nuweiba traverse the **Plateau of El-Tih** (The Wanderings) via **Nekhl** and the **Mitla Pass**, allowing you to see something of the peninsula's interior. Because of the unexploded ordnance lying around, **independent motoring** is officially restricted outside the St Catherine's–Feiran Oasis area.

Inland safaris and treks

Though most tourists are initially attracted by Sinai's beaches and reefs, even a brief trip into the interior should prove a memorable experience that'll whet your appetite for more.

Inland safaris range from half-day excursions by jeep or camel to fully fledged treks lasting up to two weeks. Travelling **by jeep** is obviously faster and makes little or no demands on your physique, but tends to distance you from the landscape and at the worst can reduce the experience to a mere outing. This is rarely the case if you travel **by camel**, which feels totally in keeping with the terrain. If you've never ridden a camel before, try a half-day excursion before committing yourself to a longer trip. Even a few hours in the saddle can leave you with aches in muscles that you never knew existed, so it is advisable to alternate between walking and riding. It's easy to get the hang of steering: pull firmly and gradually on the nose rope to change direction; a camel should stop if you turn its head to face sideways. Couching the animal – this entails thrusting one's face close to its muzzle and growling "*kkhhurr, kkhhurr*" – is best left to the Bedouin guides. See "Camels" in Basics chapter for advice on posture.

Safaris can be organized at any of the resorts on the Aqaba coast; you'll find details and prices listed under each resort. For those with more time and stamina, a third option is to go **trekking on foot**, which is the most rewarding way to experience remote areas. Treks can be arranged at the village of St Catherine's (where you can also obtain maps for one-day walks in the area from the Protectorate) or at certain points along the roads into the interior – such as the village of Sheikh Hamid – and also through many of the Bedouin who run trips from the coastal resorts. The list of destinations below is by no means all-inclusive, but should give an idea of what's on offer.

Practicalities depend on one's destination and mode of travel. Day excursions from the coast can be made on a Sinai-only visa, but to travel for any longer or explore the High Mountain Region beyond the immediate vicinity of St Catherine's Monastery and Mount Sinai you must have a proper **Egyptian visa**. To climb mountains you must also have a **permit** from the police, which can be obtained by your Bedouin guide. It is illegal – and highly risky – to go trekking without a guide. To help you select destinations and plot routes, buy the 1:250,000 *Sinai Map of Attractions* which is sold at the main resorts on the coast. Other things to **bring** are listed in the "High Mountain Region and Feiran Oasis" section (p.731).

Finally, **respect the landscape** and leave it unspoiled. Bring plastic bags to remove your rubbish when you go and burn any toilet paper left behind. Gathering firewood should be left to your guide, and gardens should never be entered without permission from the owners.

Safari destinations

The following are all shown on the map on p.676.

Ain el-Furtaga 16km from Nuweiba by road. Palmy oasis at the crossroads of trails to the Coloured Canyon, Wadi Ghazala and Ain Khudra Oasis.

Ain Khudra Oasis One of the loveliest oases in Sinai. Reached by hiking from the St Catherine's road, with help from local Bedouin, or from the south by 4WD.

Ain Kid Oasis 14km off the road between Sharm el-Sheikh and Dahab; reached via Wadi Kid, a red-walled canyon where a spring appears in rainy years. The oasis has a fresh-water well.

Ain Umm Ahmed Another beautiful oasis, accessible by 4WD or camel from Bir es-Sawa. Can serve as a base for climbing expeditions to Ras el-Qalb (see below).

Arched Canyon Sinuous gorge that's only accessible on foot; drop-off and pick-up by 4WD from Ain el-Furtaga or Bir es-Sawa.

Bir es-Sawa Small oasis with a spring issuing from a cave, beside the El-Thammed road.

Blue Valley 12km from St Catherine's. Canyon painted blue by a Belgian artist in 1978.

Coloured Canyon 17km north of Ain el-Furtaga. Two rainbow-hued canyons, great for walking or rock-climbing (no water). One of the most popular day trips from Nuweiba.

El-Haduda The biggest sand dune in eastern Sinai, reached from Sheikh Hamid (see below).

Feiran Oasis Over 12,000 palm trees, monastic remains, and access to Jebel Serbal. Wadi Feiran may have been the route taken by the Israelites to reach Mount Sinai.

Forest of Pillars Unique natural phenomenon on the cliffs of Jebel el-Tih, 15km northeast of Serabit el-Khadim (see below). Access by 4WD or camel only; guide essential.

Jebel Sabah A 2280m peak from which Saudi Arabia and mainland Egypt are visible on clear days. Experienced climbers only, with abundant food and water. Permit required.

Jebel Serbal Near Feiran Oasis. One of the loveliest mountains in Sinai, with ruined chapels lining the trail to the summit (2070m). No climbing skills needed, but guide and permit required.

Jebel Umm Shaumar The second-highest peak in Sinai, whose summit (2854m) affords a view of the entire southern horn of the peninsula. Experienced climbers only. Permit required.

Nuwamis Prehistoric site with 5550-year-old graves and inscriptions 6km from Ain Khudra. Reached on foot (2hr 30min) from Sheikh Hamid, by appointment only.

Ras el-Qalb Isolated mountain (999m) associated in Bedouin folklore with the monster Ula. For climbers only; no water. Permit required.

Serabit el-Khadim Hilltop temple overlooking the Gulf of Suez, with ancient turquoise mines and inscriptions in the surrounding valleys. Access by 4WD, then on foot.

Sheikh Hamid Bedouin settlement on the road to St Catherine's, 7km from the Dahab–Nuweiba road. Starting point for walking or camel treks to Ain Khudra, Nuwamis, El-Haduda, and remoter destinations (up to two weeks).

Wadi Ghazala Links Ain el-Furtaga and Ain Khudra Oasis. Acacia groves, dunes and gazelles.

Wadi Huweiyit North of Nuweiba. Colourful canyon with typical desert flora; easy hiking.

Wadi Mandar 40km north of Sharm el-Sheikh. Bedouin camel races occur here on January 1.

Wadi Naseb Running down from Mount Catherine towards Dahab, the verdant upper reaches of the wadi are inhabited by Bedouin. 4WD essential.

St Catherine's Monastery and Mount Sinai

Venerated by Christians, Jews and Muslims as the site of God's revelation of the Ten Commandments, **Mount Sinai** overlooks the valley where Moses is said to have heard the Lord speaking from a burning bush.

The bush is now enshrined in **St Catherine's Monastery**, nestling in a valley at the foot of the Mount, surrounded by high walls and lush gardens. As tourists have followed pilgrims in ever greater numbers the sacred mount has witnessed unseemly quarrels between Bedouin over the shrinking amount of sleeping space for the climbers at the peak, and the monastery itself shows signs of strain. Yet for most travellers it remains a compelling visit, while other seldom visited peaks offer equally magnificent views if you're prepared to make the effort to reach them.

Getting there – and moving on

Despite its isolated location, St Catherine's is one of the most accessible parts of South Sinai. You can visit on **organized tours** from Na'ama Bay, Dahab, Nuweiba, Cairo, Hurghada or Eilat, or you can make your own way by bus, car or service taxi.

The main drawback to **buses** are their variable schedules and the fact that they rarely get to St Catherine's Monastery before it shuts at noon. If you want to visit, you should consider **staying** at least one night. When last heard, you could reach St Catherine's village directly from Cairo (7hr; £E55) on a bus leaving the Abbassiya terminal at 11am via Feiran Oasis. Services from the Aqaba resorts turn off the highway between Dahab and Nuweiba; they start from Sharm el Sheikh's Hay el-Nur bus station (9.30am), Dahab (9.30am), Nuweiba (10.30am) and Taba (10am). If you are coming by bus and just want to climb Mount Sinai, ask to be dropped at the turn-off for the Monastery, 1.5km before St Catherine's village. You could also take a **guided overnight trip** from Dahab or Sharm el-Sheikh which includes a moonlit ascent of Mount Sinai, sleeping at the peak and returning to the monastery in the morning after sunrise. The village's restaurants are pick-up points for people **leaving** by bus; most depart between noon and 1pm, except for the Suez bus, which goes at 6am.

For a group of travellers, another option is to engage a **service taxi** at Suez, Dahab, Nuweiba or Taba and split the cost. Taxis usually run in the morning and afternoon if enough customers are interested, raising their fares once the last bus has left. The same goes for taxis leaving St Catherine's, which run to Dahab and other places, depending on demand.

The Monastery of St Catherine

The **Monastery of St Catherine** is a Greek Orthodox – rather than Coptic – foundation. Its origins date back to 337 AD, when the Byzantine **Empress Helena** ordered the construction of a chapel around the putative **Burning Bush**, already a focus for hermits and pilgrimages. During the sixth century, the site's vulnerability to raiders persuaded Emperor Justinian to finance a fortified enclosure and basilica, and to supply two hundred guards – half of them Greeks or Slavs – from whom the Jebeliya Bedouin claim descent.

Although the Prophet Mohammed is said to have guaranteed the monastery's protection after the Muslim conquest, the number of monks gradually dwindled until the "discovery" of St Catherine's relics (see p.732), which ensured a

726

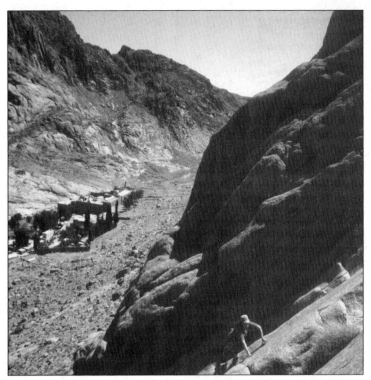
△ Climbing near St Catherine's Monastery

stream of pilgrims and bequests during the period of Crusader domination (1099–1270). Since then, it has had cycles of expansion and decline, on occasion being totally deserted. There are currently 22 monks, most of whom came here from the monasteries of Mount Athos in Greece.

Visiting the monastery

The monastery is **open** to visitors from 9.30am till noon; it's closed on Fridays, Sundays and on all Greek Orthodox holidays. There is no admission charge, but visitors must be modestly dressed.

You enter through a small gate in the northern wall near **Kléber's Tower** (named after the Napoleonic general who ordered its reconstruction) rather than the main portal facing west, which has a funnel that was used for pouring boiling oil onto attackers. Built of granite, 10–15m high and 2–3m thick, St Catherine's **walls** are essentially unchanged since Stephanos Ailisios designed them in the sixth century.

As you emerge from the passage, a right turn takes you past **Moses' Well**, where the then-fugitive from Egypt met Zipporah, one of Jethro's seven daughters, whom he married at the age of forty. Walking the other way and around the corner, you'll see a thorny evergreen bush outgrowing an enclosure. This is the transplanted descendant of the **Burning Bush** whence God spoke to Moses: "Come now therefore, and I will send thee unto Pharaoh, that thou mayest bring forth my people the children of Israel out of Egypt" (Exodus

MONASTERY OF SAINT CATHERINE

Gardens

Hostel

Charnel House

Gardens

N

0   25 m

3:10). Sceptics may be swayed by the fact that it's the only bush of its kind in the entire peninsula, and that all attempts to grow cuttings from it elsewhere have failed. The Bush was moved to its present site when Helena's chapel was built over its roots, behind the apse of St Catherine's church.

A granite basilica, **St Catherine's Church** was erected by Justinian between 542 and 551; the walls and pillars and the cedarwood doors between the narthex and nave are all original. Its twelve pillars – representing the months of the year and hung with icons of the saints venerated during each one – have ornately carved capitals, loaded with symbolism. At the far end, a lavishly carved and gilded iconostasis rises towards a superb mosaic depicting Jesus flanked by Moses and Elijah, with Peter, John and James kneeling below – unfortunately it's roped off and hard to see behind the ornate chandeliers suspended from the coffered, eighteenth-century ceiling. Behind the iconostasis is the **Chapel of the Burning Bush**, only viewable by special dispensation. The narthex displays a selection of the monastery's vast collection of **icons**, running the gamut of Byzantine styles and techniques, from encaustic wax to tempera. The church's **bell** is rung 33 times to rouse the monks before dawn.

Other parts of the monastery are often closed to laypersons. Amongst them are an eleventh-century **mosque**, added to placate Muslim rulers; a **library** of over 3000 manuscripts and 5000 books, surpassed only by the Vatican's; and a **refectory** with Gothic arches and Byzantine murals. You can usually enter the **charnel house**, however, which is heaped with monks' skeletons; the cemetery itself is small, so corpses have to be disinterred after a year and moved into

Mt. Sinai

the ossuary. The cadaver in vestments is Stephanos, a sixth-century guardian of one of the routes to the Mount.

St Catherine's village

While the monastery and Mount Sinai are the focus of interest, most of the facilities of use to tourists are in the **village of St Catherine**, 3km away. Shared taxis provide **transport** between the two, charging £E5. The road terminates at the village's main square, which acts as the bus station. On one side is an arcade containing a **bank** (Mon–Thurs & Sun 8.30am–2pm & 6–9pm), several supermarkets and restaurants; on the other side are the **tourist police** and a small **hospital**. In the vicinity of the mosque are a **post office** and **telephone exchange**.

There's little difference between the **restaurants** (6am–10pm), which do simple meals of chicken and rice or spaghetti Bolognese – the *Panorama* also runs to soup and pizzas. A **bakery** opposite the mosque sells pitta bread.

For **short walks** in the area, guide maps can be purchased from the St Catherine Protectorate visitor centre and Bedouin museum at the end of the road before the monastery If you're planning to do any trekking in the High Mountain Region, ask locals to point you towards **El-Milga**, uphill past the main square of the village, where you'll find **Sheikh Musa** (☏069/771-004 ext 457), the chief of the Bedouin guides who lead expeditions. For more details, see "The High Mountain Region and Feiran Oasis" p.731.

Accommodation

Most people on tours arrive in the early hours to climb Mount Sinai and **catch the sunrise** before descending again. Independent travellers, however, leave their packs in the monastery's storeroom (£E2) and ascend the camel path to **sleep out**. With nighttime temperatures around 10°C during summer and near zero over winter (when frosts and snow aren't uncommon), a sleeping bag is essential if you plan to do this; you can also rent blankets on the summit. Note, however, that with so many people wanting to sleep out, there is often little room at the top, and you may have to sleep further down the mountain at Elijah's Hollow (see below) and complete the journey before sunrise.

If you just need a roof over your head, the best option is the 150-bed **hostel** at the monastery (see below). Most other accommodation is a considerable distance from St Catherine's, though most places arrange transport.

Daniela Village St Catherine's village ⊕ & ℗ 069/470-379. A/c rooms with baths; plus a restaurant, cafeteria and bar (the only one in town). **⑦**

Green Lodge Near the start of the road to Wadi Feiran, 6km from the monastery ⊕ & ℗ 069/470-080. Dorm beds (£E21 per person) and tents with cots. Provides transport to and from the monastery, if you contact their office next to the post office in El-Milga. **❸**

Katherine Plaza Just outside the village ⊕ 069/470-289. Smart four-star place with a/c rooms, restaurant and bar. **⑦**

Monastery Hostel St Catherine's Monastery ⊕ 069/470-350, ℗ 470-343. Beds in dorms (£E35 per person) or triple rooms with showers (£E40 per person); simple meals included. The gates are locked at 10pm. **❹**

Morgana Land Village 200m from *Zeitouna Camp* ⊕ 069/470-404, ℗ 470-331. Dorm beds (£E25), or large rooms with showers; there's also a restaurant. **❻**

Safary Camp and Hotel 500m from the village behind *Katherine Plaza* ⊕ 069/470-085. Double rooms including breakfast or tents. Mattresses and blankets also available. **❷**

St Catherine Tourist Village By the main road, 500m from the monastery ⊕ 069/470-324, ℗ 470-323. The smartest hotel in the area, with comfortable a/c apartments; breakfast and dinner included. **⑦**

Zeitouna Camp Nuweiba road, 5km from the monastery (£E5 per person by taxi) ⊕ 069/470-409. Stone huts or tents with cots, communal showers, and a restaurant. **❷–❻**

Ascending Mount Sinai

Whilst some archeologists question whether **Mount Sinai** was really the Biblical mountain where Moses received the Ten Commandments, it's hard not to agree with John Lloyd Stephens that "among all the stupendous works of Nature, not a place can be selected more fitting for the exhibition of Almighty power". A craggy, sheer-faced massif of grey and red granite "like a vengeful dagger that was dipped in blood many ages ago", its loftiest peak rises 2285m above sea level. Strictly speaking, it's only this that the Bedouin call *Jebel Musa* (Mount Moses), though the name is commonly applied to the whole massif. Some Biblical scholars reckon that Moses proclaimed the Commandments from Ras Safsafa, at the opposite end of the ridge, which overlooks a wide valley where the Israelites could have camped.

Walking to the summit

Neither of the two **routes to the summit** requires a guide, but you shouldn't attempt the walk at night without a torch, and certainly not during winter – accidents are not uncommon.

The longer but easier route is via the switchback **camel path**, starting 50m behind the monastery. It's possible to rent a camel for most of the ascent from Bedouins hanging out at the foot of the mount (£E40; £E15 at midday; 2hr) but it's really worth the effort of walking, which takes around three to four hours. You can stock up on water at the monastery shop before setting off, and there are refreshment stalls along the way. Their prices are higher the higher you go, but it will save you carrying extra weight. Bedouin entrepreneurs at the peak rent out blankets and mattresses for the night (£E5–10).

Beyond the cleft below the summit, the path is joined by the other route, known as the *Sikket Saiyidna Musa* (Path of Our Lord Moses) or **Steps of Repentance**. Hewn by a penitent monk, the 3750 steps make a much steeper ascent from the monastery (1hr 30min), which is hell on the leg muscles. Some of the steps are a metre high.

At present, the only building on the summit is a small **chapel** sited near the cave where God sheltered Moses: "I will put thee in a cleft of the rock, and will cover thee with my hand while I pass over" (Exodus 33:22); the view over scores of arid peaks is breathtaking, particularly at sunset. A bunch of semi-permanent structures have also sprung up, offering weary travellers a place to sleep.

Many people ascend by the camel path and descend by the steps. Start your ascent around 5pm (earlier during winter) to avoid the worst of the heat and arrive in time to watch the spellbinding sunset. With a torch, you could also climb the camel path (but not the steps) by night, though not during winter. Descending the steps you'll enter a depression containing a 500-year-old cypress tree, known as the Plain of Cypresses or **Elijah's Hollow**, where pilgrims pray and sing. Here Elijah heard God's voice (I Kings 19:9–18) and hid from Jezebel, being fed by ravens. One of the two chapels is dedicated to him, the other to his successor, Elisha.

The High Mountain Region and Feiran Oasis

The area around St Catherine's is sometimes termed the **High Mountain Region**, as it contains numerous peaks over 2000 metres (6500 feet). Snow frequently covers the ground in winter and flash floods can occur at any time of the year. The scenery is fantastic, with phalanxes of serrated peaks looming above wadis full of tumbled boulders and wiry fruit trees; springs that are mere trickles in summer turn into waterfalls over winter. This harsh but beguiling land is the stamping ground of the Jebeliya and Aulad Said tribes, some of whom act as guides for **treks** on foot or by camel; with a few exceptions, the terrain is too rough for vehicles, even with 4WD. The trekking season runs from March to October. By law, foreigners are forbidden to embark on such expeditions without a Bedouin guide.

The main **starting point** for treks is the village of **El-Milga** near St Catherine's (see p.729), where Sheikh Musa will get things organized. He'll take your passport, register it with the police, purchase food and water, and work out all the details of the expedition. It costs £E55 per day to rent a Bedouin guide – who are generally helpful and reliable – plus £E30 per day for each camel. Even if you're going to walk, you'll need a camel to carry your baggage; surplus gear can be left at the sheikh's house. The ideal number of trekkers is three to five people; larger groups travel more slowly. You'll need comfortable hiking boots, warm clothes, a sleeping bag, sunglasses, sunscreen, lip alve, bug repellent and toilet paper. Though Sheikh Musa can provide eating utensils, you'll need to bring water purification tablets unless you're willing to drink from springs. To make sense of the landscape, it's essential to have a good map of South Sinai (see p.725) and a compass.

The Bedouin guides who hang out at Sheikh Hamid near the junction with the coastal highway offer **longer camel trips**.

Mount Catherine, Blue Valley and other walks

Egypt's highest peak, **Mount Catherine** (*Jebel Katerina*; 2642m) lies roughly 6km south of Mount Sinai, and can be reached on foot in five to six hours. The path starts behind St Catherine's village and runs up the Wadi el-Leja on Mount Sinai's western flank, past the deserted Convent of the Forty and a Bedouin hamlet. Shortly afterwards the trail forks, the lower path winding off up a rubble-strewn canyon, Shagg Musa, which it eventually quits to ascend Mount Catherine – a straightforward but exhausting climb. On the summit are a chapel with water, a meteorological station and two rooms for pilgrims to stay overnight. The **panoramic view** encompasses most of the peninsula, from Hammam Faroun and the Wilderness of the Wanderings to the Arabian mountains beyond the Gulf of Aqaba.

According to tradition, it was on this peak that priests found the remains of **St Catherine** during the ninth or tenth century. Believers maintain that she was born in 294 AD in Alexandria of a noble family, converted to Christianity and subsequently lambasted Emperor Maxentius for idolatry, confounding fifty philosophers who tried to shake her faith. Following an attempt to break her on a spiked wheel (hence Catherine Wheels), which shattered at her touch, Maxentius had her beheaded; her remains were transported to Sinai by angels. Others doubt that she ever existed and regard her cult as an invention of Western Catholicism, validated by "the land of her supposed sufferings" because of medieval France's demand for "holy oil" and other relics.

If climbing Mount Catherine seems too ambitious, consider visiting the **Blue Valley**, 5km southeast of the intersection of the roads to St Catherine's, Nuweiba and Feiran Oasis. You can do this as a day trip from Dahab or in half a day from St Catherine's village by renting a jeep and guide. The canyon's name owes to a Belgian who in 1978 painted its rocks a deep blue in emulation of the Bulgarian artist Christo, who hung drapes across the Grand Canyon and wrapped up the Reichstag in Berlin.

Longer treks

The two **four-day treks** outlined below give an idea of what can be done; some other possibilities are mentioned under "Feiran Oasis" (see below).

Starting off in **El-Milga**, the **first trek** begins by taking the path through the **Abu Giffa Pass** down into Wadi Tubug, passing walled gardens en route to Wadi Shagg, where you'll find Byzantine ruins and huge boulders. From there you proceed to a grove of olive trees reputedly planted by the founder of the Jebeliya tribe, where you spend the night. The next day you follow the trail through Wadi Gibal and climb one of two peaks offering magnificent views, before descending to Farash Rummana, a camping spot with showers. On the third day you strike north through a canyon to the water holes of Galt al-Azraq, pushing on to camp out at Farsh Umm Sila or Farsh Tuweita. The final day begins with an easy hike down towards Wadi Tinya, before climbing Jebel Abbas Pasha (2383m), named after the paranoid ruler who built a palace there (now in ruins). Having retrieved your gear at the foot of the mountain, you follow a path down through the Zuweitun and Tubug valleys, back to Abu Giffa and El-Milga.

The **second trek** starts at **Abu Sila** village, 3km from El-Milga, where there are some rock inscriptions. You'll probably camp out near the sweetwater spring of Bustan el-Birka. Day two involves descending into Wadi Nugra, below Jebel el-Banat, where you can relax and bathe in pools fed by a twenty-metre-high waterfall. You then press on along the path through Wadi Gharba to the tomb of Sheikh Awad, where the Aulad Gundi tribe holds an annual feast in his honour. Having spent the night here, you have a choice of three routes to Farsh Abu Tuweita, the final night's camping spot. On the fourth day you follow the same route as the final leg of the other hike, visiting Abbas Pasha's ruined palace before returning to El-Milga.

Feiran Oasis

It's thought that the ancient Israelites reached Mount Sinai by the same route that buses coming from the west use today, via Wadi Feiran and Wadi el-Sheikh. Travelling this road in the other direction, you might glimpse the **Tomb of Nabi Salah** near the **Watiyyah Pass**, where Bedouin converge for an annual **moulid** on the Prophet Mohammed's birthday. Celebrants smear themselves with "lucky" tomb dust, sacrifice sheep, race camels, bury their dead and pray, before enacting a rodeo and feasting on roast camel stuffed with lamb. Beyond the pass lies El-Tafra, a small and dismal oasis village.

Roughly 60km from St Catherine's the road passes a huge walled garden marking the start of **FEIRAN OASIS**. A twisting, granite-walled valley of palms and tamarisks, the oasis belongs to all the tribes of the *Tawarah*, who have houses and wells here. (Elsewhere, intertribal law permits the grazing of animals and pitching of tents on any land, but not the cutting of wood or building of stone houses.) Feiran was the earliest Christian stronghold in the Sinai, with its own bishop and **convent**, ruined during the seventh century but now rebuilt. More anciently, this was supposedly the *Rephidim* of the Amalakites, who denied its wells to the thirsty Israelites, causing them to curse Moses until he smote the Rock of Horeb with his staff, and water gushed forth. Refreshed, they joined battle with the Amalakites the next day, inspired by the sight of Moses standing on a hilltop, believed to have been the conical one that the Bedouin call **Jebel el-Tannuh**, with ruined chapels lining the track to its summit (1hr).

Other **hiking** possibilities in the area include **Jebel el-Banat** (1510m), further north, and the highly challenging ascent of **Jebel Serbal** (2070m), south of the oasis. This is approached via the rugged Wadi Aleyat, with a few springs at its upper end. From here you can either follow a goat track up a steep, boulder-strewn ravine called Abu Hamad (5hr), or take the longer but less precipitous *Sikket er-Reshshah* (Path of the Sweaty) to the summit. From the main peak on the ridge there's a wonderful view of the oasis, countless mountains and wadis, with a narrow ledge jutting over a 1200m precipice.

As for finding a guide, make arrangements in El-Milga; a service taxi to Feiran costs £E70 for a group. Although Feiran Oasis lacks any tourist **accommodation**, you could probably camp out somewhere in the palm groves with local consent.

The Wilderness of the Wanderings

Separating the granite peaks of South Sinai from the sandy wastes of the north is a huge tableland of gravel plains and fissured limestone, riven by wadis: the **Wilderness of the Wanderings** (*Badiet el-Tih*). Life exists in this desert thanks to sporadic rainfall between mid-October and mid-April; two or three downpours are enough to send yellow torrents surging down the wadis, rejuvenating the hardy vegetation that supports wildlife and refilling the cisterns that irrigate groves of palms and tamarisks. During Byzantine times, these cisterns sustained dozens of villages along the Sinai–Negev border; nowadays, the largest irrigated gardens are in Wadi Feiran and Wadi el-Arish.

Crossing the Wilderness via Nekhl and the Mitla Pass

The shortest route between Nuweiba and Cairo (470km; 6–7hr) crosses the great Wilderness via Nekhl and the Mitla Pass, more or less following the old *Darb el-Hadi* pilgrimage trail between Suez and Aqaba. By day the heat-hazed plateau is stupefyingly monotonous and it's hard not to fall asleep, which would mean missing a glimpse of several historic locations.

The road from Nuweiba heads north to El-Thammed before cutting west across Wadi el-Arish. **NEKHL**, at the heart of the peninsula, features a **derelict castle** built by Sultan al-Ghuri in 1516 and a big MFO observation post. South of one of the wadi's many tributaries lies **Qalat el-Gundi** (Fortress of the Soldier), a **ruined fort** built by Salah al-Din, which can also be reached by a track from Ras Sudr, on the Gulf of Suez. The fort stands atop a small mountain about one hour's climb from the road; be extremely careful when ascending the path, as there's a sheer drop on either side.

Moving west, the road descends through the 480-metre-high **Mitla Pass**, one of three cleavages in the central plateau. When Ralph Bagnold attempted this route, from Cairo, by Model-T Ford in the early 1920s, it was choked with "yellow undulating cushions" of sand that buried the wire-mesh road laid by the British during World War I. The outcome of three Arab-Israeli conflicts was arguably determined at the Mitla Pass in some of the bloodiest **tank battles** in history. During the war of 1956, an Israeli parachute battalion seized and held the road until the arrival of armoured columns from El-Thammed, which dominated the interior. Having deployed their tanks in expectation of a similar strategy, the Egyptians were wrongfooted during the 1967 War, when the Israelis advanced from Abu Ageila (in the northeast), captured the passes and then systematically annihilated their encircled foes, leaving the roadside littered with charred remains. In the October War of 1973, Egyptian forces failed to exploit their breakthrough along the Bar-Lev Line by rapidly seizing the Mitla and Giddi passes; many blamed their subsequent defeat on the cautiousness of the commander-in-chief, General Ismail.

Northern Sinai

While jagged mountains dominate the gulf coasts and interior of the peninsula, **northern Sinai** is awash with sand: pale dunes rising from coastal salt marshes and lagoons to meet gravel plains and wadis far inland. A succession of water holes along the coastal strip between Egypt and Palestine has made this *Via Maris* the favoured route for trade and invasions since late pharaonic times. However, few of the settlements have ever amounted to much, nor deserve a visit nowadays. Although the palmy beaches at **El-Arish** have spawned a popular domestic holiday resort, most foreigners just zip through on direct buses between Cairo and Tel Aviv or Jerusalem, crossing the border near the divided town of **Rafah**.

There *are* **buses** to El-Arish, although from most places you will still be reliant on **service taxis**. In Cairo buses leave from the Turgoman terminal (6 daily; 5hr; £E12–15); in Ismailiya, you can get a bus at the main terminal (6 daily; 3hr; £E10) or alternatively a service taxi (£E6). Service taxis also leave from the east bank of Qantara (2hr 30min; £E6). There are EgyptAir **flights** from Cairo to El-Arish (Thurs & Sun; 1hr; US$109 one-way) during summer only.

With no north–south transport available to foreigners across the Sinai peninsula, it's only possible to travel **between the Mediterranean and Aqaba coasts** via Cairo and Suez. It's quickest to do this by **service taxi**, changing at Ismailiya and then again at Suez (or vice versa).

Bedouin culture

Although the provision of schools, medical posts and water tanks has enticed many **Bedouin** to forsake nomadic lives, others still roam the desert with their flocks. From the El-Arish road you can glimpse girls in peacock robes with hennaed tresses, aloof boys and men, and black-garbed women in veils or leather masks spangled with coins – the colour of the cross-stitched embroidery on their robes and hoods indicates whether they are married (red) or not (blue). On the horizon you may see black tents pitched in the desert; women are responsible for weaving the goat-hair *beit shaar* ("house of hair") and striking, unloading, packing and erecting them whenever the family moves on. In Bedouin divorces the husband gets the domestic animals while the woman keeps the tent.

The Bedouin are keen observers of the Sinai's furtive **wildlife**. Hares and foxes can lead them to water holes; desert sandgrouse, gazelles and the rare mountain ibex (*bedan*) make good hunting; and flocks must be guarded against the depredations of the jackal (*taaleb*), wolf (*dib*) and hyena (*dhaba*). The last has a mythological counterpart, the *dhabia*, believed to have the power to mesmerize solitary travellers into entering its lair. Other creatures imbued with supernatural significance are the dreaded horned viper, known as *Abu Jenabiya* (Father of Going Sideways), and the fox – personifying wisdom and cunning – who is a favourite character in children's tales.

Plants are even more important to the Bedouin, who feed their camels on a prickly tribulus called *ghraghada*, and make extensive use of **herbal medicine**. Among the many remedies, *rabla* is an aromatic flower made into an essential oil that's used as a general pick-me-up; while *handl* seeds are ground into a paste, cooked in olive oil and applied in a bandage to aching joints, or mixed with garlic to treat snake or scorpion bites.

Storytelling holds a special place in Bedouin culture, where poetic imagery and Koranic rhetoric sprang naturally from the lips of shepherds exposed to a rich oral heritage since childhood. When food is lacking for guests, hospitality can still be rendered in words: "Had I known that you would honour me by walking this way, I should have strewn the path between your house and mine with mint and rose petals!". Although professional reciters of Arabic poetry are now rare, most Bedouin can reel off folk tales, which usually begin with the phrase "*Kan ma kan . . .*" (There was, there was not).

Conversation is the expected reward for Bedouin **hospitality**, which traditionally stretched to three days, each named after a stage in the ritual: *salaam* (greeting), *ta'aam* (eating) and *kelaam* (speaking). Before the rising of the morning star on the fourth day, hosts helped their guests prepare for departure; those who lingered beyond the drying of the dew were as welcome "as the spotted snake". Honour can now be satisfied by three servings of tea or coffee, and it's no longer mandatory to slaughter an animal.

The road from Suez to El-Arish

Roughly 40km along the road to El-Arish from Qantara you pass a signpost-ed turn-off for **PELUSIUM**, a fortress town that guarded Egypt's eastern bor-der for many centuries, named after the Pelusiac branch of the Nile that once watered its surroundings. Many stories are attached to what the Bible records as the "Strength of Egypt". The Assyrian king Sennacherib lost 185,000 sol-diers after swarms of rats ate their bows and quivers, while the army of Cambyses is said to have induced Pelusium's garrison here to surrender with-out a fight by driving cats (the sacred animal of the goddess Bastet) before them. Here the Roman general Pompey was murdered on the orders of Ptolemy XII, and the Crusader king Baldwin I died of ptomaine poisoning after eating putrid fish.

Although the Pelusiac branch of the Nile started to dry up in the third cen-tury AD, the city remained inhabited well into the Islamic era, before being abandoned to the sands. In recent years, moves to bring 400,000 *feddans* of land under cultivation by digging the **Al-Salaam Canal** through this region have spurred a rash of **excavations** to recover archeological evidence before it is destroyed. The sites range from Qantara by the Suez Canal to Tell el-Mahraf near El-Arish. At Pelusium, they have uncovered parts of the pharaonic town and a **Roman amphitheatre** that can now be visited by tourists (daily 9am–5pm) – though since you need a car to get there, and official permission to tour the site, it seldom receives visitors.

Overall, the dominant impression of the road to El-Arish is of a string of **new towns** consisting of huge apartment buildings, and named after hitherto insignificant villages based around wells. Whereas nineteenth-century guide-books compared the merits of vital watering holes like **Bir el-Abd** ("brackish water and some telegraph-men's huts") and **Mazar** ("it is better not to camp near the well on account of the camel ticks"), modern travellers can drive past without a qualm. Between these towns lie ramshackle villages where the local Bedouin are being induced to settle (see box), interspersed by golden **sand dunes** up to 50m high and 200m long.

El-Arish

Originally a Roman garrison town named *Rhinocolorum* ("Noses Cut Off") after the fate of dissidents exiled there, **EL-ARISH** has experienced more than its fair share of invasions. Until recently this was a popular resort for domestic tourists, attracted by the palm-shaded beaches and bracing rollers, but events over the border in Gaza and the souring of relations between Israel and Egypt have meant that many Egyptians are eschewing El-Arish for other Mediterranean resorts such as Alexandria. Westerners have been slow to sam-ple the life here, which is why the tourist poster advertising El-Arish super-imposes their images on the beach.

Whether through cause or effect, El-Arish is more **conservative** than the Aqaba coast resorts, with restrictions on booze and dress and a relatively sub-dued nightlife. However, for a group of travellers into renting a beach apart-ment and providing their own entertainment, El-Arish could be the place. Its most attractive feature is a mass of **palm groves** on the outskirts, which are unfortunately being whittled away as more and more holiday villas are built. Otherwise, the town is undistinguished and rarely makes news – the last instance being in 1995, when two mass graves of Egyptian POWs shot by the

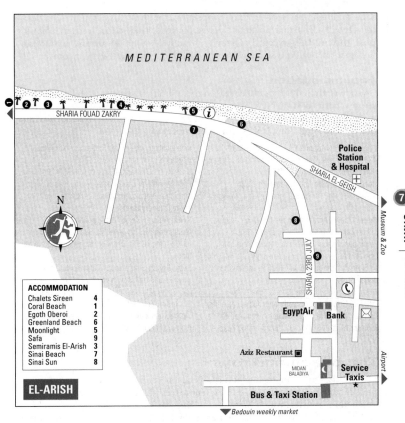

ACCOMMODATION

Chalets Sireen	4
Coral Beach	1
Egoth Oberoi	2
Greenland Beach	6
Moonlight	5
Safa	9
Semiramis El-Arish	3
Sinai Beach	7
Sinai Sun	8

EL-ARISH

Bedouin weekly market

Israelis in the 1967 war were found in the desert, causing outrage in Egypt and shrugs in Israel.

Arrival and accommodation

For details of **buses to El-Arish**, see p.735. From a visitor's standpoint there are really only two streets in town. Arriving from the west, you'll cruise along **Sharia Fouad Zakry** – parallel to the beach – until it swings inland and downhill to become **Sharia 23rd July**. This eventually turns into a **souk** of wooden-shuttered stores that look like a set from a Wild West movie, and terminates in **Midan Baladiya**, with its raucous mosque and fuming **bus station**. Minibuses (50pt) and service taxis (50–75pt) constantly shuttle between the souk and the beach, sparing you the 2–3km walk and stopping at any point along the way.

The **tourist police** (☎068/341-016) and a useless **information** kiosk (daily except Fri 8am–2pm & 7–10pm) can be found on Fouad Zakry, in front of the *Sinai Beach Hotel*; the main **police** station (☎122) and **hospital** (☎068/340-010) lie east along Sharia el-Geish, which forks off inland. There is a better equipped **Mubarak Military Hospital** (☎068/324-018) near the North Sinai Governate in Dahiya. Pharmacy Fouad (Mon–Thurs & Sun

737

8am–midnight, Fri 8am–1.30pm & 5pm) on 23rd July can recommend a doctor. One block further north and across the road, a side street leads to a **bank**, **post office** (daily except Fri 8am–2pm) and 24-hour **telephone exchange** (international calls possible, but no card-phones), and the EgyptAir office.

Accommodation

Outside of the July–September season there shouldn't be any problem **finding somewhere to stay**. New places are springing up every year, mostly aimed at middle-class Egyptians. Only if you're in a group, or you don't feel happy without a/c and mod cons, is it worth booking ahead.

Chalets Sireen Sharia Fouad Zakry ☎068/351-420, ℱ352-519. Four-person chalets with kitchen, dining room and bathroom. ❹

Coral Beach West Abu Mazrout Rd ☎ & ℱ068/331-000. Small (55 rooms) but a five-star rating. ❽

Egoth Oberoi Across from the beach on Sharia Faoud Zakry ☎068/351-321, ℱ352-352. Luxurious singles, doubles and triples; a nightclub, pool and tennis courts for guests only. The only bar in El-Arish. Non-guests pay £E25 to use the beach and pool. ❽

Greenland Beach Hotel Sharia Fouad Zakry ☎068/340-601. Rooms with fans, baths, balconies and sea views. No meals except in summer. ❷

Moonlight ☎068/341-362. An appealing beach-side location, with rooms that are being gradually upgraded to en-suite chalets. ❷

Safa Hotel Sharia 23rd July ☎068/353-798. Friendly staff, and reasonable rooms with showers and fans. Plus a rooftop restaurant with nice views. Laundry service. ❷

Semiramis El-Arish Sharia Fouad Zakry ☎068/344-166, ℱ344-168. Singles and doubles far from the beach, and Med-facing suites for a lot more. ❼

Sinai Beach Sharia Fouad Zakry ☎068/341-713. Doubles and triples with private bathrooms and a/c. Some with balconies overlooking the sea. ❺

Sinai Sun Sharia 23rd July ☎ & ℱ068/341-855. Decent rooms of all sizes with balconies, bathrooms, a/c and TV. ❺

The beach and town

Despite the huts and chalets lining several kilometres of **beach**, you can still find uncrowded stretches shaded by palm trees, the odd wrecked anti-aircraft gun adding a surreal touch. With cooler, rougher seas than the Aqaba coastline, and no reefs, El-Arish's beach is better for bracing dips and idle sunbathing than snorkelling or diving (there's no dive shop, anyway). Foreigners often get invited to join family gatherings and for women travellers this can be a good way to avoid hassle from lecherous youths. Visitors are exhorted to stay off the beach after dark and dress modestly when in town – rules enforced by the police.

For a town of 40,000 inhabitants, El-Arish offers few sights or entertainments. On Thursdays year-round a **Bedouin market** sells fruit, vegetables and Bedouin handicrafts; these are also available in the tourist shops such as Elotaify Leather Shop on Sharia 23rd July (☎068/353-311), or El-Khalily Bazaar (☎068/350-359) on Sharia Fouad Zakry. The only other attraction is a **Sinai Heritage Museum**, just beyond the UN post along the coastal road to Rafah (catch a bus or service taxi). The museum is open daily (summer 8am–8pm; winter 10am–6pm; £E4) and contains mostly stuffed wildlife and Bedouin handicrafts. Next door is a small and miserable **zoo** (same hours).

Eating and nightlife

The cheapest places to eat are the *fuul* and *taamiya* joints around Midan Baladiya or the simple **restaurants** along Sharia 23rd July. *Aziz* (below the *El-Salaam Hotel*, beside Midan Baladiya) and *Sammar* (300m up the road) do good *kofta* and salad, or chicken and chips, at reasonable rates. On the beach try

Basata, past the *Oberoi*, for good seafood. The only places serving **alcohol** are the lifeless disco on Sharia 23rd July – where you're limited to Stella – and the well-stocked but expensive bar in the *Egoth Oberoi*. If desperate for hard liquor, you could take a service taxi to the border and use the duty-free shop outside Egyptian customs and immigration.

Smoking *sheeshas* over backgammon in a café on Sharia 23rd July is usually all that El-Arish can offer in the way of **nightlife** – and that's an exclusively male pursuit. Otherwise, in the summer the *Oberoi* has a **nightclub** with live music and bellydancers, while the outdoor restaurant opposite the *Egoth Oberoi*, an unmarked dance hall on the beach nearer town, and the disco on Sharia 23rd July occasionally host **entertainers**.

Moving on

Direct buses run from the terminal beside Midan Baladiya to Cairo (£E12–15) and Ismailiya (£E10); minibus **service taxis** also run to **Ismailiya** (£E6) and **Cairo** (£E12). Over summer, there are **flights** to Cairo (Thurs & Sun) and an international service to Sharjah in the United Arab Emirates – contact EgyptAir for details.

The Red Sea Coast
and Eastern Desert

8

The Red Sea Coast and Eastern Desert

For 1250 kilometres, from Suez to the Sudanese border, turquoise waves lap rocky headlands and windswept beaches along a coastline separated from the Nile Valley by the arid hills and mountains of the **Eastern Desert**. Like Sinai, the region's infertility and sparse population belie its mineral wealth and strategic location, and there are further points in common in the wildlife, Bedouin nomads and long monastic tradition. Tourism, too, is developing along similar lines, with holiday villages proliferating along the coast, and dive boats ranging down the Red Sea as far south as Eritrea.

An entrepôt since ancient times, the **Red Sea Coast** was once a microcosm of half the world, as Muslim pilgrims from as far away as Central Asia sailed to Arabia from its ports. Though piracy and slaving ceased towards the end of the nineteenth century, smuggling still drew adventurers like Henri de Monfried long after the Suez Canal had sapped the vitality of the Red Sea ports. Decades later, the coastline assumed new significance with the discovery of oil, and its vulnerability to Israeli commando raids, which led to large areas being mined – one reason why tourism didn't arrive until the 1980s.

While Cairenes appreciate the beaches at **Ain Sukhna**, south of Suez, the real lure consists of fabulous island reefs off the coast of **Hurghada** – a booming, bold and brash resort town – and the less touristic settlements of **Port Safaga**, **El-Quseir** and **Mersa Alam** to the south. So far the international airport at Mersa Alam has only opened to charter flights from Italy, so access to points further south remains difficult unless you have your own transport. This looks likely to change in the near future, with the coast south of Quseir now subject to ambitious development plans. Dive companies are also establishing supply bases for their dive boats along the southern coastline, opening up "virgin" reefs in the south to divers, whose only option previously was a long journey by sea from Hurghada or Sharm el-Sheikh in the Sinai.

> **Warning – minefields**
>
> Large areas of Red Sea coastline and many wadis are still mined. Any area with barbed-wire fencing (however rusty) is suspect. Don't wander off public beaches or into the desert without a guide.

Crossing the Eastern Desert by bus gives little idea of its spectacular highlands. Apparently devoid of life, the granite ranges and limestone wadis harbour ancient rock art, temples and quarries, gazelles and ibexes, and Bedouin. While you might not have the inclination, stamina or money for long excursions into the interior, thousands of Copts visit the **Red Sea monasteries**, and further south, amid the **Red Sea Mountains**, truckloads of dervishes converge on **Wadi Humaysara** for the **Moulid of Al-Shazli**. If totally off-the-beaten-track destinations are your thing, the Eastern Desert has more to offer than at first appears.

The Red Sea monasteries

Secreted amidst the arid Red Sea Hills, Egypt's oldest **monasteries** – dedicated to **St Paul** and **St Anthony** – trace their origins back to the infancy of Christian monasticism, observing rituals that have scarcely changed over sixteen centuries. This tangible link with the primitive church gives them a special resonance for believers, but you don't have to be religious to appreciate their tranquil atmosphere and imposing setting – there's also scope for **birdwatching** in the vicinity.

Transport, tours and accommodation

Though neither monastery is directly accessible by public transport, they can still be reached in several ways. The main thing to realize is that a quick visit is impossible, and no one is in any hurry once you get there. If you feel OK about travelling with devout believers, it's best to join the **pilgrim tours** arranged from Cairo by the Coptic Patriarchate (22 Sharia Ramses, Abbassiya; ☎02/960-025), or the YMCA (27 Sharia al-Gumhorriya; ☎02/917-360), which dispatches a minibus every week. Coptic churches in Luxor or Hurghada may also run tours on a non-profit basis.

Commercial **tours** from Cairo or Hurghada are another possibility. Misr Travel does a tour from Hurghada to both monasteries for US$55 per person; other agencies charge less but visit only one. Depending on your starting point and number, it could work out cheaper to negotiate a **rented taxi**. A six- to eight-hour excursion should cost about £E240 from Suez, £E340 from Cairo or Hurghada; taxis from Za'farana might do a four- to five-hour jaunt for around £E150. An overnight stay for your driver adds at least £E80 more. To drive from one monastery to the other (82km) takes about ninety minutes.

The cheapest method combines **public transport, hitching and walking**. Outside of the hottest months, this shouldn't be dangerous providing you bring ample water and minimal luggage. Any bus from Cairo or Suez to Hurghada can drop you at the **turn-off for St Paul's Monastery**, 26km south of Za'farana, which is recognizable by its plastic-roofed bus shelter. Young Copts alight here, confident of hitching to the monastery, 13km uphill, for there's a fair amount of traffic along the well-paved road. If pilgrims visiting both sites don't offer you a lift, St Anthony's Monastery can be approached via service taxis running between Beni Suef and Za'farana. From the signposted turn-off 33km west of Za'farana, it's 15km uphill to the monastery, with some hitching prospects.

To stay at the monasteries' guesthouses, you *must* have written permission from their "residence" in Cairo (26 El-Kenisa El Morcosia St Kolet Beck, Cairo; ☎02/590 6025) and the offer is usually open only to religious groups.

Accommodation is in basic dormitories or family rooms. Both monasteries have cafeterias and St Paul's has a shop selling basic foodstuffs, but you might want to bring extra food. Respect conventions on dress and behaviour; smoking and drinking alcohol are forbidden.

The Monastery of St Anthony

West of Za'farana a wide valley cleaves the Galala Plateau and sets the road on course for the Nile, 168km away. Called **Wadi Arraba**, its name derives from the carts that once delivered provisions to the monastery, though legend attributes it to the pharaoh's chariots that pursued the Israelites towards the Red Sea. Turning off the road and south into the hills, it's possible to spot the monastery sited beneath a dramatic ridge of cliffs. If in doubt, ask anyone you encounter to point you towards *Deir Amba Antonyos* or *Deir Qaddis Antwan*.

Lofty walls with an interior catwalk surround the **Monastery of St Anthony** (daily 9am–5pm; closed during Lent and Christmas), whose lanes of two-storey dwellings, churches, mills and gardens of vines, olive and palms basically amount to a village. Formerly self-sufficient, the community now gets most of its food either from Cairo or its own farm near Beni Suef, but remains dependent on water from its **spring**, where Arab legend has it that Miriam, sister of Moses, bathed during the Exodus.

An English-speaking monk will give you a partial tour, which varies with each visitor; don't expect to see everything, especially as the monastery is currently undergoing a major restoration program. Highlights include the **keep**, a soot-blackened **bakery** and a **library** of over 1700 manuscripts. The oldest of the five **churches** is dedicated to the monastery's namesake, who may be buried underneath it. Be sure not to miss the wall paintings, some of which date back to the seventh century and have recently been restored to their former glory after years hidden under layers of soot, candle grease and grime. During Lent (when the gates are locked and deliveries are winched over the walls), monks celebrate the liturgy in the twelve-domed Church of St Luke, dating from 1776. Some of the churches date from the early twentieth century and there are new ones under construction. There is a well-stocked bookshop which sells books about the monastery and the Coptic Church in Egypt, as well as souvenirs and postcards. There's a small **museum** detailing the monastery's history next to the bookshop.

All of these buildings are recent compared to the monastery's foundation, shortly after Anthony's death in 356. A sojourn by St John the Short (whose body was later stolen by other monks) is all that's recorded of its early **history**, but an influx of refugees from Wadi Natrun, and then Melkite monks, occurred during the sixth and seventh centuries. Subsequently pillaged by Bedouin and razed by Nasr al-Dawla, the monastery was restored during the twelfth century by Coptic monks, from whose ranks several Ethiopian bishops were elected. After a murderous revolt by the monastery servants, it was reoccupied by Coptic, Syrian and Ethiopian monks.

Headed by Bishop Yustus, today's 65 permanent brethren are university graduates and ex-professionals – not unlike the kind of people drawn to monasticism in the fourth century AD. A typical day at the monastery begins at 4am, with two hours of prayer and hymns followed by communion and mass, all before breakfast. Despite the hard conditions, applications are increasing every year. The expansion of the guesthouse to accommodate up to three hundred people is a fair indication of the resurgence of interest in asceticism amongst Egypt's Coptic community.

St Anthony's Cave

Early morning or late afternoon is the best time to ascend to **St Anthony's Cave** (*maghara*), 2km from, and 276m above, the monastery (bring water). After passing a sculpture of St Anthony carved into the mountain rock, you'll face 1200 steps (45min) up to the cave, but the stunning views from 680m above the Red Sea reward your effort. Technicolour wadis and massifs spill down into the azure gulf, with Sinai's mountains rising beyond. The cave where Anthony spent his last 25 years contains medieval graffiti and modern *tilbas*: scraps of paper bearing supplications inscribed with "Remember, Lord, your servant", which pilgrims stick into cracks in the rock. **Birdlife** – hoopoes, desert larks, ravens, blue rock thrushes and pied wagtails – is surprisingly abundant, and you might glimpse shy **gazelles** in the early morning.

The Monastery of St Paul

The **Monastery of St Paul** (daily 9am–5pm; closed during Lent and Christmas) has always been overshadowed by St Anthony's. Its titular founder (not to be confused with the apostle Paul) was only sixteen and an orphan when he fled Alexandria to escape Emperor Decius' persecutions, making him the earliest known hermit. Shortly before his death in 348, Paul was visited by Anthony and begged him to bring the robe of Pope Athanasius, for Paul to be buried in. Anthony departed to fetch this, but on the way back had a vision of Paul's soul being carried up to heaven by angels, and arrived to find him dead. While Anthony was wondering what to do, two lions appeared and dug a grave for the body, so Anthony shrouded it in the robe and took Paul's tunic of palm leaves as a gift for the pope, who subsequently wore it at Christmas, Epiphany and Easter.

The monastery (called *Deir Amba Bula* or *Deir Mari Bolus*) was a form of posthumous homage by Paul's followers: its turreted walls are built around the cave where he lived for decades. To a large extent, its fortunes have followed those of its more prestigious neighbour. In 1484 all its monks were slain by the Bedouin, who occupied St Paul's for eighty years; rebuilt by Patriarch Gabriel VII, it was again destroyed near the end of the sixteenth century.

The monastery is much smaller than St Anthony's and a little more primitive looking. It boasts four churches, but the **Church of St Paul** is its spiritual centre, a cave-church housing the remains of the Saint. The walls of the church are painted with murals generally thought to be inferior to those of St Anthony's, though they have been well preserved. A monk will show you round the chapels and identify their icons: notice the angel of the furnace with Shadrach, Meshach and Abednego, and the ostrich eggs hung from the ceiling – a symbol of the Resurrection. The southern sanctuary of the larger **Church of St Michael** contains a gilded icon of the head of John the Baptist on a dish. When Bedouin raided the monastery, its monks retreated into the five-storey **keep**, supplied with spring water by a hidden canal. Nowadays this is not enough to sustain the seventy-odd monks and their guests, so water is brought in from outside.

There is a small shop selling supplies and a reasonably priced cafeteria just outside the monastery grounds.

Ain Sukhna

Without private transport or a firm intention to visit the Red Sea monasteries (see p.745), it's hardly worth stopping **between Suez and Hurghada**. Except for the first 30km, chewed up by tanks in the October War, the road is excellent and most of the blind corners are over by the time drivers get accustomed to speeding on the straights. Traffic is increasing, however, particularly trucks and heavy vehicles, because of major construction projects on the coast road. Heading south past the oil refineries and natural gas refineries that appear at intervals all along the coast, you'll see parched highlands rising inland. The **Jebel Ataqa** is the northernmost range in the Eastern Desert and an old Bedouin smuggling route by which hashish reached Cairo; Henri de Monfried sent his cargo this way.

Roughly 50km south of Suez, a series of beaches and coves marks **AIN SUKHNA**, where middle-class Cairenes come to picnic at weekends. Ain Sukhna's name derives from the **hot springs** (35°C) that originate in the Jebel Ataqa, but it's the sea that attracts people. Dark patches offshore indicate **coral reefs**, ideal for snorkelling, while rusty barbed-wire fences delineate areas sown with land mines (beneath the cliffs). There are paying **beaches** (£E20–40) in front of the *Ain Sukhna* and *Mena Oasis* hotels; other stretches are free. If you haven't got a car, Ain Sukhna is best reached by **bus from Suez** (see p.659; last bus back 3.30pm). The *Mena Oasis* (☎062/290-850, ℱ290-855; half-board only ❻), *Ain Sukhna* (☎062/328-488 or 325-562; under renovation at the time of writing), *Hilton* (☎062/290-500, ℱ290-515; ❾), *Palmera* (☎062/410-816 or 410-817; ❽) and *Portrait* (☎062/325-560, ℱ332-003; ❽) attract plenty of affluent Egyptians, but hardly any foreigners. There are several resorts in the area offering luxury accommodation, water sports and, in some cases, golf. *El Ein Bay* (☎02/347 0827, ℱ332 0672) even claims to offer its guests skiing on a simulated piste.

Further south, the beach at **Za'farana** has only one resort, the rather grandly named *Solymar Royal Za'farana Resort* (☎012/228 8399; half-board only ❽) approximately 10km south of the town. The *Sahara Inn* motel, a little further on near the petrol station is a cheaper option (no phone; no a/c; ❹). Its cafeteria is a good place to ask around for a lift to the monasteries. The next bus stop is at **Ras Gharib**, an oil town buffeted year-round by winds, whose sole hotel, the *Al-Alem*, is usually full – the place holds little appeal, except perhaps to mountaineers interested in tackling **Jebel Gharib** (1757m). Another 145km and you are in Hurghada.

Approximately 22km north of Hurghada lies the vast tourist resort of **El Gouna** (ⓦelgouna.com). Built on a series of islands linked by purpose-built bridges and canals, it covers 17,000 square kilometres of land, supports 10,000 staff and includes a hospital, four power plants, an international airport and several factories. There are currently twelve hotels ranging from three- to five-star (with a further three scheduled to open by 2004), several clusters of private villas and two shopping centres. The infrastructure includes a brewery that makes Sakkara and Löwenbrau beer, a winery producing Obelisque wine, a cheese factory making mozzarella, a state-of-the-art hospital and decompression chamber (ⓉT065/549-709), plus an eighteen-hole golf course and a casino. The main shopping centre has an open-air cinema, cafés, restaurants, bars (including the popular *Peanuts Bar* in the *Three Corners Rihana Resort*), nightclubs, a school, banks, two travel agencies, a museum, aquarium and a post office. There are dive centres attached to four of the hotels, and if you're still looking for something to do you can fly a microlight plane, go horse-riding, go-karting, and play tennis or squash.

The resort is already popular with the Egyptian jetset, although its Western clientele is not quite as well-heeled, being more of a middle-class package-tour crowd who pay far less than the prices below by booking in advance. Most people stay closeted within the resort's confines; however, options have been expanded by a new bus service which runs throughout the day between El Gouna, Hurghada and Safaga (see p.753). For those staying in Hurghada, there is also a free shuttle bus to the resort's disco (£E20; 10pm), the *Palladium*.

El Gouna's **accommodation** comprises properties with typical three-, four- and five-star amenities; most also offer parasailing, water skiing and windsurfing facilities. The following is a selection of places that are operational.

LTI Paradisio Beach and Golf Hotel ⓉT065/547-934, Ⓕ547-933, ⒺParadisi@link.net.eg. a/c rooms with bath, balcony or patio overlooking sea, pool or gardens, and satellite TV. Has three swimming pools, a dive centre and a 2km stretch of beach. ❽

Sheraton Miramar Ⓣ Ⓕ065/545-606, Ⓕ545-608, Ⓔsheraton.miramar.egypt @sheraton.com. Built on nine islands. 338 a/c rooms with terrace and sea view, satellite TV. Two main swimming pools, three for children, with a kids' club and a dive centre. ❽

Steigenberger Golf Resort ⓉT065/ 580-140, Ⓕ 580-149, Ⓔsteilgelg@link.net. German-owned plush hotel with 18-hole championship golf course. ❽

Three Corners Rihana Inn ⓉT065/580-025, Ⓕ 580-030, Ⓔrihana @hurghada.ie.eg.com. a/c studios for two or four people, terraces with pool or mountain views, kitchenettes and satellite TV and access to the beach and better facilities of its four-star sister hotel *Three Corners Rihana Resort* (all-inclusive only; ❽). Home to the recommended Colona Dive Centre. Half-board ❻

Hurghada (Ghardaka)

In the course of two decades, **HURGHADA** has been transformed from a humble fishing village of a few hundred souls into a booming town of over 50,000 people, drawn here from all over Egypt by the lure of making money. This phenomenal growth is almost entirely due to **tourism**, which accounts for 95 percent of the local economy. Yet it's worth taking Hurghada's claims to be a seaside resort with a handful of salt. Unlike Sinai, where soft sand and gorgeous reefs are within easy reach and women can bathe unhassled, Hurghada's public beaches are distant or uninviting, while the best marine life is far offshore.

Russians in Hurghada

The biggest change to Hurghada's tourist scene in the last decade has been the huge influx of **Russian tourists**. Their arrival in 1994 was greeted with joy by hoteliers, whose occupancy rates had plummeted following terrorist attacks in the Nile Valley. Being inured to chaos and inflation back home, the Russians weren't deterred by bomb scares and proved to be big spenders. Sadly, however, cultural differences soon soured things, and many locals now regard them all as drunks or whores, while the Russians reciprocate with equal contempt. It doesn't help that some of the Russians really *are* mafiosi or prostitutes (the latter ply their trade in hotels as "personal assistants") – nor that the Egyptians are irked by the lack of a common language in which to hustle them.

Aside from filling up the holiday villages and replacing Egyptian belly dancers in the Oriental shows, the Russians haven't had much effect on other tourists – except perhaps for the bewilderment when they first see restaurant signs advertising *borsch* and *pelmeni*. As the Russians generally have little interest in diving (being content to make descents in the *Sindbad Submarine* (see p.762), or snorkelling trips to Giftun Island), not much mixing occurs, except in Hurghada's discos.

If you're not into diving or discos, it's hard to find much to like about Hurghada – though you have to admire its commercial gusto; many of the townsfolk come from Luxor's west bank, where tourism has been a way of life for generations.

While package tourists laze in their resorts, independent travellers often feel hard done by. Paying for boat trips and private beaches is unavoidable if you're to enjoy Hurghada's assets, and although conditions for diving, windsurfing and deep-sea fishing are great, the **cost** is high, with real bargains limited to accommodation. Nor will you save much by self-catering; everything in the shops is more expensive than in Cairo or the Nile Valley. As tour groups come all year round, there's no "off" season for holiday villages, whose **peak times** are the European Christmas and Easter holidays and the Russian vacation period of August and September. Low-budget hotels are most in demand over winter, when templed-out backpackers flood in from the Nile Valley en route to Sinai.

The town itself is a hotchpotch of utilitarian structures, garish hotels and gaudy boutiques, but Egyptians love its wide boulevards and sea breezes, the spaciousness and "Benetton ambience". Nowhere else in Egypt are shorts de rigueur and holiday romances so easy. Russians (see box above) have added fresh spice to its already cosmopolitan mix of Italians, Germans, French, Brits, Aussies and Japanese, whose hedonistic potential is grasped by Saudi princes, for whom Hurghada is only two hours away by private jet. For Westerners, however, the chief lure remains underwater: a score of coral islands and reefs within a few hours' reach by boat, and many other amazing dive sites that can be visited on liveaboards.

Approaches to Hurghada

Hurghada's multiplicity of **approaches** makes it more accessible than its location suggests. Vehicles go flat out along the coastal highway and desert roads, but a full tank of petrol is essential – there are few pumps en route. Some of the desert routes from the Nile are described in more detail later on.

•**From Alexandria** Superjet (£E75) and Upper Egypt (£E60) both have one bus daily to Hurghada. EgyptAir fly on Monday and Friday (8.45am; 2hr; US$176) via Sharm el-Sheikh.

Sharm el-Sheikh

HURGHADA

Red Sea Security Dept.
& Passport Office

Police

See 'Ed-Dahar' map for detail

SHERATON ROAD

El-Fanadir Reef

El-Fanous

Islands not to scale

Um Gamar Island

EATING & DRINKING

The Chill	I
El-Masri	A
Far East Korea	H
Felfela's	J
Joker	B
KFC	K
McDonald's	E
Omar Inn	D
Papa's Beach	G
Pizza Hut	K
Spaghetti	F
Taco	C

Careless Reef

Big Giftun

See inset map
for detail

Un-Exploded
Landmines

HADABA

Small Giftun

Abu Ramada

Magawish
Island

Abu Ramada
Gota

RED SEA

Duty Free Shop

Duty Free Shop

EgyptAir

Tourist
Police

TARIQ AL-KURA

HURGHADA-SAFAGA ROAD

Arabia Beach Hotel & Iberotel Arabella

Airport

Duty Free

Police

Fedex

El Gouna Bus Office

Thomas
Cook

New
Harbour

Old Harbour

Helnan Regina

Redcon
Mall

0   500 m

SIGALA

ACCOMMODATION

Andrea's	6
Arabia Beach	3
Conrad International	21
El-Samaka Beach Club	14
Giftun Village	11
Hilton Hurghada Plaza	2
Hilton Resort	17
Hurghada Holiday Resort	7
Iberotel Arabella	4
Inter-Continental	16
Jasmin Village	20
La Perla	9
Magawish Village	18
Marine Sports Club	13
Marriott Beach Resort	8
Princess Club	15
Sindbad Beach Resort	10
Sofitel	19
Youth Hostel	1, 12

Abu Hashish
Cave

0   2 km

5 km) & El Gouna (22 km)

N

Golden Five (3km), Coral Beach (6km) & Port Safaga

• **From Cairo** Twice daily EgyptAir **flights** (1hr; US$131 one-way) need to be booked several days ahead over winter. There are eight **buses** daily from the Ahmed Helmi or Turgoman terminals, three of them a/c Superjets (£E47–60), the others Upper Egypt (£E45). During the morning there may also be **service taxis** to Hurghada (£E40) from the Ahmed Helmi depot. The newly established El Gouna Transport Company (contact via its main agent in Cairo – Egyptian Star Travel Agency, Bab el Looq, El Falaki Square ℡02/796 2660 ℱ796 3737) also runs comfortable a/c buses (7am, 1.30pm, 4.30pm, 11.30pm, 12.30am; 6hr; £E35 or £E50 including snacks and drinks) from Cairo's El-Munib bus station. You can also catch these buses half an hour later at Nasser City Station (Autostrad Road).

• **From Suez** The 410km from Suez can be covered in five hours by **service taxi** (£E25 per person), or at a less perilous speed by one of the eleven daily **buses** (£E21–26), most with a/c. Service taxis and buses leave from the new bus station on the Cairo–Ismailiya road. You should be able to get a bus ticket at an hour's notice, except during the *Hadj* season or major Muslim festivals.

• **From Sinai** Early bookings are advised for EgyptAir **flights** to Hurghada from Sharm el-Sheikh (currently departing Mon 3.30am, Sat 6am & Sun 11.30pm; US$96). At time of writing the airport at St Catherine's Monastery was closed except to private charter planes, but may reopen to scheduled flights. The ninety-minute journey across the Gulf of Suez by **catamaran** (Mon, Thurs & Sat departures at 6pm; US$40/£E200, cars from £E150) can be booked in Sharm el-Sheikh through Travco (daily 9am–3pm & 6–9pm; ℡069/660-764) or Thomas Cook (daily 9am–2pm & 6–10pm; ℡069/601-808). Schedules vary according to the season and the catamaran is liable to be out of service for several weeks in the late spring for maintenance. Catamaran bookings can also be made through Travco in Cairo (daily 9am–5pm; ℡02/342-0488), Luxor (daily 9am–3pm & 7–9pm; ℡095/383-811, ℱ374-845) and Aswan (daily 9am–3pm & 7–9pm; ℡097/316-393, ℱ315-960) – a more reliable option for advance bookings than the hotels in any of these cities. You can also buy tickets directly at the port of Sharm el-Sheikh one hour before departure, but this is risky if you have a vehicle, as space is limited.

• **From the Nile Valley** During winter, hordes of travellers come from Luxor, whence there are five daily **buses** (4hr; £E20) via Qena and Safaga. Alternatively, take a service taxi to Qena, walk to another taxi depot and catch a service taxi to Hurghada (4hr; £E15). There are three buses a day from Aswan (8hr; £E35) via Safaga, while a few service taxis cross the desert between Beni Suef and Za'farana, or Qift and El-Quseir. Weekly EgyptAir **flights** from Luxor (Wed 12.30am; US$55) should be booked as far ahead as possible.

Orientation

Despite being even more strung out than Alexandria – stretching for nearly 40km down the coast – Hurghada is easily divisible into three zones, whose salient features are mapped on p.751 and p.755.

The **town** proper – known as **Ed-Dahar** (The Harbour) – is separated from the coast by a barren rock massif, so you rarely glimpse the sea. Coming in from the north, its evolution is apparent as administrative buildings give way to hotels, shops and a maze of mud-brick homes at the feet of Jebel el-Afish. Its amorphous downtown embraces the bazaar quarter and – typical of any thriving tourist centre – a flourishing and nameless strip of restaurants, shops and hotels, which spreads from Sharia Abdel Aziz Mustafa to the Aquarium on the

Corniche and whose main landmark is The Market mall alongside the vast *Empire Hotel*. The main thoroughfare is **Tariq en-Nasr** (aka El-Nasre Way), whose busiest stretch lies between the bus station and Ed-Dahar's telephone exchange (known as the *centraal*), which acts as a terminus for local public transport. It's widely known as the Sheraton road, in reference to the now-closed landmark hotel that has long been its northernmost feature.

From Ed-Dahar, two main roads run 2–4km south to **Sigala** (pronounced "Si-*gala*"), which contains the modern **port** of Hurghada and a mass of restaurants and hotels, squeezed in wherever the terrain allows. Beyond Sigala is nothing but desert and an endless array of **coastal holiday villages** and construction sites, linked by slip roads to the Hurghada–Safaga road and dignified with the name of **New Hurghada**. This extends more than 30km south of Sigala and there seems nothing to prevent it from ultimately linking up with the resorts at Port Safaga, 50km south.

Arrival, information and transport

Most independent travellers **arrive** in Ed-Dahar at the **bus station** on the southern edge of the downtown area, though coming by Superjet from Cairo you'll be dropped at a nondescript terminal 1km north, while El Gouna buses stop at their main office on Tariq en-Nasr. Service taxis from the Nile Valley wind up at the **taxi station** midway between the two bus terminals. If you're planning to stay in Ed-Dahar it should be possible to find accommodation within walking distance of any of these points.

People arriving by boat from Sinai will disembark at the **harbour** in Sigala, whence you could walk to several mid-range places or catch a bus (£E2) or taxi (£E10) to anywhere in Ed-Dahar. Each day, forty to fifty planeloads of package tourists fly into the **airport** off the Hurghada–Safaga road, and are whisked off to their resorts in buses; arriving independently, a taxi into Ed-Dahar costs £E15.

Hurghada's **tourist information** centre is located in New Hurghada (daily except Fri 8am–2pm; ☏065/444-420) next to the tourist police and opposite the faded *Grand Hotel*. Large and airy with helpful staff, it is let down by a lack of practical information. Much more useful is the *Hurghada Bulletin*, a monthly magazine with a listings guide and area map, or the *Holiday Map* of Hurghada and El Gouna; both are free and can be found in bars, cafés and most budget hotels. Also worth checking out is *Red Sea Today*, a pocket-sized guide published quarterly by *Egypt Today*. It costs £E5 in tourist bazaars, but you might be able to pick up a free copy from its distributors, DHL, based in the Redcon Mall in Sigala. In all events, private agencies, hotels, dive centres and individual fixers are ready to help – for a price. Any information you get given in Hurghada must be regarded as suspect, since everyone earns a commission on whatever you can be induced to spend. Normally this doesn't matter too much – except when they steer you towards dodgy, potentially lethal dive centres.

Transport

While **walking** is fine for getting around Ed-Dahar, transport is needed to reach Sigala or anywhere further south. The cheapest and easiest option is the El-Gouna Transport Company's new 24-hour **bus services** between El Gouna, Hurghada and Safaga. Routes are colour-coded, with distinctive bus stops dotted all over Hurghada: the yellow route runs from El Gouna to Hurghada's Coral Beach Resort (£E5); the orange route circles Sigala (£E2); the blue route circles Ed-Dahar (£E2); and the brown route runs from Hurghada to Safaga (£E10). A one-way ticket from El-Gouna to Safaga via Hurghada is £E15.

Weekly **passes** allowing unlimited travel in El Gouna (US$5), Hurghada (US$5), between El Gouna and Hurghada or Hurghada and Safaga (US$10) are available from the company's main office on Tariq En-Nasr (☎065/541-561); El-Central, Ed-Dahar Square (mobile ☎0122 399113); Tourist Central, opposite the *Helnan Regina Hotel* (mobile ☎0123 517700), El-Corniche, at the end of Stadium Street beside El Safwa Mosque (mobile ☎0122 324567); and Dr. Hamid, Gohar district, Hafer el Batten (mobile ☎0122 283371).

Alternatively, **private minibuses** run from the *centraal* telephone exchange on Tariq en-Nasr out to Sigala (50pt), the *Sheraton* (£E1) and as far south as the *Jasmin Village* (£E5), 21km away. Running constantly from 7am to 11pm, they can be flagged down at any point along their route.

Finally, **private taxis** are happy to oblige. Expect to pay £E5–10 for a ride in Ed-Dahar, £E10 to Sigala or the *Sheraton*, and £E15–30 to the holiday villages further out. Should you need to rent a taxi for the day, £E150 seems to be the going rate for five or six hours, assuming that you don't drive any further than Safaga.

Some tourists scoot around on rented **bicycles**, which are OK in town if you can handle the traffic but are not up to trips down the coastal highway, which is often buffeted by strong crosswinds. There are lots of places around the bazaar renting bikes for £E10–20 per day; rates in Sigala are slightly higher. To really get around you could rent a car. Local **car rental** firms have lower prices than the bigger firms, but their deals tend to be for limited mileage on poorly maintained cars.

If you're into posing, El Hanouf, in front of the *Marriott*, and Seti First Travel near *Shedwan Golden Beach* both rent out US Hummers, with drivers, for expeditions into the desert.

Accommodation

Much of Hurghada consists of **hotels and holiday villages**; at the time of writing there were well over 100 in operation and more in the pipeline, with demand so high at the moment that most villages boast occupancy rates of 80–100 percent. If you're coming here to go diving, a **package deal** makes a lot of sense, as you'll pay a lot less than you would otherwise, and without having to do the rounds of the dive centres. Hotels catering to **independent travellers** get £E150 commission for each guest that they sign up for a diving course, so signing on should also improve your chances of negotiating a cut in the price of a room. As in Luxor and Aswan, many hotels make more on trips and commissions than on rooms – not to mention other transactions, at places with a liberal attitude toward selling dope.

Arriving at Hurghada's bus station, you'll be mobbed by **hotel touts**, offering free transport to their establishment (see above). In the event of having to pay, £E10 is absolute tops for a ride to anywhere in Ed-Dahar – which is where most visitors stay if they haven't booked into a holiday village beyond Sigala. If you're bent on locating a hotel on your own, bear in mind that few streets are named, and there are effectively no house numbers.

Hurghada's **water** has to be piped from the Nile Valley, so depending on your hotel's storage capacity it might be cut off for several hours a day. Profligate consumption means that others go short. Foreigners who live here strongly advise against **drinking** the tap water, and if the thought of cooling down by standing under the sprinklers that irrigate the gardens of some of the upmarket hotels appeals, think again: this (barely) treated sewage is largely responsible for the stink that blankets the town.

The map contains the following text elements.

ED-DAHAR

Passport Office (3km), New Youth Hostel (5km) & Suez (376km)

Misr Travel & Karnak Egypt Air Service

SHARIA AL-BAHR

Superjet Terminal

Papas II

Tourist Police

Esh-Shahid Mosque

Aquarium

Public Hospital

Police

SHARIA SOLIMAN MAZHAR

Service Taxis

SHARIA ABDEL AZIZ MUSTAFA

Government Store

SHARIA SHEIKH SEBAK

Banks

TOURIST BAZAAR

Jebel el-Afish

RED SEA

Public Beach

CORNICHE

Ed Dahar Mosque

MARKET

TARIQ EN-NASR

SHARIA AL-ARABI

Garage

Bus Station

El-Saffa Hospital

Main El Gouma Bus Station Office

Bank

Stop-Shop Laundry

0   200 m

Sigala & Holiday Villages

Sigala & New Hurghada Holiday Villages

EATING & DRINKING

Baron	K
Bella Riviera	F
Chez Pascal	C
Egyptian Corner	E
Juke Box Pub	B
Peanuts Bar	D
Red Sea	J
Riviera	G
Tarboush	H
1001 Nights	A
Young Kang	I

ACCOMMODATION

Andalous	10	Palm Beach	1
California	7	Ramsis	14
El-Arosa	11	Sand Beach	9
El-Gezirah	4	Sea Horse	2
Empire	5	Sea View	13
Four Seasons	8	Shedwan Golden Beach	3
Happy House	15	Sosna	16
Happy Land	12	Village	6
Hilton Hurghada Plaza	17		

THE RED SEA COAST AND EASTERN DESERT | Hurghada

8

Downtown Ed-Dahar

Most **low-budget places** cluster around the bazaar or the "strip" of cafés and shops between Sharia Abdel Aziz Mustafa and the Corniche, while **mid-range hotels** are sited off the main road near the Esh-Shahid Mosque and the coastal **holiday villages**. Many new places are currently being built on the lower slopes of Jebel el-Afish, above the public beach; the first ones to open will have large rooms and sea views, but will also suffer from the continuing noisy construction work all around. An attempt has been made to upgrade the public beach meaning a higher entrance fee, but also cafés, bazaars, palm trees and umbrellas which have gone some way to improve the atmosphere.

In general hotels are not as "luxury" as they claim to be – a good guide would be to subtract one star from their rating. All of the following places are marked on the map on p.755. Breakfast is included unless stated otherwise, and you can generally count on hot water.

Andalous on the strip ⓣ & ⓕ065/548-602. Smart, carpeted A/C rooms with bedside lamps and private bathrooms. A good option in this price bracket. ❸

California at the Corniche end of the strip ⓣ065/549-101, ⓕ548-414. Cleanish, cramped rooms, a few with baths; exotic murals adorn the corridors. You can sleep on the roof, which has a sea view. Breakfast is not included. ❷

El-Arosa on the Corniche ⓣ & ⓕ065/549-190. Nice, clean a/c rooms with baths; indoor pool and music bar. Guests can use the beach at the pricier *Geisum Village*, across the road. ❺

El-Gezirah off Sharia al-Bahr ⓣ065/547-785, ⓕ548-708. Spacious a/crooms with TV. Bar, restaurant and disco, plus free use of the pool and disco at the *Sand Beach*. Mainly German, Dutch and Russian groups. ❹

Empire off the Corniche ⓣ065/549-200/9, ⓕ549-212. Large hotel that dominates the skyline, with comfortable a/c en-suite rooms, satellite TV, balconies with seaviews. Sister hotel to the *Village* on the Corniche round the corner giving guests access to the beach. ❻

Four Seasons near the Corniche end of the strip ⓣ065/549-882, ⓕ 545-456. Simple, cleanish rooms, all with baths, balconies and partial sea views; a few have a/c (£E5 extra). ❷

Happy House between the Ed-Dahar Mosque and Tariq en-Nasr ⓣ065/549-420. Small, friendly low-budget hotel of long standing. Clean rooms with fans; one hot shower; kitchen. ❷

Happy Land Sharia Sheikh Sebak ⓣ065/547-373. Slightly shabby rooms with private bathrooms, in the noisy, funky tourist bazaar. Mostly used by Egyptians. On the downside, it's within earshot of a mosque. ❶

Hilton Hurghada Plaza south end of the Corniche ⓣ065/549-745, ⓕ547-597, ⓔhrghitw@hilton.com. Massive but isolated five-star resort perched on an arid hill between Ed-Dahar and Sigala; if you're going to stay here, you probably won't bother leaving its confines. ❽

Palm Beach Corniche Road 6km north of Hurghada ⓣ065/549-840, ⓕ549-849. Large out-of-town resort with 295 double rooms and evening folklore shows. ❻

Ramsis Sharia al-Arabi ⓣ065/549-632. Nice, colourful, clean hotel with shared or private bathrooms. ❸

Sand Beach on the Corniche ⓣ065/547-992, ⓕ547-822. Four-star holiday village with three pools, a beach and diving centre, billiards room and disco. Popular with Russians. ❼

Sea Horse off Sharia al-Bahr ⓣ065/547-016, ⓕ548-704. Comfortable rooms with private baths, a/c and balconies. Restaurant, bar, disco, billiards, backyard pool and sea views. Residents can use this beach, or the one at the *New Sea Horse*, by *Hilton Hurghada Plaza*. ❻

Sea View on the Corniche ⓣ 065/545-959, ⓕ546-779. Modern, clean a/c rooms with baths and satellite TV. Tiny swimming pool. Seafood restaurant and free use of the *Sea Horse*'s beach for residents. ❺

Shedwan Golden Beach on the Corniche ⓣ065/547-007, ⓕ548-045. Three-star holiday village with flash reception and plainer a/c rooms. Pool, beach, diving and windsurfing centres. Rates are negotiable but they start pretty high. ❽

Sosna off Tariq en-Nasr ⓣ065/546-647. Clean, carpeted rooms with fans and bedside lamps; private bathrooms are optional. Mainly used by Egyptians. Liberal atmosphere. ❷

Village on the Corniche ⓣ065/547-816, ⓕ547-514. Similar in standard to its sister hotel, *Empire*, with comfortable a/c en-suite rooms with satellite TV, some with seaviews. Less opulent than some of the other hotels on this part of the beach, but the rooms are a shade cheaper. ❻

Sigala

Despite a relatively good choice of places to eat, it's hard to see why anyone would want to stay in Sigala, since there are better mid-range options in Ed-Dahar and ritzier holiday villages in New Hurghada. However, if everywhere else is full, you could try the following options:

Andrea's ☎065/442-251, ⓕ443-388. Pleasant Italian-owned place home to Bubbles dive centre. a/c rooms, three bars and a swimming pool. Popular with young English, German and French tourists. ❺
Arabia Beach 800m north of the harbour ☎065/548-790, ⓕ548-796. Mega-holiday village that's seen better days. a/c bungalows with TV, fridge, phone and piped music; the place also boasts three pools and a marina. Popular with Gulf Arabs. ❻

Helnan Regina ☎065/442-275, ⓕ442-276, ⓔgmhrs@helnan.com. On the beach with three pools and a jetty. a/c rooms and chalets. ❼
Hurghada Holiday Resort ☎065/445-086, ⓕ445-085. A beachfront five-star complex that was formerly a *Holiday Inn.* ❽
Iberotel Arabella next to the *Arabia* ☎065/545-086, ⓕ545-090. One of the nicer-looking four-star hotels with a/c rooms, satellite TV, two large pools, extensive sports facilities and *Kalaboush* disco. Half-board only. ❼

New Hurghada

New Hurghada is the name given to the array of **holiday villages** that have proliferated for 30km south along the coast. Each is fully self-contained, so there's zero incentive to leave the complex. Though geared to package tourists, they'll take independent travellers if trade is slack. Where the clientele is mainly from certain countries, you could feel at a disadvantage if you don't speak the right language. Unless stated otherwise, all of the holiday villages are a/c, with a pool, diving centre, beach and disco. We've calculated their distance from town starting from the bus station in Ed-Dahar; for their exact locations, see the map on p.751.

Conrad International 22km ☎065/443-250, ⓕ443-258. Five-star resort with an onyx-floored lobby and an outsized pool; largely German guests but also English. Half-board only. ❼
Coral Beach 28km ☎065/447-162, ⓕ443-577. Stylish rooms with satellite TV and minibar. Two pools, tennis, squash and horse-riding. Large beach with reef. Mainly caters to Italians. ❼
El-Samaka Beach Club 16km ☎065/446-532, ⓕ442-227. Bungalows (a/c midday and evenings only) with a small beach and windsurfing lagoon; no pool. Used by German and Russian tour groups. ❻
Giftun Village 14km ☎065/442-665, ⓕ442-666, ⓔgiftunbeachresort.com Spanish-style chalets with fans, fronting a good beach and windsurfing lagoon. Half-board. ❻
Golden Five 25km ☎065/446-306. A Vegas-style combination of theme park and hotel complex, with daily shows, a replica Egyptian village and a cable-car lift. ❽
Hilton Resort 17km ☎065/442-116, ⓕ442-113. The same five-star rating as its sister *Plaza* hotel (see p.756), but a bit older and less pricey. ❽
Inter-Continental 17km ☎065/446-911, ⓕ446-910. Opulent complex of rooms with bath, bidet, satellite TV and sea views. Very large marina. One of the better luxury hotels, and home to the only casino in town. ❽
Jasmin Village 21km ☎065/446-442, ⓕ446-441. Simple rooms with satellite TV and fridge. Small beach with reef and windsurfing lagoons. Playground, zoo and aviary. Disabled access. Half-board only. ❻

La Perla 2km south of Sigala ☎065/443-281, ⓕ443-280. Pleasant enough and well-managed; has a/c rooms and a swimming pool. A bit far from the action and the beach, but still popular with English groups. ❼
Magawish Village 19km ☎065/442-621, ⓕ442-759, ⓔmagawish@link.com.eg. A former Club Med, with a big beach and good sports facilities, especially for windsurfing, plus a children's playground. Rates include half-board. ❻
Marine Sports Club 16km ☎065/444-861, ⓕ442-646. Good value a/c rooms with TV and fridge. Popular with Egyptian sport fishermen. ❻
Marriott Beach Resort 11km ☎065/446-950, ⓕ446-970. Five-star complex with a large pool and a small sandy beach; marina and residents-only disco. ❼
Princess Club 16km ☎065/443-100, ⓕ443-109. Spacious a/c rooms with satellite TV and fridge; the three-storey villas are equipped for self-catering. Small pool and windsurfing lagoon. Also rents villas across the road on a timeshare basis. ❻
Sindbad Beach Resort 13km ☎065/443-261, ⓕ443-267. Efficiently managed and family-oriented four-star complex with lots of nightlife and a huge waterchute on the beach. Home to *Sindbad Submarine* (see p.762). Half-board only. ❼
Sofitel 20km ☎065/447-261, ⓕ442-260. Classy pseudo-Moorish complex and the best hotel in town. Ex-Club Med management means events like themed dinners for which guests are encouraged to dress up. Used by Hayes & Jarvis tours. Half-board only. ❽

Camping, hostelling and apartment rental

With rooms so cheap in Ed-Dahar, saving money hardly justifies the hassle of **camping**. Would-be campers must first obtain a permission request form from the small security office behind the Esh-Shahid Mosque and then take it together with their passport to another office over the road (both open daily 8am–noon & 8–9pm). You then have to find a vacant spot to the north of Ed-Dahar or south of Sigala – which is easier said than done. All in all, it's not worth the effort.

A more feasible option is Hurghada's new **youth hostel** (℡065/544-989; £E28), on the beach 5km north of town, next to the Marine Institute of Oceanic Studies. It has separate blocks for men and women, containing spartan rooms with fans, bunk beds, and clean shared bathrooms. Non-HI members pay £E1 extra. Hurghada's other hostel (℡065/441-173; £E28) is a bit run down, but is more centrally located, opposite the *Royal Palace Hotel*. Both hostels have a three-day maximum stay.

If you're hoping to stay and work, **renting an apartment** may make sense. Most rentals are arranged through diving centres or hotels that employ foreigners, but if you put the word out, prospective landlords – and housemates – should come forward. It's also worth checking the classifieds in the *Hurghada Bulletin* or enquiring at the so-called Ceramic Building, behind the telephone *centraal* next to McDonald's, where many studios are rented out to foreigners. Expect to pay about £E800–1500 per month (excluding bills) for a two-bedroom apartment near the beach, and about £E700 in the amorphous Amal district, between Ed-Dahar and Sigala.

Diving

It is **diving** that really put Hurghada on the map, kick-starting tourism along the Red Sea Coast. The marine life here is broadly similar to that found off the coast of Sinai (see p.686), but the topography favours island corals over coastal reefs, with sharks, giant moray eels and manta rays in its deeper, rougher waters. The tide here is more dramatic, too; it drops by up to five metres from high to low tide, compared with a one-metre change in Sinai. Many islands have sheer-sided coral *ergs* (pillars) that are fantastic for drift diving, while others are shallow enough for snorkelling. There are about ten islands within day-trip range and over a score of sites that can be visited on extended dive safaris, or "live-aboards".

As ever, dive **tourism** is its own worst enemy: once-rich coral and shellfish grounds have been devastated by the sheer weight of visitors. Hurghada welcomes hordes of tourists each week, and waiting for them are over one thousand tour boats. Anchoring on the reefs does irreparable damage to fragile corals, and those closest to the port have been hit especially hard. To help combat the problem, the Underwater National Parks of the Red Sea and Protected Islands (aka Marine Park) has introduced a new daily "environmental tax" for all divers (£E3.50), snorkellers (£E2) and those on diving safaris (£E5), the proceeds of which are being ploughed back into Red Sea environmental projects, as well as clean-air projects in Cairo; this is in addition to the standard per-person charge of US$2 per day to dive the Giftun Islands and the nearby reefs (itself scheduled to rise to US$5) and US$5 per day for sites further south such as Brothers and Zabargad. The problem is also being tackled by **HEPCA** (Hurghada Environmental Protection and Conservation Association), which is installing mooring buoys and trying to raise ecological awareness – but few of the local dive centres show much interest. Tourists can help by favouring centres that belong to HEPCA and display a certificate from the Egyptian

Underwater Sports Federation – and by refusing to buy marine curios like clamshells (whose export is illegal) or stuffed sharks. You can make a difference simply by minimizing your own impact upon the dive sites you visit; don't touch the coral, don't remove anything from the sea bed, don't throw anything in the water (particularly cigarette butts) and don't feed the fish.

Your life may depend on **choosing the right diving centre**; some outfits are dangerously incompetent (leaving divers marooned at sea or lost in caves, in two notorious cases). Always check that the instructor is qualified, with valid ID and insurance, not merely photocopies. Many are freelancers who frequently change jobs, so even the best centres sometimes get bad ones (or vice versa). As a rule of thumb, however, it is safer to dive with the large outfits attached to holiday villages than with backstreet operators taking clients sent by low-budget hotels (whose recommendations *can't* be trusted). In 2001, the Red Sea Association for Water Sports and Diving was formed to increase levels of safety and service and to help market Hurghada as a dive destination; however, as membership is compulsory for all diving operators, it is not a sign of reputability.

The **courses** on offer are similar to those in Sinai. A four- or five-day PADI open-water course costs US$280–350 (including certificate); a two-day advanced course US$190–250. Beginners can expect to pay US$45–60 for an introductory lecture followed by two supervised dives. Scuba equipment is included in the price of courses, but otherwise costs extra (US$20–25); rent-

Diving centres

Of the hundred-odd centres currently operating, the only ones subject to any serious monitoring are those affiliated to HEPCA, which are listed below. We'd advise that in general you should **avoid** those that aren't members. Should you have specific marine safety or environmental concerns, contact HEPCA at PO Box 144, Hurghada, Red Sea, Egypt (℡065/446-674, ℻445-035, ℮hepca@hepca.org), or alternatively advise the EEAA Ranger (℡065/549-632), in front of the public beach in Ed-Dahar.

Aquanaut *Shedwan Golden Beach* ℡065/549-891, ℻547-045.

Aquarius Diving Club *Marriott Beach Resort* ℡065/446-950, ℻446-970, ℮hurghada@aquarius-redsea.com.

Blue Heaven Holidays *Hilton Plaza* ℡ & ℻444-738, mobile ℡010/104-1692, ℮info@blueheavenholidays.com, ⓦwww.blueheavenholidays.com.

Blue Paradise Diving Centre Ed-Dahar ℡ & ℻065/544-354.

Blue Water Dive Resort *Arabia Beach* T065/548-790, F544-888, Einfo@blue-water-dive.com.

Colona *Magawish Village* T065/408-840, F448-045. Also in El Gouna at the *Three Corners Rihana Inn.*

Deep Blue Diving Centre *Calimera Golden Beach Hotel*, 10km north of Hurghada ℡065/544-972, ℻446-724.

Dive In Red Sea *Melia Pharaoh*, New Hurghada ℡065/446-720, ℻446-724.

Easy Divers Academy El Gouna ℡ & ℻065/580-027, ℮easydive@intouch.com.

Easy Divers *Village*, Ed-Dahar ℡065/548-816, ℻443-300, ℮easydive@intouch.com.

El-Samaka *El-Samaka Beach Club* ℡065/446-532, ℻446-530.

Emperor Divers *Hilton Resort* ℡ & ℻065/444-854, ℮info.hurghada@emperordivers.com.

James & Mac *Giftun Village* ℡065/442-665, ℻442-300, ℮info@james-mac.com.

Jasmin Diving Center *Jasmin Village* ℡065/446-455, ℻446-441, ℮jasmindc@intouch.com.

Orca Tariq en-Nasr, between Ed-Dahar and Sigala ℡ & ℻065/548-048.

Sharm En-Naga Diving Centre Sharm En-Naga ℡ & ℻065/548-721.

Sub Aqua *Sofitel* ℡ & ℻065/442-473.

Subex downtown, off the Corniche ℡065/548-651, ℻547-471.

ing snorkelling gear is far cheaper (£E10–20 a day). The average rate for a day's **boat diving** is US$40–60; most trips comprise two dives, separated by lunch which, unlike in Sinai, is normally included in the price. Never hand over cash to someone on the street who promises to arrange a trip; book through a dive centre, where you can complain if things go wrong. You'll need to sign up and surrender your passport the night before; check that details are correctly noted, since wrongly documented passengers may be prevented from boarding. See the box on p.759 for a list of reliable dive centres

While day trips can be arranged at short notice through any centre, it is better to book trips on **liveaboards**, or safari boats, in advance, from home (see Basics chapter for tour operators that deal with these). Individuals who try to get one in Hurghada risk missing out, unless they can muster a group of at least six people to make it worth the captain's effort. Occasionally *Lady M* operated by Tarek El Sahwi of Hita Divers (4 Yakout El-Hamawi St, Seouf, Alexandria ℡03/502-1119, ℻502-2696, ℮info@ladym.com) will take single divers on its safari trips if there is room. Blue Heaven Holidays based at the *Hilton Plaza* (mobile ℡0101 041692, ℻065/445-300, ⓦwww.blueheavenholidays.com) can arrange liveaboards and diving packages taking you further south to sites in Safaga, Mersa Alam, Wadi Gimal and Wadi Lahami.

As in Sinai, the cost depends on the amenities of the vessel and the quality of the meals provided; expect to pay at least US$100 per person per day, though unlike Sinai, extra diving fees (see p.758) can also add US$15–70 to the final cost depending on where you dive. Most safaris last for one or two weeks, though boats going as far south as Yemen or Eritrea can be at sea for a month. Even if you're only going to Giftun Island, check that the boat has a radio, life-jackets, oxygen and a first-aid kit. Many of the dive boats lack **safety equipment**. In case of emergency, there are decompression chambers in the Hurghada area: in El-Gouna's hospital (see p.749); the Mubarak Naval Hyperbaric & Emergency Medical Centre, near the harbour (℡065/549-525 or 544-195; and at *Magawish Village* (see p.757). Thirty or so dive centres are members of the Diving Emergency Centre Organization (DECO; ℡065/443-156, ℮info@deco-international.com); those diving with them are encouraged to pay US$6 for three weeks' cover which includes free use of the decompression chambers in El-Gouna or Mersa Alam.

Dive sites

Most sites within day-trip range are to the east and northeast of Hurghada. Inexperienced divers should be wary of the northerly reefs, where the currents are strongest. While many liveaboards go as far north as Ras Mohammed, sites to the south are regarded as more prestigious. Though mentioned under other towns, they are only accessible on liveaboards via Hurghada, or through the dive centres that are appearing further south. All of the following are within day-trip range unless stated otherwise.

Abu Hashish Cave An underwater cave in the reef, once used as a dope smugglers' cache.

Abu Ramada Three coral blocks covered in psychedelic-hued soft corals, off Giftun Island.

Abu Ramada Gota (aka "Aquarium") Amazing standing *ergs* and 1500-year-old stony corals, with a profusion of bannerfish, sweetlips and spotted groupers.

Brothers Several *ergs* emerging from the deeps of the Red Sea, 80km northeast of El-Quseir. A

popular liveaboard destination, now open only to boats with permits.

Careless Reef (aka "Carless") Two *ergs* atop a plateau with a phenomenal drop-off and gardens of table and soft corals, frequented by whitetip reef sharks and moray eels, which can be seen fighting and mating by day. Only accessible in calm weather.

Dolphin House A horseshoe-shaped reef 15km south of Mersa Alam, widely used by dolphins as a nursery for their young. HEPCA has recently installed buoys to prevent boats from entering. An excellent site for snorkelling.

El-Fanadir Beautiful reef slope and large table corals, to the north of Sigala.

El-Fanous Coral gardens just off Big Giftun Island, good for snorkelling as well as diving.

Giftun Island Most of the reefs on the Big and Small Giftun have been ruined by years of dive boats dropping their anchors onto the coral, and are now mostly visited by craft packed with snorkellers (£E30–40 per person; £E90 overnight; equipment and food included). If you want to go on one of the less crowded boats used by divers, it'll cost £E5–10 extra. Two notable spots are the Small Giftun Drift (fine reef wall and lovely fan corals), and the Stone Beach on the northeast side of Big Giftun.

Shadwan Island Halfway to Sinai, so out of day-trip range. Sheer walls and deep trenches attract reef and oceanic sharks. Its lighthouse was of keen interest to de Monfried, when he navigated his boat through these waters in the early 1920s, with 600 kilos of hashish secreted in its hold.

Thistlegorm Sunken cargo ship full of jeeps, found by Jacques Cousteau off the coast of Sinai. A very popular four-day safari, albeit cheaper to make from Sharm el-Sheikh (see p.685).

Umm Gamar Island Sheer walls and caves, brilliant for drift diving. You can swim through a cave filled with thousands of silvery glassfish.

Zabargad Island Deep reefs teeming with oceanic fish and corals, 100km southeast of Berenice. A favourite long-haul destination, only open to boats with permits.

Beaches, pools and watersports

While diving is the main activity (see above), Hurghada presents itself as an all-round beach resort – a claim that's quite true, but not so great as it sounds. After years of grousing by visitors, the **public beach** in Sigala (daily 8am–sunset; £E3.50) has at last been transformed, from a wasteland where no foreign tourist would be seen dead, to a tidy shore with sunshades and a small refreshment kiosk. However, to sunbathe without unwanted attention, there's really no alternative but to go for **private beaches**. In Ed-Dahar, the *Shedwan Golden Beach*, *Three Corners*, *Geisum Village* and *Sand Beach* open their beaches to outsiders for £E25 (you can also use the pools at the *Shedwan* and *Sand Beach*). Interlopers who slip past security usually get caught on the beach because they lack the distinctive bathing mats that are issued to residents and paying guests.

Further down the coast is the cheaper option of *Shellghada Beach*, just north of the *Sheraton*, where £E10 buys a day on the sand, volleyball and use of the fresh-water showers. Eat at the restaurant and there is no entry charge. *El Saqiaa Restaurant and Beach* near the harbour offers a similar deal (£E15 including a free drink) and has a larger beach. Slightly more expensive is *The Chill* (£E30), a trendy beach bar opposite the *Roma Hotel* in Sigala, which has hammocks and sells beers. Other holiday villages allow outsiders to use their beaches and **swimming pools** for a charge that ranges from £E35 at the *El-Samaka Beach Club* to £E60 at the *Magawish Village* (which has the nicest beach). Admission policies may change, so phone ahead to avoid a wasted journey. Small coral reefs offshore from the *Shedwan Golden Beach* in Ed-Dahar, and the *Jasmin Village* in New Hurghada, offer a taste of the colourful array of fish and corals further out to sea. Buying beach or camping gear in Hurghada can be expensive; the central Government Store has a good selection at low fixed prices.

Powerful gusts make Hurghada a great place for **windsurfing**, especially the beaches at the *Magawish* and *Hurghada Beach*. Several holiday villages have lagoons and centres where you can rent boards and wetsuits, and some places offer windsurfing instruction. Happy Surf has branches at *Three Corners* (☎065/547-816), the *Sofitel* (☎065/447-261) and *Magawish Village* (☎065/446-☎450); Pro Center is based at *Jasmin Village* (☎065/446-450) and Habri/Friendly Surfing Center is at the *Hurghada Beach Resort* (☎065/443-

710). The *Arabia Beach* has facilities for **paragliding** and **water-skiing**. If you book one or two days ahead, *Marine Sports Club* (☎065/444-861/2/3) can arrange **deep-sea fishing** day trips for £E400 per boat (6–8 people) including equipment. For a few hours' **snorkelling**, try Prince Sea Trips (☎065/549-882) at the *Four Seasons* in Ed-Dahar. Run by friendly Bedouin brothers who grew up in Hurghada, you're charged just £E30 if you book with them direct, rather than the £E50–60 charged by most of the operators and commissioned agents around town.

The Aquarium, Sindbad Submarine and Aquascope

If you want a glimpse of the Red Sea's wonders without getting wet, visit the newly renovated **Red Sea Aquarium** (daily 9am–11pm; £E10, camera £E5) on the Corniche. Its tanks are labelled in English, with diagrams of where to find each species on the reef. You can learn to recognize wrasses, triggerfish, sailfintangs, angelfish and many other types, but it's sad to see them in such cramped conditions when you know that millions of others are swimming freely not far away.

Alternatively, there's the much-hyped **Sindbad Submarine** (US$50, children US$25), which can take you to depths of 22m in comfort. Disappointingly, however, the trip is more of a photo-opportunity than anything else. Half the time is spent getting to and from the sub's mooring offshore from the *Sindbad Beach Resort*, and after submerging a diver swims alongside trailing bait to attract wrasses, groupers and parrotfish past the portholes. You'd do better to go on an introductory dive – but if the sub still appeals, bookings can be made at the *Sindbad* (☎065/444-688) or other holiday villages.

Another window on the underwater world is open to you on board **Aquascope** (US$40), a sort of new-age glass-bottom boat. The two-hour trip leaves from the *Royal Palace Hotel* (☎065/446-906) near the tourist information office in New Hurghada and includes a fifty-minute tour of the coral reefs. A more traditional glass-bottom boat experience can be had on the **Red Sea Dolphin** (10am & 3pm; 2hr; US$39 including drinks), which is based at the *Inter-Continental* 3km south of the tourist information office in New Hurghada on Tariq Al-Kura.

Eating and drinking

Hurghada is good for **eating out**, with a wider choice of cuisine than anywhere else in Egypt but Cairo or Alexandria. Besides the places listed below there are dozens of restaurants in holiday villages, mostly upmarket and with **music** in the evenings. The *Aladdin Restaurant* in the *Sindbad Beach Resort* deserves an honourable mention for its *oud* player. It is also home to the only Russian restaurant and bar in Hurghada. For cheaper meals, check out the many (sometimes nameless) places in Ed-Dahar and Sigala, where new ones are opening every week. **Opening hours** are generally mid-morning until 11pm or midnight (maybe later in high season), though the choice of food dwindles after 10pm. Almost everywhere adds 10–12 percent in **service taxes** to the bill – at some holiday villages they bump things up by as much as 21 percent.

If you're keen on saving money it's worth tracking down some **street stalls**. There are two good *fuul* and *felafel* stands on the street running south of, and parallel to, Sharia Sheikh Sebak; juice bars and nut stalls are scattered around the bazaar, and there are *kushari* stands near the bus station. In Sigala, there's a pair of *felafel* stands on Sigala Square near the police station, and a place with refrigerated carcasses outside that does tasty kebab, *kofta* and pizzas. Don't miss the two excellent cake shops inside The Market mall, on the strip. For the less adventurous there are the ubiquitous *Pizza Hut* and *KFC* opposite *Sindbad Beach Resort*, and *McDonald's* in downtown Sigala.

Unless stated otherwise, all of the places listed below are in Ed-Dahar; most places close around 11pm–midnight, and nearly all are shown on the maps on p.751 and p.755.

Abo Khadega in Sigala. Small workers' café where you can get a tasty meal of soup, rice, salad, beans and grilled meat for £E8.

Baron in the bazaar. A small, simple local eatery serving chicken, beans, bread and salad for £E7.

Bella Riviera opposite *Shakespears Hotel*. Friendly café serving tasty lentil soup, spaghetti Bolognese, lasagne and salads at low prices. No alcohol.

Chez Pascal in Three Corners Empire shopping centre. Belgian-managed pizza (£E12–25) and steak (£E35) restaurant, which offers good food and service in a soothing atmosphere. Sells alcohol.

Egyptian Corner near the *Bella Riviera*. A few tables in a garden, good for a *fuul*, tomato and feta cheese breakfast (£E5), chicken with rice and salad (£E9), or *tajine* (£E8). No alcohol.

El-Arabi Sheraton Road, opposite the *Seagull Hotel*. Good-value Oriental food (£E10–20), popular with locals.

El-Masri near the police station in Sigala square. Offers kebabs, traditional Egyptian food and chicken at very reasonable prices (around £E15).

Far East Korea Redcon Mall, Sigala ☎065/445-207. Good-value Chinese-Korean restaurant with friendly staff; also offers takeaway.

Felfela's Sigala, between the *Holiday Inn* and *Sheraton* hotels ☎065/442-410. Branch of the famous Cairo restaurant chain serving decent Egyptian food at reasonable rates. Lots of space, nice atmosphere and great view of the harbour. Sells beer. Good for vegetarians. Does takeaway.

Joker near the police station in Sigala square. Excellent seafood restaurant with generous portions at very good prices (£E10–25). Try the *calamari* soup. Recommended.

Mahyma Giftun Island. A bar and restaurant for tourists visiting the island, open till 10pm. As you might expect, not terribly cheap and a limited menu. Pizza £E18, Stella £E10, coffee £E5.

Omar Inn in Sigala, opposite the *Golf* hotel ☎065/446-166. Strictly speaking a coffee shop, but serves pizza, seafood, snacks and fruit juice. Good place for people-watching. Does takeaway.

Red Sea in the bazaar, off Tariq en-Nasr. One of Hurghada's classiest seafood places, with a rooftop garden and a/c downstairs. Main dishes cost £E20–50. Sells alcohol. Takes most credit cards.

Rossi's opposite the now-closed Aquafun water-park, Sigala. Popular Italian joint with standard pizza, pasta and ice cream options.

Scruples on Tariq en-Nasr and the Corniche. Two branches of an a/c steak house serving pub food and booze at moderately expensive rates with bouts of Oriental dancing. The same firm runs Scruples Billiardeni, a pool hall on the corner of Sharia Abdel Aziz Mustafa.

Spaghetti near *McDonald's* in Sigala. Seafood restaurant with large outside seating area. Good value and popular with families.

Taco in Sigala, near *McDonald's*, and also one in Ed-Dahar. Popular fast-food outlet, famous for its *shawarma*.

Tarboush Sharia Abdel Aziz Mustafa. Small, simple pizzeria, with about fifteen not so different-tasting varieties (£E8–23) on the menu. No alcohol.

Young Kang Sharia Sheikh Sebak. Reasonable Chinese-Korean restaurant, with fair-sized portions at moderate prices. Sells beer.

Drinking

As you'd expect in a major resort, lots of **drinking** goes on in discos, restaurants and hotels – though the number of actual bars isn't that large. Most restaurants don't sell alcohol during Ramadan and before 1pm on Fridays, but holiday villages are exempt from these restrictions. There are **duty-free shops** in the AKA mall near the EgyptAir office in New Hurghada, or next to the *Ambassador Hotel* on the road to the airport. Egyptian beer and wine can be bought to take away at the *1001 Nights* (see below). If your taste for intoxicants runs in other directions, be warned that Hurghada is less of a smoking town than Luxor or Dahab – which isn't surprising given that *bango* costs at least £E50 a *talga*. The following **bars** are open till midnight.

The Chill Sheraton Road, opposite the *Roma Hotel* mobile ☎0123 820694. This beach bar has become the hangout of choice amongst Hurghada's diving fraternity and other foreign residents, with different styles of music played each night, plus dance nights at weekends.

Juke Box Pub next to *Shedwan Golden Beach* on the Corniche in Ed-Dahar. Tacky bar but good views from the rooftop beer garden. Serves food and stages sporadic Oriental belly-dance shows.

Papa's Bar next to *Rossi's* in Sigala. mobile ☎0105 129051. Another of Hurghada's popular bars for foreigners, mainly because it's Dutch-run and full of diving instructors.

Papas II below the *Juke Box* on the Corniche, Ed-Dahar. mobile ☎0122 516511. Similar to its older sister bar in Sigala, with live music on several nights a week.

Papa's Beach Bar 350m south of the harbour, Sigala. A newish *Papa* with the same atmosphere, drinks and clientele, but with the advantage of being on the beach.

1001 Nights in the *Shedwan Golden Beach* on the Corniche. Late-night café-cum-bar serving the cheapest Stella in town (£E7.50); take it away for £E7 a bottle. Omar Khayyum wine is £E27 – stick to the red and rosé versions, and avoid the white altogether. Obelisque is a good bet if available.

Nightlife

Hurghada has some of the liveliest **nightlife** in mainland Egypt, as hotels strive to outdo each other's discos and floor shows – but none are wild raves and the music is mostly mainstream. Posh places baulk at shorts or trainers; smart casual **dress** is universally acceptable. Most discos set a **minimum charge** per person, sometimes paid up front in return for a card that gets punched whenever you buy a drink – don't lose it. Drinks **prices** vary from £E8 to £E14 for a Stella, Sakkara Gold or Meister, £E20–25 for an imported beer or a cocktail. Few discos get going before 11pm, and while most are advertised as staying open till 4am, they may close earlier if things are quiet.

Discos wax and wane in popularity, with the most popular hangout at present being *The Chill* (see above), which holds parties on Thursdays, Fridays, Saturdays and full moons, sometimes hosting a DJ from Europe. Other favourites are in holiday villages; the *Dome* (10pm–4am) at the *Inter-Continental* has the best dance floor but restricts admission to mixed couples (in theory, anyway), whereas the discos at the *Sand Beach*, *Princess Club* and *Sindbad Beach Resort* put on Russian shows (see below) to pull in males. Although £E20 minimum charge is standard almost everywhere, the *Giftun Village* settles for £E15, while the discos in the *Sofitel* and *Sheraton* are free of charge, but don't have a show.

Discos aside, the main entertainments are bellydancing and Russian shows – unless you count the cringe-inducing "Animation Teams" at some tourist villages. **Russian shows** were pioneered in Hurghada, the novelty of pale-skinned Slav women in skimpy costumes soon proving to be a hit elsewhere, to the chagrin of Egyptian **belly dancers**. If this is your thing, the main venue is *Elf Leila Wa Leila* ("1001 Nights"), situated on the southern outskirts of Hurghada. Tickets including transport can be bought at most hotels, even the budget ones (US$15–18 including dinner, 8–10.30pm; $10 with soft drinks only, 8.30–10.30pm). Slightly less exotic and less expensive is the **bowling alley** at the *Sindbad Beach Resort* (☎065/442-944).

Listings

American Express Supposedly has an agent beside the garage on Tariq en-Nasr, but they'll only report stolen cards, and don't seem interested in expanding their range of services.

Banks Of the two close together on Tariq en-Nasr, the Banque Misr (daily 9am–9pm) has an ATM out-side and gives cash advances on Visa and MasterCard, while the National Bank of Egypt (Mon–Thurs & Sun 8.30am–2pm & 6–9pm, Fri 9–11am & 2–5pm) takes travellers' cheques. There is also an ATM in the *Empire* and *La Pacha Cataract* in Sigala. In New Hurghada there are

ATMs at the HSBC near *KFC* and *Pizza Hut* near *Sindbad Beach Resort*; at the *Inter-Continental* in New Hurghada and Banque Misr just north of the tourist office which also gives cash advances on Visa and Mastercard. Money transfers can be arranged through Federal Express or Thomas Cook (see below).

Books and newspapers The Red Sea Bookshop on Tariq en-Nasr, near the bus station, and *Abdoui's Internet Café and Bookshop* at the Corniche end of the strip, have the best selection.

Car rental CRC Rent-a-Car (☏065/444-885), next to Thomas Cook in Sigala, is one of the cheapest national companies and charges US$45 per day for a Peugeot 106. Cheaper still, Limo 1, at the *Inter-Continental* (☏065/446-903, ☏446-931), has Mazdas from US$29 per day or a 4WD Lada Niva at US$45. Hertz (☏065/442-884), opposite EgyptAir in New Hurghada, tends to have older cars, while Budget (☏065/442-261) at the *Sofitel* and *Marriott* has some of the newest ones, and is the only company to offer unlimited mileage with a three-day package. Other companies worth considering are Europcar (☏065/443-660) based at the *Royal Palace Hotel* in New Hurghada; Avis (☏065/447-400), which has a good range of 4WDs; and Thrifty at the *Melia Pharoah* in New Hurghada (☏065/446-723) and *Conrad International* (☏065/443-250).

Federal Express In Sigala (daily 8am–6pm; ☏065/442-444). Costly, fast and reliable worldwide express mail service. Can also wire money.

Hospitals The general hospital in Ed-Dahar (☏065/546-814) and the private El-Saffa on El-Nasr St (☏065/546-965) have improved, but the best medical treatment is available at the private hospital in El-Gouna (☏065/549-709 ext 2201/2, emergencies ext 2200), or El-Salam Hospital (☏065/548-790) in the *Arabia Village Hotel*. Less serious complaints can be treated by physicians on call at holiday villages, or check the listings in the *Hurghada Bulletin*. Diving emergencies can be dealt with either at El Gouna Hospital or Hurghada's new Naval Hyperbaric & Emergency Medical Centre (☏065/549-525 or 544-195) near the harbour.

Internet cafés These are sprouting up all over Hurghada and there should be one within walking distance of your hotel; they usually charge around £E10 per hour. *Papa's* (daily 10am–midnight; ☏065/445-230, ℮papasicc@red-sea.com), next to *Papa's Bar* in Sigala also offers international phone and fax services at competitive rates; *Aboudi Internet Café*, just along from the *Four Seasons* (daily 10am–midnight; ☏065/547-089, ℮kassem@hurghada.ie-eg.com), also has an

Internet phone service and can do scanning and printing. *Caspars Internet Café* has two branches (both daily 10am–1am):   on the Sheraton Road next to the *Mashrabiyya Village* hotel complex (☏065/442-375), the other beside the *Shedwan Golden Beach* in Ed-Dahar (☏065/540-870). *Oznet* on Sheraton Road (☏ & ☏065/540-870) has fast connections but is only open from 9am–5pm, while just up the road, *Hotline* (☏065/446-512) is open 24hr.

Laundry Stop-Shop (daily 8am–8pm; ☏065/446-609), off Tariq en-Nasr, 300m south of the bus station, charges 50pt–£E4 an item. Most hotels can have your washing sent out for £E2–8 per piece.

Passport office Entrance on the left side of the prominently signposted Red Sea Security Department building, 2km past the Esh-Shahid Mosque (Mon–Thurs & Sun 8am–2pm; ☏065/446-727).

Permits It's hard to obtain permits to travel south beyond Mersa Alam if you want to stay overnight. Put your case to the most senior English-speaking officer you can find at the Red Sea Security Department (*not* the passport office) and hope that he'll set the ball rolling. Don't be surprised if you're treated with suspicion and given the runaround for days.

Pharmacies There are several on Sharia Abdel Aziz Mustafa and Tariq en-Nasr. You can also find well-stocked pharmacies outside the hospitals.

Police The Ed-Dahar office (☏122) is on Tariq en-Nasr, out towards the passport office; the branch in Sigala (☏065/442-485) is near the main intersection. Little or no English is spoken at either; both are open 24 hours. Visitors might be disturbed to overhear suspects being beaten up on the premises.

Post office On Tariq al-Nasr, 200m north of the bus station (daily except Fri 8am–2pm). Has direct-dial phones and Express Mail Service.

Telephone calls Direct-dial phones in the 24-hour *centraals* on Tariq al-Nasr, Ed-Dahar, and in Sigala, just south of *McDonald's*, as well as at several points on the street; phonecards are sold at the *centraal*. If you're prepared to pay premium rates, many hotels and shops in the bazaar advertise international lines that may result in speedier connections.

Thomas Cook In Sigala (daily 9am–2pm & 6–9pm; ☏ & ☏065/443-500). Offers all usual services including Moneygrams, and also handles MasterCard emergencies.

Tourist police Next to the tourist office in Ed-Dahar (24hr; ☏065/546-765).

Working Distinctly feasible if you have diving qualifications (Divemaster upwards) or foreign languages (especially Japanese or Russian). Hotels and dive centres need people to work at reception or drum up clients. Ask other foreigners working here which firms are dodgy, and don't hand over your passport lightly – the biggest sharks aren't found in the Red Sea. *Do not invest any money in Hurghada.*

Moving on

Scores of travel agencies offer **excursions** to Luxor, Sinai or Cairo as day trips or overnight packages. Terms and prices vary, so shop around. Among the contenders it's worth mentioning Misr Travel (daily 8.30am–10pm; ☎065/546-600) for its day trips to the **Red Sea Monasteries** (US$55), **Mons Claudianus** (US$42) and **Wadi Hammamat** (US$25, $30 with barbecue). Other long-established and experienced agents in Hurghada include: Abu Noub Travel (☎065/442-843), Spring Tours (☎065/548-151), Travco (☎065/446-024) and Eastmar (☎065/444-581). As well as local trips, they handle tours to Cairo (two days; US$135), and day trips to Luxor (6am–11pm; US$75), and to Sinai by catamaran, including taking in St Catherine's Monastery and Dahab (US$155).

Moving on by regular transport, you've the usual choice between buses, service taxis and the odd flight, plus a sea link across the Gulf of Suez to Sharm el-Sheikh in Sinai.

Buses

For travel by **bus** to Cairo and Luxor, it's a good idea to buy your tickets in advance from the main bus station (☎065/547-582). There are five a/c buses daily to Cairo (10am, 1pm, 5pm, 11pm & 12.30am; 6–8hr; £E45–50). Suez is served by a dozen buses daily (9.30am–1am; 5–8hr; £E25–35) and tickets are sold on the bus. Buses to Luxor (12.30pm, 1am & 2am; 5hr; £E20) are routed via Safaga and Qena; those to Aswan (9.30am, 10.30pm, 11pm, 11.30pm; 8hr; £E35–40) also go via Safaga, which is also accessible by buses bound for El-Quseir (5am & midnight; 2hr; £E10–15) and Mersa Alam (4hr; £E20). Other buses travel to Safaga hourly (7am–2am; £E8). Buses to Assyut (£E20) and Sohag (£E16) in Middle Egypt run frequently but are unlikely to have a/c.

Besides the above, a/c **Superjet** buses with toilets and "in-flight" snacks and movies depart three times a day for Cairo (12pm, 2.30pm & 6pm; £E52) from the Superjet ticket office (☎065/546-768) near the Esh-Shahid Mosque, which serves as the terminal; the 2.30pm bus carries on to Alexandria (£E75). There is also a daily Superjet bus to Sharm el-Sheikh, via Suez (11.30pm; £E55). Buy tickets in advance to be sure of a seat.

New on the scene is the **El Gouna Transport Company** (☎065/541-561), which runs five buses from Hurghada, via El Gouna, daily to Cairo's El-Munib bus station in Giza (9am, 2.30pm, 4pm, 11pm, 1am; 30min later at El-Gouna; £E35, or £E50 including snacks and drinks).

Taxis

Mornings are the best time to catch seven-seater **service taxis** to Suez (5hr; £E20), Cairo (6–7hr; £E30), Port Safaga (45min; £E5) or El-Quseir (1hr 30min; £E8). Whatever the time of day, you shouldn't have to wait more than half an hour for a service taxi to Qena (4hr; £E10), whence other taxis run on to Luxor (see p.341). Don't believe anyone who says there's a "convoy charge" for foreigners. Groups of travellers can consider taking their own **taxi** all the way to Sharm el-Sheikh (about £E700) – which is one way to avoid a tedious interlude at Suez (see p.658). Plenty of taxis are prepared to take tourists to Luxor; £E180 for seven people is a fair price.

Flights

If you've got the money and book early, EgyptAir **flights** are the quickest way of reaching several major destinations (all the following prices are for one-way tickets). There are at least two daily to **Cairo** (8.45am & 6.45pm; US$115) with more laid on at weekends and public holidays. Likewise the flights to **Sharm el-Sheikh** (Mon 2.15am & 10.40am, Fri 10.40am, Sat 3.15am, Sun 2.15am; US$96) are often boosted if they are busy. The 10.40am flights on Monday and Friday both continue to **Alexandria** (US$176). There is also a weekly flight to **Luxor** (Wed 12.30am; US$55). You don't have to trek out to EgyptAir (℡065/447-503) in New Hurghada to make bookings, as everything can be handled by a subsidiary in town, Karnak EgyptAir (℡065/547-893); both are open daily 8am–8pm. The **airport** is 15km south of Ed-Dahar, off the Hurghada–Safaga road (£E25 by taxi).

By sea

Links with Sinai have been transformed by the introduction of a **high-speed catamaran** that cuts the journey to Sharm el-Sheikh to ninety minutes – as opposed to five or six hours by the old ferry, and 12–18 hours overland. The **catamaran** runs three times a week to Sharm (Mon 5am, Thurs & Sat 8am; US$40, £E200, cars from £E150). It's worth bearing in mind that the catamaran may be out of service for several weeks in the late spring for annual maintenance. The same company also operates a daily "flying boat" to Duba in Saudi Arabia (3hr; noon; US$100, £E450). You can buy tickets one hour ahead of departure at the port, from the Travco office nearby (℡065/446-024, ℻446-023), or from Amco Travel (℡065/447-571). Advance bookings can also be made through Sherif Tours at the *Sand Beach* (℡065/545-147) or El-Shaymaa Sea Trips (℡065/546-907), near the tourist bazaar in Ed-Dahar.

The Red Sea Mountains

Inland of Hurghada the barren plains erupt into the **Red Sea Mountains**, which follow the coast southwards towards Ethiopia. This geologically primitive range of granite, porphyry and breccia contains Egypt's highest mountains outside Sinai, rearing up to 2187m (over 7000ft) above sea level. During winter, peaks exceeding 1500m draw moisture from rising masses of air, while in summertime they precipitate brief, localized storms accompanied by violent lightning and flash floods. Hardy desert plants flourish in their wake, providing grazing for feral ruminants and the flocks of a few thousand nomads. Roaming their vast tribal lands, these Bedouin are perfectly at home in the wilderness – unlike isolated groups of miners and soldiers, who feel almost as exiled as the slaves who quarried here in ancient times.

Exploring the mountains

Short of befriending some Bedouin and tagging along with them, the Red Sea Mountains are most easily accessible via **day excursions from Hurghada**. The basic scenario is a half-day camel or jeep safari, timed for sundown if you want to have a barbecue with Bedouin entertainments, which will set you back around US$35. Prince Safari Trips (℡065/549-882), at the *Four Seasons* hotel, offers a sunset "safari" (£E60), which entails a half-hour journey by Landcruiser to a Bedouin village for a camel ride, followed by tea and some Bedouin music. If you haven't been to the desert before, this can be a good introduction to the Bedouin and the majestic landscape they live in – old desert hands can probably give it a miss. It also runs longer desert camping trips (£E180 per person per day, minimum five people) for the more adventurous.

The following accounts go somewhat further, to give an idea of what the mountains hold in store for travellers with the determination to embark on a trek through the region. The government is currently trying to promote **adventure tourism** in the Eastern Desert, so the opportunities for organized treks or mountain-climbing are improving. A geologist from the Netherlands, Karen van Opstal, and her partner Thomas Krakhofer run Red Sea Desert Adventures (Shagra Village, Mersa Alam mobile ☎0122 467826, ⓔdesert@red-sea.com), offering jeep and camel safaris and hikes from October to March; its six-day jeep safari from Hurghada to Mons Claudianus and Mons Porphyrites includes a visit to the prehistoric rock art in Wadi Qattar (US$700, including hotel accommodation, transport, safari, food and drink), while the six-day safari from Mersa Alam takes in Berenice, Shenshef and Wadi Sakait (from US$390). If you have less time, they can also arrange half-, full-day and overnight camel or jeep trips starting from US$30 per person.

As far as Europeans are concerned, the Red Sea Mountains were first climbed in the 1920s and 1930s, and have hardly been scaled since; as Sinai becomes increasingly commercialized, this may become the next wilderness to attract tourists.

Two Roman quarries

Twenty kilometres north of Hurghada, a piste quits the highway and climbs inland towards **Jebel Abu Dukhaan**, the 1161-metre-high "Mountain of Smoke". Anciently known as **Mons Porphyrites**, this was the Roman Empire's main source of fine red porphyry, used for columns and ornamentation. Blocks were dragged 150km to the Nile, or by a shorter route to the coast, whence they were shipped to far-flung sites such as Baalbek or Constantinople.

Round about the extensive quarries lies a **ruined town** of rough-hewn buildings with two large cisterns and an unfinished Ionic temple. Rock hyraxes (a kind of large rodent) lived in dens around Jebel Abu Dukhaan until all its trees were cut down for fuel. From the ruins, the piste follows Wadi el-Atrash and Wadi Qena down to the Nile Valley.

Mons Claudianus

Although **Mons Claudianus** is only 50km distant from Mons Porphyrites as the crow flies, lofty massifs necessitate more roundabout approaches. Coming from Hurghada, you need to follow a piste that starts between the port and Magawish Village. There are also two routes off the Port Safaga–Qena road: a well-surfaced one, 41km from the coast, and a longer, rougher piste nearer Qena.

Under the emperors Trajan and Hadrian, the pale, black-flecked granite quarried at Mons Claudianus was used to construct the Pantheon and Trajan's Forum in Rome. Around the **quarries**, beneath Jebel Fatira and Jebel Abu Hamr, you'll find numerous unformed capitals and abandoned columns. Wadi Fatira contains a cracked, 200-tonne monster, dubbed the "**Mother of Columns**" by the Arabs, while in the quarries of Hydreuma lies a giant unfinished **sarcophagus**. There's also a sizeable ruined town, **Fons Trajanus**.

Mountains and water sources

Between the two quarries rise the highest mountains in the Eastern Desert: Jebel Gattaar and Jebel Shaayib el-Banat.

Jebel Gattaar and Jebel Shaayib el-Banat

Jebel Gattaar (1963m) is esteemed by the Bedouin for its permanent springs and comparatively abundant vegetation. Umm Yasar and other wadis draining from Gattaar contain hundreds of acacia and ben trees, a remnant of once-extensive forests that were ravaged by charcoaling. As late as the 1880s, E.A. Floyer found Wadi Gattaar "thickly studded with big mimosa trees, some twenty and thirty feet high", whose reckless felling compelled the Bedouin to cut down live acacias for fodder when drought struck in the 1950s.

Further south, the loftier **Jebel Shaayib el-Banat** (2187m) rises to a summit that the geographer and mountaineer George Murray likened to a "monstrous webbed hand of seven smoothed fingers". The highest mountain in mainland Egypt, its peak was first climbed by Murray in 1922. In Bedouin folklore, Shaayib harbours a "Tree of Light" whose leaves can cure blindness; the world's only other one is believed to be in Lebanon.

The Ma'aza Bedouin, gazelles and ibexes

From St Anthony's Monastery to the Qift–El-Quseir road, 90,000 square kilometres of highland form the stamping ground of the **Ma'aza** (Goat) tribe of **Bedouin**, who migrated here from Arabia in the 1700s. As their name suggests, goats form the basis of their livelihood, although gathering plants and hunting are also important. Herbalists buy wormwood, henbane, argel and ben-tree seeds from the nomads, while hunters from the Gulf Emirates used to rent them as guides until the Ma'aza grew disgusted with their wanton slaughter of Barbary sheep (now almost extinct), ibexes and gazelles.

Traditionally the Ma'aza only hunt with dogs, rocks and knives, sprinting after their quarry. Whereas **gazelles** are regarded as everyday food, ibex meat is prized because it supposedly enables them to run up mountains without tiring. The sound of rutting **ibexes** locking horns in September attracts the foul **botfly**, which squirts its larvae into their mouths and nostrils. Smashing dead branches with rocks makes the same noise – something to remember should you camp out in these mountains, as botfly can also live as parasites in humans.

Wadi Naggaat and the Ma'aza Limestone Plateau

Early Christian hermits made their home in **Wadi Naggaat**, between Jebel Abu Dukhaan and Jebel Shaayib. *Naggaat* means "dripping place", a Bedouin term applied to a particular type of water source that falls from cliffs to irrigate maidenhair ferns, reeds and mosses, and fills pools where ibexes and people drink.

But with only four *naggaat* in the Eastern Desert and not enough rope to plumb the fifty-metre-deep well of Bir Gattaar, the Bedouin must also use surface springs and gravel seeps. These are far more common in the granite Red Sea Mountains than on the **Ma'aza Limestone Plateau** that separates the range from the Nile Valley, one reason why Bedouin dislike this "Place of Strayings". Its mysterious **Bir Shaitan** (Pool of Satan) is popularly believed to be replenished by Nile water via an underground passage but is actually dependent on rainfall; the shade from the overhanging rocks prevents evaporation.

South of Hurghada

Down the coast from Hurghada, the stream of holiday resorts becomes less dense until two belated spurts of development on the outskirts of **Port Safaga** (58km) and **El-Quseir** (a further 85km). At first sight Safaga is a total dump, but it has some charms and is within boat range of some stunning offshore reefs, while El-Quseir retains a sleepy charm unlike anywhere else on the Red Sea. From both points, connections with the Nile Valley are assured, via roads that cut across the Eastern Desert following old camel routes.

Further south, communications become tenuous and bureaucratic obstacles loom as you head **towards the Sudanese border**. From Shalateen onwards, you need military permission to proceed further south, or into the mountains. Though tourism has long been forbidden in what is still a militarily sensitive area, the authorities are now seeking to promote it, and access should become easier within a few years. Meanwhile, the allure of the far south depends on its reefs, which can be reached by dive boats operating out of Hurghada, Safaga, El-Quseir and Mersa Alam.

The highway initially runs several kilometres inland before regaining the coast. About 40km after Hurghada and 18km before Safaga, a signpost indicates the turn-off for **SHARM EN-NAGA**, a wide bay where *Sharm En-Naga Camp* (mobile ☎0101 513615; ❹) has 26 pastel-coloured tents furnished with beds and wardrobes. The tents also have 24-hour electricity and the site has hot-water showers. The main attraction here is the **beach-diving** and **snorkelling**, and day-trippers from Hurghada often come here to use the beach (£E15 fee for non-stayers). If you don't mind being away from the action, Sharm En-Naga makes an excellent alternative to overcrowded Hurghada and it is also sometimes possible to use your own tent.

The luxury development of **Soma Bay** (2km further on from Sharm En-Naga) boasts, among other things, an 18-hole golf course. There are several hotels offering similar facilities, of which the *Sheraton Soma Bay* (☎065/545-845 or 545-915, ℉545-885; ❽) is the most appealing. Further south, just before Safaga is **Makadi Bay**, a similar-style complex featuring a *Meridien* and several four and five star *Iberotel* hotels.

Port Safaga and the road to Qena

Once known for the restorative health properties of its sandy beaches, **PORT SAFAGA** (*Bur Safaga*) now amounts to very little. Coming in from the north you pass a slip road curving off to six holiday villages on a headland, which cater to groups on diving holidays. The town begins 3km later and consists of a single windswept avenue running straight on past concrete boxes with bold signs proclaiming their function, until the bus station and a final mosque, 4km south. Silos and cranes identify the port, which runs alongside (but out of bounds) for most of this distance. Safaga's only attraction is the **reefs** to the north, and if you're not going to see them, there's not much reason to hang around. As buses and taxis travelling between Hurghada and Luxor use the desert highway that turns off at Safaga, passengers can see all there is to see as they drive through town.

Accommodation

In Safaga itself, accommodation is limited to several overpriced **hotels** near the beach, a cheaper budget hotel on the main road and a couple of very cheap but basic places near the port. A better option is to stay out of town at one of the places recommended below, all of which are 3–5km north of town unless otherwise stated; minibuses (£E1) run as far out as the *Shams Safaga*, the most distant of the resort complexes.

Cleopatra opposite EgyptAir, in town ☎065/253-926. Clean carpeted rooms with baths, off dingy corridors. Caters mainly to Egyptians. ❷

El-Ezz near the port entrance and bus station ☎065/252-312. Basic rooms, mostly used by arrivals at the port rather than foreign travellers. No breakfast. ❶

Holiday Inn Resort ☎065/252-823. Safaga's most stylish tourist village, with an outsized pool and fine sea views; rooms have a/c, fridge and satellite TV. Happy hour 8–10pm for cocktails in the *Windsurf Bar*. ❼

Lotus Bay Resort & Gardens ☎065/252-443, ℉251-042. Also called *Lotus Bay Club Villas*. Spacious array of villas in a nice garden. All mod cons. Italian/Swiss clientele. Rates include half-board. ❼

Maka near the Bank of Alexandria and port entrance ☎065/253-814. Basic, semi-finished concrete box with shared bathrooms and iffy hot water. No breakfast. ❷

Menaville Village ☎065/251-760, ℉251-764. A decent place that's less flashy than the others, and reasonably priced near the bottom of the price band. Mainly Swiss, Italian and French clientele. ❼

Solymar Resort Paradise ☎065/251-633, ℉251-630. The first tourist village in Safaga has had a much needed refit, and improvements are ongoing. Half-board only. ❼

Shams Safaga ☎065/251-781, ℉251-780. Has

a private reef and better sports facilities and children's playground than the others. Used by British tour groups. Half-board only. **❼**

Sun Beach next to the *Lotus Bay Resort* ☎065/252-658, ℱ252-699. Chalets on the beach with a choice of a/c or fans, or you can bring your own tent (£E10–20 per person) and use the showers and café. Used as a stop-off by overland

adventure groups, it's also home to Orca dive centre. Rates for chalets include half-board. **❹–❺**

Three Corners Amira on the coast between the port and the town ☎065/253-821, ℱ253-825. Smart upmarket hotel, part of El Gouna's *Three Corners* chain, with its own beach. Good value though far from the rest of the tourist villages. Half-board. **❻**

Diving and snorkelling

It can be hard to just turn up and get a boat to the reefs. Boats and instructors at the main **diving centres** are fully committed to groups – though they can fit in extra people with a few days' notice. As a guide, expect to pay around US$300 for an open-water course; two boat dives, not including equipment, costs US$40. As in Hurghada (see p.758), the same extra environmental fees are levied for diving and snorkelling. If you have your own equipment, a cheaper way is to take a snorkelling **day trip** to Tubiya Island, organized by *Sun Beach* for £E30 per person with lunch.

The main diving grounds lie 6–8km offshore from the holiday villages, between Safaga Island and Ras Abu Soma. **Tubiya Island** is ringed with corals only just off its beach, while dive boats drop their clients directly over the sunken **North and South Fairway Reefs** or the twin pairs of sites known as **Tubiya Kebir**, **Tubiya Soraya**, **Gamul Soraya** and **Gamul Kebir**. Other sites include the **Seven Pillars** off Ras Abu Soma, and the **Panorama Reef** and **Shark Point**, 10km east of Safaga Island. Most of them are notable for their coral pillars and strong currents.

Among the big fish prevalent in these waters are **hammerhead sharks**, reputedly an aggressive species. Research suggests that they track their victims with two forms of biological sensor. At long range and when closing in on its kill, the hammerhead senses vibrations in the water, but in the final seconds it tunes into electromagnetic fields "bounced" off its target. It was hammerheads that caused many of the fatalities of Egypt's greatest maritime disaster, in December 1991, when a ferry returning from Jeddah hit a reef only miles offshore and 480 of the 650 passengers perished during seven hours in the water.

Other practicalities – and leaving Safaga

Such facilities as there are are all on Safaga's main drag, starting with the **police** station and **EgyptAir**, 200m south of the City Council, followed by a **hospital** 500m on. There's a **petrol station** beyond the next turn-off, across the main road from the Bank of Alexandria; further south on the other side are Banque Misr and the National Bank of Egypt, and a **telephone exchange**. Tourists staying at the holiday villages can more conveniently **change money** at banks inside *Safaga Marina* and the *Shams Safaga* or the Banque du Caire in

---

Diving centres

Barakuda *Lotus Bay Club Villas* (☎065/251-041, ℱ251-476) and Menavile Village (☎065/446-950, ℱ446-970).
Divers Inn *Three Corners Amira* ☎065/253-821, ℱ253-825.
Ducks *Holiday Inn Resort* ☎065/252-821, ℱ065/252-825, ℮ddredsea@t-online.de

Menadive *Menaville Hotel* ☎065/251-763, ℱ251-764.
Orca *Sun Beach* ☎065/242-357.
Shams Safaga *Shams Safaga* ☎065/251-782, ℱ251-780, ℮shams@internetegypt.com.

the shopping arcade near the *Holiday Inn*. The arcade also has a Fuji photographic shop. There are several cafés offering sandwiches or *shawarmas* on the main drag, but their turnover can be low so it's not a great option. The holiday villages are a better bet for food and the only place to get alcoholic drinks.

When **leaving** becomes imperative, cast about at the bus station near to the port first and then look for service taxis at the depot 500m south of the port entrance. There should be about nine **buses** daily to Hurghada (6am–11.30pm; £E5) and Suez (6am–11.30pm; £E23–35), seven to Cairo (6am–11.30pm; £E40), a dozen to Qena (8am–midnight; £E8), three direct to Luxor (1.30pm, 2am, 4am; £E13–20), and two to Aswan (leaving from the port at 4am, and the bus station at 1.30am; £E45). There is one bus daily to Alexandria (6am; £E70) and one to Sharm el-Sheikh (8.30pm; £E75). Sticking to the Red Sea Coast, two buses a day (2pm & 4pm; £E6) run down to El-Quseir, while three others (11am, 11pm & 2.30am; £E15–20) carry on to Mersa Alam. **Service taxis** run in between buses to Hurghada or Qena and charge similar rates, but it can take a long time to muster enough passengers for El-Quseir.

The road to Qena and off to the quarries

Safaga is primarily a commercial port for shipping out phosphates and importing US grain sent as food aid. The reopening of a long-abandoned freight railway has ended a windfall for the Ma'aza Bedouin, who used to feed their flocks on grain spilt along **the desert road to Qena** (161km). However, elders still spend their final years here: the pickings are good and they get to meet everybody. It's a harsh landscape of fissured rocks and canyons, with a beautiful dune cascading down the hillside shortly before you pass a small cafeteria, 85km from Qena. There are no petrol stations en route, but passengers can refresh themselves at wayside stands planted with trees, irrigated by the pipeline that conveys water from the Nile to Safaga and Hurghada.

Those with 4WD vehicles might consider two routes leading off **towards Mons Claudianus** (see p.769). The turn-off west of Safaga gets there in 25km via Bir Abd el-Wahab, whereas the rougher piste outside Qena follows its eponymous wadi to El-Heita before forking right up Wadi el-Atrash towards Jebel Abu Dukhaan (roughly 150km).

El-Quseir and the route to Qift

EL-QUSEIR, 85km from Safaga, is likewise into phosphates extraction, but has fewer inhabitants and more appeal. In pharaonic times, it was from here that boats sailed to the "Land of Punt" (thought to be Yemen or Somalia), as depicted in reliefs within Hatshepsut's temple at Deir el-Bahri. The Romans knew it as *Leukos Limen* (White Harbour), while under Arab rule El-Quseir was the largest port on the Red Sea until the tenth century, and remained a major transit point for pilgrims until the 1840s, when Flaubert caught its last flickers of exoticism. Crude pearl-fishers' *pirogues* resembling dug-out tree trunks shared the harbour with graceful Arab *dhows*, whose outsize sterns and high prows mimicked calligraphic flourishes, while Arabs and Africans jostled with Tartars from Bukhara and Crimea.

Today, El-Quseir is a sleepy place that seems mostly unaffected by tourism, despite the presence of three holiday villages on its outskirts. The town retains a charm all of its own, and locals are happy to help with directions if you get lost – not that it's necessary, as you'll soon find everything. The main **orientation** point is a traffic roundabout where service taxis drop and wait for passengers, near a Co-op garage and the *Sea Princess Hotel*.

The road bearing off to the right leads to a small **harbour** where you can watch men building boats on the beach, or stroll past shuttered and balconied houses to reach a **mosque** dating back to the thirteenth century, and a **quarantine hospital** built to screen pilgrims in the nineteenth century. This prison-like edifice is easily mistaken for the **fort** built by Mohammed Ali, whose crumbling walls enclose a watchtower and an execution chamber. It was originally an induction camp for some of the 20,000 Sudanese who were conscripted by the pasha and trained by European mercenaries in the hope of forging a modern army, but foiled his plans by sickening and dying en masse. The fort stands beside Sharia el-Gumhorriya, 200m uphill from the traffic roundabout, past a few fruit and vegetable stalls that are joined by other vendors on Fridays, when Ma'aza and Ababda Bedouin flock into town for the weekly **market**.

Practicalities

Accommodation is limited to two hotels in the centre, and three holiday villages outside town. The central *Sea Princess* (☎065/332-880; ❷) is an odd little hotel decorated with film posters and vintage banknotes, whose friendly staff and clean shared bathrooms just fail to make the rabbit-hutch rooms tolerable. A far better option is *El Quseir Hotel* (☎065/332-301; ❹), with a/c and breakfast, overlooking the sea near the harbour on Port Said Street. If you have money to spend, you're better off heading 1.5km south of town (25min walk) to the *Fanadir* (☎065/331-414, ⓕ331-415; ❼), a modest holiday village of a/c chalets and triple-person "villas", with a smallish pool, a dive centre and little shade, whose rates include half-board. The Nubian-style architecture that is popular with hotels the further south you go, is more beautifully represented on a grander scale by the *Mövenpick Sirena Beach* (☎065/332-100, ⓕ332-128; ❽), a vast five-star resort 5km north of town (£E15–20 by taxi) with every facility imaginable, including a diving centre, whose guests seldom leave its confines. Next door, the brand new four-star *Flamenco Beach Resort* (☎065/332-802, ⓕ332-801; ❼), painted a garish pink, seems representative of another, less attractive trend in hotel development in the area.

Aside from **eating** at the holiday villages, you're reliant on whatever materializes at two nameless cafés by the roundabout: soup, *fuul*, rice or chicken, if you're lucky – if not, just tea. A nicer place to pass time is the vine-shaded café overlooking the beach, which has *sheeshas* and backgammon. Alcohol and **nightlife** are confined to the holiday villages, which sometimes feature a belly dancer; non-residents may attend at the management's discretion.

The same goes for watersports, with **diving centres** deferring to guests, who may object to outside divers tagging along on sea trips. If you want to dive here, it's best to get a package deal from the start. Although the Quei and Wizr **reefs** are closer, the best sites are the **Brothers**, east of El-Quseir, and the **Elphinstone** and **Abu Dabbab** reefs, down towards Mersa Alam.

El-Quseir has few facilities. There's a **bank** on Sharia el-Gumhorriya, beyond the fort, while the road that turns right at this point leads to an old-fashioned **telephone exchange**. **Buses** leave from the unmarked bus stop just down from the *Sea Princess Hotel*, on the road to the harbour; tickets are bought on the bus. There are two a/c buses daily to **Cairo** (7.45pm & 11pm; 10hr; £E55) and two non-a/c (5am & 8pm; 10hr; £E30); all four services stop at Safaga and Hurghada. Heading south, there are two buses daily to **Shalateen** via the coastal route (4hr; 2.30am, £E30; 7.30am, £E20). There are six buses daily that head inland to **Qena**, three of which (11.30am, 1.30pm & 2.30pm; 2hr; £E8–10) also carry on to Shalateen. **Service taxis** depart from 50m south of the *Sea Princess Hotel*, bound for Cairo (£E40), Hurghada (£E8), Safaga (£E5),

Mersa Alam (£E10) and Qena (£E15). Another alternative is to get a group together to hire a **minibus** and driver from one of the tourist agencies in town. Koshar Tourist Services (☎065/331-666, ℱ331-695) will take up to eleven people to Cairo (£E600), Hurghada (£E150), Safaga (£E100), Qena (£E250), Mersa Alam (£E150), Berenice (£E300) or Shalateen (£E500).

The desert road to Qift

The modern road from **El-Quseir to Qift** (216km) follows the earliest known route across the Eastern Desert, via Wadi Hammamat (Valley of the Pigeons). Mysterious drawings of boats, humans and animals have been tentatively dated to Predynastic times, while hieroglyphic inscriptions attest to quarrying and mining from the I Dynasty onwards. Near **Bir Umm Fawakhir** (92km from El-Quseir), gold mines marked on a pharaonic survey map of c.1400 BC have been recently reopened by a Canadian mining company. Further west, the great well at **Bir Hammamat** was dug by eight thousand men for Ramses IV, to enable quarrying to continue year-round at **Wadi Hammamat**, the source of the hard dark breccia prized for statues and sarcophagi. The **quarries**, south of the road, are covered in cartouches and inscriptions, overlaying **Predynastic rock art**; hieroglyphs and boats occur at intervals as far as **El-Lakeita**. Rock art and inscriptions exist at many other places in the Eastern Desert, but access is restricted (see box overleaf).

For Bedouin, the road marks the boundary between **Ma'aza** tribal land and **Ababda** territory. Though traditional rivals, they may graze and water their flocks on each other's preserves should their own land be drought-stricken. Tribal politics are conditioned by the harsh environment and long memories; the names of wells and landmarks are often historically specific. For example, Bir Umm Howeitat, near the Umm Rus gold mine inland of Mersa Umbarak, is named after the Saudi Bedouin who harried the Ma'aza in their original homeland and later in Sinai.

To Mersa Alam and the Moulid of Al-Shazli

MERSA ALAM, 132km beyond El-Quseir, marks the southernmost point realistically of interest to divers and holidaymakers, as **military permission** is required to visit the region towards the border with Sudan. Mersa Alam's international airport, approximately 50km before the town, has been completed but is so far limited to charter flights from Italy, so access remains difficult. A new road linking Mersa Alam to Edfu has recently been completed but is not yet open to foreigners. If you do manage to get this far, accommodation is sparse and fairly expensive. That said, this stretch of the coast road (sections of which are currently being moved slightly further inland to protect the coast and wildlife) offers some of the most amazing landscape and desert in Egypt. As the road heads southwards to the Sudanese border the seemingly endless coastline is almost completely empty except for the occasional mangrove, herd of grazing camels or cluster of tanks left by the military.

Unsurprisingly, the southern Red Sea coast is growing in popularity with travellers and divers, but tourist infrastructure is far from developed. There is no telephone system in place yet – although Mobinil mobile phones work in the area – so bookings tend to be made through head offices in Cairo. *Shams Safaga* and Red Sea Diving Safari have satellite phones for emergencies (US$5 per min) and *Shagra Village* (see below) has GSM coverage so mobiles will work there.

In recent years several new tourist developments have popped up on the coastal road south of El-Quseir, but they are unlikely to be on their own for long. The first resort, 20km south of El-Quseir, is the *Utopia* (℡065/334-534, ℻330-080; half-board only ❼), an upmarket four-star place with a/c rooms, swimming pool and diving centre. A further 9km down the road is *Mangrove Bay Resort* (℡02/348 6748, ℻360 5458; half-board only ❼), a slightly cheaper tourist village. Both feature beautiful white sandy beaches with access to the 20km of coral reefs offshore.

If you have your own transport, you might head further south to the five-star *Kahramana* (℡02/360 5987, ℻349 9327; half-board ❽, all-inclusive if booked as a package from the UK), 24km north of Mersa Alam whose Mexican-inspired architecture is set against beautiful and empty sandy beaches. However, access to the sea for swimming is restricted, so guests have to use

Rock art of the Eastern Desert

The **rock art of the Eastern Desert** is one of Egypt's best-kept secrets, overlooked due to the abundance of pharaonic monuments in the Nile Valley and the difficulty of reaching many of the sites, spread over 24,000 square kilometres of desert to the east of Luxor and Edfu. Though small by comparison with the Western Desert, the dangers of this terrain shouldn't be underestimated: it's easy to get lost in the labyrinth of waterless wadis, and at least one 4WD group has died there. The **sites** vary from a single boulder to swathes of cliff-face dotted with pictures of people and animals, flotillas of boats and herds of giraffes, ostriches and elephants. While pharaonic and Roman inscriptions have revealed much about mining and trade, it is the rock art created before the unification of Egypt (c.3100 BC) that's really intriguing for the light it sheds on the origins of Egyptian civilization.

Dating Predynastic rock art is highly speculative, involving stylistic comparisons and analysis of patination (the extent to which inscriptions and rock faces darken with exposure to sunlight, dew and other factors). Since wadis often subside, some scholars date art by its height above the valley floor, assigning **spirals** to the earliest phase (7000–6000 BC), followed by **wildlife** and hunting scenes. Giraffes, crocodiles, hippos and ibexes plainly belong to a time when the region was moister than today (c.4000–2700 BC), and camels didn't reach Egypt until 625 BC; whereas elephants lived here in Predynastic times and were later imported by the Romans, so their presence can be ambiguous. **Cattle** reflect the pastoralism that took hold between 5500 and 4000 BC, and probably inspired the bovine iconography of pharaonic civilization.

The oldest **human figures** are gods or chieftains in ostrich-feather headdresses, brandishing maces; intriguingly similar to the "Conquering Hero" motif in pre- and Early Dynastic art at Hierakonpolis in the Nile Valley. They often appear standing in **boats**, which come in four types and are frequently surrounded by ostriches, elephants or cattle. Both Hans Winkler, who did seminal research in the 1930s, and David Rohl, who recently studied the rock art, believe that the oldest boats represent "**Eastern Invaders**" from Mesopotamia, who reached Egypt by the Red Sea and conquered the indigenous people of the Nile Valley, kick-starting Egyptian civilization. Boat motifs were employed throughout the pharaonic era.

In pharaonic times the Eastern Desert was an important source of gold, porphyry and breccia, so one finds plenty of **hieroglyphs**, cartouches of great pharaohs, and images of Min (the local deity of Coptos, and god of the desert). For the Romans, the road to Berenice was an important trade route, well protected with forts and scribbled with diverse **graffiti**, while Bedouin filtering in from Sinai and up from Sudan left their own tribal markers. For an **overview** of the sites, theories and questions raised, visit ⊛www.lankester.force9.co.uk.

Broadly speaking there are three areas of interest. Two are partially accessible by 2WD, using the roads between El-Quseir and Qift or Mersa Alam and Edfu, but all of the wadis between them require 4WD.

another beach 10km north, and it doesn't have its own reef. The hotel's diving centre, Pioneer Divers, run by Red Sea Diving Safari (see below), caters to divers with boat and truck trips to nearby reefs.

You'll find the first of three "ecolodges" run by Red Sea Diving Safari just past the *Kahramana*, at **Mersa Shagra**. *Shagra Village* (☎02/337 1833, ℻719 4219, ✉info@redsea-divingsafari.com; ❻) is a beachside diving centre offering a variety of environmentally-friendly accommodation, ranging from tents on the beach to rather smart bungalows, both with shared-bath facilities, and more luxurious ensuite chalets. Rates include all meals and unlimited soft drinks (beer is available at US$3 a bottle). Nearby is the new Hyperbaric Medical Centre (mobile ☎0122 935821) home to the most southerly decompression chamber in Egypt; divers are encouraged to take out cover in case they have to

Wadi Hammamat. The El-Quseir to Qift road passes lots of rock art and inscriptions, especially from pharaonic times. The quarries at Wadi Hammamat are full of beautiful **hieroglyphs**, some overlaying dancing goddesses and ibexes. Predynastic boats and pharaonic inscriptions appear on the rocks either side of the road between Wadi Hammamat and El-Lakeita. Both these localities mark the start of trails to Predynastic sites in **Wadi Qash** and **Wadi Atwani**, that require a 4WD and a guide who really knows the way.

Wadi Mineh. Accessible by 4WD from either main road, this ravishing terrain of broad wadis and dunes is impenetrable without GPS, and contains the greatest wealth of petroglyphs and rock art in Egypt. At the northern end of Wadi Mineh is everything from pharaonic boats and **Horus figures** to Roman graffiti extolling the virtues of a prostitute. Farther south in Wadi Abu Wasil, a secluded area that Winkler called **Site 26** is covered with pictures of **chieftains**, boats, ostriches and cattle. One appears to show a man bleeding a cow, a practice found among pastoralist tribes even today.

Wadi Barramiyah. The Mersa Alam to Edfu road runs straight through this wadi, where the rock-cut **Temple of Kanais**, 50km from Edfu, contains scenes of Seti I smiting Shasu (sand-dweller) and Nubian foes, and inscriptions lauding the well that he had dug along this desolate route. East of the temple, Predynastic **boats** appear on both sides of the road; some are huge, with up to seventy crewmen. Notice the pictograms of a hippo, an elephant, and a pharaonic standard resembling the hieroglyph "to bore", appropriate for a mining area. There are more boats and animals within walking distance of the road, and up side wadis. **Wadi Umm Salam** has been dubbed the "Canyon of the Boats" and also contains lines and squiggles that match up to modern maps of the wadi systems – a **Predynastic map** of the area, some believe.

Practicalities

For climatic reasons, the rock art of the Eastern Desert is best explored from mid-September till mid-May. Vehicles must travel in pairs and carry all water and fuel needed for the journey. Due to gold mining in the area and the need to protect vulnerable sites, access is only allowed from the Red Sea Coast (not the Nile Valley), and Military Intelligence and SCA **permits** for off-road travel are only issued to a single foreign operator, Ancient World Tours, in conjunction with the Egyptian firm Pan Arab Tours. Ancient World Tours has been working with Russ Ruthe and David Rohl of the Eastern Desert Survey to run "Followers of Horus" **tours** to record all the rock art in the region. For details, visit ⓦwww.ancient.co.uk, or contact ✉mra@dial.pipex.com.

use it (US$6 for 3 weeks; see p.760 for more advice). Mersa Shagra is also the base of Red Sea Desert Adventures (mobile ☎0122 467826, ✉desert@red-sea.com), which runs jeep and camel safaris and hikes from October to March (see p.768).

The town of **MERSA ALAM** itself is undistinguished, consisting of a large army base, some government buildings and new apartment blocks constructed for the expected influx of hotel staff to the area, grafted onto a fishing port where liveaboards now moor. Opposite is a coffee shop patronized by local divers. You can change service **taxis** en route between the Red Sea Coast and the Nile Valley town of Edfu, 230km inland, or use the Mersa Alam–Edfu road to visit the annual Moulid of Al-Shazli at Wadi Humaysara. Though rarely marked on maps, this site is widely known and more accessible than you'd imagine – the main problem is whether you'll be allowed through the check-points, even with a permit.

South of the town are three other camps offering basic **accommodation** for the keen divers that have made it this far. Fourteen kilometres south, one camp, *Awlad Baraka Diving Camp* (mobile ☎0123 258869), has twenty comfortable "African" huts, a restaurant and café (US$35 full board). It is run in association with Deep South Diving Centre on the beach side of the road (mobile ☎0123 258869, ✉info@deep-south-diving.com), which is close enough to go on day trips (US$45–65) to some of the best and most remote dive sites in the south Red Sea, such as **Dolphin House**, **Abu Dabab**, **Elphinstone** and **Fury Shoal**; they also offer open-water diving courses (US$290 plus US$30 certifi-cation) and liveaboards (around US$115 per person per day). There's another Red Sea Diving Safari "ecolodge" at *Nakari Village*, 18km south of Mersa Alam (contact details as for RSD Safari at Mersa Shagra), while 32km further still is *Shams Alam Hotel and Beach Resort* (☎02/417 0046, 🖷417 0158; half-board only ❼), home to Wadi Gimal Diving Centre.

The third in the trio of Red Sea Diving Safari "ecolodges", *Wadi Lahami Village*, is 130km south of Mersa Alam. This site offers boat and Rigid Hull Inflatable (RIB) diving in addition to shore diving by truck, but it caters for experienced divers only and accommodation is restricted to tents (US$40 for two people; discounts for groups and long stays).

Finally – for now at least – the most southerly hotel on the Red Sea Coast is *Zabarghad Hotel*, near Hammata some 120km south of Mersa Alam, where Orca Diving Centre has a branch. The island reefs here are home to one of the few undisturbed breeding grounds for **sea turtles** on the Red Sea Coast. Its 235m-high hill was mined until 1959 for its leaf-green coloured gems, called peridotites.

The Moulid of Abul Hassan al-Shazli

Outside Egypt, **Abul Hassan al-Shazli** (who died in 1258) is known as Al-Shadhili, hence the name of his Sufi order, the *Shadhiliyya*. According to believ-ers, Al-Shazli asked God to let him die in a place where nobody had ever sinned, and the Prophet Mohammed buried him high in the mountains at **Wadi Humaysara**. The remoteness of his grave has never deterred pilgrims, for whom the journey has become much easier since a local entrepreneur built a road to the site as a gift. It turns off the Edfu road at the tomb of another Sufi sheikh, Salim, which pilgrim trucks circle three times to avoid incurring his jealousy, before driving on to Wadi Humaysara (100km).

Al-Shazli's **moulid** starts ten days before the Muslim feast of *Eid al-Adha* and reaches its climax the day before the *Eid*. Sixty thousand Sufis from all over Egypt gather to perform *zikrs* outside his tomb, and hundreds of tents and snack stalls are pitched for the occasion. Arranging a ride there will require much palaver, but you shouldn't have any problem identifying the pilgrim trucks, festooned with banners and loudspeakers.

The far south: Berenice to the Sudanese border

A further 145km south is the town of **BERENICE**, named after the wife of Ptolemy II, on whose suggestion a trading port was established here in 275 BC. Abandoned during the fifth century AD, the site was excavated in 1818 by Belzoni, who found a Temple of Semiramis and other ruins. Nowadays, Berenice amounts to a few characterless buildings clustered together in a windswept bay, with little to interest tourists except a Bedouin museum apparently instigated by the wife of the Belgian ambassador to Egypt.

With tourism increasingly being encouraged, however, the hinterland of Berenice has several would-be attractions. For climbers, there is the challenge of Egypt's "most aggressive peaks", **Jebel Farayid** (whose highest point was reached by Murray in 1925) and the **Berenice Bodkin** – the largest rock needle in the whole of North Africa and the Middle East. Here, too, are the ancient **Emerald Mines of Wadi Sakait**, worked from pharaonic to Roman times and under the khalifs; Mohammed Ali had them reopened, but few gems remained to be found and the mines were soon abandoned. Nearby is a small Ptolemaic rock temple, dedicated to Isis and Serapis.

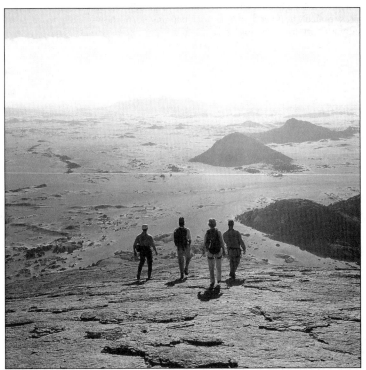

△ Walking in the Eastern Desert

The reasons why this area has long been off limits are geopolitical. Following the Iranian Revolution, the **Ras Banas air base** was earmarked for use by the US Rapid Deployment Force and war games were held in the Eastern Desert, simulating an Allied response to an Iranian attack on the Saudi oil fields. Such manoeuvres waned after Iran was embroiled in war with Iraq, and the US "forward base" withdrew to Diego Garcia – so that when Iraq invaded Kuwait in 1990, the only unit available for immediate airlift into Saudi Arabia was a single battalion of Egyptian commandos.

More recently, the **far south** has been a bone of contention between Egypt and Sudan, whose common border was arbitrarily set by the British in 1899 on the basis of the 22nd parallel. After independence, both agreed that this was unfair on the Bishari nomads whose tribal grounds straddled the border, so a slice of Egyptian territory was placed under Sudanese administration – a compromise that worked fine until Sudan granted a Canadian oil company offshore exploration rights, and Egypt responded by sending in troops to reassert its sovereignty. Since 1992, the region from **Bir Shalateen** down to **Halaib** has been under military rule, and Egypt has launched a crash programme of "development" to cement its hold on this previously neglected, potentially oil-rich region.

In May 1999, some restrictions were lifted and tourists can now travel at least as far as **Shalateen**, which has a weekly camel market. As yet there is no tourist accommodation in the area, and official permission must be obtained from police in Berenice or Shalateen if you wish to camp. An alternative is to arrange a trip with Red Sea Desert Adventures (see p.768). The area is still a very sensitive military zone and anyone not obtaining permission is likely to be treated with extreme suspicion.

Contexts

Contexts

The historical framework

The present borders of Egypt are almost identical to those in pharaonic times; territories such as Sinai and Nubia being essentially marginal to the heartland of the Nile Valley and its Delta, where Egyptian civilization emerged some five thousand years ago. The historical continuity is staggering: the pharaonic era alone lasted thirty centuries before being appropriated by Greek and Roman emperors.

Egypt's significance in the ancient world was paramount, and the country has never been far from the front line of world history. Although neither Christianity nor Islam was born in Egypt, both are stamped with its influence. In modern times, when the Arab world sought to rid itself of European masters, Egypt was at the forefront of the anti-colonial struggle, while its peace treaty with Israel altered the geopolitics of the Middle East.

Uncertainties ...

Any attempt to précis this vast span of history inevitably runs the risk of obscuring social dynamics and ordinary people amid a roll call of dynasties and great men and women. While the continuity of so many aspects of Egyptian life supports this conservative view, dramatic watersheds and subtle fluxes are also a feature of Egyptian history. Nor are the facts graven in stone. Egyptology is riddled with uncertainties, not least in its chronology of dynasties and kingdoms (not an Egyptian concept, but a modern invention enabling scholars to get a handle on three thousand years of history). Two critics have assailed conventional chronology from opposite directions. Their arguments deserve to be read in full, but can be summarized as follows.

In *A Test of Time*, **David Rohl** examines the "Four Pillars" of synchronicity between ancient Egyptian and Biblical history and judges only one to be impeccable. Anomalies such as the royal burials at Tanis and Deir el-Bahri, Israelite chariots on the Ashkelon Wall at Karnak, and evidence of their sojourn at Avaris call for a revision of the chronology of the Third Intermediate Period, with knock-on effects on earlier times. Rohl's **New Chronology** puts the Exodus in the XIII rather than the XIX Dynasty, and makes Akhenaten a contemporary of David and Saul. The sceptical response from other archeologists can be read on Ⓦhttp://members.aol.com/Ian%20Wade/Waste/Index.html.

Unlike Rohl, **Anthony West** is not a professional Egyptologist, and his *Serpent in the Sky* – propounding that the Egyptian temples embody the legacy of an older, greater civilization dating back to Atlantis – was laughed off until two geologists agreed that the erosion in the bedrock of the Sphinx shows that it was created at least 2600 years earlier than had hitherto been assumed. Egyptologists failed to refute their evidence in a showdown at the 1992 conference of the American Association for the Advancement of Science, but have since taken comfort from a study by the Getty Institute, which concludes that the erosion proves nothing of the kind.

As both debates are unresolved, we've stuck to **orthodox chronologies**, about which even mainstream Egyptologists differ and acknowledge margins of error. These are up to a hundred years in the period around 3000 BC, seventy-five years around 2000 BC, and between ten and fifteen years around 1000 BC. From 500 BC onwards, dates are fairly precise until the Ptolemaic era, when the chronology gets hazy, only firming up again in Roman times.

The beginnings

Stone tools from the gravel beds of Upper Egypt and the Uwaynat Desert attest to the presence of **hunter-gathering hominids** in the area over 250,000 years ago, when the Sahara was a lush savannah that supported zebras, elephants and other game. Between the **Late Middle Paleolithic** (c.70,000 BC) and **Upper Paleolithic** (c.24,000 BC) eras there were fluctuating wet and dry periods, when lakes rose or shrank and grasslands expanded or receded, and tribes are assumed to have moved backwards and forwards between the Nile and the oases. While most still lived by hunting and fishing, herding cattle emerged even before cereal cultivation, sheep and goat herding filtered through from the Near East (c.7000 BC).

During the **Neolithic** era, Middle Egypt and the Delta had **settled communities** that cultivated wheat and flax, herded flocks and wove linen. Although some reverted to a nomadic lifestyle after the rains of the Neolithic era checked the process of desertification, others remained to develop into agricultural societies. It was during the **Middle and Late Neolithic periods** (6600–5100 and 5100–4700 BC respectively) that human occupation of the Western Desert reached its peak, giving rise to the rock art in the Cave of the Swimmers and other sites at the Gilf Kebir and Jebel Uwaynat.

Predynastic Egypt

The impetus for development came from southern Egypt. At **Nabta Playa**, 100km west of Abu Simbel, archeologists have identified the world's **oldest calendar** of standing stones and sculpted monoliths – dating from around 6000 BC – that attests to a Neolithic culture with a knowledge of astronomy and the resources and organization to create such a site. And then there are the mysterious **boats** drawn in the Eastern Desert perhaps a thousand years later, that Rohl believes represent "Eastern Invaders" who conquered the indigenous people of the Nile Valley. However, evidence of later agricultual societies is less impressive, and there is disagreement over the categorization of cultures. The earliest is known as the **Badarian**, after the village of El-Badari where Brunton carried out excavations in the 1920s. The Badarians were farmers, hunters and miners; they made fine pottery, carved bone and ivory, and traded for turquoise and wood.

The **Naqada I** period, from about 4000 BC onwards, was characterized by larger settlements and a distinctive style of pottery: burnished red clayware with black rims or white zoomorphic decorations. Clay and ivory figurines show Naqada menfolk sporting beards and penis shields, raising a possible ethnic connection with their Libyan neighbours. More extraordinary are the narrow-necked vases carved from basalt, which can't be reproduced by twentieth-century technology, but were supposedly made by the Stone Age Naqada I culture.

In the conventional scheme of things, graves from the **Naqada II** period contain copper tools and glazed beads that signify advances in technology, and extraneous materials such as lapis lazuli, indicating trade with Asia. The graves themselves evolved from simple pits into painted tombs lined with mats and wood and, later still, brick. The development of extensive irrigation systems (c.3300 BC) boosted productivity and promoted links between communities.

The two lands

By this time, the communities of Upper and Lower Egypt existed in two loose **confederations**. As power coalesced around Naqada in the south and Behdet in the Delta, each confederation became identified with a chief deity and a symbol of statehood: Seth and the White Crown with **Upper Egypt**, Horus and the Red Crown with the **Delta**.

Later, each acquired a new capital (Hierakonpolis and Buto, respectively) and strove for domination over the entire region. The eventual triumph of the southern kingdom resulted in the **unification of the Two Lands** (c.3100 or 2090 BC) under the quasi-mythical ruler **Menes** (aka Narmer), and the start of Egypt's Dynastic period. Some identify him as pharaoh Aha, whose tomb is the earliest found at Saqqara, but if the Greek name "Menes" is derived from the Egyptian *mena* (Establisher), it may not refer to any actual individual.

The Archaic Period

The **Early Dynastic** or **Archaic Period** was the formative epoch of Egyptian civilization. Its beginnings are a mix of history and myth, relating to the foundation – supposedly by Menes – of the city of **Memphis**, located at the junction between Upper and Lower Egypt: the first imperial city on earth.

From this base, Djer and Den, the third and fifth kings of the **I Dynasty** (c.3100–2890 or 2920–2770 BC), attempted to bring Sinai under Egyptian control. Writing, painting and architecture became increasingly sophisticated, while royal tombs at Saqqara and Abydos developed into complex *mastabas*, thought to have been modelled on the palaces of living kings. At this time, royal burials were accompanied by the deceased's servants – a practice that later dynasties abandoned.

Also indicative of future trends was the dissolution of the unified kingdom as centralized authority waned towards the end of the dynasty. Although this was restored by **Raneb** (or Hotepsekhemwy), founder of a new line of rulers, regional disputes persisted throughout the **II Dynasty** (c.2890–2686 or 2770–2645 BC).

These disputes probably inspired the **contendings of Seth and Horus**, a major theme in Egyptian mythology. The Stele of Peribsen shows a temple facade surmounted by the figure of Seth, rather than Horus, the traditional symbol of kings. However, the rivalry between the two regions and their respective deities apears to have been resolved under **Khasekhemwy**, the last king of the dynasty – paving the way for an era of assurance.

During the **III Dynasty** (c.2686–2613 or 2649–2575 BC), advances in technology and developments in culture raised Egypt to an unprecedented level of civilization. The main figure of the III Dynasty was **King Zoser** (or Djoser), whose architect, **Imhotep**, built the first **Step Pyramid** at Saqqara in the 27th century BC. The pyramid's conception and construction were a landmark and later generations deified Imhotep as the ultimate sage. On the economic and political front, the III Dynasty also sent expeditions into Sinai, to seek turquoise and copper, and to subjugate the local Bedouin.

The Old Kingdom

Pyramid-building and expansionism were likewise pursued during the **IV Dynasty** (c.2613–2494 or 2575–2465 BC). The Dynasty's first king, **Snofru** (aka Sneferu), raised two pyramids at Dahshur, and made incursions into Nubia and Libya. His successors, **Cheops** (Khufu), **Chephren** (Khafre) and **Mycerinus** (Menkaure), erected the **Pyramids of Giza**, expanded trade relations with the Near East, and developed mining activities in Nubia, where a copper-smelting factory was established at the Second Cataract. Though Snofru's line expired with the death of **Shepseskaf**, his widow Queen **Khentkawes** is believed to have married a high priest to produce an heir.

This trend continued during the **VI Dynasty** (c.2345–2181 or 2465–2323 BC), when nobles were buried in their own **nomes** (provinces). While punitive expeditions carried the pharaoh's banner deep into Nubia, Libya and Palestine, domestic power ebbed to the *nomarchs*, reaching the point of no return under **Pepi II** (aka Neferkare), whose death heralded the **end of the Old Kingdom**.

The First Intermediate Period

After Pepi's death, decades of provincial rivalry and chaos ensued, with petty dynasties claiming the mantle of the Old Kingdom. The Greek historian Manetho records seventy rulers during the brief **VII Dynasty** (c.2181–2173 or 2150–2134), while an unknown number of kings vainly asserted their claims from Memphis during the **VIII Dynasty** (c.2173–2160 or 2150–2134).

When rains failed over the Ethiopian highlands, famine struck Egypt, exacerbating civil disorder. Weak principalities sought powerful allies such as **Herakleopolis**, the dominant city of the Twentieth Nome, whose ruler, **Achthoes**, gained control of Middle Egypt, assumed the throne name Meryibre, and founded the **IX Dynasty** in 2160 or 2154 BC.

Whereas most of the north came under the control of the IX and **X Dynasty** (c.2130–2040 or 2154-2040 BC) kings of Herakleopolis, Upper Egypt was contested by the rulers of Edfu and Thebes. After vanquishing his rival, the Theban ruler Inyotef Sehertowy tried to extend his power beyond Upper Egypt, founding the **XI Dynasty** (c.2133–1991 or 2134–2040 BC). The struggle between north and south was only finally resolved by **Nebhepetre Mentuhotpe II**, who reunited the whole country under one authority in 2055 or 2050 BC, establishing the Middle Kingdom.

The Middle Kingdom

During Mentuhotpe's fifty-year reign the mines and trade routes were reopened; incursions into Libya, Nubia and Sinai resumed; and arts and crafts flourished again. His successors, Mentuhotpe III and IV, were most notable for their expeditions to the Land of Punt. Inscriptions from Wadi Hammamat name the vizier in charge of the second expedition as **Amenemhat** (or

Ammenemes), who subsequently founded the **XII Dynasty** (c.1991–1786 or 1985–1955 BC).

Amenemhat returned the capital to Memphis and safeguarded the Nile Delta from raiders by constructing the Walls of the Prince, a fortified cordon sanitaire. Northern Nubia was annexed, and trade extended further into Palestine and Syria.

Under Amenemhat's son, **Senusert I** (aka Sesostris I), the administrative capital was transferred to the **Fayoum**, where massive waterworks were undertaken. Amenemhat II curbed the power of the nomarchs, while Senusert III may have abolished the office completely. These kings also built **the last pyramids**, at Lahun, El-Lisht and Hawara, where the final pyramid was erected by Amenemhat III, alongside the Labyrinth described by Herodotus.

According to Rohl's New Chronology, it was **Amenemhat III** who took **Joseph** as his vizier and let the **Israelites** settle in the Delta (c.1662 BC). Graves at Avaris suggest a large Semitic population stricken by calamities, akin to the Biblical account of the events leading up to the Exodus, which Rohl assigns to the reign of the XIII Dynasty pharaoh **Dudimose** (c.1447 BC). Both these dates are utterly at variance with the conventional chronology, which places the Exodus two centuries later, during the New Kingdom.

However, there is no disagreement that the late XII Dynasty was a **troubled time**, with the Nile flooding at record levels, bringing poor harvests and famine in its wake. The faces of the statues of pharaohs of this era are uniquely stern and careworn. Whether or not Egypt was also smitten by plagues and disrupted by an exodus from the Delta, it was obviously in poor shape to resist an invasion.

The Second Intermediate Period

Under the **XIII Dynasty** Egypt slid towards an era of disorder that archeologists term the **Second Intermediate Period**, when the pharaohs lost control of Nubia and the Delta. For the first time, Lower Egypt fell into the hands of "rulers of foreign lands" or *heka kaswt* – later rendered by Manetho as **Hyksos**. While Manetho relates that "peoples of an obscure race" appeared "like a blast of God" in the reign of Dudimose, most archeologists believe that they filtered into the eastern Delta as immigrants or slaves during the late Middle Kingdom, and only took over later. There's less doubt that they had weapons and technology which gave them an edge over the Egyptians: chariots, bronze armour, helmets and curved swords.

For a time, the western Delta remained independent, under the **XIV or Xois Dynasty**, which was contemporaneous with the **Hyksos XV Dynasty** until about 1650 BC. After capturing Memphis, the Hyksos established relations with Thebes and traded up and down the Nile, but continued to rule from the Delta city of **Avaris** and maintain links with Palestine, Crete and Persia. Relations deteriorated after the **Theban XVII Dynasty** began harassing their caravans and ships, and the Hyksos king **Apophis** sent an insult to Sekenenre Tao II of Thebes, who used it as a pretext to declare war (c.1560 BC). Sekenenre Tao's son **Khamose** continued the struggle on two fronts (after the Hyksos forged an alliance with Nubia) and was within striking distance of Avaris when he died, whereupon his brother, **Ahmosis I**, finally expelled the Hyksos from Egypt (in 1567 or 1550 BC), ushering in a new era.

Although Egyptian chronicles describe their rule as anarchic, evidence such as the *Rhind Mathematical Papyrus* suggests that the Hyksos fostered native culture, took Egyptian names and ruled as pharaohs, while their introduction of the *shaduf* irrigation device proved of lasting benefit to Egyptian agriculture. Many think that their dismissive sobriquet, the "Shepherd Kings" is a mistranslation by Josephus of Manetho's rendering of the original Egyptian name.

The New Kingdom

The **XVIII Dynasty** (c.1567–1320 or 1550-1307 BC) founded by Ahmosis inaugurated the **New Kingdom**, a period of stability, wealth and expansion, whose rulers include some of the most famous names in Egyptian history. During this era **Nubia** was brought under Egyptian control, yielding gold, ivory, ebony, gems and, most importantly, slaves. The professional armies of the pharaohs also invaded the Near East, Syria and Palestine, establishing colonies governed by Egyptian viceroys or local satraps. One result was an influx of immigrants into Egypt, bringing new customs, ideas and technology.

The effects are evident at **Thebes**, capital of the New Kingdom, where a spate of temples and tombs symbolize the pre-eminence of the god **Amun** and the power of the pharaohs. While **Tuthmosis I** (c.1525–1512 BC) built the first tomb in the Valley of the Kings, his daughter **Hatshepsut** raised the great mortuary temple of Deir el-Bahri, ruling as pharaoh (c.1503–1482 BC) despite her stepson's claim on the throne. Having belatedly assumed power, **Tuthmosis III** embarked on imperial conquests, extending Egyptian power beyond the Fourth Cataract in Nubia, and across the Euphrates to the boundaries of the Hittite empire. His successor **Amenophis II** (c.1459–1425 BC) penetrated deeper into Nubia, and **Tuthmosis IV** (c.1425–1417 BC) further strengthened the empire by marrying a princess of Mitanni, a state bordering the Hittites.

The zenith of Egyptian power coincided with the reign of **Amenophis III** (c.1417–1379 BC). With the empire secure and prosperity at home, the king devoted himself to the arts and the construction of great edifices such as Luxor Temple. During the same period, a hitherto minor aspect of the sun-god was increasingly venerated in royal circles: the **cult of Aten**, which the pharaoh's son would subsequently enshrine above all others.

The Amarna Revolution

By changing his name from Amenophis IV to **Akhenaten** and founding a new capital at Tell el-Amarna, the young king underlined his commitment to a new **monotheistic religion** that challenged the existing priesthood and bureaucracy. Since the story of Akhenaten and **Nefertiti** is related in detail on p.308, it suffices to say that the **Amarna revolution** barely outlasted his reign (c.1379–1362 BC) and that of his mysterious successor, **Smenkhkare**, who died the following year.

The boy king **Tutankhamun** (1361–1352 BC) was easily persuaded to abjure Aten's cult and return the capital to Thebes, heralding a **Theban counter-revolution** that continued under **Ay** and **Horemheb**. Though Horemheb (c.1348–1320 BC) effectively restored the *status quo ante*, his lack of royal blood and, more importantly, an heir, brought the XVIII Dynasty to a close.

The XIX Dynasty

The **XIX Dynasty** (c.1320–1200 or 1307–1196 BC) began with the reign of Horemheb's vizier, **Ramses I** (c.1320–1318 BC), whose family was to produce several warrior-kings who would recapture territories lost under Akhenaten. **Seti I** (c.1318–1304 BC) reasserted pharaonic authority in Nubia, Palestine and the Near East, and began a magnificent temple at Abydos. His son **Ramses II** (c.1304–1237 BC) completed the temple and the reconquest of Asia Minor, commemorating his dubious victory at Qadesh with numerous reliefs, but later concluding a treaty with the Hittites. At home, Ramses usurped temples and statues built by others, and raised his own monumental edifices – notably the Ramesseum at Thebes and the sun temples at Abu Simbel.

His son **Merneptah** (c.1236–1217 BC) faced invasions by the "Sea Peoples" from the north and Libyans from the west, but eventually defeated the latter at Pi-yer in the western Delta. He is also popularly believed to be the pharaoh of the **Exodus**, though the only known pharaonic reference to the Israelites describes an Egyptian victory against these "nomads". The XIX Dynasty expired with **Seti II** (c.1210 BC), to be followed by a decade without a ruling dynasty.

The XX Dynasty

The **XX Dynasty** (c.1200–1085 or 1196–1070 BC), begun by Sethnakhte, was the last of the New Kingdom. His successor **Ramses III** (c.1198–1166 BC) repulsed three great invasions by the Libyans and Sea Peoples, and built the vast temple-cum-pleasure palace of **Medinet Habu**. But strikes by workmen at the royal necropolis and an assassination plot within the king's harem presaged problems to come. Under the eight kings who followed (all called Ramses), Egypt lost the remains of its Asiatic empire, and thieves plundered the necropolis. **Ramses XI** (c.1114–1085 BC) withdrew to his residence in the Delta, delegating control of Upper Egypt to **Herihor**, high priest of Amun, and Lower Egypt to Vizier **Smendes**.

The Third Intermediate Period

This division was consolidated under the **XXI Dynasty** (c.1069–945 BC), the successors of Herihor and Smendes ruling their respective halves of Egypt from **Thebes** and **Tanis**. The two ruling houses (both designated as the XXI Dynasty) seem to have coexisted in harmony, with the Theban priest-kings acknowledging the Tanite pharaohs' superiority. Towards the end of this era, a powerful new dynasty of **Libyan** extraction was founded by **Shoshenk I**. This **XXII Dynasty** (c.945–715 BC) ruled Egypt from Bubastis in the Delta until a rival line seized power in Upper Egypt, precipitating civil war between the Bubastite monarchs and the Theban **XXIII Dynasty** (818–720 BC), which was further complicated by a brief **XXIV Dynasty** (727–715 BC) of Ethiopian kings.

The lifespan of these four dynasties – termed the **Third Intermediate Period** (TIP) – is one of the murkiest eras of Egyptian history, yet crucial to the New Chronology hypothesis, as the accepted dates for the New Kingdom hinge on the length of the TIP. Rohl contends that the XXI and XXII dynasties overlapped for generations, and that the duration of the TIP should therefore be reduced accordingly – with knock-on effects down the line. Even mainstream Egyptologists differ over the next significant dynasty, which some assign to the final phase of the TIP, and others regard as the start of the Late Period – but at least they all more or less agree on dates from this point onwards.

The Late Period

In 747 BC, Egypt's prolonged instability was brought to an end by the intervention of neighbouring Nubia. The Nubian king Piankhi advanced as far north as Memphis, while his brother Shabaka went on to conquer the Delta and reunite the Two Lands. The **XXV Dynasty of Nubian Kings** (c.747–656 BC) was marked by a revival of artistic and cultural life, and renewed devotion to Amun (as evinced by reliefs at Karnak and Luxor). The dynasty's later, Ethiopian, rulers had to contend with the Assyrians, who were thrown back from the gates of **Thebes** in 671 and eventually sacked the city in 664 BC.

Egypt became a province of the Assyrian empire, ruled by local princes who paid tribute to the Assyrians until they withdrew from Egypt to defend their empire from the Babylonians, leaving a vacuum that was filled by **Psammetichus I**, the fourth ruler of the **XXVI Dynasty** (664–525 BC). Known as the Saïte Dynasty after its capital at **Saïs** in the Delta, this was the last great age of pharaonic civilization, harking back to the glories of the Old Kingdom in art and architecture, but also adopting new technologies and allowing colonies of Greek merchants at Naucratis, and Jewish mercenaries at Elephantine.

Necho II (610–595 BC) defeated Josiah, King of Judah, at Megiddo, but was routed by the Babylonians. He is also credited with starting to build a canal to link the Nile with the Red Sea. Though **Psammetichus II** (595–589 BC) enjoyed several victories, his successor **Apries** was overthrown following defeat in Cyrenaica, the throne passing to **Amasis** "the Drunkard", who relied on Greek allies to stave off the Persian empire.

Persian rule

The **Persian invasion** of 525 BC began a new era of rule by foreigners that essentially lasted until Nasser eventually overthrew Egypt's monarchy in 1952.

Mindful of the Assyrians' mistake, the Persian emperors **Cambyses** and **Darius I** kept a tight grip on Egypt. Besides completing Necho's canal and founding a new city near Memphis, called **Babylon-in-Egypt** (today's "Old Cairo"), they built and restored temples to enhance their legitimacy. But **rebellions** against Xerxes and Artaxerxes testified to Egyptian hatred of this foreign **XXVII Dynasty** (c.525–404 BC).

Ousted by Amyrtaeus, sole ruler of the XXVIII Dynasty, the Persians constantly assailed the native rulers that followed. Though **Nectanebo I** of the **XXX Dynasty** (c.380–343 BC) managed to repulse them with Greek help, his successor's campaign in Phoenicia failed. Finally, bereft of allies, **Nectanebo II** (360–343 BC) was crushingly defeated by Artaxerxes III, and fled to Nubia. Egypt remained under Persian control until 332 BC, when their entire empire succumbed to **Alexander the Great**.

The Ptolemies

Alexander's stay in Egypt was brief, though long enough for him to adopt local customs. He offered sacrifices to the gods of Memphis and visited Amun's temple at Siwa; reorganized the country's administration, installing himself as pharaoh; and founded the coastal city of **Alexandria**; he then went off to conquer what remained of the known world. Upon his death in 323 BC, Alexander's Macedonian generals divided the empire, Ptolemy becoming ruler of Egypt and establishing the **Ptolemaic Dynasty** in 332.

Under Ptolemy I, **Greek** became the official language and Hellenistic ideas had a profound effect on Egyptian art, religion and technology. Although Greek deities were also introduced, the Ptolemies cultivated the Egyptian gods and ruled much like Egyptian pharaohs, erecting great cult temples such as Edfu and Kom Ombo. They also opened new ports, established the great Library of Alexandria and had Hebrew scriptures translated into Greek by Jewish rabbis. The first synagogue in Egypt was founded at Leontopolis in the Delta.

It was dynastic disputes that led to the loss of Ptolemaic control. **Roman intervention** in Egypt grew until, under Ptolemy XII Auletes (80–51 BC), Egypt was almost totally dependent on Rome. **Julius Caesar** attacked Egypt in 54 BC, taking Alexandria by force.

The most famous queen of Egypt, **Cleopatra VII** (51–30 BC), was also the last of the Ptolemies. Under the protection of Julius Caesar – by whom she bore a son, Caesarion – Cleopatra managed to prolong her family's rule. After Caesar's death, she formed a similar alliance with **Mark Antony** to preserve Egyptian independence. Their joint fleets, however, suffered disaster against **Octavian** at the Battle of Actium, and both committed suicide rather than face captivity. Subsequently Egypt was reduced to the status of a province of the Roman Empire (30 BC).

Roman rule and the rise of Christianity

The **Roman emperors**, like the Ptolemies, adopted many of the Egyptian cults, building such monuments as Trajan's kiosk at Philae, and temples at Dendara and Esna. Their main interest in the new colony, however, lay in its potential as grain supplier to Rome. With this end constantly in mind, trade routes were ensured by Roman garrisons at Alexandria, Babylon (Old Cairo) and Syene (Aswan). In terms of culture, language and administration, **Hellenistic influence** barely diminished and Alexandria continued to thrive as an important centre of Greek and Hebrew learning.

Although the **Holy Family's flight to Egypt** from Palestine cannot be proven, Egypt's Jewish colonies would have been a natural place of refuge, and several sites remain associated with the episode. According to Coptic tradition, **Christianity** was brought to Egypt by **St Mark**, who arrived in the time of Nero. Mark converted many to the new underground faith, founding the Patriarchate of Alexandria in 61 AD.

Politically, the most significant ruler was **Trajan** (98–117), who reopened Necho's Red Sea Canal. Trade flourished with the export of glass, linen, papyrus and precious stones. But the *fellaheen* were growing increasingly discontented with heavy taxation and forced recruitment into the Roman army.

The Copts

First-century Egypt was fertile ground for the spread of Christianity. The religion of the old gods had lost its credibility over the millennia of political manipulations and disasters, while the population – Egyptians and Jews alike – was becoming increasingly anti-Roman and nationalistic in its outlook. The core of Christianity, too, had a resonance in ancient traditions, with its emphasis on resurrection, divine judgement and the cult of the great mother.

Inevitably, as Egypt's Christians – who became known as **Copts** – grew in political confidence, there was conflict with the Roman authorities. In 202, **persecutions** began, reaching their height under **Diocletian** (284–305), when thousands of Coptic Christians were massacred. Copts date their calendar from the massacres in 284.

The legalization of Christianity and its adoption as the imperial religion by **Constantine** in 313 did little to help the Copts. The Roman leaders, from their new capital at **Byzantium**, embraced an orthodox faith that differed fundamentally from that of their Egyptian co-religionists – and persecutions continued. An attempt to reconcile differences at the **Council of Nicaea** (325) failed and the split had become irrevocable by the time it was formalized at the **Council of Chalcedon** (451), following which the Copts established their own completely separate Patriarchate at Alexandria.

The same period also saw the emergence of **monasticism**, which took root in the Egyptian deserts. The monasteries of St Catherine in the Sinai, those of Wadi Natrun and Sohag, and St Anthony's and St Paul's in the Red Sea Hills, all originated in these years.

The coming of Islam

Apart from a brief invasion in 616, Egypt remained under **Byzantine rule** until the **advance of Islam** in the seventh century. Led by the Prophet Mohammed's successor, Abu Bakr, the Muslim armies defeated the Byzantine army in 636. General Amr Ibn al-As then advanced towards Babylon-in-Egypt, which surrendered after a brief siege, to be followed by Heliopolis (640) and finally the imperial capital of Alexandria (642).

Amr built his capital, **Fustat**, north of the fortress town of Babylon-in-Egypt, in what is today Old Cairo. However, Egypt was merely a province in the vast Islamic empire that was governed from Damascus and Baghdad. As in Roman times, Egypt's primary role was as a bread basket for the empire.

Arabization and Islamicization was a gradual and uneven process, with intermittent periods of religious toleration and discrimination. Much depended on the character of the khalifs, and their own power struggles, whose impact was felt throughout the Islamic empire. In 750, the empire's ruling **Umayyad** dynasty was defeated by the armies of Abu al-Abbas (a descendant of Abu Bakr) and an **Abbassid** khalifate came to power in Baghdad, administering Egypt, along with its other territories, for the next two centuries.

The Tulunids (868–905) and Ikhshidids (935–969)

In 868, **Ahmed Ibn Tulun**, sent to administer Egypt on behalf of Khalif al-Mu'tazz, declared the territory independent. He and his successors, the **Tulunids**, ruled for 37 years, during which time economic stability and order were restored. Like previous rulers, Ibn Tulun built a new capital city, **Al-Qitai**, whose vast mosque still remains. The dynasty did not long outlive him, however. His spendthrift son, Khomaruya, was assassinated, as were his heirs, and by 905 Abbassid rule was reimposed.

Egypt remained under the direct control of Baghdad until 935, when Mohammed Ibn Tughj was appointed governor and granted the title Ikhshid (ruler or king) by the khalif. Like the Tulunids, the **Ikhshidid dynasty** functioned virtually independently of the khalifate. Severe taxation, though, led to popular discontent, and the death in 965 of Tughj's second son, Ali, combined with famine, drought and political instability, opened the way for an invasion of the **Shi'a Fatimids** from Tunisia.

The Fatimid Era (969–1171)

The early **Fatimid khalifs** ruled half the Muslim world, with Egypt forming the central portion of an empire that included North Africa, Sicily, Syria and western Arabia. **Gohar**, commander of the khalifal forces, built the city of **Al-Qahira** (the Triumphant) as a new capital in 969, its walls containing opulent palaces and the prestigious mosque-university of Al-Azhar. **Khalif al-Muizz** installed himself in the city and from there ruled the empire. Trade with India, Africa and Europe expanded, the burdensome tax system was abolished, and a vast multi-racial army that included Europeans, Berbers, Sudanese and Turks was formed.

Whereas Al-Muizz and his successor Al-Aziz were efficient and tolerant rulers, under whom Egypt's economy prospered and the arts flourished, the third khalif – **Al-Hakim** (996–1021) – was a mad and capricious despot. His laws outraged the population, while his support of Byzantine against Latin Christians, and destruction of the Church of the Holy Sepulchre in Jerusalem, later provided a pretext for the First Crusade. His mysterious disappearance (see p.146) was taken by his followers – he championed Shi'a against Sunni Islam – as proof of messianic stature.

By the long reign of Al-Hakim's grandson, **Al-Mostansir** (1035–94), decay had set in. The empire was largely controlled by army commanders, administration was chaotic and famine added to the troubles. A series of governors imposed control over the army and restored peace and prosperity to Egypt for a further hundred years, but the loss of Syria to the Seljuk Turks, and new forces in Europe, left the empire increasingly vulnerable.

The **First Crusade** (1097–99), and those that followed, were motivated as much by the desire to acquire estates as to restore Christian dominance to the Holy Land. Egypt, however, was not attacked until 1167, by which time the Crusader kingdom held the former Fatimid coastal area of Palestine. Outraged at the fraternization between Franks and Fatimids, the Seljuk Sultan, Nur al-Din, sent an expedition to Cairo to repel them. The sultan's deputy, Shirkoh, occupied Upper Egypt, while his nephew, Salah al-Din al-Ayyubi – known to Europe as Saladin – took possession of Alexandria.

The Ayyubids (1171–1250)

On the death of the last Fatimid khalif in 1171, **Salah al-Din** became ruler of Egypt. To this day he remains a hero in the Arab world, a ruler renowned for his personal modesty, generosity, culture and political acumen. Having no pretensions to religious leadership, Salah al-Din chose for himself the secular title of *Al-Sultan* (The Power) rather than that of khalif, giving his family's name – Ayyub – to the dynasty that succeeded him. Of his 24-year reign, he spent only eight years in Cairo, the rest being spent in liberating Crusader-held territory. By 1183, Syria had been won back and in 1187 Jerusalem was recaptured.

In Cairo, Salah al-Din built a fortress – today's Citadel – and expanded the Fatimid walls to enclose the city. In order to propagate Sunni orthodoxy, he also introduced the Seljuk institution of the **madrassa** or teaching mosque, thus turning Cairo into a great centre of learning. Hospitals were endowed, too, and the pharaonic canal at Fayoum was reopened.

Following his peaceful death in Damascus in 1193, Salah al-Din's eastern territories fragmented into principalities, though Egypt remained united under the Ayyubids. His nephew, **Al-Kamil** (1218–38), repulsed the Fifth Crusade. The last of the dynasty, **Ayyub** (1240–49), built up a formidable army of Turkish-speaking Qipchak slaves from the Black Sea region, and he himself married a slave girl, **Shagar al-Durr** (Tree of Pearls).

It was Shagar al-Durr who took power following Ayyub's death, ruling openly as sultana until the Abbassid khalifs insisted that she take a husband, quoting the Prophet's words: "Woe to the nations ruled by women". Jealous of her power and warned by astrologers that he would die at a woman's hands, her husband, Aybak, planned to take a second wife, whereupon she had him murdered. She herself was assassinated soon afterwards, but her henchman, **Beybars the Crossbowman**, clawed his way to power, inaugurating the Mamluke era.

The Mamlukes (1250–1517)

Beybars was a commander among the foreign troops – the Mamlukes – on whom the later Ayyubids depended. Following his accession, **Mamluke amirs** (military leaders) retained control of Egypt for the next three centuries, each sultan intriguing his way up the ranks to assume the throne by *coup d'état* or assassination.

Bahri Mamlukes (1250–1382)

The **Bahri** (River) **Mamlukes**, named after their garrison by the Nile and predominantly Turkic, formed the first of these military dynasties. The dynasty was founded by **Qalaoun**, who poisoned Beybars' heirs to inherit the throne. He sponsored numerous buildings in Cairo, and established relations as far afield as Ceylon and East Africa, concluding treaties with the Hapsburg Emperor Rudolph and other European princes. His son, **Khalil**, forced the remaining Crusaders from their stronghold in Acre in 1291.

Qalaoun's son **Mohammed al-Nasir** (1294–1340) was another great builder and power-broker. He concluded treaties with the Mongols, after defeating them in Syria, and strengthened political and trade ties with Europe. After his death a series of weak relatives were barely able to hold the throne in the face of conflicts between rival Mamluke factions.

Burgi Mamlukes (1382–1517)

In 1382 the sultanate was seized by **Barquq**, one of the Circassian **Burgi** (Tower) **Mamlukes** from the garrison below the Citadel. To finance his campaigns against the **Mongols**, who by 1387 were on the borders of Syria, he had to impose punitive taxes that beggared the economy.

Hardships were exacerbated by famine and plague during the reign of his son, **Farag** (1399–1405), and it was only under Sultan **Barsbey** (1422–37) that Egypt regained some of its power. Barsbey established friendly relations with the new power in the north, the Ottoman Turks, and expanded trade in the Indian Ocean. But although the next hundred years saw relative peace and security, the Egyptian economy remained shaky.

The country experienced a brief revival under the rule of **Qaitbey** (1468–1495), though his lavish building programme imposed a huge burden. The 46th, and penultimate sultan, **Qansuh al-Ghuri** (1501–16), suffered the loss of customary revenues after Vasco da Gama discovered the Cape of Good Hope, dealing a crippling blow to Egypt's spice trade monopoly. Worse was to come, as the **Ottoman Turks** consolidated their northern empire, defeating the Shi'ite Persians and then attacking Mamluke territory in northern Syria. In 1516, Al-Ghuri was killed in battle and his successor, Tumanbey, was executed in Cairo by the Ottomans in 1517.

Ottoman Egypt (1517–1789)

Even after the Turkish conquest, the Mamlukes remained powerful figures, running the administration of what was now a province of the vast Ottoman Empire. Government was provided by a series of **pashas**, career officials trained in Istanbul. As long as taxes were received, the Ottomans interfered little with Egyptian affairs and Cairo retained its importance as a religious, if not cultural or commercial, centre.

The Mamluke army continued to grow with the import of Caucasian slaves and by the end of the sixteenth century had become powerful enough to depose a pasha, although the Ottomans still held overall control. The growing power of the highest rank of the military corps – **the Beys** – posed a challenge to that of the pashas. Their arbitrary taxes, profligate ways and internal rivalry dominated events.

Meanwhile, economic decline, accelerated by changes in European shipping routes, and an outbreak of plague in 1719, left the country in a sorry shape. The French traveller Volney, visiting around 1784, described a depopulated country, whose capital was crumbling and surrounded by mounds of rubbish.

French Occupation 1798–1802

At the end of the eighteenth century, Egypt became a pawn in the struggle for power between France and Britain. **Napoleon** saw Egypt as a means to disrupt British commerce and eventually overthrow their rule in India. In 1798, his fleet landed at Alexandria, where he issued a proclamation that began with the

Islamic *bismillah* ("In the name of God . . ."); stated his aim of liberating Egypt from the "riffraff of slaves"; and concluded that he respected Allah, his Prophet and the Koran more than the Mamlukes did.

Although Napoleon routed the Mamlukes at Imbaba and occupied Cairo, he left his fleet exposed at Abu Qir Bay, where it was attacked and destroyed by the British under Nelson. With his grand vision in tatters, and facing a declaration of war from the Ottoman sultan, Napoleon returned secretly to France. General Kléber, whom he left in charge, had a victory over the Ottomans, but was then assassinated. When his successor, General Menou, took charge, declared his conversion to Islam, and proclaimed Egypt a **French protectorate**, the British invaded from Abu Qir and occupied Alexandria. Combined Ottoman-British forces then took Damietta and Cairo, and the French were forced to surrender. Under the Capitulation Agreement, the archeological treasures gathered by Napoleon's savants were surrendered to Britain – which is why the **Rosetta Stone** ended up in the British Museum rather than the Louvre.

Mohammed Ali and his heirs (1805–92)

After the expulsion of the French a power struggle ensued, which was won by **Mohammed Ali**, an officer in the Albanian Corps of the Ottoman forces. Widely regarded as the founder of modern Egypt, his dynasty was to change Egypt more radically than any ruler since Salah al-Din.

The Ottomans confirmed Mohammed Ali as **Pasha** in 1805, whereupon he proceeded to decapitate – literally and figuratively – what remained of the Mamluke power structure. The first time was on the occasion of his accession, where he tricked them into a coup attempt; six years later, he dispensed with the rest of the Mamluke leadership, inviting 470 Beys to a feast at the Citadel and slaughtering the lot.

Though nominally a vassal of the Ottoman sultan, Mohammed Ali's control was absolute. He confiscated private land for his own use and set about modernizing Egypt with European expertise, building railways, factories and canals. Meanwhile, his son Ibrahim led a murderous campaign to subjugate northern **Sudan**, of which the only positive result was the introduction of a special kind of **cotton** – henceforth Egypt's major cash crop.

When Mohammed Ali died insane in 1849, his power greatly reduced after disastrous adventurism in Greece and Syria, he was succeeded by **Abbas** (1848–54), who closed the country's factories and schools and opened Egypt to free trade, thus delaying the country's industrial development for the next century.

Abbas's successor, **Said Pasha** (1854–63), granted a concession to a French engineer, **Ferdinand de Lesseps**, to build the **Suez Canal**. The project was completed in 1869, by which time **Khedive Ismail** (1863–79) was in power. An ambitious and enlightened ruler, Ismail transformed Cairo, spending lavishly on modernization. However, exorbitant interest rates had to be paid on loans from European lenders. Egyptian indebtedness spiralled and, to stave off bankruptcy, Ismail sold his Suez Canal shares to the British government in 1875.

He was deposed and succeeded by his son **Tewfiq** (1879–92), whose own financial control was limited by the French and British, to the disgust of patriotic Egyptians. A group of army officers forced him to make power-sharing concessions and to appoint their leader, **Ahmed Orabi**, as Minister of War. France and Britain responded by sending in the gunboats, shelling Alexandria and landing an army at Ismailiya, which subsequently routed Orabi's forces at Tell el-Kebir and restored Tewfiq as a puppet ruler under British control.

British occupation... and nationalism

Britain's stated intention was to set Egyptian affairs in order and then withdraw, but its interests dictated a more active and permanent involvement. From 1883 to 1907, Egypt was controlled by the British Consul-General, Sir Evelyn Baring, later **Lord Cromer**, who coined the term "Veiled Protectorate" to describe the relationship between the two countries.

The emergence of the **Mahdi** in Sudan accelerated the trend towards direct British involvement in military and civil affairs. Sudan was nominally an Egyptian khedival possession – a status quo which the British, ostensibly, moved to protect. However, Britain was clearly pursuing its own interests, and dominating Egyptian government to the extent of replacing its key officials with British colonial personnel. Egyptian resentment at this usurpation of authority found expression both under Tewfiq's son, **Abbas II**, who came to power in 1892, and in a nationalist movement led by a young lawyer, **Mustafa Kamil**. To ameliorate the situation, the British made a series of reforms and allowed Orabi to return from exile in Ceylon.

Economically, however, Egypt was effectively a colony, with Britain supplying all the country's manufactured goods, and in turn encouraging Egyptian dependence on cotton exports. In order to grow cotton, the *fellaheen* had to take out loans; when prices fell, many were forced to sell up to large landowners.

Towards independence

Politically, things came to a head when Turkey entered **World War I** on the side of Germany, in November 1916. Egypt was still nominally a province of the Ottoman Empire, so to protect its interests – the Suez Canal and free passage to the East – Britain declared Egypt a protectorate. By 1917, **Fouad**, the sixth son of Ismail, was khedive of Egypt, with Sir Reginald Wingate its High Commissioner.

The **nationalist movement** flourished under wartime conditions. In 1918, its leader, **Sa'ad Zaghloul**, presented the High Commissioner with a demand for autonomy, which was rejected. The request to send a delegation (*Wafd*) to London led to Zaghloul's arrest and deportation to Malta, a decision rescinded after nationwide anti-British riots. In 1922 Britain abolished the protectorate and recognized Egypt as an independent state, but kept control of the legal system, communications, defence and the Suez Canal. In March 1922, Fouad assumed the title of king.

The years between independence and World War II saw a struggle for power between the king, the British and the nationalist **Wafd Party**. Backed by the masses, the Wafd won landslide elections, but King Fouad retained power and the backing of the British. His son, **King Farouk**, succeeded him to the throne in 1935 and a year later signed a twenty-year **Anglo-Egyptian treaty**, which ended British occupation but empowered British forces to remain in the Suez Canal Zone. In 1937, Egypt joined the League of Nations, but the outbreak of World War II halted its move to complete independence.

World War II

During **World War II**, Egypt served a vital strategic role as a British base in the Middle East. The Wafd leadership went along with support for the Allies – on the tacit understanding that full independence would be granted after the war – keeping internal tensions controlled. Cairo itself, however, became an extraordinary centre of international power-broking, with its British political-military command and exiled Balkan royals and governments.

Rommel's **Afrika Korps** came within 111 kilometres of Alexandria, but was repulsed by the **Eighth Army** under General Montgomery at the **Battle of El-Alamein** in October 1942. Thereafter the tide of war turned in the Western Desert Campaign and the Allies continued to advance across North Africa, through Libya and Tunisia.

Post-war manoeuvrings

On **conclusion of the war**, the Wafd demanded the evacuation of British troops and unification with Sudan – in opposition to British plans for the latter's self-government. Popular resentment was expressed in anti-British riots and strikes, supported by the **Muslim Brotherhood**, which led to clashes with British troops. In January 1947, British troops were evacuated from Alexandria and the Canal Zone.

Following the declaration of the state of **Israel** in May 1948, Egypt joined Iraq, Syria and Jordan in a military invasion. The defeat of the Arab forces was followed by a UN-organized treaty in February 1949 that left the coastal **Gaza Strip** of Palestine under Egyptian administration. Many of the Egyptian officers who fought in this war were left disgusted by the incompetence and corruption of their superiors: it was from the officers' ranks that many of the leading lights of the 1952 Revolution were to emerge.

The 1952 revolution

For the time being, the country experimented with democracy, holding its first **elections** in ten years. The Wafd won a majority and formed a government with Nahas Pasha as prime minister. A course for crisis was set, as the **Suez Canal** – which the British still controlled – loomed increasingly large. In 1952, Nahas was dismissed by King Farouk after abrogating the 1936 treaty with Britain, and the army was sent out onto the streets to quell anti-British protests.

Reaction was swift. On July 23, 1952, a group of conspiratorial **Free Officers** seized power and forced the **abdication of King Farouk**. General Naguib, the official leader of the group, was made commander of the armed forces and became prime minister, but real power lay in the hands of the nine officers of the **Revolutionary Command Council** (RCC), foremost amongst whom was Colonel **Gamal Abdel Nasser**.

Under RCC direction, the constitution was revoked, political parties dissolved, the monarchy abolished and Egypt declared a **republic** (July 26, 1953). Meanwhile, a struggle for power was taking place behind the scenes, as Naguib attempted to step beyond his figurehead status and moderate the revolutionary impulses of the RCC. After being implicated in an attempt on Nasser's life at Alexandria in 1954, Naguib was placed under house arrest. Nasser became acting head of state and in June 1956 was confirmed as president.

The Nasser Era (1956–70)

President Nasser dominated Egypt and the Arab world until his death in 1970, his ideology of Arab nationalism and socialism making him supremely popular with the masses (if not always their governments) from Iraq to Morocco. Under his leadership, Egypt was at the forefront of **anti-colonialism**, lending support to liberation struggles in Algeria, sub-Saharan Africa and other regions. Nasser also helped to set up the Non-Aligned Movement with Yugoslavia, India and Indonesia in 1955.

Diplomacy and war

Nasser's most urgent priority, from the start, was to assert Egyptian control over the **Suez Canal**. In 1954 he reached agreement for the withdrawal of British troops from the Canal Zone, though the Canal's management and profits were to remain in foreign hands. At the same time he was seeking credits from the World Bank to finance construction of the Aswan High Dam, and for weapons to rearm Egyptian forces, depleted from the 1948 war.

When the Soviet Union offered to supply the latter, the United States vetoed loans for the dam. Committed to the Aswan plan, Nasser had little alternative but to **nationalize the Suez Canal**, in order to secure revenue. This he did in July 1956.

His action was regarded by the West, and especially by Britain, as a threat to vital interests, and an unholy alliance was formed to combat the "Arab Hitler". Britain and France concluded a secret agreement with Israel, whose **invasion of Sinai** in October 1956 was to provide the pretext for their own military intervention. Following massive bombardment of the zone, and British paratroop landings in Port Said, the United States stepped in to impose a solution, threatening to destabilize the British economy unless their forces were withdrawn. The American motivation was to keep Britain and France from gaining control of the Middle East, and the Arabs from moving en masse into the Soviet camp. In the event, the canal was reopened under full Egyptian control and Nasser emerged from the **Suez Crisis** as a champion of Arab nationalism.

On a wave of **pan-Arabist** sentiment, Egypt and Syria united to form the **United Arab Republic** (UAR) in 1958: an unworkable arrangement that foundered within three years. Nasser also intervened in the **Yemen civil war**, supporting the revolutionary faction, to the extent of authorizing the use of poison gas against royalist forces. On a broader political front, he moved closer to the Soviet Union, accepting technical and military assistance on a massive scale, to help build the Aswan Dam and to counter an increasingly well-armed, US-supplied Israel. Meeting in Cairo in 1964, the **Arab League** set aside funds for the formation of the **Palestine Liberation Organization**.

War was again on the horizon. When Israel threatened to invade Syria in 1967, Nasser sent Egyptian forces into Sinai, ordered UN monitors to withdraw, and blockaded the Tiran Straits, cutting shipping to the Israeli port of

Eilat. Israel responded with a pre-emptive strike, destroying the Egyptian air force on the ground and seizing the entire Sinai. This **Six Day War** resulted in permanent Israeli occupation of Sinai and the Gaza Strip, the West Bank and the Golan Heights. It was a shattering defeat for the Arabs, and Nasser in particular, who proffered his resignation to the public, only resuming the presidency after vast demonstrations of support on the streets.

The Six Day War had no official resolution, merely subsiding into a **War of Attrition**, which was to drag on for the next two years. From their positions in Sinai, Israeli forces bombarded Egypt's Canal cities and even Cairo and Middle Egypt suffered bombing raids. Egypt, meanwhile, was rearming with Soviet assistance and struggling to deal with millions of refugees from the Canal Zone and the newly occupied Gaza Strip.

Progress and repression

Amid the political drama of Suez and the wars with Israel, it is easy to overlook the **social achievements** of the Nasser era. One of the first acts of the Revolutionary Command Council was to break up the old feudal estates, transferring **land** to the *fellaheen*. As a result of the **Aswan Dam**, the amount of land under cultivation increased by fifteen percent – exceeding Egypt's population growth for the first time. The dam's electricity also powered a huge new **industrial base**, which was established virtually from scratch.

Similarly radical progress was made in the fields of **education and health care**. The number of pupils in school doubled, and included both sexes for the first time. As a result of a huge programme of local health centres, and the doubling of the number of doctors, average life expectancy rose from 43 to 52 years.

The downside of Nasser's socialism was a heavily bureaucratic, often Soviet-modelled system. Political life was stifled by the merging of all parties into the **Arab Socialist Union** (ASU). Opponents of the regime were not tolerated: censorship, torture, show trials and political internment were widespread.

Nevertheless, **Nasser's death** – from a heart attack – in September 1970 came as a profound shock to the whole Arab world. His funeral procession in Cairo was the largest the country has ever seen.

Egypt under Sadat (1970–81)

Nasser's successor was his vice president, **Anwar Sadat**, whom the ASU hierarchy confirmed as president in October 1970. His role was to reform an Egypt demoralized by defeat in the 1967 war, economic stagnation and austerity. His first significant act was to announce a "**corrective revolution**", reversing the policy of centralized economic control, and expelling over a thousand Soviet advisors.

Again, however, social and economic affairs were overshadowed by military developments. In concert with Syria and Jordan, Egypt launched a new campaign against Israel. On October 6, 1973, Egyptian forces crossed the Suez Canal, storming the "invincible" Bar-Lev Line to enter Israeli-occupied Sinai. This **October War** (aka 10th Ramadan/Yom Kippur War) ultimately turned against the Arabs, but enhanced their bargaining position and dealt a blow to Israeli self-confidence. In addition, Egypt regained a strip of territory to the east of the Suez Canal.

The open door policy

After the war, extensive changes took place in Egypt. An amnesty was granted to political prisoners, press censorship was lifted and some political parties, including the Muslim Brotherhood, were allowed. Equally important was Sadat's economic policy of *infitah* or "**open door**", designed to encourage private and foreign investment and to reduce the role of the state in the economy.

Helped by Gulf Arab investments – a reward for the October War – and stimulated by the reconstruction of the Canal cities, the economy boomed. However, the benefits were distributed totally unevenly. While the number of millionaires rose from 500 to 17,000 between 1975 and 1981, and an affluent middle class developed, the condition of the urban poor and peasants worsened. Some five million families subsisted on less than US$30 a month, and one and a half million Egyptians migrated to work in the Gulf states.

In 1977, when the International Monetary Fund insisted on the removal of subsidies on basic foodstuffs, there were nationwide **food riots**. Sadat saw the crunch coming and needed a major injection of Western capital.

Camp David and afterwards

In 1977 Sadat went to Jerusalem, the first Arab leader to visit Israel. This dramatic step, accompanied by a total realignment of Egyptian foreign policy towards the United States, has been explained in two ways. One theory holds that it was solely motivated by the desire for US investment; the other, by Israel's acquisition of nuclear weapons, which rendered impossible a military solution in the region.

Under the resulting, US-sponsored **Camp David Agreement** of 1978, Egypt recognized Israel's right to exist and Israel agreed to withdraw from Sinai. This independent peace treaty, which failed to resolve the Palestinian issue, outraged Arab opinion. Meeting in Baghdad, the Arab League Council decided to withdraw their ambassadors to Egypt, sever economic and political links, and transfer the League's headquarters from Cairo to Tunis.

At home, Sadat encouraged the rise of Islamic political forces to counter leftist influences. But as the Muslim Brotherhood grew stronger and protested against the economic slump and Camp David, Sadat clamped down, with wholesale arrests of critics. In this charged atmosphere, **Sadat's assassination** by Islamic militants in October 1981 was not altogether surprising.

Mubarak's Egypt – from 1981 until the present

Sadat's policies have for the most part been continued, with rather more caution, by his successor **Hosni Mubarak**, who took office in 1981 and remains in power at the time of writing. While sheer survival counts for something, the country's situation is almost as precarious as it was in the early 1970s, when the writer Naguib Mahfouz likened Egypt to a group of drowning men struggling to reach the water's surface.

C

CONTEXTS | The historical framework

The economy

The **economy** was left in dire straits at the end of the Sadat era, and its root problems seem intractable. Only three percent of Egypt's land is useable for agriculture, while the **population** rises by a million every nine months (it currently stands at around 69 million). Since the mid-1980s, Egypt has had to import half the food it needs, and its **national debt** has reached over US$30 billion. Without **US aid** (Egypt is the second largest recipient, after Israel), the economy would collapse. It is this economic situation that has led the government to inaugurate such schemes as the Toshka Project, which aims to make 500,000 acres of desert fertile by irrigating it with water pumped from Lake Nasser (see p.477).

Domestic revenues depend on a narrow base, which is highly vulnerable to the political climate: remittances from Egyptians working abroad, crude oil production, tolls on shipping through the Suez Canal, and tourism. All of these were badly hit by the **Gulf War** of 1990–91, which led to over a million refugees returning from Kuwait and Iraq and wiped out the tourist industry for a year. The government's support for US action against Iraq was rewarded by the writing-off of US$7 billion in debts, further military and economic aid, and the promise of contracts and jobs for Egyptians in the Gulf states. However, prospects had hardly begun to improve when terrorist attacks on tourists exposed another aspect of the economy's vulnerablity. **Tourism** had only just recovered from the crippling affects of the 1997 Luxor massacre when the September 11 outrages in the US sent it plunging again.

Even before this, the economy's fragility was evident, as speculation against the Egyptian pound and a liquidity crisis in the banking system led to a six percent **devaluation** of the national currency in August 2001. Things could have been worse had Egypt not been attracting a lot of new investments from both foreign and domestic sources since the mid-1990s, while the prospect of Egypt becoming a major exporter of **natural gas** over the next decade offers some hope to economic planners.

For most ordinary Egyptians, however, living standards are no higher than in Nasser's time, and the need for housing, jobs and land is greater than ever. Discontent is also fostered by widespread **corruption**, extending from local government to central ministries and the private sector. In 2002, the ex-governor of Giza was sentenced to sixteen years' hard labour for taking over £E1 million in bribes, and charges were brought against two MPs from the ruling National Democratic Party and nine senior officials from the Irrigation Ministry, alleged to have wasted £E45 million of public funds and taken £E30 million in kickbacks. Also, while incidences of buildings collapsing due to contractors cutting corners have become all too familiar over the decades, the whole nation was shocked by a catastrophic train-fire that exposed the ramshackle state of Egypt's railways and officialdom's indifference towards the lives and safety of the poor.

Domestic politics and foreign affairs

Mubarak's cautious liberalization of the media and parliamentary politics has given a democratic gloss to an authoritarian system, essentially unchanged since Nasser's time. In 1999, a national referendum asked "Do you want Mubarak to continue as president?" The result – which saw him endorsed for a fourth six-year term – surprised no one, and mutterings about a more democratic election process were predictably subdued. Although a diverse press is tolerated, the government retains – and exercises – the right of **censorship**, banning reports on human rights violations and confiscating "atheist works" at the Cairo Book Fair. Abuses of power by the police and security forces go unpunished, while human rights activists are arrested: in 2002 **Sadd Eddin Ibrahim** of the Ibn Khaldun Centre for Developmental Studies was jailed for seven years for receiving funds from the European Union and issuing reports that "tarnished Egypt's reputation abroad"; while the authorities detained sixteen candidates for the local elections in Alexandria, who received prison terms for membership of the outlawed Muslim Brotherhood; and a student was shot dead by police during a protest about Palestine.

As the third president to have emerged from the armed forces, Mubarak is even more beholden to them than his predecessors. Ex-military and police officers hold top jobs in civilian life, and **internal security** is a constant preoccupation. Between 1992 and 1998, **Islamic militants** and the security forces fought a vicious, low-level war in Middle Egypt. Human rights organizations estimate that over 1200 people were killed and 10,000 wounded during the six-year insurgency, and about 20,000 detained under the emergency laws in 1993 alone. Ironically, the Luxor massacre that made headlines around the world proved to be the swansong of the *Gamaat Islamiya* – whose imprisoned leaders denounced the massacre and announced a ceasefire – while the other militant group, Islamic Jihad, had by this time decamped to Afghanistan, where they forged an alliance with Osama Bin Laden's Al-Qaida (see p.809).

Mubarak's **foreign policy** involves a delicate balancing act, as Egypt remains impaled on the contradictions of its relationship with America, Israel and the Arab world. The US is Egypt's prime financial underwriter and arms supplier, yet consistently favours Israel, which Arab states and peoples universally regard as the main source of instability and danger in the Middle East. While Mubarak managed to restore ties with other Arab states (which readmitted Egypt to the Arab League in 1990 and later returned the League's headquarters to Cairo) whilst maintaining a "cold peace" with Israel, the tensions and frustrations implicit in this policy are obvious. Essentially, the regime's stability hangs on the decisions of other governments, and the outcome of US and Israeli elections – as the tortuous **peace process** in the Middle East has faltered or revived.

Although the talks initiated by the US in Madrid in October 1991 soon hit deadlock, Israel's Rabin government and the PLO engaged in secret talks in Oslo throughout the first half of 1993, from which emerged a Declaration of Principles regarding Palestinian self-rule in the occupied territories, paving the way for a peace treaty between Israel and Jordan and the establishment of a Palestinian Authority widely seen as the precursor of a Palestinian state. But their failure to agree on how to go beyond Oslo, violence by rejectionists on both sides, and Rabin's assassination by a right-wing Israeli terrorist, led to the 1996 election victory of Binyamin Netanyahu, which brought negotiations to a halt.

With the election of the left-leaning Ehud Barak as Israeli prime minister in July 1999, a new set of accords were signed by the Palestinians and Israel, followed by the resumption of peace talks and an unprecedented meeting in Washington between Barak and the Syrian foreign minister. Hopes were high for a comprehensive peace, but within months the Wye accords had collapsed following disagreement over the timetable for implementation, the Syrian presidency changed hands and impetus was lost and, in September 2000, the notorious right-wing Israeli general **Ariel Sharon** sparked a new Palestinian uprising by touring Jerusalem's Haram ash-Sharif, the third holiest shrine in Islam. Within weeks Sharon had won the Israeli elections and the so-called **Al-Aqsa intifada** had become a far bloodier reprise of the *intifada* of the 1980s.

Prospects for new negotiations receded as the new US president George W. Bush announced America's disengagement from the peace process. Although the rising death toll compelled a US volte-face, it was clear that the new administration was far less sympathetic to the Palestinians than Clinton had been. The terrorist attacks of **September 11** crystallized their view of world affairs as a struggle between good and evil, where the Palestinians were seen as terrorists unless proven otherwise, while the identification of two of the hijackers as Egyptians and most of the rest as Saudis – not to mention the nationality of Al-Qaida's leaders – further undermined relations between the US and its closest Arab allies, Egypt and Saudi Arabia. While both regimes managed to keep a lid on domestic opposition to America's war in Afghanistan, they fear that an attack on **Iraq** would ignite a powderkeg.

Islam

It's difficult to get any grasp of Egypt without first knowing something of Islam. What follows is a very basic background: some theory, some history and an idea of Egypt's place in the modern Islamic world.

Beginnings: practice and belief

Islam was a new religion born of the wreckage of the Greco-Roman world around the south of the Mediterranean. Its founder, a merchant named **Mohammed** from the wealthy city of Mecca (now in Saudi Arabia), was chosen as God's Prophet; in about 609 AD, he began to hear divine messages, which were later transcribed into the **Koran**, Islam's holy book. This was the same God worshipped by Jews and Christians – Jesus is one of the minor prophets in Islam – but Muslims claim He had been misunderstood by both earlier religions.

The distinctive feature of this new faith was directness – a reaction to the increasing complexity of established religions and an obvious attraction. In Islam there is no intermediary between man and God (**Allah**) in the form of an institutionalized priesthood or complicated liturgy; and worship, in the form of prayer, is a direct and personal communication with God. Believers face five essential requirements, the so-called "**Pillars of Faith**": prayer five times daily, the pilgrimage (*Hadj*) to Mecca, the Ramadan fast, a religious levy, and – most fundamental of all – the acceptance that "There is no God but Allah and Mohammed is His Prophet".

The Pillars of Faith

The Pillars of Faith are still central to Muslim life, articulating and informing daily existence. Ritual **prayers** are the most visible. Bearing in mind that the Islamic day begins at sunset, the five daily times are sunset, after dark, dawn, noon and afternoon. Prayers can be performed anywhere, but preferably in a mosque. In the past, and even today in some places, a muezzin (prayer crier) would climb his minaret each time and summon the faithful.

Nowadays, the call is likely to be pre-recorded; even so, this most distinctive of Islamic sounds has a beauty all of its own, especially when neighbouring muezzins are audible simultaneously. Their message is simplicity itself: "God is most great (*Allahu Akbar*). I testify that there is no God but Allah. I testify that Mohammed is His Prophet. Come to prayer, come to security. God is great". Another phrase is added in the morning: "Prayer is better than sleep".

Prayers are preceded by ritual washing and are spoken with the feet bare. Facing Mecca (the direction indicated in a mosque by the *mihrab* or niche), the worshipper recites the *Fathah*, the first chapter of the Koran: "Praise be to God, Lord of the worlds, the Compassionate, the Merciful, King of the Day of Judgement. Only thee do we worship and thine aid do we seek. Guide us on the straight path, the path of those on whom thou hast bestowed thy grace, not the path of those who incur thine anger nor of those who go astray". The same words are then repeated twice in the prostrate position, with some interjections of *Allahu Akbar*. It is a highly ritualized procedure, the prostrate position symbolic of the worshipper's role as servant (Islam literally means "submission"), and the sight of thousands of people going through the same motions simultaneously in a mosque is a powerful one. On Islam's holy day, Friday, all believers are expected to attend prayers in their local grand mosque. Here the whole community comes together in worship led by an *imam*, who may also deliver the *khutba*, or sermon.

Ramadan is the name of the ninth month in the lunar Islamic calendar, the month in which the Koran was revealed to Mohammed. For the whole of the month, believers must obey a rigorous fast (the custom was originally modelled on Jewish and Christian practice), forsaking all forms of consumption between sunrise and sundown; this includes food, drink, cigarettes and any form of sexual contact. Only a few categories of people are exempted: travellers, children, pregnant women and warriors engaged in a *jihad*, or holy struggle. Given the climates in which many Muslims live, the fast is a formidable undertaking, but in practice it becomes a time of intense celebration.

The pilgrimage, or **Hadj**, to Mecca is an annual event, with millions flocking to Mohammed's birthplace from all over the world. Here they go through several days of rituals, the central one being a sevenfold circumambulation of the Ka'ba, before kissing a black stone set in its wall. Islam requires that all believers go on a *Hadj* as often as is practically possible, but for the poor it may well be a once-in-a-lifetime occasion, and is sometimes replaced by a series of visits to lesser, local shrines – in Egypt, for instance, to the mosques of Saiyida Zeinab or El-Hussein in Cairo.

Based on these central articles, the new Islamic faith proved to be inspirational. Mohammed's own Arab nation was soon converted, and the Arabs then proceeded to carry their religion far and wide in an extraordinarily rapid territorial expansion.

Development in Egypt

Islam's **arrival in Egypt**, in 640, coincided with widespread native resentment of Byzantine rule and its particular version of Christianity. By promising to respect Egyptian Christians and Jews as "people of the Book", the Muslim leader **Amr** got acquiescence, if not immediate support, from the population, in the wake of the Arab conquest. For many Egyptians who had found Christianity a more valid religion than the old pagan, polytheistic theology, Islam must have seemed a logical simplification, capturing the essence of human relationships with an all-powerful god.

Early on, the spread of Islam was accompanied by a practical conflict of interest. The Arabs wished to spread the faith, yet their administration depended on finance raised by a poll tax (*jizia*) levied on non-Muslims. A balance was maintained for a while, but towards the end of the ninth century, rulers began to use the tax as a punitive measure, alongside a series of repressive acts directed against the Christian and Jewish faiths. Khalif al-Hakim, in particular, embarked on a programme of destroying churches and synagogues. However, it was not until the eleventh century that Cairo attained a **Muslim majority**, and not until the thirteenth century for Egypt as a whole.

The original Arab dynasties of Egypt subscribed to **Sunni Islam** – the more "orthodox" branch of the religion, dominant then, as now, in most parts of the Arab world. However, the Fatimid dynasty, which took control of Egypt in 969, signalled a shift to **Shi'ite Islam**, which was to continue (among the rulers, at least) until late in the twelfth century. Under the Ayyubid dynasty that followed, Egypt reverted, permanently as it turned out, to Sunni adherence, with orthodoxy propagated through the new institution of the **madrassa** – a theological college attached to a mosque.

Orthodoxy, by its very nature, has to be an urban-based tradition. Learned men – lawyers, Koranic scholars and others – could only congregate in the cities where, gathered together and known collectively as the **ulema**, they regulated the faith. In Sunni Islam, the *ulema* divide into four schools (*madhahib*): *Hanbali, Maliki, Hanafi* and *Shafi'i* – the last two of which predominate in Egypt. The *ulema* of Cairo's great **Mosque of Al-Azhar** is regarded as the ultimate theological authority by most Sunnis outside of the Gulf Arab states, and issues *fatwas* (opinions) on a range of questions submitted by believers, from family matters to financial affairs – in person, by post or email (ⓦwww .alazhar.org, ⓔinfo@alazhar.org).

Sheikhs and Sufis

Alongside this formal religious establishment, Egypt also developed **a popular religious culture**, manifested in the veneration of sheikhs and the formation of Sufi brotherhoods – both of which remain important today.

Sheikhs are basically local holy men: people who developed reputations for sanctity and learning. There is no set process for their sanctification in Islam – only acclamation – so the names change with the locality. Similar to sheikhs are individuals revered simply as **saiyid** (lord) or **saiyida** (lady), often due to their direct descent from the Prophet's line. Important Egyptian examples include Saiyid el-Hussein, Mohammed's grandson and the son of Ali, and the Prophet's granddaughters, Saiyida Zeinab and Saiyida Nafisa.

Although the Koran explicitly prohibits monasticism and isolation from the community, Islam soon developed religious orders dedicated to asceticism and a mystical experience of God. Collectively known as the **Sufis**, these groups generally coalesced around a charismatic teacher, from whom they derived their name. The largest of these brotherhoods (*tariqas*) in Egypt are the **Rifai**, the **Ahmediya** and the **Shadhiliyya** – who can be seen at moulids ("saint's day" festivals) parading with their distinctive banners.

Towards crisis

With all its different forms, Islam permeates almost every aspect of Egyptian society. Unlike Christianity (or at least Protestant Christianity), which has accepted the separation of church and state, Islam sees no such distinction. Civil law was provided by the *sharia*, the religious law contained in the Koran, and intellectual life by the *madrassas* and Al-Azhar University.

The religious basis of Arab study and intellectual life did not prevent its **scholars and scientists** from producing work that was hundreds of years ahead of contemporary "Dark Age" Europe. The medical treatises of Ibn Sina (known in Europe as Avicenna) and the piped water and sewage systems of Fustat are just two Egyptian examples. Arab work in developing and transmitting Greco-Roman culture was vital to the whole development of the European Renaissance.

By this time, however, the Islamic world was beginning to move away from the West. The **Crusades** were one enduring influence towards division.

Another was the Islamic authorities themselves, who were increasingly suspicious (like the Western church) of any challenge and actively discouraging of innovation. At first it did not matter in political terms that Islamic culture became static. But by the end of the eighteenth century, Europe was ready to take advantage. Napoleon's expedition to Egypt in 1798 marked the beginning of a century in which virtually every Islamic country came under the control of a **European power**.

Islam cannot, of course, be held solely responsible for the Muslim world's material decline. But because it influences every part of its believers' lives, and because East–West rivalry had always been viewed in primarily religious terms, the nineteenth and twentieth centuries saw something of a **crisis in religious confidence**. Why had Islam's former power now passed to infidel foreigners?

The Islamist response

Reactions and answers veered between two extremes. There were those who felt that Islam should try to incorporate some of the West's secularism and materialism; on the other side, there were movements holding that Islam should turn its back on the West, purify itself of all corrupt additions and thus rediscover its former power.

The earliest exponent of the latter view was the **Muslim Brotherhood** (*Ikhwan el-Muslimeen*), founded in Ismailiya by **Hassan el-Banna** in 1928. The Brotherhood preached a moral renewal of Islam, established a network of schools and training centres, and later set up clandestine paramilitary groups. It was aimed as much against the corrupt feudal and khedival institutions as against Western imperialism.

Within fifteen years, the Brotherhood had spread through Egypt and spawned offshoots through the Middle East. Its terrorist activities prompted a violent state response, with its banning by King Farouk, whose bodyguards assassinated El-Banna in 1949.

After Egyptian independence, and the Revolution of 1952, the legitimized Brotherhood rapidly became disillusioned with Nasser's secular nationalism. In 1954, two Brothers attempted to assassinate him during a public meeting in Alexandria. Mass arrests followed and the Brotherhood went underground again, not surfacing in public until the Sadat era, when the government regarded it as a useful counterweight to the left.

By this time the Brotherhood had moderated its strategy, if not its aims, and its tacit cooperation with the state led to the emergence of more radical groups. One such group, *Al-Taqfir w'al-Higrah* (Repentance and Holy Flight), gained notoriety for attacking boutiques and nightclubs in Cairo during the food riots of 1977. Another faction, established within Egypt's Military Academy, planned a *coup d'état* but was nipped in the bud. Most famous – and effective – was the organization known as **Al-Jihad** (Holy Struggle), which assassinated Sadat and attempted to launch a revolution in Assyut in 1981.

Under Mubarak, the mainstream Islamic opposition was allowed to establish clinics and schools for the poor, achieving a greater influence over cultural life. During the late 1980s, **Gamaat Islamiya** (Islamic Societies) captured the professional unions, and thousands of Egyptians put their savings into Islamic investment houses, which offered higher returns than ordinary banks. When these went bankrupt amid accusations of fraud, the Islamic movement's credibility was badly dented, but its prompt distribution of aid after the 1991 Cairo earthquake redeemed its reputation amongst the urban poor.

The following year, **Islamic militants** began a terrorist campaign in Middle

Egypt, attacking tourists, policemen and Copts. The *Gamaat Islamiya* (not to be confused with the Islamic Societies, despite their overlapping membership and ideology) and the smaller *Jihad Islami* (Islamic Jihad) both claimed Sheikh Omar Abdel Rahman and Al-Jihad as their exemplars, and divine sanction for attacks on the "Pharaonic regime", "infidel" tourists, and Copts who refused to pay *jizia* – the tax that non-Muslims had to pay under the Khalifate. In practice, this involved local groups of extortionists, some of them traditional criminal families, or simply one clan revenging itself on another under the guise of terrorism.

While Copts complained that the security forces were riddled with Islamist sympathizers, Muslims in Middle Egypt were subjected to curfews, roadside searches, arbitrary arrest and torture by the security forces, badly straining communal relations. In other ways, however, the authorities deferred to the Islamist agenda, by jailing 300 Egyptians for the "crime" of converting to Christianity, and ruling that a Cairo professor found "guilty" of apostasy must separate from his wife. As recently as January 2000, nineteen Copts and two Muslims were killed in clashes at El-Qusiya that the police inexplicably ignored for two days.

However, the *Gamaat Islamiya* has not officially been implicated in any violence since its imprisoned leadership announced a ceasefire in 1998. Cynics reckon that they were simply fed up after nearly twenty years in prison, and their repudiation of past acts of violence in 2002 was a ploy by the government to deflect suspicion that terrorism is still latent in Egypt. As for the *Jihad Islami*, its leaders **Ayman al-Zawahiri** and Mohamed Atef had long ago since fled Egypt to Europe and the US before joining Bin Laden in Afghanistan (where they first met during the *jihad* against the Soviets). Having masterminded attacks against US targets in Africa and the Middle East, they stunned the world with their attack on the Twin Towers on September 11.

Although the government has variously accused Iran, Sudan and Al-Qaida of fomenting terrorism, more profound causes lie in Egypt and the wider world. Egypt's stagnant economy breeds despair, and its corrupt elite provokes anger among the vast majority of Egyptians who are struggling to get by. The appeal of Islam as a radical solution gains strength from its historic stature – by returning to the "pure" Islam of the Prophet, it is argued, Muslims can reunite and pursue their destiny, free of the arbitrary nation-states and parasitical regimes bequeathed by imperialism. While many people doubt that Islam offers a solution for *everything* – and the lifestyle-aspirations of Egyptian youth are far from fundamentalist – the Islamists' view of world events is broadly shared at every level of society, from janitors to generals. Though foreigners may deplore or deny it (or the history and assumptions on which it's based), there's universal agreement that the West is guilty of gross double standards in its policies on Palestine and the Arab world. The feeling is that while Israel has been allowed to occupy territory, ignore UN resolutions and acquire weapons of mass destruction with impunity, the US and its allies gave a crushing response to Iraq's invasion of Kuwait, and the "War against Terrorism" since September 11 seems an excuse to attack any Muslim state or group that steps out of line.

Monumental chronology

The chronology below is designed for general reference of monuments and dynasties or rulers. For simplicity, only the **major figures of each dynasty** or era are listed; likewise the monuments and artefacts.

The following **abbreviations** are used: EAM (Egyptian Antiquities Museum in Cairo), IAM (Islamic Arts Museum in Cairo) and BM (British Museum in London).

c.250,000 BC ▶ **Hunter-gathering hominids** roam the savannahs. Stone tools have been discovered in gravel beds of Upper Egypt and Nubia.

c.25,000 BC ▶ **Late Paleolithic** era. Onset of desertification, until rains of Neolithic era. Ostrich eggs and flints have been found beneath dunes of Great Sand Sea.

c.6000 BC ▶ **Middle Neolithic** era. Intensive occupation of the Western Desert by hunter-gatherers. Rock art at the Gilf Kebir; solar calendar at Nabta Playa.

Predynastic Egypt

c.5000 BC ▶ Pastoralism becomes widespread in the Eastern and Western deserts, while **Badarian culture** takes root in the Nile Valley. Pottery, jewellery and ivory excavated at village of El-Badari in Upper Egypt.

c.4000 BC ▶ **Naqada I culture** Burnished pottery and granite mace heads have been found near Qus in Upper Egypt.

Early Dynastic or Archaic Period (c.3100–2686 or 2920–2575 BC)

c.2920–2770 BC ▶ **I Dynasty** *Aha; Djer; Den.*

c.2920 or 3100 BC ▶ **Unification of the Two Lands** (Upper and Lower Egypt) by **Menes**. Foundation of Memphis; Palette of Narmer (EAM); Stele of Peribsen (BM); Scorpion Macehead (Ashmolean Museum).

2686–2613 or 2469–2575 BC ▶ **III Dynasty** *Zoser; Sekhemkhet; Huni.* Step Pyramid and Unfinished Pyramid built at Saqqara; Collapsed Pyramid at Maidum.

Old Kingdom (c.2686–2181 or 2575–2134 BC)

2613–2494 or 2575–2465 BC ▶ **IV Dynasty** *Snofru; Cheops; Chephren; Mycerinus.* Bent Pyramid at Dahshur; Great Pyramids of Giza.

2494–2345 or 2465–2323 BC ▶ **V Dynasty** *Userkaf; Sahure; Neferefre; Nyuserre; Unas.* Sun Temples and Pyramids at Abu Sir; several further pyramids at Saqqara.

2345–2181 or 2323–2150 BC ▶ **VI Dynasty** *Teti; Pepi I; Pepi II.* More pyramids at Saqqara.

First Intermediate Period (c.2181–2050 or 2134–2040 BC)

2181–2160 or 2150–2134 BC ▶ **VII and VIII dynasties** Period of anarchy and fragmentation of power.

2160–2130 or 2154–2040 BC ▶ **IX and X dynasties** *Achthoes.* Capital at Herakleopolis, near Beni Suef.

2133–1991 BC ▶ **XI Dynasty** *Inyotef Sehertowy. Nebhepetre Mentuhotpe II* reunites Two Lands in 2050 BC. Ruined mortuary temple at Deir el-Bahri; Mentuhotpe's statue (EAM).

Middle Kingdom (c.2055–1650 or 2050–1786 BC)

1991–1786 or 1985–1955 BC ▶
XII Dynasty *Amenemhat I; Senusert I and II; Amenemhat III.*
Pyramids at Lahun, Lisht and Hawara; rock tombs at Beni Hassan and Aswan; site of Medinet Madi.

1955–1650 BC ▶ **XIII Dynasty**

Second Intermediate Period (c.1786–1567 or 1650–1950 BC)

1786–1603 or 1650–1550 BC ▶
XIV Dynasty

1674–1567 BC ▶ **XV and XVI (Hyksos) dynasties** *Khyam; Apophis I and II.* Capital at Avaris in the Delta (with Minoan frescoes); *Rhind Mathematical Papyrus* (BM).

1684–1567 BC ▶ **XVII Dynasty**
Expulsion of the Hyksos by Ahmosis. Tombs at Qarat Hilwah.

New Kingdom (c.1567–1085 or 1550–1070 BC)

1567–1320 or 1550–1307 BC ▶
XVIII Dynasty Two Lands reunited; period of imperial expansion. *Ahmosis; Amenophis I; Tuthmosis I and II; Hatshepsut; Tuthmosis III; Amenophis II and III; Akhenaten; Smenkhkare; Tutankhamun; Ay; Horemheb.*
Temple of Deir el-Bahri; site of Tell el-Amarna; royal tombs in the valleys of the Kings and Queens at Thebes; Luxor and Karnak temples; Tutankhamun's gold (EAM).

1320–1200 or 1307–1196 BC ▶
XIX Dynasty *Ramses I; Seti I; Ramses II; Merneptah; Seti II.* Serapeum at Saqqara; temples at Abydos and Abu Simbel; Ramesseum and royal tombs at Thebes.

1200–1085 or 1196–1070 BC ▶
XX Dynasty *Sethnakhte; Ramses III (and eight other minor and hopeless Ramses).* Temple of Medinet Habu and further royal tombs at Thebes; some are plundered by workmen.

Third Intermediate Period (c.1069–747 BC)

1069–945 BC ▶ **XXI Dynasty**
Authority divided between Tanis and Thebes. *Smendes; Herihor; Psusennes I and II.* Capital at Tanis; Treasure of Tanis (EAM); *Book of the Dead* (BM).

945–715 BC ▶ **XXII Dynasty**
Shoshenk; Osorkon. Ruins at Tanis; Shoshenk's relief at Karnak.

818–715 BC ▶ **XXIII and XXIV dynasties**

Late Period (747–332 BC)

747–656 BC ▶ **XXV (Nubian) Dynasty** *Piankhi; Shabaka; Taharqa; Tanutamun.* Reliefs at Luxor; Kiosk of Taharqa at Karnak; statue of Amenirdis (EAM).

664–525 BC ▶ **XXVI (Saïte) Dynasty** *Psammetichus I; Necho II; Psammetichus II; Apries; Amasis.* Ruins of Naucratis; steles at Ismailiya.

525–404 BC ▶ **XXVII (Persian) Dynasty** Persian invasion. *Cambyses; Darius I; Xerxes; Artaxerxes I.* Temple of Hibis at Kharga Oasis; completion of Nile–Red Sea canal; foundation of Babylon-in-Egypt (Cairo).

404–380 BC ▶ **XXVIII and XXIX dynasties** *Amyrtaeus; Amasis "The Drunkard".* Temple of El-Ghweeta, Kharga Oasis; tomb of Amunhotep Huy, Bahariya Oasis.

380–343 BC ▶ **XXX Dynasty**
Nectanebo I and II. Additions to Philae and Karnak; ruined temple of Amun at Siwa Oasis.

Ptolemaic Era (332–30 BC)

332–30 BC ▶ **Alexander the Great** conquers Egypt and founds **Alexandria**. His successors, the **Ptolemies**, make the city a beacon for the Mediterranean world, where Hellenistic and Judaistic culture mingles. Their line expires with **Cleopatra VII** (51-30 BC), vanquished by the power of Rome. In

: kingdom of Meroe
.ts apogee. Construction (or
.cation) of temples of Edfu,
. Kom Ombo, Dendara and
.ae; catacombs in Alexandria;
.nctuary of Amun at Siwa Oasis;
ruins of Karanis and Qasr Qaroun in
the Fayoum; Valley of the Mummies
at Bahariya Oasis; temple of Dakka,
Lake Nasser.

Roman and Byzantine Period (30 BC–640 AD)

30 BC ▶ Octavian (Augustus)
annexes Egypt to the **Roman
Empire**. Tomb of Kitnes and Temple
of Dush in Kharga Oasis.

45 **AD** ▶ St Mark brings
Christianity to Egypt. Muzawaka
Tombs in Dakhla Oasis.

249–305 ▶ **Persecution of Coptic
Christians** under Decius and
Diocletian. "Pompey's Pillar" at
Alexandria.

313 ▶ Edict of Milan **legalizes
Christianity**. Foundation of monas-
teries of Wadi Natrun, St Anthony, St
Paul and St Catherine.

395 ▶ Partition of Roman Empire
into East and West; Egypt falls under
Eastern, **Byzantine**, sphere.
Necropolis of El-Bagawat at Kharga
Oasis.

451 ▶ Council of Chalcedon leads
to **expulsion of Copts from
Orthodox Church**. Numerous
objects in Coptic Museum (Cairo).

Arab Dynasties (640–1517)

640–642 ▶ **Arab conquest** of
Egypt; **introduction of Islam**.
Mosque of Amr and ruins of Fustat
in Cairo.

661–750 ▶ Egypt forms part of
Umayyad Khalifate, ruled from
the dynasty's capital at Damascus.
Ceramics and pottery (IAM).

750–935 ▶ **Abbassids** depose
Umayyads and form new dynasty,
ruling from Baghdad. In 870 Egypt's
governor, **Ibn Tulun**, declares independence, founding a dynasty which
rules until 905. Mosque of Ibn Tulun
in Cairo.

935–969 ▶ **Ikhshidid dynasty**
takes power in Egypt.

969–1171 ▶ **Shi'ite Fatimid
dynasty** conquers Egypt and seizes
the Islamic Khalifate, which it rules
from Cairo. Mosques of Al-Azhar,
Al-Hakim and Al-Aqmar,
Mausoleum of Imam Al-Shafi'i, and
various fortified gates, in Cairo.

1171–1250 ▶ **Salah al-Din** founds
Ayyubid dynasty and liberates land
conquered by the Crusaders. Egypt
returns to **Sunni Islam**. Intrigues of
Shagar al-Durr open the way to
Mamluke takeover. Madrassa-
Mausoleum of Al-Silah Ayyub and
the Aqueduct in Cairo; ruins of Shali
in Siwa Oasis. Mausoleum of Shagar
al-Durr in Cairo.

Mamluke Dynasties (1250–1517)

1250–1382 ▶ **Bahri Mamlukes**
Qalaoun; Khalil; Mohammed al-Nasir.
In Cairo: Qalaoun's Maristan-
Mausoleum-Madrassa, Mosques of
Al-Nasir, House of Uthman
Katkhuda, and Qasr Bashtak.

1382–1517 ▶ **Burgi Mamlukes**
*Barquq; Farag; Barsbey; Qaitbey;
Qansuh al-Ghuri.* In Cairo: Barquq's
Mausoleum, Madrassa and Khanqah
of Barsbey, Mosque of Qaitbey, and
the Ghuriya. Also, Fort Qaitbey in
Alexandria.

Ottoman Period (1517–1798)

1517 ▶ **Selim the Grim conquers
Egypt**. For the next three centuries
the country is ruled as an Ottoman
province from Constantinople. In
Cairo: Mosques of Suleyman al-
Silahdar and Suleyman Pasha; Sabil-
Kuttab of Abd al-Rahman
Katkhuda. Terbana Mosque in Alex.

1798–1802 ▶ French occupation of Egypt. Capitulation Agreement of 1802 leaves British in effective control of the country. Treasures shipped off to Louvre/British Museum. European graffiti left on numerous temples.

Pashas, Khedives and Kings (1805–1952)

1805 ▶ **Mohammed Ali** seizes power and begins a programme of ruthless **modernization**. Mohammed Ali Mosque in Cairo; Ras el-Tin Palace and Mahmudiya Canal in Alexandria. Belzoni, Mariette and others pioneer digs at pharaonic sites in the Nile Valley and Delta.

1848–54 ▶ Reign of **Abbas I**.

1854–63 ▶ Reign of **Said Pasha**. Suez Canal begun.

1863–79 ▶ Reign of **Khedive Ismail**. Completion of Suez Canal; Central Cairo boulevards constructed.

1879–92 ▶ Reign of **Khedive Tewfiq**. British crush the **Orabi Revolt** (1882–83). Tewfiq reinstated as a puppet ruler under British control. Howard Carter discovers Tutankhamun's tomb at Thebes (1922) at the tail end of a period of intensive excavations throughout Egypt.

1935–52 ▶ Reign of **King Farouk**; during World War II Egypt stays under British control.

1952–53 ▶ Farouk overthrown by Free Officers. **Egypt declared a republic**. Construction of Midan Tahrir in Cairo.

Modern Egypt (1952–)

1956 ▶ **Nasser** becomes President; **Suez Crisis**. Major industrialization programme, and construction of schools, hospitals and public housing.

1967 ▶ **Six Day War** with Israel; massive damage to Canal cities.

1970 ▶ **Nasser dies** and is succeeded as president by **Sadat**. High Dam at Aswan completed (1970).

1973 ▶ **October War** with Israel.

1977–78 ▶ Food riots. Sadat's trip to Jerusalem leads to **Camp David** agreement. Mohandiseen district of Cairo built, along with hundreds of new hotels, shops, etc. First line of Cairo metro completed.

1981 ▶ **Assassination of Sadat**. Presidency assumed by **Mubarak**.

1990 ▶ **Gulf War**.

1991 ▶ **Cairo earthquake** Many buildings damaged in Cairo, but the second metro line is pushed to completion.

1994 ▶ **Underwater finds at Alexandria** Divers and archeologists begin exploration of the ruins of the ancient Lighthouse of Pharos and the royal quarters in the harbour at Alexandria.

1995 ▶ Tomb of Ramses II's sons found in the Valley of the Kings.

1996 ▶ **Valley of the Mummies** Egypt's largest cache of mummies is discovered by accident in Bahariya, in the Western Desert.

1997 ▶ 58 foreigners killed by Islamic militants at Hatshepsut's Temple, near Luxor.

2000 ▶ The interior of the Red Pyramid at Dahshur is reopened after many years.

Music

As with other cultural spheres, Egypt's musical traditions date back to pharaonic times, though the primary influences are Arab and Islamic. Given Egypt's status in the Arab world, it is no surprise that Cairo is the centre of the Arab recording industry – a dominance partly acquired by the collapse of its rivals in the Lebanon, Libya and Kuwait. Egypt's sixty-nine million population makes it the most important market for Arab music, and the amazingly high proportion of youth (over thirty million Egyptians are under 25) has ensured a big demand for contemporary sounds.

The different types of folk or popular music you come across vary greatly with the region and environment: Cairo, the Nile Valley, the Delta and the desert all have their own characteristic sounds, rhythms and instruments. Often their songs reflect the rituals of everyday life: weddings, moulids, harvest festivals, old stories of village life or triumphs. What follows is the briefest of introductions to the various major forms.

Ancient Egyptian music

You won't hear **ancient Egyptian music** played anywhere – indeed, nobody is sure what it sounded like – but enough is known about the instruments for musicologists to have tried to recreate the hymns and processional songs that accompanied religious rituals and court life in ancient times. Flutes and clarinet-type instruments go back to the Old Kingdom (if not Predynastic times), as do harps (which evolved from hand-held instruments to large, freestanding ones), trumpets, cymbals and castanets. By the Middle Kingdom, harps were accompanied by the sistrum (a kind of rattle associated with the goddess Hathor and often carved with her face), tambourines, clappers and a type of guitar. The lute and lyre appeared during the Second Intermediate Period and were probably introduced by the Hyksos, while other instruments came into Egypt as a result of the various foreign invasions after the fall of the New Kingdom.

Religious music

During Ramadan and other major festivals you'll encounter **religious music** – renditions of **Koranic verses**, or praises to Allah, teased out in any number of ways.

Performers may be **munshids** – professional reciters who move from one festival to another – or simply the **muezzin** or **imam** of the local mosque. In everyday religious life, all muezzins have their individual styles of phrasing, which are sometimes jealously guarded. In a celebrated court case in the 1980s an Egyptian judge ruled that no copyright existed on any expression of the Koran, since God created it. Yet **Mohammed Gabriel** has become a superstar in this genre.

Recitals at **moulids** are often more participation than performance, with dozens of Sufi devotees chanting and swaying to the accompaniment of a drum. These recitals, known as **zikrs**, can last for days.

Classical Arabic music

Antecedents of **classical Arabic music** can be traced back to the **Bedouin** reciters and singers of the Arabian peninsula, but also to the more refined **court music** of the great khalifal cities of Baghdad and Damascus, and Ottoman Constantinople.

During the last century, the form has been characterized by oriental scales, passionate rhetoric, bravura soloists, massed orchestras and male choirs. The most famous twentieth-century exponent was **Umm Kalthoum** (aka Oum Khalsoum); until her death in 1975, she was the most popular singer in the Arab world. Her career coincided with the advent of long-distance broadcasting and she was the first Arab music star. In Egypt, she was a national institution, known as "The Mother of Egypt" and accorded a weekly concert on radio (and, later, TV). Almost as revered was **Mohammed Abdel Wahab**, who will be forever associated with the nightclubs of Cairo's Tawfiqiyya district, and composed Egypt's national anthem, *Biladi, Biladi*. Another superstar was the actor/singer **Abdel Halim Hafez**, whose film recordings are still widely loved long after his death in 1977. Fears that the genre had become ossified have been dispelled by its recent revival at the hands of **Hany Shaker**, while the Iraqi megastar **Kazem Al-Saher** (now living in Cairo) collaborated with the poet Nizar Qabbani (Umm Kalthoum's lyricist) to produce *Al Hob-Al-Mustaheel* – a massive hit that won a new generation of fans.

Regional/ethnic music

Saiyidi

The music of Upper Egypt – known, like its people, as **Saiyidi** – has a characteristic rhythm, which horses are trained to dance to. It is based upon two instruments: the *nahrasan*, a two-sided drum hung over the chest and beaten with sticks; and the *mismar saiyidi*, a kind of wooden trumpet. Performances often involve monologues, ripe with puns and wit. One of the famous names of the genre, **Omar Gharzawi**, is known for his rebuttals of the stereotyped image of stupid, hot-headed Saiyidis, while the late **Shoukoukou** has a special instrument (a joke clapping doll, sold at festivals) named after him. On a more official standing is *Rais* ("Boss") **Met'al al-I'nawi**, often chosen by the government to represent Egypt at foreign music festivals. The current popular favourite is **Mohammed El-Agouz**.

Fellahi

The northern counterpart to Saiyidi music, found in the Delta, is known as **fellahi** (peasant) music. It is generally softer, with a fondness for the *matsoum* (one and a half) rhythm, and use of instruments like the *rababa*, a two-stringed viol, and the *mismar*, a kind of oboe.

Sawaheeli

Found along the Mediterranean coast and in the Canal Zone, **Sawaheeli** music is characterized by the use of a banjo-like stringed instrument, the *simseemeya*. Another form, specific to Alexandria, also features the accordion, the result of the city's Greek and Turkish influences.

Bedouin

There are two kinds of **Bedouin** music: one found in the Western Desert, towards Libya, the other in the Eastern Desert and Sinai. Both have songs recounting old intrigues, activities and stories to a strong rhythmic accompaniment. This has been a major influence on *Al-Jeel* music (see below).

Nubian

Performed in its own language, in the southern reaches of the Nile Valley, **Nubian** music has more African than Arab roots. It relies a lot on hand-clapping and the *duf*, a kind of tambourine. More urbanized versions – found in Aswan or Khartoum – have opted for brass sections and female choruses, while **Ali Hassan Kuban** overlays the traditional percussion and *oud* framework with Western instruments such as the guitar, violin and accordian, tuned to Arabic scales. Conversely, the Nubian composer **Hamza ad-Din** has written music for classical orchestral performances.

Pop music

In Cairo and other cities, rural traditions have mixed with the more elite classical styles, and adapted to reflect urban preoccupations and the faster pace of life. By the mid-1980s two main types of music had developed: **Shaabi** and **Al-Jeel**. Nowadays, some would say that the distinction between them is moot, and artists such as Hakim can rightfully claim to have a foot in each camp, while pop idol Amr Diab has spearheaded attempts to stake a claim on the world market. In Egypt, *Shaabi* and *Al-Jeel* stars release their latest hits at peak sales periods such as Ramadan and St Valentine's Day. News and audio-clips of *Shaabi* and *Al-Jeel* stars can be found on the website ⓦwww .mazika.com.

Shaabi

Shaabi ("people") music was born in the working-class quarters of Cairo, where millions of second- and third-generation rural migrants live. It blends the traditional form of the *mawal* (plaintive vocal improvisations) with a driving beat. Its lyrics are often raunchy or satirical, politically and socially provocative. You will never hear this music via the media. It is not so much banned as beneath the contempt of the middle classes and respectable society, who see its rudeness and social criticism as coming from another Egypt. It is to be heard, however, at weddings and parties throughout working-class Cairo and at some of the nightclubs along Pyramids Road – and played on battered cassettes in taxis, buses and cafés everywhere.

The original *Shaabi* singer was **Ahmed Adaweer**, who, from 1971 on, introduced the idea of street language and subsequently broke every rule in the book. Later exponents introduced elements of rap and disco into the *Shaabi* sound, in the manner of Algerian *Raï* music. The genre is still frowned upon in official cultural circles, but commands a wide following. **Sha'ban Abdel**

Egyptian music: recommended recordings

Although CDs are catching on in Egypt, **cassettes** remain the medium of choice for recorded music, being robust, cheap and very easy to copy – piracy is such a problem that it has its own special police division in Cairo. Outlets are street-corner kiosks, small shops and market stalls, most of which tend to specialize in either *Shaabi* or *Al-Jeel*, or the old oriental musics, traditional and modern. There are no charts as such, though you will soon know when a song is the city's "number one". If it's big, producers can expect to sell up to a million copies.

The following is a highly **selective list of artists and recordings** to start you off in Cairo cassette browsing. In Britain or North America, you can find a limited range of records, too – mostly Umm Kalthoum and the like, though with a few more contemporary releases on world music labels such as Mondo Melodia, Piranha, Axiom or Mango/Island. David Lodge's *Yalla: Hitlist Egypt* collection (Mango/Island) devotes a side each to *Shaabi* and *Al-Jeel*.

Ancient Egyptian music
Michael Atherton *Ankh: The Sound of Ancient Egypt* (available abroad as a CD on the Celestial Harmonies label).

Religious music
Mohammed Gabriel Anything by the superstar of Koranic recitation.

Classical Arabic music
Umm Kalthoum *Al-Atalaal* and *Enta Omri*. Two of her greatest live recordings – among dozens of releases.
Mohammed Abdel Wahab *The Music of Abdel Wahab* (available abroad on the Axiom label).
Kazem Al-Saher *Al-Hob Al-Mustaheel*. The Iraqi-born pop star's collaboration with Umm Kalthoum's lyricist.

Saiyidi music
Ahmed Ismail and Sohar Magdy Anything by this duo is worth acquiring.

Nubian music
Ali Hassan Kuban *From Nubia to Cairo* or *Walk Like a Nubian* (both available abroad on the Pirhana label).
Hamza ad-Din *Escalay*. Classical music inspired by Nubian sounds and Sufism.
Khedr *Ya Sahabba*. Sung in an obscure Nubian dialect – and popular mainly among Nubians.

Bedouin music
You won't find cassettes in Cairo but may strike lucky in Sinai or Mersa Matrouh.

Al-Jeel music
Amr Diab *Ya Tareek*; *Awedony*; *Ya Omnena*; *Tamaly Ma'ak*; *Caravelle*. Egypt's first international crossover star, often likened to Ricky Martin. *Habibi*, the English version of his *Nour el Ain*, was a hit in Europe and the US in 1998.
Hisham Abbas *Gowa Fe* or *Habibi Da.* One of the new hot talents on the *Al-Jeel* scene.
Mohammed Mounir *Ana Qalbi Masaken Sha'abiya*. Plaintive songs of life and the city, by the master of the genre.

Shaabi music
Ahmed Adaweer *Al-Tareek* or *Adaweat*. The father of it all at his best.
Hakim *Yaho* or *Al Nazra*. Today's hardcore *Shaabi* favourite. *Shakl Tani/Remix* is a compilation of his earlier songs remixed by the British worldbeat dance group Transglobal Underground (available abroad on Mondo Melodia).
Hassan el-Asmar *Mish Hasheebak*. Classic *Shaabi* lyrics of hard urban life.

Rahim was a laundry ironer until a television appearance catapulted him to stardom. His earthy persona infuriates Egypt's cultural arbiters (leading the chief censor to propose that only singers with university degrees should be allowed to appear on TV), while his song *I hate Israel* was cited in the Knesset as proof of anti-Semitism in the Egyptian media. Meanwhile, rival *Shaabi* superstar **Hakim** has tried to reach an international crossover audience with a remix of his hits by Transglobal Underground, following the example of Amr Diab (see below).

Al-Jeel

Al-Jeel means "the generation" and followed hot on the heels of *Shaabi*, in the early 1980s. It takes disco elements a step further, using drum tracks and synthesized backing, and mixes these with Nubian and Bedouin rhythms. The latter came in large part through the influence of Libyan musicians, who had fled to Cairo in the late 1970s after Gaddafi's "cultural revolution", where he clamped down on Western musical influences. Some fans and critics now call it "Mediterranean Music", acknowledging the crosscurrents of influences within the Arab world and its European diaspora – while others simply see it as classic Arabic pop.

Whatever the name, it's big business – though not exactly as in the West. Artists receive hardly anything from sales of tapes and CDs; they earn their money from appearances at weddings and concerts. That said, Egypt's foremost pop idol, **Amr Diab**, broke into the international market after he won the 1998 World Music Award for *Nour el Ain* (released in English as *Habibi*), to become the bestselling Arab singer ever. He was also the first Egyptian artist to release a pop video, and make collaborative recordings with a Spanish flamenco group, the *Raï* star Khaled and the Greek singer Angela Dimitriu. **Mohammed Mounir** is almost as popular, and rated ahead of the rest of the pack for his plaintive songs of city life, while women singers such as **Hanan** and **Samire Saieed** have also forged successful pop careers.

Al-Jeel lyrics, in contrast to *Shaabi*, are usually about love or the country and rarely stray into sensitive areas. However, performances remain a focus for discontented youth, and stars are increasingly courted by politicians and allowed to express popular feelings. **El-Magmoaa** (The Clique) is a group of pop singers, film and TV stars, whose benefit song *Jerusalem will come back to us* is a bitter attack on Israel's treatment of the Palestinians.

Books

Most of the books listed below are in print; those that are out of print (o/p) should be easy to track down in second-hand bookstores. Books that are only published in Egypt are most easily available in Cairo; we have identified these by giving the publisher's name after the book title (the American University in Cairo Press is abbreviated to AUC).

Travel

General

Karl Baedeker *Egypt: Handbook for Travellers* (o/p). The classic guidebook, used by generations of tourists from the 1870s until World War II. Of the numerous editions, the 1929 revision – which includes the discovery of Tutankhamun's tomb – is the one to hunt for in second-hand bookshops (it sells for about £100/US$160; a facsimile edition, published in the 1980s, is also out of print but can often be found for £20/US$30 or so).

Jonathan Cott *The Search for Omm Sety: A Story of Eternal Love* (Olympic). A biography of Dorothy Eady, who believed herself to be the reincarnation of a temple priestess and lover of Seti I at Abydos (see p.330).

Robert Curzon *Visits to Monasteries in the Levant* (E. Mellen). Famed account, by a man later made Viceroy of Egypt, of youthful adventurings in Egypt, Palestine and Greece in the 1830s. Several chapters deal with Egyptian monasteries, where Curzon got the monks drunk and stole their antiquarian manuscripts.

Amelia Edwards *A Thousand Miles up the Nile* (Darf). Verbose, patronizing classic from the mid-nineteenth century. All books on Egypt have their Amelia quotes – the *Rough Guide* included.

★ **Gustave Flaubert** *Flaubert in Egypt* (Penguin). A romp through the brothels, baths and sites by the future author of *Madame Bovary*, who cared little for monuments but delighted in Egyptian foibles and vices. Skilfully edited by Francis Steegmuller.

E.M. Forster *Alexandria: A History and a Guide* (o/p UK). A foreword by Lawrence Durrell and stylishly erudite notations by Michael Haag enhance Forster's 1922 guidebook. Forster's companion piece was *Pharos and Pharillon* (o/p), a diverse collection of essays on Alexandrian life.

★ **Amitav Ghosh** *In an Antique Land* (Granta). Wry tales of contemporary life in a Delta village, interspersed with snippets of historical research which are far less absorbing.

★ **Michael Haag** *Egypt Chronicle* (Rough Guides). A pocket-size guide to Egypt's five-thousand-year civilization, with timelines on each page and sidebars on significant figures from Cheops to Nasser, and topics such as Egyptian movies, Arab music, irrigation and the Suez Crisis.

Douglas Kennedy *Beyond the Pyramids* (Abacus). A dour, Paul Theroux-ish jaunt around Egypt in the late 1980s; the Alex and Assyut sections stand out.

 E.W. Lane *Manners and Customs of the Modern Egyptians* (East-West). Facsimile edition of this encyclopedic study of life in Mohammed Ali's Cairo, first published in 1836. Highly browsable.

 Deborah Manley *The Nile: A Traveller's Anthology* (o/p). A good anthology to go for: nicely illustrated and with selections gathered from some very obscure sources.

Bimbashi McPherson *The Man Who Loved Egypt* (o/p). Edited letters of a paternalist British administrator, interesting for the light they cast on Cairo in the early twentieth century (when he headed the secret police).

Henri de Monfreid *Hashish* (o/p). A latter-day swashbuckler who followed a spell in Djibouti jail by smuggling hash on the Red Sea during the 1920s. The second half relates his dealings with the Suez underworld.

Murray's *Handbook for Travellers in Egypt* (o/p). A worthy rival to Baedeker, likewise replete with footnotes, engravings and colonial attitudes. Later editions distinguished by their coverage of Sinai sell for around £30/US$50.

Gerard de Nerval *Journey to the Orient* (o/p). Stoned on hash, de Nerval thrilled to Mohammed Ali's Egypt: splendour and squalor, eroticism and cruelty – the Orientalist fantasy that still colours perceptions today. A wacky read.

Florence Nightingale *Letters from Egypt* (Parkway). A stuffier view of

Egypt, by a 29-year-old Englishwoman who had yet to make herself famous in the Crimean War. Illustrated with paintings and drawings by David Roberts, Edward Lear and other artists of the period.

Christopher Pick *Egypt: A Traveller's Anthology* (J. Murray). Mixed bag of observers from the eighteenth and nineteenth centuries, including Disraeli, Mark Twain, Vita Sackville-West, Flaubert, E.M. Forster and Freya Stark.

 Charlie Pye-Smith *The Other Nile* (o/p). Witty and insightful account of a tour in the early 1980s, interwoven with recollections of trips into Sudan and Ethiopia, before coups and famine made them inaccessible.

 Paul William Roberts *River in the Desert* (Random House). Chiefly interesting for its eyewitness account of a *zaar* (exorcism) and a chapter on the Kushmaan Bedouin of the Eastern Desert.

 Anthony Sattin *The Pharaoh's Shadow* (Phoenix). Fascinating discourse on the "survival" of ancient Egyptian religious beliefs and practices in modern-day Egypt. Sattin's earlier book on British colonial society in Egypt is sadly out of print (see "Medieval and Modern History", p.826).

Stanley Stewart *Old Serpent Nile: A Journey to the Source* (Flamingo). Stewart managed to travel from the Nile Delta to the Mountains of the Moon in Uganda in the late 1980s, and relates his adventures in spare, taut prose.

Cairo

 James Aldridge *Cairo* (o/p). Highly readable history of the

city from ancient times until the mid-1960s, including several fine maps and photographs. Only found in second-hand bookshops.

★ **Artemis Cooper** *Cairo in the War* (o/p). Excellent account of a febrile era, with vignettes of Evelyn Waugh, Olivia Manning and other postwar luminaries.

Trevor Mostyn *Egypt's Belle Epoque: Cairo 1869–1952* (o/p). Expat highlife and diplomatic intrigue, from the time of Ismail to the revolution that overthrew King Farouk.

★ **Richard Parker** *Islamic Monuments of Cairo: A Practical Guide* (AUC). Excellent and detailed handbook to the monuments and history of seventh- to nineteenth-century Cairo.

★ **Desmond Stewart** *Great Cairo, Mother of the World* (AUC). Entertaining and erudite history of the city, from pharaonic times through to the Nasser era. Available in Cairo.

The desert

★ **Wael Abed** *The Other Egypt: Travels in No Man's Land* (Zarzora Expedition). A *tour d'horizon* of the natural wonders of the Western Desert by one of Egypt's leading safari guides and desert ecologists. Illustrated with 80 colour photos, plus rare black-and-white photos taken by explorers in the 1920s and 30s. Sold in Cairo for about £E75.

★ **Michael Asher** *In Search of the Forty Days Road: Impossible Journey* (o/p). Only peripherally related to Egypt, but well worth reading. Asher's camel journeys, in the Sudanese desert and from

Mauritania to the Nile, evoke all the hardships and magic of the desert.

★ **R.A. Bagnold** *Libyan Sands: Travels in a Dead World* (Immel); *Sand, Wind and War: Memoirs of a Desert Explorer* (Tucson). One of a band of motorized explorers of the Western Desert during the 1920s and 30s, Bagnold later wrote the seminal work on dune-formation (a book continuously in print since 1939 and used by NASA to interpret satellite photos of Mars) and led the Long Range Desert Group. Despite Bagnold's restrained prose, his exploits are compelling and the sheer range of journeys – to all the oases, Uwaynat, the Great Sand Sea and the Forty Days Road – make them essential reading.

★ **Burton Bernstein** *Sinai: The Great and Terrible Wilderness* (o/p). Mixture of travel writing and history, describing Sinai on the eve of its handover to Egypt in 1979. Dated but still the best book on the region.

Alain Blottiere *Siwa: the oasis* (Harpocrates). Slim, idiosyncratic book blending history, reportage and personal musings.

Peter Clayton *Desert Explorer* (Zerzura). A biography of the author's father, Patrick Clayton, who mapped the Western Desert at the same time as Bagnold and was likewise active in the LRDG until his capture by the Italians.

★ **Ahmed Fakhry** *The Oases of Egypt* (AUC; 2 vols.). Fakhry's unfinished trilogy is still the last word on the Western Desert Oases. Volume I, covering Siwa, is fascinating; Volume II, on Bahariya and Farafra, is heavier going, while Fakhry's death in 1973 aborted the volume on Dakhla and Kharga. Volume I has been republished in paperback; Volume II remains out of print, but can be found in Cairo bookshops.

George Murray *Dare Me to the Desert* (o/p). Despite its awful title, this is an interesting account of Murray's climbing expeditions in the Red Sea Mountains during the 1920s and 30s.

David Rohl (ed.) *Followers of Horus Eastern Desert Survey Vol. 1* (ISIS). Profusely illustrated study of the rock art of the Eastern Desert, by the Followers of Horus (see p.777). Order by post from Mike Rowland, ISIS Treasurer, 127 Porter Rd,

Basingstoke, Hants RG22 4JT, England. The editor is better known for his controversial books and TV series *A Test of Time* and *Legend* (see "Ancient History", below).

★ **Cassandra Vivian** *The Western Desert of Egypt: An Explorer's Handbook* (AUC). The best guidebook on the subject, ranging from geology to folklore and petroglyphs to safaris. It covers all of the oases and off-the-beaten-track sites, complete with maps and GPS waypoints, last updated in 2000. Fits the dashboard of a 4WD, but too heavy for a rucksack. Sold in Cairo and Bahariya Oasis for £E65–80.

Ancient history

General works

Martin Bernal *Black Athena* (Vintage). These dense, provocative works assert the "Africanness" of ancient Egyptian civilization and its contribution to Greek and Roman culture. The first two volumes (1987 and 1991) show a formidable breadth of enquiry, though Egyptologists and Classicists nit-pick holes everywhere.

Margaret Bunson *Encyclopedia of Ancient Egypt* (Facts on File). Over 1500 entries, with useful subject indexes, charts and chronologies – though not as comprehensive as the *British Museum Dictionary of Ancient Egypt* (see below).

★ **Mark Collier & Bill Manley** *How to Read Egyptian Hieroglyphics: A step-by-step guide to teach yourself* (British Museum Press). Just what the title says – and an unexpected bestseller, thanks to its clarity and the exciting sense of

knowledge that it confers.

★ **Peter France** *The Rape of Egypt* (o/p). Interesting background on the characters and personalities of the early "archeologists", and a no-holds-barred indictment of imperialist looting.

Nicholas Grimal *A History of Ancient Egypt* (Blackwell). The first detailed, reign-by-reign account since Gardiner's *Egypt of the Pharaohs* (1961), which synthesizes a mass of recent revisions, particularly chronological.

★ **George Hart** *A Dictionary of Egyptian Gods and Goddesses* (Routledge). Indispensable guide to the deities and myths of ancient Egypt, profusely illustrated with line drawings. Hart's *Egyptian Myths* (Routledge) is equally informative, covering similar ground.

T.G.H. James *An Introduction to Ancient Egypt* (o/p); *Egypt: The Living Past*; *Ancient Egypt: The Land and Its*

Legacy; *Egyptian Painting*; *Egyptian Sculpture*. James was the keeper of the Egyptian Antiquities department of the British Museum until the mid-1980s. His *Introduction* is a serious text for beginners; *The Land and Its Legacy* and *The Living Past* are coffee-table books, good for pre-visit reading; while the *Painting* and *Sculpture* volumes are accessibly written and lavishly illustrated.

Jaromir Malek *The Cat in Ancient Egypt* (British Museum Press). A charming monograph with delightful illustrations.

Geoffrey T. Martin *The Hidden Tombs of Memphis* (Thames & Hudson). A detailed account of recent discoveries at Memphis, most notably the Tomb of Maya, a contemporary of Tutankhamun.

Dimitri Meeks and Christine Favard-Meeks *Daily Life of the Egyptian Gods* (J. Murray). Scholarly study of the rituals and beliefs surrounding the gods; a TV spin-off focused on the more salacious bits.

Richard Parkinson *Voices from Ancient Egypt: An Anthology of Middle Kingdom Writings* (o/p UK; University of Oklahoma). All kinds of literature, from spells and curses to state propaganda. The material for once brings to life people rather than monuments.

Stephen Quirke and Jeffrey Spencer (eds.) *The British Museum Book of Ancient Egypt* (British Museum Press). A good general survey, lavishly illustrated with material from the museum's Egyptian collection.

Gay Robins *Women in Ancient Egypt* (British Museum Press). Interesting study of a subject largely ignored until a decade ago, focusing on queens and priestesses, fertility rituals and much else.

David Rohl *A Test of Time: The Bible – From Myth to History*; *Legend: Genesis of Civilisation* (Arrow). The former is a stimulating argument for revising the chronology of ancient Egyptian and Biblical history; the latter advances an unusual theory of Egypt's Predynastic era. Both are closely argued, and worth reading even if you're sceptical (as most Egyptologists are).

Ian Shaw *The Oxford History of Ancient Egypt* (Oxford University Press). An excellent survey taking in the latest theories and discoveries up until 2000 – though Rohl doesn't even rate a mention. Contains many fine illustrations and site plans.

Ian Shaw and Paul Nicholson *British Museum Dictionary of Ancient Egypt* (British Museum Press). Richly illustrated, paperback-sized dictionary, especially good for site plans and assessments of recent discoveries.

Robert Sole and Dominique Valbelle *The Rosetta Stone* (Profile). Relates the discovery of the crib that enabled Champollion to decipher ancient Egyptian hieroglyphs – without which, their civilization would still be a mystery.

John Taylor *Egypt and Nubia* (British Museum Press). Covers the history of Nubia from 4000 BC to the dawning of the Christian era, focusing on ancient Nubian art and relations with Egypt.

Joyce Tyldesley *Hatchepsut: The Female Pharaoh* (Penguin). Examines the life and achievements of the woman who ruled as pharaoh (depicted with male genitalia) and the sexual politics of the XVIII Dynasty. Fascinating reading.

Jean Vercoutter *The Search for Ancient Egypt* (Thames & Hudson). Pocket-size account of Egypt's "discovery" by foreigners, packed with drawings, photos and engravings.

★ **Kent Weeks** *The Lost Tomb; Atlas of the Valley of the Kings* (AUC). The former describes Weeks' discovery and excavation of the mass tomb of the sons of Ramses II, while the latter is the first volume of an ongoing magnum opus. Both are showcased on the Theban Mapping Project's website, Ⓦwww.kv5.com.

★ **John Anthony West** *Serpent in the Sky: The High Wisdom of Ancient Egypt* (Quest); *The Traveler's Key to Ancient Egypt: A Guide to the Sacred Places of Ancient Egypt* (Quest). West's New Age interpretation – postulating a connection with the mythical civilization of High Atlantis – has been greeted with derision by mainstream Egyptologists. *The Traveler's Key* is a lively on-site guide that points out inconsistencies in orthodox Egyptology and presents alternative theories.

Karl–Theodore Zauzich *Discovering Egyptian Hieroglyphs: A Practical Guide*. Profusely illustrated guide to the subject, revealing how to read hieroglyphs and their symbolic nuances.

Pyramidology

Guillemette Andreu *Egypt in the Age of the Pyramids* (Murray). Nicely illustrated study of the pyramids' evolution in the context of Egyptian life and culture, by a French Egyptologist.

Robert Bauval *The Orion Mystery* (Mandarin). Postulates that the Giza Pyramids corresponded to the three stars in Orion's Belt as it was in 10,500 BC. Archeologists are uncon- vinced, but at least the theory isn't as preposterous as Hancock's extrapolations (see below).

I.E.S. Edwards *The Pyramids of Egypt* (Penguin). Lavishy illustrated, closely argued survey of all the major pyramids, recently updated to take account of new discoveries and theories, though Mendelssohn (see below) is conspicuously absent.

Graham Hancock *Fingerprints of the Gods* (Mandarin); *The Message of the Sphinx*; *The Mars Mystery* (Heinemann); *Heaven's Mirror* (Penguin). Picking up where Bauval left off, Hancock asserts that the Egyptian and pre-Columbian pyramids, Angkor Wat temple and the stone figures of Easter Island were all created by a lost civilization propagated by Martians. Bestselling codswallop.

Peter Hodges *How the Pyramids were Built* (Arris & Phillips). As a professional stonemason, Hodges has practical experience, rather than academic qualifications, on his side. An easy read, and quite persuasive.

Britta Le Va and Salima Ikram *Egyptian Pyramids* (Zeitouna). Slim booklet of evocative sepia photos and brief accounts of the major pyramids. Available in Cairo.

Kurt Mendelssohn *The Riddle of the Pyramids* (o/p). An attempt to resolve the enigma of the Maidum and Dahshur pyramids, which postulates a "pyramid production line" and caused a stir in the world of Egyptology during the 1980s.

The Amarna Period/ Tutankhamun

Cyril Aldred *Akhenaten, King of Egypt* (Thames & Hudson).

Conventional account of the Amarna period by one of Britain's leading postwar Egyptologists.

Christiane Desroches-Noblecourt *Tutankhamen: Life and Death of a Pharaoh* (Penguin). Brilliantly illustrated, detailed study of all aspects of the boy-pharaoh and his times.

Thomas Hoving *Tutankhamun: the Untold Story* (o/p). Lifts the lid on archeological backbiting and the tomb thefts by Carter and Carnarvon.

Nicholas Reeves and John H. Taylor *Howard Carter Before Tutankhamun* (British Museum Press). Original photographs and drawings and first-hand accounts of excavations bring the irascible Carter to life.

Julia Samson *Nefertiti and Cleopatra* (Rubicon). Fascinating account of Egypt's most famous queens, by the Petrie Museum's expert on Amarna civilization. Samson concludes that Smenkhkare, Akhenaten's mysterious successor, was actually Nefertiti; her coverage of Cleopatra is rather less controversial.

Ptolemaic, Roman and Coptic Egypt

Alan Bowman *Egypt After the Pharaohs* (British Museum Press). Scholarly, nicely illustrated study of an often overlooked period.

★ **Lucy Hughes-Hallet** *Cleopatra: Histories, Dreams and Distortions* (Pimlico). Arresting deconstructive analysis of Cleopatra in history and myth down through the ages.

★ **Jean-Yves Empereur** *Alexandria Revealed; Alexandria Rediscovered* (AUC). As director of the Centre d'Etudes Alexandrines, responsible for excavating the Pharos, the Catacombs and lesser-known sites, Empereur has unearthed a mass of evidence about the ancient city. In *Alexandria Rediscovered* he writes about the problems of working in a city whose buried past is all too fragile. Both books are very readable and profusely illustrated.

★ **Roy MacLeod** *The Library of Alexandria: Center of Learning in the Ancient World* (AUC). A history of the legendary library that delves into the city's Greek heritage, the book trade in antiquity, Neoplatonist philosophers, Mystery Schools and many other topics. An introduction by the director of the new Bibliotheca Alexandrina brings the story full circle.

Otto Meinardus *Monks and Monasteries of the Egyptian Desert* (AUC). A rather turgid history and guide to Egypt's Coptic monasteries.

Dominic Montserrat *Sex and Society in Graeco-Roman Egypt* (Kegan Paul). In-depth study of sexual mores and practices in a famously licentious era.

Győző Vörös *Taposiris Magna: Port of Isis*. Many scholars disagree with his theories about this ancient port, such as the notion that its lighthouse was the prototype of the Pharos at Alexandria, not a scaled-down copy (see p.619).

Barbara Watterson *Coptic Egypt* (Scott Academic Press). Covers Coptic history and culture from ancient times to the present.

Medieval and modern history

The Crusades

Amin Maalouf *The Crusades through Arab Eyes* (Al Saqi Books). Lebanese writer and journalist Maalouf has used the writings of contemporary Arab chroniclers of the Crusades to retrace two centuries of Middle Eastern history. His conclusion is that present-day relations between the Arab world and the West are still marked by the battle that ended seven centuries ago.

★ **Steven Runciman** *A History of the Crusades* (Penguin). Highly readable three-volume narrative, laced with anecdote and scandal. Runciman's hero is Salah al-Din, rather than Richard the Lionheart, who is depicted (like most of the other traditional Western good guys) in all his murderous ferocity.

Colonial Era

George Annesley *The Rise of Modern Egypt* (Pentland). A readable survey of the period from Napoleon's invasion to the Suez Crisis, marred by Annesley's colonialist attitudes.

Corelli Barnett *The Desert Generals* (Cassell Military). An iconoclastic study that concludes that Montgomery was a less assured general than his predecessors, let alone Rommel. Still, he did win the North African campaign.

★ **George Greenfield** *Chasing the Beast* (R. Cohen, US). Evocative memoirs of the Western Desert campaign, by a Cambridge graduate who joined the infantry.

Peter Mansfield *The British in Egypt* (o/p). Interesting account of how Egypt passed from being the "veiled protectorate" to an outright imperial possession. Mansfield is also author of *The Arabs* (Penguin), a clear, perceptive and wide-ranging introduction to the Arab world from the arrival of Islam to the 1970s.

Barrie Pitt *The Crucible of War* (o/p). Blow-by-blow account of the Battle of El-Alamein.

★ **Anthony Sattin** *Lifting the Veil: British Society in Egypt 1768–1956* (o/p). A fascinating slice of social history, charting the rise and fall of British tourists and expatriates in Egypt. Classic photographs, too.

Post-Independence

A.J. Barker *Arab-Israeli Wars* (o/p). An illustrated account of the 1948, 1956, 1967 and 1973 wars, by a military historian. Photographs (and sympathies) come largely from the Israeli side.

★ **Raymond William Baker** *Sadat and After* (J. B. Tauris). Heavyweight but fascinating critique of Egyptian society from six different perspectives, including those of the Muslim Brotherhood, Nasserists, Marxists and Osman Ahmed Osman, each presented sympathetically. A *tour d'horizon* of contemporary Egyptian political thought.

Nemat Guenena *The "Jihad". An "Islamic Alternative" in Egypt* (Cairo Papers Vol. 9, Summer 1986). As the quotation marks imply, a cautious academic investigation into the beliefs and social profile of Egypt's leading radical fundamentalist group. Available in Cairo.

Mohammed Heikal *Cutting the Lion's Tail; The Road to Ramadan; The Autumn of Fury* (all o/p, though most libraries will turn up one or another). These three books cover, respectively, the Suez Crisis, the 1973 War, and Sadat's rise and fall. As a confidante of Nasser's since the Revolution, one-time editor of *Al-Ahram* and Minister of Information, Heikal provides a genuine inside view.

David Hirst and Irene Beeson *Sadat* (o/p). Revealing political biography of the man whom Kissinger described as "the greatest since Bismarck", but which stops short of his assassination.

★ **Derek Hopwood** *Egypt: Politics and Society 1945–90* (Routledge). Accessible and useful

survey of the modern era, now in its third edition.

Human Rights Watch *Hostage-Taking and Intimidation by Security Forces; Violations of Freedom of Religious Belief and Expression of the Christian Minority.* Two sobering reports of human rights abuses in Egypt during the 1990s.

Anwar Sadat *In Search of Identity* (Buccaneer). An anodyne, ghosted autobiography that reveals less about the character of Egypt's assassinated president than either Heikal or Hirst and Beeson.

Robert St John *The Boss* (o/p). Racy, anecdotal biography of Nasser, written a decade before his death. Interesting, albeit dated since its publication in 1960.

Anthropology, sociology and feminism

★ **Nayra Atiya (ed.)** *Khul-Khaal: Five Egyptian Women Tell Their Stories* (Syracuse University Press, US). Gripping biographical accounts by women from diverse backgrounds, revealing much about contemporary Egyptian life. Essential reading.

★ **Nicholas Biegman** *Egypt's Side-Shows.* Engaging colour photos of moulids, weddings and other rituals of Egyptian life. For a slightly academic treatment of the former, see Biegman's *Egypt – Moulids, Saints and Sufis.*

★ **R. Critchfield** *Shahhat: An Egyptian* (AUC). A wonderful book, based on several years' resident research with the Nile Valley *fellaheen*, across the river from Luxor.

Moving, amusing and shocking, by turn.

Joseph Hobbs *Bedouin Life in the Egyptian Wilderness.* Fascinating, albeit academic account of the Khushmaan clan of Ma'aza Bedouin living in the Jebel Galala of the Eastern Desert.

★ **Rana Kabbani** *Egypt's Myths of Orient* (o/p). An easier read than Edward Said's heavyweight *Orientalism*, this book unravels the erotic fantasies and myths which Western travellers, painters and poets built up about the East. Starting with the Crusades and continuing on through the Victorians, Kabbani shows how the East was portrayed as sexually voracious and thus intellectually and morally inferior.

Smadar Lavie *The Poetics of Military Occupation: Mzeina Allegories of Bedouin Identity under Israeli and Egyptian Rule* (University of California Press, US). Interesting study of the Bedouin tribe most affected by the changes in Sinai under both regimes, by an Israeli anthropologist.

Lila Abu Lughod *Veiled Sentiments: Honour and Poetry in a Bedouin Society* (University of California Press, US). Another anthropological study, devoted to the Awlad Ali tribe of the Western Desert.

★ Nawal el-Saadawi *The Hidden Face of Eve* (Zed). Egypt's best-known woman writer, Saadawi has been in conflict with the Egyptian authorities most of her life. This is her major polemic, covering a wide range of topics – sexual aggression, female circumcision, prostitution, divorce and sexual relationships. Visit her website at ⊛www.geocities.com/nawalsaadawi/.

Huda Shaarawi *Harem Years: Memoirs of an Egyptian Feminist 1879–1924* (Virago). A unique document from the last generation of upper-class Egyptian women who spent their childhoods and married lives in the segregated world of the harem.

Islam

★ **A.J. Arberry (trans.)** *The Koran*. This translation by Oxford University Press is the best English-language version of Islam's holy book, whose revelations and prose style form the basis of the Muslim faith and Arab literature. Arberry's scholarship is also evident in *Sufism: An Account of the Mystics of Islam* and *The Koran Interpreted*.

★ **Karen Armstrong** *Muhammed: A Biography of the Prophet* (Harper). A widely acclaimed biography which illuminates the Prophet's world and faith, and dispels many Western falsehoods and misconceptions about them.

★ **Titus Burckhardt** *Art of Islam: Language and Meaning* (o/p). Superbly illustrated, intellectually penetrating overview of Islamic art and architecture.

H.A.R. Gibb *Islam* (in the US: *Studies on the Civilization of Islam*) (o/p). Concise exposition of the historical development and nature of Islam.

Wildlife

★ **Bertel Bruun** *Common Birds of Egypt* (AUC). Slim illustrated guide, ideal for bird-watching your way around the country.

★ **Eric Hanauer** *The Egyptian Red Sea – A Diver's Guide* (o/p). A comprehensive guide to the reefs and fish, and where to find them.

Richard Hoath *Natural Selections: A Year of Egypt's Wildlife* (AUC). Enlightening and charming study of Egypt's birds, land and sea creatures, illustrated with the author's drawings.

Egyptian fiction

André Aciman *Out of Egypt: A Memoir* (Harvill). Wry, affectionate tale of a flamboyant Jewish family who emigrated to Alex at the turn of the century and left three generations later. Aciman himself came of age in Italy and France.

★ **Salwa Bakr** *The Golden Chariot* (Garnet). Absorbing novel set in a women's prison near Cairo, seen through the eyes of an Alexandrian aristocrat jailed for murder. The inmates' stories represent a microcosm of women's oppression in contemporary Egypt.

André Chedid *The Sixth Day; From Sleep Unbound* (Swallow). Another émigré author, whose metaphor-laden plots and clinical prose are not exactly beach reading.

★ **Gamal al-Ghitani** *Incidents in Zafraani Alley* (Egyptian Book Organization – only available in Egypt); *Zayni Barakat* (Penguin). *Incidents* is a highly accessible, darkly humorous read, which could be interpreted as a satire on state paranoia and credulous fundamentalism. Its ending is confused by the fact that the page order has been scrambled in the English-language edition. *Zayni Barakat* is a convoluted, elliptical drama set in the last years of Mamluke rule, which reached a wider audience at home when it was adapted for Egyptian television in 1994.

Nabil Naoum Gorgy *The Slave's Dream and Other Stories* (Quartet). The amorality of man and nature is the main theme of this collection of tales, apparently influenced by Borges and Bowles.

Gamil Attiyah Ibrahim *Down to the Sea* (Quartet). Stumbling translation mars what is by all accounts – in the original – a fascinating exploration of life in Cairo's Cities of the Dead.

★ **Yusuf Idris** *The Cheapest Nights; Rings of Burnished Brass* (P. Owen). Two superb collections by Egypt's finest writer of short stories, who died in 1991. Uncompromisingly direct, yet ironic.

★ **Naguib Mahfouz** *Adrift on the Nile; Arabian Days and Nights; Miramar; Midaq Alley; Palace Walk; Palace of Desires; Sugar Street; The Thief and the Dogs; Respected Sir; The Search; Wedding Song; The Beggar; The Beginning and the End; Autumn Quail.* Awarded the Nobel Literature Prize in 1989, Mahfouz was the Grand Old Man of Egyptian letters. His novels have a rather nineteenth-century feel, reminiscent in plot and characterization of Balzac or Victor Hugo; most are set in Cairo or Alexandria. Favoured themes include the discrepancy between ideology and human problems, hypocrisy and injustice, and taking personal responsibility.

Alifa Rifaat *Distant View of a Minaret* (Heinemann). A well-known writer in her fifties expresses her revolt against male domination and suggests solutions within the orthodox Koranic framework.

★ **Nawal el-Saadawi** *Woman at Point Zero* (Zed); *The Fall of the Imam* (Minerva); *God Dies by the Nile* (Zed); and others. Saadawi's novels are informed by her work as a doctor and psychiatrist in Cairo, and by her feminist and socialist beliefs; they range through subjects virtually taboo in Egypt. *Point Zero*, her best, is a powerful and moving story of a woman condemned to death for killing a pimp. You will find very few of her books on sale in Egypt, though *The Fall of the Imam* is the only one officially banned. Her website (ⓦwww.geocities.com/nawal-saadawi/) embraces literature, sociology and politics.

Adhaf Soueif *Aisha*; *In the Eye of the Sun* (Bloomsbury). Born in Cairo and educated in Egypt and England, Soueif's semi-autobiographical first book was acclaimed for its sensibility. *In the Eye of the Sun* is a 790-page novel exploring love and destiny in the Middle East during the 1960s and 70s.

★ **Bahaa Taher** *Aunt Safiyya and the Monastery* (University of California Press). Beautifully crafted novella set in a village in Upper Egypt, where the imperatives of a vendetta are challenged by a Muslim farmer and a Coptic monk. Taher's lapidary prose is sensitively translated by Barbara Romaîne.

Anthologies

Margot Badran and Miriam Cooke (eds.) *Opening the Gates: a Century of Arab Feminist Writing* (Virago). Mix of fiction and polemic, including a fair number of Egyptian contributors.

★ **Marylin Booth (ed./trans.)** *My Grandmother's Cactus: Stories by Egyptian Women* (Quartet). Short stories by the latest generation of women writers, including Radwa Ashour, Salwa Bakr, Etidal Osman, Neamet el-Biheiri, Ibtihal Salem and Sahar Tawfiq.

★ **Inea Bushnaq** *Arab Folktales* (Pantheon). Great collection of folk stories from across the Arab world, including many from Egypt, with interesting thematic pieces putting them in context. Highly recommended.

W.M. Hutchins (ed./trans.) *Egyptian Tales and Short Stories of the 1970s & 80s* (AUC). Includes various stories by Nawal el-Saadawi, Amira Nowaira, Gamal al-Ghitani and Fouad Higazy.

Poetry, biography and criticism

★ **C.P. Cavafy** *Collected Poems.* Elegiac evocations of the Alexandrian myth by the city's most famous poet. An excerpt from *The City* appears under "Alexandria" in this book.

Tawfiq al-Hakim *The Prison of Life* (AUC). An autobiographical essay by one of the formative figures of mod-

ern Egyptian literature, covering the first thirty years of Al-Hakim's life.

Jane Lagoudis Pinchin *Alexandria Still: Forster, Durrell and Cavafy* (AUC). Studies the influence of the city and its three most famous writers on one another. Rather dry, and strictly for people seriously into these writers.

Foreign fiction

Michael Asher *The Eye of Ra*; *Firebird* (HarperCollins). An explorer (see "The desert", p.821) with an SAS background, Asher is strong on outlaw tribes, secret elites and real mysteries like the lost oasis of Zerzura, but the paranormal twist to his thrillers lacks the chill of Easterman's *Name of the Beast* or the ingenuity of Smethurst's *Sinai* (see below).

Noel Barber *A Woman of Cairo* (o/p). Ill-starred love and destiny amongst the Brits and Westernized Egyptians of King Farouk's Cairo, interwoven with historical events and characters. From that perspective, a good insight into those times.

Gillian Bradshaw *The Beacon at Alexandria* (o/p). A woman learns medicine in secret, disguises herself as a man and practises it in sectarian strife-ridden Alexandria, and later in barbarian-haunted Thrace.

Moyra Caldecott *Daughter of Amun* (Bladud). Romanticized account of the rise and fall of Queen Hatshepsut.

Agatha Christie *Death Comes at the End*; *Death on the Nile* (Collins). The latter is a classic piece of skullduggery solved by Hercule Poirot aboard a Nile cruiser, which Christie wrote while staying at the *Old Cataract Hotel* in Aswan. *Death Comes at the End* is a lamer effort, set around Luxor and the Valley of the Kings.

Robin Cook *Sphinx* (o/p). Humdrum thriller about a secret tomb in the Valley of the Kings.

⭐ **Len Deighton** *City of Gold* (Arrow). Hard-boiled thriller set in 1941, when vital information was being leaked to Rommel. Follet's *The Key to Rebecca* (see below) concerns a later phase in the war, involving another spy.

Lawrence Durrell *The Alexandria Quartet* (Faber). Endless sexual and metaphysical ramblings, occasionally relieved by a dollop of Alex atmosphere, from one of the century's most overrated writers.

⭐ **Daniel Easterman** *Name of the Beast* (o/p). If you can swallow the notion of the Antichrist masterminding an Islamic fundamentalist coup, this fantasy-thriller grips from the beginning. The ending is a letdown, however.

⭐ **Ken Follet** *The Key to Rebecca* (Pan). Fast-paced thriller based on the true story of a German spy, Eppler, who operated in Cairo during 1942. Follet exercises artistic licence when describing the outcome, but the belly dancer Sonia, and Sadat's involvement, are largely faithful to history.

Anton Gill *City of the Horizon*; *City of Dreams*; *City of the Dead* (Bloomsbury). Gill's trilogy pits the scribe Huy against diverse conspirators during the reigns of Tutankhamun and Horemheb, in the aftermath of the Amarna era.

⭐ **Robert Irwin** *The Arabian Nightmare* (Dedalus). Brilliant, paranoid fantasy set in the Cairo of Sultan Qaitbey, where a Christian spy contracts the affliction of the title. As his madness deepens, reality and illusion spiral inwards like an opium-drugged walk through a *medina* of the mind.

Christian Jacques *Ramses the Great*; *The Battle of Kadesh*; et al (Simon &

Schuster). This over-hyped series of historical novels makes Jeffrey Archer seem like Scott Fitzgerald. Not worth reading, never mind buying.

Robert Liddell *Unreal City; The Rivers of Babylon* (Peter Owen). Two ironic novels of expat life, the first set in wartime Alexandria, the second in Cairo prior to the Suez Crisis.

Penelope Lively *Oleander, Jacaranda* (Penguin). Fond memories of growing up in Cairo in the 1930s–40s, by a British novelist whose childhood perceptions were often at odds with those of her adult contemporaries.

Norman Mailer *Ancient Evenings* (Abacus). Set in the reign of Ramses II like Jacques' stories, but far more prolix, tedious and rambling. Only enlivened by its sex scenes.

Olivia Manning *The Levant Trilogy* (Penguin). The second half of this six-volume blockbuster of love'n'war finds the Pringles in Egypt, where Harriet mopes and Guy is as crass as ever.

★ **Michael Ondaatje** *The English Patient* (Picador). The novel takes liberties with the truth when portraying Almásy and his co-explorers (see p.554) but its brilliance is undeniable, and its equal focus on Kip and Dorothy make it richer and more multi-layered than the film.

Michael Pearce *The Mamur Zapt and the Donkey-vous; The Mamur Zapt and the Girl in the Nile; The Mamur Zapt and the Men Behind; The Mamur Zapt and the Return of the Carpet; The Mamur Zapt and the Spoils of Egypt* (Fontana/Harper Collins). A series of cracking yarns set in Khedival Egypt, featuring the chief of Cairo's secret police.

★ **William Smethurst** *Sinai* (Headline). Political skullduggery, ancient history and the paranormal keep you hooked and baffled till the end. Mostly set in Sinai, so an ideal read for the beach at Dahab.

Wilbur Smith *River God; The Seventh Scroll; Warlock* (Pan). A blockbuster trilogy that crams the Hyksos invasion and liberation of ancient Egypt into one volume, before its hero, the royal eunnch Taitha, undertakes a quest into the Dark Arts in the deserts of North Africa. Enjoyable, if lines like "By the festering foreskin of Seth …." don't make you snort with derision.

Journals

Ancient Egypt Magazine Easy-to-read articles by academics from museums and universities, plus listings of lectures, conferences and events held by Egyptology societies in Britain. A subscription for six issues costs £17.60 in the UK. Back issues appear on the magazine's website, featured as a link on Ⓦ www.ancient.co.uk. For details contact: Ancient Egypt Magazine, Empire Publications, Empire House, 1 Newton St, Manchester M1 1HW (☎0161/273-7007, Ⓔ empire@ globalnet.co.uk).

Journal of Egyptian Archeology; Egyptian Archeology Published by the Egyptian Exploration Society, the *Journal* is the world's leading forum for all matters Egyptological: all the new theories and discoveries get printed here first. *Egyptian Archeology* magazine, illustrated and with a popular slant, is also published by the Society. Membership of the society costs £30 or £40 per annum (depending on whether you wish to receive one or both publications).

For details contact: The Secretary, Egyptian Exploration Society, 3 Doughty Mews, London WC1N 2PG (℡020/7242-1880, ℻020/7404-6118, ⓦwww.ees.ac.uk).

Language

Language

Language

Egyptians are well used to tourists who speak only their own language, but an attempt to tackle at least a few words in Arabic is invariably greeted with great delight and encouragement, and as often as not the exclamation "You speak Arabic better than I do!" Whatever else you do, at least make an effort to learn the Arabic numerals and polite greetings.

Although most educated and urban Egyptians will have been taught some English and are only too happy to practise it on you, a little Arabic is a big help in the more remote areas. French may also come in handy in some cities, such as Alexandria, where Greek is also spoken by older folk; German, too, is increasingly understood in tourist-related spheres.

Egyptian Arabic

Although Arabic is the common and official language of 23 countries, the spoken dialect of each can vary considerably. Egyptian Arabic, however, because of the country's vast film, television and music industry, is the most widely understood in the Arab world.

Pronunciation

Transliteration from Arabic script into English presents some pronunciation problems, since some letters have no equivalents. The phonetic guide below should help: everything is pronounced.

ai as in eye
aa as in bad but lengthened
'a as when asked to say ah by the doctor
a' a glottal stop as in bottle

ey/ay as in day
ee as in feet
kh as in Scottish loch
gh like the French r (back of the throat)

Note that double consonants should always be pronounced separately.

Basics

Yes – **aiwa** (or) **na'am**
No – **la**
Thank you – **shukran**
You're welcome – **afwan**
Please (to m/f) – **min fadlak (m) / fadlik (f)**

Come in, please (to m/f) – **itfaddal (m) / itfaddali (f)**
Excuse me – **an iznak (m) / 'an iznik (f)**
Sorry – **aasif (m) / asfa (f)**
God willing – **inshallah**

Greetings and farewells

Welcome/hello – **ahlan w-sahlan**
(response) – **ahlan bik (m) / biki (f) / bikum (pl)**
Hello (formal) – **assalaamu aleikum**
(response) – **wa-aleikum assalaam**

Greetings – **sa'eeda** (or) **marhaba**
Nice to meet you – **fursa sa'eeda**
Good morning (morning of goodness) – **sabah il-kheer**
(response – morning of light) – **sabah in-nur**

Good evening (evening of goodness) – masa'
  il-kheer
(response-evening of light) – masa' in-nur
How are you (m/f) ? – izzayak (m) / izzayik (f)
I (m/f) am fine – qwayyis (m) / qwayyisa (f)
Thanks be to God – (f) il-hamdu lilla

Good night – tisbah (m) / tisbahi (f) 'ala
  kheer
And to you (m/f) – wenta (m) / wenti (f)
  bikheer
Goodbye – ma'a salaama

Questions and directions

What is your (m/f) name? – ismak (m) /
  ismik (f) ey?
My name is … – ismi …
Do you (m/f) speak – titkallim (m) / titkallimi (f)
  Arabic? – 'Arabi?
  English? – ingleezi?
  French? – fransawi?
I speak English – ana batkallim ingleezi
I don't speak Arabic – ana ma-batkallimsh
  'arabi
I understand (a little) – ana fahem (shwaiya)
I don't understand – ana mish fahem
What's that in English? – ya'ani ey bil-ingleezi?
Where is Hotel … ? – feyn funduk il … ?
… the bus station? – … mahattat il-
  autobees?
… the train station? – … mahattat il-atr?

… the airport? – … il-mataar?
… the toilet? – … il-twalet?
… a restaurant? – … mat'am?
Left/right/straight ahead – shimaal/yimeen/
  alatool
Near/far – areeb/ba'eed
Here/there – hinna/hinnak
When does the bus leave? – il-autobees
  yissafir imta?
When does the train leave? – il-atr yissafir
  imta?
… arrive? – … yoosal?
What time (is it)? – issa'a kam?
First/last/next – il-awil/il-akhir/et-tani
Nothing – wallahagga
Not yet – lissa

Requests and shopping

Do you (m/f) have … ? – fi 'andak (m) /
  'andik (f) … ?
… cigarette(s) – … sigara/sagayir
… matches – … kibreet
… newspaper – … gurnal
I (m/f) want something … – ayyiz (m) /
  ayyza (f) haga …
… else – tanya
… better than this – … ahsan min da
… cheaper – … arkhas min da
… like this – … zay da

(but) – (wa-laakin)
bigger/smaller – akbar/asghar
How much (is it)? – bi-kam (da)?
It's too expensive – da ghaali awi
big – kebir awi
small – sughayyar awi
That's fine – maashi
There is/is there? – fi/fi?
This/that – di/da
I (m/f) don't want … – mish ayyiz (m) /
  ayyza (f) …

Accommodation

Do you (m/f) have – fi 'andak (m) / 'andik (f)
  a room? – ouda?
I (m/f) would like to see the rooms – ayyiz/
  ayyza ashuf il-owad
Can I see the rooms? – mumkin ashuf il-
  owad?

Is there …? – fi … ?
… hot water? – … mayya sukhna?
… a shower? – … doush?
… a balcony? – … balcona?
… air conditioning? – … takyeef hawa?
… a telephone? – … telifoon?
How much is the bill? … – kam il-hisab?

I (m/f) don't understand – ana mish fahem (m) / fahma (f)
I (m/f) don't know – ana mish 'arif (m) / 'arfa (f)
I (m/f) am tired/ unwell – ana ta'aban (m) / ta'abana (f)
I (m/f) am hungry – ana gawa'an (m) / gawa'ana (f)
I (m/f) am thirsty – ana 'atshaan (m) / 'atshaana (f)
I (m/f) am (not) married – ana (mish) mitgawwiz (m) / mitgawwiza (f)

It's not your business – mish shorlak
Don't touch me! – sibni le wadi!
Let's go – yalla
Slowly – baranah
Enough! Finished! – khalas
Never mind – maalesh
It doesn't matter – mush muhim
There's no problem – ma feesh mushkila
May I/is it possible? – mumkin?
It's not possible – mish mumkin

Calendar

day – youm
night – leyla
week – usbu'a
month – shahr
year – sana
today – innaharda
tomorrow – bukkra
yesterday – imbaarih

later – bahdeen
Saturday – youm is-sabt
Sunday – youm il-ahad
Monday – youm il-itnayn
Tuesday – youm it-talaata
Wednesday – youm il-arb'a
Thursday – youm il-khamees
Friday – youm il-gum'a

Money

Where's the bank? – feyn il-bank?
I (m/f) want to change ... – ayyiz/ayyza aghayyar ...
... money – ... floos
... British pounds – ... ginay sterlini
... US dollars – ... dolar amrikani
... travellers' cheques – ... shikaat siyahiyya

Egyptian pound – giney
half pound – nuss giney
quarter pound – robah giney
piastre – irsh
2 piastres – irshayn
5 piastres – khamsa irsh

Numbers and fractions

0 – sifr
1 – wahid
2 – itnayn
3 – talaata
4 – arb'a
5 – khamsa
6 – sitta
7 – sab'a
8 – tamanya
9 – tes'a
10 – ashara
11 – hidarsha
12 – itnarsha
13 – talatarsha

14 – arb'atarsha
15 – khamastarsha
16 – sittarsha
17 – sab'atarsha
18 – tamantarsha
19 – tis'atarsha
20 – ashreen
21 – wahid wa-l 'ashreen
30 – talaateen
40 – arb'aeen
50 – khamseen
60 – sitteen
70 – sab'aeen
80 – tamaneen

90 – tis'een
100 – miyya
150 – miyya wa-khamseen
200 – mitayn
300 – talaata miyya
500 – khamsa miyya
1000 – alf
2000 – alfayn
3000 – talaat alaaf
4000 – arb'at alaaf
1/2 – nous
1/4 – robah
1/8 – tumna

Numerals

١	1	١٠	10	١٩	19	٨٠	80
٢	2	١١	11	٢٠	20	٩٠	90
٣	3	١٢	12	٢١	21	١٠٠	100
٤	4	١٣	13	٢٢	22	٢٠٠	200
٥	5	١٤	14	٣٠	30	٣٠٠	300
٦	6	١٥	15	٤٠	40	٤٠٠	400
٧	7	١٦	16	٥٠	50	١٠٠٠	1000
٨	8	١٧	17	٦٠	60		
٩	9	١٨	18	٧٠	70		

Egyptian food and drink terms

Basics

'Aish – Bread
Zibda – Butter
Beyd – Eggs
Samak – Fish
Gibna – Cheese
Gibna rumi – Yellow cheese
Gibna beyda – White cheese
Murabba – Jam
'Asal – Honey
Lahma – Meat
Firakh – Chicken
Zeit – Oil
Zeitun – Olives
Filfil – Pepper
Melh – Salt

Sukkar – Sugar
Skhudaar – Vegetables
Salata – Salad
Fawakih – Fruit
Zabadi – Yoghurt
Shurba – Soup
Izzaza – Bottle
Kubbaya – Glass
Showka – Fork
Sikkeena – Knife
Mala'a – Spoon
Tarabeyza – Table
Garson – Waiter
Lista/menoo – Menu
El-hisaab – The bill (check)

Drinks

Shai – Tea
Shai bi-na'ana – Tea with mint
Shai bi-laban – Tea with milk
Shai kushari – Tea made with loose-leaf
Laban – Milk
'Ahwa – Coffee (usually Turkish)
Ziyaada – very sweet
Maazboot – medium
'Ariha – little sugar
Saada – no sugar
'Ahwa fransawi – Instant or filter coffee

Mayya – Water
Mayya ma'adaniyya – Mineral water
Beera – Beer
Nibeet – Wine
'Asir – Fruit juice
'Asiir burtu'an – Orange juice
'Asiir limoon – Lemon juice
'Asiir manga – Mango juice
Karkaday – Hibiscus
Tamar hindi – Tamarind (cordial)
'Asiir 'asab – Sugar cane juice

Soups, salads and vegetables

Shurba – Soup
Shurbit firakh – Chicken soup

Shurbit 'adas – Lentil soup
Shurbit khudaar – Vegetable soup

Salata – Salad
Salatit khiyaar – Cucumber salad
Salatit tamatim – Tomato salad
Salatit khadra – Mixed green salad
Basal – Onion
Fasuliyya – Beans
Gazar – Carrots

Bamya – Okra (gumbo, ladies' fingers)
Bisilla – Peas
Batatis – Potatoes
Ruz – Rice
Torshi – Pickled vegetables
Baytingan – Eggplant (aubergine)

Main dishes

Kofta – Mincemeat flavoured with spices and onions, grilled on a skewer
Kebab – Chunks of meat, usually lamb, grilled with onions and tomatoes
Molukhiyya – Jew's mallow, a leafy vegetable stewed with meat or chicken broth and garlic to make a slimy, spinach-like dish
Firakh – Chicken grilled or stewed and served with vegetables

Hamam mashwi Grilled pigeon
Lahm dani – Lamb
Kibda – Liver
Kalewi – Kidney
Mokh – (Sheep) brains
Dik rumi – Turkey
Samak mashwi – Grilled fish served with salad, bread and dips
Gambari – Prawns
Calamari – Squid

Appetizers and fast food

Fuul – Fava beans served with oil and lemon, sometimes also with onions, meat, eggs or tomato sauce
Taamiya – Balls of deep-fried mashed chickpeas and spices
Shawarma – Slivers of pressed, spit-roasted lamb, served in pitta bread
Tahina – Sesame seed paste mixed with spices, garlic and lemon, eaten with pitta bread
Hummus – Chickpea paste mixed with tahini, garlic and lemon, sometimes served with pine nuts and/or meat [but also just the Arabic for chickpeas/garbanzo beans – indeed, more commonly used with that meaning in Egypt]
Babaghanoug – Paste of aubergines mashed with tahina

Kushari – Mixture of noodles, lentils and rice, topped with fried onions and a spicy tomato sauce
Shakshouka – Chopped meat and tomato sauce, cooked with an egg on top
Makarona – Macaroni "cake" baked in a white sauce or mincemeat gravy
Mahshi – Literally "stuffed", variety of vegetables (peppers, tomatoes, aubergines, courgettes) filled with mincemeat and/or rice, herbs and pine nuts
Wara einab – Vine leaves filled as above and flavoured with lemon juice
Fatir – Sort of pancake/pizza made of layers of flaky filo pastry with sweet or savoury fillings

Desserts, sweets, fruits and nuts

Mahallabiyya – Sweet rice or cornflour pudding, topped with pistachios
Balila – Milk dish with nuts, raisins and wheat
Baklava – Flaky filo pastry, honey and nuts
Basbousa – Pastry of semolina, honey and nuts

Umm (or Om) Ali – Corn cake soaked in milk, sugar, raisins, coconut and cinnamon, served hot
Gelati, ays kriml – Ice cream
'Ishta – Cream
Tuffah – Apples

L

Mishmish – Apricots
Mohz – Bananas
Balah – Dates
Tin – Figs
Tin shawqi – Prickly pear (cactus fruit)
Shammam – Melon

Battikh – Watermelon
Farawla – Strawberries
Fuul sudani – Peanuts
Lib battikh – Watermelon seeds
Loz – Almonds

Some phrases

Ayyzeen el-menu min fadlak – We'd like the menu please
Sukkar aleel – With little sugar
Ihna ayyzeen … – We'd like to have …
Bidoon sukkar – Without sugar
'Ey da? – What is this?
Ma'alabtish da – I didn't order this
Ihna mush ayyzeen da – We don't want this
Da mish … – This is not …
Ana makulsh … – I can't/don't eat …
… taza – … fresh

… lahm – … meat
… mistiwi kwaiyis – … cooked enough
… beyd – … eggs
Da laziz aawi – This is very tasty
Iddini/iddina … – Give me/us …
El-hisab, minfadlak (m) / minfadlik (f) – The bill, please
… taba' – … a plate
… futa – … a napkin
Shokran – Thank you

Glossary of Egyptian terms

This is a glossary of basic Egyptian terms in everyday use, plus Islamic and architectural terms; for pharaonic symbols and terms used in temple architecture, see p.294 and p.330. Common alternative spellings are given in brackets.

Ablaq Striped. An effect achieved by painting, or laying courses of different coloured masonry (the costlier method); usually white with red or buff. A Bahri Mamluke innovation, possibly derived from the Roman technique of *opus mixtum* – an alternation of stone and brickwork.

Abu "Father of"; a term of respect.

Ain (Ayn, Ein) Spring.

Amir (Emir) Commander, prince.

Bab Gate or door, as in the medieval city walls.

Bahr River, sea, canal.

Baksheesh Alms or tips.

Baladi Local, rural or countrified.

Baraka Blessing.

Beit House. Segregated public and private quarters, the *malqaf, maq'ad* and *mashrabiya* are typical features of old Cairene mansions.

Bey (Bay) Lord or noble; an Ottoman title, now a respectful form of address to anyone in authority.

Bir (Beer) Well.

Birka (Birqa, Birket) Lake.

Burg (Borg) Tower.

Cadi (Qadi) Judge.

Caleche Horse-drawn carriage.

Corniche Seafront or riverfront promenade.

Darb Path or way; can apply to alleyways, thoroughfares, or desert caravan routes.

Deir Monastery or convent.

Fellaheen (sing. Felah) Peasant farmers who work their own land or as sharecroppers for wealthier farmers.

Felucca Nile sailing boat.

Finial Ornamental crown of a dome or minaret, often topped by an Islamic crescent.

Galabiyya Loose flowing robe worn by men.

Gezira Island.

Ghird (Ghard) Sand dune.

Gam'a Large congregational mosque, as opposed to a *masguid*.

Hadj (Haj) Pilgrimage to Mecca.

Hagg/Hagga One who has visited Mecca.

Haikal Sanctuary of a Coptic church.

Hammam Turkish bathhouse.

Hantour Horse-drawn carriage.

Haramlik Literally the "forbidden" area; ie women's or private apartments in a house or palace.

Ithyphallic Decorous term for a god with an erection; Min, Amun and Osiris were often depicted thus by the ancient Egyptians.

Jebel (Gebel, Gabal, etc) Hill or mountain.

Karkur Gorge.

Khalif Successor to the Prophet Mohammed and spiritual and political leader of the Muslim empire. A struggle over this office caused the Sunni–Shia schism of 656 AD. Most khalifs ruled from Baghdad or Damascus and delegated control of imperial provinces like Egypt.

Khalig Gulf or canal.

Khan Place where goods were made, stored and sold, which also provided accommodation for travellers and merchants, like a *wikala*. It's from *khan* that we get the word caravanserai.

Khanqah Sufi hostel, analagous to a monastery.

Khedive Viceroy.

Kom Mound of rubble and earth covering an ancient settlement.

Kubri Bridge.

Kufic The earliest style of Arabic script; Foliate *kufic* was a more elaborate form, superseded by *naskhi* script.

Kuttab Koranic school, usually for boys or orphans.

Liwan Arcade or vaulted space off a courtyard, commonly found in mosques and madrassas. Originally, the term meant a sitting room opening onto a covered court.

Madrassa Literally a "place of study" but generally used to designate theological schools. Each madrassa propagates a particular rite of Islamic jurisprudence.

Mahwagi Local laundryman or woman.

Malqaf Wind scoop for directing cool breezes into houses; in Egypt, they always face north.

Maq'ad Arch-fronted "sitting place" on the second floor of old Cairene houses, overlooking the courtyard.

Maristan The medieval term for a public hospital.

Mashrabiya An alcove in lattice windows where jars of water can be cooled by the wind; and by extension, the projecting balcony and screened window itself, which enabled women to watch streetlife or the *salamlik* without being observed. Although flat latticework partitions are strictly termed *mashrafiya*, *mashrabiya* loosely covers both types of work.

Masguid A small local mosque, as opposed to a *gam'a*.

Masr (Misr, Musr) Popular name for Egypt, and Cairo.

Mastaba Stone or mud-brick benches at the entrance to buildings. Mohammed Ali had them removed to reduce idling and speed up the traffic.

Merlons Indentations and raised portions along a parapet. Fatimid merlons were angular; Mamluke ones crested, trilobed (like a fleur-de-lys) or in fancier leaf patterns.

Mida'a Fountain for the ritual ablutions that precede prayer, located in a mosque's vestibule or courtyard.

Midan Open space or square; originally, most were polo grounds.

Mihrab Niche indicating the direction of Mecca, to which all Muslims pray.

Minaret Tower from which the call to prayer is given; derived from *minara*, the Arabic word for "beacon" or "lighthouse".

Minbar Pulpit from which an address to the Friday congregation is given. Often superbly inlaid or carved in variegated marble or wood.

Mit Village or hamlet.

Mosque A simple enclosure facing Mecca in its original form, the mosque acquired minarets, *riwaqs*, madrassas and mausolea as it was developed by successive dynasties. Large congregational mosques are called *gam'a*; smaller, local "places of prostration" are known as *masguid* – a very old distinction. Very small mosques, often associated with Sufi orders or fundamentalist groups, are known as *zawiyas*.

Moulid Popular festival marking an event in the Koran or the birthday of a Muslim saint.

The term also applies to the name-days of Coptic saints.

Muezzin A prayer-crier (who nowadays is more likely to broadcast by loudspeaker than climb up and shout from the minaret).

Munshid Professional reciter of Koranic verses and praises to Allah.

Murqanas Stalactites, pendants or honeycomb ornamentation of portals, domes or squinches.

Mustachfa The modern Egyptian term for a public hospital.

Naskhi Form of Arabic script with joined-up letters, introduced by the Ayyubids.

Pasha (Pacha) Ruler – a lord or prince. Nowadays, a respectful term of address for anyone in authority, pronounced "basha".

Qala Fortress, citadel.

Qarat Peak, ridge.

Qasr Palace, fortress, mansion.

Qibla The direction in which Muslims pray, ie the wall where the *mihrab* is located.

Qubba Dome, and by extension any domed tomb.

Ras Cape, headland, peak.

Riwaq Arcaded aisle around a mosque's *sahn*, originally used as residential quarters for theological students; ordinary folk may also take naps here.

Sabil Public fountain or water cistern. During the nineteenth century it was often combined with a Koranic school to make a *Sabil-Kuttab*.

Sahn Central courtyard of a mosque, frequently surrounded by *riwaqs* or *liwans*.

Salamlik The "greeting" area of a house; ie the public and men's apartments.

Sanctuary The *liwan* incorporating the *qibla* wall in a mosque, or the shrine of a deity in an ancient Egyptian temple.

Soffits Undersides of arches, often decorated with stripes (*ablaq*) or formalized plant designs (an Ottoman motif).

Squinch An arch spanning the right angle formed by two walls, so as to support a dome.

Sharia Street (literally "way"). Also laws based on Koranic precepts, which Muslim fundamentalists wish to see applied in Egypt.

Sharm Bay.

Sufis Islamic mystics who seek to attain union with Allah through trance-inducing *zikrs* and dances. Whirling Dervishes belong to one of the Sufi sects.

Tabut A cenotaph or grave marker, sometimes embellished with a "hat" indicating the deceased's rank.

Tariqa Sufi order or brotherhood.

Tell Another word for kom (see above).

Tir Canal.

Thuluth Script whose vertical strokes are three times larger than its horizontal ones; *Thuluth* literally means "'third".

Wadi Valley or watercourse (usually dry).

Waqf The endowment of some religious, educational or charitable institution in perpetuity. In Egypt, thousands of such bequests are overseen by the Ministry of Awaqf.

Wahah Oasis.

Wikala Bonded warehouse with rooms for merchants upstairs. Here they bought trading licences from the *Muhtasib*, and haggled over sales in the courtyard. *Okel* is another term for a *wikala*.

Yordang Freestanding, wind-eroded rock formations.

Zaar Exorcism.

Zawiya Originally a *khanqah* centred around a particular sheikh or Sufi order (*tariqa*), but nowadays used to mean a very small mosque.

Zikr Marathon session of chanting and swaying, intended to induce communion with Allah.

Ziyada Outer courtyard separating early mosques from their surroundings; literally "an addition".

Zuqaq Narrow cul-de-sac, from the Turkish word for "street".

Index

and small print

Index

Map entries are in colour

A

S

T

U

V

W

Twenty Years of Rough Guides

In the summer of 1981, Mark Ellingham, Rough Guides' founder, knocked out the first guide on a typewriter, with a group of friends. Mark had been travelling in Greece after university, and couldn't find a guidebook that really answered his needs.There were heavyweight cultural guides on the one hand – good on museums and classical sites but not on beaches and tavernas – and on the other hand student manuals that were so caught up with how to save money that they lost sight of the country's significance beyond its role as a place for a cool vacation. None of the guides began to address Greece as a country, with its natural and human environment, its politics and its contemporary life.

Having no urgent reason to return home, Mark decided to write his own guide. It was a guide to Greece that tried to combine some erudition and insight with a thoroughly practical approach to travellers' needs. Scrupulously researched listings of places to stay, eat and drink were matched by careful attention to detail on everything from Homer to Greek music, from classical sites to national parks and from nude beaches to monasteries. Back in London, Mark and his friends got their Rough Guide accepted by a farsighted commissioning editor at the publisher Routledge and it came out in 1982.

The Rough Guide to Greece was a student scheme that became a publishing phenomenon. The immediate success of the book – shortlisted for the Thomas Cook Award – spawned a series that rapidly covered dozens of countries. The Rough Guides found a ready market among backpackers and budget travellers, but soon acquired a much broader readership that included older and less impecunious visitors. Readers relished the guides' wit and inquisitiveness as much as the enthusiastic, critical approach that acknowledges everyone wants value for money – but not at any price.

Rough Guides soon began supplementing the "rougher" information – the hostel and low-budget listings – with the kind of detail that independent-minded travellers on any budget might expect. These days, the guides – distributed worldwide by the Penguin group – include recommendations spanning the range from shoestring to luxury, and cover more than 200 destinations around the globe. Our growing team of authors, many of whom come to Rough Guides initially as outstandingly good letter-writers telling us about their travels, are spread all over the world, particularly in Europe, the USA and Australia. As well as the travel guides, Rough Guides publishes a series of dictionary phrasebooks covering two dozen major languages, an acclaimed series of music guides running the gamut from Classical to World Music, a series of music CDs in association with World Music Network, and a range of reference books on topics as diverse as the Internet, Pregnancy, and Unexplained Phenomena. Visit **www.roughguides.com** to see what's cooking.

Rough Guide Credits

Text editors: Ann-Marie Shaw, Olivia Swift and Samantha Cook
Series editor: Mark Ellingham
Editorial: Martin Dunford, Jonathan Buckley, Kate Berens, Helena Smith, Ruth Blackmore, Geoff Howard, Claire Saunders, Gavin Thomas, Alexander Mark Rogers, Polly Thomas, Joe Staines, Richard Lim, Duncan Clark, Peter Buckley, Lucy Ratcliffe, Clifton Wilkinson, Alison Murchie, Matthew Teller, Andrew Dickson, Fran Sandham, Sally Schafer (UK); Andrew Rosenberg, Yuki Takagaki, Richard Koss, Hunter Slaton (US)
Production: Susanne Hillen, Andy Hilliard, Link Hall, Helen Prior, Julia Bovis, Michelle Draycott, Katie Pringle, Zoë Nobes, Rachel Holmes, Andy Turner, Dan May

Cartography: Maxine Repath, Melissa Baker, Ed Wright, Katie Lloyd-Jones
Cover art direction: Louise Boulton
Picture research: Sharon Martins, Mark Thomas
Online: Kelly Martinez, Anja Mutic-Blessing, Jennifer Gold, Audra Epstein, Suzanne Welles, Cree Lawson (US)
Finance: John Fisher, Gary Singh, Edward Downey, Mark Hall, Tim Bill
Marketing & Publicity: Richard Trillo, Niki Smith, David Wearn, Chloë Roberts, Demelza Dallow, Claire Southern (UK); Simon Carloss, David Wechsler, Megan Kennedy (US)
Administration: Julie Sanderson, Karoline Densley

Publishing Information

This fifth edition published February 2003 by **Rough Guides Ltd**,
80 Strand, London WC2R 0RL
345 Hudson St, 4th Floor,
New York, NY 10014, USA
Distributed by the Penguin Group
Penguin Books Ltd,
80 Strand, London WC2R 0RL
Penguin Putnam, Inc,
375 Hudson St, NY 10014, USA
Penguin Books Australia Ltd,
487 Maroondah Highway, PO Box 257,
Ringwood, Victoria 3134, Australia
Penguin Books Canada Ltd,
10 Alcorn Avenue, Toronto, Ontario
M4V 1E4 Canada
Penguin Books (NZ) Ltd,
182–190 Wairau Road, Auckland 10,
New Zealand
Typeset in Bembo and Helvetica to an original design by Henry Iles.

Printed in Italy by LegoPrint S.p.A

864pp includes index
A catalogue record for this book is available from the British Library

ISBN 1-84353-050-3

The publishers and authors have done their best to ensure the accuracy and currency of all the information in **The Rough Guide to Egypt**, however, they can accept no responsibility for any loss, injury, or inconvenience sustained by any traveller as a result of information or advice contained in the guide.

Help us update

We've gone to a lot of effort to ensure that the fifth edition of **The Rough Guide to Egypt** is accurate and up-to-date. However, things change – places get "discovered", opening hours are notoriously fickle, restaurants and rooms raise prices or lower standards. If you feel we've got it wrong or left something out, we'd like to know, and if you can remember the address, the price, the time, the phone number, so much the better.

We'll credit all contributions, and send a copy of the next edition (or any other Rough Guide if you prefer) for the best letters. Everyone who writes to us and isn't already a subscriber will receive a copy of our full-colour thrice-yearly newsletter. Please mark letters: "**Rough Guide Egypt Update**" and send to: Rough Guides, 80 Strand, London WC2R 0RL, or Rough Guides, 4th Floor, 345 Hudson St, New York, NY 10014. Or send an email to **mail@roughguides.com**.

Have your questions answered and tell others about your trip at **www.roughguides.atinfopop.com**.

Acknowledgements

The authors jointly would like to thank: Ann-Marie Shaw, Olivia Swift and Samantha Cook for their tireless attention to detail, Melissa Baker and Ed Wright for the maps, Sharon Martins for the photos, Andy Turner for the typesetting and Diane Margolis for the proofreading.

Thanks from **Dan Richardson** to Salah Mohammed in Cairo; Nagy and Dawn in Alex; Talaat Mola, Yehiya Kandil and Khalid Khalifa in Bahariya; Mahdi Hweiti and Martin Savage in Siwa; Omar Ahmed in Dakhla; Hagg Ibrahim, Tayeb, Hamada and Col. Hafiz in Luxor; Shukri Sa'ad and Hakeem Hussein in Aswan; Magdy Help on the Nile; Michael Ackroyd and all the crew on the Gilf Kebir expedition. Also thanks to Wael Abed, Amr Shannon and Andras Zboray, for deep-desert info.

Daniel Jacobs: Big thanks to the management and staff of the Hotel Luna, my home from home in Cairo; Hisham Youssif of the Berlin Hotel, scourge of Cairo's scamsters; Salah Mohammed; Mohamadi Mahmoud; Mr Hussein Bassir and Mme Naglat Selim of the Supreme Council of Antiquities; Mr Gamal al-Balam, curator of the Egyptian Antiquities Museum; and to the people of Cairo for their warmth, kindness and hospitality (excluding those who tried to skank me).

Jessica Jacobs: Thank you to Fatah Abbas, Sallam El Zoghby and Aadnan Shedid in Suez; Hussein Abu Ahmed, Sherif El Dardiry and Seamus Forde in Sharm El Sheikh; Constanze Conrad and Ayman Taher in Hurghada; Angela Godfrey in Nuweiba; Said Kader in Dahab; Karim Noor in Mersa Alam; and Walid and Heather Nasser in Cairo.

Readers' letters

Thanks to all the readers who took the trouble to write in with their comments and suggestions (and apologies to anyone whose name we've misspelt or omitted):

Julie Barnes; Alex Berryman; Richard Bowring; Sandi Burford-Poole; Lynne Butterworth; Giacomo Caruso; Claire Charlwood; Jayne Chater; Tony Claassens; Trevor Curnow; Jacqueline Diffey; Christopher Dyer; Sheri Eggleton; M. S. Evans; Lisbeth Fangel-Lloyd; Saffia Farr; Jocasta and Ali Fletcher; Simon Foster; Bev Handley; Simon Hancock; Tony Hardwick; Dr Sandra Harley; C Hertogh; Dr Robert Hill; John Humbach; Kerena Hutchin; Kathryn Johnson; Steve Kay; Joachim Klein; Adrian and Jill Lay; Peter Lilley; Charlotte Mabey; John Mangold; Carol and Roger Marsh; Colleen Martin; Nigel Mobey; Nadine Moeller; Linda Moore; Phil Muscutt; M. Nelhams; Eldrid Nordbo; Errol Petterson and Anna Ekdahl; Bev Roberts; G. H. Saunders; Dr Jules De Silva; Ami Skanberg; Jackie Skinner; Amanda Sloat; Natalie Smith; VC Stabler; Tania Stevenson; John Stewart; Matthew Teller; Marcus Webster; Michael Wesley; A. Whalley; Lucy Williams; Dr Tom Winnifrith.

Photo Credits

Cover credits

Main front Painted House, Luxor © Robert Harding

Small front top image Butterfly fish, Red Sea © Getty

Small front lower image Sphinx and pyramid, Giza © Robert Harding

Back top image Nile, Aswan © Robert Harding

Back lower image Karnak Temple © Peter Wilson

Colour introduction

Upper Nile Valley © Tony Howard

Bedouin man grilling meat © Mathieu Lamarre/Travel Ink

Tutankhamun funerary mask, Museum of Egyptian Antiquities © Colin Marshall/Travel Ink

Donkey cart © Mathieu Lamarre/Travel Ink

Downtown cinema hoardings featuring Omar Sharif © Abbie Enock/Travel Ink

Sign near pyramids © Sylvain Grandadam/Robert Harding

Minaret and housing, Cairo © James Morris/AXIOM

Man smoking sheesha © Jon Spaull/AXIOM

Bather against distant mountains, Red Sea © E. Simanor/Robert Harding

Diver over colourful coral © Louise Murray/Robert Harding

Statue of Ibis and the Goddess Maat ©
Roger Wood/CORBIS

Camel race © Jessica Jacobs

Bakers © Chris Caldicott/AXIOM

Things not to miss

Mural, Tomb of Ramses I, Valley of the Kings,
Thebes © James Morris/AXIOM

Belly-dancer © Robert Harding

Red Pyramid, Dashur © Daniel Jacobs

Great Sand Sea, Siwa Oasis © James
Morris/AXIOM

Cairo juice bar © Hutchison

Egyptian goose with young © Barry
Hughes/Travel Ink

The Temple of Seti I, Abydos © James
Morris/AXIOM

Great Pyramid of Cheops, Giza © Mary
Jelliffe/Hutchison

Street food stall © Doug Traverso/Robert
Harding

Elephantine Island, Aswan © Hutchison

Diver over seafan © Robert Harding

Sultan Hassan and Rifai mosques, viewed
from the Citadel, Cairo © Jeremy
Horner/Hutchison

Jeep in Western Desert © Tony Howard

Bedouin weavers, Western Desert © Sarah
Errington/Hutchison

Statue of scribe © Colin Marshall/Travel Ink

Gold jewellery booth © Carlos
Freire/Hutchison

Hands in the air & floorshow at Na'ama Bay
© Sanafir Hotel

Karkaday seller © Sylvain Grandadam/Robert
Harding

Catacombs of Kom es-Shoqafa © Abbie
Enock/Travel Ink

St Paul's monastery © James Morris/AXIOM

Feluccas on the River Nile © Abbie
Enock/Travel Ink

Dawn on Mount Sinai © James
Morris/AXIOM

Backpackers at beach café, Dahab ©
Stephen Psallidas/Travel Ink

Moray eel © Alex Misiewicz/AXIOM

Sunrise on pool deck © Andrew
Eames/Hutchison

Great Hypostyle temple, Karnak © Julia
Bayne/Robert Harding

Al-Qasr, Dakhla Oasis © James
Morris/AXIOM

Grilling fish © Jack Fields/CORBIS

Overview, Alexandria © Dorian Shaw/AXIOM

St Catherine's Monastery © Mary
Jelliffe/Hutchison

Black and white photos

Downtown cinema hoardings featuring Omar
Sharif © Abbie Enock/Travel Ink (p.84)

Islamic Old Cairo © John Hatt/Hutchison
(p.139)

Men smoking hookahs in tea shop, Cairo ©
Mary Jelliffe/Hutchison (p.239)

Elephantine Island, Aswan © Hutchison
(p.288)

Aerial of Valley of the Kings © Stephen
Psallidas/Travel Ink (p.389)

Aswan bazaar © John Hatt/Hutchison (p.443)

Jeep in Western Desert © Tony Howard
(p.480)

View through camel's legs, Western Desert ©
Mathieu Lamarre/Travel Ink (p.538)

Catacombs of Kom es-Shoqafa © Abbie
Enock/Travel Ink (p.580)

Friday prayers, Alexandria © Carlos
Freire/Hutchison (p.597)

Egyptian goose with young © Barry
Hughes/Travel Ink (p.634)

Pots and pans for sale © Gerry
Walden/Travel Ink (p.639)

Fishing boat and cargo ship, Suez Canal ©
Dorian Shaw/Hutchison (p.652)

Dawn on Mount Sinai © James
Morris/AXIOM (p.674)

Climbing near St Catherine's Monastery ©
Tony Howard/N.O.M.A.D.S. (p.727)

Diver over seafan © Robert Harding (p.742)

Trekking in Nubian Desert © Di
Taylor/N.O.M.A.D.S. (p.779)

ANCIENT WORLD TOURS

[A]WT offers fully guided tours with archaeologists and historians to all the classic [sit]es of Egypt and the truly remote and stunning delta and deep desert. AWT is the [onl]y UK company that can get you in comfort and safety to *all* the desert oases – [ev]en the remote and mysterious Gilf el-Kebir. We'll get you acquainted with the *real* [Eg]ypt, her awe-inspiring monuments and fascinating people.

[Ou]r 'Independent Traveller' service offers [ha]ssle free travel to some truly unique [de]stinations at very reasonable rates; if [yo]u want to get away from the crowds [an]d see the Egypt that lies off the beaten [tra]ck then you just can't afford to travel [wit]hout contacting us first.

AWT – THE TRAVELLER'S TRAVEL COMPANY
FOR DETAILS SEE OUR WEBSITE AT WWW.ANCIENT.CO.UK

[T]elephone: 07071-222-950   International: +44 1903 810 443

ABTA
V2607